Inclusive Early Childhood Education Development, Resources, and Practice

Fifth Edition

Penny Low Deiner

University of Delaware

WADSWORTH
CENGAGE Learning

Australia • Brazil • Japan • Korea • Mexico • Singapore • Spain • United Kingdom • United States

Inclusive Early Childhood Education: Development, Resources, and Practice
Fifth Edition
Penny Low Deiner

Acquisitions Editor: Chris Shortt

Assistant Editor: Caitlin Cox

Editorial Assistant: Linda Stewart

Media Editor: Ashley Cronin

Marketing Manager: Kara Parsons

Marketing Assistant: Dimitri Hagnere

Marketing Communications Manager:
  Martha Pfeiffer

Content Project Manager: Samen Iqbal

Creative Director: Rob Hugel

Art Director: Maria Epes

Print Buyer: Linda Hsu

Rights Acquisitions Account Manager, Text:
  Tim Sisler

Rights Acquisitions Account Manager, Image:
  Don Schlotman

Production Service: Sara Dovre Wudali,
  Buuji Inc.

Copy Editor: Tricia Lawrence

Cover Designer: Bartay Studio

Cover Image: © Cengage Learning, ECE Photo Library

Compositor: Integra

For product information and technology assistance, contact us at
Cengage Learning Customer & Sales Support, 1-800-354-9706.

For permission to use material from this text or product,
submit all requests online at **www.cengage.com/permissions.**
Further permissions questions can be e-mailed to
permissionrequest@cengage.com.

Library of Congress Control Number: 2008931217

Student Edition:

ISBN-13: 978-1-4283-2086-4

ISBN-10: 1-4283-2086-5

Wadsworth
10 Davis Drive
Belmont, CA 94002-3098
USA

Cengage Learning is a leading provider of customized learning solutions with office locations around the globe, including Singapore, the United Kingdom, Australia, Mexico, Brazil, and Japan. Locate your local office at **www.cengage.com/international.**

Cengage Learning products are represented in Canada by Nelson Education, Ltd.

To learn more about Wadsworth, visit **www.cengage.com/wadsworth**

Purchase any of our products at your local college store or at our preferred online store **www.ichapters.com.**

Printed in Canada
1 2 3 4 5 6 7 13 12 11 10 09

*To my husband, John, and
the relationship that has survived five editions
of this book, and to our children and grandchildren,
who have kept me in touch with reality.
Paige and Rudy; Michael and Suling; Jamie and Rich*

and

*Isabella Franchesca, Natalie Ann-Shin, Russell Yo-Jei,
Miles Benjamin, and Maya Grace*

Brief Contents

Contents

Chapter 4
Curriculum and Standards in Inclusive Settings   82

Chapter 5
Individualizing Planning   110

Chapter 6
Atypical Development: The Beginning   140

PART II
INCLUSIVE EARLY CHILDHOOD EDUCATION

Chapter 10
Children with Attention-Deficit/Hyperactivity Disorder   247

Chapter 11
Children with Communication Disorders   271

Chapter 12
Children who are English Language Learners   292

Chapter 13
Children with Autism Spectrum Disorders   312

Chapter 14
Children with Intellectual Disabilities and Developmental Delays   335

Chapter 15
Children Who Are Gifted and Talented   353

Chapter 16
Children with Special Health Care Needs   374

Chapter 17
Children with Orthopedic and Neurologic Impairments   407

Chapter 18
Children with Hearing Impairments   434

Chapter 19
Children with Visual Impairments   456

PART III
RESOURCES AND PRACTICE FOR INCLUSIVE EARLY CHILDHOOD EDUCATION

LIST OF ACTIVITIES   R-8

Resource Chapter   1
Social Awareness Activities: Self-Esteem, Inclusion, and Social Studies   R-11

Resource Chapter   2
Language and Literacy Activities: Speaking, Listening, Reading, and Writing   R-28

Resource Chapter   3
Discovery Activities: Mathematics, Science, and Technology   R-45

Resource Chapter   4
Wellness Activities: Health, Physical Education, and Sensory Motor   R-65

Resource Chapter   5
Creative Arts Activities: Visual Arts, Music, Creative Movement, and Dramatic Play   R-81

Resource Chapter   6
Infant and Toddler Activities: Young Infants, Mobile Infants, and Toddlers   R-97

Preface

The landscape of early childhood is changing and, with it, the fields of early childhood education and early childhood special education. The early childhood years have long been recognized as an important time of physical growth and development. Now they are also viewed as a prime time for cognitive and emotional development. Brain research confirms that the plasticity of the brain holds the potential for risk and resilience. For children with special needs the early years are critical, and the educators who work with these children need to be competent, dedicated, and passionate because they truly make a difference in the lives of children.

This book provides essential information about children with a variety of special needs and their families. It provides information about the disabilities themselves and ways to plan for children in inclusive settings. This text is written as a resource for students and developing professionals. It has something for now and something to come back to later. It is written for the educational system of the twenty-first century in which future teachers need to be prepared to have a child with cerebral palsy and several English language learners included in their class one year and next year a child with attention-deficit/hyperactivity disorder as well as some children who are gifted and talented. They need to be prepared to respond with interventions to children who are not learning in the regular educational program and to help in the diagnostic process of children who may need special education. Educators have to be prepared to do all of this while they teach and enjoy all the children in their class. There are entire books written on specific disabilities and curriculum that have greater depth in each area than this book does. However, this book offers prospective educators a foundation to work from to include children with special needs while they make themselves experts on the particular children in their classroom.

The demands of the field require that future teachers be prepared to plan for and teach children with and without special needs in the same classroom. This book covers many different special needs, but it does not stop there. It takes that information and helps educators apply it to children by providing guidelines and information on planning, adapting, and individualizing curriculum and reflecting on their practice. It helps students move from identifying the annual goals for a child to embedding those goals in the regular classroom routine. It is set up to provide information and then to ask, "So what?" It connects research, development, and practice. As a textbook it may look large, but it is designed to carry preservice teachers through their first years of teaching. It is a reference and a resource.

Organization

Part I: Early Childhood Development and Intervention

This part is designed to frame the field of inclusive early childhood education.

Chapter 1 introduces the field of early childhood education and early childhood special education, as well as the legal and educational basis for intervention with a focus on inclusion. Chapter 2 focuses on the child in the context of his family. It looks at the impact of the child on the family and the family on the child, the changing American family, and ways of working with families. Chapter 3 covers assessment and evaluation and entitlement decisions. Chapter 4 looks at curriculum and standards and how the general curriculum is influenced by state and professional standards and how curriculum and standards are incorporated into an inclusive learning environment. Chapter 5 looks at the process of individualized planning for Individualized Education Programs and Individualized Family Service Plans. Chapters 6 focuses on many of the underlying causes of disabilities, both genetic and environmental.

Part II: Inclusive Early Childhood Education

This part has 13 chapters. Chapter 7 begins by looking at infants and toddlers who are at risk for disabilities and developmental delays. It details information about early brain development and different types of risks. The remaining chapters look at a particular disability or at-risk condition. Chapter 8 focuses on children with specific learning disabilities and includes information on Response to Instruction and Response to Intervention. Chapter 9 provides information on social, emotional, and behavioral disorders, including attachment. Chapter 10 focuses on attention-deficit/hyperactivity disorders. Chapter 11 is on communication disorders including both speech and language disorders. Chapter 12 discusses children who are English language learners, with information on children in immigrant families and some of their particular challenges. Chapter 13 covers children with autism spectrum disorders. Chapters 14 focuses on children who have intellectual disabilities and those who are developmentally delayed, whereas Chapter 15 looks at children who are gifted and talented. Chapter 16 describes children with a variety of special health care needs. The last three chapters focus on sensory impairments: Chapter 17 on children with orthopedic and neurologic impairments, Chapter 18 on hearing impairments, and Chapter 19 on visual impairments.

The goal of these chapters is to take a functional approach to understanding the ability/disability, the potential for impacting the child's behavior, and guidelines for adapting the learning environment. Disability specific information is woven into the fabric of general development while acknowledging that children with disabilities have some needs that are different from their peers. Accommodations that are necessary to allow *some* children to participate are also designed to expand the learning and creative opportunities of *all* children in the class. Disabilities are viewed as part of a continuum of children's abilities.

These chapters follow a pattern that begins with a vignette and reflections to help students move beyond looking at the vignette as an interesting story to reflect on the significance of the vignette. All chapters contain information about abilities/disabilities including the definitions, prevalence rates, and probable causes of specific conditions. The chapters detail various characteristics of the disabilities as well as developmental information pertinent to early identification. They provide guidelines for including these children in the classroom as well as curriculum adaptations. Each chapter concludes with a summary, reflections, and additional educational resources for further investigation.

Part III: Resources and Practice for Inclusive Early Childhood Education

This part contains six Resource chapters focusing on information and activities to support social awareness, language and literacy, discovery, wellness, and the creative arts. The final chapter in this part addresses activities for infants and toddlers. Continuations of these chapters on the book companion website provide additional information and resources. Each chapter contains activities that focus on a particular curriculum area and include information on assessment and accommodations. The chapter on infants and toddlers is indexed by both curriculum areas and age.

The book ends with a Children's Bibliography that topically annotates books for children that relate to the understanding of special needs or related areas such as fears, death and dying, or family disruption. Age ranges are given for each book. Additional books and resources are listed on the book companion website. This is followed by an extensive glossary. The book concludes with the references followed by a combined author and subject index.

Features

The book has a variety of features that are designed to make the field come alive to preservice teachers and also to help translate research to practice. Each chapter starts with a vignette that is designed to set the tone for a chapter or provide a perspective for viewing the field. Other features that appear in every chapter include the following:

In the Field

This feature helps the text come alive with real stories from real families and dilemmas and solutions that real educators teaching real children have faced and coped with. Although I edited these, each was written or told by practicing educators, parents, administrators, or children. They offer developing educators real world scenarios, ethical and moral dilemmas upon which to reflect, and the opportunity to imagine these issues before they are faced with them.

Reflective Practice

The goal of reflective practice is to educate reflective practitioners who learn from their own practice and the practice of others. It is designed to make the book more interactive and help students think about the implications of decisions and decision makers. It helps them go beyond what was written to look at the implications of information in the context of their own teaching and where the field is.

Implications for Educators

This section is designed to help students apply the information they are learning. It helps students move from looking at a description of a particular special need to looking at the implications of having a child with that particular disability in their classroom. It is designed to help students use information and to analyze it in the context of their own practice.

The Evidence Base

Increasingly educators are using research to decide how to teach children. Research-based practice is best practice. However, learning how to evaluate and use this evidence in the classroom is challenging. Research does not always reach firm conclusions and the results are sometimes in conflict. This section presents research and research synopses as a way of educating preservice teachers about the evidence base that forms the foundation of their teaching practice.

Reflections

At the end of each chapter there are short, focused dilemmas that students can reflect on. These are designed to help students integrate information and to use the material in the chapter as a teaching tool. To become good educators, students need to reflect on their practice and what they are doing that works and does not work. They need to move from learning information to utilizing it in their practice.

Guidelines and Curriculum Adaptations

Each chapter that has a disability/ability focus has a section on guidelines that help students think about the general principles they will use to adapt their teaching style and techniques to include children with a particular special need. Curriculum adaptations looks at each curriculum area and discusses how a particular area can be used to strengthen the child's skills, or how it may need to be modified. This helps students apply the information they are learning by helping them to think more inclusively and to understand that most children can be included with adaptations.

Educational Resources

The text provides educational resources, primarily Internet-based, to help students extend their learning about particular disabilities, issues, and the supports that are available. Students are learning a lifelong skill in updating and extending their knowledge and going beyond the information provided in the text.

Activities

The text has over 300 activities to enhance students' knowledge of what and how to plan for inclusive classrooms. Of these activities, 180 are in the text and the additional 115 activities are on the book companion website. Some of the activities are designed to hone skills for children who need extra practice in an area. Others are designed to increase the awareness of the class of what it might be like to have a particular ability/disability.

Ancillaries

Instructor's Manual

Instructors will find that this manual provides them with a turnkey solution to help them teach. It includes the following information for each chapter. It begins with a chapter overview and learning objectives. A lecture outline is provided as well as discussion topics that are designed to pose dilemmas to students and encourage them to think about what they have read. There are a variety of suggested teaching strategies including many that employ problem-based learning. Possible assignments have been provided as well as Internet exercises (also available on the website) that are designed to help students use information as well as developing the skills to keep current in a dynamic field. Audiovisual materials that support each chapter have been annotated as well as sources where these can be obtained if your college or university does not currently have them. Recommended reading shares some of the most important and relevant sources that the author used to write the book. Additional or expanded websites beyond those identified in the text are also annotated. A test bank that contains multiple choice and true/false, as well as essay questions with scoring rubrics complete the package.

Book Companion Website

A book companion website at http://www.cengage.com/education/deiner, includes resources for both students and instructors. The instructor area of the book companion website at http://www.cengage.com/education/deiner offers access to password-protected resources such as an electronic version of the instructor's manual and PowerPoint® slides. The student resources include a variety of study tools and useful resources such as chapter overviews and objectives, downloadable resource chapter activities from the text along with additional resource activities, an extended children's bibliography, and more. Reflection questions are designed to help students reflect on the material and be prepared for class. Internet exercises are included to help students expand their information base and hone the skills necessary to keep current in such an active field. Additional or expanded websites beyond those identified in the text are also annotated. Tutorial quizzes include sample multiple choice and true/false questions, none that are the same as in the Instructors Manual.

Summary of Overall General Changes From The Fourth Edition

This book is the fifth edition of *Inclusive Early Childhood Education: Development, Resources, Practice*. The title of the fourth edition was *Resources for Educating Children with Diverse Abilities: Birth through Eight*. The first edition was published in 1983, the second in 1993, the third in 1999, and the fourth in 2005. The major changes in the texts are reflections of changes in our knowledge base, changes in the population identified as having special needs, changes in the legislation that underlies early childhood education, and changes in best practice in the field. The general changes include:

- Updated information on the disabilities themselves and their etiologies.

- A greater emphasis on culture, ethnicity, and language. This includes a chapter that was added on English Language Learners.

- Pairing all vignettes with some guidance on reflective practice. Adding more *In the Fields*, written by teachers, administrators, parents, and even children to look at issues from different points of view.

- New photographs that better reflect the diversity seen in today's classrooms.

- *Implications for Educators* has been expanded to ensure that students synthesize material. These sections are designed to answer the "so what" question; that is, how does this specifically apply to the classroom situation? It connects evidence to practice.

- A new section, *The Evidence Base,* has been added to all chapters to help students understand the role of research and how one uses evidence to inform practice. There is a strong evidence base for all material presented.

- Changes dictated by the passage of the Individuals with Disabilities Education Improvement Act of 2004 and the No Child Left Behind Act of 2001 have been incorporated.

- The book itself has been pared down from 21 to 19 chapters through combining and revising chapters.

Summary of Specific Changes

Part I: Early Childhood Development and Intervention

Chapter 1, Including All Children in a Dynamic Educational System, combines old Chapters 1 and 2 to more clearly focus on disability-related issues, the laws, and inclusion; information about the text has been moved to the Preface.

Chapter 2, Partnering with Families, consists of old Chapter 6, Children and Their Families and Chapter 7, Partnering with Families, which were combined and revised to focus more on families of children at risk and to include more information on diversity in families, including families with different structural configurations and those who face special challenges, immigrant families, and parents who have disabilities. These two chapters are now the second chapter in the book.

Chapter 3, Assessment and Evaluation, has a section added on: Response to Instruction.

Chapter 4, Curriculum and Standards in Inclusive Settings, is a combination of old Chapter 5, Program Planning in Inclusive Settings, and Chapter 21, Standards for Inclusion. Because of the dependence of Individualized Educational Programs on standards, this chapter now comes before Individualizing Planning.

Chapter 5, Individualized Planning, was updated based on 2004 amendments to the IDEA and its requirements. The new IEP form that was developed as a model has been added.

Chapter 6, Atypical Development: The Beginning, was refocused and pared down to just include the essentials that students need to understand the causes of specific disabilities and chronic illnesses.

Part II: Inclusive Early Childhood Education

All of the chapters in Part II have been updated to reflect what has been learned since the fourth edition.

Chapter 7, Infants and Toddlers at Risk, includes more information on early brain development as well as developmental risk. It includes more specific information on curriculum planning for infants and toddlers.

Chapter 8, Children with Specific Learning Disabilities, provides more information on specific aspects of learning disabilities including dyslexia. It also has information on Response to Intervention.

Chapter 9, Children with Social, Emotional, and Behavioral Disorders, has additional information on attachment and attachment disorders and the title has been changed from Children with Emotional and Behavioral Differences. It has been placed before the chapter on ADHD because of the high level of comorbidity with these disorders.

Chapter 10, Children with Attention-Deficit/Hyperactivity Disorder, provides additional information on medications, how they are used, and how they work and the title has been changed from Children with Attention Disorders.

Chapter 11, Children with Communication Disorders, provides more information on language disorders and the title has been changed from Children with Communication Differences.

Chapter 12, Children who are English Language Learners, is a new chapter that looks at children who come to school whose home language is not English. It looks at immigrant families and some of the dilemmas they face as well as some of the controversies on how to teach English language learners.

Chapter 13, Children with Autism Spectrum Disorders, provides more information on the research that looks into the causes of autism and why the number of children with autism is increasing. The title has been changed from Children with Pervasive Developmental Disorders.

Chapter 14, Children with Intellectual Disabilities and Developmental Delays, provides more information on how to work with children who come from families who do not provide stimulating environments and what early intervention can do to help. The title has been changed from Children with Developmental Delays and Mental Retardation.

Chapter 15, Children Who Are Gifted and Talented, continues to highlight this underserved population and new strategies to serve this population are presented.

Chapter 16, Children with Special Health Care Needs, has been expanded to include children with Tourette's syndrome and the section on obesity and overweight has been expanded. The title has been changed from Children with Health Challenges.

Chapter 17, Children with Orthopedic and Neurologic Impairments, has an expanded section on traumatic brain injury, as the number of young children with TBI is increasing.

Chapter 18, Children with Hearing Impairments, has an expanded section on cochlear implants.

Chapter 19, Children with Visual Impairments, has additional information on new lenses.

PART III, Resources and Practice for Inclusive Early Childhood Education has been divided into book- and web-based activities and the format has been changed so that accommodations and integration have been combined. The Children's Bibliography also has been updated, expanded, and the older books have been placed on the book companion website.

Using the Text

The text is designed to be used flexibly to fit professor and student needs. Although complementary, each part of the book is independent, as are the chapters. Course sequences, the availability of practicum settings, different service delivery systems, or instructor preference may influence the order in which the chapters are read.

The activities and resource materials provided in the book are just that, resources for current and future use. As such, they will be useful in both preservice and in-service education and with all educators and specialists in early childhood education and early childhood special education, and they can be shared with families. They can be referred to, used, and modified throughout one's career. Above all, this text is meant to be used. Five years from now, I hope this book is highlighted, dog-eared, and has handwritten comments in the very small margins noting where you have updated information that has changed, and noting activities that succeeded as well as revisions for those that flopped.

Acknowledgments

No author writes a text without academic and emotional support. I received support from the Human Development and Family Studies faculty, staff, graduate and undergraduate students, and my family and friends. Although each one's contribution is different, each influenced the final product.

Let me begin by thanking my colleagues in the Department of Human Development and Family Studies. Michael Gamel-McCormick is a thoughtful, sharing scholar whose expertise is particularly valued. His insights and practical ideas made a major contribution to my thinking and the content of the book. I also wish to thank Martha Buell, whose passion for quality programming for children, expertise in curriculum, and knowledge of infants and toddlers also played a major role in shaping my ideas.

I also want to acknowledge Bahira Sherif Trask who commiserated with me as only a fellow author can. She also shared and helped focus my concerns about families who are at risk in today's society and Chris Ohannessian for her interest and support. I particularly want to thank Gretchen Taylor, who can make almost everything work and do so with a sense of humor, and if it doesn't work she decides what we should sew to get our minds off the problem.

The University of Delaware Laboratory Preschool and the Early Learning Center, directed by Peg Bradley, was an invaluable resource, especially master teachers, Nancy Edwards, Tara Sutton, Laura Morris, and the support staff. In addition, Tara Sutton wrote some of the activities for the resource chapters. These teachers are inspirational as well as flexible and supportive.

I am grateful for the resources of the University of Delaware library and the reference librarians who are a source of knowledge and wisdom, particularly Rebecca Knight who continues to teach me more about tracking down references than I ever wanted to know.

Teachers taking graduate courses played a particularly important part in the revisions of this text. They contributed to the *In the Field* sections and also shared their knowledge and practical suggestions. Teachers include Tina Albanese, Cara Cuccuini-Harmon, Michelle Eichinger, Mary Gerni, Faye Gillespie, Lisa Hunt, Jennifer Janowski, Kristin Jones, Verna Milner, Melissa Neeson, Katherine Ossolinski, Emily Pettyjohn, Jessica Phillips, and Kimberly Wagner. Linda Maxwell, one of the teachers, was a marvelous source for information and practical suggestions on autism and Asperger's syndrome. Joanne Gischner continues to help me stay based in the real world of teachers and what they do on a day-to-day basis.

I would also like to extend my thanks to Donna Rafanello, Long Beach City College, Gail Laubscher Summer, Lenoir-Rhyne College, Davia Massey, Western Carolina University, Marie Brand, Suny Empire State College, Gwendolyn M. Parsons, Hillsborough Community College, Lindsey Russo, Columbia University, Sharon Hirschy, Collin College, Sylvia J. Brooks, University of Delaware, Susan S. Johnston, University of Utah, Linda Rivers, University of Tennessee at Chattanooga, Jennifer M. Johnson, University of North Carolina, Charlotte, Kristine L. Slentz, Western Washington University, Melanie J. McGill,

Stephen F. Austin State University, Jennifer E. Berke, Mercyhurst North East, and Donna Satterlee, University of Maryland Eastern Shore, for their very helpful reviews and comments.

The graduate students in Individual and Family Studies served as a constant support and played an important role in making this book possible. Kim Madey helped with the PowerPoints and the student manual, and she even enlisted her daughter Marlyn to help. Elizabeth Chambers wrote several *In the Field* sections and some of the examination questions, as well as the rubrics to grade the essays. Wei Qiu provided computer expertise and wrote vignettes in addition to increasing my cultural awareness. Working with her also increased my knowledge of online resources and how to use them effectively.

Friends play an exceedingly important role in the process. It will take me years to repay the dinners that we owe Jack and Ginger Henriksen because I was too busy writing to cook. Peggy and David Beers, Gretchen and Glenn Taylor, Ron and Donna Coffin and Bill and Sharon Crist provided support and encouragement when the going was tough.

My deepest gratitude goes to my husband John whose unwavering emotional, moral, and practical support has helped bring this book to fruition. Our youngest daughter Paige was 3 years old when the first edition of this book was published. In this edition she wrote some *In the Fields* and tried to help me keep my writing style current. And, although she has asked me on numerous occasions not to write any more books, she is now a journalist herself. Our two older children both live in California. Jamie is a speech/language pathologist and Michael works at the University of California medical center in San Francisco. Perhaps families influence their children in more ways than we think.

The production of a book such as this one is a long and complicated process. I want to acknowledge the support of Erin O'Connor who had faith that continued editions of my books were a valuable contribution to the literature. I want to thank Philip Mandl who was the initial developmental editor for this book and helped me work through many of the changes that became part of the book. As the book progressed it moved from Cengage's New York office to California and the Wadsworth imprint. Caitlin Cox adroitly managed this challenge and supported many innovative ideas to make the book shorter without losing important aspects of the resources. Ashley Cronin supported the book companion website and provided ideas to make it more relevant. Sara Dovre Wudali at Buuji helped me wade through the final details of publication. Samen Iqbal coordinated and managed the various departmental efforts that went into production of this edition.

Finally, I owe a great deal to children, my own children and their children, their peers, and the children and grandchildren of friends whom I have observed, as well as the children I taught who in reality taught me—not so much the easy ones, but the ones who challenged me.

PART

I

Early Childhood Development and Intervention

Part I provides information about early childhood education, early childhood special education, and the experiences and laws that serve as the foundation for individualized planning. It also looks at the importance of family-centered planning and partnering with families. It provides information on assessment and evaluation and the issues involved in accurately measuring what children know.

Part I also provides information about curriculum and the national standards for fields such as mathematics, technology, and music set by professional organizations. It concludes with a chapter on early development including the development of the brain.

Chapter 1

Including All Children in a Dynamic Educational System

After a struggle, another round of being the "squeaky wheel," we persuaded the principal and staff to let our son attend a traditional first grade class for part of the day—about 2 hours every afternoon. The rest of the day he remained in a segregated classroom shared by other students with orthopedic disabilities—primarily those who used wheelchairs and were for the most part nonverbal. We believed inclusion was important for Don, but also for the "typical" children—we felt acceptance of differences should start early in life and we wanted to act on our beliefs—but we were weary from the fight. . . . Don was reluctantly allowed to attend this class; however, no other child with a disability was invited even though other children were more "able" than he.

Don loved the inclusive class. At 7 he was still learning to drive a power wheelchair, and the paraeducator said that he tried to drive by the segregated classroom to get to the inclusive setting. We knew it was working for Don.

One day I came to pick Don up early for an appointment. As I walked up the hallway, a line of first graders waited to go to the cafeteria. A few of Don's classmates in the segregated classroom silently rolled by the line of chattering children. I met Don in the office and began to go with him down the hallway to the outside door. As we neared the line of kids. I prepared myself for the usual stares or pointing fingers. Instead, I heard "Look, there's Don!" "Hi Don." "See you tomorrow, Don." "Will you be back tomorrow, Don?" I couldn't believe it! Those warm greetings meant more to me than any straight A report card could have. Don smiled and so did I—through lots of happy tears on the way home. I still cry when I think about it. I felt there may be hope for inclusion.

Don attends a "typical school" now. He's just one of the gang—the kids in the school have accepted his presence as normal and he has many friends there. However, one of the staff tells me that Don still gets those stares from one group of kids. They have a program at Don's school where gifted kids come once a week for enrichment. These kids have never had the opportunity of getting to know a fellow classmate who happens to use a wheelchair. So, they still stare. . . . Will they ever get to know Don from the inside out or only the outside in? It's their loss, our loss, and society's loss. Inclusion really works.

Reflective Practice

Reflect on the value of inclusion for all children and what your role is in making inclusion work. Reflect on who you think should be included and the skills you have to make it happen.

Inclusion supports the right of all children to actively participate in natural settings, that is, the settings where they would spend their time if they did not have a disability. This position was adopted in 1993 and reaffirmed in 1996 by the Division for Early Childhood (DEC) of the Council for Exceptional Children (CEC) (DEC, 1996). However, inclusion was not always seen as best practice.

Historical Roots

To understand the challenges educators face today, it is necessary to look at how the field itself has changed and grown over time, as well as how related fields have contributed to our understanding of inclusive education.

We can also use this knowledge to learn from the past and grasp great themes. Although the history of inclusive education is relatively short, there is a long, interesting history of beliefs and decisions about children with disabilities and how they should be educated.

In the mid-1800s, little was known about disabilities or their causes. Disabilities were frequently blamed on "sinful living." People thought you could inherit lifestyle characteristics from your parents as well as genetic information (height, sex, etc.). It was commonly assumed that all disabilities were passed down through generations and that the only way to stop society from being overwhelmed with these individuals was to **sterilize** adults to stop reproduction (Berkson, 1993). This practice began in the United States in the early 1900s and continued in some states until about 1980.

Mild disabilities were not identified until the turn of the century when the work of Alfred Binet (1857–1911) allowed the identification of disabilities that impacted school performance (Berkson, 1993). He showed that the scores of children classified as mentally retarded were similar to those of younger "normal" children.

Although there have always been children with disabilities, there have not always been educational services to address their needs. The originators of special education were young, ambitious European physicians. Jean Marc Gaspard Itard (1775–1838), a French physician, is credited by some as the founder of special education based on the principles that he used to educate Victor. Victor, a boy of about 12, had been found wandering alone in the forest of Aveyron and was considered a "wild boy" or hopeless idiot. Itard did not cure Victor, but he made significant changes in Victor's behavior using a set of principles including individualized instruction, stimulation, sequenced learning tasks, a structured environment, immediate reward for correct performance, and focus on functional skills. He believed that all children could learn and, therefore, they should be educated (Safford & Safford, 1996).

Itard's protégé, Edouard Seguin (1812–1880), was also a pioneer in the field and one of the first early interventionists (Meisels & Shonkoff, 2000). He gave children detailed assessments and developed specific sensory motor activities to improve their deficits. He believed in the importance of the early years of development (Safford & Safford, 1996). Maria Montessori (1870–1951) studied Seguin's methods and adapted them. She insisted that mental retardation was an educational problem, not a medical one. Her methods were supported in the United States by Alexander and Mabel Bell (Winzer, 1993).

Elizabeth Farrell, a teacher in New York City, attempted to modify educational practices to address the needs of children and youth with disabilities. She believed that although all children can learn, some needed different educational experiences. In 1922, Farrell and special educators from the United States and Canada founded the Council for Exceptional Children (CEC), which exists today. They had a vision for serving children whose needs were not being met within the regular educational system.

Within the public school system, the first special education schools and classes were established in the early 1900s for children who were identified as "educable mentally retarded." Most of these programs were in separate schools: some private, some public. Specialists taught children with sensory impairments in residential schools. These children went to school as early as age 3 and came home only for weekends, holidays, or the summer unless the family lived near such a school (Gearheart, Mullen, & Gearheart, 1993).

During the late 1920s, classes for children with physical impairments were added to the public school system. As other disabilities were recognized in the 1950s, it became clearer that these children needed *different* educational approaches. Special education as a field has focused on "difference," and what is exceptional rather than what is the same.

Special education also traditionally focused on school-age children. It was further broken down into separate subfields such as mental retardation, learning disabilities, behavioral disorders, sensory impairments, and so on. These subfields focused on specially designed instruction to meet the unique and unusual needs of a particular group of children (Salvia & Ysseldyke, 2007). The traditional special education curriculum centered on teaching children with disabilities specific adaptive skills with teachers providing instruction one-on-one or in small groups.

After World War II, about 1945, several factors, both ideological and legal, led to a movement toward normalization in the lives of individuals with disabilities. These factors came together in the social activism of the 1960s.

Moving Toward Normalization

Normalization is an approach that ensures that children who require special services are not separated from experiences of normal life; that is, educational, social, and recreational environments are as close as possible to what they would be if children were developing typically. These are called natural settings or **natural environments**.

Schools not only impart academic information, they also impart social values. To the extent that children are segregated from regular schools and classrooms, whether because of physical impairment or skin color, they are seen as deficient. Beginning in the 1950s, the courts defended education as the *right* of every child regardless of race or disability.

Societal attitudes slowly began to change in the 1960s and the first definition of developmental disabilities was written during that time. There was a growing interest by early childhood educators in the concept of early developmental programming. Head Start was signed into U.S. law by President Johnson as part of the "War on Poverty." It began as an 8-week summer program to help low-income children catch up with their higher-income peers. It publicly acknowledged the nation's concern about the needs of young children from low-income homes, the value of early childhood education, and the concept that education begins before public school age.

Head Start was viewed as compensatory education, that is, it acknowledged the possibility that educational programs could make up for inadequate early life experiences. Head Start was community-based and was concerned not only with education but also nutrition and health. Parents were involved as planners, teachers, and decision makers. Education was being offered to children who were "disadvantaged." Parents of children with disabilities began to ask if their children, too, could profit from early education. The request of the parents of children with disabilities reflected their belief in normalization for their children.

A very different influence was also changing social attitudes and creating a demand for a solution. In the 1960s and 1970s, the cost of education had outstripped the funds available to pay for it. Constructing and maintaining separate buildings to provide programs for those with disabilities multiplied costs to parents and taxpayers. Elimination of institutions and special schools would bring tremendous savings. Further savings would be possible if, through early identification and appropriate curriculum, children with disabilities could attend regular classes and become contributing members of society.

People began to believe that individuals with disabilities were being deprived of their constitutional and human rights. In 1967, state institutions were homes for almost 200,000 persons with significant disabilities. Many of these restrictive settings provided only minimal food, clothing, and shelter (U.S. Department of Education, 2007).

The interest in normalization emerged concurrently with the increasingly high costs of institutional care, and the growing awareness of abuse and neglect in large institutions, as exposed in public scandals. Programs were and continue to be designed to reduce the rates and duration of seclusion and restraint in particular. These practices have resulted in death and posttraumatic stress disorders (Jovanovic & Johnsen, 2006). Increasingly, individuals with disabilities and their human rights became an issue.

In the Field

Allan's parents left him on the steps of an institution for persons with mental retardation in the late 1940s. By age 35, he had become blind and was frequently observed sitting in a corner of the room, slapping his heavily callused face as he rocked back and forth humming to himself.

In the late 1970s, Allan was assessed properly for the first time. To the dismay of his examiners, they discovered he was of average intelligence; further review of his records revealed that by observing fellow residents of the institution, he had learned self-injurious behavior that caused his total loss of vision. Although the institution then began a special program to teach Allan to be more independent, a major portion of his life and his vision was lost because of a lack of appropriate assessments and effective interventions (U.S. Department of Education, 2007).

Reflective Practice

Unfortunately, Allan's history was repeated in the life experiences of tens of thousands of individuals with disabilities. What does Allan's story teach you about inclusive education? How does Allan's story help you understand why inclusive education makes a difference?

Although parents viewed special education more positively than institutionalization, many still felt that there were problems with the system. Parents felt powerless in the face of school administrators who refused to allow some children with disabilities to attend public schools. Some progress was made by advocacy groups such as the Children's Defense Fund, who made their position clear about the almost 2 million children who were not being served by the public school system.

> [I]f a child is not white, or is white but not middle class, does not speak English, is poor, needs special help with seeing, hearing, walking, reading, learning, adjusting, growing up, is pregnant or married at age 15, is not smart enough or is too smart, then, in many places, school officials decide school is not the place for that child. In sum, out of school children share a common characteristic of *differentness* by virtue of race, income, physical, mental, or emotional "handicap," or age. They are, for the most part, out of school not by choice, but because they have been *excluded* (Children's Defense Fund, 1975, p. 4).

Legislative Basis for Integration

Integrating children with disabilities has followed two paths—one in the area of civil rights, the other in education. It also has three distinct eras. However, before going into these, a brief review of how laws are made and interpreted is provided.

A law passed by Congress is referred to as a Public Law (P.L.), which is followed by two sets of numbers. The first set of numbers is the Congress that passed the law; the 94th Congress passed P.L. 94-142. The second number refers to the sequential position in the laws which that particular Congress passed, in this case the 142nd law. Federal laws are often changed or amended. P.L. 94-142 was amended in 2004. These amendments change the law. Professionals in the field know the names or numbers of significant laws. When a law is passed, its meaning may not be clear. Within about 18 months of passing the law, **regulation**s are developed to make the meaning of the law clearer. These are detailed in the Code of Federal Regulation (CFR). Individual states may go beyond what is required in the regulations; however, all states have to meet the minimum requirements of the federal law.

Special Education: 1950–1970

The history of segregation because of race or disability is inextricably intertwined. The 1954 case of *Brown v. Board of Education of Topeka, Kansas*, which focused on the civil rights of black Americans, had little to do with disabilities but much to do with segregation in education. Separate education was declared not equal. Whether the separation was based on race or disability, the principle is the same:

> Separate educational facilities are inherently unequal. This inherent inequality stems from the stigma created by purposeful segregation which generates a feeling of inferiority that may affect their hearts and minds in a way unlikely ever to be undone. (*Brown v. Board of Education*, 1954)

Tinker v. Des Moines Independent Community School District (1969) furthered civil rights for students. This case focused on whether students had the right to wear black armbands to protest the involvement of the United States in the Vietnam War. The students wearing arm bands were quiet, passive, nondisruptive, and did not impinge upon the rights of others. The court ruling was interesting. It declared that children are *persons* under the Constitution of the United States and that they have civil rights independent of their parents, and further that they do not lose these civil rights when they attend school. This case set the stage for cases that used the violation of the First (right to free speech) and Fourteenth Amendments (right to **due process**) as their grounds for bringing suit.

As parents of children with disabilities became increasingly dissatisfied, they sought legal remedies to make the educational system more responsive to their children's needs. Encouraged by an increasingly receptive public and strengthened by better organization and cooperation among parent and professional groups, parents began to press their cause in court and in Congress.

The Handicapped Children's Early Education Program (HCEEP) of 1968, Public Law 90-538 was passed with a **mandate** to set up model demonstration projects. This was an official acknowledgment that the early childhood years were important and that educators did not know what system or techniques would be effective with young children. This legislation was designed to find effective programs and techniques that could be replicated throughout the country.

Special Education: 1970–1985

The Economic Opportunities Amendments of 1972, Public Law 92-424, mandated that 10 percent of the enrollment of Head Start must be children with disabilities. The move to educate *all* children without discrimination was supported by the Rehabilitation Act of 1973. Section 504 of that act focused on nondiscrimination in programs or activities receiving federal funding, this includes public schools and Head Start. The definitions used in Section 504 are far broader than those used in educational laws. This definition of a **disability** is "Any person who (i) has a physical or mental impairment which substantially limits one or more of such person's major life activities, (ii) has a record of such an impairment, or (iii) is regarded as having such an impairment." (Major life activities include self-care, performing manual tasks, seeing, hearing, speaking, breathing, learning, and walking.) The regulations governing Section 504 stipulate that

> No otherwise qualified handicapped individual . . . shall, solely by reason of his (or her) handicap, be excluded from the participation in, be denied the benefits of, or be subject to discrimination under any program or activity receiving federal financial assistance. (C.F.R. 104; P.L. 93-112)

The *Family Educational Rights and Privacy Act of 1974, P.L. 93-380,* often called the Buckley Amendment, gives parents of students younger than 18 and students 18 and older the right to examine records kept in the student's personal file and to have these explained. If found to be misleading or inaccurate, parents or students can request the records be amended by the school system. Written permission from parents is required for records to be released unless it is to other school officials (such as when students transfer).

Public Law 94-142, the Education for All Handicapped Children Act of 1975 (EHA), is the first in a series of laws focusing on the rights of children with disabilities to a free appropriate public education. The intent of this legislation has been to require schools to meet the needs of individual

students with disabilities. Legislation in this area has moved increasingly to mandate or require states to provide educational services for younger children. Failure to comply with such a mandate can result in the loss of federal funding in other programs. Legislation also supported the concept of **least restrictive environment** (LRE), meaning that children should be educated in the same setting (or as close to the same setting as possible) they would have been educated in if they did not have a disability.

Understanding the relationship between Section 504 of the Rehabilitation Act of 1973 and P. L. 94-142, the Education of All Handicapped Children Act (EHA) of 1975 is important. All children who are eligible for services under P.L. 94-142 are also covered by Section 504. However, Section 504 includes disabilities that may not interfere with learning. For example, a child who has asthma may not have a learning problem; however, he may need accommodations in physical education. Likewise, a child who tests HIV positive may have no symptoms that interfere with learning, but may need some accommodations to stay in school. Section 504 includes these children and requires that accommodations be made for them. If at some point their disability does interfere with their ability to learn, they will also be covered under P.L. 94-142.

In the Field

Mary Lee was born with spina bifida. Her parents use **intermittent catheterization** to empty her bladder because she cannot control it. As a 5 year old this was the only accommodation she needed to stay in school all day (Section 504). However, during second grade she was identified as having a learning disability. She now receives services under P.L. 94-142.

Reflective Practice

Professionals in the field use shorthand to refer to Section 504 of the Rehabilitation Act of 1973 (section 504) and P.L. 94-142, the Education of All Handicapped Children Act (EHA) of 1975 (P.L. 94-142). They might say "She is covered under section 504, but not 94-142." They will expect that you will know what this means and that she needs some accommodations to be included in the class, but that her disability does not affect her ability to learn. Reflect on what this means for you to be a professional in the field.

The passage of P.L. 94-142 in 1975 had a tremendous effect on the education of school-age children with disabilities. It had much less effect on the education of younger children with disabilities. Although children ages 3 to 5 *could* be included, that was not part of the original mandate. Educators had their hands full, and little energy was left over for concerns about younger children.

Special Education: 1985 and Beyond

By the mid-1980s, the evidence base supporting the efficacy of early intervention for children birth through age 5 was there, but there were no state-level systems of services. The need for greater interagency coordination was apparent, as was the push to serve all eligible young children (Hebbeler, Smith, & Black, 1991).

When the EHA was reauthorized in 1986, P.L. 99-457, it lowered the age of eligibility for mandated services to 36 months, increased funding for preschool children (part B), and the Infants and Toddlers Program for children from birth to 3 (part H) was established. The Infants and Toddlers Program was **discretionary** and states were allowed to develop their own definitions of "developmentally delayed" and each state could decide whether or not they would serve infants and toddlers "at risk."

The federal government also acknowledged the importance of technology when they passed the Technology-Related Assistance for Individuals with Disabilities Act in 1988 (P.L. 100-407), commonly known as the Tech Act. This act was designed to explore the potential of technology to meet the needs of individuals with disabilities including young children and the elderly. Increasingly, the field has become dependent on assistive devices to enable children with disabilities to function in regular settings.

In 1990, the Education for All Handicapped Children Act (EHA) was reauthorized and renamed the Individuals with Disabilities Education Act (IDEA). Like other laws, the Handicapped Children's Early Education Program (HCEEP) was renamed the Early Education Program for Children with Disabilities (EEPCD) in 1990.

The Americans with Disabilities Act (ADA) of 1990 extended civil rights protection and nondiscrimination requirements of Section 504 to *all* settings, not just those that receive federal funds. This opened all early care and education settings and private schools to children with disabilities. It also provides the basis for the inclusion of children and adults with disabilities in the community.

The reauthorization of the IDEA (P.L. 105-17), referred to as the 1997 amendments, provided major modifications for children in the areas of behavioral intervention, transition, assessment, the IEP, and classroom implementation strategies. The 1997 amendments also strengthened the role of the parents in the educational process and made the federal government's position on Least Restrictive Environment clearer. The reauthorization emphasized placing young children with disabilities in natural environments, such as their own homes, early care and education settings, and regular public school classrooms.

The No Child Left Behind Act (NCLB), P.L. 107-110, was signed into law on January 8, 2002. NCLB is a federal law affecting education from kindergarten through high school. NCLB is built on four principles: expanded local control and flexibility; doing what works based on scientific research; accountability for results; and more options for parents. The main goal of NCLB is to help all students reach proficiency in English language arts/reading and mathematics. Some of the tenants of NCBL impacted the reauthorization of the IDEA.

The IDEA was reauthorized again on December 3, 2004: P.L. 108-446. The final regulations for this reauthorization were published in the Federal Register on August 14, 2006. Between when the law was passed in 2004 and when the regulations were set more than 5,500 individuals and/or organizations submitted comments on how the law should be interpreted (Walsh, 2006). This reauthorization eliminated the need to use benchmarks or objectives in the Individualized Education Program (IEP) for many school-age children. Following in the footsteps of NCLB, teachers are required to be "highly qualified" in the subject areas they are teaching. As special education teachers frequently teach multiple core subjects, many saw this as a particular challenge. However, new special education teachers now have to have an academic major, advanced degree, or pass a competency exam in each subject area they teach (Mandlawitz, 2007). Another provision of reauthorization was the concept of *universal design*. The underlying concept of universal design is that products and services should be designed to be used by individuals with the widest possible range of functional capacities (Mandlawitz, 2007).

One of the major philosophical changes in the 2004 amendments is the move into the area of the possible prevention of disabilities. Early intervening services (EIS) allows school districts to spend 15 percent of the federal money they receive for children in kindergarten through grade 12, with a special emphasis on children in kindergarten through grade 3 who have not been identified as having special education needs, but who do need additional academic and behavioral interventions to succeed in the general curriculum (IDEA, 2004). EIS are about identifying children who are struggling in areas such as math and reading and intervening to provide support quickly. The use of EIS is also a way of focusing on *disproportion*. Disproportion looks at the relationship between the racial and ethnic backgrounds of the children in the school and those who are identified for special education services. Concern arises when children from some racial or ethnic groups are overrepresented in the special education population. EIS is designed to support these children early and hopefully prevent their identification as children needing special education services.

One aspect of early intervening services is response to intervention (RTI). Response to scientifically, research-based intervention only applies to children who are suspected of having specific learning disabilities. Although many feel that all good educational practices should have a strong research base and this is supported by NCLB. RTI clearly focuses on the quality of the research that is used to support educational practices. RTI is discussed in detail in Chapter 8.

The Evidence Base

Evidence is an elusive quality yet it is designed to be the basis for making decisions about how children learn. *The Center for Evidence-Based Practice: Young Children with Challenging Behavior* (Smith & Fox, 2003) has identified four different types of empirical evidence:

Type 1. *Empirical evidence (qualitative or quantitative research)* published in peer-reviewed journals that has found positive outcomes for children or reviews of empirical evidence from peer-reviewed journals that cite the original studies.

Type 2. *Evaluation reports* done by an outside source that provides data analysis that show positive outcomes for children.

Type 3. *Evaluation reports* analyzed by the system or program developer that provides evidence of positive outcome for children.

Type 4. *Survey or descriptive research* published in peer-reviewed journals that summarizes impressions of outcomes.

The center further identifies two types of consensus documents:

> **Type 5.** *Multi-authored consensus documents* that indicate evidence for the use of some practice but data to support the practice is not provided.
>
> **Type 6.** *Descriptions of system features* that are designed to provide positive outcome but evaluation data is not provided. (Smith & Fox, 2003).

Reflective Practice

As you look at the requirements for types of evidence reflect on how they are different. What is the focus of the differences? Would you feel more comfortable using Type 1 through Type 4 evidence or do you think Type 5 and 6 are equally useful? Why do you think we have different types of evidence? Do you think it is easier to have Type 1 through Type 4 evidence in medicine than education?

The IDEA has a wide-ranging impact and contains specific terminology. Detailed information about the IDEA and its requirements and implications is given in Chapter 5. Table 1–1 provides a chronological summary of the laws that relate to the education of children with disabilities.

Legislation and Litigation

The relationship between legislation and litigation is an interesting one. Litigation provides the impetus for new laws or clarifies and determines the limits or interpretation of existing laws. *Pennsylvania Association of Retarded Children v. Commonwealth of Pennsylvania* (1971), a class action suit on behalf of the parents of thirteen children, argued that the denial of a free public education for children with mental retardation was a violation of the Fourteenth Amendment of the Constitution of the United States (the right to due process). Education for *some* had to be education for *all*. In a settlement approved by the court, Pennsylvania agreed to provide education to all school-age children with mental retardation living in the state (including those in state institutions) within one year. A parallel decision, *Peter Mills v. Board of Education of the District of Columbia* (1972), added the stipulation that lack of funds was not an acceptable reason for excluding children.

Other decisions concerned children who had been misplaced by the system. In *Diana v. State Board of Education of Monterey County, CA* (1970), the court ruled that children must be tested in their primary language. Previously, children whose primary language was not English had been tested in English and sometimes declared mentally retarded. This type of litigation provided the impetus for the passage of P.L. 94-142 in 1975.

Once P.L. 94-142 was passed, litigation determined the minimum level of services that must be provided under the law. The *Board of Education of the Hendrick Hudson Central School District v. Rowley* (1982) provided guidelines on what a "free appropriate public education" means. Amy Rowley was a child with a hearing impairment whose parents thought she would do better if she had an interpreter. They were probably right. However, Amy Rowley was functioning at the same level as her peers. The Supreme Court ruled against Rowley. Their interpretation was that the EHA was not intended to require any particular level of, or intensity of, educational services. Maximizing a child's potential was too high a standard, but providing only services available to children without disabilities was too low a standard. The EHA requires the provision of a "basic floor of opportunity" consisting of "access to specialized instruction and related services individually designed to provide educational benefit to the handicapped child." If the child is educated in the regular classroom, the program should be "reasonably calculated to enable the child to achieve passing marks and advance from grade to grade."

Additionally, they defined a free, appropriate public education as personalized instruction with sufficient support services to permit a child to benefit educationally from instruction (at the public's expense) that meets the state's educational standards and approximate grade levels used in the state's regular education and conforms to the IEP.

Inclusion of children with acquired immune deficiency syndrome (AIDS) in schools has been controversial. In *School Board of Nassau County, Florida v. Arline* (1987), the Supreme Court ruled that individuals with infectious diseases including AIDS are covered under section 504 of the Rehabilitation Act. When a child needs special educational services, those will also be covered by the IDEA.

Determination of the law's meaning is an ongoing process. The laws have required that increasingly younger children with disabilities be educated, even starting at birth. Special education starts at school age. Early childhood education focused on young children without disabilities. Early childhood special education was the solution.

Inclusive Early Childhood Education

Deriving some of its characteristics from **special education,** and others from **early childhood education. Early childhood special education** goes beyond applying special education techniques to younger children. It is a unique blend that has emerged into a field of its own. It includes aspects of family relations and family therapy, the creative arts, branches of psychology and sociology, and knowledge gained from compensatory education approaches. The field continues to change and expand in response to emerging information and innovative techniques.

Early childhood education concentrates on the development and education of children from birth through age 8. It is concerned with practice, research, and theory in the field. It includes areas such as parenting and educating young children, child care, curriculum, administration, discipline, and age-based topics focusing on infants, toddlers, preschool, and early elementary school children. The field has a strong child development base, although it adheres to no single philosophy of educating children. It is committed to the principle that birth through age 8 are critical years for development and that good programs are imperative during those years. There is some debate as to whether the generally accepted, high-quality characteristics of early childhood programs for children without

Table 1–1: Public Laws Affecting Inclusive Early Childhood Education

Year	Public Law	Title and Significance
1968	90-538	*The Handicapped Children's Early Education Assistance Act (HCEEP)* established the development of model demonstration projects to serve young children with disabilities. It was renamed the *Early Education Program for Children with Disabilities (EEPCD)* in 1990.
1972	92-424	*Economic Opportunities Amendments of 1972* mandated that 10 percent of the children in Head Start have disabilities.
1973	93-112	*The Rehabilitation Act of 1973*, Section 504, mandated equal opportunities for children with disabilities in preschools and schools that receive *federal* funds.
1975	94-142	*Education for All Handicapped Children Act of 1975 (EHA)* mandated a free appropriate public education in the least restrictive environment for children and youth (5-21) with disabilities.
1983	98-199	*Education of the Handicapped Act Amendments of 1983 (EHA)* amendments supported the development of model demonstration programs for preschool special education, early intervention, and transition.
1986	99-457	*Education of the Handicapped Act Amendments of 1986 (EHA)* established (*Part B*) mandating services for children 3 to 5 years. It also established (*Part H* changed to *Part C* in 1997) an entitlement program for infants and toddlers, birth to 3.
1988	100-407	*Technology-Related Assistance for Individuals with Disabilities Act of 1988 (Tech Act)* provided adaptive devices, whether commercially available or customized to individuals with disabilities including young children and the elderly.
1990	101-336	*The Americans with Disabilities Act of 1990 (ADA)* extended civil rights protection to people with disabilities in all settings. Required that schools, employers, and government agencies provide reasonable accommodations to allow individuals with disabilities to participate fully.
1990	101-476	*Individuals with Disabilities Education Act of 1990 (IDEA)* renamed the EHA and made language changes by replacing the term *handicapped* with *disability* and used "people first language." It included services to children with autism, traumatic brain injury, serious emotional disturbances, and attention deficit disorder, as well as transition and assistive technology services.
1991	102-119	*Individuals with Disabilities Education Act Amendments of 1991* replaced the terms *language and speech* by *communication, psychosocial* by *social* or *emotional*, and *self-help skills* by *adaptive development. Case management services* are referred to as *service coordination*. Another important change is that "to the maximum extent appropriate," children are to be in natural environments, including the home, and community settings in which children without disabilities participate.
1997	105-17	*Individuals with Disabilities Education Act Amendments of 1997 (IDEA)* included the use of the Developmental Delay eligibility category, at the discretion of states, for children through age nine; funding formulas were changed to include population and poverty data. Part C (formerly Part H), infant and toddlers, allowed young children who are not eligible for services to be monitored over time. It established and implemented mediation processes. Discipline procedures were clarified; there were also changes in the IEP, assessment procedures, and a clear emphasis that children with disabilities should participate in the regular curriculum and assessment procedures.
2001	107-110	*No Child Left Behind Act of 2001* increased accountability, provided choices for parents, gave greater flexibility to states, and schools, and emphasized reading and math.
2004	108-446	*Individuals with Disabilities Education Improvement Act Amendments of 2004*. This eliminated benchmarks or objectives in IEPs and tied annual goals to state standards. It required teachers to be highly qualified in the areas they were teaching. It emphasized universal design, literacy and language skills, and intervention in natural environments for infants and toddlers. It added requirements related to early intervening services, disproportion, and response to intervention.
2008	110-325	*Americans with Disabilities Act Amendments Act of 2008* (ADAAA) continued and expanded civil rights protection to children and adults with disabilities.

disabilities are equally appropriate and effective for children with disabilities.

Early childhood special education is a blend of early childhood and special education. It focuses on children with disabilities or those who are at risk and their families. This profession emerged because neither special education nor early childhood education practitioners, while working separately, were able to effectively impact on the lives of young children with disabilities and their families. Professionals from both groups found they were more effective when they blended their expertise and used a family-centered approach.

Change in the field of inclusive early childhood education is a result of interwoven social and legal factors. Much of the change has come as a result of research and the evidence it provided. We now recognize the importance of individualizing our teaching. This has facilitated the provision of attention to individual needs that is essential when working with children with disabilities. Early brain research has focused on the potential for early intervention and the negative implications of "let's wait and see" (National Research Council and Institute of Medicine, 2000).

The importance of early life experiences has been established, as has the interactive influence of genetics and environment on the development of the human brain. The centrality of early relationships has also been acknowledged along with their potential for developing resilience or risk in children. The role of emotions in all its complexity has been increasingly explored and validated especially as it relates to motivation and aggression. The ability to increase positive child outcomes through planned intervention has been established (National Research Council and Institute of Medicine, 2000).

Most educational research has focused on how (and what) to teach rather than how children learn. Swiss psychologist Jean Piaget (whose work was published in English in the early 1950s) focused his research on *how* children learn. Piaget (1970) argued that the teacher's role is to set up an environment that a child can actively explore. Classroom activities, which are part of the environment, should incorporate both familiar and new aspects. Lev Vygotsky, a Russian researcher whose works were translated into English in the 1980s, focused on social interactions and language as the foundation for cognitive development. When examining the adult-child relationship, he looked at the range of tasks that children could not accomplish alone but could accomplish with the help of competent adults or peers. He called this the **zone of proximal development (ZPD)** (Vygotsky, 1934/1987). This concept has been every useful in teaching young children with disabilities. Techniques or strategies that adults use to allow children to accomplish more difficult tasks are called **scaffolding**. From the work of Piaget and Vygotsky, scholars concluded that to learn, a child must actively interact with the environment and that the activities in the environment must be individualized to match and then expand the child's experience.

The work of Albert Bandura (1992) and others focused on how children learn by **modeling** other children. Segregating children at an early age meant that children with disabilities had only peers with disabilities available as models. This segregation effectively resulted in teaching children to become disabled. With teacher support and exposure, children with disabilities can learn to model and play with typically developing peers. All children can gain experience in interacting with a wide range of people.

Piaget's and Vygotsky's work helped make inclusion possible by changing our philosophy and methodology of education. Bandura's work helped make inclusion imperative by demonstrating that segregation deprived children with disabilities (and those without) of a full education and a full life.

Much of the controversy between early childhood education and early childhood special education focuses around the interpretation of **developmentally appropriate practices**. In response to this controversy, the National Association for the Education of Young Children (NAEYC) published guidelines specifying what is meant by developmentally appropriate practice (Bredekamp & Copple, 2009) and operationalized this for curriculum and assessment for children with and without disabilities. The Division for Exceptional Children also put forth the DEC recommended practices for early intervention and early childhood special education (Sandall, Hemmeter, Smith, & McLean, 2005).

Developmentally appropriate practice has three distinct features: age appropriateness, individual appropriateness, and social and cultural appropriateness. Age appropriateness focuses on the relationship between the materials and methods used based on the age group that is being served. This is particularly an issue when development is either much faster or slower than average. If a second grader reads at an eighth grade level, much of the available eighth grade literature is inappropriate for him. Likewise if a second grader has the mental age of 3, many of the materials 3 year olds use are inappropriate. The concept of universal design addresses this issue. The second aspect of developmentally appropriate practice requires that the environment, materials, and interactions with adults be consistent with the ability and needs of each individual child (Bredekamp & Copple, 2009). It focuses on providing options for children rather than expecting all children to do the same thing at the same time. In early childhood education, this has frequently been interpreted as responding to

Individualized planning takes into account a child's interests and needs, supports adoptive skills, and is responsive to family background and values.

a child's interests; in early childhood special education, it is viewed as responding to a child's needs. Individualized planning should take into account both children's *interests* and their *needs*. It is not an either/or situation. The third factor, social and cultural appropriateness, relates to educating children in a way that is respectful of and responsive to their family background and values.

The DEC recommended practices focus on five direct services strands: (1) assessment, (2) child-focused practices, (3) family-based practices, (4) interdisciplinary models, and (5) technology applications. They identified a sixth strand, cultural/linguistic sensitivity, but found that it was a fundamental value that crossed all categories. They also identified two indirect supports: (1) policies, procedures, and systems change; and (2) personnel preparation (Sandall & Smith, 2005). These strands are based on the science of early childhood development and the knowledge and experience of researchers and other stakeholders (Sandall et al., 2005).

Early childhood special educators need a wide range of teaching strategies to provide education and early intervention. These strategies are individualized to facilitate learning. Partnership between families and early childhood special educators are family centered, and families play an active role in the decision-making process. Including children with disabilities in early childhood programs broadens expectations for educators' skills, and assumes that children will require more varied care and learning environments.

DEC sets forth its beliefs and values beginning with respecting all children and families and using mutual respect and appreciation as the basis for building relationships. It supports high-quality, comprehensive, coordinated, and family-centered services and supports. This is based on the research that shows that early intervention (EI) and early childhood special education (ECSE) can make positive long-term differences in the quality of life for children and their families. They endorse the rights of all children to participate actively and meaningfully within their families and communities and support the principles of normalization and least restrictive environments. However, it is not enough that children be in these environments; a child's learning needs must be identified and matched with effective intervention strategies and supports. Like NAEYC, DEC sees children with disabilities as children first, they are committed to using the guidelines and standards such as those recommended by NAEYC and Head Start that help provide quality programming for all children (Sandall, McLean, Santos, & Smith, 2005).

Labels and Labeling

Given the concerns about the power of language, leaders in the field are questioning the use of labels and the need for labeling. They argue that the challenge for both research and implementation is delivering effective, comprehensive services for all children based on their individual educational needs rather than their labeled disability.

To help the problem of mislabeling children, the IDEA allows the use of the category **developmental delay** for children from birth through age 9. This is a category that had

been available for young children (birth through 2) and became available for children 3 through 5 in 1991. The term developmentally delayed solves some of the problems related to mislabeling. The developmentally delayed label is replaced by a more specific one (e.g., intellectual disability) as the child gets older and the disability can be more clearly identified, or is dropped altogether if the delay responds to early intervention. However, if it is clear that a young child has a visual impairment, it serves no purpose to call the child developmentally delayed and the specific label may open a different array of services. Young children who are "at risk" for developmental delays can be served.

People First Language

Terminology in the field of disabilities is changing. Some of the changes are dramatic, others more subtle. However, the intent of all of the changes is to focus on people first and disabilities second. The terms **handicap** and **disability** are not synonymous. A handicap "is the cumulative result of the barriers imposed by society which come between an individual and the environment of an activity which the person wants to do" (Blaska, 1993, p. 28). An inaccessible building is a handicap for a child using a wheelchair just as reaching the top of a high bookshelf is a handicap for a short individual. A disability is a general term referring to a condition or functional limitation that interferes with major life activities such as walking, hearing, or learning. The term handicapped has been replaced by the term disability when the reference is to an individual. This change is reflected in the names of the laws passed. The Education of the Handicapped Acts (EHA) were renamed the Individuals with Disabilities Education Acts (IDEA) in 1990. The word handicapped is still used in citing laws or environmental barriers, but not in reference to people.

Another important change focuses on **people first language**. Think about how you might introduce yourself. Who are you? How would you describe yourself? The description you give will vary with the situation, making some aspects of you more relevant than others. An individual's disability is an aspect of that person. If not relevant, reference to the disability should be omitted. When used, the term disability should not be placed in a preceding adjectival phrase, nor should people and conditions be confused. Also avoid grouping individuals into categories such as "the disabled" (Blaska, 1993).

Say:	Do Not Say:
babies addicted to crack	crack babies
a child with a disability	disabled child
a child who has cerebral palsy	child who is cerebral palsied
a child who is gifted	a gifted child

When comparing children with disabilities and children without disabilities, do just that. If one refers to children without disabilities as normal children, the obvious implication is that children with disabilities are abnormal. Use terms such as **normal development, typically developing, or children without disabilities**. Be aware of the terms you use and be sure that they convey an accurate description of the child. Be wary of professionals and individuals whose language does not reflect a people first philosophy. If their language is out of date, their knowledge may be as well.

Some words used in the past to describe individuals with disabilities have negative connotations. They have created images of people who are to be pitied and who are not able. These words have been replaced with less value-laden terms, for example:

Say:	Do Not Say:
has epilepsy	is *afflicted* by epilepsy
has muscular dystrophy	*suffers* from muscular dystrophy
has AIDS	is a *victim* of AIDS
uses a wheelchair	is *confined* to a wheelchair
has Down syndrome	is *mongoloid*
is nonverbal	is *dumb* or *mute*
has a physical disability	is *crippled* or an *invalid*

Remember, it is not only what you say, but how you say it. Even appropriate language can be used in a demeaning way.

The term special has also come under scrutiny. We all like to feel special sometimes such as on our birthday, we enjoy special events such as concerts, and we may even have particular clothing that makes us feel special. However, we don't want to be special all of the time. Sometimes we want to be just like everyone else, part of the group. The question then becomes, should there be **special education**? Why not just education that meets the needs of all children?

Using people first language requires us to use more words to describe an individual. Some people find this cumbersome, some unnecessary. Words shape attitudes. They are a reflection of the timeliness and accuracy of your knowledge.

Including all Children

All children are unique, yet they have much in common. Like adults, they all have strengths as well as limitations. All children have specialized needs some of the time. One child may have a cast on his broken leg, whereas another may forget her toilet training when her baby sister is born, and another may show her anger during her parents' divorce process. Needs change during crucial periods in children's lives just as with adults.

So, if *all* children are part of regular settings and *all* children participate in the general curriculum, then *all* educators need to know techniques to care for and educate *all* children. One of the most powerful crossovers in inclusive education is that *all* educators are sharing the knowledge that *all* children are unique, that instruction needs to be individualized. Developmentally appropriate practices are important for *all* children, and what happens in classrooms is about *children*, not about math, reading, and science.

When children have diverse needs, whether temporary or permanent, there is a danger of considering only how different those needs make them: Educators may lose sight of how much they resemble other children. They may forget these children have the same basic educational and

personal needs as their classmates. They need friends, they need to develop a positive self-concept, and they need to see themselves as making a positive contribution to their class and society. The *whole* child must be planned for, not just the parts that are different. A child with a hearing loss needs to learn to speech read and use residual hearing. However, she also needs to make friends and be included in the everyday activities of the classroom.

Educational settings may be new and possibly frightening. A child who is seen as different has an added fear—fear of rejection by adults or peers. Some children may have had few experiences away from the family, and may associate school with painful experiences in a hospital or doctor's office. Parents may have had negative experiences with the school system. More than others, children with disabilities may need reassurance and may take time to develop a trusting relationship with teachers and peers. It is your responsibility to make the child feel safe and included in her classroom.

Educators can help children understand individual differences by developing an awareness of the diversity among all children as well as their commonalities. As an understanding of themselves and others grows, children can learn strategies for interacting with all of their peers—a valuable lifelong skill.

In the Field

I walked into my son's second grade graduation ceremony brimming with pride. Surrounded by camera wielding families, and children dressed in Sunday best, I sat looking forward to the performance. I walked out of that ceremony angry, sad and disheartened—not at my son, but at the system that put him in the corner. All I kept thinking was why am I here? Why is my little boy here? What is the point of this mockery?

My agonizing frustration is that my son can learn. He has an intelligence demonstrated to us all the time, especially in front of the glow of a computer screen, the great educational equalizer, and with his rapier, albeit diabolical, wit. He has the ability to participate in regular education classes, provided adaptations are coordinated with his special education teacher. I am willing to provide any necessary adaptations, from programming his communication device to providing software that will allow him to do assigned work.

We sent our son to school to learn math skills, the wonders of science, and lessons from our past; we sent our son to learn about distant lands, the joy of a good book, and to learn the "pow" that comes from putting your ideas on paper.

I am not unrealistic; I see my son's weaknesses. I just want them to acknowledge his strengths, to build upon them, to teach him to use these strengths to compensate for his weaknesses. This will give him a chance to succeed when his school years are done.

As parents of a child with special needs, we are in a constant state of angst and confrontation, eternally fighting to get services readily given to regular education children. We should not have to attend school with our son, sitting next to him with a copy of the Americans with Disabilities Act clenched tightly in one hand and the phone number of a good civil rights attorney in the other in order to assure our son's rights. I would love to be just another mom, one from whom the school administration doesn't flee upon seeing me in the hall.

Where do we go from here? I don't know. Up to this point, my husband thought we should leave him in the inclusive classroom with his peers. I think we have firmly established that it is now a moot point. According to my other son, they even moved him to another section of the cafeteria away from the kids in his grade, so even lunchtime encounters are history. I still wonder if he wouldn't do better in a one-on-one home-based program. All I am sure of at this point is that unless regular and special education are willing to work together for a functional education and believe in him, they are wasting my son's time and dooming his future.

His needs in the classroom are as basic as any medical needs. An education is about dignity and independence, and having a reason to get up in the morning. Without the proper educational foundation, attaining these goals becomes impossible. Our best hope to cure the plague of negativity that keeps my son from developing his full potential, aside from teaching him at home, is that somewhere he will meet that special, rare teacher who will look beyond the minimum legal requirements and go the extra mile to assure all children under her care are given the chance to learn. As I walked across the street to my car, tears flowing, I wondered if I would ever meet a teacher who would give him that chance.

Reflective Practice

Are you that teacher? You can make a difference in children's lives. Not just the children for whom education is easy, but for the children who require something more. You can inspire, support, and grow with the children you teach. You can identify with the families of these children. You can empathize with their frustrations. You can be an advocate for those who do not have the skills themselves, and help families find the knowledge and resources they need to meet their children's needs. You can give children a chance. Compare this family and child's experience with the one at the beginning of the chapter. The differences are obvious. How can you account for these differences? How can you make that difference?

Imagine how it might feel to be left out, excluded, from the typical activities of everyday life. Now, ask yourself, have you ever been excluded? Chosen last? Had to watch while others participated in something you could not do? How did it feel? If this were an isolated event it probably didn't impact your self-concept; however, depending on the extent that you were excluded or even made fun of and laughed at, you may have felt isolated, lonely, and uncared for. Inclusion is more than physical proximity; it requires all participants to change their values—to include everyone.

The scope of inclusion is broader than just traditional elementary school settings and includes all early care and education settings such as preschools, child care centers, and family child care homes. It offers the expectation that children with disabilities will take swimming lessons at the local Y, that they will have friends in their neighborhood, that they will attend religious services with their family, and that they will join the Boy Scouts or Girl Scouts if they

choose to do so. Inclusion creates a challenge for many adults and volunteers. It requires that they expand and modify their roles to make reasonable accommodations to include increasingly diverse children, including those with developmental delays and disabilities, and their families.

In the education of young children, the concept of inclusion requires a **paradigm** shift, "a fundamental change in the way we think about differences among people, in the way we choose to organize schools for education and how we view the purpose of that education" (Developmental Disabilities Task Force, n.d., p. 7). The hope is for an educational system in which there is no longer *special education* and *regular education*, just *education*. Inclusion is more than physically placing children in regular classroom environments originally designed for children without disabilities. Inclusion changes the care and education of *all* children (DEC, CDC, NAEYC, & ATE, 1995)

In the Field

We have been friends with Matthew for a whole school year. We call him Matt. He likes school because he loves people. . . . Matt has trouble understanding everything people say to him, so he uses lots of picture signs and some sign language. That's just the way he was born. We help him by taking turns being his buddy. When we are his buddy, Matt likes us to hold his hand firmly. He feels real sure we know what we are doing if we hang on that way. Many times he will thank us with a big hug. It's nice to be appreciated. (Zeph, Gilmeer, Brewer-Allen, & Moulton, 1992, p. 31)

Reflective Practice

This is a comment by a 7-year-old child. It focuses on her feelings. What do you think this means about children and their values? What do you think this means about inclusion? Reflect on your values and how they will affect your teaching.

Including children with diverse abilities can improve education for all—academically, as well as socially and emotionally. Designing services around children, rather than fitting children into existing services, is the goal of inclusion. When children with diverse abilities are included in a classroom setting, the child and teacher will be supported by an intervention team. This team is composed of the child's parents, the teachers (regular and special education), and any specialists who work with the child. The needs and abilities of all of the children in the classroom must be considered when incorporating an individualized program for any child. This level of planning may require a level of teamwork that is new to some teachers. It may also include a different array of services.

For inclusion to be done well, there must be support services for teachers, parents, and children. When children with disabilities were channeled off into special schools, the role of specialized services in the regular school was primarily diagnostic. As soon as a child was identified as having a disability, the child was moved; the task of the regular school support services was finished. Despite their original limited function, inclusion has expanded the roles of these professionals. School psychologists no longer just give tests, but also may do group or family counseling. Speech/language pathologists and occupational and physical therapists now work in early care and education settings and young children's homes. Social workers, adaptive physical education teachers, and home-school liaisons may all be part of a school setting. Although some of these specialists have been around for a long time, their previous practice of pulling children out of classes has changed. Now they perform some or all of their work within the classroom, and often consult with the teacher to develop a classroom program for a child that complements the individual or small-group therapy that the specialist is carrying out.

Although the field of early childhood education as a whole supports the idea of inclusion, there is disagreement about *who* should be included. Most agree that children with mild to moderate disabilities should be included in regular classes. Some believe that *all* children, including children with profound disabilities, should be included.

The 1997 and 2004 amendments to the IDEA makes the position of the U.S. Department of Education and the Congress that passed the legislation clearer on the inclusion of children with disabilities into regular neighborhood activities, schools, and classrooms. These children should be there. They should participate in the regular education curriculum and in the assessment procedures with necessary accommodations provided. When this cannot happen, there must be a rationale justifying why they cannot. This legislation supports inclusion, but does not require full inclusion.

In the Field

As a special educator working in the public school system for 11 years, I have embraced inclusive models as best practice. However, I do wonder if full inclusion gives the needed level of support and appropriate curriculum to children with disabilities. In the past, I have worked as a resource room teacher helping children learn the skills they need in the subjects in which they struggle. Some children spent every academic period with me while others may spend only one period a day in my room. I feel this has given children the support they need to survive in the world.

However, it does seem important to have more inclusion in our school. I know that the research supports this. As a result, our school has decided to start using inclusion as much as possible in the coming year. I had hoped that my school would hire more special educators and paraeducators to make inclusion successful. Unfortunately, our district does not have the money to hire the special educators or paraeducators that are going to be needed to make inclusion successful.

To solve this problem, the administrators decided to place children with learning and intellectual disabilities evenly throughout our four classrooms. One of these classrooms will be mine, while the other three classrooms will be headed by regular education teachers. None of the classrooms will have paraeducators or any other special educators besides me. Unfortunately, I will not be able to help instruct in their classrooms as I will be teaching on my own. I will be in charge of writing Individualized Education Programs (IEPs) for children I do not teach; helping the other teachers accommodate students in their rooms, and helping teachers learn to keep data for each child's IEP. All of the teachers, including me, are worried about making this work.

I am not sure this is going to give children the level of support they need. I believe we need more special educators and paraeducators to make this work. In my classroom alone, I will have children with intellectual disabilities and those who are gifted and talented. This is hard enough in itself, without another staff member in my classroom. How am I going to help children in other classrooms? It seems that each day I will be pulled in a hundred different directions. How can I work with the administrators to come up with a better plan without giving them the idea that I am lazy or not willing to make a change? Would the old resource room program be better? I want children to get as much from school as they can.

Reflective Practice

Change is difficult. This presents one of the ongoing dilemmas about inclusion. What if I believe in inclusion but it is done without the supports necessary to make it succeed? How would you feel if you were one of the other teachers in the school? How would you feel if you were this teacher?

Inclusion

Early supporters of inclusion were disenchanted with the way the traditional educational system worked. Special education itself has had limited academic success and there has been little consensus about the effectiveness of pull-out programs (Lipsky & Gartner, 1997). There is consensus, however, that children who have been labeled and segregated from their peers are often stigmatized and have low self-esteem. Pull-out programs, where children are taken out of the regular class and placed in a special smaller class to do concentrated work in subject matter areas in which the child was performing below grade level expectation, were the mainstay of mainstreaming. However, the underlying assumptions behind pull-out programs are questionable and inherently unequal. They focus almost exclusively on the child's weakest academic area. The special educators who teach these classes rarely observed the children they taught in regular education settings, thus they didn't have a complete picture of the child's academic day—which includes areas of strength as well as social interactions with peers. While the child is out of the regular class the children in the class are learning information this child will miss and will then fall behind in other areas as well. This particularistic approach rarely encourages the transfer and generalization of learning. It also requires children with disabilities to adjust to more transitions than their peers. The transition process itself identifies children who must learn in a segregated environment. Some feel this is an infringement on their civil rights (Yatvin, 1995).

Children are often identified for special educational services because they have "failed" regular education. Children who struggle, but do not fail badly enough to be labeled do not receive individualized services and may be falling between the cracks. The changes in the 2004 amendments to the IDEA are hoping to identify and support these children.

Inclusion is based on the underlying concept of equality for all.

Does inclusion work? We think so. There are so many levels of inclusion that research leading to a definitive answer is difficult. Also, it is a relatively new practice, thus there is little research to either support or refute its long-term effects. There are also concerns about what the objectives of inclusion are. How do we decide whether or not it has been successful? The impact of inclusion is difficult to assess with younger children and even for children in elementary schools.

One problem with inclusion is there is not a single definition of what inclusion is. According to the Division for Early Childhood,

> Inclusion, as a value, supports the right of all children, regardless of abilities, to participate actively in natural settings within their communities. Natural settings are those in which the child would spend time had he or she not had a disability. These settings include, but are not limited to: home, preschools, nursery schools, Head Start programs, kindergartens, neighborhood school classrooms, childcare, places of worship, recreational (such as community playgrounds and community events) and other settings that all children and families enjoy. (DEC, 1996, p. 1)

The entire DEC position statement on inclusion may be accessed online at: http://www.dec-sped.org/pdf/positionpapers/PositionStatement_Inclusion.pdf.

The Evidence Base

The National Professional Development Center on Inclusion, at the Frank Porter Graham Child Development Institute at the University of North Carolina at Chapel Hill, is funded by the U.S. Office of Special Education Programs. It summarized information about inclusion in early childhood education and provided nine synthesis points:

1. Inclusion takes many different forms; a single definition of inclusion does not exist.
2. Progress has been achieved in efforts to ensure access to inclusive programs, particularly for pre-kindergarten children (3–5). However, in the United States, universal access to inclusive programs for all children with disabilities is far from a reality.
3. Children in inclusive programs generally do at least as well as children in specialized programs. Inclusion can benefit children with and without disabilities, particularly with respect to their social development.
4. A variety of factors such as policies, resources, and beliefs influence the acceptance and implementation of inclusion.
5. Specialized instruction is an important component of inclusion and a factor affecting child outcomes.
6. Collaboration among parents, teachers, and specialists is a cornerstone of high-quality inclusion.
7. Families of children with disabilities generally view inclusion favorably, although some families express concern about the quality of early childhood programs and services.
8. Limited research suggests that the quality of early childhood programs that enroll young children with disabilities is as good as, or slightly better than, the quality of programs that do not enroll these children; however, most studies have focused on general program quality as opposed to the quality of inclusion for individual children with disabilities and their families.
9. Some evidence suggests that early childhood professionals may not be adequately prepared to serve young children with disabilities enrolled in inclusive programs. (National Professional Development Center on Inclusion, 2007).

Reflective Practice

A research synthesis provides a systematic review of research studies related to a particular topic. It looks not only at the conclusions, but how these conclusions were researched and how confident we can feel about using these conclusions. Reread the synthesis points. How do they inform what you know about inclusion? How will they influence your practice?

Concerns about Inclusion

There are a variety of concerns about inclusion that relate to the impact some children with disabilities might have on the social and learning environment of other children in the class as well as the education of children with disabilities themselves. The inclusion of children with profound disabilities, particularly children with severe behavior disorders and those who are profoundly intellectually impaired, cause the most concern. Children with severe behavior disorders may hit or bite without warning or behave in extremely violent and aggressive ways that put other children in the class at risk. These children may also display self-stimulatory or self-injurious behaviors that put them at risk and are highly disruptive in a group. The concern about children who are profoundly intellectually impaired is that they will gain little from the academic aspect of the class and will miss time they could have spent on learning basic skills. They learn best when tasks are broken down into very small steps and repeated many times. This style of teaching is rarely used in regular classrooms.

Children who are medically fragile are another group of concern. Their medical problems can be restrictive and life threatening. Although few question the social desirability of including these children in a regular classroom, the risk of infection needs to be evaluated. The concern is that a child's medical condition will worsen because of exposure to the other children in the class. This may be related to either disease or injury.

Some professionals and families feel that children with some disabilities learn better in segregated classrooms. For example, children with hearing impairments may be in segregated classrooms or at home to concentrate on learning sign language and auditory discrimination skills at a young age.

Some families may not want their children in inclusive settings. If we believe that families are partners in the decision-making process, how do we respond to families who do not want their children in an inclusive setting? Families may feel that a segregated classroom is safer and easier for them to cope with and for the families this is the "least restrictive environment."

Reflective Practice

If families are truly part of the decision-making process for their children, how do we evaluate the decisions of families of children *without* disabilities who oppose the inclusion of children with disabilities in the class? Don't they have a legitimate right to oppose the inclusion of children they believe to be potentially harmful, disruptive, or overly demanding of the teacher's time? Or, should only the families of children with disabilities be included in the decision making? These are tough questions with no easy answers. All families want what is best for their children.

These dilemmas are real and difficult to resolve. IDEA 2004 expects all children to begin their education in regular educational settings with the necessary support services. When these supports have been exhausted, children might be moved into more restricted settings.

The real crux of the issue about inclusion is its implications for the system as a whole. If one believes in full inclusion, then one supports a paradigm shift to one educational system for all. If one believes that decisions should be made on a case-by-case basis, there will be separate systems and resources will be divided between them. Underlying support of equality for all is crucial to the success of inclusion. Whether "full" inclusion happens remains to be seen. The cumulative effect of legislation and litigation clearly supports moving toward greater inclusion.

Barriers to Inclusion

Barriers to inclusion come in many forms; physical, ideological, institutional, and conceptual are just a few of the notable ones. Physical barriers are perhaps the easiest to identify and correct. If a child in a wheelchair cannot use the stairs to get to the next floor a ramp can be built or an elevator added. To change ideological, institutional, and conceptual barriers we must look at our society, the system, and within ourselves.

Lack of Awareness

Awareness of inclusion must not just lie with the families of children with disabilities but with all of the stakeholders in the educational system: families of all children, early childhood educators, early childhood special educators, administrators, paraeducators, legislators, and business and community leaders. Support staff such as bus drivers, secretaries, and cafeteria workers need to be aware

of inclusion and its purpose. Many stakeholders are not aware of legal requirements of the IDEA and the ADA to include children with disabilities in typical settings and the research that served as the foundation for these laws.

Strategies for disseminating this information vary from newspaper articles about inclusive settings to visiting model programs. Professional journals in education, early childhood, and early childhood special education all contain information about inclusion. Meetings of international, national, and state professional organizations often have presentations on this topic. Positive attitudes are at the core of successful inclusion. This does not mean that a child with muscular dystrophy will necessarily play the same sports as a child who does not have this disability, but rather, the question is "How can we include a child with muscular dystrophy in a manner that the child is physically and mentally capable of?" Disabilities are real; the intent is not to ignore the disability, but to meet the child's need to be included as a child with accommodations for the disability.

Successful programs have a shared vision that all children belong and all children can learn and have the opportunity to reach their potential. There is a sense of community that helps each child develop in her own way, with a sense of self-worth, with pride in each child's accomplishments and mutual respect (CEC, 1994).

Lack of Professional Preparation

Untrained staff and lack of consultative support is one of the main barriers to inclusion. Some teachers feel that they are not prepared to teach children with disabilities. They feel they do not have enough knowledge about disabilities per se and particularly about children with severe disabilities or those who are medically fragile. They are genuinely concerned that they might do something that will hurt the child. They also feel they lack educational strategies to effectively teach children with diverse abilities. Families, too, wonder if all educators are prepared to care for and educate their child. Educators with a background in special education feel that they may not have the management skills to teach larger groups of children and lack child development knowledge.

Inclusion has forced educators to consider new and different ways of teaching children. Educators who previously did not include children with disabilities have to develop techniques for including them; likewise, educators whose total focus was teaching children with disabilities in small segregated groups need to learn new methods of individualizing programming for these children in the regular classroom while at the same time including the child's peers.

Teacher skills are an essential part of strategies for inclusion. Often models include extensive initial training before inclusion, but research has shown that training needs to be ongoing and should provide technical assistance in order to solve problems as they arise. Strategies to change teacher attitudes are both long- and short-term. The preservice training of students in higher education needs to be evaluated against the skills needed for inclusive education. The Division for Early Childhood has agreed on a set of recommended practices for personnel preparation for early intervention and early childhood special education. The recommended practices look at the *process*, whereas the standards look at the *content* that is needed to provide services to young children (Miller & Stayton, 2005). The goal is to get institutions of higher education that train teachers to adopt these standards in their teacher preparation programs.

In the Field

I am a single father of a son with severe cerebral palsy and traumatic brain injury, which occurred during the birthing process. My wife passed away shortly after Neil was born and I have had to make decisions about Neil's life on my own.

Neil is now getting ready to enter kindergarten in a school that practices inclusion. I am concerned about his educational and health needs. I was told that this classroom will have a regular education teacher, a special education teacher, and a paraeducator. Even with all this help I worry that they do not have the expertise needed to change him, give his medication, and feed him through his stomach tube. Neil has seizures occasionally and needs proper care for this.

In a classroom that includes many children without special needs, will they help him learn the basics? Neil is functioning at 3 years below his age. Will he be given the proper help to catch up? I don't want Neil to simply be seated in a corner and not be made part of the group. Who should I contact about my concerns? Are my worries even valid? Sometimes I feel I just don't know how I can ensure that Neil receives the best education he can get.

Reflective Practice

Reflect on your personal feelings about inclusion. Who do you believe should be included? Who should not be included? Do you think inclusion works? Why or why not? Reflect on how you would explain your position on inclusion to both Neil's father and the other families.

Exclusion from Educational Assessments

When children with disabilities are included in regular classrooms, they are taught the regular education curriculum with their peers. Some states are now saying that if *all* children should be in regular classrooms then *all* children should meet the standards of the state. States need to provide testing accommodations for students with disabilities because of the requirements of the ADA. This, too, is a double-edged sword. Some students with disabilities may not graduate from high school because they cannot meet the standards (or they make take longer to graduate). However, to the extent that all children are included, more effort will be made to ensure that they meet the standards. This might provide the incentive for creative and innovative teaching. Without including children with disabilities in the assessment procedures there is no way to monitor their progress (CEC, 1996b).

Adult-Child Ratios and Class Size

Adult-child ratios and class size are significant barriers to inclusion. Many educators want fewer children per adult so they have the opportunity to individualize programming and respond to each child's needs. The assumption is that including children with disabilities will increase the time educators spend in collaboration, planning, and carrying out plans. Adult-child ratios, like many other aspects of inclusion, can be affected in surprising ways, and may result in requiring different skills.

In the Field

Rena has spina bifida (her spinal cord was not enclosed at birth) and hydrocephalus (excess cerebral spinal fluid on her brain). Rena's families want her to attend and participate in the same education setting as her older brother. Her physician supports this decision. Two early childhood educators were trained by a public health nurse to **catheterize** Rena. This allows her to attend the full-day program. Rena has large and fine motor challenges. A physical therapist demonstrated lifting techniques and positioning to all the educators at the setting as well as the support staff and volunteers. This permits Rena to move safely from her wheelchair to chairs at activity tables that have special straps designed for her. She can also join in floor activities with appropriate supports (pillow rolls). Rena's interest in drawing, painting, and gluing are facilitated by the adapted crayons and brushes recommended by the occupational therapist. The itinerant early childhood special education consultant follows up on the recommendations from the nurse, physical therapist, and the occupational therapist in his twice-weekly visit to the center. During the visit, the consultant assists the two early childhood educators who have Rena in their group to plan and implement an IEP for Rena. He also provides suggestions and support to the volunteers who work with Rena (Deiner, Hardacre, & Dyck, 1999).

Reflective Practice

Have you thought about managing the adults who might be in your classroom? How do you include and adapt to them as well as collaborate with them to educate young children? How do you see their role and yours in general? What do you think will happen when they are in the classroom? How do you plan to ensure the education of all the children while they are there?

Implications for Educators

Early childhood educators may have paraeducators or volunteers to help a child, and related services professionals (e.g., a physical therapist) as well as an early childhood special education consultant in the class. This means that early childhood educators not only have to have the techniques to teach all the children, including those with disabilities, but they also need the skills to manage the adults. This is a typical "add-on" type of problem except that not only the children, but the adults too, are being added on.

Working from an inclusive model makes some very different assumptions about the skills that teachers have and need. It may be that a different teaching model is preferable to having so many **paraeducators**. In a **co-teaching model**, there are two trained teachers, one an early childhood educator, the other an early childhood special educator. (Paraeducators, **volunteers**, and grandparents do not qualify.) The model is used when children have diverse learning abilities. The educators are there and qualified to teach; they are expected to teach all of the children in the same room at the same time. They may divide up their work differently during the course of the day. At one point one educator may take the lead, whereas the other adult floats and troubleshoots. At another point, they may divide the content to be taught and teach small groups different information while others work independently.

They may parallel teach by dividing the children in the classroom in half so the groups are smaller. Or, they may team teach as each teacher takes turns leading a discussion or modeling appropriate behavior in some area. Regardless of the model, time needs to be allocated for **collaboration** and for learning to use various teaching models.

Lack of Communication, Collaboration, and Respect

We probably all feel that we do our jobs better than others with different training and orientation. We may get territorial and think others with less expertise will lose the gains we have helped children make. Specialists often are afraid of what will happen to "their" children at the hands of educators and children without disabilities. They chose a specialty because they felt an affinity for children with disabilities and fear that others may not share those feelings.

Many educators are concerned that if they include children with disabilities they will not receive the support they need from other professionals, particularly related service professionals such as **speech/language pathologists, physical therapists, occupational therapists,** and **early childhood special education consultants.** They believe that it takes a team to meet the needs of young children with disabilities and are afraid the team will not be in place for them. Some of these fears are well-founded.

The development of mutual trust and respect is one of the core components to inclusion. Strategies for success involve ongoing discussions and the willingness to share expertise with each other as well as working as teams. Communication among professionals is often difficult. When young children have disabilities, the need to communicate may be greater and more difficult because there are many different individuals and institutions involved. The situations for these children may be tremendously complex. They may attend an early care and education setting, go to an inclusive preschool program for part of the day, and finally return to the child care setting until their parents finish work. Often they have related services such as physical or speech and language therapy on a regular basis; they may have medical needs that require both regular and specialized medical care; they need regular assessment and evaluation; and so on.

The various professionals need to talk to and respect each other to communicate necessary information in a way that all can understand. Professionals must also be able to communicate respectfully and informatively with families. Communication frequently depends on the attitudes of professionals toward inclusion. The children, too, play a very important role in making inclusive settings successful. Collaboration requires that staff, children, and their families support each other. Differences cannot be ignored but must be respected, acknowledged, and even seen as cause for creative solutions.

Lack of Supports

Strategies for achieving quality education include consideration of the supports that are necessary to make inclusion successful and communicating the value of these supports to both administrators and families. The education of all the children should be expected to meet high general educational standards (CEC, 1995).

Lack of supports can take many forms. At times supports are not available because there is no common vision of what inclusion means and requires. (Funding and budget cuts that limit money to hire trained paraeducators or to make facilities accessible make support difficult.) Lack of teaching materials or training to support inclusion, limited or no preparation or collaboration time with team members, too many nonteaching assignments (lunch duty, hall duty, etc.), large classes, and no co-planning time can all contribute to lack of support. Community supports may be unavailable due to physical location or the limited number of available professionals.

Overcoming lack of support is an administrative responsibility. The administration needs to improve leadership and to motivate and monitor commitment to the vision of inclusion. Sharing responsibilities on a setting-wide basis is necessary. The administration needs to provide a vision that all the stakeholders can believe in (CEC, 1996a). However, the vision is only the beginning. There must be a commitment to follow through on the vision.

Inclusion is not the only item on the American education agenda. However, it must be included when concerns are voiced about other topics such as literacy, math, and science. Consensus must be developed to reach *all* the goals on the agenda.

Minority Children in Special Education

The cultural composition of the United States is becoming increasingly diverse. Those who teach young children will see this diversity earlier than it is reflected in the population statistics.

Minority children are overrepresented in special education. This presents a challenge to educators. Because of the overidentification of minority children, some schools are reluctant to identify these children as needing individualized programming. Moving toward an inclusive educational system that meets the needs of all children may improve the educational opportunities for children from minority groups without the need for labeling. Some of the specific challenges are detailed below.

The federal government must be responsive to the growing needs of an increasingly diverse society. These are some of the findings cited in the IDEA (2004):

- America's ethnic profile is rapidly changing. In 2000, one out of every three persons in the United States was a member of a minority group or was limited English proficient.
- Minority children comprise an increasing percentage of public school students.
- With changing demographics, recruitment efforts for special education personnel should focus on increasing the participation of minorities in the teaching

Minority children are overrepresented in special education.

profession to provide appropriate role models with sufficient knowledge to address the special education needs of these students.

- The limited English proficient population is the fastest growing in our nation, and the growth is occurring in many parts of our nation.
- Studies have documented apparent discrepancies in the levels of referral and placement of limited English proficient children in special education.
- Such discrepancies pose a special challenge for special education in the referral of, assessment of, and provision of services for, our nation's students from non-English language backgrounds.
- Greater efforts are needed to prevent the intensification of problems connected with mislabeling and high dropout rates among minority children with disabilities.
- More minority children continue to be served in special education than would be expected from the percentage of minority students in the general school population.
- African American children are identified as having mental retardation and emotional disturbance at rates greater than their white counterparts.
- In the 1998–1999 school year, African American children represented just 14.8 percent of the population aged 6 through 21, but comprised 20.2 percent of all children with disabilities.
- Studies have found that schools with predominately white students and teachers have placed disproportionately high numbers of their minority students into special education.

Reflective Practice

Look at these bullets again. How will this information influence what children will be in your classroom? How will it influence your teaching practice? What can you do now to ensure that you are ready to teach the children you expect in your classroom?

Service Delivery Systems

Service delivery systems, individually or together, provide for the care and education of children with disabilities. Service delivery systems can be distinguished by their location, level of inclusion, focus (child or family), and whether the system is formal or informal. Children increasingly are being served by a combination of service delivery systems. Depending on the child's specific disability, medical condition, family needs, location of the community (especially rural versus urban), and available services and funding, a range of service delivery systems is possible.

Like the field itself, service delivery systems are struggling to find answers to questions such as:

- Should all service delivery systems be inclusive?
- Should service delivery systems be designed to meet the needs of the child or the total family?
- What level of participation/cooperation is expected between families and service delivery systems?
- How much input should families have in the decision-making process?
- How actively should service delivery systems pursue parent education programs?
- How is the role of advocacy divided between parents and service delivery systems?
- How much will adequate service delivery cost and who should pay?

Changing demographics are forcing service delivery systems to evaluate their policies in relation to their target population. Interagency collaboration is required to ensure quality programming for children. If parents or guardians work, whether single or married, home-based services may not be a feasible option unless educators are willing to work when families are available.

To meet the needs of the whole family, families may develop complicated "packages" based on child care, **early intervention**, education, therapy, and health services. Children with disabilities who attend school programs often need care before and after school as well as during the summer. This need extends past the time when other children can be left at home independently.

Varying theoretical differences influence the goals and supports that the delivery systems provide for children and their families. Viewing families as dynamic parts of a larger social system has brought about a change in how service is delivered. Empowering families to make choices in the best interests of both their child and family has affected delivery systems and the thoughts and actions of professionals in the field of early childhood (Sandall, Hemmeter, Smith, & McLean, 2005). Although service delivery systems vary, these systems move from the most to the least restrictive.

Hospital-Based Care and Intervention

Most hospitals are designed for high-volume, short-term acute care. Their top priority is to preserve life. The focus is primarily on medical rather than social needs. When an infant is born prematurely or critically ill, he is placed in a **critical care unit**. Not all hospitals have these units for neonates. They are staffed by **neonatologists** and **neonatal nurses**. Infants may remain in the critical care unit for only a day or two for observation or up to a year or more for some of the most fragile infants.

When infants are medically stable, they move to an intermediate unit. When the child exits critical care early intervention usually begins. Some infants who remain in the critical care unit for extended times receive early intervention services there.

Hospitals designed for the long-term care of children have their own teachers who continue the schoolwork that children would be doing if they were in school. There are many reasons why a child's medical condition may require hospitalization (uncontrolled **seizures, technology dependence**, leukemia, etc.). The length of the child's stay and the seriousness of the illness will determine to a great extent how much contact a child will have with early interventionists/educators. Larger hospitals have **child life staff** that provides stimulation and intervention to young children while they are in the hospital. They also work with children to prepare them for medical procedures.

Residential Care

A residential program is a treatment facility that is not a medical facility where young children live in order to receive intervention/educational services. Residential programs are being phased out for all children, but particularly very young children. Their use is for children with chronic and serious medical problems. Some children who are profoundly involved and whose families cannot care for them live in nursing homes or state institutions and receive care and education there.

Home-Based Early Intervention

Home-based service delivery systems usually use a consultation model. They involve an **early interventionist** (**pediatric nurse, child development specialist**, and/or early childhood special educator) visiting the family in their home on a regularly scheduled basis. This type of service delivery is frequently used for infants and medically vulnerable young children.

The **consultant's** responsibilities to the family and child include sharing information with the family about available resources and services, answering parents' questions about the child's disability, and modeling and demonstrating activities and techniques for working with the child. The consultant may serve as a liaison between the medical and educational communities (Burns, 2004).

Success for this type of system depends on families understanding and following through on the intervention. It is based on the consultant's building a relationship with the family by visiting at a scheduled time that is convenient. Most consultants work a daytime schedule; what frequently happens is that the mother, if not working, is the one who is home and then has the responsibility of carrying out the prescribed early intervention as well as interpreting for her spouse or partner (if one is part of the family system) what the consultant said. With increasing instances of both parents being in the workforce, this type of delivery system may only work for a short period, and probably only for children whose disabilities are identified at birth. Unless this program is flexible enough to schedule evening and weekend appointments, it would only be available for families who have a parent or guardian at home during the day.

Center-Based Early Intervention

Center-based early intervention service delivery systems may be situated in hospitals, schools, early care and education settings, and public or private agencies. Families are usually responsible for bringing the child to the program, although some programs provide transportation. A center-based program often has a team of specialists. Some programs are designed for children with a specific disability, such as hearing impairments, whereas others serve children with a variety of disabilities. These programs usually have specialized materials and equipment. Many of these programs are half-day, so they may represent only part of the service delivery system if the child needs full-time care. Within a dual service perspective, early childhood educators may be responsible for adapting activities to support the participation and social integration of young children with disabilities.

The staff of early intervention centers is usually well-trained in early childhood special education, and therapists not only make active contributions to the child's program but may provide needed therapy in the setting as well. This staff would also do assessments. Families often feel more comfortable leaving young children in a setting with specialists. For a variety of reasons, including both philosophy and funding, these center-based services are likely to be segregated programs.

Home- and Center-Based Intervention

Some programs are a combination of home- and center-based programs. In these programs children go to the center but are served by a home-based component as well. Early Head Start successfully uses this model. This service combines the advantages of both programs. Trained professionals are in charge of the programming, and families can consult with them on a regular basis.

Public School Programs

Public schools play a major part in the service delivery system for children 3 and older. When public schools serve children below the kindergarten level, they are faced with a dilemma. They receive funds to educate children *with* disabilities beginning at age 3, but not for those *without* disabilities. They are also required to educate these children in the least restrictive environment. If they are to create inclusive environments, they must have the families of children without disabilities pay for these public school services or they must integrate the children with disabilities into programs outside of the traditional public school. Some programs integrate children with disabilities into early care and education settings such as child care, Head Start and preschools for all or some portion of the day. Beginning with the 1997 reauthorization of the IDEA children without disabilities may profit from services designed for children with disabilities. However, it is unlikely that public schools can afford programs for 3 and 4 year olds just for the purpose of inclusion.

Early Care and Education

Many children with disabilities are included in early care and education settings. The ADA (1990) requires that children with disabilities must be accepted as any other child would be. Centers can deny admission on a case-by-case basis if the setting can show that accepting a specific child would "fundamentally alter" the services they provide or constitute an "undue burden." Otherwise, the expectation is that programs will make reasonable accommodations to include children with disabilities. A reasonable accommodation might involve adding balls with bells or other sounds inside for children with visual impairments, a specialized swing for a child with physical impairments, or not permitting class pets if a child has a chronic allergy.

Placing children with disabilities in regular early care and education care settings is not a new idea, but it has recently received a great deal of attention because of changing demographics and a changing philosophical environment.

Early care and education for children with disabilities is used in one of two ways by service delivery systems: child care before and/or after early intervention or as a primary site for the delivery of early intervention services. In the latter case, related services may be provided in the early care and education setting or elsewhere.

Programs that use child care as a **primary intervention site** typically use consultation models. The early childhood special education consultant and other professionals train the educators to function as an early childhood interventionist with the support of consultants who visit the site on a regular basis to troubleshoot and model behavior. Consultants also provide a variety of technical assistance services ranging from specialized equipment and a selection of toys to telephone consultation.

An overarching issue is whether the amount and quality of individual attention provided in early care and education is enough to meet the needs of children with disabilities. This is actually part of the much broader issue addressing quality of early care education for all young children, particularly infants.

Head Start

Head Start began in the summer of 1965 as a comprehensive service system designed to deliver health, education, and social services to children and families who met low-income eligibility criteria. Since its inception, Head Start has had a strong commitment to family involvement and inclusion. Head Start uses the state and federal definitions of disability for eligibility. In 1993, Head Start emphasized the regulations that require grantees to provide enrollment opportunities for children with disabilities as well as screening and referral services. The range of comprehensive services (medical, dental, and nutritional services) is designed to serve children with identified disabilities as well as those at risk (Meisels & Shonkoff, 2000). Head Start often uses a consultation model to provide technical assistance for children with disabilities.

Head Start programs are required to coordinate their efforts and responsibilities with the local school district. Collaboration with the public schools provides an inclusive setting for children with disabilities who do not meet Head Start income guidelines (10 percent of children do not have to be from low-income families) and the school district often provides consultative services to the program. If the child's IEP is developed by Head Start, Head Start personnel have supervisory responsibility.

Head Start programs are moving from half-day programs into programs with wrap-around child care. Head Start is increasingly moving toward a philosophy of *family* involvement and *family* (not just child) outcomes. Family outcomes relate to family literacy, adult education, substance abuse, and health (Office of Head Start, 2007).

Early Head Start

Similar to Head Start programs for 3 and 4 year olds, **Early Head Start** is designed for children birth to 3. It began in 1995 following the reauthorization of the Head Start Act. Early Head Start is a comprehensive year-round program designed to promote health; positive relationships with children, families, and staff; active family involvement; and the inclusion of children with special needs (Administration for Children and Families, 2006a). Head Start, however, has some of the same problems that other early care and education settings have relative to funding, low teacher salaries, and related concerns about program quality.

Formal and Informal Social Networks

Social networks are made up of people who are outside the home but engage in activities or supports (material and/or emotional) for the family. Research on social support for families of children with disabilities suggests that the presence of effective social supports can assist families in coping with stress and can enhance the well-being of these families. However, although families who have children with disabilities may benefit greatly from the existence of support networks, they are also less likely to have them available than are families of children without disabilities (Seligman & Darling, 2007).

Support networks can be formal or informal. Formal networks are generally made up of professionals involved with service agencies. Informal social networks are made up of friends, neighbors, and extended family members. Most families utilize informal social networks. There is concern that families with children with disabilities lack these informal networks and rely on the support of professionals (Seligman & Darling, 2007). Perhaps one role of professionals is to help families develop and rely on an informal support network rather than a formal one.

Support networks offer three major types of support: (1) providing material goods and services when needed; (2) providing emotional support by communicating the person's value and worth to them; and (3) providing information about and referrals to other, perhaps more formal, support systems. In general, social networks work best when they are reciprocal in nature (although in some extreme situations the process of having to "pay back" support can itself add stress).

Support empowers families to strengthen and add to their already existing networks. One relatively easy way for families to increase the size of their support network is to meet families of other children in their child's setting. Supporting families in building their own social support network is a lifetime skill that will continue to serve them.

Summary

Education is crossing a new frontier and changing to meet new demands. Educators are at the forefront of this change as they modify the learning environment to meet new educational standards and to include children with disabilities and those at risk. Education for children with disabilities has a history that has involved exclusion and segregation. The move toward inclusion has resulted from changing social, legal, and educational philosophies that have led to individualized programming for children. The legal requirement that all children have a free, appropriate, public education in the least restrictive environment has been a major change. In addition to including children with disabilities, their families are included as decision makers whose priorities, values, and needs must be reflected in the educational process.

Although most professionals support inclusion, they differ on who they believe should be included and how. Including children with disabilities changes the role of the educator and makes it more complex. Inclusion has a strong legal base. Whether or not full inclusion will come about is not clear.

Service delivery systems for children with disabilities are changing. Some systems are home-based, others are center-based, and some use a combination. As part of educating children in natural environments, intervention services are being incorporated into early care and education settings. Increasingly, the needs of the total family are considered when planning and coordinating services needed by children. There are many excellent services available; however, coordinating the total range of services is a challenge.

Reflections

1. Reflect on your own education. What were your best and worst educational experiences? How did these experiences influence your decision to become a teacher? How do you think education has changed since you were in an early childhood classroom? What are your feelings about these changes?

2. Legislation and litigation have made many desirable changes in the education of children with disabilities. Some cite the most important piece of legislation as P.L. 94-142, whereas others would disagree and feel that either *Brown v. Board of Education of Topeka, Kansas* (1954) or the *Pennsylvania Association of Retarded Children v. Commonwealth of Pennsylvania* (1971) was more important. What do you think is the most important piece of legislation and/or litigation in education to date? Why?

3. When teaching in an inclusive classroom, educators need to be cognizant of ways to teach the same curriculum to children needing various levels of support, accommodations, and modifications. All children need to be successful learners. How can you as an educator include all children in appropriate learning activities? Will different children be doing different activities to reach the same goals? Alternatively, will different children have different goals? What accommodations will you use to help all children learn? What other professionals can help make instruction successful? How will you know what is best for the students in your classroom? How will you become a reflective practitioner?

Educational Resources

Circle of Inclusion, funded by the U.S. Office of Special Education Programs, offers demonstrations of and information about the effective practices of inclusive educational programs for children birth through 8. http://circleofinclusion.org

Council for Exceptional Children is a professional organization that has divisions for all major disability areas and is committed to advancing the quality of education for all children. Their web page contains links to other resources. They have student chapters. (888) 232-7733; FAX (703) 620-2521; http://www.cec.sped.org

Division for Early Childhood (DEC) is a division of CEC that focuses on young children with disabilities. It has state divisions and holds international conferences as well as publishing a newsletter and journal. http://www.dec-sped.org

Inclusion Press provides links to books, workshops, online training tools, and many other resources. Great site for families and educators. http://www.inclusion.com

National Association for the Education of Young Children offers professional development opportunities to early childhood educators and publishes the journal *Young Children*. It has publications that focus on including children with disabilities in early care and education settings. It is a tremendous resource for educators and families. (202) 232-8777 (800) 424-2460 FAX (202) 328-1846; http://www.naeyc.org/

National Information Center for Children and Youth with Disabilities (NICHCY) provides resource sheets for parents, educators, or students looking for information about different disabilities. *Basics for Parents* is a publication that examines aspects of the special education processes and *News Digest* for current information. (800) 695-0285; (202) 884-8200; FAX (202) 884-8441; http://www.nichcy.org

Office of the Americans with Disabilities Act enforces Titles II and III of the ADA. It also provides publications, technical assistance, and consultation on the ADA. (800) 514-0301 TDD (800) 514-0383; http://www.usdoj.gov/

Office of Special Education Programs is dedicated to improving outcomes for children with disabilities ages birth through 21 by providing leadership and financial support to states and local districts. It reports annually on the implementation of the IDEA. http://www.ed.gov/about/offices/list/osers/index.html?src=mr

For additional resources, visit the book companion website for this text at www.cengage.com/education/deiner.

Chapter 2

Partnering with Families

I feel like a 25 year old trapped in a 55-year-old body since gaining legal custody of the children—Jessica, 3, Jeff, 5, and John, 8. It was bad when their mother left and our son had the children alone. We always knew he had a drinking problem, but we didn't want to admit he was an alcoholic and addicted to drugs. He is now in treatment for his addictive behaviors. We hope someday he will be reunited with his children on a permanent basis and that his wife will change her self-destructive patterns and form a bond with her children. Until then, I guess the children are here to stay. After a year, we are learning more about the children, ourselves, and how to cope with each other.

All of the children experienced anxiety when they first came. Although they knew us as their grandparents, we had seen little of them because they lived three thousand miles away. All of a sudden, we were thrust on each other. The two younger children adjusted more easily. John had difficulty adjusting to his new surroundings. He had fitful sleep, broken by nightmares, and he couldn't focus on his schoolwork. He seemed to get along well with his peers. He was very confused about why he and his brother and sister were separated from their parents. Probably because of the unstructured and chaotic life he was used to, he found the structure of our home both comforting and distressing. Because of the children's circumstances and the fact that our son has a learning disability, shortly after taking custody of the children we requested that they be evaluated. I lived with my son's frustration before we knew he had a learning disability. We didn't find out until he was in high school. I will not let that happen to these children.

John was evaluated first, as he was the only one in the public school system. Early in the school year, he had trouble staying focused on his work. He seemed to be in his own little world. He was frustrated with school and completed few assignments. He struggled each night with his schoolwork. The evaluation results confirmed that he did not have a learning disability. However, they did indicate that he was abnormally impulsive and distractable. We then took him to our family physician, who diagnosed him as having attention-deficit/hyperactivity disorder (ADHD). He recommended that we give him Ritalin. It seems to have helped a great deal. (I know others have had problems, but it worked for him.) He turned into a learning sponge. His difficult behaviors turned around.

I'm really glad that he didn't have a learning disability like his father. I don't think I could bear the pain and humiliation again. Now that things are settling down a little, I'm beginning to worry about the medication. Will he have to be on it forever? He is starting to lose weight, and I wonder about the long-term side effects.

Jeff was identified as "at risk" for learning disabilities and is enrolled in a public preschool where he receives speech and language therapy. Jessica, the youngest and only girl, seems hesitant and very withdrawn. She is considered at risk because of her lack of speech. She has severe articulation problems and is extremely difficult to understand, when she does talk.

The children, even after a year, still have emotional problems. They frequently have nightmares, and they openly worry when I leave to go to the store. They need constant reassurance that we will not leave them. We need support as well.

Our lives have changed. I had to quit my job to stay home with the children. I have tried to organize the household to provide a safe and structured environment, but it is hard at times. It takes a lot of energy to provide the children with good nutrition, love, and a stable environment. At times I wonder if we are doing the right thing. Although the children appear resilient, some of their behaviors worry me. Their life before was anything but normal, so it must be difficult for them to accept this new way of life.

Reflective Practice

Children are part of families and their families impact their lives. Few parents or grandparents expect that their children will have disabilities. Families who have children with disabilities face not only the ordinary tasks of family life but must also confront issues that are idiosyncratic to the disability, its severity, and the demands of the family system. Reflect on this family's needs and what community resources might help this family with the challenges they face.

The Family Life Cycle

Like the American family, the life cycle of the family is changing as it responds to the entrances and exits of its members. Looking at the family from a life cycle perspective allows us to focus on some of the **stages** and **transitions** that most affect children with disabilities.

The family life cycle conceptualizes families as a unit of interacting individuals moving through time. The family experiences some periods of relative stability (stages) and other periods of change (transitions between stages). Some changes are predictable, such as when family members are born, grow up, and leave the home. Other changes cannot be predicted, such as discovering a child has a disability, or an untimely death. The family life cycle is one way of organizing information about the family.

Regardless of variations, this model focuses on the negotiation of underlying processes of family expansion, contraction, and the realignment of relationships to support the entry, exit, and development of family members in a functional way (Carter & McGoldrick, 1999). Another value of the family life cycle approach is that it shows the different tasks family systems must accomplish at different times; how difficult it is to meet the needs of all the family members; and how patterns change based on the developmental needs of the family and as family members interact with a changing society.

Some think of the family life cycle as a kind of dance. There are times when families are very close and other times when families open up to give their members more freedom or personal space. Childbirth is one of the coming together times. Adolescence is an opening up time.

The number of stages in the family life cycle varies with different scholars, different cultural and ethnic groups, and different families. The progression from one stage to the next is marked by change. Some change can be taken care of through flexibility or adaptation. However, as the family moves through the life cycle, some changes require the family to approach things in new and different ways. The way they are currently doing things does not work, regardless of how flexible the family is or how they adapt.

The traditional family life cycle focuses on the predictable changes, such as the birth of a child. The focus of this family life cycle includes nonnormative events related to having a child with a disability. This modification of the family life cycle has more stages than the traditional life cycle. It also includes variations, such as discovering the child has a disability at birth versus learning about it later.

Families with Infants and Young Children

This stage of the family life cycle is characterized by adding a dependent member to the family. Becoming parents requires appending the role of parent to the role of partner. The adult moves up a generation and performs the task of caregiving for the young child.

Transition to Parenthood

All family life cycle transitions bring some accompanying stress, and the transition to parenthood is no exception. Becoming parents causes adults to clarify and reconsider their values and the decisions they made in young adulthood. The reality of the infant may be different from the expectation. A mother who initially planned to take a 6-week leave from work and then place the infant in child care may decide that she does not want to leave her infant in the care of others. However, if she must go back to work, her situation becomes stressful. Likewise, a mother who quit her job to be with the infant full-time may decide that full-time child care is not as fulfilling as she thought, and so she wants to return to work. As with all joint decisions, the partner may not have changed his thinking or may have changed in different directions.

The ability of the family to anticipate and respond to the ever-changing demands of an infant or young child is a central feature in this transition. When the child's demands are ambiguous or the family cannot meet the child's needs, families may become stressed. The challenge for the family is to synchronize the child's needs with the rhythm and pattern of the family (Newman, 2000). The family must also constantly adapt to the child's changing development. The first steps bring joy, but also require new vigilance, monitoring, and household adaptations. This high demand for flexibility and change may result in parental role strain and stress.

With modern technology some families learn about their child's probable disability prenatally. The extent to which the newborn is different from the family's hopes, dreams, and expectations can be stressful. Children both affect and are affected by the family in which they develop. The characteristics of the infant and the interaction of these characteristics with parenting styles are important factors.

Discovering the Disability at Birth

Parents are rarely told about their infant's condition in the delivery room, but parents often get clues: hushed voices, questions not answered, and an overall air of concern. Newborns with disabilities often spend their first days, weeks, or even months in a **neonatal intensive care unit (NICU)** (Seligman & Darling, 2007). The monitors, tubes, and atmosphere makes forming an attachment challenging.

Reactions to having a child with a disability are highly individualistic and depend on the severity of the child's condition, supports available to the family, the family's culture, and other personal factors. Parents have a variety of reactions when they learn their child has a disability. Many professionals see some type of "grief cycle" in which parents move through stages on their way to acceptance of the child. The exact stages, sequences, and the time spent in each stage are individualistic.

The relationship between disability and grief is complex. Most parents report feeling a sense of shock. Initially, they feel emotionally "numb." They may even show physical signs of shock. Shock often turns to denial; parents may deny the disability or the severity of it. For children who look "normal," this denial is easier. Denial is a way of buying time to adjust. It is psychologically highly adaptive, it cushions the blow. It allows time for parents to gather their resources. Once reality is acknowledged, life will change.

Denial may be replaced by anxiety. Most adults feel anxious when facing an unknown situation. However, anxiety provides energy that may mobilize parents to find out what the diagnosis means, to talk with other parents, and to seek new information. As parents learn more their reactions may move into fear, guilt, depression, and/or anger. Parents may feel angry at doctors, professionals, and even the infant himself. They may feel anger for the struggles that lay ahead for the child and for them. They want to know *why* and *how* it happened. For many families these answers are unknown. To the extent that they cannot find out why it happened, they cannot prevent it from happening again. If they plan to have more children they know the risk is there.

Families face challenges in adjusting to the addition of a family member with disabilities. One relates to **attachment**. When medically fragile children hover between life and death, attachment is difficult. Others may find it difficult to respond to a child who is so different from the one they expected. The establishment of trust and attachment is important to later development. These are the first of many decisions parents will have to make as they address issues of stigma and embarrassment. Sometimes parents themselves disagree about the appropriate path to take.

Grieving may continue off and on throughout a child's life. This episodic process becomes especially strong at normal transition times such as birthdays, school entry, and at traditional times when families join for reunions. Seeing how easy certain things are for other children and how difficult they are for their child can bring back the tears or the anger. Even explaining the child's disability may activate the cycle for some parents. Rather than endure this, the family may reduce its social life and withdraw from all except medical associations within the community. There is disagreement about whether the goal of family acceptance is realistic. Perhaps a more realistic goal is for families to adjust to the reality of the disability in their own unique ways (Marshak & Prezant, 2007). One parent told me that you never reach "acceptance." You love your child, but you never quite accept the disability.

In the Field

We went to the hospital early one January morning to birth our third son. He was born quickly and uneventfully. However, there was an unusual quiet in the room after his birth. They didn't give him to me but said something about cleaning him up and some other things I didn't grasp. They came back relatively soon and told us before we had time to make the first call that they thought our son had Down syndrome. I couldn't believe it. I was only 29 years old. How could this happen to us? The prenatal testing hadn't picked this up. They told us they needed to do additional testing to be sure. But they were sure. We talked before we made the call to announce the birth of our son. We decided not to tell anyone about Dillon's probable diagnosis, reasoning that if people got to know him first the disability would not influence their relationship.

Our daughter Chelsea was born with a cleft palate. We were distressed and really wanted some support. We called my parents as they were staying at our home with our oldest daughter. We told them about Chelsea's cleft palate and that although it would require several surgeries, she would be fine. My mother fainted and my father said to tell them before we brought Chelsea home so they could leave. They said they would come to see her in 2 years when she was "fixed." They live about a thousand miles away. In the 2 years after Chelsea's birth they visited several times. They always stayed in a motel and had us drop Donna, Chelsea's older sister, off. I seethed with anger. I thought it was unfair of us to not let Donna see her grandparents yet at the same time I was so resentful and hurt that my parents couldn't be there for all of us. It truly changed our relationship.

Reflective Practice

Reflect on the experiences these two families had as they welcomed their newborns into their family. Think about how different disabilities and decisions affect the welcoming process. Think about how you might respond to a friend who gave birth to an infant with a disability. Would you visit and take presents or would you avoid the situation?

Later Discovery of the Disability

For children whose disability is not identified at birth, a diagnosis is often made during early childhood. The process of identification is different for each family member. Initially the family believes they have a typically developing infant. One parent may think something is wrong, but is not sure. There is a sense of foreboding that is sometimes worse than knowing for sure that the child has a specific condition. Mothers are typically the first to sense difficulties, if these were not picked up by the physician at birth. Physicians and friends may attribute mothers' concerns to lack of experience or anxiety. Getting confirmation is often a long process: it may be months or years before they are confirmed. Sometimes learning the child does have a disability is a relief. Parents may be relieved to find their child has a learning disability when their fear was an intellectual disability (Seligman & Darling, 2007).

Parents want an accurate diagnosis that helps them plan for a life with their child. Professionals vary in how they respond to parents' quest for this knowledge. Some decide to paint the worst case scenario, others may try to be optimistic, and others are unwilling to make any prognosis without additional information. Parents have to decide who and what to believe out of what they are told, considering what they know about their child, and what they have learned on their own.

Parents adjust routines to include the care of all family members. The care for a child with a disability may be medically complicated and demanding. In the midst of day-to-day survival, personal fatigue, and self-doubt, many families identify positive contributions that the child and the disability bring to the family unit. They become aware of individual and family strengths. They value this opportunity for growth.

Parents make decisions about early intervention; specifically, what the most appropriate interventions are, given what is available, what is most useful to them, how much they can afford to pay, and what they see as the long- and short-term benefits. Parents are part of a team whose function is to develop the infant or toddler's Individualized Family Service Plan (IFSP). They decide on the role they want to take with the team and in what ways they want to participate. They educate themselves about the disability and the service delivery systems.

The service delivery systems change when a child reaches 36 months. Some children who were eligible for services from birth to 3 may no longer meet the eligibility criteria. However, for other children, where services were **discretionary** and may have to be paid for, they are now **mandated** and free. As services become more formalized, children often move from a home- or home/center-based approach to a center- or school-based system. This is a transition for children, parents, and service providers.

Siblings and extended family also have to cope with issues related to parental time and energy. Seligman and Darling (2007) noted that sibling relationships are usually the longest and most enduring of all family relationships. Siblings of children with disabilities have many of the same feelings that parents do. They are proud of each accomplishment their sibling makes. At the same time, they may wonder why this has happened to them and be sad or angry about it. There may be times when they are embarrassed by their sibling. They may feel jealous of the extra attention he receives and yet feel guilty for having those feelings. All of these feelings are normal and expected. Although there will continue to be times when they are frustrated with their sibling (as with *any* brother or sister), most children learn to accept and love their sibling.

Siblings of children with disabilities have additional needs. They need information. They want to know what's going on. Parents, in an effort to "protect" them, often don't tell them very much. Limited or poor information adds to their confusion (Turnbull, Turnbull, Erwin, & Soodak, 2006). If their brother or sister wears a hearing aid, they need to know why, how it works, and what it does and does not do to aid hearing.

They need specific information about whether the disability is transmittable, how to talk to their friends about it, how to relate effectively to their sibling, and what family expectations are for their future role with their sibling. Despite what siblings are told, many have a private version of their sibling's disability and may feel that they are the cause of it (Seligman & Darling, 2007). Someone must learn about this private version and help siblings gain more accurate information about the causes of disabilities.

All children need time to develop friendships with peers. They also need private time with parents. If there are two parents in the family, each parent needs to spend some time alone with each child. Overburdening siblings with care responsibility can result in anger and resentment rather than acceptance. A child's sense of obligation for a sibling with disabilities can be a major concern and may require professional counseling. For the most part, siblings do not expect the situation to be "fixed"; they do, however, need a safe time and place to express their feelings and to be accepted (Seligman & Darling, 2007).

In the Field

My name is Kelly and I am 15 years old. My sister, Mara, is 6 and I really love her. Mara has a seizure disorder that really messes up her life and mine. I am glad that her seizures don't happen all the time. However, the thing that really bothers me is that Mara always has a seizure when something important is happening to me. I don't mind helping Mara, but sometimes she ruins everything.

One time, I was having a slumber party at my house when Mara began to have a seizure. She had to be taken to the hospital and then all my friends had to leave. Another time Mara had a seizure on my birthday and the whole family ended up spending the day in the hospital with her. Some birthday! We don't take family vacations any more because Mara might have a seizure.

I know I sound spoiled and mean, but she seems to get all the attention. Sometimes I am tired of being the big sister. I care about my sister and I want her to be well. It just seems like everything revolves around her. What about me?

Reflective Practice

Siblings are affected by having a brother or sister with a disability. Not only because of the disability itself but also because of what it means to parental time and resources. Talk to children about their siblings and talk with siblings about their feelings both positive and negative.

Siblings may need specific support in developing their own identity. They may need the opportunity to talk with other siblings of children with disabilities. If one is available, they may want to be a part of a support group. Parents often think that siblings are coping much better than the siblings see themselves coping. Parents need to be aware of these possible differences in perception. Siblings need to be asked directly about their perceptions. Their parents cannot speak for them (Seligman & Darling, 2007).

Implications for Educators

Family members' feelings must be acknowledged as legitimate responses to difficult situations. They should not be viewed as maladaptive. Parents who are in denial for long periods must be supported in gathering resources rather than confronted with their continuing inability to face up to the situation. Professionals must learn to cope with parents' anger, whether or not it is directed at them. Professionals need to provide families with a safety zone where feelings can be expressed. This is crucial as their informal support may be small. You may have siblings of children with disabilities in your class as well as children with disabilities. Find out what they have been told, what their questions are, and be a good, safe listener for them. Extended family and friends may stay away because they feel uncomfortable or don't know what to say, do, or ask. As children reach milestones such as school entry or changing service delivery systems, professionals need to expect that there will be some grief associated with these marker events.

Families with School-Age Children

Most children with disabilities enter school with some experience in early care and education settings. However, the transition to school is still a marker event. Depending upon the area, there may be a variety of placement options. Parents, as part of the Individualized Educational Program (IEP) team, learn about these options and decide which one is the best for their child and family.

If children enter a public school, parents must learn to work with the school and the bureaucracies inherent in that system. As children become part of a school system families often become more active members of the community in which they live. They must locate community resources to arrange for after-school care, if needed, and decide on their child's extracurricular activities. They may encounter extra expenses associated with their child's disability such as tutoring or additional therapy.

In the Field

Please don't judge me. You may only have partial information. When my son was in elementary school, I volunteered to help the school nurse. During a major project she needed to call me at home frequently for input. Well … she would call at 10:00 or 11:00 A.M. and wake me up. She joked about my leisurely lifestyle. She later confided that she felt I was lazy. What she didn't know was that my autistic son rarely slept through the night. He would be up at all hours of the night (coming into my room at 2 A.M. to ask where his jeans were!).

Reflective Practice

Before making judgments about parents (even if just to yourself) ensure that you are doing it from an accurate knowledge base. Reflect on your current life style and consider how others might judge it.

Parents are adjusting emotionally to the educational implications for their child, both in the present and for the long term. Many parents worry about how their child will be treated by peers, whether he will make friends, and whether he will be included as part of the group. Siblings need to be supported in finding the appropriate words and concepts to share with their friends. There may be continuing concerns related to jealousy and the limited money available for leisure and recreation (Seligman & Darling, 2007).

Implications for Educators

Educators need to remember that even though families have been living with their children for about 5 years they may cycle into a stage of denial as they approach a marker event such as entering kindergarten. For some families, elementary school will just be an extension of preschool services, whereas others will see it as a major hurtle. For most parents, school and performance at school casts a different light on their understanding of their child's disability. This may be a difficult time for parents as they cope with these new understandings.

Parents may be wary of you, the teacher, and wonder if you have the skill and ability to educate their child, particularly if you teach in an inclusive classroom and parents have come from a more segregated setting. Parents need your assurance that their children will be safe and that you will support their child's academic and social growth.

It is not unusual to discover that what parents and educators want for children is different. Educators need to think through these differences before approaching parents. It is imperative that families decide what is important to them and the areas in which they want to focus; early childhood professionals must frame parents' focus in a developmentally appropriate way (Turnbull et al., 2005).

Families with Adolescents

As children move into adolescence, families must evaluate and establish qualitatively different boundaries than they used when children were younger. Adolescents need freedom with guidance. They want to be like their peers, thus parental authority is often challenged. Adolescence is more complex when families have children with disabilities.

For parents in this stage of the family life cycle the tasks involve adjusting emotionally to the possible chronic nature of the disability, the permanence of the disability, and the possible permanence of the adolescent's dependency (Lambie, 2000).

Parents must arrange for leisure activities that are appropriate for this age group and within the adolescent's ability range. This is also a time when parents begin planning for career and vocational development and/or postsecondary education. By this time, siblings have a better understanding of the disability and its long-term implications. For many siblings, life goals and career choices may be affected by having a sibling with a disability. Many go into fields such as teaching and social work (Seligman & Darling, 2007).

Implications for Educators

Families with adolescents are beyond the age range that early childhood educators teach. However, it is important to keep in mind that children do grow up and, as we look at behaviors and skills, we need to keep this long-term view in mind. The behavior that is cute in a young child could place an older child at risk.

Families with Young Adults

This is the longest phase in the family life cycle. The process of launching young adults is a gradual one that begins in infancy and continues into later adulthood. Children leave and return many times over the course of their lives. This is particularly true of the **boomerang generation** who may move back into their parents' home after living independently because of a poor economy, low income, divorce—or they may never have left home in the first place (Benokraitis, 2005).

Implications for Educators

As educators, our role is to prepare all children for the life they will lead when they leave school. When children have disabilities we need to talk with parents about their expectations for their children and make plans for children to acquire the skills they will need. The transition from school to work is one of the most difficult ones families will face.

Families in Later Life

Adjusting to retirement is one of the major tasks of later life. Financial insecurity and dependence are also issues that older adults face. It is a time when adults must cope with the loss of friends, relatives, spouses, and perhaps a child. As parents face their own death, they may need to review the guardianship and financial arrangements they have made in light of their adult child with disabilities.

Implications for Educators

Even when their children are young, parents may worry what will happen to their children when they can no longer care for them. Wise parents want to know about issues related to guardianship, wills, and trusts when their children are young in case something unexpected happens to them. You may be the person they ask. You are not expected to be an expert in this area, however, you should be aware of the general concerns and be able to provide sources of information for parents to explore.

Each stage of the family life cycle brings with it a unique set of decisions that have to be made. As the age of majority is reached, individuals and families have a new set of decisions thrust upon them. Decisions made by early childhood special educators and children's families have implications for their quality of life in later years. Viewing the family from the family life cycle perspective highlights some of the tasks families must perform at various stages, how these tasks change over time, and how a child with disabilities affects these tasks.

Tasks, obligations, and expectations vary with **sociohistorical time** as feelings about educating children with disabilities and the role of the family change. It is not possible to educate young children without taking into account what is happening in the world. What we know about disabilities and what is considered "best practice" changes. Today best practice emphasizes natural environments, children's ethnic/cultural background, and is family-centered.

Family-Centered Practice

A family-centered approach is the best way to deliver services to *all* young children and their families. However, defining family-centered practice is almost as elusive as defining families. One commonality in the use of the term is agreement in the centrality of the family. The family unit is the constant in the child's life and everything else comes and goes (Sandall, Smith, & McLean, 2005). Children's teachers change, therapists change, and the environment changes, but the family remains. While professionals have expertise in their fields, families have unique knowledge of their child and his environment, their values, and the consequences of their choices—past and future. The family is ultimately responsible for the child's growth and development.

The family-centered model is consumer-oriented. It is based on collaboration and open communication. It requires mutual respect and equality in relationships between parents and professionals. It is designed to meet the unique needs of a particular child and her family. It honors the diversity of families and recognizes that the family is not defined by the child's disability. Despite the support for family-centered services, many services, especially those in education, are child-centered. They don't focus on the broader context of children's lives. When the child is the sole focus, the importance of the family—its diversity, and its strengths and challenges—may be lost. Families differ in many ways that impact their children. One of the most pervasive influences is the impact of culture.

Partnering with Families and Honoring Their Culture

The United States is a multiracial, multicultural, and multilingual society. This needs to be acknowledged before effective strategies for interacting with diverse families can evolve. When trying to understand diversity it is easy to overgeneralize and oversimplify differences. Not all members of an ethnic group are alike in the way they embrace their culture's lifestyle and values (Lambie, 2000). This section is not designed to be an exhaustive view of these cultures. It is designed to raise your awareness of the importance of recognizing cultural and ethnic differences and how they influence your work with families and their children. All parents have goals and expectations for their children. However, differences in parental goals and expectations arise because parents and societies have different expectations. We as educators need to be mindful of these differences as we interact with families and educate their children.

Families' views are influenced by their cultural background. What we think, how we act, the language we speak, and even what we eat are part of our wider cultural context. Looking at cultural diversity is a balance between appreciating our common humanity and validating the differences among us.

Working with Families in a Cultural Context

Individuals do not develop their language, rituals, rules, and beliefs in a vacuum. They are part of the cultural heritage handed down to them through their family. Culture is a way of life, a blueprint for living. It is both learned and

Children grow up in families and the culture of the family influences the language they speak and the foods they eat.

internalized by being part of a particular culture (Berger, 2004). All children come to educational settings with a cultural background. They must be understood within this context.

Although the overall percentage of children in the United States population is decreasing, the proportion of children from non–Euro-American populations is increasing. In developing cultural sensitivity, knowledge about different cultural groups is necessary. However, this limited knowledge is not sufficient because all individuals and families are different and embrace different aspects of culture. Knowledge of culture has to be both generalized and individualized. To be culturally sensitive, you as a prospective teacher must accomplish several tasks:

1. Conduct a cultural self-assessment. Take a close look at your culture and how it has shaped your values and beliefs. You will view children and their families through this lens. Become aware of the biases you hold. Other than Native Americans, we are all here through past immigration. This is an important part of our personal culture. Becoming aware of your culture and its values increases the probability of becoming a culturally sensitive individual who can validate the differences among people and appreciate their commonality (Lynch, 2004a; McGoldrick, 1993).

2. Learn about the communities in which families live. Gather and analyze **ethnographic** information about the cultural community. Meet families in their space. Recognize and understand the dynamics of difference. Culture contributes to obvious and subtle differences in individuals and communities. Obvious differences include such things as the language spoken, amount of eye contact, and body language used, whereas more subtle aspects of culture may influence the amount of self-disclosure someone is comfortable with. Avoid stereotyping (Lynch, 2004b).

3. Determine the degree to which the family operates **transculturally**. Child-rearing practices are designed to socialize children into their family and culture. Daily caregiving routines reflect a family's fundamental, deeply felt values and beliefs. Since children absorb their culture as part of the caregiving process, early care and education is important to parents. Child-rearing practices may provide a key to understanding socialization practices in different cultural contexts. If early care and education reflects only the values of the dominant culture, parents may be concerned about the practices used. Children with disabilities may be deprived of a part of their own culture, or they may experience inexplicable discontinuity between home and the educational setting. Examine each family's orientation to specific child-rearing issues while acknowledging and valuing diversity. This involves the recognition that there are cultural differences and that these differences play a role in what families believe about children with disabilities and how they should be reared (Lynch, 2004b).

Acquiring Cultural Knowledge

Learning about different cultures is an ongoing process. Many books describe different ethnic groups with some focusing on practices that relate to early childhood and children with disabilities (Lynch & Hanson, 2004). This serves as the foundation to build knowledge about individual families. See Table 2-1 for more specific information.

Implications for Educators

Think about your personal background, your beliefs, and what this means in the classroom. If a child with a disability comes from a family who is poor and/or who speaks English haltingly, or the parents have little formal education, does that influence your expectations for their child? How will you support difference, not deficit; look for strength, not weakness? Many have had the strength to survive situations we cannot even imagine. How will you see families as a resource and not a liability?

Cultural Diversity in the United States

There are five main groups of racial/ethnic families in the United States: Anglo-European, Latino, African American, Asian and Pacific Islander, and American Indian and Alaska Native. In many ways they are more similar than dissimilar to the dominant family forms that exist in the larger U.S. society. Children receive their basic identity and status within the family context. Some parents subscribe to the basic achievement and mobility values that exist within the larger society; others do not.

The cultural composition of the United States is becoming increasingly diverse. The projection for 2020 shows that 40 percent of the population will be from diverse racial and cultural backgrounds. By 2050 it will be 50 percent (Table 2-2). Children from minority cultures are disproportionately identified as having disabilities (IDEA, 2004).

Demographers attribute the rising percentage to higher birth rates among nonwhite, non-Anglo women, increased immigration, and more women of childbearing age in the

Table 2–1: Acquiring cultural knowledge

- *Reason for immigration.* What was the family seeking or leaving behind? Were they fleeing from political persecution, poverty, or war, or were they brought against their will as slaves?
- *Length of time since immigration.* How many generations has the family been in the United States?
- *Place of residence.* Does the family live in an ethnic neighborhood?
- *Order of migration.* Did the family come as a unit or did one member come first and others join later?
- *Socioeconomic status.* What is the socioeconomic status of the family and what are their attitudes toward education and upward mobility?
- *Religiosity.* What are the family's religious and political ties?
- *Language.* What languages are spoken by family members and what are their levels of comfort and fluency in different languages?
- *Intermarriage.* To what extent do family members have connections to other ethnic groups and how frequently have intermarriages occurred?
- *Attitudes.* What are the family members' attitudes toward their ethnic identity and its values? (McGoldrick, 1993).

Reflective Practice

Answer these questions about yourself. Talk with your family if you are not sure about some of the answers.

The final element in cultural knowledge is using the information and insights acquired to adapt educational practices to meet the needs of children with disabilities and their families. This may challenge you to expand your definition of "family" and their participation to include grandparents and various significant others in conferences. Focus on the strengths that a particular cultural background brings to children with disabilities and work with the strengths and priorities that families have set.

nonwhite groups. Early childhood special educators need to develop cross-cultural competence, so they can better educate these diverse groups of children (Lynch, 2004a). See Table 2-3 to look at the population of people younger than 18 and the **median** ages to confirm these trends.

The following brief sketches provide some demographic information that is relevant to your teaching. The resources at the end of the chapter and the references at the back of the book can help you locate additional information. It is useful to start with a common understanding of terminology. A **racial** group is a socially defined group distinguished by selected, inherited physical characteristics. An **ethnic** group is distinguished by a sense of peoplehood or "consciousness of kind" based on a common national origin, religion, or language. If a racial or ethnic group is subordinate to the majority in terms of power and prestige (not necessarily in terms of number of members), members occupy a **minority** status as well (Eshleman, 2000).

Latino Families

Latino families constitute the largest ethnic minority in the United States with a population of 41.3 million in 2004.

This change has profound cultural and policy implications. Latinos include people from all countries in Latin America as well as parts of the Caribbean that have Latin-based languages (Halgunseth, 2004). (*Note*: I use Latino and Hispanic interchangeably in this text.) They do not share a common racial background. The population is young, diverse, dynamic, and growing rapidly. The Hispanic growth rate of 3.6 percent from July 1, 2003, to July 1, 2004, was three times that of the total population (U.S. Census Bureau, 2005a). Nationally, 7 percent of the population is younger than the age of 5. Latinos had the highest proportion of children in this age range, at 11 percent. They are a community of first-, second-, and third-generation immigrants. Many have uprooted their families and left their homes and relatives for economic, political, professional, ideological, and educational reasons (Carrasquillo, Lantigua, & Shea, 2000). Others are descendants of the native Mexicans who lived in the southwest before it became part of the United States. In the past, minority families were strongly encouraged to **assimilate** to be accepted. Assimilation required adopting U.S. customs and language as a way of being accepted

Table 2–2: Projected population of the United States: 2000–2050

Percent of Total Population	2000	2020	2050
White alone, not Hispanic	69.4	61.3	50.1
Hispanic (of any race)	12.6	17.8	24.4
Black alone	12.7	13.5	14.6
Asian alone	3.8	5.4	8.0
All other races	2.5	3.5	5.3

Source: U.S. Census Bureau, 2004.

Table 2–3: Annual estimates of the population by age and ethnic/racial characteristics for the United States: April 1, 2000–July 1, 2006

Race	Younger than 18		Older than 18		Median Age
White	56,234,845	(24%)	183,511,409	(76%)	38
Hispanic	14,966,364	(34%)	29,354,674	(66%)	27
Black	11,364,490	(30%)	26,978,059	(70%)	31
Asian	3,002,560	(23%)	10,156,783	(77%)	35
American Indian/Alaska Native	847,390	(29%)	2,005,461	(71%)	30
Native Hawaiian/Pacific Islander	151,234	(29%)	377,584	(71%)	30

Source: U.S. Census Bureau, 2007.

and ignoring or not identifying with one's home culture. **Acculturation** is different; it signifies the adoption of values of the host country but does not demand that culture values be dropped. Typically this means learning English and accepting and promoting American ideals (Halgunseth, 2004). The third option is **biculturalism. Bicultural adaptation** incorporates aspects of the home culture with the mainstream culture. Rather than replacing their home culture (their existing cultural values and behaviors), they add mainstream values and information. These individuals can function in both the home culture and the majority culture (Halgunseth, 2004). Families and settings can support bicultural adaptation by teaching children about their ethnic identity and about the special experiences they may encounter because of their ethnic background. This approach is related to higher self-esteem and proactive styles of coping with discrimination (Halgunseth, 2004).

Latinos are overrepresented in poverty groups. In 2005, 28 percent of Hispanic children lived below the poverty line. The poverty rate for all children in the United States was 18 percent at this time (Federal Interagency Forum on Child and Family Statistics, 2007). In 2005, the median income of Latino families was $35,967, whereas for all U.S. families it was $50,784. Among the Hispanic groups, Puerto Ricans (all of whom are U.S. citizens) have the lowest median family income and Cubans the highest (U.S. Bureau of the Census, 1998). The Latino population is the youngest with a median age of 27 compared to whites who have a median age of 38. They also have the highest percentage of any ethnic/racial group of their population younger than age 18 (34 percent) (U.S. Census Bureau, 2007).

Most Hispanic families have high family cohesion and flexibility. Families are important to them and they frequently have supportive kin networks. Many families have a strong ethnic identity and, despite the stereotypes, most have egalitarian decision making.

Like African American families, they face many challenges. A primary challenge is increasing their level of education and overcoming economic discrimination to gain financial resources. Less than half of the foreign-born population from Latin America comes with a high school diploma (Hernandez, 2006).

Children from Latino families do not do well in U.S. schools. Over 20 percent of children between the ages of birth and 8 are Hispanic. Although many are from immigrant homes, about 90 percent of the children are U.S. citizens. Hispanic children are five times *more* likely to have a mother who did not graduate from high school and three times *less* likely to have a mother who is a college graduate then white children (Hernandez, 2006). Hispanic children, particularly those from disadvantaged circumstances, lag behind non-Hispanic whites on measures of school readiness and school achievement. High-quality early childhood programs can contribute to greater school readiness. There is evidence that the use of both Spanish and English in early childhood programs contributes to greater school readiness for these children (National Task Force on Early Childhood Education for Hispanics, 2007).

The extended family plays an important role in Latino families. Siblings, cousins, and other relatives provide a support network that is helpful to families with young children. The overall attitude toward children is one of acceptance, putting less pressure on them to achieve milestones early. One marries to have children and children validate a marriage (Zuniga, 2004). Latinos tend to be nurturing and permissive in early childhood. Because of family values, young Latino children are less likely to be in early care and education settings. Mothers are expected to stay home and raise children. When this is not possible, extended family frequently takes over the care of young children. Some families may see sending young children to an early care and education setting as a sign of deteriorating family values. They may need home-based intervention with a bilingual/bicultural interventionist. Once trust is established they may also feel comfortable in a home/center-based service delivery system.

Latino parenting styles foster interdependence and relational learning, whereas European American parents emphasize independence and self-initiated learning. Children with disabilities may receive special treatment from their families (Zuniga, 2004). They may come to school with fewer **adaptive skills**. The major strategy that Latino parents use in teaching is modeling. If there are older siblings they may be the model for teaching younger children (Halgunseth, 2004). If a Latino parent was teaching a 5 year old to set the table she would demonstrate how to do it and where the different utensils, cups, and plates go. A European American parent would use inquiry: "Where do you think the plate goes?" Then, if the child placed the plate in the right spot the parent is likely to say, "Great, you did that all by yourself." Because of their view of modeling as a way of teaching, they talk less to their children so young Latino children have not heard as much language as others.

Maintaining harmonious relationships is important to most Latino parents. They support the development of interpersonal skills in their children. They want others to enjoy their children and find them pleasant. Negative emotions such as aggression, anger, and arguing are often distressing. They also monitor body language and facial expressions more than European American families. Being well-educated includes not only the traditional three Rs, but also a sense of inner importance that includes tranquility, obedience, and courtesy. Some of these skills may make them more passive and dependent upon adult authority (Halgunseth, 2004).

In the Field

I spent about 4 months in Costa Rica doing research and working with families who had young children with disabilities. Because I was in Latin America I was more conscious of issues relating to culture, but it was still hard. I would try so hard to figure out how to get some of the services I thought a child needed. Then when I would talk with the families about what they could do for their young children, but they did not follow through. Many mothers felt that it was a wiser use of their time to spend a half hour in church on their knees praying for their child than to use that time working with the child or going to occupational therapy. I just did not understand it.

Reflective Practice

Reflect on how you might feel if you were the one working with these families. Can you think of ways to honor cultural beliefs and to work with families whose values are different from yours while also meeting children's needs?

There are many distinctive differences among Hispanic populations. Only a few of these will be highlighted but the differences are so great that it is important to know what specific group you are learning about and what aspects of the culture the individuals you are working with embrace.

Mexican American Families

People of Mexican heritage make up about 58 percent of the Latino population in the United States (Zuniga, 2004). Over 1 million Mexican Americans are descendants of the native Mexicans who lived in the southwest and became U.S. citizens in 1848, when Arizona, California, Colorado, Nevada, New Mexico, and parts of Oklahoma, Texas, Utah, and Wyoming became U.S. territory. There was also large-scale migration in the early 1900s caused by the chaos of the Mexican Revolution and the demand for labor on cotton farms and railroads in California. The devaluation of the peso in 1994 contributed to migration. Mexicans make up over half (57 percent; over 5 million people) of the undocumented immigrants in the United States (Passel, Capps, & Fix, 2004).

High fertility rates and strong family ties typify the Mexican American culture. They often live near nuclear and extended family members and share interests and concerns about the welfare of the family unit. The needs of the family may supersede the needs of individual family members. The theme of family honor and unity is strong throughout Mexican American society irrespective of social class or geographic location.

Godparents play an important role in families. Traditionally, expectant parents select a patron, a married couple, or an extended family member to be the child's sponsor. This is considered both an honor and an obligation. The baptism ceremony establishes a social bond and godparents are thought of as being co-parents. The relationship is expected to last a lifetime, although this tradition is less strong than it has been in the past (Halgunseth, 2004).

In the past, Mexican Americans adhered to the traditional ideal of manliness (*machismo*), which is equated with authority, strength, sexual virility, and prowess. The male was the patriarch who made important decisions. He was also the provider and protector for his family. Decision making is becoming more egalitarian. In general, however, Mexican American males still exert power over their wives and the women still do the majority of child care and household tasks. Mexican American families have a high fertility rate and have an average of 3.2 children (National Center for Health Statistics, 2000). Fathers show a definite interest in their children and their behavior. Given the size of the family, along with minimal skills and low level of income, it is difficult for many Mexican American families to live above the poverty line. This is confounded by low levels of parental education. About 66 percent of fathers and 64 percent of mothers did not graduate from high school and about 40 percent completed only 8 years of formal education (Hernandez, 2006).

Puerto Rican Families

Puerto Rican families are the second largest Latino subgroup comprising about 10 percent of the Latino population (U.S. Bureau of the Census, 2000). All Puerto Ricans are U.S. citizens. Families are heavily concentrated in eastern cities, especially New York City. Many have low-paying full-time jobs, part-time jobs, or sometimes no job at all. Males came to the United States to work in manufacturing jobs that required little education and few skills. However, in today's economy there are few such jobs.

More than other Hispanic groups, Puerto Ricans form families without marriage and have a high proportion (60 percent) of female-headed households. In 1999, 27 percent of Puerto Rican households lived below the poverty line (U.S. Bureau of the Census, 2000). This poses challenges to these families. See Table 2-4 for ways of working with children with disabilities in Latino families.

Implications for Educators

Children may come to school with good language skills in both languages or with only rudimentary knowledge of English or Spanish. Communicating with Latino families who have limited English proficiency (LEP) may be challenging. Some families that speak Spanish may not read it. If the parents speak little or no English, have bilingual/bicultural support for parent-teacher conferences.
Translate forms that are to be sent home. However, translating forms may not solve the problem. Spanish has many dialectical forms just as English does and it is important to

Table 2–4: Implications for working with Latino families who have children with disabilities

- Find out about the language skills, cultural characteristics, and values that affect children's learning and cognitive development.
- Determine your experience with culturally diverse people, especially those who speak English as a second language and those who have immigrated illegally.
- Assess your style of interacting with others, especially how you think about time. If you feel the pressure of time during your interactions and that documents must be signed *now*, families may interpret this as a lack of respect or concern.
- Learn to pronounce the children's names as the family does. Do not Americanize names unless the family requests that you do so. Talk to the children.
- Appreciate the opportunity you have been given to broaden your global knowledge and to look at your culture from another perspective. Learn some of the language the family uses and appreciate the challenge they face learning English. Honor and value children's home language.
- Find out from families what they want for their children. Some families want children to be respectful, polite, and loving and are less concerned about independent thinking and problem-solving skills than most European Americans.
- Have a culturally rich classroom that includes many artifacts and activities from children's home cultures and teaches the value of respecting others and their differences.
- Find out what families believe about the cause of their child's disability. They may believe it is a result of evil in the environment, a curse, a punishing God, or something else (and the child may be wearing a amulet to ward off the evil).
- Include someone who is Latina and bilingual on an IFSP/IEP team.
- Do not assume that families who speak Spanish and/or English can also read it. They may have learned words in English, particularly in relation to their child, that they have never seen or heard in Spanish.
- Learn more about the Latino culture in general, as well as the specific country/culture from which the families come. Attend Latin American community celebrations and watch films from and about Latin America. Identify community resources that are responsive to and supportive of Latin Americans in general and specific countries in particular.

Source: Halgunseth, 2004; Zuniga, 2004; Carrasquillo et al., 2000.

have the right dialect. Additionally, there are some words families may not know in their home language that they have learned in English so the translation is not useful. Think about the concept of the IFSP or the IEP. These are particular concepts based in U.S. law. Understanding the words does not convey the underlying concept. Word-for-word translation does not solve the problem. Learn about families' culture to enrich the curriculum.

Think about how you feel about immigration and immigrants—both legal and illegal—and how this might impact your practice. Also think about what you know about different Latin cultures and how you can include what you know in working with families and curriculum planning. Use the Resources at the end of the chapter and the section in the children's bibliography on *Latino Families and Children* to share this culture with the children you teach.

Please remember that this is just an overview for you to begin to think about children at risk and those with disabilities and how families are both similar and different. You cannot assume that because a family came from Latin America that they will have the values and beliefs discussed. Work individually with families to determine what they want for themselves and their children.

African American Families

African Americans have a rich heritage with a strong sense of family, community, and culture. African Americans are the second largest distinct racial/ethnic group in the United States; they numbered about 39.2 million, or about 12 percent, of the population in 2004 (U.S. Census Bureau,

2005a). (The terms *black* and *African American* are used interchangeably in this text.) The black population has a median age of 31 compared to whites who have a median age of 38. They have 30 percent of their population younger than 18 as compared to 24 percent of whites and 34 percent of Latinos (U.S. Census Bureau, 2007). Because of their unique historical and social experiences, many African Americans have lifestyles and value patterns that differ considerably from the European American majority. The establishment and development of their domestic units took many different paths (Tucker, Subramanian, & James, 2004). One path is the support of the single-parent family (50 percent) with 48 percent of children living with single mothers; the remaining 2 percent live with single fathers. Of these single parents, 6 percent of the mothers and 30 percent of father live in a cohabitating relationship (Fields, 2003). Of mothers, 69 percent were not married at the time of their child's birth (National Center for Health Statistics, 2000). The median income for black American families was $30,858 in 2005 (U.S. Census Bureau, 2005b). In 2006, 35 percent of black children lived with two married parents. The poverty rate for black children that year was also 35 percent. In 2005, 62 percent of black children lived in families with secure parental employment (Federal Interagency Forum on Child and Family Statistics, 2007).

The migration of African Americans from rural to urban areas has followed the general population trend. With the exception of California, there are fewer African Americans in the West and more than half live in the South. African American families, like white families, fit no stereotypic view. Most do well and thrive with increasing numbers completing their education and entering the work force (Willis, 2004). Strengths such as strong family ties and flexibility in family roles, and caring parenting give some families and their young children with disabilities a strong support network. African American families have a strong work orientation and motivation as well as a strong religious orientation. The African American family is an absorbing, adaptive, flexible, and amazingly resilient mechanism for the socialization of its children and survival in society (Tucker et al., 2004).

African American families face challenges based on their history of racism and discrimination in the United States. Major disparities still exist between blacks and whites. A persistent problem is that of black females finding partners. Because black males experience higher rates of unemployment and underemployment, it is difficult to attain a family income level that allows them to provide adequately for their families. When families (regardless of ethnicity) are constantly worrying about financial problems, marital difficulties often follow.

The Evidence Base

From 1962 through 1967, at ages 3 and 4, 123 African Americans born in poverty and at risk for failing in school were divided into two groups. One group (Perry Group) received high-quality preschool education based on the High/Scope model, whereas the other (control group) received no preschool program. Of the 123 individuals, 97 percent were located and interviewed at age 40. Figure 2-1 shows the differences that were identified after 40 years.

Overall, the study documents a return to society of more than $16 for every tax dollar invested in quality early care and education. "These findings can be expected of any Head Start, state preschool, or child care program similar to the program High/Scope coordinated and then studied. Our teachers were well-qualified, they served no more than eight children from low-income families at a time, they visited these families as part of the program to discuss their child's development, and the classes operated daily for children 3 and 4 years old" said Larry Schweinhart, High/Scope president (Perry Study, 2004; Perry Preschool Study, 2005).

Reflective Practice

High-quality early childhood education works and it lasts; yet 95 percent of public investment in education occurs for children age 5 and older. How would you convince people about the importance of investing in high-quality early care and education? What would you say about the social and economic gains? What about the prevention of crime and special education? What would you say about the benefits for families and at-risk African American children?

Although African American families are primarily nuclear families, they have a much stronger social support network than white families. Such a support system is important to families who have children with disabilities. Relatives, particularly grandmothers, form a significant part of this network. The importance of religion in family life at all social levels is another difference between African American and white populations. The religious

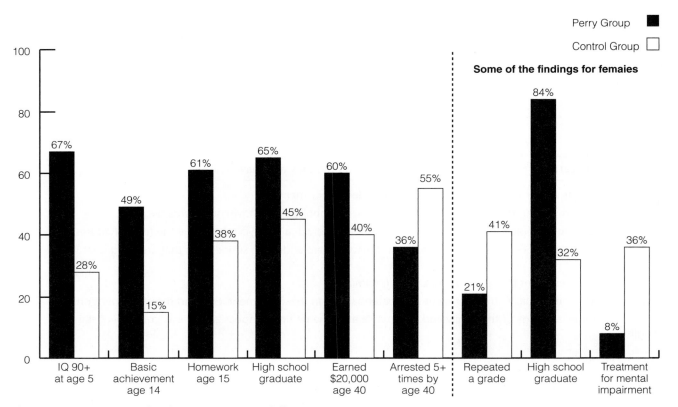

Figure 2–1: Perry Preschool Project: 40-year follow-up

community provides a social life for African American families as well as giving emotional support.

Within African American families, the typical pattern is egalitarian relationships where roles are flexible and tasks are often interchanged. Parents are often more authoritarian than in white families and encourage independence and self-sufficiency earlier. Many African American women value childbearing and child rearing as a validation of their womanhood. Education is valued for upward mobility. Most women work either out of necessity or out of desire to enhance family income. Some African Americans are asking for their differences as well as their similarities to be acknowledged and encouraged.

Implications for Educators

Like Latino families, some African American families embrace the values and lifestyles described, others do not. Learn from the families you work with what is important to them. Knowing an individual's culture does not mean you can predict their behavior (Gonzalez-Mena, 2005). Use the resources at the end of the chapter and the section in the children's bibliography on *African American Families and Children* **to enrich your classroom with literature about African American families and their culture. Develop a plan for learning more about African American families and their children. Reflect on your own comfort in working with African American children.**

Learn more about the African American culture and incorporate this knowledge into your teaching. Examine your teaching materials. Do you have stories about African American children and representative dolls available? When you discuss families do you include a wide range of family configurations including multigenerational families, those who have others living with them, single-parent families, and those with working mothers? Do not ignore ethnicity and pretend that African Americans are the same as whites and just happen to be black. Value the strengths they bring to children. Use the information in Table 2-5 to work with African American families.

Asian and Pacific Islander Families

Over 4 percent of the U.S. population (14.0 million) was characterized as Asian or Pacific Islanders in 2005 (U.S. Census Bureau, 2005b). The Asian American population has doubled each decade since 1970. Most of this growth was the result of immigration. Asian Americans are not a homogeneous group; they represent more than 28 subgroups. The major subgroups included in this category are: Chinese, Filipino, Japanese, Asian Indian, Korean, Vietnamese, Laotian, Cambodian, Thai, and Hmong. The Chinese American community is the largest Asian subgroup in the United States. Although the term Pacific Islander appears as a subcategory in the U.S. census, this does not represent an ethnic group. Included in this subcategory are Hawaiians, Samoans, and Guamanians; they constitute 980,000 people (U.S. Census Bureau, 2005b).

All of these groups had different ancestors, languages, customs, and recency of immigration. The Chinese, Korean, and Vietnamese cultures are rooted in some of the world's oldest civilizations and have been influenced by the doctrines of Confucianism, Taoism, and Buddhism (Chan & Lee, 2004). Asian and Pacific Islanders marry at the same rate as the European American population (82 percent) and there is a high level of family stability. The Asian population has a median age of 35 compared to whites who have a median age of 38. They have 23 percent of their population younger than 18 as compared to 24 percent of whites and 34 percent of Latinos (U.S. Census Bureau, 2007). They are better educated and have higher median incomes than all other groups. In 2005, the median family income was $61,094 (U.S. Census Bureau, 2005b). The poverty rate for Asian Americans was 11 percent in 2005 (U.S. Census Bureau, 2005c). Their strengths lie in family loyalty and a strong family orientation. They respect their elders and have high levels of mutual support between generations.

One challenge for those who have come more recently, such as those from Vietnam, Laos, and Cambodia, is the loss of ties with kin. They, too, face obstacles in the United

---

Table 2–5: Implications for working with African American families who have children with disabilities

- Value the strengths of kinship bonds and include extended family members.
- Work with the family's informal support network (friends, neighbors, church) whenever possible.
- Begin by addressing people formally (Ms. Wapoles) until the individual asks you to change the form of address.
- Learn about the family's beliefs relative to health and medical care and make suggestions that are congruent with their beliefs.
- Learn about the resources in the African American community.
- Evaluate assessment results with an awareness of potential bias in the assessment itself and the assessment process.
- Honor the home language of the family and child while at the same time emphasizing the importance of standard English.
- Avoid stereotyping.
- Include African Americans specialists on IFSP/IEP teams.
- Learn more about African American culture by talking and reading about it.

Source: Tucker et al., 2004; Willis, 2004.

States. They may distrust those outside of their group and have a stigma against seeking help. They have high expectations for themselves and very high academic expectations for their children, with a strong emphasis on self-control (Ishii-Kuntz, 2004).

Overall, Asian Americans value family highly and tend to solve problems within the family settings. Family needs and interdependence often have precedence over individual needs and independence. Family ties are close, divorce rates are low, and there are few female-headed households. As a culture they avoid open confrontation, and are unlikely to challenge educators even if they disagree with them. Communication is often indirect. The family is a harmonious group and anything that might disrupt this harmony, such as strong emotions, is expected to be suppressed.

In the Field

I had a difficult labor with our youngest son. I was older and the pregnancy was unexpected. I thought I was having menopause early and did not seek medical care until I was about 4½ months pregnant. When Yong was born the doctor pulled my husband aside and talked to him. When I asked him about it he said it was nothing. I was exhausted and was just pleased to see our third son. When we left the hospital I thought everything was fine. As I cared for Yong I thought he was different from the other two boys, but then I decided that maybe I was just remembering wrong. He seemed floppy and less alert than they had been. I began to get concerned and talked to our pediatrician who was also Chinese. He told me not to worry.

My mother-in-law lives two houses away and finally she voiced some of my concerns when Yong was about 2. I talked to my husband about my concerns. He told me that the doctor had told him when Yong was born that he had Down syndrome. My husband asked him not to tell me. He asked the pediatrician not to tell me either. In my culture, my mother-in-law would have blamed me for the disability. It would have been my fault; something I had done. My husband did not want to have that friction in his family. He told me that now my mother-in-law wouldn't blame me because she had learned to love Yong. Although I appreciated his caring, it took me a long time to get over his deception. I changed doctors. I think about what I could have done for Yong earlier to help him and me.

Reflective Practice

Look at this decision making from the perspective of the mother and the father. Now put this in a cultural context. Given this family's culture and history how do you think they might respond to early intervention and early childhood special education?

Over time, some of the traditional cultural norms fade, such as speaking the native language, patriarchal authority, and traditional role expectations for wives and children. By the second or third generation, children tend to accept English as their dominant language, they adopt the dress codes and musical preferences of their peers, and they pick up dating and sexual patterns that are at odds with traditional and parental values. They often intermarry with

Children living in Asian American families do well economically but still struggle with keeping traditions and deciding on the languages they want their children to speak at home and at school.

members of other ethnic groups (Chan & Lee, 2004). Children are expected to conform. To develop these values in children, parents may teach children that disobedience brings ridicule on the child and shame on the family. Traditional cultural values of patience and persistence are handed down. Family dependency is valued over independent achievement and cooperation over competition.

Parents generally show educators respect and expect their children to do the same and not to question what they say. Children may need to learn the skill of asking questions of adults without questioning the authority that adults have. Children may need support in learning skills for getting along with peers. Talk about the differences between feelings and how these feelings can be expressed. Children may need your help in learning to express themselves in ways that do not conflict with family values. As you work this out, consult with the parents for their ideas and use parents as a resource for expanding your knowledge of the Asian cultures. See Table 2-6 for ways of working with Asian American families who have children with disabilities.

Implications for Educators

Knowing what you do about Asian American culture, think about how this would influence how you would talk to a family about a child with aggressive, acting out behaviors. If you were concerned about a child's developmental level and academic achievement think about how you would approach the family and what you would show them to support your concerns. Use the Resources at the end of the chapter and read books in the children's bibliography about *Asian and Pacific Islander Families and Children* and share this with the children you teach and use these stories to increase your knowledge base. Early childhood educators need to be responsive to cultural differences and acknowledge these differences in the way they plan for children with disabilities. It is important to know about differences as well as similarities in Asian cultures and to talk with parents about the aspects of culture that are important to them.

Table 2–6: Implications for working with Asian and Pacific Islander families who have children with disabilities

- To facilitate learning and be more relevant, materials and programming need to take the child's culture into account. Be aware, however, of the differences among Asian and Pacific Island cultures. Japanese and Chinese people have both similar and different values. Even among members of one group, there is great variation. Learn about the particular families you interact with. Decide which information applies and which does not.

- When greeting (or saying goodbye) to family members begin with the oldest family member and typically greet male members first. Use the appropriate title with either the last name (Chinese and Korean) or the individual's first name (Cambodian, Laotian, and Vietnamese), depending on the country of origin. Many women retain their own family name when they marry. It is appropriate to address her as Mrs. Onn (Miss Onn becomes Mrs. Onn when she marries Mr. Kim, not Mrs. Kim).

- Initiate interactions slowly and cautiously. Ask general, not personal questions, but do not ask about U.S. foreign policy, the internal politics of their country of origin, or religion. Expect to be asked personal questions; this shows interest and concern.

- In general, avoid initiating physical contact, particularly between men and women. This includes shaking hands or hugging another individual unless they initiate it.

- Keep your language and voice reserved and polite. Control your emotions and avoid direct confrontation. Do not show anger or criticize the family.

- Focus your attention on the family as a system rather than only on the child.

- Consider the degree to which the family embraces traditional values and beliefs, particularly as they relate to spirituality and healing.

- Assess the English proficiency of the family and modify your language to accommodate their level. Speak more slowly for families who are not as proficient. Do not correct their English. Do not assume that individuals who speak with an accent are not proficient.

- Become aware of your nonverbal communication. Avoid sustained eye contact and winking or batting your eyes. Do not touch a child on the head, wave your arms, beckon, or point your index finger. These are considered to be signs of contempt.

- Learn the body language that is associated with negative and affirmative responses. Some families will say yes to you even if they disagree with your suggestions. Learn when yes means no.

- When sitting in a chair, keep both feet on the floor and your hands visible.

- If the family does not wear shoes in the house, remove your shoes before entering. Expect to be offered food or drinks and enjoy the hospitality. Do not compliment or praise a particular household object; the family may feel compelled to give it to you.

- Families may offer you gifts. This frequently poses a dilemma as many agencies do not want you to accept these. If you do accept a gift, take it in both hands, express your gratitude, and do not open it in the presence of the giver.

- Include bilingual and bicultural professionals on IFSP and IEP teams.

Source: Chan & Lee, 2004; Santos & Chan, 2004; Mokuau & Tauili'ili, 2004.

American Indian and Native Alaskan Families

There are several hundred American Indian tribes or nations with 300 separate languages and dialects. Their population at the time Columbus landed (1492) was estimated to be about 10 million (Harjo, 1993). The 2000 census showed 4,119,301 people, or about 1 percent of the population of the United States, claimed American Indian or Alaska Native origins (U.S. Census Bureau, 2002). American Indians and Alaskan Natives have a median age of 30 compared to a median of 38 for the white population. They have 30 percent of their population younger than age 18 compared to 24 percent of the white population (U.S. Census Bureau, 2007). Increasingly American Indians are moving into urban communities (78 percent) and leaving reservations, trust lands, or tribal designated areas (Kawamoto & Cheshire, 2004).

The largest group, the Cherokee, comprise about 19 percent of the American Indian population. The second largest group, the Navaho, comprise about 12 percent. Other groups, ranging from 6 to 2 percent, include the Chippewa, Sioux, Choctaw, Pueblo, Apache, Iroquois, Lumbee, and Creek tribes (U.S. Bureau of the Census, 1995). They live mostly in the western region of the United States: California, Arizona, Oklahoma, New Mexico, Washington, and Alaska. It is important to know the characteristics of the particular tribe the family belongs to, as there is much intertribal variation and danger in overgeneralization

About two-thirds of all American Indian family households are composed of married couples, with about 59 percent of mothers not married when they gave birth (National Center for Health Statistics, 2000). Interracial marriage is common. Elders play a special role. Grandparents actively participate in passing on the cultural heritage. Overall, Americans Indians stress cooperation over competition and harmony with nature as opposed to trying to control nature. Personal strength is derived from knowing oneself and one's culture. Identity is associated with family roles, responsibilities, and relationships largely passed on by their mothers (Kawamoto & Cheshire, 2004). They are adult centered as opposed to child centered, and their time orientation is present instead of future. The 2000 census found that 11.5 percent of American Indians and Alaska Natives held bachelor's degrees compared to 24.4 percent of the total population (U.S. Census Bureau, 2002).

Alaskan Natives represent approximately 16 percent of Alaska's residents, and represent a significant segment of the population in over 200 rural villages and communities. Many have retained their customs, language, hunting and fishing practices, and ways of living since "the creation times." Alaskan Native people are divided into eleven distinct cultures, speaking twenty different languages (Alaskan Native Heritage Center, 2000).

The Athabascan people live in the interior of Alaska along five major waterways. They have eleven linguistic groups. Athabascans are highly nomadic, traveling in small groups to fish, hunt, and trap. All hunters are part of a kin-based network and are expected to follow traditional customs for sharing in the community. The Alaska Natives who live in the southwest are known as Yup'ik and Cup'ik. They still depend upon subsistence fishing, hunting, and gathering for food. Elders tell stories of traditional ways of life to teach the younger generations survival skills and their heritage. The Inupiaq and the St. Lawrence Island Yup'ik People, or "Real People," are hunting and gathering societies. They subsist on the land and sea of north and northwest Alaska. Their lives evolve around the whale, walrus, seal, polar bear, caribou, and fish. The Aleut and Alutiiq peoples live in south and southwest Alaska. They are water people, whether it's the creeks and rivers near villages, or the North Pacific and Bering Sea; they depend on the ocean and rivers for food and travel. The intensity of the weather on the islands governs activities more than any other factor. The Aleut and Alutiiq cultures were heavily influenced by the Russians, beginning in the eighteenth century. The Eyak, Tlingit, Haida, and Tsimshian share a common Northwest coast culture, although there are important differences in language and clan systems. They have a complex social system consisting of moieties, phratries, and clans. The region they live in is a temperate rainforest with precipitation ranging from 112 inches per year to almost 200 inches per year (Alaskan Native Heritage Center, 2000).

The number of individuals who chose the designation Native American on census forms appeared to be growing at a rate four times the national average. One reason is because many people who have previously called themselves European Americans identified themselves as Native Americans (Eschbach, 1993). (*Note:* In collecting data, one graduate student observed that two males marked that they were Native Americans. When questioned, they said that they chose Native American because they were born here.) Individuals have the right to claim any origins they choose on forms. To the extent that individuals do not fill out forms accurately, for whatever reason, however, will cause our information to be misleading. The census now uses the designation American Indian and Alaska Native populations for their categories.

While other minorities struggled to gain a place in the United States, American Indians have struggled to avoid being subjugated and to preserve their land, water, traditions, and unique legal rights. Unlike other minority groups, American Indians have negotiated more than 600 treaties with the U.S. government and ceded billions of acres of land and untold natural resources (Harjo, 1993).

According to Harjo (1993), assimilation for American Indians has meant cultural genocide. There has been a concerted effort to destroy American Indian languages, traditions, customary laws, dress, religion, and occupations. This was done by encouraging Christian denominations to convert Indian nations, imposing an educational system that was designed to separate children from their families and instill non-Indian values, and by the federal government's breaking up tribal landholding in favor of individual landowners, and taxing the lands.

Education for American Indian children was run by the **Federal Bureau of Indian Affairs**. Traditionally, the schools were boarding schools, located far from the children's homes, with European American educators. The focus of this education was to "de-Indianize" the children. It has not worked. American Indians have, in many instances, not wanted to have their children included, but instead have wanted to foster close ties with the tribe. They want to improve the quality of education for their children by changing the standard curriculum to be more responsive to another view of American history. Until the 1970s, American Indian children were taught in school that their traditions were savage or immoral (Harjo, 1993). Educators tried actively to change and denigrate their way of life. Their school dropout rates were and still are high.

Some feel that one reason the dropout rate for American Indians and Alaska Native children is higher than for the rest of the population is because of the biased view that educators and textbooks present (Joe & Malach, 2004). For example, many American Indians view Thanksgiving as a day of mourning, not one of cooperation, celebration, and feasting. Remember that cultural diversity may impact the ways in which you celebrate holidays. Of all cultures, we tend to most misrepresent this one. See Table 2-7 for ways to include American Indian and Alaskan Native families with children with disabilities.

Implications for Educators

Reflect on the Thanksgiving holiday and how you might celebrate it in a way that is respectful of American Indians. Think about what you could do in your curriculum to help all children have a greater appreciation of the circumstances of American Indians and Alaska Natives in the United States. Use the Resources at the end of the chapter and the section in the children's bibliography on *American Indian and Alaska Native Families and Children* to learn more about these cultures and to share this knowledge with children.

Table 2–7: Implications for working with American Indian and Alaska Native families who have children with disabilities

- Ask parents whom they want to include in meetings. In some Alaska Native families, the mother's brother takes responsibility for training and socializing his sister's children so that they grow up knowing their clan history and customs. Once this is established, include and show respect for the entire group.

- Listen to the family's ideas and concerns and acknowledge and incorporate them. Provide emotional support and respect for families.

- Build trust. Many American Indian and Alaska Native families have a history of negative experiences with public agencies and hence distrust them.

- Learn about communication styles. Some families find periods of silence and reflection an important part of their interactions, move at a pace that is comfortable for the family.

- Find out what families want, particularly if they need support in interpreting an assessment and then explaining these results to other family members.

- If families speak English as a second language, offer the skills of an interpreter. Choose an interpreter with the advice of the family, sometimes an individual from the community is a good choice; in other instances, this might violate confidentiality.

- When you need a lot of information from families, set the stage by telling them you will be asking a lot of questions. Encourage them to ask for clarification if they do not understand and to feel free to consult with others before they answer.

- If you know little about the family's culture, admit it, show your respect, ask them to tell you if you offend them in some way, and make a sincere effort to learn more about the culture.

- Even after arranging to meet with families at a particular time, always check before entering to see if it is a good time; if not, honor their decision and reschedule.

- As families change and grow in their understanding of their child's situation, they may want or need information that they had previously been offered but did not seem useful then. Offer suggestions again, particularly opportunities to talk with other parents.

Source: Joe & Malach, 2004; Alaskan Native Heritage Center, 2000.

Anglo-European American Families

As with other racial/ethnic groups, we have descriptive information about this population. There were about 82 million white, non-Hispanic, family households in the United States in 2005 primarily of European American descent. Their median family income in 2005 was $50,784. In 2005 approximately 6 percent of these families lived below the poverty line (U.S. Census Bureau, 2005b). They are older than other groups with a median age of 38 and 76 percent of their population older than 18. Although they constituted almost 70 percent of the population in 2000 this is projected to drop to 50 percent by 2050 (U.S. Census Bureau, 2004).

Traditional white Anglo-Saxon Protestant (WASP) values include such personal traits as control, personal responsibility, independence, individuality, stoicism, keeping up appearances, a "hard work" ethic, and moderation. Complaining is viewed negatively. Increasingly this dominant culture is embracing the importance of individualism, especially in gender-related issues. For their children, there is an emphasis on personal development such as being independent, self-reliant, self-assertive, self-controlled, and focusing on individual achievement. In contrast, many Asian and Latin American cultures emphasize interdependence, cooperation, collaboration, and being respectful and loving (Okagaki & Diamond, 2000). There are many subcultures of the dominant culture.

The 2000 census showed individuals from the following major groups: German (15 percent), Irish (11 percent), English (9 percent), Italian (6 percent), Polish (3 percent), French (3 percent), Scottish, Dutch, Norwegian, Scot-Irish and Swedish about 2 percent each (U.S. Bureau of the Census, 2000).

Although there may be a set of values that reflects the dominant culture, it too is heterogeneous and it is just as difficult not to generate stereotypes about Anglo-European American groups as it is others. See Table 2-8 for ways of working with Anglo-European families.

Implications for Educators

Learn about your personal cultural background and reflect on how you embrace it. Value and respect the culture of others at the level at which they embrace it. Reflect on your experiences in being part of a minority or majority culture. Think about how you would be different if you were part of another culture. Talk to your parents about what they feel is culturally important to them and how that affected how you were raised. Use the resources at the end of the chapter and the section in the children's bibliography on *European American Families and Children* to learn more about the majority culture and to share this knowledge with children.

Again, a caution is in order: When discussing ethnic or cultural traits, we risk stereotyping people. My intention

Table 2–8: Implications for working with Anglo-European families who have children with disabilities

- Speak about issues directly and honestly without using jargon. Be aware of regional differences in terms and vocabulary.
- Expect families to take an active role in their children's education; they want to be informed and have input into the process.
- Acknowledge the possibility of multiple possible causes of disabilities.
- Schedule meetings to accommodate active, complex lifestyles.
- Start and end meetings on time.
- Honor and respect individual differences and preferences among the dominant culture.

Source: Hanson, 2004.

is to provide evidence of diversity. Working with families requires good communication skills and sensitivity to the needs and values of all families based on their culture and the circumstances in which they live. Early childhood special educators need to be respectful of families and read the cues the family gives them about what is important and the best way to convey information.

Working with Children with Disabilities in Diverse Family Structures

Before the 1970s, our focus was solely on *children* with disabilities. Although we were aware they had families, we rarely considered the fact that children both affected and were affected by their families. We now look at children in the context of their families with increased awareness about the impact of the family's structure, culture, and the environments in which children live and grow. Children with disabilities live in all family types. Sometimes grandparents function as parents. These variations have implications for children, their families, and how we work with these families. They increase our need to know more about families and to develop the skills to interact with all family members. The American family is changing. However, it is not the structure per se that poses the greatest challenges, but how the structure affects children with disabilities.

Family structure has changed dramatically since 1970. Fewer households have children younger than age 18. Twice as many women are in the work force. Couples are

marrying later and are choosing to cohabitate before marriage, after a divorce, or as a lifestyle choice. More single women are choosing to have children. See Table 2-9.

Family structures are evolving in the United States because of economic and social changes and immigration patterns. In 2002, 69 percent of children lived with two parents, 23 percent lived with their mother, 5 percent lived with their father, and the remaining 4 percent lived in households with neither parent (Fields, 2003). As an educator, expect that the children you work with will come from a variety of family configurations, and ensure that you are prepared to work with and honor this diversity.

Children with Disabilities in Separating and Divorcing Families

One of the largest variations from the traditional family life cycle comes through separation and divorce. Not all separations move to divorce. Of white women, 91 percent move from separation to divorce after 3 years compared to 77 percent of Latinas and 67 percent of black women (National Center for Health Statistics, 2002). Of these divorces, approximately three-fourths involve children (Berk, 2002). In divorcing families, the children are likely to be young.

Approximately 50 percent of first-time marriages end in divorce. Twenty percent of these separations or divorces happen during the first 5 years (National Center for Health Statistics, 2002). Children with disabilities who live in separating and divorcing families experience the divorce. If the separation or divorce is followed by a period of inept or under parenting by the custodial parent, the loss of the noncustodial parent, a decline in

Table 2–9: Changing structure of the American family

	1970	2001
Traditional families (husband breadwinner, wife full-time mother)	60%	30%
Unmarried couple households	19%	31%
Married women in the labor force	30%	60%
Married couples with children younger than age 18	40%	24%
Children younger than 18 living with one parent	11%	27%
Births to unmarried women	11%	31%

Source: Fields, 2003; U.S. Census Bureau, 2002.

family income, conflict between parents, and residential instability then the outcome is problematic for any child but particularly for a child with disabilities. On the other hand, if the divorce is followed by attentive and authoritative parenting, the noncustodial parent is active, the household income remains stable and there are few additional stressors then it is likely to have a minimal effect on children with disabilities. If there is a mixture, the effects on children will be a mix (Amato, 2004).

The average child spends approximately 5 years (almost a third of his childhood) with a single parent, usually the mother, but with a growing number of single-parent households headed by men. For many children this period is followed by new relationships, some informal, such as cohabitation but after 2 to 3 years approximately 40 percent of individuals remarry and an additional 20 percent are in some type of nonmarital union. About half of these remarriages will result in divorce in about 2 to 3 years (Hetherington & Kelly, 2002). However, when children with difficult temperaments or other challenges have to cope with stressful life events such as family disorganization, divorce, and remarriage, their problems are magnified (Lengua, Wolchik, Sandler, & West, 2000).

Parental conflict does not end with divorce; indeed it often escalates after a divorce. Conflicts often revolve around issues related to visitation rights and child support payments. Children with disabilities can be caught in the middle of these conflicts. Older children seem to be able to adapt and negotiate, whereas young children including many children with disabilities do not have these skills, but they do experience the stress.

Women are more likely than men to be economically disadvantaged after divorce. The economic well-being of women and children plunges when compared to predivorce levels. In addition to the loss of one income, three-fourths of divorced mothers in the United States get less than the full amount of child support or none at all (Children's Defense Fund, 2000). The economic implications of divorce may mean that families have to move from their homes, thus reducing ties with neighbors and friends. After divorce, both parents' social networks become smaller and less dense. Women, especially those caring for children with disabilities have less time, energy, and economic opportunity to build a new friendship network. Because women typically interact more frequently with kin during the marriage, they are more likely to sustain this support network than men are. Ties to kin may become the major support network if relationships are positive.

There are few issues surrounding divorce that have generated more concern than those relating to children's adjustment to divorce and its aftermath. It is difficult to make generalizations because the issue is a complex one. To some extent it is dependent upon the age, sex, and temperament of the child. The period of greatest challenge is from the separation until 2 years after the divorce. The cognitive immaturity of some children with disabilities makes it difficult for them to understand the issues related to their parents' divorce.

Three major factors impact the child's adjustments to divorce: (1) the effectiveness of the custodial parent in parenting the child; (2) the level of conflict between the mother and father; and (3) the relationship of the child with the noncustodial parent. When the custodial parent is effective, levels of conflict are low, and the relationship between the child and the noncustodial parent is maintained, the outcome can be positive for children (Hetherington & Kelly, 2002).

For children with disabilities, divorce is a loss of a way of life. The predictable patterns of everyday life are replaced by different expectations and life experiences and a profound degree of uncertainty about what is happening. Household rules and routines change, and a single parent typically experiences task overload as he or she takes on the tasks that previously were shared by two. Young children are in a particularly vulnerable position as the people they would turn to most for comfort and to mediate the stress may be unavailable (Wallerstein, Lewis, & Blakeslee, 2000).

You, as an educator, will probably be told about the divorce process when the physical separation takes place. This is when parents must make practical decisions about who will be picking children up and what emergency numbers need to be added or changed. Finding out about the divorce process may help explain a child's behavior.

Implications for Educators

Young children and children with disabilities frequently regress and lose skills they had previously attained such as adaptive skills and toilet training. They may want to be held more, or they may bring an attachment object such as a blanket that had been given up. They may need support trying new activities and materials. Children who adjusted well to the educational environment may now cry when left and become anxious when it is time to leave and someone is not there to pick them up. This is an adjustment for children. It is imperative that early childhood educators know the legal and informal agreements between parents regarding the care of the child. Children with disabilities are almost always in the custody of their mothers.

Children in their early care and education setting need stability. They need familiar toys, familiar adults, and a familiar routine. Their world seems out of their control and they seem adrift. Help them choose toys and activities that put them in control and emphasize this as you talk with them. Be supportive of children's feelings of sadness, fear, and anger. Acknowledge these feelings and find ways to deal with them. Although children may test your limits, they need to know that limits exist. "You look like you are angry. You can kick the ball two more times, but then we need to put it away."

Children need to have divorce explained to them with an emphasis on the fact that it is a permanent change. Use books in the section of the children's bibliography on *Families Who Separate and Divorce.* Read these books to all children but find time to read these books one-on-one with a child to help him talk about his feelings. Share these books with families to support them in talking with their children about the process. Support both parents in maintaining contact with their children and help them use authoritative parenting. It is not helpful if the noncustodial parent is always indulgent when he or she sees the children briefly. Children may feel that the parent would be that way all the time and it sets up conflict and erroneous ideas.

Children with Disabilities in Cohabiting Families

Cohabitation is a living arrangement in which two adults who are not married to each other live in the same setting and have a sexual relationship. Cohabitation is becoming increasingly common. By 1995, 40 percent of women 20 to 24 had cohabitated. Half of all first unions were cohabiting unions (Bumpass & Lu, 2000). Cohabiting couples are parents because they have a child together, they live with children from a previous relationship, or single women who become pregnant choose to cohabitate rather than marry.

The Census Bureau estimated that in 2002, 2.9 million children younger than 15 lived in cohabiting households (Fields, 2003). Unmarried couples living together constitute almost 9 percent of all unions (Walsh, 2003). Nearly half of all adults live in a cohabiting relationship at some time during their lives, with approximately three-quarters cohabiting before a second marriage. Cohabitation is less stable than marriage. The probability of a cohabiting relationship breaking up within 5 years is 49 percent (marriage is 20 percent) and after 10 years is 62 percent (first marriages are 33 percent) (National Center for Health Statistics, 2002).

Two out of five children will live in a cohabiting family during some of their childhood and 15 percent of children born are the biological children of cohabiting couples. Half of cohabiting unions last a year or less (Bumpass & Lu, 2000). Cohabiting fathers spend more time with their biological children than fathers who do not live in the same household, but less time than fathers who are married to the mother. Some adults may want to know the implications of including a child with a disability in a family before committing to marriage. Whether cohabiting is good or bad for children with disabilities depends upon the alternatives (Seltzer, 2000).

Cohabiting relationships cut in half the median time (7 to 3.7 years) children live in a single-parent postdivorce household (Bumpass & Raley, 1995). About half of these cohabiting unions do not last (there is either a marriage or separation). This increases the number of transitions children with disabilities experience (Seltzer, 2000). Nonmarital cohabitation appears to be difficult for many families and particularly boys. There is more cohabitation among previously married adults than never-married adults. Although this trend is too new to know what it means for children with disabilities, it does mean you are likely to have children in your setting living in cohabiting families.

Implications for Educators

Early childhood settings need to portray many family structures and provide opportunities for input from parents and significant others. When cohabiting relationships change, children need the stability of a setting that has familiar activities and people. Early care and education settings make individual decisions about whom they invite to conferences and group meetings. It is important to talk with biological parents and determine the roles of the adults in a child's life to be sure to include important figures.

Become familiar with the families of the children in your setting. If cohabiting families feel uncomfortable and judged as less than adequate they may not participate in school-related activities. When you plan activities think about having children invite a "special adult" rather than specifying a mother or father. Be inclusive rather than exclusive. Build bridges to all families regardless of their structure.

Children with Disabilities in Stepfamilies

Remarried or **blended families** are formed when divorced men and women remarry or when a divorced individual marries a single or widowed adult. About half of these remarriages include minor children and are therefore defined as **stepfamilies**. Stepfamilies are also formed when a single, never-married mother marries for the first time. A stepfamily is defined as one in which at least one of the recoupling adults has one or more children from a prior relationship and the children spend some time in the adult's household (Crosbie-Burnett & McClintic, 2000). According to the 2000 census there are 4.4 million stepchildren younger than the age of 18 (Administration for Children and Families, 2003). Three-fourths of couples who are divorced cohabitate before a second marriage.

Stepfamilies are complex and highly variable. They include more than one household unit. All family members are affected emotionally, financially, and legally by the actions of another household. The co-parenting team is large: It includes biological parents and their respective spouses and/or committed live-in partners. The new extended family includes multiple grandparents and stepgrandparents, and siblings consist of biological siblings, half, and stepsiblings from both households. Approximately half of stepfamilies have a mutual child. If the child is born after the couple has formed a solid relationship, the birth of the child makes a positive contribution to the integration of the family; if before, there will likely be increased stress.

Remarried families are different from first-married families in a variety of ways. Stepfamilies form after a process of loss and change. Members of stepfamilies come together at different phases of their individual, marital, and family life cycles. Children and adults have experienced different traditions and ways of doing things. Parent-child relationships have preceded the couple relationship, rather than followed it. One parent may have had extensive experiences with disabilities and their implications where the other (step)parent may be trying to learn about what the disability will mean for the child and family. Children have a parent elsewhere, if not in reality, at least in memory. About half of children in stepfamilies have contact with their noncustodial parent; therefore there are shifts in household membership when the children move between households. There is little or no legal relationship between stepparents and stepchildren.

Implications for Educators

Educators need to be open to discussions with children who have siblings "some of the time" or who call their mother by her first name. Conscious efforts need to be made to include diverse families in stories and celebrations. Acknowledge many types of families. Including books about stepfamilies and supporting children in making two Mother's or Father's Day presents can go a long way to helping children cope. Also, as an educator you need to be clear on who should receive notices and who should be included in conferences and invited to school events. You also need to know who is to pick up the child and under what circumstances. Know for your emergency forms whom to contact and what to do if you cannot reach the identified person.

Children with Disabilities in Single-Parent Families

Single-parent families are those with one parent and dependent children. The number of single-parent families has more than doubled since 1970. At any given time approximately 31 percent of children live in a single-parent household, more than 21 million children in 2004 (Annie E. Casey Foundation, 2006).

Single-parent families have increased because of divorce, nonmarital childbearing, and cohabitation. Most children raised in single-parent homes grow up healthy and happy. However, children raised in single-parent families face more risks than those raised in two-parent homes. Some problems relate to behavior; for boys particularly, externalizing problems such as aggression is common. Other concerns involve long-term effects such as increased risk of teen pregnancy. Single-parent homes are more likely to be economically disadvantaged and single mothers feel the strain of work and parenting (Martin, Emery, & Peris, 2004). Children with disabilities increase the stress.

Single-parent families are as diverse as two-parent families. Approximately 80 percent of all single-parent families are headed by women alone, with an additional 9 percent living with a partner. About 9 percent of children live with a single-parent father and an additional 2 percent of these fathers live with a partner. Despite the increased number of single-parent families, there is still a tendency to look at these families as dysfunctional, deviant, or unstable. Society has not focused on the strengths of single-parent families or accepted them as viable family units with variability in style, structure, and values. Given the number of children living in single-parent families, it is important to view their strengths as well as their challenges (Annie E. Casey Foundation, 2006). See Table 2-10 for the number of single-parent families.

Table 2–10: Percent of children in single-parent families in 2004

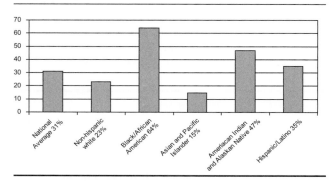

Source: Annie E. Casey Foundation, 2006.

Table 2–11: Births per 1,000 to females ages 15–19 in 2003

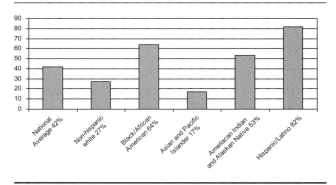

Source: Annie E. Casey Foundation, 2006.

Adolescent Single Mothers

Adolescent motherhood is a complex and serious situation. Although the national teen pregnancy rate is falling (84.5 pregnancies per 1,000 women aged 15–19) it is still the highest among developed countries. The poverty rate of children who are born to mothers between 15 and 19 who are not married and did not graduate from high school is 78 percent (Annie E. Casey Foundation, 2006). See Table 2-11 for the number of births to adolescent single mothers.

The move away from the marital dyad is increasing for all families in the United States. In 2000, 79 percent of all teenage mothers were not married at the time of delivery. Grandmothers or other family members often take on parenting responsibilities. This provides a collective responsibility for the child, but often adds stress to the household (Annie E. Casey Foundation, 2006).

Young single parent families often have fewer economic and social resoures to support their children. When children need extra care the family may be stressed.

Infants born to adolescents experience long-term consequences. They are 50 percent more likely to be born at low birth weight, 50 percent more likely to repeat a grade, and less likely to graduate from high school. If female, she is 83 percent more likely to become a teenage mother. Males are 13 percent more likely to be incarcerated. Regardless of sex, they are twice as likely to be abused or neglected and two to three times more likely to run away from home (Florida State University Center, 1997; Annie E. Casey, 2006). Early intervention and high-quality early care and education can change these statistics.

Risks do not end with the birth of a full-term viable infant. Only 1 to 2 percent of children are born with disabilities that are identifiable at birth, yet by school age we find that 10 to 12 percent of children are identified as needing special educational services. The interplay among risk factors in early childhood produces poor outcomes. The combination of low birth weight and low maternal education increases by eight times the probability that the child will need special educational services (Florida State University, 1996). Adolescent mothers are less verbal and less supportive of their infant. Negative long-term child development outcomes have been found in the areas of intellectual development, social/emotional development, and school achievement. Opportunities for learning and nurturing missed early in life cannot be fully regained; by 18 months, infants raised in impoverished environments have cognitive deficits that may not be totally reversible (Florida State University, 1996).

In the Field

Our 21-year-old daughter, Tina, lives with me and my wife Hannah. Tina gave birth to our grandson Will about 5 years ago. Tina is a single mother and she had Will when she was only 16. Hannah and I watch Will while Tina works at the supermarket and takes courses at the community college. She is trying to get ahead and we want to help her. However, taking care of Will has become very difficult for us. Will has autism. I think we have accepted this now. I'm not sure Tina has.

When Will was an infant we didn't have a lot of trouble taking care of him. We didn't want her to marry Will's father, so we agreed to help. Will is in a preschool for part of the day, but when he comes home he runs up and down the stairs for hours. We just can't keep up with him, he moves so fast. Will has trouble communicating and he gets angry when we can't understand him. Then he hits himself or us. It's getting to be too much. We tell Tina, but she doesn't want to hear it.

Tina says that she will be able to afford after-school care soon. To me it seems like soon isn't soon enough. Will is a great little boy and we love him dearly. However, my wife and I have already raised our children and we don't have the resources or energy to raise Will the way we would like. Will needs more than we can give. I'm not sure we are safe anymore. It is an awful feeling. Tina keeps saying just a little while longer, but I am afraid something terrible will happen before this all gets sorted out. I feel helpless and angry at the same time. I wish I knew what to do about all this before it is too late.

Reflective Practice

What types of services do you think would help this family? What might the preschool teacher do to support them? Do you think Tina is being unfair to her parents and son? What would you do if you were Tina?

Implications for Educators

Take time to talk with young mothers and to learn about their life and their beliefs about child rearing. Do not make judgments. Find out what kinds of support systems they have, both formal and informal. Talk with them specifically about what you do in class and why. Talk about reading to children and why you spend time doing that. Talk about talking to young children even before they can talk. Help them think about fun ways to connect. Try to be matter of fact. Do not tell them how to raise their children. Rather, try to help them think about the variables related to raising young children particularly children with disabilities. Look at the supports you might potentially provide such as a lending library. If you send homework, send home the supplies that are needed to complete the project. If children come back with incomplete projects think about the skills you expect parents to have and if these expectations are realistic relative to time, energy, and academic knowledge.

Children with Disabilities in Gay and Lesbian Families

Until recently, early childhood educators have dealt with sexual orientation by ignoring it. As more people are openly expressing their sexual preferences, the intersection between early childhood education and the gay community must be addressed (Laird, 2003). Several million gay men and female lesbians are parents. Because of the stigma associated with being identified as gay or lesbian we have little reliable data about numbers of gay and lesbian couples (Kurdek, 2004). Children of these unions often experience discrimination.

Three types of family structures typify gay- and lesbian-headed families: blended families, single-parent families, and couples having children together. As most gay fathers and lesbian mothers became parents through a heterosexual marriage, blended families are the most common type. Approximately 65,500 adopted and 14,100 foster children live with gay and lesbian parents (Gates, Badgett, Macomber, & Chambers, 2007). Lesbian partners who want to have children in the context of their relationship adopt children or use artificial insemination. This practice is new and we do not know a lot about it (Kurdek, 2004).

Contrary to concerns about children in these relationships, studies have found that children's development does not differ from that of children raised in a heterosexual relationship and that attention, love, and support seem to be more important in rearing children than the gender identity of the parents. Children seem well-adjusted and a large majority develop a heterosexual orientation (Chan, Raboy, & Patterson, 1998).

Implications for Educators

Early childhood educators need to explore their own feelings for evidence of homophobia and for the assumptions they make about the children in their classroom. It is an opportunity to also look at gender bias in general and stereotypical sex roles in particular. It is important to teach tolerance and support of those who do not follow traditional gender roles.

Working with Children with Disabilities whose Families Face Special Challenges

Regardless of family structure or culture, some families face additional challenges. Some of these challenges increase the risk of having a child with a disability and others make caring for children with disabilities more difficult. For some families the situations they are in are temporary, whereas for others they are more permanent. Poverty is a leading risk factor of negative outcomes and disabilities for young children.

Children with Disabilities in Immigrant Families

The United States is a nation of immigrants. One child out of every five in the United States qualifies as a **child of an immigrant parent**. Children are considered to be children of immigrant parents if they are younger than 18 years of age and are either themselves foreign born or were born in the United States with at least one foreign-born parent. This is the fastest-growing segment of the nation's child population. In the 1990s this population of children grew at seven times the rate of native-born children (Capps, Fix, Ost, Reardon-Anderson, & Passel, 2004). In 1900, 80 percent of these immigrants came from Europe with only about 1 percent coming from Latin America and Asia (U.S. Bureau of the Census, 1999). Today about 65 percent of immigrants come from Latin America (Capps, et al., 2004).

There were approximately 12 million **unauthorized migrants** in the United States in 2005. Most have entered across the boarder with Mexico (60 to 70 percent). Others (25 to 40 percent) entered legally but overstayed visas or violated other terms of their admission (Passel, 2006). Undocumented men come to the United States to work, and, in 2003, 90 percent of them worked, which is higher than the percent of U.S. citizens or legal immigrants who work (Passel et al., 2004). Over half of the undocumented men (54 percent) live in married couples or other families (Passel, 2006).

In the Field

I knew on our first date that José and I were going to get married. What I didn't know was how difficult that journey down the aisle would be. My husband is Guatemalan. I am from Delaware. We met at a bar in a tiny tourist town called Panajachel, in the highlands of Guatemala. He was a restaurant manager. I was a friend of one of the bands that played there frequently.

We fell in love. The only problem? We lived a continent and several countries apart. So I moved to Guatemala—living there for months at a time for almost 3 years. But then I realized that I wanted a career. I didn't want to live on $120 a month. And so I suggested that he come to the States and that we marry. Neither one of us thought the journey down the aisle would be quite as difficult as it proved to be. It took my husband almost a year for his visa to be approved. It was denied because papers were out of order, because I didn't make enough money, and because a signature didn't appear to be original.

My husband went to the U.S. embassy 16 times and lined up and stood for 7 hours in the cold (because even if you have an appointment they will only see 100 people a day) for a person who wasn't even a U.S. citizen to tell him "no." There were times when I thought our relationship would crumble. Moments when I was so angry that I wanted to scream at my government and ask them what right they have to tell me who I can or can't fall in love with. Instances when both of us said this is just too hard.

My parents watched our struggle. They mostly stayed on the sidelines, but near the end they decided to intervene. It had gotten to the point of idiocy. José's visa was being denied for no reason and their little girl was unhappy. Delaware is a small state and my parents had been active in politics. Soon our U.S. senators and representative were on a mission to bring José home. It took numerous phone calls, faxes, and emails, but with the help of a friend who is an immigration attorney and members of Congress, enough pressure was put on the U.S. embassy in Guatemala that José was granted a visa.

He came to Delaware 6 days later. He had a visa for 90 days. If we did not marry during that time, he would return to Guatemala and could not come back to the United States for 3 years. We married one day before his visa expired.

Reflective Practice

There is much concern about illegal immigrants in the United States. Have you thought much about the process of obtaining a visa to come here legally? How would you feel if you were in this woman's situation? From the first application for the visa to reapplying for a green card that will allow him to continue work in the United States and visit his family (which he wasn't able to do for 3 years) this couple paid almost $10,000. Reflect on what that means for immigrant families.

In the Field

I am an international student from China. Strictly speaking, I am not an immigrant but a "non-immigrant alien" based on the categorization by the U.S. Immigration Office. Before I came to the United States, I had a stable job in Shanghai (one of the largest cities in China) and was married to my husband, a junior scientist working in a research institute. The idea of seeking better educational opportunities in a western country was very attractive to us. A year after we got married, my husband left for the United States to study at a major university, but we never knew it would take us so long to see each other again.

Within 14 months I made four visits to the U.S. consulate to apply for a spouse visa. I was rejected the first three times because I was suspected of having immigration intentions. Each time, I cried my way back home and made tearful phone calls to my husband. I was literally hopeless when I went to the U.S. consulate for the fourth time. Luckily I was granted a visa this time. I was finally able to go to America to see my husband.

A few months after I arrived in United States, I was also accepted at the university. To enroll as a full-time student, I needed a new visa. The fastest way to obtain a visa was to apply in a U.S. embassy or consulate outside the country. Otherwise it would take several months for a visa to be approved and mailed by the U.S. immigration office. I flew to El Paso, Texas, crossed the Mexican border, and obtained my student visa in the U.S. consulate in Juarez, Mexico. Compared with my previous visa application experiences in China, this trip was easy and delightful!

So far I have studied in United States for 6 years, have had a child, and have graduated from university. If I want to stay in America after graduation, I am allowed 1 year to look for a job and change my student visa to a different one. If that 1 year expires and I still do not have a decent employer, I will have to leave America. I took the first job that was offered to me because I was afraid I would have to leave.

Reflective Practice

Both women have children born in the United States who are citizens. Reflect on these women's experiences. How are they similar to and different from each other? Do you think these are typical experiences? The home language of the children in both families is not English. How do you think this will affect their educational experiences?

Two-thirds of all children with **undocumented** parents (about three million) are U.S.-born citizens who live in **mixed-status families** (Capps & Fix, 2005). Although the children might be eligible for educational services, undocumented adults are not eligible for welfare, food stamps, Medicaid, and most other public benefits (Fix, Zimmermann, & Passel, 2001). In mixed-status families there is a concern that finding services for a child with a disability will result in the adult's undocumented status being discovered and some of the adults in the family being deported. About 5 percent of children in elementary school had undocumented parents in 2000 (Capps & Fix, 2005).

Implications for Educators

If families have immigrated recently, they may need time to adjust to the culture and to find out how they will meet their basic needs. There may be little energy left to focus on the needs of a child with a disability. Particularly if the family is not legally documented, be clear about your role. Specifically how it relates to child welfare (you are not there to take their child away) and the *United States Bureau of Citizenship and Immigration Services* (*La Migra*) (you will not inform them). In paperwork, do not reference their status. Educators need to know what resources can be used for both legal and illegal immigrants and what might

jeopardize their legal status now or in the future. Learn about the immigrants' country of origin and area of the country the family emigrated from. If the area is rural, they may need support childproofing their home and adjusting to other basic issues that are different.

Reflective Practice

Look at yourself to determine your experience with immigrant families, especially those who speak English as a second language, those who have not lived here long, and those who have immigrated illegally. Reflect on your style of interacting with others and establishing trust. Immigration, whether legal or illegal, is a controversial area. Think about your feelings and how you will provide all children with the best possible education.

Children with Disabilities Whose Families Have Few Economic Resources

One of the most pervasive adversities facing children and their families is poverty. The human cost of poverty is high. It can rob young children of their health, their education, their hopes and dreams, and even their lives. There is concern over the increasing number of children who live at or near poverty. The number of families who are totally dependent upon welfare has fallen from 2.8 million in 1976 to 960,000 in 2001. However, the number of poor children who are living in families with earned income and no public assistance has risen from 4.4 million in 1976 to 6.9 million in 2001. Of all children living in poverty, only 22 percent receive cash assistance (Annie E. Casey Foundation, 2003). See Table 2-12 for the number of children living in poverty.

Using a slightly different measure of poverty, the United Nations compared child poverty rates in the developed world. On this scale, the United States ranked twentieth out of twenty-one countries, with only Mexico having higher rates of child poverty. Another comparison using industrialized nations again found the United States at the bottom of the scale with only Russia having higher rates of child poverty (Annie E. Casey Foundation, 2003).

Poverty in the United States varies by where families live and the support systems that are available to them. Maryland and New Hampshire have the lowest rates of child poverty at 10 percent; Mississippi had the highest rate of the states at 30 percent. The District of Columbia and Puerto Rico are not ranked as states but have a 33 and 56 percent child poverty rate respectively (Annie E. Casey Foundation, 2007a)

Table 2–12: Percent of children living in poverty by race and number in 2006

Non-Hispanic White	11%
Hispanic or Latino	28%
Black or African American	35%
Asian and Pacific Islander	12%
American Indian	35%
National Average	18%

Source: Annie E. Casey Foundation, 2007b.

Table 2–13: Risks poor children face

They are

- twice as likely to be born without prenatal care, have low birth weight, and to die before reaching their first birthday.
- twice as likely to repeat a grade, drop out of school, and require special education.
- more than twice as likely to be abused or neglected.
- frequently tired in school because they can't sleep in their noisy, overcrowded apartment, house, or shelter.
- likely to fare better if they lived in another country. If they lived in twenty-three other industrialized nations they would be guaranteed health insurance, an income safety net, and a chance for a parent to stay at home with pay after childbirth.

Source: Children's Defense Fund, 2002, pp. 5, 6.

This is America's fifth child; the one child in five who lives in poverty. Contrary to public belief, this child is likely to live in a family where at least one adult works. Poverty affects all races of children; however, one in three black and American Indian or Alaskan Native children (35 percent) and one in four Latino children (28 percent) were poor in 2006 (Annie E. Casey Foundation, 2007b). Poor children face risks other children do not face (see Table 2-13).

The number of people living in poverty fluctuates. In reality, many more people are poorer than the poverty rate suggests. Families living close to the poverty line may drop into poverty because of life changes such as an illness, birth of a child, divorce, separation, or disability (Annie E. Casey Foundation, 2005). In 2007, the **poverty line** was $20,650 for a family of four and $17,170 for one parent with two children (Federal Register, 2007).

Poverty adds to the stress experienced by all families. Families who are forced to spend their resources and energy on survival often do not have additional time or energy to encourage a child with a disability to learn language and other cognitive skills. When this happens children are more likely to experience emotional trauma and sustain accidents. Poverty increases the probability that children will be born with disabilities and that disorders that are preventable with timely medical intervention may become disabilities. Families who cannot afford regular medical care may wait until conditions become severe and then seek emergency room treatment. Nine million children, most of whom live in two-parent homes and 90 percent of whom have a working parent, have no health insurance (Children's Defense Fund, 2007).

Poverty increases the probability that risk factors will be present simultaneously in the child, the parent, the parent's informal support system, and the neighborhood. The disadvantages of poverty permeate all of life, from health care and nutrition to quality of housing and neighborhoods to educational opportunities. The cycle of poverty is associated with poor maternal nutrition, increased substance abuse by pregnant women and low birth weight infants. These are all potential causes of developmental problems and additional stressors in an already stressed system.

Women with low incomes have the highest rate of depression of any group. Depressed mothers are less responsive and nurturing, less aware of their child's moods, and more restrictive. Children raised in extreme poverty are at risk for developmental problems. The causes are complicated, but include poor cognitive/language stimulation, poor nutrition, exposure to safety hazards, and poor

health care. Adverse financial circumstances affect the entire family and include increased risk of marital dissolution, family disorganization, physical abuse, and neglect (Annie E. Casey Foundation, 2006).

It appears that there may be more young children living in poverty in the future. These children may not have their basic needs met. One outcome of poverty can be homelessness.

Children with Disabilities Whose Families Are Homeless

The number of people who are **homeless** in the United States is a matter of debate. They are a difficult group to identify and definitions of homelessness vary. Homelessness can be a transient condition or long term. It is estimated that over 1 percent of the population, somewhere between 2 and 3 million people, experience homelessness during a year and that about 700,000 individuals are homeless on a given night (U.S. Department of Health and Human Services, 2003).

Most of the homeless population is adult men; however, the proportion of women, children, and youth has increased to about 38 percent of the population. Children who were members of homeless families made up a fourth of the total homeless population and were the fastest-growing segment of this population. Homeless families are diverse, but young single females with young children are the most common family configuration. About half the children in shelters were younger than 5 years of age (*A status report on hunger and homelessness in American cities*, 1998).

Many homeless families have experienced high rates of violence and report that family violence was the primary cause of the homelessness. Often the mother took the children and left an abusive situation without time, emotional strength, or financial resources to find another secure place to live. Concern about additional violence may make having a permanent address impossible. Living on the streets or in shelters impacts children and their families. There are physical health problems related to homelessness: colds, tiredness, and feelings of depression are the most frequent health problems. By 18 months, children demonstrate significant delays (Hart-Shegos, 1999).

Homeless children with disabilities may be hungry, have poor nutrition, and increased health problems. When they are homeless their parents may not have safe places to put their children; therefore, there is little opportunity for them to play and explore their environment. For a young child, becoming homeless is devastating. Conditions related to homelessness frequently lead to developmental delays;

these are most apparent in emotional, motor, cognitive, and language development. Homeless children may display problems by acting out, exhibiting aggression, depression, inattentiveness, hyperactivity, chronic tiredness, anxiety, and for younger children, regression. From toddlerhood on these delays will influence later behavioral and emotional problems (Hart-Shegos, 1999).

Parental roles may change as families move, and parents may not be emotionally available to their children when they are trying to cope with problems related to food, shelter, and finances. Poverty and homelessness are inextricably tied to the family and community. In many instances, these problems are compounded by violence.

Implications for Educators

Many young homeless children are fearful. They frequently display emotional and behavior problems such as short attention span, withdrawal, aggression, speech delays, sleep disorganization, difficulty in organizing behavior, regressive behaviors, awkward motor behavior, and immature social skills.

An increasing number of early care and education settings are including homeless children. First, and foremost, these programs need to feel safe for children. Schedules should be predictable and there should be many opportunities to use large motor skills and to participate in dramatic play. This is challenging, because although many of the children are in programs when their family is in a shelter, rules about how long a family can stay in a shelter vary, and programming is based on unstable funding sources and whether or not space is available. Some shelters have on-site child care, whereas others use settings within the community. Regardless, early care and education is seen as an essential element in helping young children whose families are homeless.

Children with Disabilities Living in Violent Environments

No one likes to think about violence and young children. When violence does occur, we want to believe that it is the exception and that it is reported to make headlines and sell newspapers. When we read these articles, we also want to believe that children don't understand what is happening and therefore won't remember the experiences. Research findings negate such optimistic views (Groves, Lieberman, Osofsky, & Fenichel, 2000).

Witnessing violence threatens a young child's basic trust in adults. Young children show their reactions in four specific areas: emotional distress, physical complaints, regression, and loss of skills, particularly in the language area (Groves, et al., 2000). Restoring the parent-child relationship, where possible, is the primary goal of intervention. The best way to help children is to help their parents. As stress to families increases, the probability for violence increases. Young children are exposed to this violence and frequently are the victims of it. Children with disabilities *do* experience violence and it influences their lives. Because they may not have the language to express their feelings, it is the professional's role to comprehend the meaning of this violence for them. In addition to being the victims of violence, children are exposed to violence on television, in their homes, and in the community. The United States is the most violent industrialized nation in the world (Zero to Three, 2007).

Parents who raise children with disabilities in violent environments may be depressed, sad, and anxious. Adults who are depressed tend to talk to children less and to be less responsive to their needs. They have difficulty controlling their emotions and their children experience more scoldings and shouts than hugs and kisses. Young children reflect this same depression and smile less and begin to withdraw into themselves. Adults may cope with violent environments in a variety of ways, such as becoming overprotective as a way of keeping their children safe. They might put children to sleep in bathtubs to avoid random bullets and rarely take them outside to play (Osofsky, 1994; Rice & Groves, 2005).

Young children who are exposed to violence think about their world differently. Repeated exposure to violence is likely to have an even more significant effect and it is likely to be more pervasive as children's understanding of events changes with increasing age. It will be difficult for such children to learn to trust others or to think about their environment as dependable and predictable. Traumatic events in infancy continue to negatively affect social, emotional, and cognitive growth into adulthood. Male children abused or neglected in early childhood were younger at the time of their first arrest and committed twice as many offences. Being abused and neglected increased the likelihood of being arrested as a juvenile by 59 percent, as an adult by 28 percent, and for a violent crime by 30 percent. Females were at increased risk of arrest for violence as juveniles and adults (Widom & Maxfield, 2001).

Unlike older children, young children have a very small repertoire of behaviors with which to show their distress. The symptoms children display are related to their age, gender, and circumstances. Some very young children who have been maltreated or exposed to violence withdraw and become depressed; others may become aggressive. Among young children who see parents fight, boys are more likely to become aggressive and girls are more likely to withdraw. Other symptoms may include disrupted patterns of eating and sleeping, fearfulness, and difficulties in attending.

Implications for Educators

Children living in violent environments need to know that early care and education settings are safe. If children cannot feel safe, they cannot participate in activities fully. Part of their energy is spent being watchful and waiting, not engaging. Children learn over time that they are safe and only then become available for learning. Activities need to be repeated to gain control and mastery. Parents need to know that their children are safe before they can be concerned about their development.

Children with Disabilities in Kinship or Foster Care

Sometimes, child rearing becomes so complicated by other stressful conditions, such as physical or mental illness, domestic violence and abuse, alcoholism or drug addiction, that the social service system decides that a child's safety is threatened. In 2005, there were more than 514,000 children in the formal foster care system (ACF, 2007). Many of these children have special needs. Of children between 2 months and 2 years in foster care over half were at high risk for developmental delays or neurologic impairments (Vandivere, Chalk, & Moore, 2003).

Abandonment and removal of children from their biological family is occurring more frequently. The increase in the number of children in out-of-home placements is related to increases in substance abuse, AIDS, homelessness, and child abuse and neglect (Green, 2004). Child removal is an emergency response for their safety. **Foster care** is a living arrangement for children who a court decided cannot safely live at home.

Kinship care occurs when children who cannot safely live at home live in a foster care arrangement with relatives. One reason why kinship care has become the preferred placement is that it can provide continuity and connectedness for children who cannot remain with their parents (Green, 2004). However, kinship caregivers receive less supervision and fewer services than non-kin caregivers do. Kinship foster parents tend to be older, have fewer resources, and be in poorer health. This makes caring for children with disabilities a challenge.

Kinship care arrangements can be informal or formal. The most common informal type, that takes place outside of the child welfare system, is referred to as **private kinship** care. In cases of child abuse and neglect a case worker may suggest that a relative take a child without the state taking custody to keep the child in a **voluntary kinship care** placement. The most common kin caregivers are grandparents. Such children are not considered part of the formal foster care system (Green, 2004). Increasingly, the child welfare system also turns to relatives to act as foster families—**kinship foster care**.

Attachment provides the framework or blueprint for future relationships. The attachment process is affected when children are removed from their homes. Attachment is based on day-to-day interactions and having needs met for physical care, nourishment, and affection. "As a practical guide, for most children between the ages of two and five, a separation for more than two months is upsetting to the degree that it may lead to psychological harm" (Solnit & Nordhaus, 1992, p. 16). Approximately 18 percent of the children in foster care are 2 years and younger. About 25 percent of children are in care for less than 6 months and another 29 percent had spent between 6 and 18 months in foster care (ACF, 2006). Concerns about attachment are one reason why kinship care is often preferred. Families who cannot meet children's basic needs place young children at risk. These young children are in double jeopardy. They live with caregivers who are unavailable to them and place them at risk, yet removing them from their homes may have negative consequences relative to attachment. Kinship care helps young children stay connected to their birth parents.

Implications for Educators

If you have a child who is living with a foster family talk to the family about the child and what types of support they receive. Find out from them how the child came into the foster care system and the child's relationship with his biological parents. Learn who you should invite to meetings. Children with disabilities are in foster care disproportionately.

Children with Disabilities in Adoptive Families

The number of children living with adoptive parents in the United States is increasing. According to the 2000 census there are 2.5 million adopted children living in U.S. households (Kreider, 2003). Of these children 87 percent were born in the United States. Of the 13 percent who were foreign-born about half (48 percent) were born in Asia, a third (33 percent) in Latin America, and a sixth (16 percent) in Europe. Korea is the largest single-source of foreign-born adopted children and accounted for 15 percent of children younger than age 6 with China contributing 3 percent. Most of the European-born adopted children younger than age 6 (82 percent) came from Russia and Rumania. Mexico accounts for a third of Latin American adoptions. However, these children have been primarily adopted by relatives or by the union of non-Hispanic whites and Hispanics who adopted stepchildren. Young children adopted from Guatemala and Colombia fit the more traditional pattern of adoption. Seventeen percent of adopted children were of a different race than their family householder (ACF, 2003). **Householder** refers to the person in whose name the housing unit is owned or rented.

The number of foreign adoptions is increasing and the situations of many of these children before adoption places them at risk for disabilities. Likewise, children from the United States who are adopted out of the child welfare system have also experienced the trauma of separation and often neglect or abuse before adoption. Over 12 percent of adopted children between 5 and 17 years have at least one identified disability as opposed to 5 percent of biological children (ACF, 2003).

The Evidence Base

When families adopt internationally they have less knowledge about the health and development of the children than do families who adopt domestically. Internationally adopted children have a range of developmental and behavioral difficulties. Seventy-five percent of children adopted from China had significant delays in at least one domain. These patterns are typical of other internationally adopted children. Children adopted from Guatemala had similar patterns of growth and developmental delays but these were milder (Miller & Hendrie, 2000). Of infants and toddlers adopted from Guatemala, those who were raised in foster care had better growth and cognitive development scores than those who were raised in orphanages before adoption. The younger the children were at adoption, the better off they were (Miller, Chan, Comfort, & Tirella, 2005).

Reflective Practice

Knowing the probability of disabilities in children who have been adopted, how will you adjust your assessment procedures to identify relative strengths and challenges for these children? Do you think this will influence how you communicate with their families?

Families who choose to adopt children have higher incomes and higher levels of education than families with biological or stepchildren (Kreider, 2003). When they adopt children with special needs they may be better informed than other parents. Families may have more realistic expectations based on education and information prior to the adoption. In addition, they may have a good external support network (Lambie, 2000).

Implications for Educators

Educators may need to support families in developing realistic expectations for their adopted children. This may be particularly true if there are no other children in the family. Children's books about adoption should be included in the classroom literature. Educators need to be aware that some projects, such as making a family tree, may be stressful. Educators also need to be watchful for social and emotional problems, particularly those relating to trust, self-esteem, and identity. Especially when children are adopted educators need to be prepared for discussions about race, ethnicity, and culture as well as about adoption itself.

In the Field

Just imagine the joy of your first anything. It is exceptionally special: your first date, your first car, your first house. We experienced an exceptionally special first last year: our first grandchild.

Our son and daughter-in-law were unable to have their own child biologically, so they began the process of international adoption. We were amazed at the amount of paperwork, visits, applications, interviews, and so on that was necessary to provide a loving, bountiful home to a child who would otherwise possibly be living in poverty. Listening to their anguish as they proceeded through this process was heart wrenching. We helped when we could. I was asked to write a letter of recommendation for the couple. I spent many hours painstakingly trying to select the correct words, terminology, and statements. I had numerous people edit and comment on this important document. After all, I did want them to be accepted as parents of our first grandchild.

Then came the home visitation. The agency was to visit their home to see if it would "pass inspection." We went up and cleaned and decorated and worked very hard to make their home seem welcoming to a child. Even their next-door neighbor offered to come out with her children so that the inspector could see that their neighborhood was "child friendly." It certainly takes a village to even get a child!

Finally the day came. I was never so excited to get this wonderful email of a child's picture and birth certificate, which I could not read. A friend helped us research the birth certificate and determined that the area was poverty stricken and that the adoption would most probably go through. That bit of information gave us some peace of mind. They sent pictures each time the child was brought to the doctor's office for a checkup. We loved this child and had never seen or held him. In the back of our minds was the ever-present fear of the parents' reneging on the decision to give José Luis up for adoption.

This adoption that was to take 4 to 6 months took 10 long months. It was one setback after another. It was paperwork and paperwork and signatures and more sign-offs. Then, at a crucial time for some paperwork to be signed, the one person (imagine, only one person in the whole country of Guatemala) who had the authority to sign the form to finalize the process decided to go to Italy for several weeks to see a soccer match.

My daughter-in-law wanted to go visit the baby, but my son was cautious because he was afraid they would become attached and then not get the baby. Finally, when things seemed certain, they went to Guatemala to spend a week with our grandson. We were ecstatic that they could bond with this beautiful boy. Still apprehensive of the situation, we sent down all sorts of gifts (perfume, jeans, soccer shirts, and cash) to be handed out to key players in the adoption process in the hopes that this might motivate them to move the process along.

But they came without the baby. My daughter-in-law's work gave her a period of 3 months to get the baby so that she would be eligible for maternity leave. Time was ticking away while the ghastly bureaucracy of adoption still crept on. The frustrations mounted each day with the insane nature of this process and the slow actions of the Guatemalan governmental agencies. We were convinced that it was a monetary issue—the longer the child stayed in Guatemala, the more money would be sent to them. Finally, the day came that my son and daughter-in-law went to Guatemala and returned with our grandson. It was wonderful and he is beautiful.

Perhaps the most frustrating of all was to see the amount of effort it took to bring this child into a loving, prosperous family when so many American children are being harmed and abandoned by their parents in the United States. International adoption was definitely a learning experience for all of us.

Reflective Practice

How do you feel about international adoptions? Do you believe that adults in the United States should be allowed to adopt children from other countries? Do you think parents should support the child's knowledge of his birth culture or just expose him to the majority culture? Do you think he will experience prejudice?

Children with Disabilities in Transient Families

The United States is a highly mobile society. Among the 287.1 million people (aged 1 and older) living in the United States in 2005, 39.9 million lived at a different address than they did in 2004. Approximately 14 percent of the population moved between 2004 and 2005. Families move for many reasons. Over 50 percent move because of housing-related reasons and more than 25 percent gave reasons related to their family (U.S. Census Bureau, 2006). Families who move frequently are diverse and range from migrant families who move with the crops, to military personnel, to high-ranking company executives, to upwardly mobile individuals following job opportunities (Plucker & Yecke, 1999). Regardless of who they are, they and their children face a common set of problems. They are frequently in a state of leave-taking and arriving at new places. This means not only looking at housing issues and friendship patterns, but it also involves looking at issues relating to continuity in medical care and educational planning. Socially, families must reestablish their support network in a new place.

Relocation disrupts social and academic continuity for all children and may impair academic achievement. The reason for the move has implications for children's adjustment. If families move because of significant life changes such as divorce, economic problems, or death of a parent, children's academic achievement is likely to be adversely affected.

The importance of family during the relocation process is paramount. Open communication and viewing the move as a common goal increases the likelihood that the transition will be a smooth one. As with other traumatic life events, a child's resilience increases when these experiences are mediated by caring adults. Helping children with disabilities reestablish familiar routines, and maintaining ties with extended family and friends helps the transition process. Children who can establish a sense of security and routine within 2 to 6 months after relocation experience less difficulty in the adjustment process (Hausman & Reed, 1991).

Migrant Families

In some situations, such as those with migrant children, it is tempting for educators to feel that it is not worth getting involved with these children because they will soon move on. There are over 2.8 million migrant children, mostly Hispanic, who live and move with their families. As a typical family of five, they may earn less than $5,000 annually (Rothenberg, 1998). Children as young as 4 may be working in the fields. These children tend to enter school later, have difficulty concentrating due to fatigue or illness, attend class irregularly, and have high drop-out rates (Davis, 1997). Migrant Head Start programs are designed to serve these children whose families are often isolated from community resources. The programs are designed to be flexible. During harvest they may be open at 4:00 A.M. and run until midnight, and may be open 7 days a week. They may run for only the 6 weeks that the families are working in their area. Health, education, and nutritional specialists may follow the children as their families follow the crops (Duarte & Rafanello, 2001).

Lack of prenatal care contributes to the poor physical and mental health of migrant children. Children have high rates of infectious diseases and chronic illnesses. Their greatest strength is their extended family. They often travel together (Duarte & Rafanello, 2001). Although some of the problems faced by migrant children are unique, others are the result of a lifestyle based on frequent relocation and poverty.

Military Families

Military families provide a unique subset of families who relocate. Military families move about three times as often as their civilian counterparts. Approximately 1.5 million children of military families attend schools other than those sponsored by the Department of Defense (U.S. Department of Defense, 2008). In contrast to the previous data on relocation, children in military families appear to experience few long-term negative effects with recurrent relocation. This may be related to the support systems available to these families. In an effort to help this transition for children, a compact was developed by the Council of State Governments, Department of Defense, and education and military family experts. The compact addresses common problems that affect military children as a result of frequent moves and deployments. States that sign on to the compact agree to work collectively with other compact states to create uniform practices regarding the transfer of records, course placement, graduation requirements, redundant or missed testing, entrance-age variations, and other transition issues (U.S. Department of Defense, 2008).

It is not only moving but deployment that affects military families. In an effort to support families with young children including those with disabilities Zero to Three has developed a variety of auditory, visual, and print resources to support families and their children. (Zero to Three, 2008)

Interestingly, military families and other families frequently try to move during the summer months so as not to disrupt their children's schooling. Children themselves are less concerned about academic continuity and would prefer to move during the school year when it is easier to establish a social network. In some instances, summer sports may fill the gap for children, if they are allowed to participate. As children increase in age, the social aspects of the move become more important. Children who moved into schools with low mobility had a particularly difficult time fitting in (Plucker & Yecke, 1999).

Implications for Educators

Early childhood settings need to have procedures in place to welcome new children whether they are entering at the beginning of a new school year, the middle, or the end. Entering children have two transitions: academic and social. Methods of obtaining information from the previous settings need to be in place. IEPs and IFSPs may need to be scanned and emailed or faxed to maintain some continuity in programming. If these processes take too long, children will have trouble with the academic transition. Socially, children may need an opportunity to mourn the loss of their previous friends before they are ready to make new friends. They may be tentative and fearful of the new setting or they may adjust quickly. This is difficult to predict because it is impacted by so many variables, including the child and his temperament, how long the family had lived in the previous location, the reason for the move, and even the response of the family and siblings to the move. Some children will need support in joining groups and becoming part of the fabric

of the class. If there have been frequent moves, children may even wonder if it is worth joining the group and becoming attached to the teacher. They need your support in reaching out.

Working with parents who have experienced several moves can be challenging. Many parents have found that the only way to get services for their children is to be a strong advocate. Most are not trying to be pushy or aggressive but are concerned that with the frequency of moving. Time lost in not receiving service can accumulate very quickly.

Children Whose Parents Have Disabilities

Parents with disabilities are as diverse as those without disabilities. They may have become disabled after their child was born or the disability may have preceded the child. Like their children, we need to view them as individuals first, parents second, and then focus on the accommodations necessary to include them. There are approximately 9 million parents with disabilities or 15 percent of all parents (Through the Looking Glass, 2007). Parents with disabilities face two barriers: physical or architectural and attitudinal. Many people judge parents with disabilities as inadequate. They may have experienced discrimination.

Specific Learning Disabilities

Given the prevalence of specific learning disabilities, it is likely that you will be interacting with parents who have learning disabilities. By adulthood, most parents know what accommodations they need and may directly ask for them. For example, they might ask you to put things in writing that you might not think necessary. There may be some fonts or colors that make materials easier for them to read. Parents may ask to tape record meetings so they can play them back when they have additional time to think about what is being said. There is a 35 to 45 percent recurrence rate for reading disabilities in families (Shapiro, Church, & Lewis, 2002). It is important to consider that some of the parents of the children with learning disabilities will also have learning disabilities whether or not they have been diagnosed. Some parents will share their knowledge of their disability with you, others will not.

Intellectual Disabilities

Parents with intellectual disabilities function at a lower level of cognitive understanding than other parents. They may live independently with support from their family or a social service agency. They need support in understanding the changing needs of their child. As an educator, you need to provide parents with information that is clear and at a level they can understand. Check the reading level of your written material to see whether it is reasonable to expect parents to comprehend it. Provide very specific information and where appropriate drawings or photographs to support the written word. Stress safety issues. Parents in these families may lack complex problem-solving strategies. They may need to be specifically told the importance of playing with and stimulating an infant as well as providing custodial care.

Early care and education settings will provide most of the stimulation that children need. Ensure that your program is strong in language and literacy and that children have many experiences in play as a support for problem solving.

Physical Disabilities

Many physical disabilities involve mobility impairments. Parents with spinal cord injuries, cerebral palsy, and other disabilities may use wheelchairs or other mobility aids. Your environment needs to be accessible to these parents. Not only do parents need to get into the building, but also you need to consider accessibility to adult restrooms and transportation. You also need to consider how you will handle a personal assistant who may come with the parent.

Other types of physical disabilities make parents fatigued or make it difficult to sit for an extended period. Obviously, some physical impairments do not interfere with communications; however, it is important to be open and inclusive with families and acknowledge how they have adapted to the tasks of child rearing. Do not exclude these families from participating in the classroom; consider how they can be included.

Psychological Disorders

Adults with psychological disorders vary as individuals and with the nature and severity of their particular situation. The National Comorbidity Survey found that 49 percent of their respondents (18 to 60+ years of age) experienced a psychiatric disorder at least once in their life and 28 percent had had such an experience within the past year (National Comorbidity Survey, 2005). **Comorbidity** refers to the presence of one or more diseases or disorders in addition to the primary disorder.

Men and women differ in the prevalence of particular psychological disorders. Men show higher rates for substance abuse (25 percent compared to 14 percent) and impulse control disorders (29 percent compared to 22 percent). Men are more likely to self-medicate with alcohol and illicit drugs as a method of coping, so their rates maybe underestimated, especially mood and anxiety disorders. Women show higher levels of **anxiety disorders** (36 percent compared to 25 percent) and **mood disorders**, which include depression (25 percent compared to 18 percent). Fluctuations in hormonal levels during the female life cycle are related to anxiety and depression. Hormonal changes during pregnancy are also related. During the major childbearing years (18–29), in any given year 22 percent of women are diagnosed with an anxiety disorder, 13 percent with a mood disorder, 12 percent with an **impulse control disorder**, and 13 percent with a **substance disorder**. Overall, 38 percent of individuals 18 to 29 years old are likely to have a psychological disorder during any 12-month period (National Comorbidity Survey, 2005).

Some parents with psychological disorders have a paralyzing listlessness, dejection, and overall feeling of helplessness that impact not only them but their children as well. Some anxiety and mood disorders manifest themselves in young adulthood. Families may have young children when parents discover the presence of these disorders.

Adults with psychological disorders, in addition to counseling and medication may need specialized help in developing and maintaining relationships with their children. The episodic nature of some mental health problems makes it particularly difficult. Illness in one parent may contribute to the other partner's problems or the partner may be able to compensate. Other problems relate to unpredictability and inconsistency. Marital discord is common as is separation and divorce.

Chronic Illnesses

Chronic illness affects all aspects of family life. Conditions that affect functioning include epilepsy, diabetes, traumatic brain injury, asthma, chronic fatigue syndrome, HIV (human immunodeficiency virus), multiple chemical sensitivities, multiple sclerosis, or environmental illness. The particular chronic illness and its severity will affect what they find difficult and what they are able to do. Learn something about the illness, in particular, if the illness is progressive, such as cancer, and whether or not it is life threatening. Find out if it is episodic and if there are times when a parent may be almost symptom-free and other times when the parent may be incapacitated or if the condition is stable. Knowing the course of a particular chronic illness will help you understand the impact on a child, some of the challenges families face in supporting their child, and better ways to work with the family. Families may or may not share this information with you. To the extent that they do, it is important to find out the accommodations they need and follow through with providing them.

Sensory Impairments

Adults with hearing impairments may wear hearing aids to help their understanding of speech. Depending upon the amount of residual hearing and when they acquired their hearing loss, their own speech may be difficult to understand. If their loss is severe or their identification is with the deaf community, they may use Signed English or American Sign Language (ASL). If they sign, it will be necessary to have a sign language interpreter at conferences or programs that depend on oral language. The parent may know someone she feels comfortable with or it may be necessary to hire a sign language interpreter. For telephone communication, TDDs (Telecommunication Device for the Deaf) or the more advanced TTYs (teletypewriters) can be used. Both locations must have the TTY. Teletypewriters consist of a keyboard that has between twenty and thirty character keys and a display screen. The TTY converts the typed letters into electronic signals that can travel over regular telephone lines. When they reach their destination the receiving TTY converts them back into letters that are displayed on the screen or printed. TTYs can be stationary or portable and can be used with digital cell phones. Depending upon the features they cost between $225 and $1,000 or more. They are easy to learn how to use. Email and instant messaging is certainly another method of communication that is useful provided both parties have computers.

Adults who have visual impairments vary greatly in their ability to use sight to comprehend their world. Again, as adults they know the mode that works best for them and the simplest thing to do is to ask. They may need written communications to be larger and bolder, or they may need information given verbally. Initially the adult may need to be oriented to the building and to where her child's belongings are to be kept. She needs to be consulted on how she prefers this orientation and under what conditions. If she uses a service dog, be clear with the children and others that the dog is working and is not there as a pet. Get her permission before approaching the dog.

Implications for Educators

The rights of parents with disabilities are protected under the ADA. Early care and education settings are required to provide reasonable accommodations to families just as they would for children. The accommodations vary with the parent's particular disability. The first and most obvious step is to learn what accommodations are necessary. This information may be obtained from parents, their partners, or other service delivery systems who work with these families. Examples of reasonable accommodations have been noted by general disability area. If more than one disability is involved more adaptations may be needed.

Educators need to challenge their own attitudes and beliefs about disabilities and inclusion. They also need to think about the assumptions they make about parents who have disabilities and how they can be included in early childhood programs.

Use the section in the children's bibliography on *Different Types of Families and their Children* to increase awareness of different types of families and the roles family members play.

Family-Teacher Collaboration

There is general consensus among all professionals that **collaboration** is important. The opportunity to set the stage for family involvement occurs during the first encounter with families. "Collaboration refers to the dynamic process of connecting families' resources (that is motivation and knowledge/skills) to an empowering context to make decisions collectively" (Turnbull & Turnbull, 1997, p. 11). With a focus on viewing children with disabilities in a family-centered way, it is important for early childhood special educators to be sensitive to the needs of families as a unit.

Communication is the key to successful collaboration. Families and educators each have history, personal style, and needs that should be acknowledged; each has different concerns, perspectives, and ideas about potential solutions. The communication skills of the teacher can increase or decrease mutual understanding.

Sharing Information with Families

Communication is the process we use to get and give information. It refers to nonverbal as well as verbal processes and includes the social context in which the communication occurs. It is an indicator of interpersonal functioning. Clear communication, both verbal and nonverbal, is essential.

Communication includes speaking, listening, reflection of feelings, and interpretation of the meaning of the message (Berger, 2004). Communication is a complicated process because it takes into account not only the words spoken, but also nonverbal information such as the tone of voice and the body language that accompanies the

Collaborating with families is a dynamic empowering process that should be child-centered.

words. The message is also filtered through the values of the receiver and his experiences in the decoding process. Once interpreted the responder sends a message back, which treads the same complicated path.

Relying only on the content of the spoken word is not effective. Researchers believe that, when interpreting communication, only about 7 percent of the meaning of a conversation is conveyed by the verbal message (spoken word). About 38 percent of the information is gleaned from the way the words are spoken (the vocal and tonal quality of the message); and 55 percent of the meaning is gathered from the visual message—the body language (Miller, Nunnally, & Wackman, 1975). As early childhood professionals we need to be conscious of these factors and monitor ourselves as communicators.

Knowledge of the communication process requires that important information be conveyed face to face with parents and that telephone conversations should be limited to nonemotional factual information. In addition to the general communication process, individuals filter messages through their culture, values, and experiences. Different people may interpret the same information differently.

Educators who are good communicators

- give their attention to the person speaking, using eye contact and body language, and focus on what is being said.
- listen to parents to gather both the feelings and meaning behind statements. They clarify, reframe or restate parental concerns, and distinguish between factual information and feelings. They do not criticize, moralize, blame, or judge.
- recognize parents' feelings and govern what they say in the context of the relationship they have with the family. They discuss the child's positive qualities before bringing up concerns.
- match their style of giving information and the amount of information they share with the family's ability to handle the information. They do not "dump" all the information on the parents at one time if they feel the parents will not be able to process the information.
- emphasize that concerns are no one's fault. They work together to solve problems and plan for the child's future.

- focus on one topic at a time and encourage families to talk and share information.
- document specific information on both concerns and progress while keeping the focus on strengths.
- become allies with parents, viewing them as partners and working to empower them to help their children (Berger, 2004, p. 208).

Words are abstractions that stand for ideas. They make communication possible but also confound it. Clarity is especially difficult when people from different cultural backgrounds communicate. Context is important in determining the meaning of words. The word *orange*, for example, can be a fruit or a color. The way it is used allows us to distinguish between the two meanings. However, as ideas become more abstract, clarity is more difficult.

Communication Techniques

The first step in this process is building rapport. Think about rapport as a process. Do you know when you have rapport with the person you are talking to? Reflect on how you know this. Be specific. Keep checking to be sure that rapport is maintained, and that there is a sense of synchronicity. Rapport is not possible where there is not trust. Do you trust the other person? Does the family trust you? If not, can you establish trust? This may mean looking at the process and stating what is going on, "When I listen to your questions, I feel that you don't think I can carry through on this. What specifically could I say or do that would increase your confidence in me?" The reply to a question such as this often relates to the past. It may start "We have been told … ." "Other professionals said … ." If families have had negative experiences with professionals in the past, you may have to prove that you are trustworthy before rapport can be established.

Until you have some feeling of rapport it is not useful to try to communicate substantive information. Much of rapport building is nonverbal. Even after rapport is established it can be lost and will need to be reestablished. Unless there is mutual respect and trust between the parties it is almost impossible to establish rapport.

There are times when you might want to break rapport. If you are developing an IEP or an IFSP with a family and everyone is feeling very cooperative, you might want to break rapport to be sure the family looks at the document itself. You might say something like "We have really worked quickly writing Elvira's IEP, now I want you to think about how this will work for her, how it will fit into your workday, and whether or not it is what you want." Then give the family the space they need to reflect on the IEP.

If a meeting has been long or complex, it is useful to present a summary at the end. Again, it may start out "Let me be sure I remember what we agreed to. I will … ." If there is an action to be taken it is also useful to write it down as you speak.

Communication, like other skills, requires practice. For some people it is easy while others need to bring techniques such as these up to a conscious level so they can be used.

Communication Techniques to Avoid

There are some ways of communicating that are likely to be counterproductive with parents—or with anyone, for that matter.

Avoid Giving Advice. It is often tempting to give parents advice on how to solve problems; it is rarely wise. It is appropriate to offer constructive suggestions, but even these should be given with care. Before giving suggestions, follow these steps:

1. Gather enough information about a situation to make the suggestions relevant.
2. Find out about the problem: when it occurs, how frequently it occurs, what parents have already tried to do to solve the problem, and whether or not these solutions were effective. Try to get as much specific information as possible before you offer any suggestions.
3. Paraphrase your perception of the problem to see whether or not it is the same as theirs.
4. Support the parents in their efforts to solve the problem by commenting positively on what solutions they have tried (if this is appropriate).

If you do find the need to offer suggestions, do so in a casual, tentative, nonjudgmental way. Offer several suggestions (optimally four) rather than just one. If you just give parents one suggestion, they are likely to come back to you and say, "I tried what you said and it didn't work."

Avoid the Word *Understand*. Sometimes educators respond to a family's problem by saying, "I understand exactly what you mean." This response is likely to trigger in a parent thoughts such as, "How can she understand? She isn't me. She doesn't walk in my shoes. She isn't the one getting up in the middle of the night," and so on. People who respond by *understanding* usually convey the impression to others that they really do *not understand*. An empathetic response is far more appropriate: "It must be difficult to get up in the night when you know you have to go to work the next day."

Avoid Judging and Blaming. Although we consciously try not to judge parents, sometimes our language gives us away. When parents feel they are being judged or blamed, they frequently become defensive. Starting out a conversation with "As you know… " is almost always offensive. Using words such as *ought* or *should* also implies judgment. Saying "You should always make sure Chunga has her medicine" is different from saying "Chunga didn't get her medicine today and that makes it more difficult for us to work with her." The former statement is likely to evoke a defensive reaction from a parent. This can end up being a no-win situation that could easily be avoided.

Avoid Mind Reading. **Mind reading** is assuming to know what another person is thinking or feeling without asking. When a parent says, "Tell me about Elizabeth's day," she is assuming that you can read her mind. If you respond to that statement, you will tell her what you find interesting or what you would want to know if you were the parent. For example, you may tell her the particular activities her daughter enjoys when what she really wants to know is whether she is a "behavior" problem. If she is not, you are unlikely to mention it. If you do not figure out what the parent wants to know, the parent will be dissatisfied with the exchange. It is more useful to help the parent clarify what it is she wants to know than to assume you can read her mind. Do this by asking the parent for more specific information: "I want to talk about the concerns you have. Can you ask me questions about certain aspects of the day?" If the parent persists in wanting to know about what you think is important, you may have to offer her choices: "Would you like to know about her activities, her eating, or how she gets along with the other children? Help me decide where to start." This will usually get a parent to at least state a preference.

Being an active and explorative listener is a good way to avoid mind reading. A parent might ask, "Do you think David is happy here?" To simply say "Yes" doesn't answer the question. It may take some exploration on your part to find out what the parent is concerned about, such as "Can you tell me more specifically what you want to know?" The parent may say, "I worry because he always cries when I leave him and I wonder if he cries all day." Then you can appropriately respond, "David continues to cry for about 5 minutes after you leave. A teacher holds him and she walks around the classroom with him as she tries to figure out what may interest him. She typically finds something and he gets involved playing. At nap time he frequently withdraws and gets a little weepy. We rub his back until he settles down. The other difficult time for him is when the other children's parents pick them up. He becomes anxious for you. I can see why you might think he was unhappy when you only see his most difficult times. Do you have suggestions for ways of comforting him that work well for you that we might try?"

Suppose, on the other hand, you had said, "David really enjoys modeling clay; that keeps him happy for a long time." Although a truthful answer, the parent might come away from the conference feeling that you didn't answer her question (even though she never really asked it).

Much of the communication that takes place between parents and teachers takes place on an individual basis in brief, daily interactions. In addition to these daily exchanges of information, regularly scheduled conferences focus on each child's long-term development. There may be other times when the parents of all the children in the class meet. This is a time to talk about general philosophy and curriculum issues and inclusion. It also provides opportunities for parents to meet other parents who may become part of informal support networks.

Productive Parent-Teacher Conferences

Traditionally, parent-teacher conferences happen two to three times a year. The first occurs near the beginning of the year, the second about the middle of the year, and the third at the end. If there is an expectation that the child will change placements in a setting or move to a different setting, another conference may be used to plan for the transition. Routine conferences use the basic technique known as the "sandwich":

- Talk about the child's positive qualities and how she has adjusted and the developmental strides she is making.
- State your concerns about the child, if there are any, and give concrete examples.
- Conclude on a positive note.

Conferences don't just happen. They require planning.

Gather and organize the notes you have about the child, including examples of activities that you plan to share with parents. Give careful thought to the child as an individual, his likes and dislikes, personality traits, temperament, and the special qualities that you enjoy. Be prepared to talk about the child's group participation and how you support this. Have some of his favorite toys or activities available so parents can see them. (This also provides them with information about developmentally appropriate materials they might use at home.) Make a short (5 minutes or less) videotape to show families how their child spends his time at the setting. Use digital photographs to support and document developmental gains if they can be pictured. They may be particularly interested in friendship patterns. Make parents physically and psychologically comfortable.

Conferencing with Families

Establish rapport. Avoid **jargon**, accentuate the positive, and talk in terms that are specific enough that parents can take action on new information if they choose.

Families genuinely want to know what their child does while he is with you. Older children bring home tests and talk about what they do in school. Younger children and those who have few communication skills cannot convey this information and they may have few "products" as examples of their activities. Families want specific information about their child. Routinely share with parents the following types of information:

- *Videotapes.* Show parents how the child spends his day. If the child has behaviors that are of concern and you want to point these out, videotape them so you can show families specifically what concerns you and when it occurs. This helps clarify the context.
- *Photographs.* Use a digital camera to help children share experiences with families that they cannot take home such as a block building, a dramatic play ensemble, or a new skill. These can be emailed if families have Internet access or printed on regular paper.
- *Work samples.* Collect samples of the child's work and share these with parents. If there are differences you want to point out to parents, show them the work of another child of a similar age and gender (obscuring his name).
- *Anecdotal records and checklists.* Have available the records (originals and your summaries) you keep on each child to share with families and to document your observations.

Sometimes, as you prepare for a conference, your concerns are heightened and you focus more closely on the developmental level of the child.

Preparing a Conference about Developmental Concerns

No one wants to be the one to suggest that a child might have a developmental problem; however, at some point, you may have to do so. The role of the educator in this instance is to provide parents with the information they need to make a decision about whether follow-up is necessary, and if so, how to do it. This type of problem-solving conference requires careful preparation, records of observations, and detailed information about interventions that have been tried and their level of success. Chapter 3 details the formal procedures necessary to make a pre-referral decision. This chapter focuses on packaging and presenting information to families.

When you first suspect a developmental problem you may have only a vague feeling of uneasiness. You may feel that something about this child's behavior is outside your category of "typical." Trust yourself and think about the steps you need to take to confirm or alleviate your concerns. Watch the child closely, and write down your behavioral observations to determine what is bothering you. These notes are for you. They need not look beautiful and they might include the questions your observations generate as well as the observations themselves, for example:

> *Shawn seems to have trouble getting along with the other children. (More often than the others) I better start counting. (frequency) (Has this always been true?) Better talk with his mother briefly when she picks him up and his teacher from last year. (context) He cannot (will not?) stay at one center for over a minute or two. I need to time this. (duration) He doesn't seem to be involved with the activities of other children. (bored? over his head?) Is he enthused about anything? (intensity) Transitions are a problem too. Are there particular times when it occurs? (time)*

Does Shawn have an emotional problem? Maybe he does and maybe he doesn't. Your role is that of gathering additional specific information, not providing a diagnosis. It is the family's decision as to what to do with the information you gather.

Your first goal is to gather the information that you need to either to talk with the family, or to dismiss the hunch. After you have gathered enough information to determine Shawn's typical or baseline information, generate (and write down) your hypotheses and potential solutions. Modify your program and instructional strategies in response to these solutions and keep records. Based on what you record fine tune what you are doing and keep doing it if you see progress. If you are not seeing positive changes, have another set of eyes look at the child. The director or administrator of the program, principal, or other teachers might have suggestions as well as additional insights and observations about the child (Salvia & Ysseldyke, 2007). Again, modify your interventions and keep records.

Gathering and Organizing Additional Information. If, after further observation and data gathering, you still believe there is a problem, the next step is to talk with the family. Prepare yourself by keeping the following questions in mind: What do I need to know? How will I use this information? What is the most effective way to gather and convey this information? Be creative and thorough in gathering your information.

To the videotape, photographs, work samples, and records and checklists, add the following:

- *Instructional modifications.* Be prepared to talk with families about the ways you have systematically modified your interventions for their child and the results of these modifications. Document and date these. As you reflect on these decide whether you have made enough modifications and tried them for a long enough period of time to ensure they had an opportunity to succeed.

- *Informal consultation*. Share with families your initial concern, how you worked through the process, the people with whom you shared your concerns, and the feedback they gave you. Be clear that this was informal, not part of the referral process.
- *Agencies, families, and other professionals*. If families share your concerns, they are likely to proceed further. They will probably ask you for suggestions about referral sources. Think about the types of services that parents may need and have the names of contact people as well as phone numbers. They may want to know about **Child Find** or other agencies that serve young children. They may also want to know about private resources. They may even want to know if there are parents or parent groups that might provide some insights for them. If they have a computer available you might want to give them some web sites to go to for additional information. (See the Educational Resources at the end of this chapter and other chapters that focus on specific problems and disabilities.)

Your role is one of expressing concern, providing information, and helping families develop a plan of action that will support their decision making about their child. This process of confirmation requires referral services. States provide free evaluation for children age 3 to 5; many states also provide these services free to children three and younger. The Child Find specialist is a contact person who knows the regulations for the state, the services provided, and the cost. Child Find is a good initial source of information.

Know going into the conference that this may be the first of a series of meetings. Most families need time to consider what you say and to look at their child in a new light. Give them time as well as information. Although you may have prepared all of the information for the conference, you may not use it all at the first conference. Conferencing is part of a process and the follow-up is as important as the conference.

Conferencing with the Families about Developmental Concerns

Welcome the family, state your general concerns, then get input from the family about their perception of their child's behavior both at home and at school. If they share your concerns and are appreciative that someone else has noticed, the conference will probably move quickly. If they don't share your concerns, you need to find out the basis for their perceptions. These are frequently based on experience with other siblings ("Jack didn't talk until he was three and he was always a loner") and/or lack of information about developmental norms or experience with other children. Sometimes learning about developmental norms can influence parents' understanding of the situation and help them differentiate between age-appropriate behavior and that which is not. They may attribute the behavior to particular circumstances ("Dottie's grandmother is in the hospital"). How you proceed depends on the parents' perception of the situation. They may provide you with information that causes you to rethink the issues.

The goal of the conference is to develop a plan of action. This plan may be additional observation and new interventions or it may be families following up on the referral process. Who is responsible for doing what and when you will conference again should be clarified. You will need to meet again to evaluate what you each have learned.

The referral process, if parents make that decision, takes time. It typically starts with a developmental screening; depending on these results, it may move to more specific assessments. Keep lines of communication open and support parents in their efforts. This is a stressful time and families may be reluctant to talk with others until they know the outcome of the assessment process. Parents themselves may disagree about whether or not to follow through on the assessment, and this may add to family stress. Support the process and the concerns that parents have. If the parents follow through on the assessment and find that their child is eligible for services under the IDEA, then the focus of concern moves more clearly into more formalized family-centered intervention.

Problem-Solving Conferences

On occasion, you will request a conference with the parents, or they with you, to discuss a specific concern. These conferences are different from the routine conferences or those about developmental concerns. They are problem-related and usually have one definite topic. A problem-solving conference should be scheduled when you notice a consistent change in a child's behavior, when his behavior in a specific area deviates significantly from the norms of development, or his particular behavior pattern consistently comes to your attention. This deviation is more than just having a bad day or behavior that is expected because of a child's disabilities.

Scheduling the Conference. Arranging a problem-solving conference is a delicate matter. You don't want to alarm parents, but they do need to know the purpose of the conference. The time frame between scheduling the conference and holding the conference should be as short as possible. Parents are likely to be anxious when you request such a conference. Plan what you will say ahead of time. State your concerns generally; for example, you might begin by saying, "I have been observing Kate for several weeks. I am concerned about the amount of time she spends sitting alone. I have tried to adapt the program to better meet her needs, but she still has difficulty getting involved with activities. She wanders around the classroom. Could we set a time to meet and talk about this?" Parents may push for additional information. Give them general information, but do not have the conference on the telephone. Explain that you have things to show them to help them better understand what is happening before you can jointly work on solving the problem. Schedule the conference as soon as possible.

Conferencing about Specific Problems. As with all conferences, being well prepared is important. In these problem-solving conferences, however, much of the preparation has to do with preparing yourself. After you have made your observations and gathered all the information you can proceed through the following steps. These steps should be thought through carefully before meeting with families; they provide guidance for the conferencing process:

- *Welcome the family and state your general concern.*
- *Define the problem.* An important aspect of this part of the conference is to separate facts from assumptions or generalizations. It is important to be specific and precise. To say that Brian "doesn't get along with the other children" is not precise enough. However, knowing that Brian bit Sally while they were both using playdough and that he hit Juan, knocking him off the tricycle, helps define the problem more clearly. It might be expressed like this: "I'm concerned about Brian's social interactions. In a typical day, he has at least three confrontations with his classmates, which usually involve hitting another child."
- *Express your concern.* At this point, it is useful to express concerns on how the behavior makes you feel: "I am worried that one of the other children will get hurt and also concerned that the program is not meeting Brian's needs."
- *Determine the parents' perception of the situation.* It is useful to describe the problem and express your concerns before you ask the parents how they feel about the situation. Parents may share your concerns or have very different ones. Some parents may respond that they do not view this behavior as a problem ("He is all boy just like his Dad!"). Another parent might be appalled that his son is being aggressive with others and want to "straighten him out at home." It is futile to try to problem solve without knowing how the parents perceive the problem. Although the "facts" might be agreed upon, how the facts are interpreted may be very different.
- *Generate hypotheses.* Ask parents their hypotheses about the child's behavior. In general, behavior doesn't have either a single cause or a single solution. It is wiser to think through the problem fully the first time than to have a second conference over the same issue, having made no progress toward the solution. Problem solving generally involves generating hypotheses about the cause of the problem and potential solutions. Generate some hypotheses of your own before the meeting. If your hypotheses are different from the parents', include them in the discussion. Ensure that you and the family have an agreed upon plan of action when the conference ends.

Summary

One way of understanding families is looking at the family life cycle and the developmental tasks families must perform at different stages. Educators need to understand how families affect children and likewise children affect families. Educators need skills to adapt their programming to children's special needs, their family, and cultural context. Educators need to be knowledgeable about the changing demographics of U.S. families and children. They need to develop cultural competence and the ability to design and implement an antibias curriculum that welcomes and includes children from diverse cultural backgrounds. Educators need to be aware of the special challenges some families face in addition to rearing a child with a disability. They need to reflect on the implications of living in poverty, in foster care, or in violent environments and what this means to a child's development and his behavior in the classroom. They need to adapt to families with structural, functional, cultural, and ethnic diversity that have children with disabilities.

Partnering with families is an essential part of early childhood education. Families are the experts on their children and through collaboration educators build early childhood programs that meet the parents' goals in a developmentally appropriate way. To provide appropriate service, educators need to find out what families want for their children. They need to coordinate and deliver educational services in a respectful way to all families. Educators need a repertoire of good communication skills to establish rapport with families, gather the information they need, and then summarize the information and clarify action plans. Professionals need to be supportive of the family's values and work to provide a culturally rich curriculum that includes and honors diversity.

Teachers and parents schedule routine conferences as well as conferences devoted to solving specific problems and developmental concerns. The latter conferences require more preparation and more detailed follow-up.

Reflections

1. School populations in the United States are becoming increasingly diverse. Although most educators embrace and celebrate cultural/ethnic differences some inequities remain. Some studies have shown that teachers call less on African American males and are more controlling with these children than others in the class. Some teachers give less praise to Latino children. Other teachers praise those who are quiet and follow the rules in contrast to children who are more outspoken.

   As a reflective practitioner think about diversity and gender issues. Will you give everyone the same chances and treat each child fairly? Will you discipline some groups of children more than others? Will you give less attention to one gender or cultural/ethnic group? Do you expect less from some groups of children? How will you know if you are treating a cultural/ethnic group fairly? If you find you are not, what can you do about it?

2. To be a good communicator in a time when best practice focuses on working with the whole family, educators must be familiar with the customs, verbal language, and body language of families from different cultures. Do you feel comfortable working with families from many different cultures? How important is it to be able to work well with families and children from a different cultural background than your own? How can you become more successful working with families whose culture is not familiar to you?

3. A child's disability truly affects a whole family. Many families have difficulty coping with this reality especially when the disability is severe or the child has multiple disabilities. As an educator, family members may come to you to seek advice, look for help, or simply to talk. How will you support family members? How can you help them find the services they may need? Do you believe that it is sometimes important simply to listen to problems? How can you be as much service to the family as you are to the child?

Educational Resources

Annie E. Casey Foundation has a variety of research and information about current topics including **Kids Count,** which provides benchmarks of child well-being by the state and nation. http://www.kidscount.org

Beach Center on Families and Disability is a federally funded research and training institute that focuses on families and the successful functioning of families who have members with disabilities. (913) 864-7600; FAX (913) 864-7605; http://www.beachcenter.org

Family Village at the Waisman Center is a global community that integrates information, resources, and communication opportunities on the Internet for persons with cognitive and other disabilities, for their families, and for those who provide them services and support. It is easy to navigate and has resources and links. http://www.familyvillage.wisc.edu/index.html

Institute for Urban and Minority Education at Teacher's College provides online publications dealing with the education of minority families. It also provides links to other sites concerning minority families. http://iume.tc.columbia.edu/contact.asp

National Black Child Development Institute was founded to improve and protect the quality of life of African American children and families. It publishes a variety of pamphlets and magazines with information about parenting and child health. (202) 387-1281 FAX (202) 234-1738; http://www.nbcdi.org

National Task Force on Early Childhood Education for Hispanics provides information about the Latino culture and the early childhood education of Latino children. http://www.ecehispanic.org

Native Americans – Internet Resources provides links to a variety of internet resources about American Indians. http://falcon.jmu.edu/~ramseyil/native.htm

Parents with Developmental Disabilities shares information on the struggles parents face in raising their children. Videos make this site come alive and provide good information for discussing the rights of parents. http://www.developmentaldisability.org/parents_with_disabilities.htm

For additional resources, visit the book companion website for this text at www.cengage.com/education/deiner.

Chapter 3

Assessment and Evaluation

I probably wouldn't have kept the appointment except that I forgot to cancel it and felt guilty when they called. I had made the appointment to get Diana's hearing checked several months ago when she was having a bout of ear infections and I was concerned about her hearing.

Because we weren't worried, my husband went fishing, and Diana, then almost 3, and I went to the audiology clinic. We entered a soundproof room about the size of an elevator, and I sat slightly behind her so she couldn't see me. The audiologist conditioned her to place a ring on a spindle each time she heard a noise. She learned easily. Then the testing actually began. I didn't pay much attention to what was going on until I realized that I could hear sounds but Diana wasn't doing anything. Then I began to pay close attention. She really couldn't hear the sounds. I could hear them, but she couldn't. I was dumbfounded. I didn't have to be told that she had a hearing loss. Next, they tried to get tympanic responses and said that her ear canals had fluid in them. They recommended that I take her to an ear doctor. I heard what they said but didn't really absorb it. All I kept thinking was that I was her mother and I didn't know she couldn't hear. Somehow I should have known.

I was dazed as we left. I couldn't decide whether to take her to the child care center or not. She couldn't hear. Rationally, I knew that she went the day before and couldn't hear then, but now I knew. How could I have let this happen? Where was my husband when I needed him? I pulled myself together and decided, given my current state, that my daughter was probably safer at the child care center than she was with me and I really needed some personal space. I took her into the center and explained very briefly that I'd just had her hearing tested and that she had a hearing loss of about 60 decibels. I turned as the tears began to come and ran to the car. I just sat there and cried for awhile. Then I decided there were a lot of things I needed to do. I went home and made an appointment for Diana with the otologist. I cried some more. Then I began to wonder why there was fluid in her ears. What caused it? Was it my husband's fault? He had allergies, so she probably had allergies. And where was he anyway? Wasn't our daughter's health more important than his fishing? I called the pediatric allergist and made another appointment. By now, it was time to go get Diana. I was early and the director met me at the door and invited me to come in and talk. The tears that were close to the surface welled up again. I felt ridiculous because it was almost certain the hearing loss was temporary and getting the fluid out of her ear canal would solve the problem, but this knowledge didn't seem to register with me. By the time Diana and I got home, the family was there, home from the activities

of their day. I thought that now I would have the support system I needed.

I told my husband, Jim, and the two older children, Anne, 15, and Seth, 13, what had happened. No one believed me, but as I was preparing dinner, I could hear the older children hiding and calling Diana from another room to see if she could hear them. The hiding and calling seemed to go on forever. Jim followed me into the kitchen and wanted me to repeat in exact detail everything that happened. He also found the whole thing hard to believe. How could she talk if she couldn't hear? It made no sense to him. The assessment must be wrong. We'd find another audiologist. He'd go with me this time. Probably the best thing that happened to me was that by this point I was too mad to cry.

We finally sat down to dinner with Diana still being asked questions amid the general uproar of a typical dinner. Midway through dinner, there was a big storm with lightning and thunder. The thunder was loud and startled everyone; everyone but Diana, that is. More questions: Did she hear the thunder? What thunder? It came again, but there was no response. Dinner was very quiet after that. I think the family finally realized what I already knew.

Reflective Practice

When assessment has unexpected results it is often difficult for families to accept the results of the assessment. What would you do if you were Diana's teacher to accommodate her intermittent hearing loss and probable allergies and to support her family during this process?

The Assessment Process

Many of us have had the nightmare in which we have a final examination and we arrive at the class with only 5 minutes left to take a 2-hour exam, and all we have on is our underwear. Fear and apprehension accompanies most testing situations. Even if we have prepared well for the test, we will probably experience some apprehension prior to it. Now, try to imagine the level of apprehension parents might feel when an assessment may indicate that the child of their dreams is no more and that another child has taken her place.

Young children are delightful, unpredictable, and difficult to make conclusive statements about. The child who "acts out" daily is angelic when you ask someone to come and observe; the child who is withdrawn cooperates beautifully during the observer's visit. Parents face similar problems when having their child assessed. A child who shuts his eyes during an eye examination makes it difficult to determine accurately what he sees. If another cries when earphones are put on, it is difficult to determine what she hears. The difficulty in getting representative behavior from children on a scheduled basis makes the role of early childhood professionals important. They can provide baseline information about behavior and how typical it is.

"Assessment is the process of collecting data for the purposes of making decisions about individuals and groups" (Salvia & Ysseldyke, 2007, p. 4). **Assessment** is designed to determine a quality or condition, whereas **evaluation** uses the assessment information to make decisions. Assessment should be broad-based and include a wide range of methods such as observations, checklists, rating scales, portfolios, samples, or documentation of children's work as well as criterion and norm-referenced tests (NAEYC, 2003). The National Association for the Education of Young Children recommends:

> To assess young children's strengths, progress, and needs, use assessment methods that are developmentally appropriate, culturally and linguistically responsive, tied to children's daily activities, supported by professional development, inclusive of families and conducted to specific beneficial purposes: (1) making sound decisions about teaching and learning, (2) identifying significant concerns that may require focused intervention for individual children, and (3) helping programs improve their educational and developmental interventions (NAEYC, 2003, p. 10.)

Implications for Educators

Assessment is a complex topic. Educators have a major role in the early identification of young children with disabilities. The first part of this chapter focuses on using assessment for identification purposes. Children who are receiving special educational services will already have been through the identification and assessment process. When there are concerns about children, but no diagnosis, the assessment process provides four major decision-making points for educators. The initial one is a pre-referral decision.

Pre-Referral Decisions

After the first week of school, you may reflect on the children in your class. Different children come to mind, with different incidents that make them stand out: your mind's-eye snapshot creates what each is like, both high points and those not so high, as well as triumphs and concerns. Sometimes, the concerns focus on a particular child. They start out small but then niggle in the back of your mind, stay there, and grow. The scenario often goes something like this:

> Natasha is one of the youngest children when she enters your class. She is not as advanced as the other children, but that is expected. She doesn't seem to catch on as quickly as the other children; she seems small for her age. Informal conversation with her family reveals that she was a preemie weighing in at only 2 pounds. You casually inquire if her parents have any concerns. They don't. They did when she was younger, but when she started to walk they knew that she had finally "caught up." Her behavior is a puzzle to you, and your concern increases. You are convinced that there is something different that you should be doing with Natasha, but you aren't sure what.

All of us have some expectations about what normal, typical, or developmentally appropriate behavior is. Trust yourself. Watch the child more closely; noting what bothers you. The first decision you must make is whether a child's behavior is typical for her age. That is, "Is the behavior that you are observing so different from the norm that it will require different educational methods and materials?" There are a variety of ways of making this decision, all require observation, instructional assessment and modifications, and record keeping. You need to be sure you are responding to a pattern of behavior that extends over time. Answer the following questions for yourself:

- What do I need to know?
- How will I use this information?
- What is the most effective way to gather this information?

If you have a system of record keeping in place, use it; if not, some suggestions for informal assessments follow. Observation and record keeping are essential parts of the assessment process.

Record Keeping

There are many different systems of record keeping. Older children have test scores and report cards. Younger children provide more of a challenge. Especially at the beginning of the year, a combination of record-keeping methods is most effective.

In the Field

When I began my job as an early childhood educator a few years ago, I had little idea about how to keep accurate records about my students' learning. I felt my progress reports were based on limited reliable data. To solve this problem I asked for help.

I began speaking to colleagues about how they handled record keeping in their classrooms. I soon learned that I did not have to reinvent the wheel. My coworkers helped me learn some easy tips for keeping accurate records on children's learning. This made my job much easier and less stressful. My colleagues gave me some checklists they used in their classrooms and showed me how to use them. I reprinted these and my paraeducator and I changed them to work with our children and what they were learning. I also learned that I had to have a schedule that would allow me to track their learning goals on a regular basis. This took some adjustment, but soon worked. Finally, I learned the importance of clipboards. I have checklists on clipboards in appropriate areas throughout the classroom.

I now feel as though I have my record keeping together. When it is time to do progress reports, I can give an accurate assessment of what each child has learned and can do. Good record keeping also allows me to be more reflective about my teaching practices. I now change instructional strategies and activities to fit the needs of each child.

Reflective Practice

Assess your skills in the area of record keeping. How do you plan to document children's learning? When and how will you collect it?

Anecdotal Notes

Probably the most common form of nonsystematic observation is keeping anecdotal notes. For each child you might have a card, a page in a notebook, or a folder. In a class of twenty, some educators write notes about four children each day. There are some problems with this system: significant events happen to children on "other" days. If your order of writing is random, on Friday you may have put off writing notes on four children because you don't know what to write and what you really want to do is go home. Frequently, going home wins. Additionally, one tends to write about interesting events as opposed to developmentally important information; the age-old question of "What's cute? What counts?" It is useful to note whom you have the fewest notes on and try to figure out why. These may be the children that you need the most information on.

Anecdotal notes are for you. They need not look beautiful and they might include questions your observations generate as well as the notes themselves. Your notes may resemble these:

> (4/7) *Suzy spilled her milk (more often than the other children?). She did not (cannot? will not?) put a simple puzzle together. She did not sit through group time (bored? over her head?). She played with Nathan in the dramatic play area but this ended when she couldn't be the baby. She ran to her cubby and stayed there until a teacher helped her reenter the group. (Was this a bad day?) (I better check and see if anything is going on at home.)*

> (4/8) *Talked to Mom and she said everything was fine at home.*

To make anecdotal notes more useful, you might ask yourself why you observe the children. What is the purpose of observation? Typically, observations are used to make academic and social decisions. When things are going well, they provide the information you need for parent conferencing. When you begin to develop concerns about a child, you need to refine your note-taking system and combine it with behavior observations to help you target children and specific behaviors.

Behavioral Observations

Behavioral observations are useful ways of recording information on behaviors that draw your attention (such as hitting). They are less useful as an everyday program assessment or as an assessment of social patterns and what children are learning. The usual purpose of behavioral observation is to target behaviors that need intervention or that indicate a child's development is not following the usual track. Behavioral observations include information about the situation as well as specific characteristics relative to behavior: duration, latency, frequency, intensity, context, and time (Salvia & Ysseldyke, 2007).

Duration. Behaviors have discrete beginnings and endings. It is relevant to know how long Suzy played in the dramatic play area before leaving and how long she remained in her cubby before a teacher helped her reenter the group. Think about how she spends her time. Picture her in your mind's eye; where do you see her? If you picture her sitting in her cubby, find out how much time she spends there each day. Most digital watches have timers. Use yours for several days to record the amount of time she spends in her cubby. Duration also provides important information about children who wander or who remain at activities for a short or long time.

Frequency. Frequency relates to how often a particular behavior happens. In this case, it is relevant to know how often Suzy goes to her cubby during a day and for how many days. If you record how many times a day she seeks refuge there and the amount of time she spends each time, you can build a database. Compute a weekly and daily average using the frequency and duration data for the episodes.

Intensity. Intensity has to do with the magnitude or severity of the behavior. Some children whimper, others scream; sometimes a temper tantrum involves lying on the floor sobbing, other times screaming, flailing arms and pounding legs. Find some consistent way to calibrate intensity. Perhaps a scale of one to four, where one is low intensity, nondisruptive; two disrupts a small group of children nearby; three disrupts most of the class; and four disrupts the entire class and those in the hall or perhaps in adjoining rooms. Adding intensity to duration and frequency data provides additional insights.

Latency. Latency is the length of time between a request and the child's response to the request: Asking children to put away their materials and when they actually start to do so. This is a relevant variable when children are asked to do tasks that require higher-order thinking, tasks that require change, and tasks children do not want to participate in.

Context. Context refers to what is happening in the classroom before, during, and after an event. Context provides information about probable causes for the behavior: what influences the duration of the behavior and what role the response to the behavior has in maintaining the behavior. If the behavior occurred during group time, one might explore different possible solutions than if the behavior occurred during **transitions.**

It is useful to find out whether behavior is consistent across settings and contexts (Salvia & Ysseldyke, 2007). It is particularly useful to know if you are seeing the same behavior as the parents. If the behavior is consistent across contexts, you need to focus on the behavior itself. If it is inconsistent, there may be something in the environment that is triggering the behavior.

Time. Time refers to when during the day a particular behavior occurs. It is important to note if the behavior happens at specific times of the day or if it seems to occur randomly throughout the day.

In the Field

Ronnie had a temper tantrum every day, starting on the first day of school. I checked with his mother and found that he "never" had temper tantrums at home. I observed his behavior and found that he only had one temper tantrum a day; it seemed unrelated to the children he was playing with or the activity itself, and it lasted about 10 minutes and disturbed most of the class. After trying a variety of different interventions, all of which failed miserably, I talked with his mother again and asked her to tell me about a typical day. His day began about 4:30 A.M., he had breakfast at 5:00 A.M., played until lunch, which he had about 10:00 A.M., took a nap and played, had dinner at 4:00 P.M. and was in bed by about 6:00 P.M. Based on this information, I noted the time of the temper tantrums: 10:00 A.M. I decided the cause of the temper tantrums was hunger, I had a snack ready earlier or had an open snack set up at a center where children could eat when they were hungry. The temper tantrums stopped.

Reflective Practice

Good record keeping and communication with the family solved this problem in an unexpected way. Reflect on how you can use assessment techniques as behavior

management tools and how creatively you need to think about potential solutions to problems.

Behaviors that are targeted for observation and intervention are those that are harmful to the child or others (hitting, biting), behavior exhibited in an inappropriate context (using an outside voice inside, running inside), infrequently displayed desirable behavior (sharing, turn-taking, and other prosocial behavior), and stereotypic behavior that draws negative attention to the child (hand flapping and rocking) (Salvia & Ysseldyke, 2007). Anecdotal notes are typically done at the end of the day; behavioral observations are made during the day. They require planning and organization. Behavioral observations focus on particular children and specific behaviors, checklists collect general information on all children in a short time span.

Checklists

At the beginning of the school year, checklists can help you learn children's names, focus on general patterns of adjustment and behavior, and learn where and how long children play in different areas. Use a checklist such as the one in Figure 3–1 several times during free play for about a week. If there are other adults in the classroom, encourage them to fill out the checklist as well. The recorder initials the form and fills in the time and date. First divide the room into areas and write a brief description of what is in each area on a given day. (If the dramatic play area is a hospital, note that.) Write the first names of the children in alphabetical order on the side. Use the form adapting it as you need. When you have it the way you want it duplicate it and use it.

This checklist is most useful at the beginning of the year. After you name each different area add areas beyond the heavy line where children might be (bathroom, wandering around, cubbies, nurse's office, and therapy, if this is not in the classroom). If events such as these happen frequently, add them to the checklist; if they are unusual, they are not worth including. Indicate the theme, if any, and place a brief reminder of the day's activities below each designated area. Use the checklist by placing a check in the box beside the child's name to indicate where each child is in the room. Use a checklist like the one in Figure 3–1 several times a day. It helps to have it on a clipboard in various places in the room.

Assume that in a week you have been able to fill out this form ten times. What can you learn from the data you've generated? First, put it all on one form. Some

Recorder_____									Time _____	
Unit/theme _____									Date _____	
Activity Areas Checklist										
	Area	Art	Manipulative	Water/Sand table	Books	Blocks	Dramatic Play	Cubbies	Wandering	Bathroom
Child's name	Day's activities									

Instructions: Place a check mark in the areas where you observe child.

Figure 3–1: Checklist: Activity Areas
Use this form at the beginning of the school year to determine where children are playing, with whom, and for how long.

implications are immediately apparent. Some children play in many areas, some in only one or two. You might identify small groups of children who play together. If you haven't noticed them yet, children who appear in the last three columns (cubbies, wandering, and bathroom) frequently are of concern. These are children who are walking around without purpose and not engaging in activities. They probably need your help. At this stage, you are asking more questions than generating answers. If you become interested in how long children are staying at activities, try to use the form at short intervals for a few days, and look at children who are in the same area of the room on at least two consecutive observations as well as those who are never in the same area twice. This allows you to generate some information about interest span. These data, coupled with other observations, begin to give you a foundation for looking at the children in your classroom in a more systematic way. You can do all this record keeping and teach at the same time. You may now decide that you need more specific data on some children's skills.

Checklists can also help focus attention on specific skills. Some you can more appropriately fill in after school is over. Useful examples and rationale for some of the checklists have been included. Especially with younger children, adding their age (in years and months) to a general skills checklist often is important, as children in a given class have a range of 12 to 18 months in age. For 4 year olds, this is a fourth of their lifetime. It is a reminder that children are appropriately different. Try to add information to these charts a few times a week. Children who are inconsistent or need work in an area will become more evident. These are the children to observe more closely (see the General Skills Checklist, Figure 3–2).

Transitions are a good time to collect information about children's skills. For example, as children move from a group situation to centers, it is easy to dismiss them while you assess their learning. With planning, you can ensure that all children are successful, and that you have accurate records. If you are concerned with number and letter recognition, consider using the record-keeping forms in Figure 3–3, Group Time Transitions. Include color and spatial concepts in your assessment as well. To do this effectively, you can use a calendar for number identification ("Put your finger on the 12 and then you

may go to the block area") or recognition ("Tell me the name of this number [point to a number on the calendar] and you may go to center time"). If your calendar is magnetic or is designed in a way that something will stick to it (tape on the back of the object works), ask the child to put an object in different spatial configurations relative to a specific number on the calendar. ("Put the circle above the number 21.") This exercise allows you to tap both spatial and numerical concepts. You can modify this form to gather information that is important to you. With an alphabet available, you can pose similar tasks. As children learn the capital letters, introduce lowercase letters.

Checklists are quick and efficient to use. They can be used on your schedule, and they include all of the children. They can be designed to fit your particular purpose. If you were interested in the quality of children's play you might design one similar to Figure 3–4. The disadvantage is that you have to prepare them ahead of time, and it may take a few attempts for you to develop checklists that fit your needs.

Work Samples or Portfolios

Work samples or portfolios are another form of assessment particularly applicable to young children and are being viewed as an alternative assessment for children with disabilities of all ages (Salvia & Ysseldyke, 2007). There are many different types of portfolios: showcase portfolios use a child's best work; working portfolios allow children and teachers to communicate about a work in progress; assessment portfolios are holistic and are scored or rated (Columba & Dolgos, 1995). Portfolios include examples of children's writing, art, and so on, photographs of projects including skills children display, friendships, and construction projects. To be useful, the collection of samples needs to begin the first week of school so you can see growth, and also so the children learn that putting some of their products in the folder is part of the system, both yours and theirs. The following guidelines will help you decide what should go in the portfolio. Items or representations that

- reflect what you want children to know and learn.
- reflect authentic assessment of what children are expected to do in the real world.
- reflect learning strategies and problem solving.

| Recorder _____ | | | | | | | Date _____ |

General Skills Checklist

Child's name	Age yr./mos.	Language		Approach + or –	Social		Motor	
		Receptive	Expressive		Assertiveness interaction child	Assertiveness interaction adult	Small	Large

Key: 1 Above average   2 Average   3 Seems inconsistent   4 Needs work

Figure 3–2: Checklist: General Skills
Decide what skills to monitor. Language and motor skills have norms and social skills that relate to inclusion are critical. Use children's age in years and months as it may vary by 12 to 18 months. This span causes a significant difference in skill development and expectations.

Child's name _____

Numbers

	Code	Date	Code	Date
0				
1				
2				
3				
4				
5				
6				
7				
8				
9				
10				

Letter concepts/capitals

	Code	Date	Code	Date
A				
B				
C				
D				
E				
F				
G				
H				
I				
J				

Letter concepts/lowercase

	Code	Date	Code	Date
a				
b				
c				
d				
e				
f				
g				
h				
i				
j				

Spatial concepts

	Code	Date	Code	Date
Above				
Below				
Between				
Inside				
Outside				
Behind				
Under				
At the top				
At the bottom				
Across from				
In front of				
Up				
Down				
Beside				
Beneath				
Nearest				
Right				
Left				

Shapes

	Code	Date	Code	Date
△				
○				
□				
□				
⬭				

Sizes
Materials: Three sizes of shapes

	Code	Date	Code	Date
Small				
Smallest				
Little				
Littlest				
Medium				
Big				
Bigger				
Large				
Larger				
Largest				

Body parts

	Code	Date	Code	Date
Ankle				
Arms				
Back				
Cheeks				
Chest				
Chin				
Ears				
Elbow				
Eyes				
Eyebrows				
Eyelashes				
Feet				
Fingernails				
Fingers				
Hair				
Head				
Hips				
Jaw				
Knee				
Mouth				
Neck				
Nose				
Legs				
Lips				
Teeth				
Tongue				
Toes				
Thumb				
Waist				
Wrist				

Key: Response
R = Recognition (point to the)
I = Identification (What is this? Where is this?)

Key: Accuracy
+ = Correct
⊕ = Correct with help
○ = Incorrect
NA = Not attempted

Figure 3–3: Checklist: Group Time Transitions
Transitions from group time provide the opportunity to assess and keep records on individual skill levels. Double coding (R+) provides information that a child correctly recognizes a particular item.

- show cooperative learning and engaging with peers.
- show patterns of learning and reflection as part of the learning process.
- show the relationship between assessment and instruction (Salvia & Ysseldyke, 2007).

Chose items that meet the above criteria rather than those items that are "cute." Talk to the children about their portfolio and give them the opportunity to add items and reflect on the items that are included. Establish early that there are short- and long-term items for the portfolio. Long-term items would include children's first drawings and paintings of the year, as well as work that illustrates particular skills (or lack of them). Short-term items might be stories that are then replaced by other stories.

| Recorder _____ | | | | | Time _____ |
| | | | | | Date _____ |

Level of Play

Child's name	Unoccupied	Onlooker	Solitary	Parallel	Associative	Cooperative

Key: Write initials of playmates in space. For cooperative play, note the leader.

Figure 3–4: Checklist: Level of Play

One goal of inclusion is to have children play together. It is useful to know the level of children's play to suggest appropriate peers. A child's level of play is developmental and it is helpful in transition planning. Forms such as this make observations more systematic.

Definitions. *Unoccupied:* **Child is not participating in an activity or watching other children.** *Onlooker:* **Although not participating, the child is actively watching other children.** *Solitary:* **The child is playing alone with materials that are different from other children's.** *Parallel:* **The child is playing alone with materials that are the same as other children nearby.** *Associative:* **Children are playing together but the play is not goal oriented and there is no leader.** *Cooperative:* **Children are playing together, the play is goal oriented, and there is a leader (Parten, 1932).**

Use the portfolio with the children. Let them enjoy their personal growth by looking at work they have done earlier and comparing it with what they can do now. Talk about how much they have learned. Invite a photographer or designer to come to the class, share a portion of her portfolio with the class, and explain its use in her profession.

For each artifact collected it must be clear what specific curriculum goal the child was working toward and how this work clearly documents progress (or lack of progress) toward meeting the goal. The role of the teacher is to provide commentary about the context and process (Gronlund, 1998). To streamline this process develop a checklist similar to Figure 3–5.

In addition to work that is the outcome of various activities, it is important to include work in the portfolio that helps you focus on specific areas such as language, math, science, and so on. You might design some activities in each area that you do consistently several times each year. For example, make up a short story with specific details at the beginning of the year and then have the children draw a picture about the story. (This is not an art project; it is assessment.) Tell the same story about 4 months later and again at the end of the year. Look for personal growth and also at the level of detail in the drawing across the group. This story should have details, familiar animals and modes of transportation, and a very simple plot. Tell a story something like this:

One day a dog and a cat met. The dog said, "I like to run, I'll race you home." "Okay," said the cat. "One, two, three, go!" The dog raced past the cat. The cat saw a boy on a bicycle. "Can you go fast?" "Yes," said the boy. "Can you catch that dog?" "Sure." The cat

As children complete tasks such as identifying the letters of the alphabet and placing them in a puzzle documentation should be kept about the number of letters correctly identified and the number of puzzle pieces correctly placed.

Portfolio Artifact Checklist

Child's name _____ Date _____

Curriculum goal:

Activity:

Initiation:	child	peer	teacher
Task:	new	emerging	mastery
Support:	adult	peer	independent
Involvement:	little	average	great
Time:	short	average	long
Requirements:	not met	met	exceeded

Figure 3–5: Checklist: Portfolio Artifacts

jumped on and off they went, up and down hills and across bridges. Finally, they caught up to the dog. The dog was mad. If the cat can play tricks, so can I. He met a horse and asked if the horse could go as fast as the bicycle. The horse said "Yes." The dog jumped on his back, and off they went. They went through the woods, jumped a stream, and finally caught up with the boy on the bicycle. The boy on the bike hit a rock and the cat fell off. The dog raced by on the horse. The cat shook himself off. The dog said to the horse, "I'm glad we don't have to run as fast now." Just then they saw the cat go flying past on an airplane. "Oh, no!" said the dog. And when he got home he said to the cat, "Let's race again tomorrow." "Okay," said his friend the cat.

Feel free to use this story or modify it. By having the children draw pictures about the same story over time; it is easier to see change. It is important that the story be original, as some children might know a published story and others not.

Other areas about which you may begin to gather some systematized data are fine and gross motor skills. One way to do this is to have your own (noncompetitive) Olympics. Develop the Olympic events from criterion-based assessments. One of the most useful is the *HELP for Preschoolers Charts* (VORT Corporation, 1995). The three-page charts are organized by domain areas (social, gross and fine motor, cognitive, and so on) and by age. They also provide a time span during which skills should emerge. The *Learning Accomplishment Profile*, Third Edition (Sanford, Zelman, Hardin, & Peisner-Feinberg, 2004) also provides relevant information. For 3 year olds, the Olympic events (with appropriate norms noted) might include:

- Broad jump (mark off 2 feet) to the next line.
- Push or pull a wagon to the next line (10-foot distance).
- Walk (10 feet) on a 4-inch-wide taped line.
- Catch a ball thrown from 5 feet away.
- Put the ball down, take two steps, and kick it.
- Gallop back to the starting line.

These are all skills that 3 year olds are expected to be able to do. The Olympics provides the motivation and learning opportunities that make this part of the curriculum. You have made assessment fun and interesting as well as informative.

Implications for Educators

You now have some ideas about how to collect the informal data you need to confirm or disconfirm your concerns about a particular child, as well as to monitor the development of all the children in your classroom. Use this information in two ways: First, to look at the development of a particular child over time; second, to compare children to a norm or average for the age level you are teaching. Next, look at the birth dates of the children in the class. If there is a child you are concerned about, find other children who are within a month or two of the child's age and compare their work samples and observational results. The intention is not to make judgments, but to see the range of behaviors and to determine whether a particular

child is outside of this range. Then compile information from your behavioral observations, checklists, and the child's portfolio. You may decide at this point that the behavior that caught your attention was unusual for the child and just the result of a temporary problem; or you may decide that you need additional information to reach a decision. You might begin to generate some hypotheses about what is causing the behavior and how you can modify your curriculum to better meet this child's needs.

As you modify your curriculum and instruction, documentation is extremely important. You have now made a commitment about your concerns and have developed a plan of action. Put your concerns in writing and list your hypotheses about probable causes. Decide on your modifications, the period in which you will use them, and the outcomes that you expect. If your hunch is right, you will need this documentation for the next step. At this point your concerns relate to a child who needs additional help in a particular area or a child who appears bored and needs enrichment. Document your results. If you feel the concern has been dealt with, continue to monitor the situation intermittently to ensure it stays solved. If the problem is still of concern, there is another decision to make: Is it time to call in additional support, to try different methods of remediation or enrichment, or to make substantial changes in the child's program?

Response to Instruction

If your planned instruction and interventions were not successful, the next step is to seek assistance. Some educational settings have formal intervention assistance teams that are designed for this specific purpose; other intervention assistance works on friendship patterns or an informal organization. With these additional sets of eyes and insights, new methods of evidence-based instruction may be suggested and tried and again judged as successful or unsuccessful. If the problem is still of concern, it is time to talk with the parents and share your concerns with them. What you are trying to do in the pre-referral stage is to eliminate the environment as the source of the problem or as a solution to the problem.

Response to instruction (RTI) is a concept with multiple meanings but the focus is on how effective the instruction is for all children in the classroom. With the implications of the No Child Left Behind Act and the 2004 reauthorization of the IDEA there is an expectation that all instruction is evidence-based. Therefore response to instruction (RTI) measures how much all children are learning in the core instruction in the classroom. That is, if there is specific content the majority of the children in a classroom are expected to master the question, are they in fact learning the material? They need to be monitored on a regular basis to ensure that learning continues and that it is effective. As part of this process some children will be identified as not learning at the expected rate. Based on their response to instruction something else needs to be done to ensure their success. Their instruction needs to be enhanced, modified, or changed in some way to ensure they will progress at the expected rate. This requirement highlights the circular relationship between instruction and assessment and the modification of instruction and additional assessment to make data-driven decisions (Salvia & Ysseldyke, 2007).

If children are not learning at the expected rate, instruction is intensive, individualized, and assessed more frequently. Tell parents about your concerns and what you have done to lessen them. This is particularly true if the intensive instruction you designed did not make a difference. What you are doing is comparing a child's rate of learning from regular classroom instruction to his rate of learning with intensive instruction. Children who do not respond to intensive interventions based on the RTI model are referred for further evaluation to determine if they are eligible for special education services based on the requirements on the IDEA. If children are not learning at the expected rate, you need to talk with their parents.

Conferencing with Parents

Using the guidelines from Chapter 2, schedule a conference with the child's family. Explain your concerns, how you have reached your conclusions, and why you believe the child will benefit from a formal screening. You need the *information* an evaluation provides (not the *label*) to meet this child's needs. If the family does not agree with your concerns and conclusions, this process may take several conferences and some structured observation. Some families may never agree.

If the family agrees to a diagnostic assessment, the exact procedure depends on the age of the child, whether or not the child is in a public or private school, and the nature of the problem itself. The child may be assessed by the school psychologist, educational diagnostician, Child Find specialist, or other professionals. If concerns are more medical in nature, the child's physician would do an initial assessment and provide necessary referrals.

Your role (with family permission) is to share your written data with the specialists of their choice, and to support that person's observations in your classroom. If the family does not agree to an assessment, your role is to continue to provide intensive individualized programming in your class and to use your support network for ideas and interventions. If parents do agree, you move into a set of decisions related to **entitlement**.

Entitlement Decisions

Entitlement decisions are made to determine whether or not children are eligible for certain types of services. The first step in entitlement decisions is screening.

Screening

The goal of screening is to identify children who are currently experiencing delayed development and who will continue to experience delays and academic challenges without intervention. The underlying assumption behind screening is that children can be divided into two categories: those who are at risk and those who are not at risk.

We have all been screened at one time or another. School districts screen children prior to their entering kindergarten. Scheduled hearing, visual, and dental screenings are done throughout the school years. Adults are screened for vision and knowledge of driving safety before receiving a driver's license.

Children enter the screening process in different ways. Some physicians have concerns about children and encourage parents to have them screened. Some parents themselves are concerned and initiate the process. You, as an educator, may express concerns to parents about their child's need for screening.

Screening instruments vary. Some require highly trained professionals while others use trained volunteers. The goal of a screening instrument is to identify all children who have certain characteristics, called "hits," and none of the children who do not have the characteristics. For screening to be effective the process needs to be simple. That is, it needs to be easy to complete and quick. It also needs to be accurate. There needs to be clear criteria, and the measures used need to be sensitive enough to identify as many children as possible who have delays or disabilities, as well as specific enough to distinguish between children with delays and those without delays. Measures need to be comprehensive and cost effective. They need to be done in partnership with families. There are three screening outcomes:

- The results look typical; that is, development seems to be proceeding at the expected rate.
- The results are inconclusive and the child should be monitored or rescreened.
- The results indicate the possibility of atypical development and the child should be referred for further, more in-depth assessment.

The criterion used in making screening decisions varies from state to state; however, the following concerns are typically addressed in screening decisions: development that is more than 1.75 **standard deviations** below the **mean** (that is, below the eightieth percentile) medical history that shows risk, parental concerns, environmental concerns, and professional judgment (Salvia & Ysseldyke, 2007).

In the Field

After teaching for many years, I have concerns with the screening procedures used to identify young children with academic problems. One of my concerns is that the screening tests are not identifying children with intellectual disabilities. The testing measures are not accurate when dealing with at-risk children. Many of the measures are inappropriate for some populations. Several of the children I now work with passed the screening tests at age 3 and later, when they entered kindergarten, were found to have IQ scores in the range of 50 to 55.

My other concern compounds the problem of the poor predictability of screening tools. This concern relates to the inadequate training of teachers to identify developmental problems in the children they teach. Teachers in some programs are required to have an associate's degree (2-year degree) in child development. This lack of training adds to the problem of identifying children who need early intervention. It is a disservice to the children. The earlier these children receive intervention, the more likely they are to overcome their delay. Proper training and knowledge of developmental delays is crucial to identifying these children and providing appropriate services for them.

I have found that taking anecdotal notes and doing observations can help to identify any problems that the child may be exhibiting. Assessment techniques should be a part of all programs that train early childhood educators. They assist in meeting children's individual goals but they also help detect problems that screening measures miss. Screening children who live in poverty doesn't seem to work. However, when I use my checklists it is clear that some have a pattern of delays. These children are at risk for academic failure and deserve the best possible services to ensure their success.

I am committed to the children I teach, but they would be so much better off if they had been identified when they were younger. They come to me expecting to fail. I have to spend the first part of the year working on what they know to give them the motivation to begin to work on the material that we are supposed to cover in kindergarten. There has to be a better way to identify these children at a younger age.

Reflective Practice

The potential that early intervention holds has made early identification imperative to support the best outcomes for children. What do you think the qualifications for early childhood teachers who teach in Head Start, child care, private preschools, and other programs should be? As you look at your own program do feel you have the skills you need to identify young children whose development is on an atypical path and who could profit from early intervention?

For young children, screening should consist of a range of activities that include information about the child's health, physical and motor development, social interactions, emotional expressions, social competence, concept development, and adaptive skills. It should also include an interview with the child's family so that relevant information about the child's medical history, family health concerns, and the family's perception of the child's development and their concerns, if any, are available. Screening is a brief assessment designed to identify children who may have a condition that requires further diagnosis. Screening should not be used as a diagnosis, particularly not with children who are English language learners (NAEYC, 2003).

Guidelines for Developmental Screening and Assessment

Assessing young children is very different from assessing adults or even older elementary school children. It requires different skills for those who are doing the assessment. The following guidelines highlight recommended practices:

- **Assessment should be based on an integrated holistic developmental model.** Children's functioning is interdependent; it is not a collection of isolated areas such as cognitive, sensory, or motor abilities. Assessment needs to focus on the child's level and pattern of organizing experiences and his functional capacity. Assessment needs to take into account not only what the child can do and how he does it but also the child's motivation and the context in which the behavior is or is not displayed. It needs to be gathered in natural settings that reflect what the child knows and can do.

- **Assessments need to include multiple sources of information and multiple components gathered over time.** Information from the family and different members of the assessment team obtained in different contexts provides different perspectives and allows a more comprehensive profile of the child to emerge. Assessment is a collaborative process.

- **Assessment requires establishing working alliances with the significant individuals in a child's life and the child.** Professionals need to develop rapport and trust with families and respect them as members of the assessment team. This alliance is the first step in the assessment process; it includes the relationship between the family and child, family and professional, and child and professional. It requires families and early childhood educators to learn about assessment tools, what they do, and how they are appropriately used.

- **Assessment of the child's relationship with her most trusted caregivers forms the base for assessment.** The parent-child relationship forms the blueprint for later relationships to build upon. When this is well grounded, professionals can develop methods of intervention that are congruent with the child's preferences and interaction patterns. If the parent-child relationship is maladaptive then it needs to be a focus of the intervention, whether this involves teaching families new patterns or providing other potential attachment figures.

- **Assessment is appropriate for the child's age and characteristics; what is assessed is developmentally and educationally significant.** Assessment should be aligned with early learning standards and should be broad-based rather than focusing on a narrow set of skills. The instruments should be valid for the children based on their age, culture, abilities, home language, and other characteristics.

- **Assessment processes should identify the child's current and emerging strengths and competencies.** The focus is on what children can do, as this forms the basis for intervention. Assessment should increase early childhood educators' knowledge about children, improve the educational program, and identify resources and teaching techniques needed to support learning.

- **Assessment is not dependent upon norm-referenced tests.** The use of norm-referenced tests should be limited and provide only part of the information needed about a child's development, such as identifying potential disabilities.

- **Assessment should be viewed as a service.** It is the first step in a potential intervention process, not merely a means for identification and measurement. Assessment should be viewed as a recursive process that informs intervention and is informed by intervention.

- **Assessment measures and procedures should be relevant and used for their intended purpose.** The measures should be reliable, valid, and unbiased. Those who participate in the assessment process should have extensive and comprehensive training as well as be familiar with the child (Meisels & Atkins-Burnett, 2000; NAEYC, 2003; Salvia & Ysseldyke, 2007).

If the screening determines that a child is at risk, further assessment is designed to confirm or refute the existence of a problem. (This should sort out the children who were mistakenly referred for screening or assessment.) Development is more a matter of degree than a yes or no answer. For example, a child with 20/40 vision may not profit from wearing glasses; a child with 20/100 would. The question really becomes, "Is the problem so serious that intensive intervention is required and do the interventions need to be designed by specialists?" Diagnosis also is designed to clarify the nature of the problem. "Is a hearing loss the result of fluid in the ear canal, nerve damage, or both?" Formal diagnosis is a long process.

If the results of the screening indicate that a child is at risk, developmental assessments are the next step in the process. **Referral** is a formal process and requires parents to fill out specific forms requesting assessment by a team of professionals to determine whether their child's academic, behavioral, or physical development qualifies him for special education services. This team is frequently called a Child Study Team. The makeup of the assessment team varies depending on the age of the child, the particular concern, and how the child entered the screening process. For example, if the early childhood educator expressed the concern to the family she would be on the team.

However, if the parents were following up on their own concerns, there might be an early childhood educator on the team but that educator would not necessarily be the child's teacher, particularly if the child were not in a preschool program.

The assessment team must decide whether or not the child meets the state's eligibility criteria for services by either having a documentable disability or by being gifted and talented. State criteria differ. This is especially true for children birth to 3. Additionally, the team must decide whether the child has special learning needs. Children can have a disability and not have special learning needs. Likewise, children can have special learning needs and not meet the state criteria for special services. Children must meet both criteria to receive mandated services.

Standardized Tests

As an early childhood professional you need to be able to interpret the results of standardized tests, convey these results to others and understand how they will affect curriculum planning. You should know how standardized measures are selected and evaluated, and the purpose of the measures used. Educators should have a course in assessment; this chapter is not meant as a substitute for such a course, but rather to highlight the role of assessment in the educator's decision-making process.

Standardized testing is complex—there are many different types of tests for different purposes. The tests you are most likely to encounter fall into two broad areas: **norm-referenced** and **criterion-referenced**.

In a norm-referenced assessment, a child's performance is evaluated relative to the performance of other children of the same age. We use norm-referenced tests to compare the performance of a child to a sample of children who are similar to him. To the extent that he, and the children in the sample, are representative of the population as a whole and the test was designed for the purpose we are using it, the test results should provide valuable information for decision making (Salvia & Ysseldyke, 2007).

Criterion-referenced measures rely on an absolute standard for determining scores. Children are asked to perform certain tasks and the score is based on the level at which they respond. Criterion-referenced measures are more useful for curriculum planning. It is more helpful to know that Linyu can read beginning second-grade material with 70 percent accuracy than that she has an **intelligence quotient (IQ)** of 90.

The measures you encounter also fall into categories depending upon the purpose of the test. **Developmental tests** are age-related, norm-referenced measures of skills and behaviors that compare the scores of children of a given age. For younger children they typically have **developmental quotients (DQs)** which, like intelligence quotients (IQs), the norm is 100. Children taking these tests are compared to the norm. Those scoring more than 100 are considered to be developing faster than the norm and those with DQs less than 100 are developing slower than the norm. The norm was established by testing and retesting many children. Developmental norm-referenced tests are part of most screening and diagnostic workups.

Curriculum-based assessments are used in schools to determine the instructional needs of children, whereas **achievement tests** measure the extent to which a child has mastered a certain body of knowledge after having received instruction in that area. **Objective-referenced assessments** look at how a child is performing relative to specific objectives that have been designed for that particular child (Salvia & Ysseldyke, 2007).

Assessment provides us with baseline data. If one wishes to monitor change, the first thing that has to be established is change *from what*. The initial assessment provides this starting point. The second purpose of assessment is *prediction*. We not only want to know what the child is doing now, and at what rate he is learning, but we also want to be able to predict how the child will be learning when he enters school or at some other future time. The assumption is that if the assessment is representative of the child's behavior, then the child will continue to develop at the predicted rate (Salvia & Ysseldyke, 2007). If, however, an external force (early intervention or child abuse) impacts the child, the principle of continuity may not hold and the assessment will not accurately predict future behavior.

Post Entitlement Decisions

When children between the ages of 5 to 9 are identified as needing services, it is frequently because of lack of academic progress. For younger children, it is more likely the failure to reach developmental milestones at the appropriate time. These differences are what must be addressed in curriculum planning. There are a variety of decisions that need to be made: What to teach (content), how to teach it (methods, teaching techniques, or strategies), and realistic expectations (Salvia & Ysseldyke, 2007). Consideration also needs to be given to the setting in which instruction will take place, and the additional supports necessary for success. Agreement must also be reached on how to evaluate progress or learning on a regular basis. Chapter 5 focuses on individualized planning.

Issues in Assessment

Assessment affects all children, and since assessment and curriculum are inextricably tied together, curriculum is part of the issue. As a nation we are concerned about what our children are learning (or not learning). The **No Child Left Behind Act (P.L. 107–110)**, signed into law on January 8, 2002, is a reauthorization of the federal Elementary and Secondary Education Act. This law affects schools, school districts, and state Departments of Education. The No Child Left Behind Act of 2001 and the 2004 reauthorization of the IDEA continues the federal agenda for education. It creates strong standards in each state for what children need to know particularly in the areas of literacy and math. These laws have a strong focus on reading, particularly for children in kindergarten through third grade who are at risk for reading disabilities (learning disabilities). The hope is that early identification of these children will result in interventions using evidence-based instructional strategies that will increase reading skills and reduce the number of children in special education. The law increases state and local flexibility while at the same time holding them responsible for failing schools, particularly schools that serve low-income and minority families. It gives parents the right to move their children out of "failing schools" to other public schools including charter schools (Salvia & Ysseldyke, 2007).

How will we determine whether children are *ready* to learn? Assessment. Concern about the use and abuse of assessment is not new and it stems from many different areas: the tests themselves, the testing process, and the use of the test results. Concern about the assessment process is primarily focused on the use and misuse of standardized tests and testing procedures.

Although No Child Left Behind does not focus on children below kindergarten it has generated concerns about the increasing academic pressure brought to early childhood settings. If public schools are being judged on their ability to teach children to read, they want children to enter school with basic pre-reading skills. Skills that may have been taught in kindergarten or even first grade are now expected of entering kindergarten children. There is concern that if children do not have these skills they will not be considered "ready" to enroll in kindergarten. We are particularly concerned that black and Hispanic children come to kindergarten with fewer skills in math and reading than white children. Differences in vocabulary, letter recognition, and early reading and math skills are apparent by age 3 (Haskins & Rouse, 2005).

When a teacher reads to a child one-on-one she has the opportunity to show the child how the words and sounds go together. By using her finger to identify each word this teacher is supporting prereading skills.

The Evidence Base

Black and Hispanic children enter kindergarten already behind their white peers. The question is what is the size of the gap and what does it mean. Because different tests are used to measure learning and readiness statisticians typically use a tool called the standard deviation for measuring the spread of scores around a bell-shaped distribution. The assumption is that 68 percent of all scores will be 1 standard deviation above or below the mean score and 95 percent will be within 2 standard deviations.

- The Early Childhood Education Longitudinal Study, Kindergarten Cohort (ECLS-K), a nationally representative sample of almost 23,000 kindergartners, shows that black and Hispanic children score more than half a standard deviation below white children at the beginning of kindergarten on math and reading achievement.
- The Family and Child Experiences Survey (FACES), an assessment administered to children entering Head Start, shows that the program's children, disproportionately minorities from low-income families, already are up to one standard deviation, (15 points on an IQ test) below their white peers in vocabulary, early reading, letter recognition, and early math at ages 3 and 4. Using representative data from the National Longitudinal Survey of Youth–Child Data, Jencks and

Phillip (1998) found that about 85 percent of black 3 and 4 year olds scored lower on a vocabulary test than did the average white child of the same age.

What does a gap of one standard deviation mean?

1. Choosing one white and one black child randomly the white child will have higher scores 76 percent of the time, the black child 24 percent of the time.
2. Eighty-four percent of white children will perform better than the average black child and 16 percent of black children will perform better than the average white child.
3. If half of the class is white and half black the students in the lower performing group will be 70 percent black and 30 percent white.
4. If the top 5 percent of children are identified as gifted there will be 13 times more white than black children.
5. If the bottom 5 percent of children are identified as having special needs 72 percent of the children will be black. (School populations are 17 percent black.)
6. If a reading textbook is written so the average white student has a 75 percent comprehension rate the average black child will read at 53 percent comprehension (Rock & Stenner, 2005).

A gap of 1 standard deviation or even half a standard deviation matters. The reasons for the gap are complex and not well understood. Future research is designed to learn more about this gap, what it means.

Two types of programs hold promise—those that help parents learn the behaviors that promote child development and school readiness and those that directly teach poor and low-income children school readiness skills, both intellectual and behavioral, that will help close the gap (Haskins & Rouse, 2005).

Reflective Practice

This research highlights the importance of the years from birth to 5 in the learning process and school readiness. Early intervening has not been used with children from birth to 5. If you were going to design an early intervening or prevention program for young children how would you go about it? What goals would you have and how would you expect to accomplish them? How would this program change if the focus were just on infants and toddlers and it was an intervention program?

Standardized Testing

Standardized tests are used frequently in current educational practice. Your scores on a standardized test influenced whether you were accepted at the college of your choice or whether you got into kindergarten. Many question the role of standardized tests in refusing children admission to kindergarten or in deciding if a child has a disability.

Over reliance on standardized testing is viewed as a major problem. Although there are many alternatives to standardized tests, these tests are used because they are the same everywhere and so allow comparison (but not responsivity to different program goals), they are inexpensive, and they are relatively fast to give. When properly designed and used, they give information about groups of children that can be compared to a standard (Salvia & Ysseldyke, 2007). They also tend to make assumptions about learning. For example, they are designed to view learning as incremental; that is, a child first learns the name of one color, then a second, and so on. They do not account for a child's discovering that colors have names and properties and becoming intrigued with learning color names so that one day the child does not know any colors but a few days later he may be able to name twenty colors. Depending on the day the test was given, the results would be very different for this child. Because young children change quickly and their growth may be uneven across domains, standardized tests may over- or under-evaluate what is learned. The results of standardized tests may be misleading for some children.

Some assessment characteristics influence the quality of the measure regardless of what is being measured. **Psychometric issues** relate to the quality of measurement. The question here is how one differentiates between "good" measures or tests and "bad" ones.

Reliability focuses on the consistency of a measure, that is, the degree to which the scores are consistent, dependable, or repeatable. One way of determining if a measure is reliable is to give it again and compare the results. If the measure is reliable, the results should be the same or very close to the same. The child who obtains a score of 100 on Tuesday should get the same score or one very close to it on Wednesday. The underlying question is to what extent differences in scores on a given test can be attributed to actual differences in the individuals taking the test or to errors of measurement in the test itself. If tests are not reliable, we do not know whether differences are related to the children being tested or the test.

Validity has to do with whether a test measures what it claims to measure. Reliability is related to validity. If you cannot consistently get the same results each time you measure something (reliability), it cannot be valid. On the other hand, just because you can consistently measure something doesn't mean that it is valid or even worth measuring. There are degrees of validity, and so the question really is whether or not it is valid for a particular use (Salvia & Ysseldyke, 2007). Actually, tests themselves don't have validity; rather, it is how the test is used that determines whether or not it is valid. There are many aspects to validity. **Content validity** is concerned with the relationship between the items in the test and the intended use of the test. If the course you are taking uses this text and your midterm examination consists of twenty math problems, you would question the content validity of the examination. With children, we are frequently concerned with the relationship between the test and the content of the curriculum.

Other issues relate to the difficulty of the test. A single, group administered test is likely to be too difficult for 10 to 20 percent of the children and too easy for another 10 to 20 percent (Rock & Stenner, 2005). This creates floor and ceiling problems. If some children get almost all of the items correct (ceiling) it is difficult to measure their learning. Likewise, if children miss most of the items (floor) it is hard to measure what they have learned. Individualized, one-on-one testing can adapt to these issues.

Achievement tests are designed to measure the content children have learned as a result of instruction. That is, the content of the test ought to reflect the content of the curriculum. There is concern that this sometimes works the other way around; that is, the content of the curriculum is driven by the content of the test. If educators believe they will be judged by how well the children in their class do on achievement tests, they may "teach the test." They may also put pressure on the teacher in the previous age/grade level to have children come to their class better prepared. This has resulted in many kindergartens becoming "watered-down" first grades, which are developmentally inappropriate for 5-year-old children (Bredekamp & Copple, 2009). In a trickledown effect, programs for 3 and 4 year olds may be designed to get children ready for kindergarten. Children who do not come to school "ready" influence later test results. Some children were denied admission until they are ready or, alternatively, placed in a readiness class where their scores were reported separately. This is not an appropriate practice and hopefully no longer used.

With young children, we are also concerned with **predictive validity**. Predictive validity is concerned with the ability to predict the same or related characteristics in the future. We are concerned with how children will perform in the future and how their diverse abilities will impact that future. This is especially important for diagnosis and placement. If we identify a child as having delayed language development at age 3, we want to be able to assume that she will have delayed language development when tested again at age 8 without intervention. If, however, the child had a language delay at age 3, received no intervention, and was identified as having superior language development at age 8, we would question the predictive validity of the test. This particular issue has arisen with children whose home language is not English and for whom it is a misuse of the test. Much of early intervention is based on the predictive validity of assessments given at young ages.

Objectivity is important in the administration and interpretation of tests. To the extent that the requirements of a specific measure are not adhered to and that subjective assessments are used, a test is less valid and/ or reliable. A related issue is **bias.** There is concern about individual bias in a testing situation and cultural bias in the test itself. If clean, attractive, cooperative, and highly verbal young white children consistently score higher than minority or white children who are dirty, poorly dressed, shy, or disruptive, bias might be operating. Construct bias can occur if all children taking a particular test have not had equal exposure to the material, that is, the items tend to be more familiar to one group than another. One way of looking for bias is to determine if groups of white and minority children who have the same score have a similar breakdown of right and wrong answers. If this is not true the test may be sorting by race/ethnicity not ability. Prediction bias looks at the relationship between the ability to predict third grade performance in kindergarten for children of different races. Research over 30 years has not identified bias as the reason for identified black-white difference in achievement (Rock & Stenner, 2005). Newer assessment tools hold the potential of being more developmentally appropriate and technically adequate (Ford & Dahinten, 2005).

Concerns about Standardized Testing

There are concerns about standardized testing, whether for screening or diagnosis, and its use and misuse. Some of these revolve around the use of tests to determine school entry. The practices include:

- inappropriate use of screening and readiness tests;
- discouragement or outright denial of school entrance to eligible children;
- the use of segregated transitional classes (prekindergarten or pre–first grade) for children who are felt to be unready for the class they should be enrolled in;
- the increasing use of retention (National Association of Early Childhood Specialists in State Departments of Education [NAECS/SDE], 2000).

These problems seem to revolve around whether or not children have the capability of coping with the kindergarten curriculum. Many believe that it is not the children who should be capable but the program that should be flexible, and if the children aren't capable they should not be denied admission to the place designed to teach them these skills. There is particular concern that male children, those of racial and linguistic minorities, and low-income children are disproportionally denied entrance to school when they are legally entitled to enroll. More disconcerting is that at the end of the primary grades children who delayed entrance to kindergarten did not perform better than peers who entered on time (NAECS/SDE, 2000).

Although retention seems like a good short-term solution when children are deemed to have not mastered required materials, the long-term consequences must also be addressed. "Children who have been retained demonstrated more social regression, display more behavior problems, suffer stress in connection with being retained, and more frequently leave high school without graduating" (NAECS/SDE, 2000, p. 6).

Some issues surrounding assessment have to do with the application of standardized tests to children with disabilities in general and to the child being tested in particular. One is that assessment tools are usually standardized on children without disabilities, so the validity of using those same tests on children with disabilities is questioned. Standardized tests assume that children have had equal opportunities to learn, which may not be accurate. Traditional assessments may also result in little information on functional skills. For instance, a child with severe motor problems may not be able to use his hands well enough to manipulate objects. Because many items assessing development at young ages require this type of fine motor coordination, the child would not be fairly assessed. Assessments results need to be used with caution.

Culturally Sensitive Assessment Procedures

The first step in any assessment process is establishing rapport with both the child and the family. When the people involved are from different cultures this makes the process more difficult. Professionals need to be culturally sensitive, open and nonjudgmental. To the extent that professionals decide that all children and families should fit a single mold and a single set of interventions is offered, it is likely that families will refuse to participate. There is no blueprint for cultural sensitivity. However, culturally sensitive screening and assessment procedures start from a family-centered perspective. Professionals need an understanding of the family's values, the group with which the family identifies, and their degree of transcultural identification. Then they need to act and respond in ways that are congruent with this understanding (Lynch, 2004).

Assessments that compare children to a standardized sample (norm-referenced) or on the basis of their mastery of specific skills (criterion-referenced) could result in biased assessment of children from minority cultures and ethnic groups. Assessment is complicated by the fact that knowledge and behaviors valued by one culture are not necessarily those valued in another culture. If tasks are not valued then it is unlikely that families have encouraged their children to perform these tasks. This often means that children have not had the same opportunities to learn the required skills, an assumption that most standardized assessments make. This can be further complicated when the family speaks a language other than English. Although some assessment tools are translated into languages other than English, they are often direct translations and they do not have separate norms (Iglesias & Quinn, 1997). Functional assessments can be very useful in these circumstances. They too should be conducted by bilingual-bicultural professionals. Although ideal and what we should be striving for, if this is not possible there are other options, including assistance from a bilingual paraeducator or professional, a family member or friend, or someone from the community.

If the assessment finds that the child is eligible for services, interventions that are individually tailored for each child and family are necessary. Families are more likely to participate in interventions that are congruent with high-priority family goals and those that are compatible with their values and beliefs.

Young English Language Learners

Assessing children with limited English proficiency can be a daunting task especially in the early childhood years. It isn't just about knowing or not knowing the English language, but about demographic, linguistic, and cultural development. More than three-quarters of the children whose home language is not English speak Spanish (Salvia & Ysseldyke, 2007). And, even in these broad groups children speak different dialects, and those who speak the same language do not necessarily have a shared culture and history.

How families came to the United States and why they came impacts the language proficiency of the parents and the resources the family has. To the extent possible children's assessments must be administered in their home language. Special education is not an appropriate way to deal with children whose only problem is **limited English proficiency (LEP)**.

Some tests may be available in the child's home language. When tests are translated we assume the child can understand the directions and the questions (which may or may not be true); we cannot assume that the child has had the same experiences as children growing up in the United States. An interpreter can be used to administer a test and can translate directions or test content. Again, this is still problematic. Ideally, those assessing young English language learners are bilingual and bicultural, they know assessment, and they know the child (NAEYC, 2005). Or, we can just assume that the child has enough English to make the test valid. Or, perhaps the better answer: Do not test.

For some disabilities it is obvious, regardless of language, that a disability is present. This is true for sensory and physical impairments. It is more difficult with specific learning disabilities, communication and language impairments, social, emotional and behavior disorders, and cases of mild intellectual disabilities. Observations, portfolio assessment, and locating an interpreter who cannot only provide some information about testing but also interview families and find out about the child's experiences are necessary.

Standardized Achievement Tests and Accountability

Standardized achievement tests are used not only to assess children but also the teachers and schools in which these children learn. Assessing and teaching are inextricably combined. You need to know what children have learned in order to know what they are ready to learn. Accurately accessing young children is more difficult than accurately assessing older children or adults. Inappropriate testing of children can lead to unfair and harmful decisions. The most frequent abuses of testing in early childhood occur when a test designed for one purpose is used for another or when testing procedures appropriate for older children are used with younger children (NAEYC, 2003).

Although it is apparent that infants and toddlers do not have the language or motor skills to "bubble in" answers, the question arises as to when children do have these skills. According to the National Association for the Education of Young Children (2003) and Shepard, Kagan, and Wurtz (1998):

> Before age eight, standardized achievement measures are not sufficiently accurate to be used for high-stakes decisions about individual children and schools. Therefore, high-stakes assessments intended for accountability should be delayed until the end of third grade (or preferably fourth). (p. 52)

There are specific problems that relate to giving younger children standardized achievement tests. Developmentally it is difficult for children to sit still for the allotted amount of time and their depth of knowledge can rarely be tested through this methodology. This brings into question the validity of this type of testing for young children (Popham, 2000). Testing itself is stressful for children. The nature of standardized test construction requires that tests be constructed so that they discriminate among children. If teachers did a marvelous job teaching an important concept and 98 percent of the children taking the test got the answer right, this question would have little testing value because it does not discriminate and it would be removed (note the same would be true if 98 percent gave incorrect responses). Those who construct tests are looking for items that about 50 percent of the children get right (Wesson, 2001). What this means to the young child taking the test is that she is confronted with many items for which she does not yet know the answer. Teachers face the dilemma in a different way. To the extent that teachers agree on what is important for children to learn and teach it well, those items will be removed from the test because they no longer discriminate.

If teachers become better at helping children learn to the point that most children have mastered concepts, then testing these concepts will no longer discriminate among children. There is some concern that what is happening, and may happen more, is that test developers will choose items that reflect what children learn *outside* of the classroom rather than *inside* the classroom. Such tests may lead to what Wesson (2001) calls the "Volvo effect": higher correlations with family income, education, and occupation than what goes on in classrooms. Knowing a child's zip code may be a good predictor for how well the child will do on the standardized tests.

To the extent that the dominant culture's *outside* experiences help in taking standardized tests, children who come from different cultures and ethnic groups are disadvantaged. And, they are disadvantaged in a way that good teaching cannot make a difference. Young English-language learners face additional challenges in the testing arena. As one might predict, in homes where Spanish is spoken, children perform better on test items in mathematics than they do on items that are more heavily language-based (Wesson, 2001).

Implications for Educators

If teachers are judged based on children's standardized achievement scores, then the tests may set the curriculum. Achievement tests require that all children at a particular age/grade level learn the same material (Kohn, 2001). This idea flies in the face of what we know about the role of motivation in children's learning, multiple intelligences, anti-bias curriculum, and a constructivist approach to curriculum. As achievement tests primarily focus on language arts, science, mathematics, and social studies, there is concern that other areas of the curriculum such as social skills and the fine arts will no longer be an important part of the early childhood curriculum. Many of the experiences that transform children's learning cannot be measured in this way. A related problem exists among children with disabilities. They too may have had different experiences both inside and outside of the classroom. Their particular disability may impact how they can participate in the assessment process.

Assessment of Children with Disabilities

Children with disabilities, until recently, were excluded from school reform activities that relate to curriculum standards and state assessment programs. Measuring educational outcomes for children with disabilities has been inconsistent, at best, among states. The No Child Left Behind Act requires all states to report each year on the progress of *all* children. The reporting leads to two types of accountability: **student accountability,** which is designed to motivate students to do their best; and **system accountability,** which is designed to improve educational programs. The focus of federal education reform efforts are at the systems level (Salvia & Ysseldyke, 2007).

If all children are to be assessed then accommodations need to be designed to allow children to participate

without compromising the technical aspects of the test. The matter of accommodations for testing individual children with disabilities is covered as part of the IEP and should be used for all testing situations, not just state and national tests. There are four general areas in which accommodations are made:

- presentation of the test material (oral, interpreter, and so on)
- response format (oral, computer, and so on)
- setting (individual or small group)
- timing/schedule (allowing breaks and more flexible time limits)

The most common accommodations include individual or small-group administration, dictating responses, large print or Braille, extended time or testing breaks, having an interpreter for instructions or clarifying the directions, computer responses, reading the test aloud and marking the answers in the test booklet (Thurlow & Bolt, 2001; Salvia & Ysseldyke, 2007). The particular accommodation is made on an individualized basis and is stated as such in the child's IEP. These accommodations need to be available for all testing situations, not just high stakes standardized tests.

Play-Based Assessments

Professional organizations, such as the National Association of School Psychologists and Zero to Three, advocate the use of dynamic play-based approaches for the assessment of young children. Transdisciplinary play-based assessment is an integrated approach to assessment based on research showing that play encourages children's thinking skills, communication and language abilities, movement proficiency, and social-emotional development. It also lends itself to intervention (Linder, 2008a). Despite concerns about testing young children using formal measures, they still seem to be the standard.

To develop a naturalistic curriculum assessment, the following steps need to be taken:

- First, conduct an ecological assessment. This involves looking at the environments in which the child spends his time, and how he performs in these environments.
- Establish priorities for goals; determine which areas of development hold the greatest potential for intervention and what is most important to families.
- Determine the child's present level of academic achievement and functional performance (PLAA).
- Identify measurable annual goals in the context of state and professional standards.
- Develop an instructional plan (for eligible children this will be an IEP or IFSP).
- Develop an instructional schedule. That is, answer the question, How will the child's instructional objectives be incorporated into the daily schedule?
- Put the plan into motion and provide the required instruction based on the schedule that was set up.
- Finally, assess the skills learned and monitor the level of attainment, retention, and generalization (Ford & Dahinten, 2005).

Transdisciplinary Play-Based Assessment (TPBA) and *Transdisciplinary Play-Based Intervention* (TPBI) (Linder,

2008a, 2008b), is a curriculum-based criterion-referenced assessment and also an intervention system. It is designed for use by a team of different professionals (early childhood educators, early childhood special educators, physical therapists, occupational therapists, speech and language pathologists) and the parents. Transdisciplinary teams require a high degree of coordination and trust. The goal of TPBA is to look at the child as a whole so that each professional can see her particular area from the view of others, particularly the family. It is also designed to be a more normal, natural situation in which to assess a young child. One professional typically takes the lead while the others sit around in a circle and watch, sometimes asking questions or making requests or suggestions. Done well, this is an excellent way for professionals and families to assess and plan for young children with disabilities.

Assessment Teams

The first team that parents typically encounter is called a "child study team" although it may be called different names. This team decides whether the child meets the eligibility criteria of the IDEA, the designated disability category, and the child's special learning needs. The amount of collaboration varies greatly among child study teams. In some cases, members of a team are not aware of who else is on the team.

Working as a Team

There is consensus that it takes a team to educate a child with disabilities. It is important to know what each team member (specialist) does and there are often many team members. In inclusive settings, most professionals will come into the classroom and work with a particular child or a small group of children. Specialists working in the classroom give educators an opportunity to observe what they do and gain additional skills. They can then help children generalize and transfer the skill that the specialists initiated. Educators and peers have the opportunity to learn about the therapy and to ask questions. In cases where the therapy cannot be done in the classroom, the educator should try to observe the child in therapy and request a description and explanation of the activities that occur during therapy. Specialists can help educators understand how a child's therapeutic needs will affect behavior in the class. Educators need to know how to follow through with the therapists' goals in the class, and should invite the therapists to visit the class whenever possible.

Conversely, the early childhood special educator can help the therapist understand what is happening in the classroom with the child and why (specialists may not know why play is important). Educators should also see the specialist as a consultant available to share her expertise concerning any child in the classroom.

Knowing what specialists do is important, especially when you need advice about a problem. The next part of this chapter discusses types of specialists who work with children with disabilities. When consulting a specialist, an effective communication strategy is to confirm or clarify points, restate what you think the specialist said in your own words, and ask if that interpretation is accurate. Demonstrations are often effective. Say "Let me show you and tell me if I am doing right." The role of the early childhood educator is to help children learn and generalize concepts and behaviors by using them in a variety of situations.

Implications for Educators

Once you read and analyze a specialist's report, you must translate it into strengths and challenges for which you can program. The process might work like this: The occupational therapist reports that "Mike fell off the nystagmus board following rotation." After doing some checking in the medical dictionary, you decide that Mike was dizzy! Mike probably needs practice in changing directions and starting and stopping to better develop the sense of balance, which is located in the inner ear—his vestibular sense. Now, check with the medical report and parents to figure out why Mike might be dizzy and if you need to avoid or limit these activities. You might need to plan some creative movement activities with slow turns, as well as working on body awareness, flexibility, and static and dynamic balance.

Potential Team Members

I have included an alphabetical listing of specialists who provide services for young children with disabilities. More detail is provided for the less familiar specializations. These specialists are members of the teams that work with early childhood special educators in meeting the holistic needs of the child.

- **Administrators** are individuals who provide leadership to organizations and are charged with ensuring organizations run smoothly, goals are being met, and the place works. This would include school district level administrators, school principals, center directors, and others.
- **Child development consultants** usually have a master's degree and are trained in developmental principles and in the use of assessment measures for young children. These consultants work in a home-based setting and provide consultation to families, as well as in early care and education settings. They may serve as a liaison between the parents and medical and educational setting.
- **Developmental psychologists** know about various aspects of child development and usually have a doctorate degree. They conduct assessments of children and families, are knowledgeable about behavior management, counseling, and intervention strategies. They use educational and psychological tests to aid in the diagnostic process and are often on the multidisciplinary assessment teams of young children.
- **Early childhood educators** provide care and education for children birth through age 8. They informally and formally assess children's development, plan curriculum, and select activities and experiences to support children's development in the areas of social/emotional, cognitive, language and literacy physical/motor, and aesthetics. They may work with children and families in their home, in centers, or in schools. Increasingly these educators are graduating from blended degree programs where they also have

skills in early childhood special education and early intervention.

- **Early childhood special educators** have training in child development, early childhood materials and methods and special education. Increasingly there is state certification for this position. This specialist has in-depth knowledge of specific disabilities and strategies for learning and accommodation. She may team teach with an early childhood educator. Increasingly students are earning dual certification in early childhood education and early childhood special education including early intervention.

- **Educational diagnosticians** usually work under the supervision of a psychologist, testing and observing children referred to them for suspected disabilities. They write the formal reports that are required for special educational services. They can discuss the test results with parents and educators and are usually knowledgeable in other areas such as behavior management, counseling, and intervention strategies.

- **Family support workers** offer home-based services to families of children with developmental delays and disabilities. They provide emotional support, assistance with obtaining appropriate services, and information on issues that relate to the child. They also act as advocates for the family and child and assist in coordinating services.

- **Medical specialists** are frequently consulted when children have disabilities. The exact nature of the problem and the complexity of it determine the specializations required. Frequent specialists include those in the fields of allergy and clinical immunology; arthritis and rheumatology; cardiovascular diseases (heart); dermatology (skin); endocrinology and metabolism (glandular diseases); gastroenterology (stomach and intestines); hematology (blood); nephrology (kidneys); neurology (nervous system); oncology (cancer); ophthalmology (eyes); orthopedic (bones); otolaryngology (ear, nose, and throat); physical medicine and rehabilitation; psychiatry; surgery; and urology (urinary tract). When specialists further focus their specialty on children, the word **pediatric** precedes the specialization; for example, a pediatric rheumatologist.

- **Nutritionists** have training in the area of foods, the essential nutrients for a balanced diet, and the amount of nutrients necessary for energy, maintenance, and growth. They are concerned about all the processes by which the body uses food for energy and growth. Children with feeding problems, food allergies, and children who fail to thrive are likely to have a nutritionist on their team.

- **Occupational therapists** (OTs) work from a developmental rather than a medical base. They hold bachelors or advanced degrees from an accredited school with course work in biological and psychosocial sciences, foundations of medicine, sensory integration, psychiatry, and prevocational skill development. Their therapy emphasizes vestibular (balance), tactile, kinesthetic or proprioception (sensory knowledge of one's body movements), and perceptual motor (mental interpretation of sensation and movement based on these sensations) development, fine motor

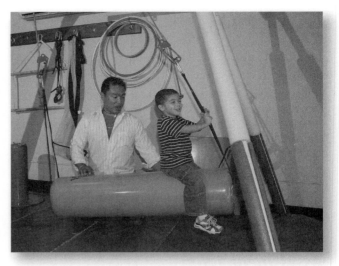

Therapists are important team members. They provide guidance for working with particular children relative to activities and positioning.

coordination, and self-help/adaptive skills. The therapist's role includes assessment, intervention, and consultation in the areas of adaptive behavior and play, and sensory motor integration. OTs may adapt the environment (limiting distractions, combining gross and fine motor activities, making a task achievable) and provide devices to help develop functional skills such as eating, dressing, and playing, and minimizing the impact of a disability.

- **Paraeducators,** paraprofessionals, teacher's aides, educational assistants, instructional assistants reflect the variety of roles and responsibilities of this member of the special education team. Paraeducators are present in most educational settings under the supervision of the teacher. They have skills and contributions that make them important in the education of young children particularly those with disabilities.

- **Parents and family members** are important specialists. They determine the priorities for their child and family. They know what their child wants and needs and how they want these needs addressed. Families give other team members information on how their child functions at home and help team members see the whole child in the context of the family and the culture in which they live. They update the team on an ongoing basis.

- **Pediatric nurses** are registered nurses who have training in developmental screening tools as well as additional training in family counseling, evaluation, and children. They work out of hospitals, community-based setting, or a state department of health. The pediatric nurse often makes home visits to help parents learn to better care for and meet the medical needs of their young child with a disability, in addition to monitoring the child's health status. Nurses often work with child development specialists for developmental intervention or infant stimulation.

- **Pediatricians** are physicians who specialize in the medical treatment of children from birth to about age 12. They are probably the most familiar professional to families with young children. Pediatricians may be the first to express concern about a condition or the first person to whom parents turn to express their concern.

- **Physical therapists** (PTs) are state-licensed health professionals who have completed an accredited educational program, largely medically based, which includes the study of biological, physical, medical, and psychosocial sciences, as well as course work in neurology, orthopedics, therapeutic exercises, and treatment techniques. Physical therapy is directed toward preventing disability; that is, developing, improving, or restoring more efficient muscular functioning and maintaining maximum motor functioning. PTs work with any child requiring **prosthetic** management training, wheelchair mobility training, or measurement for or use of other medically prescribed mobility devices. PTs evaluate the child's range of motion, posture, muscle tone, strength, balance, and gross motor skills. Treatment usually focuses on increasing strength, improving balance skills, and facilitating gross motor development. PTs are responsible for monitoring a child's orthopedic needs and assisting the family in obtaining adaptive equipment, if necessary. They provide families and educators with information about optimal ways for positioning and carrying the child for different activities.

- **Physicians** are medical doctors who may be pediatricians, in family practice, neurologists, or another specialist. Their role includes determining medical needs and referring the family to specialists and programs that can provide needed services.

- **Psychologists** roles vary with the setting and the level of training they have as well as their specialization. A school psychologist is state certified and has typically completed either a master's or doctoral degree in school psychology. Course work varies from state to state, but generally includes psychology, counseling, standardized testing and its interpretation, child development, disability studies, and education. Most psychologists must complete an internship or practicum under a practicing psychologist. The duties of a psychologist in a school setting vary with the number of psychologists in the district and their individual skills. Most school psychologists test and observe children referred to them because of a suspected disability. They write formal reports that are required to place children into any special education program. They may consultant with teachers or families to discuss test results or make observations and suggestions. Some psychologists emphasize individual therapy others work with the child as part of the family unit.

- **Social workers** usually concentrate on the adults in the family unit. They may well look at family needs in relation to child-rearing or coordinating the social service network. They are knowledgeable about resources and referrals to community services (Medicaid, **respite care**). Social workers usually work in the home and are often the best source of information about the types of intervention families are most likely to use. They are trained in family relations, counseling and advocacy skills, and working with agencies. Increasingly, public schools have social workers as part of their staff.

- **Speech/language pathologists** are state licensed and have completed a degree program with an accredited college. Course work includes psychology, education, and anatomy, with an emphasis on speech and language development. The role of the speech/language pathologist in early intervention includes assessment and intervention with oral-motor disorders (difficulties in feeding and swallowing as well as speech production) and communication delays and disorders. Their work includes social communicative competence during preverbal and verbal development, receptive and expressive language (both speech and nonverbal means of communication), and speech production and perception. Many children with disabilities have associated problems with muscle tone that may affect the movements of the tongue and lips needed for feeding and speech.

The role you as educator will play on the team is largely determined by how the team defines itself, but your role is extremely important. You have the opportunity to talk formally and informally with families on a regular basis and you see the child almost every day. Few other team members will have that amount of contact. Although team assessment is necessary, professionals may choose to operate in several ways: as a multidisciplinary team, an interdisciplinary team, or as a transdisciplinary team.

Multidisciplinary Teams

The multidisciplinary team sorts the child's condition into component parts. The parents take their child to different professionals for assessment and intervention, and the professionals then funnel their input back to the parents, primary care physician (and hopefully the service coordinator), who must sort it out. A strength of this model is that people from different disciplines are involved and parents have more input in the choice of team members (they can choose the physical or occupational therapist they like best). However, separate disciplinary assessments, reports, and goals written by each professional may contribute to confusion, fragmented services, and lack of coordination of services to children and their families.

Professionals may present conflicting diagnostic and intervention strategies. Because team members rarely meet it is often left up to parents to decide what to do, who to believe, or what further information they need. Despite the obvious drawbacks, with strong, knowledgeable parents, this type of team has the potential for providing good programming for children. This is the only option available to some families, especially those who live in rural areas. For professionals, this is the least time-consuming type of team. No time needs to be allocated for interacting with team members and for many professionals that is an important consideration.

Interdisciplinary Teams

Traditionally, interdisciplinary teams have specified members as a core team and add members as needed. Core team members include those who are most directly responsible for the child and who work together to plan, implement, and evaluate a child's educational program. Core members usually include the child's early childhood educator and early childhood special educator, paraeducators, therapists, and family members (Snell & Janney, 2000). They meet on a regular basis (e.g., once a month). With young children who are severely involved, the service coordinator is frequently a pediatric nurse. A **service coordinator** is a designated individual who, in addition to being part of the team, has the specific role of communicating with the family to set up meetings and to convey information. She is responsible for organizing the team and ensuring that outcomes do not conflict with one another. She is the main contact for the family when the assessment process is completed. The IDEA requires that identified children between birth and age 3 have a service coordinator. Parents, if they choose, can function in this capacity. For less involved children the service coordinator may be the early childhood special educator.

It is possible for interdisciplinary teams to have some specialists who do not meet with the group but send in written reports. Drawbacks to this method include problems in communication and interaction when team members do not have comprehensive understanding of the expertise of other team members. Scheduling of meeting is frequently a problem.

Transdisciplinary Teams

Transdisciplinary teams have the highest level of coordination and integration. All members of the transdisciplinary assessment team, including the parents, provide information regarding the child's strengths and needs. Ideally, this process helps each discipline see the interrelationships among developmental areas. What emerges is an individualized program based on the child as a whole that can be implemented in a setting following the regular routines.

Once the child is assessed, the team develops an integrated service plan and decides on one team member to carry out the plan with the family. One major concept in the transdisciplinary approach is that of **role release**. Role release is "a process of transferring information and skills traditionally associated with one discipline to team members of other disciplines" (Rainforth & York-Barr, 1997, p. 19). For example, the PT may coach the speech/language pathologist on working with positioning a particular child and thus function in both roles in this instance. Role release requires trust that another professional will follow through and seek more advice when necessary. A developmental psychologist may work with a child in the areas of OT and speech therapy in addition to psychology. This does not mean that the developmental psychologist has become an instant occupational therapist, but rather that the skills necessary to intervene with this particular child can be transmitted to the psychologist so that the child and family can receive three types of therapy in an integrated approach from one person.

The potential for communication and a more accurate diagnosis exists because parents and professionals can ask questions of each other during the assessment process rather than relying on written reports. This highly desirable approach is also a costly one. Considerable time needs to be allocated for sharing, planning, coordinating, and training team members. Coordinating schedules so that all are available at the same time necessitates an ongoing regular commitment. However, more agencies are seeing the worth of this model. From parents' perspective, one possible drawback is that once they choose the team, they lose the ability to choose individuals, so that if there is one member of the team they do not like or respect, they must adapt.

Implications for Educators

As part of the assessment team, you will often find yourself in the position of needing to get or give information about a particular child. There are several points to remember when you are part of an assessment team. Without meaning to, other professionals may use terms that are unfamiliar to you. Stop and ask them to define words that you don't understand. If you disagree with something that other professionals have written or said, ask them to talk more about it and ask why they made that particular determination. Often if you pair something that you like about what they did or said with something you are concerned about, they will listen more attentively. For example, "I'm very pleased with the progress Victor's been making since he began physical therapy, but I don't understand why it is so important for him to sit this particular way during group time."

Remember that you know the child well. You certainly see the child more often than the specialist you are talking with, and you have important information to share. It is helpful to be specific and to base your comments on direct observations of the child and your written records. For example:

- When you know that a child can perform some skills that specialists report she did not perform during the assessment, share that information with them. They may still want the child to perform the particular skill for them as well, but your input is helpful.
- Whenever you notice dramatic changes in a child, it is important to report them to the child's family and other professionals on the team especially if they are trying to determine the usefulness or appropriate amount of medication needed. (Also, ask that others inform you if a child's behavior or medication has changed.)
- Keep other team members informed when you've observed that a child is able to master goals written on her individualized plan. This will let others know that it is time to write new goals and suggest some new activities.
- A child's needs are best met when all individuals working with the child, including parents, educators, doctors, therapists, and child care providers, are well informed.

Program Evaluation

Assessment and evaluation includes program evaluation. Programs must be regularly evaluated to determine whether or not they are meeting their goals and whether children and their families are benefiting from the program (NAEYC, 2003). In the past, it was often simply assumed that if children went to school they were learning. But teaching, like other professions, must be accountable—not to only principals and other administrators, but to children, their parents, taxpayers, and the legal system as well.

As with assessing children, multiple indicators of progress are used and all components of a program evaluated. Parents and legislators are increasingly concerned about how well educational settings are doing in educating the young citizens of the country, particularly those at risk. Without accountability assessments, it is difficult to know which aspects of a program are doing well and which are not. Accountability decisions are usually made at the district, state, or national level.

The Evidence Base

The emphasis on evidence-based early childhood educational programs has made us look at programs differently. The problem is that there is often conflicting evidence or researchers come to different conclusions about programs based on the same data. To address these problems we as educators must become better consumers of evaluation information. The National Forum on Early Childhood Program Evaluation (2007) has identified five key questions that should be asked about early childhood programs.

1. **Is the evaluation design strong enough to produce trustworthy evidence? (2007, p. 2)**

This question really asks "how are children different because they attended xyz program?" To answer this question a comparison group of children who did not attend xyz is needed. Ideally, children are assigned randomly to intervention and non-intervention options. If this is not possible a comparisons group must be used and the research must be designed to ensure that the comparison group is similar to those who are attending the program.

2. **What program services were actually received by participating children and families and comparison groups? (2007, p. 3)**

The way programs are designed and the way the services are actually delivered can differ. Sometimes programs are not implemented as intended or families may not participate in the expected way. It is important to know whether families and children availed themselves of the services offered, that is, how many of the children and families participated and how much service did they receive. Similar information is needed about the comparison group.

3. **How much impact did the program have? (2007, p. 5)**

Impact is the difference between the treatment and comparison group on selected outcomes. This is frequently expressed as "effects sizes." In general, the larger the effect size, the better. Program impact may be different for different subgroups of children and for those who used the program more.

4. **Do the program's benefits exceed its costs? (2007, p. 7)**

If very effective programs have a large effect but are tremendously expensive they may not be practical. It is a balance between costs and benefits or return on investment. But return for whom? Is the value quality of life for the participants and/or economic productivity for society? In early childhood the benefits are typically longitudinal relative to fewer children in special education, fewer children in the juvenile justice system or fewer obese children needing health care.

5. **How similar are the programs, children and families in the study to those in your constituency or community? (2007, p. 8)**

To the extent that you decide to use a particular program or practice you need to find out how similar the children and families served are to the children and families you work with (National Forum on Early Childhood Program Evaluation, 2007).

Reflective Practice

Program evaluation that meets the gold standard is difficult, expensive, and needs long-term follow-up. However, the basic principles can be used to focus thinking in all programs.

Using evidence to improve programs is an important part of program evaluation. However, all programs need to be evaluated formally or informally on a regular basis.

Informal Program Evaluation

The major reason for evaluating a program is to provide information to those involved with the program about what is working well and what needs attention. One obvious question most programs want to answer is, "Does the program meet the needs of the people it serves?" The answer to this question requires information. What are the characteristics and needs of the children and families served in the program? Different children in different types of families have different needs, although they may all be in the same program or classroom. Program evaluation needs to be sensitive to both group and individual differences.

It is important to know the purpose of the evaluation at the beginning. When the evaluation is being done to decide whether to continue a program or eliminate it, those involved may have very different agendas. If the purpose of the evaluation is to determine whether or not early intervention decreased the number of children requiring special education services, then the data necessary for evaluation are very different than if the purpose of the evaluation is to decide which is more effective, full- or half-day kindergarten. Without having decided on the purpose of the evaluation, one cannot proceed in any meaningful way.

Sometimes program evaluation is used to help solve a particular problem a program or class is having. This type of evaluation focuses on a single aspect of a program or a classroom that has been identified as a problem. Although the problems may vary, the procedure for evaluation is similar:

1. Identify the problem in a way that it can be solved. "They should not have violence on children's television shows" is not a solvable problem. It is a value judgment. Instead: "Some children watch superheroes on television and come to school and play out what they have seen. How can I set up my classroom to discourage superhero play? What rules do I need to develop to regulate this play?" is a solvable problem.
2. Review relevant literature and talk to people in other programs or classes to see how they have dealt with similar problems. (Although problems may seem unique, it is unlikely that you are the first person to encounter the problem.)
3. Develop a system for dealing with the problem. Share this system with all those involved (especially families) and gather their input. Modify the system.
4. Field-test the system for an appropriate period of time (perhaps 2 to 4 weeks).
5. Evaluate the results, modify the system if necessary, and retest or keep the system in place.

You may have used this procedure informally when you were coping with superhero play and not realized that in reality you evaluated your program as having a problem, explored the dimensions of the problem, looked at what others had done and developed a system to solve the problem, evaluated that solution, and modified your approach.

Some program evaluation is extensive and ambitious. You may be asked to participate in evaluation projects by providing specific input. Some evaluation projects are long-range as well as short-range. Knowing long-term goals for children can help focus a curriculum in early childhood.

Implications for Educators

People who fund programs want to know how effective they are, and administrators may need the information to defend programs or to get additional programs or classrooms. Educators, however, may feel threatened by the evaluation process or feel that it is not relevant to them. They may feel that the obligations of teaching are already enough. "You hired me to teach, leave me alone and let me teach!" Program evaluation is not likely to succeed without teacher support.

At the very least the process of evaluation describes the population you serve and exactly what you are doing. At a minimal level, all programs and individual classrooms need this information. If you are not clear about what you are doing and why you are doing it, you cannot effectively present your classroom to parents or administrators.

Evaluation is essential to improve programs. Administrators need to know how you evaluate your program and how satisfied you are with your job. To the extent that you are not an active participant in the process, things that do not satisfy you are unlikely to change, and you may be unhappy in your job. Know that you are one of the stakeholders; you have a vested interest, and you need to know enough about the evaluation process

to make it work for you and your program. You also need to be sure the evaluation process does not interfere with your teaching.

The less intrusive and less burdensome the evaluation process is for teachers; the more likely it is to go smoothly and to be completed. You need to remind others this is a primary consideration, not a secondary one. Data collected must be used, and the people who collect the data need to be informed of its use. If you perceive the information you collect going into a "black hole," you are unlikely to continue collecting it in a careful manner, if at all.

When children have individualized programs with measurable goals these need to be evaluated as well. Individualized plans should be grouped for evaluation, and you should aim for an 85 percent achievement rate. A higher rate may show that you aren't stretching yourself or the families; a rate of 50 percent or less means that expectations are not realistic or the program is not effective.

Today, we need to ask different questions because we no longer must "prove" the efficacy of early intervention. We are now fine-tuning the system. We need to learn about the effectiveness of different models of programming for different populations: "What types of services, in what combinations, using what models are most effective?" Applied research is concerned with why a program works or fails to work and for whom it works.

Summary

Overall, assessment provides the basis for eligibility for special educational services and the individualized program planning that is part of these services. The referral process typically begins informally with families or educators having concerns about a child. They use interventions that they think will help the child and may call in colleagues for additional ideas. A response to instruction plan is developed. If these interventions are not successful, a more formal process is used that typically begins with the administration of screening measures and may be followed by functional assessments and standardized tests. Information from these measures and the information gained from the pre-referral process are used to determine whether or not a child is eligible for special educational services. If the child is eligible a team that includes the parents or guardian makes decisions about the instruction and placement that will best meet the child's needs. As part of a team, the early childhood special educator must learn the roles of other team members and methods of collaborating with them, and open up her classroom to them

At a broader level assessment is concerned with the quality of education for all children and whether the quality of education meets specific standards. There are concerns about how standardized tests are used, particularly with children from minority groups and children with disabilities. Because of the importance of the assessment process no single person or test is used to place children, but rather an assessment team is assembled. Assessment teams are organized in a variety of ways depending on the particular team members and the roles that various professionals play. Programs are evaluated as well as the learning that children do in these programs.

Reflections

1. Assessment can help children in many ways. However, some educators and parents use assessments to look at what a child cannot do and then try to "fix" the problem. Assessments can show a child's areas of resilience, or what the child can do. With this information educators can take a strengths-based approach to teaching by identifying what the child can do and building on these competencies. This may make learning easier and enjoyable for the child. Do you plan to focus on resilience and use a strengths-based approach in instruction? How will you keep from falling into the trap of only focusing on what children cannot do? How can you get better at using a strengths-based approach in teaching?

2. An educator's job is to help all children become contributing members of society. However, children are held accountable for what they learn by taking standardized tests. These tests affect children with disabilities. Even with accommodations many children with disabilities will not pass some of these tests. As a result, many fail grade levels and may eventually drop out of school. How do you feel about this type of testing in schools? Do you think it is fair to make a high school diploma hinge on a few tests? Or, do you think it is important that students are competent enough to pass a test to move to the next grade or earn a diploma? What if the child does fairly well in classes and gives an outstanding effort but cannot pass the test. Should this child be left behind or not allowed to graduate? Do you feel the content of the tests will drive instruction? If so, is this a bad or good thing? Is it probable that raising standards and requirements will help students achieve more? Will tests negatively affect children with disabilities? All early childhood special educators are struggling with answering these questions.

Educational Resources

American Psychological Association (APA) has specific sites for testing and assessment. The APA publishes journals and holds annual conferences that relate to assessment as well as other developmental issues. http://www.apa.org; http://www.apa.org/science/testing.html

Association of Test Publishers provides good basic answers to why testing is useful. Good site for educators and parents. http://www.testpublishers.org

ERIC Clearinghouse on Assessment and Evaluation provides links to tests and test selection kits and information on assessment, evaluations, and research information. Good resource for educators and providers. http://www.ericae.net

National Center for Research on Evaluation, Standards, and Student Testing (CRESST) focuses on the assessment of educational quality, design problems, and the use of assessment systems to serve multiple purposes. CRESST conducts research that improves assessment, evaluation, technology, and learning. http://www.cse.ucla.edu/

National Center on Educational Outcomes (NCEO) provides leadership in the participation of students with disabilities in national and state assessments. Has an online bibliography with research on the effects of various testing accommodations for students. http://cehd.umn.edu/nceo

Wrightslaw provides accurate, reliable information about special education law, education law, and advocacy for children with disabilities at http://www.wrightslaw.com/. It provides information on Understanding Tests and Measurements for parents that explains the law and the meaning of tests. Also links to other sites about advocacy and IEP planning at http://www.wrightslaw.com/advoc/articles/tests_measurements.html.

For additional resources, visit the book companion website for this text at www.cengage.com/education/deiner.

Chapter 4

Curriculum and Standards in Inclusive Settings

The most difficult thing for me when I first began teaching was to figure out how to set up and run my classroom. I remember going into my room for the first time and seeing this huge pile of stuff in the middle of the floor. The pile contained all of my classroom furniture, desk, and other random materials. I had no idea where to start, so I just dug in and started laying out my classroom.

When I began designing lessons, I realized there was no curriculum to follow and no resource materials to provide ideas. I was overwhelmed! I asked my principal about the kindergarten curriculum; he told me that whatever I wanted to do was fine by him as long as the class wasn't too noisy. That was not the answer I was looking for. I went to a teachers' store and began gathering and reading resource books for ideas—even for ideas about how to begin school on the first day.

I remember being frustrated and thinking that college did not prepare me to design and develop a curriculum. There were very few materials to work with in the room—no manipulatives, construction paper, or even paint. I quickly found out how much my budget was going to be, grabbed all the catalogs the school had, and ordered my materials. I felt much better knowing that I would have some materials to start the year.

When we had our first open house, parents thought my paraeducator was the teacher, not me. I looked far too young to be a teacher. That was difficult and I felt I had to start earning the parents' and my coworkers' respect. They didn't take me seriously because I was so young and new to the classroom. When I held my individualized educational plan (IEP) meetings at the beginning and end of the year, I felt the need to prove myself as a professional, and to be seen as the authority in my classroom. Even after my 3 years in the classroom, parents still refer to my paraeducator as the teacher; I quickly cleared up the mistake.

The first year ended quickly, but when I look back on those hectic first days I wonder how I endured the stress. I had a very good mentor who helped me when things got hairy and I owe her a great many thanks. She helped and guided me whenever I had questions about IEPs or anything else related to the classroom. I don't think I would have survived without her mentorship and patience.

Reflective Practice

Do you feel ready to set up a classroom and greet children the first day of school? You probably have additional coursework to take and student teaching. As you continue your education reflect on this new teacher's dilemma and what you need to do and learn to feel more confident on your first day.

Planning Inclusive Curriculum

Developing a program that (1) meets the needs of all the children in your classroom, (2) falls within the guidelines of your current workplace, (3) follows the dictates of both state and federal laws, and (4) fits your personal philosophy and beliefs is a difficult task at best. To do it on a daily basis, year after year, may seem daunting. Given the importance of the task, it is necessary not only to do it well but also to do it efficiently. Designing a classroom experience that is enjoyable for you and the children is flexible enough to support both short- and long-term change, and has a flair of creativity is a challenge.

Curriculum involves decisions about how children learn, when learning takes place, and what is to be learned. It requires you to "Implement curriculum that is thoughtfully planned, challenging, engaging, developmentally appropriate, culturally and linguistically responsive, comprehensive, and likely to promote positive outcomes for all young children" (NAEYC, 2003, p. 20).

Some children with disabilities take longer to learn some concepts than their peers. They need activities that are self-motivating within a prescribed set of IEP goals. Planned activities and experiences must also cover all the strands that are traditionally part of the developmental domain (cognitive, adaptive [self-help], physical [fine and gross motor], sensory, communication, social, and emotional) and also part of the general curriculum (mathematics, science, language and literacy, and so on). Where possible, activities need to teach more than one skill at a time.

Including children with diverse abilities in regular classrooms has a legislative base. However, your personal feelings about inclusion will influence how you proceed. Once you are clear about your feelings, you can move on to the next stage and look at the strategies you will use to be inclusive and the personal supports you need to make inclusion a positive experience for all the children.

There may be some children and some disabilities you will find easier to include than others. Although all of us like to think we like all children equally, this is rarely true. We may treat children equally, but personal feelings are different. Try to move yourself away from the specifics and figure out the generic aspect of a child or disability that influences you—the part that will be repeated with other children.

Reflective practice is the foundation of competence in early childhood education. It emphasizes the importance of thoughtful analysis and continual revision of effective approaches to teaching and learning. The competent educator is characterized by habits of mind that emphasize critical thinking, experimentation, and openness to change. Reflective practice encourages educators to become confident in applying a flexible array of skills that at times may seem automatic. Understandings are constructed, not given, and these understandings must be continually adapted, revised, and revisited. Reflection is different from description. Reflection requires asking "what if . . . " types of questions. Reflection is a complex process that needs to be broken down into smaller units. It needs a model or an organizational framework that makes clear the steps in the process. Reflection is a skill that becomes more refined with practice; it is a growth experience that leads to continuous improvement in teaching.

Developmentally Appropriate Practice

What is developmentally appropriate practice? How do you know it when you see it? To explain developmentally appropriate practice, the National Association for the Education of Young Children (NAEYC) developed a position paper and guidelines in 1986, updated them in 1987, revised them in 1996, and again in 2008. These revisions reflect new knowledge, particularly in neurobiology; the inclusion of children with disabilities in regular classrooms; and the increasing number of infants and toddlers in group care. They also reflect a field that is changing and

a professional commitment to keep up with these changes (NAEYC, 2006b).

Developmentally appropriate practice has three basic components: (1) knowledge about development and learning, (2) knowledge about individual children, (3) and knowledge about the social and cultural context in which children learn and grow (NAEYC, 2006b).

Knowledge about child development and learning requires you to understand patterns of growth and development. Knowing about child development is essential but it is also necessary to know about the strengths, interests, and needs of the individual child. This knowledge allows you to adapt to and be responsive to individual variations including children with diverse abilities (NAEYC, 2006b). Knowledge of age-related characteristics helps you predict where children are developing within an age range so you can design experiences and activities and choose materials that are interesting and that will also challenge them (NAEYC, 2006b). Children live in families. Meaningful and relevant learning experiences are respectful of children and their families. They must take into account the children's culture, language, and social context (NAEYC, 2006b).

Principles Underlying Developmentally Appropriate Practice

The principles underlying developmentally appropriate practice are based on what we reliably know about child development and learning. The principles are given below and a brief explanation follows each principle. These principles influence the beliefs and philosophy of education for all children. Principles of development and learning inform developmentally appropriate practice (NAEYC, 2006b).

1. *Domains of children's development—physical, social, emotional, and cognitive—are closely related. Development in one domain influences and is influenced by development in other domains.*

The younger the child the closer the curriculum is tied to the child's experiential base. Scholars are focusing more on functional interrelationships among developmental **domains.** This multidomain approach increases the complexity of thinking about children's development, which is further complicated by looking at the child as part of a family and cultural system that embraces certain values and lives in a specific geographic area at a particular time. Thinking about multiple domains helps organize learning.

2. *Development occurs in a relatively orderly sequence, with later abilities, skills, and knowledge building on those already acquired.*

Predictable changes occur in all developmental areas. Knowledge of these patterns provides the basis for designing the environment and planning for children. Information about developmental patterns helps determine the types of materials to use as well as whether children are showing delayed or atypical patterns of development.

3. *Development proceeds at varying rates from child to child as well as unevenly within different areas of each child's functioning.*

All children are unique, yet they share commonalities in their sequence of growth and development. Children come "prewired" to grow and develop in a predictable pattern. Individual variation is expected and valued.

4. *Early experiences have both cumulative and delayed effects on individual children's development; optimal periods exist for certain types of development and learning.*

Children's early experiences, both positive and negative, affect their development. Isolated events may have a minimal impact, but events that occur frequently can have powerful lasting effects. Research supports the idea of broadly conceived *sensitive periods or cycles* when the child is more susceptible to change or where the impact of events is more pervasive. Birth to 3 years is the optimal period for the development of verbal language skills. Although children can learn language later, it requires specific intervention and more effort.

5. *Development proceeds in predictable directions toward greater complexity, organization, and internalization.*

Young children learn through hands-on experiences. They begin to acquire symbolic knowledge and move into thinking that can take place in the present, remember the past, and anticipate the future. Children grow in their ability to regulate their own behavior. The adult's role is to present a curriculum that motivates and challenges them and social situations that require high levels of peer interaction.

6. *Development and learning occur in and are influenced by multiple social and cultural contexts.*

Changing social patterns affect families and children. Most children spend large parts of their day with adults other than their parents. We must become more aware of families and culture; the role they play in early growth and development and assure that curriculum and planning is responsive to this knowledge base. This diversity is forcing us to investigate the roles of nature, nurture, culture, and the complex intersections of these.

7. *Children are active learners, drawing on direct physical and social experience as well as culturally transmitted knowledge to construct their own understandings of the world around them.*

Environments that support children as active learners encourage the construction of knowledge by offering experiences that are at the edge of a child's knowledge base and that encourage a child to generate and test out their hypotheses. Well-chosen new experiences help children modify, adapt, expand, and reorganize their working model of the world. When educators help children plan, act, and then reflect on experiences, this process is enhanced.

8. *Development and learning result from interaction of biological maturation and the environment, which includes both the physical and social worlds that children live in.*

Information about the relationship between early experience and the brain has focused on early childhood as a "prime time" for development. An enriched environment helps brain cells form synapses and stabilizes these connections to support learning. Genetics may establish the upper and lower limits of development but the environment determines where within this range a specific trait falls.

9. *Play is an important vehicle for children's social, emotional, and cognitive development, as well as a reflection of their development.*

Most early social interactions center on play and play activities. The quality and level of interaction that occurs among children in play activities develops sequentially, increasing with age and maturation. As children's play develops, their social interactions move from adults to peers. One of the greatest aspects of play is that is that it is unpredictable. When children play, they do not know where it will lead. They have to respond to what happens. This means they have to put their cognitive processes in gear as well as using their social and emotional skills.

10. *Development advances when children have opportunities to practice newly acquired skills as well as when they experience a challenge just beyond the level of their present mastery.*

Curriculum continually moves from what children know to the acquisition and consolidation of new knowledge. It moves from what children can do themselves to learning that requires adult scaffolding. Children come to learning experiences with different backgrounds; some have had a variety of experiences, others relatively few. Good curriculum and responsive adults meet children where they are and provide the scaffolding for them to take the next steps. Curriculum and experiences need to be flexible and allow for different learning experiences with the same activity. Experiences must be modified (made easier or more difficult) to meet the needs of children with diverse experiences and abilities.

11. *Children demonstrate different modes of knowing and learning and different ways of representing what they know.*

Children come to understand their world in different ways. Over time, children develop preferred learning modalities and different styles of learning. They represent their world differently. They are good at different things. Sometimes this is due to personal experience and preferences. Other times it is because of sensory or motor impairments. Knowing how children represent their world, adults can present information in ways that make it easier for them to learn; likewise, they can give children opportunities to strengthen other areas.

12. *Children develop and learn best in the context of a community where they are safe and valued, their physical needs are met, and they feel psychologically secure.*

Children need to be in environments where they can develop trusting relationships with adults, establish their autonomy, and be empowered to continue to learn. They need to feel safe in early childhood settings both psychologically and physically. Prosocial behavior needs to be encouraged and supported (adapted from NAEYC, 2006b; pp. 1–8).

Strategies for Individualizing Learning

Regardless of content or age, there is a cycle of learning that takes place as new information becomes part of a child's repertoire. This learning framework has four broad aspects: awareness, exploration, inquiry, and utilization (Bredekamp & Rosegrant, 1992).

1. *Awareness* is the initial stage in the learning cycle. Awareness grows out of experience. As children notice differences among themselves, questions arise: "Why does Ian have those things on his legs?" "Why is my skin black and Justine's white?" When children are at an awareness level, they want a simple, straightforward answer. "Ian's legs aren't strong enough to hold him so he needs braces to help" may be all the child wants to know. Often we tell children more than they really want to know.

2. *Exploration* is the next level and requires children to examine and try to make sense out of an event or experience by exploring materials, gathering additional information, poking, prodding, or doing whatever seems to make sense to the child. Although it is tempting to "explain" the situation, it is rarely useful; children need to find their own meaning for information. Explaining fosters dependency. Asking open-ended questions fosters exploration.

3. *Inquiry* involves the understanding of classes of information, the ability to generalize information, and call up previous learned information for comparison. Adults can help children with more focused questions at this stage.

4. *Utilization* is a functional level of learning where information can be used in a variety of settings and applied to new information and situations. Children who understand the concept of one-to-one correspondence can count objects accurately and decide that six chairs are necessary for six children to sit on.

This cycle occurs repeatedly as children learn. It is important to know where individual children are in the cycle. When a child encounters information for the first time, he begins at an awareness level. Children with previous experiences may be generalizing the same information. Some children with disabilities will have less broad experiential backgrounds. They need to be given time to experience and explore before they can be expected to participate in higher level skills. Programs must be designed that allow children to profit from experience at all places in the learning cycle.

Young children encountering a wheelchair for the first time will go through these stages in the learning cycle. Rent or borrow a wheelchair so children can explore it. Initially, they will be curious about the wheelchair and they might want to sit in it and see how it works. This is exploration; they need this time. When they have their own understanding of the wheelchair, try to broaden and generalize this information so they can figure out what activities are difficult or easy to do in a wheelchair and the relationship among wheelchairs, crutches, and walkers. As they integrate this information, have them think about the world outside the classroom, the utility of curb cuts, why bathrooms can be difficult to negotiate, and the problem with table heights.

Continium of Teaching Techniques

Teaching techniques need to be adapted to meet children's learning needs. These techniques range from more directive to less directive, with many degrees in between. The goal is to match the technique to the material being learned and the child who is learning it. *All* teachers need *all* of these techniques. Starting from the least directive to the most directive, the techniques are as follows:

- *Withholding attention* or planned ignoring is frequently used when adults know a child can accomplish a task without assistance, or as part of a behavior strategy for handling undesirable but nondangerous behavior. It can also be employed during the latency period between making a request and the child's response. Be sure to give young children enough time to respond.

- *Acknowledging* reinforces children's behavior, particularly when the goal is to have the behavior continue. Done intermittently and for pointing out specific aspects of behavior, it is a useful way to shape behavior. When overused or when acknowledgment is too general, it is less useful.

- *Modeling,* whether conscious or unconscious, is a way of teaching children which behaviors are appropriate and which are inappropriate. By their actions, adults show children how to interact with others or how to use a new material.

- *Facilitating* involves providing temporary assistance to a child. This can involve verbal support, such as giving a suggestion for a different way of approaching a problem or reattaching a piece of paper that has come loose. It is specific and time-limited and enables a child to continue independently.

- *Supporting* is similar to facilitating, but it is more general and lasts longer. The goal is independence, but the expectation is that it will take longer to achieve.

- *Scaffolding* is associated with Vygotsky's work and implies working on the edge of a child's knowledge base. It provides the link between what a child can do independently and what she can accomplish with adult help. It is more directive than the previous techniques in that the adult provides more focus for the child's activity.

- *Coconstructing* involves actually doing a project with or collaborating with a child. This is a more directive technique and one that is useful when children don't know how to use particular materials. It is also useful to join with children. One can move momentarily from scaffolding to coconstruction and back.

- *Demonstrating* is more directive as the teacher does the project and the children watch. There are times when this is extremely useful and appropriate and other times when children can appropriately construct their own knowledge. Demonstrating is often followed by less directive techniques. One problem with demonstrating is that children may assume there is only one way to do an activity rather than actively constructing a method of approaching a task.

- *Directing* involves telling a child specifically what to do. It also implies that there is a correct way to do something and that there is a outcome desired. This technique is frequently used when less directive techniques have not taught a desired task (adapted from Bredekamp & Rosegrant, 1995).

An educator's philosophy reflects how much time she spends at each place on the teaching continuum. Early childhood educators are frequently criticized for being too nondirective to meet the needs of children with disabilities while special educators are criticized for being too directive. The solution is to be aware of the continuum and continually move from less directive to more directive techniques as children need more support learning, but then to move into less directive strategies as children begin to master tasks. The goal is an appropriate match so that the strategy that provides the most learning for the child is employed.

Contextual Planning

Planning is dependent upon your philosophy, the setting you work in, the age of the children you teach, and the children who are included in your class. Planning starts with the children you teach. Find out what topics interest them, and then evaluate these topics for the goals you have for the class and the standards children are striving toward, both academic and developmental. Then, think about yourself. Does the topic interest you? What do you know about the topic? What resources do you have to support it? Then think about its potential for meeting children's individualized educational program (IEP) goals. If you work through this process the themes or units you choose are likely to be successful.

For children the curriculum is based on their individual needs, the places (home, school, child care, or some combination) where they spend time, and the priorities of the child's family. Good curriculum is responsive to the cultural background of the children and their geographic location. For example, if transportation was the theme, a class of children from an urban area studying transportation might graph the number of children who walk to school, take the bus or subway, or are driven by families. Children in a rural agrarian area may focus on cars, trucks, and tractors, whereas those who live near the shore might look at boats and ships, including tugboats, freighters, and container vessels.

Schedules, Routines, and Transitions

Schedules refer to who will do what and when they will do it. The key to schedule planning is flexibility and organizing general time blocks that respond to children's needs. Ideally, timing is flexible but sequences are predictable. This helps children learn what will happen next. **Routines** are events that must be completed on a regular basis and often involve a series of responses. Some routines offer an opportunity for spending time individually with a child and provide chances to communicate. Routines give children a sense of security and trust, as their most basic needs are being met in a consistent caring manner. Thinking about routines as part of the learning environment incorporates planning into the caring aspect of routines.

Transitions are the time between the end of one event and the beginning of another. Transitions offer unique opportunities for growth as well as challenges to educators.

Children need hands-on experiences and to have the opportunity to experience and express knowledge in a variety of different ways.

This can be the time between activities, the beginning and end of the day, before and after lunch, or moving from inside to outside. Transitions are particularly difficult times for children, as well as adults. At home, the times before meals, bedtime, and the like are stressful. As there are many transitions in a single day, and the stress created in these transitions can carry over into the next event, it is important to plan transitions to both increase learning and decrease stress.

The younger the children, the wider the age range of children, or the more children with severe disabilities, the more likely it is that transition periods will be longer. (Compare the time it takes for a 5 year old versus a 3 year old to put on boots and a snowsuit.) With younger children, the transitions may be more obvious to the adult than to the child. Transitions are important learning times for children, as many tasks involve adaptive skills. Teaching these skills (dressing and undressing, toileting, hand washing, eating, and settling for a nap) consumes a large portion of the day. It is sometimes tempting to just do things for the children rather than support them in learning these skills. Learning adaptive skills is a legitimate part of the curriculum and should be planned and valued in that light, not just as a daily necessity.

Standards in Early Childhood Education

As leaders have focused on what children know and are able to do, they have becoming increasingly aware of **standards** and curriculum content. Neither early childhood education nor special education had been included in the early part of the standards movement; that has changed.

The federal government supported the efforts of professional organizations to develop national standards. This standards movement was part of the Goals 2000: Educate America Act of 1994 and continues with the No Child Left Behind Act of 2001. No Child Left Behind is a sweeping reform of the Elementary and Secondary Education Act (ESEA). It targets reading and math standards in particular and has a strong emphasis on assessment. Children with disabilities are included in the general curriculum and are expected to meet state standards. States are required to report assessment information for four subgroups: children who are economically disadvantaged, children from racial/ethnic minorities, children with identified disabilities, and children who have limited English proficiency. In the past, many of these children were not included in the assessment system, or if they were, their scores were not reported and not counted.

Standards in and of themselves are neither good nor bad. Because children in elementary school are held accountable for meeting standards, teachers want children to come into their classes with a broad academic knowledge base. Thus there is pressure to teach more academic material in kindergarten and during the preschool years. Standards can transform the early childhood curriculum even when they do not directly apply to preschool.

Early childhood educators are challenged to teach children in a developmentally appropriate way and meet recognized standards, whether the standards are those developed by professional organizations, the federal or state government, or the school district. These standards, plus the 2004 amendments to IDEA, influence the development of individualized programs must be seen as guiding and building on each other to develop successful programs for all children in all educational settings.

Different people mean different things by standards. Not only could we not agree on what standards to support, but there was little real agreement on what standards are. This is changing. Thus, standards are affecting early childhood educators through pressure from the top down and through the inclusion of children with identified disabilities in the assessment process.

In all early childhood programs there are agreed upon characteristic of high-quality programs. The NAEYC has developed a set of standard to acknowledge and improve the professional practices in early childhood education and early childhood special education and to increase public knowledge about the importance of quality in early childhood education. The NAEYC (2006a) program standards focus on four areas: children, teaching staff, family and community partnerships, and leadership and administration. See Table 4–1 for the focus of the standards and the program standards under each foci.

Content or Performance Standards

Some see standards in terms of specific content based on subject matter areas; others see it as the ability to perform certain tasks. In reality, the two are intrinsically related (Kendall & Marzano, 1996). **Content standards** specify what children should know and be able to do; **performance standards** specify at what level children need to know and demonstrate their understanding of the concept to meet the standard, that is, the quality of the child's performance. In elementary school, report cards typically indicate how a child is meeting performance standards.

The emphasis of this book is on content standards. The expectation is that content standards will be used to determine the annual goals that are on children's individualized programs. Before talking about specific standards, let's talk about standards in general and try to answer the following questions:

- What led to the decision to develop standards?
- What are the sources of expertise in determining what the standards should be?
- How are the standards implemented in the classroom?
- What skills transcend standards?

Table 4–1: Standards for early childhood programs

Focus Area: Children

    Program Standard 1: Relationships: the focus is on developing positive relationships among all children and adults.

    Program Standard 2: Curriculum: the focus is on curriculum that has consistent goals for children and promotes learning and development in cognitive, emotional, language, social, and aesthetic development.

    Program Standard 3: Teaching: the focus is on adherence to developmentally, culturally, and linguistically appropriate teaching that results in children learning.

    Program Standard 4: Assessment of Child Progress: the focus is on ongoing systematic formal and informal assessment to document children's learning and development and to make sound decision about children, teaching, and programs.

    Program Standard 5: Health: the focus is on the health, safety, and nutrition of children and staff.

Focus Area: Teaching Staff

    Program Standard 6: Teachers: the focus is on educationally qualified and committed staff.

Focus Area: Family and Community Partnerships

    Program Standard 7: Families: the focus is on establishing and maintaining sensitive collaborative relationships with families.

    Program Standard 8: Community Relationships: the focus is on knowing about and establishing relationships with resources in the community to support young children's growth and development.

Focus Area: Leadership and Administration

    Program Standard 9: Physical Environment: the focus is on a safe healthful environment both indoors and outdoors.

    Program Standard 10: Leadership and Management: the focus is on having effective policies, procedures, and systems for children, families and staff to have positive experiences.

Source: National Association for the Education of Young Children, 2006a.

The Evidence Base

There is great concern about the widening gap between children who live in low-income families and those who have more economic resources. Seven- to 8-year-old children in low-income families obtain math scores that are five test points lower than their middle class peers. Their reading scores are four test points lower. They are twice as likely to repeat a grade, 3.4 times more likely to be expelled from school, 3.5 times more likely to drop out of school, and half as likely to finish a 4-year college (Children's Defense Fund, 2002).

Reflective Practice

How do you see this information affecting your teaching? Do you think it should be your problem to ensure that these children meet the standards? Do you think that helping these children will take so much of your time that middle class children will learn less? How can you teach all children and have them meet the standards? Reflect on how this evidence will affect society and your likelihood of collecting social security if no one acts on this information.

Developing Standards

The push for standards began at the national level in January of 1992, when National Education Standards and Testing (NEST) called for the development of national standards and assessment in core subject matter areas (math, English, science, history, and geography). Professional organizations were awarded federal funds for this project. Funding for the arts followed. Regardless of subject matter area, these are voluntary standards that describe the knowledge, skills, and understanding that all students should have. Professional organizations responded to this in a variety of ways.

The impetus to develop standards was based on the performance (or lack of performance) of children in certain subject matter areas. For example, some children could execute required mathematical calculations, but couldn't solve similar problems when presented as word problems. That is, they could calculate but they could not apply and comprehend when to use specific applications. In addition, children from families with lower socioeconomic status had fewer math skills than their higher-socioeconomic peers (Clements, 2002).

Our growing knowledge that learning during the early childhood years lays the foundation for future brain development has led many to question whether we are using these years wisely. But what is wise? Does early childhood curriculum sufficiently exploit the potential of this crucial period in the brain's development? Does curriculum adequately emphasize cognitive development, language, and literacy? Or will standards eventually overemphasize cognitive development, language, and literacy at the expense of development in other areas?

One way of looking at standards is by looking at the content to be mastered and the level at which it must be mastered to reach the standards. Does everyone have to be an expert at everything? **Literacy** and expertise form a continuum of competence, with literacy being the minimum that all students need of knowledge and skills in a particular area to continue moving toward becoming competent adults of the twenty-first century. Literacy requirements are different in 2010 than they were in 1990. To be literate in today's world, one needs to be able to read varied material, fill out forms, and access technology.

Expertise includes the level of mastery and content options that should be available to children who want to become mini-experts in a field (Kendall & Marzano, 1996). This text focuses on the literacy end of the scale, the skills that all children need to attain.

A related area is teacher preparation. Are teachers prepared to use a standards-based curriculum? Do you as a potential teacher understand what standards are and how to incorporate them in your curriculum planning? It requires us to look at designing activities to help children meet content standards. Child outcomes are first; activities make meeting those outcomes interesting, provide a context, and make them applicable to the real world in which children live and grow.

Who should decide on the standards? Professional organizations took the lead in making decisions about standards. Some are concerned that professional organizations include professionals who know the subject matter area, but may not know much about young children and how they learn. They may have unrealistic expectations for children. Some are concerned that school districts may set standards low so that everyone will meet them so they will look good on paper. It truly is a dilemma. Because this text is used in many states and different nations I have chosen to use the standards of professional organizations, rather than state standards. I use other standards to illustrate specific points.

Some organizations do not like the term *standards*, so the terminology varies. Some choose to call them *guidelines*. Head Start has a child *outcomes* framework while others prefer the word *goal*. The intent is to ensure that curriculum is planned and designed to help children master increasingly more complex material in relevant areas.

In the Field

I once had a student teacher who wanted to do a 2-week unit on chocolate. It was well thought out, although the unit had some problems. But I thought that, given what children needed to learn, it was not a wise use of their time. The student teacher pointed out the merits of what she had done, and in many cases, she was right. I did not have problems with the activities, but whether it was worth 2 weeks in kindergarten to learn about chocolate. I persisted. She was very angry with me.

Reflective Practice

What do you think? Would you have let her do it? If you were a parent how would you have responded to this unit?

Implementing Standards

Are standards the curriculum? No! Standards guide curriculum: they provide parameters about what children should know and be able to do. You cannot say, "I am teaching literacy, phonological awareness, indicator three (progresses in recognizing matching sounds and rhymes in familiar words, games, songs, stories, and poems) during group time today." Rather, you choose, based on your unit or theme, a story, poem, finger play, or rhyme that uses these concepts. You may dismiss children from the group by asking them to name a rhyming word to one you give. And, you would note which children can and cannot do this. Then you reflect on who did not succeed at the task and decide how to work with them, within the context of the unit, to meet this indicator. This also alerts you to look at the bigger picture. This was one indicator of phonological awareness. Does the child know the other four indicators for phonological awareness? What about literacy in general? Used well, standards help us think about children, their special needs, and their level of competence in important areas of learning.

Some skills are part of all standards but are difficult to quantify in any standards. Virtually all content areas require (or should require) skills related to thinking and reasoning. The question is how these skills should be articulated in the standards. Some standards developed by professional organizations have specifically included these standards: Math standards include mathematics as problem solving, reasoning and proof, communication, connections, and representation (National Council of Teachers of Mathematics, 2004). Others are implied in the standards themselves, such as in the visual arts: choosing and evaluating a range of subject matter, symbols, and ideas (Consortium of National Arts Education Associations, 1994). Professional standards are written by different groups, and they include skills in ways each group feels are most appropriate. When you try to use the standards in curriculum planning, it is clear that they have some commonality that transcends content areas. It is important to maintain a holistic approach to the curriculum and not lose the child or lose sight of the child's special needs in the struggle over the standards the child should meet.

Regardless of the discussion about standards, there is a need to have appropriate content in all domains, a method for determining the order in which this content should be presented, some parameters for the scope of what content is covered, and the determination of some minimal level of performance. At the least, standards can guide our thinking about curriculum. They provide the impetus for continued reflection about developmentally appropriate practices and assessment during the early childhood years.

In most states, there are more detailed standards in mathematics and reading than other curriculum areas. State standards pay little attention to the creative arts and to social and emotional development, which is a major concern. There are professional standards for some areas of creative arts (visual arts and music). Head Start is an exception because they include both creative arts and social and emotional development in their outcomes. Because standards for creative arts and physical education are not required, and areas such as social-emotional development are not always required, there is concern that they will be seen as less relevant and that time spent in these areas will diminish as educators focus on the standards they are required to meet.

The educational standards developed by professional organizations are included by content area. In some cases, just an abstract of the standard is used; in other cases, more details are given. This was done because of the complexity and applicability of some of the standards and because some standards did not include children below kindergarten. I strongly recommend that you read the standards developed, not to jump into the fray over their use, but as part of your reflective learning and growth and to clarify what you believe is important. As a field, early childhood education has not strongly embraced specific standards but have focused on developmentally appropriate practices and play as the base of learning.

Because of the link between curriculum standards and curriculum, the order below reflects the organization of the Resource Chapters. Where there are more holistic standards, they have been included.

Self-Awareness Standards

There are not national standards in some areas such as self-awareness even though it is an important aspect of the early childhood curriculum. There are many standards that focus on social studies.

Self-Esteem

Conflict and its resolution are at the core of many of society's problems. The conflict between the child's growing need for autonomy and self-esteem and the adult's need to inculcate values and socially acceptable behavior is classic.

Conflict appears first in toddlerhood, and parents and caregivers make a conscious or unconscious choice about where they stand. The issues that need resolving are the forerunners of the conflicts in adolescence and even in later adult life. When put in perspective, especially if one believes that conflict resolution patterns learned as toddlers set the groundwork for adolescence, some solutions are more expedient than others are.

Many of us use the words discipline, guidance, or punishment as though they were interchangeable synonyms. However, each means something slightly different, and their use affects children differently. Gartrell (2002) defines discipline as behavior that is designed to encourage self control. **Discipline** is any actions or words that help children self-monitor their behavior so it is appropriate and acceptable. Discipline is a form of teaching. One assumption is that young children misbehave out of lack of knowledge. Discipline supplies information about the appropriateness of actions.

Punishment and guidance are two forms of discipline. **Punishment** involves the infliction of a negative consequence for a behavior that is inappropriate or wrong (Gartrell, 2002). Punishment usually succeeds in stopping behavior that is unwanted, but it may have negative effects on some children. Children may learn that they can "get away" with negative behavior without the presence of the controlling adult. Or, they may come to fear adults as harsh and uncaring.

Guidance, or positive discipline, facilitates the development of self-esteem, prosocial behaviors, and the ability to control one's own behavior (Gartrell, 2002). It is a process approach to guiding children's behavior rather than an isolated act of punishment. Positive discipline involves awareness of children's feelings, developmental levels, and the ability to set and keep sensible limits. When children's behavior is unacceptable, they are presented with the logical consequences of their behavior in a way that preserves their self-esteem. As children learn there are consequences for their behavior—positive ones when they are acting appropriately, and negative ones when they act inappropriately—they begin to learn to act responsibly and control their own behavior.

Typically, adults begin to discipline children at the end of the first year, when children become mobile. Young children behave—they don't misbehave. Misbehavior is an interpretation by adults. Setting limits is part of an adult's commitment to a child, not just a reaction to the child's immediate behavior. The discipline should fit the child and should be accompanied by a conviction that setting limits is an important part of caring for young children. When caring accompanies discipline, it is guidance; when there is no caring, it is simply punishment.

The goal of discipline is to help children learn socially acceptable limits and develop internal controls to implement these limits. As such, discipline involves facilitating children's social development and prosocial skills. The objectives of discipline are twofold. One is immediate: to stop inappropriate behavior as it occurs. The second involves the development of inner controls for behavior. Adults can facilitate the development of these inner controls in children if they use positive discipline effectively.

Discipline is influenced by several factors, including how the child usually acts or responds to social situations. Children's temperaments and the goodness of fit between adult and child is particularly important when considering young children with disabilities. A child's temperament may influence the teacher's expectations of the child, and thus influence instructional and disciplinary decisions. In addition to the child's temperament, his disability, care demands, behavior, and social responsiveness play a part in how adults handle discipline situations.

Implications for Educators

Setting classroom rules, and behavioral expectations, is as important as the arrangement of the classroom. In any classroom, it remains extremely important to take time to teach classroom rules and procedures. This is particularly important when working with children who may have behavioral challenges. Children need to learn appropriate behavior, social skills, and positive character traits. The behavioral expectations and classroom routines you set for the children in the first few weeks of school will affect how well your classroom runs the remainder of the school year.

When developing rules for the classroom, you should consider three or four rules that are very important to you and phrase them in a positive manner. Then, on the first day of school, have a class meeting with children to discuss other rules that they feel are important. Help children to come to an agreement about which rules deserve to be classroom rules, and phrase them positively. Add these to your rules chart in both word and picture form. As children have played a role in developing the rules, they should feel a sense of ownership for both the rules and the classroom. When establishing classroom rules in this manner, children are more likely to respect and follow the rules, especially if you adhere to them consistently.

Take this opportunity to teach, model, and role-play the rules in appropriate situations. For example, if one rule you and the children have chosen is "Listen quietly when the teacher speaks," you will want to model and discuss how one listens quietly, discuss and role-play situations in which this rule applies, and, finally, practice as a whole class. Practice each rule consistently the first few weeks of school. Also, reinforce children who follow the rules by being specific about the rules and the exact behaviors they demonstrate.

Classroom procedures, the manner in which activities and daily routines are followed, should be taught concretely through the first few weeks. For example, you should discuss, model, and then have children repeatedly practice the procedures for lining up at the door, washing hands, changing centers, and walking in the hallway. Discuss why those routines are important and give specific reinforcement to children who follow routines well. Continue practicing until all are running smoothly. By practicing, modeling, discussing, and role-playing rules and procedures, children know what to expect from you and their environment. Once these are established, you will have more time to focus on other areas.

Behavioral Standards

We usually don't think of behavior in relation to standards. Rather, concerns about behavior are related to terms like *safety, stricter discipline, zero-tolerance policies,* and *violence prevention approaches.* We rarely think about discipline as being a major issue in early childhood. Times are changing. There is a goal to establish safe schools. To have safe schools, children in schools must abide by its rules.

The Evidence Base

The National Prekindergarten Study of almost 4,000 prekindergarten classrooms was published by the Yale University Child Study Center. One report from this study looked at the number of prekindergarten children who were expelled.

> "Results indicated that 10.4 percent of prekindergarten teachers reported expelling at least one preschooler in the past 12 months. Nationally, 6.67 preschoolers were expelled per 1,000 enrolled . . . 3.2 times the rate for K–12 students. Rates were highest for older preschoolers and African-Americans, and boys were over 4½ times more likely to be expelled than were girls." (Gilliam, 2005, 1)

Reflective Practice

To the extent that preschool programs expel the children who most need to learn prosocial behaviors, children are not likely to develop these skills and their behavior will continue to be problematic. What solutions do you see for teachers and children? How might you help these children learn social skills and increase their self-awareness and self-esteem?

Disproportionately, poor, male, minority students, and students with disabilities are identified as discipline problems (Palley, 2002). The hope is that through early identification and intervention behavioral issues will be dealt with at an early age so they are not problematic as children become older.

One concern is whether children with disabilities violate these behavioral standards in disproportionate numbers. Students with disabilities are overrepresented in the juvenile justice system (U.S. Department of Education and U.S. Department of Justice, 1999). According to the Office of Special Education Programs 30 to 50 percent of the children in juvenile corrections facilities are identified as having a disability. Some of these disabilities were identified during children's school years. Others, although present during the school years, were not identified until later. The reality of the disability (whether or not it was covered by the IDEA) was that children fell behind academically and repeated several grades. Many were functionally illiterate. As you read the discipline section of the 2004 amendments to the IDEA you may have felt that these requirements were irrelevant to early childhood education. Reflect on that decision.

Inclusion

Social competence is another aspect of social studies in the early childhood years. It involves the ability of the child to successfully select and carry out his interpersonal goals. It includes the child's effectiveness in meeting his goals, and the appropriateness of these goals in social situations. Different social situations require different competencies. The three major categories of social competence include adult-child interactions, social play relationships, and peer interactions. Inclusive classrooms place high demands on social competence.

Children with disabilities are often expected to have interpersonal competence because of their experience with a wide variety of adults. However, children may be competent with adults on a one-to-one basis because adults do the compensating and adapt their expectations. The same compensation rarely occurs with peers. Competence with peers is important. Success with social tasks such as making friends and gaining entry into groups is imperative not

only now but for later adjustment. Inclusion of all children in the same classroom makes this more challenging because inclusive settings provide opportunities for many levels of play, including more complex play behavior.

Mildred Parten (1932) was one of the first scholars to point out the dramatic changes in children's play behavior as they progress through the preschool years. She identified a three-step sequence that we still use to categorize children's play. Children's play typically starts with nonsocial activity and consists of **unoccupied play**, **onlooker play**, and **solitary play**. They move into a limited form of social interaction that Parten called **parallel play**. Children play near other children using similar materials, but the children don't really influence each other's behavior. She also identified two types of true social interaction. In **associative play**, children engage in separate activities but they exchange toys and influence each other. In **cooperative play**, children have a common goal or are interacting using the same materials. Although nonsocial play decreases as children increase in age, it continues to be part of children's repertoire throughout their preschool years. What does change is the quality of the nonsocial play. This play should reflect children's increasing cognitive maturity. If, however, the nonsocial play is made up of aimless wandering, looking, and repetitive motions, there is some cause for concern (Rubin & Coplan, 1998). Solitary play in and of itself is not a problem. It is the level of play that is of concern and the ability of the child to join a group if the child chooses to do so.

Social competence is the key to social acceptance. Peers make judgments based on data (Jorge can't climb, looks funny, and so on). Children enter a new group with a clean slate, but they develop a personal social history within the group. Children with disabilities often use strategies of approaching other children that make it difficult to make friends. They are often less socially competent. As clusters of children form, more complex entry skills are required to join groups; if children lack these skills, a reputation for lack of social competence is established, and a pattern of social separation and reduced social status can result. Social networks become narrower and more difficult to enter as children get older; therefore, it is imperative that children learn these skills early.

If a child uses inappropriate social strategies she is treated differently by her peers and other individuals with whom she interacts. This may result in a child having fewer opportunities to practice social skills. There is some evidence that there are characteristic patterns of social behavior depending upon a child's type of disability (Guralnick, Connor, Hammond, Gottman, & Kinnish, 1996). Nonsocial play is a characteristic of children with severe developmental delays even in inclusive classrooms (Hundert, Mahoney, Mundy, & Vernon, 1998).

Children with disabilities face challenges in social play situations. Children with communication difficulties have decreased access to peers. The ability to communicate is important in developing social competence. Children with communication disorders participate in fewer positive social interactions and use speech less frequently. They were not as successful as their typically developing peers in getting positive responses to their social overtures. They could, however, sustain play and respond to others' social bids (Guralnick et al., 1996). Children with hearing

All children need to be included. Ensure there is enough room for children to stand and sit so children can play together.

impairments, too, have trouble joining groups and tend to wait and hover on the edge of an activity (Brown, Remine, Prescott, & Rickards, 2000). Children with visual impairments have also been shown to initiate social interactions less frequently (Crocker & Orr, 1996). Disorders that affect children's behavior, such as attention-deficit/hyperactivity disorder (ADHD) and autism, lead to difficulties in social situations (DuPaul, McGoey, Eckert, & Vanbrakle, 2001). Children with ADHD have fewer social skills and display more negative social behaviors than their typically developing peers. Our knowledge about the influence of ADHD on younger children is limited because few children have been diagnosed with ADHD during the preschool years (DuPaul et al., 2001).

Given the problems that some children with disabilities have in social relationships, it is useful to try to pinpoint where in the interaction children are having problems:

- Gaining attention—before a child can join a social group she has to get the attention of the children in the group she wants to join.
- Initiating interaction—once it is clear to others that the child wants to join the child must make an overture to the children in the group.
- Responding to others—children need to develop skills that allow others to join their groups.
- Sustaining interactions—to participate in ongoing social play children need to be able to continue interactions and develop the give and take necessary for play to continue.
- Shifting the focus of an interaction—as play continues and becomes more complex, children need to be able to change roles and refocus the play.
- Ending an interaction—children need to find ways to close interactions rather than just walking away when they lose interest.

Intervention aimed at supporting the social integration of children with disabilities has been approached from two very different frameworks. Educators with strong developmental backgrounds have assumed that physical proximity to other children, plus using open-ended, process-oriented activities in a free play setting, would result in social integration. This has not been the case. Others, from a more behavioral orientation, have observed the lack of social competence and have developed very structured skits and specific exercises for children to repeat (Strain, 1990). For example, children are paired, and one child says, "Hello, my name is Dayonn. I like your shirt." The other child responds, "I'm glad to meet you. My name is Min." Dayonn then responds with "I'm glad to meet you." Other than using different names, all of the children in the class use the same procedure and the same words. The exercise might be repeated several times. Activities such as these have resulted in increased integration, but have not been generalized to nonstructured situations and are not representative of how young children interact with each other in the real world. The problem is that the structured behavioral approach is an overly narrow solution to a complex problem. It is viewed as developmentally inappropriate by some early childhood educators. They find it stilted and not easily incorporated into their existing teaching style.

Social Studies

Social studies is a subject with specific activities and learning, but also one in which observation and modeling are important learning tools. The National Council for the Social Studies (1994, 2008) developed national standards for social studies. Several related areas that are included under social studies during the early childhood years—geography, civics and government, and history—also have standards. The Geography Education Standards Project (GESP; 1994) developed the *Geography for Life, National Standards;* The Center for Civic Education (CCE; 1994) provided the *National Standards for Civics and Government* and the National Center for History in Schools (NCHS; 1994). *National Standards: History for Grades K–4: Expanding Children's World in Time and Space.*

Although the social studies standards provide guidance on what to teach it is up to the early childhood educator to determine how to teach the content. Ensure that the content reflects an anti-bias approach and includes the roles of men, women, and minorities. Highlight ways that social studies is inclusive particularly as it relates to children with disabilities.

Social Studies Standards

There are ten social studies standards. For the standards and complete information about these expectations, go to The National Council for the Social Studies at http://www.socialstudies.org. They revised these standards in 2008 and included information that children should learn during the early elementary years. They identified learning expectations for each standard. They also provide information on the purpose of the standard, key questions for exploration, knowledge (the learner will understand), processes, (the learner will be able to), forms or products (learners will demonstrate their knowledge, skill and dispositions by) (National Council for the Social Studies, 2008). This additional information makes it easier for early childhood educators to adapt some of the content for younger children. They also provide snapshots of practice to show how to implement the standards in the classroom.

- I—Culture. Social studies curriculum should include experiences that provide for the study of culture and cultural diversity.
- II—Time Continuity and Change. Social studies programs should include experiences that provide for the study of the ways human beings view themselves in and over time.
- III—People, Places, and Environments. Social studies curriculum should include experiences that provide for the study of people, places, and environments.
- IV—Individual Development and Identity. Social studies curriculum should include experiences that provide for the study of individual development and identity.
- V—Individuals, Groups, and Institutions. Social studies programs should include experiences that provide for the study of interactions among individuals, groups, and institutions.
- VI—Power, Authority, and Governance. Social studies programs should include experiences that provide

for the study of how people create, interact with, and change structures of power, authority, and governance.

- VII—Production, Distribution, and Consumption. Social studies programs should include experiences that provide for the study of how people organize for the production, distribution, and consumption of goods and services.
- VIII—Science, Technology, and Society. Social studies programs should include experiences that provide for the study of relationships among science, technology, and society.
- IX—Global Connections. Social studies curriculum should include experiences that provide for the study of global connections and interdependence.
- X—Civic Ideals and Practices. Social studies curriculum should include experiences that provide for the study of the ideals, principles, and practices of citizenship in a democratic republic (National Council for the Social Studies, 2008).

History Standards

The history standards were developed by the National Center for History in the Schools (2005). The history standards are divided into two broad areas: historical thinking skills and historical understanding. The standards for children kindergarten through fourth grade are given below.

A. *Historical thinking skills* enable children to differentiate past, present, and future time; raise questions; seek and evaluate evidence; compare and analyze historical stories, illustrations, and records from the past; interpret the historical record; and construct historical narratives of their own.

Standard 1: Chronological thinking
Standard 2: Historical comprehension
Standard 3: Historical analysis and interpretation
Standard 4: Historical research
Standard 5: Historical issues—analysis and decision making

B. *Historical understandings* define what students should know about the history of families, their communities, states, nation, and world. These understandings are drawn from the record of human aspirations, strivings, accomplishments, and failures in at least five spheres of human activity: the social, political, scientific/technological, economic, and cultural (the philosophical/religious/aesthetic), as appropriate for children.

Topic 1: Living and working together in families and communities, now and long ago.

Standard 1: Family life now and in the recent past; Family life in various places long ago.
Standard 2: History of students' local community and how communities in North America varied long ago.

Topic 2: The history of the student's own state or region.

Standard 3: The people, events, problems, and ideas that created the history of their state.

Topic 3: The history of the United States: Democratic principles and values and the peoples from many cultures who contributed to its cultural, economic and political heritage.

Standard 4: How democratic values came to be, and how they have been exemplified by people, events, and symbols.
Standard 5: The causes and nature of various movements of large groups of people into and within the United States, now and long ago.
Standard 6: Regional folklore and cultural contributions that helped to form our national heritage.

Topic 4: The history of peoples of many cultures around the world.

Standard 7: Selected attributes and historical developments of various societies in Africa, the Americas, Asia, and Europe.
Standard 8: Major discoveries in science and technology, their social and economic effects, and the scientists and inventors responsible for them.

For more information about the history standards go to the National Center for History in the schools at http://nchs.ucla.edu/standards.

Geography Standards

The *Geographically Informed Person* knows and understands

I—The World in Spatial Terms
- How to use maps and other geographic representations, tools, and technologies to acquire, process, and report information.
- How to use mental maps to organize information about people, places, and environments.
- How to analyze the spatial organization of people, places, and environments on Earth's surface.

II—Places and Regions
- The physical and human characteristics of places.
- That people create regions to interpret Earth's complexity.
- How culture and experience influence people's perception of places and regions.

III—Physical Systems
- The physical processes that shape the patterns of Earth's surface.
- The characteristics and spatial distribution of ecosystems on Earth's surface.

IV—Human Systems
- The characteristics, distribution, and migration of human populations on Earth's surface.
- The characteristics, distributions, and complexity of Earth's cultural mosaics.
- The patterns and networks of economic interdependence on Earth's surface.
- The process, patterns, and functions of human settlement.
- How forces of cooperation and conflict among people influence the division and control of Earth's surface.

V—Environment and Society
- How human actions modify the physical environment.
- How physical systems affect human systems.
- The changes that occur in the meaning, use, distribution, and importance of resources.

VI—The Uses of Geography
- How to apply geography to interpret the past.
- To apply geography to interpret the present and plan for the future.

(National Council for Geographic Education, 1994; 2008)

To view these standards, get some ideas for implementing them, or take a tutorial go to the National Council for Geographic Education http://www.ncge.org. The National Geographic provides lesson plans and additional information at http://www.nationalgeographic.com/xpeditions.

Young children's study of geography begins with digging in sand, being fascinated by the stars, and getting wet from the rain. The standards provide you with a range of content areas you need to think about relative to the geographic knowledge children need. The process of *doing* geography can guide the curriculum. The skills are in asking questions and acquiring, organizing, and analyzing the information necessary to answer these questions (Seefeldt, 1995).

Civics and Government Standards

The Center for Civic Education developed National Standards for Civics and Government in 1994. Five of the standards relate to children in kindergarten through fourth grade.

I – What is government and what should it do?

II – What are the basic values and principles of American demography?

III – How does the government established by the constitution embody the purposes, values, and the principles of American democracy?

IV – What is the relationship of the United States to other nations and to world affairs?

V – What are the roles of the citizen in American democracy?

Center for Civic Education (1994; 2007). For additional information about these standards go to http://www.civiced.org.

Taken together, these social studies standards and principles require early childhood educators to take a very close look at how they present the social studies curriculum. This is an area that is frequently neglected in early childhood but has more standards than other areas. It will take a skillful teacher to implement social studies standards in a developmentally appropriate way.

Implications for Educators

There are no standards for self-esteem and self awareness and many standards in social studies. Does that mean self-esteem and self awareness are not important? If standards focus educational practices what do you expect will happen to areas such as these that lack standards?

Successful social inclusion of children with diverse abilities requires thoughtful planning and programming. Think about social inclusion as you do math or language and literacy. Think about the learning cycle and use this to plan for social inclusion: work from awareness to exploration to inquiry to utilization. Start by increasing the awareness of all children about differences including cultural and ethnic differences and disabilities.

Allocate time for children to ask questions, explore, and experiment. If this involves a simulation, do not have the child with a disability play the part of the child with the disability. He already knows what it is like. The goal is for others to learn; he might, however, be a good coach.

Have children discuss the feelings they had during the simulation and have them evaluate the strategies they used to cope. Help them decide what was easy and what was difficult. Discuss how these would vary from the classroom, to home, and in the community. Repeat the process on another day, helping children generalize and use the information they learned earlier. Support them in generating additional solutions and alternative explanations for behaviors. Encourage children who are ready to think in a broader context.

In early childhood, social studies is usually taught through daily organization and decision making: deciding what to name the new goldfish, what to do when someone knocks down the blocks, and how to share special materials. This is all part of the social learning that occurs at this age.

As children and their families enter your classroom, they learn something about how you respond to inclusion and how you teach social studies. They will look at the pictures and bulletin boards to see if they represent the culture and language of the children you teach as well as those in the community. They will look at the books on display to see if you support a bias-free approach or if you reinforce racial and gender stereotypes that are current or in the past. They will evaluate the room to determine whether or not it allows diversity in play. As their eyes wander, they will note whether the dolls represent the diverse cultures reflective of the children and how you will promote equity. They will look for the possibility of language differences, not only Spanish or Chinese, but also American Sign Language and Braille. They might even note whether there are pictures and books about children with disabilities. All children need to feel they are part of the class. It is important that they become aware of themselves both as unique human beings and as people who are similar to, as well as different from, others.

Children learn through social studies about the situational aspects of behavior. Behavior that is appropriate in one situation or time is not necessarily right in another. Children in the process of learning to take turns wonder whether or not they will actually get their turn if they postpone it or let someone ahead of them. If they do lose their turn, they will be less likely to take turns in the future. Start with your setting. Help children feel comfortable knowing their way around both indoors and out. Take short walks in the area. Focus some part of your curriculum on the community itself as well as communities in general—why we have them, what they do, and how they help the people who live there. Discuss the differences between rural and urban communities.

Field trips are one of the most common ways of making abstract ideas concrete to young children. Resource people can be invited to visit and resource media such as film, television, videotapes, compact discs, and the Internet can also be used to include the social studies standards in your curriculum.

Language and Literacy Standards

Learning to communicate and understand communications is one of the major tasks of childhood. Learning language is a dynamic process that is affected by the language heard and the way that adults respond to emerging language. In situations where children have rich language models and are supported in producing speech, they are more open to new opportunities to expand their language skills. In addition to a strong experiential base to provide something to talk about, children also need to feel the urge to communicate. If no one listens and responds, children are less likely to talk. Children who spend many hours watching television have little incentive to talk because television is a noninteractive media.

Language and literacy is a particular concern in early childhood special education as many children, particularly those with specific learning disabilities, struggle in this area. The 2004 amendments to the IDEA place particular emphasis on learning to read. Having a broad understanding of the principles involved in learning to read helps you design curriculum and identify children who are not learning at the expected rate.

Speaking, listening, reading, and writing although highlighted individually, are interrelated and interdependent. Although there are designated language and literacy activities, the language and literacy curriculum should be part of all curriculum areas. In addition, the goals for language and literacy, such as increasing vocabulary, appear in the math and science area as well as language.

Speaking

Speaking, or expressive language, is a major component of the early language and literacy curriculum. To match language and literacy activities to the level of the children in your class, it is important to know each child's present level of language functioning. This can be compared to what the typical child of that age can say (vocabulary and **mean length of utterance**), and the types of activities that increase children's vocabulary and sentence length.

There is some professional debate about the role language plays in learning. Some focus on children's active role in language learning as they construct language (and knowledge) for themselves to meet their needs to communicate. The child is viewed as a producer of knowledge, not a recipient of it (Piaget, 1967). The process itself is interactive. Others place more emphasis on the social function of language and view speech as a vehicle for self-organization (Vygotsky, 1978). The core of young children's language and literacy development is to convey meaning through speaking and writing and to interpret meaning through listening and reading. Whether children invent language or use it as a vehicle for social interaction, it is an important part of the development of

communication and knowledge. The role of the teacher is to ensure that children have a rich base on which to build communication skills and to support children in using these skills.

It is imperative that children have a vocabulary large enough to express their wants and needs and to enable them to understand the wants and needs of others. Children must also learn the rules that govern how language is used. Understanding language enables them to function effectively in their environment. They also need to learn that language can be both spoken and written. Most professionals feel that children use their own language system to make guesses about words they cannot read. The more specific and complex their spoken language is, the better their guesses will be as they learn to read.

Listening

Listening is a relatively recent addition to the language and literacy curriculum. It was obvious to most people that children learned to talk and must be taught to read and write, but listening was taken as a given. The belief was that all children knew how to listen; they just needed to "pay attention."

Listening is a complex component of learning. It involves hearing that allows for auditory identification and discrimination. There is both a short- and long-term memory component. Listening or auditory processing is also part of attending and sensory motor integration. If you ask a child "What is your name?" the child must hear the message, interpret the meaning, formulate an answer, and respond to the question. We do not assume children are listening unless they respond to our requests.

Listening, or at least making sense out of what is heard—taking in information—has a developmental base. It is the role of the adult to match the language base of the child. The following list highlights the steps in moving along the listening continuum:

- No information intake via language. Initially, the verbal aspects of language (words) have no meaning for children; they use nonverbal cues by looking at what is being done or the tone of the voice to gain information.
- Information intake if language is redundant with the experience. This is like the play-by-play broadcast: Adults put into words what children are seeing or experiencing.
- Information intake if language complements or extends the ongoing experience.
- Information intake if language complements or extends the context of the experience, that is, paints a broader scene.
- Information intake if language complements or extends a topic or activity a child has initiated.
- Information intake if language reminds the child of past familiar experience and extends that experience.
- Information intake if language is about a new topic the child has neither experience with nor any particular interest in (French, 1996).

Much teaching in public schools is about new topics some children may have had little experience with, and perhaps no interest in. If children have not had the previous developmental experiences, they may not gain information through listening.

As with speaking, children are most likely to develop good listening skills if you are a good model. If you always repeat what you say, children learn *not* to listen the first time. When you are listening to a child, *listen*. Although we don't often think of listening as a school subject, children spend more of their school time listening than doing any other single task. They listen to the teacher, they listen to peers, they listen to the intercom, and they listen to recorded sounds. For younger children, we have fingerplays that help them "zip their mouths closed" so they can listen, or they put on their "listening cap." The goal is to have the children be quiet. Despite the preparation for listening, the focus is still on speaking rather than the skills involved in listening. One of the questions we as teachers must evaluate is how much of what we say is worth listening to? Would we be willing to sit spellbound for several hours each day listening to boring information? For children to practice good listening skills, they need something stimulating to listen to. Interest helps them focus on listening as a process.

Reading

Educators are becoming more interested in and concerned about literacy. Although there is agreement that no one teaching method or approach is likely to be effective for all children all the time there is agreement that it builds on what children already know and is part of both direct teaching of key literacy skills as well as being incorporated into play (NAEYC & IRA, 2005). There is also agreement that the teacher is an important variable. Your enthusiasm for reading and valuing it as a skill are important as children struggle to learn this complex task. Although the formal teaching of reading usually begins in elementary school, early literacy skills which set the foundation for beginning reading begin in infancy. The International Reading Association (IRA) and the National Association for the Education of Young Children (NAEYC) issued a

Reading includes being able to choose a book and share it with a friend.

joint position paper about learning to read and write. The statements below are based on that position statement (IRA & NAEYC, 1998; NAEYC & IRA, 2005).

Children come to school with diverse literacy experiences. Some children have been exposed to many different types of reading materials at home or in an early care and education environment. Others come with few literacy experiences.. Reading needs to build on what children know and can do.

Phase 1: Awareness and exploration (infancy though preschool)

During this phase children are exploring the environment and build the foundations for learning to read and write (IRA &NAEYC, 1998). Read to infants and toddlers and preschool children. Establish a literacy-rich environment. As they become preschoolers ask them questions about the characters and the plot, and have them retell the story. Expose children to concepts about print. Help them connect written and spoken language. Label materials in your classroom and model how the label helps you know what something is. Help children understand that there is a systematic relationship between letters and sounds (alphabetic principle). Linguistic awareness develops through rhyming activities such as nursery rhymes. **Phonemic awareness** "refers to a child's understanding and conscious awareness that speech is composed of identifiable units, such as spoken words, syllables, and sounds" (IRA & NAEYC, 1998, p. 4). During the preschool years direct training in phonemic awareness is inappropriate. Sensitizing children to sounds that form predictable patterns while enjoying being read to is more appropriate.

Phase 2: Experimental reading and writing (kindergarten)

Kindergarten children are developing basic concepts about print and are beginning to engage in and experiment with reading and writing (IRA & NAEYC, 1998). In kindergarten, one focus is on enhancing children's vocabulary. This can be achieved by listening to stories if children are asked predictive and analytic questions before and after reading the story. It is not something that happens automatically. Repeated readings seem to help children extract the way different genres are structured. Reading then becomes an interactive experience, not a listening activity. Language-experience stories help children clarify the concept of word. Writing down what children say helps focus on the connection between speaking and writing but also on the fact that there are spaces between words, different words have different letter configurations, and words differ in the number of letters they have. Letter naming is an important first step in literacy, and by the end of kindergarten most children can recognize and discriminate letter shapes with ease. Phonemic awareness (connecting the sound to the letter) follows, but it takes time and practice. Rhyming words can be used to extend children's vocabulary. Some children develop phonemic awareness through reading. However, approximately 20 percent will not without additional training (IRA, 1998).

Kindergarten children will read some words and are building a sight vocabulary. The relationship between reading and writing ability is a strong one at this age. Children can engage in independent reading and writing. Educators help children focus on concepts of print related to understand left-to-right and top-to-bottom orientation. Children are learning to segment spoken words into individual sounds and blends. Strong programs in early literacy are not as obvious in preschool and kindergarten as they are in the primary grades.

Phase 3: Early reading and writing (first grade)

Children are beginning to read simple stories and write about meaningful topics (IRA & NAEYC, 1998). Reading instruction in the primary grades is often based on a basal or literature anthology series. Successful approaches to reading have "some type of systematic code instruction along with meaningful connected reading . . . " (IRA & NAEYC, 1998, p. 7). Children are building a sight word vocabulary as teachers introduce new words and teach spelling strategies. As children are learning to read, their reading is likely to be slow and deliberate, but as they become more confident, their fluency increases, as does their comprehension. Attempts at punctuation and capitalization are becoming part of their writing. Reading and writing are used for a variety of purposes. Children need to be read to as well practice their reading skills.

Phase 4: Transitional reading and writing (second grade)

Children are beginning to read more fluiently and to write using simple and more complex sentences. Good readers use metacognitive strategies that help them prepare for what they are going to read. Then they read and reread a passage and ask questions if necessary. Children need to practice reading to others. They also profit from integrating reading and writing. Children can now write stories, poems and use other forms of writing. They can read a range of texts and their writing has become part of a process of writing, editing, and proofing. They can spell more difficult words and have new spelling strategies. Invented spelling, although still acceptable, is phasing out as spelling instruction is increasing the number of words children can spell accurately.

Phase 5: Independent and productive reading and writing (third grade)

Children continue to refine and extend their reading and writing skills and modify them to suit varying purposes and audiences. Third graders are capable fluent readers who have a range of strategies to draw meaning from text (IRA & NAEYC, 1998). Identification strategies are becoming more automatic and writing and spelling easier and more accurate. Instruction is not focused on teaching children to read and write, but using reading and writing as tools to learn other material.

- Children need to be exposed to a wide range of print and nonprint material to acquire information about themselves and the world they live in. Texts should include works of fiction and nonfiction as well as classic and contemporary works.

- Children need to read literature chosen from many periods in many genres.
- Children need to develop a wide range of strategies to use texts, including knowledge of the English language and life experience.
- Children need to learn the structure and conventions of language and to adjust their language usage (written and spoken) to their purpose and audience.
- Children need to use a wide range of strategies as they write for different audiences and purposes.
- Children need to apply their knowledge of language structure and conventions (spelling, punctuation) to create, critique, and discuss written material.
- Children need skills in conducting research, that is, they need to identify a topic, pose problems, gather, evaluate, and synthesize data from a variety of sources and communicate this knowledge to an appropriate audience.
- Children need to be able to use a variety of information technologies (libraries, databases, videos, the Internet) to obtain and synthesize information and to convey it to others.
- Children need to respect diversity in languages and communication patterns.
- Children with limited English need to use their first language to increase their competency in English and to understand content.
- Children need to be part of a literacy community.
- Children need to use spoken, written, and visual language to accomplish their purposes (adapted from IRA & NCTE, 1996, p. 3).

For more information about reading and writing go to http://www.naeyc.org/about/positions/learning_read write.asp.

Some children have difficulty learning to read. Although this book suggests many activities to make learning the underlying concepts of reading more fun, it is your role to put the magic in reading. The best way to do that is to read to children. Read literature, poetry, and plays. Read to children even after they can read. Their ability to read and what they enjoy as literature may be on different levels. My favorite third grader announced after the first week of school that she liked all her teachers but one, the librarian. When asked why, she said, "She doesn't read to us." Reading is difficult; it requires many skills and complex tasks. These should be learned because of the elation of reading, not the drudgery and discipline of learning letter sounds and blends.

Writing

A classroom that provides the space, materials, time, and rewards for writing is a classroom in which children will write. Although we think of writing as beginning later than other communication skills, such thinking is due more to our inability to interpret the writing of children than to their lack of interest. From the time a toddler picks up a marker and puts the first stroke on the page, that child has become an author. Over time, with appropriate materials and encouragement, that author will go from scribbling, to drawings that may contain letters or words or tell a story, to writing words using invented spellings, to fluent writing that may involve editing and publication. Although some information about writing was included in reading, this section highlights other relevant areas.

For children with fine motor problems learning to write is challenging. Some of the challenge is in the writing itself, not the conceptualization. Support children in the way you teaching writing by using a variety of tools, adaptive grips, and computers. Reading and writing support each other. Help children see this connection.

One of the first things that children want to write is their name. However, even before children can write, they need to see you write. As you write, verbalize for the children why you are writing: "I am writing your name on the paper so I know that it is yours," "I am making a list of the things we need at the store so I don't forget," "I am writing a note to your mother so that she knows why you have a bandage on your finger." Children need to be aware of the purpose of writing from an early age. If a classmate is sick, suggest that the children write a get well note to her. In the age of the television and the telephone, it is important that children appreciate the value of writing.

Writing, like most other skills, progresses through developmental stages. Thus, writing a name, for example, typically progresses from "scribbling a name; writing a name in mock letters; copying a name; writing a name that is illegible; writing a first name legibly, but misspelled; writing a first name correctly with some letter reversals; writing a first name correctly; writing a first name with last initial; writing a first and last name legibly and correctly spelled" (Lamme, 1985, pp. 48–49).

The requirements necessary for writing vary with age. Very young children need both stand-up and sit-down places to write (Lamme, 1985). For young children, a chalkboard with large chalk, an easel with thick markers, or just a large piece of paper taped to the wall or any other flat surface can make a mural so that writing is a social event.

Although children can write almost anywhere, having a designated place in your classroom increases the likelihood that they will do so. Choose tables large enough for at least two and no more than four children. Tape the alphabet letters on the table so each child can refer to them as she writes. Think of writing as a social process, not an isolated experience. Children can ask each other questions about their writing. After writing, children need an audience for their written work if they choose to share it. An author's chair, where children can read to others what they have written, is part of the process.

As children become more experienced writers, the materials needed to be more diverse. The writing center should be equipped with a variety of paper: manila paper, wide-lined paper that covers the entire sheet as well as some that covers only half the sheet (which allows space for illustrations), and plain white paper. Add paper that is folded in half, small notepads, paper cut into interesting shapes, colored paper, and even stationery. Rubber stamps allow children to print their own stationery. Almost any light-colored paper will do; it is having a variety that is important. The writing tools need to be selected to match both the paper and the children using them. The youngest children (18 months to about 3 years) need water-soluble markers and large crayons or crayons with knobs on the top. They also need large paper. As children gain experience and proficiency, add thin markers and pencils that

have erasers, as well as a supply of interesting erasers. A pencil sharpener is a must; the small handheld ones are fine if they don't "walk home." Colored pencils add interest also. As children get older, you might add some of the writing and illustrating media that are more difficult to control, such as oil pastels, chalk, watercolors, and charcoal. One solution is to place the writing center near the art area so that children can freely use art materials to illustrate their writing.

Children need to think of writing as a process, and certain materials can help make that possible. Rewriting is often slow for children, so they need to have scissors and tape available for changes. Glue or paste is also helpful, as well as a stapler, hole punch, and brads to hold pages together (provided there are not younger children around). Add a ruler, gummed stickers, and other accessories. Although you might have all of these materials available, it is not necessary to have them all out at any one time. The particular materials and accessories used can vary with the theme or unit that is being studied and even the season of the year.

Increasingly, children and adults use the computer to word-process written work rather than to write it out by hand. This is particularly helpful for children with fine motor problems and specific learning disabilities. Because of this, it is important to separate your writing goals from your penmanship goals. Children do need to learn to write; however, when the content is the goal, I believe children should use whatever method helps them put their ideas into a print format. Therefore, in addition to the art table, I would have the computers located near the writing table with appropriate software to support writing, such as My First Amazing Diary or Diary Maker.

Implications for Educators

Children do not automatically become literate. It takes careful planning and instruction to support young children as they learn to speak and build their vocabulary, to listen and follow directions, and to become fluent readers and writers by the end of the preschool years. Building vocabulary is a particularly important aspect of speaking in early childhood. Think about how you can teach to ensure that the children you teach learn at least one new word every day and that they can use that word in appropriate contexts. Think about how much you and other adults talk in the early childhood classroom. Particularly think about English language learners and how much they will learn by listening (or not listening). Evaluate your expectations about how children learn and how much of the day they will listen. Think of the methods you can use to make information more relevant by tapping into prior knowledge and by presenting information in a variety of formats.

Look at the skills needed for reading such as letter recognition, phonemic awareness, segmenting words into sounds, and decoding printed text. Think of ways of teaching these skills to instill in children a love of reading while making learning the necessary skills fun and interesting. Reflect on the 20 percent of children who may not learn to read easily. How will you identify these children early before they see themselves as struggling readers and what will you do to help them?

Writing is a difficult skill for many young children. Reflect on how you can provide opportunities to support children's interest in writing as they work to master the skills. Think of ways to make language and literacy important to children and how to integrate it into other curriculum areas.

Discovery Standards

Discovery describes both curriculum and an approach to a curriculum area. The approach is one of *doing* math, *doing* science, and *working* with computers. This is not drill and practice but developing an understanding of underlying concepts.

Mathematics

Mathematics is an area that causes concern for many people. When children have trouble remembering math facts at whatever level, adults usually try to intervene, perhaps by getting flash cards or writing numbers for children to count, copy, add, or subtract. Such an approach is rarely effective, even though the facts are reviewed over and over again.

Some children with specific learning disabilities find math particularly challenging. Building a strong sensory motor base helps them as they move into the more abstract areas of mathematics. Finding out specifically what children know and starting there helps children develop a solid foundation.

The National Council of Teachers of Mathematics (NCTM) discussed their ideas about math in a document called *Curriculum and Evaluation Standards for School Mathematics*. After these standards had been used in the field, the NCTM evaluated their effectiveness and decided to rethink some of their expectations to ensure that children could not only do math but use math. The outcome was six principles and ten standards that apply to all children from prekindergarten through grade 12.

The six principles, or overarching themes, include:

- *Equity.* All students need good mathematics skills.
- *Curriculum.* Mathematics is more than work sheets; there must be a coherent plan in which skills build upon each other across the grades.
- *Teaching.* Educators need to know what children know and need to learn, and challenge and support them to learn it.
- *Learning.* Children need to learn mathematics in the context of prior knowledge and experience.
- *Assessment.* Assessment should support learning and provide useful feedback to children and teachers.
- *Technology.* Technology is essential in mathematics, as it influences what is taught and enhances learning (NAEYC & NCTM, 2002).

The standards are divided into five content standards: numbers and operations, geometry, measurement, algebra, and data analysis and probability. There are also five process standards: problem solving, reasoning and proof, communication, connections, and representation. Although these apply to all grade levels, the expectation is that the standards receive different emphasis at different grade levels. For prekindergarten to grade two the major emphasis is on numbers and operations, followed by geometry and measurement. By high school, the major emphasis is algebra (NCTM, 2003).

Numbers and Operations

Children need to do the following:

- Understand numbers, ways of representing numbers, relationships among numbers and number systems.
- Understand meanings of operations and how they relate to one another.
- Compute fluently and make reasonable estimates (NCTM, 2003).

Children need to learn the basic computational skills: addition, multiplication, subtraction, and division. They need to develop computational fluency. That is, they need to be able to conceptualize what operations are needed, to do them proficiently, and to judge whether or not the results of their calculations are reasonable. They also need to know which tools (mental calculations, paper and pencil, or a calculator) to use. By the end of second grade, children should know the basics of addition and subtraction for two-digit numbers (NCTM, 2003).

One of the major understandings children need during the early childhood years is that a number can be decomposed and thought about in a variety of ways (NCTM, 2003). That is, children need to know that the number thirty-three is three tens and three ones and it is also three sets of eleven. Many children understand the relationship among numbers up to ten during kindergarten and can often count as high as 100. They may not understand, however, that in our base ten system, there are eight tens in eighty, although they may be able to count to 100 by tens. Children need to learn about odd and even numbers and why this is relevant. All of this is to say that understanding mathematical concepts requires far more than identifying numbers and young children need many concrete mathematical experiences.

Geometry

Children should be able to do the following:

- Analyze characteristics and properties of two- and three-dimensional geometric shapes and develop mathematical arguments about geometric relationships.
- Specify locations and describe spatial relationships using coordinate geometry and other representational systems.
- Apply transformations and use symmetry to analyze mathematical situations.
- Use visualization, spatial reasoning, and geometric modeling to solve problems (NCTM, 2003).

Geometry helps children focus their reasoning, but has a strong concentration on properties and their relationships. Children can learn some of this informally through form boards and block building. During the preschool years the focus is primarily on concrete reasoning and looking at the relationship between shape and function. Children need to learn the language of relative position (under, over, behind, near, and so on) and to learn to look at things from different perspectives. In the early years, help children look at a block structure from different angles and discuss what they see. You can extend this by using a digital camera to take a picture of the structure from different angles and perspectives and talk about it again.

Children learn basic geometric shapes during the preschool years. By kindergarten, children can usually identify basic shapes such as triangles, circles, squares, and rectangles, although the latter two may be confused. Although children can see differences in types of triangles, they cannot usually articulate these differences. With experience, they discover the relationships among these figures and what makes each unique. Children need exposure to many different shapes: plain, colored, large and small, and even embedded in each other to sort out the qualities that remain stable.

Measurement

Children should be able to do the following:

- Understand measurable attributes of objects and the units, systems, and processes of measurement.
- Apply appropriate techniques, tools, and formulas to determine measurements (NCTM, 2003).

Measurement is practical and pervasive in many aspects of everyday life. Young children enjoy measuring and comparing what they have measured. They learn about length and the concepts of shorter and longer. Children have to measure concrete materials before they get into weight, time, area, and volume.

Understanding relative size and the vocabulary that goes with it is a necessary math skill. The vocabulary of size is part of all of our lives. We want a "little" more to drink and the "largest" piece of pie. Children are curious about how "big" they were when they were born and how "tall" they are now. Children like compare their height over a span of months and years. However, children grow slowly compared to bulbs and seeds that can also be sized, measured, and charted. Have children predict whether things will be bigger or smaller than others and then have them check out their estimates.

Children can measure length, weight, area, and volume. Before children can be expected to use standard units of measurement, such as feet and inches or meters and centimeters, they need to understand that measuring describes things in small increments. Children can use their hands, feet, books, popsicle sticks, blocks, or whatever is handy to measure length; scales and balances are used for weight; squares for area; and marbles or liquids to ascertain volume. Standard measures hold little meaning for children. It is only when two children measure the same item and get different results that the need for a standard becomes apparent. One child may claim that the water table is eleven hands long, another that it is really thirteen. Obviously, their hands are different sizes or their spacing was different.

Children need to learn number and measurement concepts before they can understand basic time concepts. (Telling time usually is not taught until the end of the early childhood years.) Children begin to learn underlying time concepts by using a calendar and by discussing time sequences for class activities: "We will have a snack, go outside, and then it will be time to go home."

Algebra

For young children, algebra focuses on understanding patterns, relations, and functions. Children need to have experience classifying objects and ordering them. They need to identify, make, and extend patterns. Playing "before and after" games is helpful. Just playing "What number comes before or after X (seven)?" is helpful, as is having children produce sequences or patterns. Patterning can be done with silverware, crayons, markers, or anything that you have enough of to manipulate. Children enjoy counting backward as well as forward, especially if they are jumping or "blasting off."

Board games in which children toss dice or spin to determine the number of spaces to move help establish knowledge of patterns and relationships, especially if one can be "sent back." Card games such as Fish, War, Hearts, Solitaire, Concentration, Skip-Bo, and Uno are also fun and great ways to learn. Dominoes and Double Nines are other excellent activities to teach matching, patterns, and addition and subtraction.

Data Analysis and Probability

Children need to formulate questions that can be answered with data and to collect, organize, and display relevant data to answer them. Children may take a survey of their classroom to see who likes avocados after they have all tasted them and graph their results.

Because math requires few formal props, play math games while waiting or during transitions. Children learn as much from fun activities as from those that seem "academic." The math problems we commonly associate with school are a formalization of experiences that relate to numbers, geometry, measurement, time, and money.

The recommendations set forth in a joint position paper of the NAEYC and NCTM identify characteristics of high-quality mathematics education for children 3 to 6 years. In these programs educators attempt to do the following:

- Enhance children's natural interest in mathematics and their dispositions to use it to make sense of their physical and social worlds.
- Build on children's experience and knowledge, including their family, linguistic, cultural, and community backgrounds; their individual approaches to learning; and their informal knowledge.
- Base mathematics curriculum and teaching practices on current knowledge of young children's cognitive, linguistic, physical, and social-emotional development.
- Use curriculum and teaching practices that strengthen children's problem-solving and reasoning processes as well as representing, communicating, and connecting mathematical ideas.
- Integrate mathematics with other activities and other activities with mathematics.
- Provide ample time, materials, and teacher support for children to engage in play, a context in which they explore and manipulate mathematical ideas with keen interest.
- Actively introduce mathematical concepts, methods, and language through a range of appropriate experiences and teaching strategies.
- Support children's learning by thoughtfully and continually assessing all children's mathematical knowledge, skills, and strategies (NAEYC & NCTM, 2002, p. 3).

It is beyond the scope of this book to detail all the standards and processes that have been developed by the National Council of Teachers of Mathematics, but I strongly urge you to visit their web site. Not only do they have the standards there, but they have ideas for implementing them at http://www.nctm.org. You can see the complete position statement on Early Childhood Mathematics: Promoting Good Beginnings at http://www.naeyc.org/about/positions/pdf/psmath.pdf.

Science

Science, or sciencing, is a process, a way of knowing about the world. Science facts will change, but the process of generating these facts is relatively stable. Science is both knowledge about specific phenomena and the strategies or processes used to collect and evaluate the information. The application of science to human problems (technology) is part of science (National Center of Improving Science Education, 1990; National Science Teachers Association, 1996).

Science is particularly relevant to children with disabilities. Much of what we know about disabilities is based on science and the hopes that we have for discovering more is through the scientific process. Some children may need support in being curious about their world and others may need parts of their world brought to them. Technology, simple and sophisticated, promises opportunities that were not available 30 years ago.

Three goals are recommended for *sciencing* with young children, which include:

- To develop each child's innate curiosity about the world.
- To broaden each child's procedural and thinking skills for investigating the world, solving problems, and making decisions.
- To increase each child's knowledge of the natural world (National Center of Improving Science Education, 1990).

For children in kindergarten to fourth grade, National Science Education Standards have been developed by the National Academy of Sciences. They are available on the web at http://www.nap.edu/readingroom/books/nses/html/6c.html. The ones relevant to young children are detailed as follows:

Grades K–4 Standards

Content Standard A: Science as Inquiry

- Abilities necessary to do scientific inquiry
- Understanding about scientific inquiry

Content Standard B: Physical Science

- Properties of objects and materials
- Position and motion of objects
- Light, heat, electricity, and magnetism

Content Standard C: Life Science

- The characteristics of organisms
- Life cycles of organisms
- Organisms and environments

Content Standard D: Earth and Space Science

- Properties of earth materials
- Objects in the sky
- Changes in earth and sky

Content Standard E: Science and Technology

- Abilities of technological design
- Understanding about science and technology
- Abilities to distinguish between natural objects and objects made by humans

Content Standard F: Science in Personal and Social Perspectives

- Personal health
- Characteristics and changes in populations
- Types of resources
- Changes in environments
- Science and technology in local challenges (National Academy of Science, 1995)

To learn more about the national science standards go to http://www.nap.edu/readingroom/books/nses/html.

Children need to develop a respectful curiosity about the beauty, orderliness, and balance of the world. They need to develop skills to gather data; this requires observation. The next step requires that these observations be organized in some useful way so information can be classified and hypotheses can be generated. These hypotheses need to be tested through experimentation and the results recorded. The last step in the process is the sharing and application of the knowledge gained.

Children need the opportunity to explore materials on their own, with minimal adult supervision. Initially, children need to be asked questions such as "What do you think will happen?", "What else could you try?", and so on. Such questions aid children in exploring materials and learning about their properties. Your goal is to have children discover as many properties as they can and to encourage their discovery of more subtle aspects of materials. Give as little guidance as possible to promote the most learning. Children are not just learning facts; far more important, they are learning how to learn.

Technology expands children's worlds especially when it is a shared experience.

Technology

Technology is part of today's life. The question is how to use it in a developmentally appropriate way as an optimal learning experience for children. Computers offer children a source of communication and a way of exerting control over their environment. Children can make a plan, carry it out, and see the outcome of their actions. Children need to be exposed to a variety of technologies including computers, the Internet, email, digital cameras, tape recorders, calculators, and so on. In early childhood technology should be a social experience. Computers should have at least two chairs around them for children or a child and adult to work together. Software needs to be chosen that facilitates the interactive use of technology (NAEYC, 2006).

Work in adapting computers to serve as a resource for children with disabilities is an important part of the field's growth. Computers can be customized for children with severe physical or sensory impairments using switches, voice and music synthesizers, robots, and other peripherals.

The key to using computers in early childhood is selecting appropriately designed software and modifying the hardware to be responsive to the developmental needs of the child. The criteria for evaluating software set forth by Haugland (2002) in the *Haugland Developmental Software Scale and the Haugland/Gerzog Developmental Scale for Web Sites* are useful for determining the developmental appropriateness of web sites and software. Both scales have ten criteria. A summary of the criteria follows:

1. *Age appropriateness:* Think about the age of the children. Regardless of the computer, would you expect children this age to do these types of activities? The focus is on one or more valuable learning objectives. Do the teaching methods meet the needs of children rather than requiring the child to adapt to the software or web site? Any software used should support curriculum objectives.
2. *Child control:* Does the computer request responses from the child or does the child control the computer? The computer is only a tool. Control should be with the child. She should set the pace and return to the main menu when she desires. There should be visual or verbal prompts to assist her as she moves throughout the site.
3. *Clear instructions:* How easy are the instructions for young children who do not read? To the extent that directions are dependent on the teacher's reading to the children, children are being taught dependence in a medium that should foster independence. Directions should be simple, precise, and verbal, or have picture choices.
4. *Expanding complexity:* Software should start where the child is and grow with her. It should be designed to provide increasingly challenging tasks, not solely repetition, and it should have the potential to teach powerful ideas.
5. *Independence:* The goal of computers is to make children independent of adults. Software must be selected to support this concept. Using a computer independently or with peers supports self-esteem, confidence, and learning. That does not diminish the teacher's responsibility to supervise computer activities; it means that their role is to enrich and expand learning, not choose and load the software. Children should be encouraged to work together to solve problems.
6. *Nonviolence:* Violence in software is a particular concern because frequently it is the child who initiates and controls the violence. They are not just seeing it, they are doing it. Children don't experience the results of their violent behavior when they use software. When they start it again, everything and everyone is as good as new. This is not true in real life. Software can and should enhance positive social values both on the screen and off.
7. *Process orientation:* Computers are discovery-oriented media; the reward is in the process.
8. *Real-world model:* In the real world, houses are larger than children and eyebrows fit on faces. Look at the software to see if the images on the screen reflect this orientation. Children need to learn how the real world works; software should present accurate information.
9. *Technical features:* Graphics and sound should support the program. Cluttered designs and too much sound detract. The program should load quickly, and the disks need to be sturdy. The software and web sites should be colorful and allow children to control the animation. It is important that programs are consistent so children learn when they do X, Y happens. Printing allows children to share their experiences and use them in off computer applications. It also allows them to be part of a child's portfolio. Software should also allow children to save their work so they can start where they left off as opposed to starting at the beginning again.
10. *Transformations:* Computers have the potential for making changes at the stroke of a key. Children can make designs and re-create them without the redrawing necessary in other media.

The final element of the scale is an anti-bias deduction, which is designed to ensure that software accurately reflects the diversity of the global society in which children live (Haugland, 2002).

Much of the software that is on the market today for young children is not developmentally appropriate. In 2006 the National Association for the Education of Young Children issued a revised position statement on Technology and Young Children—Ages 3 through 8. They believe that "Educators must use professional judgment in evaluating and using this learning tool appropriately; applying the same criteria they would to any other learning tool or experience" (NAEYC, 2006c, p. 1). They offer the following guidance for using technology with young children:

- Used appropriately, technology can enhance children's cognitive and social abilities.
- Appropriate technology is integrated into the regular learning environment and used as one of many options to support children's learning.
- Early childhood educators should promote equitable access to technology for all children and their families. Children with special needs should have increased access when this is helpful.

- The power of technology to influence children's learning and development requires that attention be paid to eliminating stereotyping of any group and eliminating exposure to violence, especially as a problem-solving strategy.
- Teachers, in collaboration with parents, should advocate for more appropriate technology applications for all children.
- The appropriate use of technology has many implications for early childhood professional development (NAEYC, 2006c).

If you don't have enough time to do all the footwork, use web sites like http://www.childrensoftware.com for their reviews of software for both home and school.

To make traditional computers work, children must be able to implement a single keystroke. Without this skill, typing looks like this: *ppppppppppppppppp*—and the computer cannot interpret it (the sensitivity of the keyboard can be controlled to make this easier). Once children can make a single keystroke, they need to build keyboarding skills. These skills involve learning to locate keys, reading and selecting from a menu, and giving commands. Additionally, children need to learn about the computer itself and how to make it run. They also must develop the necessary fine motor and sensory integration skills. Computers have tremendous potential for positive change for children with diverse abilities. They need adult scaffolding to make the system work. As we begin to think about the area of computing with children, it too has a set of standards that relate to what children should know and be able to do.

The International Society for Technology in Education (ISTE) took the leadership in establishing the National Educational Technology Standards for Students. They identified six categories that apply to students of all ages. These include

1. Creativity and Innovation
2. Communication and Collaboration
3. Research and Information Fluency
4. Critical Thinking, Problem Solving, and Decision Making
5. Digital Citizenship
6. Technology Operations and Concepts (ISTE, 2007)

Technology literate children between ages 4 and 8 are expected to engage in the following types of activities:

- Write and illustrate ideas and stories using digital tools.
- Identify, research and collect data on a topic and propose solutions.
- Engage others through email and other electronic means.
- Work collaboratively to produce a digital presentation or product.
- Find and evaluate digital information about people, places, and things.
- Use simulations and graphical organizers.
- Demonstrate safe, responsible, cooperative use of technology.
- Communicate about technology accurately.
- Navigate virtual environments such as electronic books, software, and web sites. (ISTE, 2007).

The expectation is that by the first or second grade, children should be able to recognize a web site and work in that site using links. They should be able to use the basic tools of a browser to go forward, back, and home. By grades three or four, they can be expected to recognize the components of a URL (web site address) and to access a web site by using a URL. They should be able to use a children's search engine (such as Yahooligan) to find information. Additionally, they should be able to send and receive email. Appropriately used, computers hold potential for helping all young children, particularly children with disabilities. Your role is to help children see technology as a natural part of everyday life.

Implications for Educators

It is important that children develop positive attitudes toward mathematics, science, and technology and view themselves as competent in these areas. During their early years, children learn about math informally. Adults help children connect their experiences to mathematical knowledge. Educators set the stage by providing children access to books and stories with numbers and patterns, and they integrate math with music and language. They provide children with the opportunities to count, sort, categorize, match, and so on. They help children make comparisons and learn the language of mathematics. Math includes activities such as counting, measuring, using blocks, playing games, and so on. Children need opportunities to solve problems and talk about their solutions. Both computers and calculators play a role in learning math. Children need to learn when and how they are best used.

Children sometimes know more about math than is conventionally tested. Teachers need to use a variety of assessments to find out what children know so they can plan appropriately for each child. Numbers and operations form the basis for most mathematics curriculum, whether it is using them to solve simple problems, such as how many crackers we need so each child has one, or complex data analysis. Numbers are for more than counting. Children need to know that numbers can be represented with objects or numerals, they need to know how to use numbers and operations to solve problems and that numbers are part of a rule-based system.

Children write numbers less frequently than they write letters or words, so they may be less skillful in writing numbers than letters. Reversals of numbers in the preschool years are common, with the numbers two, three, six, seven, and nine the most frequently reversed. These numbers continue to be reversed even after children are consistently writing all of their alphabet letters correctly (Lamme, 1985). In addition to signaling inadequate left-right orientation, reversals may be one sign of a problem with patterns and relationships.

Exposing children to informal science and experiences is not enough to build necessary concepts; but it is a necessary first step. Many activities in this area require at least two days and often more. The second time the materials are out, some children will continue to explore the materials; others will need more structure to expand their explorations. It is important that children view science as part of their world and that they see the cause-and-effect relationships rather than "teacher magic."

Think about the discovery standards. What qualities make them relevant and good examples of best practice? As you think about the mathematics you will do in the classroom, how do they guide what you will plan and expect from children? What concepts might support you in other curriculum areas? What can you do in your teaching to help children see themselves as scientists? To build scientific concepts your curriculum has to support the process. What will you do to ensure this happens? Why do you think science has such a strong discovery base? Think about how you will use technology to put children in charge, not the other way around. Children are intrigued with technology. However there are concerns about the types of technology children are using and what they are learning from it. How will you choose software wisely for young children and what advice will you give parents as they support their children in this area?

Wellness Standards

Wellness is an overriding concern for all children. It goes beyond the lack of illness to a way of looking at well-being. Children who are hungry, who live in unsafe environments, and who struggle with tensions at home may not come to school ready to learn. They may lack energy, motivation, or attention. School needs to be a safe haven for children, one in which they can feel free to devote their energy to learning.

Health and Safety

Health and safety are areas of study as well as states of being. When young children become aware of what it means to be unhealthy and have the knowledge and vocabulary to describe their symptoms, there is less likelihood of serious, undetected illness. When they have learned to recognize signs of danger and act appropriately, the environment will be less threatening to them. Children need to refine their awareness and skills in these areas. Only children who are healthy and feel safe are free to enter into your program fully. Children learn basic health practices as part of routines (such as washing their hands after toileting and before snack).

The Joint Committee on National Health Education Standards (1995) developed the National Health Education Standards: Achieving Health Literacy. Young children achieve health literacy through experience and related learning activities (Hendricks & Smith, 1995). The abstracted standards include concepts relating to health promotion and disease prevention; accessing health information, products, and services; practicing health-enhancing behaviors and reducing health risks; using interpersonal communication skills to enhance health; learning skills in setting goals and making decisions to enhance health; and advocating for personal, family, and community health.

In early childhood, most of the emphasis is placed on the development of a healthy lifestyle, including good hygiene and nutrition, the prevention of infectious diseases and injuries and participating in structured and unstructured physical activity. Safety education focuses on self-awareness and the prevention of injuries in the classroom and at home. Common accidents for young children include falls; burns; eating small, sharp objects or poisonous substances; choking; smothering; traffic accidents; and water accidents. Children need skills to avoid these situations and to cope if they have not avoided them.

Proper nutrition is an important part of being healthy. Childhood obesity is a concern. About 20 percent of children and adolescents between 6 and 19 are overweight, and almost 15 percent of young children 2 through 5 years are overweight. These rates are increasing and have tripled for all age groups between the NANES 1971–1974 and the 2003–2004 survey (CDC, 2007b). Between 10 and 12 percent of infants' birth to 23 months are overweight based on the CDC growth charts (CDC, 2007c).

Increases in overweight after age 2 suggests that the infant and toddler years provide a window of opportunity to target nutritional messages and to initiate healthful eating practices (Mennella, Ziegler, Briefel, & Novak, 2006). With the current concerns about obesity, there is a renewed interest in nutrition for very young children. Nutrition during the first three years in interaction with genetics and activity level helps determine growth patterns and can prevent some diseases. The patterns established during these years may program preferences into the brain that influence adolescent and adult nutrition.

Obesity prevention involves maintaining a healthy weight while meeting health and nutritional needs. Energy balance means that energy input is equivalent to energy expenditure. Young children need a slightly positive energy balance to grow. With young children, the goal is healthy eating. The other part of the energy equation is energy output or physical activity. The goal is for children to become physically active for life. For this to happen they need to develop fundamental motor skills as young children.

Physical Education

The National Association for Sport and Physical Education (NASPE) published its national education standards in 2002. The standards are for *all* children. The role of the teacher is to include *all* children in meeting the standards. The content standards for a physically educated kindergartner are as follows:

- Demonstrates competency in many movement forms and proficiency in a few movement forms.
- Applies movement concepts and principles to the learning and development of motor skills.
- Exhibits a physically active lifestyle.
- Achieves and maintains a health-enhancing level of physical fitness.
- Demonstrates responsible personal and social behavior in physical activity settings.
- Demonstrates understanding and respect for differences among people in physical activity settings.
- Understands that physical activity provides the opportunity for enjoyment, challenge, self-expression, and social interaction.

The content standards are the same at the early childhood age level; the assessment guide reflects increasingly complex motor activities and thinking.

Structured physical activity for young children is "planned and directed by the parent, caregiver, or teacher and is designed to accommodate the infant, toddler, or preschooler's developmental level" (NASPE, 2002, p. 18).

When physical activity is adult directed children obtain significant amounts of moderate and vigorous physical activity (Ward, Saunders, & Pate, 2007). **Unstructured physical activity** is "child-initiated physical activity that occurs as the child explores his or her environment" (NASPE, 2002, p. 18).

Most children do acquire **fundamental movement skills** in unstructured physical activity. However, they never achieve an advanced level without instruction, practice, and encouragement that are available only in structured physical activity (NASPE, 2002). These early skills provide the foundation on which later skills are built. Children who lack these skills often choose not to participate in physical activities as they get older and games become competitive (Graham, Holt-Hale, & Parker, 2005).

During the preschool years, children should be encouraged to practice movement skills in a variety of activities and settings. Instruction and positive reinforcement is critical during this time to ensure that children develop most of these skills before entering school (NASPE, 2002).

There are no recommendations for the amount of physical activity infants need. The National Association for Sport and Physical Education (2002) has recommended five physical activity guidelines for toddlers and preschoolers:

1. Toddlers should accumulate at least 30 minutes daily of structured physical activity; preschoolers at least 60 minutes.
2. Toddlers and preschoolers should engage in at least 60 minutes and up to several hours per day of unstructured physical activity and should not be sedentary for more than 60 minutes at a time except when sleeping.
3. Toddlers and preschoolers should develop movement skills that are building blocks for more complex movement tasks.
4. Toddlers and preschoolers should have indoor and outdoor areas that meet or exceed recommended safety standards for performing large muscle activities.
5. Individuals responsible for the well-being of toddlers and preschoolers should be aware of the importance of physical activity and facilitate the child's movement skills.

For both structured and unstructured physical activities to happen they need to be incorporated into the schedule and embedded in routines and transitions.

Implications for Educators

As we become increasingly concerned about health and safety related issues these too come into the standards mix. If standards show what is important for children and their well-being, reflect on the need for nutrition standards and the relationship between nutrition and disabilities. When you think about snack do you think about juice and crackers? Neither are wise choices. Do you think obesity is a disability? Think about how you would arrange a schedule to include the recommended amounts of structured and unstructured physical activity in an early childhood program. How will you go about rethinking the areas of physical activity and nutrition in light of this information?

Creative Arts Standards

All children are creative. Some are more creative than others. Some children are more creative in one area than in other areas. As children interact with the environment, the response they get to their creative efforts plays a large part in their creative development.

As children get older, they are increasingly rewarded for convergent thinking. Children also need to be supported in divergent thinking. The world is changing too quickly to predict the kinds of knowledge children will need in 20 years. They need to develop processes that allow many potential solutions and methods for figuring out how to solve problems. This approach to problem solving begins now. Children who know only how to acquire facts and who are rewarded for conformity and neatness may not be equipped to solve tomorrow's problems.

What is creativity? Creativity is a process of thinking, acting, or making something that is new or different. It doesn't mean that a person has to be the first one to produce a product, but it does mean it is a new experience for that particular person.

The creative process can be thought of in two stages. The first is the thinking or idea stage: Children play with what they want to do in their mind. The second stage is the implementation stage. This is the "doing" stage: Children try out their ideas. This process is probably best thought of as a circular rather than a linear process, as children change their thinking and actions as they get feedback from the process.

Children gain many benefits when their creativity is fostered. Rewarding creativity helps develop a positive self concept. It supports children's finding alternative solutions to problems and expressing their own ideas. Children learn to take risks to develop new skills and also learn about their own uniqueness. These are particularly positive qualities for children with diverse abilities.

Educators can support creativity in two major ways: by supporting the creative process itself; and by providing the time, space, and materials necessary to foster creativity. The Consortium of National Arts Education Associations (1994, pp. 122–127) developed national standards for arts education including the visual arts, music, dance, and theater. To see all of the content and achievement standards for the arts go to http://www.artsedge.org/teach/standards.cfm. The arts are a mainstay in the early childhood curriculum. The visual arts offer opportunities for individual participation as well as for being part of a group.

Visual Arts

Visual arts for young children are messy, fun, and exploratory. They range from squashing sponges and watching how much paint drips, to rolling and pounding playdough; from gluing paper, cloth, and macaroni, to coloring or scribbling with water-based markers, chalk, or crayons. Art is actively engaging materials. It is not making something that looks like everyone else's; nor is it gluing precut objects in the same place as does everyone else. Art is an experience, a process. The best art may never hang on the refrigerator door. It may remain in the child's mind.

The visual arts help children learn about color, texture, moods, and ways to use this information to display what they know and can do.

Art helps young children understand the properties of materials. Children's first response to any new medium is one of exploration. What can it do? What are the limits? What do I like to do with it? Curiosity abounds. Allowing children to explore these differences and helping them figure out the variables to test is far more useful than explaining to them that objects stuck with glue will stay when turned upside down, whereas paint is unlikely to hold objects together. They learn thin paint runs down a page faster than thick paint.

At 12 months, children can begin to do simple art projects. By 3 years, these patterns begin to have more structure and children can tell you about them. With increasing age, products become more important, and this is the time when reinforcing the process aspect is imperative. If children decide they don't draw well, they may decide not to draw. Some children will have better products than others. However, the process is as important as the product.

The content standards for children in the visual arts for kindergarten through grade 4 follow:

- Understanding and applying media, techniques, and processes.
- Using knowledge of structures and functions.
- Choosing and evaluating a range of subject matter, symbols, and idea.
- Understanding the visual arts in relation to history and cultures.

- Reflecting on and assessing the characteristics and merits of their work and the work of others.
- Making connections between visual arts and other disciplines (Consortium of National Arts Education Associations, 1994).

Music

Music can be soothing or stimulating; it can promote social activity; it can be used anytime anywhere. Traditionally, music has not been integrated with the rest of the curriculum. It has been restricted to a "music period" and taught without any goal beyond the vague one of teaching children music. Music can be used to meet a number of educational goals. It can teach and reinforce skills that are part of other curriculum areas. Music is also an academic field in and of itself, with its own standards established by the Music Educators National Conference (1994a). This organization has a very child-centered approach to learning. Their standards are based on the following beliefs:

- All children have musical potential.
- Children bring their own unique interests and abilities to the music learning environment.
- Very young children are capable of developing critical thinking skills through musical ideas.
- Children come to early childhood music experiences from diverse backgrounds.
- Children should experience exemplary musical sounds, activities, and materials.
- Children should not be encumbered with the need to meet performance goals.
- Children's play is their work.
- Children learn best in pleasant physical and social environments.
- Diverse learning environments are needed to serve the development of many individual children.
- Children need effective adult models (MENC, 1994b, p. 9).

As with other areas of the arts, music educators have included children below kindergarten. Content standards for children 2 through 4 years include

- Singing and playing instruments
- Creating music
- Responding to music
- Understanding music (National Association for Music Education, 2002).

Content standards for children five through eight years have more detail and show that children are increasing their confidence and skill.

- Singing, alone and with others, a varied repertoire of music.
- Performing on instruments, alone and with others, a varied repertoire of music.
- Improvising melodies, variations, and accompaniments.
- Composing and arranging music within specific guidelines.
- Reading and notating music.
- Listening to, analyzing, and describing music.
- Evaluating music and music performances.

- Understanding relationships between music, the other arts, and disciplines outside the arts.
- Understanding music in relation to history and culture (National Association for Music Education, 2008).

Music is a multisensory experience. Music can foster learning skills without sacrificing the goals and objectives or the standards of a music education program. The goal of music is to "acquire a disposition for lifelong musical interest" (Andress, 1995, p. 107). Children learn new words and develop memory skills as they recall songs from one time to the next. They develop a sense of rhythm as they sing and listen to music.

Musical experiences need to match the developmental level of the child. By one year, children begin to actively participate in musical activities. They clap and hit drums or xylophones in a purposeful way. They dance for their own pleasure, as they often continue after the music stops (Mayesky, 2002). About age 2, children enjoy learning simple songs, especially those that include movement. Songs need to be short. By 3, children may have favorite songs and can recognize some tunes. They may want to add words or motions to songs for a new verse. They learn longer songs. By age 4, children participate in singing games and more actively participate in selecting musical experiences. With increasing age, children can sit longer and enjoy songs and dances that have rules (Mayesky, 2002). By 7 or 8, children can read the words to songs, and some become interested in more formalized music training.

The overlap of music and listening skills is obvious. Children learn to differentiate pitch, rhythm, and intensity. As children become older, they enter into some of the more visual aspects of music, such as visually discriminating the musical notes and symbols and then integrating this information into auditory output. Pairing music with movement can use both gross and fine motor skills and supports sensory integration. The mood of the music can set the pace for the movement.

Creative Movement

Movement helps children become aware of their bodies. This awareness helps them express feelings and moods, improve self-control, and learn how to relax at will. Children discover ways to relax and to work off excess energy. Movement activities develop rhythm and balance. Creative movement and dance can provide sensory integration and an opportunity for creativity and expression.

The Consortium of National Arts Education Associations also developed content standards in the area of dance for children kindergarten to fourth grade:

- Identifying and demonstrating movement elements and skills in performing dance.
- Understanding choreographic principles, processes, and structures.
- Understanding dance as a way to create and communicate meaning.
- Applying and demonstrating critical and creative thinking skills in dance.
- Demonstrating and understanding dance in various cultures and historical periods.
- Making connections between dance and healthful living.

- Making connections between dance and other disciplines (The Kennedy Center, 2008).

Creative movement and dance are particularly helpful for children with behavior and emotional disorders as they can participate without fear of being judged. It allows you to meet autistic children when they are and help them into more functional movement patterns.

Creative movement and dance is not a child-sized version of calisthenics with a "no pain, no gain" philosophy. It is the way young children learn how their bodies work. Creative movement is a personal statement about one's inner self. This is what differentiates it from functional movement, which usually has a practical purpose such as running to get a ball. Creative movement is a way of supporting classroom management and obesity prevention. Get music with a fast beat and have a dance party. Count children as you jump and reach, march, and move.

Dramatic Play

Dramatic play is spontaneous, self-expressive play through which children can learn to understand themselves and their relation to others and to the world around them. In dramatic play, children construct a world in which they can make up for defeats and frustrations and experiment with different ways of working out fears, feelings, and uncertainties. Dramatic play can help children grow in social understanding and cooperation; it provides a controlled emotional outlet and a means of self-expression.

Dramatic play for young children starts out with what they know the best: domestic scenes. Children cook, clean, care for younger children, leave for work and return, have visitors, and so on. They begin with familiar roles. A second theme is superimposed upon the first and involves a rescue mission. The baby is sick, someone has fallen and broken a leg, and the children focus their play around solving the problem presented. Once solved, a new "problem" is likely to occur. The third theme is sudden threat. A monster appears to carry off a victim, wild animals threaten to attack, and villains must be beaten off. Children reenact these themes over and over again. The setting changes, and with increasing age, the play becomes more sophisticated, but the themes remain. The play itself, however, often is chaotic, violent, noisy, and difficult to manage. It sometimes involves children who "don't want to play" as unwilling victims. It needs firm guidelines to work for all the children in the class.

As play becomes more sophisticated and children are older dramatic play turns into more planned and formalized play called theater. This may involve assigned roles and a written script. The Consortium of National Arts Education Associations also developed content standards in the area of theater for children kindergarten to fourth grade:

- Script writing by planning and recording improvisations based on personal experience and heritage, imagination, literature, and history.
- Acting by assuming roles and interacting in improvisations.
- Designing by visualizing and arranging environments for classroom dramatizations.
- Directing by planning classroom dramatizations.

- Researching by finding information to support classroom dramatizations.
- Comparing and connecting art forms by describing theatre, dramatic media (such as film, television, and electronic media), and other art forms.
- Analyzing and explaining personal preferences and constructing meanings from classroom dramatizations and from theatre, film, television, and electronic media productions.
- Understanding context by recognizing the role of theatre, film, television, and electronic media in daily life (The Kennedy Center, 2008).

Implications for Educators

With standards and legislation so clearly focused on literacy and math there is concern that the creative arts will systematically be eliminated. The arts provide a lifelong means of expressing feelings and gaining enjoyment. Art allows children to be part of a group while at the same time expressing their feelings and creativity without being judged different or strange. Children can react to art and talk about the characteristics that appeal to them or do not in a particular work as well as in their own art. Children can explore materials and express themselves in a visual form, and they can look back at past artwork and see how they have changed.

To support the visual arts in your program schedule time for children to paint, draw, glue, color, and use dough or clay each day. Do *not* provide a model for the children to copy. When children request a model, help them visualize what they want to draw and emphasize the process, not the product. Differentiate between art and fine motor development. Keep art activities for art. Teach academic tasks like letter printing or coloring within the lines for other times. Show interest in what the children are doing and display everyone's original artwork regardless of quality. Instead of asking, "What did you make?" say, "Tell me about your picture."

Audiovisual equipment can be used both as a source of creativity and as a method of capturing creativity so that it can be shared or viewed at a later time. Consider videotaping a creative movement experience or the dramatic play area and then showing it to the children. Children can use digital cameras and record the events of a field trip with photographs. Encourage children to record their voices and play them back, or record the group singing and then listen. Children are intrigued with technology. Use it to encourage and support creativity.

Music supports language development especially for children with fluency disorders and is a way of building memory and vocabulary for children with specific language disabilities. As children vocalize sounds and words, they may create new verses to familiar songs. Music is also a social experience. Include music from many cultures, folk music, classical music, and contemporary selections. Think about music as a content area and what music can teach children. Reflect on its overlap with reading and math and how it supports those areas as well as having its own standards.

Creative movement has no right or wrong movements but the potential for moving can encourage children to think about situations and integrate that cognitive information with what their body does. Reflect on how you can use this knowledge to support movement and learning.

You can use dramatic play as an index to measure children's development. By observing dramatic play you can assess small and large motor coordination, language development, social skills, concept formation and their developmental progression. Reflect on dramatic play and where it fits in with the standards movement. If early childhood theory supports children learning through play how do you see the amount of time devoted to play changing based on standards? Do you think you can justify play as a way of meeting standards? Be prepared to defend the time spent on creative arts in the early childhood curriculum and why they should be maintained.

Summary

Curriculum planning is complex and challenging. It requires looking at the relationship between one's personal philosophy, principles underlying developmentally appropriate practices and, how these fit with national, state, and district standards.

There is a concern about the level of educational attainment that all children are achieving in schools. In response to this concern, many professional organizations have developed national standards for children in a variety of areas. The standards impact education for *all* children. As children with disabilities are included in regular classrooms, they too will be assessed in these content areas.

Social studies is a broad area that looks at the child and the world in which he lives. There are many different sets of standards that are applied to social studies. Language and literacy is being emphasized and the requirements for pre-reading and reading skills permeates all curriculum areas. The mathematics and science curriculum focuses a hands-on approach to learning content and the underlying principles of the discovery process. Computers are part of the technology that supports discovery. Movement underlies many activities in early childhood as children learn to master the large and small muscles of their bodies. There is an emphasis on an early commitment to health and physical fitness. Creative arts has long been a focus of the early childhood curriculum. The standards in the visual arts support creativity and experiencing many different media. Music standards emphasize that all children have musical ability. The combination of music and movement leads to an integration of sensory experiences.

When these area standards are translated into activities that are flexible enough to meet the needs of all the children in the classroom and they are placed in the context of a relevant, developmentally appropriate theme or unit, the integrated curriculum emerges.

Reflections

1. Reflect on the impact of the standards movement. How do you think standards will influence what you teach and what children learn? How do you think they will affect children with disabilities, English language learners, and those who are eligible for a free lunch? How will you help all children meet the standards?

2. As an educator interested in professional development and successful teaching strategies, one must constantly use reflection as a tool for growth. What does reflective practice mean to you? What exactly does a reflective practitioner do? Are you a reflective practitioner? If not, how can you become one, and how can this help your teaching skills?

3. People in the United States are concerned about education and the level of achievement that children are reaching. They are particularly concerned about math, science, and reading. Among other industrialized nations the United States is tenth in eighth grade science scores and twenty-first in eighth grade math scores. Do you believe that requiring teachers to use standards is the way to solve this problem? If so, how? If not, what would you do instead? How could we as educators improve the system from within?

Educational Resources

Early Connections: Technology in Early Childhood Education provides research, information, and best practices regarding technology use to benefit children through age 8. http://www.netc.org/earlyconnections/index1.html

International Society for Technology in Education has the National Educational Technology Standards and provides information on the standards for students and teachers. http://cnets.iste.org

National Association for Music Education provides information on music standards and additional information on how to meet these standards. http://www.menc.org

National Center for History in the Schools is dedicated to improving history education in K–12 schools via its challenging, yet easy to use, curricular materials and assisting with the professional development of K–12 teachers. http://www.sscnet.ucla.edu/nchs/

National Council of Teachers of Mathematics provides information on the mathematics standards as well as ideas for lessons at different levels to incorporate mathematics into the curriculum. http://www.nctm.org

National Council for Geographic Education provides information on geography standards as well as lesson plans for teachers and ideas to implement these standards by developmental levels. http://www.ncge.org/

National Council for the Social Studies helps social studies educators teach students the content knowledge, intellectual skills, and civic values necessary for fulfilling the duties of citizenship in a participatory democracy. Its mission is to provide leadership, service, and support for all social studies educators. http://www.socialstudies.org/

Project Intersect at The Institute for the Study of Exceptional Children and Youth, University of Maryland (UM), looks at how special education and charter schools coexist, updates and expands the knowledge base regarding access and delivery of special education and related services to students with disabilities in charter schools. http://www.education.umd.edu/Depts/EDSP/ProjectIntersect/index.html

Public Broadcasting Service has a link, From the Start, which is funded in part by U.S. DOE. It gives teaching ideas (lesson plans and activities) linked to PBS shows, organized by grade level and topic. http://www.pbs.org/teachers/

Yahooligans is a searchable index of the Internet that focuses on content designed for children. http://kids.yahoo.com/

For additional resources, visit the book companion website for this text at www.cengage.com/education/deiner

Chapter 5

Individualizing Planning

I left for the meeting alone at 7:00 A.M. Jack wanted to come, but with three kids, someone had to get them off to school. I arrived at the school for my first individualized education program (IEP) meeting. I wasn't sure what to expect, but I knew there would be a lot of *them*. Having gone through all the assessment and evaluation procedures, we were convinced that Charlene had a learning disability. More specifically, she was probably dyslexic.

After the introductions (where was her classroom teacher?), they gave me the IEP. I was appalled, as I thought this was something we did together. I would talk about what Charlene could do and liked to do, and then we would figure out how to use what she could do to help her learn to read. It seemed clear that they did not want my input because the form was typed and there were seven copies of it (one page of her IEP is shown in Figure 5–1).

I tried to get myself back together and at least look at the information on the form. The annual goal was fine. We too wanted her to improve her reading skills. The rest of the form made little sense. It was like a code that teachers use to keep parents out. How could I ever tell if she mastered the critical objectives for her grade when they were given as 01, 02, and so on? When I looked at the evaluation procedure it said that she was to get at least a 75 percent accuracy rate. Why not a 100 percent? How were they going to teach her to read: Structural analysis, phonics, and kinesthetics? How individualized was that? What had they been doing up till now, trying osmosis? I was not a happy camper. Then I looked at who was responsible. Staff! What if I have a question? Do I call up the school and say, "Hello, I'd like to speak to staff to see if my daughter is mastering her cm 04s yet?" Again, I tried to get my act together.

I asked them what they liked most about my daughter. There was silence. The educational diagnostician finally spoke up. She was the only one in the room who would even recognize Charlene. I asked where Charlene's classroom teacher was. They said she wasn't necessary as they began to explain why Charlene would be better off in a special education class. I explained that my husband and I had both observed in this class and didn't find it appropriate for our daughter. After some discussion, they said that there was a marvelous teacher at another school in the district who would just love to have a little girl like Charlene in her class and they were sure it could be arranged to bus her to that school. At this point, the meeting seemed pointless. As I got up to leave, one of the individuals reminded me that I hadn't yet signed the IEP. I left the meeting and I didn't sign the IEP. I wondered if that meant that Charlene didn't have a disability.

Reflective Practice

This happened in 1988. Do you think the process has changed and is more family friendly today? How would this meeting be different if it happened now? How could you make it different?

Planning for Individual Children

In the years since 1988 the law and the educational system have changed. Current laws more clearly support the decision making role of parents and they keep most children, especially those like Charlene, in regular education classrooms. These changes have impacted classrooms and how we prepare teachers. All teacher need to be prepared to teach all children.

We no longer believe that one size fits all. The concept of individualization is strongly supported by law.

| Student _Charlene_ | School _West End School_ | Page _2_ of ____ |

Annual goal _1.0 To improve reading skills_

Short-term objective	Criteria and evaluation procedures	Specific educational services	Dates		Staff responsibilities	
			Begin	End	Name	Position

1.0 Charlene will master four critical objectives for grade.
 	
Reading vocabulary   Comprehension
VC 01   CM 01
  02   02
  03   03
  04   04
  05   05
  06   06
                07
 	
Study/ references   Sentences
SR 01   SN 01
  02
	1.0
	—Teacher test } at least
	—Textbook test } 75%
	—Observation } accuracy
	—Other
	
	Methods to include:
	—Structural analysis
	—Phonics
	—Kinesthetic
		Level I	11/88	6/89	Staff	

Parent's signature		Teacher's signature _Ms. Vandivere, E.D._				

Figure 5–1: Annual Goal from Charlene's Individualized Education Program (IEP)

Individualized planning is a mainstay of early childhood special education. The idea of appropriateness comes from developmentally appropriate practices and looks at whether planning is appropriate for the child as a individual based on his age and culture. If a child with a disability reads at a pre–first grade level but is 8 years old, the content of the reading material should reflect the child's age, whereas the reading level should match the child's ability. To understand planning for children with disabilities one must understand the law that guide this planning: Individuals with Disabilities Education Act (IDEA). The rules set forth by the IDEA determine which children are eligible for services, the sources of paying for these services, the roles parents and professionals play in deciding which services should be offered, how frequently they are given, and where these services are delivered.

The IDEA requires that all children identified as eligible for services have an individualized plan for their education. Infants and toddlers have an individualized family service plan (IFSP) and older children have an individualized education program (IEP) to guide adults when they work with these children. This plan is an acknowledgment that each identified child needs individualized special educational services and supports to learn. Family goals and expectations for their children are part of the plan.

Individuals With Disabilities Education Acts

The Individuals with Disabilities Education Acts (IDEA) are a set of laws that ensure services to children with disabilities throughout the United States. The IDEA governs how states and public agencies provide early intervention, special education, and related services to more than 6.5 million eligible infants, toddlers, children, and youth with disabilities (U. S. Department of Education, 2006b). It has four parts. Part A defines the terms used in the law. Part B gives money to states to provide special education and related services for eligible children and youth (3 to 21 years) with disabilities. Section 619 of part B focuses on services for preschool children (3 to 5 years). Part C provides for early intervention programs for infants and toddlers (birth to 3 years) with developmental delays, disabilities, or who are at risk and their families. Part D helps state education departments and other agencies improve how they work with children and youth with disabilities. When professionals in the field talk about services for children 3 to 5 they might refer to them as either 619 or Part B. The shorthand for services for children birth to 3 is Part C.

The IDEA 2004 defines key terms and concepts and sets minimum federal standards that must be met to achieve **compliance**. The following definitions apply to children from birth through 8 and those who educate them. This information is organized conceptually here rather than as it actually appears in the law. However, it is taken directly from the law to give you a feel for how the law reads.

General Definitions

The first thing to establish is who we are talking about. The IDEA 2004 defines what the important terms mean. This section identifies the specific disabilities included under the law and exactly what **a child with a disability** means. Note that children with ADHD are not included. Although the law continues to use the term mental retardation, people in the field believe that the term intellectual disability is a more appropriate term. I agree and use this term unless I am referring to the law. The law defines each of the disability terms used. Rather than defining them here, they are defined in the chapters where they are covered.

(3) Child with a disability.—

(A) In general.—The term 'child with a disability' means a child—

(i) with mental retardation, hearing impairments (including deafness), speech or language impairments, visual impairments (including blindness), serious emotional disturbance (referred to in this title as 'emotional disturbance'), orthopedic impairments, autism, traumatic brain injury, other health impairments, or specific learning disabilities; and

(ii) who, by reason thereof, needs special education and related services. (Title I/A/602/3, U.S. Department of Education, 2006b)

There is concern about mislabeling young children and the term developmentally delayed allows for the provision of services rather than requiring a more specific diagnosis, such as learning disability or intellectual disability for children between 3 and 9. The expectation is that during these years the delay will have responded to early intervention or a more specific diagnosis will have been established. States vary in how they use this provision of the law.

(B) Child aged 3 through 9.—The term 'child with a disability' for a child aged 3 through 9 (or any subset of that age range, including ages 3 through 5), may, at the discretion of the State and the local educational agency, include a child—

(i) experiencing developmental delays, as defined by the State and as measured by appropriate diagnostic instruments and procedures, in 1 or more of the following areas: physical development; cognitive development; communication development; social or emotional development; or adaptive development; and

(ii) who, by reason thereof, needs special education and related services. (Title I/A/602/3, U.S. Department of Education, 2006b)

The law also defines what is meant by special education.

(29) Special education.—The term 'special education' means specially designed instruction, at no cost to parents, to meet the unique needs of a child with a disability, including—

(A) instruction conducted in the classroom, in the home, in hospitals and institutions, and in other settings; and

(B) instruction in physical education. (Title I/A/602/29, U.S. Department of Education, 2006b)

The area of related services is an interesting one. The goal of related services is to ensure that children are available for a free appropriate public education and its provisions are designed so that the school is not a provider of medical services but does provide supportive services. The 2004 amendments clarify that medical services required for daily functioning are not related services. For example, school personnel could help set the volume and check the batteries but not adjust the electrical stimulation levels of cochlear implants nor pay for doing so (Mandlawitz, 2007).

(26) Related services.—

(A) In general.—The term 'related services' means transportation, and such developmental, corrective, and other supportive services (including speech-language pathology and audiology services, interpreting services, psychological services, physical and occupational therapy, recreation, including therapeutic recreation, social work services, school nurse services designed to enable a child with a disability to receive a free appropriate public education as described in the individualized education program of the child, counseling services, including rehabilitation counseling, orientation and mobility services, and medical services, except that such medical services shall be for diagnostic and evaluation purposes only) as may be required to assist a child with a disability to benefit from special education, and includes the early identification and assessment of disabling conditions in children.

(B) Exception.—The term does not include a medical device that is surgically implanted, or the replacement of such device. (Title I/A/602/26, U.S. Department of Education, 2006b)

The law defines what is meant by a **free appropriate public education**.

(9) Free appropriate public education.—The term 'free appropriate public education' means special education and related services that—

(A) have been provided at public expense, under public supervision and direction, and without charge;

(B) meet the standards of the State educational agency;

(C) include an appropriate preschool, elementary school, or secondary school education in the State involved; and

(D) are provided in conformity with the individualized education program required under section 614(d). (Title I/A/602/9, U.S. Department of Education, 2006b)

The increasing role of assistive technology in supporting children with disabilities is acknowledged in the law as is the need for educational institutions to provide and maintain these devices as well as provide training on their use. An **assistive technology device** is any item, piece of equipment, or product system, whether acquired commercially off the shelf, modified, or customized, that is used to increase, maintain, or improve functional capabilities of a child with a disability. On a case-by-case basis children may use school-purchased assistive technology devices at home or in other settings if it is on the child's IEP.

(2) Assistive technology service.—The term 'assistive technology service' means any service that directly assists a child with a disability in the selection, acquisition, or use of an assistive technology device. Such term includes—

(A) the evaluation of the needs of such child, including a functional evaluation of the child in the child's customary environment;

(B) purchasing, leasing, or otherwise providing for the acquisition of assistive technology devices by such child;

(C) selecting, designing, fitting, customizing, adapting, applying, maintaining, repairing, or replacing assistive technology devices;

(D) coordinating and using other therapies, interventions, or services with assistive technology devices, such as those associated with existing education and rehabilitation plans and programs;

(E) training or technical assistance for such child, or, where appropriate, the family of such child; and

(F) training or technical assistance for professionals (including individuals providing education and rehabilitation services), employers, or other individuals who provide services to, employ, or are otherwise substantially involved in the major life functions of such child. (Title I/A/602/2, U.S. Department of Education, 2006b)

This part of the law focused on children three years and older. Part C of the law defines the aspects of the law that relate to **infants or toddlers with disabilities**.

(5) Infant or toddler with a disability.—The term 'infant or toddler with a disability'—

(A) means an individual under 3 years of age who needs early intervention services because the individual—

(i) is experiencing developmental delays, as measured by appropriate diagnostic instruments and procedures in 1 or more of the areas of cognitive development, physical development, communication development, social or emotional development, and adaptive development; or

(ii) has a diagnosed physical or mental condition that has a high probability of resulting in developmental delay; and

(B) may also include, at a State's discretion—

(i) at-risk infants and toddlers; and

(ii) children with disabilities who are eligible for services under section 619 and who previously received services under this part until such children enter, or are eligible under State law to enter, kindergarten or elementary school, as appropriate, provided that any programs under this part serving such children shall include—

(I) an educational component that promotes school readiness and incorporates pre-literacy, language, and numeracy skills; and

(II) a written notification to parents of their rights and responsibilities in determining whether their child will continue to receive services under this part or participate in preschool programs under section 619. (Title I/C/632/1/6, U.S. Department of Education, 2006b)

Other definitions and parts of the IDEA are discussed where they apply in the text.

Requirements of the IDEA

Sections of the IDEA require states to do a variety of different things to ensure that children with disabilities are provided with the services they require and the safeguards they need. The following highlights some of these requirements:

Identification. States must make extensive and well-publicized efforts to screen and identify all children and youth with disabilities. **Child Find** agencies typically fulfill this role.

(3) Child find.—

(A) In general.—All children with disabilities residing in the State, including children with disabilities who are homeless children or are wards of the State and children with disabilities attending private schools, regardless of the severity of their disabilities, and who are in need of special education and related services, are identified, located, and evaluated and a practical method is developed and implemented to determine which children with disabilities are currently receiving needed special education and related services. (Title I/B/612/a/3, U.S. Department of Education, 2006b)

Least Restrictive Environment (LRE). To the maximum extent possible children must be educated in the **least restrictive environment** that is consistent with their educational needs and as much as possible with children without disabilities.

(5) Least restrictive environment.—

(A) In general.—To the maximum extent appropriate, children with disabilities, including children in public or private institutions or other care facilities, are educated with children who are not disabled, and special classes, separate schooling, or other removal of children with disabilities from the regular educational environment occurs only when the nature or severity of the disability of a child is such that education in regular classes with the use of supplementary aids and services cannot be achieved satisfactorily. (Title 1/B/612/a/5, U.S. Department of Education, 2006b)

Due Process. Parents' informed consent must be obtained before a child is evaluated, labeled, or placed. Parents who disagree with the school's decision have the right to mediation and to an impartial due process hearing.

(f) Impartial Due Process Hearing.—

(1) In general.—

(A) Hearing.—Whenever a complaint has been received under subsection (b)(6) or (k), the parents or the local educational agency involved in such complaint shall have an opportunity for an impartial due process hearing, which shall be conducted by the State educational agency or by the local educational agency, as determined by State law or by the State educational agency. (Title I/B/615/f, U.S. Department of Education, 2006b)

Mediation. In an effort to resolve issues between families and schools without requiring a due process hearing, the IDEA supports mediation.

(e) Mediation.—

(1) In general.—Any State educational agency or local educational agency that receives assistance under this part shall ensure that procedures are established and implemented to allow parties to disputes involving any matter, including matters arising prior to the filing of a complaint pursuant to subsection (b)(6), to resolve such disputes through a mediation process.

(2) Requirements.—Such procedures shall meet the following requirements:

(A) The procedures shall ensure that the mediation process—

(i) is voluntary on the part of the parties;

(ii) is not used to deny or delay a parent's right to a due process hearing under subsection (f), or to deny any other rights afforded under this part; and

(iii) is conducted by a qualified and impartial mediator who is trained in effective mediation techniques. (Title I/B/615/e, U. S. Department of Education, 2006b)

Highly Qualified Special Education Teachers (HQT). This part of the law is new in 2004 and related to the No Child Left Behind Act (NCLB, 2002). Highly qualified teachers apply to special education teachers teaching core academic subjects in public elementary or secondary schools. Fully certified general education teachers who earn full special education certification or licensure are considered new special educators teachers for purposes of HQT. There are alternative routes to certification and additional requirement for teaching children in grades five and higher. The requirements of the law for new teachers are abstracted below. To see the full requirements go to http://www.idea.gov.

(10) Highly qualified.—

(A) In general.—For any special education teacher, the term 'highly qualified' has the meaning given the term in section 9101 of the Elementary and Secondary Education Act of 1965, except that such term also—

(i) the teacher has obtained full State certification as a special education teacher (including certification obtained through alternative routes to certification), or passed the State special education teacher licensing examination, and holds a license to teach in the State as a special education teacher, except that when used with respect to any teacher teaching in a public charter school, the term means that the teacher meets the requirements set forth in the State's public charter school law;

(iii) in the case of a new special education teacher who teaches multiple subjects and who is highly qualified in mathematics, language arts, or science, demonstrate competence in the other core academic subjects in which the teacher teaches in the same manner as is required for an elementary, middle, or secondary school teacher under section 9101(23)(C)

(ii) of such Act, which may include a single, high objective uniform State standard of evaluation covering multiple subjects, not later than 2 years after the date of employment. (Title I/B/615/e, U. S. Department of Education, 2006b)

Reflective Practice

The law is not very exciting reading. However, it impacts what you do in the classroom, the education that you are receiving, and what you will be qualified to do when you graduate. Reflect on how the IDEA and laws beginning with Public Law 94–142 passed in 1975 have transformed the profession.

Individualized Education Program Teams

The individualized education program (IEP) team is responsible for the identification, assessment, design, and implementation of the individualized program. The federal law provides information about the individuals who need to be on this team, their respective roles, and necessary skills.

(B) Individualized education program team.—The term 'individualized education program team' or 'IEP Team' means a group of individuals composed of—

(i) the parents of a child with a disability;

(ii) not less than 1 regular education teacher of such child (if the child is, or may be, participating in the regular education environment);

(iii) not less than 1 special education teacher, or where appropriate, not less than 1 special education provider of such child;

(iv) a representative of the local educational agency who—

(I) is qualified to provide, or supervise the provision of, specially designed instruction to meet the unique needs of children with disabilities;

(II) is knowledgeable about the general education curriculum; and

(III) is knowledgeable about the availability of resources of the local educational agency;

(v) an individual who can interpret the instructional implications of evaluation results, who may be a member of the team described in clauses (ii) through (vi);

(vi) at the discretion of the parent or the agency, other individuals who have knowledge or special expertise regarding the child, including related services personnel as appropriate; and

(vii) whenever appropriate, the child with a disability. (Title I/B/614/d/1/B, U.S. Department of Education, 2006b)

The IEP team can be a formidable group. Parents have an extremely important role as they will ultimately accept or reject the IEP. Regular education teachers are required because children are included in regular classrooms. The special education teacher or consultant is part of the team. Someone must be on the team who has the authority to commit resources. If the team wants something, such as having an assistive technology device included in the IEP, someone has to have the authority to say the school system will pay for it. There is a requirement that at least one individual on the team knows specific instructional techniques for this particular child as well as an individual who is knowledgeable about the general curriculum. Someone on the team must understand and be able to interpret evaluation results. There is an option for others to be part of the team at the request of either the parents or the educational setting. The goal is to have all the stakeholders on the team. Some team members might fulfill multiple roles.

Additional IEP team members frequently include specialists who work with the child, but they can also include advocates, representatives of agencies and community programs that the child has attended or might attend, friends, previous teachers, parents of children with disabilities, or anyone the family or school feels would provide emotional support and practical assistance.

One of the initial responsibilities of the IEP team is to ensure parents understand the process itself and their rights under the law. Team members have responsibilities to talk with families about the range of services and service delivery settings available and to arrange for meeting times and locations that are convenient for families and other team members. This is a time to organize and evaluate information about the child that has been gleaned from assessment data and other sources. It is a time for parents to talk about their child's strengths and their desires for their child. The IEP meeting also is a time to develop individualized criteria for assessing progress toward goals and giving family-initiated outcomes and goals priority and to explore necessary accommodations for children to be part of the general curriculum.

In the Field

I had a boy named Jake in my 4-year-old class. Jake was labeled as severely intellectually disabled. His older brother and sister are developing typically and his sister Jane is in the gifted and talented program. His parents are well-educated and hold good jobs.

Most of the time Jake's parents are calm and giving. In fact, they gave the school a computer and each classroom some toys. However, when it was time for an IEP meeting, Jake's father's demeanor changed dramatically. Mr. Taylor sent a note saying he had a list of things he wanted addressed at the meeting and individuals he wanted to attend. I was able to get the various people to the meeting, but as far as his list went, he would not tell me anything except that he wanted a certain car seat for Jake to use on the bus. Needless to say, I reflected a lot on my teaching and wondered what I was not doing for this child and his family.

At the IEP meeting Mr. Taylor had a checklist in front of him and made sure to check it frequently and say things like, "Only 16 more things to address." For me, it was very intimidating. Eventually, the IEP meeting ended and because his father had not asked for anything too unreasonable, the school district was able to accommodate Jim's wants in Jake's program. I assumed that Jake's father was happy and it would be smooth sailing for the rest of the school year. It was smooth until the home visit.

Immediately after I scheduled the home visit the daily notes in the communication book had a different tone. Mr. Taylor was critical of the way I ran my classroom and of the methods I used to teach his son. He also felt that we were not providing Jake with everything he that was entitled to, specifically, a portfolio. Mr. Taylor added that he was not afraid to get his lawyer involved and that he had done it before.

Before the home visit I sent home a copy of the functional curriculum to show him how I was teaching based on the curriculum goals and Jake's IEP. Additionally, I explained the portfolio was not officially started until kindergarten but I would be willing to bring the portfolio of Jake's progress that I was keeping. I let him know that I was open to suggestions and would be willing to incorporate his ideas. At the home visit, I took some time going over everything I had sent home. My teaching and organizational methods were explained as well. Mr. Taylor seemed to feel better.

For the next few months, Jake's parents seemed happy with the school and program. When it was time for school to end and Jake to go on to kindergarten, his father started writing not-so-nice notes again. He questioned our motives for sending Jake to kindergarten and not retaining him. Mr. Taylor also threatened to sue because the assistive technology referral from the IEP was taking too long. Once again, I explained the philosophy of the program and why the assistive technology was taking longer than expected.

After the year ended, I really started to think about Jake and his family. It occurred to me that the only time his parents had issues with the school was before a transition and before a meeting directly related to Jake and his progress. I think scheduling these meetings really triggered some emotions for his family. They start to think about all the things that Jake will not be able to do and how they are going to accommodate him later in life. I believe that if we had a social worker in the school who could help families many of these threats would end. Instead of taking their feelings out on the teachers and school they would be able to handle them more appropriately and effectively.

Reflective Practice

What do you think about this teacher's reflections? Can you think about how you might work with this family based on what you have read? Do you think that the skills required fall more in the line of a social worker than a teacher?

Individualized Education Programs

When a child is identified as having a disability, certain procedures and requirements must be followed. Many of these are determined by federal and state laws. All states individualize programming for eligible children with disabilities. Information about the IEP is given first because the IFSP was developed based on the IEP.

The law requires that an IEP be designed *in writing* for each child with a disability, and as noted, the program must be developed *jointly* by teachers, specialists, parents or guardians, and, if possible, the child. Putting the program in writing is meant to ensure that it will be carried out and that agreement has been reached by all members of the IEP team about its contents.

The 2004 amendments to the IDEA require that the IEP include the following information:

(A) Individualized education program.—

(i) In general.—The term 'individualized education program' or 'IEP' means a written statement for each child with a disability that is developed, reviewed, and revised in accordance with this section and that includes—

(I) a statement of the child's present levels of academic achievement and functional performance, including—

(aa) how the child's disability affects the child's involvement and progress in the general education curriculum;

(bb) for preschool children, as appropriate, how the disability affects the child's participation in appropriate activities; and

(cc) for children with disabilities who take alternate assessments aligned to alternate achievement standards, a description of benchmarks or short-term objectives;

(II) a statement of measurable annual goals, including academic and functional goals, designed to—

(aa) meet the child's needs that result from the child's disability to enable the child to be involved in and make progress in the general education curriculum; and

(bb) meet each of the child's other educational needs that result from the child's disability;

(III) a description of how the child's progress toward meeting the annual goals described in subclause (II) will be measured and when periodic reports on the progress the child is making toward meeting the annual goals (such as through the use of quarterly or other periodic reports, concurrent with the issuance of report cards) will be provided;

(IV) a statement of the special education and related services and supplementary aids and services, based on peer-reviewed research to the extent practicable, to be provided to the child, or on behalf of the child, and a statement of the program modifications or supports for school personnel that will be provided for the child—

(aa) to advance appropriately toward attaining the annual goals;

(bb) to be involved in and make progress in the general education curriculum in accordance with subclause (I) and to participate in extracurricular and other nonacademic activities; and

(cc) to be educated and participate with other children with disabilities and nondisabled children in the activities described in this subparagraph;

(V) an explanation of the extent, if any, to which the child will not participate with nondisabled children in the regular class and in the activities described in subclause (IV)(cc); (VI)(aa) a statement of any individual appropriate accommodations that are necessary to measure the academic achievement and functional performance of the child on State and districtwide assessments consistent with section 612(a)(16)(A); and

(bb) if the IEP Team determines that the child shall take an alternate assessment on a particular State or districtwide assessment of student achievement, a statement of why— (AA) the child cannot participate in the regular assessment; and (BB) the particular alternate assessment selected is appropriate for the child;

(VII) the projected date for the beginning of the services and modifications described in subclause (IV), and the anticipated frequency, location, and duration of those services and modifications. (Title I/B/614/d/1/A, U.S. Department of Education, 2006b)

Put in more straight forward terms the IEP must include the following:

- A child's *present level of academic achievement* (PLAA) and functional performance.
- *Measurable annual goals (MAG)*, including academic and functional goals.
- Information about a child's *progress* toward meeting the annual goals, which must be provided at the same time as regular report cards.
- *Special education and related services* and supplementary aids and services, based on peer-reviewed research to the extent practical.
- Expected participation with children without disabilities. The extent to which a child is *not participating* needs to be explained.
- Appropriate *accommodations* or modifications necessary to measure the child's academic achievement and functional performance on state and district assessments.
- If using an *alternative assessment*, why, and why the alternative assessment selected is appropriate.
- A projected *time frame* or date for services and modifications to begin and the anticipated frequency, location and duration of these.
- *Transition services* must be included when a student is age 16.

No additional information is required to be included in a child's IEP beyond what is explicitly mentioned. To see the law, go to http://idea.ed.gov.

Parents have the right to examine all relevant school records regarding the identification, evaluation, and educational placement of their child. This right enables parents to examine the data that decisions are based on. Parents are now entitled, on request, to see test results and receive copies of reports. Families are equal members of the IEP team and are invited to all team discussions of their child and access to data encourages them to actively participate in the IEP process. Therefore, documents need to be jargon-free (or, at least necessary technical terms should be defined) so that all team members can understand them. Families need to know the current laws that regulate this process and what is considered best practice in the field.

The school district must provide parents with information *in writing*, in a language they can understand, about the identification, evaluation, and placement of their child. The parents must be notified in writing of contemplated program changes as well. In the past, some parents were not informed when their children were placed in or removed from special education classes.

In developing a child's IEP, the IEP team considers the strengths of the child, the goals and concerns of the parents, and the results of the evaluations of the child. As you are learning the elements of an IEP, you may ask yourself, "Is this worth the effort for just one or two children?" Yes! In the process of complying with these legal requirements, you can learn a great deal about individualizing instruction for all children and about getting the maximum benefit from the resources you have. For other children in the class, especially those you have some concerns about, you can incorporate the planning and principles used to design IEPs.

The U.S. Department of Education designed a model IEP form that provides guidance about how the form should look and how to ensure that the needed elements are included. This form (Figure 5–2) documents the legal requirements for each section. Although states use this model to ensure compliance most states have developed their own forms.

Requirements for Annual Goals

The 2004 reauthorization of the IDEA no longer requires measurable instructional objectives or benchmarks as part of the IEP for most school-age children. This decision was made in an effort to reduce paperwork. Rather, the annual goal is measurable and is tied to state standards for each grade level. State standards provide the needed guidance for instruction. Unlike the national standards discussed in Chapter 4, state standards are specific and reflect the scope and sequence used for all children in a grade level. Families are concerned about how they will know if their children are learning the required material if objectives and benchmarks are eliminated. They are concerned that if the state standards are used to meet annual goals there will be no individualization of instruction as these standards apply to all children.

Implications for Educators

Think broadly about measurable annual goals, state standards, and the scope and sequence that support the attainment of these goals. Be prepared to tell families how you know their children are progressing toward their annual goals and the techniques you are using to individualize instruction.

Writing Annual Goals

Annual goals are statements of long-range, measurable behaviors. They are based on the child's strengths and areas of need and on both informal and formal assessments of the child, developmentally appropriate practice, knowledge about the child's developmental profile, and regular educational standards. Annual goals relate to a particular developmental/educational area such as gross or fine motor development, language and literacy, mathematics, and so on. Within that domain, they are more specific. An appropriate annual goal in the area of mathematics based on the National mathematics standards could be *to understand numbers and operations*. For preschool children this could be broken down into benchmarks such as: *To improve number sense and numeration* and *to understand concepts of whole-number operations and computations* and activities could be designed to support these benchmarks or objectives. For kindergarten and elementary grades the expectation is that the state standards have quantified this statement and instruction will be based on these standards.

One school district's standards for kindergarten mathematics are as follows:

Kindergarten Mathematics
STUDENTS WILL:

- Recognize and write numbers 0–20.
- Use objects to show number combinations up to five ($2 + 3 = 5$ and $1 + 4 = 5$).
- Identify at least four basic shapes (circle, square, triangle and rectangle).
- Sort and group objects by shape, color or size.
- Order a group of objects from smallest to largest and largest to smallest.
- Recognize, describe, copy and continue patterns (red, blue; red, blue, or ▲❤∅; ▲❤∅).
- Use objects to solve story problems.
- Tell time to the hour.
- Select pennies, nickels, dimes and quarters from a set of coins.

Source: Christina School District, 2005–2008.

In the case of kindergarten and older children these district standards would serve as instructional objections if mathematics skill was one of the annual goals and the curriculum in general and the IEP in particular would be designed to facilitate children meeting these objectives.

The first step in writing annual goals is to determine what the child can do independently, and what can he do with scaffolding from an adult.

Present Level of Academic Achievement and Functional Performance

A statement of the child's present levels of academic achievement and functional performance (PLAA), including how the child's disability affects the child's involvement and progress in the general education curriculum (i.e., the same curriculum as for children without disabilities) provides the starting point. For preschool children the emphasis is on developmental milestones, functional performance, and pre-academic skills and how the disability affects the child's participation in these types of activities. Annual goals are the educational focus for a year, so they are broad, but measurable.

Individualized Education Program

The Individualized Education Program (IEP) is a written document that is developed for each eligible child with a disability. The Part B regulations specify, at 34 CFR §§300.320-300.328, the procedures that school districts must follow to develop, review, and revise the IEP for each child. The document below sets out the IEP content that those regulations require.

A statement of the child's present levels of academic achievement and functional performance including:

- How the child's disability affects the child's involvement and progress in the general education curriculum (i.e., the same curriculum as for nondisabled children) **or** *for preschool children*, as appropriate, how the disability affects the child's participation in appropriate activities. [34 CFR §300.320(a)(1)]

_____

_____

_____

_____

A statement of measurable annual goals, including academic and functional goals designed to:

- Meet the child's needs that result from the child's disability to enable the child to be involved in and make progress in the general education curriculum. [34 CFR §300.320(a)(2)(i)(A)]

- Meet each of the child's other educational needs that result from the child's disability. [34 CFR §300.320(a)(2)(i)(B)]

_____

_____

_____

_____

For children with disabilities who take alternate assessments aligned to alternate achievement standards (in addition to the annual goals), a description of benchmarks or short-term objectives. [34 CFR §300.320(a)(2)(ii)]

_____

_____

_____

_____

A description of:

- How the child's progress toward meeting the annual goals will be measured. [34 CFR §300.320(a)(3)(i)]

- When periodic reports on the progress the child is making toward meeting the annual goals will be provided such as through the use of quarterly or other periodic reports, concurrent with the issuance of report cards. [34 CFR §300.320(a)(3)(ii)]

_____

_____

_____

_____

A statement of the *special education and related services* and *supplementary aids* and *services*, based on peer-reviewed research to the extent practicable, to be provided to the child, or on behalf of the child, and *a statement of the program modifications or supports* for school personnel that will be provided to enable the child:

- To advance appropriately toward attaining the annual goals. [34 CFR §300.320(a)(4)(i)]

- To be involved in and make progress in the general education curriculum and to participate in extracurricular and other nonacademic activities. [34 CFR §300.320(a)(4)(ii)]

- To be educated and participate with other children with disabilities and nondisabled children in extracurricular and other nonacademic activities. [34 CFR §300.320(a)(4)(iii)]

_____

_____

_____

_____

An explanation of the extent, if any, to which the child will not participate with nondisabled children in the regular classroom and in extracurricular and other nonacademic activities. [34 CFR §300.320(a)(5)]

_____

_____

_____

_____

A statement of any individual appropriate accommodations that are necessary to measure the academic achievement and functional performance of the child on State and districtwide assessments. [34 CFR §300.320(a)(6)(i)]

_____

_____

_____

_____

If the IEP Team determines that the child must take an alternate assessment instead of a particular regular State or districtwide assessment of student achievement, a statement of why:

- The child cannot participate in the regular assessment. [34 CFR §300.320(a)(6)(ii)(A)]
- The particular alternate assessment selected is appropriate for the child. [34 CFR §300.320(a)(6)(ii)(B)]

_____

_____

_____

_____

The projected date for the beginning of the services and modifications and the anticipated frequency, location, and duration of *special education and related services* and *supplementary aids* and *services and modifications and supports.* [34 CFR §300.320(a)(7)]

Service, aid or modification	Frequency	Location	Beginning date	Duration

Transition services
Beginning not later than the first IEP to be in effect *when the child turns 16, or younger if determined appropriate by the IEP Team*, and updated annually thereafter, the IEP must include:

- Appropriate measurable postsecondary goals based upon age-appropriate transition assessments related to training, education, employment, and where appropriate, independent living skills. [34 CFR §300.320(b)(1)]

_____

_____

_____

_____

- The transition services (including courses of study) needed to assist the child in reaching those goals. [34 CFR §300.320(b)(2)]

Transition services (including courses of study)

_____

_____

_____

Rights that transfer at age of majority
- Beginning not later than one year before the child reaches the age of majority under State law, the IEP must include a statement that the child has been informed of the child's rights under Part B of the IDEA, if any, that will, consistent with 34 CFR §300.520, transfer to the child on reaching the age of majority. [34 CFR §300.320(c)]

Figure 5–2: Part B Individualized Education Program

Source: U. S. Department of Education (2006b). Building the Legacy: IDEA 2004. Accessed on August 19, 2008 from http://idea.ed.gov/static/modelForms

Implications for Educators

Where does one begin writing goals? The only way to answer that question is to know what the child is able to do now in different content areas. With older children, achievement tests are often used to provide this information; with younger children, it is more of a challenge. If mathematics was a potential annual goal it might be: *To improve understanding of numbers and operations.* The next step would be to look at the benchmarks that relate to the national mathematics standards:

> number sense and numeration
> geometric and spatial sense
> measurement concepts
> estimation skills
> two-number operations and computation
> fractions and decimal
> patterns and relationships

Let's use patterns and relationships as the example. Find out if the child can continue a simple pattern? (If you start a pattern of black, white, black, white ... and then ask the child to continue the pattern, can he? If not, check to be sure he can match the colors.) If he can match the colors but cannot repeat the pattern, his present level of academic achievement and functional performance is *can match colors but cannot identify simple repeating patterns.* You know where to start and in the process you have identified other strands related to understanding mathematics.

Think of the IEP as a useful system of keeping track of information about children. Help families to think about it that way as well. As you talk about annual goals, discuss what you do in the classroom to ensure the child meets the goals and the types of experiences families might work into their routines at home that would enhance their child's learning. (Setting the table can teach simple patterns and relationships.) Families may not be aware of underlying math concepts and might not think of this as supporting math. This is a team effort and all members of the team can help the child reach annual goals.

Choosing Annual Goals

After the child's present level of academic achievement and functional performance is determined, the IEP team must develop measurable annual goals. Research on the quality of IEP goals and objectives for young children shows that the goals and objectives have been poorly written, with little attention to the context or activity in which the skill will be taught. Also, many goals are not developmentally appropriate nor do they target functional skills. **Functional skills** are those skills the child needs to function independently in the environment and that can be taught during activities in the classroom or in routines at home (Grisham-Brown & Hemmeter, 1998). Rather, many IEP goals reflect isolated skills. If children with disabilities are to be included, IEP goals need to be written in such a way that they can be part of the ongoing curriculum.

To develop goals for an individual child within this context, you need to know the demands of the school setting (or other settings where a child spends his time); that is, "What is the child required to do?" You need to find out from the child's family about their priorities

Choose annual goals that increase the probability that children will develop the skills they need to function well in the world in which they live.

for his skill development and behavior. Determine the developmental level of the child, where he is in the developmental sequences, and expected behaviors as the child progresses.

Family priorities may be very different from the ones you might set for a child. A family might want their child to have friends and play with other children. Your goals might revolve around specific communication skills. Although on the surface these may look different, it may mean that the communication skills you focus on are those that are likely to increase communication with peers and the ability to join groups. If a family wants to toilet train a child, and you see fine motor skills as a priority, again, practice fine motor skills in the context of toileting. Before writing goals, the families with the IEP team must identify the skills that are critical for a particular child.

Determining Critical Skills

Although critical skills for each child will differ, the following guidelines offer a way of thinking about skills that are useful for all children. Identify skills that, for example:

- Are emerging or are present in some contexts but not in others.
- Will permit the child to participate in daily routines and become more independent.
- Will allow the child to accomplish the greatest number of tasks.
- The child is highly motivated to learn.

- The family wishes the child to learn.
- Will support the child's participation in future environments.

Annual goals for school-age children are related to academic skills and behaviors, based on the regular education curriculum and the state standards. For children ages 3 to 5 they can be developmental skills that will have an impact on educational ability. National standards and state-developed performance indicators provide guidance for these goals. The annual goals in this text are based on the national standards developed by professional organizations and necessary developmental skills. All measurable goals need to be based on the child's present level of academic achievement and functional performance. In addition, the key is sequential learning.

Writing Measurable Goals and Objectives

Measurable objectives and benchmarks are written in such a way that anyone can tell whether the child has learned a skill and is making appropriate progress toward attaining the goal. To help satisfy this empirical requirement, there are rules for writing measurable goals that include identifying a measurable goal, describing the behavior that shows the goal is being met, and establishing a criteria for acceptable performance.

With young children the measurable part is a challenge. This is difficult because you must be able to measure (see) what is done. This means that some words—such as *understand, know, appreciate, try, feel, discover,* and *think*—cannot be used. Early childhood special educators have more difficulty with this step than other educators because young children have a smaller repertoire of behaviors. Traditional words—such as *write, list, translate, read, predict,* and *compare*—represent skills the children may not yet have achieved. A starter list of words that allow skills to be measurable follows:

point to	match	select	tell	order
say	label	repeat	name	pick out
choose	find	color	copy	dramatize
dictate	set up	state	arrange	locate
define	look at	draw	circle	hop
run	jump	walk	cut out	count

The evaluation criteria are also challenging. How well or how often does this goal need to be achieved for you as the teacher to decide that it has been mastered? In education, we frequently decide a child has to be correct four out of five times to have mastered an objective. This is 80 percent. Because of human variability, it is unwise to anticipate a 100 percent performance, even when you think this can be achieved. For a variety of reasons, children often decide not to comply with requests. You need to build flexibility into your evaluation criterion. You also need to give some thought to what you specifically need to do to figure out whether the goal has been met. How will you know it is 80 percent of the time unless you allow the child at least five trials (you can convert four out of five trials to 80 percent; if you choose 90 percent you have to use ten trials)? Will this get "old" for you and the child? Think about it before you write it down.

Goals should have enough flexibility to allow for individual differences and lend themselves to variety in programming. Once you begin to think more broadly about the goals themselves, you need to expand that thinking to the settings where potential behaviors can happen. Children need many opportunities to practice these goals. Think about how to build them into routines in the classroom and into the routines that the child's family already uses. Inclusion of a goal in several settings increases the probability that the skill itself will be generalized. It also increases the opportunities the child has to practice the skill.

As you reflect on writing and implementing annual goals and objectives, it becomes clear that it is much simpler to write trivial goals than important ones. Furthermore, some of the qualities you value most are almost impossible to put into measurable terms, for example, empathy, creativity, cooperation, joy, and interest. Finally, it is clear you will have to develop a system of record keeping to determine whether or not these goals have been met or are in the process of being met.

Setting priorities, or deciding what to do first, is sometimes difficult. Parents' choices and children's preferences are a primary consideration. However, parents may not be aware of the many steps it takes the accomplish a particular goal. If parents want their child to read, yet the child cannot identify letters and letter-sound relationships, you need to be prepared to help parents understand some of prerequisite skills. And, that "learning to read" is not a measurable goal as stated. This doesn't mean that the goal is inappropriate; it means that it may take a long time to reach and you and the parents need to be clear about prerequisite skills that lead to the attainment of the goal. Additionally, the goal needs to be reframed so it is measurable: *Read at the beginning second grade (2.0) level as measured by the STAR (Standardized Test for the Assessment of Reading) Early Literacy test.* This is an important and measurable goal.

Find out the family's priorities, and then ask about each annual goal: How difficult will it be in the future if the child does not learn _____? The more the child will need this skill, the higher the priority you could assign the annual goal and its prerequisite skills, and the more time designated to work on the standards or benchmarks needed to meet this goal. Goals should reflect knowledge of child development, the child's abilities, and the importance of the goal.

Embedding Annual Goals

The process of embedding goals requires you to identify when and where a child's goals will be addressed in the classroom and who will be responsible for implementing them. To imbed annual goals successfully, you might try the following:

1. Identify the structure of the day including the daily schedule, routines, transitions, and activities or experiences.
2. Review each child's IEP or IFSP and annual goals.
3. Identify possible times during each day when a child's goals and objectives or standards can be incorporated into the program.
4. Starting with the child's present level of academic performance and functional behavior (PLAA), determine the next steps in the process by breaking the goal down into prerequisite skills.

5. Determine what types of activities—specify which activities—can be planned during the identified routines to foster the acquisition of the necessary skills and objectives. The extent to which you include them in daily routines and transitions will increase the likelihood of meeting the goals.

6. Determine what teaching strategies best support the acquisition of these skills.

7. Decide which adults in the classroom are going to support the child learning these prerequisite skills and ensure that they are aware of both the skill and the teaching techniques necessary to ensure the acquisition of the skills that will help the child meet the annual goals.

8. Ensure that the adults discuss the child's learning and chart his accomplishments so that needed skills increase in complexity or are replaced with different prerequisite skills.

If more than one child has an IEP in your classroom, or you have closely embedded your goals within the routine of the program, it is useful to include them in the daily schedule. Put the skills or objectives you plan to meet for each child across from the designated routine and code the objectives from each child's IEP that you plan to meet. If you embed skills in the activities that you plan, be clear what skills you are going to emphasize for different children as part of the planning process (Pretti-Frontczak & Bricker, 2004).

Schedule	Saul
Arrival (8:30)	A.2 Respond to "yes/no" questions
	A.3 Respond to "tell me about" questions
	Stella
	B.2 Name members of the class
	C.1 Initiate communication with peers and adults

Reflective Practice

Notice how easily these objectives fit in with regular routines and planning. What is takes is the reminder to do this everyday on a regular basis. The questions vary in content but not in intent.

Goals and their prerequisite skills can also be incorporated into activities. You need to think in terms of the underlying principles of how children learn developmentally appropriate practices, and how you plan for children. Do not think in terms of particular activities but in types of activities that support the skills children need. If children are struggling with reading, one aspect of reading is vocabulary. If adults know the goal is to increase vocabulary, this can be done through such activities as synonyms (2–52w), singing Jenny Jenkins (2–38w), using materials in the water table (2–41w), identifying initial sounds of different body parts (3–12), or even talking about fractions (3–2).

Goals are met when adults build the skills into each day multiple times and in multiple contexts.

Part Three of this text is designed to help you embed annual goals and their supporting skill in activities. The numbers given above are for specific activities that are designed to increase vocabulary. The List of Activities details additional activities that support this goal. You would have to decide which activities to use in what particular progression and how to vary them to meet an individual child's needs.

With increased emphasis on academic areas, some of the skills that make children available for learning, increase their self esteem and their self awareness, and support social inclusion are becoming rare on IEPs. Whether or not children's goals include skills related to self-regulation and social interactions, they are important aspects of school competence. If children have trouble joining groups then a plan must be developed to scaffold joining groups. Families, educators, and specialists should participate in developing and carrying out the plan. Although this skill cannot logically be carried out as part of a transition, it can be scaffolded several times each day, thus providing opportunities for social interaction. It is up to adults to design environments to promote active engagement, learning, participation, and membership (Wolery, 2005). To program inclusively, you must meet the learning needs of all children who are functioning at a variety of developmental and academic levels, not just those for whom you have an IEP.

In the Field

As a first-grade teacher in an inclusive classroom, I have often struggled with how to embed the teaching of IEP goals into the regular routine of my classroom. When I began teaching, I simply had a paraeducator pull the children receiving special education services out of the lesson to teach a particular IEP goal. This did not seem fair. However, I continued this practice for several years until I realized that this was not truly inclusion.

After taking a graduate class that focused on inclusion, I learned many other ways to embed teaching of annual goals into the classroom. I actually incorporated the skills and goals into classroom instruction by adding these to my lesson plans and I found time to make each IEP goal fit in with the general curriculum. During every unit I identified which activities lent themselves to teaching the skills needed for the annual goals.

Further, I identified what routines and schedules needed to be changed and which would work with the skills I needed to teach. I used my paraeducator's help to involve children in an activity instead of pulling out the children with disabilities; at times, the paraeducator may be working on IEP goals within the whole class activity. I also had to identify different teaching strategies to help each child learn her goals.

Having really focused on embedding the IEP goals into the regular curriculum, I realize that I am teaching more effectively in this inclusive classroom. Now I know that I am truly planning for the individual needs and differences of each child.

Reflective Practice

Including IFSP/IEP goals on a regular basis ensures that the goals are accomplished requires planning and practice. It also requires evaluation to determine if what is planned is being learned and if what is learned in one context is being generalized in other contexts. How would you plan to do this in your classroom?

Universal Design for Learning

Universal design for learning (UDL) is a research-based educational framework that promotes the development of flexible learning environments that can accommodate individual learning differences. It means that instructional materials and activities are designed so that children with wide differences in their abilities can achieve learning goals. Universal does not mean one size fits all. Instead, it is meant to underscore the need for multiple approaches to meet the needs of children with diverse abilities.

The 2004 amendments to the IDEA emphasize this concept as a way of supporting the learning of all children. This is achieved by using flexible materials and activities that allow children to display their learning in a variety of ways. The materials and activities are designed this way from the beginning; they are not additions or modifications. Flexible digital media makes it easier to provide these multiple alternatives and customize teaching and learning. Although technology can make the process easier, the underlying concepts apply to all areas. Information should be accessible, should support skill development, and above all, what is learned should be important (Stahl, 1999).

More specifically, UDL helps educators accommodate individual differences by providing (1) multiple means of representation of the information presented, to give learners various ways of acquiring information and knowledge, (2) multiple and modifiable means of expression and control, to offer learners alternatives for demonstrating what they know, and (3) multiple or modifiable means of motivation or engagement, to tap into learners' interests, challenge them appropriately, and motivate them to learn (CAST, 2007; Rose & Meyer, 2002; Stahl, 1999). Research in neuroscience has shown that each brain processes information in a different way. The way we learn is as individual as our DNA or fingerprints.

The Evidence Base

In its research, CAST (2007) has identified three primary brain networks and the roles they play in learning:

- **Recognition networks involve gathering facts. They look at how children identify and categorize what they see, hear, and read. Identifying letters, words, or sounds are recognition tasks—the "what" of learning.**
- **Strategic networks are used in planning and performing tasks. How children organize and figure out how to perform new tasks (motor or cognitive), express their ideas and solve math problem are strategic tasks—the "how" of learning.**
- **Affective networks are the ways in which children are engaged and motivated. How they are challenged, excited, or interested. These are affective dimensions—the "why" of learning.**

UDL principles help educators reflect on their teaching for individual differences in each of these three brain networks. Because all students use the same materials, there is no stigma related to special materials or methods. (CAST, 2007).

Reflective Practice

UDL is a challenge for educators because it requires them to design multiple means of representation, expression, and engagement. Do you feel ready to do this? What aspects of UDL will challenge you?

Implications for Educators

As you think about applying the principles of universal design to activities and materials that support annual goals, remember to:

1. **Choose activities that use as many senses as possible (vision, taste, touch, hearing, smell). Be clear that these senses are available for both input and output of learning experiences.**
2. **Choose activities that reinforce goals but have many variations. Repetition helps children master a concept but repeating the same activity is boring. If you are working to improve measurement concepts, have children measure both wet and dry materials (water, cooking oil, coffee beans, cornmeal, etc.). Have many different types of measuring devices and talk with children as well as show them the relevance of being able to measure materials. This provides a broad base for learning about a variety of concepts including measurement, as well as fitting into a variety of themes that support generalization and contextual learning.**
3. **Use variety when presenting the same information. Color, for example, can be shown through clothing, painting, bingo, gelatin, and nature walks, to name just a few.**

Record Keeping

Good record keeping is indispensable for implementing an IEP. Much of your record keeping will be similar to that described in Chapter 3 on assessment. However, for children with an IEP, in addition to the records that you keep on all the children, you must keep records on children's progress toward meeting annual goals and benchmarks or standards.

A one-page outline that corresponds directly to the child's annual goals and the skills needed to meet these will be a reminder to ensure children have many opportunities to practice skills and that you are keeping track of their progress on a regular basis. In an outline report, numbers and key words identify the goals (Figure 5–3). Checks, plus, and minus signs are helpful shorthand for daily notes.

Figure 5–4 shows how anecdotal notes can be used for the same record keeping. The choice of how you keep records is yours, but you must keep records.

IEPs are individualized plans, but as you plan for your class, it is important that you include all of the children's goals in your planning on a regular basis. To do this it may help to put goals on one planning form such as the one illustrated in Figure 5–5. You may have one chart such as this with all the child's goals stated in a generic sense, and then individualized to fit into your class routines (Pretti-Frontczak & Bricker, 2004).

Name	Tinea B.	Evaluation criteria		Date	Date	Date
				10/13/08	10/20/08	10/27/08
1. Fine Motor						
1.1 Stringing beads		10 beads		2 beads	2 beads	
1.2 Copy shapes		3 of 5 correct		2 shapes	3 shapes	
1.3 Block tower		5 blocks high		3 blocks	4 blocks	
2. Language concepts						
2.1 Colors		6 of 8	R	3 red, yellow, green	3 red, yellow, green	
2.2 Numbers		1 to 5	E	1, 2	1, 2	
2.3 Prepositions		6 of 8	R	on, under	+ in	

Key: E = Expressive
R = Receptive

Figure 5–3: Checklist: Weekly IEP Report
There are a variety of ways of keeping records. Some teachers like checklists others prefer anecdotal notes. Both work.

As you plan an activity or unit, think about a child's IEP goals. Determine which of them can be met during an activity. Then, focus on what changes or adaptations you need to make to meet the goals. Finally, determine what you will need to adapt (materials, equipment, procedures, instructional style, or peer behaviors) to ensure that the child's goals are met in the context of what all children are learning.

Tinea B. 10/20/08

Fine motor: T. is still demonstrating needs in this area. She can now build a 4-block tower, copy three shapes, △○□ Bead stringing is not improving. I think I'll try sewing cards and see if that helps

Language: T.'s language has improved since September. Sentences have 3 to 5 words. She can identify red, yellow, and green when I give her a pair of colors and ask her to show me (red). We are working on blue. She can say the numbers 1 through 5 but I'm not sure it means anything. It is sort of like singing the alphabet song. She can follow one-step directions containing the prepositions: on, under, in. Starting to work on beside.

Figure 5–4: Anecdotal Records: Weekly IEP Report
This figure contains the same information as Figure 5-3, but in an anecdotal format

Implementing an IEP in a Theme Plan

The next step in planning is to decide how to implement the theme. Start with your learning goals. Themes make learning fun and facilitate children's learning. They are a means to the end, but not the end itself. Focus on how themes support the content of the general curriculum. Literacy and vocabulary are still goals; the themes provide guidance and continuity for the books you read, the topics children write on, and the vocabulary words they learn. Children are excited and motivated about themes that grow out of their interests and are presented in a developmentally appropriate way.

There are many ways to incorporate individualized planning in a theme or unit. One way is to make a chart. Put each of the child's annual goals in the middle and the areas around the room at the sides. If the theme was *transportation* and the annual goals were *to improve receptive and expressive communication and increase vocabulary,* the chart would look something like Figure 5–6 for 4 year olds. It is not difficult to incorporate individualized planning in a theme, but it is necessary to think it through and plan it.

In many ways, the theme makes some of the planning easier. The vocabulary to stress is more obvious and is more easily reinforced because it is maintained for at least

Child	Communication	Cognitive	Gross motor	Fine motor	Social skills
Ali	B.1 Request desired transportation objects.	C.2 Identify different methods of transportation.			A.1 Initiate conversation with a peer about transportation.
Mario	A.1 Respond to a yes/no question about transportation.			B.1 Move small trains and buses on a path.	
Carol	C.2 Respond to "what" or "how" questions about transportation.			A.1 Move from a lying down to a sitting position and maintain that position while using transportation manipulatives.	

Figure 5–5: Embedding Children's Objectives in a Theme-Based Curriculum

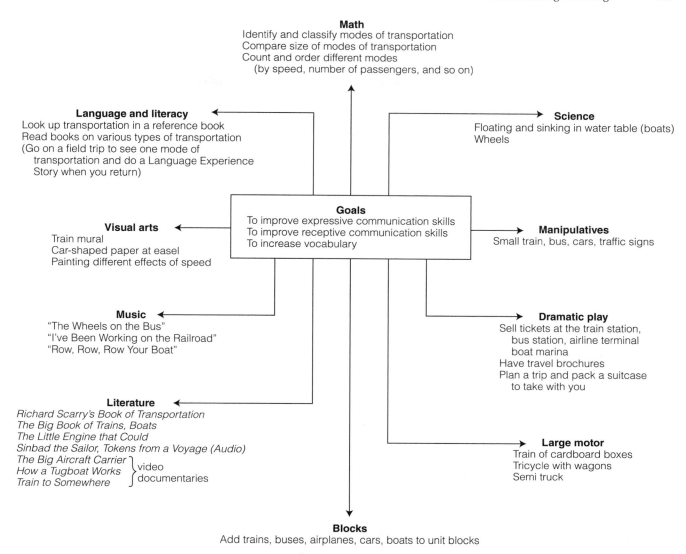

Math
Identify and classify modes of transportation
Compare size of modes of transportation
Count and order different modes
(by speed, number of passengers, and so on)

Language and literacy
Look up transportation in a reference book
Read books on various types of transportation
(Go on a field trip to see one mode of
transportation and do a Language Experience
Story when you return)

Science
Floating and sinking in water table (boats)
Wheels

Goals
To improve expressive communication skills
To improve receptive communication skills
To increase vocabulary

Visual arts
Train mural
Car-shaped paper at easel
Painting different effects of speed

Manipulatives
Small train, bus, cars, traffic signs

Music
"The Wheels on the Bus"
"I've Been Working on the Railroad"
"Row, Row, Row Your Boat"

Dramatic play
Sell tickets at the train station,
bus station, airline terminal
boat marina
Have travel brochures
Plan a trip and pack a suitcase
to take with you

Literature
Richard Scarry's Book of Transportation
The Big Book of Trains, Boats
The Little Engine that Could
Sinbad the Sailor, Tokens from a Voyage (Audio)
The Big Aircraft Carrier
How a Tugboat Works } video
Train to Somewhere } documentaries

Large motor
Train of cardboard boxes
Tricycle with wagons
Semi truck

Blocks
Add trains, buses, airplanes, cars, boats to unit blocks

Vocabulary
Types of transportation
Train (station), bus (station), airplane (terminal, hanger), car (garage), boat (marina, slip, dock)
Freight train, passenger train, subway
School bus, city bus, long distance bus
Sedan, station wagon, convertible, SUV, truck
Speedboat, tanker, tugboat, sailboat

Figure 5–6: Theme Plan: Transportation

a week. As children expand their concepts, use analogies from one form of transportation to another to help them learn. The purpose of theme-based planning is contextual learning. Children can learn more, faster, and in greater depth if materials are related and relevant.

Implications for Educators

The principles of contextual learning can be applied to the home as well. If parents want to work on language concepts at home, use the house as your context. Have parents decide what they will do in each room of the house to help children learn contextually. Make a chart similar to Figure 5–6, but instead of having developmental domains, have rooms of the house. In the bedroom, children might

learn the names of clothing; in the kitchen, eating utensils and foods; in the living room, furniture. Parents are more likely to remember if they can put the sheet of paper on the refrigerator instead of in a notebook. Change charts as children master concepts.

Discipline and the IDEA

The 2004 amendments to the IDEA made some modifications to disciplinary actions.

Schools must decide on a case-by-case basis whether to change a placement for a child who violates the code of student conduct. The goal is that the same rules apply to children with and without disabilities. Children can be removed from their current placement to an appropriate

interim alternative educational setting (IAES), another setting or suspended for not more than 10 school days and for additional removals of not more than 10 consecutive school days during the school year for other incidents as long as these do not constitute a change of placement.

Whether or not the behavior is a manifestation of the child's disability when a child is removed, he must continue to receive education services to help him progress toward IEP goals and participation in the general education curriculum. As appropriate, he also must receive a **functional behavioral assessment** and behavioral intervention services and modifications. There is a concern that children who are removed from school because of behavioral problems will also experience academic failure. If the removal is a change of placement, the IEP team determines appropriate services.

One requirement of the process is to determine whether or not the conduct was a **manifestation of the disability**.

(I) if the conduct in question was caused by, or had a direct and substantial relationship to, the child's disability; or

(II) if the conduct in question was the direct result of the local educational agency's failure to implement the IEP.

(ii) Manifestation.—If the local educational agency, the parent, and relevant members of the IEP Team determine that either subclause (I) or (II) of clause (i) is applicable

Most children test rules some of the time. When a child has a disability it is important to find out if the behavior is a manifestation of the disability or if it is related to the environment. A behavioral intervention plan can be designed to decrease the undesired behavior.

for the child, the conduct shall be determined to be a manifestation of the child's disability. (Title I/C/636/d, U.S. Department of Education, 2006b)

If either applies, the conduct is seen as a manifestation of the disability. If the IEP is not being implemented the LEA must remedy this problem. If it is related to the child's disability, the IEP team must either conduct a functional behavior assessment (FBA) if this had not been done previously, and implement a **behavioral intervention plan** (BIP) or review the previous plan and modify it as needed. The child then returns to his previous placement unless the violations involved weapons, drugs, or serious bodily injury, or there is agreement that the placement should be changed.

Functional Behavioral Assessment and Behavior Intervention Plans

The IDEA amendments of 1997 and 2004 focus attention to the connection between behavioral problems and learning in the creation of individualized education programs (IEPs). Analyzing this connection involves assessing the function of problematic behavior. Understanding what a student gains through his actions is critical to behavior modification efforts. The functional behavioral assessment (FBA) involves determining the cause of a behavior in order to formulate an appropriate intervention. It reviews how a child functions in different settings such as school, home, and in the community, and uses this information to develop a plan that addresses the underlying causes of problematic behavior (Mandlawitz, 2007). IEP teams use a variety of techniques to investigate whether biological, social, affective, and environmental factors contribute to the origin, maintenance, or cessation of the targeted problematic behavior.

The IEP team must first identify the behavior(s) that cause(s) problems in the designated setting. They must describe the behavior in concrete detail so that it can be easily identified, measured, and recorded. Assessment procedures may include structured interviews with the child, parents, teachers, and other involved adults, or direct observation of the child in varying contexts. They record the antecedents, behavior, and consequences of the problem behavior and analyze them to determine if they are linked to a skill deficit, specific setting, or context.

Once the FBA sheds light on the function of the behavior in question, the IEP team can focus on creating a BIP that will appropriately address the problematic behavior. Although the long-term goal may be to decrease or eliminate a specific behavior, this plan may focus on positive interventions that build the skills needed to perform desired behaviors and increase the student's motivation to use these skills consistently. Positive interventions that address student needs and foster appropriate behaviors will be more successful than plans focusing strictly on controlling the problematic behavior in question. As with other areas of an IEP, the BIP should be evaluated, revised, and updated annually, or when a member of the IEP team feels it is necessary.

Section 504 and 504 Plans

In addition to the IEP and the IFSP, another plan exists, a 504 plan. Section 504 of the Rehabilitation Act of 1973 as well as the Americans with Disabilities Act (ADA) addresses issues of equity and access. Some children who have disabilities but do not qualify for individualized education programs under the IDEA do require individualized accommodations. The definition of a disability under Section 504 is different and more inclusive. Section 504 defines a person with a disability as any person who has or is thought to have a physical or mental impairment that substantially limits one or more major life activities. This definition does not require that the child needs to have special education and related services, but that the environment needs to be modified to provide access to learning.

Like the IEP, this is an individualized plan with a lengthy list of potential modifications. For example, the physical education curriculum for a child with asthma may be adjusted, the school day may be shortened, or rest periods may be provided. There may be a tutor provided at home if the child is out of school frequently. There may be changes in classroom management, curricula, or instructional procedures to accommodate these children. Like the IEP, these are individualized plans designed to make school accessible for all children. I have included a sample 504 plan so that you can see the ways in which it might be used, and how it is different from an IEP (see Figure 5.7 for a sample 504 plan).

In addition to the public school setting, the ADA extended the right to access for all children to early care and education settings, preschools, charter schools, and private schools. It also applies to activities that occur outside of the school, ensuring that libraries and recreational facilities are accessible to all children.

Reflective Practice

Children with special health care needs may need 504 plans to help accommodate limitations in energy, problems relating to the environment, or other ways to make learning accessible. They do not need special instructional methods as much as accommodations to allow them to come to school and for continuity of instruction. How would you feel about having a child with a 504 plan in your class? What if a child had an episodic illness such as asthma or cancer? What about epilepsy? Would you have to learn new techniques? 504 plans can impact a very different part of the educational system and they require you to develop different skills and ways of thinking.

Individualized Family Service Plans

The IFSP is one component of Part C of P.L. 108–446, the 2004 amendments to the IDEA. Identified infants and toddlers (birth to 3) will have an IFSP. There are differences between the IEP and the IFSP, and in the approach of professionals who work with infants and toddlers and their families. The purpose of the IFSP is to identify, organize, and facilitate the attainment of families' goals for their children and for themselves to support their children. The process of interacting and joining with families in their exploration of their strengths and goals for themselves and their children may be more important than the IFSP itself. The IFSP requires professionals to add new skills to their repertoire and to go beyond the traditional boundaries of their disciplines. In many ways, the IFSP addresses not only intervention in the child's development

but the relationship between families and professionals. The family-centered model is based on collaboration and partnership. The relationship depends upon mutual respect, understanding, and empathy. In a family-centered approach, parents and professionals are viewed as equals. This is very different from the paternalistic view of the past, when professionals were seen as having both knowledge and power. However, now the family defines the role the professional will play. The role can be an active or passive one and it may change over time. The role of the professional is to empower families to make the choices that best fit their current strengths and needs.

The central idea of an IFSP is that services should be family-based instead of child-based. The IFSP changes as the family and child change because the process and resulting product are *family-driven*. Families decide what they want as outcomes on the IFSP. Four major themes are part of the recommended practices:

1. Shared responsibility and collaboration
2. Strengthened family functioning
3. Individualized and flexible practices
4. Strengths- and assets-based practice (Trivette & Dunst, 2005).

These themes provide professionals with a framework for thinking about and supporting families. Although it is the process that is important, sometimes the product tells us about the process. Because infants and toddlers are not the same as *small preschoolers*, the IFSP does not bring to it the behavioral, child-focused approach of the IEP.

Content of the IFSP

The IDEA determines the requirements of the IFSP, and it specifies that the early intervention services must include a multidisciplinary assessment and a written IFSP to be developed with the family. The 2004 amendments to the IDEA stipulate the following relative to the content of the IFSP.

(d) Content of Plan.—The individualized family service plan shall be in writing and contain—

(1) a statement of the infant's or toddler's present levels of physical development, cognitive development, communication development, social or emotional development, and adaptive development, based on objective criteria;

(2) a statement of the family's resources, priorities, and concerns relating to enhancing the development of the family's infant or toddler with a disability;

(3) a statement of the measurable results or outcomes expected to be achieved for the infant or toddler and the family, including pre-literacy and language skills, as developmentally appropriate for the child, and the criteria, procedures, and timelines used to determine the degree to which progress toward achieving the results or outcomes is being made and whether modifications or revisions of the results or outcomes or services are necessary;

(4) a statement of specific early intervention services based on peer-reviewed research, to the extent practicable, necessary to meet the unique needs of the infant or toddler and the family, including the frequency, intensity, and method of delivering services;

Public School District
504 Plan

Name: Russell Johnson   DOB: 10/6/00   Phone: 555-5555

School: Woods Elementary   Grade: 3   Teacher/Counselor: Dovre

Parent(s)/Guardian(s): Debra Connor, Harold Johnson

Date of Conference: 11/5/08   Reevaluation Date: 6/09

Conference Participants: We, the undersigned, have participated in a discussion of this child's eligibility for services under Section 504 and designed this plan.

Title	Name	Signature
Parent(s)	Mr. Johnson	
Teacher	Ms. Dovre	
School Counselor	Mr. Wudali	
Asst. Principal	Ms. Agazadian	

Eligibility statement: (Explain the nature of the disability which determines this student's eligibility for 504 services) Russell's second-grade teacher referred him to the Pupil Support Committee (PSC) last April because of his inability to concentrate on tasks requiring attention for more than five minutes. Russell was also calling out in class without raising his hand and not waiting his turn, which was becoming a problem. Russell's parents were noticing impulsive behavior at home and had him evaluated by a physician. At that time, it was determined that Russell has ADHD–Hyperactive Subtype and he began taking medication. Although the medication has helped, Russell is still experiencing difficulty in the classroom and may need further intervention and support.

Goals/objectives:
General goals for Russell include interacting with peers in an age-appropriate manner, remaining focused on his work during class and homework, and following classroom rules.

Services to be provided:

Service	Person responsible	Duration
Telephone Contact	Parent and Teacher	Ongoing
Teacher "good day" notes (with subsequent reward at home)	Teacher/Parent	11/08–6/09
Monthly meetings for first 3 mos. then meetings every other month	Parent, Teachers, 504 Coordinator	11/08–6/09
Referral to School Counselor (will include in social skills groups as appropriate)	Counselor	11/08

Classroom Modifications:
Use of computer time as reward
Use of a one-person table
Leadership responsibilities
Cooperative learning with older students
Use of agreed-upon signal to remind Russell to remain calm and think before acting

Evaluation:

Procedures	Date
Teacher and parent evaluate at monthly meetings	Monthly
PSC contact	Beginning 11/08
Teacher/student conference (self-evaluation)	Once every 2 weeks
504 Coordinator to remain in contact with parent, physician, and teachers	Every 6 mos. (more frequently if needed)
Parent/Guardian attended meeting: Y N	

_____
504 Coordinator

Figure 5–7: Sample 504 Plan

(5) a statement of the natural environments in which early intervention services will appropriately be provided, including a justification of the extent, if any, to which the services will not be provided in a natural environment;

(6) the projected dates for initiation of services and the anticipated length, duration, and frequency of the services;

(7) the identification of the service coordinator from the profession most immediately relevant to the infant's or toddler's or family's needs (or who is otherwise qualified to carry out all applicable responsibilities under this part) who will be responsible for the implementation of the plan and coordination with other agencies and persons, including transition services; and

(8) the steps to be taken to support the transition of the toddler with a disability to preschool or other appropriate services. (Title I/C/636/d, U.S. Department of Education, 2006b)

The IDEA stipulates also that the contents of the IFSP shall be fully explained to the parents and informed written consent from the parents shall be obtained prior to the provision of early intervention services described in such plan. If the parents do not consent to a particular early intervention service, that early intervention service will not be provided.

In the 2004 revisions to the IDEA, some changes were made to the Act. Table 5–1 summarizes relevant changes to Part C.

The areas of evaluation and assessment have changed in the IDEA 2004 as well. There is an increased emphasis on assessments being timely, comprehensive, and multidisciplinary.

- Child assessment refers to reviewing a child's pertinent records (health status and medical history), observing the child and assessing him to identify his unique strengths and needs, including his level of functioning in cognitive and physical development, including vision and hearing, communication development, social or emotional development, and adaptive development. These assessments must be based on objective criteria and must include informed **clinical opinion**.

- Family assessment, typically a voluntary personal interview with the family, involves the identification of the family's resources, priorities, and concerns, and the supports and services necessary to enhance the family's capacity to meet the developmental needs of the family's infant or toddler with a disability, as determined through child assessment.

- Service needs assessment, if the infant or toddler qualifies as a child with a disability, includes reviewing the assessment of the child and family as well as pertinent records and observations to identify the early intervention services appropriate to meet the child's unique needs in each developmental area.

- Evaluation is the method used to review the assessments of the child and the family to determine if the child is eligible for services and his continuing eligibility (Keilty, Walsh, & Ziegler, 2007; U.S. Department of Education, 2006b).

IFSP Process

Although all agencies will have slightly different procedures, eligibility criteria, and organizational frameworks, it is expected that the process will be something like this:

1. Families are referred by a physician, agency, or are self-referred to early intervention services.
2. Families then talk about their likes and dislikes, wants and needs, preferences, and priorities. This may be the first time some families have had any interaction with early intervention. It may also be the first time they have been asked what *they* want for their family as well as for their infant or toddler. They may need support to think about the needs of the family instead of just the child. This process may take more than one meeting. Because families' preferences set the stage for the IFSP, it is vital.
3. Assessment planning then analyzes the information-gathering process. It clarifies the family's preferences for involvement and their priorities for both the family

Table 5–1: Changes to Part C of the IDEA 2004

1. Emphasizes identifying underserved populations of infants and toddlers who have or are at risk of having developmental disabilities and new screening regulations
2. Clarifies that the IFSP is implemented as soon as possible once parent consent to intervention is obtained
3. Increases accountability for the success of early intervention services
4. Ensures a seamless transition for children and families when they exit from the Part C program to other appropriate programs with planning and descriptions of available services at least 9 months prior to the toddler's third birthday
5. Provides states with flexibility to provide early intervention services to children with disabilities who are age 3 and older
6. Provides states with alternatives to dispute resolution under Part C's procedural safeguards
7. Clarifies certain definitions, including specific early intervention services, qualified personnel, and emphasizes that intervention services should be provided in natural environments

Source: Keilty, Walsh, & Ziegler, 2007; U.S. Department of Education, 2006b.

Infants and toddlers need to be observed in their natural environments as part of the assessment process

and child. Information about the infant or toddler's characteristics and additional information from other assessments should be included. One role of the service coordinator is to help support the family in deciding on their role and the level of participation. Families have an active voice in the assessment process, scheduling the assessment, determining appropriate assessment measures and when and how the assessment information will be shared. Planning the assessment around the parents' work, the child's most alert time, and the schedule of professionals can be a challenge. Parents participation in the process makes the assessment more accurate and more relevant.

4. Before formal child assessment begins, it is imperative to determine the parents' perceptions of their infant or toddler. Find out what they consider to be the child's strengths and needs, likes and dislikes, what are their specific areas of concern, and what they want for their child. It is often useful to find out what a typical day is like in the family; be sure to include all family members to understand how they share roles as well as the role the infant or toddler plays in the family.

5. Child assessment serves different functions at various points in the process. Initially the assessment focuses on diagnosis to determine whether the child meets the eligibility criteria for the program. Information is also necessary to develop the IFSP.

6. Identification of family values and preferences involves clarifying with families what aspects of their family life are relevant to their child's growth and development. There are a variety of measures available to help families identify their strengths, needs, resources, and supports. These measures come in many different formats. However, the most efficient way to learn about what families want and how they want to participate is to ask them. If they want further clarification, offer them some options.

Developing outcomes to meet child and family needs requires the interpretation and synthesis of formal and informal assessment information in light of the family's priorities. It may involve some rethinking, and will certainly necessitate choosing among strategies, activities, and services to meet desired outcomes. Do not assume all families with a child with a disability have the same needs, wants, desires, or values.

IFSPs are designed to be a family-based collaboration. When this does not happen, the results can be devastating to families and children.

In the Field

I was concerned about Bobby's language and decided to take him to Child Development Watch. It was horrible. I have never had such a bad experience in my life. I called to get an appointment and waited to hear from them. They called on Friday to confirm the appointment for Monday. I decided not to say anything even though they scheduled it right at his naptime.

It didn't go well. Bobby and I were the first people there. It was a doctor's office with all kinds of cabinets and stuff. He was tired and he played with the stroller until we put it outside. Then they gave him toys and instead of doing what they asked he would put the toys in the cabinets.

There was a developmental nurse and a speech/language pathologist. The speech and language person could not get him to engage. They called him Bob and that is my husband's name and then they said he didn't respond to his own name. I was getting upset and I forgot to tell them that we called him Bobby. I would have told them if they asked if he had a nickname. They gave him the Peabody Picture Vocabulary test, but they couldn't get him to sit still to look at the pictures. He kept pulling at my hand, because he wanted to go home. We were there for over 2 hours. We were both exhausted. When we got home, he slept for 3 hours.

They kept saying things like "Well, we know he's different." And "He likes music maybe he could do something in that." He's only 2 years old and they are already feeling that he's not going to make it. They didn't listen to anything I said. I told them that he doesn't do what you tell him to do. But in 10 minutes she "knew" what was wrong with him. She kept pooh-poohing everything I said he could do. I was irrelevant in a doctor's room. Just because something happens in one situation does not mean it is true in all settings. The environment was producing some of this.

I was frustrated. I knew that he had some problems but not all the problems they were saying. I told them that he could go down four stairs independently (we have a split-level) so they took him to the top of this long dark staircase and the speech/language pathologist stood at the bottom of the stairs and called to him. He shook and cried and grabbed me and she only said. "Well, sometimes we see what we want to see when it is our child." I know he is not perfect—his temperament makes it difficult for him to sit still, he is just 24 months old, and he needed a nap. He knows what he wants to do and he does it. I do a lot of incidental teaching at home. He moves to learn, because he is not a sitter. Bobby likes to play with his toys by running them on the couch or windowsill. When he was playing with the toys there, they said to me, "Don't you ever put toys on the floor for him?" Of course I do.

What did they think? This was a strange place and his style is to explore it all.

When he is free to explore he is like this. He likes his stroller and when we go to the grocery store, everyone in the store knows him. I went here for 8 years before we had Bobby and I never knew anyone. They say things like "Here comes the boy." Everyone knows him. He really likes grown-ups, especially the Grandpas and Uncles, and tries to get their attention. Sometimes I'll hear him belly laughing and see some guy down at the end of the isle making faces at him. He's very outgoing.

They gave me the results right there. They said they would give me the results in writing later, but they wanted me to know right away so we could get started. He is 24 months old and they said his adaptive skills were at 24 months; his cognitive skills were only at 11 months. He got two out of twelve questions on the Bayley. His receptive language was at 10 months and his expressive language at 13 months. His fine motor skills were at 10 months and gross motor 21 months. His social and emotional skills were at 18 months.

I was devastated. I cried for 2 weeks and then I got angry. They wouldn't listen to me. They felt they knew more about my son than I did. They told me he needed a neurologic evaluation and they gave me a card telling me when it was scheduled on my way out. They didn't even ask me if I wanted one. They told me he needed speech and language therapy, occupational therapy, and a feeding evaluation (I guess that was because I said he was a picky eater.) He also needed a hearing test. That was supposed to be done that day as well but when we went to the audiologist she looked at us and asked if I was really worried about his hearing. I said I wasn't. She asked how likely it was that Bobby would cooperate. I said he wouldn't. She suggested we come back on another day.

I walked out of there shaking like a leaf. I wanted to shout "How can you do this to parents?" I wanted to throw up for a week. My God, is there nothing you can do for me? If we give kids early intervention, they can do more. Is there no hope? Kids are not a textbook. We know more now and how to help them better but that was not how I felt when we left. We are doomed. I kept saying, "Don't worry about the tests, they are just test results." I felt like I needed to defend him. At 2 he looks like everyone else because they are all throwing tantrums. It is very disturbing; these people are going to identify all the kids who need help. Their goal seems to be to scare people. They do not say things like "Based on what we see today ... " "Or "he qualifies for help" because he does need help. I wanted someone to affirm what I was feeling. I wanted them to do it at my house. This felt like a medical model where they were making a diagnosis rather than trying to figure out what we could do to help him learn. My academic field is early childhood special education and I sought them out because I was concerned about his language development. I didn't need this.

Reflective Practice

Reflect on how this process compares with the seven points documented under the IFSP Process and the four recommended practices. If you were the mother

what would you have done? What could the professionals have done differently that would have changed the outcome for both the mother and Bobby? What conclusions can you draw about Bobby and how he functions in his world? Think about his scores on the Bayley Scale of Infant Development III. Where do these scores place him developmentally?

The IFSP's expected outcomes should be the changes that families want for themselves and their child. The IFSP does require a statement of what is going to occur to produce the desired outcome. Because the IFSP is developed collaboratively with parents it may require new skills for professionals. The IFSP should reflect the values and priorities of the family, not the professionals. The role of professionals is to help families identify relevant strengths. Professionals need to use listening and interviewing techniques as well as negotiation skills. They also need to know the resources available in the community.

Implementing the IFSP requires another round of decision making. Families need to know the range of options available to them and decide which of the options best fit their needs. This range should start with the options that the family would choose from if their infant or toddler did not have a disability. If the parents' first choice is that the toddler should be in the same family child care home as his older sister, that should be the first option explored. If this setting is chosen, the question for the team becomes how to support the toddler in that setting. Assistance might include the provision of necessary related and support services as well as training, technical assistance, and perhaps specialized equipment for the family child care provider.

Different families have different desires. For some, placement in an early care and education setting is most appropriate; for others, a home-based program or even a segregated early intervention program will best fit the family's needs. Or, families may find that a combination of these options works best. The role of the professional, particularly the service coordinator, is to ensure that families make choices from the full range of options in both settings. Facilitating linkages among professionals, available resources, and program options is a major role. Creativity is required to meet families' needs.

Young children change quickly. Informal IFSP reviews need to be made on an ongoing basis, and more formal ones should be called for when necessary. At the beginning, reviews need to be made early for troubleshooting, if necessary. The IFSP must be evaluated annually with a formal review every 6 months.

IFSP Case Studies

Families are different. Case studies have been included to help to clarify these differences and the roles necessary for positive interaction. Because the IFSP process is more flexible than the IEP process, I provided all the relevant parts of the IFSP for one child and portions of IFSPs for other children. I have used a variety of formats as there is no set form. The first IFSP is for Bobby (Figure 5–8). You read about his Child Find experience in the In the Field included previously in this chapter.

Section 4. Developmental strengths and concerns for the child plan	Date: 9/18/08	Child's name: Bobby
Present levels of functioning	**Strengths/resources**	**Concerns/needs/priorities**
1. Cognitive (thinking and solving problems): Date: 8/14/08 Age at evaluation: 24 months Test tool: Bayley Scale of Infant Development III Developmental age: 11 months	1. Will repeat an activity to get a laugh. Very inquisitive—wants to know how things work. Good problem-solving skills. Loves books. Imitates adult activities—engages in imaginary play.	1. None
2. Adaptive (self-help skills): Date: 8/14/08 Age at evaluation: 24 months Test tool: Early Learning Accomplishment Profile Age: 24 months	2. Can pull off and put on pants. Uses a spoon; learning to use a fork. Can brush teeth. Can put on shoes.	2. None
3. Social/emotional (interacting with others): Date: 8/14/08 Age at evaluation: 24 months Test tool: Early Learning Accomplishment Profile Age: 18 months	3. Great sense of humor. Does things to make people laugh. Good socially. Gets along with others at preschool. Can be independent and he engages in parallel play.	3. None
4. Communication (understanding and using language): Date: 8/14/08 Age at evaluation: 24 months Test tool: Preschool Language Scale 4th Edition Receptive language: 10 months Expressive language: 13 months	4. Makes his needs known by making sounds, pointing, eye contact, some signs, and can use some words. He seems to understand what is said. He has just started singing. No problem with food textures—balanced diet— loves fruit and eats meat.	4. Bobby should be saying more at this age and we would like Bobby to express himself appropriately.
5. Physical (large body movement and ability to use hands): Date: 8/14/08 Age at evaluation: 24 months Test tool: Bayley Scale of Infant Development III Fine motor: 10 months Gross motor: 21 months	5. Good gross motor skills—runs, jumps, kicks ball— loves to roughhouse. Can unlock and open sliding glass door. Colors. Puzzle play is emerging. Plays with play dough. Loves to dump/pour—loves to play with water.	5. None to motor skills but have concerns about sensory integration.

Section 5. Health strengths and concerns for the child plan	Date: 9/18/08	Child's name: Bobby
Present levels of functioning	**Strengths/resources**	**Concerns/needs/priorities**
Primary care physician	Dr. Amy Groll	
Vision:	Vision was tested: appropriate	
Hearing:	Tested 9/8/08: appropriate	None
Nutrition:	Picky eater—but has a balanced diet—takes a vitamin—typically two	
Significant medical findings: Cognitive Communications Motor		

Figure 5–8: Individualized Family Service Plan

Section 6. Strengths and concerns for the family plan		Date: *9/18/08*		Child's name: *Bobby*
Current family information		**Strengths/resources**		**Concerns/needs/priorities**
Bobby currently lives at home with his mother and father and two dogs.		*Supportive family with some family in the area and others in Florida.*		*None*
		Mom gets to work part-time and be at home with Bobby.		

Section 7. Child and family outcomes plan		Date: *9/18/08*		Child's name: *Bobby*
Major outcomes (to address concerns/needs priorities)		**Steps toward outcomes**		**Review dates/outcomes**
1. *Bobby will speak at an age-appropriate level.*		1. *Refer for speech and language therapy. Parents will convey all of the wonderful things they are doing.*		
2. *We will explore sensory integration*		2. *Refer to an occupational therapist for a sensory integration evaluation. Mom will read Raising Your Spirited Child.*		

Figure 5–8: Individualized Family Service Plan (continued)

Reflective Practice

Think carefully about this IFSP. Consider the discrepancies between the test results and the parents concerns. If this 2-year-old were in your classroom, what concerns would you have? How would you plan to work with this child to support his needs and the parents' concerns? How would you decide to work with the differences between the assessment information and the parent's concerns as reflected in the IFSP? What do you see as Bobby and his family's strengths?

The Dee Family

The Dee family consists of a single mother with six children. The mother, a full-time homemaker, is pregnant with twins. The two oldest children have been identified as having learning disabilities and receive special education services. Alvin is 1 year, 8 months old and attends a child care center full-time, along with his 2½-year-old brother. Alvin was observed informally at the child care center where staff was holding an in-service training. Upon learning about developmental norms, a child care provider became concerned about Alvin and asked if she should talk to his mother. At 20 months Alvin was not walking, standing, eating independently, or talking. He had strong temper tantrums. He had to be fed and used a bottle. He had limited social interaction skills and few purposeful play skills.

Public health nurses were involved with the family. They made appointments for the family, but the mother did not keep them (sometimes appointments conflicted with one another, sometimes she forgot). The mother reported that all the children have behavior problems. The family lives in a rural area and transportation is a problem. The mother feels overwhelmed. The father is available but not living in the home.

The amount of child support payments makes the family ineligible for Temporary Aid for Needy Families (TANF); however, payments are frequently late or too little. While there is no money for utilities, heating bills are $400 in the winter months. The children experience frequent illnesses, but the mother cannot locate a doctor willing to treat the children because no local doctor will accept new Medicaid patients; therefore, illnesses go unattended.

A graphic outline of the coordination services facilitated by the staff between the family, the early care and education center, and the service providers is shown in Figure 5–9. Initial involvement with this family required assisting the mother in meeting her priorities, including getting financial assistance for child care, food, and utilities. This assistance was gained through agencies listed under the economic category, and included accessing emergency utility funds and budgeting help, applying for special needs child care funding, and accessing the regional food bank.

Once some basic resource issues were attended to, the mother became more receptive to tackling child issues. Arrangements were made to have the two younger boys assessed for intervention purposes. The family was channeled to the Early Childhood Center for an evaluation. Developmental evaluation results indicated Alvin was functioning cognitively at about 50 percent of his age expectations, and his brother had a significant language delay. The Early Childhood Center assisted in the provision of speech and language therapy and behavioral intervention. Therapy was provided at the child care center. Behavioral intervention was provided at home with consultation. The public health system was accessed for evaluations including the hearing clinic, vision clinic, and medical clinic. Transportation was arranged when possible, and efforts were made to prevent appointment conflicts.

Meetings were set up between the child care center and service providers to facilitate a coordinated intervention program. The child care center was able to implement activities involving language stimulation and behavioral management. When the mother did not come to the meeting, the early childhood consultant made a home visit to gain input and share the information. The result of these efforts was a coordinated intervention system for Alvin (see Figure 5–10 for a portion of Alvin's IFSP).

Service coordination for the Dee family was complex. It required an unusual variety of skills on the part of the service coordinator in addition to a broad knowledge of available community resources, far beyond that expected of most early childhood educators.

The Monroe Family

The Monroe family consists of a dual-earner, professional couple and their two biological children and one daughter from the husband's previous marriage. Their youngest child Cathy was diagnosed with Down syndrome (**mosaic trisomy 18**) at birth. Cathy was enrolled in a program when she was 25 months old. She is severely delayed in all areas of development, and is currently functioning at levels of 12 to 14 months in all areas. The Monroes heard about the early intervention program from another parent at a workshop sponsored by the Parent Information Center and contacted the program staff. When services began, the Monroe family had their daughter enrolled in a child care center, but were not satisfied with the level of care. They thought the center was too large. The Monroe family located a family child care provider who agreed to participate in training and also enrolled their daughter in an early intervention program two afternoons a week. (Transportation provided by the early intervention program made this possible.)

This family is functioning well. The parents are aware of their daughter's disability and are seeking ways to provide her with the best opportunities possible. Their concerns have been to find the best public school option for Cathy and to plan wisely for her future. Staff provided the family with information on financial planning for families with children with disabilities. A staff member attended the family's meeting with the school district as part of the transition process to public school services, as well as observing in potential classrooms and talking with the teachers.

The service coordinator made a few visits to the early intervention site to coordinate the services Cathy was receiving there with the care she received at the family child care provider's home. She also arranged for Cathy's physical therapist to visit the family child care provider to demonstrate positioning and carrying techniques. In the beginning, monthly home visits were scheduled, but once the program for Cathy was in place, visits were replaced by monthly telephone contacts at the family's request (Figure 5–11).

Some families need far less coordination. They are aware of their personal resources and those in the community. However, they, too, need to have a service coordinator available, especially as children transition from one setting to another. Such families might find an informal narrative statement of their strengths/resources and desired outcomes the most workable for them. Figure 5–12 is an example of part of the Monroe family's plan.

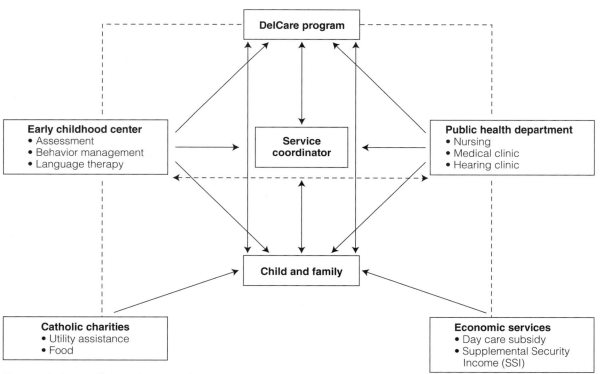

Figure 5–9: Family Service Coordination: Dee Family

For some families service coordination is complex. It requires the service coordinator to be knowledgeable about early childhood special education and also public and private services and resources. When service needs are complex family needs may take priority over child needs.

Child's name: Alvin Dee	DOB 4/8/07	Date 10/10/08

Child's strengths and functioning levels:

Alvin is a relatively happy undemanding child who seems to be able to occupy himself. His mother reports that he enjoys watching television but has a "terrible temper" like the other children in the family. She has not encouraged him to stand or walk because he is easier to care for when he stays put in the playpen. He likes his bottle so she has encouraged him to use it. He shows some initial interest in toys but this is only momentary and if in the crib he throws them out. At the child care center he can focus on toys for 2 to 3 minutes with adult support. He can hold his bottle and will crawl toward it when hungry.

Family's strengths, concerns, and priorities:

Alvin's mother is a full-time homemaker. She is concerned about all the children but her priorities now relate to basic needs rather than whether or not Alvin has a developmental delay. She is concerned about them turning off the utilities as it is getting cold. The children need warm jackets. She wants to keep the two younger children in child care but is afraid her benefits will run out and with her pregnancy she doesn't have the energy to care for them all day. She needs money for some basic expenses and information on money management as well as the services she might have available. She would like to focus on skills that will make Alvin more independent as she is worried about the time she will have to devote to his care once the twins are born.

Child assessments

Note: There have been few assessments as Alvin's mother's priorities are in other areas at this time.

Skill area Language	Chronological age	Functional level	Skill area Developmental	Chronological age	Functional level
Receptive	18 months	12 months (9–13)	Mental age	18 months	13 months (11–16)
Expressive	18 months	8 months (6–9)	Motor age	18 months	9 months (6–11)

Child's name: Alvin Dee		Date 10/10/08				
Major outcomes	**Supports/ resources**	**Action plan**	**Comments**	**Family eval. Date**	**Status**
Alvin's receptive language will improve	*Mrs. Dee, siblings, Ms. Taylor (teacher) Mr. Janis (service coordinator)*	*Mrs. Dee and his teacher Ms. Taylor will make a list of words and concepts that would be most useful for Alvin to understand. Then Ms. Taylor will develop a plan. Mr. Janis will show Mrs. Dee and the other children how to use it at home.*		*10/10/08*	*1*
Alvin's expressive language will improve	*Mrs. Dee, siblings, Ms. Austin (speech therapist) Mr. Janis*	*Mrs. Dee and Ms. Austin (speech therapist) will generate a list of words based on Mrs. Dee's priorities and Ms. Austin will refine the list based on the difficulty of the words and sounds and suggest alternatives for important ones if necessary. Ms. Austin will develop a plan and Mr. Janis will convey, model, and monitor the plan at home and in the child care setting.*		*10/10/08*	*1*

Family evaluation status: 1 = Implementation not yet begun   2 = Outcome partially accomplished; continue current strategies
3 = Outcome partially accomplished but need different strategies 4 = Outcome partially accomplished but needs practice
5 = Outcome predictably accomplished to family's satisfaction

Figure 5–10: Individualized Family Service Plan: Alvin Dee

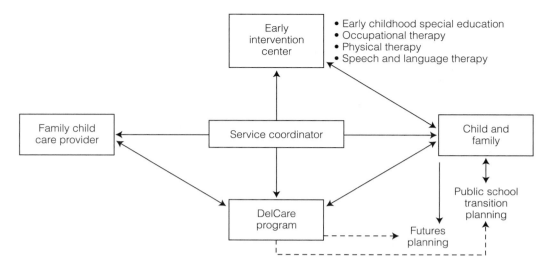

Figure 5–11: Family Service Coordination: Monroe Family
Some families need far less coordination. They are aware of their personal resources and what is available in the community. They still need a service coordinator especially during transitions.

> **Individualized Family Service Plan**
>
> *Family's strengths, concerns, and priorities*
>   The parents are aware of Cathy's disability and are actively planning for her present and future. They are willing and able to read and understand complex material and participate actively in both short- and long-term planning for Cathy.
>   Their long-term goal is to find the best public school placement for Cathy. Their other major concern relates to long-term financial planning.
>   Because they both work they would like the service coordinator to coordinate services between early intervention and the family child care provider. More specifically, they would like to help the family child care provider understand the importance of positioning for Cathy. They would also like some references on long-term financial planning.

Figure 5–12: Individualized Family Service Plan: Monroe

Family Goals

Some families do not want family goals as part of the IFSP; others feel having stated outcomes for the family can help them justify what they need but frequently neglect. Figure 5–13 shows family goals for a couple who want to spend more time together.

Transition Planning

Moving from one educational setting to another can be stressful. Increasingly, kindergarten is not the first educational setting young children encounter. Most children have had previous experience with "school." Based on the requirements of the IDEA and common sense, we have begun to look more critically at the transition from one setting to another and what this means to children, parents, educators, and related service providers. The transition from infant and toddler programs (Part C) to preschool programming (Part B, Section 619) has regulations in the law. It is also a move from discretionary services into mandated services that changes eligibility requirements and entitles children to a free appropriate public education.

However, the principles underlying transition planning are the same for transitions between other settings such as preschool to kindergarten or between grade levels.

Transition planning begins when toddlers are about 28 months old to allow time for exploring options, determining the most appropriate placement, and working on the skills necessary to make the transition a smooth one. To support children in transitions, infant and toddler

> **Family Goals/Outcomes**
>
> **1. Goal/Outcome:** Lee and Joe will spend more time together as a couple.
>
> Objective: They will be together alone for an outing 1/month
>   Strategy: Ask Joe's mom or friend to babysit
>   Persons responsible: Lee and Joe
>   Criteria: They go out 1/month
>   Review date: 1 month
>
> **2. Goal/Outcome:** Lee will be provided with more information on prognosis of microcephaly
>
> Objective: To obtain information about microcephaly and on children with microcephaly, especially long-term effects.
>
> Strategies:
> 1. Ask questions of medical personnel involved with Justin (i.e., pediatrician, pediatric neurologist, or early intervention program).
> 2. Provide reading material on specific disability.
> 3. Provide phone number of Parent Information Center, where Lee may talk with other parents as well as get information she wants
>
> Persons responsible: Lee and Celeste (service coordinator)
> Criteria: Parent is satisfied with information she obtained
> Review date: 3 months

Figure 5–13: Individualized Family Service Plan: Family Goals/Outcomes

Transition planning can be difficult for parents, teachers, and children. It requires all involved to learn about different people and to develop new skills and encounter new challenges.

and preschool teachers need open communication patterns throughout the year. Teachers, parents, and children should visit the other program. Joint in-service workshops can facilitate the development of both informal networks as well as the exchange of information.

The critical goal for toddlers is to provide the support and skills necessary for them to have a successful experience in the new setting. They should approach preschool with motivation and openness to a new experience that is a validation of their growing achievement and confidence. If toddlers are to approach this setting positively, parents, too, must feel confident about their child's ability and the ability of the setting to meet their child's needs.

The IDEA sets forth transition requirements for toddlers moving from infant and toddler programs into the mandated programs that begin at age 3. To ensure a smooth transition for toddlers receiving early intervention services under Part C to preschool Part B, Section 619 or other appropriate services the lead agency has some specific responsibilities.

(ii) the lead agency designated or established under section 635(a)(10) will–

(I) notify the local educational agency for the area in which such a child resides that the child will shortly

reach the age of eligibility for preschool services under part B, as determined in accordance with State law;

(II) in the case of a child who may be eligible for such preschool services, with the approval of the family of the child, convene a conference among the lead agency, the family, and the local educational agency not less than 90 days (and at the discretion of all such parties, not more than 9 months) before the child is eligible for the preschool services, to discuss any such services that the child may receive; and

(III) in the case of a child who may not be eligible for such preschool services, with the approval of the family, make reasonable efforts to convene a conference among the lead agency, the family, and providers of other appropriate services for children who are not eligible for preschool services under part B, to discuss the appropriate services that the child may receive. (Title I/C/637/a/9/A/ ii, U.S. Department of Education, 2006b)

The written transition plan looks something like Figure 5–14. For teachers to support the transition they need to know the individual child and the differences and similarities between their program and the one the child will enter. Key elements to successful transitions for young children include the following:

- providing program continuity through developmentally appropriate curricula;
- maintaining ongoing communication and cooperation between staff;
- preparing children for the transition;
- involving parents in the transition.

To the extent that the programs are developmentally based, the transition between the two is easier. It is also easier to meet the individual needs of children with disabilities, because this type of programming allows for a wide range of developmental differences within the same class. To the extent that the preschool has a very academic orientation, the transition is likely to be more difficult.

Even preschools with a developmental base have some significant differences from most programs for infants and toddlers. Preschool children are older and can do more things. They are interested in the broader community, they have better gross and fine motor skills, they play for longer periods and at the associate and cooperative level.

Preschools that include children with disabilities may be public or private. They may be part of the public school system, Head Start, early care and education centers, church preschools or family or center child care. The group size is typically larger and the number of teachers is smaller. Time schedules may be more strictly adhered to because there may be only one time when specific groups of children can use the playground, or they may have a schedule for "specials" such as gym or music.

Implications for Educators

Early interventionists prepare for the transition by visiting preschools, perhaps sharing a snack with the children, or by making a videotape of what happens in preschool. It is important that you show toddlers several different

Transition Plan

Child: _____   Expected transition date: _____

Service coordinator: _____   Target receiving site: _____

Reason for transition: _____

_____

_____

Transition event	Person responsible	Dates achieved	Comment
1. Parents informed of possible options	Service coordinator		
2. Receiving agencies contacted	Parents Service coordinator		
3. Parents visit agencies	Parents Service coordinator		
4. Transition conference to determine appropriate placement	Parents Service coordinator Receiving agency Intervention team		
5. Transfer of records	Receiving agency Sending agency		
6. Written transition plan developed	Parents Service Coordinator Receiving agency		
7. Placement	Parents Child Receiving agency		
8. Follow-up	Sending agency Service coordinator		

Figure 5–14: Transition Plan

preschools if you do not know the school or class they will be entering or if they will go to different preschools. Because teachers may be moved or hired in August, this exposure is a good idea even if you feel confident you know what will happen. Talk about the differences and similarities between preschool programs and between preschool and infant and toddler programs.

Encourage parents to visit the preschool class they would like their child to attend. They may want to visit early in the year (October) to get a feel for the expectations teachers have of incoming children and then perhaps all the classes during the latter part of the school year to look at teaching styles. Some schools are responsive to suggestions from parents about particular teachers with whom they feel their child would do well while others are not. Most are willing to listen to why certain teachers might be a mismatch.

Talk with parents about what records they want forwarded and those they do not. Tell parents about the other children in the class or children that you know who will be attending the same setting. Encourage parents to invite that child over to play and perhaps arrange a time when parents could get together to talk as well. Be sure that parents know what their rights are and help them stand up for them, if necessary. If a child who was served under Part C (birth to 3), at the parent's request, the Part C coordinator or other representative can be present to ensure a smooth transition.

Summary

Over the past two decades individualized programming has moved from being an oddity to a place where curriculum is universally designed to include children with a wide range of abilities. IEPs are designed with measurable annual goals that are tied to state standards for the education of all children at a particular level. Increasingly technology is used to support children with disabilities.

With young children, the efficacy of including families and the needs of the family instead of focusing solely on the needs of the child became apparent. For younger children with disabilities, an IFSP is required. It focuses on the strengths and resources of the family as well as the child. Because children are receiving intervention services earlier, they are moving from one program to another. Transition planning is an important and vital part of the process.

Reflections

1. The Individuals with Disabilities Education Act of 2004 has many purposes, sections, and requirements that early childhood educators should be familiar with. However, it seems that after college, if you do not refer back to the act itself, you may forget some of the important points of this very salient piece of legislation. For example, are you familiar with exactly what a free appropriate public education entails? Do you know about requirements for assistive technology? What about IEP and IFSP requirements? Are you knowledgeable about mediation and due process? Would you be intimidated if you were called to one of these meetings? Can you answer the previous questions? Do you have a plan for keeping up with new legislation? Do you see this as a part of being a reflective knowledgeable practitioner? How will you do it?

2. Early childhood special educators play a significant role in writing goals for IFSPs and IEPs. A child's learning is directed by how well the goals are written and whether or not they are appropriate for the child. Therefore, it is necessary that educators are highly skilled at writing goals. How will you go about learning this skill? As a competent and reflective practitioner, you must be able to write and implement goals that help children learn the skills they need in the sequence in which these skills should be taught and how to embed these in the curriculum. Can you do this? Remember, the reflective practitioner reflects not only on children, lessons, and curriculum, but also on her own knowledge and skills.

Educational Resources

Association for Persons with Severe Handicaps (TASH) is an advocacy organization that disseminates information to improve the education and independence of those with severe disabilities. http://www.tash.org

Disability Rights Education and Defense Fund (DREDF) provides information, technical assistance, and referrals on laws and rights. (510) 644–2555, (510) 644–2626; ADA Hotline: (800) 466–4232; http://www.dredf.org

IDEA: Building the Legacy of IDEA 2004 is designed as one-stop shopping for information about the IDEA. This site is sponsored by the U. S. Department of Education and is an ideal place to keep current on the law and its regulations. http://idea.ed.gov

National Center to Improve Practice in Special Education through Technology, Media and Materials provides information on the effective use of technology; video profiles of children using assistive and instructional technologies, both high and low tech. It provides links to other special education and technology resources. http://www2.edc.org/NCIP/

SERI Inclusion Resources is a good site to start with as it provides essential information plus links to other resources. http://www.seriweb.com/inclu.htm

Through the Looking Glass (TLG) disseminates research and information to family members who have a disability or medical issue. The **National Parent Network on Disabilities,** an advocacy group that publishes a newsletter and legislative alerts regarding federal policy that affects children with disabilities is accessed on this site. It serves as an information and referral source for organizations and parents. Publishes a newsletter called Parenting with a Disability. Voice/TTY (800) 644–2666 or (510) 848–1112; FAX (510) 848–4445; http://lookingglass.org/index.php

For additional resources, visit the book companion website for this text at www.cengage.com/education/deiner.

Chapter 6

Atypical Development: The Beginning

He sat on the floor of the cement terrace, a joint dangling between his fingers, his eyes full of tears, as he began his story. "I was so stupid," he said. "Laura and I would get drunk and high and then we would just do it. I never thought of condoms; I never thought of consequences. It was just you know . . . good. It's different when you're in college, you're studying, you're partying and that is your world. I didn't know . . . no I did know, but I didn't care if she got pregnant . . . that's what abortions were for. But then she did and everything changed . . . And then again it didn't. . . ."

"I didn't know she was pregnant until the third month . . . and we kept partying and having sex, night after night, until she finally told me she was pregnant. I remember we had done coke the night she told me. And afterward I drank and drank; I just couldn't believe she was pregnant . . . I didn't even really know her. All I knew was that she refused to have an abortion and that I was going to be a father."

"What did I know about being a dad; it's not like I had the best childhood. But I knew that babies cost money . . . and that was something I didn't have and Laura wanted us to live together, to be together. . . . All I had wanted was sex . . . not a relationship, just sex."

Robert pulled the joint in his mouth and inhaled for what seemed to me to be forever. Then he looked at me glassy-eyed and said with a conviction I had never heard from the notorious party boy, "Elaine always, always make sure he uses a condom. . . . Don't be stupid like me."

"Anyway, Laura went to the gynecologist, and stuff. Everything was going ok. I thought that at least the baby would be normal and maybe life wouldn't be so bad. I got my head together, quit school. I started working and getting ready for the big B."

"But four months later . . . Laura went into labor and the baby was born 3 months premature. I can't say that Carena was a beautiful baby . . . no baby is beautiful with tubes and IVs and stuff. She was so little, and deformed . . . and at that moment I regretted every time I had ever slept with Laura. I wanted a different life and it seemed that the nightmare was just beginning."

"Doctors explained that my little girl would probably never walk, would never be able to eat without tubes, and might never sit up. A normal life was completely out of the question for Carena."

"Laura became a full-time mom. She got up every time Carena cried; she was attuned to her every movement. I tried, I really did, but I couldn't bond with my baby. She had no idea who I was and she cried constantly. Sometimes I felt she cried just to annoy me . . . but I know that wasn't true."

"The doctors' bills for Carena were incredible. Seventy percent of my paycheck went to paying for her health care. Thank God, Medicaid paid for some of the expenses or it would have been 100 percent. Laura stayed home with the baby and I started to hang out at bars more . . . I couldn't deal with the two women in my life, one who I didn't love but had to support because she was the mother of my child and the other the baby girl who I couldn't understand."

"Life hit an all time low when Carena became really, really sick when she was 18 months old. The doctors told us she was going to die and they pushed us toward hospice to help us. Laura was hysterical. She never slept. She worried constantly that Carena was in pain and when she wasn't worrying, she was grieving."

"I didn't know what to do when I knew my baby was going to die. I discovered that I loved her, but at the same time it was a relief to know that she wouldn't have to suffer anymore. Now that she's dead . . . it's hard. Laura and I have nothing joining us . . . but I feel guilty about ending the relationship . . . and then I still grieve for Carena and also for the way life might have been. I wish that I had used a condom . . . I wish that I had been more careful . . . but maybe it was good. For 2 very short years I learned how to be a dad to a very special little person."

Robert snuffed out the joint on the concrete floor, stood up, leaned over the iron banister, and started to cry.

Reflective Practice

Building and maintaining relationships is challenging. Men and women frequently respond to the birth of an infant with a disability differently. How would you work with this family before Carena's death? How would your work with this family change after her death? Do you think Laura and Robert's relationship continued?

Pregnancy

The United States does little in the way of educating its young women and men to think about the life skills and healthy living habits needed before, during, and after pregnancy. When pregnancies are planned, the prospective mother and father can make positive changes in their lifestyle. Such conscious decisions are crucial because prenatal development dramatically impacts the infant.

A healthy lifestyle is a positive step, but it does not guarantee a successful pregnancy outcome; however it should be a goal of all prospective mothers and fathers. Many prenatal risks can be prevented; others can be monitored or managed. Planning gives a woman time to ensure that her diet meets the nutritional demands of pregnancy. It provides time to stop using tobacco, alcohol, drugs, and caffeine, and to avoid harmful environmental exposure. These decisions are designed to increase the probability of having a normal, healthy, happy baby. Unfortunately, some prenatal risks are unknown. They cannot be prevented and may not be discovered until birth or after.

There are many factors that influence the development of the fetus before birth. These factors come from the genetic matter that forms the fetus, the environment in which the fetus grows and develops, and the developing fetus himself. These factors interact and influence each other and shape the developing organism.

The time from conception to birth is called **gestation** and usually lasts 40 weeks or about 9 calendar months. The most common way to think about the duration of a pregnancy is to divide the 9 months into three trimesters. This is an outside-looking-in approach. In this section, we will focus on periods that are more significant to the developing organism: the germinal, embryonic, and fetal periods. This approach still breaks down the 9 months into three periods, but the duration of each period is different: the germinal and embryonic periods correspond to the first trimester, and the fetal period corresponds to the remaining two trimesters.

Germinal Period

Each of us starts out as a single cell, the ovum or egg. To develop from this single cell into the person you are today, several processes had to take place: first, the egg had to be fertilized by a sperm; cells then divided and increased in number; they differentiated to create different body parts (skin, bones, heart, and so on); finally, the cells initiated the systemic function of metabolism.

Women are born with all of their reproductive cells. About 2 million eggs or immature **ova** are present in a female's ovaries at birth; however, only about 500 to 600 are used. The mature unfertilized ovum is the largest cell in the female's body. It is about the size of the period that ends this sentence. The ovum is large because of the nutrients it contains. These nutrients nourish the cells during their initial growth and development. Approximately once a month during a female's reproductive years, an egg ripens, is pushed from the **ovary**, the female reproductive organ, drops into one of the **fallopian tubes,** and is available for fertilization. If the egg is not fertilized in 10 to 14 days, the woman's menstrual flow begins, washing away the egg and the lining of the uterine wall. This cycle repeats itself on a regular basis unless fertilization takes place (Haffner, 2007).

Although females are born with immature eggs, males do not begin producing sperm until puberty and continue into old age. Sperm are composed of a large head and a long tail. The head contains the cell nucleus, and the tail, or flagellum, is used for propulsion. During intercourse, hundreds of millions of sperm are mixed with seminal fluid and deposited into the female vagina. Sperm travel the remaining length of the vagina and push through the cervix into the uterus. Midway into the menstrual cycle, mucus secretions of the vagina and the thinning of the cervix make it easier to penetrate, so fertilization is more likely. Women are fertile for approximately 5 days before ovulation and the day of ovulation, which is the day that conception is most likely to occur.

Once in the **uterus,** the 300 million sperm must travel to the correct fallopian tube and then swim up the tube to meet the egg. Only about 200 reach the fallopian tubes. Sperm must travel approximately 7 inches to reach the egg, a journey of about an hour. When one sperm penetrates the outer layer of the egg, the successful sperm prevents others from penetrating the egg. The unsuccessful sperm die within 24 hours (Haffner, 2007). Once inside the egg, the sperm's tail detaches, and the nucleus from the sperm and ovum migrate toward each other and then unite creating a **zygote.** Fertilization restores the number of **chromosomes** to twenty-three pairs and initiates cell division or **cleavage.** In humans, of the twenty-three pairs of chromosomes, there are twenty-two twin chromosomes called autosomes and one pair of sex chromosomes. Chromosomes are very long continuous pieces (or molecules) of DNA that contain many genes and other regulatory material. The sex chromosomes are designated X for female and Y for male. The sex of the child is determined by the father. If the child is a girl, she will have two X chromosomes; if it is a boy, he will have an X and a Y chromosome.

All of the cells in the body divide. However, they divide at different rates ranging from once every 10 hours, in skin cells, to once a year, in liver cells (Batshaw, 2007). All cells except sex cells divide through the process of **mitosis**. Mitosis is the process by which a cell duplicates its genetic information (DNA) and generates two identical cells. These two daughter cells are formed from one parent cell and are exact replicas of the original cell. Cells also divide through **meiosis**. Meiosis is more complicated than mitosis and results in more abnormalities. Unlike mitosis where two identical daughter cells are formed, during the first division in meiosis, the chromosomes that come from the mother and father intertwine, allowing genetic material to be exchanged. Meiosis recombines the twenty-three chromosomes from each parent and fuses them with the set from the other parent to make the forty-six chromosomes necessary for sexual reproduction. This union results in four daughter cells (Batshaw, 2007). This complexity increases the likelihood of genetic disorders but it also enables children to be similar to, but not exactly like, their siblings.

The fertilized cell continues to replicate itself. By 3 to 4 days, this solid mass is called a **morula**. The morula is the earliest stage of development and this egg mass continues to multiply as it moves down the fallopian tube. After 5 days, fluid begins to accumulate between the cells and it begins to change in size and shape, becoming a **blastocyte**. The blastocyte is the second stage of development with an inner and outer cell mass. Once in the **uterus**, it rests for about 2 days before it attaches. This is the formal beginning of pregnancy (Haffner, 2007).

Following ovulation and fertilization, hormonal changes begin. **Progesterone**, a hormone that supports pregnancy, levels increase and that, in combination with other hormonal changes, causes the lining of the uterus, the **endometrium**, to become thick, spongy, and ready for implantation. The endometrium is the inner membrane of the uterus whose glands and blood vessels increase in number and size during pregnancy. The follicle from which the egg was released increases in size and secretes progesterone to help maintain the pregnancy until the placenta is capable of producing enough progesterone on its own. The placenta is formed from the endometrium and supplies the embryo with oxygen and nutrients and takes away wastes.

Of all fertilized eggs, only about half survive and reach the uterus; the body reabsorbs the others. Although it is possible for the blastocyst to implant, or attach, itself to the uterine wall in many places, it normally does so in the upper back portion of the uterus. The site of implantation is critical. If the blastocyst attaches itself to the bottom of the uterus it may cause complications in the delivery or the placenta may detach too early. Sometimes implantation takes place outside the uterus, usually in the fallopian tube. This is called an **ectopic pregnancy** and results in miscarriage.

Until implantation is complete, about 12 days after conception, the developing organism absorbs nutrients directly from the mother's cells. The developing organism is called an **embryo** from the time of implantation through 8 weeks. During the time leading up to implantation, a woman may not even suspect that she is pregnant. Her suspicions usually begin once her menstrual flow is due but does not occur. The embryo produces a hormone, **chorionic gonadotrophin**, which prevents the mother from menstruating.

Exposure to **teratogens** during the germinal period usually leads to a spontaneous abortion or does not impact the embryo. There are so few cells at this stage it tends to be all or nothing (Haffner, 2007).

Embryonic Period

The embryonic period lasts from week 3 to week 8 after fertilization. The 5 weeks of the embryonic period are crucial. For the embryo to survive, a complex infrastructure must be developed to protect and nourish the growing organism. These changes are generated through cell differentiation. Although the cells were originally unspecialized, the membranes now begin to develop into three distinct layers: the **ectoderm**, which evolves into skin, spinal cord, and teeth; the **mesoderm,** which becomes blood vessels, muscles, and bones; and the **endoderm**, which develops into the digestive system, lungs, and urinary tract (Batshaw, 2007). The changes they evoke include thickening of the uterine lining, the development of the **placenta**, the **umbilical cord**, and the **amniotic sac.** The amniotic sac consists of a pair of tough thin membranes that hold the embryo and then fetus during pregnancy.

The placenta is a highly specialized disk-shaped organ through which the fetus makes functional contact with the wall of the uterus. The embryo is connected to the placenta by the umbilical cord, which is hose-like and contains blood vessels. The **amnion**, a sac-like membrane is filled with a clear liquid called **amniotic fluid**. The amnion is the inner membrane of the amniotic sac containing amniotic fluid and the embryo. This membrane allows the embryo to move freely within the uterus, and protects it from injury.

The mature placenta develops rapidly after implantation and covers about 20 percent of the uterine wall. There is a fetal and a maternal portion of the placenta, and although these intertwine, they do not intermingle. Once implantation is completed, the embryo experiences a period of rapid growth receiving nourishment from the mother's blood through the placenta, which is more efficient than absorbing nutrients from the mother's cells.

A placental barrier keeps the blood supplies of the mother and embryo separate. Even though small molecules can pass through this barrier, large molecules cannot. The exact exchange of substances is complex, but in general, nutritive materials from maternal blood—oxygen, water, and salts—cross the placental barrier and digestive waste products and carbon dioxide from the developing embryo can cross back the other way toward the mother. However, large molecules, like red blood cells, most bacteria, maternal wastes, and many dangerous toxins and hormones, cannot pass.

Earliest development occurs in the head, brain, and sense organs, followed by the trunk area (**cephalocaudal**). After 2 months of gestation, the head accounts for about half of the total body length; by birth, the head comprises about one quarter of the newborn's body length. In adults, the head is only about 10 percent of a person's height. Growth moves from the middle outward. Structures that are near the **midline** of the body, such as the spinal cord and heart, develop before the arms and legs, which develop before the fingers and toes (**proximodistal**).

The rate of growth is faster during the embryonic period than at any other time: all body tissues, organs, and systems develop. While all this is happening, a woman may not yet realize that she is pregnant. For this reason many physicians recommend that women who are planning to become pregnant begin taking prenatal vitamins and that all women of childbearing age take folic acid to protect against **congenital malformations**. Congenital malformations are medical conditions that are present at birth. The embryo is very susceptible to the influences of disease, drugs, radiation, and other substances. Exposure to **teratogens** during this period usually leads to structural abnormalities or miscarriage. Changes are so precise and predictable it is possible to determine when a certain problem occurred. If a child is born with a cleft palate, we know the defect occurred between the seventh and eighth week, when the palatal arches normally close (Haffner, 2007).

During the second month, the embryo becomes markedly less curved and the head increases in size; a face develops with a primitive nose, eyes, ears, and upper lip; and the neck lengthens. The tail-like projection almost fully disappears. Fully formed, but extremely small, arms and legs, hands and feet, and even fingers and toes appear. The heart and circulatory system begin working, and by the end of the second month, the kidneys take over the function of concentrating and excreting urine. Although not yet functional, digestive and respiratory systems develop. The reproductive system also forms. A skeleton of cartilage develops, as do some finer features such as eyelids. The embryo is recognizable as a human being by the end of the second month of development, although it is somewhat strange looking (Haffner, 2007).

Fetal Period

The developing organism becomes a **fetus** when all the major structures and organs have been formed, about 8 weeks until birth. The early part of the fetal period is characterized by the development and growth of true bone. During the third month, the main organ systems (cardiovascular, neurologic, digestive, and so on) are established and differentiated. The fetus is about 3.5 inches long and weighs about an ounce. By the fourth month, with the fetus growing to about 6 ounces and measuring 10 inches, the mother can begin to detect movement. Tissues and organs continue to develop; the heart can be heard with a stethoscope, or by placing an ear on the mother's abdomen. During the fifth and sixth months there are more refinements in development (fingernails) and continued growth. By the end of the sixth month the fetus is about 12 to 14 inches long and weighs about 1.5 to 2 pounds. With the support of neonatal intensive care nurseries, infants born at 22 weeks or later are considered viable (Lowdermilk & Perry, 2003).

The major function of the third trimester is fetal weight gain. The fetus starts storing fat, and life support functions develop more fully. The brain continues to develop rapidly. The lungs begin to be capable of some limited gas exchange. The fetus grows to about 20 inches in length, usually weighs between 6.5 and 8 pounds, and is ready to be born (Lowdermilk & Perry, 2003).

Multiple Pregnancies

Usually the female releases only one ovum at a time. If two mature eggs are released and they are both fertilized (by separate sperm), fraternal **or dizygotic twins** will develop. Dizygotic twins occur when two fertilized ovum are implanted in the uterine wall at the same time. The term dizygotic refers to the fact that there are two zygotes as well as two amnions, two chorions, and two placentas. Genetically, fraternal twins are no more alike than other siblings. They are the result of different eggs and different sperm, yet they share the same uterine environment.

Identical or **monozygotic twins** develop from a single fertilized ovum that divides into two separate embryos. These twins will be of the same sex and have the same **genotype**. The cell division resulting in monozygotic twins usually occurs between 4 to 8 days after fertilization. When this division is early there will be two amnions, two chorions, and two placentas that may be fused (Lowdermilk & Perry, 2003).

In 1980 the rate of twining was one in fifty-three per 1,000 live births; it rose to one in thirty-two births per 1,000 births in 2002 (National Center for Health Statistics (NCHS), 2007). The rate of triplets and other higher order births rose from one per 2,703 to one per 543 total births, representing an increase of 65 percent and 497 percent respectively since 1990 (Martin, Kochanek, Strobino, Guyer, & MacDorman, 2005). Multiple gestations accounted for 3.3 percent of all births in 2002 (Brown & Satin, 2007) and the rate is increasing. The incidence of fraternal twins varies with the age of the mother, whether or not there were previous births, racial background, and the use of assisted reproductive techniques. Mothers having babies later and the use of fertility drugs increase the number of multiple pregnancies or multifetal gestations. When couples use in vitro fertilization more than one embryo is typically implanted. Multiple gestations pose short- and long-term risks. Regardless of how the embryo is implanted, it contains the genetic material for future generations.

Heredity and Genetics: Just the Basics

Heredity influences the growth and development of human beings. It was once believed that hereditary factors were the only influences on development. Research has since indicated that this is not true (Travers, 2006). The genetic makeup within each individual plays a strong role in dictating specific developmental outcomes. The color of our eyes, our height, the size of our feet, the color of our skin, and even the diseases that plague us are influenced by the genes we inherited from our biological parents. However the environment too plays a role in the expression of many genes. Most traits that humans are interested in are not located on a single gene, but are actually the interactions among different genes and the environment. Personality and intelligence fall into this category. Genetics is a complex field and knowledge about inheritance patterns varies with particular traits.

Human development is complicated. Because the process of development from conception to birth usually occurs without incident, we do not think about the complexities. However, the more we know about this process and the potential problems that can occur, the more amazing it is that most babies are born healthy, happy, and demanding attention from those who care for them.

Chromosomes

The human body is made up of cells, approximately 100 trillion cells. There are a variety of different kinds of cells including skin cells, liver cells, nerve cells, and so on. In the center of most of these cells (but not blood cells), there is a nucleus. The nucleus is a membrane that encloses the genetic material of the cell, whereas the cytoplasm is a watery-like substance that fills the rest of the cell. The cell nucleus houses the deoxyribonucleic acid (DNA). DNA is formed in thread-like double-helix strands called chromosomes and contains the genetic blueprints or instructions for development (Batshaw, 2007). Its main role is the long-term storage of information. Humans have forty-six chromosomes arranged in twenty-three pairs. To help identify the chromosomes they are numbered. Chromosomes one through twenty-two are called **autosomes**. Autosomes are nonsex chromosomes. Although different in size, each is a matched pair. The twenty-third pair of chromosomes is the sex chromosomes. The female chromosome is larger and in the shape of an X whereas the male chromosome is smaller and looks like a Y with a short tail. Females have two XX chromosomes, whereas males have an X and a Y (National Human Genome Research Institute, 2007). During one state of cell division (**metaphase**) the chromosomes can be seen as distinct cell bodies that can be counted and grouped. This process is called **karyotyping** and is used in the identification of some disabilities (see Figure 6–1).

Chromosomal errors account for 3 to 5 percent of disabilities that are identifiable at birth. The actual number of these problems is much higher; approximately 25 percent of eggs and 3 to 4 percent of sperm have an added or missing chromosome. Approximately 95 percent of fetuses with these chromosomal disorders do not survive to term

(Batshaw, 2007). Most chromosomal abnormalities occur during cell division: meiosis. Damage can happen to parts of a chromosome or to the whole chromosome. There are two basic types of chromosome abnormalities: numerical and structural (Figure 6–2).

Numerical Abnormalities

In numerical abnormalities, one chromosome from a pair is missing or a chromosome pair has an additional chromosome. In most instances this results in a miscarriage. When it does not infants have developmental disabilities. In trisomy 21, the most common form of Down syndrome, children have three 21st chromosomes (hence the "tri", the somy comes from chromosome), or, a total of forty-seven chromosomes instead of the usual forty-six. The extra chromosome causes some of the distinctive features of children with Down syndrome, including a small head, flattened face, an upward slant of the eyes, and small ears, mouths, hands, and feet. Children with Down syndrome are born with developmental delays, and often have medical conditions requiring ongoing treatment, and typically need extra support throughout their lives (Roizen, 2007).

The Evidence Base

Down syndrome (trisomy 21) is the most common chromosomal abnormality in the United States. The risk of this chromosomal abnormality increases with maternal age:

Level of Risk	Maternal Age
1 in 1,250	25 years
1 in 1,000	30 years
1 in 400	35 years
1 in 100	40 years

(American College of Obstetricians and Gynecologists, 2001)

Screening for chromosomal abnormalities cost about $60, an ultrasound averages $150, genetic testing about $400 per test, an amniocentesis about $300, chorionic villus sampling about $350, and genetic counseling $40. The *lifetime* cost of live-born infants with Down syndrome (figured on medical, developmental, special education, and lost productivity based on 1988 cross-sectional data) was estimated at about $1.8 billion dollars in 1992 dollars (CDC, 1992). The value of lost workdays for caregivers was estimated at $252,000 in 1993 dollars (Kelly, Haddix, Scanlon, Helmick, & Mulinare, 1996; Campbell, Grosse, & Chattopadhyay, 2006).

Reflective Practice

Looking at the economic cost of disabilities is not something we do frequently especially when termination of the pregnancy is the only method of prevention. Reflect on your personal values in this area and how you might view others with different values. How does looking at disabilities from a cost-benefit perspective feel to you? Do you believe one of the reasons that many tests are covered by insurance is because it is cost effective?

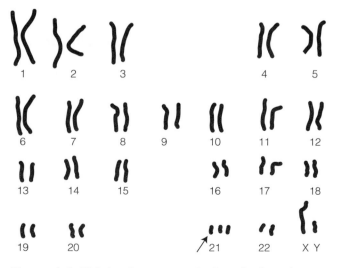

Figure 6–1: This is a karyotype of a boy (look at the X Y chromosomes) with Down syndrome (look at chromosome 21; there are three chromosomes instead of two). An actual karyotype is more difficult to decipher than this one.

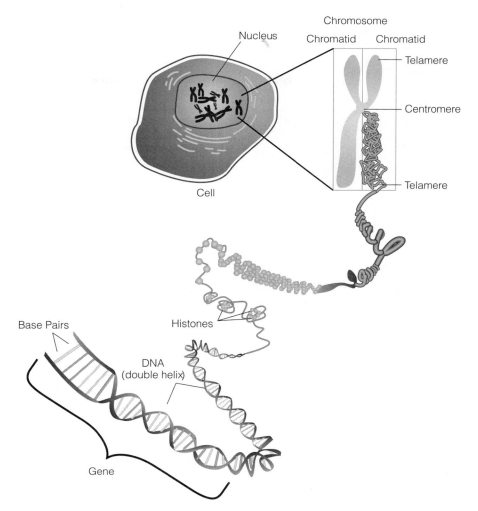

Figure 6–2: Chromosomes are found in the cell nucleus. Humans have 23 pairs of chromosomes which are made up of threadlike packages of genes and DNA. DNA is formed as a double helix composed of sugar and phosphate. The rungs of this twisted ladder are made up of chemicals called nucleotide bases (C for cytosine, G for guanine, A for adenine, and T for thymine). The sequences of these bases form one's genetic code. To pass this code on, the DNA unzips. At that point, uracil (U) substitutes for thymine and messenger RNA is formed. It is possible for transcription mistakes or mutations to occur during this process. Genes are pieces of DNA. Courtesy of the Human Genome Project.

In the Field

We hadn't planned on my getting pregnant. We weren't married and we were struggling with the decision. Although we had lived together for 8 years we just couldn't make that final commitment. It wasn't like there was anyone else. It was just that we both did things that annoyed the other. However, it was clear that I was pregnant.

At first we decided not to tell anyone until after the first 3 months. But after a visit from my parents, I told. I was really feeling guilty because I didn't plan to get pregnant. I was drinking and not taking great care of myself when I found out. I spent a lot of time feeling guilty because I couldn't undo those first few weeks.

I liked the doctor. She was a woman and seemed to care a lot about me and understood some of my concerns. They did some routine blood work and then she wanted me to have an ultrasound. It seemed early to me. Although I had never been pregnant I had many friends who were. Actually, I was worried about my biological clock and I figured this was why it was done. I was concerned listening to the conversation when they were talking about the neck and that it was thick or something. It seemed strange to me.

Then, the unthinkable happened. Just when we were beginning to cope with the idea of having a baby I had a miscarriage. It was awful, not so much physically as emotionally. Having just accepted being pregnant I was no longer pregnant. When I talked to the doctor she told me that one of the things she was concerned about was the possibility that the baby might have had Down syndrome. She was going to suggest an amniocentesis. This hit me hard. She said that one reason I had the miscarriage was that he had a problem. It was a he. What if he had had Down syndrome? What would I have done? I know how I feel about this issue, but I don't know how I feel about it when it is me.

Children with Down syndrome have forty-seven chromosomes instead of forty-six. With early intervention these children are active participants in the inclusive classroom.

Reflective Practice

An unexpected pregnancy does not allow couples time to plan for a baby. Do you believe her lack of planning influenced the miscarriage? Do you think this woman could profit from counseling? If so, what topics do you think need to be covered? How do you think this will impact her having another child?

In other cases, a chromosome is missing. Turner syndrome is an example of a disability caused by a lost chromosome (resulting in forty-five chromosomes). The lack of one X chromosome is usually from the father. Girls have one X chromosome rather than the pair, XX. These mistakes cause girls to be sterile; short in stature; have webbing at their neck; broad chests; compromised throat, trachea, and sinus; and often have heart and middle ear problems. Turner syndrome occurs in one in 5,000 live births per year (Batshaw, 2007).

Structural Abnormalities

In some cases a portion of the chromosome and hence the genetic information is missing (deletions), in other cases, genetic material may be duplicated, which results in extra genetic material (duplication); in other cases, a portion of the chromosome has broken off, turned upside down, and been reattached (inversion). Sometimes information that should be on one chromosome is put on a different chromosome (insertion), and in other cases parts of two chromosomes are switched (translocation);

some of chromosome 20 ends up on chromosome 4 and likewise some of chromosome four becomes part of chromosome 20 (National Human Genome Research Institute, 2007). In still other cases a portion of a chromosome is broken off and forms a circle or ring. Depending upon the particular genetic material this may or may not influence development (see Figure 6–3).

Most chromosomal abnormalities are accidental and are present in the egg or sperm at the time of fertilization. When this happens the abnormality is present in every cell of the body. If the problem happens later, after conception, some cells will be abnormal and others will not. This results in **mosaicism**. Mosaicism is abnormal chromosome division that results in two or more types of cells containing different numbers of chromosomes. Because not all of the cells are affected, children who are affected will have a milder version of the abnormality.

Genes

Chromosomes are made up of genes. Each chromosome has between 250 and 2,000 genes. Genes contain genetic material (DNA) that directs the body through the developmental process, one protein at a time. The human genome contains about 30,000 to 40,000 genes. In April 2003, the human genome was mapped. This mapping facilitates the study of hereditary diseases and the identification of single-gene disorders (National Human Genome Research Institute [HGP], 2007).

Genes have two core functions: they serve as a reliable template or blueprint for development and they have a transcriptional function. As a template, some genes regulate the development and functioning of the body while others make specific products such as enzymes and hormones. Their transcriptional function is less well-known. The transcriptional function allows the gene to impact the structure, function, and other biological characteristics in which it is expressed (Jensen, 2006). Every cell has the genes for your whole body. However, only a small portion of the gene is activated in a particular cell: Only the kidney-related function of a gene is expressed in the kidney cell and the other parts of the gene are repressed. It is gene expression that translates genetic information into action. Everyday factors such as emotional states, stress, exercise, and nutrition influence gene expression. The environment in which one lives and how one feels can impact gene expression. This is the basis for early intervention and the cause for concern about toxic environments. Although genes provide the blueprint, like the blueprint for a house, there can be modifications in the structure and the house can be remodeled later. Brain structure is highly experience dependent (Jensen, 2006).

A **mutation** is a change in a gene that occurs by chance. Changes occur at various steps in the process for a variety of reasons. Some changes or errors are irrelevant; there are enough checks and balances in the system to take care of them. Other errors, like those in the gene itself, disrupt subsequent steps. About 1 percent of the population has a congenital malformations caused by a single-gene defect (Batshaw, 2007).

A genetic mutation can lead to a genetic disorder (Batshaw, 2007). The larger the gene affected, the greater the probability of a mistake. Older parents have higher mutation rates. Some mutations occur spontaneously,

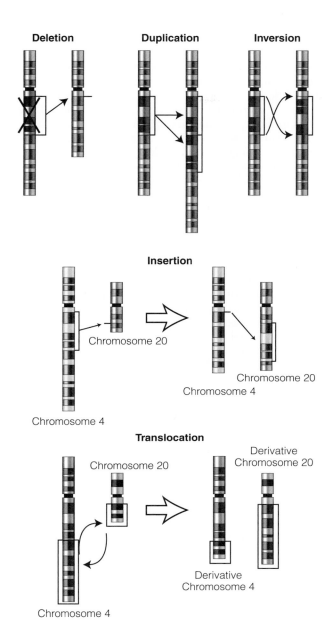

Figure 6–3: Types of Mutations
Chromosomes can mutate during cell division. In some cases information is deleted, duplicated twice, or inverted. In other situations parts of one chromosome are inserted on a different chromosome and other times parts of two chromosomes are traded. Courtesy of the Human Genome Project.

others are related to radiation, chemicals, and viruses (HGP, 2007). The most common mutation is called a point mutation where a single chemical is replaced with another chemical. In sickle cell anemia, a single substitution in the DNA base tells the cells to produce valine instead of glutamic acid at one spot on the hemoglobin protein. This leads to a painful disability where red blood cells are shaped like sickles instead of disks.

Now that you have a basic understanding of how chromosomes and genes work and the role they play in development. The next step is to put this knowledge in the context of heredity and the children who may be in your classroom.

Genetic Transmission

Some genetic traits follow a Mendelian pattern, so called because they were discovered by the Austrian botanist Gregor Johann Mendel. His findings were first published in the late 1800s. He did not study animals, but the laws he formulated while working with plants provided the basis for understanding inheritance patterns. Mendel was fascinated by green and yellow plants and he did not understand why, when he genetically mixed green and yellow plants, he did not get a chartreuse plant. Instead, he continued to create green and yellow plants, but he always had more green plants than yellow plants.

He concluded that some traits (green in this instance) are dominant, whereas others are recessive or hidden (yellow in this case). Scientists found that these same principles of dominant and recessive genes apply to human beings and they help us understand how some traits and disorders are inherited (HGP, 2007).

Before getting into this let's talk about the language of genetics. When we talk about genetics we use a lot of prefixes. Breaking the words down makes it easier to understand what we are talking about. Let's start with the prefix *homo*. Homo means the *same*. Think about words you know that begin with homo. Homogeneous is an adjective that generally means composed of the *same* kind of parts. We homogenize milk to break up the cream so the fat globules are all the *same* size. And we are homo sapiens because we are all the *same* species. Thus when you encounter the prefix *homo* you can assume that it means the *same*.

Obviously there is a flip side to this: *hetero*. Hetero means different. Heterogeneous groups are different from each other. The term zygote is used for the developing individual who was created by the union of the egg and sperm. Think about eye color. Both the mother and father contribute a gene (or genes) related to eye color. If they both contribute the *same* eye color (both blue) the child will be **homozygous** for that trait. If they contribute different colors (brown and blue) the child will be **heterozygous** for that trait. Armed with this information, let's tackle heredity.

Two basic concepts will help you understand how inheritance patterns work: how genes are passed from parents to children and the dominant and recessive characteristics of genes. Genes, or **alleles**, always occupy a specific location on a chromosome. An allel is a DNA sequence, usually a gene. The genes for eye color from each parent are in the same location on their respective chromosomes. Although the genes are in the same location, they may be for different eye colors.

Let's start with the assumption that you have blue eyes (we'll get to brown eyes soon). Your blue eyes are somewhat of a mystery because both of your parents have brown eyes. If you inherited the same coding, alleles, from each parent (blue eyes) you are homozygous for that trait. If you inherited different codes (brown eyes from one parent and blue eyes from the other) you would be heterozygous for the trait and you would have brown eyes. So, obviously this didn't happen. Something else is going on.

We use capital letters (A) to indicate dominant forms of genes and small letters (a) to indicate recessive forms. There are two ways to be homozygous: you can inherit two dominant (AA) genes or two recessive (aa) genes. Knowing you have blue eyes, your parents have brown eyes, and that brown eyes are dominant, we know that you received recessive genes from both your parents. We also know that your parents are heterozygous for eye color. When there is one dominant and one recessive gene in a pair (Aa), the individual is heterozygous.

The basic genetic makeup of an individual transmitted from the specific genes of the parents at conception is called a person's genotype. This is the sum total of the genes transmitted to you from your parents and the genes that you will pass on to future generations. However, you can't tell a person's **genotype** by looking at her. Think about your mother and father. Because of the dominant and recessive quality of genes they were able to pass the gene for blue eyes on to you. So what you see is not necessarily what you get. The observable characteristics of an individual, both biological and behavioral, are a person's **phenotype**. The phenotype is partially the result of the interactions within the genotype of dominant and recessive genes. However, phenotypes can be determined by multiple genes and influenced by environmental factors. Knowing one or a few known alleles does not always enable prediction of the phenotype particularly for more complex traits. The distinction between genotype and phenotype is important in understanding genetic transmission (Figure 6–4).

Reflective Practice

If you have two brown-eyed parents and you have brown eyes (phenotype) what are the possible genotypes you could have?

Humans have twenty-three pairs of chromosomes. Twenty-two of these are autosomes. The third pair is the sex chromosome. Because genes can be either dominant or recessive and there are two different types of chromosomes, three different inheritance patterns are possible: autosomal dominant, autosomal recessive, or X-linked. The X-linked refers to those genes on the sex (X Y) chromosomes. Single genes control some of these characteristics (unifactorial inheritance). Single gene disorders are caused by a change (mutation) in one gene. There are over 6,000 identified single gene disorders. Although each disorder does not affect that many children when grouped together they account for about one in 300 births (Centers for Disease Control and Prevention [CDC], 2007e). Other disorders are caused by a variety of factors (multifactorial inheritance) including genes interacting with the environment.

Understanding inheritance patterns is a bit like gambling: trying to figure the odds. We want to understand the probability of someone inheriting a particular genetic trait. If individuals understand the probability of a particular trait being passed on to their children they can make informed decisions before deciding to have children. When you think about applying for college you may have been playing the probability game. You may have applied to one university that you really wanted to attend, but didn't think you could actually get in. Then you may have applied to other colleges where you thought your odds were 50-50. And, to be safe you applied to one school

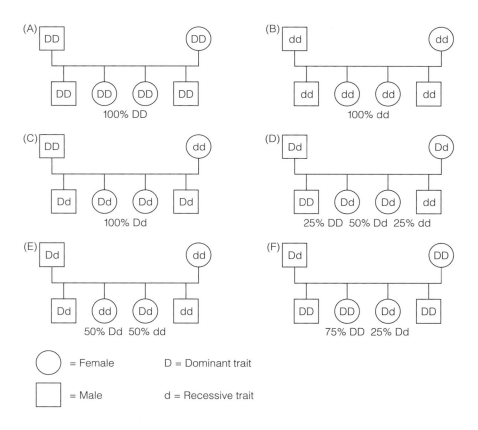

Figure 6–4: Mendelian Inheritance Patterns
Mendelian inheritance patterns are based on the predictable relationship between dominant and recessive genes on the autosomes and the probability of different inheritance patterns.

where you thought you had 100 percent probably of getting in. Some inheritance patterns have known probabilities. The focus in the next sections is on the inheritance of genes that cause disabilities in children.

Autosomal-Recessive Disorders

There are approximately 1,700 different autosomal-recessive disorders (McKusick et al., 2005). Generally, dominant genes determine traits. However, if an infant receives a dominant gene (A) for a particular autosomal-recessive disorder from one or both of her parents, she would not inherit the recessive disorder. For a child to inherit this type of disorder, she must receive an abnormal-recessive gene (a) from both her father and her mother. The child would therefore be homozygous (aa) for the autosomal-recessive trait. Autosomal-recessive disorders typically relate to enzyme disorders. Enzymes break food down into fats, proteins, and carbohydrates. Children with phenylketonuria (PKU) lack the enzyme to convert phenylalanine to tyrosine. The phenylalanine is toxic to the brain and, if not treated, will cause intellectual disabilities. In autosomal-recessive disorders the parents do not have the disorder but they are heterozygous for it.

Autosomal-Dominant Disorders

Autosomal-dominant disorders relate to structural abnormalities in the individual. Unlike someone who is heterozygous (Aa) for an autosomal-recessive disorder (and would therefore only be a carrier and not have the disorder), those who are heterozygous for an autosomal-dominant disorder, will be a carrier of *and* be affected by the disorder.

There are approximately 4,500 autosomal-dominant disorders that have been identified (McKusick et al., 2005). Achondroplasia, a form of short-limbed dwarfism, is an autosomal-dominant disorder. If only one parent has a dominant gene (Aa) for an autosomal-dominant disorder (e.g., one parent with achondroplasia has a child with a person who does not have this disorder), the probability that the child will have the disorder is 50 percent. However, the probability is also 50 percent that the child will not be affected and not be a carrier (aa). If both parents are heterozygous for the trait, the pattern would predict that the child has a 50 percent chance of having achondroplasia, a 25 percent chance of being unaffected, and a 25 percent chance of receiving two copies of the dominant gene. If the child receives two dominant genes (AA), the disorder will be more severe and may result in death. Autosomal-dominant disorders affect men and women equally and most frequently involve structural (physical) abnormalities. About half of these disabilities result from mutations (Batshaw, 2007).

Reflective Practice

You have just been told that a child with achondroplasia is going to join your classroom. You know this means the child will be disproportionately short in stature. You also know that it is an autosomal-dominant pattern of inheritance. What will you expect when you meet the parents? How will you understand what happened if the parents are not what you expected?

X-Linked Disorders

Approximately 900 X-linked disorders have been identified. X-linked disorders typically result in physical disabilities and cognitive impairments (McKusick et al., 2005). They include such disorders as hemophilia, Duchenne muscular dystrophy, fragile X syndrome, and red-green color blindness. These disorders are passed between generations by carrier mothers. That is, they are carried on the female sex chromosome (X), and they typically involve mutations of genetic information that are found on this chromosome. These disorders occur mostly in males because the pairing of the XY chromosomes means that there is no second X chromosome in males to cover the problem. Approximately 25 percent of males with intellectual disability and 10 percent of females with learning disabilities are affected by X-linked disorders (Batshaw, 2007).

If a carrier mother who reproduces with an unaffected male passes along the X-linked trait, the female offspring will either be a carrier (50 percent) or not be affected (50 percent). A male child's situation is different. He has a 50 percent chance of getting the disorder and a 50 percent chance of not being affected. He cannot become a carrier, either he has it or he doesn't. In the situation where both parents are carriers, male children still have a 50 percent chance of inheriting the disease or being unaffected. But, in this instance, the females have a 50 percent chance of being a carrier and a 50 percent chance of actually being affected by the gene (Figure 6–5).

Multifactorial Inheritance

Genes from one or both parents may interact with each other and may be interfered with by environmental factors. The exact cause isn't known and we understand less about these problems than single genes. These factors are more challenging to identify and beyond the scope of this book (Lowdermilk & Perry, 2003). Many common congenital malformations are a result of multifactorial inheritance such as cleft palate and neural tube defects. Depending upon the number of genes affected, these malformations can be mild or severe. In families in which this pattern of inherited disorders occurs, it usually favors one sex more than the other. Many traits not related to disabilities are also inherited in this way. Height is an obvious example of multifactorial inheritance. It is a result of genetics but also environmental factors such as diet.

Genetic Counseling

Genetic counseling is the process of advising individuals of the consequence of a disorder, the probability of developing it and transmitting it, and ways in which the disorder can be prevented or ameliorated. A range of individuals provide genetic counseling, depending upon the complexity of the situation. Most obstetricians and others such as family doctors, nurses, midwives, and social workers feel comfortable providing information about chromosomal abnormalities and common conditions that follow the Mendelian pattern. Beyond this, they may refer individuals to a clinical geneticist.

Genetic counseling before conception can often identify genetic disorders within a family and the risk of occurrence. The goal is to reduce the probability of serious

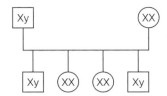

(A) Unaffected male and female

No males or females will be affected

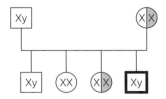

(B) Unaffected male, carrier female

50% of the females will be carriers
50% of the males will have the disorder

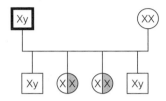

(C) Affected male, unaffected female

No males will be affected
100% of females will be carriers

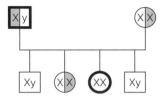

(D) Affected male, carrier female

50% of males will be affected
50% of males will not be affected
50% of females will be affected
50% of females will be carriers

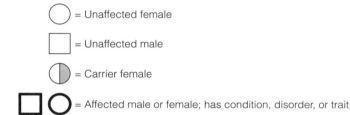

○ = Unaffected female

□ = Unaffected male

◐ = Carrier female

■ ● = Affected male or female; has condition, disorder, or trait

Figure 6–5: X-linked Inheritance Patterns
Traits carried in the X sex chromosome follow a different pattern of inheritance that is influenced by the sex of the offspring.

life-threatening disorders occurring or reoccurring in the same family. Parents who have, or who have had a child with an inherited disease might seek genetic counseling before deciding to have more children. Genetic counseling might be particularly appropriate for couples from groups with a high incidence of an inherited trait, women older than 35 years of age, individuals who have had excessive exposure to drugs, chemicals, or radiation, and close relatives (first cousins) who plan to marry (Schonberg & Tifft, 2007).

Often genetic counseling begins with a family tree, genogram, or pedigree that carefully identifies people in the family who may have the disease or are carriers of the disease. This pedigree includes close family relatives and is done over several generations. For genetic counseling to be effective, hereditary information obtained needs to be precise and comprehensive enough to make an exact diagnosis or estimate of risk. Decision making lies with the individual receiving the information. Genetic counseling should be nondirective and supportive. It can happen before conception or be part of the prenatal screening process. The most common reason for obtaining genetic counseling is advanced maternal age. The risk of trisomy 21 and all other chromosomal abnormalities increases markedly after age 35.

Fetal Therapy

The ultimate goal of prenatal diagnosis is to prevent severe disabilities by treating them before birth. Although fetal therapy is an exciting field, it is so new that there are many complications. Because of these complications, work is being done primarily in areas where the child's early death is almost a certainty or when the fetal condition will worsen as the pregnancy progresses (Schonberg & Tifft, 2007). Prenatal screening serves a variety of purposes. When results of diagnostic tests show that the developing fetus has a major abnormality, parents must make a decision about whether the infant will be carried to term, or the pregnancy will be terminated. In addition to genetics, other conditions influence the developing fetus.

Implications for Educators

Although it is not expected that you are an expert on hereditary and genetics it is expected that you will be able to talk with parents and understand what they are saying about genetic disorders. And, if you have a child in your class with a genetic disorder that you understand the implications of the disorder and what it will mean in your classroom.

Maternal Diseases, Disorders, and Illnesses

There are many different maternal diseases, disorders, and conditions that affect the unborn infant. Pregnancy alters the natural course of some infectious diseases. Group B streptococci are rarely associated with infection in nonpregnant women, but can cause infectious diseases during pregnancy. Additionally, some noninfectious chronic diseases of the mother, such as diabetes, may require different management techniques because of the physical demands of pregnancy. With good prenatal care, negative effects of these risk factors may be avoided, cured, or birth outcomes improved. Maternal infection and chronic illness account for 3 to 4 percent of congenital malformations (Hill & Haffner, 2002). Only the most common conditions are discussed.

TORCH and Other Infections

Researchers group together a number of infectious agents that cause similar disabilities and refer to them as TORCH syndrome. The acronym TORCH refers to toxoplasmosis (T), other congenital infections HIV, syphilis, varicella, and others (O), rubella (R), cytomegalovirus (C), and herpes simplex virus (H). When a mother contracts one of these agents, the infant may be born with visual or hearing impairments, damage to the central nervous system (CNS), or heart defects (Bell, 2007).

Toxoplasmosis

Toxoplasmosis is caused by one of the most common protozoan parasites in humans, *Toxoplasma gondii*. It is contracted through the fecal matter of cats, infected meat, or protozoan eggs. Most people with toxoplasmosis are asymptomatic. Prevention is the best strategy—stay away from cats if you are pregnant. If you have cats, determine your exposure to the protozoan before you become pregnant. An estimated 4,000 cases of toxoplasmosis occur each year (Montoya & Liesenfeld, 2004). Infants are usually asymptomatic at birth but many will have neural pathway impairments. Other impairments can result in cerebral palsy, including hydrocephalus or microcephalus, intellectual disability, visual and hearing impairments, and other problems such as anemia, low birth weight, and liver and spleen enlargement.

Other Infections

Syphilis is a venereal disease that once appeared to be virtually eradicated with the advent of antibiotics. However, it is becoming a problem again with thirty cases per 100,000 in the United States (Bell, 2007). If it is detected and cured with antibiotics (penicillin) before the sixteenth week of pregnancy there are few adverse effects. A single injection of penicillin can prevent 98 percent of congenital cases. The particular spirochete (*Treponema pallidum*) that causes syphilis is passed from human to human and can cross the placenta. Before penicillin, 60 percent of infected infants were stillborn or died during the first month or had severe brain damage (Golden, Marra, & Holmes, 2003). The risk to the fetus is influenced by the severity of the infection. Many affected infants die before birth or shortly after birth. Those who live have a variety of problems, from skin rashes and edema to malformation of the eyes, hearing impairment, growth retardation, CNS problems, seizures, intellectual disability, and other effects. The diagnosis of syphilis is dependent upon blood tests (Bell, 2007).

Varicella, or chicken pox, has been associated with malformations. The abnormalities it causes are less severe and less common than most other uterine infections. When it does occur (about 2 percent risk), it results in limb, facial, skeletal, and neurologic abnormalities. There is a vaccine for this virus. Women should determine whether or not they have had chicken pox, or be vaccinated before they plan to become pregnant.

Human immunodeficiency virus (HIV) is a retrovirus that infects cells in the immune system making it vulnerable to infection (Bell, 2007). The HIV virus can be transmitted in utero, during delivery, or through breast milk. Active treatment with zidovudine (ZVD) in pregnant women has reduced the vertical transmission of HIV.

Approximately 25 percent of infants born to mothers with HIV infection will become infected without intervention. Aggressive treatment with a highly active antiretroviral treatment (HAART) is recommended as soon as infants are diagnosed. If it is suspected, infants should be tested within 48 hours of birth, at 1 to 2 months and again at 4 to 6 months. If negative at 6 months, the infant has a 99 percent chance of not being infected with HIV. HIV enters the CNS in the early stages of infection. It damages the neurons and glial cells making children vulnerable to developmental brain injuries as well as the typical opportunistic infections of childhood (Bell, 2007).

Rubella

During a 2-year period in the 1960s there were 11,000 fetal deaths and 20,000 infants were born with birth defects caused by rubella. With vaccination and surveillance programs it is now about twenty infants a year (Atreya, Mohan, & Kulkarni, 2004). Rubella is caused by a virus that is transmitted through body fluids, including mucus and saliva. If a woman is infected during the first trimester, there is a 90 percent rate of fetal damage, including hearing and visual impairments, heart defects, cataracts and malformed retinas, brain calcification, CNS damage with long-term neurologic impairment, and thyroid dysfunction (Bell, 2007).

Cytomegalovirus

Cytomegalovirus (CMV) is a virus from the herpes family, a double-stranded DNA genome of more than 200 genes and is the most common cause of intrauterine infection. Infections of adults and children are asymptomatic or flu-like, with few or no side effects. A majority of adults (50 to 80 percent) are latently (hidden, inactive) infected. It occurs in 1 percent of live births but only one in 1,000 of these infants will have CMV disease. The greatest risk is to women who acquire a primary CMV infection during the first half of pregnancy. The most common effect of CMV disease is CNS damage. Of initially asymptomatic infants, approximately 10 to 15 percent will develop a sensorineural hearing loss, significant intellectual disability, and behavior problems. Overall, the most common symptoms are progressive hearing loss and intellectual disability (Bell, 2007). Women of childbearing age should be tested for CMV exposure; if not immune, they should avoid infection. A vaccine is being researched but is not yet available.

Herpes Simplex Viruses

The herpes simplex virus (HSV) causes a variety of diseases in humans from "fever blisters" to genital infections. Orolabial herpes is primarily a disease of childhood. Adult herpes is transmitted through sexual contact. About 5 percent of neonatal HSV infections happen in utero with 85 percent occurring during the birthing process (a cesarean delivery is recommended). The remaining 10 percent are acquired from environmental sources (Bell, 2007). Like CMV, herpes is difficult to diagnosis because about 50 percent of the women do not have genital lesions. There is no cure for these infectious diseases. However, if it is known that a woman has CMV or herpes the pregnancy can be managed in such as way as to reduce the probability of neonatal infection. Without proper management the outcomes are much less positive. Untreated the infant mortality rate is 70 percent. Antiviral therapy reduces this to about 30 percent. Even with treatment infants are likely to have CNS involvement and may have blindness, deafness, or significant intellectual disability (Bell, 2007). Some congenital infections such as influenza, mononucleosis, malaria, parvovirus, and enterovirus result in increased maternal anemia, low birth weight, intrauterine growth retardation, premature deliveries and infant mortality, but they do not seem to cause fetal malformations (CDC, 2007c). Group B streptococcus is one of the most common infections in the developed world.

Group B Streptococcus

Group B streptococcus (GBS) was recognized in the 1930s and 1940s as a cause of postpartum infection, but it was not until the 1970s and 1980s that the impact of the mother's infection was related to the prevalence of the **perinatal** infections in infants. Although not part of TORCH infections, Group B streptococcus is a leading cause of **sepsis,** a serious blood infection, and **meningitis** during the first 2 months of neonatal life. Meningitis is an infection of the fluid and lining (membranes) of the brain and spinal cord.

Approximately 30 percent of pregnant women have GBS in their genital tract and 1 to 2 percent of their infants develop blood poisoning (sepsis). When this occurs there are two patterns. In about half of the cases the infant becomes ill in the first week of life. The newborn may get sepsis, pneumonia, and meningitis. In other cases the onset is later (a week to several months after birth) with meningitis more common (CDC, 2007d).

Women should be screened routinely between 35 and 37 weeks gestation for this infection. If GBS is discovered, the infected woman is treated with antibiotics (penicillin). Because GBS can cause women to have a fever during labor or their membranes to rupture 18 hours or more before delivery, women who experience these symptoms should also be screened for GBS, and if it is detected the infected women should be given antibiotics before birthing (CDC, 2007d).

Chlamydia

Some sexually transmitted diseases (STDs) pose serious threats to the fetus. One of the most common, yet least well known is chlamydia. Chlamydia is the most commonly reported bacterial sexually transmitted disease in the United States. The Centers for Disease Control and Prevention (CDC) estimate that 2.8 million people are infected each year (CDC, 2006). The infection is silent: Three-quarters of the women who have the disease have no symptoms. Chlamydia is potentially highly destructive, and difficult to diagnosis. The fetus is most likely to be affected during the birthing process. Outcomes range from conjunctivitis (eye inflammation) to pneumonia but also increase the risk of acquiring HIV infection. It increases the risk of prematurity, stillbirths, and infertility. Chlamydia is responsive to antibiotics (CDC, 2006). Overall, 26 percent of female adolescents (14 to 19 years of age) in the United States, about 3.2 million females are infected with one or more STDs (CDC, 2006).

Maternal Weight and Weight Gain

The fetus is dependent upon the mother for all of his nutrition. Her diet is his diet. Prepregnancy weight is a given and not amenable to change. There are few standards by which to evaluate weight as a risk factor. When a woman is either significantly overweight or underweight before becoming pregnant or when the weight gain during pregnancy is too low or too high there is concern (Lowdermilk & Perry, 2003). Women who are overweight are more likely to have high blood pressure, hypertensive disorders, problems regulating blood sugar and insulin, and urinary tract infections.

Gestational diabetes is a form of diabetes that affects pregnant women who have never had diabetes. It is probably caused by hormones produced during pregnancy. Overweight women are also likely to have infants who are large for their **gestational age.** Dietary manipulation is not advocated during pregnancy as it is viewed as having no benefit to the mother at this time and may be harmful to the fetus. The risk of having a child with a major problem that is present at birth (congenital) is double that of a woman in the normal weight category (Prentice & Goldberg, 1996).

Weight gain during pregnancy is a common concern for many women. A pregnant woman needs to consume about 300 additional calories a day (Haffner, 2007). Recommended weight gain is dependent upon the appropriateness of the prepregnancy weight. For a single fetus the recommendation would be between 25 and 35 pounds. Overall, a weight gain of about 17 to 20 percent in body weight is the goal (Abrams, Altman, & Pickett, 2000). Thus a woman with a prepregnancy weight of 100 would be considered fine even if she gained only 17 to 20 pounds, whereas a woman weighing 150 pounds might expect to gain 26 to 30 pounds. If the mother is underweight, she should gain between 27 and 40 pounds and if overweight, at least 15 pounds and up to 25 pounds (Lowdermilk & Perry, 2003).

Optimal rates of weight gain depend on the stage of the pregnancy. At the beginning of pregnancy the weight gain is primarily in the mother (amniotic fluid, placenta, breast tissue, extra stores of fat, blood, and fluid). By the third trimester it is the fetus who is gaining the weight. During the first trimester a woman may gain about 5 pounds. In the second and third trimester it may be about a half a pound a week.

Chronic Maternal Illnesses

Some women become pregnant already possessing conditions that may affect the fetus; in other situations the pregnancy itself can precipitate risk conditions. Pregnancy causes complex metabolic changes in a woman that can alter previously controlled conditions, such as diabetes, lupus, cardiovascular disorders, anemia, and hypertensive disorders. These conditions affect both the mother and the child.

Diabetes Mellitus

Women with diabetes do not produce enough insulin. Before insulin was discovered in 1921, little was known about diabetes or its effects on pregnancy. Synthetic insulin has resulted in higher pregnancy rates in women with diabetes, but managing insulin during pregnancy is challenging. Pregnancy influences the amount of synthetic insulin a women needs. Early in pregnancy, diabetic women may have periods of **hypoglycemia** because of the fetuses' heightened demands for glucose (sugar). Hypoglycemia is having lower than normal amounts of sugar (glucose) in the blood. Hormones produced by the placenta alter the mother's metabolism, and in general, increase her need for insulin. Changes in the mother's metabolism produce periods of maternal **hyperglycemia**, high levels of sugar in the blood. Uncontrolled diabetes can place the fetus at risk; too much sugar (glucose) results in large babies (excessive fetal growth) and places the infant at risk for hypoglycemia at birth when less insulin is required. Controlled diabetic women who receive optimal prenatal care do well; those whose diabetes is not controlled or who do not receive this level of care are more likely to experience sudden and unexplained stillbirths and an increased risk for major birth anomalies (Brown & Satin, 2007).

Women who are not diabetic may become so during pregnancy, particularly if they are overweight. This is called **gestational diabetes**. This usually occurs late in pregnancy. Diabetes is diagnosed though urine and blood samples taken from pregnant women between 24 and 28 weeks of pregnancy. If well-managed, birth outcomes are generally positive (Brown & Satin, 2007).

Hypertensive Diseases

Some women (1 to 5 percent) have **hypertension**, or elevated blood pressure before conception or before 20 weeks of gestation. Hypertension is blood pressure that is chronically elevated (greater than 140/90 mmHg) (Brown & Satin, 2007). These women may have high blood pressure because of personal heredity factors, excessive weight, or medical problems. Hypertension is one of the most common medical complications of pregnancy. These women are monitored carefully because the fetus is at risk for intrauterine growth deficiency and premature rupture of the placenta.

When hypertension develops after the twentieth week of gestation and is accompanied by the accumulation of fluid in the tissue (**edema**) and protein in the urine, it is called **preeclampsia**. This form of hypertension occurs most frequently in first pregnancies and complicates 7 percent of pregnancies (Creasy, Resnik, & Iams, 2004). The cause of preeclampsia is unknown, but for women with this condition the risks are the same as those for women who enter pregnancy with high blood pressure. Preeclampsia is a concern for the fetus because there may be a low blood supply to the placenta, which is the fetal source of food and oxygen (Haffner, 2007). If preeclampsia is not treated, seizures (**eclampsia**) may develop. In some cases, labor will be induced or a cesarean section if the mother's life is threatened by the probability of having seizures.

In the Field

As soon as they knew I was having twins they told me to expect to have a cesarean. The babies weren't due until October but I was ready to have them in August. I felt like a beached whale. Me, who likes to swim and hike, me who eats organic food and who takes such good care of myself. I gained 70 pounds. Can you believe it? The doctor was so pleased with me and I was so miserable.

They became concerned about my blood pressure during the seventh month. By the beginning of the eighth month I had to see the doctor twice a week. His nurse would take my blood pressure. He would come in and shake his head and then send me to the hospital for blood work and a urine sample. It took hours and I began to dread sitting in the hospital just waiting and waiting.

The third time we went through this we were sitting and sitting and sitting. Me, with my fat tummy and swollen feet, trying to find a way to get comfortable. I told my husband we should just leave. Suddenly there was all this activity and I knew something was wrong. I looked around to see what all the commotion was about and realized they were heading our way. Apparently, my tests results suggested that I could easily go into seizures. We didn't go home to pick up my nicely packed bag; we went directly to the operating room. Less than an hour later, I was the mother of twins.

Reflective Practice

Women who are older and those with multiple gestations are more likely to have hypertensive disorder. How would you feel about going to the hospital for testing twice a week? How do you think this would be impacted by having a toddler, or several other children? Do you think they could continue to work? How might a job impact hypertensive disorder?

Trauma and Abuse

Approximately 10 to 20 percent of women experience some form of trauma during pregnancy (Cunningham et al., 2005). Motor vehicle accidents, falls, and assaults cause the most common form of blunt trauma to the abdominal area. The most likely outcome is preterm labor that occurs in as many as 28 percent of the cases (Brown & Satin, 2007). The placenta can become detached placing the mother and fetus at risk.

Teratogens

Teratogens are nongenetic, extraneous substances implicated in causing malformations in the developing fetus. They adversely affect the development of the fetus, causing death, malformations, growth deficiency, or functional deficits. Common teratogens include alcohol, nicotine, and prescription and illicit drugs. The effects of many specific teratogens are known. Some teratogens have more effect at specific times during prenatal development,

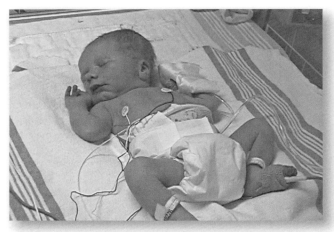

Teratogens adversely affect the developing fetus. Although they work in different ways, most affect the physical growth of the fetus and many are born too soon, and too small.

whereas others have debilitating effects throughout fetal development. This section focuses on the major teratogens that directly affect the fetus.

Among pregnant women, 5 to 10 percent abuse alcohol, 20 percent smoke cigarettes, 10 percent use marijuana, about 1 percent use cocaine, and 0.5 percent use opiates. Three quarters of individuals who abuse one substance are likely to abuse others as well (Center on Addiction and Substance Abuse, 1996). Polydrug use makes it difficult to determine the exact impact of a specific substance on the fetus. Additionally, pregnant women who use drugs rarely have adequate prenatal care or good nutrition, and they may have STDs.

Alcohol

Alcohol use during pregnancy is the most common cause of preventable intellectual disability. Alcohol is abused more than any other drug in the United States. In the United States, and in many parts of Europe, fetal alcohol spectrum disorders (FASD) are the leading cause of intellectual disability. They are more frequent than Down syndrome, spina bifida, or fragile X syndrome. Fetal alcohol syndrome (FAS) is the most severe end of fetal alcohol spectrum disorder. Although prevalence varies among different populations the CDC estimate that FAS occurs in 0.2 to 1.5 cases per 1,000, and that FASD is approximately three times that rate, putting it at 0.6 to 5.5 per 1,000 live births in the United States. Combined they constitute 0.8 to 7 cases per 1,000 live births (CDC, 2007a). Binge drinking early in pregnancy produces the worst birth outcomes (Burbacher & Grant, 2006).

FAS is defined by four criteria: maternal drinking; prenatal and postnatal growth deficiency (low birth weight and poor muscle tone); facial anomalies (thin upper lip, flat mid-face, short nose, low nasal bridge, small head, droopy eyes); and brain damage (CNS dysfunction, irritability, hyperactivity, attention deficit, and intellectual disability) (Wunsch, Conlon, & Scheidt, 2002). Timing of alcohol consumption affects fetal outcome. If alcohol abuse occurs during the first trimester of pregnancy, there is an increased probability of miscarriage and the physical signs of FAS are likely to be present. Alcohol abuse during

the second trimester affects physical and intellectual growth, but there are no physical malformations. If abuse occurs in the third trimester, cognitive development alone is impaired. Children exposed to alcohol show learning and behavior problems and poor impulse control.

In a survey of American mothers, about 30 percent reported drinking alcohol at some point in their pregnancy (U.S. Department of Health and Human Services, 2003). When a pregnant woman drinks alcohol, her blood alcohol content and that of her fetus increases. They increase at the same rate, but the blood alcohol level of the fetus remains high longer because the mother's liver must remove the alcohol from her own blood before removing the alcohol from the fetus. The ethanol in alcohol crosses the placental barrier and goes into both the fetus and the amniotic fluid. Ethanol impairs the placental function of channeling essential nutrients to the fetus and it also interferes with carbohydrate metabolism, resulting in growth retardation. By causing fetal malformations through chemical imbalances, alcohol affects the cells and the DNA of the fetus. Alcohol also affects fetal breathing and therefore levels of oxygen in the blood. If a woman drinks one drink per day throughout her pregnancy (270 days) she will have exposed her fetus to 135 ounces of absolute alcohol. This would be the equivalent of feeding the baby sixteen bottles (8 ounces each) of absolute alcohol (Burd, n.d.a).

Nicotine

Exposure to tobacco smoke is the number one preventable cause of low birth weight infants. The birth weight is directly proportional to the number of cigarettes smoked per day or the length of time a woman is exposed to passive smoke (Klesges, Johnson, Ward, & Barnard, 2001; Wunsch et al., 2002). If a woman smokes one cigarette per day throughout their pregnancy (270 days) she will have exposed her fetus to thirteen full packs of cigarettes. If she smokes ten cigarettes per day it is equivalent to 135 full packs of cigarettes (Burd, n.d.b). Approximately 25 percent of pregnant women smoke (Fried et al., 2003). The CDC found that 3 to 13 percent of women not covered by Medicaid smoked during pregnancy compared to 14 to 38 percent of women on Medicaid (CDC, 2005). **Medicaid** is a health insurance program for individuals and families with low incomes and few resources funded by the state and federal government and administered by states. A recent CDC study showed that the less education a woman had the more she was likely to smoke during pregnancy. That same study also showed that white women are far more likely to smoke than black, Latina, or American Indian (CDC, 2005).

The Evidence Base

Women who smoke during pregnancy are 83 percent more likely to deliver a low-birth-weight infant, 129 percent more likely to have an infant who will die from SIDS, 30 more like to deliver an infant with respiratory distress syndrome, and 41 percent more likely to have an infant with a perinatal respiratory condition (Marks, Koplan, Hogue, & Dalmat, 1990). In 2003, 12.4 percent of all women, 13 percent of Latinas, and 20.2 percent of black women who smoked during pregnancy delivered a low-birth-weight baby (U.S. Preventive Services Task Force, 2003). Up to 8 percent of all neonates who die in the week after birth are due to problems related to their mother smoking during pregnancy (CDC, 2005). Smoking is correlated with education: 2 percent of college-educated non-Hispanic white women smoked during pregnancy whereas 42.7 percent of non-Hispanic white women with 9 to 11 years of education smoked during one of their pregnancies (U.S. Department of Health and Human Services, 2004).

Specific counseling tailored for pregnant women increase smoking abstinence rates during pregnancy and leads to increased birth weight. Of women who received less than 3 minutes of physician counseling 10.5 percent quit, of those receiving 3 to 10 minutes 12.1 percent quit, and of these receiving over 10 minutes of counseling 18.7 percent quit. In 1996, maternal smoking accounted for 2.3 percent of all neonatal medical expenditures, an estimated $367 million dollars. Pregnant smokers incurred an additional $704 in health care costs (in 1996 dollars) (Berg, 2003). Clinical trials show that $6 in health care cost are saved for every $1 invested in smoking cessation programs for pregnant women (Campbell, Rosenthal, & Chattopadhyay, 2006)

Reflective Practice

Given the evidence, how would you go about designing a prevention program? Who would be your target audience? What facts would you use that you feel are the most salient for this population?

Almost 60 percent of U. S. children between 3 and 11 years, 22 million children, are exposed to **secondhand smoke**. One in 4 of these children live in households with at least one smoker (Department of Health and Human Services, 2007). Children whose parents smoke have more respiratory illness, bronchitis, and pneumonia than children of parents who do not smoke. The California Environmental Protection agency estimates the secondhand smoke caused 430 children to die of sudden infant death syndrome (SIDS), was responsible for 202,300 asthma episode and 790,000 ear infections that required medical attention (Department of Health and Human Services, 2007)). Children of fathers who smoked were twice as likely to develop cancer in adulthood as those whose fathers did not smoke (Huncharek, Kupelnick, & Klassen, 2002). When a woman smokes, the carbon monoxide from her bloodstream crosses the placenta and reduces the amount of oxygen available to the fetus. The nicotine causes the blood vessels to become smaller (constrict). In response to this, both maternal and fetal heart rates increase and fetal movement decreases. Cigarette smoking also interferes with the assimilation of essential vitamins and minerals. Nicotine has been found in breast milk, although the impact on the infant has not been well documented. Long-term follow-up has shown impaired intellectual and emotional development. Infants born to smoking mothers are more likely to display hyperactivity and impaired school performance. Prevention involves explaining the risks of maternal smoking and advising women to stop or at least reduce the number of cigarettes they smoke.

In the Field

As a special educator whose school draws from a mostly low socioeconomic area, I know that many of my students' parents smoke. While I know this could cause respiratory problems, I always held my tongue when I conferenced with these adults. I am young and I don't want to be judgmental. However, on one occasion I scheduled a conference with the mother of one of my students. I knew she was pregnant. Ethically, I felt I should talk to her about smoking and its dangers during pregnancy. I thought about this as I watched her outside my window having her second cigarette while she waited for the school buses to leave. Smoking is not allowed on school grounds, but the signs did not seem to deter her. I didn't want the conference to start off badly so I didn't mention it as she put out the cigarette before she entered the school.

In the days before the meeting, I had learned that this mother lived in a very poor trailer park; she had one other child in addition to Ellen, who was in my class. My colleagues told me that she herself had attended this school and had dropped out at 16. They remembered that she had learning problems but that was in the days before we knew much about learning disabilities. Her school experiences had not been positive.

The mother was very polite during our meeting and seemed very interested and concerned about Ellen. She wanted to know if she could do anything to help her. We discussed how she could help her at home. I wondered if she would be as happy to help her unborn baby by quitting smoking.

Throughout the meeting, all I could look at was the pack of cigarettes hanging out of her purse. I wanted more than anything to tell her about the dangers of smoking, not only for Ellen, but also for the unborn baby. Because of her economic situation I figured she did not receive the best prenatal care. Also, I surmised that she didn't know much about the dangers of smoking to unborn babies because she probably never completed crucial high school classes, such as health education. I never got up the nerve to bring up the topic. To this day I think about it.

Reflective Practice

This teacher had an ethical dilemma. She wanted to talk with the mother about smoking but did know if it really was her job. Do teachers need to educate parents too? Would it be overstepping her boundaries to discuss this matter at a student progress conference? By the end of the conference, she hadn't gotten up the nerve to discuss this issue. Should she have talked to her about the smoking? Would you?

Drugs

Drugs are another commonly abused substance. Of those who use drugs, some pregnant women use illicit drugs, whereas others use only prescribed drugs. In the United States, the Food and Drug Administration (FDA) is considering methods of testing drugs to collect information about their effects on pregnant women to provide information about safety. The FDA uses potential fetal risk as its criterion for establishing guidelines for prescribing drugs to pregnant women. General concerns related to drug use during pregnancy are birth defects, spontaneous abortion, preterm labor, low birth weight, and fetal death. Drugs taken by the mother pass through her system to the fetus via the placenta. Some over-the-counter drugs such as aspirin can cause problems. Aspirin interferes with blood clotting and leads to increased bleeding. High doses of aspirin can lead to more serious problems.

Illicit Drugs

Some pregnant women are recreational drug users (those who use narcotics sporadically), and others are addicted (they have a tolerance to the narcotic and show signs of withdrawal when they stop using it). When pregnant women were asked if they had used illicit drugs during the past month, 9.6 percent reported that they had. Eight percent of younger women (15 to 25 years) reported using drugs, whereas only 1.6 percent of those between 26 and 44 reported they had used illicit drugs (Substance Abuse and Mental Health Services Administration [SAMHSA], 2005a). The actual incidence of use during pregnancy is much higher, ranging from 5 to 32 percent depending upon whether the results are based on self-report or urine testing (Mason & Lee, 1995; SAMHSA, 2005a; Huestis & Choo, 2002). If a woman uses illicit drugs, the specific drugs and the magnitude of use must be determined. Women are routinely asked about their drug use, but about 25 to 50 percent deny using drugs even when they know they have just given a urine sample that will be tested for drug use (Mason & Lee, 1995). Given social desirability, the expectation is that the higher numbers are more accurate. The price for the infant is high. More that 75 percent of infants who have been exposed to drugs in utero will have major medical problems compared to 27 percent of unexposed infants (Huestis & Choo, 2002).

Marijuana. Marijuana is the most commonly used illicit drug among middle class women of childbearing age and, after alcohol and tobacco, is the most commonly used drug during pregnancy. Of young adults between 18 to 25 years, 17.3 percent state that they have used marijuana in the past month (SAMHSA, 2005b). It is estimated that 10 percent of pregnant women use marijuana. More use it in the first trimester than in the third, but these rates vary throughout the population.

Marijuana increases the carbon monoxide level in the blood. Carbon monoxide levels while smoking a "joint" are five times higher than those found during cigarette smoking (Wunsch et al., 2002). There is some indication that infants of marijuana users might be born preterm and have low birth weights; however, this is not conclusive. Effects after birth are that the infants cry more and are difficult to console. There is disagreement about the effects of marijuana on the development of the fetus. When confounding variables of race, education, income, marital status, and alcohol and tobacco use were controlled, many findings about the detrimental effects of marijuana did not hold up (Kandall, Doberczak, Jantunen, & Stein, 1999; Lester, 2000). Prenatal marijuana exposure did not appear to have an important impact on postnatal development when it was used in isolation.

Cocaine. Cocaine is one of the most frequently used illicit drugs and one of the most addictive. Of young adults between 18 and 25 years, 2 percent state that they have used cocaine in the past month (SAMHSA, 2005b). Although its use is not as prevalent as alcohol and marijuana, fetal exposure occurs in 1 to 3 percent of pregnancies (Chiriboga, 1996). Although this drug is generally labeled "cocaine," it may take many forms, the concentrations vary, and it is used in different ways: inhaled, smoked, free-based, or injected making conclusive states about its effects difficult.

The effects of cocaine are both direct and indirect. Cocaine affects the CNS as a stimulant and causes the blood vessels to constrict, which decreases the amount of blood and oxygen that can reach the fetus. The lack of blood and oxygen circulation then interferes with development and the effect is magnified if the mother also smokes cigarettes or drinks alcohol. Structural defects associated with cocaine use are caused by the interruption of the blood flow to developing structures or previously developed structures (Covington, Nordstrom-Klee, Ager, Sokol, & Delaney-Black, 2002). Cocaine has been associated with prematurity and low birth weight, as well as neurobehavioral abnormalities (Wunsch et al., 2002). It can also cause contractions of the uterus and premature birth or spontaneous abortion. The constriction of the blood vessels can result in growth retardation, intracranial hemorrhage, malnutrition, reduced oxygen (intrauterine hypoxia), and microcephaly (Espy, Kaufman, & Glisky, 1999).

Children who have been exposed to cocaine prenatally are at biological and environmental risk. However, these risks may be overstated. With differences in instruments used and inconsistencies in results it is difficult to reach conclusions. Some of the differences that appear shortly after birth fade by 7 months or so (Wunsch et al., 2002). Some abnormalities are not apparent until school age (Singer et al., 2002).

Opiates. Opium and its derivatives (heroin, morphine, and codeine) can be ingested, injected, or absorbed through mucous membranes. Heroin addiction has decreased since the 1990s. Most heroin users administer it intravenously because of the immediate effect. The only drug available to treat pregnant heroin-addicted women is methadone. This can be taken orally, is long acting, and helps women maintain fairly consistent blood levels. The use of other opiates tends to produce rapid swings from intoxication to withdrawal and this adversely affects the fetus. The most common signs of neonatal narcotic withdrawal syndrome in infants reflect the disregulation of the CNS and include irritability, restlessness, sleep disturbances, sweating, vomiting, diarrhea, high-pitched cry, tremors, seizures, **hypertonicity,** and uncoordinated suck. Withdrawal symptoms are more severe and prolonged for methadone than heroin (Haffner, 2007).

Environmental Teratogens

There are many factors found within the environment of the pregnant mother that can affect the developing fetus. Some of these environmental effects include radiation, hyperthermia, mercury, and lead. Prenatal environmental factors account for 2 to 3 percent of disabilities (Hill & Haffner, 2002). Environmental factors often lead to congenital malformations. For infants, exposure to environmental toxins during the first few days after conception seems to have an all-or-nothing effect. That is, the embryo either dies or is unaffected. Later in the pregnancy, these toxins may affect the size of the fetus, either causing microcephaly or low birth weight. There are individual differences in susceptibility to these toxins as well as a threshold effect. Below a certain level, some toxins may not be harmful.

Radiation, Mercury, and Lead

Radiation is one of the most common toxins. Low doses of radiation have been found not to be harmful. The effect of radiation depends on the amount and timing of exposure. During the first weeks of pregnancy the embryo is either unaffected or its effects are lethal. During the next 2 months, if not lethal, exposure to radiation produces growth retardation. During the second trimester, excessive radiation can cause central nervous sensitivity, microcephaly, and eye abnormalities. Pregnant women should avoid x-rays when possible. All females should wear lead capes when exposed to x-rays to protect their supply of eggs from radiation. Radiation is energy in the form of waves or particles.

Maternal exposure to mercury can lead to severe disabling conditions in the infant, including cerebral palsy, congenital malformation, and intellectual disability. Methylmercury is a heavy metal that is found in some fish, however, other nutrients in seafood may mitigate its potential adverse effects (Davidson & Myers, 2007). Ingestion of **lead** during pregnancy has been shown to cause brain damage in infants. Prenatal exposure to lead also predisposes children to develop ADHD (Stein, Efron, Schiff, & Glanzman, 2002). Lead is also a heavy neurotoxic metal that accumulates in soft bones and tissue. Lead levels as low as 10 micrograms per deciliter are associated with lower IQ scores. Fetal exposure to many different environmental pesticides, cleaners, paints, and other toxic substances increases the risk for developmental disabilities.

The Evidence Base

High levels of lead affect the **cardiovascular**, **renal** and **hepatic** systems and can produce neurological complications that can result in disability or death. The neurological complications are irreversible. A rise in blood level from 10 to 20 µg/dL reduces a child's IQ by an average of two points. It is estimated that 310,000 children between 1 and 5 years have elevated blood levels. The prevalence of elevated has declined 98 percent since 1976–1980. Critical factors were the reduction of homes with lead-based paint, lead-soldered pipes, leaded gasoline, and industrial emissions.

The estimated cost for a birth cohort of 5 year olds (children born the same year) was estimated at $43.4 billion in 1997 (Landrigan, Schechter, Lipton, Fahs, & Schwartz, 2002). Because of falling blood lead levels since the late 1970s it is estimated that the average IQ of children in the late 1990s was on average 2.2 to 4.7 points higher. Each IQ point raises worker productivity 1.76 to 2.38 percent. The estimated economic benefit in 2000 dollars for each year's cohort of 2-year-old children ranges from $110 to $319 billion (Grosse, Matte, Schwartz, & Jackson, 2002). The cost of blood lead screening averages $30 per specimen. Children at risk for lead exposure should be screened at or before 12 months of age and again at 24 months if the risk continues. The main treatment is to stop exposure by removing the environmental or dietary source of lead (Brown & Chattopadhyay, 2006)

Reflective Practice

Evidence about the affects of lead were used to make societal changes. Although there is concern about the welfare of children it is sometimes the economic impact that is the impetus for change. How do you feel about that? Do you believe that one of the reasons universal preschool may be implemented is because it is cost effective not that it is good for children?

Hurricane Katrina brought a lot of the concerns about environmental toxins to the fore, including concerns about carbon monoxide because of power outages, the chemicals in floodwaters, and even the use of insect repellent. There are not enough studies to know if DEET is safe for pregnant women (CDC, 2007b). It should not be used on infants.

Hyperthermia

Exposure to high temperatures (over 102°F), especially during the first trimester, is related to neural tube defects (Liptak, 2002). In hyperthermia the body absorbs more heat than it can get rid of so the body temperature rises. Because of the negative effects of hyperthermia, spas and hot baths are not recommended for pregnant women.

Summary

Every human being starts as a single cell. This cell contains the genetic information that will shape that individual and the genetic material that individual will pass on to future generations. Sometimes there are problems in the process of cell division and chromosomes are added, lost, or moved to different locations. Some of these changes have significant consequences, whereas others do not.

An individual's traits, whether positive or negative, are passed on in predictable ways. When these traits can result in developmental disabilities, families sometimes seek genetic counseling to determine the probability of their children inheriting these traits. We use a variety of different screening methods to identify prenatal disorders and help families understand what these conditions mean. Some developmental disabilities can neither be prevented nor diagnosed prenatally.

In utero, the fetus has predictable patterns of development. Sometimes, however, maternal diseases, disorders, or illnesses interfere with this path. Other times, biological factors such as maternal malnutrition and chronic illness impact the developmental trajectory. At other times, teratogens such as alcohol, nicotine, and drugs interfere with development. Additionally, there are teratogens in the environment. Despite all of these problems, the vast majority of infants are born without developmental disabilities. With advances in knowledge about the brain and its development, and early intervention, children born with disabilities face new opportunities.

Reflections

1. As an educator, your class may include children who have disabilities that could have been prevented. These children may have been exposed to teratogens resulting from substance abuse during the prenatal stages of development. Some mothers may have used these substances before they realized they were pregnant, some without knowing they could harm the unborn fetus, whereas others knew but did not change their behavior. Do you think you will feel differently about mothers whose drug or alcohol use or smoking caused disorders in their children than about mothers who did not use these substances? Will you treat these mothers differently? If so, is this fair? Is this discrimination or just a normal feeling? How could you overcome your feelings? Is it your job to do so?

2. As an educator you should have some knowledge about the causes of disabilities. To what extent do you think you need to be knowledgeable about prenatal causes of disabilities? Isn't your job just to teach the children, not to figure out the causes? Do you think that knowing about prenatal causes of disabilities will make you more successful in teaching these children? In conferencing with their parents? Reflect on your knowledge base. Do you need to know more? If so, how will you learn?

Educational Resources

Centers for Disease Control and Prevention is a government funded source that contains a wealth of health information and up to date information about a variety of diseases and conditions. http://www.cdc.gov/

Kids Health supported by the Nemours Foundation is a nonprofit organization supporting child and family health. It had an extensive searchable database on issues relating to prenatal development and risk factors, as well as other information. It has places for parents, teens, and children. http://www.kidshealth.org.

National Human Genome Research Institute supported by the National Institutes of Health provides educational materials including definitions, a talking glossary, and fact sheets as well as information about the Human Genome. http://www.genome.gov.

National Library of Medicine (NLM) is part of the National Institutes of Health and is the national resource for all health-related materials. (888)346-3656; http://www.nlm.nih.gov

National Organization for Rare Disorders, Inc. (NORD) is a clearinghouse for information about rare disorders (e.g., inborn errors of metabolism). It encourages research, represents people with rare diseases, and educates the public about these diseases. (203) 746-6518; (800) 999-NORD; http://www.nord-rdb.com.

Smart Moms, Healthy Babies was developed by UMHS Health Education Resource Center and the Women's Health Resource Center developed to provide information about pregnancy, prenatal testing, and a variety of conditions that affect fetal development. http://www.smartmoms.org.

For additional resources, visit the book companion website for this text at www.cengage.com/educatio/deiner.

PART

II

Inclusive Early Childhood Education

This part of the book focuses on educating children with disabilities in inclusive settings. It begins with a chapter on infants and toddlers who are at risk. It details some of the conditions that place infants at risk. It also provides information on early brain development and the role that experience plays in shaping the brain. It provides information about curriculum in general as well as ways of including infants and toddlers with disabilities in the curriculum.

Chapters 8 through 19 each focus on including children with a particular disability (such as a specific learning disability or a visual impairment) or a special need (such as English language learners or children who are gifted and talented) in an educational program. Each chapter provides a definition of the disability or special need as well as information on the prevalence and cause. It also provides information on assessment and early identification. All chapters include guidelines and curriculum adaptations.

Chapter 7

Infants and Toddlers At Risk

We were older parents—I was 34 years old—so I asked my obstetrician about some of the newer tests. He told me I was healthy and in good shape, and I shouldn't worry. I decided not to. My water broke in the middle of the night. I went to the bathroom, Jack laid towels on the floor and called the doctor. He said we should come to the hospital. When we arrived, Jack calmly asked the nurse, "Is she pregnant?" They told him to sit down for a few minutes. They swept me away, telling him they would be back for him in a few minutes.

We had decided to try to have the baby as naturally as possible. I knew about fetal monitors and decided if it lost the heartbeat, Jack would lose it. I refused the monitor. We had the baby in the birthing room of the hospital. Having gone to the birthing classes, my husband was helping me breathe. Later, a nurse commented that what we were doing was asthmatic breathing as my husband has asthma. I had what I later learned was "back labor." That meant it hurt all the time, not just when the contractions came. I had to put my hand on my stomach to feel the contractions.

I was tired. After 20 hours of labor, I overheard the nurses say that I was "only 8 centimeters dilated." Given my feelings about medication, the doctor apparently resigned himself to the idea that I would hold out. He told me to push; the nurses murmured; I pushed. I might have had better luck pushing a BMW toward a wall 10 feet away. At some point I heard my husband and the doctor talking as the face emerged; they were guessing about whether it would be a boy or girl. I pushed again. It was a girl.

They held her up and I looked. She had the right number of fingers and toes and they put her to my breast. I was cold and trembling, but elated. She looked so perfect. I felt wonderful. I had entered the hospital about 4:30 A.M. I am not a hospital person and wanted to leave.

My obstetrician released me the next day but said only the pediatrician could authorize my daughter's release. He did. As we were leaving the hospital they stopped us—they needed a name. When we told them we'd get back to them, they made it very clear that there would be a lot of complications if we didn't name her. My husband filled out the papers. As we got in the car I asked him what he had named her.

We are a blended family. When we got home our new addition enthralled the two older children. My mother arrived to help. Things went normally. I breast-fed her. I am an academic and in those days there was no maternity leave. I taught my

first course when she was 9 days old. When I couldn't go to the classroom for meetings, the students met at my house. She nursed on my left breast while I graded and wrote comments on student papers. It was more difficult on the right side—I had to remember what I was going to say and, when she finished, write the comments all at once.

Things seemed to be going well. We had a large circular table and we just put her in the middle of it when we ate. She was the entertainment. I knew she wouldn't sleep through the night as an infant. That was okay. My husband and I adjusted, taking turns when we could. As an infant, she slept near us in a converted hall; but, when she could walk independently and climb out of her crib, we put her in a bedroom next to the other two children. No longer in a crib, she slept on a trundle bed.

There were pros and cons to this arrangement. She could not fall out, but she could get out.

And she did. She would wake up, walk through the house and over to our bedroom and call us. We would walk her back to bed, and then she would go to sleep. And then it would happen again, and again. It was a very long year. From age 1½ to 2½ she woke up between two and twenty-two times a night. The year is deeply imprinted on my mind. We tried different things. If she called for me, Mark went. We even bought a king-size bed in hopes that the one who minded the child would not wake the other. We thought it was a phase; she would get over it; we would live through it. The pediatrician suggested locking her in her room. I couldn't do that. Life was a blur.

Then someone suggested she might have allergies. Mine were seasonal, and my husband did have asthma, but anything seemed worth a try. As it turned out, she was allergic to everything. The doctor explained that she got up during the night because she was stuffy and couldn't breathe. When she got up the substances drained, allowing her to sleep, which is why she got up—and so went the endless cycle. This explained why our attempts to control her behavior didn't work.

Perhaps it also explained why she took off her clothes at every opportunity. Each night I zippered her into sleeping pajamas and every morning she woke up naked. She only wore clothes that dropped from the shoulders. Other parents must have thought I was strange because she never wore pants, only soft dresses. Her bare legs must have been cold in the winter months, but she would not give in.

The reality of the situation finally hit after I took her to an allergist and then took the resulting prescriptions to a pharmacy. Over the years I had gotten many prescriptions for the children. This time they gave me a quart bottle with twelve refills. And, this was only one of the prescriptions. She also needed weekly allergy shots. We were in it for the long haul, and only at the starting line. We built a platform bed, put a plastic cover over the mattress, removed the rugs, and took down the curtains. But most difficult of all was moving all her stuffed animals to the attic. And there was the laundry. I changed her bed daily, and all clothing pieces that went over her head had to be washed. But she finally slept.

We thought we were survivors. We knew how to deal with allergies. But we had yet to learn of the relationship between allergies and learning disabilities.

Reflective Practice

Stories such as these are not uncommon. What seems like a minor issue, sleeping, can be a major source of familial stress. It can disrupt the family for a long time before it is resolved. In this instance the solution was medical, but that was not obvious initially. What do you think about having a toddler with allergies means in a classroom? Will you have to make modifications to the cleaning, pets, even lawn mowing? Can something as seemingly simple as allergies put a toddler at risk for other disabilities? How do you know when an infant or toddler is at risk?

Pregnancy to Birth

The move from pregnancy to giving birth is dramatic, and one that brings many biological, social, and emotional changes to mothers and fathers. The process of giving birth to a baby, which has changed dramatically over the centuries among industrialized societies, has remained quite personal for millenia. New methods of fetal monitoring and delivery practices have made childbearing safer for both mother and infant. Complications during labor and delivery account for less than 10 percent of cases of severe childhood disabilities (Brown & Satin, 2007).

The average pregnancy lasts 280 days or 40 weeks. Figuring out when those 280 days begin is sometimes challenging, but about 85 percent of women deliver within 7 days (before or after) of their due date. Most of the factors that cause labor to begin are chemical in nature, and the expectant mother is unaware of them. Some chemicals like **oxytocin** stimulate uterine contractions; others such as **epinephrine** cause uterine relaxation. Basic knowledge of the role of different chemicals has allowed doctors to control the onset of labor to some degree. However, they are still uncertain about the role of *every* chemical or the interactions between chemicals.

Labor and Delivery

Dating a pregnancy is a crucial step in prenatal care. A pregnancy is full term if the baby is delivered between 38 and 42 weeks. The fetus is still small enough to fit through the birth canal and mature enough to cope with the extrauterine environment. Deliveries before 37 weeks are consider **preterm** and those after 42 weeks are **postterm**.

An early sign of labor is **lightening**, which is the initial descent of the fetus and uterus into the pelvic cavity. The decrease of pressure makes breathing easier. This is followed by **engagement** as the fetus moves farther down the pelvic cavity into position for birth with his head low in the mother's abdomen and close to the mother's cervix. As the cervix thins and dilates, tiny blood vessels break and give the mucus a bloody appearance, which may be seen on a mother's underwear as bloody spots. Also, the mother's "water" may break. This water is the clear amniotic fluid that that surrounds and protects the fetus while he is in the womb. **Contractions,** or the movement of the muscular walls of the uterus that push the fetus through the birth canal and out of the woman's body, may also alert her to the impending birth. Initial contractions may be cramp-like and come at irregular intervals. With time, these contractions become more intense, regular, and closer together.

The process of bringing an infant into the world is called **labor**. Most women who have had children approve of the name. Labor is defined as regular uterine contractions leading to progressive cervical changes. Technically, it involves discharging the fetus, placenta, and umbilical cord from the uterus. Labor is a dynamic personal experience.

The **first stage of labor** begins with the onset of regular contractions and continues until the cervix is completely dilated (about 10 centimeters). As the fetus descends, doctors and nurses check on the dilation of the cervix and the station of the fetal head. Uterine contractions and the fetal heart rate are also monitored. A normal fetal heart rate ranges between 120 and 160 beats per minute, and varies within these limits during childbirth. A fetal heart rate that slows beneath this range is cause for concern, and unless the cause is found and the heart rate returns to the normal range, the delivery is made by cesarean, forceps, or vacuum extraction, depending on considerations of safety and expediency (Brown & Satin, 2007).

During the **second stage of labor**, the constriction of the abdominal muscles and the straightening of the fetal body push the fetus into the birth canal. Each contraction also decreases the placental blood flow for a short time. For most fetuses, this decrease is not a problem. However, **hypoxia** (deprivation of oxygen to the brain) may be a problem for premature or at risk fetuses. Contractions also compress the umbilical cord and the fetal head. When the fetal head encounters the pelvic floor, the chin tucks, presenting a smaller diameter for the descent. The fetus then rotates and the head extends to permit passage through the vulva. The crowning head, then face and chin, are delivered. While awaiting the next contraction, the obstetrician applies suction to remove fluid from the newborn's mouth and nose. Following the delivery of the head, the fetus rotates, allowing the shoulders and the rest of the body to pass out of the birth canal. The umbilical cord is then clamped and cut (Lowdermilk & Perry, 2003).

The **third stage of labor** involves the separation and expulsion of the placenta or afterbirth, which happens about 5 minutes after the birth of the baby (Lowdermilk & Perry, 2003).

A **cesarean section** is the delivery of the fetus through an incision in the abdominal wall and uterus. The purpose of the cesarean birth is to support the life and health of the mother and the fetus. A fast delivery is particularly important when the fetal supply of oxygen is diminished (Lowdermilk & Perry, 2003).

Complications in the Birthing Process

Complications arise from a variety of sources related to the health of the mother, the placement of the placenta, the presentation of the fetus, multiple gestations, and birth injuries. Many of these conditions result in preterm labor and delivery. Preterm birth, delivery before 37 complete weeks, places the fetus at risk. It is the major source of long-term complications and accounts for 85 percent of complications around the time of birth (Norwitz, Robinson, & Challis, 1999; Lowdermilk & Perry, 2003).

At birth, infants must make the transition from the dark, watery womb that was warm and constant (almost 99°F) to a world of variable temperatures, light, and air. The wet infant enters the world with a large surface area and little body fat, which is why he needs to be warmed immediately. He must move from a pulmonary (lung) and cardiovascular (heart and blood vessels) system dependent on the mother and the placenta to one that is independent. The passage through the birth canal usually rids the lungs of fluid and the first cry usually inflates the lungs. The chemical surfactant helps the lungs maintain their shape (Gaitatzes, Chang, & Baumgart, 2007). The pattern of blood circulation changes allowing the lungs to oxygenate the blood. These changes are tenuous during the first few hours and even days after birth. When the umbilical cord is clamped, additional circulatory changes allow the blood to pass through the liver for detoxification before entering the infant's heart. The transitions are challenging for a full-term infant; prematurity can make the birth process daunting.

Newborns at Risk

The neonatal period refers to the first 4 weeks of life. **Infant mortality** (death) in the United States is comparatively low: 6.8 per 1,000 live infants in 2004 (Forum on Child and Family Statistics, 2007). Of infants who die during the first year, more than half die during the first month (Hoyert, Freedman, Strobino et al., 2001). **Morbidity** refers to the occurrence of complications such as disease, disability, and chronic illness. Both term and premature infants are at risk for morbidity, but the nature and the frequency of conditions varies.

Some infants are born with conditions that place them and their future development at risk. The purpose of this section is not to identify all such conditions, but rather to increase your awareness of them and to help you think about how these conditions will impact how you will educate and care for these infants and toddlers.

Birth weight and gestational age are used in determining neonatal risk. The preterm infant comes into the world at a disadvantage. The immature organs may not be ready to perform the necessary tasks of independent living. Neonates weighing less than 2,500 grams (5½ pounds) are considered *low birth weight (LBW),* those weighing below 1,500 grams (3⅓ pounds) are *very low birth weight (VLBW),* and below 1,000 grams (2¼ pounds) *extremely low birth weight (ELBW).*

The relationship between gestational age and size is an important one. Infants who are born **small for gestational age** (SGA) are particularly at risk. These are infants whose birth weight is below the tenth percentile for their gestational age. Infants below the fifth percentile are particularly at risk. The size of the infant indicates fetal growth retardation unless the infant is simply genetically small. An infant born at 40 weeks gestation and weighing 4 pounds would be considered small for gestational age, as he ought to weigh about 7.5 pounds. If born at 34 weeks gestational age, he would just be considered low birth weight and preterm, as his weight would be appropriate for his gestational age. About half of SGA infants are attributable to maternal illness, smoking, or malnutrition (Rais-Bahrami & Short, 2007). SGA infants are at greater risk for complications.

Preterm and Low Birth Weight Newborns

Thirteen percents of infants are born before 37 weeks and 8.1 percent are born weighing less than 5½ pounds (National Center for Health Statistics, 2007). Preterm births and low birth weight babies occur in 11 percent of all pregnancies, yet they account for the majority of **neonatal deaths** and almost half of all neurodevelopmental disabilities that are present at birth (Hoyert et al., 2001). These figures are not distributed equally: the percent of black low weight births (13.4 percent) is 72 percent higher than any other group and the infant mortality is double the national average (14.0) (Annie E. Casey Foundation, 2003, 2006). The most common causes are maternal infections and adolescence, or both (Rais-Bahrami & Short, 2007).

Being born too soon means that not all systems are ready. Premature infants face risks that other infants do not face. Their immature immune system makes them more susceptible to infection. They have problems regulating body temperature, coordinating sucking and swallowing, absorbing nutrients, they may not breathe regularly, and their heart may not beat rhythmically. They also look and sound different than term infants. They typically have fine hair, or *lanugo*, over their body (disappears by 38 weeks), their skin is more translucent and has a reddish tinge because the blood vessels are closer to the surface, and they may lack breast buds, skin creases, and cartilage in their ear lobe. They may be floppy because their muscle tone is not well-developed. These preemies may appear passive and disorganized (Rais-Bahrami & Short, 2007).

Respiratory Problems

Their respiratory system does not work as easily or predictably as term babies. Their lungs may not expand because of the lack of the chemical surfactant. Supplemental oxygen is given to infants until their system can produce enough surfactant. In more serious cases, infants are given surfactant replacement therapy, which works almost immediately (Rais-Bahrami & Short, 2007).

Cardiovascular Problems

For some premature infants, necessary changes in the circulatory system do not take place. One of the most important is the closure of the ductus arteriosus, which the fetal circulatory system used to bypass the lungs. In **patent ductus arteriosus**, which affects about 30 percent of premature infants, this closure does not take place. A higher blood oxygen level stimulates closure, but if the premature infant has respiratory distress, the opening may not close. This exacerbates the problem of oxygenating the blood. Medication exists to stimulate closing of this duct (Rais-Bahrami & Short, 2007).

Neurologic Problems

The preemie is also troubled by an immature central nervous system (CNS) that controls respiration and circulation. Getting oxygen into the lungs is a challenge. **Apnea** is a respiratory pause of 15 to 20 seconds; **bradycardia** is a fall in the heart rate to below 80 to 100 beats per minute Apnea and bradycardia are problems for about 10 percent of low birth weight infants. The smaller the infant the more likely the problem (Rais-Bahrami & Short, 2007). Although apnea of prematurity is not a major predisposing factor for SIDS, infants who have persistent episodes of apnea and bradycardia are sent home from the hospital on an **apnea monitor**. Theses monitors sound an alarm if the infant stops breathing.

In The Field

I had an emergency c-section and Harvey only weighted 5 pounds 2 ounces at birth. I was in my thirty-fourth week. He was in the neonatal intensive care unit for a week. We begged to bring him home. They finally agreed after we had taken a course in infant CPR. He came home with an apnea monitor. It has been a nightmare. I feel like I have my own little corner of the world. One of us sits here and watches him day and night. I watch during the day and we take 3-hour shifts at night. We know we can't keep doing this, but now it is the only way we have any peace. I know it would wake us up as it is loud, but it is so scary. What if we didn't wake up, what if we didn't get to him in time. I heard about a woman who took a shower and didn't hear the monitor; her baby died.

It goes off all the time, but then he starts to breath again or his heart beats or whatever is supposed to happen does. Only once did we have to press on his heart. They told us that he self-stimulates. If it stops for too long it will start again. But it is always there, because he is connected to a machine. I can't decide if it gives me comfort or anxiety.

Reflective Practice

How would you feel about having an infant with an apnea monitor in a child care setting? Do you believe he should be there? Do you think you have the skills to provide early intervention for an infant on an apnea monitor? If not, what do you need to learn?

In addition to heart and respiratory problems, premature infant's blood vessels are very fragile. Problems occur when the blood vessels that go to the ventricles break. This causes bleeding or hemorrhaging in the brain. Most preemies have some degree of **intraventricular hemorrhage (IVH)** within a few hours after birth. Intraventricular hemorrhaging is bleeding into or near the normal fluid spaces (ventricles) of the brain. The lower the birth weight and the younger the gestational age, the greater the probability of hemorrhaging. When hemorrhaging is limited, there are no adverse outcomes. Severe hemorrhages lead to neurologic impairment such as cerebral palsy and intellectual disability. Ultrasound is used to diagnose and classify intraventricular hemorrhage. Medication is used to reduce the incidence of IVH (Rais-Bahrami & Short, 2007).

Ophthalmologic Problems

Premature infant's eyes should be checked for retinopathy of prematurity (ROP). ROP occurs when abnormal blood vessels grow and spread throughout the **retina,** the tissue that lines the back of the eye. These fragile blood vessels can leak, scarring the retina and pulling it out of position, which causes the retina to detach resulting in visual impairment and/or blindness This occurs most frequently in newborns weighing 2¾ pounds or less (National Eye Institute, 2006).

Gastrointestinal Problems

Many low birth weight babies cannot coordinate the sucking reflex and swallowing mechanism. This coordination is possible by about 32 weeks gestation. Before this the infant wears himself out sucking without getting the necessary calories and nutrients. A special high caloric formula or tube feeding may be used. Some premature infants have a life-threatening intestinal disease called **necrotizing enterocolitis,** which may be cured by managing feeding and suctioning, but in about half of the cases surgery is required to remove the diseased section of the bowel. Additionally, preemies often have problems with **gastroesophageal reflux;** the contents of their stomach regurgitates into the esophagus. Treatment involves medication and positioning the infant so his head is higher than his feet when sleeping (Rais-Bahrami & Short, 2007).

Other Physiologic Problems

Some problems directly relate to prematurity, others relate to the infant herself. Preterm neonates are more susceptible to problems such as **hypothermia, hypo-** and **hyperglycemia, anemia,** and **jaundice.** Hypothermia occurs because the preemie does not have much subcutaneous fat and his higher ratio of body surface to body weight causes faster heat loss. Premature infants have smaller reserves of **glucose** (sugar), which puts them at risk for hypoglycemia. This may cause lethargy, vomiting, and seizures. These infants have early feedings, their glucose levels are monitored, and glucose may be administered intravenously. An immature liver may cause **bilirubin** to build up in his system, giving him a yellow, jaundiced appearance. Treatment involves phototherapy. The newborn's eyes are shielded and he is put under a light source. Anemia decreases the oxygen-carrying capacity of the red blood cells and may be treated by transfusion or medication (Rais-Bahrami & Short, 2007). Premature newborns are assessed to determine if they could profit from early intervention and to help their parents understand their behavior.

Long-Term Implications of Prematurity

Socioeconomic factors have a significant impact on the predicted outcome for all at-risk infants. The stresses of coping with premature infants are exacerbated by limited parental resources (money, transportation, education, and so on). Problems of developmental delays and neurologic problems are greater for very low birth weight infants whose mothers are 17 years or less, have less than a high school education, and are not married, than for infants born to middle class families (Moore, 2003). Premature and low birth weight infants have a far greater risk of being abused by parents or caregivers during childhood even when social class is held constant (Sullivan & Knutson, 2000).

The possibility of developmental delays also looms. Overall, there is a correlation between birth weight and developmental delay: the lower the birth weight, the greater the probability of a developmental delay. Delays appear more likely in the perceptual-motor areas than in verbal areas (Allen, 2002; Msall & Tremont, 2002). **Perceptual-motor development** is the ability to mentally organize and interpret sensory information and respond to it. Birth weight itself is not the major factor, but rather the complications such as hemorrhaging and other medical risk conditions.

Infants born prematurely typically develop at a rate based on their expected due date, not their birth date. Their motor skills lack the coordination of infants born at term. Most infants who weigh 3⅓ pounds or more show few differences from their peers by age 5. The prognosis is not as positive for infants who were born very premature or those who weighed less than 3⅓ pounds. By age 2 some of these toddlers show signs of attention-deficit/hyperactivity disorder (ADHD) and language delays that are often precursors to learning and behavior problems. Infants born weighing less than 2¼ pounds are at greater risk. Approximately a fourth of these children will be identified as having developmental disabilities in intellectual and motor development (Rais-Bahrami & Short, 2007).

Carefully assessing at risk infants over time, as well as working closely with their families, is necessary, because risk factors are cumulative and interactive. One must evaluate the infant and the socioeconomic and familial factors that influence developmental outcomes. Without assessing biological and environmental factors, it is not possible to determine whether intervention will be helpful or appropriate.

Medical risk factors are the best predictors of developmental risk during the first year while environmental risk factors are more useful predictors at older ages. Early intervention programs have positive effects on child outcome. However, this is not a cure. Many children will continue to need speech and language therapy, special education, and supports around behavior and emotional development through their school years to maintain gains from early intervention (Guralnick, 2005).

Bringing a Preterm Infant Home

As threatening as an intensive care nursery is, parents may be more frightened of bringing their baby home. Most premature infants come home around their due date. This is not the same as bringing a full-term infant home. Preemies are not well-organized internally and they may not give clear signals when they are hungry, sleepy, or overstimulated. They may go from soundly sleeping to loudly screaming in a matter of seconds. It takes full-term infants several weeks to begin to establish predictable patterns of eating and sleeping. It takes preemies even longer.

Because the infant is not well-organized, the adults need to be. The easiest way to do this is for families to keep a chart of what the infant does 24 hours a day. This may seem unreasonable given the total situation, but the long-term payoffs are high. After 2 or 3 days a pattern may emerge. With a pattern families may be able to predict what the infant's needs are and how to meet them before the situation becomes disorganized.

Preterm infants usually sleep 18 hours a day or more. However, if they have been in an intensive care unit (ICU) there has been no attempt to mold their sleep preferences into a pattern of day and night. It may be necessary to experiment with the environment to help infants adjust. Some infants like the new peace and quiet; for others the adjustment is too great. Some infants may need to have the lights on and the radio playing softly when they go to sleep.

Neonatal Assessment

The most widely used neonatal assessment tool is the Neonatal Behavioral Assessment Scale (NBAS) developed by T. Berry Brazelton in 1973, revised in 1984, and again in 1995 (Brazelton & Nugent, 1995). It is used with infants from the first day of life up to 2 months. The scale evaluates the infant's potential for self-organization and his ability to control his state of arousal (alertness) as a response to the environment. The NBAS focuses on four major areas: the autonomic system, the motor system, state regulation, and social interaction (Brazelton Institute, 2005).

The measure is based on several key assumptions:

- Newborns have 9 months of experience to draw on.
- Infants are capable of controlling their behavior to respond to their environment.
- Infants communicate through their behavior.
- Infants are social beings who shape and are shaped by their caregiving environment (Brazelton Institute, 2005).

Unlike most previous measures, the NBAS is an interactive assessment and the role of the examiner is to draw out the neonate's organizational skills and strengths. The emphasis is on establishing the newborn's capacities and limits, especially as they affect interactions with a caregiver. The infant's best scores are used, rather than his average performance. The examination takes 20 to 30 minutes and the examiner does the testing with the infant's parents or guardians, who help the examiner assess the infant's level of skill. The examiner must be knowledgeable about infants while administering the test. The assessment assesses the infant's capabilities and determines if she may need extra caregiving in some areas (Brazelton Institute, 2005).

One of the first challenges newborns face is to regulate their temperature, breathing, and other parts of the autonomic system. High-risk infants may spend most of their energy just doing this and not have energy left over for other developmental tasks. They may be overtaxed by noise and visual stimulation. Infants also need to inhibit random movements and control their activity level. This includes the infant's muscle tone, activity level, and reflexes. Swaddling helps infants control random movements.

State regulation is the next challenge. State is the term used to describe levels of consciousness that range from quiet sleep to active crying. The ability of the infant to control her state determines how available she is to respond to her environment. The examiner looks at an infant's state, state changes, and the predominant state of the infant during the assessment process. Some infants can ignore stimulation or **habituate** to it. Caregivers need to evaluate the environment and regulate the amount of stimulation if infants cannot.

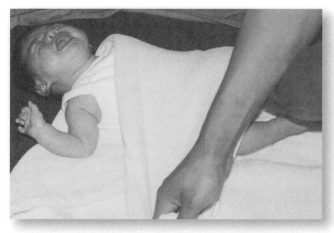

One of the first challenges infants face is regulating their state. Sometimes infants get out of control and cannot lower their state. When young infants are crying swaddling them helps them get organized and lowers their state.

Finally, the ultimate developmental task: social interaction. The examiner looks at how infants respond to faces, voices, and even a ball. Because the parents or guardians are present at the assessment, they see what their infant can do. The examiner gives them a profile of their infant that they can use to better care for her (Brazelton Institute, 2005).

Developmental Risk

Before deciding that an infant is "at risk," it is important that the term be clarified. It is also important that parents be informed of the criteria used to determine risk and how their child's situation will differ based on this label. As children change, grow, and develop, risk needs to be re-evaluated. Caution should be used before labeling a child as developmentally at risk, and when this labeling is used it should consider not only the child, but the family as well.

The term *at risk* does not mean that a child will inevitably be delayed or affected, but rather that the probabilities are higher than normal. Children can be placed in this category because of biological conditions, the family in which they live, or the physical environment in which they are raised. Children with established biological problems (e.g., Down syndrome) who may be functioning within the normal range at an early age are considered "at risk" for later developmental delays because experience has shown that their rate of development will be slower.

Families have the potential for increasing or decreasing child risk. Families who abuse or neglect children put them at medical, psychological, and educational risk. Infants born prematurely and infants with disabilities are particularly vulnerable to abuse and neglect. On the other hand, families who love and respond to their infants, spend time playing with them in developmentally appropriate ways, and keep the infants safe and healthy decrease child risk.

Environments can also cause infants and toddlers to be at risk. Some environments are conducive for developing motor delays or patterns of behavior that make learning difficult. Substandard housing, crowded conditions compounded by poor nutrition, and lack of medical treatment increase the risk of developmental problems among young children. Environments that reduce risk are settings where infants and toddlers can safely and freely explore inside and outside, where a wide selection of toys and materials are available for them to play with, and where adults support and facilitate play and learning. Environments affect not only the infant but the architecture of the developing brain.

The Developing Brain

Because of the importance of the brain and its role in early development, this section is detailed. In early fetal life the brain starts from the ectoderm, the outer layer of the embryo. The fetal brain undergoes a complicated process of development. Through cell migration a solid rod is formed down the midline of the embryo called the **notochord**. By day 18 chemical signals cause the ectoderm to begin maturing and eventually become nerve cells. They start replicating at a rate of 250,000 neurons per minute (Al-Chalabi, Turner, & Delamont, 2006). The nerve cells differentiate into inner and outer layers that are called the **neural plate**. These plates begin to fold over each other because of their fast rate of growth, and become the **neural fold** that becomes the **neural tube**. The head portion of the neural tube becomes the brain and the tail portion the spinal cord (Haffner, 2007).

The **central nervous system** (CNS) consists of the brain, the spinal cord, and the nerves that control voluntary and involuntary body functions. The development of the CNS affects the actions of the muscles, glands, and organs of the body, as well as motor and cognitive activities.

Between 3 and 5 months gestation, **neurons** from the neural tube rapidly divide and migrate toward the outer cell layers of the brain to form the **cerebral cortex**. Neurons are the specialized nerve cells that make up the CNS. If something interferes with this process, brain development will be impeded and the child will experience developmental delays.

The fetal brain consists of only one layer, whereas the adult brain is arranged in six layers. It is through the process of proliferation and migration that additional layers form. The sequence and timing of new layer formation are crucial. Brain cells must find their way up the cerebral walls using **glial cells**. In addition to 100 billion brain cells there are at least ten times that many glial cells. Glial cells provide support and protection for neurons. Some glial cells are able to move around the brain consuming dead neurons, others form the **myelin sheath** around neurons and others direct information flow as they come into contact with various genes, which define the neuron's identity, location, and mission (O'Shea, 2005). As brain cells migrate they can receive "misinformation" and die, or they can go to the wrong place, at the wrong time, and form the wrong synapses. A **synapse** is a small space separating neurons.

The brain is divided down the middle into two hemispheres: left and right. Each hemisphere plays a major role in some behaviors. The hemispheres communicate with each other through a bundle of 200 million nerve fibers called the **corpus callosum** (McDowell, 2004). The corpus callosum is a broad band of nerve fibers, **axons** of cells in the cerebral cortex that connect the left and right hemispheres of the brain. It permits the exchange of information between the two hemispheres. If this does not develop properly, or is damaged, this communication function is impaired. Other nerve fibers also connect the hemispheres. Figure 7–1 shows the cerebral cortex and the lobes of the brain.

The Cerebral Cortex

The **cerebrum** is largest part of the brain. It resides in both hemispheres of the brain. The outer layer of the cerebrum is called the cerebral cortex. Looking at the brain in cross section there are two distinct regions: the **gray matter** and the **white matter**. The gray matter is nerve cell bodies, which are grayish in color. They cover the white matter and together make up the cerebral cortex. The white matter is the axons, which are covered in a protective fatty coating of glial cells called a myelin sheath. The **myelin sheath** is an electrically insulating layer of glial cells that surround the axons of many neurons. It allows the rapid conduction of nerve impulses. Axons of newborns have little or no myelin. Development of the myelin sheath is necessary for the development of voluntary fine and gross motor movement. Myelination moves the newborn from the primitive reflexes present at birth to the ability to walk, run, and pick up small objects (Figure 7–1).

The Four Lobes of the Cerebral Cortex

The cerebral cortex is further divided into four regions: the frontal, parietal, occipital, and temporal lobes. Each of the four cortical lobes is responsible for specific activities and functions. This is a simplistic view of the brain as there are far more areas of the brain used than those most identified with particular behaviors (Al-Chalabi, Turner, & Delamont, 2006). Each cortex lobe has many folds, which do not mature at the same time. The brain releases chemicals in waves, which govern maturation; therefore, different areas of the brain evolve in a predictable sequence (Jensen, 2006; Shore, 1997). This helps explain why there are prime times for certain types of learning and development.

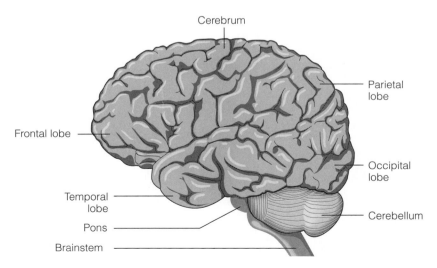

Figure 7–1: **The Brain**
The brain had two hemispheres and four lobes.

Frontal Lobe. The **frontal lobe** contains the motor areas of the brain. The left hemisphere controls the right side of the body and vice versa. The frontal lobe lies at the front of each cerebral hemisphere and plays a role in reasoning, judgment, impulse control, planning, language, memory, emotions, and problem solving. Humans have large frontal lobes relative to other species (McDowell, 2004). The frontal lobe is where high-level abstract thinking, planning, and organizing for the future takes place. The frontal lobe is one of the slowest areas for myelination to be completed (Jensen, 2006). The frontal lobe is separated from the parietal lobe by the motor strip or the primary motor cortex. It controls the planning and execution of movements and the intricate muscles necessary for speech such as the tongue, fine motor coordination, and muscles in the shoulders, knees, and trunk (Yaun & Keating, 2007). For motor activity to occur, a nerve impulse is sent from the primary motor cortex down the **pyramidal** or **corticospinal tract** that connects the cortex to the spinal cord, and ultimately to the appropriate muscles. The corticospinal tract is a massive collection of long motor axons that go between the brain and the spinal column. Damage to either the motor cortex or the pyramidal tract can result in spasticity (cerebral palsy) or seizures.

Parietal Lobe. The **parietal lobe** is the primary sensory area. It is concerned with the perception and integration of sensory input. There are distinct areas for vision, hearing, and smell. The parietal lobe also houses the sensory areas of perceived touch, pressure, temperature, and pain (McDowell, 2004). The parietal lobe is responsible for integrating other stimuli. Children with visual-perceptual problems and trouble with fine motor coordination, including children with specific learning disabilities and ADHD, may have abnormalities in this area of the brain (Yaun & Keating, 2007).

Temporal Lobe. The temporal lobe is involved with sensation and communication. It also enables auditory processing and verbal and visual memory. The dominate hemisphere (for right-handed people it is the left hemisphere) is responsible for the production and comprehension of speech. The **limbic system**, also located in the temporal lobe, consists of the structures of the brain involved in the emotions associated with memories and motivation. The limbic system reacts to stress and controls emotions (McDowell, 2004). The hippocampus and amygdala are small structures at the base of the temporal lobe, and are part of the limbic system. The **amygdala** controls emotions that are fundamental for self-preservation, the "fight or flight" response. It is the center for basic feelings, particularly fear and sexual response, and plays a crucial in control of major emotions such as love and rage. The **hippocampus** plays an important role in memory, the ability to learn new information rapidly, and processing and packaging the context of memory (McDowell, 2004).

Occipital Lobe. The **occipital lobe** houses the primary visual receptive cortex and the visual processing center of the brain. Damage to this area causes defects in the visual field (Yaun & Keating, 2007).

Brain Stem

The **brain stem** is the lower part of the brain that connects to the spinal column. The brain stem controls reflexive and involuntary activities such as blood pressure, heart rate, and regulation of body temperature, breathing, and other automatic processes. It is made up of the midbrain, pons, and medulla oblongata (Yaun & Keating, 2007). The **midbrain** serves as the nerve pathway of the cerebral hemispheres and contains auditory and visual reflex centers. The **pons** plays a role in relaying messages in the brain. It controls arousal and regulates respiration. The **medulla oblongata** is the lower portion of the brainstem. It deals with autonomic functions.

Some parts of the brain are not involved in either movement or sensation. These are called association areas. It is these areas that are believed to give individuals personality and a sense of humor (McDowell, 2004).

Connecting the Brain

Infants don't start with a small brain that just gets bigger and fills up with information. The brain is made up of nerve cells called neurons (Figure 7–2). Neurons are different and distinctive from each other in physical and biochemical features. During early childhood the brain has amazingly plasticity or **malleability**, that is, if one area of the brain is damaged another part may be able to take over the function. For example, if a young child loses her language skills due to a stroke, she may recover these language skills because the brain cells move this function to another area of the brain. This is more likely in a younger brain than an older one. In a young brain there are areas of the brain that are not yet committed to a particular function. There is an overproduction of synapses that are not in use and not yet designated for a particular use (Jensen, 2006).

Brain cells are like all other body cells in that they contain a nucleus and cytoplasm. However, they are not the rounded shape we think of. They differ because they have an **axon**, a long snake-like fiber, which reaches out from the cell body that conducts electrical impulses away from the cell body. **Dendrites** are short spider-like branched projections of a neuron that conduct electrical impulses to the cell body. Axons carry impulses away from the nerve cell body while dendrites receive impulses from other neurons and carry them the short distance to the cell body. The tip of each axon, the **growth cone**, provides guidance for the growing axon and helps it reach its destination. As axons grow, the dendrites respond by increasing the number of spines along their surface. This increased surface area allows for more elaborate and sophisticated communication between neurons. Individuals with intellectual disabilities have fewer dendritic spines (Yaun & Keating, 2007).

The axon of one cell body does not actually touch the dendritic spine of another cell body; there are spaces, **synapses,** which separate the two. There are two types of synapses: chemical and electrical. Electrical synapses are closer together and there is communication between the cytoplasm of the neurons. This makes electrical transmission rapid and bidirectional (Yaun & Keating, 2007).

Neuron

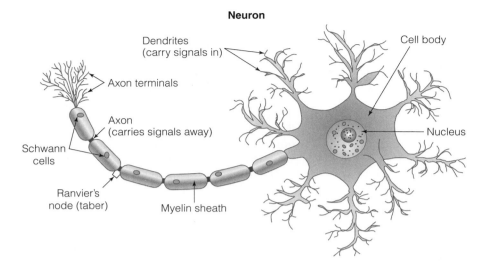

Figure 7–2: Neuron
This simplified drawing of a neuron shows the cell body with the axon surrounded by the myelin sheath and the dendrites. Courtesy of the Human Genome Project.

With chemical synapses the gap between the neurons is larger. Transmissions stop at the end of the axon, there are small vesicles in the neuron that hold neurotransmitters. **Neurotransmitters** are chemicals that relay, amplify, or modulate electrical signals between cells. The neurotransmitter affects the postsynaptic cell by either exciting it or inhibiting it. The signal is unidirectional (Yaun & Keating, 2007). Exposure to teratogens such as drugs, alcohol, radiation, intrauterine infection, and poor nutrition can derail this process. Depending on the timing and nature of the problem, the child might develop a specific learning disability or a neurologic disorder such as epilepsy, autism, or schizophrenia. In general, the earlier that the derailment occurs the more severe the effects (Jensen, 2006).

If this process seems long, complicated, and laborious, with many steps, it helps explain why speed is important. Infants have immature dendrites and the process is very slow. It takes a long time for them to perceive sensation, send a message to the brain, process it, return with a message, and respond. This is why infants seem to react in slow motion. As children grow the number of neurons remains stable, but each one becomes bigger and heavier due to the increasing number of dendrites. The key task in early development is the growth of these connections in the brain. One neuron can connect to as many as 15,000 other neurons (Yaun and Keating, 2007).

Connections form based on the child's experiences in the world and attachment to family and caregivers. In these early years, the child's brain forms twice as many synapses as it will need. If synapses are used repeatedly and are reinforced, they become part of the brain's permanent circuitry. If they are not used repeatedly, or often enough, they are eliminated or pruned. Experience plays a crucial role in "wiring" the young child's brain. The brain works on a threshold level—when a part has been activated so many times (it is different for different parts of the brain) it becomes exempt from elimination and is retained into adulthood. Much of the brain has a "use it or lose it" status. By age 3, a child's brain has about 1,000 trillion synapses. By late adolescence, about half of these synapses have been pruned, leaving about 500 trillion. Experience determines which synapses become hardwired and which are pruned (Shore, 1997).

The brain runs on **glucose.** Glucose is a simple sugar that cells use as a source of energy. Between birth and age 4, the cerebral cortex's use of glucose rises to more than twice the level of adults' brains and stays that way for 10 years (Chugani, 1998). Young children also have higher levels of some neurotransmitters. Children are biologically primed to learn. Some areas are getting hardwired, whereas roughly thirty-three synapses are eliminated every second. The brain responds constantly and swiftly to conditions that promote (or inhibit) learning. Brain activity surges when a child addresses a difficult problem. It is virtually nondetectable when a problem is easily solved (Shore, 1997).

Neurotransmitters play an important role in this process. Each neuron uses specific neurotransmitters. There are many different neurotransmitters; some of the most important include **serotonin, dopamine,** and **norepinephrine.** The neuron's neurotransmitters are stored in pouches, **synaptic vesicles,** which border the synaptic membrane. When a depolarizing electrical current passes through the presynaptic membrane of the axon, these pouches open and release the neurotransmitters. The released neurotransmitters move across the **synaptic cleft** to the postsynaptic membrane of the dendrite with an excitatory or inhibitory neural impulse, much like an on-off switch. This process goes on and on until it reaches its destination. Each neurotransmitter also has an inactivator that can stop the transmission (McDowell, 2004). Problems related to neurotransmitters are implicated in a variety of disabilities such as autism, attention-deficit/hyperactivity disorder (ADHD), and some inborn errors of metabolism. Many of the drugs that are used to treat these disorders as well as seizures, movement disorder, and depression act by altering specific neurotransmitters, their receptor sites, or what happens to the neurotransmitters that are released but not needed for the transmission (Yaun & Keating, 2007).

Experience and the Brain

At birth, the infant's brain is still under construction. Experience is the architect that determines how blueprints are turned into reality. Brain development is an interplay between the genes the child was born with and the experiences he has. These early experiences shape not only the child's behavior, but the child's brain itself.

Unlike other primates, who are born with the brain more completely formed, three-quarters of the human brain develops outside the womb. This is both an asset and a liability. How the brain develops is based on the interplay of nature and nurture. It seems obvious that trauma, disease, and abuse and neglect can change the brain. However, positive influences can change the brain as well. An enriched, stimulating environment can change infants' brains not only in the area of cognitive development but in social development as well (Jensen, 2006).

The brain's ability to change and recover lost functions is remarkable during the first 10 years of life. Early intervention takes advantage of the brain's plasticity. These are prime times for optimal development as the brain is particularly efficient at specific types of learning. In physiologic terms, there are times when the brain's neurons create synapses more efficiently and more easily than at other times. This requires not only energy and neurotransmitters, but space. For example, the increased metabolic activity in the frontal cortex during the second half of the first year coincides with the ability of the infant to form attachments.

Although we use the plasticity of the brain to enhance the development of children, early experiences of trauma and abuse can interfere with growth and impair brain development. Negative early relationships can lead to a lifelong limited ability to regulate the intensity, frequency, and duration of primitive states such as rage, terror, and shame. It is related to antisocial behavior and personality disorders. Factors that increase the activity or reactivity of the brainstem (chronic stress) or decrease the moderating capacity of the limbic or cortical areas (neglect) will increase the child's aggressiveness, impulsivity, and capacity to display violence. Violent behavior is most likely to occur when there is lack of stimulation to the cortex and overstimulation of the limbic system.

Implications for Educators

Early intervention is based on the malleability of the brain and methods of changing neural pathways to benefit children. To get the brain to pay attention we must teach in a way that is congruent with brain development.

- **Children must be active participants in their learning. (The brain doesn't change from observation.)**
- **Experiences must be novel, challenging, and meaningful for children to learn. (The brain doesn't change by repeating what children already know, meaningless experiences do not produce change.)**
- **Experiences must have both complexity and coherence. (The brain doesn't change from chaos or boring experiences.)**
- **Children need to strive for attainable goals. (The brain does not form new synapse when uncomfortable and overwhelmed.)**
- **Children learn in the context of positive social relationships. (Unsafe environments cause the brain to be over-vigilant and develop synapses that do not support learning.)**
- **Children need good nutrition to grow their bodies and their brains. (Both too little and too much food is not good for the brain.)**
- **Children need time and repetition with minor variations. (The brain rarely changes by just one experience unless it is traumatic.) (Jensen, 2006).**

The potential for early intervention is high. Individual experiences specifically designed for young children can help them develop new capacities and change their brain. Using the principles given, think about how you could design an experience for a child that you think will change his brain. Start small, look at what the child is playing with. Decide what you could do to add a novel touch. You can and will make a significant difference in children's brains. Identifying children who need additional support early and working within these prime times can and does make a difference.

The brain changes when young children actively participate in a safe and interesting environment with adults they can trust. Knowing how they develop helps you plan better and more effective activities and learning environments.

Curriculum for Infants and Toddlers at Risk

Infants move through three major developmental stages during their first 3 years. From birth until about 6 to 8 months, the focus is on developing a sense of security. With mobile infants (8 to about 18 months), internal needs focus on moving and exploration. Between 16 and 36 months, the focus changes again. Now, toddlers need to explore is replaced by a drive to define the self. "Interactions and negotiations with others lead to learning about themselves as independent, dependent and interdependent beings" (Lally & Mangione, 2006, p. 17). The

To learn the infant must participate in novel experiences. A trip to the beach provides a variety of interesting and novel sensory experiences for young children who grow up in urban areas.

role of the educator and interventionist must change with the infants' development. With toddlers, the adults' role is setting boundaries to help them learn about themselves and the societal rules that govern interactions. Adults must be supportive while providing security for the toddler and enforcing boundaries that are set. Development and appropriate interventions are highlighted.

Including Young Infants: Birth to 9 Months

Experiences and materials for very young infants are chosen because they are interesting to look at or listen to. By about 2 to 3 months, infants begin to reach for and grasp small toys. For infants older than 3 months, materials and experiences are designed to withstand active exploration, particularly mouthing, as well as constant washing. For infants to practice skills, having a variety of similar toys is helpful and varying their use is the key for planning. Observe infants and respond to their changing skills.

Implication for Educators

If you want to play with a 6-month-old infant, start by observing him. He is sitting on the floor and you notice that he looks at a particular toy. Voila! You get the toy and hold it slightly out of reach (motor). You encourage him to reach for it. Tell him what it is (cognitive) and verbally support his exploration of the toy (language). When he tires of the toy, you show him a different way to use it (cognitive). He led; you followed (social). Look at the activities in Resource Chapter 6. Choose one based on your knowledge of what infants can and like to do. Try it out. Challenge yourself to think of variations for tummy time. Also think about how much time infants are spending in car seats, swings, and other "containers." What can you do to decontainerize these infants and support their development?

Think about the process you used. You did not expect him to get the toy because you knew he could not crawl yet, but his sitting was stable enough that he could lean, reach, and manipulate the toy (physical/motor). You supported his choice of object and you provided him with experiences responsive to his interests (emotional). You encouraged his exploration by talking about what he was doing (language) and provided additional ways to play, which enriched his cognitive experience. Reflect on how this interaction is respectful and responsive to infants' development. Think about the types of interactions that are intrusive. How would you expect infants to respond to these?

The nonmobile infant is dependent on the adults in her environment to choose developmentally appropriate experiences. Planning is very individualized and developmentally based. Activities, usually one-on-one, are planned for a particular infant, and are executed when that infant is interested. Because of the individualistic nature of planning, including young infants with disabilities requires few adaptations. Infants have such a small repertoire of behaviors that a single activity with variations can be repeated until the infant reaches another developmental level. For example, an activity such as "Rattle" (6–44w) can be repeated many times, simply by using different rattles and talking about their characteristics.

Planning for young infants is more holistic than planning for older children. Their ability to attend to a task is dependent on their state, and your ability to choose the appropriate time and activity to engage them. The ability to excel as a teacher is dependent on accurate observations of the infant, knowledge of development, and the ability to bring these two sets of information together.

The best materials are those that encourage active involvement of the infant. Active involvement differs; just looking is active involvement for a very young infant, but not for an older infant. Many interventions for infants are variations on caregiving routines or are implemented during routines. Build interventions into routines. It is important to think of these as experiences and vary them; otherwise care can become solely custodial.

Routines are events that the must be completed on a regular basis and often involve a series of responses (Ostrosky, Jung, Hemmeter, & Thomas, n.d.). Much of the time spent providing care to infants is made up of important and essential routines such as changing diapers, preparing meals, giving bottles, or helping infants settle down for a nap. These routines offer an important opportunity for spending time individually with an infant and provide chances to communicate how much you like that infant by making eye contact, talking, singing, imitating the infant's sounds, or saying nursery rhymes. Routines give infants a sense of security and trust, as their most basic needs are met in a consistent and caring manner. Routines are part of the learning environment. If infants have an individualized family service plan (IFSP), the goals for the infant should be planned for and incorporated into routines. Tying intervention to routines ensures that there are many opportunities during the day for intervention to occur.

The learning environment changes during the day as infants play on the floor, are picked up and carried, are rocked in a rocking chair, are walked outside in a stroller,

Tummy time is any activity that keeps infants from lying flat on their back in one position on a hard supportive surface. Tummy time changes as infants grow and gain strength. Infants who need to develop upper body strength may use a ball to develop strength and to work on balance.

and are set to bask on a blanket in the sun. Infants need a variety of learning environments. Their environment should contain both soft and hard elements, such as pillows and mirrors. Infants like bright, high-contrast colors and interesting patterns to look at. They need cheerful, friendly pictures of infants, children, and adults hung at different levels. The learning environment should include equipment and materials that are developmentally appropriate, and these materials should be organized in a useful way so that they are readily available, but rotated so they are not all out at once.

The interaction of development, experiences, and learning is the foundation for planning for young infants. The infant's development is the given; the adult selects experiences or activities within the infant's **zone of proximal development,** and when the match is accurate, learning takes place. This learning is then "grooved" to a level of mastery through variations of the experiences, and new and more complex experiences are introduced with adult scaffolding.

Young infants need materials that can be held, dropped, thrown, mouthed, and shaken. They need materials of different textures, colors, weights, and sizes. Adults must choose appropriate materials to support infant learning. Figure 7-3 depicts this process of materials-methods interaction. This is part of how you teach young infants.

Including Mobile Infants: 8 to 18 Months

Planning for mobile infants is different from planning for either young infants or toddlers. Mobile infants want to move! Developmental milestones emphatically mark this transitional time: the first step and the first word! Mobile infants have a growing sense of self and an increased interest in their peers. They are interested in listening to adult language, but may not be happy around unfamiliar adults. Sitting is old hat; crawling is being replaced by creeping and standing. Walking is emerging, to be followed by the infant's version of running.

Receptive language far outstrips expressive language. Mobile infants are moving from one- to two-word utterances and their vocabulary is increasing. There are often long babbled sentences that "ought" to make sense, but it is as if they are in a different language. Adaptive skills are emerging as children want to dress and feed themselves, although they may be happier undressed and self-feeding is often messy. Emotions are becoming more specific. There are smiles and hugs for affection, anxiety at separation, and anger at people and objects that do not do what they are "supposed" to do.

Mobile infants have a heightened awareness of the world around them and the ability to explore more of that world. But they lack experience. Planning concentrates on the consolidation of emerging skills and building a foundation of trust in the world around them. Adults are responsible for setting the stage for mobile infant's play. To provide quality play experiences, adults must arrange time, space, materials, and preparatory experiences. Mobile infants need space to play in order to practice emerging large-motor skills. A good program has areas for mobile infants to create messy art work, a dramatic play corner for simple familiar play (variations on housekeeping), a block corner for constructive play, a cozy book and language area for quiet reading, a fine motor manipulative area, and a sensory area for exploring the properties of materials.

Mobile infants need a combination of materials and experiences that are nearby. Toys should be arranged on low shelves so they can go to them and choose the ones that attract them. Be sure that toys are accessible, as mobile infants will creep to an area, sit, make a choice, and then play. Be prepared that this process may be repeated several minutes later (if that long). When the infant initiates the choice of materials, play will probably take place on the floor; if an adult prepares an experience, older infants may be at a low table, but it will be their choice to be there.

Mobile infants learn through active exploration of materials and objects. They learn using all their senses. They continuously absorb the sights and sounds of the world around them, whether events are planned or happen spontaneously. Building on what they have previously learned, they add new ideas, words, and thoughts. This building process results in learning when adults provide the scaffolding to support learning.

Mobile infants need more than nice toys and equipment to play with. They need to have warm, caring interactions with adults. Knowledgeable adults join infant's plan and expand it through imitation, modeling, and scaffolding. They demonstrate and talk about cause and effect actions. If a mobile infant is using playdough, the adult might expand the play by initially manipulating the playdough and then making a pancake, snake, or little balls out of it. The infant can decide whether or not to add these actions to his repertoire of playdough behaviors.

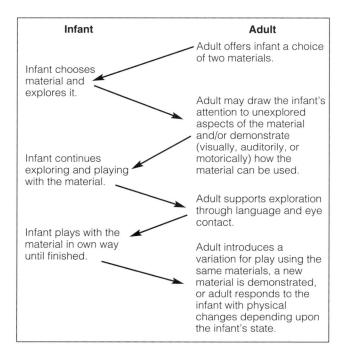

Infant	Adult
	Adult offers infant a choice of two materials.
Infant chooses material and explores it.	
	Adult may draw the infant's attention to unexplored aspects of the material and/or demonstrate (visually, auditorily, or motorically) how the material can be used.
Infant continues exploring and playing with the material.	
	Adult supports exploration through language and eye contact.
Infant plays with the material in own way until finished.	
	Adult introduces a variation for play using the same materials, a new material is demonstrated, or adult responds to the infant with physical changes depending upon the infant's state.

Figure 7–3: Materials-Methods/Adult-Infant Interaction

Implications for Educators

Inclusive programs are the norm. Expect mobile infants with disabilities in the classrooms they would be in if they did not have a disability. Teaching in an inclusive classroom requires additional skills. Social interactions may not occur spontaneously. You may need to facilitate positive social interactions between children with disabilities and those without. Ways to encourage positive interactions include supporting the achievements of all infants, even when these accomplishments are different; modeling appropriate behavior for infants; and encouraging empathy and prosocial behaviors in children. When teaching mobile infants:

- Say the infant's name, this serves as a marker for getting his attention, then tell him what he has done in short, simple language, and that it pleases you.
- Be responsive to cues from mobile infants that indicate understanding, interest, frustration, or fatigue.
- Provide many opportunities to manipulate and explore objects and materials. Give mobile infants time to explore materials before expecting them to use the materials.
- Provide experiences that are developmentally appropriate for the skills and goals of each mobile infant in the program.

Including Toddlers: 16 to 36 Months

With predictable mobility, mobile infants move into toddlerhood. The changes that occur between 16 and 36 months are dramatic. Toddlers move from tentative walking to running, climbing, jumping, and twirling around. They learn to throw and sometimes catch a ball, to pick up small objects with their fingers, to scribble, and to feed themselves. They learn to dress themselves in easy-to-put-on and take-off clothing and most learn to use the toilet. They can talk and they are learning to share and take turns. They know they can impact their world and they want to. Most of all they are learning about themselves.

Toddlers use two-word phrases and finally full sentences. By their second year, most toddlers are capable of holding conversations with adults. With the advent of language skills, play becomes richer and more imaginative. They begin to "pretend play" with toys and imitate the adults in their world, often playing "Mommy" or "Daddy." They begin to understand themselves as separate individuals with rights and privileges; however, they are only beginning to see that others have these same rights. They are more aware of their own feelings than the feelings of others. This is the stage of increasing independence and possessiveness. You'll hear exclamations such as "Mine!" and "Me do it!" and "No!" as children try to assert control over their environment. They notice other children in their world and struggle with building social play skills; they are sometimes eager to share toys with another child and sometimes hoard all the toys.

They are emotional beings who are learning to identify, label, and demonstrate their feelings. They display a range of emotions, from pure delight to utter frustration and sadness, from open curiosity and gregariousness to extreme shyness, from happy cooperation to obstinate

noncompliance, and from tender loving to hurtful anger. Physical development has slowed down, but language, cognitive, social, and emotional development are in full swing. It is a period of rapid changes and amazing growth. Toddlers need adults who can accept the inconsistencies in their behavior with loving care and serenity.

Toddlers are challenging to adults in different ways than infants. Some adults feel very comfortable working with toddlers. For these adults, it is like being able to watch a person unfold and develop, with all of the trials and tribulations that are inherent in the process. Others prefer to work with infants; they like the dependency and the caring of this age more than the budding autonomy of toddlerhood.

Curriculum and setting up learning environments for toddlers is different from planning for young or mobile infants. Although developmentally based, planning for toddlers is typically experience-related and organized along more traditional subject matter. A good toddler curriculum provides toddlers with choices of experiences. Toddlers play with what interests them at any given moment and might reject a particular experience an adult has planned. If given choices, the toddler can choose the toys or materials she wants to play with from the preselected, developmentally appropriate experiences the adult provides. This is most easily accomplished by having low open shelves with safe toys that toddlers can use. Choices also provide toddlers with the opportunity to assert their independence and autonomy. Choosing for oneself builds self-esteem.

Good toddler curriculum provides experiences that are self-paced and open-ended. A toddler is finished playing when he wants to leave an area. Forcing or coaxing a toddler to "finish" his art project only causes frustration for the adult and the toddler. Toddlers have different interests and attention spans. Some toddlers paint for 20 minutes, others for 20 seconds. The same toddler might paint for a long time one day and not show any interest in painting the next.

Implications for Educators

Toddlers learn through sensory, creative, physical, and problem-solving experiences. Experiences are the building blocks of planning. As you think about experiences, think about areas of development and how these can be incorporated into your plan in a developmentally appropriate way. One way to do this is to label the different areas of the room such as dramatic play or language arts. Allocate space for sensory play, easel painting, creative arts, playdough, simple dramatic play, books, blocks, music, language, and manipulative experiences. There should be enough materials for toddlers to use without causing undue frustrations; that is, there should be at least duplicates of popular toys and enough other materials so sharing is not a problem. Toddlers need:

- Warm, personal contact with adults (verbal and nonverbal) who are active, enthusiastic, and enjoy playing with toddlers.
- Experiences that are mostly self-directed and a few that are teacher-directed including active physical play.

- **A comprehensive program that includes developmentally appropriate experiences that meet the interests of individual children as well as the group. Planning includes physical, emotional, social, language, creative, sensory, and cognitive areas of development.**
- **A regular and stable schedule that allows for flexibility in meeting the needs of toddlers, including planned times for quiet and active periods.**
- **Consistent rules and guidance techniques that preserve self-esteem.**
- **Opportunities to play alone, near peers, with peers, and with adults.**
- **A safe classroom environment that encourages active play.**

Including Infants and Toddlers With Disabilities

Some infants are vulnerable because of their environment or their biological makeup. Infants born to parents living in poverty, infants born too soon, and infants who do not weigh enough are at risk for developmental disabilities (Guralnick, 2004). Some infants are doubly vulnerable, as they have identified disabilities and other risk factors.

States differ in the eligibility criteria they use for early intervention services. We classify infants as having a developmental delay rather than trying to pinpoint a specific disability unless a specific disability is apparent such as Down syndrome. Unless the infant is being monitored because of risk factors, or the delay is serious, it is unlikely that an infant will be identified before 9 months. It is often unclear whether delayed development is just an individual growth pattern and the infant will "catch up" in his own time or whether the delay is of a more permanent nature. However, if an infant cannot hold his head up when on his tummy, or he cannot push up with his arms by 3 months, encourage parents to consult their pediatrician or contact the local Child Find. Infants identified as having a developmental delay can have an early intervention team and an IFSP. This team provides guidance in planning for these infants.

Toddlers are becoming aware of the ways in which they are similar to and different from each other. It is the skill of a sensitive teacher that determines the long-term outcome of this awareness. Children look to you as a model. Examine your feelings about including young children with disabilities in early childhood programs. Also, reflect on your feelings about having children from different ethnic, racial, and language backgrounds, and your expectations based on gender, to discover if you have personal values that might make working with some children difficult.

If you pity toddlers with disabilities or are overprotective or condescending toward them, the other children will react the same way. If you celebrate only holidays that a majority of the children share, then those who have different beliefs may feel excluded. If you always choose boys to go to the block area and expect girls to use the dramatic play area, you are supporting stereotypic gender differences. Awareness is important for *all* children. Toddlers are egocentric. They need support in viewing events from another's perspective.

Adults can successfully facilitate the inclusion of infants and toddlers with disabilities into their programs if they plan to meet the individual needs of all the children in their group. Sometimes special toys or materials are needed to support a toddler with a disability in learning a new skill. Often, all the children in the program can use the special toys. By including young children with disabilities in a setting, there is potential gain for all children.

Infants and Toddlers with Developmental Delays and Intellectual Disabilities

For infants and toddlers the category of developmental delays is a broad one and will include some children who will later be identified as having other disabilities and some whose development has moved into the typical category.

Young Infants

Early intervention can change the trajectory of development and it begins shortly after birth with disorders such as Down syndrome or fetal alcohol syndrome. Accommodations are easy to implement because working with infants is so individualized. Early intervention increases the probability that low birth weight and premature infants will catch up to their peers. Use infants' adjusted age for planning. A 5-month-old who was born 2 months prematurely is appropriately planned for as a 3-month-old infant.

Infants born prematurely have an especially limited repertoire of skills, so a variety of materials at the same developmental level is important. Although many low birth weight infants catch up with their peers, at this young age there are predictable differences. The cues that these infants give are often subtle. With practice, these can be interpreted and responded to. The task of interpretation and response may not be easy.

- Provide a visually stimulating environment, particularly mobiles, until the infant begins reaching and grasping. (Watch the infant—what is stimulating to some is overstimulating to others.)
- Monitor premature infant's level of stimulation. An active early care and education setting may tax their system. When they become fussy and irritable, try less, as opposed to more, stimulation. Decrease the stimulation as much as you can. Swaddling is a good way to help them get organized.
- Use variation and repetition of experiences, especially those that intrigue the infant; it is likely to take these infants longer to "groove" an idea or skill.
- Help premature infants establishing a pattern of wake and sleep.
- Help disorganized premature infants become more organized. Remember they often cry 6 hours a day. (Full-term newborns cry 2 to 3 hours a day for several months.) Colicky crying typically begins right after feeding and frequent burping helps. Random patterns of crying are difficult to interpret. They may be just a discharge of excess energy, boredom, or overstimulation.
- Encourage the efforts that all infants make.

Mobile Infants

With increasing age, differences among infants become more apparent. Infants with developmental delays may have deficits in a variety of areas so that a particular disability is not yet apparent. Mobile infants with intellectual disabilities may also have deficits in other areas but it is clear that intellectual functioning will be involved. They require some modifications in your planning and activities, but these are minor and usually easy adaptations. Depending upon the specific infant, there are also areas that you will want emphasize more than for other infants. Embedding these needed skills into routines ensures that they are taught.

- Use simple, direct language and directions.
- Break down difficult activities into small steps. (If you are playing with pop beads start with two and see if the infant can pull them apart. It is far easier to pull them apart than to put them together.)
- Model what you want the infant to do. Then give her a turn and support her attempts at imitating you. Reflect on her response and decide how effective your scaffolding was. That will determine your next response.
- Emerging skills need to be honed by working on variations of that skill. If the infant has learned to roll an orange rubber ball, then have her roll a tennis ball, a wiffle ball, a yarn ball, a soccer ball, a football, a beach ball, and any other balls you have.
- Keep activities short. Infants with developmental delays have short attention spans and need more support and redirection. They may need more cues to interact with materials.

Toddlers

Involve toddlers actively in the learning process but expect to repeat this process with variations many times for learning to take place. Have toddlers crawl *under* the table when you are teaching that concept. Point out when he is using an obstacle course that he is *under* the ladder. You may need to use more direct teaching, rather than assuming the toddler will discover what to do or learn from observing others. You may have to provide more scaffolding for learning to occur:

- Keep a consistent daily schedule so toddlers will know what will happen next. Provide a picture chart to support the schedule.
- Limit choices to two or three experiences during free play time or provide some guidance in choosing appropriate experiences.
- Add cues such as carpet squares to indicate where toddlers should sit.
- Provide safe outlets for the release of excess energy and feelings. Toddlers may need punching bags, dance parties, or silly time to use up excess energy.
- Sequence tasks from easy to hard to match the toddler's developmental level. Use **backward chaining** where appropriate.
- Be specific about rules for experiences and post these with pictures. Show the toddlers the rules as well as telling them.

- Toddlers with developmental delays may have a limited repertoire of behaviors, and modeling can increase this repertoire. Point out the salient features you want them to attend to.
- Help toddlers organize their experiences. For example say, "What will you do first? . . . What comes next?"

Infants and Toddlers with Mental Health Challenges

Infants with social and emotional disorders cover a broad area and with young children it is sometimes difficult to accurately identify all of the important variables. These problems and disorders fit in the broad area of infant mental health and, at these ages, are frequently related to sensory integration and self-regulation.

Young Infants

It is very difficult to identify young infants who are having problem with mental health issues. Partly, we don't expect it. It may be manifest in feeding issues, lack of attachment, or inappropriate response to touch. These infants may cry more and be more difficult to comfort, not make eye contact and generally seem unhappy. They may truly be. Thus, you can:

- Help infants develop secure relationships with their caregivers.
- Actively explore the types of problems infants may be having from allergies to formula and gastrointestinal reflex, to living in an environment where their needs are not being met either physically or emotionally.
- Look into both internal and external sources of stress and do what you can to decrease the stress.

Mobile Infants

The goal of programming is to identify an infant's internal response to sensory input and then to program in a way that is compatible with their internal being. Children can have either high or low sensory thresholds and within these limits, some overreact to small stimuli, whereas other children try to avoid stimulation. Some children with high sensory thresholds take a lot of stimulation to get their attention, whereas others seek stimuli. Consult with families, a psychologist, and/or an occupational therapist on the best ways to adapt programming to include mobile infants with mental health challenges in your program. You may need to look at the "goodness of fit" between the child's needs and your environment (Anzalone, 2006). Some helpful guidelines include:

- For mobile infants with a very low threshold for sensory input the littlest thing can bother them, such as a tag in their clothing. They are distractible, their affect is often negative, and they are impulsive. (Does this sound like a feisty child with a difficult temperament?) If a child is overly sensitive to stimuli, evaluate your environment in this respect. A loud heating and cooling system or other children playing noisily may disturb mobile infants with this type of social/emotional disorder.
- Other mobile infants with low thresholds for stimuli may try to avoid sensory input. They are often

quiet and hypervigilant, scanning the environment for someone who might come too close or touch them. Respect the infant's concerns and create areas that are safe for him to play without other children getting in his space. Be sure to find ways of letting this infant know you like him. Verbal support such as saying "Brett, I'm glad to see you this morning" is wiser than a hug. If you do touch the infant, do it firmly.

- Some infants have high thresholds of arousal. These mobile infants may be difficult to arouse and may miss opportunities because they do not engage. Their affect may appear flat or depressed. We often miss these infants because they are "good." A light touch may alert this child. Loud music with a varied intensity might get their attention as well.
- Other infants with high thresholds seek sensory input. They may be impulsive and take risks for the sensory feedback. They can become over-excited. These are the mobile infants who pull up on shelving, not to see what is on the shelf, but to get to the top. For these children, classical music is a better choice, swinging and rhythmical rocking decrease stimulation. A pacifier also can decrease sensory input.

Identifying mobile infants and meeting their needs is a challenge and takes skill. Too often, these children are not identified as having a genuine problem, but seen as unusual or difficult children.

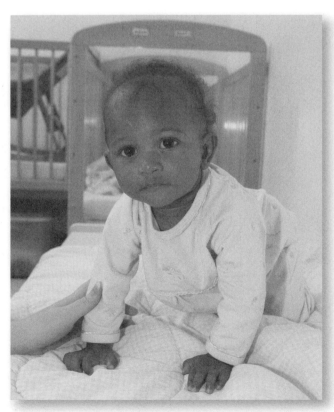

Mobile infants desire different levels of sensory input. When infants become concerned think about decreasing rather than increasing the level of stimulation.

In The Field

Laura had difficulties with feedings around 3 weeks of age. She would cry for food and then when drinking her bottle, she would scream and claw at the bottle as if in extreme pain. My husband and I took her to the doctor who diagnosed our child with gastrointestinal reflux. The solution was to hold her high on an incline when feeding her, give gas relief drops, and try to get as much air out of the bottle as possible before feeding. This alleviated some of the crying, but not all.

She continued to cry while eating for 6 more weeks. This was extremely stressful to me. Listening to her cry for hours on end was frustrating and anguishing because I could not do anything about it. She hurt, I hurt. When she began eating solid foods she no longer cried when drinking her formula, but now made strange noises when eating the baby foods. The noises sounded as if she was not enjoying the food, but she never made any gestures to avoid the food or refused to eat it. This continued from when she was around 5 months old to a little over 2 years of age. I think there was something else going on. I attribute this behavior to her having sensory integration issues. She had problems with loud noises and too many people in one room. She had extreme responses to new and different environments, and adults she didn't know getting too close to her. Her response would be to cry and try to escape.

Reflective Practice

With the information you have what do you think? If Laura were to join your classroom of toddlers what would you expect? How would you prepare for her? How would you adapt your program for her?

Toddlers

A predictable, safe environment helps toddlers become better organized. A consistent structure provides stability. Toddlers need adult support, warmth, and attention. They may have the same problems as mobile infants related to sensory integration and self-regulation. Try to help them get organized with the following ideas:

- Provide toddlers with many opportunities to run, jump, climb, and swing in a secure environment.
- Develop with the parents a consistent plan for handling disruptions and targeting behaviors to concentrate on.
- Give toddlers positive feedback and help them develop the skills necessary to enter small groups and play with others.

Infants and Toddlers who are English Language Learners

The infant's first language, or home language, is the language that the infant heard and overheard her parents speak before and after her birth (Genesse, Paradis, & Crago, 2004). It is the language she was exposed to. Infants and toddlers exposed to two languages at the same time are called **dual-language learners** (Genesse et al., 2004).

Young Infants

Young infants depend upon familiar schedules, routines, and relationships to feel safe. To the extent that these are extremely different infants can become confused and disorganized. Creating some level of continuity is important and yet challenging when the infant's home language is not English. It is more of a challenge when neither the parents nor the caregivers are fluent in a common language. In situations where many infants come from homes where the caregivers do not speak English, it is imperative to have at least one child care provider who speaks the home language. Although it is helpful to send important information home in both English and the home language, it may not be possible. Additionally, adults may not be literate in either their home language or English. To support young English language learners:

- Find out about the infant's routines at home and, if possible, ensure there is continuity between home, early care and education, and/or intervention settings.
- Be honest about your desire to communicate with families and be creative about making this happen. Find out from parents what works for them.
- Celebrate the ways in which infants and families are alike and different.

Mobile Infants

Locomotion makes all infants able to explore their world. This provides greater potential for learning as well as greater challenges. If families are recent immigrants to the United States, they may have come from regions where the threats to a mobile infant's safety were very different. Mobile infants in immigrant families are more likely to live in crowded housing (more than one person per room) and in households that include people in addition to their parents and siblings (Hernandez, 2004). Crowded conditions may make it difficult for mobile infants to explore their environment safely.

Evaluate the learning environment to ensure it is supportive of the children in the setting. The early childhood classroom provides messages about what the program values and who is valued, from what hangs on the walls to the experiences educators offer. Bilingual teachers are a tremendous asset in language learning and in communicating with families. Research supports infants' ability to learn two languages simultaneously. Settings make decisions about how they support second language learning. The choices made are dependent on the goals and philosophy of the program and available resources (human and material). To support infants who are English language learners and their families:

- Provide information about childproofing environments and child safety for mobile infants.
- Ensure that mobile infants are encouraged to explore their environment. Provide safe places to crawl, creep, and explore.
- Play CDs that celebrate different cultures, languages, and styles of music.
- Sing songs and use finger plays in the language of the infants in the setting.
- Develop effective ways to communicate with families. This may include sharing photographs as a method of communication and assessment.

Toddlers

As mobile infants move into toddlerhood, language becomes a more important vehicle of communication and learning. Supporting early language learning is an important aspect of all early childhood programs. When toddlers are learning two languages, the process is more challenging, but also more rewarding. How this process actually works is dependent on how particular programs are set up. In some settings, the toddlers spend their day in the second language. Depending on the multicultural commitment of the program, there may be few cultural supports for children whose first language is not English. This situation is both stressful for toddlers and not supportive of the home language; it devalues the home language. Culture and language are part of the curriculum for toddlers.

Ideally, programs have bilingual educators who are representative of the languages and cultures in the setting. It is easier to build relationships and to understand schedules, routines, and transitions in the home language. If one teacher speaks each toddler's home language and other teachers speak English, all children are immersed in a rich language environment. However, this may not be possible where children speak five or six different home languages and no educators can speak the language. If toddlers are not taught in their home language then it is imperative that the setting reflect the cultures of the toddlers who attend. A play-based environment and small groups support language learning. A long large-group time in one language does not support language-learning goals in addition to being inappropriate for toddlers (DeBey & Bombard, 2007).

As toddlers are learning two languages, there may be words they know in one language but not in the other. It is natural for them to use the words they know from both languages (**code switching**). As you talk with them, include the words they are trying to learn. Provide a language-rich environment.

- Provide board books in the home language, and other picture books that show different cultural and ethnic groups.
- Support both the home language and English in the classroom; do not comment when toddlers switch between English and another language.
- Encourage families to talk with you about what they want for their toddlers.
- Discuss childproofing the house, given the toddlers' increased mobility skills.
- Provide time for active play inside and outside.

Infants and Toddlers with Physical and Neurologic Impairments

The back-to-sleep initiative reduced cases of Sudden Infant Death Syndrome (SIDS) by 40 percent, but infants no longer get the 12 hours of tummy time they used to get during sleep. This tummy time stretched and strengthened the back and neck muscles. One in 40 babies is diagnosed with an early motor delay, and 400,000 babies a year are at risk. These numbers are increasing and lack of tummy time exacerbates early motor delays. Pathways Awareness Medical Roundtable is trying to establish standards for tummy time. It supports having children attain at least one hour of tummy time by the time and infant is three months old. This should not be all at once but spaced throughout the day (Pathways Awareness, 2008)

Other motor delays and physical disabilities involve damage to the CNS. Although these cannot be cured through early intervention, alternative pathways may be developed through exercise, massage, appropriate positioning, and the use of prostheses.

Young Infants

It is difficult to identify young infants with physical impairments until they begin to miss developmental milestones. Try to help them with the following activities:

- Provide toys that are interesting to look at and listen to.
- Bring objects to the infant and experiment to see if there is a way she can hold or control the object herself.
- Use soft or textured objects that are easier to grasp.
- Use toys with suction cups so the toys stay in one place if the infant has coordination problems.

Mobile Infants

Mobile infants with physical impairments need materials that support the development of their large and small muscles if this is appropriate. When other children are beginning to crawl and walk, it is important that you think about other forms of mobility, such as a creeper of some kind. Scaffolding motor tasks may be challenging. Talk to families and other professionals working with the infant to find the best way to do this. Holding and positioning children with physical impairments is important. Specific information should come from the infant's family or the physical or occupational therapist. To help mobile infants progress, use these guidelines:

- Encourage mobile infants to use all the movements they are capable of.
- Be alert to subtle movements that indicate communication of thoughts or feelings.
- Movement is both internal and external. Infants whose muscles do not move as they want can observe other children moving in ways they want to move. They can use these models for motor planning and visualization.
- Support children's exploration of materials. Ensure that they can reach, touch, and explore the materials.
- Talk with the families and therapists about positioning. Infants should be positioned based on the task they are trying to accomplish.

Toddlers

Toddlers need materials that encourage the development of large- and small-motor skills and to work on the skills that have potential functionality for them. The adult's role is to provide an adequate supply of a variety of materials that encourage functional movements and reflect a developmental progression for skill building. The nature of the disability will determine the most appropriate accommodations. Try the following ideas to support a toddler's motor skills:

- Use adaptive equipment to support toddlers' participation.
- Use larger lighter versions of manipulative toys.
- Be aware of equipment in the classroom that can easily tip or roll.
- To encourage adaptive skills, attach a carry-all or basket to the child's walker or have the child wear a back or front pack if he is using crutches.
- Encourage the toddler to use her motor skills. Children may shy away from art or manipulative experiences because these are difficult for them. It is your job to make these areas fun and intriguing.

Infants and Toddlers with Hearing Impairments

Be aware of infants who pull on their ear. They may be pulling on their ears because they discovered them or because they hurt. Some infants begin to have middle ear disease at a young age. Also be alert to infants and toddlers who don't seem to respond to sound appropriately and infants who stop babbling around 6 months.

All children need exposure to language. If a child's home language is American Sign Language this needs to be respected and included in the curriculum as you would any other language. Learn as much ASL as you can and use it correctly. It confuses young children when you make motions with your hands that look like they are signs but are really just made up or random signs. Integrate ASL across the curriculum if that is what families are teaching their infants and toddlers. Increasingly we are using signs with all infants as a method of communication before they have the coordination to speak. Take advantage of this opportunity to teach all infants and toddler signs. Early intervention can help infants and toddlers use residual hearing. Infants with identified hearing impairments who are in families that use American Sign Language (ASL) see signs in much the same way hearing infants hear conversations. With the support of parents these signs should be encouraged as one would encourage babbling.

Young Infants

With most states adopting universal hearing screening of newborns more infants with hearing impairments are identified earlier. Once identified they are likely to be prescribed hearing aids as young infants. To help young infants with hearing problems, try the following:

- Support infant's signs and learn the meaning of gestures that the infant and his family typically use for communicating.
- Offer stimulation through other senses in addition to hearing: sight, smell, taste, and touch.
- Find out what residual hearing the infant has, what the hearing aids supplement, and what you should do in the context of this knowledge.

Mobile Infants

If a hearing impairment has not been identified at birth it is often during this period that it is suspected. When infants and young toddlers do not meet milestones in the area of speech and language they are referred for a hearing evaluation. Consult with the child's family and the speech/language pathologist for additional information on how to accommodate and adapt your programming. Clearly, the degree and cause of the loss determine the needed accommodations. Families decide how they plan to have their child educated and the form of language they wish to pursue. If the infant has a profound hearing loss, the family may decide to have a cochlear implant during this time. To help mobile infants progress, try the following:

- Use vision and visual cues as input sources with appropriate verbal information. Show the child what you want her to do. Model behavior.
- The sense of hearing and balance are related. Give infants many opportunities for experiences that require and develop balance.
- Provide activities that encourage the child to use the hearing she has. Find out what the child is most likely to hear and incorporate these sounds into your curriculum.
- Sing songs and use finger plays that have motions to go with the words. If you can sign songs in ASL, do so. If not, ensure that the motions are not confusing to a young child learning ASL.
- Be aware of extraneous noise in the classroom. Hearing aids amplify all noise, so the child may actually have a hard time concentrating on specific sounds if there is loud background noise.
- Use signs with all infants to communicate some information. Many infants who do not have hearing impairments do not have the language skills to tell you what they want or need.

Toddlers

Families decide how they want their toddler to be taught communications skills. Your role is to support this decision. When possible, incorporate the toddler's preferred communication mode into regular experiences. To help toddlers with hearing impairments, try to:

- Remove barriers that may block the child's vision of the classroom, provided such removals do not create runways. Encourage toddlers to look over activity choices before deciding what to do.
- Encourage toddlers to attend to a speaker's face. Look at the toddler when you talk to her, remind the other children to do the same. "Look at Sofia when you talk to her, it makes it easier for her to understand you."
- Place the toddler in a good visual position during small group time or snack time; across from you, and not looking into the sun.

Infants and Toddlers with Visual Impairments

In infancy the role of vision is to motivate and guide behavior. It also plays a major role in incidental learning and it extends the infant's world beyond his reach. Because infants with severe visual impairments do not use eye contact to express and maintain interest, caregivers must use other senses to motivate infants and toddlers to explore their world.

Young Infants

Unless an infant has a severe visual impairment, it is not likely to be identified at this age. Intervention begins in early infancy for infants with severe visual impairments. It is important in preventing **blindisms** or secondary autistic-like behaviors. Physical stimulation is necessary during the critical periods of 2 to 3 months and 7 to 9 months in order to develop attachment behaviors. To encourage infants with visual impairment, try the following ideas:

- Find out the infant's degree of vision and under what distance and lighting conditions she sees best.
- High-contrast colors such as black and white are usually easiest to see and developmentally appropriate for this age.
- Use real three-dimensional objects to support concept development.
- Work through the infant's strengths by offering stimulation through other senses: sound, smell, taste, and touch.
- Keep in verbal contact with the infant as she will use your voice to know you are near if she cannot see you. Be sure to identify her by name when you talk to her.
- Provide as much verbal stimulation as the infant can adapt to.
- Work with the family and **orientation and mobility specialist** to ensure that the infant has an environment that meets her needs.

Mobile Infants

With the advent of locomotion, infants with visual impairments may need additional accommodations. Consult with a vision and orientation and mobility specialist about room arrangement, appropriate experiences, and so on. These specialists have information about long-term expectations for the child; that is, whether the child will read using large print or Braille, and useful information as well. Try the following ideas for mobile infants with visual impairment:

- Use materials that make sounds when manipulated. Toys that make a noise when they move help children focus on and reach for them.
- Help children locate sound. Make a noise, and when the child turns to the sound encourage him and give him the noisemaker. Verbally encourage him as well. "Friedrich, I can't fool you. You know where that noise is coming from, don't you. Here is the ball." This supports locating skills through sound.
- Use whatever sight the mobile infant has available. If she can make distinctions only among toys with high contrast like black and white, be sure you have toys like this.
- Locomotion is challenging for infants with visual impairments. They frequently walk later than other children and they often use **hitching** as a means of locomotion instead of creeping or crawling. (Children hitch when they scoot on their bottom while using their legs for propulsion.) This is very adaptive, as they run into things with their feet, not their head.
- Provide materials such as large manipulative toys that require two hands or activities that prohibit self-stimulation behavior, if this is a problem.

Toddlers

Help the toddler locate the different areas of the room and help her develop safe ways to get to each (no toys lying around). Keep these areas consistent to encourage independent movement. Providing consistent routines helps children know what to expect and supports their independence. Try the following ideas for toddlers with visual impairment:

- Be aware of the toddler's location in the room.
- Use objects the toddler can feel and pair words with the objects she is feeling. "Chunga, this is a ball. Feel how round it is. Drop it and it bounces back up." Use of pictures of objects is dependent upon the child's level of vision.
- Be aware of lighting needs. Some toddlers see better in dim settings. If she sees better in some lighting conditions than others, adapt your classroom.
- Use language that is comfortable for you. Don't eliminate the words "see" and "look" from your vocabulary, but describe what you see to the child in the most concrete way you can.

Adapting Materials for Infants and Toddlers With Disabilities

Most of the toys and materials you would use for any mobile infant or toddler can be used with infants or toddlers with disabilities; others may require minor modifications. If there are major modifications, families or specialists will typically provide this equipment or the information for adaptation. If there is no need to modify an experience, don't. When modifications are necessary, the toys and materials should be appropriate for the child's developmental level and chronological age, promote age-appropriate social and communication skills, and not interfere with regular routines or call undue attention to the child. Although alternative activities may be used, they should be interesting, varied, and available to all the children in the class. In reality they are activities that are good for all children, not just alternative activities. Adaptations are useful to all infants and toddlers who are challenged by any activity. Try using some of the following adaptations:

- Slightly deflated beach balls are easier than regular rubber balls for mobile infants and toddlers to grasp, throw, and catch.
- Hang toys above an infant or toddler who is not moving independently but can reach for and grasp toys. Hang them from the upright handle of an infant seat, above a changing table, or (if you are ambitious!), attach a pulley to the ceiling and hang toys from a rope. The use of the pulley allows you to adjust the height of the toys. Be sure that this equipment is strong enough to be safe when infants grasp and pull toys.
- Toys with several parts (such as simple puzzles) can be adapted by gluing magnetic strips onto the back of each piece. Use a cookie sheet as a base. Moving the pieces and taking them on and off the cookie sheet provides some resistance.

- Cut pop beads open and put them over small handles, such as those on a jack-in-the-box, to make them easier to hold. Foam hair curlers can be placed over paint brushes or crayons to make them easier to hold.
- Experiment with different adaptations to see what works. Remember young children change and grow quickly, so monitor and evaluate adaptations to ensure they are developmentally and socially appropriate and are still necessary.
- Suction-cup toys are valuable because they stay put when a child who is working on eye-hand coordination tries to manipulate them.
- Velcro™ wrist bracelets can aid an infant who is unable to hold a rattle independently.
- Pop beads or bristle blocks are good for putting things together, but for a child who needs to work on strength, pulling them apart is great.
- Inflatable toys that haven't been inflated all the way are easier to grasp.
- Place Dycem™ (a nonslip plastic) on the table to keep toys from rolling away and to anchor cups and plates. You can also put Dycem on chair seats to keep children from slipping off.
- Hook up a toy to a capability switch (a device the child uses to manipulate something. The child activates the switch and something happens, encouraging cause-and-effect reasoning). Capability switches are very sensitive and will respond to slight movements from any body part. Switch selection should be based on the mobile infant's or toddler's most consistent and reliable body movement. There are switches that will respond to sipping or puffing, voice, sideswipes, pinches, touch, movement of the tongue, chin, nose, and so on. Lighted switches help children with hearing impairments; others are gravity-sensitive so that tilting a body part will activate them. Photosensitive switches are activated by any body movement that creates a shadow. Switches can control robots, trains, fire engines, pigs, bears, and rabbits. They can be attached to music boxes, toy radios, toy TVs, and tops. They help children with disabilities gain control over their world.

Individualizing Planning

Individualized planning is a circular process. It starts with a designated outcome: what is it the infant or toddler's family want the child to be able to do? Also ask for input from early childhood and other professionals to frame the goal. For example, if a goal for a toddler is to increase his receptive vocabulary one of the first steps in the process is to decide when and how frequently you are going to incorporate this goal into your programming. Start with routines. They occur several times each day, ensuring that the child has many opportunities each day for practice. Identify the routines and the types of receptive language that can logically be a part of each. When the toddler arrives at school, you might decide to comment on articles, colors, and patterns of clothing. You might say, "You have a *shirt* on today. Let me look at that *shirt*. I like the buttons on your *shirt*." As the toddler's receptive vocabulary increases this might change to "Let me see what *shirt* you are wearing today," with the expectation that the toddler will show off his *shirt*. If the toddler can do this successfully, you know this technique works to build receptive language. When you share this information, it is useful to identify both the techniques you are using and the vocabulary and receptive language you are supporting.

To broaden the context of receptive language you might think of including a broad-based theme such as "my family and me," and then incorporate the words you want the child to identify into that theme to increase contextual learning. If you are interested in children learning household words, you might set up the dramatic play area as a house, choosing the specific household items based on the receptive language you plan to teach. Then consider how you will incorporate the teaching into the play. You might begin by labeling the objects for the infant or toddler and demonstrating what each does. Support the mobile infant or toddler using the objects and again verbally labeling the objects and what the child is doing. Finally, request that the child discriminate between the desired object and others: "Show me the blanket." "Can you wrap the baby in the blanket?"

The process you develop might look something like the one in Figure 7–4. You might begin by identifying the desired IFSP outcomes and frame them in the context of the theme you are working on. You then determine the procedures you will use to implement the goal, choose the appropriate materials, and implement the experience or activity with the infant or toddler. Once implemented, you reflect on the effectiveness of the process. If it was effective you would use it again with variations until the infant or toddler reaches the necessary level of performance. If the process is not effective you try to determine the aspects that were not working well, modify them, and use the activity again.

Once you have worked through this process on an individual basis several times you will begin to get a feel about the match between what the mobile infant or toddler can do and the goal that was set. With this new insight you share your information with the team. You would let them know that you were working toward an achievable goal, or, if things were not progressing, that the goal itself might need to be modified.

The Evidence Base

The age at which infants and toddlers begin early intervention (EI) influences the outcome. The National Early Intervention Longitudinal Study (NEILS) had a sample of 3,338 infants and toddler who entered early intervention before 31 months of age and their families. One aspect of the research focused on the process of getting into the early intervention system and beginning to receive services. Table 7–2 shows the data from when families were first concerned about an infant's health or development until the IFSP was developed. The data are given in months. Both the mean (arithmetic average) and median (the middle figure) meaning that half of the infants and toddlers were younger and half older than the month given are included.

The differences between the mean and the median are significant. It is clear that some children entered early intervention early and others much later. This is particularly true for the difference between first concerns and the development of the IFSP. In trying to sort out this problem, the researchers divided the infants and toddlers into three groups: developmental delay, diagnosed condition, and risk condition (see Table 7–3).

Approximately three times as many infants and toddlers with developmental delays receive early intervention services. However, on average, infants and toddlers with developmental delays did not have an IFSP until they were 20 months old, whereas infants with diagnosed conditions or risk conditions had an IFSP at 7.1 and 5.9 months. Adults did not become concerned about their delays until they were close to a year old whereas adults were concerned about the health of those with a diagnosed or at risk condition at 2 months. (Hebbelere et al., 2007).

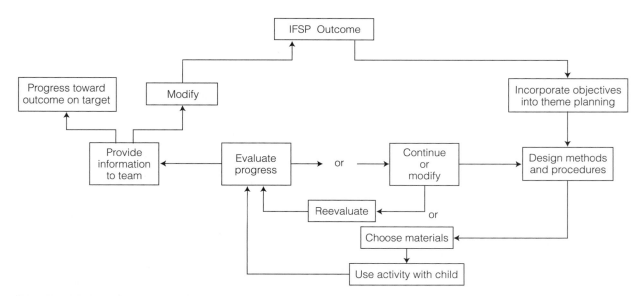

Figure 7–4: IFSP Child Outcomes

Table 7–2: Ages for identification of infants and toddlers and service provision

Situation	Ages in Months Mean	Ages in Months Median
First concern about health or development	7.4	4
First diagnosis or identification	8.8	6
First looked for early intervention	11.9	11
Referral received by early intervention program	14.0	14
Age at which IFSP was developed	15.7	16
Difference between first concerns and IFSP	8.3	12
Number of children	3,056–3,235	3,056–3,235

Table 7–3: Identified delays, disability, or risk and age

Situation	Developmental Delay Mean Age in Months	Diagnosed Condition Mean Age in Months	Risk Condition Mean age in Months
First concern about health or development	11.1	2.3	2.1
First diagnosis or identification	12.9	3.5	2.5
First looked for early intervention	16.0	5.7	5.2
Referral received by early intervention program	18.2	7.8	6.1
Age at which IFSP was developed	20.0	9.4	8.0
Difference between first concerns and IFSP	8.9	7.1	5.9
Number of children	1,826–1,923	638–675	436–463

Reflective Practice

Look at Tables 7–2 and 7–3 carefully. Entering into early intervention is dependent upon someone noticing a problem, perhaps something very subtle in the infant's or toddler's development. How will you hone your skills to be aware of developmental differences that may require early intervention? What do you think caused the difference in ages among the groups?

Implementing an IFSP

Because so much of infant and toddler programming is individualized, incorporating the goals of the IFSP into your daily plans is relatively easy. As you work from the IFSP, you may find it useful to develop your own format for planning.

Sometimes, the easiest way to individualize programming is to work it into your daily routine on a regular basis. This process ensures that it is done and supports contextual learning. Serving a cut up fresh fruit snack is an easy way to help children practice using a spoon. Likewise, talking about body parts and pointing to objects is easy when a child is arriving: "You needed to wear a sweater today to keep your arms warm. Please hang your sweater in your locker." "Show me what you have on your feet. What are these?" You can easily incorporate these steps in your planning, but you need to remain deliberate

about what you are doing and why. Schedule when you will work on specific outcomes with a toddler. Short-spaced work is more effective than attempting to sit a toddler down for half an hour and "do it all."

Because routines take up so much of the day, it is often useful to develop a chart like the one in Figure 7–5 that focuses your attention on the goals themselves as well as when you plan to implement them. Generalize this concept to home and other settings.

Adaptive Skills

The development of adaptive skills is important for the growing independence of infants and toddlers and they also (long term) reduce the amount of time parents spend in caregiving. Parents often have conflicts regarding self-help skills. They want their children to be more independent, yet logical times for learning these skills are often stressful. Logically, children could learn to dress themselves in the morning before going to school, but this is a high demand time for parents. This does not mean that parents do not value dressing skills. It means they need your help in finding other times and ways to support this adaptive skill.

Adaptive skills are repetitive and predictable if they are done effectively. They require adaptations for some children, but overall, the procedure is similar. Young children with disabilities may find these tasks difficult when adults try to "hurry" them. It helps children to experience success with a small part of a task rather than expecting completion

Child _____   Date _____

Routines

Outcomes	Arrival	Morning snack	Diapering	Play	Lunch	Special time	Play	Outside
Point to or touch named objects	X	X		X		X		
Touch and name body parts	X		X		X	X		
Follow simple directions	X			X	X	X		X
Use a spoon		X			X			
Drink from a cup		X			X			

X indicates when you plan to work on the desired outcome behavior.

Progress toward attaining outcome: AU – Attempted very little success
AS – Attempted successfully   NA – Not attempted
A –   Attempted with some success

General Comments: _____
_____
_____

Figure 7–5: Embedding Goals and Objectives in Routines
Because so much of infant and toddler curriculum revolves around routines it is essential to incorporate their IFSP goals into these routines. A chart such as this one makes it clear what the desired outcomes are and when they will be addressed.

of the whole task. One of the most effective ways of teaching these skills is through a **task analysis**. This breaks down a task into its component parts. There are many commercially available sources for this information. However, it is easy to create your own task analysis. Pick a skill—hand washing—and write down the steps involved. Number each step. Then, wash your hands using the identified steps. Did you forget anything? Does your chart look like this?

1. Turn on water.
2. Press the liquid soap container.
3. Rub soap on hands.
4. Rub hands together and sing "Mary had a Little Lamb" while scrubbing.
5. When song finishes, rinse hands.
6. Turn off water.
7. Dry hands.
8. Throw paper towel away.

Knowing the parts of any task is the first step involved in teaching it. The next step is chaining. **Chaining** is the process of taking a task analysis and deciding where to begin teaching it. Chaining can be forward (start teaching the first step in the task and work through it step-by-step to the end) or backward (start teaching the last step of the task and work backward through the steps to the beginning). In **backward chaining**, a child can feel successful after having to complete only the last step in the process. Gradually, earlier steps are added until the child is able to complete the entire task. For backward chaining, then, you would *help* the child turn on the water, *help* use the soap, *sing* with her while she rubs, *help* rinse, *help* dry hands, and teach the child how to throw away the paper towel. You would then say something like, "Cheri, now put the towel in the trash. Great job! You did that by yourself." Praise the child for doing it well. When Cheri can predictably throw the towel away you would teach her to dry her hands. For some tasks to begin at step one is discouraging because the teacher, not the child, accomplishes the final step. Task analysis is useful in making you aware of the steps involved in a particular task. It also becomes clear what the prerequisite skills are. If a child lacks the prerequisite skills, it is doubtful that the task will be completed.

Guidelines

1. *Discuss important issues.* Provide an atmosphere where issues about race, culture, gender, and disability can be freely discussed. Young children are becoming aware of these differences. Toddlers learn respect and caring for others who are different from themselves by modeling adults' interactions with the child.

2. *Support diversity.* Provide activities, materials, and curriculum planning that allows children to learn about differences by firsthand experience. If a toddler wears braces, the other children may want to try on the braces. Under supervision and perhaps with the support of a physical therapist, children can explore and experiment with braces and other adaptive equipment, but they should not be the child's actual aids. The goal is to create awareness and to have a positive, rather than a negative, experience.

3. *Teach ways to cope with unkind words.* Teach specific ways of handling situations involving staring or making unkind remarks. Make toddlers aware of how children who are stared at feel. If other children tease or make unkind remarks about a child with a disability, serve as the child's ally. Stop the teasing and explain that words can hurt people's feelings. Give correct information: "Camille is not stupid. It just takes her longer to learn new things." Over time, help children build the skills necessary to stand up for themselves. Teach all children socially acceptable ways of learning about others.

4. *Teach how to approach others.* There are specific skills used in approaching others and entering groups; some children do not know these skills.

5. *Facilitate social inclusion.* Help infants and toddlers find roles to play and facilitate adaptations and accommodations that allow children to play together.

6. *Keep a consistent daily schedule.* Infants and toddlers know what will happen next when the sequence is consistent. Provide a picture chart to support the schedule.

7. *Add cues.* Carpet squares or marks on the carpet indicate where toddlers should be.

8. *Limit the potential for distraction.* During small-group experiences, seat the child with a disability close to you and facing away from busy areas. If you have large group activities with older toddlers, they should be limited to 5 to 10 minutes.

9. *Use planned energetic play.* Provide safe outlets for the release of excess energy and feelings. Lead toddlers in jumping or marching or dancing for 2 to 3 minutes frequently during the day.

10. *Use a variety of teaching techniques.* Match your teaching techniques to the information you want the child to learn and the particular infant or toddler. Mobile infants and toddlers often learn appropriate behavior by imitating others.

11. *Use shaping.* Help shape a mobile infant or toddler's behavior by breaking an activity down into smaller steps and then leading the toddler through progressively more of the steps, providing many prompts until she can do the task independently.

12. *Use fading.* The opposite technique of shaping is fading. As the mobile infant or toddler begins to master a skill, gradually give fewer cues and less information so that he becomes more responsible for doing the skill independently.

Summary

The first 3 years of life pose risks and potential that will not appear again. There are risks to being born into the world. The risks increase if infants are born too small or arrive too soon. They may have problems in a variety of systems: respiratory, neurological, cardiovascular, gastrointestinal, and ophthalmologic.

Physical and motor skills develop at a rapid rate. The brain itself is not fully developed and, through interacting with the environment, some parts become hardwired while unused synapses are pruned. The CNS gains maturity and speed in the transmission of impulses. Rates of development are assessed, and interventions prescribed if development is not proceeding along a typical path.

Delays in reaching developmental milestones are one way children with disabilities are identified. Good programming provides varied opportunities for children to practice identified goals and incorporates them into routines and themes.

Reflections

1. Technology has changed the birthing process and the survival rates of very small newborns. Reflect on the changes that have occurred from the perspective of the child and family's quality of life, rather than from the perspective of the medical community. What issues will you consider and how will you evaluate them?

2. With new knowledge about brain development and the importance of early experiences, how should we spend our money? Should we concentrate our time and effort in learning more about early development, when the brain is more plastic, or should we continue to support research across the life span?

3. As an early childhood educator, you will meet families who have different values, beliefs, and ways of life. How will you work with these families and adapt your program for their infants and toddlers?

Toddlers need to be taught skills of approaching other children and how to maintain play once contact has been initiated.

Educational Resources

Child Find has a variety of resources for the early identification of infants and toddlers who may have developmental delays or disabilities. http://www.childfindidea.org

Early Head Start Nation Resources Center at Zero to Three supported by the Administration of Children and Families has a variety of information available about Early Head Start as well as health and safety and useful multimedia. http://www.ehsnrc.org

Healthy Child Care America sponsored by the American Academy of Pediatrics (AAP), in collaboration with the Department of Health and Human Services, the Child Care Bureau, and the Maternal and Child Health Bureau, sponsors the Healthy Child Care America Campaign and has resources for parents and early childhood educators. http://www.healthychildcare.org

High/Scope Educational Research Foundation support an Infant-Toddler Curriculum based on the principle that children learn best through direct, hands-on experiences with people, objects, events, and ideas. Learning and development are anchored by long-term, trusting relationships with caregivers. Adults scaffold further learning as they interact with infants and toddler throughout the day. http://www.highscope.org/Content.asp?ContentId=62

March of Dimes provides information about birth defects and related newborn health problems. (888) 663-4637 or http://www.marchofdimes.com/

Pathways Awareness Foundation has produced an inexpensive compact disk, *Is my baby OK?*, which highlights typical and atypical development in the young infant. It also has other resources. 1-800-955-2445 or http://www.pathwaysawareness.org

World Bank Early Child Development focuses on early childhood from a global and economic perspective. It has resources and links to international and regional sites, and data from international organizations. http://www.worldbank.org/children

Zero to Three provides information and advocacy for professionals and parents for children birth to 3; including links to resources, training, and conferences. http://www.zerotothree.org

For additional resources, visit the book companion website for this text at www.cengage.com/education/deiner.

Chapter **8**

Children with Specific Learning Disabilities

I never thought that I would have to call a lawyer to see that my daughter got the education she deserved. I was wrong. I would like to share my experience with you. It will show how far we have come, or have not come. I am sharing it in the form of letters I sent. The first letter was written to her second grade teacher in November; the second letter, a year later, was to update our lawyer.

November 8, 1995
Dear Mrs. Brown,

We appreciate being able to talk with you about Pat. We know you will have many conferences during the day, and thought it would help if we could share our major concerns with you. We would like to know whether our perceptions of the problems are the same as yours and also which of our solutions are feasible.

We would like to concentrate on the area of **reading**. We appreciate and notice that you are going out of your way to help Pat learn to read and we also notice that she is consciously trying hard. However, she is not learning at the level her ability suggests is appropriate. (Our assumption is that she is average to above average in intelligence.) We have tried to figure out why she is not performing at grade level.

1. Problem: Hearing. As part of Pat's allergies, her ears fill up with fluid. When this happens she experiences a 50–60 dB bilateral conductive hearing loss. This condition can change on an almost daily basis. We had tubes placed in her ears when we discovered the condition. They were replaced once. After that, the medical decision was that they were probably not necessary as the medication she was taking should control the condition.

    Implications: Pat has irregularly experienced hearing losses since infancy. She does not trust that sense and has not developed it well. Because she does not trust her hearing, she frequently asks questions for clarification, perhaps out of habit as much as necessity. There is a possibility that she may still be experiencing hearing problems, especially as we have been trying to adjust

her medication to make it more responsive to her needs.

Potential solutions: Is it possible to have her hearing tested by the school nurse something like every 2 weeks? Although she has regular medical examinations, this does not indicate how well she hears on a given day. (The dark circles under her eyes are the single most visible indication that her allergies are out of control.) Pat is finally on her new medication, so she will not miss any more Monday mornings.

Given Pat's history of hearing losses, is it possible to use a different basal reading series or a different approach to teaching her reading? I would not expect you to do this in your classroom. However, could/should she be part of some reading group even in another class? Could you suggest something that you feel would not interfere with the program that is used in the class? We could do this at home so that she could experience some success.

2. Problem: Auditory Processing Problem. Another potential cause of Pat's difficulties is that she has an auditory processing problem. Her auditory memory appears to be well developed. But, she seems to have problems connecting a visual stimulus such as a letter to an auditory sound.

    Implications: If she does in fact have an auditory processing problem it is unlikely that any amount of effort on either your part or her part will result in success in reading.

    Solutions: A diagnostic workup would be needed to determine whether or not this is in fact a problem. This workup should probably include a general intelligence test, as well as specific measures of visual motor skills, spatial relations, and an occupational therapy evaluation (given her level of performance).

3. Problem: Dyslexia. Pat has many of the characteristics commonly associated with dyslexia. She still has letter and number reversals. Although reversals may be common until age 7, she is getting to the stage when she should be outgrowing this. She is left-handed and a lot children who are dyslexic are lefties (at least that is what people have told me). She appears to be bright, but still does not grasp the essentials of reading, and in math seems to have particular problems with one-to-one correspondence.

    Implications: If dyslexia is the problem, we need to work on keeping up her self-concept while we develop an educational program that is appropriate for her.

    Solutions: Again, she would need an educational workup similar to the one mentioned above, but with a particular test designed to pick up dyslexia. If the results are positive, she would need a specific educational program for dyslexia.

    There may be other potential problems, and probably other solutions you can suggest. The three mentioned above occurred to us as possibilities. We are not concerned that Pat is not in the "highest" reading group, but rather that she learn at a pace she can feel good about.

    We would appreciate any help you can give us regarding your perceptions of this problem, as well as potential solutions. Our biggest concern is not Pat's lack of achievement, but rather the struggle she is going through. We want to find ways to maintain her current enthusiasm for school and learning.

Sincerely,
Ellen and Jim Hastings

The second letter was written to their lawyer in December. Pat was in third grade.

December 21, 1996
Dear Mr. Hart,

An update on Pat as requested. I have also enclosed copies of the child study team meetings that we attended and a copy of the letter and attached information we received today from the cluster coordinator.

I would like to add just one word of special thanks to you. For a long time I believed in the school system and that it works for all children. In the "ivory tower" approach, I guess I wasn't willing to entertain the idea that I should go ahead on my own. You helped me see that, so whatever the outcome, this has made a tremendous difference in Pat's life.

Thanks.
Ellen and Jim

Re: Teacher assignment

After talking to you at the end of August, I called Mrs. Truck's (principal) office on August 25th to make an appointment sometime during the week of August 29th. I was told by the secretary that this was not possible, but that she would try to get Mrs. Truck to call me. She called on August 30. I briefly explained the problem and, after a long lecture on the problems of having parents request teachers and so on, I was told, and I quote "I have been in special education for 18 years. Your daughter is not identified and I will call Special Services to see what I *have* to do for her." I called the cluster coordinator the next day and explained to her what happened. (It appeared that she expected my call.) She felt that I should talk with the superintendent about the situation. She agreed to call him and to prepare him for my request. I called but did not get him on Wednesday and left a message. I called again on Thursday and did not get him but after I told the secretary my name, she told me "you got what you wanted" and hung up.

I decided to take Pat to school the first day just to see what was happening. I took her to Mrs. Lee's third grade room (the class I had requested) and she was not on the list. Mrs. Lee graciously added her and I stopped by the nurse's office to see if I could get a class list to see what was happening. Given Pat's recurring illness, I knew the nurse well. Pat was assigned to Mrs. Nola's class. I retrieved Pat, apologized, and took her to Mrs. Nola's classroom (either teacher was fine with me, but the reading teacher had recommended Mrs. Lee). She has been in Mrs. Nola's classroom since.

Re: Memorandum of agreement concerning Pat Hastings, Grade 2, East Park School

I met with Pat's teacher, Mrs. Nola, on September 20, 1996, at my request. At that point, I began to talk with her about the letter of agreement you had written to the school district. She had not seen it nor did she know that it existed.

Dr. Cole called the evening of September 21 to set up an appointment for a child study team conference.

The conference was held on 10/27/96. Relative to that conference the following is in place:

- Pat will not get Project Assist, the reading help we requested, as it is not in the school and will not begin until January; however, the reading resource teacher, Mrs. Fewell, feels that Pat should not be in the program as so many other children have a greater need for the service.
- The reading resource teacher, Mrs. Fewell, learned about the letter of agreement at the conference (10/27/96). She said that she can do nothing for Pat as she is now reading at grade level and all of the children she works with are below grade level.
- She is continuing to receive instruction in the District basal.
- The report card appears to be the measure used to determine progress.

Re: Current status

Currently, Pat has been changed into the highest reading group and is at the end of the 3.2 reader. Her classroom teacher, Mrs. Nola, expressed some concern about this move and worried that her grades in reading would go down. Her first marking period grades are all As. Her reading, spelling, language and math are all at the 3.1 level.

At this point, the school's accommodations do not require her to write her spelling words three times, twice a week, although, as she has an A in spelling, she would not be asked to do that anyway. The school is providing no supports for her.

What we are doing:

We have developed a rigorous and intensive therapy program for Pat in addition to the academic work we do with her. Homework is a struggle. Jim and I take turns. We also try to read to her at least a half an hour a day. She struggles so much with learning to read that we want her to experience the joy of books, thus the struggles are worth it for her.

Perhaps I should give you the rationale for what we have done. I started to do a lot of reading on sensory integration. I found that the brain is programmable up until about 8–10 years. The more I read, the more I was convinced that her problem was dyslexia and something they call "clumsy child syndrome." I decided to focus on her postural stability/flexibility, balance, and motor planning and control. (This was based on the occupational therapy report.) I tried to think of fun ways to begin to work on these and, given her age, we had a very definite time frame; time was not on our side. I guess I am telling you all of this because we are putting a tremendous amount of time, energy, and money into this and I think we are getting amazing results. The school system seems totally uninterested in what we are doing.

Project Assist is based on the Orton Gillingham theory of dyslexia. Both Jim and I have taken the training. The course is 4 hours a week for 10 weeks. Although we don't formally sit Pat down on a daily basis, we do use the techniques to teach her spelling and to help her with her reading.

Sensory Motor Therapy: This is the occupational therapy that Pat gets 30 minutes each week. Our Blue Cross/Blue Shield pays for that. With driving time, that is about an hour a week of our time.

Recreation: This is one of the related services listed in the rules and regulations, and it is through the interpretation of the occupational therapy report that the additional evaluations were completed and the specific recreations chosen.

Therapeutic Horseback Riding: We had Pat evaluated for this program and found, through the occupational therapy evaluation, that this particular program should help her in the area of balance. They are also working on the rotational skills she needs while she is riding. This is a half hour a week at the state park. It is officially through 4-H. We pay $14.00 for each lesson and with driving time, it takes 2 hours a week.

Ice Skating: As I analyzed Pat's evaluation, I thought that as a sport, ice skating had the potential to help her in all of the six areas she has needs in:

- Monitor response to movement
- Postural stability/flexibility
- Balance
- Gross motor planning and control
- Fine motor planning and control
- Tactile and kinesthetic perception.

I have worked with her skating coach to emphasize that the skating is not competitive, but to work on related issues. With lessons and practice, she currently skates 5 to 6 hours a week. Between the lessons and the ice time, this costs about $40.00 a week. Since an adult has to take her and stay with her during this time, in parent time this is about 7 to 8 hours a week.

Is it worth it? Yes! However, my concerns are twofold. In many ways, I am the one who both diagnosed and remedied the problem. I don't think most children have parents with this knowledge and I think these children are not being served. The tragedy is that what I have found about Pat is that some of her problems can be permanently helped through what we are doing. Others could be as well, but when the brain is no longer able to be programmed in this way, the only thing that therapy can do is teach compensatory skills. I think the school system has failed to identify the problem.

The second area that is still of concern to me is that she is currently functioning very well in a regular third grade class. If she were identified as having dyslexia she would not be in that placement. We know she has a disability. We are not in denial, but we are unhappy about the range of services offered by the school if we allow her to be identified.

Interestingly, now the school seems convinced that there is nothing wrong with her. We, however, feel that we have a lifetime challenge.

Again, we thank you for your time and effort on our behalf.

Reflective Practice

If you were the teacher, how would you feel about these parents? How would you respond to them? What would your expectations be? Would you feel threatened by the letter? This happened a long time ago before the parts of the IDEA supporting children in their natural environments were emphasized as part of the law. Think about the time commitment this family made to their daughter's education. Reflect on what they did and how they used normalized recreational experiences to support her development. Think about what you might do in a classroom to support children with specific learning disabilities in addition to what is required by the IEP. What will you need to know about what other professionals do to work with them effectively?

Specific Learning Disabilities

Children with specific learning disabilities are as smart as their classmates. However, one or more of their information processing systems does not work efficiently, making academic work challenging (LD OnLine, 2007). Most children with learning disabilities struggle with learning to read.

Learning disabilities were recognized by the federal government in 1969 as a group of disabilities requiring special educational services. At that time the identification of children with disabilities was very medically based. The problem with learning disabilities was that they could not identify them medically. Although children showed the behavioral signs of children with brain injury, there was rarely neurologic evidence of the damage. Many of the old labels reflect this confusion: minimal brain dysfunction, information processing disorder, central nervous system (CNS) disorder, brain damage syndrome, and on and on. The focus of many of the terms related to the CNS, as it was assumed that learning disabilities were caused by damage or injury to the brain. The problem was finding the part of the brain that was damaged. When this couldn't be found, the medical profession saw it as less of a priority.

Teachers, however, still saw it as a major problem as they watched children struggling to learn. In the educational community these were underachievers. Some saw this perplexing problem as a "school disability" because children seemed to be fine before they went to school and then they had problems. The assumption was also that when they got out of school they were fine. We know far more about specific learning disabilities than we did 50 years ago, and we are still learning.

Defining Specific Learning Disabilities

In addition to not agreeing on the actual nature of learning disabilities, confusion also resulted from different definitions used by the educational, legal, psychological, and medical fields. It is easier to determine what learning disabilities *are not* rather than what they *are*. This is further confounded because learning disabilities can coexist or be **comorbid** with other disabilities. It is estimated that about 10 to 40 percent of children with specific learning disabilities (SLD) have other disabilities including

attention-deficit/hyperactivity disorder (ADHD), conduct disorder, oppositional defiant disorder, major depressive disorder, and others (APA, 2000; Silver, 2002).

The clearest agreement seems to be that learning disabilities are neurologic in nature and they impede a child's ability to store, process, and produce information. The federal government's definition of SLD governs academic programs and determines our estimates of the number of children with learning disabilities. Not all children with learning disabilities qualify for special educational services. The term *specific learning disabilities* is used in educational settings and in this text. However, the American Psychiatric Association (APA) uses the term *learning disorders* (APA, 2000).

According to the federal government IDEA 2004:

(30) Specific learning disability.—

(A) In general.—The term 'specific learning disability' means a disorder in 1 or more of the basic psychological processes involved in understanding or in using language, spoken or written, which disorder may manifest itself in the imperfect ability to listen, think, speak, read, write, spell, or do mathematical calculations.

(B) Disorders included.—Such term includes such conditions as perceptual disabilities, brain injury, minimal brain dysfunction, dyslexia, and developmental aphasia.

(C) Disorders not included.—Such term does not include a learning problem that is primarily the result of visual, hearing, or motor disabilities, of mental retardation, of emotional disturbance, or of environmental, cultural, or economic disadvantage. (TITLE I/A/602/30, U. S. Department of Education, 2006)

The National Joint Committee on Learning Disabilities (NJCLD) defined learning disabilities in 1985 and revised their definition in 1990. Their definition is broader and looks at the lifetime implications of learning disabilities. NJCLD defines learning disabilities as

a heterogeneous group of disorders of presumed neurological origin manifested differently and to varying degrees during the life span of an individual. These disorders are developmental in nature, occur prior to kindergarten, and continue into adult life. Various manifestations of LD may be seen at different ages and as a result of varying learning demands. (NJCLD, 2006, p. 1)

The American Psychiatric Association (APA) in the Diagnostic and Statistical Manual of Mental Disorders IV-TR (DSM IV-TR) defines learning disorders in the following way:

Learning Disorders are diagnosed when the individual's achievement on individually administered, standardized tests in reading, mathematics, or written expression is substantially below that expected for age, schooling, and level of intelligence. The learning problems significantly interfere with academic achievement or activities of daily living that require reading, mathematical, or writing skills. (APA, 2000, p. 49)

The reason the term *specific learning disabilities* is used is because there are different types of learning disabilities. Most of these fall into three broad academic categories:

reading disorder (dyslexia), writing disorder (dysgraphia), and arithmetic disorder (dyscalculia). Because of the overlapping aspects of speaking, listening, reading, writing and arithmetic, as well as the brain functions that support these skills, some children have problems in all of these areas (LD OnLine, 2007). The APA (2000) refers to this overlapping disorder where a child might not meet the criteria for any specific disorder such as reading disorder but together the problems from each area interfere with academic achievement as *Learning Disorder Not Otherwise Specified*. **Not Otherwise Specified (NOS)** is a code you will see frequently in relation to many disabilities. It is used when a child does not meet the specific criteria set forth by the APA, but is identified as having the particular disorder.

Prevalence of Specific Learning Disabilities

The federal government began keeping records on children with SLD during the 1976–1977 school year. At that time, 8.3 percent of children in the public schools were identified as having a disability. Of these children, 1.8 percent had a specific learning disability. In the 2005–2006 school year, 13.8 percent of children were identified as having a disability with 5.6 percent of these children having a specific learning disability (Table 8–1). The number of children identified with learning disabilities had been steadily increasing and reached a high of 6.1 percent in 2000–2001 (National Center for Educational Statistics [NCES], 2006). This caused concern and required educators to look at how these children were identified and what could be done to prevent this problem.

Some are concerned that the rise in the number of children identified as having SLD is a result of misclassification; others believe that it indicates an improved ability to identify these children, others see it as a reflection of the stresses of the times, and child's response to stress. Other schools of thought propose a biological explanation for the swell in SLD numbers, such as substance abuse by pregnant women. Others looked at the relationship between the number of children who were identified as having mental retardation (in 1976–1977 it was 2.2 percent, whereas in 2005–2006 it was 1.1 percent) (NCES, 2006) and felt that some of the change could be attributed to classifying children who might previously been identified as having intellectual disabilities as having SLD.

There are few estimates of how many preschool children are identified as having SLD. Many professionals believe SLD exist during the preschool years, or precursors to the problem are present. When the focus is on prevention there is efficacy in identifying children during the preschool years if there are interventions that could effectively prevent children being labeled SLD in elementary school (Coleman, Buysse, & Neitzel, 2006). Changes in the early identification system are moving into the area of prevention and the preschool and early elementary years are viewed as a time to support young children in learning the skills they need before they experience failure.

Causes of Specific Learning Disabilities

In many cases, the causes of learning disabilities are not known, although we do have some clues, and science is making further discoveries at an ever-increasing rate. There are two fundamental ways of looking for causes of learning disabilities: medical models and educational models. The medical model looks for causes in the child's biology and the makeup of the CNS. The educational model looks at the interaction of the learner and the environment and looks at changing the learning environment and using behavioral reinforcement to shape behavior.

Scientists are providing us with insight into how biological factors may cause learning disabilities. There is growing evidence that genetic influences play a role in some learning disabilities. Since the human genome has been mapped, there are increased investigations into genetic causes of SLD. Loci on chromosomes 1, 2, 3, 6, 13, 14, 15, and 18 have been related to SLD and dyslexia (Démonet, Taylor, & Chaix, 2004; Fagerheim, et al., 1999; Raskind, 2001). Dyslexia may be caused by a misaligned gene on chromosome number 6 (Howard, 2000). These factors can be inherited and may be related to family genetics, as there is a 35 to 45 percent recurrence rate for reading disabilities in families (Shapiro, Church, & Lewis, 2002).

Another hypothesis is that learning disabilities are the result of subtle disturbances in the functions and structures of the brain. These differences begin in utero. Brain development is complex and disruptions or errors in cell makeup, location, or connections can occur. This means that the brain has some "faulty wiring" in its cortex. The problem becomes obvious when the miswired area of the brain is needed to process information (Silver, 2002). Intervention, then, involves developing learning strategies to compensate for this problem. These errors show up as SLD in children.

There has also been a great deal of research in the areas of both short-term and long-term memory. The research reveals that children who experience difficulty learning to read often demonstrate deficient short-term memory, but intact long-term memory (Wong, 1998). While we continue our efforts to pinpoint the causes of SLD, we accept the fact that they are real and that a child with a SLD will often need more time, understanding, and encouragement from early childhood educators. Indeed, educators may

Table 8–1: Percent of children with disabilities, specific learning disabilities, and Intellectual disabilities

Year	Children with Disabilities	Children with Specific Learning Disabilities	Children with Intellectual Disabilities
1976–1977	8.3%	1.8%	2.2%
2005–2006	13.8%	5.6%	1.1%

Source: National Center for Educational Statistics, 2006.

need to concentrate efforts on preliminary assessments of a child suspected of having a learning disability.

Early Identification of Specific Learning Disabilities

Early signs of potential learning disabilities appear during the preschool years. These are seen in pronunciation problems, slow growth in vocabulary, and a lack of interest in listening to stories and in telling them. Children also have poor memory for routines. They have trouble learning numbers, the alphabet, and the days of the week, especially when asked questions like, "What day comes before Wednesday?" They often show signs of restlessness and lack the ability to persist at tasks, particularly those they do not enjoy. They may have trouble sitting still and employing self-help skills. They have trouble with tying shoes, buttoning buttons, and getting zippers to work. Overall they appear to be clumsy. They may be reluctant to draw, especially if they have received negative feedback about the relationship between what they think they have drawn and others' perceptions. They may show difficulty playing with peers and demonstrate weakness in other social skills. They also have problems with learning directionality (left and right).

Although it is difficult to identify children during the preschool years who may later be identified as having

The signs of learning disabilities are apparent during the preschool years. Changes in early intervening may prevent some children from being identified as having learning disabilities.

SLD, there are some areas that signal risks for later academic problems:

- Perinatal conditions: low Apgar score, low birth weight, 24 hours or more in a neonatal intensive care unit, difficulty sucking and swallowing, intermittent middle ear disease;
- Genetic or environmental conditions: family history of learning disabilities or language problems, limited exposure to language, exposure to environmental toxins, being adopted, living in poverty;
- Delays in reaching developmental milestones such as the following:
  - Delays in cognitive skills: not understanding means-end relationships, object permanence or lack of symbolic play;
  - Delays in comprehension and/or expression of spoken language: limited receptive and expressive vocabulary, immature syntax, speech that is difficult to understand, little spontaneous communication, and trouble following directions;
  - Delays in emergent literacy skills: names fewer objects and colors, limited print awareness or interest in print, little phonological awareness (rhyming);
  - Delay in perceptual-motor skills both fine motor (coloring, cutting, stringing beads) and gross motor (hopping, running, jumping).
- Attention and behavior
  - Shows distractibility, impulsivity, hyperactivity, preservation (constantly repeats actions or ideas) and has problems with change (NJCLD, 2006).

Before the 2004 amendments to the IDEA it was difficult to identify a child with a learning disability until he was in second or third grade and had experienced failure. States identified children with learning disabilities by looking at the difference (discrepancy) between a child's IQ on a standardized intelligence test and the child's academic achievement. This was done by comparing the child's mental age from the intelligence test to the grade-age equivalent of a standardized achievement test. States developed formulas for how far a child had to be behind to qualify. In some states, if the child's achievement scores were 2 years below his mental age, the child was identified as having a learning disability.

The American Psychiatric Association (2000) criteria used by the medical profession uses essentially the same approach. They consider "substantially below" as a discrepancy of two or more standard deviations between achievement and IQ. For cases in which the IQ may be unreasonable (for reasons of ethnic, cultural, language differences, or comorbid conditions), a smaller discrepancy (between one and two standard deviations) may be used.

There are a variety of problems with this practice, including:

1. The discrepancy requirement made it virtually impossible to identify young children as having a learning disability.
2. Discrepancies may exist for a variety of reasons that may or may relate to having a learning disability.
3. Disproportionately children from diverse cultural and ethnic groups were identified as having learning disabilities.

4. The discrepancy model required that children have repeated experiences with failure until the gap between IQ and achievement was large enough to meet the criteria for identification.
5. Children who fail academically often develop behavior problems, low self-esteem and have problems with peer relations.
6. IQ scores are not good predictors of a child's ability to recognize words and do phonological decoding—the basic skills involved in reading (Coleman, Buysse, & Neitzel, 2006; Shapiro, Church, & Lewis, 2002).

It became clear that if the goal was to prevent so many children from being identified as having SLD then the criteria would have to change. According to the regulations for IDEA 2004, states must do the following:

1. Add procedures for identifying children with specific learning disabilities.

A State must adopt, consistent with 34 CFR 300.309, criteria for determining whether a child has a specific learning disability as defined in 34 CFR 300.8(c)(10). In addition, the criteria adopted by the State:

- Must not require the use of a severe discrepancy between intellectual ability and achievement for determining whether a child has a specific learning disability, as defined in 34 CFR 300. 8(c)(10);
- Must permit the use of a process based on the child's response to scientific, research-based intervention; and
- May permit the use of other alternative research-based procedures for determining whether a child has a specific learning disability, as defined in 34 CFR 300.8(c)(10). (U.S. Department of Education, Office of Special Education Programs, 2006)

The regulations specify that if a child is suspected of have a SLD, specific people must be part of the IEP team:

2. Require additional group members.

The determination of whether a child suspected of having a specific learning disability is a child with a disability as defined in 34 CFR 300.8, must be made by the child's parents and a team of qualified professionals, which must include:

- The child's regular teacher; or if the child does not have a regular teacher, a regular classroom teacher qualified to teach a child of his or her age; or for a child of less than school age, an individual qualified by the State educational agency (SEA) to teach a child of his or her age; and
- At least one person qualified to conduct individual diagnostic examinations of children, such as a school psychologist, speech-language pathologist, or remedial reading teacher. [34 CFR 300.308] [20 U.S.C. 1221e-3; 1401(30); 1414(b)(6)] (U.S. Department of Education, 2006b)

The regulations add criteria for determining if a child has an SLD:

3. Add criteria for determining the existence of a specific learning disability.

The group described in 34 CFR 300.306 may determine that a child has a specific learning disability, as defined in 34 CFR 300.8(c)(10), if:

- The child does not achieve adequately for the child's age or to meet State-approved grade-level standards in one or more of the following areas, when provided with learning experiences and instruction appropriate for the child's age or State-approved grade-level standards:
  - Oral expression.
  - Listening comprehension.
  - Written expression.
  - Basic reading skills.
  - Reading fluency skills.
  - Reading comprehension.
  - Mathematics calculation.
  - Mathematics problem solving.
- The child does not make sufficient progress to meet age or State-approved grade-level standards in one or more of the areas identified in 34 CFR 300.309(a)(1) when using a process based on the child's response to scientific, research-based intervention; or the child exhibits a pattern of strengths and weaknesses in performance, achievement, or both, relative to age, State-approved grade-level standards, or intellectual development, that is determined by the group to be relevant to the identification of a specific learning disability, using appropriate assessments, consistent with 34 CFR 300.304 and 300.305; and the group determines that its findings under 34 CFR 300.309(a)(1) and (2) are not primarily the result of:
  - A visual, hearing, or motor disability;
  - Mental retardation;
  - Emotional disturbance;
  - Cultural factors;
  - Environmental or economic disadvantage; or
  - Limited English proficiency.

To ensure that underachievement in a child suspected of having a specific learning disability is not due to lack of appropriate instruction in reading or math, the group must consider, as part of the evaluation described in 34 CFR 300.304 through 300.306:

- Data that demonstrate that prior to, or as a part of, the referral process, the child was provided appropriate instruction in regular education settings, delivered by qualified personnel; and
- Data-based documentation of repeated assessments of achievement at reasonable intervals, reflecting formal assessment of student progress during instruction, which was provided to the child's parents.

The public agency must promptly request parental consent to evaluate the child to determine if the child needs special education and related services, and must adhere to the timeframes described in 34 CFR 300.301 and 300.303, unless extended by mutual written agreement of the child's parents and a group of qualified professionals, as described in 34 CFR 300.306(a)(1):

- If, prior to a referral, a child has not made adequate progress after an appropriate period of time when provided instruction, as described in 34 CFR 300.309(b)(1) and (b)(2); and
- Whenever a child is referred for an evaluation. [34 CFR 300.309] [20 U.S.C. 1221e-3; 1401(30); 1414(b)(6)] (U.S. Department of Education, 2006b)

The regulations describe where the child must be observed and what should be observed:

4. Describe the required observation.

The public agency must ensure that the child is observed in the child's learning environment (including the regular classroom setting) to document the child's academic performance and behavior in the areas of difficulty.

The group described in 34 CFR 300.306(a)(1), in determining whether a child has a specific learning disability, must decide to:

- Use information from an observation in routine classroom instruction and monitoring of the child's performance that was done before the child was referred for an evaluation; or
- Have at least one member of the group described in 34 CFR 300.306(a)(1) conduct an observation of the child's academic performance in the regular classroom after the child has been referred for an evaluation and parental consent, consistent with 34 CFR 300.300(a), is obtained.

In the case of a child of less than school age or out of school, a group member must observe the child in an environment appropriate for a child of that age. [34 CFR 300.310] [20 U.S.C. 1221e-3; 1401(30); 1414(b)(6)] (U. S. Department of Education, 2006b)

The law specifies the documentation needed to determine whether a child has a SLD:

5. Specify documentation required for the eligibility determination.

For a child suspected of having a specific learning disability, the documentation of the determination of eligibility, as required in 34 CFR 300.306(a)(2), must contain a statement of:

- Whether the child has a specific learning disability;
- The basis for making the determination, including an assurance that the determination has been made in accordance with 34 CFR 300.306(c)(1);
- The relevant behavior, if any, noted during the observation of the child and the relationship of that behavior to the child's academic functioning;
- The educationally relevant medical findings, if any;
- Whether the child does not achieve adequately for the child's age or to meet State-approved grade-level standards consistent with 34 CFR 300.309(a)(1); and the child does not make sufficient progress to meet age or State-approved grade-level

standards consistent with 34 CFR 300.309(a)(2)(i); or the child exhibits a pattern of strengths and weaknesses in performance, achievement, or both, relative to age, State-approved grade-level standards or intellectual development consistent with 34 CFR 300.309(a)(2)(i); or the child exhibits a pattern of strengths and weaknesses in performance, achievement, or both, relative to age, State-approved grade-level standards or intellectual development consistent with 34 CFR 300.309(a)(2)(ii);
- The determination of the group concerning the effects of a visual, hearing, or motor disability; mental retardation; emotional disturbance; cultural factors; environmental or economic disadvantage; or limited English proficiency on the child's achievement level; and
- If the child has participated in a process that assesses the child's response to scientific, research-based intervention:
  - The instructional strategies used and the student-centered data collected; and
  - The documentation that the child's parents were notified about: (1) the State's policies regarding the amount and nature of student performance data that would be collected and the general education services that would be provided; (2) strategies for increasing the child's rate of learning; and (3) the parents' right to request an evaluation.

Each group member must certify in writing whether the report reflects the member's conclusion. If it does not reflect the member's conclusion, the group member must submit a separate statement presenting the member's conclusions. [34 CFR 300.311] [20 U.S.C. 1221e-3; 1401(30); 1414(b)(6)] (U. S. Department of Education, 2006b)

These changes are a result of the passage of the 2004 amendments to the IDEA. They are new and the profession is trying to figure out exactly what they mean. There is a new model for identifying children with SLD that includes younger children and there are requirements in place that must be fulfilled before this identification can happen. The first criterion is that the child must have had "appropriate instruction in reading and math" (appropriate is based on the child's age). Obviously children who have had little or poor instruction cannot be expected to learn reading and math. The second criteria is that the process must be based on the "child's response to scientific, research-based intervention." These criteria have given rise to the concept of early intervening services (EIS) and response to intervention (RTI).

Early Intervening Services

Early intervening services (EIS) are designed for children in kindergarten through grade twelve (with a particular emphasis on K–three) who are not identified as needing special education services but who need additional academic and behavioral support to succeed in the general educational environment (U.S. Department of Education, 2007). States are allocated funds for EIS that can be used in a variety of different ways:

(2) Activities.—In implementing coordinated, early intervening services under this subsection, a local educational agency may carry out activities that include–

(A) professional development (which may be provided by entities other than local educational agencies) for teachers and other school staff to enable such personnel to deliver scientifically based academic instruction and behavioral interventions, including scientifically based literacy instruction, and, where appropriate, instruction on the use of adaptive and instructional software; and

(B) providing educational and behavioral evaluations, services, and supports, including scientifically based literacy instruction. (Title I/B/613/f, U. S. Department of Education, 2006)

Response to Intervention

The acronym RTI is used to refer to response to intervention or response to instruction. **Response to instruction** is use to refer to core programming or what is happening everyday to all students. **Response to intervention** refers to responses that are made when there are major or substantial changes in programming for some or all students (Salvia & Ysseldyke, 2007). The RTI model for school-age children allows and supports early and intensive intervention before children fail. The underlying assumption of RTI is that early intervening services hold the potential of preventing academic problems for children with learning difficulties. It emphasizes the general curriculum and holds potential for helping all children (Coleman et al., 2006).

There is general agreement that the model is a tiered approach and that the first tier is regular education and the top tier is special education. There is less agreement about the middle tier(s) (Reschly, 2005). The bottom of the tier or the foundation of the triangle is high-quality instruction for all children. The assumption is about 80 percent of children in a class should be making progress at the expected rate. If this is not true then the intervention would be to improve the quality of the classroom instruction until this goal is met. Tier one is also designed to determine which children need additional instructional interventions to progress at the expected rate (Coleman et al., 2006). The second tier is targeted to the small group of children who did make adequate progress in tier one. Teachers intervene with these children using differentiated instructional methods such as modifying the curriculum, using small-group instruction, standard treatment protocols, or other methods of presenting material in different ways that support learning and have a research base. It is expected that an additional 15 percent of children will progress at the expected rate with these modifications in instruction. A small portion of the children, perhaps 5 percent, will not make sufficient progress with these modifications and will move on to tier three. These children will receive intensive individualized interventions. If this intensive instruction does not produce learning at the expected rate, the children are referred for formal evaluation (with parent consent) (Reschly, 2005). The approach is a collaborative one between classroom teachers and specialists that uses assessment data to guide curriculum, teaching, and interventions.

There is an emerging body of literature that says that RTI is a potentially effective method of identifying children at risk for learning disabilities. However, there is less agreement about the intervention strategies that are most effective and about how RTI could be implemented for 3 and 4 year old children. There is even less information about children who have problems in areas other than reading (Coleman et al., 2006). RTI presents an instructional approach for identifying school-age children who are at risk for learning disabilities. It provides intervention without the need to label children until it becomes clear that they need a different method of instruction and that they are likely to meet the IDEA criteria for SLD.

Professional organizations including the Learning Disabilities Roundtable (2002) and the National Joint Committee on Learning Disabilities (NJCLD) (2006) recommend that preschoolers be screened for early language and readings skills just as they are for vision and hearing. As with other areas prevention may need to begin during the preschool years.

Reflective Practice

Reflect on the concept of RTI in the context of the definitions of specific learning disabilities. Are the definitions wrong about SLD having a much broader scope than the ability to read? Or, have we been misidentifying children who did not get appropriate reading instruction? How do you think this will impact what you do in the classroom?

Recognition and Response

Recognition and Response is an early intervening system being developed for preschool children at risk for learning disabilities. It has its base in the RTI movement, but applies the principles to younger children and the contexts in which young children grow and learn (Coleman et al., 2006).

Program standards and guidelines have been developed to guide early care and education practice. High-quality early care and education settings are expected to construct and implement a thoughtfully planned comprehensive system of curriculum that aligns with early learning standards and program standards and make sound educational decisions for all children (NAEYC, NAECS/SDE, 2006). The National Institute for Early Education Research (NIEER) (Barnett, Hustedt, Friedman, Boyd, & Ainsworth, 2007) has developed a quality standards checklist for prekindergarten programs. Table 8–2 on the following page highlights the policy, the benchmark needed to meet the policy and the number of states actually meeting the policy in 2007.

Reflective Practice

The lowest ratings (other than providing meals) are in the level of education required of teachers and assistant teachers. What does this mean in the field and in what is happening in preschool classrooms?

As of 2007, twelve states had no ratable state-funded programs for three and four year olds and only two states, Arkansas and North Carolina, met all 10 of NIEER's quality benchmarks (Barnett, et al., 2007). This reflects

Table 8–2: Number of states meeting prekindergarten initiatives

Policy	Benchmark	Of the 49 State Pre-K Initiatives, Number Meeting Benchmarks
Early learning standards	Comprehensive	41
Teacher degree	BA	27
Teacher specialized training	Specializing in pre-K	36
Assistant teacher degree	CDA or equivalent	11
Teacher in-service	At least 15 hours/year	37

Maximum class size
   3 year olds
   4 year olds
	20 or lower	41

Staff-child ratio
   3 year olds
   4 year olds
	1:10 or better	42

Screening/referral and support services	Vision, hearing, health; and at least 1 support service	35
Meals	At least 1/day	24
Monitoring	Site visits	38

Source: Barnett, Hustedt, Friedman, Boyd, & Ainsworth, 2007, p. 5.

tremendous variability across states and probably within states as well. Looking at a combination of state, local, federal, and TANF spending per child, approximately $4,134 for preschool, for Head Start it moves up to $7,860 and for children in kindergarten through grade 12 it is $11,286 (Barnett, et al., 2007). As we look at the preschool year as having the possibility for prevention of learning disabilities we are beginning to look more closely at the allocation of resources, teacher-child interactions, and how children are spending their time during the preschool years.

The Evidence Base

Measuring quality in early child classrooms is challenging. It is easier to count ratios, class size, and qualifications than what is going on in the classroom. The National Center for Early Development and Learning (NCEDL) at the Frank Porter Graham Child Development Institute conducted the Multi-State Study of Pre-k in six state-funded prekindergarten programs. It included 240 randomly selected state-funded programs with more than 900 pre-K children who were representative of over 211,000 pre-K children participating in the sites. Overall the class size and teacher-child rations met or exceeded standards. The Pre-K teachers, on average, were better educated and better paid than teachers in nonschool settings (FPG Child Development Institute, 2005a).

Although two of the states in the study (Georgia and New York) were moving toward universal pre-k, most of the children were from poor families or those at risk for learning delays. A large proportion of the children's mothers (42 percent) had only a high school education or less and 23 percent of the pre-kindergarten spoke a language other than English at home (FPG Child Development Institute, 2005a).

Researchers developed two measures of quality that looked at "Emotional Climate" which "indicates how positive, sensitive, and responsive the classroom is" and "Instructional Climate" which "indicates how well time, materials, and teacher-child interactions are managed to optimize children's learning (FPG Child Development Institute, 2005b, p. 21).

Trained observers spent two day in each classroom using the SNAPSHOT. This measure looked at the main intended activities, the content areas the child was engaged in and the frequency of teacher-child interactions. Overall, children spent the most time (13%) in social studies which included dramatic play and blocks, closely followed by literacy (12%), art and music (9%), science (8%), motor (7%), and math (6%). However, 44% of the time the child was engaged in none of these. Teacher-child interactions were also coded. Distressingly there was no teacher-child interaction during 73% of the time children were in preschool. Teacher-child interaction was minimal 18% of the time with elaborated interactions coded only 8% of the time. They occurred mostly during whole-group activity. Routine interactions occurred about 1% of the time. Only about 3% of the time was devoted to teachers helping children move from less complex to more complex understanding of math and literacy and less than half of the children experience this (FPG Child Development Institute, 2005c). What were the children doing? They spent a lot of time waiting in line or eating.

Reflective Practice

If prevention of learning disabilities is going to move into preschool how do you see that happening? What will have to happen to preschool programs and curriculum? What

will you do to change your pattern of interacting with children and supporting literacy and math in a developmentally appropriate way?

The Recognition and Response system is being designed to help preschool teachers identify children who are not learning at the expected rate and who require more focused intervention. It can provide guidance by offering teaching strategies and approaches for monitoring and evaluating the effectiveness of instructional approaches. The Recognition and Response system is expected to be beneficial for children enrolled in all types of prekindergarten programs including child care centers and family child care homes, Head Start, and private and public preschools. It also holds the potential, because of its research base, to improve the quality of early childhood programs for all children (Coleman et al., 2006).

To establish the evidence base, a research synthesis on Response to Intervention was conducted. It shows that specialized interventions could either potentially help children learn the skills they need or could prevent the occurrence of learning disabilities. Research results varied based on who delivered the intervention, how long children participated, the intervention approach used, the outcome measures, and even the function of RTI (Coleman et al., 2006). However, most of the studies focused on children in grades one to three rather than preschool children. Additional research with preschool children is needed to expand the research to younger children and to answer some of the important variables, such as what instructional methods, for which children, and for how long, which produces what outcomes. The Recognition and Response system is trying to answer some of these questions.

The essential components of the Recognition and Response system include:

- An intervention hierarchy (three tiers).
- Screening, assessment, and progress monitoring.
- Research-based curriculum, instruction, and focused interventions.
- A collaborative problem-solving process for decision making (Coleman et al., 2006).

Recognition and Response is similar to RTI in its tiered approach. Tier one focuses on the early childhood research-based curriculum to ensure that most of the children (about 80 percent) are making progress at the expected rate. Children who are not move to tier two. In tier two, educators provide interventions and curriculum modifications to targeted groups of children that require minor adjustment to classroom routines. For example, before a story is read to the entire group, a small group of children who are not making progress at the expected rate would be gathered. The story might be discussed briefly to activate prior knowledge, vocabulary might be reviewed, or other strategies would be used to make the experience more meaningful. As with tier one, decisions would be guided by assessment. Tier three would provide more intensive individualized instruction. A teacher might work one-on-one teaching rhyming concepts, letter recognition, or whatever the assessment shows that the child needs. If children do not make adequate progress in tier three they would be referred for formal testing (Coleman et al., 2006).

The overarching goal of the Recognition and Response system is for teachers to use assessment as part of an integrated instructional system to make improvements in the general early education program and to plan more focused interventions for children who may be at risk of developing learning disabilities and who require additional supports to learn (Coleman et al., 2006, p. 33).

Young children who are at risk for learning or reading disabilities need a carefully planned environment that supports their development and prevents learning difficulties from occurring later. Risk does not mean a child will have a learning problem. Protective factors will help. These include high-quality responsive learning experiences and the availability of multiple supports if children are identified as having a problem. However, protective factors do not rule out the possibility of a child actually having a disability.

Implications for Educators

We know more about techniques that support all children in learning to read that can be incorporated into the early childhood curriculum.

- Before reading a story activate prior learning. After reading a story, discuss it. Stop some stories and see if children can anticipate what might happen next. Have children retell stories using the pictures as clues. Have children "play read" books. Share your joy of reading with them and continue to read to them.
- Teach children about the structure of books and the vocabulary that goes with it. They need to know the title of a book (after you have read it) and to point to it on the book itself. They need to know where the story begins. Additionally, they need to know the front and back of a book, the first and last page, and the bottom and top of the page. Children need to be able to find individual words and to point to words as you read. (This is best done individually, with a child on your lap.)
- Help children recognize rhyming words. Many nursery rhymes have rhyming words at the end of lines. Change one of the words and see if the children notice. If they understand the concept of rhyming, see if children can generate rhyming words to match those you say.

Children also need to be taught about parts of words and how sounds blend into words. If their name has more than one syllable, this is a place to start. Say the first syllable and pause before saying the second: Mi-chael. Sometimes, compound words help children get the idea: play-ground, bed-room, air-plane. Don't belabor this, but do introduce it regularly.

A beginning phonetic skill is the association of initial sounds with objects or pictures. Begin with small objects and initially agree on what each is called (apple, cup, key, pencil, toothbrush). Then, ask the child to give you the object that begins with the sound /a/ (be sure it is the *sound*, not the letter name). Make it a guessing game: "I'm thinking of something that begins with /p/. What am I thinking of?" Then, ask for the remainder of the items. Ask for some more than once, and put the items back so the child cannot use the process of elimination. Then, have the child be the "thinker" (teacher) who requests the information. Start with real objects, then use pictures for some sounds that are difficult to find objects for.

Foundation skills and motivation are important in learning to read. To help determine a child's skill level do the following:

- Read a book with a child one-on-one. Choose a simple yet unfamiliar book with clear illustrations. Ask the child what the book is about. (Does the child use the illustrations and other clues to make a guess?) Read the story together with the child. Can the child use context to make sense of the story? Does the child go back and reread part of a sentence once she has worked out the meaning? Does the child hesitate over misreading? Can the child comment on characters and events in the story? Children need to learn to use contextual cues combined with the knowledge of phonemes to figure out what a word might be. If they don't have these skills, you need to teach them while you read to individual children.
- Children need to be able to read and write single-letter sounds. Particularly look for the following errors: b/d/p/q, u/n, m/w, and f/t. When children have associated sounds with lowercase letters, they need to make the same associations with uppercase. (Note: Children also need to know the alphabet names of letters, but for reading, the concern is about the sound-letter association, not the name-letter association.)

Keep records for each child on the alphabet letters the child can identify (upper and lower case) and their single letter sounds as well as the number of words in their word bank. Look carefully at the children who are in the lowest 20 percent. Something is not working for these children and they are going to need more individualized and intensive instruction in this area.

It is often difficult for children with specific learning disabilities to interpret what they see (**visual perception**). A child may not be able to judge size, shape, location, movement, and color, because to the child these properties keep changing. Because of the difficulty they have in sorting out foreground and background, they often focus on irrelevant details. It is difficult for them to recognize similarities and differences (**visual discrimination**). Their problems are magnified when they try to learn to recognize numbers and letters, as the differences are slight. The letters that are reversible are especially difficult (*b, d*), as are the ones with "tails" (*p, q, j, g*). See Activity 2–12 Alphabet Lotto.

Visual tracking is the ability to focus the eyes on one point and then move them rhythmically from side to side, up and down, and diagonally. Some children have jerky eye movements, or move their whole head instead of just their eyes. Part-whole relationships (**visual closure**) cause problems. The children may have trouble identifying missing parts; a picture of a three-legged chair appears normal to them. They may have trouble remembering what they see. (Place four objects on the table, cover them, remove one, ask them to name the missing one.) Poor **visual memory** also makes it difficult to remember sequences. Needed memory skills can be built by games that require

children to remember the original order of objects that have been moved. See Activity 2–17 Changing Objects. To support visual skills teachers can

- Play visual tracking games by having children follow a flashlight or pointer with their eyes.
- Hide objects or pictures so they are partially visible and have children find them.
- Help children learn to observe detail. Have children think about the parts of a flower while they are looking at it, and then from memory.

Assessment of Specific Learning Disabilities

Although many are reluctant to identify young children as having learning disabilities, there may be indications in young children that learning is not progressing in some areas at the predicted rate. These may include:

- Delays in speech and language development
- Lack of motor coordination
- Problems with perceptual reasoning
- Immature social interactions and achievement
- Premath and preliteracy skills (NJCLD, 2006).

More specifically, young children who struggle with reading often have problems with **phonemic awareness** (the ability to identify and manipulate the sounds in words) and they usually have a small **sight vocabulary** (words they can read without sounding them out).

The Evidence Base

Assuming that children are being taught prereading skills, if by January children do not know letter names, this may be a sign that there will be reading problems. If a child gets to first grade and does not have letter-sound knowledge, this also signals reading difficulties (American Federation of Teachers, 2004). Based on this information, the Committee on the Prevention of Reading Difficulties in Young Children (1998) looked at 1,000 kindergarten children's letter identification skills. They looked at the children who were designated as at risk in kindergarten (the bottom 10 percent), that is, they did not know their letter names, and who were in the bottom 20 percent of teacher's ratings in first grade (did not have letter-sound knowledge). This method correctly identified sixty-three children as having reading disability and falsely identified thirty-seven children.

Reflective Practice

Screening mechanisms, even ones as simple as these, are the first step in the assessment process and the basis on which EIS can prevent learning disabilities. With this information one could begin to target these children in kindergarten and move into a RTI that would increase their probability of learning to read before they experienced failure in first grade. If you were a kindergarten teacher how

would this knowledge impact your assessment and teaching practices? If you were teaching 3 and 4 year olds, how might this impact you assessment and teaching practices?

If EIS are not successful, the formal assessment process begins. There is agreement that assessment must be multimodal. It typically includes the use of standardized tests of intelligence and standardized achievement tests combined with teacher ratings. Although the exact battery of tests may differ, it should include testing of the eight areas identified by the 2004 amendments to the IDEA (oral expression, listening comprehension, written expression, basic reading skills, reading fluency skills, reading comprehension, mathematics calculation, and mathematics problem solving) (Salvia & Ysseldyke, 2007).

Cognitive functioning (IQ) and executive function should also be assessed. **Executive function** involves the ability to maintain appropriate problem-solving procedures to attain future goals. It is a broad area that involves the ability to plan, to wait, to control one's impulses, to store relevant information for future use, to think creatively, and to problem solve (Pennington, 1991). The need for executive function increases with age, particularly as children get to middle school and more independence is required. A medical/health history should be obtained and the child should have a complete medical examination to rule out other possible causes, such as hearing loss or poor vision.

In the past, formal assessment did not begin until a child's reading age was significantly below grade level, and this could not be accounted for by delayed general development or a sensory or communications impairment. This method is better at identifying bright children who have dyslexia, but often misses others who are also not reading well. If we do not intervene with children who are having problems reading before the third grade, the probability of successful remediation drops to about 25 percent (Shaywitz & Shaywitz, 1991). Early intensive remediation has a much higher probability of success. Hence, the 2004 IDEA supports identifying all children with early reading problems and using EIS to prevent future reading problems for most children.

The National Joint Committee on Learning Disabilities recommends a four-step ongoing assessment:

1. Describing learning problems prior to referral for formal assessment particularly as they relate to a child's strengths and problems. This step involves interviewing key participants, gathering and analyzing information, observing the child in the classroom, and looking at alternative explanations for the problem. It also focuses on monitoring the interventions and accommodations and their effectiveness.
2. Identifying children as having learning disabilities involves looking at the information from step 1 and deciding how pervasive and severe the problems are and how they relate to other areas of development. If the decision is made to proceed, a comprehensive evaluation should be conducted. Information should also include the areas of listening, speaking, reading, writing, reasoning, and mathematics. Decision making should be sensitive to both over- and under-identification by looking at linguistic and cultural differences, adequacy of general instruction, and the occurrence of other disabilities.
3. Determining eligibility for special education and related services that involves a collaborative decision-making process, taking into account the requirements of the IDEA.
4. Bridging assessment to specialized instruction and accommodations involves using the information gleaned from the entire assessment process to develop an IEP that is responsive to the child's current strengths, weaknesses, learning styles, and input from the parents, educators, and therapists (NJCLD, 2006).

Formal assessment of learning disabilities is likely to include a measure of cognitive functioning, such as the Wechsler Preschool and Primary Scale of Intelligence–III (WPPSI–III, Psychological Corporation, 2002). The WPPSI–III has two scales: one for children 2 years and 6 months to 3 years and 11 months. The other scale begins at 4 years and goes to 7 years and 3 months. Both scales have verbal and performance subtests as well as some supplemental subtests. One supplemental subtest, Picture Naming, can be used with the other verbal subtests to compute a General Language Composite IQ. The Wechsler Intelligence Scale for Children–IV (WISC-IV, Wechsler, 2003) is used for children from 6 years to 16 years and 11 months. The WISC-IV provides a full-scale IQ as a measure of general intellectual functioning. It also provides four index scores: Verbal Comprehension Index (VCI); Perceptual Reasoning Index (PRI), Working Memory Index (WMI), and Processing Speed Index (PSI). The index scores provide information about aspects of general intelligence that are helpful in understanding how a child views his world.

Achievement tests are used frequently in education settings to evaluate knowledge and understanding in different curricular areas. Some tests are group-administered while others must be administered individually. Some serve as screening tests while others are diagnostic devices. Some focus on a single content area such as reading or math, whereas others cover multiple areas. Some are norm-referenced while others are criterion-referenced (Salvia & Ysseldyke, 2007). Without knowing what the results will be used for makes it difficult to select an appropriate measure. The Iowa Tests of Basic Skills-C (ITBS) (Hoover, Dunbar, & Frisbe, 2007) includes subtests for children kindergarten through grade eight. Applicable subtests include vocabulary, word analysis, reading/reading comprehension, listening, language, and mathematics. For kindergarten and first grade, the tests are untimed and read aloud by the teacher.

Measures specifically designed for reading may be used as well. The Woodcock Diagnostic Reading Battery (WDRB; Woodcock, 1997) has ten subtests that focus on reading, which are combined to provider cluster scores. It can be used for children age 5 and older. The subtests include letter-word identification, word attack, reading vocabulary, passage comprehension, incomplete works, sound blending, oral vocabulary, listening comprehension, memory for sentences, and visual matching.

Teacher rating scales can be informal or formal scales such as the Conners Rating Scale-Revised (CRS-R) (Conners, 2000). The Conners Teacher's Rating Scale is an observational measure used by teachers (there is also a parent's version) to rate children's behavior. It looks at factors such as daydreaming-inattention, hyperactivity, conduct problems, anxiousness-fearfulness, and social-cooperation. The actual battery of tests will be determined by the child's pattern of strengths and weaknesses and the school and examiner's preferences.

Informal assessment methods may involve having a child read a particular passage that has a known age-to-grade-level equivalent and noting the mistakes the child makes. In the hands of a skilled educator, this can be a good assessment tool; in the hands of a less-sensitive educator, it may be meaningless information.

Additional assessments include trained observers and a behavioral event sampling that targets behaviors in specific situations. Peer rating may also be used, as children with SLDs often find peer relationships challenging. Overall, the goal of assessment is to focus on the particular problems and strengths the child shows and to develop an individualized curriculum to work through the strengths to build needed skills. The most common specific learning disability and the one we know the most about is dyslexia.

Developmental Dyslexia or Specific Reading Disability

Developmental **dyslexia** or specific reading disability is the most common type of learning disability, affecting approximately 80 percent of all those identified as having a specific learning disability (Roush, 1995). Because children are frequently classified as having a learning disability rather than having a reading disability, these figures are less reliable, but the American Psychiatric Association (APA) (2000) estimates are similar. It estimates that 4 percent of the school-age population or four out of five cases of learning disorders relate specifically to reading. Developmental dyslexia is a chronic, persistent condition and one that is both familial and heritable. Boys are more frequently diagnosed (60 percent to 80 percent) than girls (APA, 2000).

The Board of Directors of the International Dyslexia Association (2002) has adopted the following definition of dyslexia, which states:

> Dyslexia is a specific learning disability that is neurobiological in origin. It is characterized by difficulties with accurate and/or fluent word recognition and by poor spelling and decoding abilities. These difficulties typically result from a deficit in the phonological component of language that is often unexpected in relation to other cognitive abilities and the provision of effective classroom instruction. Secondary consequences may include problems in reading comprehension and reduced reading experience that can impede growth of vocabulary and background knowledge.

This is clearly a medical definition of dyslexia, but it is one that is supported by genetic research and how we know the brain works. Reading is a dynamic complex process that changes with experience. Early reading instruction focuses on **decoding**.

Children with dyslexia need one-on-one time to actively participate in reading.

In the Field

I was initially appalled when my daughter's teacher allowed her, a second grade student, to do her spelling homework on the computer. (She is dyslexic and was a very poor speller and had even poorer handwriting.) I predicted gloom and doom. Apparently, the computer pointed out her mistakes again and again without the frustration we experienced over her continuing problems. Her spelling improved and she got an A in spelling.

Reflective Practice

Be open to trying a variety of different ways to reach children. Be creative and reflect on what works, why, and how you can use this knowledge in the future.

Children with dyslexia have problems with the decoding process. They seem unable to segment the written word into its phonologic elements (Shaywitz, 1998). The phonologic-deficit hypothesis for dyslexia posits that children with dyslexia have a neurologic inability in this area. This is supported by functional brain imaging studies that show differences in the temporo-parietal brain regions between those with dyslexia and those without (Shaywitz & Shaywitz, 2005). This is the area of the brain that is used to analyze the written word, which is called decoding. This lower-order linguistic block prevents access to higher-order linguistic skills. Until children can decode and identify words, they cannot look at meaning and comprehension. Their skills in other areas of language (syntax, semantics, etc.) are comparable to their peers.

Dunst, Trivette, Masiello, Roper, and Robyak (2006) have identified overlapping areas of skills necessary for reading in their framework for developing evidence-based practice in early literacy. These skills and variations of them can be categorized as print-related skills, linguistic processing skills, and visual processing skills (Dunst, Trivette, & Hamby, 2007). These skills are later predictors of decoding, spelling, and comprehension (see Table 8–3).

Although the above skills are necessary for early literacy, it appears that a shotgun approach to teaching all of these skills is not supported by the evidence. Rather interventions that focus on one skill or a set of interrelated targeted skills are more likely to be effective (Dunst et al., 2007).

Further research looked at the efficacy to reading instruction practices showed that active reading experiences were most effective with 3 and 4 year olds, although young children benefited as well and shorter reading episodes (15 minutes or less) were more effective than longer ones.

than deadpan and to choose books that are at children's developmental level, but are there techniques that work better than others, especially for children who may struggle with reading? The answer is yes. The degree to which children are actively involved in the process matters. It starts with the child and their interest in the topic as the basis for the book choice. Then comes the how question, which appears to be more important than in the sheer amount of reading (Trivette & Dunst, 2007). In **shared reading** an adult reads a book to one child or a small group of children. In **interactive shared reading** the adult reads a book to a child or a small group of children and asks *Wh_____* questions. In **dialogic reading**, the adult and child switch roles so the child learns to become the story teller with adult support. The adult functions as an active listener and questioner. Both interactive shared reading and dialogic reading are more effective than passive approaches (shared reading) and reading for 15 minutes or less is more effective than reading for 30 minutes or more. Apparently, how one reads is more important than the length of time spent reading (Trivette & Dunst, 2007).

Implications for Educators

Children need a literacy rich environment and they need to be read to. Do you think there are better ways to read to children? Obviously, it is better to be expressive

Reflective Practice

As you think about reading do you expect parents to read to their children? Do you expect in-class reading to be a large-group activity? How might this knowledge change

Table 8–3: Print, linguistic, and visual literacy skills

Print-related skills	
Alphabetic Knowledge	Ability to recognize and name letter of the alphabet and translate graphemes (units of print) into units of sound (phonemes).
Print Awareness	Ability to recognize that print has rules and properties based on the written language and what children can see in print they can say.
Written Language	Ability to represent ideas or concepts in a printed or written format consisting of letters, words, and sentences.
Linguistic processing skills	
Phonological Awareness	Ability to recognize, manipulate, and use sounds as distinct from meaning. Includes rhyming, blending, and segmenting sounds into syllables and words.
Oral Language	Ability to understand the rules for combining sounds and organizing sounds into words and words into sentences as well as understanding the meaning of words and using words to communicate with others.
Listening Comprehension	Ability to understand the meaning of the spoken word by decoding words and sentences and making meaning of what is heard.
Text Comprehension	Ability to understand the meaning of the written word by decoding words and sentences and making sense of what is read.
Visual Processing Skills	
Visual Memory	Ability to remember visually representations such as letters, words, and pictures.
Visual Motor Skills	Ability to integrate visual information with fine or gross motor skills.
Visual Perceptual Skills	Ability to accurately interpret what is seen and make it meaningful.

The print-related skills and the linguistic processing skills have been identified by literacy experts, literacy centers, and professional organizations as important for reading literacy. The visual processing skills do not yet have that level of research support.

Source: Dunst, Trivette, Masiello, Roper, & Robyak, 2006; Dunst et al., 2007; Robyak, Masiello, Trivette, Roper, & Dunst, 2007.

what you tell parents about reading to their children and how you spend your time reading in the classroom? How can you use this information to develop a method of early intervening for young children. Where would you start? How would you plan to focus your intervention?

In the Field

My son, Rob, was identified last spring as having a learning disability. I had always known that Rob learned differently than other children and was happy when his problem was identified so he could receive services to help him.

Unfortunately, Rob's problem didn't only consist of a learning disability. Since the time Rob was an infant, I have had many problems with Rob's behavior, both in and out of school. One of Rob's most disturbing behaviors is his inability to follow directions and complete simple chores. It seems that he simply forgets what he has to do. Rob is easily distracted. He has trouble completing a task and concentrating on what he is doing. I took him to a doctor to find out if he had ADD or ADHD, but he didn't. He also seems awkward and a bit clumsy. He constantly had skinned knees from tripping, and other children laughed at him. Because this makes him feel bad, he quit participating in the games and sports he used to play. I know he is young, but I see him starting to gain weight.

I decided to ask for a meeting with Rob's teacher to see if she had some ideas for me. I learned that some of Rob's behavior problems are normal for children with learning disabilities. I really thought it was just that he couldn't learn to read and struggled with math. I didn't realize how much it affected other areas of his development. This has helped me deal with these behaviors differently. Knowing that these are normal characteristics for kids with learning disabilities has made me a better parent. I learned that he is not being naughty, and now I try to help Rob instead of losing my cool. If only I could teach the rest of the family.

Reflective Practice

Think about how you might help families understand children with specific learning disabilities and what this means in the big picture. Could you share ideas with families that might work at home? How might you support a child such as Rob in learning the fundamental motor skills necessary to play sports and help other children to include him?

Dyscalculia or Mathematics Disorder

Unlike some of the other specific learning disabilities discussed, dyscalculia has no clear-cut cause. It is frequently found in combination with reading disorders or disorders of written expression (APA, 2000). The number of children identified with a mathematics disorder fluctuates between 1 and 6.5 percent of the children enrolled in school (APA, 2000; Geary, 1999). One study identified 6 percent of children as having some difficulty in grasping one or more established standards from one grade level to the next (Geary, 1999). Like a reading disorder, it is identified by mathematical ability that is significantly below that expected, given the child's age and intellectual level. It is seldom diagnosed before the end of first grade. For children with high IQs it may not be identified until fifth grade or later (APA, 2000).

Dyscalculia is the inability to understand the processes associated with mathematical calculation and reasoning. Like some other learning disabilities, it has little to do with IQ, motivation, or other factors that might influence learning. Although there are many aspects of math relating to problem solving, measurement, time and so on, it is defined by lack of mastery of mathematical facts and lack of fluency in calculations (Jordan, Hanich, & Kaplan, 2003). Children with dyscalculia may never grasp the fact that $5 + 7 = 12$, or that $4 \times 6 = 24$. These children will work feverishly for years using everything from fingers to pieces of paper to assist them in their quest to arrive at the correct answer to a math problem without understanding that the problem calls for subtraction and not addition (Garnett, 1998).

Identifying a specific mathematics disorder is challenging because there is more variation in teaching mathematics than reading. Poor math skills may be related to lack of adequate instruction. If this is the case, RTI should impact these children. Mathematics encompasses a variety of skills and neurologic processes. Some of these skills may be impaired and others not (Shapiro, Church, & Lewis, 2007). Some children may have problems with math because they have a reading disability or because of lack of executive function and inattention. Inattention causes mathematics to be problematic. Of a sample of children with dyscalculia, 17 percent also had a reading disability and 26 percent had ADHD (Gersten, Jorden, & Flojo, 2005). The neurobiological evidence of dyscalculia is evolving, but different types of math skills require different brain functions that activate different brain areas (Shapiro, et al., 2007).

Although the inability to decode the written symbols of math is part of dyscalculia, it goes far beyond that. Dyscalculia also includes the inability to understand the visual spatial aspects of math and the language of math (Garnett, 1998). Dyscalculia may affect children in very different ways. One may not be able to add; another may be able to add; however, division is a notion that is simply unattainable. Some have problems similar to dyslexia, such as approaching problems in a left to right manor, forgetting to carry, or misplacing signs or digits (Shalev, 2004). There is far more unknown about math disorders than is known about them. However, like dyslexia, dyscalculia seems to be genetic and heritable in nature. The parietal lobe is implicated in the cause of this disorder, although other areas of the brain can compensate for this impairment in some children (Shapiro, et al., 2007). As is the case with all SLD, research continues to find ways to improve the quality of life and education for children with these disorders.

The Evidence Base

The ability to determine what mathematic difficulties are persistent and lead to mathematics disorders is the first step in the process. If these learning needs could be identified early, then interventions could be designed to prevent failure in math. One component identified by Jordan, Kaplan, Oláh, and Locuniak (2006) is number sense. They identify the key elements of number sense in children as counting, number knowledge, and number operations. Engaging young children in simple number games helps build number sense. Their sample included 411 kindergarten children in six schools, all of whom used the Trailblazers kindergarten math curriculum. Based on a number sense battery of tests, they found three distinct classes of children in kindergarten and first grade, which showed their skill and growth curve: low/flat (139 children), middle/steep (173 children), and high/flat (102 children). Low/flat patterns had children coming to kindergarten with few skills and showing little improvement. Middle/steep patterns showed children coming with some skills but showing rapid learning. High/flat patterns showed children coming to kindergarten with most of the needed skills but not acquiring many additional skills. They tracked children's development of number sense at four points during kindergarten and into first grade. Although almost all children learned some math skills, low-income children fared poorly compared with middle-income children with 50 percent in the low/flat category. They came to kindergarten with fewer skills in number sense and gained very little in kindergarten and first grade. Story problems were a notable exception. Low-income kindergarten children showed almost no growth from the beginning of kindergarten to the end of the year. A similar pattern was observed in number combinations. Gender differences were small but emerging, with boys showing an advantage over girls; these differences extended into first grade. Reading proficiency at the end of kindergarten predicted performance on all number sense measures. Children who began kindergarten at an older age and were more advanced in reading at the beginning of kindergarten continued that advantage. Screening children for number sense in kindergarten might be a way of identifying children who may struggle with math and may be an opportunity to provide intervention (Jordan, Kaplan, Locuniak, & Ramineni, 2007). Based on their research Jordan, Glutting and Ramineni (2008) have develop a 33 item streamlined assessment tool for identifying number sense in children.

Reflective Practice

In this study, children in free and reduced lunch programs entered kindergarten with fewer skills in the area of number sense. They had particular problems in the area of story problems and number combinations. With this knowledge, what might you do to help children in these areas as either prevention or intervention?

Dysgraphia or Disorder of Written Expression

Dysgraphia is also a neurologic disorder; it is generally characterized by the profound inability to form meaningful symbols. The child with dysgraphia produces distorted or incorrect letters in his attempt to write (National Institute of Neurological Disorders and Stroke (NINDS), 2007). Many children who are identified as having dysgraphia also have dyslexia. A disorder of written expression is more than just poor handwriting (which would be classified as a developmental coordination disorder); it involves problems related to grammar, punctuation, and poor paragraph organization, as well as excessively poor handwriting. There is some evidence that perceptual motor and language deficits may be part of this disorder. Prevalence rates for dysgraphia are difficult to establish because it is almost always accompanied by other learning disorders (Richards, 1999). It is seldom diagnosed until the end of first or second grade when children are required to do more writing (APA, 2000). See Table 8–4 for tell-tale signs of dysgraphia.

Fatigue and frustration impede the child's learning process, and may lead to low self-esteem. It is not that the child cannot learn, but that so much time may be spent on the writing process that much of the information is missed (Jones, 1996). The child is able to associate sounds with meaning, and therefore able to develop appropriate verbal skill; however, sound-letter recognition appears to be lacking in many children who have a writing disability.

There are a variety of strategies used to help children with dysgraphia and the most important thing is to find the strategy that best fits each child's needs. Some children's handwriting will improve with additional instruction. Other children do better when they are provided with alternatives to written expression and avoiding the area of weakness (NCLD, 2008)

Word processors are utilized in many educational settings to aid children with dysgraphia. Although computers greatly aid children with dysgraphia, understanding and time are still the greatest gifts a teacher can give. The following poem (found on the Internet) may help you to better understand the problem of not developing proper sound-letter identification.

(Author unknown)

Eye Halve a spelling chequer

It came with my pea sea

It plainly marques four my revue

Miss stakes eye kin knot sea.

Eye strike a key and type a word

And weight four it to say

Weather eye am wrong oar write

It shows me strait a weigh.

As soon as a mist ache is maid

It nose bee fore two long

And eye can put the error rite

Its rare lea ever wrong.

Eye have run this poem threw it

II am shoe your pleased two no

Its letter perfect awl the weigh

My chequer tolled me sew.

Table 8–4: Signs of dysgraphia

Illegible slow handwriting (in spite of appropriate time and attention given to the task by the child) and tiring quickly while writing

Inconsistencies—mixtures of points and curves, improper use or mixture of upper- and lowercase, irregular size, shape, or slant of letters

Unfinished words or letters, or omitted words in sentences

Inconsistent position on the page with respect to lines and margins, messy and unorganized

Inconsistent spaces between words and letters

Poor fine motor skills

Problems copying

Tight awkward pencil grip and body position

Avoidance of writing or drawing activities

Saying words out loud while writing

Problems with syntax structure and grammar

Problems organizing thoughts on paper

Large gap between expressive language and what is produced in writing

Source: International Dyslexia Association, 2003; National Center for Learning Disabilities, 2008.

Implications for Educators

There are a variety of ways of supporting children with dysgraphia in the writing process. Using paper with raised lines may help children stay within the lines. Different pens and pencils and pencil grips may make the process work better. Experiment until you find a match. Air writing letters and numbers with big arm movements helps improve motor memory. As children are beginning to write ensure that they use an appropriate grip and that their posture and the position of the paper supports the writing process. These are very difficult to unlearn later on. Talking about letter shapes and how they are formed may make this process easier. Each letter may have a consistent story that goes with it (NCLD, 2008).

Problems in the Learning Process

One way to look at learning is to break it down into four different processes. The first step in the process is *input*, recording information in the brain. The second step, *integration*, requires the organization and understanding of this information. The third step has to do with recording and retrieving this information using *memory*. The final step, *output*, requires that the information retrieved be packaged in a way to communicate with others or to be translated into behaviors. Problems in any of these areas can cause problems in learning. When you think about a child who isn't learning at the rate you expect, explore the following areas to see if there is a pattern (Silver, 1995). Looking at learning in this way can be helpful for all children, not just those with SLD.

Input Problems

Information enters the brain through the senses. For educational purposes, we are primarily concerned with seeing (visual) and hearing (auditory), and kinesthesis (tactile).

When there are problems in this area, we refer to these as perceptual problems and identify the sense.

Visual Perceptual Problems

Children who have problems in this area confuse visual input. They have difficulty identifying letters of the alphabet, confusing such letters as *b*, *d*, *p*, and *q*. They might read *pat* as *tap*. They might have problems copying designs and copying from a vertical surface such as the chalkboard to a horizontal one such as their desk.

Other types of visual perceptual problems relate to organizing the child's position in space. The child might confuse left and right or misjudge distance. Some children have problems with figure-ground distinctions; it is difficult for them to focus on a particular aspect or figure as distinguished from the entire page. In reading, they might skip words or lines. In games where children are to find one object in a picture with many details, they are unlikely to find it.

At a younger age, visual perceptual problems might be displayed in visual-motor tasks such as putting puzzles together, catching or hitting a ball, jumping over a rope, and related activities that require visual motor coordination.

Auditory Perceptual Problems

Some children have difficulty distinguishing subtle differences in sounds and confuse words like *plan* and *plane*, *play* and *place*. They may also have problems focusing on a voice, such as the teacher's, when there is background noise like children talking, a CD playing, or even the heating or cooling system running. We often accuse these children of not listening or not doing what they are told, when, in reality, they may not have heard us.

Kinesthetic/Tactile Problems

The tactile system is the largest sensory organ and covers the body and the external surface of the internal organs (Williamson & Anzalone, 2001). Young children can either over- or under-react to touch. Children who are hyposensitive may not feel pain from bumps and bruises, and also may not be able to manipulate materials well. Children who are hypersensitive may avoid tactile input and not want to be held or cuddled and not participate in tactile activities such as sand and water play. Vestibular information helps to regulate attention as well as posture and balance. Children who don't process enough information about their own movements may have trouble maintaining balance and need to spend conscious energy just to sit in a chair. Those who process too much movement information may become fearful or overstimulated.

Integration Problems

Perception is the cognitive process in which the information received from the senses is organized and interpreted by the brain. Executive functions involve using information to problem solve. Perception is dependent on motivation and memory. Once information enters the brain it must be placed in the correct order or sequence, it must be understood in the context in which it was used (abstraction), and then it must be integrated with other information that is also being processed (organization) (Silver, 1995).

Impairments in Executive Function

When children's executive functions are impaired they have less ability to wait for a turn and they have problems inhibiting responses that involve self-control and delayed gratification. They struggle with formulating sequential plans. They also have problems encoding the information that is relevant for current or future problem solving (focusing on shoe color rather than facial expression). Executive function involves awareness of what skills, strategies, and resources to call upon to perform tasks efficiently and effectively and having the self-regulation to complete tasks (Shapiro, et al., 2007). Children lacking these skills may use the first solution that occurs to them and may have errors because they are more interested in just finishing (if they do) rather than doing it correctly.

Abstraction Problems

At young ages, problems with abstraction are developmentally appropriate. Children live in a literal world. As they approach the elementary school years, this becomes more problematic and they misunderstand jokes and puns. These children literally believe "I have eyes in the back of my head" rather than understanding the message that you are aware of their behavior even when you are not looking at them. Children who cannot make these distinctions are easy victims of teasing because they respond so literally.

Organization Problems

Some children can process information but can't integrate the information to form a whole. As long as they are asked for specific pieces of information, they can answer questions (What was the mother's name?). But they often miss the big picture (What was the story about?). Their lack of organization is frequently general: Their desks are a mess, they forget to take things home or bring them back, they might do work but can't find it to turn it in, they forget their lunch or snack, and so on.

Sequencing Problems

Children with sequencing problems may hear and understand a story, but they confuse the sequence of events; they don't know what comes first or last. They may be able to say the letters of the alphabet, days of the week, or months of the year in order, but they can't tell you what letter comes after *l*, the day that comes before Monday, or the month that follows July. If they can, they will start with the beginning of the sequence and go through it until they come to the needed information. They may also have problems with numerical sequences, seeing "35" but writing "53."

Memory Problems

Once information is in the brain, it must be stored. The brain stores information in different ways. The two most important for learning are short- and long-term memory. Short-term memory is limited temporary storage, perhaps 5 seconds at most; for example, looking up a phone number and then walking to the phone to dial the number. Distractibility makes short-term memory difficult. Long-term memory is more permanent and seemingly unlimited. Retrieving information from long-term memory requires remembering where the information was stored; much like remembering what label you put on a document in your computer. Many children with specific learning disabilities have a pretty haphazard labeling system. They function better using divergent retrieval (talking about a topic they generated) rather than convergent retrieval (answering a question).

Usually, the child's ability to transfer information is good. That is one reason why contextual learning is so important; it gives them a system for not only learning, but storing information. Rote learning and isolated facts tend to be stored randomly; this may account for the unevenness of responses in memory tasks. Memory may also be affected by whether the input was visual or auditory. The inability to remember information or effectively retrieve it limits sequential problem solving (Shapiro, et al., 2007).

Implications for Educators

Activating prior knowledge is a strategy you can use with children in a large or small group, and you can even teach them this strategy to help them remember new information, especially in reading. Before reading a story, ask children questions what they know about the subject of the story. (One of the *Wh_____* questions). For example, if you are reading a story about a picnic, ask children if they have ever been on a picnic and what they remember. Have children share with the class their descriptions of previous picnics. When reading, refer back to what the children said about picnics or their own experiences with picnics. They will make connections between what they already know and the new information. As a result, they will be more likely to remember the story or the new information.

This seems to work because new information coming into short-term memory only stays there briefly if it is not processed into the long-term memory. By connecting new information in a story or lesson to information already stored in long-term memory, the new concepts are also likely to "hook onto" or be stored in long-term memory.

Children will therefore remember and understand stories and other lessons to a greater degree.

This can also be used in other domains, such as science. If you are teaching about tigers and want children to remember that all tigers have a different set of stripes, first discuss the children's own unique fingerprints. This has something to do with them and is probably already in the long-term memory. Then, when you introduce the concept of each tiger's unique stripes, they will have a previous concept to latch onto, and will be more likely to remember and understand the new concept.

Without actually naming the memory strategy, teach older children about activating prior knowledge. Simply tell them that before they learn about a new concept or read any story, they should think about what they already know about the subject or story, or what they have experienced. You may want to tell them that by doing this they are getting their brains ready to remember new information from the lesson. You might even show them a simple diagram of what this might look like (Figure 8–1), explaining that for the little bits of information not to drop out (be forgotten), they have to join up with other information to get into long-term memory.

Remember to activate prior knowledge before every read-aloud and reading lesson. This is especially important during guided reading. **Guided reading** is a process where the teacher introduces a book and guides the children through it. The teacher takes the children through a "book walk" or a "picture walk." Children think about the story and what will happen in the book. The teacher introduces key vocabulary in the context of the story and discusses reading strategies. Children read the book independently, with a partner or in a small group. The goals is to make children successful readers. After they have read the book the teacher discusses the book with the children

Motor planning and motor output are challenging for some children with learning disabilities.

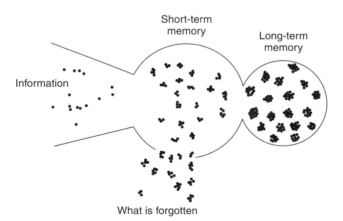

Figure 8–1: Short- and Long-Term Memory
The brain receives an enormous amount of information. If this information seems random or not related to other information it is dropped out of short-term memory. To retain information, move it to long-term memory, and store it so it can be retrieved it needs to be connected to other information the child knows. Interactive reading activates prior knowledge and helps children make connections to new information.

to assess their level of understanding. The children then re-read the book.

Output Problems

Once information is integrated, the next step is to communicate a response through words, behavior, or motor activity.

Language Problems

Language is related to memory: When language is spontaneous, the words flow; when the demand is to speak on a particular topic or answer a specific question, the language system may break down. The question may need to be repeated; frequently, children need extra time to search their memory for the needed information before they can answer.

Motor Problems

Some children have either gross or fine motor problems, or both. Children with large motor problems are clumsy, bump into things, have poor coordination. Children with fine motor problems have trouble tying, zipping, and buttoning, as well as printing and writing. Handwriting might be slow and difficult to read, with uneven pressure.

Guidelines

The following guidelines should be useful when including children with specific learning disabilities. Two key words to keep in mind are *consistency* and *preparation*.

1. *Be consistent.* Establish class rules and classroom management/guidance techniques and use them consistently, but also keep the daily schedule and sequence of the program the same.

2. *Prepare for questions about changes in the routine.* Announcement of a change will set off a flood of questions. The third time you hear the same question, you might respond, "I hear your concern about the trip to the orchard. You are asking that question a lot. Can you tell me the answer?" If the child cannot give you the answer, give the child the words and then ask her to tell you the answer.

3. *Keep the classroom orderly and organized.* Use color coding or numbering of bins and shelves to identify groups of materials.

4. *Give frequent feedback.* Verbal feedback may be the least salient. Find out what works, but try visual (smiles, stickers) and tactile (a touch, a hug) feedback.

5. *Use self-correcting materials.* These materials provide feedback to the child. It is immediate and it will not embarrass the child.

6. *Move from simple to complex.* Begin with simple activities dealing with one concept and move to more complex concepts as the child seems ready; for example, move from *taking turns* to *friendship*, from *counting* to *estimating*.

7. *Give directions simply.* Make directions simple, brief, and clear; state them in a positive manner, with eye contact maintained. If necessary, give them a step at a time. "It's cleanup time" may not be enough. Try "Put the doll clothes back in the drawer;" when that is completed, continue with "Put the dolls in their bed," and so on. When the child has done as you requested, be sure to reinforce the behavior: "I liked the way you folded the doll clothes and put them away." A specific and concrete reinforcement is more effective than one as general as "good job."

8. *Check for prerequisite skills.* If a child has problems learning a particular task, check if she has mastered the prerequisite skills. If a child can't pick out the square from a group of circles, she probably can't find the *p* among similar looking letters. A task analysis is necessary.

9. *Use concrete objects when teaching.* Count children, fingers, boys, girls, windows, and teachers—but don't just count. Count for a purpose that you share with the children. Use manipulatives such as blocks to count during activities. Each child can touch her own manipulatives as she counts.

10. *Identify learning styles.* All children have a preferred way of learning information (visual, auditory, or kinesthetic/tactile). If possible, give children a survey about learning styles at the beginning of the year so that you can appropriately adapt your lessons. It is helpful to know and use the child's preference or use all three, including:

    - *Visual.* Have a poster in the block corner demonstrating the proper and improper use of blocks. Put a big line through those that are not safe.
    - *Auditory.* Tell the child, "Blocks are to build with," "You may not throw the blocks."

    - *Kinesthetic/tactile.* Take the child to the block corner and show the child what to do, then have the child demonstrate the appropriate behavior to you.

11. *Provide processing time.* Be cognizant of processing problems in all learning styles. Give children time to process verbal, visual, and kinesthetic information.

12. *Use differentiated instruction.* Provide children of different abilities and learning styles with similar, but different, tasks to teach the same lesson. This will allow children with different abilities to learn the same concept in a manner appropriate for them. This also works with different learning styles.

13. *Teach rules.* At the beginning of the year, teach your schedule, rules, and procedures. Model and practice these with the children. Some teachers like to have children develop one or two of the rules. This allows children a sense of ownership in the classroom.

14. *Provide varied learning experiences.* Teach the same concept in many different ways numerous times. Teach body awareness through art, movement, listening, music, and health activities.

15. *Alternate quiet and active times.* Children need periods of quiet time and relaxing activities as well as active or hands-on work. Some children may also need to take a few minutes "off" between activities. Have some times each day when children participate in structured moderate to vigorous activity.

16. *Use planned energetic play.* Provide activities that encourage movement, especially during large-group times. Don't expect children with SLD to sit as long as their peers might. Have children march or jump for the number of children in the class. Jump and count or do calisthenics and count. This works well at the beginning of a group time.

Group time is often a difficult time for all children; for children with specific learning disabilities, it can be challenging. Experiment to find out what works best for you: Seat children in a semicircle and place the child with a learning disability across from you where you can easily maintain eye contact. Have children who are good role models sit on either side of the child. Be sure to rotate these children so they take turns.

Sometimes, children need more structure in learning tasks than is typically provided in early childhood classrooms. Skilled teacher can provide more structured, individualized learning tasks. Use the basics of RTI:

1. *Assess* the child's knowledge base in the specific area.

2. *Describe* the procedure, what is going to happen, giving the child a rationale for the procedure.

3. *Model* the procedure. As you demonstrate, state aloud the procedure and the thought processes.

4. *Use verbal rehearsal.* Have the child state the procedure aloud.

5. *Practice* the "easiest version" of the task with your assessment and feedback.

6. *Modify* the task to make it more difficult until it reaches age-grade expectations. Provide assessment and feedback.

7. *Evaluate* the child's learning and begin generalization.

8. *Promote generalization* so the child becomes aware of situations and strategies for using the learned material.
9. *Communicate* with the parents. Change can take place daily, and knowing that a child had a "good day" may be the support a parent needs.

Curriculum Adaptations

Children with specific learning differences require some adaptations. The particular adaptations and emphasis are determined by children's individual needs. If you adapt your programs to include children with specific learning differences and meet their needs during the early childhood years, you may prevent a secondary disability, such as oppositional defiant disorder, that may be based on repeated social and academic failure. Help children build necessary academic and social skills, so they can meet the continuing challenges of the educational system.

SLD is not a single problem but rather a combination of problems. SLD are diverse. Be alert to patterns of behavior and clusters of needs that indicate areas to concentrate on. (If a child is clumsy, has poor eye-hand coordination, and has balance and rhythm problems, concentrate on working with this child in the motor skills area.) Keep in mind the developmental level of the child. (Is the attention span really short for a 3 year old?) Look for uneven development characterized by average to above-average development in some areas, but noticeable developmental lags in other areas. (The child can discuss trains, the roles of the various people on the train, and how trains work, but cannot put a toy train beside, in front of, or above a block.)

Social Awareness: Self-Esteem, Inclusion, and Social Studies

All children need to form relationships with other children and adults. They need to be aware of how they are similar to and different from others. Encourage children with SLD to use a variety of solutions to problems; they have a tendency to get stuck. They require guidance and practice. The skills of taking turns and sharing are especially critical.

Children should be taught concrete methods for dealing with problems. For example, if children have a "small" problem, they could be taught to choose to apologize, compromise, or ignore something that bothers them. For a "big" problem, they can be told to speak to a trusted adult. Some of the activities in the Resource Chapter 1 are specifically designed to support children who have specific learning disabilities. Activities such as 1–4 One More help children think about a variety of solutions to problems. Activities 1–41w Cutting Cardboard and 1–43 Noisy Tasks help all children learn more about how difficult it can be to accomplish certain tasks and may set the stage for understanding individual differences.

Self-Esteem

Identifying learning needs early benefits both you and the child. Once children have already experienced failure, you have to deal with poor self-esteem in addition to the specific learning disability. You can help children become aware of their individual strengths even while working on challenging areas.

1. Children with learning disabilities often show poor knowledge of their body, whether they are asked to label parts on a doll or identify a body part of their own. Increase body awareness and value the uniqueness of each child.
2. Point out what children do well and the contribution each makes to the class.
3. Highlight children's creativity and divergent thinking.

Inclusion

Help children feel they are part of the group. Appreciate their uniqueness as human beings and the contributions they make to the group.

1. Help children become aware of the situational aspect of socially acceptable behavior. In the classroom, there are rules that all children need to abide by.
2. Help children develop skills to be part of a group some of the time as well as skills to be and do things alone.

Social Studies

Social studies can be used to create awareness of other people and the roles they play.

1. Set up a "society" in your class based on the strengths and needs of the children: "Gina will take the messages to others because she is a good runner. Barbara will print the messages. Kenzi will call us together because he has a good strong voice."
2. Explore varied occupations such as plumber, computer programmer, baker, physicist, producer, professional athlete, and pest exterminator. Let the children's interest guide your choices. Be sure to give a nonsexist presentation of occupations.

Language and Literacy: Speaking, Listening, Reading, and Writing

There is concern about the language and literacy development of the children in our schools. There are too many children who do not communicate effectively or read and write at the level that today's society demands. Some question whether all of the children who are identified as having dyslexia are truly dyslexic or whether they have not been taught well. Good preschool programs that provide different levels of intensity of instruction to children can provide a solid foundation for reading. This may mean that for all children you assist families and caregivers to increase their interactions with children. Encourage interactive book reading, conversations, trips to the store, library, and playground to stimulate cognitive and linguistic development. If families have few books, develop a lending library.

Children with dyslexia will find this a particularly challenging area. Make it a positive experience. Most children with SLD find some aspects of language difficult. Sequencing activities and memory games may be difficult for some while making auditory distinctions is difficult for others. Children with dyslexia will need more practice than others in literacy skills. If these skills are difficult, they may try to avoid them. Emphasize activities that intrigue them while teaching the necessary skills at the same time. Your job is also to provide excitement and motivation.

Speaking

Encourage children to verbalize their feelings as well as to communicate ideas. When they do not have the words, provide them.

1. Support children in their verbalizations with picture cues. Ask children to tell you about specific items in a picture. This helps focus their attention as they talk.
2. Give children a sequence of pictures that displays a familiar action, such as getting ready for bed, and have the children tell you what is happening in the sequence.
3. Give children pictures of the sequence of your day at school and have children put these in order and describe the sequence.
4. Play a sentence completion game, such as "I draw with a. . . ." To make it more difficult, ask what else they can draw with.
5. Play "Say What I Say." You can make sounds, words, sentences, or nonsense. See Activity 2–7 Say It.
6. Play rhyming games to increase children's phonological awareness. See Activity 2–4 Rhyming Words.
7. Play word games. See Activities 1–1 Synonyms, 2–31w Same and Different, and 2–32 Never.

Listening

Listening is made up of many different auditory skills. **Auditory discrimination** is the ability to tell the difference among sounds. Children with SLD often have trouble recognizing differences in sounds or words; hence, they often misinterpret meanings (*rat, rap*). They also have problems identifying the rhyming elements of words.

Auditory memory requires children to keep in mind what was said. Sometimes, children forget the beginning of a sentence by the time you get to the end of it. The second request in two-step directions may not be remembered. Some children have problems with spatial awareness and the parts of speech in relation to position such as prepositions (*in, on, over, under, beside*). Give children practice following your directions by showing what they mean both with their own body and with a block or doll. Children need to develop auditory skills, thus choose topics that are of particular interest and reinforce their attempts at communicating. Work to increase attention span and concentration. Shorten sentences and give directions one step at a time.

1. Play games such as "Find the. . . ."
2. Play direction-following games such as "Put the block under the table," "Simon Says," and "Mother, May I?" Add steps. Don't eliminate children who make mistakes; they are the ones that need the most practice.
3. Play musical chairs. Don't eliminate any chairs; this is a listening game.

4. Use sound tapes and have the children identify the sounds. See Activity 2–8 Sound and Tell and 2–9 Sound Cues.
5. With the child blindfolded or looking away, have the child guess who is talking or where in the room the person is speaking from. See Activity 2–51w Where Is It/Who Is It?

Stories can be entertaining and enlightening for children. Choose them carefully, introduce them to the children and read them with interest, expression, and interactively. Remember to ask the *Wh_____* questions before, during, and after reading.

6. Choose stories that deal with individual differences.
7. Tell stories and read poems so that the children's only cues are auditory.
8. Read rhymes and poems that help build phonemic awareness.

Reading

Because many children with specific learning disabilities have problems learning to read, it is imperative to make language arts and literacy enjoyable. To be motivated, they need to know reading can and *will* be fun. Begin by building strength in literacy skills. Children are expected to be ready to read when they are about 5 or 6 years old. However, some children don't seem to be ready when their peers are. This doesn't mean that reading instruction should be delayed; it means it may have to begin in a different place. Challenge, but don't overwhelm, children with the necessary visual and auditory skills that are prerequisites to reading. (Note: There are many different approaches to teaching reading. It is beyond the scope of this book to decide among these. However, the basic foundation skills given below are a place to start. A reading specialist will provide additional help.)

During the early development of reading:

1. Take children on a "book walk" before reading the story. Look at the pictures and make predictions about the story.
2. Spend some time reading to children at their interest level, not at the level at which they read. Read above what they can read independently.
3. Have children put words they can read in a word bank or personal dictionary.
4. Play memory games such as Concentration with increasing numbers of cards. Identify and match shapes and colors before proceeding to letters and numbers. See Color Concentration Activity 2–20.
5. Have a set of wooden numbers and letters. Encourage children to feel the letters and numbers and match them to outlines of the same letters. Start with letters that look different or those with significance (letters in the child's name).
6. Play sequencing games using picture cards.
7. Encourage children to read by having a wide selection of books available on many different reading levels and on many different topics, including books that have only pictures.
8. Have a quiet reading area that has private soft space for children to get away and encourage looking at books alone or with others.

Writing

Most young children love to write until someone tells them they aren't "really" writing or that they can't spell. They may stop writing. Seeing oneself as an author during the early childhood years provides some insulation for the future.

Writing involves legibility (someone has to be able to read what is written), fluency (writing flows smoothly without breaks within words), and speed. Some problems in this area relate to lack of stamina (poor muscle strength) and lack of fine motor coordination. Left-handed children have additional problems.

There is disagreement about whether children should begin with script (printing) or cursive (joined writing). Those who favor script look at the relationship between reading and writing and feel that it strengthens this connection. Others feel that if children are likely to have problems writing, one shouldn't waste time on teaching them to print when it is easier to write in cursive. This decision belongs to you and the educational setting in which you work. One method of teaching cursive has all the lowercase letters start on the line. This helps children with spatial problems. If they have learned script first, they can print the capital letter and follow with this method of cursive (Figure 8–2).

1. Set up a writing center and stock it with a variety of writing instruments (pencils, fine and thick colored markers, crayons) and many types of paper to write on (plain and colored, cards, envelopes). Talk about writing. See Activity 2–29 Writing Center.
2. When you read a book, talk about the author who wrote the book and the illustrator who drew the pictures.
3. Show children books that other children have written. If children say they can only scribble, support their efforts and ask them if they would like to entitle their book *Anasha's Book of Scribbles*. Get children "hooked" on writing. It is a necessary but often difficult skill for them. Start a child library section in the classroom in which only child-authored pieces are kept.
4. If children want to write a book with words, have them dictate it to you and write it for them. They could also "write" it verbally on a tape recorder to be transcribed later or have them type it on a computer.

5. Encourage children to "read" their book to others. Let them know that writing is a process that includes writing, editing, rewriting, and publishing. When children are not pleased with their work, talk about editing. This is a way to deal with spelling, as it is an obvious time to correct it and it provides a life-long skill of not stopping with a first draft.
6. As children become concerned about spelling in their written work, write out the words they need to spell on cards and develop a spelling bank. Put the words in the bank alphabetically so they can find them. Or, you can help them with the process, but you don't need to rewrite the words. Looking words up that are in alphabetical order is challenging for children, but it ties together the reading and writing process.
7. Encourage children to write stories on the computer, spell-check them, and print them.

Discovery: Mathematics, Science, and Technology

Children with specific learning disabilities may not have as much general knowledge as other children. This is especially true in the area of cause-and-effect relationships. They may not understand that it is hotter in the sun than in the shade, or that if you don't water plants, they will die.

Children need practice in logical reasoning. Demonstrate first with objects and then by drawing attention to the child's own behavior that it is possible to make predictions about what will happen. In this way, they will gradually improve cause-and-effect reasoning skills. Start with short, obvious examples, such as putting weights on a balance. Work toward tasks requiring higher-level reasoning skills. Include activities in which children can cause change: the harder they press their crayons, the darker the color. Help children learn how they cause their environment to change. Children need skills to understand and organize their world. They need to recognize relationships, classify items, compare and contrast objects, and solve problems. Children need a broad foundation in exploration without their products being judged. They need help learning how to develop compensatory skills that will serve them as math and science become more formalized.

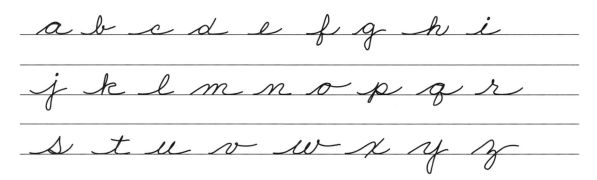

Figure 8–2: Lowercase Cursive Letters
In this system of cursive writing all of the letters begin on the line. This helps children who cannot remember where to start to form letters.

Children need to learn concepts basic to both mathematics and science. Fundamental mathematics and science concepts include observing, comparing, classifying, measuring and communicating. Process skills support children in learning new information through concrete experiences (Charlesworth & Lind, 2003). Use real materials and situations. For children with dyscalculia, work on number sense including counting, one-to-one correspondence, estimation, and copying and extending patterns.

Mathematics

Help children develop a sensory motor experiential awareness of math. *Doing* math, not just looking or hearing about it, is the key.

1. Use concrete objects to teach number sense and numeration, and employ as many variations as you can think of. Use snack time and food (raisins, whole grain cereal, small whole grain crackers) for teaching these concepts: same/different, numbers, sets, equal, one-to-one correspondence, and more/less/same. (Somehow, children learn faster when another child is going to get "more" than they are!) Play Activity 3–3 100's Game.
2. Play number concept games, such as counting objects, naming numbers when shown the number, matching numbers to groups of objects, and games that require matching, sorting, and selecting numbers, colors, or pictures. Use charts, lists, and graphs to organize and classify information. See Activity 3–1 Matching Symbols and Activity 3–33w Spacey Dots.
3. Create situations where children must use mathematical reasoning to solve problems: "What if you run out of large blocks and you need to make another wall the same length as the first?" Discuss relative length. See Activity 3–34w Variations on Block and Activity 3–35w Variations on Cuisenaire™ Rods.
4. Play size comparative games with children: "Give me the big ball" or "Give me the biggest triangle."
5. Help children identify, construct, and predict patterns and relationships of colors, objects (shoe, shoe, sock, shoe, shoe, sock), and numbers. Have a pattern party.
6. Emphasize the vocabulary children need to communicate mathematical concepts (two- and three-dimensional geometric shapes, relative size, numbers themselves, spatial relations, measurement).
7. Have children keep a math journal in which they write about math problems and triumphs.
8. Give large-grid paper to children to help them complete math computations.
9. Work with children on story problems and have them play them out to make them more concrete.

Science

Science activities can create enthusiasm in children with specific learning disabilities if a basic discovery approach is taken. Children can use basic science concepts to organize and understand the natural world.

1. Use science to teach general information, such as cause and effect (the relationship between temperature and the state of water: liquid, steam, ice); the relationship between structure and function (how do snakes move?); continuous and discontinuous properties (pitch, and how it changes on various instruments from water glasses to violins); and diversity (how leaves of various trees are alike and different). See Activity 3–54w Planting and 3–55w Scrambled Eggs.
2. Let children examine items (orange, cup, mirror) and describe as many details of the item as they can (color, shape, size, texture, function, parts). This is a great way to teach comparison. Two items are alike in some ways and different in others.
3. Because children with SLD often have gaps in their knowledge, remember to repeat the learning cycle (awareness, exploration, inquiry/experimentation, and utilization) when you introduce new ideas and concepts and tie it to previous knowledge.
4. Teach older children science process skills and the basics of the scientific method.

Technology

Computers have infinite patience, their energy is inexhaustible, and they don't get upset with children who forget. Some programs are even designed to support children as they get closer to the right answer or have increased their scores, no matter where they started. Computers are under the control of the children who use them. They can be turned off or their plug can be pulled. This is empowering to children who are in charge of so little. Computers can provide personal instruction to children at a speed that suits their learning process and in a time frame that accommodates the child's attention span. Children can participate at their own pace.

By age 3 children can begin to use a computer and discovery-based software with the help of an adult or an older peer. Limit screen time (television, computer, DVD, or VCR). Children's attention jumps to flashing images or moving graphics. Young children's attention span is short and naturally jumps from thing to thing. However, some forms of electronic media may support and prolong this level of immature development (Early Connections—Preschool, n.d.). To be effective and developmentally appropriate, technology must be planned for and be a part of the curriculum. Plan to use all the senses when working on the computer. Software and technology use should support educational goals. Think carefully about the experiences you want children to have or the learning goals you want to support and select software to encourage these learning experiences.

1. Choose software that is compatible with the child's learning needs, supports her interests, and is open ended. Ask open-ended questions about children's work. Ensure that two or three chairs can fit around the computer and plan activities that require the help of peers.
2. Although older children might profit from some of the drill and practice in the areas of spelling and math, for younger children, the idea that computers are interactive and that children can learn cause-and-effect (if-then sequences) reasoning is far more compelling. Talk with children about what is happening on the screen. "When you click the mouse here, the person moves."
3. Becoming comfortable with computers at a young age is critical for children with SLD. Computers can compensate for poor handwriting, they can check

spelling, and as children get older, there are programs that can analyze their grammar and composition.

4. Software can support emerging literacy skills by helping to link words to pictures. Children can create their own stories (on the computer or dictated into a tape recorder) and illustrate them.
5. Software can be chosen that helps children work on emerging math skills such as patterning, classification, seriation, and numerical relationships (Early Connections–Preschool, n.d.).
6. Software can influence behaviors such as cooperation and motivation and how children interact with each other.
7. In an inclusive classroom, the computer is an excellent tool for individualizing instruction.

Wellness: Health, Physical Education, and Sensory Motor

All children need to find ways to be safe and healthy in their world. Children with SLD are at risk because of impulsive behavior, lack of planning, and problems in processing information about their environment. They may also experience complications when understanding directions or taking appropriate actions during an emergency. They may show an impaired ability to integrate information about space and distance in relation to their movement.

Children need to refine the movements of both their large and small muscles in addition to coordinating these muscles with information they receive from their senses. Children with SLD need to develop a physically active lifestyle. It is critical that children develop strength in their core muscles to provide trunk stability as a prerequisite for doing fine motor skills. (Children cannot concentrate if they are worried about falling off their chair.) Children who are not good at these motor activities may avoid them. It is the teacher's role to support children, but also to make activities so intriguing that children want to participate. Some children with SLD have related sensory motor integration problems.

Health and Safety

Children with learning disabilities may have had many prior experiences with health care professionals. They may have had a history of early ear infections and may have been seen for mild trauma care. Their difficulty following safety directions and poor sensory motor integration place them at risk.

1. As these children are more likely than others to become lost, teach them to state their name and learn what information parents want them to give in this situation.
2. Talk about injury prevention. Help children see the relationship between actions and results (what may happen if someone runs in front of a tricycle or bicycle).
3. Talk about the health problems common to children (colds, ear infections, stomachaches, headaches) and ask children to identify the symptoms of each. Talk with children about ways to prevent illness, and how illnesses are treated. See Activity 4–3 Symptoms and 4–34w What would you Do If?

Large Motor

Children with learning disabilities may have been late (or at the end of the normal age range) in reaching developmental milestones such as sitting, crawling, and walking.

Some lack body control and rhythm. While walking or running, these children appear disjointed. They get where they want to go, but they are inefficient and they don't move smoothly. Some lack necessary fundamental motor skills such as hopping, jumping, and skipping. Before children can participate in fine motor skills they must be able to stabilize the large muscles in their trunk and shoulders. The activities you choose should be based on the developmental levels of the children you teach. Obviously some activities that are challenging for preschool children are

Learning about nutritious food and the self-help skills to support independence are important for all children.

too easy for children in the primary grade and too difficult for infants and toddlers. Extract the principle behind the activity and adapt it to the developmental levels of the children you are teaching. The following activities are designed to strengthen the core muscles of the neck and trunk, which include:

1. Have children crab walk to get items and carry them back on their stomach. Vary the type of walking and the way they hold the object on their return. Vary the walk based on the developmental level of the children.
2. Play crab soccer with a small group of children or have children try to keep a beach ball up in the air using their feet while maintaining the crab position. This is challenging.
3. Do bent-knee sit-ups and give children puzzle pieces that they reach for with each sit-up. Some children will only be able to get their shoulders off the floor at the beginning.
4. As part of an obstacle course, tie a rope between two stable objects and have the children lie on a scooter on their back and pull themselves from one end to the other. See Activity 4–8 Obstacle Course.
5. Have children lie on their backs and throw beanbags at a target. Then have them do the same thing while lying on their stomachs. You might provide a bolster for under their chest to increase their range.
6. Encourage children to draw on a chalkboard at shoulder level.
7. Include activities that develop the lateral muscles of the trunk: crawling, climbing, and crashing. Children can't control a tool such as a crayon or pencil until the lateral muscles are sufficiently developed. See Activity 4–35 Variations on Creeping and Crawling.

To increase balance skills, try the following:

1. Play "Freeze and Thaw" but have children hold their position for 5 seconds or more.
2. Tape a line on the floor and have children do a variety of activities while staying on the line: pick up puzzle pieces, catch beanbags or beach balls, walk forward toe/heel, backward heel/toe, tiptoe, and so on. See Activity 4–9 Variations on Balancing.
3. Tape a square onto the floor and have children hop on two feet while staying in the square, then on one foot. Play catching and throwing games with the child staying in the square. Play hopscotch.

Some children will have problems with tasks that require bilateral movement (using both arms and hands at the same time) such as lifting or throwing. Cross-lateral movements (using opposite arm and leg at the same time) such as crawling may be difficult. It may be hard for them to control their balance while moving, and they may frequently trip, bump into things, or drop things. They may also have poor spatial orientation and may find the relationship of objects to each other difficult to understand. They may not know how high to step to get over an object or how to fit their body under a rope. These children also have trouble catching a ball, especially if it bounces first. It is difficult for them to decide when the ball will reach them and how high the ball will be when it does. Hence, they rarely catch it.

Some children will need your encouragement to participate in large motor activities, especially if others have teased them in the past about their lack of coordination. Plan opportunities both indoors and outdoors for children to practice large motor skills, including the following:

1. Help children develop concepts of space and direction by having them pace off distances, or see how far they can run in 5 seconds compared to walking or crawling.
2. Have children do variations on skills that they already know: walking, jumping, throwing, rolling, and crawling. See Activities 4–6 Variations on Jumping, 4–7 Variations on Running, 4–10 Variations on Hopping, 4–12 Variations on Throwing, 4–38 Variations on Body Rolling.
3. Use under-inflated beach balls as well as large balls to increase the possibility for successful throwing and catching.
4. Help children learn sequencing by using the large muscles of their body. Design an obstacle course that children must do in sequence. After the child can successfully navigate the two or three obstacles in sequence, add another obstacle.
5. Help children become physically fit. Preschool children need an hour of structured moderate to vigorous physical activity each day. Put on the music and plan 4- to 8-minute dance parties several times a day. Build these into your routines and transitions. These work well before group times because they help children settle down. To be effective children need to dance (or jump, or march, or . . .) until they are breathless. See Activity 4–13 Fitness Course.
6. Help all children understand and respect differences among children who participate in physical activities.

Small Motor

All young children need practice in fine motor skills. Children with specific learning disabilities may need extra motivation in this area. They may avoid small motor activities. However, they need the practice, and it is your role to make it fun. Children with poor fine motor skills are clumsy in handling small objects that require finger and wrist movement. They may not be able to button, snap, or tie. An underdeveloped **pincer grip** may make it hard to pick up small items.

1. Flick a ping-pong ball into a container placed on its side using the index fingers, thumbs, and then other fingers.
2. Squeeze a bulb syringe so that the air pushes a ping-pong ball across the table. See if they can get the ball to cross a line for a goal.
3. Roll putty or playdough into a log shape, place it around the fingers, and spread the fingers to stretch the playdough; include the thumb. Make small balls by rolling the playdough between the first two fingers and the thumb.
4. With older children use different sizes and shapes of rubber bands to encircle geoboards and objects.

Coloring inside the lines and pasting in a specific area may be difficult. Cutting with conventional scissors can be challenging. Large crayons, large chalk, and simple designs all help. Your concern is to ensure that these children experience success in this area so that they do not quit trying. These skills can be encouraged by the following:

1. Pick some activities that may especially intrigue a particular child. If the child likes cars, provide a car drawing to color. (This is not creative art, but rather practice in small motor skills.) Provide a maze for small toy cars to follow. Have the child practice lining the cars up in specified patterns. Magnets can be used to attach metal cars to a jelly roll pan.
2. Have children practice adaptive skills like buttoning, snapping, and tying. Discuss the pride of being able to "do it myself." Plan extra time so this is functional, that is before going outside, when coming inside, or when going to the bathroom. See Activity 4–42w Caterpillars.
3. Encourage children to participate in board games that combine fine motor skills with other skills; such games include bingo, dominos, checkers, and Chinese checkers. See Activity 4–41w Game Board.
4. Use hand and finger puppets to increase dexterity.
5. Have a variety of different types of scissors available (including left-handed ones), so children can choose scissors that will enable them to cut. There is a fine line between scissors that are safe and those that are sharp enough to cut. If you can't cut easily with them, the children won't be able to. Ensure that you include scissors with small holes for small children, spring-loaded scissors, scissors with four finger holes (so the teacher can help), and scissors attached to a block (so that a child needs to just press down on scissor handle).
6. Supply smaller materials that connect together in a variety of different ways to improve fine motor skills. Have a large supply so children can work together.

Sensory Motor Integration

Children get information from their senses—including touch, sight, sound—and from movement, body awareness, and the pull of gravity. The process by which the brain organizes and interprets this information is sensory integration. The integration of this information with motor activities is called **motor planning**. For some children, motor planning is easy and natural, but children with SLD may find it difficult. When this process is disordered, children may have problems in learning new skills, development, and behavior. They may under- or overreact to touch, movement, sight, or sound; they may be clumsy or appear careless; their activity level may be inappropriate; and this combination may lower children's self-esteem. Motor planning skills increase when children do such things as finger plays and songs that require sequential motions. Obstacle courses in which children move through different types and sizes of objects require planning, as does using different parts of their body to keep an object in the air. Children also work on motor planning when they do variations on familiar activities like rolling, walking, hopping, and when a particular pattern is requested (two steps forward, one to the side). Ask children to march in a circle with their eyes closed, and so on. Have children work their way through mazes. Motivation plays a critical role in sensory integration. Children must be actively involved and exploring in a goal-directed way to become an efficient organizer of sensory information. If the activity is not goal directed it does not increase motor planning.

1. Roll playdough into logs, make letters, and help the child spell his name or initials.
2. Play *Hot and Cold*. Hide an object and have the child try to find something by telling the child whether she is hot (close to object), hotter (even closer), or cold (going away from the object).
3. Play *Do What I Do* while sitting still. You do something (clap twice, tap your head with one hand, and hit your thighs with both hands). The children imitate what you do. Play *Follow the Leader* as well. See Activity 4–22 Mirroring.
4. Include activities that require children to use both sides of their body at the same time, such as underhand throwing or catching a large ball with both hands, hopping or jumping with both feet together, clapping, and doing jumping Jacks or Jills.
5. Include activities that require children to use both sides of the body alternately, such as going up steps with alternate feet on each tread, climbing a ladder, riding a tricycle, walking a line or balance beam, running, walking, and skipping. Place a string or tape on the floor in various configurations (straight, curved, with angles) and have the children walk on this.
6. Include activities that require children to cross the **midline** (the imaginary line through the center of the body, which divides it into right and left sides). Have children throw balls or beanbags while standing sideways to the target. Have them touch the toes of the opposite foot while standing. See Activity 4–20 Hand Clapping.
7. Encourage children to draw a design on paper (with adult support) and then make this design with blocks or other small manipulatives.
8. Introduce yoga.

Creative Arts: Visual Arts, Music, Creative Movement, and Dramatic Play

Creative arts provide an opportunity to practice skills in a safe place before using them elsewhere and to learn more about the world. Children with specific learning disabilities may find in the visual arts an emotional release, an opportunity to integrate the visual and tactile senses, and to make a creation that will not be judged by others as right or wrong.

Music can help improve sensory motor integration; adding creative movement helps children express emotions and increase body awareness. Use dramatic play to help children become more aware of roles and feelings. Help them express caring and happy feelings as well as sad, angry, and unhappy ones. As holidays and special events are stressful for some children, playing them through may help.

Visual Arts

For children with specific learning disabilities, the major focus of art should be on the *process*, not the product. Allow children freedom to be spontaneous and creative.

When they begin to feel that their work should "be something" or look like something specific, and the emphasis is on a product, the potential for failure is greater.

1. Use large paintbrushes; these require less eye-hand coordination than small brushes. As children become skillful with the large brushes add smaller ones.
2. Colored marking pens are easier to use than crayons, because either light or heavy pressure leaves an impression. As children become skillful add crayons, chalk, and colored pencils.
3. Make your classroom an attractive place. Use reproductions of art to connect art to culture and the real world of artists.
4. Give children time to explore a wide variety of art materials. Help them build the vocabulary that supports art—colors, shapes, textures.
5. Use art to develop children's observational skills. Help them think about art and how it is created by asking questions. What did the artist use to make the creation you are displaying? What are the processes involved?
6. Tie illustrations in books to the art you have encouraged children to think about. Don't make models for children, but do teach them techniques to control the medium with which they work.

Music

Music contributes to a child's physical, aesthetic, and intellectual development. It provides pleasure and creative experience, develops auditory skills, encourages physical development, and increases the range and flexibility of the voice. Use a wide variety of musical experiences: listening, singing, moving to music, and playing instruments.

1. Have a variety of different instruments available. Help children explore and evaluate the sound of an instrument when it is held and played in different ways. See if they can identify the instruments they know in a recording.
2. Incorporate music and language experiences; have children make up new verses to songs. Play unusual instrumental recordings and ask children to describe what they imagine while listening. See Activity 5–13 Mood Songs.
3. Put stories to music. Have children choose background music for stories; encourage them to think about how the mood of the music relates to their story.
4. Have children make musical instruments (glasses with different amounts of water, coffee-can drums, and wax paper over combs). As they participate in this process, they will gain an understanding of how sounds are made, where they come from, and how to change them. See if they can make sounds with different parts of their body.
5. Introduce children to the concepts and vocabulary of music, including pitch, loudness, tempo, and duration. See Activity 5–16 Conductor.
6. Expose children to music of various genres, styles, time periods, and cultures.

Creative Movement

Movement that is not judged on quality, but rather on creativity, offers potential for children with specific learning disabilities. Children can experiment with movement and their interpretation of what it should be like without being judged. Movement also provides an opportunity for sensory integration.

1. Have the children walk through imaginary substances, such as gelatin, deep sand, flypaper, a swamp, or quicksand. Have the others guess what the substances are.
2. Combine music and movement to give children the opportunity to translate an auditory stimulus (music on CD) into movement. Be sure to discuss the mood of the stimulus and the types of action this mood evokes.
3. Have a daily dance party using music from different cultures and encourage children to explore different types of dancing.

Dramatic Play

Dramatic play allows children to try out roles and the potential to work through new experiences. It also gives them the opportunity to rehearse new roles and to be in control.

1. Special and unusual events may be stressful. Help children play through field trips, visits to the doctor, and so on. Discuss what could happen as well as what behavior is expected of them. (You gain some insight into what children expect to happen.) See Activity 5–28 Doctor's Office.
2. Because children with SLD often have as much trouble expressing pleasure as pain, have them practice being happy and sad. Discuss how others know you are happy. Have the children pretend to open a package that contains something they really want. Have older children role-play various social interactions.
3. Encourage children to play the role of therapists or medical professionals and pretend to tell other children what to do. Provide them with the necessary supports.

Routines and Transitions

Some children with SLD dislike change. Special school events can be stressful, and children may have trouble handling feelings of anticipation. In addition to the challenge, transitions provide another opportunity for helping children feel the same as others, yet unique as individuals. Be sure children understand what you want them to do during transitions, especially at the beginning of the school year. Routines and transitions, a difficult time for many children, make up approximately 20 percent of the school day. Structure them well and ensure that they are times of learning.

1. Plan enough time to prepare children for the upcoming transition; try a warning of "5 more minutes" or singing a particular song. Tell children about the next activity and the motivating aspects of it. Use code words, songs, or visual cues to help children anticipate transitions.
2. Employ auditory or visual cues to signal change in the daily routine itself. Let children know specifically how and what needs to be done to move to the next activity.

3. Reinforce and acknowledge a child's completion of an activity.
4. Without being obvious about it, dismiss children with SLD early in the transition; this should be thought of as prevention, not favoritism.
5. Use transitions to increase body awareness and feelings of being part of the group: "All children with brown eyes and black hair may *jump* to their centers."
6. Play the "I'm thinking of someone" game to dismiss children: "I'm thinking of someone with blond hair, blue eyes, and a striped top. Yes. Lisa, you can get your coat."
7. Ask older children math facts or spelling words; they can get in line after giving answers.
8. Use planned energetic play (PEP) during transitions to help children burn off calories and focus. Play music (3- to 5-minute songs) with a fast beat and model for children different ways of moving to the music. Keep your movements in the moderate to vigorous range.

Summary

Children with SLD are the largest categories of children identified as needing special education services. Although learning disabilities are probably present at birth as they are increasingly tied to a hereditary, genetic base, they are often not identified until the early elementary school years. However, the 2004 amendments to the IDEA focus on identifying children earlier and providing individualized programming as a way of decreasing the number of children identified as having SLD in elementary school.

Of children identified as having a SLD, reading disability or dyslexia is the most prevalent and best understood. Other disabilities include dyscalculia and dysgraphia. Many children experience problems in the learning process. Some of these relate to visual or auditory perceptual input problems. Other problems relate to sequencing, organizing, and integrating information in the brain. Memory, both short and long term, challenges many children with SLD.

Early identification and intervention helps children work on issues related to their learning differences before these become confounded with issues related to academic failure and poor self-esteem. Children who have specific learning disabilities may need more support, structure, fewer distractions in their environment and require more direct teacher instruction, especially in the area of literacy, than other children the same age.

Reflections

1. Reflect on your skills in the area of teaching reading and what the emphasis on the early identification of children with potential reading problems means relative to the self-evaluation of your skills. Another facet of this process is recognizing some of the behavioral characteristics of children with potential learning disabilities. Your job therefore includes being able to effectively use an array of behavior

management strategies to handle such behaviors and run your class smoothly. How will you handle all these expectations?
2. Learning can be broken down into four different processes. These processes include *inputting* information, *integrating* or organizing information in the brain, recording and retrieving information using *memory*, and packaging information for communication or *output*. As an educator working with children with SLD, you must be cognizant of how problems in any of the preceding areas can cause problems in learning. How do you plan to observe children in a way that you can identify where in the process children are having problems?

Educational Resources

Center for Early Literacy Learning (CELL) is a research-to-practice technical assistance center funded by the U.S. Department of Education, Office of Special Education Programs, Research to Practice Division. CELL's goal is to promote the adoption and sustained use of evidence-based early literacy learning practices in early childhood education. http://www.earlyliteracylearning.org/

Division for Learning Disabilities (DLD), Council for Exceptional Children (CEC) concentrates its efforts on specific learning disabilities, producing a journal and newsletters. They also have state divisions. http://www.dldcec.org/

Dyslexia, The Gift is a site maintained by the Davis Dyslexia Association International and has information about dyslexia and other learning disorders. Great for parents and teachers. http://www.dyslexia.com/

Handwriting without Tears provides resources and information on handwriting and literacy. http://www.hwtears.com or email Jan@hwtears.com

International Dyslexia Association focuses exclusively on helping children with specific reading and language learning disabilities. It has publications for parents, educators, and physicians. http://www.interdys.org

LD OnLine website offers information on learning disabilities for parents and educators, as well as children and adults with learning disabilities. This site is well-organized and easy to navigate. It has lots of information for anyone wanting to learn more about learning disabilities. http://www.ldonline.org

Learning Disabilities Association of America (LDAA) is a nonprofit organization of volunteers including individuals with learning disabilities, their families, and professionals. This site is well-organized and has fact sheets and online publications. http://www.ldanatl.org/

National Center for Learning Disabilities provides information, referral, and resources to children and adults with learning disabilities. This is a good site for parents, adults with learning disabilities, professionals, and children (teens) dealing with learning disabilities. http://www.ncld.org

For additional resources, visit the book companion website for this text at www.cengage.com/education/deiner.

Chapter 9

Children with Social, Emotional and Behavioral Disorders

I wonder about Julie. She used to be such a happy, outgoing little girl, and now it seems like she'd rather sit in her locker than do anything else. Even the other children notice it. They ask me what's wrong with Julie. I'm probably overreacting; after all, what could be wrong with a 4 year old?

Reflective Practice

That's a good question. What could be bothering a 4 year old? As you contemplate your own problems and worries, the things that might bother a 4 year old seem so inconsequential that you may decide the child's concerns are not worth worrying about. Therefore, you tell the child not to worry. That is like a millionaire telling you not to worry about your inconsequential rent, bills, and so on. Your response would probably be a silent or spoken, "You don't understand."

To go back to Julie, she has lost interest in everything, including playdough, which used to be her favorite activity. Trying to interest Julie in the playdough is one way you show her you don't understand. Julie has been spending more time just sitting in her locker, and that worries you. Rather than enticing her away, you show concern by saying, "Julie, *I'm* worried because you are sitting in your locker and not playing with the playdough and talking with your friends the way you usually do." Compare the preceding statement with this one: "Julie, *you* shouldn't be sitting here in your locker, especially when I put out your favorite activity." In the first instance, you make an "I" statement, which reflects your concern about the situation. It requires nothing of Julie, not even a response. In the second statement, you seem to be both judging and blaming Julie for her behavior. "*You* shouldn't" really means "*she* shouldn't because *I* don't want her to." You would be better off admitting your discomfort than blaming it on her. After expressing concern, give the child permission to talk about her feelings: "Sometimes when I'm sad I want to be alone. I wonder if you're sad about

something now?" While still expressing concern, you can offer an opportunity, or invitation, for Julie to talk.

Whether or not she responds, the next move is to tell her how you are willing to help while giving her some control over the situation: "Would you like to talk about how you feel? (Pause) I can listen now. I'd like to come and sit beside you for a few minutes whenever I can. Is that okay with you?" Be careful not to make an offer you can't follow through on. Don't offer to sit beside the child all morning even if you think that would be helpful. Your duties as a teacher make an "all morning" offer impossible to fulfill.

Is Julie just having a temporary bad time? If you were this teacher what approach would you take? How would you go about finding out what the problems are?

Social, Emotional, and Behavioral Disorders

Increasingly, children come to educational settings with the stress that is part of living in a struggling family. Both parents may be working and trying to balance work and family issues. Some families may be living in poverty, going through a separation or divorce, or just too stressed to cope with life due to situational or maturational crises. Educators have the opportunity to help children by modifying the learning environment to meet children's needs as well as helping children develop skills to cope with these diverse situations.

Helping children deal with mental health problems has not traditionally been a school responsibility. However, current thinking is that all school personnel should be part of a team engaged in an effort to help children develop coping skills to live with stressful situations. Teachers are key figures because they see children daily. They need the training to provide psychological first aid to children. However, this is no longer enough. There needs to be a follow-up system to open lines of communication between the home and school and mental health agencies.

Stress can be viewed as an event or a pileup of events that is perceived as threatening and that the child does not have the resources to cope with. Developmentally, events that are stressors to young children might be coped with by older children. Sensitive adults can serve as mediators in lessening the impact of stress on children (Finkelhor, 1995). Stressors can be caused by a variety of different situations. The definition is determined by the child, and the impact of the stress is related to the coping strategies and resources of that child. For example, one might believe that a child who has just moved with his mother to an apartment because of a marital separation would feel stressed. If they moved because the father was abusive and now they feel safe, this actually may have reduced stress.

Stress for young children can be internal, arising from such factors as gas pains in a colicky infant, a painful ear infection in a young child, or the episodic pain of a child with juvenile rheumatoid arthritis. Stress can also result from external factors such as being placed in child care, the arrival of a new sibling, domestic violence, or living in a distressed neighborhood.

Stress can be unique, based on a single situation such as an injection, a single incidence of sexual abuse, or a fire. Stress can also be habitual, chronic, and cumulative, based on living in poverty with a parent who consistently uses drugs or alcohol or abuses the child. A child with a chronic illness may have pain so continually that others tend to see it as the norm and forget that it is still real and stressful to the child.

Stress can be overt or covert. Overt stress, such as a home fire or a death in the family, may create fewer problems because others are aware of the situation and are a potential resource for helping the child cope with the problem. Children can talk about their fears and others

can respond. When stress is covert others may not know about it. It may be a family secret. Habitual abuse of a child is typically not talked about with others. If children are threatened, particularly by adults they are entrusted to, they have no one to mediate the situation and few resources to cope. Sometimes it isn't clear whether stress is real or imaginary. From the standpoint of the child, that is irrelevant; the child's perception of stress is very real. For children, stress may result in irritability and disorganization. Children who have developmental disabilities may have mental health disorders related to that particular disability in addition to being vulnerable to the same range of stressors and illnesses that typically developing children encounter (Robb & Reber, 2007).

Defining Social, Emotional, and Behavioral Disorders

Social, emotional, and behavioral difficulties exist on a continuum ranging from short-term problems that may produce acute, disruptive, and challenging behaviors to long-term serious mental health problems (O'Brien, 2005). This may be a single problem or it may be related to other disabilities. Disorders in this area are divided in a variety of different ways. **Social disorders**, or anxiety disorders, focus on issues related to attachment, separation, and social situations. **Emotional disorders** focus on mood disorders. **Behavioral disorders** focus on disruptive behavior (Robb & Reber, 2007).

Social, emotional, and behavioral development highlights the emergence of an accurate and positive sense of self and the ability to develop and maintain meaningful relationships with other children and adults. Children with social, emotional, and behavioral problems experience an abrupt break, a slowing down, or a delay in the development of these processes. It is the level and duration of disruption that distinguishes between social, emotional, and behavioral problems and disorders.

Social, emotional, and behavioral actions are difficult to classify accurately. Some children have not had the opportunity to learn the expected social and school-related skills. Other children have had to learn early how to fend for themselves to survive in their environment. Some families have values and expectations for their children different from the traditional white middle class because of their cultural and ethnic heritage. Children's emotional and behavioral development needs to be evaluated in the context of their early environment. Children with emotional and behavioral problems and disorders occur in all ethnic groups and at all socioeconomic levels.

In 1997 the IDEA changed the term *serious emotional disturbance* to *emotional disturbance* in an effort to take away some of the stigma of this diagnosis and also to acknowledge that the manifestation of emotional disturbance changes with age. According to the IDEA 2004:

> (4)(i) *Emotional disturbance* means a condition exhibiting one or more of the following characteristics over a long period of time and to a marked degree that adversely affects a child's educational performance:
>
> (A) An inability to learn that cannot be explained by intellectual, sensory, or health factors.

(B) An inability to build or maintain satisfactory interpersonal relationships with peers and teachers.

(C) Inappropriate types of behavior or feelings under normal circumstances.

(D) A general pervasive mood of unhappiness or depression.

(E) A tendency to develop physical symptoms or fears associated with personal or school problems.

(ii) Emotional disturbance includes schizophrenia. The term does not apply to children who are socially maladjusted, unless it is determined that they have an emotional disturbance under paragraph (c)(4)(i) of this section. [34 CFR 300.8 (c) (4) (i)] (Electronic Code of Federal Regulations, 2007).

All of the disorders discussed fall into the emotional disturbance category of the IDEA. I use the term *problems* to refer to less serious social, emotional, and behavioral situations that are very real, but would probably not meet the requirements of the IDEA. The section on social, emotional, and behavioral *disorders* describes those that meet the requirements of the law. Table 9–1 summarizes the signs of social emotional and behavioral disorders.

Some behavioral problems are more common at certain stages of development. When they appear during expected periods, they are considered normal behaviors. When these behaviors persist beyond expected ages and/or the behaviors become excessive in nature, they are considered emotional and behavioral disorders. Definitions related to specific psychiatric disorders are given in the text when the disorder is described.

Prevalence of Social, Emotional, and Behavioral Disorders

There are no universally accepted criteria for determining which children have social, emotional, and behavioral disorders. This chapter acknowledges the emotional aspect of the problem but focuses on the disordered behavior. As you might assume, if we cannot define the term we do not have a good idea of how many children fit the definition. Much of what is diagnosed is a matter of the degree to which behaviors occur. It is almost always subjective and falls in the category of **clinical judgment**.

According to the National Center for Educational Statistics (2006) for children between 3 and 21 years of age they found 7.4 percent of children eligible for services under the IDEA were identified as having an emotional disturbance in 2004–2005. This rate has been relative stable since 1976–1977 with a high of 8.4 and a low of

Table 9–1: Signs of social, emotional, and behavioral disorders

Medical/Physical
History of abuse and/or neglect
Does not like to be touched

Behavioral
Aggressive—hits, throws things, kicks, or bites as first response to frustration
Destroys other children's materials and/or property
Is withdrawn, moody

Interpersonal
Fearful, anxious, excessively shy, uncomfortable around new adults and in new situations
Insecure attachment
Hurts others deliberately, shows no remorse
Defiant
Blames others
Displays attachment problems
May be a bully or victim

Cognitive/Language
Lower than average intelligence
Has problems communicating with others

Family
Parental history of chronic antisocial behavior or other emotional disorders
Dysfunctional family environment (poor parental supervision)
Economic disadvantage

7.4 percent. Prevalence rates also vary by disorder and they will be given with the discussion of that disorder.

All children have problems sometimes; it is the length, severity, and unacceptability of the behavior that determines whether or not it is a problem or disorder. Some behavior problems are learned behaviors that affect children's ability to participate in activities with adults and other children. They are considered situationally specific responses; examples include attention-seeking behavior, pinching, and temper tantrums. Emotional and behavioral disorders involve pervasive changes in the child's behavior and mood states exhibited across many situations and settings. They interfere with interpersonal relationships and with development and learning. They can be harmful to the child and others.

Classification of Social, Emotional, and Behavioral Disorders

Professionals concerned about social, emotional, and behavioral disorders are primarily in the field of mental health (e.g., psychologists and psychiatrists). The focus of mental health for young children has been on prevention and an attempt to identify long-term risk factors. This is a fast-growing field and one that is different from adult mental health. From its inception, the field has been multidisciplinary.

One of the challenges to the profession is the task of classifying disorders in this area. Problems must be classified with a developmental orientation, because young children change so quickly that what is normal at one time may be atypical at another. Classification must also be done with an understanding of the dynamic exchange among the child, the family, and the environment. This requires a systemic and multigenerational point of view.

Several different organizations have developed classification systems, including the American Psychiatric Association (APA), the World Health Organization (WHO), and the National Center for Clinical Infant Programs (NCCIP). The APA (2000) has a section devoted to disorders first diagnosed in infancy, childhood, or adolescence. This text uses the categories developed by the APA and information from the NCCIP. Only the most prevalent problems and disorders are discussed.

Causes of Social, Emotional, and Behavioral Disorders

The causes of most social, emotional, and behavioral disorders are complex interactions among biological factors, including genetics, the environment in which the child lives and grows, and psychosocial factors (Robb & Reber, 2007). Single risk factors generally represent no more than 10 to 20 percent of the total risk (Rutter, 1994). Problem behaviors that are restricted to a few environments are likely to be caused or maintained by specific contingencies in those particular environments. Those that are generalized across many environments have multiple causes, may have a biological base, and are more difficult to modify (Salvia & Ysseldyke, 2007).

Overall risk factors include the child, the family, the school, and the society in which the child lives. The complexity of human behavior, the range of potential influences, and the diversity of behaviors represented by behavior disorders preclude simple answers. There are factors that predispose children to these disorders.

Child Factors

The temperament of a child influences the way he relates to the world. Children with difficult temperaments are likely to show more behavioral problems and are more likely to be referred for treatment for aggressive behaviors and tantrums (Chess, 1990). Although not all children who are aggressive during early childhood develop behavioral disorders, behavior in early childhood is one predictor of later disruptive behavior disorders. Evidence suggests that neuropsychological deficits and difficulties early in life place a child at risk for subsequent conduct problems and delinquency (Moffitt, 1993).

Also, neurologic dysfunctions may reflect and partially explain the impact of child behavior on other influences such as the pre- and postnatal exposure to toxic agents. Early neurologic dysfunctions predict subsequent disruptive behavior disorders in adolescence and adulthood (Kazdin, 1995).

Childhood behavior disorders tend to be relatively stable over time. If young children show consistent patterns of **antisocial** and **aggressive behaviors** toward others it is unlikely that they will just "grow out of it" (Kazdin, 1995). These children become antisocial youths and adults. A well-developed pattern of antisocial behavior during the early school years is perhaps the single best predictor of adolescent delinquency, and, in turn, the best predictor of adult criminality (Walker, Ramsey, & Gresham, 2004).

Academic deficiencies and below-average intellectual functioning are associated with disruptive behavior disorders. The association does not necessarily mean that academic dysfunction represents a risk factor but that reduced time at school (e.g., truancy and expulsion) and less attention from teachers, may lead to poor academic performance (Walker et al., 2004).

Some types of maladaptive behaviors are found primarily among children who have severe and profound levels of intellectual disability and may be the direct result of biochemical abnormalities (Robb & Reber, 2007). Overall, children with intellectual disabilities have higher levels of psychiatric disorders. Gillberg and colleagues found 57 percent of children and youth with mild intellectual disability and 64 percent of those with severe intellectual disability met the diagnostic criteria for a psychiatric disorder (Gillberg et al., 1986).

Family Factors

Evidence has emerged in support of the role of genetic factors in placing individuals at risk for disruptive behavior disorders. Twin studies show the risk of delinquency, criminality, and conduct disorder are significantly stronger for monozygotic than dizygotic twins. Parental psychopathology places any child at risk for psychological dysfunction. The risk for disruptive behavior disorders increases if either parent has this disorder or a related disorder (Kazdin, 1995). The risk greatly increases if both genetic and environmental influences are present. Within family relationships deviant mother-child or father-child relationships, no father in the home, mental health problems of the parent(s) or other family members and deviant parental relationships were viewed as factors that placed children at risk (Aronen & Arajarvi, 2004).

Parental disciplinary practices and attitudes influence child behavior. In homes of children with disruptive behavior disorders, punishment practices have been found to be extreme. These children are also more likely to be victims of child abuse and to be in homes where domestic abuse is evident (Frick, 1998). Although severity and consistency of punishment contribute to aggressive behavior, some evidence suggests that parental punishment may be a response to child aggression rather than an antecedent to it (Frick, 1998). Parents of antisocial children are less likely to monitor their child's whereabouts or to make arrangements for child care when they are temporarily away from home. In general, the quality of the parent-child relationship is low. There appears to be less warmth, affection, emotional support, and less attachment (Frick, 1998). Research has consistently demonstrated that unhappy marital relationships, interpersonal conflicts, and aggression characterized the parental relations of delinquent and antisocial children. Whether or not the parents are separated, it is the extent of discord and overt conflict that is associated with the risk of disruptive behavior disorders and childhood dysfunction (Nichol, Stretch, & Fundudis, 1993).

Poverty, overcrowding, unemployment, receipt of social assistance, and poor housing are among the salient measures of socioeconomic disadvantage that increase family risk for disruptive behavior disorders and delinquency. The effects appear to be enduring. Socioeconomic disadvantage can be viewed as a risk factor. However, once all other associated features are controlled, the precise role of economic issues is not always clear.

> Look behind an aggressive child and you may well find parents who are preoccupied, incompetent, or negligent. Or you may find parents who recognized trouble but prayed that the child would "grow out of it." You may find parents who asked for help and were told there was nothing wrong or that it was their fault; or confused, frustrated, disappointed parents who have tried to follow through on expert advice and failed, even seen the problem grow worse. What you're certain to find is an ignorance of the fact that aggressive adults often start out as children who hurt others, children whose social ineptitude already reflects destructive interactions between the brain and an environment that is threatening, unfulfilling or incomprehensive. (Niehoff, 1999, pp. 281–282)

Young children are dependent upon the adults in their world to fulfill their basic needs; they are vulnerable in ways that older children are not. They can easily become victims of inappropriate adult-child relationships. As children grow and develop they both acquire and lose characteristics that put them at risk for atypical social development (Finkelhor, 1995).

In an effort to move beyond the literature that focused solely on child abuse and neglect and to find a developmental framework for viewing social situations in which children are at risk Finkelhor (1995) proposed the concept of "victimization." He saw the need to develop a means for understanding social traumas within a developmental framework.

The most clearly dependency-related form of victimization is neglect (Finkelhor, 1995) and parents are the adults responsible for such neglect. Even when others are aware of neglect it is the parents' responsibility to care for their children. Young children are also victims of child abuse, homicide, and abductions by parents.

This view of victimization uses the disruption of developmental tasks of childhood as a basis for understanding vulnerability (Finkelhor, 1995). Development of attachment to a primary caregiver is a major social task of infancy. Victimization interferes with this task when abuse is perpetrated by the caregiver. The result is disorganized attachment and the expectation is that the effects of this insecure attachment will be carried into later phases of development and other relationships. There may also be physiological alterations in endocrine functioning and neurologic processes that permanently affect cognitive and behavioral development (Putnam & Trickett, 1993). The effects of abuse don't end in early childhood. Infants and toddlers who have been maltreated show more symptoms of anxiety and depression in adulthood (Kaplow & Widom, 2007).

Preschool children are capable of mental representation and they develop the ability to dissociate. **Dissociation** is a mental state where certain thoughts, sensation, or memories are compartmentalized because they are too overwhelming for the conscious mind. Therefore children fantasize, developing imaginary playmates, and deny things they clearly have done. Young children use dissociation as a defense mechanism and can develop chronic patterns of dissociation, such as memory loss, a tendency for trance-like behavior, and auditory or visual hallucinations (Putnam, 1991; Macfie, Cicchetti, & Toth, 2001).

Assessing the results of victimization for young children is different than adults. When adults are victimized, they typically display posttraumatic stress symptoms that are relatively short term and primarily affect the behavior associated with the experience. Young children, too, show such behaviors as fearfulness, nightmares, avoidance of violence on television, fear of adults who resemble the offender, and fear of returning to the place where the victimization occurred (Finkelhor, 1995). Almost all traumatic situations result in some increased sense of fearfulness. In addition to traditional posttraumatic stress symptoms with very young children, victimization interferes with normal developmental processes. Although specific developmental problems vary, the effects of victimization can result in impaired attachment, problems relating to others, poor peer relationships, often in the form of aggression toward peers with lack of remorse, and problems coping with stress and anxiety (Briere, 1992; Cicchetti & Lynch, 1993).

School Factors

Characteristics of some schools place children at risk for disruptive behavior disorders. Schools that use and support harsh discipline and provide poor child supervision place children at risk. For many children, school is no longer a safe haven. School shootings have brought this to our attention vividly. There is not a single profile of boys who turn to violence in schools. What we do know is that, in an analysis of 37 school shootings, all the attackers had come to the attention of someone (school officials, police, other students) for disturbing behavior (Dedman, 2000).

Few had histories of diagnosed mental illness or drug and alcohol abuse, but over half had a history of feeling extremely depressed or desperate. In his journal, Luke Woodham, a 16 year old who killed his mother, two students, and wounded seven others, wrote "I am malicious because I am miserable" (Dedman, 2000, p. 9).

The motives for the shootings were typically revenge for a known or imagined act. In many cases the attackers felt persecuted, bullied, or threatened—tormented (Dedman, 2000). Although young children do participate in violent acts, they rarely result in the death of themselves or others. However, the seeds of disruptive behavior are evident during this time as are the opportunities for prevention.

The Evidence Base

Character education is a newcomer to curriculum interventions. It emphasizes concepts such as respect, fairness, caring, responsibility, trustworthiness, and citizenship. The What Works Clearinghouse looked at 93 studies in this area. Eighteen studies of 13 programs met their review qualifications; 7 without reservations and 11 with reservations. The program that had the highest evidence rating was Positive Action. Positive Action is designed for children kindergarten through grade 12. The kit contains instructor's manuals with 15 minute lessons designed to be taught several days a week throughout the school year.

Children participating in the Positive Action program improved an average of 19 percentile points in areas such as being supportive, friendly, and helpful; honest, rule-abiding, and respectful; and had less fighting. Interestingly, the children's standardized achievement scores in reading and math increased an average of 16.5 percentile points. Positive Action has no lessons designed in these areas (What Works Clearinghouse, 2007).

Reflective Practice

How do you explain the increase in math and reading when there was no instruction in these areas? What do you think this means in the broad context of education?

Well-meaning teachers who are not aware of different behavioral, disciplinary, and communication styles of different ethnic and socioeconomic groups in their classrooms can misperceive and misunderstand children's behaviors.

Teachers may:

- *Perceive behavior problems that do not exist.* Many African American children express emotions much more intensely than European American children; too often teachers assume children are much angrier than they really are.
- *Not notice problems that do exist.* Teachers who are not tuned in to the ways students from other cultures communicate can miss a request for help or assistance. For example, some Asian Pacific American children believe that to ask for help would insult their teachers.
- *Misunderstand the causes of children's behavior problems.* Educators may mistakenly attribute different

causes to behavioral problems that are culturally determined. A teacher may assume that an Asian child who smiles when reprimanded has no respect for authority. Asian children tend to "camouflage" their embarrassment by smiling.

- *Use inappropriate techniques to deal with children's behavior.* Even when teachers recognize that a child's behavior problem might be culturally determined, they may still respond inappropriately. Hispanic parents tend to speak more politely and indirectly when they criticize or discipline their children. If teachers are gruff and direct with children they may see this as indicating they are not worthy of a proper relationship (Lynch, 2004).

Societal Factors

Society's social and economic problems spill over into the schooling process and greatly complicate the task of educating young children. We are a violent nation. The United States has the highest rates of violence of all industrialized nations, and children and youth are more involved in violent behavior at ever younger ages (APA, 2000). The cost of disruptive behavior disorders is high. First, there are the personal costs to the child. These children are often victims of abuse, neglect, and insensitive caregiving. The dysfunctions of early childhood are likely to continue into adulthood without intervention. The children tend to victimize others. They may use coercive acts to attain short-term gains, but they experience long-term losses. They are victimized by their own behavior and need assistance to break out of this behavior pattern. Schools and teachers play a pivotal role in this process (Walker et al., 2004).

School may not feel like a safe place for some children.

Societal problems related to bias and discrimination are concerns in identifying children with disruptive behavior disorders. There are a disproportionate number of male, black, and Hispanic children in special education and they are especially overrepresented in the category of emotional disturbance (IDEA, 2004). Ultimately, nearly all behavioral standards and expectations—and therefore nearly all judgments regarding behavioral deviance—are culture-bound; value judgments cannot be entirely culture-free.

Early Identification of Social Problems and Disorders

The identification and detection of atypical social development is difficult with young children. Diagnosis includes a subjective judgment of what is inappropriate. Assessment must consider cultural and child-rearing differences. The first signs of atypical social development are identified as children try to master basic developmental skills or social responses. There is concern when an infant cannot be comforted, when a toddler does not talk, when a child continues to show extreme anxiety around strangers, or when a child does not demonstrate any responsiveness to adults. These responses are warning flags for social development.

Shyness and Selective Mutism

All children like and need to be alone some of the time. Children who are alone most of the time or who seem uncomfortable when they are with groups of people cause concern.

Occasional shyness is expected, and typical of slow-to-warm-up children. It is characterized by an ambivalent approach/avoidance quality. Shyness is different from wariness and social disengagement; those behaviors do not share the ambivalent characteristics of shyness. In young children, shyness is often in response to new adults and is often characterized by thumb sucking or alternately smiling and hiding. Avoidance of gaze, an unwillingness to respond to friendly social overtures, and even blushing are also associated with shyness.

Some aspects of shyness are learned by children, some appear to be culturally based, and others are genetic. When shyness is a temporary solution to a novel or overwhelming social situation, it may be adaptive. Extreme shyness may be related to poor self-image or lack of social skills. Shy children may not be noticed and may not have the opportunities or skills to interact with other children or to gain an adult's attention (Hyson, 2004).

Selective mutism may be an extreme form of shyness, if the child displays different behavior in the family setting (APA, 2000). In selective mutism the child can talk and is familiar with the spoken language, but does not talk in specific social situations, such as school, when there is an expectation that the child will talk. It cannot be diagnosed during the first months of school, but it must last at least a month. It interferes with the child's social and academic development.

Shy children need to be given time to warm up in new situations. They may need to be taught skills for joining peer groups and support in feeling good about themselves and the talents they have to offer. They need the subtle support of caring adults who encourage them, but don't take over and act for them.

Shy children may need to learn skills to gain access to groups and maintain group membership. Children who grow up in authoritarian families are more likely to be shy. Caregiving styles that support democratic decision making and respect may help young children; making children feel attractive, supporting them in small groups after teaching them social entry skills, and teaching them muscle relaxation games helps.

Fear, Anxiety, Phobias, and Anxiety Disorders

All children have times when they are fearful. Sometimes this begins with a single incident such as being frightened by a dog. This fear may then generalize to all dogs and perhaps to all animals; in extreme cases, even to pictures of animals or animal crackers. When the focus is on a single object, place, or situation (dogs, school, going to a sleepover) it can be the beginning of a phobia. These passing fears are normal in children; it is their persistence and ability to limit the child's daily routine that are of concern. A phobia is a marked and persistent fear that is excessive or unreasonable, and set off by anticipating, seeing, or coming into contact with the object. For example a child may be afraid of dogs. Upon seeing a dog the child may cry, tantrum, freeze, or cling (APA, 2000). Children may try to avoid these situations. It is not a problem unless it interferes with academic functioning or social activities.

Of particular concern is **social phobia** that involves marked and persistent fear of situations that expose a child to strangers or in which she feels she might be embarrassed. This may be a social situation such as a birthday party where the child may cry, have a temper tantrum, freeze, or shrink away from unfamiliar people. This child might be afraid to go to school, not speak up in class, not use the restroom, and not eat in the cafeteria. To be a social phobia it needs to last for 6 months, take place in multiple settings, but not take place at home with familiar adults (Robb & Reber, 2007).

Anxiety is more generalized. Children worry, become upset easily, and may become extremely anxious about participating in new activities. They may be worried that they can not do things right and actually become perfectionists. They may have more problems than other children at their developmental level in distinguishing between the real world and the one that is make-believe. Monsters may be very real and a threat to them. Transitions and unstructured situations may increase their anxiety. Their anxiety to try new experiences may delay their mastery of new skills and interfere with their memory and concentration. Help anxious children by giving them clear explanations of what is expected and reassuring them about what is happening and your confidence in their ability to cope. They need praise and support and may be oversensitive to criticism.

Anxiety disorders are among the most common and are associated with feelings of emotional uneasiness, fear, and maladaptive worry. A **generalized anxiety disorder** is excessive anxiety and worry about a variety of things and results in fatigue, restlessness, difficulty concentrating, irritability, tension, and sleep disturbance. Generalized anxiety is more prevalent than had previously been thought; however, these disorders are difficult to diagnose (Robb & Reber, 2007).

Posttraumatic stress disorder can result from exposure to an extreme traumatic stressor, such as when the situation involves actual or threatened death or serious injury. It may involve feelings of intense fear, helplessness, or horror. In young children this may result in disorganized or agitated behavior (APA, 2000). Young children may repeatedly reenact the experience. They may have physical symptoms such as stomachaches and headaches. They may feel that they are not going to grow up. Increasing numbers of children experience this disorder.

Posttraumatic stress disorders are classified based on the number of events: A single event (acute, single event) or a connected series of traumatic events (chronic, repeated). A child who was in an automobile accident and broke her arm and had to be taken to the emergency room would be expected to have short-term disturbances such as nightmares and probably be fearful of riding in cars for a time. A child who is repeatedly abused or neglected is at risk for more pervasive interference with developmental tasks.

Attachment and Attachment Disorders

Some children fail to develop secure attachment patterns with adults. They do not respond as expected to social stimuli. They may be irritable, not easily comforted, dislike affection, and withdraw. These children may have difficulties in their signaling systems that interrupt the early attachment process. They may cry continuously, have a piercing scream, arch their bodies to physical touch, and show no response to soothing interactions from adults. They may have poor eye contact and lack interest in social interaction. They are frequently described as "difficult" children. The presence of these behaviors can cause adults to think the child does not like them. They may also find it unpleasant to be around the child due to these behaviors. The result may be the failure of the adult and the child to develop secure attachment.

Attachment is the development of the human bond between infant and adults. The underlying assumption of attachment is that young children use attachment as an internal working model for relationships. Its purpose is to make the relational world more predictable, meaningful, and shareable (Bretherton, 2005). Attachment has been studied in more detail than any other early childhood relationship. Some see the development of attachment as the most important early social event to occur in a child's life. For the attachment process to operate efficiently, the infant must have information about himself and the attachment figure. He needs to know how likely the other is to respond as environments and conditions change. By the end of the first year, the infant has a considerable amount of knowledge about his world and organizes this knowledge to form a "working model" that includes models of self and adults in interaction with each other (Bowlby, 1989). The infant uses these models to plan his behavior. When caregivers abuse or neglect infants, or when the relationship is disrupted by events such as death or foster care placement, the model does not function as intended (Dozier, Dozier, & Manni, 2002). The more accurate and adequate the infant's model, the better adapted his behavior.

Stages of Attachment

Attachment develops in several stages. **Indiscriminate attachment** is present from birth to approximately 4 to 6 months. The infant enjoys being handled, being approached by people, and engaging in social interactions. Once the infant develops the ability to identify familiar adults (3 to 4 months), the process of **discriminate attachment** begins. During this stage children show a marked change in social behavior. They respond differently to one (or a few) familiar individuals than they do to strangers.

The third stage builds on earlier attachment behaviors but is characterized by the infant's initiative in seeking proximity and contact with the attachment figure. This is referred to as **active initiation** and begins around 8 or 9 months (Ainsworth, 1969). Bowlby (1989) identified a final stage as **goal-directed attachment** which usually appears in the third year.

Patterns of attachment in children appear to be far more stable over time than specific behaviors. However, they are less stable for infants from economically vulnerable families or in families where mothers entered into employment during the attachment process. It appears that the mother-child relationship has to be renegotiated at this time. The picture emerging is one of developmental complexity (Sroufe, et al., 2005). Infant attachment alone does not predict later relationships but in the context of other information provides important information. Secure attachment histories provide a base for toddlers to accept parents' limit setting. When there is insecure attachment or anxious attachment parents have greater problems setting limits, boundaries and providing the support for the struggles that children have with autonomy (Sroufe, et al., 2005).

One way of looking at attachment is through the strange situation developed by Ainsworth (1963). It works something like this:

- A mother and child (between 12 and 24 months) enter an unfamiliar room that contains two chairs and a few appropriate toys for the child to play with. The mother stays with the child for 3 minutes and then leaves.
- A stranger enters and stays for 3 minutes.
- The mother returns and the mother and infant are reunited (Honig, 1993).

Much of our knowledge about attachment is based on research done using the strange situation.

Types of Attachment

Four different types of attachment have been identified.

- **Secure attachment.** Young children showing secure attachment protest at being left alone, or with a stranger in an unfamiliar place. They may show the obvious distress of crying or fussing, the disruption of play behavior, or unwillingness to be comforted by a strange adult. When the parent returns, the child calms quickly, seeks proximity, and returns to play and exploration. Parents of securely attached children appear to be sensitive and responsive to their child's signals. Children who are securely attached seek out their parent for comfort when they are scared, hurt, or hungry. These children use their parents to help them settle down (Dozier, Dozier, & Manni, 2002).
- **Avoidant Attachment.** Young children who display avoidant behavior neither protest when their parent

leaves nor do they immediately acknowledge her return. Rather, they become busy exploring the surroundings and making overtures toward the unfamiliar adult. At first glance, these look like mature behaviors. However, most feel that this is a strategy for dealing with the stress of separation rather than lack of stress per se. It is viewed as an organized defensive strategy. Parents of these infants tended to minimize or dismiss the importance of attachment and to avoid confronting negative affect. When children come to their parents because they are scared they may be told "There is nothing to be scared of," or "You have to grow up, this is silly," or "Don't bother me." If parents consistently do not comfort and reassure their young child he learns that they do not respond to his concerns. He may look and then turn away based on his memory of previous experiences. The child's behavior may be adaptive for the situation he is in (Dozier, Dozier, & Manni, 2002).

- **Resistant Attachment.** Toddlers displaying this type of attachment are distressed at separation from the parent and contact her when she returns, but the contact is one of anger. They don't seem to be comforted by the parent's return and they don't seem to be able to resume play. This behavior has been interpreted as the child's response to inconsistent caregiving. Parents of ambivalent children showed similar ambivalent feelings about their own parents and appeared preoccupied with attachment relationships (Dozier, Dozier, & Manni, 2002). Avoidant and resistant attachment patterns are seen as organized consistent strategies of response to stress that are adaptive for the young child in some situations.
- **Disorganized/Controlling Attachment.** Young children with disorganized/controlling attachment lack a consistent pattern in response to stress. This behavior is typically in response to caregivers whose behavior is frightening to them. Parents' behavior can be frightening for a variety or reasons. They can be based on abuse or neglect or they can be responses to threats of abandonment. Children's responses may be idiosyncratic, but typically includes alternations of approach and avoidance of the parent. They lack an organized way of seeking comfort and security when stressed. Parents of these children appeared stressed and seemed to be dealing with unresolved loss or trauma. Parents who are depressed, abusive, alcoholic, or having serious psychosocial problems may respond in ways that frighten young children and make them unable to respond in a consistent way. Some researchers feel that these children are at the greatest risk for later psychopathology (Dozier, Dozier, & Manni, 2002). Children with both avoidant and resistant attachment have figured out a system that works for them, not ideal but workable. Children with disorganized/controlling attachment are vulnerable for both internalizing symptoms such as anxiety and depression as well as externalizing symptoms such as acting out (Lyons-Ruth, 1996).

Reactive Attachment Disorder. Failure to develop appropriate attachment patterns may lead children to withdraw or shun social interaction. They may exhibit cranky and whiny behaviors. Social responsiveness may be limited.

These children fail to develop appropriate interaction patterns with adults and peers. They do not respond as expected to social stimuli. The combination of these behaviors typically results in further isolation, as both adults and peers tend to ignore or dislike these children and refrain from interacting with them.

Although rare, children who experience markedly disturbed and inappropriate social relatedness before age 5 can be diagnosed with *Reactive Attachment Disorder of Infancy or Early Childhood* (APA, 2000). The main characteristic of this disorder is the lack of social relatedness that occurs before the age of 5. There are two different types: inhibited and disinhibited. In the inhibited type, the child does not express age-appropriate signs of social responsiveness. The child does not respond appropriately to social interactions and may be excessively inhibited, hypervigilant, or show approach/avoidance responses. In the disinhibited type, the child is indiscriminately social, relating to strangers with excessive familiarity but showing no selectivity in attachment figures.

The reactive attachment disorder is caused by extreme neglect and grossly inadequate or inappropriate caregiving. Children with this disorder respond well to positive nurturing and caregiving. Although the emphasis in intervention is typically on parent-child relationships, it is possible that a child who is distressed in an early care and education setting would show a disorder in this category. Adults can be helped to read children's cues more accurately and respond to them quickly as well as increase the order and predictability in the child's environment and the availability of a primary caregiver.

Separation Anxiety Disorder. As the name suggests, anxiety results from separation from familiar people, usually parents, or from leaving home. The reaction is excessive and usually occurs regardless of the general intellectual level of the child. Separation anxiety and generalized anxiety are strongly associated (Warren, 2004). Separation anxiety may be a precursor to adult anxiety.

All young children react to separation. Some children cry, others want their parent to stay, some withdraw and some act out, some hesitate to enter a new setting and, when left, keep returning to the door, some look stressed, and some bring attachment objects. It is the recurrent excessive distress on separation and persistent and excessive worry about losing or having harm befall the attachment figure that characterize this disorder. It may involve sleep disturbances, both not wanting to go to sleep as well as having nightmares about separation. It may involve physical symptoms such as vomiting, headaches, or nausea upon separation or knowledge of separation (APA, 2000). The condition must last at least 4 weeks to be considered a disorder.

In the Field

When you teach 2 year olds you expect separation problems. We have a goodbye window where children can watch their parents leave and look in anticipation of their return. We have had some difficult separations, but not in the same category as Rebecca. She started school in September, and her mother stayed in the classroom with her on the first day, which is pretty typical. The next day her mother planned to leave, but Rebecca protested so violently that her mother stayed. I tried to coach the mother to have her say goodbye, leave for 5 minutes, and then return so Rebecca would get used to the separation. She cried the whole time her mother was gone. The next day, Rebecca came with her father. This was more difficult, and we again tried the 5-minute routine. The family was desperate for her to be in school because they were expecting another child in several months. Rebecca's father did mention that she and her mother were very close. Rebecca didn't like her mother to close the door when she went to the bathroom. And although Rebecca had her own room, she cried to the point that she either slept with her parents or one of them slept with her in the double bed in her room. Her father said they were always tired. As long as he stayed and talked with us, Rebecca was fine. When he left, she cried. We tried variations on leaving, bringing attachment objects, and everything else we could think of. It was difficult to tell at the beginning if this was a power struggle or if it was a genuine separation anxiety disorder. By the end of the third week we were all exhausted. We had a parent-teacher conference and mutually decided that Rebecca would be withdrawn from the program. I suggested that some family counseling might be helpful. They were noncommittal. I feel a bit guilty, but I felt like the other children were paying such a high price and I really thought that I had done all I knew how to do. This situation required more skill than I had.

Reflective Practice

Separation is an issue with some children. Think about the skills you have to apply to this situation. What might you do that was not done by this teacher? How would you have handled this situation? How long would you let it continue?

Eating and Eating Disorders

Many children go through stages in which eating certain foods is problematic, often more a problem for adults than for children. Typical eating problems involve "finicky" eaters who go through phases when they will eat only certain foods like hot dogs, peanut butter and jelly, and candy. They may refuse to eat most table foods, and they may eat on the run, grabbing an apple slice or cracker. For most children, these finicky habits are just phases that they experience and pass through.

For some children, eating problems are more severe and can lead to nutritional problems that affect development. Some infants develop a pattern in which they refuse to eat, turning their head away from nursing, the bottle, and cereal. As we are learning more about children's eating behaviors, it appears that food allergies may play some part in the child's behavior. Infants who are allergic to milk or soy formulas may be diagnosed as "failure to thrive," when in reality the child is having an allergic reaction to the food offered. In recent years, more children seem to be developing severe food allergies.

If children have eating problems, a medically based approach such as blood tests to determine food allergies should be suggested. If the child is allergic to particular foods or additives, a special diet can be recommended. Ensuring that children are not hungry, reinforcing appropriate eating habits, establishing consistent eating routines, and suggesting behavior modification techniques can help to overcome most eating problems. However, some children fall into the category of "failure to thrive."

Failure to Thrive

Undernutrition is more common in children with disabilities than typically developing children. It is caused by inadequate calorie intake, calorie expenditures that exceed calorie intake, or the body's inability to use the calories for growth and development (Eicher, 2007). The most frequent cause of failure to thrive is that the infants do not get enough food. It is, in effect, more of a symptom than a diagnosis (Beker, Farber, & Yanni, 2002). In infancy, it also means deficits in nutrients to the brain and diminished physical energy for exploring and learning. Malnutrition reduces the number of brain cells.

Failure to thrive can be a result of organic (biological) or nonorganic (psychosocial/behavioral) reasons, or the interaction of these. It is more common among children living in impoverished environments, but not exclusive to them. In these cases, it may relate to lack of available food, lack of parent knowledge, or lack of parent involvement. It can also be related to the child's refusal to eat, or to eat only certain foods. Children with developmental disabilities are disproportionately represented in infants who fail to thrive (Isaacs, 2007). As children become older, around 2 years, failure to thrive is less of a problem because children can obtain food for themselves by asking for it or finding it in the home.

Early Identification of Emotional Problems and Disorders

Although the basic processes by which children learn about and develop emotions are similar, there are vast individual differences in the display of emotions and emotional states in children. Temperament is one aspect of emotional development that has received much attention. Each child has a unique personality. Part of an individual's personality is his temperament. Temperament affects how a child relates to his world. Temperament includes the child's predictable pattern of response and preferences.

Temperament

All children exhibit the following characteristics to some extent; it is the extremes that characterize children who show emotional and behavioral vulnerability. It is the pattern of these dimensions that make up temperament (Thomas, Chess, & Birch, 1968)

- **Activity Level.** This refers to the amount of time a child is active or not active. Children who are always on the go and can't sit still are at one end; children who are inactive and just sit are at the other extreme.
- **Regularity.** All children have an internal biological clock that can be either regular or unpredictable. For those children who are *very* regular (they get up at the same time, eat at the same time), it is important to look at the match between adult expectations, programmatic demands, and the child's typical pattern. To the extent that these are mismatched, these children can be more difficult than the unpredictable child. Unpredictable children do not have a strong internal rhythm.
- **Approach/Withdrawal.** Children have a typical response to new experiences. The extremes are to approach

without caution or to avoid at all costs through crying or clinging to adults. Most children approach new experiences with some degree of caution. For children who have had many or recent new encounters that were painful, the avoidance response may be predominant.

- **Adaptability.** Some children find it easy to adapt to change; others find it very difficult. Children who are change resistant find new routines, a substitute teacher, a new sibling, or even a new child entering the class extremely stressful. Especially at celebrations, holidays, and transitions, slow-to-adapt children need extra time and support.
- **Physical Sensitivity.** Some children are aware of slight changes in the environment; others respond only to major physical changes. Children who are highly sensitive can become overstimulated by too much noise, touch, light, and so on. They need support in regulating their environment.
- **Intensity of Reaction.** Many situations evoke reactions in children; it is the intensity and length of the response in relation to the event that needs to be evaluated. One child may cry violently for 20 minutes when another child takes a toy, whereas another child may fuss only briefly.
- **Mood.** Children have a range of moods that are a balance of happy and less positive moods. Some children are in a predictable mood most of the time; others vary considerably. Children who are predictably negative may make adults feel guilty or angry. Rather than receiving the extra attention, love, and support they need, these children may be avoided.
- **Persistence.** Persistence is the amount of time a child attends to or persists with a task. It is related to how difficult the task is and how interested the child is in the task.
- **Resistance/Distractibility.** Resistance measures the ability of the child to return to an activity after an interruption. Resistance focuses on longer breaks for such things as toileting. Distractibility relates to momentary interruptions and how the child reacts to extraneous stimuli. Distracting sights and sounds cause some children to lose concentration while others can continue.

Table 9–2 provides a method of assessing temperament in children and adults.

Temperament Styles

Thomas and his colleagues (1968) have organized these dimensions of temperament into three basic temperament categories (see Table 9–1)

1. *Easy or flexible children* are those who rate moderate in intensity, adaptability, approachableness, and rhythmicity, and have predominantly positive moods. They are usually calm and predictable and tend to eat and sleep on a schedule, although they can adapt the schedule to some extent. They smile frequently, typically approach new experiences positively, and show little negative emotion. They tend to be easygoing and highly sociable. They adapt quickly to change, and have low-to-medium intensity of reactions. Their biological rhythms are regular, they are (or were) easy to toilet train, and they sleep through the night. Chess and Thomas (1977) classified about 40 percent of their sample as easy children.

Table 9–2: Assessment of temperament

Activity Level				
Quiet	1	3	5	Active
Regularity				
Regular	1	3	5	Irregular
Approach/Withdrawal				
Approach	1	3	5	Withdrawal
Adaptability				
Adaptable	1	3	5	Slow to adapt
Physical Sensitivity				
Sensitive	1	3	5	Not sensitive
Intensity of Reaction				
Low intensity	1	3	5	High intensity
Predictable	1	3	5	Not predictable
Mood				
Positive	1	3	5	Negative
Persistence				
Long attention	1	3	5	Short attention
Resistance				
Returns to task	1	3	5	Doesn't return
Distractibility				
Not distractible	1	3	5	Highly distractible
Temperament Style:				

Flexible (40%); Feisty (10%); Fearful (15%); Typical (35%)

2. *Difficult or feisty children* are at the other end of the temperament scale. Difficult children often display negative emotion. They cry a lot and are fearful or withdrawn in the face of new experiences. They are unpredictable, have mood shifts, and are easily distracted. Although they set their own eating and sleeping schedule, they do not have a predictable schedule (Chess & Thomas, 1990). They shift states quickly and may go from sleeping to screaming in seconds. These children are slow to adapt and change, are nonrhythmic, have intense reactions, and often have negative moods. Their biological rhythms are irregular and they have difficulty sleeping through the night; toilet training also is a challenge. They are typically movers: they crawl, walk, or run, rarely staying in the same place for long. They are less sociable than other children. Chess and Thomas (1977) found about 10 percent of their sample to be difficult or feisty children.

3. *Slow-to-warm-up or fearful children* share some of the characteristics of difficult and easy children. They initially appear to have the characteristics of difficult children, but do not show the intensity or persistence. Initially, their response to new events is negative, but, given time, they do in fact "warm up," although it takes them longer to adapt than easy children. They have negative moods, but the intensity is low or mild. They can have either regular or irregular biological rhythms. Fifteen percent of Chess and Thomas's (1977) sample fell into this category.

Children with easy temperaments are flexible, moderate, and usually in positive moods.

Approximately 35 percent of children did not fall into any of these categories and were classified as typical.

A child's temperament is sometimes a challenge to adults. Some parents find it comforting to know that children are born with different temperaments and that they are not the cause of their child's temperament. Temperament affects the child's development because it impacts how the child approaches her environment, as well as how the environment responds to the child. Difficult children and easy children evoke different responses from adults. However, they don't get the same response from all adults. The key is the interaction pattern between the child and the adult, or the "goodness of fit" (Thomas & Chess, 1980).

Goodness of Fit

The concept of goodness of fit looks at the match between the expectations and interactions of the adult and the child's behavior in relationship to these expectations. A parent or educator who is up and on the go, wants to do things and not sit around, and isn't disturbed by crying and temper tantrums might be delighted with a difficult child and find an easy child boring. A parent or educator who has a cautious approach to new ideas and patience may find a slow-to-warm-up child enchanting, whereas with either a difficult or easy child, she may feel overwhelmed or unnecessary. It is not possible to evaluate child outcome on temperament alone. Chess (1983) stresses that the interaction between the adult's expectations and the child's responses is a key factor in assessing the quality of the adult-child relationship. Concern focuses around children who are "slow to warm up" and those with difficult temperaments who need

extra adult understanding but who may actually receive fewer positive responses from adults who do not understand and know how to work with these children.

Implications for Educators

Using Table 9–2, observe and record the behavior of a particular child for parts of several days or as long as you feel you need to establish a pattern. If possible, ask the child's teacher or parents for their input about the child's temperament. Compare your observational results with their perceptions and reflect on the similarities and differences. Identify the child's temperament style. Decide how this might impact your programming for this child or a child with his temperament. Now do the same thing for yourself. What is your temperament style? Which children do you like to teach most? Which children are you most comfortable working with? Which children are most difficult for you? Which children have the best goodness of fit in your teaching? Once you know this, do some hard thinking about children who may not fit as well. The adult and the environment need to be as flexible as possible to include children of all temperament types.

Educators need to be observant of and responsive to children's temperament. The goal is not to change their temperament (which is genetic and not likely to change), but to work with children in ways that are supportive of their development. This means finding time to give the easy child attention, supporting the fearful child as she learns to join groups, and setting limits, and finding ways to help the feisty child calm down. It also means acknowledging that young children do have issues that impact their emotional and mental health, and being knowledgeable about the resources to support these children.

The Evidence Base

Bulotsky-Shearer, Fantuzzo, and McDermott (2008) studied 3,799 Head Start children in 233 urban classrooms. Annual income for 93 percent of the population was below $15,000. The children were 73.5 African American, 16 percent Latino, 7 percent Caucasian, and 3.5 percent Asian or other. The children ranged in age from 36 to 69 months with 51 percent of the sample female.

The focus of the first study was to identify situational classroom dimensions where behavior problems most frequently occurred. All children were given the Adjustment Scales for Preschool Intervention (Lutz, Fantuzzo, & McDermott, 2002), which is based on teachers' observation and consists of 122 items reflecting problem behaviors and 22 reflecting positive behaviors. These reveal five behavioral dimensions: aggressive, oppositional, inattentive/hyperactive, withdrawn/low energy, and socially reticent behavior. Three situational dimensions were identified: problems in structured learning, problems in peer interaction, and problems in teacher interaction. Problems in structured learning included such things as involvement in class activities, playing games, paying attention, free play, and maintaining friends. Problems in peer interaction involved getting along with peers, behavior, respecting other's belongings, reaction to being corrected, telling the truth, and standing in line. Problems in teacher interaction included general manner with teacher, talking to and answering teachers' questions, greeting the teacher, seeking her help, and helping with jobs.

The findings revealed a clear developmental sequence with the youngest children (3 year olds) having the greatest difficulties in all situations, and the 5 year olds the least difficulties with 4 year olds in the middle of the scale. Boys had greater adjustment difficulties across all situations compared to girls.

The second study looked at the relationship between school readiness and these situational dimensions. Data was obtained from another group of 747 children at the same urban Head Start programs with similar demographic characteristics. Behavior problems in each of the three situational dimensions (problems in structured learning, problems in peer interaction, and problems in teacher interaction) were associated with low social or learning outcomes. Children with early problems in structured learning situations had a greater disconnection from peers and lower classroom learning competencies at the end of the year. Children who have problems engaging learning opportunities within the preschool setting are more likely to demonstrate both lower social and academic readiness outcomes. Children who had early problems in peer or teacher interactions had greater peer social difficulties at the end of the year (greater disconnected and disruptive play).

Children who struggled behaviorally in structure learning situations at the beginning of the year increased their levels of socially reticent behaviors and their cognitive skills and social engagement declined. Problems in peer interaction intensified when children exhibited inattentive/hyperactive problems. Knowing both the behavior problem (what) and the situational problem (where) increases understanding of what is going on in the classroom and possible interventions.

Reflective Practice

This study looked at the interaction between the demands of the classroom and the child's capacity to respond to these demands. How does this knowledge change what you might do in the classroom? Might you look at the demands you place on children during group time? How might you help children who are having problems and ensure that they are available for learning? How could you change what you do?

Introversion, Extroversion, and Mood Disorders

Children differ in how introverted or extroverted they are. Children who are introverted need more time to be alone, whereas children who are extroverted like lots of social interaction. Respect the rights of children to be introverts, but be wary of a pattern of excessive withdrawal, characterized by the inability to develop relationships with parents or peers, inactivity, excessive social isolation, and lack of affect. Children may have a favorite place in the room where they feel safe. When approached, they may react by moving away and not interacting. If these characteristics occur individually or in combination, there is a cause for concern. Children may need to be taught social skills and reinforced for social initiatives. Consistent lack of interaction will cause a child to miss experiences that lead to improved social competency, better self-esteem, and increased overall development. Settings that emphasize warmth, caring, and consistency can help children overcome feelings of insecurity. Children who are withdrawn learn from observation. If they are not part of the group, ascertain what they can see from their vantage point and maximize their opportunity for learning.

There are three significant mood disorders: **dysthymia**, **depression**, and **mania**. Dysthymic disorder is characterized by being sad or "down in the dumps." For children this has to happen for a year. This becomes the way the child is in the world and is associated with poor eating or overeating, low energy, low self-esteem, poor concentration or difficulty making decisions, and feelings of hopelessness (APA, 2000). These symptoms can go unrecognized because they are so chronic. Major **depressive disorders** can appear as a single event or a repetitive series of discrete episodes. They are more obvious than dysthymia, and more extreme. The differences are based on severity, chronicity, and persistence (APA, 2000). Children who are depressed emotionally withdraw, have little interest in the activities of daily life, have problems sleeping and eating (failure to gain expected weight), have poor concentration, often feel worthless and guilty, and may have thoughts of death or suicide. In young children it can also be seen as an irritable mood.

A **manic episode** is characterized by an abnormally and persistently elevated, expansive, or irritable mood. This is accompanied by inflated self-esteem; a need for little sleep; being talkative, flighty, and distractable; and excessive involvement in pleasurable activities that have a high potential for painful consequences (APA, 2000). **Bipolar disorder** is a condition where a child has episodes of mania and also periods of depression. Bipolar disorder has a strong hereditary base. Symptoms of bipolar disorder can emerge in infancy or early childhood. In retrospect, mothers report that their children were difficult to settle, slept erratically and seemed extraordinarily clingy. Even at a young age they had uncontrollable seizure like tantrums out of proportion to the issue, even the word *no* could trigger these episodes. Some children with ADHD may have early onset bipolar disorder or this may be in addition to ADHD (Child and Adolescent Bipolar Foundation, 2002). When bipolar disorder begins in childhood it may be a different and possibly a more severe form of the illness. It is often characterized by a continuous, rapid-cycling, irritable, and mixed symptom state that may co-occur with disruptive behavior disorders (Robb & Reber, 2007). At this point there are not separate criteria for diagnosing children with bipolar disorder. The concern is that early intervention might have helped and that the symptoms worsen and the child becomes progressively impaired.

Overall, children with emotional disorders are either too sensitive or not sensitive enough to the stimuli in their world. Their sensory systems over- or underreact to stimulation, and sometimes they do so inconsistently. Their functional development is uneven, that is, they may walk within the normal range but not talk. Children who talk may have an appropriate vocabulary, but not use it to convey meaning in a conventional sense. They may confuse words that are associated (hat and coat) or use unique code words when most children have replaced these with conventional words. They may have favorite toys they want to use and find it difficult to use others or to change tasks. Their body language communicates isolation and confusion, often lacking a social smile, eye contact, and social approach skills.

They may use their bodies in unusual ways (rocking, flapping) but also as a way of comforting themselves. Some children also use their bodies to express strong feelings by banging their head against the wall or floor and hitting or biting themselves until they are stopped. They don't seem to function in an integrated way. It is difficult to develop an accurate picture of these children, as they are difficult to assess. Educators need to be firm and kind and, above all, consistent. Keep routines the same and favorite toys and materials in the same locations.

Early Identification of Behavior Problems and Disorders

Before deciding whether or not you think a child has a behavioral problem, look at the child's environment and lifestyle. There is a difference between being "streetwise" and having a behavior problem. Some children may have *learned* to be aggressive as a way of surviving. I have taught children who would not have made it safely home if they had followed the same rules I enforced in our classroom

In the Field

A 6-year-old inner-city boy once told me: "Lady, you wouldn't last 1 hour on my block." I responded, "Germane, you're right. In fact, I probably wouldn't last 5 minutes."

Reflective Practice

This is the time to emphasize the situational aspects of behavior. Think about how you can reinforces class rules while at the same time ensuring the safety of the children you teach.

Assertiveness is a valuable asset for children. When it moves into aggressiveness, it causes concern, particularly if it becomes the child's typical way of interacting with others. Aggressive children hurt others with or without provocation. Some children become aggressive under stress when they cannot get what they want, they explode. They use aggression as a means of communication, but what are they trying to communicate?

Children who are aggressive may be fearful and anxious and use aggression as a way of responding to an inner self that also feels hateful and suspicious. These children often have poor self-images. Trying to identify the situations that provoke aggressive behavior is one place to start. However, it isn't useful to waste time on what you cannot change. You can, however, control where the child sits in the classroom, the children you sit next to him, as well as the space available for large motor activities when it rains. You need to set and enforce the boundaries of acceptable behavior in your classroom.

Start by gathering information by behavioral observations, including information about the situation as well as specific characteristics relative to behavior: duration, latency, context, frequency, intensity, and time (Salvia &

Ysseldyke, 2007). You want to answer the questions: When, where, and how often does the behavior happen? and What causes or triggers the behavior? You will also need to answer questions that are more specific to the particular situation:

Who is the victim? Is the victim anyone who happens to be there, or is it usually a particular child or a certain few children? If it is a variety of children, check if they are mostly boys or girls; bigger or smaller; older or younger; aggressive or timid. Or are the victims adults?

How does the child act after the behavior? Does the child deny the behavior or admit it? Is the child upset by the victim's crying (if that is what happened)? Does the child get upset if the victim returns the behavior (bites or hits back)? Does the child look to see if an adult is watching before proceeding with the behavior? Does the child walk away? Or does the child apologize and show concern for the victim?

Children who are aggressive in early childhood are at risk for loneliness and lack of peer support. A high level of aggression is predictive of serious problems in adulthood. Half of the children who displayed persistent aggressive behaviors at an early age were heading toward a path of adolescent delinquency and later adult criminality (Webster-Stratton, 1998). Children with these behaviors may continue a cycle of violence, including severe punishment of their own children, domestic violence, and antisocial and violent criminal behavior (Lewin, 1999). Bullying is one of the common forms of aggression children face.

Bullying

According to the Multidimensional Bullying Identification Model (Marini, Fairbairn, & Zuber, 2001), there are three components to bullying: the characteristics of bullying, types or forms of aggression, and roles involved in bullying. Bullying is used with the intent to control and harm. Bullying behavior is purposeful and repetitive in nature. The intent is to cause damage either psychologically or physically. Bullying is secretive in nature. It usually occurs in areas that lack adult supervision (Olweus, Limber, & Mihalic, 1999). The bully puts substantial effort into concealing bullying from parents and teachers. The harm that results from bullying is recurrent. Victims fear the bullying because they know that it will happen again and again. This is a significant and devastating aspect of bullying. A power differential between the bully and the victim is a component of bullying behaviors. The power from bullying can be knowledge of the victim's sensitive issues or vulnerabilities, higher intelligence, or better physical strength. This power creates fear, anxiety, and intimidation in the victim (Marini et al., 2001).

Bullying can be physical, social, cognitive, or emotional in nature. The most common type of bullying is physical. Physical contact between the victim and bully comes as kicking, hitting, shoving, hair-pulling, or punching. In social bullying, a group or gang of peers pick on a particular child. Other types of bullying use verbal threats or insults or nonverbal gestures such as glares or hand gestures to cause harm to the victim. Excluding peers from play or spreading rumors is another form that bullying can take. The goal of this bullying is to exclude or isolate the victim. Talking about someone, spreading rumors, and making obscene phone calls are just a few examples of emotional bullying (Marini et al., 2001) (Figure 9–1).

Types of aggression

	Instrumental/physical	Relational/psychological
Direct	**Physical** Shoving Punching Kicking	**Cognitive** Teasing Insulting Threatening
Indirect	**Social** Involving groups or gangs Daring, Instigating Ordering attacks	**Emotional** Spreading rumors Excluding Ostracizing

Modes of attack

Figure 9–1: Types of Aggression
Bullying can take many different forms. It can be physical, the most common type, or social, cognitive or emotional. It can be either direct or indirect. But all bullying creates fear, and anxiety and has the goal of intimidating the victim.
Source: Marini, Fairbairn, & Zuber, 2001, p.178

The final component of bullying looks at the roles children take during a bullying situation. The three specific roles are bully, victim, and bystander. Each one is affected and part of the act of bullying (Marini et al., 2001). The role of bully is the perpetrator or instigator who directly or indirectly causes harm, physically, or psychologically to the victim. Bullies tend to chose victims who are significantly weaker cognitively and social-emotionally (Marini et al., 2001). Victims are on the receiving end of the bullying behavior. Victims can commonly be described as insecure with low self-esteem, socially isolated, lonely, and having deficits in psychological and physical strength (Olweus, 2001). The third role in bullying is the bystander. These children are the largest group in the bullying situation, but may not be directly involved. Their contribution to the bullying situation can range from detached observer, to supporters of the bully, or defenders of the victim (Olweus, 2001). Although bullying seems like a minor problem, it impacts the lives of many children.

Of the behavior disorders that occur in early childhood, those identified by the DSM-IV-TR (APA, 2000) are oppositional defiant disorder, conduct disorder, and disruptive behavior disorder not otherwise specified. These disorders may co-occur with other disorders, but are characterized here as single disorders to highlight their characteristics.

Oppositional Defiant Disorder

The essential feature of oppositional defiant disorder (ODD) is a recurrent pattern of defiant, disobedient, negativistic, and hostile behavior toward authority figures (APA, 2000). This behavior is evident before age 8 and typically begins in the home but appears in other settings as well. For some children it is a precursor to a conduct disorder. Depending upon the population studied and the methods used, the prevalence rate ranges from 2 percent to 16 percent (APA, 2000).

Beneath the observed behavior is a child who does not know how to deal with the discomfort or pain of stress. They project their problems onto others and do not take responsibility for them. Someone else always starts the fight and the adults are at fault. Children who externalize stress do not accept responsibility, therefore they do not appear anxious or depressed even though the adults around them do (Silver, 2004). These children are difficult to help because they see others as the source of their problem.

Oppositional behavior is common in preschool children and should be diagnosed with care. Oppositional behavior should be markedly greater and more persistent than expected by developmental norms. Depending upon the age of the child, these characteristics play out in different ways. During the preschool years, these children often have difficult temperaments with high reactivity and are difficult to soothe. They frequently have high levels of motor activity. They may have low self-esteem or an overinflated self-esteem. As they reach school age they show low frustration tolerance and precocious use of alcohol, tobacco, or illicit drugs as well as changeable moods (APA, 2000). ODD is more common in boys than girls until puberty, but equals out after that. As expected, there are frequent conflicts with parents, teachers, and peers. Boys have more confrontational behaviors and more persistent symptoms (APA, 2000) (see Table 9–3 for diagnostic characteristics of ODD).

There are some familial patterns that relate to children having ODD such as at least one parent with the disorder or a related disorder such as a mood disorder, conduct disorder, or attention-deficit/hyperactivity disorder. It is also more frequent with maternal depressive disorder, but it is not clear whether this is a cause or result (APA, 2000). The occurrence is also higher in families with serious marital discord and in families where harsh, inconsistent, or neglectful child-rearing practices are common (APA, 2000). It has been related to inconsistent caregiving.

In some instances the oppositional behavior only occurs in the home setting and it is more evident with familiar adults and peers, making diagnosis difficult. Usually children with ODD do not consider themselves defiant, but see their behavior as a legitimate response to unreasonable demands or circumstances.

Table 9–3: Diagnostic criteria for oppositional defiant disorder

A. A pattern of negativistic, hostile, and defiant behavior lasting at least 6 months, during which four (or more) of the following are present:

    1. often loses temper

    2. often argues with adults

    3. often actively defies or refuses to comply with adults' requests or rules

    4. often deliberately annoys people

    5. often blames others for his or her mistakes or misbehavior

    6. is often touchy or easily annoyed by others

    7. is often angry and resentful

    8. is often spiteful or vindictive

Note: Consider a criterion met only if the behavior occurs more frequently than is typically observed in individuals of comparable age and developmental level.

B. The disturbance in behavior causes clinically significant impairment in social, academic, or occupational functioning.

Source: American Psychiatric Association, 2000, p. 102.

Children with ODD show persistent stubbornness, noncompliance to requests, and an unwillingness to compromise or negotiate. They deliberately and continually test limits. These children frequently ignore requests, argue, and do not accept blame for misdeeds. In fact, they often blame others for their mistakes and are angry, spiteful, and vindictive. They deliberately annoy others, but this is usually done verbally, not physically. These behaviors interfere with their social and academic functioning.

In the Field

The most difficult child I ever taught was a 6-year-old boy with defiant behavior. His antisocial behavior kept many of his classmates from associating with him, and this led to his inability to make and keep friends. He was in a vicious cycle.

Justin hated school, he hated home, and he especially hated women in authority. He would swear and kick if he was told to do something he didn't want to do. He wanted to love and he wanted to be loved, but he didn't have the social skills to do so. Justin was a loner and he had a difficult time fitting in. Children and adults avoided him and kept a safe distance.

We quickly learned that Justin hated change and that he did not like to be interrupted from an activity. We arranged the classroom so that we could decrease the likelihood of an outburst during transition. We always gave Justin a countdown so that he could prepare himself. A 5-minute warning was used and then we basically counted down. This gave him time to get accustomed to the change.

Since our centers are self-selected, we knew that Justin would always go to the art table first and get "hung up" on the activity. We modified his self-selection by stating that he had to do three other centers first and then he could spend as much time as he wanted at the art table.

We have an open snack and it is one of our centers. We always kept snack last for him because he had a difficult time eating with other children. He could handle two or three but five was overwhelming. Most of our children like to go to snack first or second so the majority of the children were done before Justin ate.

We learned to recognize the signs when Justin was going to get out of control. By getting to know his behaviors, we could often distract him or remove him before he would lose his cool.

Justin needed a structured environment. We made sure that he knew exactly what was expected during the day. After meeting with his parents several times, it became evident that Justin had no set routines at home. His house was chaotic. He seemed to relax in a structured environment. He liked knowing that a certain type of behavior would result in a particular consequence. Justin liked consistent rules and discipline. Naturally we always had to pick up the pieces after a long weekend or winter break.

Justin hated waiting times but he loved fingerplays. During transitions we always kept him busy until the last possible minute. When we had to wait in line for buses or other such necessities, I often asked Justin what he would like to sing or which fingerplay he wanted. If he didn't get to pick, I stood close to him so that he would not feel left out.

Justin was a ball of fire during circle time. He constantly pushed or leaned on children. I quickly learned that he liked to have his back scratched during sitting activities. This really calmed him down. Of course you cannot provide that constantly, but Clifford (stuffed dog) helped as did other children. Once during a lesson I noticed two of my very bright young children sitting beside Justin. Justin was attending and very calm. I was glad to see that and I continued my lesson with ease. I started to notice that this little boy to the right of Justin and the little girl to the left of Justin were putting their hands behind his back. I thought that they were holding each other's hands behind him or poking Justin to agitate him. I continued my lesson, watching curiously what was going on. I soon realized that both children were rubbing Justin's back together in a very pleasant way. I was so pleased to realize that Justin may have finally made some friends.

I believe that the most important way to deal with a difficult child is to get to know that child. You must be patient, and try to figure out what will work. Be positive because change is difficult, and the child may be living with the negative daily. It is also important to be positive with the parents. They are probably sick and tired of hearing how terrible their child is. It may be a difficult road to follow, but it is worth the journey.

Reflective Practice

Do you think Justin would qualify as being ODD? What do you think of the accommodations the teacher made for him? What might you do in addition to or instead of these?

Conduct Disorder

The essential aspect of a conduct disorder is a repetitive and persistent pattern of behavior that violates the basic rights of others and does not follow rules or age-appropriate societal norms (APA, 2000). The American Psychiatric Association (2000) identifies four specific areas of concern: aggression to people and animals, destruction of property, deceitfulness or theft, and serious violation of rules.

Conduct disorders have increased in frequency and are higher in urban areas. Prevalence rates vary widely and are reported ranging from 1 to more than 10 percent of the population (APA, 2000). There are concerns that children will be identified as having a conduct disorder when their undesirable behaviors actually have protective value. The occurrence of conduct disorder is higher in males than females and has become the most frequently diagnosed condition in both outpatient and inpatient mental health facilities for children (APA, 2000). This text only deals with childhood-onset type (Table 9–4).

Table 9–4: Diagnostic criteria for conduct disorder

A. A repetitive and persistent pattern of behavior in which the basic rights of others or major age-appropriate societal norms or rules are violated, as manifested by the presence of three (or more) of the following criteria in the past 12 months, with at least one criterion present in the past 6 months:

Aggression to people and animals

1. often bullies, threatens, or intimidates others
2. often initiates physical fights
3. has used a weapon that can cause serious physical harm to others (e.g., a bat, brick, broken bottle, knife, gun)
4. has been physically cruel to people
5. has been physically cruel to animals
6. has stolen while confronting a victim (e.g., mugging, purse snatching, extortion, armed robbery)
7. has forced someone into sexual activity

Destruction of property

8. has deliberately engaged in fire setting with the intention of causing serious damage
9. has deliberately destroyed others' property (other than by fire setting)

Deceitfulness or theft

10. has broken into someone else's house, building, or car
11. often lies to obtain goods or favors or to avoid obligations (i.e., "cons" others)
12. has stolen items of nontrivial value without confronting a victim (e.g., shoplifting, but without breaking and entering; forgery)

Serious violation of rules

13. often stays out at night despite parental prohibitions, beginning before age 13 years
14. has run away from a parental or parental surrogate home at least twice (or once without returning for a lengthy period)
15. is often truant from school, beginning before age 13 years

B. The disturbance in behavior causes clinically significant impairment in social, academic, or occupational functioning.

Conduct Disorder, Childhood-Onset Type: onset of at least one criterion characteristic of Conduct Disorder prior to age 10 years.

Severity:

Mild: few if any conduct problems in excess of those required to make the diagnosis **and** conduct problems cause only minor harm to others

Moderate: number of conduct problems and effect on others intermediate between "mild" and "severe"

Severe: many conduct problems in excess of those required to make the diagnosis **or** conduct problems cause considerable harm to others.

Source: American Psychiatric Association, 2000, pp. 98–99.

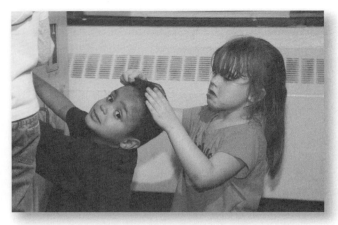

Children with conduct disorders repeatedly and persistently violate the basic rights of others.

Children with conduct disorders show little empathy and have little concern for the feelings, wishes, and well-being of others. They frequently misperceive the intentions of others and respond with aggression, which they feel is justified but may not be an accurate representation of the situation. Although there is bravado displayed, these children usually have low self-esteem. Conduct disorders are most frequently diagnosed in adolescent children (Robb & Reber, 2007). In addition to a diagnosis of conduct disorder, children may have other disorders.

Disruptive Behavior Disorder Not Otherwise Specified

Disruptive behavior disorder not otherwise specified (NOS) is usually diagnosed when it is clear there is a significant impairment, but the behavior does not meet the requirement for a conduct disorder or oppositional defiant disorder (APA, 2000).

This diagnosis may be given because the behavior itself is not severe enough to meet the qualifications of a conduct disorder or oppositional defiant disorder, because not enough of the criteria are met (e.g., a child was physically cruel to people and animals but lacked their third criteria), or because it has not lasted for 12 months. When it is clear that a child's behavior impairs his social and academic life and it is persistent the goal is to get the child help and this diagnosis allows that to happen. With intervention, the diagnosis may be changed or removed or it may show the clearer pattern of conduct disorder or oppositional defiant disorder.

Comorbidity

Comorbidity literally means an additional "morbidity" or disability. Definitions of **comorbidity** have ranged from "dual diagnosis" when a psychiatric or medical disorder occurs with substance abuse, to increased relative risk of one or more disorders occurring in the presence of an index or primary condition (Frick, 1998). Disruptive behavioral disorders rarely occur in isolation. Some disorders result from the same underlying causal factors, such as dysfunctional family processes, and may lead to both depression and disruptive behavior disorders. Likewise, there may be a relationship between two disorders such as ADHD and conduct disorder. That is, the ADHD disrupts

the family functioning, leading to a conduct disorder. Or, it may be our inability to classify disorders accurately (Frick, 1998). Despite the reason, it is important to recognize that comorbidity is the rule rather than the exception for children with disruptive behavior disorders. More importantly, the co-occurring conditions are important because they influence how we treat and educate children with these disorders.

ADHD is the most common comorbid diagnosis for children with conduct disorder, with rates of ADHD ranging from 65 to 90 percent in clinic-referred children (Sholevar, 1995). There are more children with ADHD who do not have conduct disorder than there are children with conduct disorder who do not have ADHD. This suggests that there may be different causal factors involved in the development of the two disorders. There is no widely accepted explanation to account for this overlap. However, children with ADHD are difficult to parent, making it more likely that parents will use inappropriate parenting strategies. These ineffective parenting practices may result in a child who develops a conduct disorder. Children with both ADHD and conduct disorder are at high risk of developing substance abuse problems, developing antisocial personality disorder, and being involved in criminal activity than children with just ADHD (Pliszka, 2003). The ADHD is likely to be treated with stimulant medication, but behavioral disorders respond better to behavioral therapy (Robb & Reber, 2007).

A second common comorbidity with conduct disorder is the presence of an anxiety disorder. In community samples, between 22 and 33 percent of children with conduct disorders also had an anxiety disorder, whereas the rates range from 60 to 75 percent in clinic-referred children with conduct disorder (Zoccolillo, 1993). Depression is another common co-occurring condition. As with anxiety, the children referred to clinics have higher rates (15 to 31 percent) than those in the community (4 to 9 percent) (Zoccolillo, 1993). The comorbid condition needs to be acknowledged and educational programming must take this into account to be successful. Interventions must not simply focus on eliminating or reducing the conduct problems, but also focus on providing treatment for the comorbid conditions.

The Evidence Base

Chase and Eyberg (2008) studied 64 children with oppositional defiant disorder (ODD) including 15 children who also had separation anxiety disorder (SAD), and an additional 26 who experienced a clinical level of internalizing behavior problems. There were 42 boys and 22 girls. The population was predominately Caucasian (77 percent), with 6 percent African American, 2 percent Hispanic, 1 percent Asian, and 14 percent biracial (Caucasian and African American). Comorbidity is high in psychological disorders and raises treatment questions. Parent involvement and early intervention are key aspects of treatment of externalizing behavior problems. **Cognitive behavior therapy** is typically used with child anxiety disorders in school-age children. Parent-child interaction therapy is an evidenced based treatment for families with young children with externalizing behavior problems. It has two phases. In the child-directed interaction (CDI) phase the parents learn to follow their child's lead in play situations to enhance parent-child relationships. Once CDI skills are mastered the parent-directed interaction (PDI) is introduced. Parents learn ways to lead their child's activity and provide consistent consequences for their child's cooperation or lack of compliance (Brinkmeyer & Eyberg, 2003). Pretreatment demographics for the SAD and no-SAD groups were not statistically significantly different. The only statistically significant difference between the internalizing and no internalizing groups as a comorbid condition was that the internalizing group children had a higher comorbid rate of conduct disorder resulting in higher externalizing scores.

Parents in the CDI phase of the treatment needed 5.65 sessions to attain skill mastery. Treatment continued until parents reached mastery criteria for the PDI skills and they reported that their child's behavior problems were within ½ standard deviation (SD) of the norm. Overall, the number of treatment sessions varied with a mean of 14.04 (SD=7.2) and had an average length of 18.9 weeks (SD=11.1). Children with and without SAD did not differ on these variables.

The presence of SAD did not affect the initial presentation of ODD and did not differentially influence the children's decrease in ODD symptoms during treatment. And, 15 (73 percent) of the children with SAD did not meet the diagnostic criteria at the end of treatment. Externalizing behavior decreased significantly for both the internalizing and no internalizing groups, but the children with the elevated internalizing scores continued to have higher externalizing scores.

Reflective Practice

Reflect on the results of this study. What conclusions can you reach? Do you think that some element of parenting skills might underlie the psychological disorders? If children with conduct disorders are more "severe" than those with oppositional defiant disorders does that shed any light on the results? What else would you need to know to use this information in your classroom?

Assessment of Social, Emotional, and Behavioral Disorders

The development of social, emotional, and behavioral skills is influenced by many factors. Assessment is necessary to determine if children's development in this area is harmful to themselves or others or if it is displayed in inappropriate contexts. There are a variety of ways of assessing problem behavior. Systematic observation of children in natural settings is one of the best ways. When this needs to be quantified, rating scales or check lists are used. They offer more structure to the assessment and provide focus. Mental health professionals typically use interviews to gain insight into behaviors and issues that are troubling. There are standardized measures as well (Salvia & Ysseldyke, 2007). Often a variety of these measures are used to provide a broader perspective of the situation.

One of the most frequently used assessments of child emotional/behavioral functioning is the Child Behavior Checklist series. There are profiles for children 2 to 3 years (Achenbach, 1992) and for children ages 4 to 18 (Achenbach, 1991). For the youngest children, behaviors are divided into internalizing and externalizing problems, sleep problems, and **somatic problems**. It is divided into sections that look for competence as well as problems. For older children, additional items relate to social and school functioning, and problems in the areas of social, thought, and attention.

The Devereux Behavior Rating Scale – School Form (Naglieri, LeBuffe, & Pfeiffer, 1992) is a 40-item scale that can be completed within 5 minutes and helps evaluators determine whether a child's behavior falls within the normal range or whether a child might be experiencing an emotional or behavioral disturbance. The scale focuses on interpersonal problems, inappropriate behavior/feelings, depression, and physical symptoms/fear.

Models for Understanding Disruptive Behavior Disorders

How you approach children with behavior disorders will probably be influenced by the theoretical model you used to determine the cause of the disorder and how the family decided to treat the disorder. For example, if they believe in a biophysical model, they would believe that the cause of the problem lies within the child. This model typically has a medical basis. The expectation is that the cause of the disorder is genetic, developmental, neurologic, biochemical, or temperamental. The solutions are primarily medical (often psychopharmacological) and your role as the teacher would be to daily monitor the prescribed interventions and serve as a liaison with families and specialists.

If they take a psychodynamic view, the focus would be on helping the child in the development of his personality and the process of emotional growth and change in individuals. This model would see therapy, including group therapy and class meetings, as the preferred approach. As the teacher your role would be to promote a humanistic and therapeutic school environment in which affective issues and personal growth are as important as academic success.

Behaviorists view disturbed behavior as learned responses that are subject to laws that govern all behavior. Behaviorists assert that the only difference between most disordered behaviors and normal behaviors are the frequency, magnitude, and social adaptiveness of the behaviors; if certain behaviors were less frequent, less extreme, and more adaptive, they would not be labeled disordered. Classical or operant conditioning and social learning are the three major divisions of the behavioral model. Because behaviorists place the utmost importance on the setting in which the behavior occurs, and on the events immediately preceding and following the behavior, your role as the teacher would be to manipulate environmental events to support change in behavior. You would use methods such as **shaping, modeling,** and **contingency contracting** to increase desired behaviors and **extinction, reinforcement** of incompatible behaviors, and **punishment** to decrease undesirable behaviors. You would keep track of this information using checklists, rating scales, and observation and regular recording of this information.

An ecological model would focus on the interaction of the child with others in the environment. It would view deviance from a culturally relevant perspective and acknowledge that behaviors and traits that are deviant or abnormal in one setting (school) might be relevant and highly desirable in another (the street). The model implies that it is meaningless to discuss problems of behavior in isolation from the contexts that define the behavior as a problem. Behavior is viewed as disturbing rather than disturbed, and the emphasis is placed not only on the child but also on the individuals and factors in the child's immediate environment. As a teacher, your role would be to assess and intervene in the various environments in which the child lives and interacts, such as the home, school, classroom, community, and so on.

In many instances, some aspects of several of these models are combined. For example, someone using an ecological model can develop a home behavior management program using behavioral principles.

Behavior Management/Guidance

Children with social, emotional, and behavioral disorders, whether temporary or long term, need a warm, relaxed, and secure environment. They need to be accepted as they are with the educator's attention focused on the behavior that needs to be modified. Allow children to work at their own pace. Until children can cope with the world, they may not have the energy to forge ahead academically, even if tests show they have the ability.

Many of the principles that are used to manage disruptive behavior are based in behaviorism. John B. Watson (1926) wrote about and did research on the uses of behaviorism. His work was extended by B. F. Skinner (1953) and many of the principles of operant conditioning are used regularly in the early childhood classroom. Positive reinforcement occurs when the child does something the teacher wants to continue and she rewards the child for her behavior. "I like the way you are sitting, Mia." This is done to positively reinforce this way of sitting and it is typically done intermittently. When the goal is to decrease a behavior the consequences are negative. "If you play with the hamster too roughly, I will have to put him back in his cage." And, if the behavior continues, follow through and put him back. Another way of decreasing some behavior is called **extinction**. In this instance the behavior produces neither positive nor negative consequences. Although there are many ways of coping with challenging behavior it is important that you understand the principles so you are clear how your behavior management techniques will cause some behaviors to continue and others decline.

When children have social, emotional, or behavioral problems or disorders, it is important to fine-tune your classroom management techniques. Be consistent, set clear limits, and state the necessary rules as briefly and directly as possible. However, be prepared to reinforce rules that you have. Make children aware of both positive and negative consequences. *If you don't think you can enforce a rule, don't make it a rule.*

If a rule states that everyone who plays with the blocks must help to clean them up, you need to know who played there. If a child is reluctant to help, you need to say, "Mae, you played with the blocks, so you need to help clean them up." If there is no response, you might make an offer: "It's time to pick up the blocks. Do you want to do it by yourself, or would you like me to help you?" If necessary, physically help Mae by opening her hand, placing a block in it, closing her hand, walking with her (or carrying her, if need be) to the block shelf, and helping her deposit the block in the right place; then thank her for helping. The rule was not that children had to clean up *all* the blocks. Time and physical limitations might make such a rule unenforceable. The children are only required to *help,* and even one block put away is a help.

When a child does something that you want continued, reinforce the child's behavior. Decide what specific behavior you want to reinforce (such as sitting through group time). Tell the children they can have or do something they value if they do the specific behavior you've decided on. The trick in using reinforcement is to discover what is rewarding to a particular child. Encouragement, attention, a hug, or some time alone to read in the book corner may be the answer for different children. Make your best guess and then try it. (If the positive behavior continues, you are doing something rewarding.)

When dealing with children with social, emotional and behavioral problems, be cautious about being demonstrative at first. Some children find this frightening, and some find it difficult to handle praise. Some children may not consider a hug or praise at all rewarding. An obvious ploy is to ask a child what he finds rewarding and do what he likes. Some children will prefer rewards that you don't personally like. Start with rewards you both agree are acceptable until the behavior is established. Then decide how to change the reward system. If the child finds food rewarding and you want to use verbal encouragement, use the following procedures: When Doyle does well, verbally encourage him, then give him food he desires. Over time increase the time span between when you verbally encourage him and giving him the food. Then, gradually stop giving him the food at all but continue to verbally encourage him when he does a behavior that you want to continue. The principle that you used was to present the new reward just before you present the old one that you know works but that you want to change.

Reward children's behavior each time only until the behavior becomes established, then reward intermittently. This is the way to have desired behavior continue. If you *always* reward behavior, then forget a few times, the child will decide you don't want that behavior to continue—if you did, you would keep rewarding it as in the past. (Note that the child's age and cognitive level will influence your decision about reinforcement. Some children who are young either chronologically or developmentally may not "get it." Be prepared to be flexible.) Intermittent reinforcement is a proven method for establishing a new behavior. (Regretfully, the same principle works in reverse for setting limits. If you uphold the limits sometimes and not others, the children will *always* test them. It is important to always reinforce limits!)

If you think a child is acting out to get attention, purposefully ignore the behavior—*providing the behavior isn't dangerous to the child or other children.* Make a mental note to give attention when the child does something that is desired. Give the child cues for acceptable ways of getting your attention: "If you want me to watch you while you use the computer, you need to ask and I'll come over."

The problem in an inclusive setting is how to deal with the other children. What if another child complains that when he paints a lovely picture all he gets is a hug? You need to talk about differences. You need to talk about the fact that for some children, some things are difficult that for other children are easy. Then enlist the children to find rewards that are reinforcing for all. If what Sean really wants to do is play with Steven, will Steven play with him for 10 minutes? This can be a win-win situation and inclusion rather than exclusion.

Demonstrating behavior in situations, **modeling**, is also effective, but it can be a double-edged sword. Children tend to model meaningful people, which in a classroom means they will probably model you over classmates or volunteers (and model parents over you). You are always on display. If you combat aggression with aggression, you may then serve as an aggressive model for children regardless of your intentions. Be a good model by behaving in a way you would like the children to copy. If you don't want children to yell at each other, then you need to talk in a normal voice even when you are angry.

Warning children before they are expected to do something, **cuing**, is another effective means of changing behavior. You use cuing when you flick the lights to tell the children it is cleanup time. More specifically, if Amy looks longingly at Nancy's truck, warn her by saying, "Ask Nancy if she is using the truck." Don't wait until Amy has clobbered Nancy and then say, "Nancy was using the truck. It hurts her when you hit her." If you can anticipate that the child is about to do something undesirable, try to act *before* it happens. When you sense trouble, just moving into the area may prevent a child from misbehaving. Giving a child a "teacher look" is another way to cue a child that something the child is doing or plans to do is not appropriate. These nonverbal techniques (frowns, eye contact, throat clearing) are most effective when a child is just beginning to act out. To work, they require a relationship with the child and eye contact.

When these approaches don't solve the behavior problem, you need to take a more systematic approach to changing the behavior. Write down the information that you gathered through informal observation. Then check with the parents to see if the behavior is happening at home. Gather some baseline data on frequency. That is, if hitting is the problem, wear an apron with a pocket and keep a paper and pencil in it. Put a mark for each time the child hits during the day. (This can be adapted for whatever behavior is the problem.) You can get more elaborate and write down the time, place, victim, and reaction if you want. However, the first step is determining how often this behavior occurs. Do this for 3 days in a week and put it on a chart. Mark where you begin to intervene. By using a chart such as shown in Figure 9–2, you can tell if you are making a difference. If necessary, you can show the parents your documentation of the problem.

Implication for Educators

Teach all children the turtle technique. Although there are many variations, the basic steps are the same. First the child has to recognize her feelings to know that she needs to use the technique. Think "stop" to use the analogy of a red light. Put your hands across your chest (right hand to left shoulder, left hand to right shoulder) to go inside your shell, and then take 3 deep breaths (caution, yellow light). Come out of your shell when you are calm, say what the problem is, how you feel and think of a solution (go, green light). You need to teach children how to "turtle." Initially you will be the one to issue the command "turtle." When this is done often enough children will learn to do it themselves.

Your goals are to strengthen or reinforce appropriate behavior and to redirect inappropriate behavior. Let's start with the strengthening goal. It is easy to reinforce children who do the right things. A smile, a "thank-you," a hug, or even a token reward works, but with children who don't do the right things, where do you start? Start with a principle called successive approximation. Reinforce the child at each step that brings him closer to the goal. For example, if a withdrawn child like Julie sits in her locker and cries during group time, encourage her when she doesn't cry. Then encourage her when she progresses to sitting on a chair beside her locker, a chair at a table, a chair nearer the group, a chair behind the group, then on the floor a little separate from the group, and finally with the group. Reward each stage, but don't expect her to go

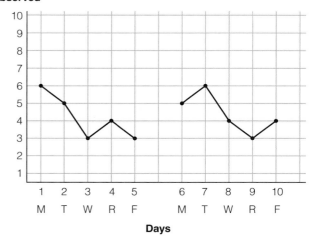

Figure 9–2: Behavioral Frequency Chart
The chart shows a pattern of occurrence that appears to be high at the beginning of the week and decreases toward the end of the week. More data would be needed to see if this is accurate. If accurate it can be used to generate hypotheses about potential causes.

directly from her locker to the middle of the group. **This process may take days, weeks, or perhaps months. Discuss with Julie where she'd like to sit. After you and she reach an agreement, reinforce behavior that conforms to the agreement. As children do things closer to what you want, keep intermittently rewarding that behavior until you achieve the goal.**

Guidelines

One important thing you can do for children with social, emotional, and behavior problems is to help them accept themselves as good individuals with behaviors that need to be changed. The most effective ways to do that are to teach children to control the behaviors that cause other children to avoid them and to provide successful experiences for them. Arrange the environment to decrease the likelihood of behavioral problems.

1. *Structure the environment for behavioral success.* Have a sensory area with water, sand, or other materials to relax a tense child. Have a punching bag and playdough to release aggressive feelings. Arrange traffic patterns to prevent congestion and long runs; make lighting less harsh; and remove toys or objects that create problems. (Make a rule that if a child brings a gun-like toy from home, it must stay in the child's locker and should not return.) Balance active and passive activities. Give children choices and warn them before changes.

2. *Plan a very motivating activity.* If children have trouble focusing at the end of the day or before lunch this will help. Children will be more cooperative and feel more in control.

3. *Maintain consistent rules and discipline.* Set limits and enforce them. Children need to know what your expectations are for them. Write them down for yourself, tell the children, and post them both in writing and in picture form. For example, draw a stick figure of a child with a block in a raised hand and put a large X over it. Place the picture in the block area. Your reminders for yourself might be to be positive and to say, "You may build with blocks, but you cannot throw them." If necessary, add, "If you throw a block again, you will need to pick something else to play with." If the child throws the block again, follow through. Physically guide the child to pick up the block and return it. Then remove the child from the block area and help her choose another area to play in. Repeat the rule: "Blocks are for building, *not* throwing." Make as few limits as possible, but if children violate these, there need to be natural and logical consequences.

4. *Teach rules and procedures at the beginning of the year.* Although you may feel this is a waste of instructional time, it is not. Having children understand the rules and procedures saves instructional time in the future.

5. *Have a consistent plan that all educators and paraeducators use to respond to particular types of behavior.* Deal with situations directly and at the time they occur. Do not ignore the situation.

6. *Communicate clearly, using language the child can understand.* Be clear about your expectations.

A child's definition of sharing the blocks may be very different from yours. Ask questions to determine the child's perceptions. Be specific. For example: "Which blocks are you sharing with Misha?" (The child points to three small blocks.) "You need to give him some of the big blocks, too, so that you each have some. Help me count yours. Now count Misha's."

7. *Teach children to distinguish between feelings and behavior.* Provide them with socially acceptable outlets that are accessible. Teach prosocial behavior and social interaction skills. Support children in practicing these skills with small groups of children who accept different behaviors. Use stories, dramatic play, and puppets to teach ways of expressing positive and negative feelings.

8. *Give children choices.* If a child is acting out or not following directions, give him the choice of doing whatever it is you are asking or, for example, sitting in the thinking chair for a few minutes. Often children will choose to cooperate instead of choosing the negative consequences.

9. *Learn more about the children in your class.* Watch how each child waits for a turn, plays with others, and interacts in a small group. Learn to read children's body language. Be aware of who is sitting beside whom. Some combinations of children provoke trouble. Intervene before a conflict occurs.

10. *Control children's behavior by obtaining and maintaining eye contact, standing close by, or gently touching the child.* Use positive, firm, supportive language.

If you use a thinking chair ensure that the time children think is appropriate for their age.

11. *Intervene early.* If a child cannot cope with a situation, take her out of it early, before it worsens. If children are having problems playing together and your several solutions to sharing aren't working, say, "There are too many children in the dramatic play area now. Who would be willing to play in another area?" If no one volunteers, ask a child. If that doesn't work, close down that area for the day. This prevents the need for more drastic measures.

12. *Insert activity breaks.* If you have planned a long story or listening time and some of the children are having problems listening, change the pace. Break for something active; for example, have the children stretch as high and as low as they can, then come back to your quiet activity. Put on some music with a beat and have a dance party.

13. *Keep waiting times to a minimum.* When it is unavoidable, make waiting interesting by singing songs, doing fingerplays, and so on. Often, behavior problems develop when children are unoccupied and expected to wait for long periods.

14. *Evaluate the structure and sequence of the class day,* especially if children seem to have problems at the same time each day. If large-group time is at 10:30 and this is a bad time for the children, consider rearranging the schedule so that the class is outside at 10:30 and in group time at 9:30 or 11:30.

15. *Evaluate yourself and the children objectively.* Are there particular behaviors that "bug" you? What is your temperament style? What is the match or mismatch between the children you find most difficult and your temperament? What can you change about your own behavior?

16. *Mediate.* Children rarely think about how what they do affects others. Children need to be told that being hit with a block hurts and perhaps told that other children might not want to play with them if they do that.

17. *Give children a warning.* Sometimes children do not realize what they are doing is wrong or irritating. For example, children may not realize they are tapping on the floor while you are reading to them, or humming while you are discussing a lesson.

18. *Make four positive statements for each negative or corrective one.* Count! It may seem to you that you are being positive, but the reality may be different. Make positive statements to children's parents on a regular basis.

19. *Be patient.* Change is difficult, both for children and adults. When you become discouraged, try to think of *one* time when the desired response occurred. If even that does not work, pretend it did and think through the result. The struggle is long and hard, but the development of children is worth it.

20. *Overall, simplify, shorten, and structure activities.* Plan to specifically teach skills other children might learn informally. Make learning meaningful and be respectful of children's work.

21. *Use timers.* If they are visual children can see how much time they have left.

22. *Use behavior management techniques.* If children are asked to do a task they don't want to do (cleaning up) follow it by something they like. First we are cleaning up, then we'll have snack.

There is one area that I think should be part of the guidelines, but I feel conflicted about it. Many people feel that a child who hurts another child should apologize. My problem is this: When a child tells me he isn't sorry he hurt Allen and he'd like to do it again, I am not clear what to do. If I make him apologize, then I am teaching him to ignore his own feelings. On the other hand, I believe that an apology is an appropriate response. My compromise has been to find out what the child is sorry about and require the apology, but not the expected one. For example, "I'm sorry I have to sit in the thinking chair because I hit you." A compromise, but consider it.

To be effective, all educators and paraeducators must use the same procedure when rules are not followed. This is particularly true when someone is hurt. Consistency works and must be established before the behavior becomes a problem. One scenario might look like this:

1. Quickly check on the victim. If possible, have another adult do this.

2. Tell the aggressor firmly but quietly that you will not tolerate the behavior (think through this statement so you know exactly what you will say ahead of time). For example, as you are walking with the child to the thinking chair, say, "I will not allow you to hurt other children." Ask the child how long he needs to sit in the thinking chair to get himself back together. (Children have little concept of time, so their responses may not make a lot of sense, but you want the children to learn techniques of getting in control of themselves and this is part of the process.) If the child's response is unrealistically long, state that you will set the timer for a specific time to come and check on her.

3. Note the time or set a timer, turn your back on the child, and walk away. Do not talk to the child or make eye contact with the child during this time. If other children approach the child, simply state, "TR needs to be alone for a few minutes. He needs to think about what he has done."

4. Thinking time needs to be developmentally appropriate for the child. A useful guideline is one minute for each year of the child's age: 2 minutes for a 2 year old, 4 minutes for a 4 year old, and so on. (Although this seems like a short time to adults, a child's perception is very different. It is far better to keep it short than to deal with the child's behavior during a long "thinking time.") In addition to chronological age, children who have developmental delays may need shorter times as well.

5. When the time is up, go to the child and ask, "Are you ready to get up now?" If yes, talk with the child about what happened very explicitly. If no, give the child another minute or so. If the answer is no again, tell the child you will help her get ready. Then take the child to a private area and talk about what happened. This is the time to talk about the incident. It is imperative that children know exactly what they have done wrong and why it is not allowed. The incident needs to be addressed. The goal is to bring closure to the incident so that both you and the child can continue your day without this hanging over you.

If particular children are especially difficult, remember that you can get help: You don't have to solve all problems on your own. Sometimes, someone outside of your setting can be more objective about the situation than you are. Ask another teacher or an administrator to observe the situation and offer suggestions. Or seek the advice of a school or community mental health professional.

Positive behavior management requires respectful treatment of all children. Your consistent modeling of respect for the children in your care is probably the most powerful behavior management tool you have. Positive relationships between adults and children and among children are the foundation for each person's feeling good about herself. Children who feel loved and respected are more likely to help and follow your rules.

Curriculum Adaptations

The number and degree of adaptations depend on each child's needs. Your awareness of short-term needs will do a lot toward the child's long-term adjustment.

Social Awareness: Self-Esteem, Inclusion, and Social Studies

For children with social, emotional, and behavioral disorders, this area is paramount. Some children may not be tuned into the world around them, and they need to be. They often lack social skills and perhaps even display an unwillingness to approach others, and because they do not deal with reality well, there may be safety risks. The classroom and community need to become familiar and safe places for them. Do a lot of preparation for field trips as well as follow-up. Make sure you have plenty of adults on trips so that all of the children can be safely supervised. Take care to keep routines a consistent part of the program for all children. Some of the activities in Resource Chapter 1 are specifically designed to support children who have social, emotional, or behavioral disorders. Activities such as 1–5 Family Book may help children who are having separation problems. Activity 1–8 Share Your Feelings encourages children to talk with others about how they feel and learn ways to share feelings.

Self-Esteem

Children need to feel good about themselves. Before children can learn to control their feelings, they must become aware of their emotions and how they respond to them. It is important to ask a child how he feels: "When I see you wandering around the classroom, I wonder how you are feeling." Don't tell a child, "You're lonely"; the child may not be lonely—he may be sad or angry. Help children learn that they are the only ones who know how they feel. Once children are aware of feelings, they can be taught to express them. If you, as a teacher, accept the feelings and don't judge them, then the children will probably continue to talk. If children are told that it is silly or stupid to feel the way they do, they are likely to quit talking about how they feel.

1. Talk to individual children about their similarities to other children; at the same time, talk about what makes them unique (hair, skin, eye color, and so on).

2. Write children's names on the chalkboard and discuss the names and nicknames of children and members of their respective families.

3. Include children's names in songs and stories.

4. Have children share some of the great things that happen to them. (Children may need support in sharing and these great things may need your help to happen at school.)

5. To help raise a child's self-esteem, mention to the class a particular skill she does well. Or point out something she has accomplished. Your statements should be sincere. Over time, do this for all children.

6. Building good character is difficult. Children who demonstrate good character traits such as honesty, respect, fairness, and so on should be rewarded. Choose this child as student of the week or whatever reward system you use. Let him do special classroom jobs that use his special trait.

Inclusion

It may seem clear to you by this point that including some children with social, emotional, or behavioral disorders will be a challenge. You are right. Children need help to feel that they are part of the group. They need to be aware of individual differences, know the other children, and know that they too are accepted and belong even when they are isolated or have conflicts with others. Plan some activities that don't demand a great deal of social interaction yet allow children to see themselves as part of the group. For example, have each child paint or color an area of a mural, or have each child contribute a page to a class book.

1. Discuss appropriate behavior with the entire class. Point out when a child is engaging in an appropriate behavior. This will be helpful in prompting children with social, emotional, or behavioral problems to engage in the behavior. Keep your eyes open for children with these disorders to "catch them being good." It is especially important to point out good behavior at the beginning of the year.

2. Talk to children about aggressive or withdrawn behavior (or whatever specific problem you have) and discuss the dimensions of that behavior: how people behave when they feel different ways. The purpose is to discuss the behavior, not the child and to generate alternative behaviors.

3. Ask all the children to think about times when they felt or acted this way (aggressive, withdrawn). If they don't respond, ask them to pretend what it would be like. Encourage them to role-play the different general behavior patterns.

4. Then ask them how they felt when they were role-playing the behaviors. (They will usually say "lonely," "angry," "mad," and so on.)

5. Ask them what they really want from others when they feel that way. Talk about how children can help each other. Give them the words: "I'm feeling lonely, may I play with you?" Some children may not be willing to include others in the play. Help them with the skills of negotiation: "You can play when we finish this game"; "You can watch and we'll talk to you." All children need skills to include others and to request inclusion.

6. Ask other professionals for help with building social skills and appropriate behaviors and friendships in your inclusive classroom. Often the school counselor or child development specialist are willing to come to your classroom to teach lessons on a problem that could be occurring (such as name-calling or swearing). This colleague may also spend time during the school day to target specific behavior problems.

7. If a child's behavior looks like it is becoming unacceptable, send them to a "Chill Out Corner." In this corner, provide short, meaningful, easy activities. When the child calms down let her return to the group. Some children know when they need to chill out and will actually ask to go. This is prevention, it is not the "thinking chair."

Social Studies

As children move into the preschool and elementary years, interactions with peers and the community at large become more important.

1. Some adjustment problems have their basis in the family. Talk about many different types of families: those with one or two children, those with many children, those with single parents, step- or blended families, families with relatives living in the home, mixed racial families, families that are cohabitating, and families with adopted or foster children. Emphasize the functional components of families.

2. Expand the concept of families by talking about different roles family members have: mother, friend, daughter, teacher, sister. Help the children see their own various roles: son, friend, brother, student. See Activity 1–31w Photograph Story.

3. Talk about the roles of community helpers. (Note that some children may be frightened of police because of a previous experience with them.) They may need a neutral ground to learn about the variety of roles community helpers play. Role play such situations as being lost, seeing a fire, and visiting a friend. Follow this up with having some helpers visit the class (children usually like the K-9 police squad the best).

4. When giving directions to get a paper signed or when telling a child to complete a project with an adult, include many different family members. For example, tell children they must get the paper signed by the adult who takes care of them, whether that be mom, dad, grandmother, or uncle. If you only mention parents, you may be leaving much of the family out of the picture. Do, however, know who can legally sign permission slips. Learn the caregivers of the children in your class and include these roles when you speak of family. Respect all family structures, don't leave children feeling awkward or left out.

Language and Literacy: Speaking, Listening, Reading, and Writing

The language arts area can help children develop the skills to talk about situations they find difficult and the feelings these situations bring about. Through literature, children learn how other children have dealt with similar feelings and situations. Children with social, emotional, and behavioral disorders require a vocabulary that helps them verbalize their feelings and communicate with others.

Some children may have learned to tune out their environment because it seemed negative, irrelevant, or scary. They will need your help in learning how to tune you in and listen again. These children may find reading and writing less threatening than field trips or spoken language. They can expand their knowledge at a time when other options are not available. Allow them time to do these activities. Writing and illustrating are potential outlets for feelings and expression. Help children take advantage of these.

Speaking

Although children with social, emotional and behavioral disorders speak, they may need to learn to focus on using language for social interaction.

1. Teach the vocabulary for expressing feelings. Use words the child understands: *mad, sad, happy, tight, hit, tense, excited.* Expand on these words to place them in a preventive framework: *before, going to be, want, ready to,* and so on.

2. Encourage children to use words to solve problems: "May I play in the hospital with you? I could be the nurse."

3. Demonstrate words, especially those associated with feelings. Pretend to be a statue or fashion model. Have the children tell you how to arrange yourself to show a specific emotion. Give them some clues about the areas to address: "I'm angry. Should my hands be open or closed? Should I look up or down? How should my mouth be?"

Fingerplays are beneficial for children because they provide opportunities for peer group acceptance and positive role models.

1. If a child has a characteristic behavior such as hand waving, incorporate it into a fingerplay or a set of motions done to music. Do this in a way that helps the child feel part of the group but that doesn't draw attention to him: "Shake, shake, shake your hands, shake your hands together." Then do something that is incompatible with hand shaking: "Clap, clap, clap your hands, clap your hands together." Ask for other suggestions.

2. Use fingerplays to "settle" children. Practice fingerplays ("Open, Shut Them") that finish with the hands in the lap. Whether a fingerplay merely quiets the children or has them keep their hands in their lap, they will be less likely to poke others.

Listening

Use listening to increase children's awareness of their behavior.

1. Give children short, simple, and specific one-step directions until they can predictably follow them.

2. Reassure children with your words and your tone of voice.

3. Tell children what to do, followed by what not to do. Children with social, emotional, and behavioral

problems need both. Give children feedback about their behavior: "Walk more slowly. You are walking too fast." (Put a hand on the child and walk with him.)

4. If children seem to listen but not understand, think about the content and whether the child has the experiential background for understanding.

As many listening experiences happen during group time, be aware of some of the inherent problems for children in groups.

1. Interestingly, aggressive children are often fearful of attack by others. This is particularly true when their personal space is invaded by sitting next to others. Try to seat these children between the most non-threatening children in the classroom. However, keep a careful eye out for warning signs of aggression. (Always placing a child next to an adult externalizes their control and contributes to dependency.) Rotate the children so that it is not always the same children sitting next to each other.

2. Frequently calling on a child who is very active, or just mentioning the child's name helps focus attention. (Do this for all the children, but mention that child's name more frequently, if necessary.) Do not pay undue attention to the child. Keep activities short and focused, give directions frequently, and intersperse moderate and vigorous physical activities with those that require only listening. For example, count the number of children in the class then jump once for each child's name. Then, do it again.

3. Children who are anxious may be afraid of talking in front of the whole class. Give them the opportunity to talk, but don't force them to respond. If this is a concern, tell them that you will not call on them unless they give a particular signal such as raising a hand, or allow them to say "pass" if they are uncomfortable or don't know an answer.

4. Children who are withdrawn may not participate in the group at the beginning. Initially, they may need to watch and listen from the fringes. As children show signs of becoming part of the group, encourage them as well as their participation.

Reading

Mastering reading readiness skills requires children to make fine auditory and visual distinctions. Although the needs of all children are similar when learning to read, choose subject matter that is relevant to the adjustment needs of the child.

1. Distinguish and label facial features. Play Lotto by matching faces. Even in simple line drawings, focus attention on the face and help children attach feelings to expressions (Figure 9–3).

2. Have children discuss moods. Write language experience stories using moods as themes. Discuss what might happen to make children feel different ways. Move beyond the obvious happy and sad.

3. Cut pictures of people and situations out of magazines (those with obvious themes are easiest). Have the children make up a story about what might have happened and how the people involved may have felt. Invent a variety of endings and discuss which aspects of situations could change.

4. Read aloud a story that has a pertinent problem situation. Stop before the problems gets solved and ask the children to predict what the character will do to try to solve the problem. Then, ask the children what they would do to solve the problem. Compare their ideas to what the character does to solve the problem and discuss it or have the children to finish the story by drawing illustrations, or in writing. Ask children to share their responses and discuss the appropriateness of solutions.

Use stories to help children increase skills in dealing with themselves and others. See the Children's Bibliography for suggested resources.

1. Read stories dealing with angry feelings and peer conflict.

Figure 9–3: Facial Expression Lotto

2. Select stories that have problem situations pertinent to the child's.
3. Tell stories about a child who learns to deal with feelings: "Once upon a time, there was a girl named _____ who. ..." (Be careful not to pinpoint a particular child or social/emotional/behavioral problem.)
4. Read *Social Stories* (by Carol Gray) or write your own.

Writing

Like other fine motor activities, writing is challenging for some children. Focus on the process, not the product. Some children may find it is easier to convey ideas graphically than verbally or using a word processor rather than a pencil.

1. Have a variety of materials available, especially large paper and large markers and crayons.
2. Help children focus on the communicative aspect of writing as opposed to fine motor skills or art.
3. Praise their efforts and call children authors and/or illustrators. Any attempts they make at communication in any media need to be encouraged.
4. Securing paper with a clipboard or taping it to the table may be helpful.
5. Scribe, or write children's stories as they orally tell them. Let them revise and edit this way. Help children use a computer to write, edit, and illustrate their stories.
6. When older children are producing a specific writing piece give them a rubric for how it will be graded. If the emphasis is on content write the rubric so no or few points are deducted for spelling and grammar mistakes.
7. As children become more skillful, begin a communication journal with them. This provides a private outlet for children to share their feelings. You can also use the journal to practice specific forms of writing such as letter writing, poetry, and so on.
8. Help children focus on a topic for their writing pieces. Then, during a writing conference, help them choose the correct form for what they want to write and teach them how to use this form.

Discovery: Mathematics, Science, and Technology

Children need positive, successful learning experiences. Encourage participation and the process regardless of the outcome. Break tasks down into small steps that can be done in a short amount of time. Science and mathematics demand little social interaction, yet they hold the potential for it. Children with emotional and behavioral disorders may be more willing to participate in small groups. The emphasis on discovery may make this area less threatening for them. Choose computer software that allows children to be in control.

Mathematics

Math skills can be taught for their own sake, but when taught as part of other activities, they can also be used to increase a child's general awareness.

1. Use math to point out likenesses and differences and to create a sense of group belonging: "There are *three* boys with brown hair, but only *one* boy with brown hair and a red shirt."
2. Incorporate math skills into turn-taking and sharing: "You can play with the truck for five minutes, then it is Lance's turn." (Set a timer.) "You can ride the tricycle around the play yard four times, then give it to Carlos." (Incorporate children into the waiting process by helping them count the four trips.)
3. Use simple card games like Go Fish to encourage peer interaction.
4. Do not play whole-group competitive mathematics learning games like clock bingo too often. These games do not promote peer interaction and may cause competition and anger in the room. Some children become upset when they lose.
5. Use manipulatives to support math.
6. Create math problem-solving activities for children to solve in small groups. This will promote peer interaction and cooperation. You may want to teach, model, and practice guidelines for working well together in a small group. If children can read, post these guidelines in words; if not, add pictures of the guidelines.

Science

A discovery approach has great potential for teaching science to children with social, emotional, or behavioral problems. They can be doing what they prefer, yet still be included.

1. Help children to understand cause-and-effect relationships as they learn the physical properties of materials: "Snow melts when it gets warm." Help them to think about this in relation to their behavior and consequences.
2. Encourage children to make predictions about experiments before they actually do them: "What will happen to the balance when you put the cup on it? Let's try it and see." Eventually, you can expand this skill to personal situations: "What might Brad do if you take his book?"
3. Teaching children how to perform an experiment while working in a group will promote cooperation and peer interaction. You may want to assign jobs for children in each group. One child may be the recorder, one the speaker, one may be in charge of the materials while another actually does the experiment. Rotate jobs during the next experiment. Remember that this will take practice, discussion, and modeling. Plan and test the experiment ahead of time to avoid problems.

Technology

Computers offer the potential for communication without the need to cope with people. For some children, this is much less threatening.

1. Start with simple programs where the children are in control and a single keystroke makes something happen. Talk with children about what they are doing. Help them begin to focus their behavior and make it

more purposeful. If necessary, adjust the touch of the computer keys to make them easier to control.

2. Children can work with the same software with little need (but many opportunities) for personal interaction.

3. If computers are limited, be sure to create a list of children's names so that each child gets an equal chance to work on the computer. Put two to three chairs at a computer so that children can work on the computer together.

4. Choose software that promotes positive relationships and social skills.

5. Encourage children to work in pairs on the computer to promote social skills, friendships, and positive peer interactions.

6. Take pictures of children with a digital camera when they are part of a group or doing something you want to reinforce. Talk about the picture with the child.

Wellness: Health, Physical Education, and Sensory Motor

Before children are available for learning they need to feel safe, trust the environment, have nutritional needs met, and develop relationships with caring adults and peers.

Motor activities help develop gross and fine motor skills and provide opportunities for peer interaction and opportunities to learn spatial and temporal concepts. Help children learn to monitor their level of activity. Children with social, emotional, and behavioral disorders can use large motor activities as a way of venting energy and participating in a group experience. A noncompetitive organization allows you to individualize activities without focusing attention on a particular child.

Children need to become more aware of their bodies and the relationship between their feelings and what they do with their bodies. They need help learning to recognize tension in their bodies and how to release that tension in a way that doesn't infringe on the rights of others. Children need to know how their bodies feel just before aggressive interactions; once this knowledge is attained, you can help children learn to substitute other behaviors. (It is much like toilet training in that respect.) Children need to become aware of their bodies before they can control them.

Health and Safety

Help children learn that your classroom is a safe place. Provide predictability and consistency so children can plan on what will happen.

1. Help children develop independence and self-esteem by teaching adaptive (self-help) skills. To teach dressing, use buttoning and zipping frames as well as natural opportunities such as coming and going home from school or outside or when playing with large dolls. Teach children hygienic toileting behaviors: Be sure children learn to wipe themselves, flush, and wash and dry their hands after using the toilet.

2. Provide children with a variety of experiences with different nutritious foods for snacks or lunches to help them learn to use different eating utensils.

3. Use cleanup time to help all children feel that they are contributing members of the group. Create a sense of responsibility for keeping the room neat.

4. Teach lessons on nutritious foods and have healthy snacks for the children to try. Talk about the importance of drinking milk and water (not juice or soda) and eating fruits and vegetables and lean protein.

5. Teach simple safety lessons about fires, electricity, stoves, and more. Many children may not receive these important lessons at home. See Activity 4–31w Not to Eat.

6. Make personal safety lessons part of your curriculum. Such lessons might include discussions about good and bad touch. The guidance counselor, nurse, or child development specialist may be helpful with these topics. Also, discuss safety in general. See Activities 4–32w Traffic Sign Hunt and 4–33w Warning Sounds.

Large Motor

Large motor activities should not be equated with being out of control. Teach children to use large motor play to run off excess energy and frustration. The benefits are obvious to adults who clean house or jog or work out in a gym when angry or upset. Children have yet to learn this.

Structured times such as group times are difficult for children with behavioral problems.

Prevent the need for discipline by encouraging children to run, climb, or ride tricycles. Encourage them to play hard until they are tired; breathless, but not exhausted.

1. If children have a long ride to school, do some large motor activities early. Work on developing fundamental motor skills.
2. Make exercise an important part of the school day. Plan 60 minutes of structured moderate to vigorous physical activity for preschool and elementary school-age children (30 minutes for toddlers) in an all-day program. The structured part means that it is planned as you would plan a literacy lesson and that you are responsible for ensuring that it happens and that you participate with the children. Preschool children do not have the stamina to do 60 minutes at one time so it needs to be spaced throughout the day. Incorporate 3 to 4 minutes of vigorous activity into classroom routines. This ensures that they happen on a regular basis.
3. Structure some outdoor time to ensure that children actually participate in moderate to vigorous play. Children with emotional and behavioral problems may become overly rough during unstructured recess and may get angry at other children who touch or tease them. Your presence and structuring some of the time decreases these problems.
4. Large motor play may let an aggressive child be part of a group and accepted.
5. Consider adding a punching bag or an inflatable Bobo doll to your room. When children feel like hitting something, encourage them to hit the punching bag—hard. Comment positively on this behavior: "You really can hit that punching bag hard." (A commercial punching bag that is on a spring attached to a wooden base can be moved to different locations, even outside. Be sure to develop rules about its use.)

Small Motor

Be aware of the timing of small motor activities for children with social, emotional, and behavioral problems. If a child is already feeling frustrated, problems connected to small motor development may increase the frustration. However, children should not just avoid what they find frustrating; rather, educators need to provide motivation, encouragement, and support for the child.

1. Encourage the independent use of small motor materials when children can concentrate on them most easily. At other times, promote success by making the activity more interesting or easier, or shorten the time expectation.
2. Use a wide variety of materials, including some of the *large* small motor toys designed for toddlers.
3. If a child appears frustrated by a particular material or activity, help the child finish the step of the task that she is doing, label for the child what this step is ("After you add the eyes, we'll put the puppet away"), and then tell the child that she can finish it another day. Children need to understand that they need to finish tasks (often they don't), so start by completing one part and on another day a little more until the

project is completed. They learn both self-control and a sense of completion.
4. Include materials in your fine motor area that children find motivating. These will vary with the group of children, but often include tangrams, puzzles, and math manipulatives. Making small motor practice fun decreases discouragement.

Sensory Motor Integration

Children need practice integrating sensory information. Some children are hyper- or hyposensitive to touch, sound, or other sensory input.

1. If children are hypersensitive to touch, allow them to wear a sweater or jacket when contact is likely. Designate personal space, and be sure all children know the rules of the game before you start. Stop the game, if necessary, to remind all children of the rules. It is imperative that children feel safe.
2. Avoid competitive games, especially chase-type games. Add a cooperative, or at least noncompetitive, component to games.
3. Adapt games so children are not eliminated. If you play musical chairs, don't remove any chairs. When the music stops, all children will have a place to sit.
4. Be sure children have good control of their hands and fingers before expecting them to control tools. Build this strength through using clay, spray bottles, hole punches, holding on while swinging, and so on.
5. Warm water has a calming effect and is useful for hypersensitive children. For children who are hyposensitive, use cold water and add ice cubes for variation.
6. Encourage children to increase their body awareness and how their body feels at various points in time. See Activities 4–25 Freeze and 4–26 Tense Me.

Creative Arts: Visual Arts, Music, Creative Movement, and Dramatic Play

Encourage children with social, emotional, and behavioral disorders to use art as a way of expressing feelings. Strong feelings can be expressed through the use of bold colors, pounding clay, and tearing paper. Draining angry feelings in these ways helps children keep themselves in control. Use music to help children relax (play soft music at rest time) and to release feelings (encourage them to beat a drum to express anger). Provide plenty of movement and large motor activities to help children express pent-up emotions. As long as there is no right or wrong movements, children can participate and learn about their bodies. Dramatic play can help children work through their fears and anxieties about specific issues. If talking directly about situations produces anxiety, have the child dress up and pretend to be someone else or talk through a puppet. Blocks can be a solitary or group experience; there are no right or wrong buildings. Encourage both boys and girls to use this area, but establish clear safety rules with both words and pictures.

Visual Arts

Art can teach children about their bodies and how to express their feelings.

1. Use activities that incorporate the child's body or name. Make body pictures. Trace the outline of the child on a large sheet of paper. Have the child color and cut it out to make a life-sized paper doll. Use water to paint the child's shadow on the sidewalk. Use face- or body-shaped paper for painting or coloring. Make a Name Book, a book about the children and what each child does and likes. Take a photo of the child doing the activity and add this to the book. Make posters or books using pictures of the children in the class. Do foot or hand printing or painting. See Activity 4–19 Body Pictures.
2. Help children use three-dimensional art media such as clay to work through feelings. Let them pound, roll, and tear clay.
3. Encourage children to paint their feelings and to use the paintings to talk about these feelings. See Activity 5–12 Mood Montage.
4. If children are reluctant to try messy activities, start with "clean" messy activities.
5. Encourage children to use art programs and games on the computer. These are motivational and allow children to express themselves through art. Help children print their creations and take them home or hang them in the classroom.
6. Have children create simple picture books about themselves. They are the author and illustrator of a book about themselves, their lives, and their feelings.
7. If you use a "Chill Out Corner," have children paint or draw their negative feelings while they are there and let these out through art.

Music

Music can be used to teach the relationship between feelings and sound. Combined with movement, it is good for energy release.

1. If children are particularly wound up and you need to calm them down, start out with a vigorous tune and work toward a slow one. Make a tape or compact disk of selections ranging from very loud and active to quiet and restful. Tape only a part of each piece rather than the whole piece so that the recording is not too large.
2. Once children have learned songs, use them often to promote a sense of predictability in a changing world. Teach new songs after singing old favorites.
3. Particular rhythms can be very enjoyable to children with social, emotional, and behavioral disorders. Encourage children to request particular songs.
4. Talk about the different moods that music conveys and how different music can make children feel. See Activity 5–13 Mood Songs
5. Music can be exciting to children. Be sure to use quiet music at the end if you expect children to participate in quiet activities.
6. Play quiet and/or classical music during quiet activities. This may help keep some children on task and promote a calm atmosphere.

Creative Movement

Children need to learn to control their bodies, be aware of their internal feelings, and develop socially acceptable behaviors that respond to these feelings.

1. Help children learn to tense their bodies like wooden soldiers and to relax like rag dolls. See Activity 5–24 Rag Doll and 5–25 Relaxation Stories.
2. Teach children that dance can be a way of letting out emotions or releasing energy. Play a variety of music with a fast rhythm for children to dance to.
3. Movement requires space. Music activities with movement are good for helping children learn how much space they require to avoid bumping into each other.

Dramatic Play

Dramatic play can be used to help children build successful peer relations and work out fears about specific issues.

1. If a child wants to play with another child or a group of children but does not know how to join the group, you might join the group with that child, play until the child becomes involved, and then slowly lessen your own involvement.
2. If a child is afraid to join in the play when many children are present, arrange some times when only two or three children may use a specific area at one time.
3. Let children see how they fit into the various roles and relationships in a family, school, store, hospital, or fire station. Let them try different roles.
4. Help children reenact fearful experiences in a supportive class atmosphere, where they can come to grips with the experience. Read children the story of the "Three Little Pigs." As children play the role of a pig, have them make a safety rule when the wolf knocks on the door; for example, never answer the door without asking who it is (look through a window); call 911 if the Big Bad Wolf is breaking into the house or hurting someone; don't take candy (drugs) from the Big Bad Wolf (stranger); don't run off with the Big Bad Wolf (stranger). Videotape the role play and encourage children to draw or paint it.
5. Encourage children to talk about things they are afraid of and discuss what to do in various situations such as seeing a snake or getting stung by a bee. You may need to include some areas that you will need some preparation for, such as what to tell children about domestic violence and drug dealing, and how to remain safe when drugs and alcohol are being abused in the family. This helps children gain some control and some strategies as well as the knowledge that they are not alone.
6. Use puppets as a way for children to talk indirectly about experiences.
7. Have pretend telephones available. Children may talk more freely when not face to face with their partner. Encourage them to write, type, or draw feelings and share them with someone.
8. Watch and listen to children's dramatic play to help guide them to act appropriately in certain situations.

Routines and Transitions

Transitions are difficult for many children. Consider the number of transitions in the day. Can any of them be eliminated (e.g., can you have an "open" snack that is available during free play rather than a time specified when all children must participate)? Keep transitions to a minimum. Provide warnings before they happen and support for children who have difficulty with them. Incorporate planned energetic play into routines by having children dance or move to a song.

1. Follow a regular routine for arrivals, departures, and moving among activities. If the adults are disorganized, the children will feel even more confused.
2. Gradually reduce the support you offer during routines to match the child's learning.
3. Some children have a difficult time coping with noise and movement and have little internal sense of time. For them, transitions may be incomprehensible and overwhelming. Adult support is necessary during these times until the child adjusts.
4. Use transitions to single out children and build their self-esteem. When you dismiss children from large-group time or while you wait for others to join the group, try:

   Singing the children's names.
   Calling last names or initials (children often are not aware there are so many different ways of referring to themselves).
   Describing an important event or fact about the child. Calling children by hair color, eyes, or type of clothing.

5. Practice, teach, and model routines and transitions. Focus on this at the beginning of the year, but continue throughout the year. Post times for different activities if possible.

Summary

We live in a complex world where children are being asked to cope with a variety of situations from very young ages. Some of these situations are stressful to families, children, and educators.

Social, emotional, and behavioral problems and disorders exist on a continuum ranging from short-term problems that may produce acute disruptive and challenging behavior to serious mental health problems. Intensity of reaction and duration influence the continuum. Social, emotional, or behavioral issues may be a child's only problem or they may be related to other disabilities. Disorders in this area are divided in a variety of different ways. Social disorders, or anxiety disorders, focus on issues related to attachment, separation, and social situations. Emotional disorders focus on mood disorders. Behavioral disorders focus on disruptive behavior. Oppositional defiant disorder (ODD) and conduct disorder are increasingly occurring in the early childhood population.

Comorbidity is common when children are identified with social, emotional, and behavioral disorders. Attention deficit/hyperactivity disorder (ADHD) is the most common comorbid condition. Interventions involve helping children learn self-regulation skills and supporting adults, educators, and parents to learn skills in behavior management.

Reflections

1. As I think about the children whose behavior has been particularly challenging for me, I find that many of them are boys. I don't like to think I am prejudiced, but it concerns me. I know there are gender and cultural differences in what is acceptable, but I feel like I need to ensure that my classroom is safe for all of the children. Perhaps I need to learn more about why children are behaving the way they are and why these particular behaviors are a trigger for me. When you think about challenging behaviors what do you envision? Who are the children? What are the issues? How will you deal with them?
2. When you teach in a classroom that includes children with social, emotional, and behavioral disorders, you are likely to have a paraeducator working with you. It is great to have the extra help, but it can also be a challenge to work with other adults as well as children. One of the issues you need to clarify for yourself and the paraeducator is the role you expect each of you to play, particularly as it relates to the child who has a disruptive behavior disorder. How do you see your role? What do you see the paraeducator doing in the classroom? How will decisions be made? Reflect on these questions, because you must have a plan when you enter the classroom.

Educational Resources

American Psychiatric Association offers information for both professionals and parents. The site is well-organized and allows for searches on specific subjects. It also has the latest press releases on mental health subjects. http://www.psych.org/

National Alliance for the Mentally Ill (NAMI) is a nationwide network for family advocates on behalf of individuals with severe and chronic mental illness. It has local chapters and also publishes and annotates books and pamphlets. Their web page is for networking with people working to improve the lives of those with mental illness; many resources are available. (703) 524–7600 FAX (703) 524–9094; http://www.nami.org/

National Mental Health Association refers individuals to local affiliations, directs a research program and a public information program, and acts as a liaison with governmental and private organizations. It has specific information for children and families. http://www.nmha.org

Pendulum Pages is a non-profit source for information on bipolar mood disorders. http://www.pendulum.org

Research and Training Center (RTC) on Family Support and Children's Mental Health is designed to promote the transformation of mental health care by increasing knowledge of supports, services, and policies that build on family strengths; are community-based, family driven, and youth-guided; promote cultural competence; and are based on evidence of effectiveness. http://www.rtc.pdx.edu

What Works Clearinghouse (WWC) was established in 2002 by the U.S. Department of Education's Institute of Education Sciences to provide educators, policymakers, and the public with a central and trusted source of scientific evidence of what works in education. WWC reviews and reports on existing studies of interventions (education programs, products, practices, and policies) in selected topic areas. They have a section on early childhood. http://www.ed.gov/about/offices/list/ies/ncee/wwc.html

For additional resources, visit the book companion website for this text at www.cengage.com/education/deiner.

Chapter 10

Children with Attention-Deficit/Hyperactivity Disorder

Jack was the firstborn child in a family with six children. He was a very happy baby. I stayed home with him while his father went to work Monday through Friday. Jack developed through infancy just a little on the early side: sitting independently at 4 months and 3 weeks, crawling just before his 6-month birthday, and walking 1 week before his first-year birthday. He was a very curious toddler. He was given developmentally appropriate toys, many of which we made: a crib mobile, plastic orange juice cans strung across the crib on elastic, at approximately 3 months of age; soft plastic books he could chew, around 9 months; yogurt cups to stack and later practice putting on the lids, a plastic container to drop small toys into, and for his first birthday his dad made a wooden box with cutout shapes to push through the appropriate holes. Jack was allowed to explore the small home in which we lived. He often opened cupboards to pull out Tupperware or pots and pans and played quietly in the living room where all breakables were kept out of sight and the electric outlets were plugged with safety caps.

In the summer he played in a small swimming pool while I sat close by and he loved to ride the lawn tractor on Daddy's lap as they cut grass together. He really enjoyed picking strawberries from the home garden just before his second birthday. Although Jack was very active, he cooperated with a schedule that included age-appropriate nap times and 10 to 12 hours of sleep each night. He ate well and grew steadily, although he remained at the tenth percentile for height and weight consistently. His most outstanding feature was an insatiable appetite for climbing. The higher he could go, the happier he was. He seemed to be "all boy." He was not uncontrollable, but very active. As an infant and toddler, if Jack for any reason missed his normal naps or nightlong sleep, he was very restless, "bouncing off the walls."

While he never attended a child care or early education setting before age 6, he did attend Sunday nursery school, where he was noted as being well behaved, but a "wanderer." He liked walking around the room and touching things. At age 5, it was clear that Jack really preferred balls, bicycles, running, and jumping to paper and pencil (which he liked for about 5-minute stretches). We decided to delay school for 1 year because his birthday was in late summer, making him one of the youngest children in the classroom. I often "wondered" if Jack might have attention deficit/hyperactivity disorder (ADHD) or just "all boy" and slow to mature. Because I had grown up with a very severe ADHD child as a neighbor,

and the fact that Jack slept peacefully through the night and took naps, I thought "no."

Jack was in private school through the fourth grade, homeschooled for 4 years, and entered the public school system for the first time as a freshman in high school. Most teachers really liked him and he was cooperative, but he was *always* losing things, flustered, not completing assignments, and for the first time failed a class: Math. At first the teachers thought he was lazy, unfocused, or just too busy with sports and girls to accomplish the tasks required of high school. But as time went on, he did not get along well with the kids on the soccer team (on which he dearly loved playing), received low grades for incomplete work and test scores, and just generally appeared to be helpless and increasingly depressed. He didn't want anyone to do the work for him, or help him with it, he just let things go. During Jack's junior year in high school we finally turned to the pediatrician for help. His younger brother was also struggling in school: easily distracted, inattentive, poor grades, and difficulty with social behavior. I began investigating attention-deficit/hyperactivity disorder. Jack seemed to fit the bill for ADHD (hyperactivity), while his younger brother was being diagnosed with ADHD (inattentive) and possibly with a learning disability. There was also a family history of schizophrenia and bipolar disorder two and three generations prior. Both boys were prescribed Adderall with great results in schoolwork and behavior. I still have some worries about the side effects, but right now I have put that aside.

Reflective Practice

Often, parents are the ones to seek a diagnosis, which often occurs *after* a child has entered school, and sometimes not even until high school. Educators also may be the first to suggest a screening for attention-deficit/hyperactivity disorder (ADHD) or possibly a learning disability when children struggle to progress (or even "tune out") in the educational setting. Mild or moderate cases of ADHD can look normal especially in young boys. Although some girls with ADHD do exhibit hyperactive behaviors, more often they are seen as "dreamy" or "air headed." Some educators and educational settings make it easier for children with ADHD to survive in the classroom. Nontraditional educational settings such as home-schooling or schools specifically designed to work with children in nontraditional ways may prolong a diagnosis or make it unnecessary. Both boys mentioned in the vignette were diagnosed with ADHD, but they did not each have the same symptoms. The second child was not as active, but was much more obviously "lost" in the classroom. He also has a learning disability, which is common among children with ADHD. The same medication was prescribed for both boys and produced positive results for each of them. Because the understanding is that the problem is caused by neurotransmitters in the brain, the medicine worked for both boys. How do you think this scenario would have been different if these boys had been in an early care and education setting during their early childhood years? When would their behavior have called attention to their learning needs? What would you have needed to do to help identify their learning needs before they failed?

Attention-Deficit/Hyperactivity Disorder

Although attention-deficit/hyperactivity disorder (ADHD) is one of the most prevalent neurodevelopmental/mental health disorders in childhood (Glanzman & Blum, 2007) there is still some debate about whether the disorder actually exists. The consensus seems to be that it does in fact exist even though there is not an objective, conclusive test for it. Because children identified with ADHD are at greater risks for academic, behavioral, and social problems and early identification and intervention helps improve these outcomes, most scholars want to move on from this debate and serve children who seem to be vulnerable to academic risks (Weyandt, 2007).

Defining Attention-Deficit/ Hyperactivity Disorder

ADHD has had many other names in the past and has many variable characteristics today. This makes it difficult to give a simple definition, but reflects both its complexity and our gradual understanding of the symptoms, causes, and interventions for ADHD over the years. The changes in terminology over time provide clues as to how we can and cannot define ADHD. In the 1950s

and 1960s **minimal brain damage** was coined to address the symptoms of inattention, impulsivity, and overactivity in children. This inferred that brain damage was the cause. This "damage" could not actually be identified so the term was changed to *minimal brain dysfunction*, again inferring a biological base in the child's brain, but not necessarily caused by damage to the organ. By the mid-1960s, doctors focused on the hyperactivity of these children, so the name changed to *hyperkinesis*. In the 1970s, the term was changed to *attention-deficit disorder* as focus was moved from activity to the short attention span as the primary condition. The *Diagnostic and Statistical Manual of Mental Disorders, 4th Edition, Text Revision (DSM-IV-TR)* (APA, 2000) uses the term "Attention-Deficit/Hyperactivity Disorder" and identifies four subtypes: predominantly inattentive type, predominantly hyperactivity-impulsivity type, combined type, and not otherwise specified.

To be identified as having ADHD, specific criteria must be met:

> *ADHD, Combined Type:* requires six or more symptoms of inattention and six or more symptoms of hyperactivity. Most children and adolescents with the disorder have the combined type.
>
> *ADHD, Predominantly Inattentive Type:* requires six or more symptoms of inattention and fewer than six symptoms of hyperactivity-impulsivity.
>
> *ADHD, Predominantly Hyperactivity-Impulsivity Type:* requires six or more symptoms of hyperactivity-impulsivity and fewer than six symptoms of inattention.
>
> *ADHD, Not Otherwise Specified (NOS):* is used for children who have a significant impairment but do not meet the criteria for the other subtypes.

The symptoms have to have persisted for at least 6 months to a degree that is maladaptive and inconsistent with the child's developmental level and the behaviors must happen frequently (APA, 2000). Table 10–1 summarizes the symptoms of inattention and hyperactivity-impulsivity.

Children with ADHD do not meet the criteria for special educational services because they are diagnosed with ADHD. It must be shown that they also have an inability to learn using regular educational methods. To be eligible for special educational services under IDEA, children may be categorized as having a specific learning disability; if their behavior interferes with their ability to learn, they might receive services as children with emotional disturbances; or they might meet the criteria for "other health impairments." These criteria are:

> [I]f the ADD or ADHD is determined to be a chronic health problem that results in limited alertness that adversely affects educational performance, and special education and related services are needed because of the ADD or ADHD. (The note clarifies that the term "limited alertness" includes a child's heightened alertness to environmental stimuli that results in limited alertness with respect to the educational environment.) (IDEA, 2004)

Children who are not eligible for services under the Individuals with Disabilities Education Act (IDEA) may

Table 10–1: Diagnostic criteria for attention-deficit/hyperactivity disorder

Symptoms of Inattention

- Fails to give close attention to details or makes careless mistakes in schoolwork
- Has difficulty sustaining attention in tasks or play activities
- Does not seem to listen when spoken to directly
- Does not follow through on instructions and fails to complete schoolwork, chores, or duties (not due to oppositional behavior or failure to understand instructions)
- Has difficulty organizing tasks and activities
- Often avoids, dislikes, or is reluctant to engage in tasks that require sustained mental effort (such as schoolwork or homework)
- Often loses things necessary for tasks or activities (toys, school assignments, pencils, books, or tools)
- Is easily distracted by extraneous stimuli
- Is often forgetful in daily activities

Symptoms of Hyperactivity-Impulsivity

- Fidgets with hands or feet or squirms in seat
- Leaves seat in classroom or in other situation
- Runs about or climbs excessively in situation where it is inappropriate
- Has difficulty playing or engaging in leisure activities quietly
- Is "on the go" or often acts as if "driven by a motor"
- Talks excessively
- Blurts out answers before questions have been completed
- Has difficulty waiting for his turn
- Interrupts or intrudes on others (butts into conversations or games)

Source: American Psychiatric Association, 2000.

be eligible for accommodations under Section 504 of the Rehabilitation Act. This act defines a disability differently and refers to a physical or mental impairment that limits one or more major life activity. Academic performance is a major life activity for children and youth. Section 504 is not an education act and does not provide additional funding for qualified children. However, it does protect their rights to reasonable accommodations and they may have a 504 Accommodation Plan rather than an individual educational plan (IEP).

In The Field

At one point in my life, when I was younger, more naïve, and perhaps more creative, Beth was in my 4-year-old class. The problem was that we had an open snack as one of the centers and Beth came in and went directly to the snack center and ate most of the snack. Other children came later and there was nothing for them. Had Beth been undernourished I might have dealt with this differently, but Beth was, if anything, overweight. I was initially subtle and talked about sharing equally, taking turns, exploring all the centers, but it was ineffective to say the least. I had heard about family meetings and class problem solving but had never tried it. With little thought, I decided to broach the topic of snack. At a group time I said "I'm concerned about the snack center because by the time some of you get there, there isn't anything left."

I called on a child who had dutifully raised his hand and he said "Yea, Beth eats it all." I was unprepared for this directness and unable to think of a way out. Everyone was nodding. I hadn't thought they noticed. "Well, I said, what do you think we should do to make sure everyone gets a snack?" The first response was "Kill Beth." Well, obviously I was out of my league. I described Beth's good points and tried to refocus the discussion. The children were adamant. I started this and apparently I would have to finish it. We agreed that killing Beth was not an acceptable solution. The children came up with a variety of solutions and then settled on one. We had a chart that showed which children were responsible for certain activities during the day (leading the line, setting up snack, and so on). Remember that Beth is sitting here during this. I was wishing I had decided to become an accountant like my father wanted. The children's decision was that Beth should be put on the chart and that one child should be assigned to watch Beth each day so that she didn't eat the entire snack. I was mortified, but I had backed myself into a corner that I couldn't get out of. So, we put Beth up on the chart and children were assigned to watch Beth on a rotating basis.

I had apparently missed a lot. Beth had no friends and no one to play with. The children on the roster were conscientious and played with her. She became more a part of the classroom and began to play with others. The snack problem was solved. She was later diagnosed with Prader-Willi syndrome (a disability that includes behavior problems and an insatiable appetite). This explained our problem. The parents were concerned, and knew something was wrong, but no one seemed able to tell them what it was.

Reflective Practice

Children are observant and they know what is going on in a classroom. Although this eventually worked out well, in retrospect what do you think this teacher could have done to control this situation better? How might you have handled it and gotten the positive outcome that this eventually got? Do you feel this was an acceptable solution?

Prevalence of Attention-Deficit/ Hyperactivity Disorder

The American Psychiatric Association (2000) estimates that between 3 and 7 percent of the school-age population has ADHD. Prevalence rates vary depending upon the population assessed, the exact definitions used, and who is doing the rating. Nolan, Gadow, and Sprafin (2001) found a prevalence rate of 15.8 percent when teachers rated children ages 3 to 18 using the *Diagnostic and Statistical Manual of Mental Disorders, 4th Edition (DSM-IV)* criteria. Prevalence rates were higher for African American children (39.5 percent) than white children (14.2 percent). Other studies have also found more African American children identified than white children (Reid, Casat, Norton, Anastopoulos, & Temple, 2001). This suggests that children are at risk of over identification and black males are probably being over identified as having ADHD (Weyandt, 2007). It is difficult to decide if the number of children identified with ADHD is increasing because the diagnostic criteria have changed confounding comparisons. The Centers for Disease Control and Prevention (2005) estimated that 4.4 million youth ages 4 to 17 have been diagnosed with ADHD by a health care professional. In 2003, 7.8% of school-aged children were reported to have an ADHD diagnosis by their parent (CDC, 2005). There is also a discrepancy between males and females, with males more frequently diagnosed. In 2003, half of those identified as having ADHD—2.5 million youth ages 4 to 17—were receiving medication treatment for the disorder (CDC, 2005).

Reflective Practice

Reflect on your background, values, and expectations. Evaluate your teaching philosophy particularly as it relates to male children. Think about the fit between these and how you might need to adapt your expectations in relationship to the children you teach.

The Evidence Base

There is concern about the number of children who are identified as having ADHD and some factors associated with this diagnosis. This study used a nationally representative sample of 9278 children in the 2002 follow up of the Early Childhood Longitudinal Survey-Kindergarten

Cohort. In 2002 most of these children were in the third grade. According to the parents' report 5.44 percent of these children had received a diagnosis of ADHD. Overall, girls, black children, and Hispanic children were less likely to have a diagnosis of ADHD. Children who lived with their biological father were also less likely to have been identified. Children who had older teachers had higher diagnosis rates. Stricter state-level performance accountability laws were also associated with higher rates of diagnosed ADHD. Children living in the western regions of the U.S. had lower incidence of ADHD. Lower rates were also associated with having a white teacher. There was no significant difference found for larger class size or the ability of school personnel to talk about ADHD treatment options (Schneider & Eisenberg, 2006).

Reflective Practice

Reflect on this information in the context of the other information in this chapter. What does this mean to you? Do you think that the move toward stricter state-level performance standards will increase the number of children identified with ADHD? How do you make sense out of this information?

Comorbid Disorders

When children have more than one disability they are referred to as **comorbid** or coexisting. Comorbidity requires that children with ADHD meet the criteria for diagnosis for ADHD and also the criteria of the other disorder. There are cases in which children experience anxiety or impaired learning but the criteria for the second disorder are not met. Researchers estimate that as many as two-thirds of children diagnosed with ADHD also have at least one other condition. Because of the numerous conditions that can coexist with ADHD and their implications for education, it is important to identify these as well. Approximately 30 to 50 percent of children diagnosed with ADHD also have an externalizing or disruptive behavior disorder (Waxmonsky, 2003).

The Evidence Base

This nationally representative Canadian study followed ten cohorts of approximately 1,000 children (N = 10,658) over 6 years. They identified three distinct developmental trajectories of children between 2 and 11 years of age based on their physically aggressive behavior. About a third of the children (31.1 percent) rarely used physical aggression as toddlers and used virtually no physical aggression by pre-adolescence. The majority of the children (52.2 percent) showed moderate physical aggression as toddlers but used it infrequently by pre-adolescence. One sixth of the children (16.6 percent) followed a high stable trajectory of high levels of physical aggression that continued on into pre-adolescence. Analysis found that these children were more likely to be boys, from low income families where the mother had not completed high school and who reported using hostile/ineffective parenting strategies (Cote, Vaillancourt, LeBlanc, Nagin, & Tremblay, 2006).

Reflective Practice

The results of this study identify a group of children, as young as toddlers, who are at risk for developing physical aggressive behavior that will continue on into preadolescence. How does this knowledge affect your response to these children and what might you talk with their parents about? What could you do to change this trajectory?

There is considerable overlap with ADHD and mood disorders (depression, anxiety), estimates range from 14 percent to 83 percent. Overlap with bipolar disorder is only now being studied, and estimates range from 10 percent to 20 percent. Anxiety disorders occur in about 25 percent of children with ADHD. There is debate about the overlap with specific learning disabilities and these estimates range from 10 percent to 40 percent (Spencer, Wilens, Biederman, Wozniak, & Harding-Crawford, 2000; Glanzman & Blum, 2007; Weyandt, 2007; Kronenberger & Dunn, 2003). Although these disorders may accompany a primary diagnosis of ADHD, they also may be found alone or in various combinations without ADHD.

Implications for Educators

In addition to ensuring that your personal values and expectations do not influence the identification of children with ADHD, educators need to develop the skills to adapt curriculum for children with ADHD and possible comorbid conditions whether or not they reach the criteria for identification.

Causes of Attention-Deficit/Hyperactivity Disorder

It is estimated that between 60 to 90 percent of children with ADHD inherited it from their parents (Kuntsi et al., 2005). No specific gene or combination of genes has been identified as causing ADHD. However, there is much research going on in the field looking for such a connection. Many studies have found a relationship between genes involved in the production, regulation, and functioning of the neurotransmitter dopamine and behaviors related to ADHD (Asherson, Kuntsi, & Taylor, 2005). **Dopamine** is involved in the ability to modulate attention and behavioral regulation in the frontal cortex. **Norepinephrine**, another neurotransmitter, plays a role in orienting attention and regulating alertness, which is also in the frontal cortex (Glanzman & Blum, 2007).

Clearly the **cerebral cortex** of the brain is involved, the **limbic system**, the **basal ganglia**, and the **reticular activating system** are involved in ADHD (Silver, 2004). As scientists learn more they may be able to identify the specific sites and neurotransmitters that are causing the problem.

Conditions that predispose the brain to develop ADHD include prenatal exposure to lead, alcohol, nicotine, and possibly cocaine; prematurity or low birth weight; brain infections; and certain genetic syndromes. Complications during labor and delivery and infancy seem to impact the brain, but how this happens is not clear (Glanzman & Blum, 2007).

The frontal lobe of the brain processes incoming stimuli and coordinates it with appropriate responses. This part of the brain in children with ADHD is different in subtle ways and this area of the brain may be compromised (Glanzman & Blum, 2007). Neuroimaging technology has enabled researchers to compare the brain activity of individuals with ADHD to those who are not identified. They can also see the effect that specific medication has on parts of the brain. Specifically, they have found that certain structures in the right prefrontal region of the brain are smaller in individuals with ADHD. Interestingly, maturation in these circuits continues into the third decade of life, which could account for the fact that many children with ADHD show progressive improvement in symptoms as they enter their 30s and 40s (Castellanos et al., 2001).

Many people assume that, because glucose is the energy source used by the brain, an excess of sugar would lead to an excess of brain activity, perhaps leading to hyperactivity. Empirical studies have not found food additives or sugar to be a cause of ADHD. Allergies to specific foods and dyes and reactions to refined sugar have not stood up to scientific evidence in spite of the advocates who claim their effect on the attention and behavior of young children (Weyandt, 2007).

Effective parenting makes a difference in all children. Lack of parenting skills does not cause ADHD, however, it can exacerbate the condition. Researchers have found that difficult children tend to evoke more commands and negative feelings from parents. Being consistent and following through to the resolution of conflicts is difficult. Parents may be challenged much more often and with greater intensity by a child with ADHD. Conduct disorders and oppositional defiant disorders are more common in children with ADHD than in the general population, further confounding the relationship between parenting and ADHD. The presence of these disorders in children stresses the parenting process. However, all children diagnosed with ADHD will not look alike due to comorbidity, personality, temperament, and environmental influences. We have tantalizing pieces of the puzzle related to ADHD, but we have yet to find all of the pieces and know what the puzzle will look like when it is put together. Educators find themselves trying to assemble this puzzle beginning with questions about whether a child might have ADHD.

Early Identification of Attention-Deficit/Hyperactivity Disorder

It is unlikely that children birth to 3 would be identified as ADHD as it is difficult to determine the difference between very active infants and toddlers who are displaying developmentally appropriate behaviors for their age and those who might have ADHD. However, the peak age of onset is between 3 and 4 years of age (Barkley, 1998). Yet, most children are not referred for diagnosis until between 7 and 9 years of age (DeWolfe, Byrne, & Bawden, 1999).

Implications for Educators

As an educator, you and the child's family are likely to be part of the early identification process. Thus, knowledge of the identification process and characteristic behaviors is important. Identifying children with ADHD is difficult,

because during the early childhood years, many of the characteristics of ADHD are characteristics of normally developing children. It is more a matter of degree than whether or not a behavior is present. However, children with a *difficult* temperament may be at risk. Children who have a high activity level, do not adapt well to changes in the environment, have intense reactions, have unpredictable routines, and have difficulty sleeping and eating are challenging to even the most competent parents.

If pediatricians began to routinely screen for children with difficult temperaments, we could begin to provide parents with resources to increase their competence in parenting, whether or not the child was later identified as having ADHD. To the extent that families, educators, or caregivers become anxious, irritated, and angry at these children because of their inability to manage their behavior, problems will be exacerbated.

As children move into the preschool years, power struggles between parents and children escalate. Predictable patterns of eating and sleeping have not emerged, and frequently toilet training has not been completed. As children move into group settings, the child may be labeled immature. The characteristics of ADHD during the preschool years frequently leads to judgment of immaturity. Whenever this label is used, the question should be asked, "Is the child immature or does he display some characteristics of ADHD?"

There are other warning signals in the medical realm. Children later identified as ADHD have frequent ear infections; there is also a high incidence of allergies, asthma, and other respiratory problems. Early care and education settings allow and expect a wide range of social, emotional, and cognitive development. A child's inability to master specific age-expected tasks may have been unnoticed or attributed to immaturity.

Although there is a lack of agreement about what ADHD actually looks like in preschool children they are increasingly being diagnosed and treated for this disorder (Connor, 2002). Key factors in children being diagnosed in the preschool years are

- Displaying symptoms of ADHD very early and at a much more severe level than is developmentally expected.
- When symptoms are apparent in a variety of contexts (school and community) not just the home.
- When symptoms continue after a developmental stressor (the birth of a sibling) (Connor, 2002).

Implications for Educators

Identification of children with ADHD may be confirmed during the preschool years. Three year olds, who are very intense in their reactions to the environment, particularly when these reactions are usually negative, are of concern. Also, children identified as having speech and language problems are at risk for ADHD. Other at-risk children are those who lack good problem-solving strategies as well as those who cannot delay their response to an inviting stimulus, whether a toy another child has or a cookie. These children don't seem to develop the early skills necessary for making and keeping friends. Children who are impulsive, noncompliant, and fearful may also be at risk.

Children who seem unable to plan or accept limits. Motor clumsiness may become apparent as children take over more responsibility in dressing, toileting, tying shoes, cutting, coloring, and writing.

As children reach elementary school, some of the characteristics of ADHD become more apparent and the implications more obvious. The demands on children to perform specific skills at specific times and in specific ways may be daunting to the child with ADHD. Teachers give tests and grade them and send the results home on report cards (if they wait that long). Some children do not perform well in school, often fail to finish assignments, may become disruptive in class, may experience poor social relations, and may be easily frustrated. They may have a very short attention span and show some aggressive or even oppositional behavior. Children frequently are moved to the lowest math and reading groups. If they become disruptive, they lose instructional time because they are in the principal's office. The hyperactive child may become a bully. The inattentive child may be perceived as weird. Because of impaired social skills, the child with ADD (frequently girls) may be lonely, isolated, and lack friends. Organized extracurricular activities begin to play a role in children's development. For some children, sports such as soccer and baseball may be an opportunity for success and acceptance. For others, it will be another area of failure and rejection. Look at the whole child in the context of where he lives and grows.

When children spend tremendous amounts of energy keeping themselves under control during school hours, they may let it all out when they come home. Battles ensue

Girls with attention deficit disorder may appear lonely, dreamy or just not paying attention.

over homework, chores, mealtime, bedtime, and so on. As children get up to face another day, they dawdle to keep from having to go to school while parents are trying to get themselves off to work and other children off to school as well. It may be only 8:30 A.M., but parents may feel that they have already put in a full day's work.

Assessment of Attention-Deficit/ Hyperactivity Disorder

Although there is no one way to diagnose ADHD, most professionals use multiple measures to tap into its various aspects. These include behavioral rating scales, structured interviews, measures of attention, and hyperactivity and impulsivity and structured observations (Smith & Corkum, 2007).

Typically, parents are interviewed to obtain information about the child's developmental, medical, and family history, as well as information about the child's behavior, academic progress, and psychosocial relationships. Parents are also asked to fill out rating scales. Additional information would be obtained by interviewing the child, his self-report, a medical/neurologic examination and a psychoeducational assessment (Stein, Efron, Schiff, & Glazman, 2002). The psychoeducational assessment is designed to look for overlap with specific learning disabilities. Most clinicians use the diagnostic criteria developed by the APA (2000) and published in the **DSM-IV-TR** as the starting point for diagnosis.

A history will typically be gathered from the parents. Parents, early childhood educators, and others who have observed the child's behavior in different settings may be asked to fill out formal observation scales. There are a variety of formal rating scales and behavior checklists used to help in this process including the Conners' Teacher Rating Scale (Conners, 1997); the ADD-H Comprehensive Teacher's Rating Scale (Ullman, Steator, Sprague, & Metritech Staff, 1996); and the Child Behavior Checklist for Ages 4–18 (Achenbach, 1991). These tools are useful, but teachers and others may have a different view of behaviors, and the child may display different behaviors in different settings. Early childhood educators view the child in the context of the children in the classroom, whereas the parents may see the child only in the context of the home and with siblings or neighborhood children. The different perspectives add both confusion and information.

In addition to the information obtained in the checklist the focus should be on three tasks:

1. The child's ability to seek out what he wants and then attend to and focus on it.
2. The child's ability to maintain this focus.
3. When finished, the child's ability to stop attending and to move on to something else (Sliver, 2004).

Implications for Educators

As a teacher, you may be one of the first to suspect that a child may have ADHD. The question is when does a child exhibit enough of the characteristic behaviors for a long enough time for you to talk with the parents? Before approaching parents, look at the cultural background of the family and learn something about the family's expectations. Information about any child needs to be evaluated within the context of the family and the culture.

If further information sheds no light on the behavior, observe the child over a span of time to get a representative look at his behavior. Then construct a simple behavioral checklist that focuses attention on areas identified by the APA as criteria for identifying children with ADHD. First, decide how much a particular behavior describes the child on a given day. Then note the behaviors that you observed to form that opinion. Do this for several days and ask other adults in the classroom to do the same. Also observe one child of the same gender who is about the same age whom you think is developing typically. Your form may resemble Figure 10–1.

Your observations should be systematic and the behavior observed should have necessary detail: "Sheila knocked over the juice while reaching for the crackers with her left hand." Write down the details as you see them. Keep your facts objective. The most important part of observing is to look for patterns. You will have to observe for several days or weeks to get enough data for patterns to emerge. Whether or not you decide to talk with the parents about your observations, you will have a more accurate picture of the child. This information is useful in targeting program goals.

It is also useful to include peers in the evaluation process, as ultimately it is the peers who will decide who they are willing to include in their play and who they are not, as well as who they choose to be friends with. Teachers may accept some aggressive behavior as being part of the syndrome a child has, whereas peers are less forgiving—hitting is hitting!

Attention Disorders and Associated Problems

Children with ADHD have challenges monitoring their behavior. This inability to prioritize and inhibit responses interferes with their academic achievement. They may also have problems in the area of sensory motor integration, which interferes with the development of adaptive skills and the attainment of skillful locomotion.

Executive Function is the system within the brain that uses cognitive control and future-oriented processes to make decisions (Shapiro et al., 2007). It underlies good organization. Successful people use schedules, organize time, set priorities, concentrate on complex tasks, and minimize inefficiency. People who have dysfunction in this area are inefficient and often nonproductive. Children who have problems in executive function have trouble organizing and prioritizing information, sustaining attention, planning, self-monitoring, and inhibiting responses (Shapiro, Church, & Lewis, 2007). Academically they are underachievers even if they have a high IQ (Denckla, 2003). They acquire skills but do not use them effectively.

Academic Underachievement is one of the markers of ADHD during the school years and more than 50 percent may require academic tutoring (Barkley, 1998). Although children may not reach the criteria for a specific learning disability, they frequently have problems learning to read and dealing with the mechanics of writing. They may struggle to figure out what is important.

Developmental Coordination Disorder or just clumsiness in general may make a child the last chosen for teams

ADHD: Inattention	Perceived frequency	Actual frequency*
1. Makes careless mistakes		
2. Does not follow through		
3. Disorganized		
4. Loses things		
5. Inattentive		
6. Distractible		
7. Does not seem to listen		
8. Avoids challenging tasks		
9. Forgetful		
ADHD: Hyperactivity–Impulsivity		
10. Fidgets, squirms		
11. Leaves large, small group activities		
12. Runs, climbs excessively, inappropriately		
13. Trouble playing quietly (books, manipulatives)		
14. Seems always "on the go"		
15. Talks excessively		
16. Blurts out answers		
17. Trouble taking turns, waiting for turn		
18. Interrupts, butts into activities and conversations		

#1-1	Antecedent behavior	
	Behavior	
	Consequences	
	Comments	

#1-2	Antecedent behavior	
	Behavior	
	Consequences	
	Comments	

Key:
M = Frequently, more than other children
S = Sometimes, same as other children
R = Rarely, less than other children

*Use numbers to count actual frequency and put numbers in the comments section and clarify the antecedent behavior, the behavior itself, and the consequences.

Figure 10–1: ADHD Observation Form
When children's behaviors are irritating or cause problems in the classroom, it is sometimes difficult to sort out their actual occurrence from perceived occurrence. It is important to differentiate between these two, particularly when you are responding to questions about the effects of different medications and/or behavioral interventions. Before you begin using a form such as Figure 10–1, start by reflecting on your class as a whole and then the particular child relative to the class. Then fill out the perceived frequency in Figure 10–1. Over the course of several days or a week, look at the relationship between your perceptions and the actual occurrences and the behavior itself, what preceded it, and what happened afterwards. These insights will provide information to respond to questions and to develop a plan of action.

and may make sports a challenge. This also places the child at greater risk for accidental and nonaccidental injuries. Children may get themselves into difficult situations more frequently and have fewer skills to get out. Some of their behaviors may irritate adults and peers and put them at risk for abuse (Stein et al., 2002).

Adaptive skills may be slower to develop; rather than waiting for children to perform certain tasks, parents may decide that it is just easier to do it for them. This is a good short-term solution, but has serious long-term implications.

Impulsiveness means acting quickly, without planning and thinking about the consequences of actions. Children seem to have a short fuse. They act before they think, and they rarely learn from past experience, because they don't give themselves time to reflect on previous experiences and their outcomes.

Distractibility—is having problems attending to a task. Children's attention and even their bodies seem to be drawn elsewhere. They do not have the ability to redirect their attention back to the original task once it has wandered. Children's seeming disinterest and inability to complete tasks is not always a disadvantage; sometimes, they notice new connections and come up with imaginative solutions to problems.

Short attention span—means children do not stay at tasks for long. They rarely finish tasks or get satisfaction from them.

Inability to follow directions—can relate to a lack of understanding the directions or understanding, but then forgetting what was asked.

Hyperactivity—is too much activity or motion that is not goal-oriented. Children seem distracted by and need to respond to all environmental stimuli. Even when sitting, these children are not quiet; they may twitch, jerk, or rock. As they get older, the hyperactivity may be displayed in nonstop talking as well as nonstop moving. The hyperactivity is chronic and unrelated to specific events.

Hypoactivity—is too little activity. Children appear to move in slow motion. They may seem listless, bored, or sleepy. Every movement seems to require a lot of effort.

Perseveration—is starting a task without the ability to stop. A child rolling a playdough snake may roll snakes all morning long if not interrupted. It is as if the child is not capable of refocusing attention once it has been focused: The child can't change channels. This may be a way of coping with distractions.

Awkwardness—is clumsiness where children frequently bump into things or people, knock things over, and trip over their feet or other objects.

Social problems—may occur because children may do things that irritate others. They are more likely than other children to be in conflict with their peers. They have difficulty recognizing social cues and using social skills. They don't read others' body language accurately and hence make wrong assumptions and act inappropriately.

Family problems—lack of social skills is apparent in the home as well. Children's frustrations and failures affect families and family relationships. Parents may disagree on how to cope with troubling behavior, causing additional stress on relationships. Siblings may feel that there is a double standard applied to behavior and chores. Even as they begin to understand about learning disabilities, they may feel both guilt and anger (Shapiro, Church, & Lewis, 2002; Shapiro et al., 2007; Silver, 2004).

Overall, in evaluating a child with ADHD, one has to take into account the child's developmental level, the context in which he lives, and the possibility of both a variety of comorbid disabilities and the reality of those that are problematic but do not reach criterion.

Medical Treatment of Attention-Deficit/Hyperactivity Disorder

When a child is referred to a medical professional, the process focuses on four aspects of the diagnosis: (1) the symptoms of ADHD, (2) whether other conditions might

be causing the symptoms, (3) comorbid conditions, and (4) associated conditions that might not have enough symptoms to be diagnosis but could interfere with the child's life and should be part of the treatment plan (Glanzman & Blum, 2007). Although the process may vary, it should be a multimethod assessment (Weyandt, 2007). The presence of associated problems also needs to be explored.

Many factors can cause children to have symptoms similar to ADHD. A number of physical and psychiatric problems should be ruled out before a diagnosis of ADHD is made. Inattentiveness, impulsivity, and underachievement can be found in children with emotional and behavioral disorders and those who are depressed. Children should have a medical examination to rule out medical problems such as sensory problems, motor disabilities, seizures, thyroid disease, allergies, intellectual disability, and pervasive developmental disorders (Glanzman & Blum, 2007).

The evaluation team for determining ADHD usually involves the family, the family physician or pediatrician, a child psychologist or psychiatrist, a neurologist, a family counselor or therapist, and a teacher or early childhood educator. Research indicates that diagnostic certainty is increased by the number of informants (Weyandt, 2007). Accurate diagnosis is important because it dictates follow-up treatment. It is important to rule out conditions that mimic attention disorders.

Although a direct cause for ADHD has not been found, there is agreement that it has a physiological base and that some of the problems are related to neurotransmitters. In addition to educational interventions, about half of children identified with ADHD also have a pharmacologic intervention (CDC, 2005).

Medication

Twenty years ago, medication was considered a last resort for treating ADHD. Today, medication is recognized as a first line of treatment for ADHD children, and the emerging consensus is that medication should be used sooner rather than later. Mental health professionals consider medication the most effective treatment. A greater variety of drugs are now prescribed. More precise diagnostic practices enables individually tailored multimodal approaches that combine the use of medication with behavioral interventions (Weyandt, 2007). Stimulant medications are most commonly prescribed for children with ADHD.

Let's begin with the medication itself and how it works. **Stimulants** increase the level of arousal of the central nervous system (CNS). Although this may seem strange, research suggests that children with ADHD are underaroused and that their hyperactivity is a way of increasing arousal (Weyandt, 2007). Stimulant medications interact with the biogenic amine transporters (**dopamine, norepinephrine, and serotonin**). Their actions increase the availability of these neurotransmitters, primarily dopamine (Stein et al., 2002). Research shows positive effects of stimulant drugs on decreasing impulsivity and hyperactivity. The short-term and intermediate-term effects remain positive. The long-term effects are not as well-studied (Glanzman & Blum, 2007).

There are primarily two kinds of stimulants: **methylphenidate stimulants** and **amphetamine stimulants**. Although similar, they act on the brain in slightly different ways. The methylphenidate stimulants block the dopamine transporter; because there are fewer available transporters, there is increased dopamine at the synapses. The amphetamines work by increasing the release of biogenic amines in general. Methylphenidate (Ritalin, Concerta, Metadate) is the most commonly prescribed stimulant for children (Zito et al., 2003). Most stimulants are available in two forms: short-acting (given twice or more a day) and sustained-release (given once a day). The sustained-release form can be given to a child before he goes to school. This eliminates the need to have medication taken at school and ensures some confidentiality. The dosage and type of stimulant used should be individually determined (Weyandt, 2007). Medication is increasingly being prescribed for preschool children (Zito et al., 2000).

Implications for Educators

As an educator it is important that you know when and if the medication has been taken and how long it is likely to be effective. You should also know about the specific side effects and what to look for. Families make decisions about whether or not their child should be on stimulant medication and the medical community tries to select the most appropriate medication for the child. Your role is to observe the child and provide accurate feedback about the child's behavior in the classroom.

In The Field

As a special educator who teaches 7 and 8 year olds, I have worked with many children who have attention-deficit/hyperactivity disorder. I have learned to work with most of these children very successfully over the years. I currently have a student in my class, Nikki, who displays all of the symptoms of attention-deficit disorder without hyperactivity. Nikki often loses focus during lessons and cannot work on an assignment or an activity for a sustained period of time. She also has problems keeping her hands out of her desk. Nikki's main difficulty, however, is staying focused during reading and writing times; she usually only sits quietly.

Nikki only has a minor learning disability, but I feel that her attention problems are seriously affecting her grades and learning. She cannot pay attention long enough to master new concepts and skills. As a result, I have contacted her parents and discussed the issue with them. Nikki's mother mentioned that it takes about 4 hours a night to complete homework—and this is when she sits right by Nikki's side. (Most other children report completing the homework in less than an hour.) Nevertheless, they downplayed any concern and said that sometimes Nikki just doesn't feel like doing work. I suggested they take Nikki to the family physician and to mention my concerns. I even sent home an ADD/ADHD checklist that they could also take to their physician; the checklist did substantiate my theory that Nikki had a problem with paying attention. However, the doctor visit never happened.

Nikki's parents will not consider the fact that Nikki may have ADD. Even after mentioning the subject at our many meetings, the parents have not acted in any way to help their daughter. Nikki's father did once mention that he did not believe in medication for children. I wanted to scream out loud at him, "If your daughter had diabetes, would you provide her with insulin?" To me ADD is the same as any other disease or disorder. This child will continue to suffer, learn less, and get very poor grades until these parents decide to help their daughter. I feel a mind is being wasted.

Reflective Practice

How do you feel about the use of medication for young children who may have ADHD or ADD? Do you think this teacher is justified in her feelings? What might you do in her situation? How would you respond to a parent who asked you about the efficacy of using stimulant medication on her 6-year-old child who was diagnosed with ADHD? Could you explain to her how it works?

Efficacy of Medications

There are few studies of the efficacy and safety of stimulant medication for preschool children. With school age children and older who have average intelligence, the drugs have been effective. However, parents in particular are concerned about the side effects of taking stimulant medication. The major side effects include weight loss, sleep disturbances, headaches, stomachaches, and mood changes (Weyandt, 2007). There is some concern that preschool age children might be more susceptible to the side effects than older children (Connor, 2002).

If stimulant medication is recommended for a child, it typically starts with a low dose and is increased gradually (perhaps every couple days or over the course of a week) until a response is evident or until side effects develop. Other protocols use different dosages and compare the results. During this time teachers may be asked to fill out daily or weekly behavior rating forms. (The teacher does not know the medication regimen.) Often one week on and one week off are compared. Stimulants work immediately; they do not need to build up in the body. Families need to make decisions about when they feel the benefits of medication outweigh the concerns. Some children do not receive medication after school, on weekends, and during the summer. This is particularly true if children's rate of growth begins to decelerate. Children need to be monitored on a regular basis (every 3 to 6 months) to ensure proper growth and nutrition and to determine if the medication is still required (Glanzman & Blum, 2007). Although the short-term benefits seem to be well-documented, many questions remain about the long-term effects.

In The Field

I am a boy in first grade in Mrs. Michael's class. Sometimes I am bad in school but I can't help it. I try to be good for Mrs. Michael, but I always seem to get put in time-out. It isn't fair. She picks on me. Sometimes when my Mommy forgets to give me my medicine I have lots and lots of energy in school. It is hard to sit still. I get yelled at for talking. I am not a bad boy and I want to be good. Sometimes I just cry.

Developing a 504 Accommodation Plan

Children with disabilities recognized by the IDEA are entitled to an Individualized Education Program (IEP). Children with ADHD are not included in the disabilities served under the IDEA. They may receive special education because of comorbid conditions (e.g., specific learning disabilities or emotional disorders) or under "other health impairment" (IDEA, 2004). If these conditions do not exist, a child may qualify for a 504 Classroom Accommodation Plan. The Rehabilitation Act of 1973, an antidiscrimination law, requires public schools to provide accommodations for children with ADHD (all subtypes). The definitions of disabilities that receive services under the Rehabilitation Act of 1973 are different from those in the IDEA. ADHD is included because it is a "physical or mental impairment which substantially limits a major life activity" (learning).

There is a three-step process for creating a classroom accommodation plan (Blazer, 1999).

1. *Talk with the parents and child.* Children as young as 5 years of age can be included in creating their plans. They often know better than others what would make school easier. At this point, you may have to give parents some guidance on the types of accommodations available under Section 504.

   - Physical accommodations may include the following: posted class rules, color codes, preferential seating, reorganized work space, an extra seat or table, a standing workstation, a quiet area to study, and so on.
   - Instructional accommodations may include the following: repeated and simplified directions with additional directions provided in written form; individualized homework assignments that reduce the volume of work and extended deadlines, alternative assignments, and an extra set of textbooks; assignments requiring technological learning aids (e.g., tape-recorded assignments, word-processed assignments, and multisensory manipulatives).
   - Behavioral accommodations may include the following: to promote consistency with posted rules—positive reinforcement, verbal or written feedback, reward systems and incentives, private signals, role playing, and clearly articulated rewards and consequences for actions; to promote leadership and accountability, assigned jobs that can be performed well (e.g., line leader), clearly defined goals with incentives and reinforcements (through student contracts, an incentives chart,

and reward system), and communication between parents and teachers (phone calls, email, daily or weekly book or diary, and so on).

Use a form that children are familiar with, such as a webbing, draw a chart or create a poster, and have children decide what they want and what would make it easier for them to learn (Figure 10–2). Children may keep this form (perhaps laminated) so they know the accommodations to which they are entitled.

2. *Teacher input/agreement.* This is a more formal step that is written by the teacher(s) and appropriate school personnel. It involves not only listing the accommodations, but also determining whether or not they are achieving their purpose. Teachers provide input about the accommodations they are currently using, how successful they are, and what is still challenging. If, for example, the teacher has allowed the child to do her spelling homework on the computer, and spell-check it, and the child is getting 100 on the Friday spelling test, the accommodation would be considered very effective. On the other hand, if the child continues to fail the spelling test, a different accommodation would be needed. The effectiveness of an accommodation is related to child outcomes. Children with ADHD are not expected to learn less; they may need to approach learning by a different route.

3. *Parent follow-up, coordination and advocacy.* At this point, the parent formally sends a letter to the school requesting a "504 Classroom Accommodation Plan." Included in this request are the accommodations developed by the child, the family, and the educators. Once agreed upon, this becomes part of the child's permanent file and will not have to be renegotiated each year, just modified and updated.

Intervention Strategies

There is no cure for ADHD, but just as there is a multimodal assessment plan, there is also a multimodal intervention plan. Intervention typically involves parent education in behavior management, an appropriate educational setting (typically, with a teacher who knows behavior management techniques), individual and family counseling when necessary, and frequently medication.

Education and training of parents of children with ADHD is an essential component of most intervention plans. Informed parents are more likely to comply with medication regimens and pursue effective child management (Glanzman & Blum, 2007). Educators also need training in modifying their classroom behavior management methods. Consistency between home and school in behavior management is a tremendous asset for the child. Techniques focus on maintaining the child's attention on tasks, improving behavior, teaching organizational skills, and adapting programming to specific learning disabilities if they coexist (Glanzman & Blum, 2007).

Intervention should be multimodal. The intervention team may need to act like detectives, assembling clues to provide ideas about effective intervention strategies. Start with the setting itself. Look at the child's strengths and where he functions most competently.

The teacher will check I wrote my assignments correctly before I leave school.

My math work is coded red; my language is coded yellow.

If I don't call out and wait for my turn I can use the computer for 15 minutes.

I can work at my desk or at the standing table.

I can wear my weighted vest during group time if I need it.

Jake's accommodations

I can play with my fidget toy during group time.

I can sit directly across from the teacher during group.

When we work in small groups I don't have to be the scribe.

I can walk at the end of the line.

I can run on the playground.

Figure 10–2: My Accommodation Plan
This is an accommodation plan for Jake, a 6-year-old, in first grade, who has been diagnosed with attention-deficit/ hyperactivity disorder, hyperactive/impulsive subtype. Using a format that children are familiar with helps them become more independent in their learning and ensures that if there is a substitute teacher that they will receive their needed accommodations.

See Table 10–2 for what this might look like for some children with ADHD.

Although these variables may not always be under your control, it is important to think about them and know that children are facing challenges. Space should be arranged to offer children opportunities to work individually, in small groups, or in large groups. Ideally, the classroom provides a variety of well-defined learning-action stations. If children have coexisting conditions, look at the guidelines for those chapters to expand your teaching strategies.

Table 10–2: Strengths and Challenges for Children with ADHD

Challenges	Strengths
group times	one-on-one
novel tasks/situations	familiar/frequent recurring tasks/situations
infrequent feedback	frequent feedback
delayed consequences	immediate consequences
less obvious consequences	noticeable consequences
unsupervised work	supervised work
afternoon	morning
tasks paced by others	self-paced tasks
noisy environment	quiet environment
larger class	smaller class

Working with Challenging Behaviors

Challenging behavior is difficult for teachers to deal with. However, it is not the same for all teachers. What is challenging behavior for me may not be challenging behavior for you, and vice versa. Challenging behavior is in the eye of the beholder. Challenging behavior is behavior that makes us feel inadequate because we don't know how to deal with it. Challenging behavior is behavior that challenges the teacher (Marion, 2002).

As with all behavior, it is important to look for patterns and to try to examine the roots of the challenging behavior. The first thing to consider is developmental level. Is the behavior appropriate for the developmental age/level of the child? It is difficult for young children to take the perspective of others and to understand that it hurts to get hit. Young children typically focus on one thing at a time and that may be getting the toy they want.

Think about the children and the purpose of challenging behavior. Is it something that starts out as fun that children do not know how to end or is there an underlying cause?

Or, is there a skill that a child needs that he lacks? Some children have unmet needs. If the child needs attention, is this the only way he can get it? Is this the only way he knows how to get it? Look at the context (the environmental aspects) of the situation. Does the environment support this behavior? Look at the room arrangement, the available activities, and the sequence of activities to determine if these contribute to the behavior.

Implications for Educators

Figure out specifically what you want. Often it is easier to know what we don't want than what we do want. If the problem is cursing, what do you want? I know you want it to stop; me too. Is there an appropriate place for a child to curse? Is there a safe place for this to happen? If you can provide an uninteresting place for a child to go, this may be part of your solution. (After you have tried a variety of other things that you hoped would work.) It is important to teach the child that behavior is situational and there are things you can say and do in some situations and not in others. Be creative. The more skills you have, the fewer challenging behaviors you will encounter.

It is important, however, to be able to differentiate between children whose behavior challenges you and requires educational intervention, and children who need therapy. You are probably not a therapist, but you should know how to get the support of one. Be authoritative, unrelentingly positive, and reflect on your behavior and your practice with challenging behaviors (Marion, 2002).

Behavior Management/Guidance

Discipline, or classroom management, is rarely easy; including children with ADHD presents additional challenges. Because their behavior is inconsistent, it is difficult to know whether these children are refusing or are unable to behave as requested. (Parents have the same dilemma.) Children often take medication in the morning before school. It takes about half an hour for it to work which may mean that mornings are a challenge for families. Children with ADHD, even young ones, can control the family. If they want attention and aggressive behaviors gets attention (even if it is negative attention) their need may be rewarded.

Implications for Educators

The development of a behavior management/guidance plan is part of the multimodal method for working with children with ADHD. If you already have a plan that works, use it. There are a variety of ways to plan. Some teachers use a token system. This involves token rewards for appropriate, or on-task, behavior and loss of token rewards for inappropriate behavior. Others successfully use logical consequences. For example, if a child knocks all the plastic blocks off a table, he needs to help pick them up; if he spills milk, he should help clean it up. (If the child spills milk persistently and purposefully, you might try not giving any more. If the child is thirsty, give him water.) Impulsive children who act before they think and only then remember the consequences of their actions may not profit from this approach. A combination of the two methods often works best. You want the child to learn internalized self-control and to stop inappropriate behavior.

Any behavior management plan has two basic principles

1. Rewarding desired behavior is more effective than punishing undesired behavior.
2. There must be agreement on what behavior is acceptable and unacceptable and the responses to the behavior must be consistent (Silver, 2004).

The first step is to collect information. One easy model to use is the ABC chart. The chart has four components: the date and time, then the antecedent (what happened before the behavior occurred) (A), the behavior itself (B), and the consequences of the behavior (C) (Silver, 2004). If parents are doing the recording, have them do it separately. The same goes for teachers if there is more than one in the classroom. Table 10–3 shows a typical ABC chart.

As data is collected, patterns should emerge. They may be related to time of day, specific antecedent behaviors leading to predictable unacceptable behaviors, routines change, medication is wearing off, and so on. Data often clusters to make an impossible list more possible. Most unacceptable behaviors fall into one of three categories: physical abuse (hitting someone, breaking things, or threatening to do so); verbal abuse (yelling, cursing, taunting, and so on); and noncompliance (not completing a task or complying with a request) (Silver, 2004).

Once the patterns have been identified, an initial plan is designed. The family, including siblings if any, and educators should be part of the plan. The plan involves rewarding positive behavior and withholding rewards for negative behavior—every time it happens. For children the day is too long to be one unit. It should be divided up into three or four time units, such as (1) getting up until getting to school, (2) getting to school and until lunch, (3) from lunch until getting picked up or leaving school, (4) returning home and until bedtime.

Remember the purpose is to reward positive behavior. However, the first step is to determine what the unacceptable behaviors are. There are two types of unacceptable behavior: ones in which a child does not receive points toward a reward (if that is the system) and those that require removal from the group. Behaviors that physically hurt other children or adults typically fall into the latter category. Agree on the consequences.

Table 10–3: ABC chart for Daria

Date/Time	Antecedent	Behavior	Consequences
10/6/08			
10:30	Don't know	Had a temper tantrum screaming, fell on floor	Moved furniture out, redirected children
11:00	S took her book (end of clean-up)	Bit S	Time out, 5 minutes & talked to her
11:20	Spilled juice	Knocked pitcher to floor	Made her clean it up

Ignoring challenging behavior (especially when you think that getting attention is the child's purpose) is ideal when it works. However, it doesn't always work, and it is inappropriate if the child is doing something dangerous or is hurting others. Then, removing the child from the situation is probably the best solution. But that is only the first step in the process.

The use of "time out" for children with ADHD has its proponents and opponents. If it is used it should be only one of a variety of methods of guidance and there should be clear guidelines as to when it is most appropriate alternative. If removing a child is necessary, I prefer the concept of "thinking time," which involves removing the child from the ongoing activities to a specified location off to one side of the room or playground. It is designed to give children time to think about what happened and regain their self-control. The child may know better than the teacher when he is back in control. Ask him. The space can be designated by placing a chair in a taped-off square. When a child is out of control, it may be necessary for him to leave the classroom. This option should be used as just one of the tools in behavior management/ guidance. Its effectiveness is diminished when used continually or exclusively. It also reduces the number of social interactions that occur between peers. Using incentives, behavioral reinforcers, and modeling opportunities may be more effective. When it is used, it is important to ask the child three questions before allowing the child to leave the thinking area: (1) What happened? (2) What should you have done? (3) What will you do next time?

Guiding the child in ways to handle issues for the next time is beneficial. However, until the child is emotionally available it is a waste of time. It may take children 5 to 10 minutes to emotionally recover to the point that they can think about what happened (Goleman, 1995). This is the time to talk with them about the behavior, the choices they made, and could make. Help them think about alternatives. Ultimately, the goal is to have the child do the thinking before the action.

Implications for Educators

It is important to find out what is rewarding to the child. If the reward is irrelevant, there is no incentive to work toward it. The best rewards are those that involve time with adults. Food is not a good reward. For young children, using stickers or stars often works. The child may earn the right to borrow a favorite book, have 5 minutes of special one-on-one time with the teacher, or whatever that child finds rewarding. If your system does not seem to be effective, see if there are unexpected snags. All systems need fine tuning once they are in place.

In The Field

I once taught a little girl who was particularly disruptive during group time. I had a student teacher take her out into the hall when she acted up. Instead of decreasing, the disruptive behavior increased, and it began to occur closer to the beginning of group time. I decided to see what was happening. The next time Andrea created a disturbance, I took her out into the hall. Once there, she told me to sit down, plopped herself in my lap, and said, "This is the book I want to read today." She then hauled out her book, and I read it. Now I knew why this child disrupted my group! The next day, Andrea went to the hall with *no* book, and the student teacher was instructed to ignore her. By the end of the week she sat through most of group time!

Reflective Practice

Make sure your consequence is not rewarding, or the behavior will continue. It is important to think about what behaviors are being rewarded and whether or not those are the ones you want to continue and to develop a system to ensure that you move to intermittent rewards to establish the behavior.

Satiation is another way of dealing with challenge behavior. The child is made to continue a behavior when he no longer wants to. This is particularly effective for something physical, like falling off a chair. If a child is required to sit down, fall off, and get up repeatedly this behavior lost its charm. To discourage acts that are likely to be contagious in a classroom, satiation may be more effective than ignoring.

An additional method of stopping a behavior is to set up incompatible alternatives: consider the child who frequently masturbated in class. After all attempts had failed in discussing the difference between private and public behavior, reviewing the program to see if the child might be bored, checking to see if his pants were too tight, and asking his mother if he had a rash—tactics were changed. The teachers planned a program of messy table activities requiring two hands. It really is difficult to fingerpaint with both hands and masturbate at the same time!

Guidelines

1. *Seat a child with ADHD in the area where the teacher spends the most time.* If children sit in rows, place the child close to the front with his back to the rest of the class to keep other children out of view; surround the child with good role models (ensure that this does not become a problem for these children or rotate seats), and seat the child away from auditory distractions such as pencil sharpeners, heat and air-conditioning units, or open doors and windows.

2. *Assign a child with ADHD two chairs or a chair and a standing work place.* When children are required to sit in chairs, he can move between them (within reasonable limits). Allow the child (or any child) to sit astride the chair (backward); this will keep the chair from rocking or tipping and provides a more stable base.

3. *Present information from a location where physical and visual reinforcement can be maintained.* Do not have a group activity in a place where the child can look outside and see others playing. Children's ability to selectively ignore stimuli varies. Reducing external visual and auditory distractions is usually helpful.

4. *Keep the classroom orderly and organized.* This can be done through color coding or numbering bins and shelves.

5. *Keep lessons brief, fast-paced, and break up information into manageable "chunks."* Present information sequentially, a step at a time rather than all at once. Model tasks to make them easier to follow and improve recall.

6. *Decrease waiting and increase on-task time.* Plan ahead.

7. *Encourage cooperative/collaborative learning.* Have children work in small groups with a common goal.

8. *Require a daily assignment notebook.* Make sure each child correctly writes down all assignments each day. If a child is not capable of this, help her. Sign the notebook daily to signify completion of homework assignments. (Parents should also sign.) Use the notebook for daily communication with parents. For younger children, teachers may write the comments to the family and include children's illustrations or photographs of what they did during the day.

9. *Modify assignments as needed.* If the child has an IEP use the information to determine the child's specific strengths and challenges. Provide extra time and opportunity for certain tasks. Children with ADHD may work slowly. Do not penalize them for needing extra time. Make sure you are assessing knowledge and not attention span. If a child has a 504 plan base modifications on the plan.

10. *Decrease frustration.* Stress, pressure, and fatigue can break down their self-control and lead to poor behavior.

11. *Give feedback frequently, using visual, verbal, or tactile methods.* Verbal reinforcement is often the least salient. Find out what works and use it.

12. *Avoid ridicule, criticism, and sarcasm.* Remember, children with ADHD have difficulty staying in control.

13. *Enforce classroom rules consistently.* Have pre-established consequences for behavior. Remain calm, state the infraction of the rule, and avoid debating or arguing with the child. Administer consequences immediately, monitor and support appropriate behavior frequently, move on.

14. *Determine the child's preferred learning style.* Get information from educational, psychological, and/or neurologic testing to determine if the child has a preferred learning style (auditory, visual, kinesthetic) and use this information to frame instruction.

15. *Decide which of the smaller characteristics typical for children with ADHD you can ignore* (fidgeting, swaying, rocking, and so on). Try redirecting behaviors you cannot ignore into more purposeful actions. This may take some creative planning. If fidgeting during groups time is something you want to address provide all children with "stress balls" to fidget with during group time. Initially all children will probably use them over time; however, some children will continue to use them while others will not.

16. *Ensure belongings are labeled.* As homework plays a larger role, if parents can afford it or the school is willing, obtain a second set of books. This means the child has a set at home to do her homework and that she can also write in the book or highlight it. For some children this is a very effective learning strategy.

Curriculum Adaptations

Children with ADHD require some adaptations. For those with impulsivity and hyperactivity it may be in the area of increasing the time available for learning and helping them focus on tasks. The social skills necessary to do cooperative learning may have to be taught. In general, the accommodations are behavioral in nature or are designed to support the child's organization and minimize distractions. Because so many children with ADHD have coexisting conditions, these also need to be taken into consideration when adapting the curriculum.

Social Awareness: Self-Esteem, Inclusion, and Social Studies

All children need to form relationships with others. The skills of taking turns and sharing are especially critical. The behavior of children with ADHD is variable; they are often unaware of how they feel, and so they need to identify their feelings and learn to control them while developing a sense of self-worth and group belonging.

Impulsiveness is one of the hallmark traits of ADHD. Children with ADHD have poor self-control. This negatively affects their behaviors in the classroom and also with their peers, which impacts their social development. Social and organizational skills that we take for granted may have to be specifically taught. Experiences in starting and stopping an action on a signal and in self-pacing or regulating their responses will help them develop self-control. Learning of this nature can be initiated in the classroom, provided some activities have definite starting and ending points. Practice the starts and stops on a signal. Visual and tactile clues will help the child mark passages of time.

Some of the activities in the Resource Chapter 1 are specifically designed to support children who have ADHD. Activities such as 1–4 One More help children think of many different solutions for a problem. Activity 1–12 Feelings helps children identify their feelings. I'm Thinking of, Activity 1–40w, is like the game "20 Questions" where children ask yes-no questions until they can answer the question. It increases children's awareness of not having enough information.

Self-Esteem

Help children feel comfortable seeking assistance (many children with ADHD will not ask for help). Gradually reduce the amount of assistance, but keep in mind that these children need more help for a longer time than typically developing child. Evaluate your own behavior: do you reward more than you discipline? This ratio impacts self-esteem. Support children immediately for any and all demonstrations of good behavior until those behaviors are well-established. Encourage children in a variety of ways; change rewards that are not effective in motivating behavioral change. Teach the child to reward herself. Encourage positive self-talk ("You did very well remaining in your seat today, how do you feel about that?"). This encourages the child to think positively about herself.

Children need to increase their awareness of their own feelings and those of others. They also need experience in differentiating between feelings and behavior: "It's okay to be mad at Chunga; it is not okay to hit her." Help them learn to express both positive and negative feelings in socially acceptable ways. They can run, poke playdough, or hit a punching bag. They need to consciously decide how they will deal with their feelings. They may also need to learn expressions and gestures that show others that they are happy and like them. They need help making and keeping friends.

1. Work on identifying feelings. Help children learn the specific facial configurations of different emotions. Go beyond happy and sad to angry, hurt, surprised, scared, jealous, embarrassed, and so on. Discuss when children might have these feelings and what they want to happen.
2. Encourage children to make books about their feelings: "When I felt. . . . " See Activity 1–12 Feelings.
3. Support positive self-talk: "I can . . . ," "I like . . . ," "I'm good at. . . . "

Inclusion

All children need to feel they belong. They need to appreciate and learn from differences as well as similarities. They all need to feel that they contribute to the group.

1. Help children view events from various perspectives. Increase children's awareness of the uniqueness of self.
2. Support children as problem solvers. Encourage children by sharing problems about broken crayons, markers that dry out, and other current problems. As children begin to see themselves as problem solvers, begin to talk about problems in the classroom and brainstorm about how these problems might be resolved.

Social Studies

Children construct their understanding of the world based on their experiences. They try out their ideas in social situations and get feedback: positive or negative. Sometimes objects or events challenge the child's working model of his world and he is then forced to adjust the model and alter the mental structures that support that sociocultural model (Bredekamp & Copple, 2009). Children need to be presented with diverse social situations and a culturally rich classroom to get an accurate working model of the global world in which we live. Social skills are the foundation of being a successful part of groups and establishing friendships. These skills develop during the early childhood years and lay the foundation for social relationships throughout life. As concerns about school violence increase, it becomes imperative that we teach children about their immediate social world as well as the larger one in which they will live and grow.

1. As children play with others, teachers need to help children see the perspectives of others and the consequences of social actions.
2. Emphasize group belonging and the courtesy extended to other group members: property rights, space to play, and including others. Discuss how children feel when they are not included, their toys are taken, or their space is invaded. Also, discuss ways of dealing with these feelings.
3. Teach children to read social cues and when and how to join groups.
4. Use vignettes, puppets, and dolls to pose problems to children and ask what they might do if they were the child in the vignette. Get at least four responses for each scenario. As you get each response look at it from the children's point of view and discuss how they might feel. Have children role play. The goal is to help children develop a repertoire of skills for assessing and joining groups, and for figuring out which skills to apply under what set of circumstances.
5. Once children have figured out how to join the group, there is a different set of skills necessary for maintaining group membership. Teach these as well.

Language and Literacy: Speaking, Listening, Reading, and Writing

Communication is important to all children. This is the information age. Communication, whether spoken or written, formal or informal, English or Spanish, using paper or electronic means, is the cornerstone for conveying information. Children need skills in both expressive and receptive language. These skills develop in the context of social interactions and are based on the child's cultural experience. Effective communicators master the skills of both speaking and listening in the context of turn taking. Some children with ADHD have problems with the listening part. For children with a high activity level, having to *just* listen may seem close to punishment. Children also need to develop print awareness and skills in reading and writing.

Speaking

Help children with ADHD develop the words to connect their speech and language to their behavior. Encourage them to use self-talk as a way of regulating and making sense out of their behavior. Support them in learning to talk through situations based on anticipation of what may happen and as a way of reflecting on what did happen.

1. Encourage children to ask questions and help them focus their questions.
2. Encourage children to restate directions for each other.
3. Talk to children about oral histories and why they are important. Ask children about their own oral histories with questions like "What do you remember about being little?" "What stories does your family tell about your being little?" "Why aren't these written down?" Invite children to talk to their parents and grandparents about their memories and to tape record or write their responses. Encourage children to expand on this and to talk about family customs and the holidays they celebrate.
4. Support children's speaking by active listening. Paraphrase and summarize what children say.

Fingerplays are great for children with ADHD. The children are actively involved and able to learn through the kinesthetic/tactile sense. Also, children whose hands are busy doing fingerplays are less likely to be bothering the person next to them.

1. Use fingerplays to teach concepts.
2. Quiz the children in a way that is fun but that also makes them think about what they are saying. Sing "Where Is Thumbkin?", but instead of holding up your thumb when you sing "Here I am," hold up your index finger. Ask them what is wrong with doing it that way. Ask them for another word for thumbkin (thumb), pointer (index finger), tall man (middle finger), ring man, and pinkie. Ask children to tell you how the fingers got these nicknames.

Listening

Listening is difficult, especially for children who are ready to move. Gain the child's attention before speaking. Speak slowly, but not so slowly that it is exaggerated. When giving directions to children with ADHD, maintain eye contact and make verbal instructions clear and concise. Be consistent with daily instructions. Simplify complex directions. Avoid multiple commands. Make sure children comprehend the instructions before beginning the task. If they don't, repeat instructions in a calm, positive manner. Recognize when a child is tired and give him a break. This may be the wrong time for concentrated listening.

1. Use gestures when they support what you are saying, but are not distracting.
2. Use words that guide behaviors such as first, next, and last, and help children pick these out while they listen.
3. If children don't seem to understand, restate what has been misunderstood rather than repeating all of the information.
4. Check for comprehension by asking the child questions, then go to a new topic.

Some children find listening stations a great way to listen to books, other children find them difficult.

Stories can be entertaining and enlightening for children. Choose them carefully and read them interactively with interest and expression.

1. Keep stories short. It is better to read a five-page story that the children sit through attentively than to read a 20-page story with 20 interruptions.
2. During group times, use physical signals to help children organize their bodies as they listen. A carpet square or "X" made with masking tape may help. As children become more competent, replace these with verbal reminders. Children need to learn to control their bodies without external cues, so they don't become dependent on them.
3. Use stories that support participation. Children can move the flannelboard characters to follow the story As well as make predictions about what will happen.
4. Read stories in small groups, where you can individualize the story and your attention.
5. Choose stories that deal with feelings, including hostile or unhappy feelings as well as happy ones. See the Children's Bibliography.

Reading

Children need to be literate in many aspects of reading and they need to learn about the function that written language serves. They need to know about environmental print, such as stop signs, price tags, schedules, and so on. Occupational print might be a menu for a waiter or health records for a medical professional. Informational print is found on calendars, newspapers, and reference books. Recreational print is used for leisure such as novels, magazines, and poetry. Children need to be exposed to a variety of print sources and to understand their functions.

1. Help children name pictures and/or discuss what is happening in pictures. Give children time to formulate their answers. Add to the picture by saying such things as "What do you think will happen if someone appears and. . . . ?"
2. Help children reflect on their feelings after a book has been read. Encourage them to think about what they might do if they were one of the characters in the story.

3. Encourage children to respond to reading through the arts, dramatic play, building, and so on.
4. Provide opportunities for children to learn a sight vocabulary. Begin with their names.
5. Expose children to a variety of **genres**. (A genre is a category of language that is used to classify its form and content.) Genre is shaped by the purposes of the writer and the needs of the audience. It helps children know what to expect. If you know someone is a chef, it helps to narrow down what the possible words are. Stories are an important genre during early childhood, but children should also be exposed to story telling, poems, rhymes, and so on.

Writing

Encourage children to think of themselves as writers from an early age. Writing is a difficult, complex task. And initially, there is little satisfaction until others can read what is written. Support prewriting skills as well as alternative writing procedures like word processing. Have a variety of materials (pencils, markers, crayons, rubber stamps, papers of many sizes and colors, cards, and so on) so children can find materials that both appeal to them and are easy for them to use.

1. Support children's attempts at writing. Like language, writing is culturally based. If children see a written language other than English at home, their writing may look different from children who have seen only written English.
2. Attach a visual strip of letters and numbers to the writing area or, as children become older, each desk so that children have a visual model.
3. Teach children how to use the index finger of the nonwriting hand to identify the letter or word they want to copy.
4. Place an arrow → on the writing desk and have the child put his paper below the arrow. Explain that you move in the direction of the arrow.
5. If children want to write, but have trouble with spacing; draw a space on the paper for each letter or word. This is easier if children know what they want to say because you can space out the letters and the distance between words.
6. Encourage children to use the keyboard if they find writing to be a laborious process. Children can use software such as My First Amazing Diary (ages 5 to 9) with which children can fill in facts and answer questions as well as write. It gives some structure and variety to the writing experience. As children reach age 8, there are many programs that teach typing and other forms of writing. See Activity 2–57 My Diary.

Discovery: Mathematics, Science, and Technology

Children are curious about their world. They want to understand it and how their actions impact it. Discovery needs to be integrated all through the curriculum, especially dramatic play. The underlying concepts of math and science can be found throughout the early childhood

classroom. Number symbols can be on price tags, play money, shoe sizes, or rulers. You can count the grocery store items purchased, chairs at the table, or the number of items at the sand or water table. Children can classify blocks, beads, or buttons. Part-whole relationships can be taught as children slice an apple or eat a piece of whole wheat pizza. Children with ADHD often participate in more risk-taking behaviors than other children. Use science and math processes to help them grasp the sequences of behaviors and also the consequences of actions that may be unsafe.

Children learn about science through cooking, by watching a liquid turn into a solid, watching what happens when heat is applied, or by watching the ice or snow melt. Science and math are all around. Children can be helped to remember the sequence of these activities through the use of a digital camera. Computer software and the Internet can bring science to children. They can visit the Exploratorium in San Francisco (http://www.exploratorium.org) or the Franklin Institute Science Museum in Philadelphia (http://www2.fi.edu/) even if they live in North Dakota.

Mathematics

The underlying concept of mathematics is problem solving. This is not a narrow definition that looks at $2 + 4 = 6$ as the problem to be solved, but rather takes a broad definition of problems to be solved. Children can work in groups on problems generated by both the teacher and the children. Math needs to be real for young children.

1. Provide running commentary whenever possible to help children make connections between mathematics and its use in the real world: "You've had half of your water," "You have one piece of cheese yet to eat," and "We have two empty chairs at this table."
2. Help children develop concepts of patterning and seriating starting with simple repeating patterns (red, yellow, red, yellow) not only by showing them blocks but also by looking at clothing for check patterns and more complex patterns like plaids. See if children can repeat these patterns with blocks or Unifix™ Cubes. Help them see the utility of patterns in their daily life as a method of organization.
3. Provide children with picture sequences of the class routine. Ask children what is going on in each of the pictures. Then mix up the sequences in silly ways (go home *before* you come to school, wash your hands *before* you go to the bathroom) and talk about this with children. Help children develop sequences in their own behavior; an after-school sequence that incorporates getting necessary work done and going outside to play (or vice versa).
4. Teach children the vocabulary of time (such as age, morning, soon, next, calendar, weekend) and use time informally by incorporating it into art (drawing a night picture) and social studies (special occasions and holidays). Encourage them to use timers in dramatic play or outside, to see how far they can run before the timer goes off. Again, use time as an organizational device. Setting a timer to work on a particular project provides boundaries and may make tasks doable. Consider the developmental level of the child

as you consider the time span. It is better to get great concentration for a short time than to struggle to keep it for a longer time. Gradually increase time based on positive experiences.

Science

Like math, science is based on problem solving. Sciencing, a verb, might be a more accurate description of science during the early childhood years, and perhaps after. Children need to learn the basic processes of science, such as observing, comparing, classifying, measuring, and communicating. These extend into inferring, predicting, hypothesizing, and defining and controlling variables (Charlesworth & Lind, 2003).

1. Encourage children to use their senses in isolation and combination. Observation involves all of the senses. Children need to become accurate observers. Encourage children to look at photographs and pictures in books and to tell you what they see. Help them look for additional items in the picture. You want children to pick up details as well as the major event. Then make them into picture *detectives,* using clues to interpret what is going on in the picture. Do the same thing with hearing; encourage them to close their eyes. As you play a piece of music, have them describe what they hear. Talk about tone, tempo, and pitch. Using their kinesthetic sense, have children reach into a bag and describe the object in the bag or have them choose between two objects and ask them to describe the objects. Keep the task simple and short at the beginning. Support the development of specific vocabulary.
2. Classification skills underlie both science and math skills. For children with ADHD, one purpose in teaching these skills is to help keep children safe. Classify food-type items as to whether or not they are safe to eat or drink. Classify people who are safe to talk to if a child is lost (this is tricky, as in many cases a woman with a child may be the first choice). Think about the environment and what is geographically and culturally safe. Classify behavior as safe (piling blocks) and unsafe (throwing blocks).
3. Cause and effect reasoning, or learning the predictable consequences of events, is important. It may help children develop inner controls and control impulsivity in some situations. Encourage children to answer questions such as "What happens if . . . ?" "What could you do about . . . ?" "Is there anything else you could do?" And, if possible, have them test out their responses. Help children think through actions before performing them and predicting the consequences.
4. Children will get wrong answers and make inaccurate predictions. One way to handle this is to frame it as part of the scientific method. This does not mean that the answer was right, but places it in a framework of scientific investigations. Talk about the scientists who work to come up with solutions and get many wrong answers before they get the right one. Help children see mistakes as a natural part of the learning process.

Technology

Technology offers children opportunities to explore, learn, and play, either alone or with friends. It enables them to have a sense of control and do extraordinary things. They can make decisions, change decisions, and develop the skills to work cooperatively with others. Technology can capture moments that children want to remember; digital pictures can support children's memories of events and share with their families what they have done at school. Technology supports many accommodations for children with disabilities: speech synthesizers allow the computer to talk to the child, switches can take the place of the keyboard, and alternative keyboards can be used. Touch windows can control the computer. Children like technology. We, as adults, may have our doubts, but children do not share them.

1. Modify computers and other input devices to meet the needs of the children in your classroom.
2. Identify software and websites that support children's learning. Share this information with families if they have computers at home. If they do not have computers at home, encourage families to go to the public library and use their computers.
3. Encourage children to use a word processor or computer for schoolwork. Help them use spell and grammar check as a way to learn which words they have misspelled, to see their mistakes, and to learn the accurate spelling and use of words.
4. Use the digital camera to enhance children's memory skills and to encourage complexity in their development. Instead of just building blocks, see if they can replicate what they built in the past and then decide on the changes they want to make.
5. Use the digital camera to talk about perspective taking. Start with the concrete. Take a picture of a child from the front and back and each side. Print the picture. Talk about the differences from each angle. Use this to segue into talking about behavior. Take pictures of a child with a toy or material and a picture of a child who wants this toy or is grabbing it (or use other situations that occur in your classroom). Have children pose for these pictures so you are not singling out children who engage in this behavior. Talk about the picture from each child's perspective. The power in this technique is that it is immediate; it uses the children in your classroom to illustrate the points you are making, and it does not involve the specific children who typically engage in such behavior. Instead of being a one-on-two discussion of what is going on, use it to talk to the class at a time when people are not emotionally involved in what is going on.
6. Many well-known magazines and programs have websites designed for children:

   - *National Geographic* has a kids section (http://www.nationalgeographic.com/)
   - *Owl Kids* is a science site for children and *OWL* is a Canadian nature magazine for children younger than age 8. (http://owlkids.com/)
   - *Reading Rainbow* is designed to encourage a love of books and reading among children ages 4–8. (http://pbskids.org/readingrainbow/)

This is just a small sample. There are many more and many categories of sites as well.

Wellness: Health, Physical Education, and Sensory Motor

Moving is part of life. Movement increasingly comes under the child's control and gradually become more efficient and skillful. Children learn adaptive skills, allowing them increasing independence and control of their bodies. With independence comes increased risk. As children move farther and faster, they can place themselves in situations in which they need to make judgments about what is safe and healthy. Children with ADHD need to be aware of specific practices that place them at risk. They need to learn to use the muscles in their bodies in concert with their senses to explore their world.

Health and Safety

This is an important curriculum area for children with ADHD, who, even at an early age, may have seen a variety of specialists, perhaps had an electroencephalogram (EEG) and taken medication, and who may have some fears about health professionals. Children must cooperate in testing and report their reactions to medicine they may be taking, so developing good rapport between children and medical personnel is important. Increase body awareness so children can locate body parts and then respond about how specific parts feel.

1. As children may become lost, teach them to state their name, telephone number, and parents' names early in the year, if this is what parents want them to do. Use the Activity What Would You Do If? 4–34w.
2. Work on traffic signs and teach children to control impulsive behavior that may lead to accidents. Use activities such as Stop and Go 4–4 and 4–5 Warning Signs to teach children about safety signs and their implications for behavior.
3. Talk about injury prevention. Help children see the relationship between actions and results (what may happen if someone runs in front of a tricycle, bicycle, or car).
4. State and post class safety rules, especially those in which children could be hurt (standing on chairs and tables, running with scissors, throwing blocks).
5. When children initially engage in some unsafe practice, such as climbing the fence instead of the jungle gym, make your limits clear, but situational: "*At school* you may not climb on the fence. If you want to climb, you may climb on the jungle gym." Be prepared to reinforce this statement physically if necessary: Help the child climb down from the fence and walk her over to the jungle gym.
6. Integrate food preparation into the curriculum through snack and lunch. Discuss nutrition. Help children learn about the relationships between growth, food, and health. Include cultural variations of good food. Use foods that are familiar to the children, as well as some that aren't. Serve fruits and vegetables for snack that the children help prepare such as Fruit Kabob 3–27.

7. Discuss where foods grow and compare fresh foods with canned or frozen foods. Talk about food additives and food allergies. See Food Forms 1–34w.
8. Talk about common health problems of children (colds, ear infections, stomachaches, headaches) and ask children to identify the symptoms of each. Talk with children about ways to prevent illness and how illnesses are treated.
9. Talk about healthy lifestyles and the need for nutritious eating and exercise. Discuss the role of doctors and the medicine they prescribe in helping children stay healthy and helping them return to health after they have been sick.
10. If children are on stimulant medication for ADHD, one of the side effects may be loss of appetite. Be sure that your snacks are nutritionally sound. Evaluate them based on calories and nutrition. Add low-fat cream cheese to crackers or rice cakes and put cut-up vegetables on them to make faces. In a group snack, children might eat this, whereas they may not at home. Dip fruit or vegetables in yogurt or low-fat salad dressing. Make choices that are good for all children.

Large Motor

Children with ADHD may use large motor activities to release frustration, tension, and anger. If they do not do this independently, encourage them. Participating in these activities helps children develop feelings of belonging to a group. Practice fundamental motor skills. Children need many and varied opportunities to practice.

1. Obtain a punching bag and encourage children who feel like hitting to hit the bag (not just to hit it once or tap it lightly, but to hit it hard and frequently).
2. Provide balls for throwing and kicking. Encourage children to kick the ball and then run after it and kick it again, or to kick the ball at a target like a plastic milk bottle. See Activity 4–11 Target Bounce, 4–12 Variations on Throwing, and 4–36w Variations on Dribbling.
3. Spot children who are using equipment to climb high. Teach them safety rules. Ensure that the surfaces beneath equipment children could fall off of are padded.
4. Encourage cooperative sports.
5. Motor skills need to be practiced and, over time, refined and mastered. They develop in a predictable order. Locomotor skills that young children are working on include walking, running, hopping, skipping, galloping, sliding, leaping, climbing, jumping, and chasing/fleeing. Incorporate these skills into your everyday planning. See Activity 4–7 Variations on Running, and 4–10 Variations on Hopping.
6. Habits of lifetime activity can be developed during the early childhood years. Help children develop a physically active lifestyle.

Small Motor

Small motor skills are challenging for many children. Developmentally, these skills need the large muscles of the trunk to have developed to provide the stability that

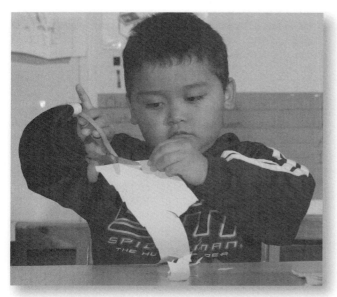

Fine motor skills, particularly cutting is challenging for many children with ADHD.

allows the use of the small muscles. Small muscles are used for writing, manipulative, and adaptive skills.

1. Teach adaptive skills in naturally occurring situations: dressing and undressing when it is time to go outside, when coming to or leaving school, during toileting; using utensils at snack and mealtimes. Allow time for children to learn the skills—they are part of the early childhood curriculum.
2. To the extent that fine motor skills are challenging, ensure that children participate in these activities. This is the only way the skills will develop. Have children participate for several short times over the course of the day rather than an extended time once a day.
3. Encourage children to try using their fine motor skills in a variety of positions such as standing, sitting, and lying down. Vary heights of tables.
4. Use adaptive equipment to make skills easier. Adaptive handles on scissors, spoons, and pencils make them easier to hold, but consider this an interim step. As children become more proficient, gradually stop using the modification.
5. Integrate fine motor skills into program areas that children enjoy. If children like the computer, they will be motivated to develop the skills necessary to use it. If children particularly like dramatic play, then include activities that require fine motor skills as part of what is going on in that area.

Sensory Motor Integration

Sensory integration requires children to use the information they receive from their senses to understand where their body is in space and to understand what is heard in the environment, to coordinate both sides of their body, to develop fine motor skills including eye-hand coordination, to process movement, and to respond to touch. Sensory integration encompasses quite a list, but it is possible to modify the level of sensory motor integration required in

many activities. Before you modify an activity for a child, decide on the value of the activity for the child. Is this something the child really needs to learn how to do, in and of itself, or is it a basis for later essential skills? If so, then modify the activity; if not, let it go.

1. Observe the skill level of the children by playing simple games that children should have the skills to do. If they cannot, try to analyze where in the system the process is breaking down. If it is in understanding the directions, give them directions one at a time. If it is motor planning, model or physically help children move through the actions.
2. Children come with different skill levels. Focus children who are more advanced in a skill on the next step in the developmental process. If children can catch large balls, then decrease the size of the ball for these children. If children are struggling with a skill, coach them. If they are jumping, coach them to bend their knees, move their arms, and take off from the balls of their feet. Although almost all children learn basic motor skills, they do not perfect them without coaching. Activities that are too easy or too difficult tend to elicit disruptive behavior.
3. Find out from children what is more important to them: the process or the outcome. If the outcome is important, use this knowledge to build their motivation and persistence. Help children understand the steps necessary to achieve the outcome and support the accomplishment of each step in the process.
4. Use activities that require coordinating both sides of the body, such as hand clapping. Provide opportunities for hands and fingers to work together with Legos, pop beads, stringing beads, sewing, cooking, woodworking and so on.
5. For some children, organizing personal belongings is challenging. Try to limit the number of items children have at school. Color-code containers for specific objects. Add weight (fishing sinkers work well) to containers to make them more stable. Talk about strategies for organizing personal belongings.
6. Encourage children to pour at the sand or water table. The emphasis here is on accuracy. Can they pour different amounts of sand, seeds, or liquid from a pitcher into a smaller container? This requires them to use eye-hand coordination and to control the force and angle of their pouring.
7. As children develop prewriting and writing skills, have them practice in a variety of ways: writing with finger paint, sand, aluminum foil, stencils, and so on.

Creative Arts: Visual Arts, Music, Creative Movement, and Dramatic Play

Creative arts allow children to develop and practice necessary skills and movements in a safe way. An emphasis on creativity encourages children to think outside the box and allows them to explore and take chances, because there is little possibility for failure—difference, yes, failure, no—creative arts allow children to experiment and practice.

Visual Arts

Children need to be exposed to a variety of art forms and processes. They need to work on individual projects and to be included with others on murals and collages. They need to see art and learn about artists. They need to look at illustrations in books and learn about illustrators. Help them see themselves as artists and illustrators.

1. Talk about art. Not just about the picture, but about what they like and don't like about a particular picture. Bring in sculpture and share it with them. If possible, bring in very good art (certainly borrowed, reproduced, or from the web) and compare it to other art (not art that children create, but not from well-known artists, either).
2. Use three-dimensional materials such as clay and playdough. These can be good for releasing tension and are reusable and easily stored; they are available on short notice.
3. Include some art materials that accommodate expansive work. Color or paint on very large paper without restrictions, use fingerpaint on the table, then print the pictures.
4. Encourage art that does not require cutting with scissors or precise fine motor skills. Tear paper, use larger brushes, bigger paper, markers, sparkle glue, and so on. See Activity 5–8 Torn Paper Flowers.

Music

Music is an essential part of who we are as a people and as a nation. It is also a way to explore other cultures. Music is a field of its own, yet it provides many opportunities to learn about other areas. Integrating music with other curriculum areas encourages the development of concepts, but provides interesting and varied ways of practicing skills.

1. Paint to music. Be sure the music has a distinctive mood. Talk about this with the children. Ask how it influenced the colors they chose and what they painted. See Activity 5–39w Mood Colors.
2. Sing songs with motions ("My Bonnie Lies Over the Ocean," "Hey, Betty Martin") and those that create body awareness ("Put Your Finger in the Air," "Head, Shoulders, Knees, and Toes"). See Activity 5–19 Sequencing Songs.
3. Sing songs and play music (vocal and nonvocal) that are stylistically different from traditional "American" music. Include chants, bells, drums, and so on. Help children focus on the differences and similarities. Or, listen to music that depicts natural events that may be less familiar to children. They might listen to the CD *African Rainforest* by Putumaya Kids and draw pictures of what they think the sounds represent.
4. Include music from different parts of the United States and from different cultural/ethnic groups. Help children think about the differences in the music and why the specific groups might have developed different music.
5. Sing songs to practice vocabulary. Listen to the song first so that you know what words children will need to know, and go over them briefly before singing the song. For example, sing along with "Shake Something," which uses the vocabulary words: shake, up and down, round and round, bend and unbend, twist back and forth, side to side, fast and slow. "Circle Game" practices the vocabulary: around, inside, out of, over, above, below, to the side, between, behind, in front, forward, backward, under, through. Both of these songs are on the CD titled *Getting to Know Myself* by Hap Palmer.
6. Use music to release energy. If bad weather has kept children indoors, play salsa music or a Sousa march.
7. Use music to help children settle down. If children are excited before a quiet time, encourage them to march, then jump, then twirl and repeat it all again for 3 to 5 minutes. When they are tired help them relax with some "easy listening" music.
8. Encourage children to find patterns in the songs they sing at group time. In the song "Good Morning," the pattern is AAB: Good morning, good morning, good morning to you. The CD title is *We All Live Together*. "Number Rock" on the same CD includes counting forward and backward by Greg and Steve.

Creative Movement

Creative movement incorporates movement into a series of movements for a particular purpose or in response to a stimulus such as music. It often requires children to take an experience that is familiar to them and to interpret it with their bodies.

1. Encourage children to dance to music with different tempos. Include dances and music from a variety of cultures and those that are stylistically different (waltz, country line dancing, ballroom dancing, tango, calypso). Help children analyze the differences.
2. Show children ice melting and have them be ice that is melting in the sun. Or, they could be a snowman that melts. You can also have them freeze. Talk about the fact that this is a gradual process and have them think about what parts melt or freeze first.
3. Do animal walks. Talk about the characteristics of different animals and how they move. Discuss the relationship between movement and body type (turtle versus cheetah) and how movement is adaptive.
4. Encourage children to think about different surfaces and how they would walk through or on them (sand, water, a mattress, a hot surface, a very cold surface, a slippery surface, a gooey surface, a moving surface). Have children think about how they will move and then have all children demonstrate their version of it. Talk about the characteristics that influence their choices. Have them think about the shoes they might like to have as they traverse these surfaces.

Dramatic Play

Dramatic play supports children in learning about their world in a safe environment, an environment in which they can be in control. They can rehearse new roles and they can replay familiar ones. They can camp in a tent, construct a beaver dam, or play "house." The area is driven by the children's interests and the teacher's philosophy.

1. Encourage children to build structures for various climates and uses. Ask them to suggest supplies they need for the construction area, such as fabric, dowels, netting, and so on to build their structures. Have them design:

   - A house for a climate that is hot and rainy.
   - A school in a climate where it is almost always cold and often dark.
   - A store where the temperature changes seasonally.

2. Help children role play different medical roles and what these professionals do and look for. Provide the necessary supports. Incorporate technology using web sites such as http://www.uniquely-adhd.com/add_adhd.html to provide pictures of the brain.

3. Use dramatic play to help children learn social skills. Teach children skills to enter groups and maintain group membership.

Routines and Transitions

Routines and transitions are challenging and often a difficult time for children. Structuring them well helps children with ADHD.

1. Employ auditory and visual cues to signal change in the daily routine.
2. Decrease the number of required transitions as much as possible; plan those you must have carefully.
3. Try using code words, songs, or visual cues to help the child anticipate and make the transition.
4. Plan enough time to prepare the child for an upcoming transition. Try a warning of "5 more minutes" or a song to begin the transition. Let the child know about the next activity and the motivating aspects of it.
5. If children need to take medication build it into a routine or transition so it is seen as a natural part of the day.
6. Let the child know specifically how and what needs to be done to move to the next activity. Express positive reinforcement and recognition of the child's ability to finish and make the transition.

Summary

Children with attention-deficit/hyperactivity disorder (ADHD) can have problems with attention, hyperactivity, impulsivity, or both. Somewhere between 2 percent and 7 percent of children are identified as having ADHD. For most children, ADHD is an inherited genetic problem. The problem itself has to do with how neurotransmitters work in the brain. Some children are prescribed stimulant medication that acts on the neurotransmitters. The use, and misuse, of medication has stirred controversy in the field. ADHD alone is not covered by the IDEA, unless there are comorbid conditions such as learning disabilities or emotional disorders. It may be classified among "other health impairments" if the child meets these criteria he will have an IEP. ADHD is covered by Section 504, and children may have an accommodation plan.

It is difficult to diagnose children with ADHD when they are very young because the behaviors that mark ADHD are typical for young children. Effective interventions include behavior management plans both at home and at school. If children have other disabilities, they must be included in the intervention plan to meet the child's needs.

Reflections

1. As an effective educator, how will you deal with learning processing problems in the classroom? How will you support a child with ADHD who is bright but not learning at the rate you expect? What general guidelines will you follow to help make learning and classroom routines as positive as possible? What adaptations will you make in the curriculum for children with ADHD? Where will you find resources to make your classroom successful?

2. Whether or not medication is prescribed for children with ADHD, it is only part of the process of making the child available for learning. Some form of behavior modification and alternative teaching strategies are required for children with ADHD both at school and at home. Some professionals recommend that educators have an accountability plan for children who have challenging behaviors. What systems would you use to help the child control his behavior? What behaviors would you allow or choose to overlook, and what behaviors would you consider to be most important to establish or eliminate? Reflect on how these decisions relate to your philosophy of teaching.

Educational Resources

American Academy of Child and Adolescent Psychiatry is designed as a public service to support the understanding and treatment of children with developmental, behavioral, and mental disorders. It is designed for professionals and families. http://www.aacap.org/

Attention Deficit Disorder Association is a national organization that provides information on education, research and public advocacy. Although useful, it provides little information on young children. http://www.add.org

CD Baby Independent Music. Hap Palmer pioneered the integration of music and movement in the area of early childhood education. His songs enhance the development of motor skills, language acquisition, reading readiness, and math concepts as well as nurture the imaginative process and encourage creative problem solving. The CD *Getting to Know Myself* is on this site. http://cdbaby.com/cd/happalmer21

Children and Adults with Attention Deficit Disorder (CHADD) emphasizes family and community support, as well as encourages scientific research. It is a great resource for parents and professionals with many fact sheets and provides many useful links. (800) 213-4050; FAX (945) 587-4599; http://www.chadd.org/index.html

Greg and Steve have as their goal to "Educate, Motivate, Enrich, and Entertain" young children. http://gregandsteve.com/cds_videos.php

Putumaya Kids is committed to introducing children to other cultures through fun upbeat music from around the world. In additions to having CDs like *African Rainforest* they have a section on teaching tools to help use their music in the classroom. http://www.putumayo.com/en/putumayo_kids.htm

School and Me with ADD! is a national organization that supports parents, teachers, and children with attention-deficit disorder, with special pages for home-school interactions. http://www.add.org/main/kids/school.htm

For additional resources, visit the book companion website for this text at www.cengage.com/education/deiner.

Chapter 11

Children with Communication Disorders

I didn't talk as a young child. Well, I said things, but no one could understand what I was saying. My sister Mary was 10 months older and they would use her to interpret what I was saying. I am one of five children. We are each separated by about a year. I am the middle child. I remember the debate over whether I'd be allowed to go to preschool. I also remember people being so mean and teasing me saying, "Can't you speak English? Are you speaking German?" At the time, I neither knew what "German" meant nor "English," but what they made me feel came across loud and clear. I did not speak for a long time, even when I had needs. I showed someone. Often my parents didn't have the time to wait and told me to "Just say what you want." Then I did without.

I don't know why they finally decided to take me to a specialist. With five kids, we rarely saw doctors of any kind. To this day I remember what the room looked like as well as the person who administered the test; I even remember some of the room's windup toys. What's interesting is how they arrived at the conclusion that I was not "retarded." My receptive language skills were not in sync with the expressive ones. I not only misplaced words, but apparently mixed up letter placement as well. Even now, I often will put words in the wrong order.

I remember, vividly, stopping before I opened my mouth and thinking of the action and the steps involved before I could tell an event in the right order; it wasn't that I didn't know the order, but I skipped to the end and then returned, "outside the box," to the next thing. I felt I was living in a world where I could produce sounds, but not put them in an order that could be understood.

One day, when I was having a bad day and getting nowhere, my Gram, who was living with us at the time, took me aside. She pulled out a book and tried to explain how the pages went in order. She was the only one who noticed my frustration. She could not speak English when she moved to this country, and told me I was not alone and it was nothing to "cry about," just "do something about." I came back with, "But NO ONE is listening!" She got down at my eye level and said, "I am, even if I don't have a clue what you want. Show me." Perhaps this is why I always ask kids who don't understand, and even my dog, to "show me." The visual part of my brain must kick in.

Because I could not get the words out, I was unable to defend myself when blamed for stuff I didn't do. The more stressed out I became, the worse things got. I do not remember going back for any type of follow-up therapy. Apparently, knowing that I wasn't "retarded" was all they were concerned about.

I remember trying so hard, and knowing exactly what I wanted to say. I would try, and get these blank stares, and I would have to wait until Mary got home from school to translate, if she felt like it. When my parents took the time to tell me to "slow down," rather than "hurry up, we don't have all day," I had time enough to order the words or letters, once I knew which letters went with what words.

The last time the other kids on the block teased me about my speech was when I clobbered Pammy Pantalo over the head with Anne's book bag. She had been teasing me so much and was much larger than me. Anne (my oldest sister) was in kindergarten, I was about three. After a number of, "Look at the baby, she can't even talk yet—can't talk, stupid, stupid, stupid," I took Anne's red-and-black-plaid book bag and hit her over the head with it. I distinctly remember her mother bringing Pammy to the house and wanting to speak to Mom. I hid behind the stairwell until her mother accused my sister of picking on her charming Pammy, and wanted to know why Anne didn't pick on someone her own size. (Our family was tall; Pammy was average from what I can remember.) When Mom ordered Anne to come and "fess up," Anne said, "Oh that wasn't me, I gave Paula my book bag because I would have missed and I knew she would hit her." When Pammy's mother found out it was me, she dragged Pammy home, scolding her daughter for making her look stupid, because I was so much younger and not even Pammy's size yet. I guess I learned early that I needed to stand up for my rights. I remember well the loneliness and isolation. It helps me still today to read aloud to no one, or to the dog if I find my mind racing, as it probably redirects the nerve pathways to a slower route.

I remember needing to put a great deal of effort into talking. Gram would help by repeating what she thought I was trying to say, or part of it, and asking me to fill in the blanks. When we moved to Maryland, I was placed in speech class, but that had more to do with my strong New York accent—compounded with the Irish brogue I learned from Gram—and specific sounds I couldn't say. I was relieved that two others kids in my class, both boys, had the same problem. We all froze up when asked to read to the rest of the class. All through third grade we encouraged one another. None of us had a problem understanding one another's "skip talk."

Reflective Practice

How would you accommodate this child in your class? What would you do about peer relationships? What would you talk to the family about? Reflect on the ways this child's lack of communication skills impacted her life.

Communication

Some children come to school as "talkers." They immediately want to know where the crayons are, why they are in school, why they can't go outside now...until you think you may change your profession if you hear one more question. These children stick in your mind from day one. Then there are the children who appear shy and immature and of whom you probably still won't have a clear picture even after a few weeks. This group is difficult, as it is hard to determine whether these children choose not to communicate or do not have the ability to communicate. A third group is composed of children who have a diagnosed language or communication disorder.

One of the first questions to ask when you are concerned about communication is: Can this child communicate in an age-appropriate way that can be understood by others? Then think back over events of the week. When you dismiss the children from group time by the color of their clothes, does this child need to be prompted? When you give simple directions, can this child follow them? How about more complex directions? Does this child volunteer comments? Does the child speak up during group time? When this child speaks, can you understand most of the words or only some of them? Given free choice, does this child seek out activities requiring language, or does he avoid them? How can you tell whether the child falls in that wide range called typical or if he has an impairment?

The next concern relates to how representative what you hear is of the child's speech?" Children are very adaptable in their communication styles and use language differently when talking with a peer or an adult, as well as adapting their speech to a variety of situations. Young children's language in school differs from that at home. When at home, the child typically displays more frequent, longer, and more balanced conversations over a wider range of topics than at school. Children who are quiet at school may be nonstop talkers at home. Given this, it is important to find out from a child's family how representative the speech is that you are hearing.

Communication is a complex process that involves different regions of the brain that regulate, integrate, and formulate communicative messages (Stuart, 2007). Communication is also dependent upon the lungs, larynx, vocal cords, throat, nose, mouth, lips, and other body parts. Communication involves many areas of the brain, some more than others. Broca's speech production area is in the frontal lobe. Wernicke's speech comprehension area is located in the temporal lobe, which also contains the primary auditory areas. The primary visual area is located in the occipital lobe. The parietal lobe contributes to the integration of stimuli to promote a "whole" picture from the variety of sensory inputs (Yaun & Keating, 2007).

Sound enters primarily through the ear and travels through the auditory nerve to the auditory cortex, which signals Wernicke's area where the neurons for that combination of sounds are activated. Neurons can store a variety of information about a particular sound combination. If the combination was "book" the neurons might have a visual representation of a book, while other neurons might store more conceptual or functional information about books. These ideas would then be transmitted to the speech area of the brain (Broca's area), then converted into patterns of motor movement, referred to the motor strip, which then sends the impulses for the muscle movements needed to produce sound (Hegde, 2001).

Children also have to learn the rules of a language. Language, any language, is composed of a set of rules that govern its form and function. Form is concerned with the rules that determine which sounds and words are combined to express meaning. The form of any language relates to the rules that govern **phonology** and grammar (Stuart, 2007). **Phonemes** are the smallest units of a language that distinguish meaning (vowels and consonants). The meanings of c*a*t and c*a*p are distinguished by the phonemes /t/ and /p/. Phonology uses the rules for combining types of phonemes, pauses, and stress to form words (Stuart, 2007). One phonemic rule of the English language is that *q* is always followed by *u*. Other rules relate to whether vowel sounds are short or long.

Grammar is concerned with the rules for using the smallest units of language that contain meaning (*morphemes*) and word order (*syntax*) to convey meaning. **Morphemes** are words or meaningful word parts. **Prefixes** and **suffixes** are morphemes. **Morphology** looks at how adding or deleting parts of words change their meaning. An example would be the difference between *disorder* and *order* or changing book to book*s*. **Syntax** refers to the linguistic rules that govern the arrangement of words into phrases or sentences and the relationship between these elements in a sentence. Syntax establishes the requirements that all sentences have a subject and verb, and that different word orders change the meaning; that is, "André hit the ball" is different from "The ball hit André."

Function relates to the rules that govern the meaning specific words convey (*semantics*) and the sociolinguistic use of language (*pragmatics*). **Semantics** is the psycholinguistic system that governs the relationship between words or phrases and their meanings—the intent and meaning of utterances. It relates to the meaning conveyed by words, phrases, and sentences. Semantics has a cognitive base and involves underlying skills such as memory, mental imagery, and concepts (Stuart, 2007). Sometimes children have problems in this area because of lack of an appropriate knowledge base. **Pragmatics** relates to rules that govern the use of language in personal situations and social interactions. The emphasis is on the functional use of language rather than the mechanics of it. Children need language to convey their needs to others and to interact with them.

Defining Communication Disorders

I have purposefully used language, communication, and speech as if they were interchangeable. Although there is much overlap, there are also some important distinctions. Communication is the process by which information is transmitted between two or more individuals. It involves a sender, who encodes information, and a receiver, whose job it is to decode the information. This information can be verbal or nonverbal, symbolic or nonsymbolic, widely understood or colloquial, human or nonhuman. Language has functions other than communication. It is a cognitive tool that is used to organize information and influences thinking and memory skills. Speech is an aspect of language: spoken language. Disorders of spoken language include speech disorders, articulation disorders, and fluency disorders

The definition according to IDEA 2004:

Speech or language impairment means a communication disorder, such as stuttering, impaired articulation, a language impairment, or a voice impairment, that adversely affects a child's educational performance.

Expressive Language Disorder

The American Psychiatric Association (APA) (2000) is more specific. Although the actual diagnostic feature vary with age, they see an *expressive language disorder* as one in which expressive language development is substantially below the norms for a given age based on a measure of nonverbal intellectual capacity and receptive language development. These requirements ensure that it is viewed separately from an intellectual disability, a speech-motor or sensory deficit or environmental deprivation. They also caution about the relevance to linguistic and cultural groups. Symptoms of an expressive language disorder would include limited vocabulary, making errors in tense, having problems recalling words, and using sentences that lack length and complexity based on the age of the child. And, these problems interfere with academic or social communication (APA, 2000).

Mixed Receptive-Expressive Disorder

In a *mixed receptive-expressive language disorder* both receptive and expressive language are below the norms on a standardized test. In addition to the characteristics described for expressive language children with receptive language impairments have difficulty understanding words and sentences or specific types of words. Because the development of expressive language is dependent upon receptive language, a purely receptive language is almost never identified. What differentiates this disorder from the expressive language is the comprehension deficit (APA, 2000). These communication disorders vary depending upon severity and the age of the child. Again, these problems must interfere with academic or social communication.

Phonological Disorder

Phonological disorders are the failure to use developmentally appropriate speech sounds based on the child's age and dialect. This was formerly called developmental articulation disorder (APA, 2000). In this disorder there are errors in sound production, use, representation, or organization. In some cases, one sound is substituted for another or sounds are omitted from words. And, these phonological problems interfere with academic or social communication (APA, 2000).

Fluency Disorder

Stuttering is a disturbance in normal fluency and the time patterning of speech that is developmentally inappropriate. It is characterized by one or more of the following:

- Sound syllable repetitions
- Sound prolongations
- Interjections
- Broken words (for example pauses within a word)
- Audible or silent blocking (filled or unfilled pauses in speech)
- Circumlocutions (word substitutions to avoid problematic works)
- Words produced with an excess of physical tension
- Monosyllabic whole-word repetitions (for example, I-I-I see him) (APA, 2000, p. 69)

These problems vary in frequency and interfere with academic or social communication.

Prevalence of Communication Disorders

Problems with the overlapping of categories of communication disorders impacts our ability to identify how many children actually have communication disorders. Depending on the definition used, children with communication disorders (including speaking, listening, reading, and writing) constitute 21.7 percent of children receiving services based on the IDEA (National Center for Educational Statistics, 2005). This rate has decreased since 1976–1977 when 35.2 percent of children receiving services were identified as having a speech or language impairment.

The APA (2000) estimates that 10 percent to 15 percent of children younger than 3 have an expressive language disorder and that from 3 percent to 7 percent of the school age population have this disorder. A mixed receptive-expressive language disorder is less frequent occurring in about 5 percent of preschool children and 3 percent of school age children. Articulation or phonological disorder affects approximately 2 percent of 6 and 7 year olds. This drops to 0.5 percent by age 17. Almost all cases of fluency disorders (stuttering) begin before 10 years of age with a peak at age 5. The onset is typically gradual affecting three times as many males as females. It occurs in about 1 percent of children and drops to 0.8 percent in adolescents (APA, 2000).

Causes of Communication Disorders

Communication differences can have a genetic, neurological, structural, physiological, psychological, emotional, or cognitive base (Stuart, 2007). They can be related to late maturation or an unstimulating environment. They can also be related to cultural and language differences. Although English is the primary language of the United States, there are a variety of regional differences and dialects such as African American English, which use a different set of linguistic rules, as well as other languages.

There are two major types of concerns that are related to communication: communication delays and communication disorders. Children with communication delays have normal or close to normal speech and language form and function (phonology, grammar, semantics, and pragmatics) but are delayed in their development. Children with communication disorders are impaired in their ability to generate or interpret language and their speech may be impaired. These disorders may appear singly, or be part of other disorders, such as intellectual disability, autism, apraxia, and aphasia. Communication differences are further divided into those that affect language, speech, or both.

Speech and language therapy are often provided to a wide range of children with other disabilities such as hearing impairments, intellectual disability, specific learning disabilities, and behavioral and emotional disorders. Language is rarely the only target for intervention in young children.

In the Field

As a special educator who teaches 6 and 7 year olds, I always thought I would consistently reinforce the use of standard English in all situations. This was until I began teaching in a rural area. I soon learned that the language students and many parents in this area used was far from what I would consider to be standard English. Suddenly, I was drawn into a personal debate over the extent to which I should require standard English in the classroom. The language of children in this area commonly included the use of double negative, the word "ain't," the changing of consonants and vowels in certain words such as "bafroom" for "bathroom," the use of "me" rather than "I," "done" rather than "finished," and so on. While I know it was my job to teach standard English, I realized that their speech was the accepted way to speak in their area and neighborhoods. Most of the adults and friends in their lives spoke this way. What should I do about this?

After giving much thought to the subject, I decided that I would teach the students standard English and that they should always use this in the classroom. I also informed them that when they went on a field trip and when they got older and applied for a job, standard English was the way to go. I realized that they would probably never use standard English at home; it would be inappropriate and may even make them stand out. I hope I have fulfilled my responsibilities as a teacher of language, reading, and writing.

Reflective Practice

Do you think this teacher made the right decision? What would you have done in her situation? If you go beyond this situation to the larger one of culture and children's whose home language is not English, how do you think these children should be taught? Reflect on this as you continue reading this chapter.

Early Identification of Communication Disorders

Identifying children with communication delays early is critical. Communication plays an important role in children's cognitive development, social interactions, and overall well-being. Children with communication delays may also be at risk for other developmental disabilities that affect school performance.

Unless it is related to a high visibility disorder, such as severe intellectual disabilities or neuromotor abnormalities, it is difficult to diagnose a communication disorder at an early age. Communication disorders are high-incidence, low-visibility disorders and often not identified in very young children. Table 11–1 highlights behaviors that should make you look more closely at a child's speech and language development.

Because communication has such a strong developmental base knowing age-appropriate behavior is essential.

Infants and Toddlers

Young infants respond to speech by looking at the speaker. From birth until about 2 to 3 months, the infant's communication consists of reflexive reactions to internal and external stimuli. At about 2 months, cooing is added to the infant's repertoire. By 4 months, laughter is added to the infant's inventory of sounds, and by 5 months, infants produce vocalizations that bridge between cooing and true babbling. Infants who do not respond to environmental sounds or voices by 6 months should be referred for evaluation as should children who do not make cooing or comfort sounds (but only cry) by 4 months (Wang & Baron, 1997).

Between 8 and 12 months infants use communication, gestures, and vocalizations to show intentionality. Infants point to objects they want and shake their head when they don't want something. Near their first birthday, they respond with gestures to words such as "Hi," "Bye-bye," and "Up," as well as by stopping actions when told "No" firmly (Hulit & Howard, 2006). They enjoy taking turns with adults and will vocalize after an adult vocalizes. They can communicate meaning through intonation and the attempts to imitate sounds. Their first word appears at about 12 months.

Between 1 and 2 years, toddlers go from several one word utterances to being able to put two words together. Toddlers can get familiar objects on request: "Bring me the ball." They begin to understand prepositions such as *on*, *in*, and *under*. They respond to simple commands like "Close the door," and to simple "where" questions: "Where's José?" They enjoy listening to simple stories. About a fourth of their speech is comprehensible to non-family members.

Table 11–1: Signs of Communication Disorders

Medical
History of ear infections
Mouth seems abnormal

Language
Does not talk
Makes no attempt to communicate with words
Has difficulty putting words and sounds in a sequence
Does not appear to understand when others speak
Small vocabulary for age

Speech
Cannot imitate sounds or words
Speech is difficult to understand, words are mispronounced
Uses echolalic or parrot-like, repetitive speech
Voice is unusual: breathy, hoarse, too loud or soft, too high or low, or nasal

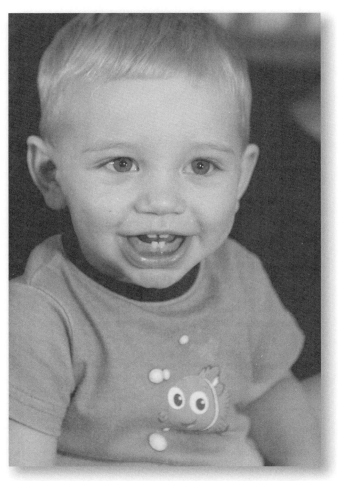

Between 1 and 2 years of age, most children move from a few single words to two-word utterances and make major increases in their receptive language.

Toddlers' sounds become more word-like and meaningful. They now refer to themselves by name, and they are very clear about the use of "my" and "mine" to indicate possession and are beginning to use the pronouns "me," "I," and "you." Toddlers use successive one-word utterances and begin to make two-word utterances: "All gone." All vowel sounds are learned, plus the consonant sounds /h/, /p/, /b/, /m/, and /n/. Toddlers can answer routine questions, say the names of familiar objects in pictures, and identify body parts on a doll as well as on their own body. They like to ask "what" questions and have a vocabulary of about 50 words. Once children hit the 50-word mark (about 18 months) they tend to experience rapid growth in vocabulary, especially nouns (Hulit & Howard, 2006). About half of their speech should be comprehensible to nonfamily members.

Implications for Educators

Children need many opportunities to build vocabulary in the context of learning.

Children who speak fewer than 10 words and do not seem to comprehend simple directions or requests by age 2 should be referred. By 2-and-a-half, concern arises about children with very limited vocabularies, those who have no phrases of two or more words, those who cannot answer simple questions, and those whose speech is entirely unintelligible (Wang & Baron, 1997).

Preschool Children

By 3 years, children can point to pictures of familiar objects when they are named, identify objects when told their use, and understand questions relating to what and where. They also clearly understand the negations "no," "not," "can't," and "don't," and they enjoy simple stories again and again and again. Expressively, they can now name many common objects and use language as a way of communicating thoughts. They usually enjoy using language, gain satisfaction from expressing themselves and being understood, and show frustration when they are not understood. The consonant sounds /k/, /d/, /f/, /ng/, /y/, /t/, and /w/ have been added to their repertoire, as well as the use of plurals. They use early forms of negation: "No," "No want," and "Can't open it." They understand and use abstract words such as "up," "down," "now," and "later." They are beginning to refer to themselves as "me" instead of using their proper name, and they can now state their first and last names. Words are combined into short phrases, and they are starting to ask primitive questions.

Children's understanding of relationships is increasing. They can use words like "because" and contingencies such as "if" and "when." They also understand size comparatives (large–larger). They are less concrete and are beginning to understand the vocabulary of time (tomorrow) as well as the concept of "pretend." They can carry out a series (two to four) of related directions. Although children often talk to themselves while playing, language is becoming more socially directed. Children are beginning to ask questions for information and for social contacts. They use simple sentence structures and can repeat at least one nursery rhyme. They are beginning to use the simple future tense, "I will," as well as pronouns that refer to others (he, his, and so on). They have added the consonant sounds /g/, /s/, /r/, /l/, /sh/, and /ch/, and their vocabulary increases rapidly. They love new words. By age 4, all of their words should be intelligible (Hulit & Howard, 2006).

Children's language skills increase in many different areas. They can follow three unrelated commands and listen to longer stories. They understand three levels of comparatives (big, bigger, biggest) as well as the sequencing of events: "First we have group time, then free play, snack, stories, outside play, and then we go home."

Children now talk a lot—not always to tell or ask something important, but to seek attention and companionship. They love silly language. They use a variety of sentence structures and use almost all pronouns appropriately. They can explain why they want to do something a certain way as well as asking "when," "how," and "why" questions. They have added the consonant sound /th/ and their vocabulary has grown to about 1,200 to 1,500 words by around age 4 (Hulit & Howard, 2006).

Implications for Educators

By 3 years, the average child has a vocabulary of 250 to 900 words. Three year olds who cannot engage in simple conversation, have no short sentences, and whose speech is largely unintelligible are of concern (Wang & Baron, 1997). When 4 year olds have difficulty learning new concepts, explaining events, and following two-step directions, there is concern. Likewise, when their speech is unclear or they are still simply echoing speech with no complete sentences, a referral is indicated (Wang & Baron, 1997).

School Age Children

Between 5 and 6 years of age, children demonstrate many pre-academic skills. Except for the understanding of complex vocabulary, they function at an adult level in

understanding communication. They are curious and ask many questions. They use complete sentences and give full information and thus need opportunities to talk with someone who is interested and who will listen attentively. They have added the consonant sound /v/, use different verb tenses, and have a vocabulary of about 2,000 words.

By the time children enter school they demonstrate academic skills and function at an adult level in understanding communication. They understand more complex vocabulary. The language structures are mastered and are being refined for irregulars. The consonant sounds /z/ and /j/ are added, and their vocabulary has grown to about 2,600 words. Children are adding reading and writing to their communication skills.

Implications for Educators

Children entering school meet with different language expectations than at home. Language at school relies less on the context of environment, which is less familiar than at home, and less on the context of past conversations and events. The teacher in many elementary school classrooms does most of the talking, giving the children fewer opportunities to initiate conversation. Teachers also have less knowledge than parents about individual children. Finally, the school culture may make demands on the child that are not parallel to the home culture (Howard, Shaughnessy, Sanger, & Hux, 1998). These are some of the distinctions between social and academic English.

Assessment of Communication Disorders

Language is a very personal thing, and language styles are different depending on the individual and her cultural or ethnic identification. Certainly, we would expect language differences in children who are learning English as a second language. However, there is also much variation in individuals who are native English speakers. Some children who did not speak and write standard American English have previously been diagnosed as having a language disorder (Salvia & Ysseldyke, 2007). The 2004 amendments to the IDEA are designed to ensure that this does not happen. Although there is debate about acceptance of nonstandard English, there is agreement that children who speak nonstandard English should not be classified as having a language disorder. In some instances, there are regional as well as cultural uses of language. Think of such terms as *hotdog, frankfurter,* and *wiener.* If only one of these is an acceptable answer on a language assessment, then some children are penalized not for their lack of vocabulary, but for using a regional label.

Informal Language Assessment

If you are concerned about a child's speech and language, begin informally. First, look up the child's birth date. This alone might resolve the problem. If this child is one of the youngest in the class and your basis for comparison is older children, the difference between them may be a developmental one that will disappear with time. In early childhood, even a few months has a considerable effect. As a further check, find out if this child was premature and is developmentally even younger.

If you are still concerned, assign the child to a small group with several others who are close in age. (Do not include children who are cognitively delayed or advanced.) While doing language activities with the children, note who volunteers the most and least often. Take language samples from each child and compare them for sentence length, sentence structure, vocabulary, concepts, and articulation (note omissions, distortions, or substitutions of sounds). An easy way to obtain language samples is by recording small-group time. Do this on at least two occasions to allow for a child's having a bad or good day. If the child is in the top to middle of this group, there is probably no cause for concern. If the child is at the bottom, continue gathering information.

As you continue your observations, note how the child uses materials not related to language. How many different materials are used? Are the materials used appropriately? This information will help you decide if the child is delayed in other areas. If so, the child's speech and language problems may have an underlying cause, such as a developmental delay or lack of an experiential background.

The next step is to determine the gap between the child's comprehension and production of language. During the early childhood years, children have a greater ability to understand language than to speak it; you are looking for a significantly wider gap between the two than is expected.

Analyze the child's speech carefully. If the child is having trouble pronouncing words, note exactly which sounds are difficult. Vowels and the consonants /p/, /b/, /m/, and /w/ are easiest for a young child to pronounce, followed by /t/, /d/, /n/, /k/, /g/, /f/, and /v/. The more difficult sounds are /s/, /z/, /l/, /ch/, /th/, /sh/, /j/, /b/, and /cr/. If the child only has problems with the last set of sounds, which children normally take longer to learn, reevaluate a few months later. Be sure to look for the obvious. If the child doesn't have front teeth, some sounds will not be possible.

After carefully observing the child alone and with others, if you still feel there is a problem, schedule a conference with the parents. Alert them to your concerns, and then accept whatever they say. Your goals in the first conference are to gather more information and to begin to make the parents aware of your concerns. Schedule a class visit for them in about 2 weeks; if this isn't possible, make a videotape to show them. Have them observe (or show them) their own child with an age-mate, just as you did. At your second conference, discuss and compare their observations with your own. (Their opinions may have changed as they became more conscious of their child's speech and language and listened more carefully.)

Consider making a home visit. You will have an opportunity to watch and listen to the family interact more informally. You may learn that the child's speech or language is modeled after the family pattern, which means you are unlikely to convince the parents there is a problem. If you still feel the problem exists, discuss it. Even if parents do not share your concerns, there is still much you can do with classroom programming to foster this child's speech and language development.

If you and the parents agree the child has a problem, you might suggest that the child be assessed. The family physician is probably the best choice to begin, as there may be a medical reason for the problem. The physician might then refer the child to an audiologist to test hearing, to a speech/language pathologist, and to a psychologist for testing in social and intellectual development.

No matter how the parents choose to obtain further information about the child's needs, there will be a lag between your initial concern and a final conclusion. Young children can be difficult to assess, test results may be inconclusive, and many times the decision is made to "wait and see." In the meantime, you can develop ideas for helping this child in your classroom.

Formal Language Assessment

The goals of assessment are to determine whether, in fact, there is a communication impairment and in what area or areas this disorder lies. The next step is to determine the goals for intervention and then to establish a plan to meet those goals and implement the plan. The final component is to develop a method for monitoring progress toward goals.

To determine whether a child has a communication and/or language disorder, we typically use standardized tests. Most tests differentiate between receptive language, comprehension, and expressive language, production (Salvia & Ysseldyke, 2007). *The Test of Language Development, Primary:* Third Edition (TOLD-P: 3; Newcomer & Hammill, 1999) is a norm-referenced, individually administered test used for children ages 4 through 8. It measures expressive and receptive language, identifies children's language strengths and weaknesses, progress in language development, and language problems. *The Goldman-Fristoe Test of Articulation,* Second Edition (GFAT-2; Goldman & Fristoe, 2000) is one of the most frequently used tests to assess phonology. It is a norm referenced test designed to measure articulation for individuals 2 through 21 years of age.

There are some concerns with the assessment of language. One is whether the formal assessment actually reflects the child's spontaneous language. Testing situations may be new and frightening for children. To the extent that children's response to this situation influences their language, the measure will not be an accurate reflection of their spontaneous language. A second concern relates to the use of standardized tests of language. The step from getting the results of a language test to generating goals and ways to implement them is a large one. Parents may want to focus on a fundamental social vocabulary to allow them to better understand what their child wants and needs. Speech/language pathologists may want to work on particular articulation problems or other specific areas of language, whereas the early childhood specialist may feel the most appropriate goal is to increase the number, complexity, and length of children's sentences in spontaneous conversation. A third concern of assessment is whether or not the child being assessed has the same characteristics as the sample on which the measure was standardized; in other words, are test norm results valid for this child (Salvia & Ysseldyke, 2007)? If they are not, then it is difficult to figure out what to do.

The Evidence Base

The Peabody Picture Vocabulary Test III (PPVT-III; Dunn & Dunn, 1997) is a measure of receptive language. It is frequently used as a screening measure because it is short, easy to administer and score and correlates with intelligence scales. The Expressive Vocabulary Test (EVT; Williams, 1997) is a measure of children's expressive one word vocabulary. It is often used in conjunction with the PPVT to measure expressive language. There is some concern that these measures might be biased against certain groups. To look at the issue of bias 210 children (range 4.0 to 5.2 years) attending public school prekindergarten programs (one rural, one urban) were given the PPVT-III and the EVT within the first 45 days of the school year. Although an item analysis of the PPVT-III did not find evidence of ethnic bias against African American children the performance of these children as compared to European American children was significantly lower across most maternal education levels. Using the PPVT-III as a diagnostic measure 24 percent of African American children were identified as having a significant vocabulary problem as compared to 4 percent of European American children. For mothers who had a high school education or less 24 percent of the children were identified as having a significant vocabulary problem as opposed to 4 percent for mothers who had a bachelor's degree or some college. No gender bias was evident.

Using the EVT only 5 percent of African American children were identified as having a significant language problem and no European American children were identified. For mothers who had a high school education or less 4 percent of the children were identified as having a significant vocabulary problem as opposed to 1 percent for mothers who had a bachelor's degree or some college (Restrepo et al., 2006).

Reflective Practice

Why does this matter. The concern is that African American children and children whose mothers have a high school education or less may be misdiagnosed as having a potential language disability if the measure of language used is the PPVT-III. What does it mean in your classroom and how you will evaluate the results of these measures? How can you use this evidence to inform your practice?

Language Disorders

Language has a developmental base. What is appropriate for children at one age is inappropriate and considered dysfunctional at other ages. Additionally, language does not develop in isolation, and the interaction between language and cognitive development is difficult to unravel. There are also many ways of classifying language disorders. Some look at the rate and sequence in which language develops, whereas others focus on the cause or related conditions, and still others break language down into subsystems (phonology, morphology, syntax, semantics, and pragmatics). In general, a child's language is impaired when there are deviations in the formation, expression, or understanding of language. Characteristics of impaired language include poor concepts, inability to follow directions, speechlessness, speech confusion, and poor word comprehension.

According to the American-Speech-Language-Hearing Association (ASHA) (1997–2007) language is made up of socially shared rules that include the following:

- What words mean ("star" can refer to a bright object in the night sky or a celebrity)
- How to make new words (e.g., friend, friendly, unfriendly)
- How to put words together ("Peg walked to the new store" rather than "Peg walk store new")
- What word combinations are best in what situations ("Would you mind moving your foot?" could quickly change to "Get off my foot, please!" if the first request did not produce results)

When a person has trouble understanding others (receptive language), or sharing thoughts, ideas, and feelings completely (expressive language), then he has a language disorder (ASHA, 1997–2007).

There are two major categories of language disorders: those that are present from birth (**congenital**) and those that arise after a child has been developing language at a typical rate (**acquired**). Congenital language disorders usually have some organic base. Hearing loss is a primary consideration.

Developmentally Delayed Language

Infants are born communicating. Initial communication is not intentional, but does function as a signaling system. It is up to the adults in the environment to figure out what the signal means. Despite variations in the timing of language acquisition, like motor and cognitive development, there are major milestones that occur in a predictable sequence. When milestones are not reached there is concern about delayed language development and whether children have the underlying skills to develop language (Table 11–2).

Communication does not develop in isolation; it is truly a joint venture. Adults provide most of the modeling and examples for young language learners. Parents who respond to a toddler's communicative attempts support and encourage these attempts. When adults do not respond to a toddler's sounds and gestures, they send a message that communication behaviors are not valued. It is important that the toddler's communicative efforts be responded to so they continue to communicate. Lack of reinforcement extinguishes behavior. Adult interaction is necessary for the development of the child's language abilities.

Parents are rarely the cause of delayed language. However, making disparaging remarks about children's language has negative effects on children's language development. Focusing on their deficits and not allowing children time to respond reduces children's self-esteem as well as their language output.

Language delays are the failure to acquire language skills at the typical rate and within expected age ranges. Children with language delays acquire language along the same developmental patterns as typically developing

Table 11–2: Skills required to develop speech and language

Children need to be able to

- attend to speech
- discriminate among speech sounds
- discriminate among intonational patterns
- remember a sequence of speech sounds and the order they were presented
- discriminate between sequences of speech sounds
- compare a sequence of speech sounds to a model stored in memory

Source: Owens, 2005.

children, but the acquisition of skills occurs over a longer period of time. A language delay can include a general delay in all dimensions of language or it can relate to skills in specific areas, such as **semantics** or **syntax**. Causes for delay in the acquisition of language can include physical or structural problems, such as a hearing impairment, and physiological or neurologic problems, such as cerebral palsy, intellectual disability, or mental health problems. Some language delays have no specific cause and may be environmental.

The two most common organic causes of language delays are intellectual disability and hearing impairment. Brain damage, also organic, can interfere with a child's ability to receive, understand, remember, and recognize communicated information. These types of disorders are referred to as receptive language disorders. The child can hear adequately and has no expressive disorder, but the messages, once heard and transmitted to the brain, encounter interference and the message is not understood.

Physical disabilities can also affect both speech and language development. Motor impairments that prevent children from becoming involved with their environment—that is, they are unable to actively manipulate materials and receive sensory input—will result in fewer experiences to build semantic language skills. Children with these impairments may be delayed in language acquisition and will require assistance in acquiring the knowledge or experiences to compensate. Physical disabilities can also affect the oral motor structures and musculature of the body. These children are capable of developing language, but may be unable to verbally express themselves in ways that others can understand. Alternative methods must be developed for these children to express and communicate their thoughts and wishes.

Emotional disturbances can lead to language delays. Young children who exhibit moderate and severe emotional disorders often have problems with language expression. Emotional disorders may slow a child's development of expressive language skills, or stunt the development of an inner language with which to think about received information. Some children with emotional disorders may develop their own language form, one that is unintelligible to the outside world. Children with autism and severe psychotic disorders typically demonstrate severe language disorders, even though they may not experience speech difficulties.

Increasingly, researchers are searching for a better means of classifying language disorders, especially related to brain function, as a means of providing better intervention. One disorder, called a fundamental processing impairment, or auditory processing problem, falls into this category.

Auditory Processing Disorder

Auditory processing is what happens when the brain recognizes and interprets sound. The disorder part means that something is happening in the brain that interferes with the process. Children with processing impairments are unable to integrate auditory stimulation despite having normal hearing. For these children, the learning of meanings, sound combinations, and the specific order of words is flawed; hence, the child's internal models of language are inaccurate (Stuart, 2007). What you say is not necessarily what they hear. This is worse in noisy environments or with complex information (National Institute on Deafness and Other Communication Disorders [NIDCD], 2004).

The cause of congenital auditory processing disorders is usually unknown. The most common cause of acquired language disorders is traumatic brain injury. The part of the brain that is injured will determine the severity as well as the type of the disorder. Children with auditory processing problems have normal hearing and intelligence. Characteristics of children with auditory processing problems are listed in Table 11–3.

Auditory processing problems may appear alone or they may be associated with other language impairments, dyslexia, or developmental delays. Because of the elusive nature of auditory processing disorders, a medical diagnosis begins by ruling other things out and the most obvious is hearing loss. Audiologists may suggest ways to adapt the listening environment to improve the child's learning.

Aphasia

Aphasia is caused by damage to one or more of the language areas of the brain. Although it can happen at any age most adults acquire aphasia from a stroke. When blood doesn't reach part of the brain and it is deprived of oxygen and nutrients brain cells die. Other causes of aphasia include blows to the head, brain tumors, brain infections, and other conditions of the brain. The disorder impairs the expression and understanding of language as well as reading and writing (NIDCD, 2002b). Some children with aphasia will have mild problems; others will be severe. Damage to the left side of the brain causes aphasia for most right-handed people and about half of left-handed people (ASHA, 1997–2007b).

Table 11–3: Characteristics of children with auditory processing problems

Children with auditory processing problems have some of the following challenges:

- Paying attention to and remembering information presented verbally
- Carrying out multistep directions
- Listening
- Processing information quickly
- Learning in general and reading, comprehension, spelling, and vocabulary in particular
- Behaving appropriately
- Understanding language; they confuse syllable sequences and find it hard to increase their vocabulary

Source: National Institute on Deafness and Other Communication Disorders, 2004.

The area in which the brain is damaged determines the nature of the particular problem. Even older children with expressive aphasia will speak only in single words or short fragmented phrases. Words are omitted or put in the wrong order and nonsense words and jargon are mixed with words making it difficult to make sense out of utterances. For children with receptive aphasia, spoken words are difficult to understand, it's a struggle to follow fast speech, and many meanings are taken literally. Children can have both expressive and receptive difficulties in varying degrees (ASHA, 1997–2007b). Treatment depends upon the needs and goals for the child.

Speech Disorders

The production of speech sounds involves the manipulation of the mouth, tongue, cheeks, and throat, along with the shaping and control of air, to produce specific vowel and consonant sounds. Problems with any one of these variables can result in atypical sound production or a speech disorder. In general, a child's speech is impaired when it deviates so far from the speech of other children that it calls attention to itself, interferes with communication, or causes the child to be self-conscious.

Speech is the verbal means of communicating. Speech consists of the following:

- Articulation: How speech sounds are made (children must learn how to produce the "r" sound in order to say "rabbit" instead of "wabbit").
- Voice: Use of the vocal folds and breathing to produce sound (the voice can be abused from overuse or misuse and can lead to hoarseness or loss of voice).
- Fluency: The rhythm of speech (hesitations or stuttering can affect fluency).

When a person is unable to produce speech sounds correctly or fluently, or has problems with his voice, then he has a speech disorder (ASHA, 1997–2007a).

Articulation

The ability to produce, orally, any one of a variety of vowels, consonants, and/or vowel-consonant blends is articulation. The inability to produce these sounds can be physiological: lack of tongue or mouth control, oral musculature difficulties, or a hearing loss. Articulation errors occur when sounds are omitted, added, distorted, or substituted. Take, for example, *spaghetti*:

paghetti	(s is omitted)
spaghettiti	(extra *ti* is added)
speghetti	(*a* is distorted to *e*)
basaghetti	(*ba* is substituted for *p* and put at the beginning)

Articulation errors can happen at the beginning, middle, or end of a word. They may be the result of indistinct articulation. Slow, labored speech and rapid, slurring speech are both articulation problems. Some articulation problems are a natural part of a child's development. Although children may, in fact, outgrow some problems, care must be taken to determine whether therapy is indicated.

Voice

A voice disorder involves abnormalities in pitch, volume, voice quality, and/or duration of speech. The cause can be attributed to physical, learned, or psychological problems. Voice disorders occur less frequently than other speech problems. Children's *pitch* should be appropriate for their age, sex, and size; mismatches can lead to social and emotional difficulties. *Volume* concerns the children's ability to monitor the loudness of their voices; hearing losses can result in a child's using a louder voice than normal. *Quality* refers to the general character of the voice such as hoarse, nasal, breathy, or normal. Extremely harsh or hoarse quality speech can be related to vocal cord nodules or excessive screaming; nasal quality speech can be the result of cleft palate disorders. *Duration* refers to how much or little a child talks. Most problems encountered in voice disorders are treatable medically or through speech therapy.

Fluency

Fluency disorders are the abnormal flow of verbal expression which is characterized by impaired rate and rhythm that may include labored speaking. The most common fluency disorder is stuttering. Stuttering occurs when the normal flow of speech is interrupted by abnormal repetitions, hesitations, and prolongations of sounds and syllables and avoidable struggle behaviors. Associated with stuttering are characteristic body motions such as grimaces, eye blinks, and gross body movements (Stuttering Foundation, 2007).

Children with fluency disorders may experience some tension as they talk.

Most children experience some dysfluency between the ages of 2 and 5. In normal dysfluency, there is no struggle and the dysfluency is effortless. Normal dysfluency is also situationally specific: It increases when children talk with someone who speaks rapidly, when language use is more formal, or when they ask questions, use more complex sentences, or use less familiar words. Dysfluency is episodic and may occur because the child is upset, anxious, under pressure to communicate, or has a lot to say. Approximately 20 percent of children go through a stage of development when they stutter enough to concern their parents (Stuttering Foundation, 2007). Boys are three times more likely to stutter than girls. Most children outgrow stuttering and it is estimated that less than 1 percent of adults stutter (NIDCD, 2002a).

The question is "When should a child be referred to a speech and language pathologist based on stuttering?" Young children who stutter may recover naturally without intervention so there is some reason to wait and look for changes in the child's speech. If, after 6 months there are not significant improvements, or if the child shows signs of becoming distressed by the disorder, the child should be referred. See Table 11–4 for ways of working with children who stutter. During the early childhood years, treatment for stuttering is very effective and can result in children speaking as if they have never stuttered (Onslow, 2000).

Developmental Apraxia of Speech

Developmental apraxia of speech (DAS) occurs in children and is present at birth. It affects more boys than girls. Although children speak later, their language does not follow the typical pattern of children with delayed language development (NIDCD, 2002c). Children with apraxia of speech have trouble saying what they want to say consistently or correctly. This problem is not based on weakness or paralysis of the muscles necessary for speech. Although the cause or causes are not known, it is likely to be a neurologic disorder that affect the brain's ability to send the proper signals to the muscles involved in speech. However, brain imaging has not found differences in the brains of children with DAS. They frequently have family

Four factors most likely to contribute to the development of stuttering: genetics, over half of those who stutter have a family member who does also; having other speech and language problems or developmental delays increases the likelihood of stuttering; neurophysiology, research shows that people who stutter process speech and language in different areas of the brain than those who do not; and family dynamics where there are high expectations and fast-paced lifestyles (Stuttering Foundation, 2007).

Table 11–4: Guidelines for Working with Children who Stutter

Do not imply that stuttering is a bad habit.

Do not tell children to stop and start over or to stop and think what to say.

Do not help them with words with which they are having trouble. Wait for the children to get it out for themselves.

Do not tell them to talk slowly unless they speak too rapidly to articulate.

Do not tell them to talk faster, in a low voice, high voice, to swallow, to take a deep breath first, and so on.

Do not call on them when they don't volunteer or when they are tired and harassed.

If children do not know they stutter, do not call it to their attention.

If they are aware of their stuttering, do not protect them by pretending that their speech is normal.

Try not to make the tempo of home and school life too strenuous.

Do not make children compete for a chance to talk; let them have their turn at activities or during group discussions.

Do not let other children feel they can "catch" stuttering. Stuttering is not a disease.

Do not require children to participate in competitive activities that require rapid verbal responses (reading flash cards, spelling bees, and so on).

Source: Guitar & Conture, 2007; Rind & Rind, 2003.

members who have communication disorders or learning disabilities suggesting that genetics may play a role (NIDCD, 2002c).

As infants, they do little or no babbling and have difficulty imitating sounds and words. They may have limited vowel and few consonant sounds. They frequently leave out or substitute incorrect sounds in words. And, frustrating for them and others, their speech errors are unpredictable and inconsistent. Together, these problems result in a small vocabulary, incorrect grammar and difficulty organizing spoken information. These problems frequently spill over into reading, writing, spelling, or math.

Additionally, they may not accurately vary the rhythm, stresses, and inflections that are used to convey meaning. Children have better receptive language than usable speech (NIDCD, 2002c). Diagnosis is difficult because there is no single factor or test that is used. There is not agreement on the significant symptoms that define the disability. Much is left to clinical judgment. Like most disabilities, this can vary from mild to severe. Some children may need the help of alternative or additional communication methods.

Augmentative and Alternative Communication

Some children have such severe communication disorders that normal spoken communication is not a long-range option for them. Augmentative communication is an alternative communication system that is used to supplement the expressive communication skills of a child either temporarily or permanently. Augmentative and alternative communication (AAC) is categorized in two ways: unaided and aided. Unaided communication systems use only the child's body to communicate. Sign language, gestures, vocalizations, and facial expression are examples of unaided communication. Aided communication methods employ tools or equipment to help the child expressively communicate such as picture communication boards, object symbols and high- or low-tech speech-generating devices (Stuart, 2007).

To work effectively, aided augmentative communication must be designed for an individual child. The creative software that is being designed for microcomputers is greatly impacting augmentative communication and has tremendous potential. Even for young children, the use of touch-sensitive control pads can facilitate communication. Voice synthesizers are relatively inexpensive and plug into the printer port of most computers. Rather than printing what is typed, the synthesizer "speaks" it. If the child touches the color red on an adapted keyboard, the word "red" is said.

Children may use a variety of AAC systems depending upon the activities they are participating in, the situation, and how familiar they are with the people involved. Speech/language pathologists play an important role in deciding on the most effective system and in helping children learn to use it.

In the Field

As a vice principal at an elementary school, I fully support speech and language therapy for children in the school.

However, speech class has led to some scheduling and organizational problems. First, it is very unfortunate that the school district does not provide our school with a full-time speech and language pathologist. The speech/language pathologist who works at our school is sometimes here only 1 or 2 days a week. This means children who are tested for possible communication disorders, and those receiving speech therapy, spend less time than they should with the therapist.

Further, because of scheduling problems and the large number of children receiving help in speech, many children are pulled out of academic classes for their therapy. This bothers some teachers. They tell me that the children who are consistently pulled out of the same subjects are falling behind in these areas. (By county policy, we do not pull children out of specials such as art and gym for speech.) Further, some teachers complain that they are constantly interrupted by the speech and language pathologist, who comes to the classroom throughout the day to walk students back to the speech room. In classes where the speech therapist stays in the room with a group of children, teachers find that she is late, or early, and constantly disrupts class schedules. Although most teachers are understanding, some are not.

Over the summer, I will devise a plan to help the situation for next year, but I am not sure if I can assuage teachers' concerns while at the same time providing the necessary therapy these children require.

Reflective Practice

We rarely think about disabilities from an administrative perspective. How would you feel about working with a speech/language pathologist who did take children out of the classroom or came consistently late? Can you think of ways to handle this that would not penalize the children who need the therapy but also would contribute to positive relationships and optimal learning for all children?

Instructional Strategies

The following language modeling techniques can be used at any time in the early childhood classroom. They can be used with all children throughout the day to stimulate language. If the concern is with infants and toddlers, use parentese. *Parentese* is a way of speaking that has a slower rate of speech and exaggerated intonation and stress with more variation in pitch and loudness. It uses a limited vocabulary with short, simple sentences. Parentese helps focus the infant's attention on language and the same words are repeated frequently enough for the young child to understand their function as well as learning the words themselves. This is a tremendous help to the infant who is trying to figure out when speech stops and starts and the role different words play (Hulit & Howard, 2006).

Using **parallel talk** the adult gives words to the child's behavior. As the child plays the adult describes what the child is doing, seeing, or hearing. In **self-talk**, the teacher describes what she is doing while the child watches. Like parallel talk, it is an effective way to model vocabulary and grammatical forms.

Expansion is the process of extracting the meaning of a child's utterance and putting it into a more complex form. For a child using telegraphic speech such as "Me go," the expansion might be "Where do you want to go?" or "Are you ready to go now?" The objective is to provide a language model, not just answer "okay." **Extension** involves putting the child's statement in a broader context; that is, extending the meaning of the phrase. If a child says "Me go out," the adult might respond, "If you want to go outside you need to put your coat on." Using these techniques is particularly effective as the child has initiated the "conversation" and is prepared to listen to the response, as it is meaningful to him. Adults can also extend children's language through intonation and emphasis (What do you want to *do* outside?). Expansion and extension encourage young children to use more complex language structures (Hulit & Howard, 2006).

Language stimulation can be either direct or indirect. In **indirect language stimulation** the adult provides labels for objects, people, and actions without requiring the child to respond. In **direct language stimulation**, the adult questions the child. These questions should be phrased in such a way that the child cannot answer with a "yes" or "no."

In **repetitions,** the adult repeats all or part of the child's phrase. This is a good strategy when a child has made an incorrect utterance. The adult repeats the utterance, correcting the mistake. **Fill-ins** require that the child complete the statement. This is frequently done when reading a familiar story or when dealing with rhyming words or analogies.

Guidelines

If a child has been diagnosed with a communication disorder, read the child's file. Talk with the parents and gain their perceptions (this is in addition to formal individualized education program (IEP) team conferences). Find out what the diagnosis means to the child's total development. (Is the language delay part of another disorder?)

Ask the child's speech/language pathologist when she expects to be in your classroom and the kinds of activities you can do that would be helpful. Whether a child has an official diagnosis or not, you must assess where in the language process the problem is, its severity, and how you will adapt your programming to meet this child's needs. As you listen to children throughout the day, look for their most and least comfortable times with speech. Most children show a pattern. Although each child's situation will be different, the following guidelines are helpful:

1. *Use simple, concrete language and lots of repetition.* Simplify your grammar and vocabulary and use shorter sentences. Children will have fewer problems processing information in this form. If you talk fast, slowing down your rate of delivery may help.
2. *Ask few direct questions, especially during group times.* Questions place high demands on a child for speech even when the response requested is just a short one.
3. *Allow children to, on occasion, "pass" answering a question* if they feel uncomfortable or cannot verbalize the answer. This will reduce fear of embarrassment and may lead to more interaction in the long run.

4. *Give short, simple, clear directions.* Start with one-step directions; gradually work up to more complex directions. If necessary, have the child repeat or verbally "walk through" the directions before doing an activity. Reward children for following through on the directions given.
5. *Use appropriate "wait time"* when asking children a question. Some children need more time to form or articulate their answers. Don't rush answers.
6. *Plan for language development.* Set aside time each day that specifically emphasizes language development. (The activity may vary, but the intent shouldn't.)
7. *Encourage children's desire to communicate.* Increase their interest in themselves and their environment. Find out what children find interesting. If a child with a communication disorder in your class likes biking, discuss the topic with her. She may be eager to talk about a subject that is important to her.
8. *Provide a secure, consistent, well-organized environment.* Set up activities to provide noncompetitive peer interaction.
9. *Include children with communication disorders in group activities.* Children need not have a speaking role if that provokes anxiety. Nonverbal group participation may be a prerequisite to verbal participation. Participating with puppets may come before participation without props.
10. *Create a need for speech.* If the child uses gestures instead of speech, deliberately (but not obviously) misunderstand briefly and name other objects. Before the child becomes frustrated, give the child what was requested, but use the word in one- or two-phrases or sentences. Gradually increase the number of misunderstandings and incorrect guesses until the child is slightly frustrated by your "stupidity."
11. *Give a lot of running commentary.* Give a play-by-play description of what either you or the child is doing. One way that children learn to talk is by listening and imitating.
12. *Be a good listener.* Give the child your undivided attention or explain that you cannot listen then, but will soon. Arrange to do it as soon as possible.
13. *Reward the child for correct speech,* but do not criticize lack of speech or incorrect speech.
14. *Model good speech and language.* Rephrase what children say to reinforce appropriate speech and to let them know that you care about what they are saying.
15. *Differentiate between speech and language and reinforce appropriately.* For example, you might tell a child, "I'm glad you want to tell me about your picture. I'm having trouble understanding what you are saying. Can you tell me with different words?"
16. *Post rules and routines in a visual manner with pictures and/or words.* Reinforce learning through visual and tactile experiences.
17. *Structure lessons to provide children with more successes than failures.*
18. *Reinforce spontaneous language* independently of the quality of the speech. Respond to the meaning of children's communications.
19. *Help children develop the skills to handle teasing independently.* Some children may imitate speech

problems or make fun of the way others talk. Do not reinforce the children, and tell them clearly that you find their behavior unacceptable. The imitation problem is usually a short-term one that goes away without reinforcement, but teasing may continue indefinitely.

Language and cognition are related. For children to use their language, they need something to talk about. Expand children's awareness of the environment. Lack of stimulation may be a factor in underdeveloped language. Children cannot be expected to talk about something they have no knowledge of. Given opportunities to explore the environment, children often need several experiences to gain the necessary information. Remember the learning cycle—awareness, exploration, inquiry/experimentation, and utilization—and provide children with opportunities for different levels of learning.

Curriculum Adaptations

Children with communication disorders require few curriculum adaptations. Rather, they may need some areas of the curriculum expanded to meet their needs.

Social Awareness: Self-Esteem, Inclusion, and Social Studies

Children with communication disorders may not have good skills at joining groups. Help them develop the language necessary to be included. Think about the priorities in language development: broaden language skills through field trips, followed by language experience stories. This sequence supports both the social studies and language aspects of the experience. Include listening skills and following directions: "Show me what you do when you see a red light." Work on vocabulary to go with the actions. As children's vocabulary expands, help them become more detailed and specific in their speech. Some of the activities in Resource Chapter 1 are specifically designed to support children who have communication disorders. Activities such as 1–15 Tongue Twisters help children learn that some things are difficult to say. The activity 1–22, Talking demonstrates different ways of talking and some frustration if they are not understood.

Self-Esteem

As children learn more about themselves, their self-awareness increases. Give them the support to use their language skills to communicate their wants and needs. As they build skills, teach them ways to be assertive.

1. Incorporate a broad base of communication skills into your curriculum to increase children's background about communications. Include different written and spoken languages, American Sign Language, computers with voice simulators, communication boards, and so on.
2. Have children make their own communication board. Discuss what to include and talk with them about what is important to be able to communicate. Then discuss the limitations and the frustrations of not

being understood and especially how the person who is not understood might feel.
3. Help children learn about their body and how it reacts in different situations and how this impacts their speech and language. (How do they feel when asked a question in a group situation? When someone calls them names?) Talk about how children can handle these situations. Initially, the plan may involve your intervention; however, as children learn and grow, they should take increasing responsibility.
4. When children with speech disorders speak out in class, do not correct them in front of the other children. They may not speak up again. Correctly rephrase what they say and encourage their good content or answers.

Inclusion

Children with communication disorders may not seek out other children; they may play alone or near another child. Encourage cooperative play so that children can learn to interact comfortably with peers. When they do play with others, these children are rarely leaders; they often receive instructions from classmates rather than give them, and because they are often reluctant to argue with the leader as others might, they may end up with the least-desirable roles. It is important for all children to feel they belong. Children need to know they are all similar in some ways and different in others. Language may be an area in which they are different.

1. Have children play with language, perhaps by mispronouncing an unfamiliar word. Ask children how they feel and how they would feel if others criticized or made fun of them. Ask them if they would try to pronounce the word again and how they would feel.
2. Discuss the importance of taking turns in language as well as on pieces of equipment. Point out that sometimes they may need to wait for others to have time to say what they want to communicate. It is important for them to wait, as well as you.
3. Use books without words.
4. Discuss teasing and treating others appropriately with the whole class. Do not focus on speech but on being respectful in general. Many children, especially older children, will understand that this also pertains to speech disorders.
5. Talk about different languages and some of the commonalities and differences in language and culture and how one might feel if he didn't speak the same language as others in the classroom.

Social Studies

Speech and language skills can be integrated into the social studies curriculum through conversation and role playing. Help children identify similarities and differences throughout the immediate environment, the region, the country, and globally. Your goal is to promote the concept of diversity. At the same time, you are promoting the children's awareness of differences and similarities in speech and language.

1. Names are different in other languages. Some common names can be discussed that translate well: John in Spanish is Juan; in French, Jacques; in German, Johann.

However, there are some names for which there are no equivalents. Discuss these as well.

2. Make a tape recording of people from different regions in North America (with the characteristic accent). If possible, have them all say the same sentences so that the children can more readily grasp the differences. Make a similar tape of people from different countries or those for whom English is a second language. Have a person comes who speaks another language. See Visitor 1–46w.

3. Help children act out situations that require roles that have different speech patterns associated with them, for example, teacher, police officer, father, mother, baby.

4. Teach lessons that introduce children to famous figures such as Helen Keller. Introduce sign language, Braille, and other methods of communication such as pantomime. Talk about communication in languages other than English. Help children to get a more global concept of communication.

Language and Literacy: Speaking, Listening, Reading, and Writing

The language and literacy curriculum consists of speaking, listening, reading, and writing, and it is the area most emphasized for children with communication disorders. Communication skills cannot be viewed in isolation, but rather are related to the acquisition of all language skills. Children who do not acquire a complex expressive sentence repertoire are at high risk for problems in reading and writing, which are language-based skills.

In particular, children need to develop and refine listening, attention, and memory skills. Language arts can be used to increase spontaneous language as well as to develop readiness skills. Check with the child's speech/language pathologist for specific advice and additional activities. Children with communication disorders must concentrate on the development of underlying language skills by participating in many firsthand experiences. If children are reluctant to speak, create a need for them to talk. Instead of asking children yes-no questions ("Do you want to play with the blocks today?"), use forms such as "Where do you want to play today?" to elicit more speech. For children who need work on specific speech sounds, read stories and ask questions that require them to practice those sounds. Some children have articulation problems because they do not have good speech models. Their speech reflects what they hear. It is important that you provide a good model for them. Highlight the interrelationship between expressive and receptive language and reading and writing. Children with weak listening and speaking skills may be reluctant to participate in reading and writing activities. Negative feelings about spoken language may carry over into these areas. Children need to be encouraged and rewarded for participation.

Provide the child with firsthand experiences followed by discussions and opportunities for internalizing concepts and expanding key ideas. Using a farm as an example, you might:

- Visit a farm.
- Generate a language experience story about the trip to the farm.
- Read a book about a farm at story time and have other books available for individual reading.
- Play farm animal lotto.
- Sing "Old MacDonald had a Farm."
- Learn about different types of farms. Discuss the equipment and animals on these farms, their purpose, and imitate the sounds that farm animals make.

These suggestions are ordered on the principles that children learn contextually rather than in isolation, they learn the concrete before the abstract, and gradually increasing exposure to a concept increases the depth of learning.

Speaking

Children with communication disorders may speak only when absolutely necessary because of the negative feedback they have received in the past: "You talk funny." Speaking in front of others may be a threatening experience for these children. When asked questions in a group situation, they may respond with a shrug or "Don't know." It is easier for them not to know something than to risk ridicule by the other children. Encourage speech in one-on-one situations and in small groups before you work on large groups. Which speech skills to emphasize will depend on the needs of each child; areas include fluency, voice, resonance, and articulation, especially as they relate to intelligibility of speech. Provide many opportunities to practice in nonthreatening situations. Speaking requires practice and information to communicate.

1. Use puppets to encourage children to talk. Give the child cues to encourage speaking when necessary. As children become more confident, have them play together using the puppets.
2. Have telephones available and encourage children to talk on the telephone with you and with each other.
3. Practice reading poems and rhymes out loud from a poster, the board, an overhead projector, or computer with a projector. This will enhance reading and speech skills. Use activities such as Synonyms 2–1, and Rhyming Words 2–4 to expand vocabulary.
4. Have the whole class write a story or letter together, which you record on a large piece of lined paper. Practice reading these as a whole group out loud.
5. Include poems that match a current language arts theme or celebration. Make these appropriate for the children and have them practice reading these at home and out loud to you on an individual and group basis. This promotes fluency.

Fingerplays are good for children with communication disorders. Although done with a group, finger plays cause children to lose their self-consciousness, in part because they can participate in the motions without speaking. The motions also provide visual cues that help children understand the words. Fingerplays that rhyme are good for ear training. Those that have the sounds the child is working on are also useful.

1. Use fingerplays to stimulate body awareness. Those that involve the face and mouth area are especially beneficial.
2. Fingerplays such as Teensy, Weensy Spider facilitate eye-hand coordination as well as motor and manual control.

Listening

Provide varied listening experiences to help children discriminate and associate sounds. Read books to expand the child's world as well as provide an opportunity to practice different sounds. Begin with stories about familiar events, including books about children, families, and animals.

1. Read stories that emphasize specific sounds, ones that are easy or hard for the child, depending on your objectives. *Sammy Snake* is an example of a story emphasizing the *s* sound.
2. Read stories that emphasize rhyming words (e.g., *Each Peach Pear Plum*), voice control (*The Whispering Rabbit and Other Stories),* and listening skills (*What I Hear in My School*).
3. To foster ear training, read stories and do fingerplays that have rhymes until the children are familiar with them. Then read the stories with pauses to let the group fill in the rhyming word. Children also enjoy nonsense rhyming games. You say a word and have the children call out real and made-up rhyming words for you to write on the board.
4. Encourage children to use listening centers and following along in a book. This is a very motivating activity.

Reading

Young children with communication impairments are likely to have difficulty learning to read. While they are concentrating on pronunciation, their comprehension of the reading material goes down. Their reading rate may be slower than average and their phrasing may be poor. In fact, reading may become so unpleasant they may avoid it whenever possible. Particular care should be taken to develop their reading literacy skills to forestall these problems.

When you teach reading literacy skills, you will most often use visual and auditory means. Children need to see and say letter sounds and blends regardless of where they are positioned in the word. Ear training, the ability to listen well, is one prerequisite that children with speech and language disabilities may find difficult to master, yet it is essential to the development of literacy.

Matching and sorting tasks can be either perceptual or conceptual in nature or combine elements of both. Perceptual matching requires the children to match like letters to each other. They don't need to know what the letters stand for. When the task is a conceptual one, the children are required to abstract the idea and generalize it to another instance, for example, when going from lower-case letters to uppercase letters or when going from script (printing) to cursive. Conceptual matching can be used not only in reading literacy but also in other curriculum areas. Examples of both are presented in Figures 11–1 and 11–2.

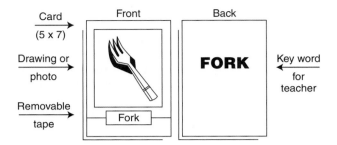

Figure 11–1: Picture File Card
A picture file can be used to identify words as well as beginning, medial, and ending consonant sounds.

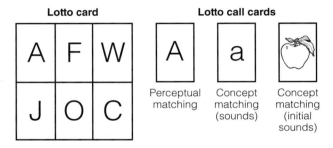

Figure 11–2: Alphabet Lotto with Perceptual and Conceptual Matching
Alphabet lotto with upper and lower case letters and initial sounds provides important literacy skills.

A picture file set up in a flexible format allows for later expansion. Divide the file into three sets: beginning consonant sounds, medial (middle) consonant sounds, and ending consonant sounds. Include the consonant blends (*bl*ouse, pu*m*pkin, sta*nd*) in each set. Vowels may be omitted because children rarely have problems with them. Organize the sets alphabetically and store them in three file boxes. Once you have developed the three basic sets, you are prepared for a variety of activities.

1. Have children find all the pictures with a specified beginning sound. (When ending an exercise, call out the sounds in alphabetical order. The pictures will automatically be organized for putting away.) Do the same thing for beginning consonant blends. Repeat the process for the middle and final position. When you introduce this activity, you might have the name on the front of the card; the activity is easier when the child can match the initial letters as well as the sound. See activity 2–12, Alphabet Lotto 2–12, and Body Sounds 2–13.
2. Set out four picture cards (three of which have the same ending sounds), say the words, and then have the children identify the one that is different. Gradually give the children more responsibilities, thereby increasing the level of difficulty. You might have the children say the words, have them create sets for each other, and so on.
3. A more challenging and creative activity is making sound books. Introduce one sound at a time. Write the sound at the top of a piece of paper. Have the children find pictures of objects that have that sound

Ensure that all children are included. Talk about language differences and similarities and verbal and nonverbal communication.

and paste the pictures on the page. When the child has a page for each sound, make it into a book.

4. Alphabet Lotto (or variations of bingo) is a fun way to teach letter recognition (see Figure 11–2). When children can match identical letters, add pictures as well as lowercase letters to the game. Play Sound Bingo 2–14 as well.

5. Make a set of alphabet cards or use letter tiles with multiple copies of each letter. Encourage children to play games and make words.

6. The development of letter memory or letter sounds can be facilitated by making two sets of the Lotto call cards and playing Concentration. Start by turning four to six pairs of cards face down. If this is too easy, add more pairs.

7. Create or buy games for learning centers that focus on learning words and vocabulary. For example, you may want to use sight word bingo, or have the children play games in which they create words using word families.

8. Incorporate reading into other areas where children need to read the directions to complete a project. Support the written word with pictures.

9. Because reading is connected to speech and if you are testing comprehension or content, you may want to read tests out loud to children with communication disabilities or for English language learners.

Writing

The focus in early writing is on meaning. If the initial focus on written work is on the spelling and punctuation, young writers can become discouraged. Allowing children to spell creatively (how it sounds or looks to them, regardless of accuracy) increases their fluency and allows writing to serve as an outlet for children who are not comfortable speaking. Correcting children's spelling as they are just beginning to write causes some of the same problems

as correcting their speech. If the task becomes onerous, children try not to participate; if children do participate, they take as few risks as possible.

Writing provides both challenges and solutions for children with communication disorders. First, they need to establish the connection between the written and spoken word. Do this informally by pointing out to children that you cannot see words if their hand is over them, or that you cannot read the book if it is upside down. Write down what they say, but do not hesitate to ask them to slow down, pointing out that you cannot write as quickly as they can talk. Use language experience stories and support all of children's attempts at writing, regardless of the quality of the letters or the spelling.

1. Write their names on their papers and point out to children that you do this so they will not get mixed up. Compare two pictures and then explain that if you forget who made them, you can look at the name.

2. Support children's verbalizations by writing down what they say and then reading it back to them. Again, point out the advantage of a written language by reading what the children said at a later date.

3. Discuss writing as a symbol system and point out that the English language uses the alphabet they are familiar with but some other languages do not. Illustrate these. Have the children create a syllabary (a type of dictionary); they can decide on the written configurations that stand for words or syllables. They can use this to write to each other. (In this instance, spelling is irrelevant.)

4. Have a writing center and support writing as a process that involves authorship, illustration, editing, and publishing. Support children in each stage of the process.

5. Scribe or write for a child when testing for content, not writing skills.

Discovery: Mathematics, Science, and Technology

For children with only speech problems, the discovery area is not likely to be different from other children in the classroom. Like others, they need to start with concrete experiences to learn best. Emphasize the vocabulary that goes with the experiences of learning math and science: taller, shorter, more, less, the same, equal, one more, one less. Children can learn through science how sounds are made and which parts of the body are involved in making various sounds. They can learn to use objects such as a feather or pinwheel to observe the effect of their breath. Technology offers another opportunity for communicating without the need for speaking while it can also reinforce communication.

Mathematics

Children with communication problems usually have math skills comparable to their classmates. They often enjoy math, as it can be learned with a minimum of speech. Math, then, can give these children a feeling of achievement.

1. Use math concepts to facilitate speech and language development. Have children count and sort objects that make sounds and objects that don't. Have them count the number of times a sound is made.

2. Make number books by having children cut out a specified number of pictures beginning with the same sound. You might have, for example, one /T/, two /Rs/, three /Ss/, four /Ts/, and so on.

3. Apply the math vocabulary (big/little, more/less, equal) to sounds and body awareness. Tell children to make their bodies as big as they can, then as little. Have them find pictures of an animal with a big tail and one with a little tail. Do those animals make big/loud sounds or little/soft sounds?

4. Present pictures of geometric shapes and have children draw these shapes in the air with various parts of their bodies. Once they have shown they understand by tracing the shapes with their hands, have them outline the shapes with their jaw, head, tongue, and finally by moving only their eyes.

5. Put a word wall up in the classroom that includes math words. Practice saying these words with the whole class and send a sheet home to be read out loud. Include definitions on the worksheet you send home.

6. Compare the chest measurements of children after they inhale and after they exhale. This can be done with string or measuring tape; string is more effective with younger children because they can see which string is longer.

Science

Science can enhance children's understanding of the mechanics of speech and language. Although fewer verbal skills are required by science than by some other subjects, interest is usually high and it stimulates language use.

1. Teach some anatomy, especially the organs that produce sound (lips, tongue, teeth, throat, diaphragm, and so on).

2. Put up a word wall in the classroom that includes science words. Like math, practice saying these words with the whole class and include the words and their definitions for children to take home.

3. Use mirrors to help children see the articulatory organs while exploring the concept of mirror images (reversals).

4. Discuss the sounds different animals make and how they make them. (Crickets, for example, rub their legs together.) Have children experiment making sounds by using different body parts (clap, stomp, slap thighs). Make a tape recording of animal sounds and pair the picture of the animal with the sound.

5. Talk about how sound is made in nature (thunder, water moving, wind) and how humans make noise (music, talking, working). Discuss how noise cues us about what is happening in our environment. These sounds may be presented on tapes or compact discs. Use pictures to present the sounds; the visual reinforces the aural learning.

6. Discuss the properties of air and its function in speech. Use a beach ball or fan to make air more tangible.

Technology

Computers require no verbal input, yet are capable of verbal output. Children who will later depend on computers for communication need to be interacting with them from the preschool years on. Most computers are designed with internal features that can be modified to make them easier for children to use. The manufacturers have this information and willingly share it. Use digital cameras and videotapes or tape recorders to communicate information.

1. Have a computer with a voice synthesizer in the classroom so children can become familiar with it.

2. Help children become familiar with computers. If necessary, modify a keyboard to match the child's needs. See Activities 3–28 Alphabet Keyboard and 3–29 Computer Bingo.

3. Encourage children to learn that computers are part of their life and that they are in control of computers.

4. Encourage children with communication disorder to regularly play on the computer with another classmate. They often will be eager to play, speak while playing, and develop friendships.

5. If children are nonverbal or not proficient in English, take digital pictures and use them to talk with children and to share information with families.

6. Videotape field trips and class experiences so you can reflect on experiences with the children.

Wellness: Health, Physical Education, and Sensory Motor

Work on language skills that will increase the child's safety and/or auditory identification of warning signals. Use large motor activity to build self-esteem and to support children's inclusion. Talk about their skills and what they are doing.

Sensory motor activities support the communication process by increasing body awareness. They provide opportunities for communication but are not dependent on it. Supply words for what children are doing in the motor area. Focus fine motor activities on those movements associated with speech, such as breath control and lip and tongue action, in addition to those necessary for visual discrimination, writing, and adaptive skills. Help children increase their body awareness, particularly to learn when they are tense. Many speech problems increase with tension.

Health and Safety

Speech and language production requires the coordination of muscles from the waist up, the speech organs, and the brain. It is one of the most complicated human processes. Children need to be made aware of the body parts involved. Listening to someone who has nasal congestion helps children learn the nose's function; a sore throat demonstrates the throat's contribution to speech.

Teeth—Discuss how to care for teeth. Invite a dentist to visit the class. As children lose their baby teeth, discuss what sounds become difficult. Have them discover the role teeth play in making sounds.

Jaw—Use scissors to illustrate the hinge-like action of the jaw. Have children use their fingers to feel the bones and muscles as they drop their jaw. Again, experiment with sound as the jaw lowers and rises.

Tongue—Do tongue exercises with the class. Let the children use mirrors to watch their tongue move. Have them pair off and watch each other. Make it fun.

Vocal Cords—Have children place their hands on their throat to feel the vocal cords vibrate. See if they can feel a difference in sounds. Use a rubber band to show how the vocal cords work, stretching it tight for high sounds and only slightly for low ones.

1. Teach children the language of safety: Stop/go (red/green), fast/slow, quickly/slowly, carefully, quietly, and so on. Children not only need to know the words but need to have a sensory motor understanding of the behaviors.
2. Teach children how to talk about their needs and wants. This is one of the most important reasons for language. Also, tell children how to verbalize that they need help or have a problem.
3. Go on imaginary walks with children to demonstrate language safety concepts. Children need to know that moving quietly means walking on tiptoes very carefully without talking. See Traffic Sign Hunt, Activity 4–32w.
4. Talk about voices and how they are used and where they are used appropriately. Talk about what happens when children shout, scream, or talk loudly for too long.
5. Discuss times when it is appropriate to scream or speak loudly. Also, discuss times when it is appropriate to speak quietly and wait for your turn to talk. Introduce "6-inch voices"; this means speaking as if you were 6 inches tall during quiet times.
6. Help children learn about the various health problems related to the speech-producing parts of the body, how to describe their symptoms, and what is typically done about them.
7. Blowing an object like a pinwheel helps develop the muscles of the mouth, gives children practice in closing off the palate and throat, and teaches breath control. Your role is to make this fun.

Large Motor

Large motor play is usually a pleasure and should be encouraged. Because children's language problems rarely interfere, this may prove to be one of their strengths.

1. Use large motor play to foster a sense of group belonging.
2. Help classmates see children's strengths in this area.
3. Play cooperative not competitive games. As cooperative play increases, children talk more to each other. See Activity 4–40w, Circle Ball.
4. Use structured games during outdoor time or recess that can give children with speech and communications differences a chance to be part of a team and to participate with a group without high language demands.
5. Include games using balls, from playground balls to soccer balls, to beach balls.

Small Motor

Children may need to focus on the small muscles of their body; eye movements are necessary for reading, the hand and fingers for writing, and the facial muscles for speaking.

Activities like blocks and trains allow children to build and play together with few demands for speaking but many opportunities to expand language concepts and talk.

1. Finger strength is necessary for holding a crayon or pencil. Start with large writing tools, then provide many opportunities for children to pick up small items.
2. Use drawing or painting to communicate feelings or events in children's lives. The child may want to talk about his art or you may ask questions about the child's feelings as he was working on it.
3. Encourage children to draw or scribble by providing a variety of paper and drawing utensils and many varieties of manipulative toys.

Sensory Motor Integration

Children need to listen in coordination with seeing, hearing, and touching.

1. Use activities that pair listening skills with visual or tactile skills: "Turn the page when you hear the tone."
2. Use activities that help establish a hand preference (coloring, turning nuts on bolts, eating). (It is irrelevant which hand is preferred.) Play hand clapping games. See Activity 4–20, Hand Clapping.
3. Play games like bingo. Children must listen intently to what is being called. Many children with communication disorders have trouble with this. Also, children are likely to speak out and ask a question if they missed a call or won bingo.

Creative Arts: Visual Arts, Music, Creative Movement, and Dramatic Play

Creative arts offer children the ability to develop skills with much less emphasis on the specific product. Children may become so absorbed in the creative arts that they forget their reluctance to talk as they discover they want to share their work with others. Music can provide a nonthreatening atmosphere for using expressive language. Through music, you can encourage children to attempt speech and to imitate other children and adults. Include songs and activities that concentrate on sounds that are difficult for them to produce. Creative movement allows children to participate without speech and also provides the potential for increasing body awareness. Through dramatic play, children can practice situations before encountering them. They can use puppets, talk on the telephone, or dress up and pretend they are another person as they participate in situations that provide the opportunity for communication.

Visual Arts

Children have the opportunity in the arts to develop fine motor skills. Visual art activities provide a nonverbal way of expressing feelings and working off energy.

1. Children can learn to recognize differences in how pencils, crayons, markers, paint, and chalk sound, feel, and look, and are used.
2. Encourage children to talk about their pictures (not in response to "What is it?" or, as a naïve graduate student once asked a 3 year old, "What does this picture represent to you?"). Start out with a comment such as, "I like the way you use red in this picture." That's an invitation—you may have shown enough interest to get a response. You might ask, "Does your picture have a story?" Be prepared for the fact that it may not!
3. Have children create pictures or art together such as murals or collages. Children may talk when working on a task they can make a real contribution to.
4. Discuss murals and how they have been used to express feelings that people could not talk about.
5. Make puppets to be used in dramatic play. Often, shy children will vocalize more with puppets.

Music

Music requires children to develop and use different vocal patterns. Blowing instruments and singing stimulate the palate and musculature of the mouth. Because some speech problems don't carry over into singing, this vocal activity can be especially rewarding.

1. Have children make musical instruments to develop listening skills. Make paper plate tambourines filled with beans or rice. They can be played in a group as well as paired according to the different sounds they make. Have children make and use musical instruments that emphasize mouth movements. See Activity 5–41w, Making Tambourines and 5–42w, Reeds.
2. Children become more aware of their voices as they whistle, hum, and sing high and low, loud and soft. Help them note tension in the lips and the feel of air coming in and out. Help them relate what they learn to speaking.
3. Music is a natural way to teach the concepts of high and low. Reinforce the concepts by having the children stretch their bodies high for the high notes, crouch low for the low notes, and be somewhere in between for the middle notes.
4. Holding notes for long or short periods of time increases breath awareness and improves breath control. See Activity 5–16, Conductor.

5. The rhythm of music also applies to speech and language, especially for children who are dysfluent. Interestingly, these children can often sing things they cannot say. To create more awareness of rhythm, you can have children lower their jaws (as if chewing), or even click tongues to a rhythmical pattern.
6. Songs with action allow children to participate whether or not they know the words. Actions provide visual cues for learning the words.
7. Tapes, and compact discs enhance listening skills, but they should be used with visual aids and an informed adult to help children comprehend the content and purpose.
8. Use simple musical instruments to play along with a recorded song.

Creative Movement

Use movement to increase body awareness (especially of speech organs) and to provide relaxation.

1. Have children pretend to be clothes fluttering on the line in a gentle wind. To relax the throat and neck, have the children drop their heads forward (chin toward chest). Have the wind pick up a bit and then die down. Talk with children about the differences. Use a variable speed fan if children seem to have trouble understanding the concept, and hold a piece of clothing in front of it as you change the speeds. Be sure the fan is one that is safe for children to be around.
2. Encourage games and movements that use pantomime, like charades, and discuss how frustrating it is not to be understood.
3. Music with movement provides an avenue for interpreting or expressing moods. See Activity 5–14, Mood Songs.
4. Use movement to help children relax. See Activities 5–24, Rag Doll and 5–25, Relaxation Stories.

Dramatic Play

Dramatic play provides a safe outlet for energy and an opportunity for children to try out roles without fear of judgment. It also allows children to be a part of a group.

1. At the beginning of the year, the dramatic play area should be an easy, familiar, nondemanding place. Children may drift toward this area, as it represents a tie with home. (This is particularly true of younger children.)
2. Children may be fearful of new situations and the demands this may make on their language skills. Take advantage of dramatic play to have children rehearse potential experiences beforehand to gain knowledge of what to expect.
3. Puppets encourage speech in a nonthreatening way. Play a recording of characters with very distinctive speech patterns (such as Donald Duck and Mickey Mouse) as a way of reassuring children that puppets can and do sound different.
4. Join children in dramatic play and take a minor role in their play. This allows you to facilitate some children's play without obvious intervention.

Routines and Transitions

As children end one activity and prepare to go on to another, there is often some confusion. Turn the confusion into opportunities for learning by taking advantage of routines and transitions to build language.

1. Combine movement and sound to help children get from one area to another: "Walk like a duck and quack as you go to the art area." Ask children to walk as quietly or to make as much noise as they can while going to the learning center of their choice.
2. Increase body awareness and sense of self. Dismiss children by having them make a particular sound.
3. Ask children to line up by asking them questions about words and letters.

Summary

Approximately 20 percent of all children who need special educational services either have a primary or a secondary communication disorder. For some children, it is a temporary articulation problem, for others it is a major delay in language development itself, for still others it is a secondary disorder related to another disability, and for some, English is a second language.

Children's language development includes several distinct aspects. Including children's ability to make and understand speech and speech sounds, to change meaning, to use language in a social environment, and to understand and use words appropriately.

Because language has such a strong developmental base, it is sometimes difficult to discern what is problematic and what is part of the normal language development sequence. Assessment of language development is typically broken into specific subareas that have some overlap and also must be understood within the context of both expressive and receptive language. Language is assessed both formally and informally. When formal assessments are done, they often focus on the separate subareas of language, so early childhood educators have to translate these results into overall goals and to plan for children.

Reflections

1. Many children whose speech is dysfluent will be teased or made fun of at some point in their lives. This could seriously hurt their self-esteem and confidence. How would you deal with a child or children in your classroom who tease or taunt the child with a dysfluency? Would you discipline the children? Would you take the children doing the teasing aside and speak with them privately or would you speak to the whole class? Which would be the least embarrassing for the child who is dysfluent? What would you do to make the child who is dysfluent feel more comfortable in your classroom? What would you say to her?
2. Some children with communication disorders use augmentative communication systems. These children may use communication boards and/or computers with speech synthesizers. What would you do if you found out that a child using an augmentative communication system was joining your class? Would you seek support from a colleague in the area of speech, an administrator, another teacher, or the child's parents? Do you think it would be important to conference with the child's parents before the first day of school? What if the communication system was computerized? Would you worry about whether the program's software will be difficult to master? Would you feel qualified for the job? How could you learn more about the child, his needs, and the actual communication used?

Educational Resources

Ablenet provides a mail-order catalogue of communication aids; also produces videotapes and conducts technology workshops. (800) 322-0956; FAX (612) 379-9143; http://www.http://ablenet.org/

American Speech-Language-Hearing Association (ASHA) site is divided into specific information for professionals, parents, and students. Some of the information is useful to all. http://www.asha.org/

Australian Stuttering Research Centre provides reports on research related to preschool children and stuttering. http://www3.fhs.usyd.edu.au/asrcwww

Center for Applied Linguistics serves as a national and international research and resource center in the application of linguistic science for social and educational problems. http://www.cal.org/

CLAS: Culturally and Linguistically Appropriate Services is an early childhood research institute that collects and describes early childhood/early intervention resources that have been developed for children with disabilities and their families and the service providers who work with them. The materials and resources available reflect the intersection of culture and language, disabilities and child development. Parts of the site can be read in Spanish. http://clas.uiuc.edu

Learn English Effectively is a site for learning English as a second language. The site has the symbols for the International Phonetic Alphabet which some speech and language pathologists use. http://www.antimoon.com

National Stuttering Association has information for parents, professionals, adults, teens, and children. It is easy to navigate and offers information on books, newsletters, and conferences on stuttering. http://www.nsastutter.org/

Stuttering Foundation of America offers many on-line resources to help parents, professionals, adults, and children deal with stuttering. The information is plentiful and also links to international programs. http://www.stuttersfa.org/

For additional resources, visit the book companion website for this text at www.cengage.com/education/deiner.

Chapter 12

Children who are English Language Learners

I live in fear. Every time I pull out of the driveway I wonder whether the police will stop me for driving without a license. I can't set up a bank account. I worried when I registered Diego for school because I don't have a social security number. I am undocumented.

For me the risks of being deported are worth it. My country was engulfed in a civil war when I came to the United States. The war disrupted not only the economy—so much so that unemployment was higher than 60 percent in my village and those that found work only made $2 a day—but also made traveling, going to the market, or even attending church services unsafe. Death was a way of life, and a day didn't pass when we didn't hear that someone we knew—a friend, a family member, had either been found dead or had simply disappeared.

I was 18, and my 9-month-old son Rodolfo and I were starving. I walked from Guatemala to the border of Mexico with the help of a coyote. There I train hopped through Mexico, dodging gangs and the unforgiving wheels of the train that claimed more lives than I care to remember. It took two harrowing months to get from Villa Nueva, Malacatán, Guatemala to Houston, Texas.

I stayed in a shelter in Houston—Casa Juan Diego—until I had enough strength to work. Then I found employment as a nanny, tending to other children as I wept for the child I'd left behind.

Two years later, I fell in love with a man from El Salvador. He had also fled a Civil War and knew what it meant to live in fear—his friends had been shot or tortured by guerrillas. He fled El Salvador knowing he would never return—and left with a heavy heart knowing he was leaving his teenage daughter behind. We married in Houston, but soon found work to be scarce. So moved to the east coast, where jobs are plentiful in the poultry industry.

I think the schools are good here, but it is hard for me to know because I speak little English and there is no one at the school who speaks Spanish. My son Diego broke his glasses and he needs them for school, but we don't have enough money to buy new ones. He gets headaches and has trouble seeing the board. In Texas, the children qualified for Medicaid but in Delaware, the requirements are different. We are trying to save the money to buy Diego new glasses, but with two U.S.-born children here and two children still overseas it is difficult.

I have not seen Rodolfo for 10 years. It is hard to be a mom over the phone. You can't hold your son or kiss him good night. I dream that one day he will be able to come to the United

States. Rodolfo lives with my parents. They are in their 80s and my mother has diabetes. I wonder what will happen to him when they die. I cry when I think about him.

Maria our youngest is 3 and she stays home with me. I thought about Head Start but I am too afraid to enroll her. Diego is 6. He is having problems in school and we can't help him because we can't communicate with his teachers or understand his homework. Kindergarten was okay, but a struggle. I know he is a smart boy but first grade is difficult for him. He is trying to learn English. They want to test him to see if he has a disability. They keep sending papers home. Even when they are in Spanish they don't make any sense to me. I wish there was someone at the school I could talk to. I want him to learn English and succeed that is why we came here. I didn't think it would be so hard.

Reflective Practice

Children come to school with different cultural and linguistic experiences. Their families too bring different challenges and experiences to the teacher-family partnership. How would you work with this family? What resources do you have, does the school have, and does the community have to include children whose home language is not English and whose mother is undocumented?

English Language Learners

English language learners (ELL) are children who have had experience with a language other than English. As a group, these children are diverse. They speak 460 different languages (Hepburn, 2004). They also have a tremendous range of educational needs. Some parents with limited proficiency in English, are highly educated, and provide their children with excellent role models in their home language. Other parents with limited English proficiency face challenges related to literacy, poverty, and legal status. Some parents are bilingual and value having two languages, and want to pass this gift on to their children. Some parents cannot read or write proficiently in their home language or English. Not all of these families will have children who are considered English language learners, although all are learning English. In addition to children who are identified by the schools as limited English proficient there are many more children whose home language is not English and the number is increasing.

Children who are English language learners (ELL) have problems speaking, reading, writing, and understanding English, which interferes with their ability to learn academic information. The first school-related policies came with The Bilingual Education Act, Title VII of the Elementary and Secondary Education Act of 1968. This law established federal policies for bilingual education for economically disadvantaged language minority children and allocated funds for innovative programs including teacher training. Title VII was eliminated and was rolled into Title III of the No Child Left Behind Act of 2001. The word bilingual has been removed from the law and the Office of Bilingual Education and Minority Language Affairs has become the Office of English Language Acquisition, Language Enhancement, and Academic Achievement for Limited English Proficient Students (OELA). The mission of this office is two-fold:

> "Provide national leadership to help ensure that English language learners and immigrant students attain English proficiency and achieve academically and, assist in building the nation's capacity in critical foreign languages." (OELA, 2008)

Historically, English language learners have been excluded from the statewide assessment process. However, with the passage of the No Child Left Behind Act of 2001 (NCLB) states are required to show that all children are making yearly progress toward reaching the "proficient" level on states' language arts, mathematics, and science assessment by 2014. No Child Left Behind requires states to assess the English proficiency of English language learners annually. Limited English proficiency is viewed as a temporary condition. The expectation is that these children will learn English and once they have reached proficiency they will no longer be classified as limited English proficient, and hence they will meet the same requirements of No Child Left Behind as their peers whose first language is English (United States Government Accountability Office [U.S. GAO], 2006a). Although federal funds are still available to support English language learners this money will be spent in different ways (Crawford, 2002). One way that schools will be judged is on the percentage of English language learners who are reclassified as fluent in English. This is expected to discourage instruction in other languages. It is also likely that the money to support English language learners will be spread more thinly. According to Crawford's (2002) calculation it resulted in providing only $149 per eligible student in 1999–2000. This is a concern.

The requirements of No Child Left Behind (NCLB) hold the potential for improving the education of young English language learners, because they are required to learn the same content and pass the same assessments as other children, and the schools are held accountable for their English proficiency. This may lead to more of an investment in early education programs with strong educational underpinnings in order to serve these children and to begin to close the achievement gap before kindergarten. The requirement that teachers are highly qualified and hold a degree or have significant expertise in the subject areas in which they teach also has the possibility of impacting the education of English language learners (Capps, Fix, Murray et al., 2005).

Like all other aspects of No Child Left Behind there is an emphasis on using evidence to make decisions. We do not have a strong evidence base on how to best teach English language learners.

Defining English Language Learners

Language is one of human's highest achievements. All civilizations have developed a symbol system that allows them to express their ideas and concepts, to share their feeling and emotions, to remember the past, discuss the present, and plan for the future. However, cultures have varied in the approaches they have taken to language and literacy. The written forms of language are as diverse as the spoken ones. Language and literacy served different purposes and social functions at different times and in different places. In the past the ability to encode and decode written language has often been reserved for those with privilege and power. However, in highly literate societies such as the United States, the ability to read and write affects all people's lives on a daily basis (Ada, 2002).

English language learner (ELL) refers to children for whom standard academic English is not their first language (Houk, 2005). Limited English proficiency (LEP) is the term used in both the No Child Left Behind Act of 2001 and the Individuals with Disabilities Educational Opportunity Act of 2004. There are a variety of other terms that are also used to refer to this category of children: English as a second language (ESL), limited English speaking (LES), second language learners (SLL), potential English proficient, and non-English speaker. I have chosen to use English language learners as I feel this designation is more positive than the term used in the federal law. It also supports the concept that some children may be learning English as a third or fourth language. In this text, English language learner refers to children learning the academic English that is used in schools in the United States for teaching and learning (Houk, 2005).

There is a difference between being able to use a language socially and academically. Socially, it is enough to be able to be polite and greet others, say thank you and ask and respond to requests about concrete situations. An academic language requires a far more complicated set of skills. Academic language requires the ability to understand abstract thought, to use inductive and deductive reasoning, and to create and critique ideas and concepts (Fineberg, 2002). Think about how many years you studied English in school.

According to most research, it takes more than 6 years for non-English-speaking children to compete academically with their English-speaking peers (Ada, 1993). Although they learn to speak the language before this, to be able to use English as a tool for learning requires in-depth knowledge not only of speaking and comprehension but also reading and writing.

Young children who are just learning language have a fragile hold on their home language and if their language development is not supported they can lose their home language. Parents who speak limited English use their home language to hand down traditional family values and to communicate within the home. Loss of the home language can be damaging to children's self-esteem and may make mastery of their home language and English more difficult (Fineberg, 2002).

In The Field

I came to United State at the age of 23. After more than a decade in this country, I still speak English with a Chinese accent. When I was pregnant with my son, I had planned to teach my son the Chinese language, that which is spoken by a fourth of the population on earth. I asked my family in China to send me children's books so that I could read to him even before he was born. I wanted to make sure that he would immerse himself in the Chinese language and culture. My plan was to speak and read to him only in Chinese. Good plan, right? Good luck to me.

It was not too difficult in the beginning. When he was little, I could read him anything and he would not protest. I have read all the Chinese children books and classics that my dear sister could afford to send me. I read to him while he was nursing, I read to him before bedtime, and I sang to him in Chinese. He was happy to hear my voice. Those were the happy, easy days. I was so sure that my son would be speaking Chinese as his first language.

My husband, who is not Chinese, however, speaks to my son only in English alone. Even though English is not my husband's first language, he is more comfortable with it than his mother tongue, which is Urdu. I think that my husband's intention is to make sure that our son will be speaking English without a foreign accent like us. We have been teased and frowned upon more times than we care to remember.

My son is 2 and a half years old now. Every morning he greets me in English, he asks for his breakfast and milk in English, and he wants to watch the Barney DVD. I think his first word was "DVD," and his second was "TV." When I drop him off at the child care center, he will not respond to me unless I talk to him in English. All day long, he spends his time in an English-speaking environment. When I pick him up and start to converse with him in Chinese, he only responds to me in English. Then it starts—my desperate effort to engage my son in Chinese for a few hours

before he goes to sleep. I know that he understand my Chinese because he can follow my commands and smiles at my praises of his good behavior. But somehow, it is so difficult to get him to speak the language. When I try to read to him bedtime stories in Chinese, he will cover his head with the blanket or cover my mouth with his hand. By the time he falls asleep, he may have heard about 10 minutes of Chinese spoken to him.

Every night I feel frustrated and wish that I had spoken a few more words in Chinese to my son. Now he can speak English in full sentences, but only phrases in Chinese. What happens to the assumption of acquisition of the "mother tongue"? He seems to pay more attention to me when I speak English. To be fair, I do speak English all day long until I pick him up from the child care. How can I expect him to speak Chinese since I don't speak it very often myself?

Despite the resistance on my son's side, I am still very committed to teaching him Chinese. The majority of the rest of the world can speak more than one language. Why can't we? In the meanwhile, I am just going to press on and not give in. It feels almost like a battle between my son and me. The problem I am facing is that there is no environment that my son can practice Chinese. I just have to keep trying and not lose faith. When I have the time and money, I will take him back to China to spend a few months with my family. Perhaps he will pick up the language quicker this way.

I do hope that we can get more encouragement from society. Every time when I speak to my son in Chinese, the child care providers would ask me what I said. I do not want to appear rude or inconsiderate; therefore, I do not speak to my son in Chinese in public any more. It is also extremely difficult to find any books or videos in Chinese. These are the difficulties I am facing. The challenges are mine, and forward-minded shall I be.

Reflective Practice

How do you feel about raising children bilingually? If you were in this child care setting, how would you respond to her language dilemma? As you think of yourself as a professional in the field, what do you believe about bilingualism in early childhood? As you think about the possibilities of bilingual education, where do you place yourself?

Prevalence of English Language Learners

The United States is a nation of immigrants many of whom came as English language learners. In the 19th and 20th centuries the large number of immigrants caused concern and fear. The nation's response was to assimilate these new immigrants into American culture and language.

During the 1980s the population of foreign-born residents increased by 40 percent with most of this population having some difficulty with English (Saracho & Spodek, 2004).

In 1980, because of the Mariel boatlift that brought younger and poorer Cubans to Dade County, Florida, the voters passed an anti-bilingual ordinance that prohibited spending money or supporting any language other than English or promoting cultures other than mainstream U.S. culture (Saracho & Spodek, 2004). In a U.S. Supreme Court decision in 1982, *Plyler vs. Doe*, the court denied states' right to exclude children of **illegal immigrants** from public schools.

In 1994, California passed Proposition 187 making it illegal for children of **undocumented immigrants** to attend public schools. The federal courts ruled Proposition 187 unconstitutional. In 1998, California voters overwhelmingly approved Proposition 227 which eliminated the state's bilingual education programs and required that all instruction be conducted in English. Arizona passed a similar law, Proposition 203, in 2000 (Saracho & Spodek, 2004). The education of English language learners is growing and is controversial.

It is difficult to put a firm figure on the soaring number of culturally diverse children in the schools, particularly the number of children with limited English proficiency. In 2000, there were 10.5 million **immigrant children**, that is, children of **foreign-born parents** and children of **immigrant parents**, enrolled in grades kindergarten through 12. This is an 84 percent increase in a 10-year period (Hood, 2003). The rapid growth of the Hispanic population is related to a high and sustained level of immigration, the large number of young adults who are in their family-formation years, and the relatively high fertility rate among Hispanic women (primarily immigrants). In 2004, 23 percent of the 4.1 million babies born in the United States had Hispanic mothers. By 2050, Hispanics are projected to number 100 million and be one-fourth of the nation's population (National Task Force on Early Childhood Education for Hispanics, 2007).

Between 1990 and 2000 the number of students classified as limited English proficient increased by 105 percent while the overall student population increased by 12 percent. Children whose home language is not English are the fastest growing segment of the population. English language learners make up nearly 10 percent of the national student population in pre-kindergarten through twelfth grade and disproportionately (44 percent) these children are in pre-kindergarten through third grade (Kindler, 2002).

Economically, politically, and socially English language learners, Hispanic children in particular, will play an important role in the nation's future. In 2000, there were 106 workers for every 100 non-workers. It is projected that by 2050 there will be only 90 workers for every 100 non-workers (Toossi, 2002). Given the projected number of Hispanic children, they and their education is critical for our nation's future. Most young Hispanic children were born in the United States and hence are U.S. citizens. It is important that they become informed, engaged citizens with skills that promote their strengths (National Task Force on Early Childhood Education for Hispanics, 2007).

Information about limited English proficiency is gathered by both the U.S. Census Bureau and the U.S. Department of Education. Their figures are different because of how the data is collected, the use of different definitions, and the inclusion or exclusion of undocumented children. According to the 2000 U.S. Census, nearly one in five people, or 47 million U.S. residents age 5 and older, spoke a language other than English at home. To determine languages spoken and English ability the 2000 census included the following questions about residents and children:

A. Does this person speak a language other than English at home?

(For those who speak another language)

B. What is this language? _____

C. How well does this person speak English?—very well, well, not well, not at all.

The number of individuals who spoke a language other than English in the home, according to the 2000 census, reached almost 9.8 million. When asked about the language ability, 55 percent of the respondents reported that the children spoke English "very well." The schools and the census have different definitions of "very well."

Reflective Practice

Reflect on how a parent might answer the questions of how well a 7 year old speaks English versus how her teacher might answer the same questions. What might this mean relative to different perceptions about language skills and implications for policy?

During the 1996–1997 school year approximately 3.4 million children were classified as limited English proficient (U.S. GAO, 2001). During the 2003–2004 school year approximately 10 percent of the total school population, or 5 million children, were identified with limited English proficiency (LEP). Although they speak over 400 languages, 80 percent of children with limited English proficiency speak Spanish (U.S. GAO, 2006a). However, even within these broad groups, children speak different dialects, and those who speak the same language do not necessarily have a shared culture and history.

The Evidence Base

About 4 million children in the U.S. public schools were designated as English language learners in 2003–2004. They accounted for 8 percent of public school enrollment that year (National Center for Educational Statistics, 2006). Five states educate almost 70 percent of English language learners: Arizona, California, Florida, New York, and Texas. Data from these states was used to look at the role schools play in the English language learner achievement gap (Fry, 2008). In all five states English language learners were much less likely than white children to score at or above the state's proficient level.

This research focused on the schools that educate English language learners. About half the elementary schools in the nation educate English language learners. Almost 70 percent of English language learners are enrolled in 5,000 public schools. This is about 10 percent of the nation's 50,000 elementary schools. Although these schools served 70 percent of English language learners they accounted for only 13 percent of elementary school children (Consentinode Cohen, Deterding, & Clewell, 2005). These schools are identified as "high-LEP" schools. These schools are mostly located in urban areas, where there are a majority of English language learners and many of the children are economically disadvantaged, embedding the discussion in the context of poor, minority, immigrant-serving urban schools. The other 30 percent of English language learners are educated in "low LEP" schools in which they are a minority population. (Remember that the U.S. Department of Education uses the term Limited English Proficiency, hence LEP.)

There are significant differences between High-LEP and Low-LEP schools in principal and teacher demographics, training, and experience. With the exception of Florida, the High-LEP reporting schools tend to be located in central cities, the schools themselves are larger and serve more children, there is a higher child-to-teacher ratio, they have more children qualified for free or reduced-price lunch, and they have fewer white children (Fry, 2008).

When English language learners and white children attend the same schools the differences in proficiency are less. (In Arizona the differences in white and English language learners overall is 35 points but this dropped to 27 points for children in Low-LEP schools, in California it went from 32 to 21 points.) (Fry, 2008). Math proficiency rates are lower for LEP reporting schools for all children who attend the school, not just English language learners. Overall, English language learners do better in schools with enough white children to report the results of white children separately and sufficient black children to report the black results. English language learner's math achievement is lowest when schools report the results of English language learners and black children but there are insufficient white children to report white results (Fry, 2008).

Reflective Practice

Reflect on the implications of high and low LEP schools and what this means for the education of all children. We frequently think about individual children and classrooms but rarely the influence that schools per se have on children. What does this information mean in a practical sense? Will this influence the schools you might want to teach in? How do schools impact children's education and what might be done to bring about change?

In The Field

In 2000–2001, 6 percent of the children in my school were identified as having limited English proficiency (LEP). By 2007–2008, that number has grown to more than 40 percent. This makes very different demands on my staff. Unfortunately, my budget is decreasing. Seven years ago, funding was $530 for each student with limited English proficiency. It has dropped to $212. That doesn't cover the need. I have to use local money and take resources away from other children to support this program. I keep moving money around to hire the teachers I need for the LEP children. I apply for grants for before school and after school instruction and to help in the summer. I think I spend more time writing grants and begging for money than I do being principal. We have to change how money is allocated or we are going to have a massive population of limited English proficiency children and no money to serve them or the other children.

We place LEP children in different classes depending on what they need. If children have very little English they are placed in self-contained classrooms for first and second grade with Spanish as the language of instruction. We use a small group pull out program for some children from the regular class whose comprehension is good but need additional help, usually in reading and writing English. What we are doing works but I don't know how much longer we can keep doing it.

Reflective Practice

English language learners can be a challenge for administrators. When there is a finite amount of money, they are the ones who decide how the money will be divided. What do you think of this principal's decisions? If you were he would you make the same decisions? What would you tell parents if they challenged your decision making?

Causes of English Language Learners

Children are born into families and families lives are part of a culture that determines what language will be spoken in that family. Shared behavior helps children know how to act with others and establishes broad social patterns that determine what is appropriate or not appropriate in a particular culture. Culture and families are adaptive, creative, and dynamic (Perez & Torres-Guzman, 2002).

Schools, in general, have not done a good job teaching children who are from different linguistic, cultural, and social backgrounds. Studies have documented apparent discrepancies in the levels of referral and placement of limited English proficient children in special education (IDEA, 2004). In 2004, students with limited English proficiency performed below progress goals in two-thirds of the 48 states that reported data. There are some problems obtaining separate test results for limited English proficient students. There is also concern that the U.S. Department of Education is using flawed data to distribute funds to states to support English language learners (U.S. GAO, 2006a).

Children of Immigrant Parents

One out of every five children in the United States is an immigrant or the child of an immigrant parent (Capps, Fix, Ost, Reardon-Anderson, & Passel, 2005a). Children are considered to be **children of immigrant parents** if they are younger than 18 years of age and are either themselves foreign-born or were born in the United States with at least one foreign-born parent.

Place of Origin of Immigrant Families

In 1900, 80 percent of immigrants to the United States came from Europe with only about 1 percent coming from Latin America and Asia (U.S. Bureau of the Census, 1999). Today immigrants come mainly from Latin America. See Table 12–1 for the place of origin of current immigrant families.

Growth and Location of Immigrant Children in the United States.

In the 1990s, the population of immigrant children grew at seven times the rate of native-born children (Capps, Fix,

Table 12–1: Place of origin of immigrant parents of children younger than age 6

- 64% (3.7 million) are from Latin America and the Caribbean
- 39% (2.3 million) are from Mexico
- 25% (1.4 million) are from other Latin American and Caribbean countries
- 23% (1.4 million) are from Asia
- 7% (423,000) are from Europe and Canada
- 6% (363,000) are from Africa and the Middle East

Source: Capps, Fix, Ost, Reardon-Anderson, & Passel, 2005.

Ost et al., 2005). Although immigrants make up 11 percent of the total U.S. population, children of immigrants make up 22 percent of the 23.4 million children younger than 6 in the United States and 20 percent of children 6 to 17 (Capps, Fix, Ost et al., 2005b).

Two-thirds of children of immigrants are concentrated in six states: California, Texas, New York, Florida, Illinois, and New Jersey. However, immigrants are increasingly moving to other states. Between 1990 and 2000, the number of young children in immigrants families in some states increased by over 200 percent (Capps, Fix, Ost et al., 2005) (see Table 12–2).

The rapid growth of this population of young children in many different states has moved this from a concern for a small number of states and cities to a national concern (Capps, Fix, & Passel, 2002).

Status of Immigrant Children

Most children in immigrant families are born in the United States and are American citizens (93 percent). Seven percent of children younger than 6 have foreign citizenship. See Table 12–3 for the status of children younger than 6 years of age. The status of other family members is more complex. Most of these children live in **mixed-status families** with one or more noncitizen parents (Capps, Fix, Ost et al., 2005).

English language learners come from many different cultures and homes. During the preschool years they may have a good command of their home language and little English or they may have few skills in either language.

Table 12–2: Percentage of children in immigrant families and the increase of children younger than 6 in immigrant families from 1990 to 2000 in selected states

State	Percent of Children in Immigrant Families: 2006	Percent Increase 1990 to 2000
North Carolina	13	270
Nebraska	12	269
Arkansas	8	244
Nevada	35	236
Georgia	16	210
Iowa	7	182
Tennessee	7	165
Oregon	19	159
Colorado	20	155
Idaho	12	151
Texas	31	76

Source: Capps, Fix, Ost, Reardon-Anderson, & Passel, 2005; Annie E. Casey Foundation, 2007.

Table 12–3: Status of children younger than 6 years of age born to immigrant parents

- 19% are citizen children of naturalized citizen parents
- 48% are citizen children of legal noncitizen parents (permanent residents, people who have been granted asylum, and those with work permits)
- 26% are citizen children of undocumented parents
- 4% are legal noncitizen children (children who came to the United States due to a parent's work, people who have been granted asylum, or those awaiting citizenship)
- 3% are undocumented noncitizen children

Source: Capps, Fix, Ost, Reardon-Anderson, & Passel, 2005; Schmidley, 2003.

Half of the children of immigrant parents younger than six have a parent who came to the United States during the past 10 years. Of these children, 86 percent have only foreign-born parents (Capps, Fix, Ost et al., 2005; Schmidley, 2003). You might ask why this matters. It matters because many federally funded programs are not available to legal immigrants until they have lived in the United States for 5 years or longer. If one member of the family is undocumented, the family may fear dealing with federal agencies even though the child is eligible for services. It also means that the home language may not be English.

Children whose parents have limited English proficiency face not only language barriers, but health barriers. Parents with limited English proficiency are three times more likely than parents who speak English well to have children in fair or poor health. Of parents who report that they speak English not at all, 27 percent were uninsured (Flores, Abreu, & Tomany-Korman, 2005).

Over half of immigrant families with young children are poor, with access to fewer formal supports. This increases the probability of food insecurity and inadequate or crowded housing. These children may be facing extreme hardships and they have at least one parent in the workforce. The major reason for their poverty is the hourly wage the parent earns. These hardships are one reason why Latino children enter kindergarten with fewer skills than other children and are disproportionately placed in special education (Takanishi, 2004). The lack of formal schooling of children's parents is another reason why they are overrepresented among low academic achievers and why the potential of high quality early childhood education has the possibility of having such a positive impact (National Task Force on Early Childhood Education for Hispanics, 2007). Of Mexican American children in immigrant families, only 4 percent had a mother with a bachelor's degree or more while 64 percent had a mother who had not completed high school (Hernandez, 2006).

Early Identification of English Language Learners

A child's first language, or home language, is the language that the infant heard and overheard her parents speak before and after her birth (Stechuk, Burns, & Yandian, 2006). It is the language she was exposed to. Infants and children exposed to two languages at the same time are called **dual-language learners** (Genesse, Paradis, & Crago, 2004).

Dual-Language Learners

Adults often believe that learning one's home language is effortless and that trying to learn two languages would get in the way to learning a single language. They may believe that learning two languages will delay language acquisition or cause confusion in language use and linguistic representation. These beliefs may be different from children's internal processing of language. We really can't identify how children represent their language or experiences and why some are retained and others are lost (Petito et al., 2001).

Infants exposed to two languages babble and use the same number of vocalizations as monolingual infants (Oller, Eilers, Urbano, & Cobo-Lewis, 1997). Children who have good language models in two languages meet the same milestones as monolingual children relative to first words, two-word utterances, and the achievement of 50 words. Children's vocabulary was similar and they spoke in the language of their communication partner (Petito et al., 2001). There are different ways to count vocabulary. When counting the vocabulary of a bilingual child, the vocabulary in each language is counted then combined for a total. This may actually be an underestimation if the child knows the translational equivalents (zapatos in Spanish and shoes in English) of many words.

We know more about the development of monolingual children than bilingual children. At 24 months, children average 200 to 300 words in their expressive vocabulary. By about 30 months, it grows to 400 words (Hulit & Howard, 2006). One explanation for the child's ability to acquire so much information about so many words is the concept of **fast mapping** (Carey & Bartlett, 1978).

In fast mapping when a child first encounters a new word, she uses the surrounding language and the context to gain some clues about the meaning of the word. She stores these bits of information. When the word is next encountered the child adds to her knowledge base about the word. This process works best when children hear the same word over a period of time. Drilling a child on a word is not effective because the context within the drill is the same each time and it is more difficult for the child to extract the bits of information necessary to form meaning. What this means in the context of word knowledge and vocabulary building, is that children may have bits and pieces of information about a word, but not a complete understanding of it (Hulit & Howard, 2006). This is why so much programming for children is theme- or unit-based. This is one reason why culture and context are so important for children learning a first or second language.

There is some concern that young children do not understand that they are learning two languages. This is especially true when they code switch or mix the two languages. As children are learning two languages, there may be words they know in one language but not in the other. It is natural for them to use the words they know from both languages (**code-switching**). However, their switches are grammatically correct. Think about your language. What if you wanted to use the word "simultaneous" but you couldn't think of it so you said "at the same time." That is how young children code switch. They use a word they know in one language to substitute for a word they don't know in the other. As their vocabulary grows this becomes less frequent. As you talk with them, include the words they are trying to learn. Provide a language-rich environment.

Young children who are raised in a bilingual environment may show language delays. Communication differences based on learning English as a second language should not be confused with communication disorders. Children who speak languages other than English can have language delays. However, it may take a native speaker, ideally a bilingual speech/language pathologist, to pinpoint areas of concern.

Second Language Development in Young Children

The changing demographics of the early childhood population demand that educators have some knowledge about second language acquisition and culturally sensitive instruction as well as first-language learning (Hepburn, 2004).

Some aspects of second language acquisition are the same as first-language learning, others differ. The stage the child is in may determine the most appropriate teaching strategies. Carrera-Carrillo and Smith (2006) identify five stages in this developmental process with corresponding teacher strategies:

- *Preproduction.* As with first-language acquisition when children start the second language learning process they understand few words and may have no verbalizations. To show they understand they do such things as nod or shake their head, point to objects, or categorize them. Children need a language-rich environment, including many different and varied learning and listening opportunities with an emphasis on physical movement, art, and music. Mixed ability groups work well as does shared interactive reading.
- *Early Production.* Children have limited comprehension and can use one and two word responses. They can identify people, places, and things, repeat some language, and listen with greater understanding. Context helps children understand the meaning of language. This is the time to ask who, what, where questions, give either-or choices, and ask yes-or-no questions. Encourage children to label and actively manipulate objects. Before shared reading or other activities that are new activate children's prior knowledge to provide a context for learning and ensure that the reading is interactive.
- *Speech Emergence.* Children at this stage have good comprehension and can make simple sentences that may have errors but are understandable. This is the time to have children build vocabulary, define new words, and describe people places, and events. Encourage them to retell information in their own words. Now teachers should move to more open-ended questions as well as modeling, restating, enriching, and expanding children's language. Continue to provide and use context in learning and create language experience stories and books. Small groups work well.
- *Intermediate Fluency.* Children at this stage have excellent comprehension and few grammatical errors. They can express and defend views, behaviors, and actions. They can negotiate with others and give their own opinions. Teachers can begin to use larger groups and provide more complex language. Children need a variety of realistic reading and writing opportunities. Children should actively participate in the writing, editing, and publishing process with appropriate reference materials.
- *Advanced Fluency.* Children have oral and written language comparable to native English speakers of the same age. Teachers continue to use and support an integrated language arts program.

In reality, although the stages have been identified, there is little evidence to support a separate set of "second language" learning experiences for young children (Stechuk. Burns, & Yandian, 2006). However, if you reflect on the earliest stages they are very similar for what you would do with all young children.

International Children Adopted into English Speaking Homes

The number of children living with adoptive parents in the United States is increasing. According to the 2000 census, there are 2.1 million adopted children living in United States (Administration for Children and Families [ACF], 2003). Of the 13 percent who were adopted from foreign countries, about half (48 percent) were born in Asia, a third (33 percent) in Latin America, and a sixth (16 percent) in Europe. Korea is the largest single source of foreign-born adopted children but accounts for 15 percent of adopted children younger than age 6, with China contributing 3 percent. Most of the European born adopted children younger than age 6 (82 percent) came from Russia and Rumania. Seventeen percent of adopted children were of a different race than their family householder (ACF, 2003). Although adopted from different countries, they share one commonality: They are all English language learners. Their situation is different from children whose home language is not English.

We may not think of the challenges these children face as English language learners. They are leaving familiar surroundings and immediately thrust into an environment where the language and culture is unfamiliar. We know little about how these children best learn English as a second language.

Supporting Second Language Learning

Some children come to school proficient in their home language but with no knowledge of English. These children can express themselves at home, get their wants and needs met, and communicate their joys and sorrows.

They come to school and must not only master the content of the curriculum but learn English and a new set of cultural expectations. They may feel different. They have lost some of their identity—personal and cultural—and their ability to express themselves. There is concern that these young children may find the totality of this experience overwhelming and withdraw.

There are a variety of ways in which adults support children's language learning. One strategy is that of *saying* the word in English and in the child's home language. For example, if a child were playing with a train, the adult might point to the train and "tren"(Spanish) and then say, "train." This may be followed by a request *asking* the child, "Can you say train?" A response to this question is hopefully followed by reinforcing statements such as, "that's close, good for you," or, "you certainly can."

At a later time there might be follow-up about the train where the adult *talks about* the properties of the train or the phonemic aspect of the word: "This train is moving on the track. I wonder where it is going?" Or, "Train starts with the sound /t/ like your name: /t/rain, /T/omas." Other times, adults *define* the word: "All of this [*gesturing*] is the train. This front part of the train that makes it move is called the engine. It pulls the other cars. The last car is the caboose." Sometimes adults *explain* a word by adding details and tying them into the children's experience: "When you come to school, you cross over the railroad tracks. Have you ever had to stop and wait for a train to pass? Some trains are long and others are shorter. Some of the trains go very fast, but others seem to go back and forth and they take a long time. But, all of the trains have to stay on the track. They can only go where there are train tracks" (Han, Roskos, Christie, Mandzuk, & Vuklich, 2005). Obviously what you would use from these techniques is dependent upon the age of the child, the child's interest in the topic, and your assessment of the child's language skills.

Speaking is one aspect of language. An academic language also requires reading and writing. To be successful readers, children need to have a stock of about 6,000 root words by grade two. To do this requires them to acquire about two new word meanings per day from 1 year of age (Biemiller & Slonim, 2001). If children do not have a strong English vocabulary, they are unlikely to become successful readers. So, an important part of early childhood education for all children who are English language learners is the development of vocabulary, particularly root words.

Root words are common words and are defined as basic vocabulary as opposed to rare words that are specific and used infrequently. A root word is a real word and one you can make new words from by adding prefixes and suffixes. For example, the root word "use" can become useful, useless, using, user, usable, misuse, used, and so on. Together these words form a word family. **Word families** share the same root word, part of the spelling, and have a shared meaning. Using word families is a way of increasing vocabulary. One responsibility of the adults in all children's environments is to ensure that there are many opportunities for the development of vocabulary and that the adult and child jointly focus their attention on the same object or event at the same time (Owens, 2005).

Assessment of English Language Learners

The intent of the IDEA (2004) is to ensure that children's abilities are tested. It reads:

> "Materials and procedures used to assess a child with limited English proficiency (must be) selected and administered to ensure that they measure the extent to which the child has a disability and needs special education, rather than measuring the child's English language skills."

It is difficult to assess young English language learners as it is challenging to sort out what they know from their misunderstanding a question because of language barriers (U.S. GAO, 2006b). Even if assessments are translated, they are not necessarily equivalent. A word that is difficult in English may not be the same level of difficulty in other languages (U.S. GAO, 2006b). Children may be given accommodations to help in the testing situation or an alternative assessment. These too may impact the validity of the measure unless it can be demonstrated that the assessments are equivalent. No Child Left Behind requires that limited English proficient children must be provided with reasonable accommodations and must be tested "in the language and form most likely to yield accurate data." If children have been in U.S. public schools for 3 years or more, language arts must be assessed in English. States must establish English language proficiency standards and these standards must be aligned with their academic content standards. They are required to measure all English language learners' oral language and skills in reading and writing English annually from kindergarten through grade 12 (NCLB, 2001).

Implications for Educators

It takes approximately 2 years for children to become socially competent in a language and 5 or 6 years for academic competence. Thus, it is unlikely that children will be academically competent during the early childhood years. What further confounds the issue is that children may know information in one language and not in another. For example, if a child whose home language is Spanish attended an English-only preschool at ages 3 and 4 and the assessment is given at the entrance to kindergarten, what language should the child be tested in? He might actually know colors and numbers and other things better in English but if a question involved problem solving or complex thinking he would do better in Spanish. Look at the results of testing very carefully in the context of what you know about the child and his language development and make decisions based on multiple sources of evidence gathered over time, not just test scores.

English Language Learners in Early Care and Education

High-quality early childhood education holds the potential for helping all young children enter kindergarten with skills to get along with others and the prereading and premath skills that are vital to success in kindergarten and beyond. They particularly benefit low-income children and those at risk of school failure (Matthews & Ewen, 2006). Children born to immigrant parents face multiple risks that would make participation in quality early childhood education programs beneficial, yet these children are less likely to participate in these programs than native-born children (Matthews & Ewen, 2006).

Quality early childhood programs can help children increase school readiness and accelerate language acquisition as well as serve as a transition to public school. They also increase the probability of identifying children with special needs and starting early intervention. In programs with a broad array of services, families might participate in literacy programs, improve their English, and gain skills that increase their employment opportunities (Matthews & Ewen, 2006).

Children of immigrants face multiple risks. They are more likely to live in households characterized by poverty, low parental education, and low maternal employment. Approximately 29 percent of young children of immigrants live in households that are below the federal poverty level and another 27 percent have incomes between 100 and 200 percent of poverty (Capps, Fix, Ost et al., 2005). Of U.S.-born citizens of young children, only 8 percent of parents have less than a high school degree compared to 30 percent of children of immigrants (Capps, Fix, Ost et al., 2005). Over half of all young children of immigrants have at least one parent who has limited English proficiency and almost one-third live in homes that are linguistically isolated. Homes are considered **linguistically isolated** if no one older than the age of 13 speaks English fluently or exclusively (Capps, Fix, Ost et al., 2005).

Mothers in immigrant families are more likely to be married but not work. They are more likely to stay home with their children, and, like all non-working mothers, their young children are less likely to be in early care and education settings. Children of immigrants are less likely to participate in any type of non-parental care arrangement than children who are born of citizens of the United States (Matthews & Ewen, 2006). Children of immigrants compose 22 percent of children younger than age 6, yet they compose only 16 percent of children attending preschool (Capps, Fix, Murray et al., 2005). Additionally, federal restrictions and fear of government makes these families less likely to use public benefits and may increase the hardships associated with poverty.

Mexico is the country of origin for 39 percent of immigrant families with young children. The next country, India, accounts for 2.8 percent of immigrant families with young children (Capps, Fix, Ost et al., 2005). Three- and 4-year-old children of Mexican origin and children of native-born families with Mexican origins have the lowest preschool enrollment of any group of immigrants. This is also true for kindergarten enrollment (Matthews & Ewen, 2006). Because Mexican immigrants constitute such a large proportion of the immigrant population, the experiences of children of Mexican immigrants drive national trends among all young children of immigrants (Capps, Fix, Murray et al., 2005).

The Evidence Base

By fourth grade, 35 percent of English language learners are behind in math and 47 percent are behind in reading when compared to their white counterparts (Fry, 2007).

Table 12–4: Percent of fourth grade children by achievement level for reading and mathematics

	Reading Grade 4	Math Grade 4
English Language Learners		
Advanced	1	1
Proficient	6	11
Basic	21	43
Below Basic	73	46
White Children		
Advanced	10	7
Proficient	30	40
Basic	35	42
Below Basic	25	11
Black Children		
Advanced	2	1
Proficient	11	12
Basic	29	47
Below Basic	59	40
Hispanic Children		
Advanced	2	1
Proficient	13	18
Basic	29	48
Below Basic	45	33

Source: National Assessment of Educational Progress, 2005.

The National Assessment of Educational Progress (NAEP), begun in 1969, keeps nationally representative assessments of educational achievement. The data Fry (2007) analyzed was from this source. He looked at a sample of about 172,000 fourth graders to document these findings.

The gap between English language learners and white learners is clearly apparent in reading in the fourth grade. The gap between white children and all other children in math is apparent. The number of children classified as English language learners begins to decrease in second grade as children exit programs that are designed for English language learners and move into other classrooms. The pattern continues in every grade thereafter (Fry, 2007).

Reflective Practice

Look at these numbers carefully, what do they tell you about what children have learned in school during the early childhood years? Do some subtraction. How far behind are the groups identified from white children? What does this mean relative to what you do in the classroom and how you teach children?

Educational Approaches for English Language Learners

Language is an important vehicle of communication and learning. Supporting early language learning is an important aspect of all early childhood programs. When children are learning two languages, the process is more challenging, but also more rewarding. How this process actually works is dependent on how particular programs are set up. In some settings, the children spend their day in the second language. Depending on the multicultural commitment of the program, there may be few cultural supports for children whose first language is not English. This situation is both stressful for children and not supportive of the home language; in fact, it devalues the home language. Culture and language are part of the curriculum for young children.

See Table 12–5 for a summary of different ways in which programs teach English language learners.

Reflective Practice

Reflect on the different types of program options and the implications of the requirements of No Child Left Behind. Also, reflect on your own preparation to teach English language learners and how comfortable you would be teaching in these different models. What do you think will be the most popular models based on the requirements of No Child Left Behind?

Implications for Educators

Ideally, programs have bilingual educators who are representative of the languages and cultures in the setting. It is easier to build relationships and to understand schedules, routines, and transitions in the home language. If one teacher speaks the children's home language and other teachers speak English all children are immersed in a rich language environment. This way both teachers are considered pure language models (Carrera-Carrollo & Smith, 2006). However, this may not be possible in settings where there are five or six different home languages. In

Table 12–5: Methods of teaching English language learners

Structured immersion: The entire day is in English with little support or use of the child's home language; the goal is for children to learn English. Research has shown that this slows down academic learning and achievement.

Culturally and language-enriched environments: Although the entire day is in English as in the structured immersion program, there is an effort made to increase the linguistic and cultural awareness in the classroom.

English as a Second Language (ESL): The entire day is in English with an emphasis on teaching the English language during specific school periods or having children pulled out of the classroom once to several times a week for additional supplemental English language instruction or to help with specific content areas. This is the second-most common approach used in the United States.

Dual immersion bilingual education: This format uses both English and another language. Depending on the program approximately 50 percent of the day is in English, with times or days specified for each language. The goal is for English language learners and English-proficient children to become bilingual.

Early-exit or transitional bilingual education: This approach supports the child's home language to teach both English and academic subjects as well as emphasizing English language development and academic learning. Children are usually in these programs for 1 to 3 years. This is the most common model used in the United States.

Late-exit or developmental bilingual education: This method emphasizes full bilingualism by varying the amount of instruction given in the home language as children progress academically in their knowledge of English and subject matter areas. Children are in these programs for approximately 6 years before moving into a more traditional English-based classroom. This model shows the highest progressive academic achievement in the long term.

Dual-language programs: This approach supports children in developing proficiently in their home language and in English. Typically one teacher, a native English speaker, teaches in English, and the other teacher, a native speaker of the home language, teaches in the home language in a culturally and language-rich environment.

Source: DeBay & Bombard, 2007; Saracho & Spodek, 2004.

some cases, no educators who are from the child's culture speak the language. If children will not be taught in their home language it is imperative that the setting reflect the cultures of the children who attend. A play-based environment and small groups support language learning. A long large-group time in one language does not support language-learning goals (DeBey & Bombard, 2007).

Regardless of the philosophy of the program, children and their families need to be valued and feel positive about their home language and their culture. They need to be encouraged to communicate and never threatened. Code-switching should be accepted and not criticized. Children live in homes and need to be supported in learning their home language, particularly if that is the way they communicate with their parents and extended family.

The Evidence Base

An expert panel was convened by the Institute of Education Science to summarize and evaluate the evidence available on teaching literacy to English language learners in kindergarten through fifth grade (Gersten, Baker, Shanahan, Linan-Thompson, Collins, & Scarcella, 2007). They identified five essential concepts and have provided recommendations on how to implement these concepts as well as information on the level of evidence to support the practice.

1. **Screen and Monitor Progress:** Conduct formative assessments to screen for reading problems and monitor progress (Evidence Strong). Children need to be assessed in the areas of phonological processing, letter and alphabetic knowledge, and word and text reading. These data can be used to identify children who require additional instructional support.
2. **Provide Reading Interventions:** Provide intensive, small group reading interventions for English learners at risk for reading problems (Evidence Strong). Reading interventions should be timely, occur in a small group format, be provided in addition to the regular reading and cover the five components of reading: phonological awareness, phonics, reading fluency, vocabulary, and comprehension. Instruction should be fast-paced, explicit, and direct.
3. **Teach Vocabulary:** Provide extensive and varied vocabulary instruction throughout the day (Evidence Strong). Vocabulary should be taught throughout the day. Essential content words should be taught in depth and children should have opportunities to acquire vocabulary from a language-rich setting. Instructional time should address the meaning of common words, phrases and expressions not yet learned.
4. **Develop Academic English:** Develop academic English competence beginning in the primary grades (Evidence Low). Academic English focuses on the formal aspects of the language including understanding the structure of language and the precise way in which words and phrases are used.
5. **Schedule Peer Learning:** Schedule regular peer-assisted learning opportunities, including structured language practice (Evidence Strong). Students of different ability or proficiency levels should work together on structured academic tasks at least 90 minutes a week. These activities should be designed to allow children to practice what has been taught and to extend to their learning.

Source: Gersten et al., (2007).

Reflective Practice

Reflect on how this is similar to or different from your expectations about teaching reading to children in grades 1 through 3. How do you feel about these practices? Would you like to know what they are based on? I strongly encourage you to go to the references and the What Works website and see for yourself.

Multicultural Education

Multicultural education encompasses all of the issues young children encounter in their lives that can potentially create stereotypes and bias: race, ethnicity, handicapping conditions, language differences, class, gender, age, religion, and so on (Williams & Cooney, 2006). Multicultural education uses age-appropriate materials and activities, incorporating the strengths of children's families and communities to enrich the curriculum.

There are a variety of ways of looking at classroom diversity. Morey and Kitano (1997) identify three levels of curriculum transformation: exclusive, inclusive, and transformed.

The *exclusive* level has a low level of diversity with a focus on the four "f's"—food, folklore, fun, and fashion. Basically, the tourist approach. The *inclusive* level adds diversity content, but focuses of comparing other cultures and knowledge to the majority culture. A variety of methods are used to relate new knowledge, for children to construct their own knowledge, and to think critically with peers about issues related to diversity.

The *transformed* curriculum challenges traditional views and encourages the reconceptualization of issues and new ways of thinking. Diverse perspectives are shared and problem-solving is the focus. Moving from an exclusive to a transformed curriculum is a developmental process for both teachers and children (Kea, Campbell-Whatley, & Richards, 2006). Utilizing children's literature is certainly a key as is inviting families not only to come to class but to provide input into the decision-making processes.

Developmentally children as young as 3 notice and ask about physical characteristics and specific cultural acts. They are trying to learn more about themselves and others. Four-years-olds are constructing an understanding of gender, racial, and ethnic identity and constancy. They see themselves as part of their family, absorbing the rules and language of their home culture. They are influenced by societal norms and vulnerable to negative societal messages about themselves. They develop theories about how people are grouped.

Guidelines

The modifications that you will need to make in your classroom depend on the needs of the particular children you have and your approach to teaching English language learners. The following guidelines are divided into two sections. The first includes guidelines and techniques to support culturally sensitive instruction as a context for teaching English language learners. It includes some information on working with families, particularly those who have come to the United States recently. The second section provides guidance in how to develop and use specific strategies for language acquisition.

Culturally Sensitive Instruction

The early childhood classroom constantly provides messages about what the program values (and who is valued) from what hangs on the walls to the curriculum teachers implement with the children. Regardless of the particular approach to bilingual education used the programs should support a multicultural philosophy. The question is how you would know one if you saw one and how you could ensure that all classrooms support multicultural values. Williams and Cooney (2006) suggest a culturally sensitive approach.

1. *Promote sensitivity and appreciation for cultural diversity.* If children do not feel safe and develop positive relationships they will not be available for learning.
2. *Focus on many different cultural groups* through literature, music, and environmental planning.
3. *Instill creative and critical thinking skills.*
4. *Value families' cultural and linguistic practices* and does not try to "fix" them.
5. *Respect and learn about the children's culture* and how they spend their time at home.
6. *Understand what is important to parents* in terms of cultural values.
7. *Ensure that pictures, photographs, and artifacts represent diverse racial, ethnic, and ability groups.*

Interacting with Families

1. *Provide information about childproofing environments and child safety.* When children become independently mobile families may need to learn ways of keeping their children safe.
2. *Develop effective ways to communicate with families.* This may include a translator or teachers learning the language of the children in the class if no teachers speak the languages of the children.
3. *Use a digital camera and photographs to share with families what their child is doing during the day.* Encourage families to bring you (or email you) photographs about how they do things at home. If they do not have a camera, loan them one if possible. Photographs give you a common ground on which to base a discussion, even one that may consist of a lot of nodding and smiling.
4. *Value all languages spoken in the classroom,* whether or not you can speak them. As children are learning first words, learn with them. Ask parents to write down the words children know and how they use them. Develop your own pronunciation code.
5. *Ensure that children are encouraged to explore their environment.* Provide safe places indoors and outdoors for children to play.
6. *Ensure that the music you play, the picture books you look at, and the toys and materials that are available reflect the cultures of the children* in addition to the dominant culture.

Second Language Acquisition

1. *Determine where children are in language learning* relative to speaking, listening, reading and writing. If possible do this for both their home language and English.
2. *Label objects in the classroom in the languages the children speak.* Color code the labels so that each language is in a specific color. As you add labels point these out to all children. Help children connect the written and spoken word.
3. *Support teaching and learning with visual cues.* Use real objects, pictures, photographs, role-playing, maps, and diagrams to help set the context of learning. Knowing what is being talked about helps English language learners make better guesses about content and language and helps increase vocabulary. Post class rules in written and picture form. Model, show, and demonstrate a variety of ways of doing things.
4. *Make language more understandable* for children by using simpler speech, shorter sentences, and slowing your rate of talking. Use children's names when you talk to or about them. Avoid using slang or idiomatic expressions. When you do use them, teach the children what they mean.
5. *Repeat and restate language enunciating clearly and emphasize key words.* Check frequently to see if children actually comprehend what is happening. Give clear directions and ensure children understand them by having them demonstrate what you asked.
6. *Pair children and use cooperative strategies for teaching and learning.* Teach children how to work together using verbal and nonverbal strategies. Ensure that all children's ideas are valued and respected. Pair children with different ability levels or different levels of English proficiency. Rotate the pairs.
7. *Focus on the meaning and comprehension of language rather than correcting grammatical errors.* Developmentally, young children do not understand the structure of language even when they use it well. Modeling language until children self-detect and self-correct is more useful.
8. *Build vocabulary.* Provide opportunities throughout the day to increase children's vocabulary. Give children the words for what they are doing, how they are doing it, and what they are doing it with. Don't give so many words that it is difficult to connect the words to the meaning and know that children rarely learn a word the first time they hear it.
9. *Provide language instruction in small groups.* Short language group times highlight the importance of both languages and help all children feel like part of the group. Use small groups in addition to other times when you focus on language. If some children are struggling with particular concepts use small groups to focus on these concepts and explicitly teach them.
10. *Drill and practice is not a developmentally appropriate way to teach young English language learners.*

Curriculum Adaptations

The number and degree of adaptations depend upon the children in your classroom, including the diversity of languages and language skills, and the program philosophy. A thematic approach to content instruction may help English language learners learn content as well as usable vocabulary.

Social Awareness: Self-Esteem, Inclusion, and Social Studies

As children in classrooms are more diverse in background and ability spend time developing a community of learners. Help children have a forum to share artifacts that shed light on their joys, passions, experiences, and home culture. Despite obvious differences, one of the conclusions is how much children are the same. Some of the activities in the Resource Chapter 1 are specifically designed to support children who are English Language Learners. Activity 1–7 Hello Poem is designed to teach children to say "Hello" in a variety of different languages; and Activity 1–18 Foreign Languages increases awareness of other languages. International Snack 1–24 introduces children to a variety of different foods and Charades 1–35w helps all children focus on nonverbal communication.

Self-Esteem

Children need to feel good about themselves, their families, and their culture. They need to be part of social interactions. They need to be valued as individuals.

Children may be tentative about joining groups if they do not know how they will be received and they do not have the language skills to negotiate entering the group.

1. Provide time for children to learn about themselves and their culture.
2. Help all children feel positive about their speech, language, and communication skills.
3. Encourage children to communicate whether in their home language, English, or a combination of the two.

Inclusion

Not speaking the same language is a barrier to inclusion. It is also a concern relative to discrimination. Children who are English language learners not only need to be included, but valued as contributing members of the group.

1. Use many centers and small group experiences as language is learned; children want to be part of a group and to be included. Use few large groups and keep them short.
2. When a child is playing use similar toys or materials to copy and observe his behavior. If he leads expand on what he is doing, and add an innovation to see if he will follow. Join the child first nonverbally, then talk about what is going on.
3. Pair children for some activities. Encourage children to be "coaches" and "players." Pair them based on expertise and experience. Then reverse the roles.
4. Celebrate ways in which children and families are alike and different.

Social Studies

We are all members of a global community. Including English language learners stretches us to learn more about different cultures and different places.

1. Create a cultural democracy in which children's language and cultural differences are viewed as a resource not a liability.
2. Educate children about social justice.
3. Discuss with children how decisions are made in the classroom and in governmental agencies.
4. Show children safety signs or other significant signs they are familiar with (stop, go, bathroom, etc.) in another language. Talk about how confusing and even scary it might be to not understand written language. Expand this to talk about immigrants to the United States and children with dyslexia.
5. Talk about spoken language and how difficult it might be to communicate and meet one's wants and needs if one can't understand what is being said. Again, bring this back to the classroom and children who speak English as a second language and children who have auditory processing problems.

Language and Literacy: Speaking, Listening, Reading, and Writing

Create a literacy-rich environment that includes multicultural materials, resources, and interactive learning. Partner with families to identify their language goals for their child and the interface of their goals with the program. Use books that are multicultural and nonsexist showing different family structures, races, and ages and include individuals with disabilities. Include books with families of various cultures living in the United States (see Children's Bibliography). Have a variety of books in the classroom include some books in Spanish, Chinese, and other languages, even Braille. As you work with and observe children who are English language learners look at both their English language proficiency and how well they are reading. Some English language learners profit from additional support in this area.

Speaking

Learning to speak academic English is a challenge. It requires a language-rich environment and a commitment to teach English more formally even during the preschool years.

1. Provide language input. In some Latin American cultures, the expectation is that young children learn by modeling the behavior of others. In these cultures, children may not have been exposed to as much spoken language as European American children.
2. For English language learners, use visual cues, repeat and restate language, use simpler language.
3. Support both the home language and English in the classroom.
4. Support children's talking and do not comment when they switch between English and their home language.
5. Language learning is a social experience. Provide many demonstrations on how to use language.
6. Use small conversational groups where children are expected to talk and receive feedback on how to use their skills.
7. Talk to children about topics they are interested in and revisit these topics on different occasions.
8. Introduce new vocabulary (root words) that is relevant to the child. Help him learn to use prefixes and suffixes to make new words. See Activity 2–1 Synonyms and Activity 2–4 Rhyming Words.
9. Help children learn to compare words across languages. A simple conversation may include the following exchange:
   Teacher: "Que es esto?" (Pointing at a book)
   Child: "Es un *libro*."
   Teacher: "En ingles es un *book*."
10. Invite a native speaker to talk to the children about her culture and language particularly if she speaks a particular dialect of that language.
11. Teach all children to speak Spanish or another foreign language.

Listening

Being expected to listen when you cannot understand is difficult and being the only one who does not understand makes it more difficult. Children quit listening if they are put in frequent situations where they cannot understand most of what is happening.

1. Provide many opportunities throughout the day for children to listen to language. However, most of this should be one-on-one or in small groups.
2. Learn to read the children to see if they are agreeing because everyone else is or because they understand what is happening.

3. When children are listening, pair what you are saying with a physical response. Ask them to do something: follow directions, stop or go, turn, twirl, sit down, and so on.
4. Provide multiple opportunities for children to respond to questions.
5. Play games like "Simon Says."

Reading

Learning to read is a challenging task for all children. To be learning English and learning to read is more challenging. Support all children as they are learning to read by reading to them at their level of interest and understanding rather than the level at which they can read independently.

1. Label materials in the classroom in the languages of the children in the setting. This is not because you expect children to read, but because you are respecting their language and honoring your commitment to support first- and second-language literacy.
2. Provide simple board books in the home language and help children read them to each other.
3. Provide bilingual visual and word dictionaries so children can look up new words.
4. Use picture books that show different cultural and ethnic groups and have children make up stories to go with the pictures.
5. Teach phonological processing by helping children identify the individual sounds that make up words (phonemes) and identifying the words that those sounds combine to make. Play Sound Bingo, Activity 2–14 and Body Sounds 2–13.
6. Teach the alphabet and letter sounds. See Activity 2–12 Alphabet Lotto and 2–16 Letter Day, and 2–19 Alphabet Line.
7. Provide multiple opportunities for children to read words and sentences in small groups or with a peer.
8. Give clear feedback about errors as children increase in age and when it is part of formal language learning.
9. Read many different alphabet and number books.

Fingerplays are beneficial for children because they provide opportunities for combining language and movement. They can be done many times which increases the possibility of connecting the language and the movements.

1. Start with short simple fingerplays that involve the child's body such as "Where is Thumbkin?"
2. Use fingerplays that teach concepts. If children don't understand the abstraction provide models. Get three different-sized balls and point out the difference in size and the label that goes with each size. Then move to making ball shapes with your hands while saying the following fingerplay:
   A little ball, a bigger ball, a great big ball I see.
   Now let's count them one, two, three.

Writing

Provide many opportunities to write and many examples of why writing is a necessary and useful skill. Show examples of many different types of written work. Include examples of different alphabets such as the Chinese and Cyrillic

Academic English is dependent upon reading as well as speaking. Children need many opportunities to look at and read books.

alphabet (base for Slavic language including Russian), and even Braille, fingerspelling, and Morse code. Discuss the different purposes of writing.

1. Encourage children to use thinking maps and webbing as graphic organizers for their work. See Activity 2–25 Mind Mapping.
2. Have children air write letters with the large muscles of their dominant arm. Pair this with the letter name and the sound of the letter. As children become better have them write whole words. See Activity 2–26 Air Writing.
3. Set up a writing center with a variety of writing tools and different types of paper. Include an English alphabet as well as others in the languages of the children in the class. Have bilingual picture dictionaries.
4. Cultures vary in the emphasis they place on writing and the skill it takes to write beautifully. In some languages writing is almost an art form as well as the written word. Discuss this with children and provide examples.
5. Encourage children to use the computer to write. Help them learn about some of the supports the computer can provide, such as spell checking, grammar, and other languages using various fonts.
6. Create a bilingual word wall.

Discovery: Mathematics, Science, and Technology

English language learners do less well in math than their native-born peers and need to be supported to learn the necessary skills. They need to become intrigued with science and the potential it holds for change and solving global problems. They also need to become competent users of technology to be part of the information age.

Mathematics

English language learners need to learn the language of math as well as the computational skills. Word problem are particularly problematic for all young children. Children need the skill to use math, not just do it.

1. Teach the math vocabulary (numbers, plus, all, round, square, etc.) so children become familiar with the terms and what they mean. See Activity 3–41 Big and Little Pairs.
2. Use manipulatives to teach math. See Activity 3–3 100's Game. Also use informal opportunities to teach math skills such as one-to-one correspondence during snack, and when putting blocks away. See Activity 3–34w Variations on Blocks.
3. Use visuals to teach math concepts. See Matching Symbols Activity 3–1 and Spacey Dots 3–33w.
4. Accentuate the visual side of math. Use graphs and charts.
5. Talk about symbols and abbreviations and ensure that children know what they mean before being expected to use them.
6. Give children practice in writing numbers. All children write numbers far less frequently than letters.
7. Sing songs about math and read stories about math (counting books).

Science

Children need to learn about the world they live in and what they can do to change it and what the implications of those changes are. They need the skills of astute observers, and from these observations the ability to classify information and generalize it.

1. Whenever possible show as well as tell children what is happening. Demonstrate science, do experiments, and encourage children to participate in the experiments.
2. Sciencing should be experimental learning supported by field trips and other experiences to establish a common experiential base to work from. This can be followed by language experience stories as well as diagrams of what the children found interesting.
3. Use illustrations and graphics to teach concepts.
4. Use word study and word sorts to help children expand their vocabulary in a particular area and their understanding of relationships within that category.

Technology

Technology is an important resource and knowing how to use technology is a necessary skill. If children come from families in which there is little technology in the home, they will need to develop these skills at school.

1. Help children gain the skills they need to independently use the keyboard effectively. In addition to contributing to keyboarding skills this also is a motivation for alphabet learning. See Activity 3–25 My Keyboard, 3–26 Spell It, and 3–29 Computer Bingo.
2. Although it may be tempting to use computer programs that provide drill and practice, particularly in areas of English language and math, these are not developmentally appropriate for young children.
3. Young children need interactive programs they can gain control over. They need to learn cause-and-effect reasoning and that they can cause the computer to do something.
4. Encourage children to work on the computer in pairs. Given the variety of skills the computer requires it is a great way to teach and learn and to help children develop friendships.
5. Educational Freeware has free educational software in Spanish at http://www.educational-freeware.com/language/Spanish.aspx. The company also has many children's programs that run in Spanish, as well as software that teaches Spanish.
6. Take photographs of children with a digital camera so they can share with their family what they have been doing and learning in school.

Wellness: Health, Physical Education, and Sensory Motor

Children need to feel safe, trust the environment, have nutritional needs met, develop relationships with caring adults and peers, and to feel that they and their family and culture are respected to be available for learning. Culture impacts the food they eat, the games they play, and maybe even how safe they feel.

Health and Safety

The legal status of children and their families impacts their health and safety. If families are here without documents, they are often reluctant to seek medical care until children become very sick. Even if families are here legally, if they are recent immigrants, they may not be eligible for many social and medical services.

1. The food in the United States may be very different from what the children are used to if they were not born here, or if their families cook traditional foods at home. Find out what children eat at home and check to see if there is anything that you are serving that could be problematic for them because of dietary or religious reasons.
2. Observe what children wear. If they come from a climate that was determined by altitude, had rainy and hot seasons, or was always cold, they may not know about appropriate seasonal clothing or concerns related to sun and wind burn and what to do about these. See Activity 4–1 Seasonal Clothing.
3. Teach children what safety signs mean and what to do when they see them. Do not just tell them, but play games in the classroom and outside where they must respond to different signs and warning sounds. See

Activity 4–4 Stop and Go, 4–32w Traffic Sign Hunt, and 4–33w Warning Sounds.
4. Teach children body parts and some medical terms so that if they are sick they can describe what part of them hurts and how much. This is particularly important if their parents have limited English and the medical profession is unlikely to speak their language.

Large Motor

Provide time for active play inside and outside. This is particularly important if children live in crowded housing conditions and there are few safe outdoor play areas.

1. Find out about the sports that are played in the child's country of origin and the fundamental motor skills needed to participate. Think about how you can support these skills if they are not part of your traditional program.
2. Young children need 30 minutes of structured moderate to vigorous activity. Plan to incorporate this into your day, especially if children do not have safe places to play at home.
3. Ensure children get opportunities to develop fundamental motor skills such as ball handling. (See Activities 4–11 Target Bounce, 4–12 Variations on Throwing, 4–23 Big Balls, 4–36w Variations on

Toys and experiences that are familiar to most children may be new to English language learners.

Dribbling, 4–40w Circle Ball, and 4–44w Variations on Tossing). They also need locomotor skills. (See Activity 4–7 Variations on Running).

4. In order to ensure the moderate to vigorous activity time is structured, you have to participate. Lead the way in helping children improve their large motor development during this time.

Small Motor

Fine motor skills are necessary for writing, keyboarding, and adaptive skills. Find a variety of interesting ways for children to practice these skills.

1. Ensure that puzzles are multicultural and nonsexist. Include some with and without knobs and use simple form boards as well as multi-piece puzzles.
2. The development of small motor skills are an essential component to adaptive skills. Be sure that the dress-up clothing you have available has the type of fasteners children are most likely to encounter and that some of the clothing is representative of the types children in the class might wear. Build vocabulary by talking about the clothing children are putting on and taking off. See Activity 4–15 Progressive Dress Up and 4–42w Caterpillars.
3. Encourage children to play with and use a wide variety of tools for a particular purpose. Tools can be paintbrushes or crayons used in art or tweezers and needle-nose pliers to pick up small things, or forks and chopsticks to eat with. Include the vocabulary necessary for children to identify all the tools used.

Sensory Motor Integration

Combining information from the senses and translating this information to motor activity is an important part of many academic and sports activities. It requires both hemispheres of the brain to work together to accomplish tasks.

1. Encourage children to play follow the leader and other games where children can lead and follow. Pair children and have them take turns. See Activity 4–22 Mirroring.
2. Individuals in different cultures carry objects in different ways. Talk with children and show them photographs of people carrying objects on their head, back, in slings, wraps, and pouches. Encourage children to try a variety of ways to carry different objects and evaluate their effectiveness. See Activity 4–21 Balance It.
3. Help children develop their tactile sense by matching material and identifying objects without seeing them. See Activities 4–27 Feely Bag and 4–30 Pick-a-Pair.

Creative Arts: Visual Arts, Music, Creative Movement, and Dramatic Play

Encourage children to share their culture through creative arts. Ensure that you have the necessary materials and equipment to allow this to happen. Evaluate your visual arts materials, for example, music—both singing, playing and listening, and the equipment you have for dramatic play to ensure that it reflects the global community, particularly the cultures of the children in your class.

Visual Arts

Show children a variety of art and sculpture from different countries. Encourage them to look at the style of painting as well as the particular type of paint used. Ask them questions about the art to help focus their attention on its particular features. Show them different types of visual art, such as murals and talk about how murals are used to document events and even to protest.

1. Make a mural with children. Decide on the topic of the mural, what its purpose is, and how they can each contribute to the mural.
2. Have children make handprints and talk about similarities and differences in their prints. See Activity 5–9 Hand Print Mural.
3. Talk about different countries, different climates, and how structures are related to where they are built. Choose a country and find out about its climate and, using papier-mâché, create a community for that country with each child contributing to the community. See Activity 5–1 Creature.
4. Show children rubbings from temples, churches, and other surfaces and discuss how and why they are made. Have children identify objects in the classroom that would be interesting to make rubbings of. See Activity 5–4 Crayon Rubbing.
5. Look at the relationship between celebrations and art. Identify relevant celebrations, talk about their significance, and help children use art to celebrate the occasion such as Dia De Los Muertos or the Chinese New Year. See Activity 5–33 Chinese New Year Dragon.

Music

Music is a multisensory experience. It can teach listening skills and help develop vocabulary and basic concepts. Children can be part of a group or children can perform individually. Music is also part of culture and language. Musical notation may be new to many children and learning the meaning of that symbol system and integrating it with auditory output is a great literacy skill for all children. See Activity 5–14 Color Notes and 5–40 Notes Collage.

1. Use tapes and compact disks that celebrate different cultures, languages, and styles of music.
2. Sing songs and say fingerplays in more than one language.
3. Ensure that the music you play reflects the languages and cultures of the children in the class.
4. Use music (singing and compact discs) to support play and language learning.
5. Help children learn about the musical instruments used in different cultures and how they are played. Use maracas and castanets and other instruments.
6. Teach children the hand signals that conductors use when they lead a band. Talk about rhythm of music and the rhythm of different languages. See Activity 5–16 Conductor.

7. Sing songs with movements. See Activity 5–44w Movement Songs.

Creative Movement

Creative movement encourages children to move in response to ideas, music, or imaginary circumstances. It challenges children to find different ways to move and to get in touch with their body.

1. Pair music and movement and have a dance party. Be sure to include traditional dance movement from different countries. Demonstrate for children dancing from different eras as well as different styles: swing, jitter bug, tango, line dancing and so on. Don't forget the chicken dance.
2. Provide props to support movement such as scarves and fans that can be twirled and moved.
3. Increase body awareness by moving different body parts in different ways and at different speeds.

Dramatic Play

Use dramatic play to help make the unfamiliar familiar. Provide safe places for children to learn about experiences they might encounter and to replay those they have. Use dramatic play to expand children's knowledge.

1. Set up the dramatic play area in a variety of different ways. If children want to play through medical experiences set it up as a doctor's or dentist's office. See Activity 5–27 Dentist's Office and 5–28 Doctor's Office. If children are interested in stores, have a grocery store, shoe store, clothing store, and so on. See Activity 5–29 Shoe Store. If children are interested in food production have a sushi bar, tea house, taco stand, and so on.
2. Have a variety of clothing available for children to try on. Help children explore different types of traditional dress and talk about the utility of the clothing and why people wore that clothing. Also look at the fabric the clothing is made of and why particular types and colors of fabric are used in some places and not others.
3. Ensure that the dolls are male and female and ethnically diverse, and that other huggables represent the cultures of the children.

Routines and Transitions

Children depend upon schedules and routines to feel safe. To the extent that these are extremely different children can become confused and disorganized. Creating some level of continuity is important and yet challenging when the child's home language is not English. It is more of a challenge when neither the parents nor the caregivers are fluent in a common language. Create a bilingual learning environment by learning helpful phrases in the child's home language that support daily routines and transitions. Routines and transitions emphasize the social aspects of language.

In situations where many children come from homes where the caregivers do not speak English and speak a common language, it is imperative to have at least one educator who speaks the home language. Although an obvious strategy is to send important information home in both English and the home language, it may not be possible. Additionally, adults may not be literate in either their home language or English.

Be honest about your desire to communicate with families on a daily basis and be creative about making this happen. Find out from parents what works for them. Provide them with their own take-home learning tools that support their native language and English (Hepburn, 2004).

1. Use routines to build adaptive skills and the language that goes with the skill and what the child is doing. It is a natural time to say (and point) "that is your hat." "You are putting on your hat."
2. Use meal and snack time to initiate purposeful communication. It also communicates values "Good, you are using your spoon."
3. Routines are also the source of indirect experiences as children listen to conversations of other children as well as observe other adult-child interactions.
4. Use transitions to teach prepositions like on, under, in front of, behind, and so on.

Summary

The number of children who are English language learners is increasing dramatically. Although they speak over 400 languages almost 80 percent speak Spanish. Many of these children live in immigrant families. When one or more members of the family is undocumented children are more likely to be poor and arrive at kindergarten with fewer academic skills.

Accurate assessment of English language learners is challenging because it is difficult to know whether children do not know the answer to the question or did not understand it. Even if tests are translated into the child's home language, if the test is based on mainstream U.S. culture, children may not have had the same experiential base. Also, children may know some information in their home language and different information in English especially if they have attended preschool.

How English language learners should be educated in a controversial area. Some believe that they should just be taught English and others that they need to be taught in some combination of their home language and English. The passage of No Child Left Behind has influenced this controversy. Most believe that the classroom should be language-rich and teaching should be culturally sensitive.

Reflections

1. Working with children and families who are English language learners poses some challenges and opportunities for educators. No Child Left Behind clearly supports the learning of English so that children become English proficient. The research says that it may take as long as six years for children to become proficient in academic English. How do you feel teaching English language learners and

working with their families? How do you think they should be taught?

2. Illegal immigration is a concern in many areas of the United States. Reflect on this issue from the point of view of those who come to the United States, those who hire the adults, those who educate their children and citizens who are not involved with this population. What do you see as the major issues of agreement and disagreement? What do you see as potential solutions?

Educational Resources

Bebop Books have a selection of child-centered stories that support literacy learning and provide multicultural content for beginning readers in guided reading and intervention settings. (202) 779-4400; http://www.bebopbooks.com

Early Child Development (ECD) by the World Bank focuses on early childhood from a global and economic perspective. It has links to international and regional sites; resources, and links to data and statistics from various international organizations. http://www.worldbank.org/children

International Reading Association (IRA) lists culturally diverse books for children, and provides professional development resources. IRA has position statements on reading instruction, as well as resources on teaching strategies for teaching in diverse classrooms. http://www.reading.org

Multicultural Kids is a great source of multicultural books, videos, puzzles, music, dolls, puppets and other educational resources in a variety of languages. (800) 711-2321; http://www.multiculturalkids.com

National Center for Cultural Competence (NCCC), based at Georgetown University, is dedicated to increasing the capacity of health and mental health programs to design, implement, and evaluate culturally and linguistically competent service delivery systems. It has checklists for self-assessing one's cultural competence. http://www11.georgetown.edu/research/gucchd/nccc/

Oyate offers books, music, curriculum materials, and lesson plans that authentically portray the lives of many different Native American tribes and people. (510) 848-6700; http://www.oyate.org

Pan Asian Publications offers multicultural, multilingual, and bilingual books and materials. They have original, translated, or bilingual materials in 36 languages. (510) 848-6700; http://www.panap.com

Shen's Books offers a large selection of multicultural and multilingual books for children in a variety of different languages. It has Cinderella stories from many nations. (800) 456-6660; http://www.shens.com/

For additional resources, visit the book companion website for this text at www.cengage.com/education/deiner.

Chapter 13

Children with Autism Spectrum Disorders

The most difficult child I ever taught was severely autistic. Carlos was 4 years old with no language abilities. We were unsure of his mental abilities because he often refused to do any type of class work. He was a very heavy child and often threw temper tantrums that resulted in him throwing himself onto the floor and screaming. Carlos could not handle any type of change in his routine and often had a tantrum if we altered anything in our class schedule.

This was Carlos's first experience in a school setting and he had a difficult time understanding that there were rules and consequences for inappropriate behaviors. At school he was given breakfast, lunch, and a snack. He would only eat peanut butter and jelly sandwiches and refused any other foods. Carlos only drank milk and would often tantrum if he did not have his "usual" lunch.

We developed a picture exchange system for communication. Carlos had never been required to use any form of communication; when he wanted something he either pointed or simply grabbed. By the end of the year, Carlos understood that he needed the pictures to get what he wanted rather than being his usual bossy and demanding self. He also understood that his picture schedule would keep him aware of upcoming events throughout the day, so he was prepared.

Carlos's mother was a single parent with two other children. I often did respite care for her after school since her parents refused to watch him because of his behaviors. Carlos would come home with me and we would play with whatever held his interest. Once, I left the room to use the bathroom and I thought I had locked all the doors in the house, but he found one that was open. When I went back into the room he was not there. I looked all over the house yelling his name, but since he wouldn't speak, I got no response. I lived on a little back road and he loved going to the playground behind the house. I quickly went there, but he was nowhere to be found. I was in such a panic and was totally flustered when I saw him walking near my driveway. I quickly checked for any scratches or injuries and, thankfully, there were none. Carlos was laughing and didn't seem bothered. I brought him in the house, gave him a huge hug, and made him a huge peanut butter and jelly sandwich, his favorite.

Working with him was so difficult because he was the most violently temperamental child I have dealt with and I would be physically exhausted by the end of the day. There were many

funny incidents that occurred with Carlos that I can now look back on and laugh about, but at the time, they seemed terrible. Even though I used to pray for his absence the next day at school, I still wonder how Carlos is doing and hope that he is improving year by year. That year I learned many things from Carlos. I needed to be patient and to give him space when he needed a break, and to be more understanding than frustrated when he refused to do activities.

Reflective Practice

How would you feel if Carlos was in your classroom? Reflect on how this teacher molded his behavior from the beginning of the year to the end. Think about the challenges of parenting Carlos and his two siblings. Reflect on the skills you will need to teach Carlos and partner with his family.

Autism Spectrum Disorders

The term autism spectrum disorders (ASD) refers to a continuum of neurodevelopmental disorders related to impairments of social interaction, communication and narrow repetitive patterns of behavior (Matson & Minshawi, 2006). The American Psychiatric Association (2000) uses the term pervasive developmental disorder (PDD), which includes autism, Asperger's syndrome, Rett syndrome, and childhood disintegrative disorder. Pervasive developmental disorder–not otherwise specified (PDD-NOS) is used as a classification when symptoms are present but do not meet the criteria for a particular category. These disorders are grouped because they share an essential feature of all PDDs: impaired social reciprocity. Children with these disorders also have problems with communication and repetitive behaviors. The social limitations usually result in limited play skills. PDDs may coexist with other disorders and there is often some degree of intellectual disability (APA, 2000; Hyman & Towbin, 2007).

Defining Autism Spectrum Disorders

For purposes of education the IDEA 2004 defines autism as follows:

> Autism means a developmental disability significantly affecting verbal and nonverbal communication and social interaction, generally evident before age three, that adversely affects a child's educational performance. Other characteristics often associated with autism are engagement in repetitive activities and stereotyped movements, resistance to environmental change or change in daily routines, and unusual responses to sensory experiences.
>
> Autism does not apply if a child's educational performance is adversely affected primarily because the child has an emotional disturbance.
>
> A child who manifests the characteristics of autism after age three could be identified as having autism if other criteria are satisfied.

The American Psychiatric Association (2000) has developed diagnostic criteria for autistic disorder. To be diagnosed with autistic disorder, its onset must be before age 3, with abnormal functioning in one of the following areas: social interaction, language as a communication skill, or symbolic play. To meet the criteria, the child must display six or more items from the list in Table 13–1, with at least two coming from A and one each from B and C.

The diagnostic criteria for Asperger's syndrome requires that there is not a general or significant delay in language, but the disturbance does cause problems in social, occupational, or other areas of functioning. Additionally, children must display at least two criteria from A and C given in Table 13–1.

The term *pervasive developmental disorder–not otherwise specified* (PDD–NOS) is a source of confusion for parents and professionals. It is a vague designation that does not have specific criteria. Some use it as a diagnosis for children who have a basic impairment in relating and communicating, but do not meet the criteria for autistic disorder. Others use it when it is not clear whether the criteria (before age 3) have been met or when the child is too "mild." Some professionals do not like the term *PDD–NOS* and would prefer to use the term autistic spectrum disorder.

Table 13–1: Diagnostic criteria for autistic disorder

A. Qualitative impairments in social interaction

- marked impairment in using multiple nonverbal behaviors such as eye-to-eye gaze, facial expression, gestures, and body postures to regulate social interaction
- inability to develop appropriate peer relationships
- lack of spontaneous sharing of enjoyment, interests, or achievements with others
- lack of social or emotional reciprocity

B. Qualitative impairments in communication

- delay in, or lack of, spoken communication
- inability to use speech to initiate or sustain conversation
- stereotyped and repetitive use of language or idiosyncratic language
- lack of spontaneous make-believe play or social imitative play

C. Restricted, repetitive, and stereotyped patterns of behavior, interests, and activities

- preoccupation with stereotyped patterns of interest (intensity or focus)
- adherence to specific nonfunctional routines or rituals
- stereotyped and repetitive motor mannerisms (hand flapping)
- preoccupation with parts of objects

Source: American Psychiatric Association (2000).

Greenspan and Wieder (2006) particularly object to this label. They prefer to use the term *neurodevelopmental disorders of relating and communicating*. They feel that this term more accurately defines the regulatory-sensory processing problems with the significant developmental delays and dysfunctions that derail the child's ability to relate and communicate.

Greenspan and Wieder's research (2006) shows a different pattern of development than that noted by the American Psychiatric Association (2000). Their research shows children having seemingly normal development for about the first 12 to 15 months. At this time, the toddler begins to show oversensitivity or becomes less reactive to sounds and touch. Language development stops and existing language seems forgotten. Greenspan and Wieder (2006) see these behaviors as falling along a continuum rather than fitting into clear diagnostic categories. They see each child as having a unique profile relative to sensory reactivity, sensory processing, muscle tone, and motor planning or sequencing.

Prevalence of Autistic Spectrum Disorders

Autism is diagnosed at the rate of 2 to 20 cases per 10,000 individuals with a median rate of 5 cases per 10,000 individuals (APA, 2000). Autism is generally diagnosed before age 5. Autism occurs more frequently in males at a ratio of 4:1 (Hyman & Tobin, 2007). Looking at the entire spectrum of autistic and pervasive developmental disorders Chakrabarti and Fombonne (2005) estimate the rate to be 35 to 60 per 10,000. Other estimates have concluded prevalence is 1 in 150 children, supporting the higher rate (Autism and Developmental Disabilities Monitoring Network, 2007).

The number of children being identified with ASD is increasing. It is difficult to tell specifically by looking at the data from the National Center for Educational Statistics (NCES, 2005) as they combined autism with traumatic brain injury. They began keeping prevalence rates on these disabilities in 1992–1993. At that time autism and traumatic brain injury constituted .04 percent of the special education population. This percentage has shown a steady increase and in 2003–2004 it reached 2.8 percent. There have been a variety of explanations offered for this increase. Some focus on the definitional issue. With a possible diagnosis of PDD–NOS, not all of the characteristics for PDD have to be met. Additionally, more disabilities (Asperger's syndrome, Rett syndrome, and Childhood Disintegrative Disorder) were added to the PDD category by the American Psychiatric Association in 1994. Another possibility is that children who had previously been diagnosed as having intellectual disabilities are being served on the autism spectrum (Matson & Minshawi, 2006). The services are typically better for children with autism than intellectual disability so, given a choice, parents would rather have this designation. This is supported by the decreasing number of children identified as having intellectual disabilities (1976–1977, 26 percent of the special education population; 2003–2004, 8.9 percent) (NCES, 2005). The number of children diagnosed with autism served under IDEA increased by more than 500 percent between 1995 and 2005 (U.S. Government Accountability Office, 2005).

There are many unanswered questions about autism spectrum disorders. To help answer some of these questions the Combating Autism Act of 2006 was signed into law on December 19, 2006. It mandates the expansion of autism research and the development of a national research agenda, and the education of physicians and the public about autism with the goal of early identification and intervention.

Causes of Autism Spectrum Disorders

Autism spectrum disorders (ADS) encompass a variety of different disorders and there is not a single etiology. There seems to be general agreement in the field there is a biological base and a significant genetic influence in ASDs (Hyman & Towbin, 2007). Scientists have isolated several abnormalities on chromosomes 2, 7, and 15 associated with ASD (Muhle, Trentatcoste, & Rapin, 2004). There is interest in the role of neurotransmitters, particularly serotonin, in children with ASD. In Rett syndrome, the relationship is clearer as it is associated with a mutation of a gene on the X chromosome. It is predominately seen in girls as male infants usually die (Huppke & Gartner 2005).

Although it seems clear that genetic influences are an important risk factor, environmental factors influence gene expression. Research also shows that autism tends to run in families, although not in a clear-cut way. Siblings of children with autism have a higher rate of autism than expected in the general population and if one twin has autism the other twin has a 65 percent chance of having autism and others will show some autistic symptoms (Hyman & Towbin, 2007).

Advances in diagnostic testing including the Comparative Genomic Hybridization (CGH) array have allowed scientists to identify subtle duplication or deletions of genetic materials (Hagerman, 2007). These changes affect the development of synapses early in development or synaptic plasticity and environmental responses. Mutations in genes that guide inhibitory and stimulatory connections also contribute to autism. Environmental stimuli such as emotional trauma can impair synaptic connections and likewise targeted educational programs can enhance synaptic connections (Hagerman, 2007).

There are some drugs, which if taken during pregnancy, can increase the probability of having a child with autism. Thalidomide, a drug used in the 1950s and 1960s to treat morning sickness is one such drug (Newschaffer et al., 2007). Clearly, our environment has changed with both natural and manmade toxins. Pregnant women and children are exposed to pollution, nuclear waste, food additives, household chemicals, and pesticides at levels no other generation has faced (Interactive Autism Network, 2007). There is no single, simple answer.

Greenspan and Wieder (2006) feel the disorder is triggered by the environment and that two events derail the child's development between 16 and 24 months. The first is the child's emerging capacity of higher-level presymbolic, symbolic, and cognitive functioning. These new capacities are built on a weak foundation. They overwhelm the child and cause him to regress in the areas of self-regulation, behavioral organization, interpersonal patterns, motor control, and language abilities. At the core of this regression is a weak capacity for intentional two-way affective communication. Although this alone may impact development, a second event that stresses the child such as the loss of a caregiver, a parent's return to work, or the birth of a sibling may be overwhelming. The more difficult the child becomes, the more frustrated the parents feel. They feel that it is a biologically based problem in forming an early sensory-affect-motor connection that leads to the challenges and symptoms observed in autism spectrum disorders.

There has been a lot of controversy about whether the measles, mumps and rubella (MMR) vaccine caused autism or the ethyl mercury-based preservative thimerosal that was used as a preservative for pediatric vaccines before 2001 could be associated with the rise in cases of ASD. At this point there is not scientific documentation for a causal relation between these variables, although clearly some parents believe this is true (Hyman & Towbin, 2007).

In the Field

Our son has autism. He was a marvelous well developing toddler until he had his MMR. Several weeks after he had his vaccination his behavior began to change. He quit talking and looking at our eyes. He became self-absorbed. We told his pediatrician who made light of it. His older sister was very advanced for her age and he told us not to make comparisons. We didn't, we worried. We talked to people. My wife is a nurse and she began to talk to people and we began to believe that Tony was developing autism. We changed pediatricians. We told our new pediatrician that we believed our son has autism and that it was caused by the thimerosal in the MMR. Over time and with a lot of observations, surveys to fill out and so on he eventually diagnosed Tony with autism. We were angry and we now talked to other parents who were angry. At first we were so consumed with our anger that we almost forgot about Tony. We were going to get lawyers and sue. We were going to march. We were going to do all kinds of things. Then it hit us that as we were focusing on our anger our son was slipping farther and farther away from us.

Finally, we refocused and used our energy to learn about how to teach children with autism. We decided that the Applied Behavior Analysis (ABA) made the most sense for us. My wife got the training and then we started. We really thought about what we wanted for Tony and then how to get it. Depending on the year we spent between $60,000 and $100,000 doing the training. That isn't counting our time (daughter included) and the friends that came to help. I haven't changed my mind about what I believe caused my son's autism, but I did change how I used my time and money.

Reflective Practice

How would you work with a parent that had these beliefs? How could you support this family? Do you think the thimerosal in the MMR vaccination could be the cause? Can you put yourself in this family's place? How does it feel?

Early Identification of Autism Spectrum Disorders

Identification of children with autism spectrum disorders is typically determined by their behavior in three areas: social reciprocity, communication, and repetitive behaviors (APA, 2000). Delays of abnormal functioning in social interactions, not using language as a tool for social communication, and not participating in symbolic or imaginative play serve as markers (APA, 2000).

One finding that may help in the early identification of infants is that their pattern of brain growth, as measured by head circumference, shows a different pattern than other children. Although normal at birth, brain growth accelerated between 1 to 2 months and 6 to 14 months (Courchesne, Carper, & Aksoomoff, 2003). There are a variety of theories about the impact this has on development. One theory focuses on the synaptic pruning process where synapses that are used stay and that those that are not used are pruned. If this pruning does not happen than the neural structure of the brain may be disorganized (Mundy & Burnette, 2005). In addition to differences in brain structures there also seem to be differences in the connections between various parts of the brain. The abilities that are most characteristic of autism, social interactions and language, require a high degree of integration among various parts of the brain (Minshew, Sweeney, Bauman, & Webb, 2005).

Parents often notice lack of speech by 15 to 18 months. However, deficits in the areas of communication can be noted before in prespeech behavior. Infants will lack appropriate gaze and the turn-taking pattern that characterizes adult-infant communication. They do not recognize their parents' voices or respond to their name, yet they are aware of environmental noises. They also don't have a gesture system that typically supports vocalizations. Approximately 25 to 30 percent of infants with ASD begin to say words, then stop speaking and using gestures between 15 and 24 months. Although children do regress based on environmental stressors, ASD should be one of the possibilities considered (Johnson, Myers, & the Council of Children with Disabilities, 2007).

Parents seem less aware of the social aspects of children's early development than motor milestones. Infants with ASD do not seek connectedness, they seldom make eye contact, and ignore their parents' bids for attention. They seem content being alone. Deficits in joint attention are one of the most distinguishing characteristics of very young children with ASDs (Johnson et al., 2007).

The importance of early identification and early intervention is imperative. If children are identified early and intervention is begun, the outcome for children and families can be positively impacted.

The Evidence Base

As we move toward more evidence-based decision making it becomes clear that in some instances we lack evidence. As a result of the Children's Health Act of 2000 the Centers for Autism and Developmental Disabilities Research and Epidemiology (CADDRE) Network is undertaking a 5-year multisite collaborative study: *The Study to*

Explore Early Development. The goal of the study is to identify what might put children at risk for autism spectrum disorders and other developmental disabilities. The study will include 2,700 children, 2 through 7, and their parents in six states: California, Colorado, Georgia, Maryland, North Carolina, and Pennsylvania. They are looking at the following factors:

- Reproductive and hormonal features of mothers
- Smoking, alcohol, and drug use during pregnancy
- Parents' occupation
- Sociodemographic features
- Genetic features
- Biomarkers
- Physical and behavioral characteristics
- Infection and immune function, including autoimmunity
- Select mercury exposures
- Gastrointestinal features
- Sleep features
- Hospitalizations and injuries (CDC, Centers for Autism and Developmental Disabilities Research and Epidemiology [CADDRE], 2008)

To keep updated about this research go to http://www.cdc.gov/ncbddd/autism/seed.htm.

Reflective Practice

As you reflect on what you know about autism, are these the factors you would be looking into? Are there others you would add? How do you think this information would inform your practice in the classroom? What research would need to be done to guide your practice? What are the factors involved?

Assessment of Autism Spectrum Disorders

Assessment begins with a multimodal view of the problem. It may begin with a family medical history, a detailed history of the child's social development and general information about the family and how it functions. Typically, the child's hearing and language development are assessed. A test of intelligence is used to determine overall cognitive functioning. More information is obtained through a neurologic examination, an **electroencephalogram** (EEG), and blood studies (Hyman & Towbin, 2007).

Observations of the child are made in different settings at multiple times. Rating scales are often used to assist and organize evaluation information. Scales like the Childhood Autism Rating Scale (CARS; Schopler, Reichler, & Renner, 1993) developed in North Carolina for use in the TEACCH (Treatment and Education of Autistic and Communication-Handicapped Children) clinic rely on comprehensive observations and are summative for children older than age 2.

The Autism Diagnostic Interview-Revised (ADI-R; Lord, Rutter, & Le Couteur, 1994) focuses on five different areas: (1) opening questions about parents' or caregivers' concerns; (2) early and current communication skills; (3) social development and current play skills; (4) repetitive and restricted behaviors; and (5) behavioral problems. Questions were added that are designed to differentiate between different disorders on the spectrum. Mothers typically serve as the informants and the interview takes 60 to 90 minutes to complete and requires someone who is a competent interviewer and knowledgeable about ASD (Matson & Minshawi, 2006). This is often used in conjunction with the Autism Diagnostic Observation Schedule-Generic (ADOS; Lord et al., 1989, 2000). This tool has eight standardized tasks the examiner and child participate in. During the tasks and throughout the observation, the examiner rates the child's behavior as within normal limits (0); infrequent or possible abnormality (1); or definite abnormality (2). These tools are used with children during their preschool years.

Because of the importance of early intervention waiting until the preschool years for diagnosis is seen by many as too late. Although parents become concerned about their child's behavior around their child's first birthday, children are rarely assessed by a pediatrician or psychologist for ASD until their second or third birthday or later. The Checklist for Autism in Toddlers (CHAT) was initially developed to be used by parents and pediatrician at regular 18-month check-ups as a screening tool (Baron-Cohen, Allen, & Gillberg, 1992). A modified version, the M-CHAT (Dumont-Mathew & Fein 2005) is a screening tool for children ages 18 to 36 months.

Although other disabilities have batteries of tests used in the early identification process mental health professionals have relied primarily on unstructured clinical interviews and clinical judgment based on guidelines from the American Psychiatric Association's *Diagnostic and Statistical Manual of Mental Disorders* Fourth Edition-Text Revision (APA, 2000) to make decisions (Matson & Minshawi, 2006). In general, medical testing is not helpful, although a detailed medical history should be taken and other potential causes of the behavior ruled out. One major concern with the diagnosis of autism is differentiating it from other disorders.

It is unusual to have a child with Asperger's syndrome diagnosed during the early childhood years because they mask the severity of their difficulties with social interaction with verbal skills. Asperger's disorder may not be diagnosed until school age when the social demands of the classroom make the symptoms apparent (Hyman & Towbin, 2007).

Disorders on the Autism Spectrum

Like most children with disabilities children on the autism spectrum have different disabilities and different levels of involvement. Disorders that are considered part of the autism spectrum include autism, Asperger's syndrome, Pervasive development disorder–not otherwise specified, Rett syndrome, and childhood disintegrative disorder.

Autistic Disorder

Autism was first described by Kanner (1943) as infantile autism. He documented with detail and accuracy such children's lack of interest in people, stereotypic behavior, and problems with language, which are still part of the diagnostic assessment today. Given Kanner's sample of 11 children, he did not believe that autism had such a high overlap with intellectual disability as today's research supports. His research also led to a misunderstanding of the parent-child relationship. The reciprocal nature of parent-child relationships was not explored and reports looked to parents' psychopathology as one of the causes of autism, identifying, for example, the "refrigerator" mother who could not relate to her child. Recent research (Wamboldt & Wamboldt, 2000) found that although family problems can exacerbate child problems, it is often the other way around. Autism is not caused by lack of parenting skills.

Children with autistic disorder are usually identified when they are toddlers or during the preschool years. As infants their characteristic behaviors may seem unusual, but by age 2, the failure to develop nonverbal aspects of social behavior (facial expression, looking at the speaker) and lack of interest in peers become apparent. Deficiencies in communication skills are also noted, particularly the lack of spontaneous communication, and the inability to use language symbolically. If there is language, it may be immature or idiosyncratic so that only those familiar with the child know what is meant.

Asperger's Syndrome

Asperger's disorder or syndrome is a neurobiological disorder in which children have a marked deficiency in the area of social skills. This impairment in social interaction is obvious and sustained. Children with Asperger's syndrome have trouble with transitions and change. They want things to stay the same. Because they may become preoccupied with a particular object or subject, they can be misdiagnosed as autistic. Unlike autistic disorder, there is usually no intellectual disability or impairment of language acquisition. Children may have mild motor clumsiness and even signs of overactivity and inattention. There is considerable overlap between the diagnosis of high-functioning autism (no intellectual disability) and Asperger's disorder (Hyman & Towbin, 2007).

This impairment centers on social skills. Children with Asperger's syndrome have an impairment of social interaction, social communication, and social imagination; that is, flexible thinking and imaginative play (Cumine, Leach, & Stevenson, 1998). These impairments may be subtle but they are nonetheless real.

Children with Asperger's syndrome may be socially isolated, but this rarely bothers them. They may become tense and distressed when they are trying to cope with the approaches and social demands of others. Although children with Asperger's syndrome may have perfect spoken language, they often use language in a way that tends to be formal and even pedantic. The use of language will set the child apart from others. The child's voice may lack expression and he may have problems getting meaning from the tone of someone else's voice. Children may need a visual signal to know that you are unhappy with their behavior. They have problems interpreting nonverbal communication and may understand others in a very literal way. To say "I could have died laughing" would be very confusing to the child because you are not dead. Children also fail to get the implied meaning of language. If you said "The telephone is ringing" the child wouldn't understand that you intend to answer the phone or that you may want someone else to answer the phone (Cumine et al., 1998).

A child with Asperger's syndrome may have an all-absorbing interest in something his peers find unusual. He may have a schedule or routine that he insists be observed. This may be anything from a bedtime ritual to how he puts on his clothes. He is limited in his ability to think and play relatively. He also has problems in generalizing and in transferring skills from one setting to another (Cumine et al., 1998). Children with Asperger's syndrome often have difficulty in motor skills. The child may be clumsy, awkward, and gauche in his movements. Organization is a challenge. A child may have problems getting all his belongings together or finding his way around. Writing and drawing neatly is also problematic, as is finishing tasks (Cumine et al., 1998).

In the Field

My brother Paul was born in 1962. We knew he was different, slow, his speech was weird, but we lived on a small farm in Alberta, Canada. When my parents tried to enroll him in school, he was not admitted. He worked some on the farm but mostly he stayed at home and cleaned things. It took him a long time, but he loved to clean. Canada passed new laws about children with disabilities and, in 1978, when Paul was 16 he entered school for the first time. Our family grows them big. At that time Paul was almost 6 feet tall and weighed close to 160 pounds. He was formally tested and identified as having Asperger's syndrome. He was placed in a first grade class. Can you imagine? He cried, he fought, and he didn't want to go to school and the school didn't want him. He scared the teachers and the children.

He was then enrolled in a residential school in Edmonton, about 2 hours away. He lived with my aunt during the week. We expected him to have adjustment problems and he did. However, when he started defecating in all of the corners of my aunt's house, she had had it. He was once again home on the farm. My father died when Paul was in his thirties. At his funeral I told my stepmother that I would have Paul spend a week with me as soon as I could arrange it. About 2 months later Paul came to visit me. When the week was up I called to make arrangements to take him back to my stepmother. She said that she had packed his things up and she planned to have them delivered to me, and that he would be staying with me. That was 10 years ago.

Reflective Practice

We knew very little about autism 50 years ago. How would Paul's life be different if he had been born this year instead of 1962? What impact might that have had on his family?

Pervasive Developmental Disorder–Not Otherwise Specified

The diagnosis PDD–NOS has no minimum number of criteria to be met, but it does represent a functional impairment. It is referred to as a **subthreshold condition**. Children diagnosed with PDD–NOS are a heterogeneous group that may have comorbid symptoms of cognitive,

Children with autism spectrum disorders are frequently more interested in things than in playing with other children.

language, and behavioral symptoms in addition to symptoms of autism (Hyman & Towbin, 2007). These children typically are identified later than children with autism and are less likely to have intellectual disability. Whether or not a child is diagnosed with autism or PDD–NOS, the treatment and interventions are individualized but essentially use the same principles.

Rett Syndrome

Rett syndrome is a neurodevelopmental disorder that begins with a period of normal development through the first 6 to 18 months of life. Then there is a deceleration of head growth resulting in intellectual disability. There is progressive neurologic involvement, which results in the loss of purposeful hand skills (replaced by hand wringing or hand washing behavior) and spasticity in the legs. Social engagement is lost. The child has a severe impairment in both expressive and receptive language and has a poorly coordinated gait and trunk movements. The disorder eventually stabilizes. In toddlers, it has the same characteristics as other autistic disorders; however, by preschool age, the differences are evident. Rett syndrome has only been diagnosed in females and is much less common than autistic disorder (Hyman & Towbin, 2007).

Rett syndrome is caused by a mutation in the MECP2 gene on the X chromosome (Huppke & Gartner, 2005). This gene contains instructions for the synthesis of a protein MeCP2 that tells other genes to turn off or stop producing their own unique proteins As girls have two X chromosomes, only about half of the cells in the nervous system use the defective gene. Boys with the MECP2 mutation die shortly after birth (National Institute of Neurological Disorders and Stroke [NINDS], 2008).

There are four stages to the syndrome. In stage I, early onset, the disorder may be somewhat vague and autistic-like if noticed. This stage lasts for a few months and possibly up to a year. Stage II, rapid destructive stage, begins between ages 1 and 4 and lasts for weeks or months. It is during this time that the characteristic hand movements appear, head growth slows, and rapid or gradual purposeful hands skills and spoken language are lost. Stage III,

plateau or pseudo-stationary stage, begins between 2 and 10 and can last for years. **Apraxia**, motor problems, and seizures are prominent, but the child may show more interest and alertness, and some skills improve. Girls may remain in this stage for most of their lives. Stage IV, late motor deterioration stage, can last for years or decades and is characterized by reduced mobility (NINDS, 2008).

Childhood Disintegrative Disorder

The essential feature of childhood disintegrative disorder (CDD), as the name implies, is a marked regression in multiple areas of function following a period of at least 2 years of normal development. After 2 years, but before 10 years, the child loses previously acquired skills in the areas of expressive and receptive language, social skills, and adaptive behavior including bowel and bladder control, motor skills, and play skills (APA, 2000). At some point the disorder stabilizes, leaving children with many of the characteristics of autistic disorder (Hyman & Towbin, 2007). CDD is usually associated with severe intellectual disability. It is a very rare condition and no single cause has been identified.

Associated Conditions

There is a close connection between autism and intellectual disability, which confounds diagnosis. It is estimated that two-thirds to three-quarters of children 3 to 10 years of age with autistic disorder also have intellectual disability (Yeargin-Alsop et al., 2003). The overlap appears to be only about 40 percent with preschool children (Chakrabarti & Fombonne, 2001). The developmental trajectory of this group of children who have autism but do not have intellectual disability can be greatly impacted. With early intervention to improve language, play, and the motivation to socialize with peers during the preschool years they will appear more like children with Asperger's syndrome than autism (Attwood, 2007).

Sleep disturbances are very common in children with ASDs with 50 percent to 70 percent of children reported to have problems in this area. These appear most problematic during the preschool years but persist for many years (Wiggs & Stores, 2004). Approximately a fourth of children with autistic disorder also have epilepsy (Tuchman, 2000).

Characteristics of Children with Autism Spectrum Disorders

Like all children, children with ASD have a variety of characteristics with a range of severity. Some of these behaviors are close to what other children their age might do while others are more severe. There are three central domains affected: social, communication, and behavior.

Social Reciprocity

Social interactions form the core of getting along with others. Social interactions are complex. They involve being able to read and respond accurately to the cues of others. These social skills emerge as children learn about themselves as individuals and, eventually, about the thoughts and feelings of others. Children with ASD are inept at learning these skills. They may not respond, have limited responses, or be clumsy in their attempts. Thus, they do not have good social interaction skills. Overall, depending upon the level of involvement, they may

- show little interest in making friends and playing with other children; are indifferent to peer contact.
- would rather play alone than play with others.
- have difficulty being with and interacting with peers.
- may not imitate behavior or model what other children or adults are doing even when this is one-on-one.
- may not show age-appropriate play behaviors.
- may not make eye contact.
- may not smile at people or family members.
- have difficulty interpreting social cues.
- seem unaware of the existence of other people and may not respond to family members differently than unknown adults.
- show socially and emotionally inappropriate behaviors (Attwood, 2007; Powers, 1989).

Communication Skills

Children with ASD have some degree of communication impairment. Expressive language may show more echolalia (repetition of what is spoken) than spontaneous speech. Personal pronouns are often confused. Speech may be high pitched, and have an unusual rhythm and intonation pattern (Hyman & Towbin, 2007). Receptively, children may have problems with more complex communication. Traditionally, they are visual learners. Overall, depending upon the level of involvement, they may

- have delayed speech development.
- have difficulty maintaining a conversation even if they have good speech skills.
- reverse pronouns such as "I" and "you."
- have echolalic speech or "parrot" words others say either immediately or after a delay.
- have little or no imagination, cannot understand symbolic or creative interactions, and cannot pretend.
- misinterpret literal or implied meanings.
- not use traditional symbolic gestures such as waving; have limited facial expression.
- cannot communicate well with words or gestures.
- Have expressive language that may be superficially perfect and formal (Attwood, 2007; Powers, 1989).

Stereotyped Behavior

Children with ASD don't know how to play, especially when children get into pretend play. They often get into rituals, routines, and schedules, but spontaneity is beyond their capability. They often become upset if their routines are disturbed. They may display stereotyped movements and self-stimulating behaviors such as arm flapping, pacing, running in circles, rocking, hand waving, and so on. They may have sleep disturbances, mood changes, and unusual responses to sensory input. Overall, depending upon the level of involvement, they

- be passive or physically inactive and may not respond to requests.

- have a narrow range of interests to the exclusion of other activities.
- be picky eaters.
- throw temper tantrums when there is not an obvious cause.
- behave aggressively and may physically attack others.
- practice self-injurious behavior such as head banging or eye gouging.
- have a compulsive need for routines which affects themselves and others (Attwood, 2007; Powers, 1989).

Instructional Models

There is no one accepted way to teach children with ASD, although all believe that early intervention is essential and that this intervention should be intensive, continuous, and multidisciplinary (Hurth, Shaw, Iseman, Whaley, & Rogers, 1999). Most agree that early intervention for children with autistic spectrum disorders needs to have a high degree of structure; materials must be presented in a planned, predictable manner, and environmental stimulation needs consideration (Gammeltoft & Nordenhof, 2007). However, professionals disagree over how this should happen. Educational approaches are diverse and there does not seem to be compelling information to support one method. All, however, agree that intervention needs to be individualized.

Some professionals believe that children with ASD should be included in regular classrooms while others feel that this is inappropriate. Still others feel that early intervention needs to be individualized and segregated but that children do need to be included as they get older and/or for some part of the day, although maybe not the entire day. The programs and methods detailed below are designed primarily for segregated programs and focus on individualized planning.

In the Field

Children with autism can be quite challenging to teach, which is what makes their success that much sweeter! Knowing what to teach preschool children with autism is very important. Some parents may want academic rather than functional skills on their child's individualized education program (IEP). I cannot stress enough the importance of functional skills. If a child has not already mastered these skills, then she should be working on them. The critical skills include responding to yes–no and choice questions, using the bathroom, dressing, personal appearance, mobility in familiar locations, eating without drawing attention, occupying self while waiting, responding to greetings, requesting what she needs, indicating when a task is finished, and gaining attention. When teaching children these critical skills, teachers must present them in a functional way. Having a child get dressed just because it is 10:00 A.M. and that is what you do in school at 10:00 A.M. is not functional, but having a child change into "messy play clothes," or having children practice dressing themselves after going swimming, is very functional.

Reflective Practice

What do you think of this teacher's analysis of critical skills? Are there skills you would add or subtract from the list? Do you think parents would agree with the skills chosen?

Applied Behavior Analysis (ABA), the Lovaas Method

Lovaas (1987) developed a model of intensive, comprehensive one-on-one training. It involves teaching many discrete lessons. Children usually start a 40-hour-per-week program at age 2. The approach is based on principles of behavior modification. It uses a model of introduction, prompting, and reinforcement of behavior. The curriculum focuses on language, academic skills, and social behavior. Although not as simple as this, the approach involves the following steps.

- Deciding on the behavior you want to change, replace, or initiate. Take a baseline (how frequently does it occur, what happens before it occurs, when and where does it occur).
- Make a hypothesis about the purpose of the behavior you want to change or replace. State the goal in positive terms (what the child will do, not what the child will not do). Think about the components of the behavior.
- To initiate behavior, break the goal down into its component parts, and design a drill. Speech is a good area to start in.
- After each intervention use positive reinforcement. Because drills are short and frequent, rewards must be small and fast and something the child finds reinforcing, such as food, hugs, verbal praise, and so on. Some programs use negative reinforcers for undesired behaviors.
- Assess the effectiveness of the intervention and modify it if necessary (Waltz, 1999).

This is a very intensive program and most frequently is a home-based program run by parents who are trained in the method, with family, friends, and students as volunteers. Generalization of the skills learned is an important component of the treatment plan.

In the Field

Data collection is a very important part of evaluating a child's programming. Classroom staff needs to collect data on each IEP goal one time per week to determine how well the child is progressing. If the child is not progressing, the team needs to review the data to decide what changes should be made in how goals are presented. A data sheet needs to include, at the very least, the name of the child, goal or benchmark, key, reinforcement schedule, and parameter details. We also include the initial stimulus, target stimulus, error correction procedure, task format, prompt strategy, and the target level. Data collection can be very time-consuming and works best when it is built into the daily classroom routine. For example, many children have hand washing as an IEP objective.

Since children have the opportunity to wash their hands at least three times per day, data should be taken at one of those times. Do not just decide out of the blue that you are going to take a child to wash his hands just because you need to collect data.

Reinforcement is very important for children's success. Before an activity, each child should have the opportunity to choose what he wants to work for. You will often hear me say in my classroom, "If you want _____ , then you need to _____." It's amazing the change in behavior I find when children are reminded of what they can receive if they complete a task. It is often difficult for some parents to realize the effectiveness of this approach. Of course, fade the reinforcement as much and as quickly as possible. If a child does a good job and likes pretzels, don't give him 10 pretzels, one is just fine. We have to remember that adults need reinforcement, so why wouldn't children? It is just that our reinforcement is usually a paycheck, or an evening out.

Reflective Practice

How comfortable are you with a behavioral model? What about food as a reinforcer? Do you think like this teacher does that we all work for external reinforcement?

Children with autism appear to be developing normally until about 12 to 18 months when their failure to develop nonverbal aspects of social behavior and their lack of interest in toys and peers becomes apparent.

Developmental Individual-Differences Relationship-Based Approach

The Developmental Individual-Differences Relationship-Based (DIR) Approach was developed by Greenspan and Wieder (2006). They identified six fundamental developmental skills they feel should form the foundation of all intervention:

- the dual ability to take an interest in the sights, sounds, and sensations of the world and to calm oneself down
- the ability to engage in relationships with other people
- the ability to engage in two-way communication
- the ability to create complex gestures, to string together a series of actions into an elaborate and deliberate problem-solving sequence
- the ability to create ideas
- the ability to build bridges between ideas to make them reality-based and logical (Greenspan & Wieder, 1998, pp. 3–4).

Greenspan and Wieder (2006) place autism spectrum disorders in the broader context of Neurodevelopmental Disorders of Relating and Communicating (NDRC). They have proposed four types of clusters, or clinical subtypes that they feel have implications for diagnosis and treatment. They base these on four developmental pathways that characterize how individuals process information:

- Sensory modulation—the ability to modulate or regulate sensation as it is coming in
- Motor planning and sequencing—how we act on our ideas or what we hear and see
- Auditory processing and language—the way in which we receive information and comprehend and express it
- Visuospatial processing—the ability to make sense of and understand what we are seeing (Greenspan & Wieder, 2006, p. 236).

Their approach is very different from a behavioral approach but just as intensive. Children and their parents engage in emotional interactions that use emerging but not fully developed capacities for communication and relatedness. Working from this hypothesis, they feel that intervention should "involve children in dynamic, emotionally based, problem-solving interactions that are likely to foster abstract thinking and the very ability to generalize itself" (Greenspan & Wieder, 1998, p. 478). The intervention, sometimes called "Floor Time," begins with establishing attention, engagement, and intimacy, and then moves on to two-way communication, feelings and ideas, and logical thinking (Greenspan & Wieder, 2006). In a comprehensive program they see spontaneous, follow-the-child's-lead floor time happening 8 to 10 times a day with 20- to 30-minute sessions in addition to semistructured problem-solving and spatial, motor, and sensory activities. They are far more optimistic about outcomes for children, but feel that approaches that do not pull the child into spontaneous, joyful relationship patterns may intensify rather than remediate the problem (Greenspan & Wieder, 2006).

Treatment and Education of Autistic and Related Communication-Handicapped Children (TEACCH)

Treatment and Education of Autistic and Related Communication-Handicapped Children (TEACCH) was established in the early 1970s by Eric Schopler at Chapel Hill, North Carolina and was one of the first disorder-specific educational programs that developed an intensive, structured, coordinated approach to developing communication abilities for children with autism. The approach involves parents as co-therapists and uses behavioral strategies to enhance communication and social interactions. It heavily supports the use of visual organizers and cueing (Mesibov, Shea, & Schopler, 2005).

In the Field

I implement some TEACCH strategies in my classroom. Each day, I assign children "basket work," which is basically an individual work system. Work systems should always answer four questions: (1) what work, (2) how much work, (3) when is the work finished, and (4) what's next? Basket time allows the children to work independently on tasks with a work schedule. I have set up "basket work" so that each child has a sentence strip with three cards on it. The child takes the first card on his strip and matches it to a basket that is found in the same place each day. When the child returns to his desk and completes the work in the basket, he places it in a "finished" basket and gets the next card on his strip. These steps continue until the child has completed all his tasks. On the strip, after the third card, is a picture of a preferred activity. The children know that when they have completed all three tasks, they can participate in the preferred activity. I usually have the children complete basket work while I am working with children individually. Basket work is also a good activity for the kids to work on when they first arrive in the morning, while I am reading communications books and taking children to the bathroom. It is exciting to see the children's progress from completing one task with assistance to completing three or four tasks independently for 15 minutes or more!

Shoebox tasks, or task boxes, are wonderful to use in basket work. These activities can be made using shoeboxes (what else?) and Velcro™. To make a task box for a child who needs to improve fine motor skills, attach an ice cube tray to the top of the box and then place 1-inch cube blocks inside each of the cube holders. Cut a hole in the shoebox for the children to put the cubes into. The child has to use a pincer grasp to take the block out of the ice cube tray and put it in the hole. Children know the task is complete when all of the blocks are gone. When cleaning up, simply take the ice cube tray off the top of the box, put it in with the blocks, and it is done. I like shoebox tasks because they contain all the materials in the box, so there is no need to go searching around for the manipulatives you need. It is also nice that you can use your imagination to make the task boxes meet the needs of your children. You can also purchase shoebox tasks online at http://www.shoeboxtasks.com. I think they are rather expensive, but you can also use the website just to get ideas for making your own task boxes.

Reflective Practice

Can you check out the shoebox tasks and make one? At a more global level, you have read about a variety of methods of teaching children with autism. Which do you think you would try if you had a child with autism in your class?

Assistive Technology

Much of the focus of assistive technology for children with ASD is on augmentative and alternative communication. Some of these devices are made by parents, and children are able to point to pictures to let others know about their wants and needs. Some of the communication devices actually "talk" and with current technology there is even a choice in the voice that will be used. In the past, the voice was typically that of an adult male whether the user was a female or a child.

Many schools use the Picture Exchange Communication System (PECS), which is commercially available. The pictures in this system are specifically designed to represent words and concepts. PECS was developed in 1985 to teach children and adults to initiate communication. It has seven phases and works well with approaches that use behavior analysis. Briefly:

Phase I: Teaches children to initiate communicate by exchanging a single picture for a highly desired item.

Phase II: Teaches children to be persistent communicators by actively seeking out their picture and traveling to someone to make a request.

Phase III: Teaches children to discriminate pictures and to select the picture that represents the item they want.

Phase IV: Teaches children to use sentence structure to make a request in the form of "I want. . . ."

Phase V: Teaches children to respond to the question "What do you want?"

Phase VI: Teaches children to comment about things in their environment both spontaneously and in response to a question.

Phase VII: Expanding Vocabulary: Teaches children to use attributes such as colors, shapes, and sizes in their requests (Frost & Bondy, 2002.)

In the Field

I cannot say enough about the importance of communication skills. The most common reason that adults with disabilities are fired from jobs is their lack of communication skills. The Picture Exchange Communication System (PECS) can be used not only with children with autism, but with children who have other disabilities as well. Children beginning to learn to communicate via PECS start with requesting a desired item by placing a picture of the item in an adult's hand, with full assistance. Gradually, assistance is faded and children are presented with a variety of pictures from which they need to discriminate what they want. Children go on to use an "I want _____" sentence strip and often use the sentence strip as a visual cue for how to request an item.

One key thing to remember with PECS is that adults should not be asking children what they want; rather the child should initiate communication with the adult. Children begin PECS training with requesting because they will find it motivating to receive an item they have asked for. Once a child becomes proficient at requesting, staff will begin helping the child to comment on things in the environment. Having previously taught at a school that did not implement PECS I can vouch that children who have learned the PECS as an alternate form of communication have enjoyed many more opportunities at school, home, and in the community. If a child is having a tantrum and I don't know why, it is very nice to know that if I gesture toward their communication book, they can usually tell me what it is they want.

Reflective Practice

Using the PECS as a model, make a picture communication system and try it. Decide on the most important things you want to be able to communicate and how you will portray these.

The Evidence Base

This synthesis of practice-based research focused on the effectiveness of the Picture Exchange Communication System (PECS) for improving the functional communication skills of children with autistic spectrum disorders. Eleven articles (13 studies including 125 participants) met the selection criterion (Tien, 2008).

In all of the studies participants who received PECS training experienced positive gains in functional communication skills. The most commonly reported outcomes included (a) successful use of PECS as a communication tool (100 percent of studies); (b) an increase in overall level of communication and language (62 percent of studies); (c) an increase in spontaneous language/speech imitation (46 percent of studies); (d) an increase of initiations of communication (31 percent of studies); and (e) an increase in mean length of utterance (23 percent of studies) (Tien, 2008). Studies that included follow-up assessments found that the gains were maintained at posttest.

Reflective Practice

This research synthesized the studies that had been done using PECS to determine the effectiveness of this particular approach to teaching language skills to children with ASD. They set up selection criteria, analyzed the studies, and then proposed rival explanations. They looked at threats to internal validity such as observational coding and the fact that the changes could be related to maturation and ruled out these possibilities. They concluded that PECS is a tool for teaching functional communications skills for children with ASD and that it can be easily integrated into the school and home. They caution that these results cannot be generalized to other disabilities. As you look at yourself as an educator who uses evidence-based research what doe this mean to your practice? How might you use this information? What does it suggest about ways to determine best teaching methods?

Therapies and Interventions

There are a variety of different therapies that are used with children with ASD. Speech/language therapy is a major intervention for children with ASD. The issue is typically one of lack of speech and functional communication skills. When children are nonverbal some advocate the use of **total communication**, a combination of speech and sign language. They feel this may lay the groundwork for oral speech and it takes advantage of the visual skills many of these children have (Waltz, 1999). Other focuses of therapy may be on **echolalia**, the repetition of words or phrases just heard, and **palilalia**, the repetition of one's own words. Sometimes dance, music, or art therapy is used with children who have ASD. These therapies do not appear to have curative value, but children can develop skills and enjoy the process.

For children with ASD an occupational therapist (OT) would develop an individualized program based on the particular child and his needs. It might focus on helping the child learn to suck through a straw, put on and take off clothing, and work on balance and developing the vestibular sense. The OT might also work on building up specific muscles, teaching techniques for self-relaxation, and techniques for dealing with sensory overload. Occupational therapists might also work with body awareness using massage and brushing the limbs. Most children with ASD will need occupational therapy. Some children will need physical therapy to work on issues like gait problems, low muscle tone, strengthening muscles, and other related issues.

In the Field

Communication with parents is key! I found that each day I was writing home to parents basically the same information and it was taking up a lot of time. I modified a "Daily Report" from a fellow teacher to send home. On the daily report there is space to circle what the child ate at school, the activities and therapies in which she participated, and what her mood was like. Each day, the paper goes home with the child and the parents are expected to complete the same type of information on the back of the paper and return it to school. I really like knowing what the children did at home the previous night so we can talk about it at school the next day. In addition to this, we also send home a communication book, in case the parent or teacher has a question or comment.

Reflective Practice

Do you have a plan for regularly communicating with families? Do you think this level of communication is needed in an inclusive classroom?

Sensory Integration

Sensory integration is the process by which individuals receive information from their senses, process that information, and then act on it. Some feel that one of the problems that children with ASD have is interpreting the world around them. Sensory integration problems can be fundamental because they interfere with the development of basic skills. These skills can be used in both segregated and inclusive settings.

Children demonstrate individual variations in how they respond to their world. One reason for this is differences in the ways they interpret it. **Registration** refers to awareness, the point at which we know we have touched or smelled something. People have different thresholds for awareness and, to further confound things, these levels change relative to our levels of stress and fatigue. People can also have a low threshold for some things and high for others. If you are concentrating on reading this book, you may not hear approaching footsteps until someone is beside you. If, however, you are listening for someone to come you might pick up the footfalls much earlier. Until the input registers, it cannot be acted upon (Myles, Cook, Miller, Rinner, & Robbins, 2000).

After registration, *orientation* can occur. This typically results in a shift of attention—from the book to the footsteps. *Interpretation* takes place as we relate what is happening to our past experience. What does this mean? If nothing, the response may end. If it is determined that a response is necessary, then internal *organization* occurs to determine what response will be made. Finally, the *response* will be executed (Myles et al., 2000). In real life this process happens so quickly it may seem like a single action.

Modulation is the ability to regulate responses in the context of what is happening. If there is an exam the next day, you might continue to read the book. If you are reading ahead, you might benefit by taking a break with a friend. To stay awake driving you might sing, open the window, or chew gum. When you arrive, you might read a boring story, or play soft music in order to calm down to make sleep possible.

Effective sensory process feeds into motor planning or praxis, which is necessary to respond and execute motor actions. This is particularly important in analyzing new actions and in adjusting to variations in old ones. It involves the cognitive process of representing the action, knowing where the body is, starting the action, proceeding with the necessary sequence of steps, making adjustments, and then knowing when the action is over. Something as simple as getting out of a different chair requires praxis. Think about how you would get out of a deep, low-slung chair as opposed to a straight-backed wooden chair. Different motor planning and adjustment is required.

Some children have ineffective sensory processing. They have trouble learning to ride a bike. Some children may refuse to wear some types of clothing that feel uncomfortable, due to their unusual responses to sensory input. They may experience unpleasant sensations when others do not. Children with ASD often have unusual sensory reactions. These reactions vary with the sensory input involved.

Children with ASD tend to have reactions either greater or less than one would expect from the situation. This has to do with the central processing of the child's brain. The hypersensitive child's brain registers sensation too intensely, which causes the child to misinterpret information (Kranowitz, 1998). He may view a touch as a life-threatening blow and hence try to avoid being touched. Children who are hyposensitive are underreactive. This child's brain registers too little sensation, so the child seeks stimulation to maintain a "normal" arousal level. This child may be constantly touching and feeling things. He needs to act but he may lack coordination and organization. He misses cues other children get. He may not understand nonverbal cues. Some children are a combination of hyper- and hyposensitive. This can vary with the particular stimulus or it can vary with the place or time of day (Williamson & Anzalone, 2001).

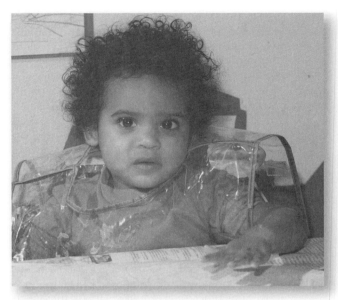

Children with autism can have unusual reactions to tactile stimulation. Some children are hypersensitive to touch and approach sensory experiences tentatively.

In the Field

Children with autism need sensory input. It is a good idea to set aside a specific time each day to incorporate sensory activities into your classroom. The most common thing to do for sensory time is to play in the bean/sand/rice/water table. Although this is a great idea and fun for them, there are many other types of sensory activities that are as much or more beneficial for the kids. For example, children in my class love the "hot dog game," which is when they lie on a sleeping bag and we roll them up tightly. They also enjoy vibrating pillows and having their back, arms, legs, hands, and feet brushed with a fingernail brush or surgical cleansing brush. To get children moving more, try having them bounce on a therapy ball or jump on a trampoline. Oral-motor stimulation can occur when a child brushes his teeth with an electric toothbrush, or by using straws for pudding and applesauce. Some occupational therapists have recommended using a weighted vest with children. I have found this to be very helpful. The vest will be on the child for 15 to 20 minutes and then off for 15 to 20 minutes. The times will vary depending on the child. The weights used should be no more than one-tenth of the child's body weight.

Reflective Practice

Think about how you traditionally ensure that children have needed sensory input. What kind of support do you think you would need to move more clearly into the sensory stimulation done by occupational therapists? Are you comfortable going there?

Tactile

Children with ASD can be overreactive (hypersensitive) or underreactive (hyposensitive) to tactile stimuli.

Tactile Hypersensitivity. Children who are hypersensitive to touch, sometimes called tactile defensiveness, often refuse to participate in messy activities. They may only wear certain clothing (dresses that fall from the shoulders), or certain fabrics (cotton), or only clothes that have been washed in a certain detergent. They may have problems with some food textures. They may not feel safe when close to other children because they don't want to be touched. Work with these children and their families. Some children need to wear sweaters or jackets so they can modulate the experience of touch. Find out what type of touch is best tolerated.

Tactile Hyposensitivity. Children who are hyposensitive to touch may not notice touch until it is firm or intense. Children may not react to scrapes or bruises or know when or how they received them. They may touch others in line or even lean on them and not know it or understand the problem. If accompanied by low muscle tone they may be clumsy and tire easily, becoming exhausted after physical activity. They may run into the door jam as they walk through the door. Because they need sensation, they may crave tactile input, which may result in hitting or biting themselves. Or, they may bite their fingernails to the quick or prefer clothing that is tight (Myles et al., 2000).

Vestibular

The vestibular system is involved with movement, posture, vision, balance, and coordination between the sides of the body.

Vestibular Hypersensitivity. Children who are hypersensitive have a low tolerance for activities that involve movement. They like their feet on the ground. They don't like to play games that involve changing direction, speed, or other than upright body positions. Children who have problems in this area may not participate in sports and may have some problems with requirements in physical education. Some school tasks are challenging, such as copying from the board and keeping their place when reading. The child may move his whole body rather than just his head to look at something.

Vestibular Hyposensitivity. Children who are hyposensitive often rock back and forth in their chair. They are clumsy and have trouble starting and stopping movement.

They cannot sit still, wiggle, and constantly reposition themselves (Myles et al., 2000).

Proprioception

This system helps us keep our balance and to rebalance based on feedback from our muscles and joints. It also helps us move, sit, and hold things. When the proprioception system is not working well, children may slump, display left/right confusion, and have problems completing obstacle courses. Fatigue is common.

Visual

Compared to other sensory systems, vision is a relative strength. With concentration and motivation, this system usually works well. It is difficult, however, for children with ASD to maintain both concentration and motivation.

In the Field

Children with autism are visual learners. These children need visual supports throughout the school day. Children often respond better to a picture symbol that displays "sit down" than to the verbal command "sit down." It can be hard to limit "verbage" (verbal garbage)—basically it is easy to talk too much, leaving children completely lost. For example, instead of saying, "Johnny, you need to sit in your chair like your friend Matt," it's much better to simply say "sit," or better still, show the child a "sit" picture. Visuals can be easily implemented into morning circle songs as well. For the song "If You're Happy and You Know It," teachers should have on hand pictures of various actions so the children have a visual representation of the actions they are expected to follow. This works best if the pictures are made on a large scale, laminated, and bound into book format in the order you sing. (Digital cameras are a godsend.) Organization is very important when teaching preschoolers in general, especially preschoolers with autism. The last thing you'll have time to do is gather a bunch of different pictures from a variety of places!

Reflective Practice

How will knowing that children with autism are visual learners impact how you teach?

Auditory

Children with autistic spectrum disorder do not seem to process auditory information the same way that other children do. Children with ASD typically have unusual sensory preferences. Three- and four-year-old children with ASD do not show a preference for parentese or child directed speech over acoustically modified nonspeech (Kuhl, Coffey-Corina, Padden, & Dawson, 2005).

The Evidence Base

The purpose of this study was to investigate the auditory preferences of children with ASD. A sample of 53 children 3 and 4 years of age who met the criteria for ASD were identified and were matched with comparison groups of (a) 32 toddlers matched for language-age (b) 44 typically developing age-matched infants, and (c) 30 typically developing younger children (12 to 15 months) who were at the same receptive language level and gender ratio as the children with ASD (Paul, Chawarska, Fowler, Cicchetti, & Volkmar, 2007).

Four set of comparisons with two subsets of stimuli were used. The target pattern was language or a language pattern that typically developing children who are learning English as a first language preferred (For example, in one set the subset had an adult female native English speaker reading *Little Red Riding Hood*). The second subset was similar but the sound was different in the nontarget pattern (The comparison subset had an adult female native Mandarin Chinese speaker reading *Little Red Riding Hood* in Mandarin).

Children with ASD are able to participate in auditory preference tasks. Findings suggest that children with ASD show a reduced preference for child-directed speech, compared with typical age-mates, but few differences from children with developmental delays. Children with ASD perform differently from typical peers in auditory preference paradigms and that may be related to their language development (Paul et al., 2007).

Reflective Practice

Does this research provide you with clues about communicating with children with ASD?

Auditory Hypersensitivity. Loud noises can be unbearable to some children. Even small noises can be irritating. Some children cannot tolerate specific sounds, and others have problems with noises that seem quiet to us.

Auditory Hyposensitivity. Some children seem not to hear what is going on around them, not even when their name is being called. Others seem to drift off in the middle of a conversation.

Gustatory

The sense of taste can be problematic for some children with ASD. They often have strong likes and dislikes.

Olfactory

Apparently, many children with ASD have a type of olfactory sensory sensitivity (Myles et al., 2000). Schools have many smells, from the materials used to build them to the unique body odor each of us possesses. For some children and adults, these smells can be overpowering and even problematic.

Medication may be used as part of the intervention for children with ASD.

Medication

Once an education program is in place medication may be considered as part of a treatment program for specific target behaviors or comorbid conditions. Stimulant medications might be used if the child has symptoms of hyperactivity or inattention. If there is concern about neurotransmitters, serotonin reuptake inhibitors might be used to treat repetitive behavior. Other medication is being researched but medication is not seen as a cure for ASD (Hyman & Tobin 2007).

Many families, in their search to understand and help their child, turn to complementary and alternative medicines (CAM). The National Center for Complementary and Alternative Medicine divides these approaches up into five categories:

- Whole medical systems (homeopathy or Chinese medicine)
- Mind-body interventions (meditation, dance therapy, auditory integration)
- Biologically based therapies (using herbs, food, and vitamins)
- Manipulative and body-based methods (deep pressure and craniosacral therapy)
- Energy therapies (reiki, electromagnetic fields and so on) (National Center for Complementary and Alternative Medicine, 2007)

Dietary treatment (often eliminating wheat and milk proteins) are tried. Vitamins may be taken in mega doses. There is little support for these therapies, but they are frequently used (Hyman & Tobin, 2007).

Inclusive Settings

People have very different feelings about the inclusion of children with ASD into regular classrooms. Although most feel that children should spend *some* time in a regular classroom, many feel that only children with mild impairments should be significantly integrated into inclusive classrooms. They feel that the structure and organization most children with ASD need cannot be provided in an inclusive setting. Others disagree. Regardless of location, many experiences need more structure and a clearer purpose than other young children require.

Organizing games for children with ASD is different than thinking about playing with other children. If the games involve social interaction it has to be set up for that to happen. Playing is vital to children's social development. However, playing is not spontaneous for children with autism; it needs to be organized and planned. Gammeltoft and Nordenhof (2007) suggest thinking through the following

- *Where will the game take place?* Choose a table or some place that can be delineated using tape or mats.
- *What are we sharing?* Children need to know exactly what they will be doing and for how long. Begin with several short games rather than one long one.
- *Who is playing the game?* It may be easier if another child initiates the play. Give participating children numbers and the child whose number is one begins the game.
- *Whose turn is it?* A cap may be used to identify whose turn it is at the beginning.
- *How should the materials be handled?* Be clear what materials belong and how they should be used.
- *Where does the game start and end?* Clear indicators help determine when the game is completed.

In the Field

Play skills are very important for young children to acquire. Children need to be taught to play appropriately with a variety of toys. This is especially important if a child is in an inclusive classroom with typical peers. Play skills are best taught in a systematic manner by first selecting a new toy or activity, establishing objectives, analyzing the task, teaching one step at a time, and finally, gradually expanding the play period. Cause-and-effect play skills should be taught first. Toys in this category include pop-up toys, rain sticks, bubbles, and so on. Closed-ended activities may be taught next. These activities are puzzles, shape sorter, stringing beads, and so on. Open-ended activities (for example, playing with playdough, blocks, dolls, dress-up clothes, and paints) may be more difficult for children to learn because there is no end product or sequence. Visual supports may help with open-ended activities. Children can be given a doll and clothes along with a picture of a doll all dressed and be told to dress the doll like the picture. Or, children can be given a visual model to guide them in stacking blocks to make a bridge or a train. Once a child has developed a repertoire of play schemes, the child is ready to move on to parallel play activities where he is expected to play with his own toys beside another child, and finally the child should progress to group play activities.

Reflective Practice

Decide how you will go about teaching a child with autism to play. Pick an activity and decide on the materials you will need and construct the script you will use. Does this challenge your concept of play?

Support Personnel

Frequently, when children with ASD are included in regular classrooms, support staff are included as well. This means that the teacher not only has additional support for the child who is in her classroom, but that she also has to manage other adults in her classroom. In general, support staff do one of three things: they provide one-on-one support for a particular child, they provide support for the children in the class who have special needs either directly or making or modifying special curriculum materials, or they support the delivery of curriculum.

Support staff have the potential for enriching the classroom and but also of stigmatizing the child. It should be clear in what way the support staff will make a difference, and what form it should take. To determine this, teachers, parents, and children need to be consulted. Sometimes the greatest support can be to modify lessons to include children with special needs or to collect data about what is happening. In other instances, team teaching is the goal. It is important for all to know the goal of additional support and to agree about what is needed. This goal impacts the job description of the individual, the required training, the status, and the expected support. Thus, the role of the support person can take shape in many different ways. This person can be a consultant, an observer, a problem solver, a person who sits beside the child, and so on. What is important is what the role is relative to the teacher, that it is clearly defined, and is agreed upon by all. The role of the support person should also be clear to children in the classroom.

In the Field

Children with autism do best when their time is structured. They do not do well with a lot of downtime. File folder activities work well with children. Since they are easy to make, the file folders can be adapted to meet the individual needs of children. I also like to make theme- and holiday-related file folders. File folder books can be purchased at teacher supply stores, but I have found them to be too challenging for most of my children, so I make them myself or ask one of my support staff to help. We use colored file folders, index cards, library book pockets, and stickers/stamps/picture symbols. For example, if you have a child who is working on matching numbers, you can make a file folder match. Begin by gluing or stapling eight library pockets on a file folder. On the pocket you can place number stickers, number stamps, or just write the numbers the child is working on matching. On the index card, write the same numbers, or use stamps or stickers, whatever was on the pocket. Laminate all materials, cut them apart, and the student is ready to match. If your school does not have the library book pockets, you can use index cards in place of the pockets. I attach the loose card to the cards glued on the folder with Velcro™ so I can check the child's work before the cards end up all over the floor.

As I said before, children need a structured school day. In addition to structure, children also need predictability. Providing children with a picture schedule provides them with both structure and predictability. Children with autism have trouble with transitions because they do not know what to expect next. Tantrums and noncompliance due to difficulty with transitions is dramatically reduced if a picture schedule is used consistently. Some people may question the use of schedules, stating that children become too dependent upon them. I usually respond to such questions by asking people what they would do without a calendar, which usually puts things in perspective for them. Depending upon ability, some children will come to the table for the arts. I will have a mini schedule that shows children that they will first color, then cut, then glue. Many parents find schedules useful at home as well. Educators should visit homes to teach families how to incorporate a schedule, and to determine what picture cards are needed.

Reflective Practice

Make a file folder game or a picture schedule. Is it more difficult that you thought once you actually do it? How do you relate this to a task analysis?

Guidelines

Children with autism spectrum disorders cover a wide range of disorders with different levels of involvement; however, the following guidelines are useful in working with all children with ASD. The way in which you will use these guidelines will be determined by the particular child you are working with and the setting he is in.

1. *Ensure visual and auditory congruence.* When you discipline or correct a child, show him your facial expression and say, "Look at my face. Am I happy?" "Look at Tyrone's face. He is sad; you just hurt him." It is very confusing for a child if you use your "happy face and voice" when you are telling him something negative.

2. *Make auditory messages congruent with task.* When you need to discipline a child, use a stern voice so he knows you are not happy. Then find a child who is doing something good and use your happy voice to offer positive reinforcement. This way children know that you are not mad at the entire class. Once the child's behavior has changed, immediately "catch him being good" and provide positive reinforcement so he knows that the entire day is not ruined because of one problem. This also forces you to deal with the situation and move on.

In the Field

At the beginning of the year, my children help me draw a paper plate puppet to show what I look like when I am happy and when I am "grumpy." The happy side shows me smiling, eyes open, hair neat. Then we write the word "Happy Teacher" on the plate. On the other side we draw what I look like when I am mad (grumpy). My face is red, eyes squinted, hair is a mess, and we write the words "Grumpy Teacher" on the plate. We then talk about what happens when the "grumpy teacher" comes to class: no treats, lost recess, observer chair. We then attach a craft stick and hang it on the chalkboard with a magnet. When some children do not respond to verbal directions, I ask them if they want the grumpy teacher to come visit. I then hold the puppet to my face and we see if I am happy. It sounds crazy, but it works. It also lets them know that I do not like it when I need to use my grumpy tone, and they need to change their behavior.

Reflective Practice

Do you think something this simple might work for you? How might you use this or a similar concept in your classroom?

3. *Define tasks.* Make clear the meaning of any task. Don't assume that a task, situation, activity, or event is clear to a child. Try to see it from his perspective.

4. *Define the child's role.* Alert the child to his role in tasks, situations, or events. Even if he is clear about what is happening, he may not understand his role in the event.

5. *Forewarn children.* Some children with ASD are tactile sensitive; therefore, you need to check with them to ask if they want a pat on the back. Ask, "Are you ready for a pat on the back for being good?" This allows the child to have control of the situation and also get used to positive touch. Use deep pressure where possible. Encourage the child to initiate touch.

6. *Be explicit.* Don't assume that the context will help make the meaning of directions clear. Don't assume, for example, that if you have a table set up with large paper and markers, the child will know he is expected to draw.

7. *Identify beginning and end points of tasks.* List the steps involved in the task or have pictures or diagrams.

8. *Use visual clues.* Pictures help to highlight meaning.

9. *Help children generalize knowledge.* Build in opportunities for children to generalize what they know. Add variety to children's work by varying the materials they use to achieve a particular goal. Help children use skills in a variety of different situations.

10. *Activate previous knowledge.* When presenting new material, identify the main point and make connections between previous knowledge and skills explicit; help children see the whole picture rather than just the details.

11. *Individualize instruction.* Remember that each child is different and what works for one child may not work for another. Children themselves are also variable, so what works for a child one day may not necessarily work another day.

12. *Present tasks visually.* Make expectations clear and highlight the important information.

13. *Be patient.* Learning and relationships take time to build.

14. *Provide boundaries.* Visual or physical boundaries for sitting (tape, carpet squares, and so on) or working at a table (tape) are useful.

15. *Provide fidget items.* Give children a fidget item to play with as they listen. This can be a pillow, a stuffed animal, a stress ball, or something related to what is going on.

16. *Eliminate visual distractions.* Assess your room for visual distractions such as cluttered walls or work surfaces. If the play space is visually confusing or very complex, make modifications to decrease visual distractions.

17. *Eliminate auditory distractions.* Check the room for auditory distractions such as noise from the street, hall, or playground. In some cases there is nothing you can do about these distractions. If you can predict the timing of auditory distraction, however, try to schedule your class to make these times less problematic.

Curriculum Adaptations

Curriculum adaptations involve relating your interpretation of class activities to children with ASD and focusing the children on their specific tasks and roles. Things that may come automatically to other children may need to be taught. Including children with ASD in your class may challenge some of your beliefs about how children should be taught. Some of the recommendations given are different from what I would do if I did not include a child with ASD. For example, I am against giving children models to copy in art; however, that is one of my suggestions for a child with ASD. For children who cannot picture what a picture looks like, provide an example

or two. Some of the suggestions may be a stretch for you. Know they are available as additional resources if needed. Think about yourself and what you believe. You need to be calm, positive, consistent, and to maintain your sense of humor!

Social Awareness: Self-Esteem, Inclusion, and Social Studies

It is difficult to think about teaching levels of social behaviors that we have never needed to learn. They are just part of what we are. For children who have ASD, this is not true. They have to learn what we take for granted. We cannot just deal with the surface behaviors, but need to get to the fundamental deficits. Social skills need to be specifically taught. They will not develop on their own. Learning the social skills necessary to be included in a classroom is a demanding and stressful task for a child with ASD. It may take so much concentration that the child is not available for academic learning. Give children time to get to know you and the other people in the classroom and school. Don't expect too much too fast.

Self-Esteem

All children need to develop self-knowledge. They need to have some understanding of themselves before they can understand others. Help children gain this knowledge by providing feedback about what the child likes and dislikes and what he does well.

1. Use specific strategies to develop the child's sense of self.
2. Help children become aware of their own feelings and beliefs and then those of others.
3. Help children think of themselves as problem solvers; use visual methods of promoting self-reflection and self-recognition.
4. Teach children to make choices.
5. Teach children how to respond to criticism.

Inclusion

Children with ASD are being placed in regular classes; the challenge is to include them. Adults must make conscious efforts to guide them so that children play together. Educators must explain behavior that other children might find unusual. Children need simple explanations and adult models.

1. Understand that for a child with ASD, being part of a classroom is a challenge.
2. Teach children to identify emotions as physical, auditory, and visual expressions. Draw their attention to the emotions of others. Be specific. Clarify why another child may be having these emotions.
3. Teach other children how to approach and interact with a child who has ASD.
4. Identify what children like and dislike socially, and use this information when including the child and helping other children to include him as well.
5. Be sure the child does not become a victim of teasing, exclusion, or other more subtle forms of relational violence.

6. Focus on individual similarities and differences and what children like and dislike. Use this as a frame for discussing why there may be different rules for different children and some children are taught differently than others.
7. Engage children in the problem-solving process. Let them help decide what is reinforcing and what they can do to facilitate the education of all the children in the class.
8. Allow all the children to be alone some of the time. Talk about why children want to be alone.

In the Field

If a child is having a bad day, I take him aside and ask him if he wants his pals to help him be good. If he says yes, we ask the class to give him a thumbs-up when they see him being good and a thumbs-down when the behavior is inappropriate.

Reflective Practice

This practice identifies a particular child who is having problems to all the class. Do you think they already know the child is having problems? Is this a practice you would be comfortable using?

Social Studies

Social studies is a challenging area for children with ASD. Because of the subtle and pervasive nature of these disabilities, those who work with them must provide a level of scaffolding that is more extensive than other children need. If you have animals in your classroom, teach children how to hold and stroke them. Some feel that because animals do not talk but do communicate, children with ASD who do not have useful communication skills will find the relationship therapeutic.

1. Meet the child at his social developmental level—you need to start where the child is, not where you expect him to be.
2. Do not assume that children can identify your intentions from your behavior.
3. Draw the child's attention to the use of gesture, facial expression, eye direction, and proximity as social cues that convey meaning. Identify specifically what these mean.
4. Expect to teach basic social skills such as taking turns, sharing, waiting in lines, and working in small groups.
5. Discuss how different animals communicate without using words.
6. Children may need to be taught a specific script to repeat if they bump or annoy another child.

Language and Literacy: Speaking, Listening, Reading, and Writing

Communication is the foundation for social interaction. It is also an area that is very challenging for children with ASD. For many children, it is not that they cannot speak; it is that they do not use speech for communication. In addition to building speech skills, children need to develop the intentional use of speech for communicating with others, particularly peers.

Speaking

Be careful of your word choices and avoid absolutes, such as always, never, all, none, and so on. When children have problems, you can build on a vocabulary that allows exceptions. Children with ASD need support in initiating and maintaining a conversation, and in developing techniques for understanding the meaning of conversation. Think about their communication level rather than their ability to speak.

1. Try to use words such as *most* or *some* of the time. If you *always* eat lunch at school and then have a half day, children become upset. "*Sometimes* when we have to wait we sing." Work with children on this concept to build the idea of several alternatives.
2. Teach children how to use language socially; specifically teach such skills as making eye contact, entering a group, listening to replies, and responding to others.
3. Be aware of the difference between a child's ability to use language and his ability to communicate. They are two different functions of speech and children may be on very different levels for each.
4. Simplify your language.
5. Give instructions one at a time, not in an entire sequence. If necessary, support these with visual cues.
6. Keep your facial expression and gestures clear, simple, and congruent with your speech.
7. Teach metaphors and be aware of them in your own speech.
8. Help children vary their tone and volume to match situations.
9. Children may use self-talk to support task completion. If this does not interfere with other children, support it. Teach the child to do this quietly.
10. Encourage peers to be involved in the Picture Exchange Communication System if this is what children use.

Listening

Children with ASD may have trouble just listening, so be sure to use facial expressions and gestures to support what you are saying. Encourage children to look for nonverbal cues and body language.

1. Teach children to listen and not interrupt.
2. Give children time to respond.
3. Develop a code so that if the child does not understand he can tell you without disrupting the class and calling attention to himself.
4. Support children's auditory discrimination skills by playing games such as bingo, comparing sounds, associating sounds with the materials that made them, and so on.
5. Some children may have problems with loud noises or the specific pitch and frequency of some sounds. If possible, warn children that the noise will occur, so they can prepare. If the noise cannot be eliminated, try exposing the child to the noise in small increments or for limited periods. Pair the noise with a preferred activity or use another more pleasing noise (music) at the same time.

Reading

Reading can be both an individual and a group activity. Preview books with children. Help them connect what is in the book with the real world.

1. Read books about being different.
2. Read children books about children who have autism. Use this as a springboard to talk about ASD.
3. Teach stories using picture sequence cards. Draw the child's attention to the cause-and-effect aspect of the book, identify the plot, and make the motives of the characters in the story explicit.
4. Use social stories to help children learn necessary social skills.
5. Carol Gray has developed a social skills program for children with autism. She has published books of social stories. These stories describe social situations in terms of relevant social cues and these can be used to teach necessary social skills. There are now many social skills books available or you can make your own.

In the Field

I find social stories beneficial for the children I teach. Books of social stories can be purchased, or a social story can be written by the classroom team, based on the needs of the children. The suggested formula to use for writing a social story is three to five descriptive and perspective sentences and one each of directive and control sentences. A descriptive sentence explains who, what, where, and/or why. An example of a descriptive sentence would be, "My teacher changed her mind in school today." A perspective sentence describes the feelings and reactions of others in a situation. For example, "This means that she had an idea, but then had a different idea." A directive is an individualized statement of what the child needs to work on. An example would be, "I will work on staying calm when my teacher changes her mind." The last type of sentence found in a social story is a control sentence. A control sentence could be, "When my teacher changes her mind I can ask to take a break to give me time to adjust to the new idea." Due to their complexity, social stories work best for higher functioning children. Some teachers write their own social stories and illustrate them with photographs of the children in situations corresponding to events in the story. When I use pictures of the children, they feel a stronger connection to the story.

Reflective Practice

Try writing a social story using the information given. Choose an incident and write a story about it. Was it easier or more difficult than you expected?

6. Read joke books. Try to cultivate a sense of humor.
7. Help children extend their understanding by using the pictures to predict what will happen or to add context.
8. Be sure to have nonfiction as well as fiction books.
9. Use computer programs to support learning. Programs such as Edmark's Reading Program Software Series, Levels 1 & 2 (Riverdeep) for grades K–three is designed to help children with developmental disabilities and those who are learning English as a second language. It helps children practice words used in basal readers. The software is very straightforward with few multimedia perks, which is good for children with ASD.
10. Adapted books.

In the Field

My favorite books are books I adapt. These books have picture symbols added to them to help children identify and understand the concept illustrated. Children can use the symbols to tell someone who or what is in the pictures, or what is happening. The books you adapt should have clear pictures, with not much writing on each page. The teacher should read through the book and write a list of words to be emphasized on each page. After creating the corresponding symbols to go with the words you want to emphasize, laminate, and attach them with Velcro™ to a file folder or piece of tag board. Place a piece of Velcro™ near the picture in the book you will be emphasizing. As you read the story, have the children identify the matching picture. Many children enjoy "reading" these books by themselves. I like to adapt board books due to their sturdiness. If I do not use a board book, I always laminate the paper books.

Reflective Practice

Choose an appropriate board book and adapt it. Reflect on the process and what you learned by doing this.

Writing

Encourage children to write, either with a pencil or through word processing. An inability to think creatively may impede children's progress in writing. Use a copy of the alphabet, pictures for each letter, and small pictures that can be used instead of words.

1. Encourage children to write about real things they have experienced, then introduce a "What if . . ." to help them extend their thinking and writing.
2. Start with the child's interests, even if they are narrow, and build from there. If it is animals, use this, and extend it into where they sleep, what they eat, and so on.
3. Give children a visual cue, such as a picture to write about.
4. Children may have a difficult time learning to write; have them trace and copy letters. Help children form letters and connections between them. Use their strength in memory skills (if this is true) to learn this.
5. If children hold markers and pencils with just their fingertips they will have trouble controlling them. They may lack finger strength or the writing implement may feel uncomfortable to them. Try adding different grips or use deep pressure on the palm of the child's hand (rubbing it with your thumb) before writing.
6. Help children write in the air, on textured surfaces, and with a variety of tools. See Activity 2–26 Air Writing and 2–27 Sand Printing.

Discovery: Mathematics, Science, and Technology

Make math and science concrete. Use practical examples and emphasize the utility of the process. Take advantage of technology to help children. Use the digital camera to take pictures to help the child structure his environment. Technology can also provide support in the area of organization. A computer can take some of the tedium out of writing while providing visual support.

Mathematics

Make math relevant to children. Use objects and pictures that are of interest to children to teach math. If children are interested in trucks, they can sort them by color, size, material, function, and design. They can count them, pair them, and even add them. If you include people with the trucks, you can do one-to-one correspondence. Children with ASD need to apply math. The more you teach it as part of problem solving and relating to real issues, the more likely math will be useful.

1. If a child asks the same question over and over, decide on a limit (perhaps three times) or a place where he can pursue this.
2. Teach children the language of math. Write the words on cards. Have children sort cards and identify different words that mean the same thing (multiply, times; add, sum).
3. Teach math concepts visually and with three-dimensional objects.
4. Use word problems.

Science

Science is not about memorizing isolated facts but about making observations, asking questions, and gathering, organizing, and analyzing data (Charlesworth & Lind, 2003). Framing science in this way makes the process more challenging and more beneficial to children with ASD.

1. Science uses observation as a fundamental skill. Have children observe on walks, on the playground, in the classroom, and at home. Help children use observational skills to anticipate events so they can be prepared for them.
2. Help children sharpen their observational skills by identifying the main idea and the supporting parts. Connect this information to previous learning.
3. Encourage children to make charts and lists as methods of organizing information.
4. The Sammy's Science House (Edmark) pre-K–two program helps children with part-whole relationships in "The Workshop" and they can sort plants and animals at "The Sorting Station."

Technology

Technology can be a tremendous asset in working with children who have ASD. Your ability to think about creative uses of technology can support their learning and ability to function in the classroom. Technology can help children handle change. It can be modified to the needs of particular children and it can support their learning (with infinite patience). It also provides opportunities for children to work together. The task is defined and children can be together without a great demand for social interaction.

1. Explore a variety of assistive technologies and encourage children to use technology to help with writing, spelling, grammar, and so on.
2. Children can use a digital camera as a support for sequencing activities and the events of the day.
3. Use the computer and programs such as PowerPoint to present material to the class. This can provide visual support and if there is a sequence, the child can recheck the necessary information independently. If the family has a computer, you can email the presentation to the family so they know what you are teaching and can support the concepts at home.
4. Because of their need for visual input, encourage children to develop their own website. Use an easy program such as Complete Web Studio or Sierra On-line (Havas). This supports children's learning and their self-concepts.

Wellness: Health, Physical Education, and Sensory Motor

Children may need support to participate in physical activities. They may avoid them because of concern about being touched, anxiety about their skill level, or to avoid unpleasant sensations. Be sure the environment provides opportunities and places to vigorously exercise and to calm down.

Health and Safety

Health and safety are particularly important areas for children with ASD. If children are more tuned into themselves than their surroundings, they can place themselves in dangerous situations. Their concern with the textures of foods as well as personal likes and dislikes may make eating a balanced diet a challenge. Some health and safety practices that other children learn from observation have to be specifically taught.

1. Children need to learn techniques of grooming and adaptive behaviors. They need a visual sequence or checklist to ensure that all the steps are completed.
2. If children don't button or fasten coats and other garments, it may be because they have trouble doing so. Encourage the use of Velcro™ fasteners or large fasteners. Be sure that children look at what they are doing.
3. If a child has problems eating a variety of foods, find one food the child likes and present it in a different form. If the child likes fruit, try fresh, dried, and canned fruit. Add small amounts of different fruits in very small bites.
4. If children have problems using utensils to eat, work on fine motor skills to ensure this is not the problem. Then encourage activities that use the mouth such as bubbles, blowing through a straw, blowing ping-pong balls across the table, and so on.

5. Self-care practices have to be specifically taught: "After five bites, wipe your mouth with a napkin."
6. Evaluate the environment for safety. Is the outside area fenced? How close is traffic? What are the surfaces made of under the equipment?

Large Motor

Activities in this area need to be more structured, especially if there is an unstructured recess or outdoor playtime. Without support, the child may be isolated and stand around, as opposed to playing.

1. Organize cooperative games or games where there are no winners or losers.
2. Use obstacle courses and, using a digital camera and printer, provide pictures of the next piece of equipment with a child demonstrating how to move through that piece of equipment.
3. Provide children with "large motor breaks" where you encourage all children to work the wiggles out.
4. Support underlying concepts of physical fitness and provide opportunities for children to participate in activities that will develop these skills.

Small Motor

Children, especially those with low muscle tone, may need to develop strength in their fine muscles. To do this, they need to use them. The trick is to find things they enjoy doing so that practice is fun.

1. Children may lack hand strength. Hide objects that need to be found in putty, clay, or playdough.
2. Encourage children to use their hands in a variety of different textures such as birdseed, sand, and so on. (If children may eat the materials use rice and beans instead.)
3. Support children in using their hands to explore materials, especially to hold objects with one hand and investigate them with the other.

Sensory Motor Integration

Organizing sensory information so that it can be regulated and acted upon challenges all young children. Some children require a great deal of assistance in processing sensory input and achieving the levels of self-regulation necessary to explore and interact with their environment. Children respond to their environment in unique ways. The guiding principle is "to modify the environment to provide motivating, sensory-enriched surroundings that require repeated, complex coordinated action by the child" (Williamson & Anzalone, 2001, p. 106).

1. Some children may be oversensitive to certain smells. If this is true, try to make your environment as fragrance-free as possible. Use unscented detergents and shampoos. Don't wear perfumes or aftershave lotions.
2. Have a swing or rocking chair available for children to use. Use beanbag chairs if children need stability to read or to do fine motor activities.
3. Vary traditional activities. Have children walk across or jump on a mattress or crawl over and around cushions.

4. Children with ASD may take longer to learn motor activities than other children. Give them the time and opportunities to repeat and practice, even if the behavior may appear perseverative. Then introduce variation.

Creative Arts: Visual Arts, Music, Creative Movement, and Dramatic Play

Children with ASD are rarely creative on their own. They need adult support to play and pretend. They need to be encouraged and provided with more structure than other children. Rather than the child generating the script, the adult may have to provide the script and help the child work through it. Because of the children's deficits, you have to work with them very differently than you do with other children. You need to be more directive in areas where you would normally follow the child's lead.

Visual Arts

Encourage exploration of a variety of media. Allow children to approach tentatively and find ways to increase their exploration of new and different materials. Start with what they like and what is familiar and add variations a little at a time.

1. If a project has several steps or it is the first time the child has used a particular media, show the child a model or picture of the end product so the child knows what is expected or possible.
2. Introduce activities in which children can participate by using just their fingertips, such as fingerpaint or lotion. As children become comfortable with the various textures, encourage them to use their whole hand, and both hands.
3. Encourage children to use putty, clay, and playdough.

Children with autism may need adult support to participate in creative arts activities. They can become overwhelmed by the situation and stimulation.

Music

Use music to create a mood, to help focus attention, and to help children get in touch with the auditory world.

1. Add music to tasks to give them a beginning and an end.
2. Sing songs with children's names and reinforce the child for responding to it.
3. Experiment with using background music in the classroom. For some children this is calming.
4. Sing songs with motions.
5. Provide pictures of some of the things you will sing about.

Creative Movement

For children with ASD, the best thing about creative movement is not that it is creative but that movement is not judged; even repetitive and self-stimulating movement is acceptable.

1. When you do creative movement, do join children in their idiosyncratic movements as a teacher and as a class and then introduce variation on that movement. Change the rhythm, range of motion, speed, and so on. Bring the movement up to a more conscious level.
2. Have children move to music. Discuss the music first, and how it relates to the type of movements that fit with the music.
3. Provide pictures and have discussions if you want children to move in specific ways. Try to make pretense as real as possible.

Dramatic Play

Children with ASD do not pretend-play well. This is something they have to be taught.

1. Teach children to pretend-play and help them discriminate between what is pretend and what is real.
2. Role-play. One way of managing change is to make it more familiar. If you are going to do something new and different, role-play it. Point out the salient features.
3. Write a script and play it with the children. Provide specific directions on how things are done.

Routines and Transitions

Transitions are difficult for many children. For children with ASD, they loom even larger. Use the child's strengths to help with transitions.

1. Have as few transitions as possible.
2. Have a predictable routine that you keep as consistent as possible.
3. Introduce change gradually.
4. Use visual supports to manage change. Provide children with a picture sequence of the day (a digital camera makes this easy). As each part of the day is completed, have the child take that picture off the sequence.
5. Give children time to prepare for change. A specific signal about five minutes ahead of time is useful.

6. When it is necessary to line up, ask the child to be first or last.
7. Select a locker or cubby for the child that is at the end of the row to decrease unintentional physical contact.
8. Consider having children do jumping jacks or touch their toes before or during a walk in the hall.
9. Develop a system to ensure enough space between children when they walk.

In the Field

We have a mailbox outside our classroom. Every day, we check for mail from our friend Myron the Mouse. Myron is at home sick and is unable to come to school. His sister, Myra (a white stuffed mouse who sits in class on her own carpet square) comes to school and goes home each day to tell Myron what she has learned. Each day, Myron writes a letter, reviewing what we have learned, asking questions, and most importantly, telling the children if there are any changes in the schedule. (Myra sneaks around the class at night so she knows things before Mrs. Wells does. She knows when we have assemblies, or any change in the schedule.) Several aspects of this strategy work well: Myron tells the children when there is a change, so it is not Mrs. Wells' fault that things are different, and Myron uses question marks and exclamation marks. The children count the different punctuation marks and then determine whether he is "more excited" or he has more questions. To recognize an exclamation mark, we say, "the line was so excited it jumped up and down on the period." We then make simple math sentences. They love this! Myra will be included in our class photo this year. Last year we forgot her, and they were upset.

Reflective Practice

What do you see as the utility of a technique such as this? What you see as the academic and behavioral merits of using a technique like this? Is it one you could incorporate into your repertoire?

Summary

Children with autism spectrum disorders or pervasive developmental disorders may have autism, Asperger's syndrome, pervasive developmental disorder–not otherwise specified, Rett syndrome, or childhood disintegrative disorder. Although each disorder is different and each child is affected in a different way, the essential feature of all ASDs is impairment in social reciprocity, communication, and repetitive behaviors. Social limitations result in limited play skills.

Children with ASD require more structure in their environment and more one-on-one instruction to learn skills. Teachers need strength in behavior management and a good understanding of sensory motor integration issues to work effectively with these children. Some early childhood practices that work for many children are not effective in working with some children with ASD.

Remarkable advances in early identification and early intervention have made a tremendous difference in the lives of children with ASD and their families.

Reflections

1. As an educator, you will probably work with many children who are on medication for ASD or a related disorder such as ADHD. How much do you know about the effects of medication? Do you think it is necessary to know not only the symptoms and behavior management techniques for these problems, but to also know about medications some children may take? Where would you find information about these medications? Should you know how each works? Further, to successfully help children with each of these disorders, do you feel you should have some background on the proposed **etiologies** of each disorder?

2. People have very different ideas about how children with autism should be educated. Some very clearly espouse a strong behavioral approach, while others feel that this is not effective. Reflect on your own feelings. What do you believe about the education of children with autism? What do you see as the role of the teacher? The parents? The support staff? Should children with ASD be included in regular classrooms? If so, when and how?

Educational Resources

Augmentative and Alternative Communication (AAC) assists people with severe communication disabilities to participate by providing access to a wide range of information and resources related to the AAC effort. http://aac.unl.edu/

Autism–PDD Support Network has a large website with information on diagnostic criteria, the IEP process, and helpful hints for working with schools and specialists. It also provides information about state agencies. http://www.autism-pdd.net

Autism Research Institute provides information about current research projects and methods of working with individuals with autism. http://www.autism.com/index.asp

Autism Society of America answers many common questions about autism, particularly those related to causes, types, and diagnosis. It also looks at different approaches and news and events related to autism. It provides links to state resources and local chapters. http://www.autism-society.org

Do 2 Learn provides picture schedules and tips on how to structure your classroom, pictures that you can print, and children's games. http://www.do2learn.com

First Signs website provides a wealth of vital resources, covering healthy development, to concerns about a child; from the screening and referral process, to treatments for autism spectrum disorders. http://www.firstsigns.org

Interactive Autism Network (IAN), is a project of the Kennedy Krieger Institute and is funded by Autism Speaks. IAN's goal is to facilitate research that will lead to advancements in the treatment, cure, and prevention of autism spectrum disorders. It provides information about current research and findings in the area of autism. http://www.ianproject.org/

Tinsnips—Special Education Resources for Autism contains tools for teachers of children with ASD, related developmental disabilities, and children with special needs. It contains ideas, themes, snippets, readings for teachers, and strategies and links to other related sites. http://www.tinsnips.org

Treatment and Education of Autistic and Related Communication Handicapped Children (TEACCH) provides information on a structured program that integrates methods and services in a systematic way. http://www.teacch.com/

For additional resources, visit the book companion website for this text at www.cengage.com/education/deiner.

Chapter 14

Children with Intellectual Disabilities and Developmental Delays

Watching André, you would guess him to be one of the youngest children in the class, yet he is actually one of the oldest. He rarely has much to say and what he does say is difficult to understand. His parents say they are not talkers and they understand him and are not worried. I thought by 4 years old more of his speech should be understandable. He doesn't seem to get involved in his play. He plays alone most of the time. Most things seem difficult for him. It is hard for him to sit through our group time and he rarely participates. He struggles with adaptive skills but with help and time he usually succeeds. His parents say he dawdles so they just do things for him. Many things seem to be beyond him. He just seems like he is slower developing than the other children. He is not as animated and seems confused. I have tried to talk to his parents but when I bring up these issues they don't seem concerned and often don't follow up. I really can't decide if it is just the environment he lives in or if he is not as capable of learning as the others. Or is my program not matching his knowledge base?

Reflective Practice

How do you feel about André? A majority of children who cause concern for teachers look like other children but don't seem to be learning as quickly in one or more areas. We're not as accurate in identifying children with mild delays as we are children with more serious delays. It may not be until a child enters an intellectually demanding environment that adults become concerned about his level of functioning. On what basis would you decide to follow up with children like André?

Intellectual Disabilities and Developmental Delays

Intellectual disability is a failure to meet age-appropriate neurodevelopmental milestones based on the typical sequence of development in the areas of language, motor, and social-adaptive development (Batshaw, Shapiro, & Farber, 2007). Most children with intellectual disabilities follow the same sequence of cognitive skill acquisition as other children, but the rate of acquisition is slower.

Defining Intellectual Disabilities and Developmental Delays

Intellectual disabilities is a broad term that can refer to children of all ages and with differing degrees of delays and differences in cognitive development. Within this are two broad categories of children: those who are classified as developmentally delayed (children birth to up to 9 years) and those who are classified as having intellectual disabilities or mental retardation. I prefer the term intellectual disability and use it in this book except when quoting, referring to the work of others particularly the IDEA, or for historical reference.

Professionals today are reluctant to classify young children as having an intellectual disability. The requirements for this diagnosis are more stringent than they have been in the past. Misdiagnosis is a concern because of the stigma attached to this particular label and because of the overidentification of children from ethnic/cultural minorities (Individuals with Disabilities Education Inprovement Act [IDEA], 2004). Concern relates to the child developing a poor self-concept, the negative view of others, and the belief that intellectual disabilities are a socially constructed condition. That is, children who are relatively high functioning do not *become* "mentally retarded" until they enter school. (Many children who in the past were classified as having an intellectual disability are now classified as having a learning disability.) Also, we no longer view an intellectual disability as a permanent condition.

American Association on Intellectual and Developmental Disabilities (AAIDD) formerly the American Association on Mental Retardation (AAMR) has developed the following definition: Intellectual disability is a disability characterized by significant limitations both in intellectual functioning and in adaptive behavior as expressed in conceptual, social, and practical adaptive skills. The disability originates before the age of 18. (AAIDD, 2008, p.1)

Concerned about labeling per se, and also wary of the assessment process, AAIDD requires professionals to

- Evaluate limitations in present intellectual and adaptive behavior functioning within the context of the individual's age, peers and culture;
- Take into account the individual's cultural and linguistic differences as well as communication, sensory, motor, and behavioral factors;
- Recognize that limitations often coexist with strengths within an individual;
- Describe limitations so that an individualized plan of needed supports can be developed; and
- Provide appropriate, personalized supports to improve the functioning of a person with intellectual disability (AAIDD, 2008, p.1, 2).

Previously, the definition of mental retardation was based almost exclusively on IQ scores. Now, although an IQ of 70 to 75 or below is considered below average, there is consensus that additional measures must be used to verify these results and that the results should be reviewed by a multidisciplinary team.

According to the IDEA 2004:

Mental retardation means significantly subaverage general intellectual functioning, existing concurrently with deficits in adaptive behavior and manifested during the developmental period, that adversely affects a child's educational performance.

As with many other disabilities, intellectual disability is further divided into levels. These are based on the theoretical assumption that intelligence is normally distributed. The levels generally indicate the intensity of services that are needed for the child. The levels are assigned after formal assessment of the child's intellectual and adaptive functioning skills. A traditional breakdown of the levels of intellectual disability is given below. Because of the error of measurement of the assessment instruments, we assume that scores can vary by about 5 points, so we use a range (i.e., an IQ of 70 may be 65 or 75, given the error of measurement, see Figure 14–1).

Using only IQ as a way to determine intellectual functioning assumes that 95 percent of the population is in the "average or normal" range, with 2.5 percent on either end being above or below "normal." Some question the validity of using IQ to determine intellectual disability with young children because of the poor predictive validity of infant psychological tests and concerns related to cultural bias. The American Psychiatric Association (APA, 2000) continues to use IQ scores. The American Association on Mental Retardation (2002) focuses their subcategories on the patterns and intensity of supports individuals will need. This is a move away from looking at disability to ability. In this text, the definitions of the subcategories given combine the two approaches. The designated categories are determined by the APA categories, but the focus is on the needed supports.

Mild Intellectual Delays (IQ 50–55 to 70–75)

For educational purposes, children in this category were often referred to as educable mentally retarded (EMR). This category constitutes about 85 percent of children with intellectual disabilities (APA, 2000). Children develop sensory motor, social, and communication skills during early childhood, but these may be consistently at the lower range of the developmental norms. They generally attend regular early care and education settings and neighborhood public schools. These children may be identified as needing additional educational services during the early elementary years. Their learning process

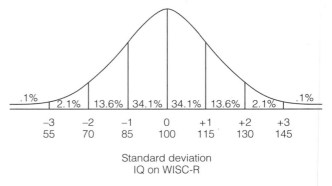

Figure 14–1: Theoretical Distribution of IQ

is usually slower than other children, often requiring concrete learning procedures. The focus is on learning basic academic skills. Most will live independently in the community with intermittent supports and hold jobs after schooling is completed (American Association on Mental Retardation [AAMR], 2002).

Because schools have been criticized for improperly identifying minority children as having an intellectual disability, professionals are now reluctant to identify any children as mildly retarded. Because the term *specific learning disability* is more acceptable to both parents and administrators, borderline children are more likely to be placed in this category. This solves some problems but creates others.

Moderate Intellectual Delays (IQ 35–40 to 50–55)

This group constitutes approximately 10 percent of the population of individuals with intellectual disabilities. These children are frequently identified during the preschool years because of their delayed pattern of development. They develop sensory motor and communication skills but at a much slower rate. There is increasing focus on the development of their social skills for inclusion. The learning process typically focuses on adaptive skills, functional academic skills, and prevocational skills. Individuals require limited support (AAMR, 2002). Our past expectation was that these children would reach an academic attainment level of about second grade (APA, 2000). Again, as these children are identified during the early years, the success of early intervention makes us question these expectations.

Severe Intellectual Delays (IQ 20–25 to 35–40)

Individuals in this category constitute approximately 3 to 4 percent of individuals with intellectual disabilities. Children are identified as infants or toddlers and may not reach early communication and physical/motor milestones until their school years (APA, 2000). Their learning may progress to learning some sight words and survival skills. These children need extensive support (AAMR, 2002)

Profound Intellectual Delays (IQ below 20–25)

Children who are classified as profoundly retarded constitute approximately 1 percent to 2 percent of individuals with intellectual disabilities. They are delayed in all areas of development and require intensive services and pervasive supports. They usually have an identifiable neurologic condition that accounts for the intellectual disability (APA, 2000). Identification occurs early, and intervention generally focuses on self-help or adaptive skills, mobility, and basic cognitive development. As adults, they can perform uncomplicated vocational tasks and live in supervised settings (AAMR, 2000).

Prevalence of Intellectual Disabilities and Developmental Delays

Given our difficulty in defining intellectual disability, it is not unexpected that prevalence figures vary. They are dependent upon the definition used, the method of assessment, and the population studied. The identification figures peak at 10 to 14 years of age, when most children with mild impairments have been identified (Yeargin-Allsopp, Drews-Botsch, & Van Naarden Braun, 2007). Overall intellectual disabilities occurs more frequently in boys than girls. Approximately 12 to 16 of every 1,000 school age child has an intellectual disability, or about 1 in 83 children had an IQ of 70 or below in 2000 (CDC, 2008).

During the 2003–2004 school year, 8.9 percent of the children receiving special educational services were identified as having mental retardation. This is in contrast to 1976–1977 when 26 percent of school children who were identified as needing special education had mental retardation. (NCES, 2005). Look at Table 14–1 to see the relationship between children identified as having mental retardation and learning disabilities. It seems clear that there is a relationship between the two and how children are being classified.

Causes of Intellectual Disabilties and Developmental Delays

Intellectual disability can begin anytime before a child turns 18. Some causes happen before a child is born such as those that are genetic in nature. Other causes happen during pregnancy and can relate to the way embryonic or fetal cells divide and grow. The cells can be affected by alcohol or infections like rubella. Other problems can happen during the birthing process such as lack of oxygen to the infant's brain. Other problems happen after the child is born. Problems after birth can be caused by infections such as meningitis or measles (National Dissemination Center for Children with Disabilities [NICHCY], 2004). In general, the earlier the cause the more severe the effect (Batshaw et al., 2007).

Overall, causes of intellectual disabilities fall into two overlapping categories. Children who fall in the mild category (about 87 percent) (NICHCY, 2004), those needing intermittent supports, are most frequently from families of lower socioeconomic status, have fewer environmental resources, there may be neglectful or abusive parenting, and there is less likely to be a biological cause. Disabilities

Table 14–1: Percent of children receiving special educational services by year

	1976–1977	1980–1981	1990–1991	2003–2004
Learning disabilities	21.5	35.3	45.2	42.7
Mental retardation	26.0	20.0	11.3	8.9

Source: National Center for Educational Statistics, 2005.

that require more extensive supports, those in moderate to profound categories, are usually linked to biological causes (Batshaw et al., 2007). These account for about 13 percent of children with intellectual disabilities (NICHCY, 2004). Many causes of intellectual disability are not known.

The causes of mild disabilities are known in less than 50 percent of children identified. When the intellectual disability is severe a biological cause can be identified in about three quarters of the cases (Aicardi, 1998). When the causes of intellectual disabilities are known, approximately 5 percent are hereditary, such as Tay-Sachs disease. Another 30 percent are due to chromosomal mutations during the development of the embryo (for example, Down syndrome trisomy 21), or to damage to the embryo due to toxins (such as alcohol, drugs, or infections). Another 10 percent occur during the fetal period and include such problems as malnutrition, trauma, hypoxia (lack of oxygen), and prematurity. After birth, another 15 percent to 20 percent are related to environmental influences such as neglect and lack of stimulation, as well as related disorders such as autism. Approximately 5 percent are related to infections such as meningitis, traumas such as head injuries, and poisoning due to lead (APA, 2000).

The environment in which a child is raised is a big factor in facilitating intellectual development. Some limitations may be present that prevent a child from acquiring specific intellectual skills, such as advanced abstract thinking abilities. Appropriate stimulation and early intervention is a key ingredient to a successful educational program.

In the past, intellectual disabilities present at birth were viewed as a given, a nonpreventable disability. Increasingly, causes of intellectual disability are preventable. Some prevention is based on health procedures that ensure that children receive inoculations in a timely manner (CDC, 2005). Others relate to accident prevention and environmental stimulation. The fastest-growing prenatal causes of intellectual disability are preventable.

Children experiencing intellectual disabilities are as different from each other as those who have more typical developmental patterns.

Early Identification of Intellectual Disabilities and Developmental Delays

Depending on the level of the impairment, intellectual disabilities are identified at different times during early childhood. Concern may arise because infants were born prematurely, had low birth weight, or there were perinatal complications (Batshaw et al., 2007). During the first months of life concerns arise because of inadequate sucking, floppy or spastic muscle tone, and/or lack of response to visual or auditory stimuli. Infants may show little interest in the environment and not be as alert as other infants. As infants grow older and approach developmental milestones, it may be determined that the infant is not developing as quickly as most infants his age. It is often unclear whether this is just an individual growth pattern and that the infant will "catch up" in time or whether the delay is of a more permanent nature. Gross motor skills such as walking and language development

are key indicators. The most obvious signs of intellectual disability are that children are slower to talk than other children, may seem immature, and may also have been slower to walk (after 15 months). (Batshaw et al., 2007). They may have a short attention span, and some are highly distractible. Language skills are delayed, as are basic daily living skills (feeding, toilet training, and dressing). Children with more severe delays lack social interaction skills, motivation, and a striving for independence. Infants and toddlers exhibiting extremely delayed development or for whom there is a known cause or etiology may be diagnosed before age three. Because of the success of early intervention, if you suspect delayed development, talk with parents and support their seeking medical and educational intervention.

Mild delays may not be noticed during the preschool years, although you may begin to suspect something as you watch these children. Perhaps a 4 year old with a mild delay acts more like a 3 year old. Preschool children with developmental delays have a slower rate of learning, poor memory skills, poor generalization skills, and lack higher-level learning strategies (NICHCY, 2004).

Even during preschool children with moderate cognitive impairments show noticeable delays in intellectual development, especially speech and language, and motor development. They may need assistance in self-help skills. They may not be toilet trained, or if they are, they may not be able to manage taking off and putting on their clothes independently. In some cases, these children will look different from other children (if they have fetal alcohol

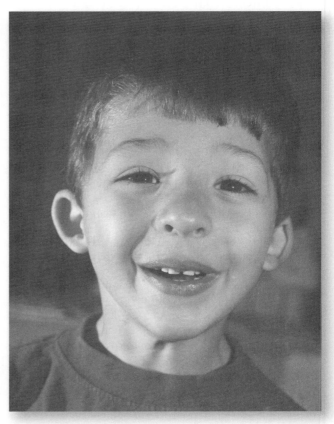

Sometimes intellectual disabilities are suspected because they are part of other syndromes.

syndrome). In other cases, they won't. A 4 year old needing limited support may act more like a 2 year old. Most likely, parents will know that their child is cognitively delayed. Children needing extensive support show marked delays in all areas of development and, at the preschool level, have few verbal communication skills.

Implications for Educators

Increasingly, children needing extensive supports are being cared for and educated in regular early care and education settings. Young children may be in regular settings for part of the day and in a setting designed for intensive early intervention for the other part of the day. Here, the emphasis is more on developmentally appropriate curriculum and fundamental activities, focusing on adaptive skills to support the development of independence. Social skills to foster peer interaction are also stressed.

During the early elementary years, the focus is on early literacy skills and abilities that are prerequisites for later learning. They include behaviors such as learning to sit and attend to teachers, following directions, and learning the names of the letters of the alphabet. Children with delayed development need support developing small motor skills, which are necessary to hold a pencil and cut with scissors. They will need continuing support on adaptive skills and developing skills to interact with peers. The focus is frequently on fundamental academic skills that are necessary in life as well as skills that allow them to communicate.

In the Field

My son Roberto was identified as a toddler with delayed development. I feel that he has received some of the best early intervention possible. I kept thinking that he would catch up, but he did not. Then I struggled to accept a diagnosis of mental retardation. At first it seemed so cruel, but I finally realized that it is something I must deal with. Since I have gotten divorced I worry more about money and the future. While I am blessed to have Roberto in my life and I love him dearly, I wonder what will happen to Roberto if anything happens to me. My husband Tomas left because he couldn't deal with Roberto. Would Tomas raise Roberto?

My main goal now is to help Roberto receive the best education and the best services possible. I am happy to say that Roberto receives all the support he needs in his classroom from his teacher and therapists. I don't see them as much as I used to, but it seems to be working. He is learning to use his small muscles better and he is easier to understand. What is important to me is that he is so much better at dressing himself and he can even go to the bathroom alone. He is getting too old to bring to the ladies' room with me, so going out with him was getting to be a problem.

In the next few years I hope that Roberto will learn the skills to live independently. I truly worry about his future and his happiness. Will Roberto ever be able to live on his own?

Reflective Practice

As educators we frequently focus on what children can learn in the time they spend with us. Parents often have a long-term view and concerns for the future. Reflect on how these concerns would impact what you would do in the classroom and when working with parents.

Assessment of Intellectual Disabilities and Developmental Delays

There are two major aspects in the assessment of intellectual disability: intelligence and adaptive behavior. Adaptive behavior is the ability an individual has for self-care. In young children, we are concerned with self-help skills; in young adults, we focus on the ability to understand currency, pay bills, and so on.

Assessment of Intelligence

The assessment of intelligence is a controversial issue. What is intelligence? We can't see it, we can't hear it, and we can't agree on a definition. We use the concept of intelligence to explain differences in behavior.

Two major dimensions relate to the accuracy of measuring intelligence in very young children; the first has to do with issues relating to the test, the second is the child herself. In general, when we talk about intelligence testing for children under age 3, we don't end up with an intelligence quotient or IQ; rather, we talk about a developmental assessment and a developmental quotient or DQ.

One reason for assessing an infant is to determine whether there might be long-term problems that could respond to intervention. In this case, the concern is the test's ability to detect problems that have potential long-term negative outcomes. Infant developmental tests do a good job of identifying infants and toddlers with severe and profound delays. They are not as effective in identifying infants and toddlers with mild to moderate delays.

One critical issue concerns the relationship between scores obtained on infant developmental tests and intelligence tests given at a later age. What we consider intelligence in infancy is not the same as intelligence in elementary school children or adults; different patterns of cognitive activities constitute intelligence at different ages

Norm-referenced measures such as the Battelle Developmental Inventory, Second Edition (BDI-2; Newborg, 2005), and the Bayley Scales of Infant and Toddler Development, Third Edition (Bayley III) *Screening Test* (Bayley, 2005) often form the core of a diagnostic assessment. These measures are used to get an overall picture of the infant or toddler and to determine whether further, more specialized assessment is necessary. Given the lack of high-quality screening measures for young children, norm-referenced measures may also serve a screening purpose. These measures are standardized and require a trained examiner.

As children increase in age, other assessments are used. For children older than 2 years, the Stanford-Binet Intelligence Scale, Fifth Edition (SB5; Roid, 2003) may be used. During the preschool years, the Wechsler Preschool and Primary Scale of Intelligence–III (WPPSI–III; Psychological Corporation, 2002) is an option. School-age children may be evaluated using the Wechsler Intelligence Scale for Children, IV (WISC-IV, Wechsler; 2003).

Criterion-referenced measures such as the Learning Accomplishment Profile, Third Edition (LAP-3; 2004) for children 36 to 72 months and the Early Learning Accomplishment Profile, Third Edition (E-LAP; 2002) for children birth to 36 months, are often used after screening and diagnosis have been completed. These measures are useful in curriculum planning and in measuring increments of development.

Regardless of the test, one test alone should never be the only source used to determine whether or not a child has a developmental delay. This information needs to be included with information from behavioral observations, medical history, and information obtained from the parents to gain a more accurate picture of a child's functioning.

Assessment of Adaptive Skills

To classify someone as having an intellectual disability, a test of intelligence and a test of adaptive skills are required. Assessing adaptive behavior is also useful for curriculum planning.

The assessment of adaptive skills relies on the report of a respondent or observer. In the case of young children, this is primarily their parents and/or caregivers; for older children, a teacher might also be a respondent. The respondent is expected to be both truthful and knowledgeable in answering questions about the child's behavior. Having more than one respondent helps reveal the situational aspects of behavior (home and school).

The Vineland Adaptive Behavior Scales, Second Edition (VABS II; Sparrow, Cicchetti, & Balla, 2005) is an individually administered scale for individual's birth through 90 years. There are a variety of forms that can be used by parents, caregivers, or teachers to appraise a child's development. They vary in the amount of information obtained. All three assess communication, daily living skills, motor skills, socialization, and maladaptive behavior.

The AAMD Adaptive Behavior Scale–School: 2-(ABS–S2; Nihira, Leland, & Lambert, 1993) is an individually administered, norm-referenced scale for individuals 3 to 21 years. It looks at five main factors: personal self-sufficiency, social adjustments, personal adjustment, personal-social responsibility, and community self-sufficiency.

Two elements are important to note. One is that a child must be well below average in *both* measured intelligence and adaptive behavior. The second is that we no longer regard intellectual disability as irreversible, especially for those who are in the mild range. We now believe that with appropriate early intervention, some children will no longer be identified as having an intellectual disability, and with early intervention, some children who would have been categorized as having an intellectual disability will not be so classified. Hence the use of the term *developmentally delayed* with young children and *intellectual disability* with older children.

For children with mild intellectual disabilities (those needing intermittent supports), this is often their only impairment. Children needing more supports are more likely to have other disabilities such as cerebral palsy, speech and language impairments, sensory impairments, seizure disorders, psychological or behavioral impairments, and learning disabilities (Batshaw et al., 2007). These may make it challenging to identify children and the supports they need.

Intellectual Disabilities and Syndromes

There are many different identified intellectual disabilities and syndromes. Only the most common are detailed.

Down Syndrome

Down syndrome was one of the first syndromes associated with intellectual disabilities. The number of infants born with Down syndrome is decreasing. Prevalence of Down syndrome is associated with increased maternal age. At age 30 a woman has about a 1 in 900 chance of conceiving a child with Down syndrome. Those odds increase to about 1 in 350 by age 35 and rise to about 1 in 100 by age 40. Therefore, the incidence of Down syndrome is dependent upon the maternal age distribution and age specific pregnancy rates. In the early 1970s Down syndrome occurred in 1.33 per 1,000 live births; currently it is stabilized at 0.92 per 1,000 live births (Roizen, 2007). One reason for the decrease in the number of children born with Down syndrome is the number of couples who have decided to terminate pregnancy when the fetus is identified as having Down syndrome.

There are three types of chromosome abnormalities associated with Down syndrome. The most common, trisomy 21 accounts for about 95 percent of children with Down syndrome. In this case the problem relates to **nondisjunction** of chromosome 21 and which results in three copies of chromosome 21 instead of two (Batshaw, 2007). In **translocation**, which accounts for about 4 percent of Down syndrome, chromosomes break and exchange parts with or attach to other chromosomes. In Down syndrome part of the long arm of the chromosome 21 breaks and usually becomes attached to chromosome 14. These children have two copies of chromosome 21, one copy of chromosome 14, and one chromosome 14/21 (Batshaw, 2007). In **mosaic trisomy**, about 1 percent, the problem occurs in some but not all of the cells (Roizen, 2007).

Children with Down syndrome are typically identified at birth because of characteristic features that include a small, relatively flat head, an upward slant to the eyes that have **epicanthic folds** at the inner corners, and a broad neck. The ears, mouth, feet, and hands are relatively small, fingers are unusually short and broad, and there is a simian crease on the palm of the hand (Roizen, 2007). Chromosome analysis determines if Down syndrome is an accurate diagnosis.

Children with Down syndrome have an increased risk of abnormalities in almost every organ system (Roizen, 2007). They usually have decreased motor tone and appear floppy. This may result in feeding problems because the tongue is usually thick. They reach motor milestones later than other children. Some will not walk independently or speak their first words until about age 2. Language delays become evident during the preschool years. Most of the motor problems are overcome by school age, but the cognitive deficits become more obvious. With the success of early intervention and educational inclusion, some children with Down syndrome are doing exceedingly well. They have graduated from high school and are seeking advanced vocational training.

Children with Down syndrome often have other health-related problems. Almost half of children born with Down syndrome have congenital heart disease, vision problems such as cataracts, amblyopia, **refractive errors,** or **strabismus**; hearing problems (often related to chronic middle ear infections) or structural problems with the ear itself (KidsHealth, 2008). Although this list may sound long and negative, many of the problems are treatable. The vision problems respond to corrective lenses, and most of the problems that relate to the heart and gastrointestinal system are solved through surgery or medication. Most children with Down syndrome are included in regular early care and education centers and in the public schools.

Implications for Educators

Children with Down syndrome are usually enrolled in an early intervention program by 3 months of age. Initial intervention may focus on maintaining antigravity

Children with Down syndrome are active participants in the activities of inclusive classrooms.

postures, **such as sitting, and working on other motor skills, if the young child has low muscle tone. Children with Down syndrome usually respond to educators who arrange tasks sequentially, and break up complex tasks into smaller and simpler ones. A speech/language pathologist can often help with feeding as well as speech and language.**

Fragile X Syndrome

Since its recognition as a genetic disorder, fragile X is the most common inherited cause of intellectual disability worldwide (Down syndrome, although genetic, is not inherited) (Meyer, 2007). An unusually large number of genes critically important to brain development, nerve cell functioning, learning and memory reside on the X chromosome (Inlow & Restifo, 2004). In Fragile X there is an abnormality in the X chromosome that causes the bottom tip of the large arm to become threadlike and "fragile." Although there are other X-linked disorders that cause intellectual disability fragile X (FXS) is the most common. It is one reason why more males have intellectual disabilities than females. It is estimated that 2 to 6 per 1,000 live births have X-linked intellectual disabilities (Stevenson & Schwartz, 2002).

The problem in Fragile X is a chemical one. The FMR1 gene influences the expression of many other genes and may be related to the development of autism. The FMRP (the protein missing in fragile X) is inactivated and it is essential for early brain development. Both males and females can have the full mutation or a permutation which is more variable and less severe (Meyer, 2007). The overlap of fragile X and autism is an interesting one and one that has the potential for helping researchers understand both conditions better. Approximately 2 percent to 6 percent of children with autism spectrum disorder have fragile X syndrome; the cause is the fragile X gene mutation. About a third of children with Fragile X show some degree of autism. Fragile X is the most common single gene cause of autism known (National Fragile X Foundation, 2008).

Although there are common physical features these are not pronounced during childhood. Delays are apparent in cognitive ability, communication, behavior patterns and low muscle tone. Approximately 80 percent of males with this syndrome will have mild to moderate intellectual disability (Loesch et al., 2002). These children are likely to be identified as infants or toddlers. Sensory integration issues are common and children often become overwhelmed with noisy environments. They have a tendency to be tacitly defensive. Most females do not show the significant delays that are apparent in males. Children having fragile X who don't show intellectual delays may have learning disabilities or behavior problems (Meyer, 2007).

Unless suspected, children with fragile X are often difficult to identify in early childhood because they may meet developmental milestones; however, their ability to meet milestones on time gradually declines. There are some behavior patterns that are typical of children with fragile X. Although all the behaviors alluded to are typical of young children, it is the frequency, duration, and intensity that indicate a problem. When excited or frustrated, children may flap their hands or bite them or have other autistic-like behaviors such as a fascination with spinning toys or other unusual objects. Speech patterns are unusual, and speech may be high-pitched, repetitious, and cluttered. They may be hyperactive or inattentive, with low levels of frustration tolerance, which can lead to temper tantrums. Some may overreact to light touch (Meyer, 2007).

Implications for Educators

Be aware of some of challenges that children with fragile X face and of the behaviors that characterize this disorder as early childhood educators may be some of the first to suspect a disability. Work through their strengths. They tend to process information as a whole rather than step by step. The have good visual matching as well as adaptive functioning. They may have problems with executive functioning and sequential learning (Loesch et al., 2002; Meyer, 2007). Look for autistic-like behaviors. Provide children with functional skills as well as academic challenges and match their level of learning with an enriched environment.

Fetal Alcohol Spectrum Disorders

Alcohol ingested by a pregnant woman can have a variety of physical and neurodevelopmental effects on the developing fetus. They range from death of the fetus to physical malformation, intellectual disability, or learning and behavior problems. This range of disorders is known as fetal alcohol spectrum disorders (FASD) (CDC, 2006). Fetal alcohol syndrome (FAS) is the most severe of these. Children with FAS have three characteristic anomalies: interuterine and postnatal growth deficiency, including low birth weight and poor muscle tone; facial anomalies (thin upper lip, flat midface, short nose, low nasal bridge, small head, droopy eyes); and central nervous system (CNS) dysfunction, including irritability, attention deficit, hyperactivity, and intellectual disability (CDC, 2006). The most severe effects happen early in the pregnancy and are related to maternal binge drinking (four or more drinks) (Davidson & Myers, 2007).

The prevalence of FAS and related disorders is difficult to estimate for a variety of reasons. One is the ability to confirm exposure to alcohol during fetal development. Depending upon the population studies, estimates range from 0.2 to 1.5 per 1,000 live births for FAS and three times that frequency for FASD (CDC, 2006). One of the most frustrating aspects of FASD is that, theoretically, it is 100 percent preventable. The savings in human terms is obvious in quality of life. However, society bears to a great extent the cost of raising children with FAS through the health care and educational systems.

The Evidence Base

Using data from North Dakota it was estimated that the health care costs for a child with FAS were $2,842 annually compared to children without FAS, which were approximately $500 a year. Assuming these costs are stable between birth and 21, health care costs alone run about $50,000 more than that of a child without FAS. Prevention of one case of FAS per year for 20 years results in a cost savings of $491,820. If one were to take into account the costs of special education and foster care, and then add in potential costs (or savings) by corrections and mental health, the potential savings grow from the prevention of just one case of FAS (Klug & Burd, 2003).

Reflective Practice

It is very different to look at the prevention of disabilities from a societal and economic perspective than from early childhood education. What do you see as your role in the prevention of fetal alcohol syndrome? How would you go about doing it?

Children with FAS often have feeding problems, which can lead to failure to thrive. As young children they tend to be short and thin, although they are likely to attain a typical height and weight. Developmental delays become apparent early, particularly in the area of speech and recall. Although they have motor delays, these seem to show themselves as clumsiness and lack of fine motor coordination (Wunsch, Conlon, & Scheidt, 2002). Although children with FAS display a range of IQ scores, most of them fall in the mild intellectual disability range. Part of their intellectual challenges are in the areas of planning, sequencing, self-monitoring, and goal-directed behaviors. These can lead to problems in routine activities, such as self-help skills, and can appear as behavior problems. Behavior problems such as hyperactivity and impulsivity are common. Children with FAS may also display oppositional defiant disorder or they may have a conduct disorder with increasing age.

Children with FASD tend to function in the borderline average range and have fewer behavioral problems. Their impairments are more subtle. In school they seem to have particular difficulty with reading and math. They do not necessarily have the global delay that is often associated with intellectual disability (Wunsch et al., 2002).

Implications for Educators

Children who are exposed to alcohol prenatally often live in families who have problems nurturing their children. In addition to inborn risks, children are often raised in homes where there is biological, psychological, and environmental risk. Infants and young children in such an environment are at increased risk for abuse and neglect. Many will be placed in foster care for this reason. Others will enter the foster care system because their parents died of alcohol-related causes, such as cirrhosis of the liver, car accidents, suicides, and overdose.

In the Field

My daughter, Grace, couldn't have children and she and her husband desperately wanted a child. They considered many alternatives and finally decided on a private adoption. They hired a lawyer who specialized in adoption, sold their boat, got a second mortgage on their home, and waited. They received the call when they were on vacation. They flew back to New York City in the midst of a raging snowstorm. Rented a car and started into

the city. It took them 5 hours. My daughter kept calling, reminding them that one of the conditions of the adoption was that they could speak with the birth mother before she left the hospital.

The birth mother assured her that the baby's father was Dominican even though the baby boy was blond with blue eyes. (Grace's husband is Cuban.) She also said that she didn't use drugs or alcohol while she was pregnant (another condition). The weather made going home impossible. They checked into a hotel that was close by with provisions provided by the hospital. I called and my daughter was deliriously happy. The baby was beautiful. Her husband was downstairs with the chef trying to figure out how to make formula. (Thank God the chef had children). And, the baby was crying. Grace didn't know much about babies, but I had had four children. I started to worry when he was a week old. By the time he was in preschool he was identified as having neurologic problems that affected his behavior and his learning. They said he had fetal alcohol effects. I was angry that the birth mother had lied about the father and about drinking. I kept telling my daughter she should do something. But, she loves him.

Reflective Practice

What would you do? When you have children in your classroom with FASD find out more about their families and how they are coping. Whether or not this is the birth mother, blaming her for the problem is not productive. Can you think of ways of support these families and children?

Cultural-Familial Delays

This term is used to refer to children with mild intellectual disabilities when the cause of the delay is thought to be an unstimulating environment and/or general genetic factors.

We are back to the nature-nurture issue but still seem to maintain the position that nature provides the broad parameters in which nurture plays out its role. Studies consistently show that mild intellectual disability without a known etiology or cause is highly correlated with lower socioeconomic status (Drews et al., 1995).

The Evidence Base

To the extent that early intervention in the form of high quality preschool could influence outcomes for children whose families are "poor" the question is "How many of them attend preschool?" Barnett and Yarosz (2007) attempted to answer this question by using data from the 2005 National Household Education Survey. They made no attempt to measure quality, only participation. The data are interesting and the differences between 3 year olds and 4 year olds is quite revealing.

Overall, children in poverty have lower participation rates in preschool than families who make more money with families making between $20,000 and $30,000 having the lowest rates. These are the working poor. Despite the compensatory efforts of government to support these families almost half of 4 year olds and the vast majority of 3 year olds do not participate in preschool. It is not until income levels rise to more than $85,000 that over half of 3 year olds attend preschool (see Figure 14–2).

Another way to look at concerns related to cultural-familial intellectual delays is based on the mother's education (see Figure 14–3). This relates both to the concept of valuing early childhood education and the level of stimulation that one might expect in the home environment.

There is a strong link between mother's education and preschool participation. The children who could be expected to gain the most from high-quality preschool programs

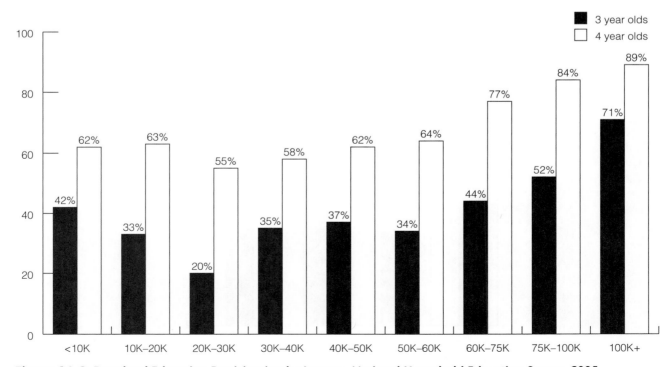

Figure 14–2: Preschool Education Participation by Income, National Household Education Survey, 2005

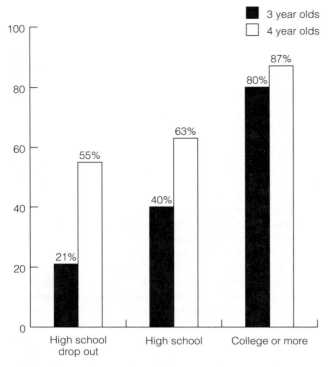

Figure 14–3: Preschool Education Participation by Mother's Education, National Household Education Survey, 2005

are the least likely to attend. These may well be the children who are identified as having mild intellectual delays when they reach kindergarten. And, families in which the mother dropped out of high school have children who are likely to reach kindergarten with 2 years less of high-quality preschool than mothers who went to college.

A third way of looking at preschool participation is by ethnicity. Clearly, Hispanic children are less likely than other children to attend preschool (see Figure 14–4). Data suggests that lack of access is the most likely reason for this low rate (Barnett & Yarosz, 2007).

Reflective Practice

Although two-thirds of 4 year olds and 40 percent of 3 year olds were enrolled in preschool education, the children participating do not represent the population equally. As you reflect on this data do you believe that lack of participation in high-quality preschool programs might be one reason why some children come to school and are identified with mild intellectual disabilities? How do you see poverty, mother's education, and race interacting? How might this impact how you teach these children? What are the implications for public policy?

Children born to women who have fewer resources are more likely to have had little prenatal care and poor nutrition and are less likely to have received social and cognitive nurturing in early childhood. Women who haven't completed high school are four times as likely to have children with mild developmental delays (Mendola et al., 2002). African American children are twice as likely to be categorized as having mild developmental delays; this may be related to the disproportionate number of African American families who live below the poverty line. Early intervention services have improved the expected outcome for children with mild developmental delays (Batshaw et al., 2007).

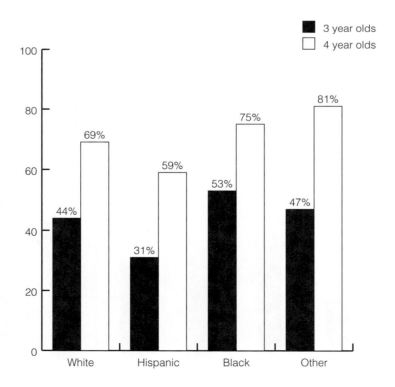

Figure 14–4: Preschool Education Participation by Ethnicity, National Household Education Survey, 2005

Implications for Educators

When children who live in impoverished environments are identified as having intellectual disabilities they need a program with many hands-on experiences. You cannot assume that they have been exposed to the same experiences as other children. Do not assume that they are incapable of doing a task until you ensure that they have the necessary prerequisite tasks to participate. These children need to go on field trips and to experience a variety of materials and media. They need to role play and to have good language models. They need an enriched environment, but one that starts where they are.

Instructional Strategies

In general, teach from simple to complex. Be specific! Where appropriate, simplify information, but not to the point that it loses its meaning. Use a variety of teaching techniques.

Task Analysis

A task analysis is the process of breaking a task down into its component parts, sequencing these, and then teaching them. A great deal has been written on the use of task analysis. However, if you understand the basic principles involved in a task, you can do the task analysis yourself. Start with something the child must do frequently, like putting on a coat. If, after your task analysis, the child still has a problem, review your analysis for both order and possible missed steps. Change it and try again.

Figure 14–5 presents a sample task analysis, including a filled-in chart that shows the child's progress. Task analysis and tracking of progress should be done on a weekly basis.

Backward Chaining

In some cases, the technique of backward chaining is useful. Using the example of putting on the coat, offer the most help with the first steps and the least help with the last step in the chain. The first step you would expect the child to do without assistance is step 8 (zip up the coat). This means the child gets some satisfaction for task completion instead of needing help to finish. (Backward chaining is easier when the component parts are of about equal difficulty.)

Modeling

Teachers may need to model the particular behavior while verbally describing it. Provide opportunities for the child to practice and verbalize what the child is doing; also, provide reinforcement and specific feedback.

Guidelines

Because it takes longer for children with intellectual disabilities to learn, it is important that you adapt your teaching style to meet the needs of these children.

1. *Use all the senses.* In your teaching, use as many of the senses as possible. Even if you are teaching concepts that are primarily visual, such as colors, have children reinforce the visual with other sensory experiences. Have them: *see* the red ball; *sit on* the red square; *add* red food coloring to the finger-paint; *eat* a red tomato; and *listen* to a red fire truck. Like most children, they don't learn the first time; teach the same concept in different contexts.
2. *Promote overlearning.* Keep going over the same concept until they have *overlearned* it, but not to the point of boredom—theirs or yours. Use variations to maintain interest. Because children may easily forget, they need to overlearn and review information until it is firmly established. Also, teach skills in different areas and situations to ensure generalization.
3. *Use spaced practice.* Teach a concept for a short time each day for many days, rather than for a long period of time on fewer days. Spaced practice is always more effective than massed practice, as those who "cram" for an exam know.
4. *Choose materials that teach several skills.* Because learning is challenging, determine the learning value of specific materials and use those that are most efficient or those that teach two necessary skills at one time. For example, buttoning sequences where children must duplicate a pattern of colors teaches buttoning, a necessary self-help skill, and the patterns and relationships necessary for reading and math, as well as color names.
5. *Generalize concepts.* When you teach concepts, try to make them as close as possible to the setting where they will be used. Keep activities relevant, short, and to the point. Be clear with directions. Be wary of cute shortcuts. One school I visited decided to teach children to say "three-teen" instead of thirteen because it was easier. Some of those children are now about "three-teen and five-teen," and their peers make fun of them when they say how old they are.
6. *Use many examples.* If you use only one example when teaching the concept red, it is likely that the children who learn this one particular red will have difficulty generalizing to other red objects.

	M	T	W	TH	F	M	T
1. Take coat off hook.	P	V	V	V	N	N	N
2. Put coat on floor inside up.	P	P	V	V	N	N	N
3. Stand at neck of coat.	P	P	V	V	V	N	N
4. Bend over.	P	P	P	V	V	N	N
5. Put hands in armholes.	P	P	P	V	V	V	V
6. Flip coat over head, pushing arms into armholes.	P	P	P	P	V	V	V
7. Start zipper.	P	P	P	P	V	V	V
8. Zip up coat.	P	P	P	P	P	P	P

Be sure to praise the child for his efforts.

Key: P = physical help
     V = verbal help
     N = no help

Figure 14–5: Task Analysis and Tracking Chart

7. *Reinforce appropriate behavior*. Set your sights realistically. Reinforce effort and steps accomplished toward a goal. Don't wait until the goal is accomplished, or the child may lose motivation. Reinforce children for zipping up the last part of their jackets; don't wait until they can put their jackets on and get the zipper started.

8. *Focus on essential skills*. Don't try to teach the whole curriculum at a lower, slower, simpler level. Rather, concentrate on what is important for children. What skills will be essential later for the children that need a base developed now? Depending on the child, you will teach basic academic skills, and also functional living skills, and/or vocational skills. Teach safety and health skills necessary for wellness. Children need to learn to wash hands after toileting, not to get into the path of moving objects (whether swings, tricycles, or cars), and to wear clothing appropriate for the weather.

9. *Teach vocabulary*. Children need the vocabulary to express basic wants and needs whether they learn words or signs or use a communication board. Children need a way to communicate that they are hungry, thirsty, tired, and need to go to the bathroom. Practice on a daily basis. Incorporate vocabulary learning into all curriculum areas on a daily basis.

10. *Use universal design*. Provide activities that can be used at many different levels by individuals and groups of children and provide adult scaffolding to support children's learning.

11. *Evaluate Progress*. Evaluate the progress of children with intellectual disabilities against their own development, as well as in the context of the general curriculum and what all children in the class are learning.

Curriculum Adaptations

Adapting the curriculum, in general, consists of simplifying some tasks, focusing on essential tasks and omitting others, and including tasks that other children may learn more informally through incidental learning such as toileting, feeding, and early language skills.

Social Awareness: Self-Esteem, Inclusion, and Social Studies

Children learn about themselves and their environment by building on familiar experiences. Begin with them and their immediate surroundings — family and school — then expand into the larger community. Help children evaluate situations, including your classroom, relative to their health and safety. Make good health and safety practices part of their routine. Focus on making all children part of the group and teaching them social skills that will be appropriate throughout their lives. Some of the activities in the Resource Chapter 1 are specifically designed to support children who have intellectual disabilities. Activity 1–47w Our Town provides a concrete way for children to think about the community.

Self-Esteem

All children need to learn about themselves. Teach children the names of their body parts. Use songs as well as direct instruction and questioning to teach this. Remember, you want to include all children: Do not act surprised when a child with intellectual disabilities can do something or praise him inordinately.

1. Help develop a positive self-concept by pointing out to the child and others what she can do and how much she *has* learned, just as you do with all children. Be truthful.

2. Focus on and support strengths where possible. Use these to work on necessary challenges.

3. Support children's expansion of learning at the level at which they are capable.

4. Support children in learning age appropriate adaptive skills.

Inclusion

All children need to be part of society. As you help children join groups, model and teach the skills they need; gradually fade your support so children will not be dependent on your intervention.

1. Teach children the courtesies of everyday living. Be sure children know how to greet you (say "Hello" and look at you while they say it). They also need to learn to use "Please" and "Thank you" appropriately and not to interrupt conversations.

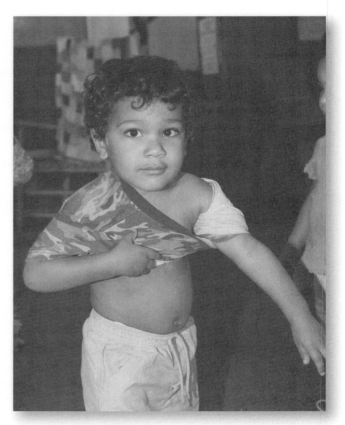

Build time in the curriculum to teach adaptive behavior. Use naturally occurring opportunities to teach needed skills.

2. All children need to be contributing members of the class. Give children tasks they can do.
3. Be sure to have easy and difficult, but age-appropriate, options available so children can easily participate in group play. Mix age groups for some activities if this is possible.

Social Studies

Like all children, those with intellectual disabilities need to learn about the community in which they live. Concentrate on roles the children may need to know or can readily identify with.

1. Discuss the roles of police, firefighters, and mail personnel. Go on field trips to see them at work, then follow up with role-playing. Be practical. Have children mail letters or postcards home to see their address. Talk about the implications of writing the wrong address.
2. Help children learn about many different roles: cafeteria worker, bus driver, or therapists they are likely to encounter. Have them play games in a one-on-one situation with a teacher or paraeducator. Discuss how the teacher also learns from these specialists.
3. Explore varied occupations. Be sure to include *some* occupations that require limited skills (teacher, farmer, baker, factory worker, janitor, clerk, construction worker, worker in fast-food chain, and so on). It is important that a range of occupations be included and that they be valued.
4. Take children on field trips to different areas in the community. Teach skills they need to interact in the community. Encourage parents to take children on the bus, to restaurants, and to the library. Teach prerequisite skills for these trips.

Language and Literacy: Speaking, Listening, Reading, and Writing

Language, both expressive and receptive, may be the child's weakest area but one of the most essential. Children with intellectual disabilities have smaller vocabularies and use simpler sentence structures than their peers. Their language may be difficult to understand and used less frequently than that of other children. Lack of competence in communication can lead to frustration and may result in crying, hitting, or other means of nonverbal communication.

Children with intellectual disabilities learn more slowly than other children, so they may need extra repetitions of vocabulary and help generalizing words to a variety of situations. They will spend most of their time mastering the concept of a symbol system and developing a functional vocabulary. They need time to practice literacy skills. They may need to repeat and copy sounds before these become connected to words. These skills may be learned in conjunction with such necessary small motor skills as patterned eye movement (left to right), following a line of print with a finger, and turning pages. Children need to work on these skills, and it is your role to motivate them and capture their interest. Do this in short periods, and be sure prerequisite skills have been attained before going on to more difficult tasks. Children with intellectual disabilities may just be mastering the initial stages of reading and writing during the early elementary years. If the prerequisite motor skills are not developed, it is useless to continually practice skills such as name writing if they can not effectively use a spoon or cup.

Children who have intellectual disabilities need first-hand experiences to translate into language and literacy. They need to build a strong experiential base before they can use concepts in language and literacy activities. Start with the concrete and gradually work toward the more abstract. Children need to explore a ball, roll, throw, and kick a ball before reading about a ball makes sense.

Speaking

Like all children, those with intellectual disabilities depend on communicating with others to have their needs met.

1. Work on vocabulary. Start with a nucleus vocabulary that focuses on the child. Teaching body parts teaches not only vocabulary but body awareness as well. Next, focus on health care, the family, clothing, and aspects of the school and home environments. Emphasize nouns and verbs first. They are essential for communicating needs. If necessary, begin with words that allow children to express their basic needs and wants. These may include words such as *yes, no, thirsty, hungry, please, bathroom,* and *tired.*
2. Encourage children to communicate in some way. Start conversations with an obvious frame of reference: "I like your hat." Pictures or videotapes taken during field trips can be used later to help children talk about what happened on the trips. The children can also sequence pictures. A sequence of a trip to the apple orchard might look like this:

   Picture 1:   Getting into the cars
   Picture 2:   Arriving at the orchard
   Picture 3:   Eating apples at the orchard
   Picture 4:   Taking off coats back at school, with the apples in the picture

   Using a digital camera that provides instant pictures allows you to show the sequence quickly without having to wait for the film to be developed. Printing the photographs on regular paper rather than photographic paper saves money.

3. If you are going to set up a grocery store in the dramatic play area, take a field trip to a grocery store so they have this experience to build on. Point out the similarities in the two situations.
4. Use simple nursery rhymes and rhyming in general to develop vocabulary.

Fingerplays can help teach concepts, improve fine motor coordination, and keep children interested and occupied. Using fingerplays also engages the tactile mode for learning and may make the necessary repetition less monotonous.

1. Set aside time to repeat simple fingerplays, songs, and stories.
2. Use fingerplays, songs, and stories to teach basic concepts, such as numbers and to follow stories, field trips, and other activities. A good source for songs and fingerplays is http://www.enchangedlearning.com.

Listening

Listening is difficult. Where possible, use props. Speak clearly at a normal speed with simple, direct statements.

1. Provide concrete examples of the items that you are talking about so children can both see and hear the information.
2. Give the child practice following one- and two-step directions.
3. Be sure that children understand the interactional quality of listening and speaking and that they don't see it as a passive experience (as they might with television).

At the beginning, use short, simple stories that have a familiar theme. Remember, the group experience may be new to children.

1. Use stories with repetition, rhythm, and rhyme, such as Dr. Seuss books like *Go Dog Go*. If you have the resources, start a read-at-home program. Send books home and have children read, and reread them, with their families.
2. Animal stories with big pictures and few words, alphabet books, and those with simple rhymes are good. Have children write simple books to connect reading with writing.
3. Before you read a story, it is helpful to discuss the meaning of some words beforehand. For example, before reading the story *Caps for Sale*, establish that caps are hats.
4. Use flannelboard stories. They have simple plots and children can participate in the story and repeat it as they manipulate the pieces.

Reading

Children with intellectual disabilities may require more practice to develop early literacy skills. Build a solid base and do not push children before they are ready or spend so much time on rote drill and practice that children lose interest in learning to read. First establish basic skills, then use these skills to teach the integration of higher-level skills.

1. Read to children. When you read, especially one-on-one, follow the words with your finger so children develop the connection between written words and reading. Make reading fun and exciting. Read more books rather than fewer.
2. Concentrate first on auditory and visual identification. Don't assume that children can label all the sounds and objects in their environment. Then work on discrimination skills. Once identification skills have been established, work on visual and auditory memory. For example, have children first match objects, then alphabet letters, then label them by name or sound.

Writing

Writing begins with marks on the page and ends with the understanding of a complex symbol system. Work initially with the fine motor aspect, as the symbol system will take time.

1. Help children enjoy the process of making marks on paper. Give them a variety of tools (crayons with knob ends, large markers, thick chalk) to mark with and varying sizes of paper, cardboard, and poster board to mark on.

2. Have large wooden alphabet letters available. Spell out the child's name and have the child trace the letters with two fingers (index and middle fingers of dominant hand).
3. Have children imitate you as you make large arm circles in the air with the dominant arm, first in one direction and then the other. When children can make circles, begin to make letters with your arm (it is important that this is a large motor activity). This is air writing. See Activity 2–26 for more details.

Discovery: Mathematics, Science, and Technology

Support the discovery approach with verbalizations about the process. Allow time to repeat experiences and to do variations on themes. Children may need help generalizing knowledge or may do so at a slower rate than their age mates. As activities become more difficult, ensure that they can be done at different levels. Children with intellectual disabilities will need concrete experience even after their peers are dealing with more abstract concepts. Use real objects that can be touched and manipulated. Modify the keyboard of the computer or be sure children have prerequisite skills such as the ability to use a single keystroke before expecting them to interact with computers.

Point out similarities and differences within classification systems (e.g., cars and trucks both have wheels). Increase attention span by programming for what the child likes and praising the child for staying with projects to completion. However, don't avoid areas that are challenging, as this may be where he needs the most practice. Make it interesting.

Mathematics

Children with intellectual disabilities need a foundation in basic mathematical skills to function in society.

1. Teach number concepts, such as counting, with real objects that can be moved or touched. Count children, blocks, chairs, and tables. Use an abacus and relate the beads back to real objects. See Activity 3–31w Abacus.
2. Choose math experiences that also teach other skills. Pegboards are useful for facilitating small motor skills while teaching counting and one-to-one correspondence. Pegboards can also be used to teach sequential patterns and relationships. You can make up a pattern and ask the child to copy it, identify the pattern, and then count the number of pegs used in the pattern. Stringing large wooden beads offers a similar opportunity for learning about numbers and patterns while also teaching eye-hand coordination. Geoboards are also useful for teaching counting, area, and multiplication.
3. Use real objects such as cups, napkins, and fruit pieces to teach one-to-one correspondence. A good activity for snack time is to have a child put a glass and piece of fruit or vegetable in front of each chair (children without something to eat or drink usually make this known, and thus you have a teachable moment).

Science

Science should focus on first-hand knowledge and give information that is relevant for future learning and well-being.

1. Use field trips, especially those dealing with nature and the environment, to teach children about the world around them.
2. Discuss the seasons and the predictable changes that occur with the changes in nature. Discuss how the seasons affect clothing and activities. What you do is dependent on where you live.
3. Encourage children to test simple cause-and-effect reasoning. State a relationship and have the child test it. "The color is darker if you press harder" may be obvious to you, but children may not realize they cause the change systematically.
4. Plant a garden for first-hand experience with growth and learning the necessary conditions for growth.
5. Tie science lessons to safety knowledge. Science lessons can also provide an important opportunity to teach everyday living skills, such as the relationship between being out in the sun and getting a sunburn, and stopping the spread of germs by such things as hand washing.

Technology

Technology holds great potential for teaching cause-and-effect reasoning, and the "patience" with repeated learning is infinite. It is an absolute must.

1. Look at various keyboard options and choose ones that best meets the children's needs.
2. Choose software carefully. It needs to be developmentally appropriate and simple to operate.
3. Encourage independent use of the computer itself. This is tremendously impressive to others. Parents may be encouraged and surprised that their child can turn on and operate a computer. Some of the skills are easy and sequential, and some of the software (especially those with picture menus) are very user-friendly.
4. Encourage children to work at the computer in pairs.

Wellness: Health, Physical Education, and Sensory Motor

Children with intellectual disabilities may not be as proficient as other children because their pattern of large motor development may have been slower. Plan activities that are at the child's developmental level, with variations to allow mastery and more challenging ones to provide growth. Children must devote time to mastering small motor activities, so provide many different opportunities and make these intriguing. They need simple and more complex activities and many opportunities for practice. Begin with relatively large objects with few pieces: program for success. Try to include as many adaptive skills as you can (dressing boards, doll clothes with Velcro™ fasteners, and so on).

Health and Safety

It is important for children to make good health habits part of their routine. They may not have learned some of the things that seem obvious: toileting, washing hands, blowing and wiping their nose with a tissue, eating with utensils, and grooming.

1. Teach safety skills. Emphasize dangers with the greatest likelihood of occurrence and those that are most dangerous, such as traffic, electrical outlets, and poison. Teach safety signs, warning signs, and warning words. See activities such as 4–4 Stop and Go and 4–5 Warning Signs.
2. Concentrate on building good food habits. Help children learn to choose healthy snacks like water and milk, vegetables, fruit and low-fat yogurt rather than juice and soft drinks and cookies and crackers.
3. Role-play with children what to do if they get lost. Make address and identification cards with a phone number on them if that is the parent's choice. Have children memorize these. A task analysis may be useful.
4. Break complex skills down into simple tasks the child can do. Teach the necessary skills in different curricula. Toileting involves the ability to dress and undress oneself, so be sure to teach buttoning and snapping as part of fine motor skills.

Large Motor

Large motor skills help develop stamina and increase body coordination and awareness. Provide opportunities for children to participate in skills that require locomotion (creeping, running), manipulation (throwing, bouncing, catching), and stability (stretching, rolling, balancing). Encourage children to develop game skills (kicking, throwing, catching, jumping, batting). Participation in cooperative games where no one wins or loses and no one is eliminated works best.

1. Emphasize basic fundamental motor skills and their variations; walking forward, backward, sideways, fast, slow and so on.
2. Help children build physical stamina by daily participation in moderate to vigorous activity, active games, and an active lifestyle.
3. Use large, lightweight blocks, which are easy to manipulate.

Small Motor

When you plan for small motor play, think of the skills that both help the child develop the necessary small muscles in the body and serve as a foundation for later skills.

1. Start with beginning grasping and manipulation. Provide a variety of objects so that the child can practice many styles of grasping. Encourage the child to use the pincer grasp (thumb and forefinger apposition) once it has been developed.
2. Use many different activities that require fine motor skills (formboards, pegboards—rubber ones for strengthening finger muscles—plastic blocks, or beads that fit together). Start with relatively large, preschool-size objects. Gradually add more pieces and smaller objects (be sure they cannot be swallowed). Use this opportunity to teach color and number skills also. Have children sort and group various materials. Older children can use the arts to promote small motor skills.

3. Code your sorting and matching tasks by number (use *1* for easy tasks, *2* for more difficult, and so on). This means that all the children can do the same activity but at different levels. Provide a variety of levels of sorting activities such as
    (a) Sort identical objects from a mix: round beads from crayons or wooden clothespins from small wooden blocks.
    (b) Group the same objects by size: big from small, plastic clips or big blocks from small ones.
    (c) Sort the same objects in different colors: red from green beads or red from white Legos®.
    (d) Group the same objects with differing shapes: round from square from cylindrical red beads.
    (e) Have a mix of objects that can be grouped in two or more ways. First, demonstrate the system and have the child follow it; later, encourage the child to group and regroup independently. A mix of large and small cars of different colors, large and small blocks of different colors and shapes, and large and small beads of varying colors and shapes may all be sorted into two containers of large and small, three if they sort by object, and more if they sort by color.
        Within each step, you can make the task more difficult by adding more objects, colors, sizes, and shapes. Start with two items and work up to perhaps ten. A more difficult version is grouping different objects by color, size, and shape.

4. Often, it is hard for children to hold a pencil or crayon in an appropriate writing grasp. Larger implements are easier to grip. Provide a variety of pencils, crayons, and brushes of different sizes. Add grips, tape, or foam curlers to make them easier to hold. (An occupational therapist can provide advice on these accommodations.)

Sensory Motor Integration

Provide many opportunities for children to use motor skills in coordination with their senses.

1. Provide materials and activities that require the use of two hands: clapping, lacing beads onto string or pipe cleaners, lacing cards with various-sized holes (some large and easy to string, others small), putting together snap-construction toys, and placing blocks in containers.
2. Provide puzzles at different levels of difficulty. Puzzles with knobs attached to the pieces are easier to manipulate.
3. Provide activities that require different motions of each hand (such as a jack-in-the-box, where a child must hold the box with one hand while turning the knob with the other). It is easier for children to do the same thing with both hands or to use only one hand. Some fingerplays do this as well.

Creative Arts: Visual Arts, Music, Creative Movement, and Dramatic Play

As long as there is no competition and children are not required to do the "same" thing, children with intellectual disabilities need little accommodation in this area. Through the manipulation of various art media, they can learn about texture, shape, and size. Expect them to choose to sing favorite songs over and over. They may not show a lot of imagination in moving. If you use costumes, provide realistic ones. Start with large motor movements and encourage children to move their whole body to bold music. Gradually work on small motor movements. The practice of moving and the opportunity to be part of the group is important.

Visual Arts

Art for children with intellectual disabilities, as with all young children, should focus more on the process than the product. Children learn by doing, especially if a thoughtful teacher is providing guidance.

1. Use a variety of art media.
2. Cutting is often difficult; it may be helpful to use easy-grip or "training" scissors with a loop or a spring handle or tear paper. See Activity 5–8 Torn Paper Flowers.
3. Encourage children to participate in the visual arts each day. Provide feedback on what they do and how they are doing it.

Music

Music can be used in a variety of ways. Repetition makes it easier for children to learn songs. Teach families songs so children can hear and sing them at home as well.

1. Use music to teach basic concepts such as numbers, colors, and body parts.
2. Music can expand a child's vocabulary and increase auditory memory.
3. Music can also help children establish a rhythm pattern. Vary the pattern so that children can learn to match it.
4. Using songs that call children by name can increase self esteem and create a sense of group belonging.

Creative Movement

Movement is a must for all children. Nonjudgmental movement is an added plus. Support all attempts at movement.

1. Encourage children to move to music that has an obvious beat, but don't require the child to follow the beat.

Provide children with many hands on experiences. If they are approaching an experience for the first time provide them with support and encouragement.

2. Encourage children to move specific body parts. Be sure to have these parts moved long enough so you are sure the children know the part indicated: "Everybody move your arms in circles."

3. Help children recognize speed by having them move quickly or slowly. Children gain sensory motor integration as well as necessary concepts through movement.

Dramatic Play

Dramatic play is a way to make strange experiences more familiar and is a good way to teach appropriate behavior.

1. Visit a real store, then set up a play store (department, grocery, pet). Play through the essential features. Setting it up for one or two days isn't enough; keep adding features throughout the week so it doesn't get boring.

2. Playing with other children in this area might also provide the child with information about how roles are played in society. Children, especially those with disabilities, may be given little realistic feedback, yet feedback is necessary for their development. It can be realistic without being judgmental: "You can't reach that." Acknowledge reality, but help children think about alternatives (a taller friend or a stool might be the solution).

3. Play should be fairly concrete with realistic props. Children with intellectual disabilities are typically less imaginative than their peers. Have a lot of props available to facilitate play: a garage, for example, needs cars, trucks, a block structure, hose, gas pumps, and so on.

Routines and Transitions

Routines and transitions can be used to promote independence and prevocational skills as well as teach colors, numbers, and body awareness.

1. Have a sign-in and sign-out board. Use this for roll call some days. Have children find their own name tag and put it on, or move name cards from one side to the other. This reinforces name recognition and independence.

2. Children may need more help with toileting and dressing. Dismiss them at a time when they can get the help they need.

3. Use transitions to reinforce concepts the child has learned. For example, call children to line up after they have correctly spelled a word or answered a math question. Vary the difficulty of the questions to match what the children are learning.

4. Allow time for transitions so children can be successful. It is easy for children with intellectual disabilities to get distracted and to feel rushed when others are waiting.

5. Sitting too long for the sake of sitting, although helpful to the teacher, is not a useful skill for a child. Use finger plays or listening games while other children are finishing, or teach children to independently get and use readiness materials (puzzles, books, or small motor materials) while they wait.

Summary

Increasingly, we are seeing intellectual disabilities as conditions that can be changed or modified through early intervention. Hence, we are reluctant to label children as mentally retarded, and most young children with intellectual disabilities are classified as having developmental delays. These delays are apparent in infants and toddlers by missed motor and language milestones, the quality of their movements, and lack of interest in the environment. In the preschool years, they are characterized by a short attention span and poor memory skills. By school age, the children may not have readiness skills necessary to pursue learning at the expected rate. The milder the cognitive delay, the later it is likely to be identified. To be classified as mentally retarded, children must be assessed and shown to have delays in both intelligence and adaptive skills.

There are many different causes of intellectual disabilities, some of which are unknown. Genetic factors such as Down syndrome and fragile X cause delays. Environmental factors are related to cultural-familial delays and fetal alcohol spectrum disorders.

Children with intellectual disabilities may need more repetitions and more direct teaching techniques such as task analysis, backward chaining, and modeling. Teaching goals for children with intellectual disabilities focus on motor and language skills as well as thinking and reasoning skills, particularly social awareness and adaptive living skills. Adaptations include working from simple to complex and concrete to abstract.

Reflections

1. Fetal alcohol spectrum disorders are preventable. We in society pick up the expenses for these children's health, education, and sometimes even foster care. What do you feel our role is in prevention and how would you go about preventing FASD? What do you think would be effective? Do you see this as a single problem or one that is more deeply embedded in poverty and poor neighborhoods? As a taxpayer, how do you feel about these mothers? Would this influence how you would teach their children?

2. Reflect on the supports we provide to severely involved children with intellectual disabilities. We have few expectations that they will become productive members of society. Is this a wise use of resources? Should these children go to school with children without disabilities? Is this a service to children and their families? In the past these children lived in institutions. Should that practice be put in place again? What do you see as the pros and cons of institutionalization for young children?

Educational Resources

American Association on Intellectual and Developmental Disabilities (AAIDD) is a national organization for professionals interested in the general welfare of individuals with intellectual disabilities and the study of their causes, treatment, and prevention of mental retardation. (202) 387-1968; FAX (202) 387-2193; http://www.aaidd.org/

ARC of the United States is an organization with a strong advocacy commitment to meet the needs of those with mental retardation and their families. (817) 261-6003; FAX (817) 277-3491; http://www.thearc.org

Division on Developmental Disabilities of the Council for Exceptional Children is a national organization. Its goal is to enhance the competence of individuals working with those with cognitive disabilities/mental retardation, autism, and related disabilities, to address emergent and critical issues in the field and to be advocates. http://www.dddcec.org/

Family Village integrates information and resources on the Internet for people with disabilities and their families. (608) 263-5973 TDD; (608) 263-0802 FAX (608) 263-0529; http://www.familyvillage.wisc.edu/

National Down Syndrome Society provides information about Down syndrome, including the topic of inclusion. (212) 460-9330 (800) 221-4602; http://www.ndss.org

National Fragile X Foundation provides information about fragile X and supports research to better understand who it affects and how it affects them. http://www.fragilex.org/html/home.shtml

Pregnancy and Alcohol is a nonprofit site sponsored by the University of Wisconsin that provides information about pregnancy and the use of alcohol as well as information about fetal alcohol syndrome and related conditions. (800-752-3157); http://pregnancyandalcohol.org/index.asp

For additional resources, visit the book companion website for this text at www.cengage.com/education/deiner.

Chapter 15

Children Who Are Gifted and Talented

Chevaneese stacked blocks before her older brother. She walked early and she spoke in sentences when her peers were still saying one or two words. Chevy was smart. But being labeled as "gifted and talented" eventually became more of a burden than an accolade.

"I've always had more stress in my life because I was 'smarter,'" she said. "Teachers put me in groups with 'troublemakers' and 'nongifted' children, somehow hoping my influence would encourage them." But making Chevy the example, and letting everyone know that she was smarter than others, strained relationships with her peers. "Many children would purposely not interact with me, and if I received a less than perfect grade on something, taunts of 'Why did you get that grade if you're so smart?' followed," she said.

This caused her to not only regret her "smartness" but also feel emotionally unstable. "There's a serious problem when you get sick and you're scared to miss school for fear you'll get behind," she said

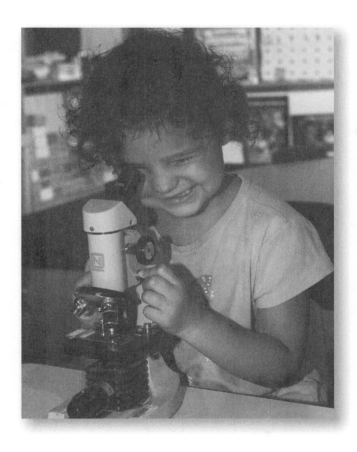

Reflective Practice

Children who are identified as gifted and talented have the same needs as other children and sometimes these gifts become a burden. Reflect on how you include and think about children who are gifted and talented. Do you expect to take advantage of their skills and make them into helpers or to find ways to enhance their development?

Sometimes we focus so much on children's differences we forget that, regardless of their ability or disability, they have the same needs as other children.

Gifts and Talents

If we are committed to inclusion and equal educational opportunities for all children, then what do we do about children who are intellectually advanced in their development? Some see gifted children as a precious national resource that is being wasted. Others feel that these children should be able to succeed very well without special services. Gifted education has been criticized as being "elitist," not open to children from diverse ethnic groups, those with disabilities, and those who exhibit gifts and talents in only one area.

In the current educational climate, the energy of the nation is focused on closing the gap between learners who have access to resources and those who do not. The No Child Left Behind Act of 2001 has helped focus this commitment and also made clear the emphasis on math and reading literacy. The 2004 amendments to the IDEA also focus on literacy, particularly providing early intervening services for children who are not progressing at the expected rate. Standards have been developed to ensure that children learn appropriate content. However, little is said about developing a conceptual framework to understand how gifted children learn, how and what they should be taught, and how schools should be supporting their development (VanTassel-Baska & Stambaugh, 2006). Some feel that No Child Left Behind leaves gifted children behind, or that no child is allowed ahead.

Many feel that the instructional needs of gifted and talented children are not being met. That is, there is little curricular differentiation to accommodate their learning needs. Further, few preservice teachers are receiving training to teach gifted and talented children. We are more concerned that teachers who have children with disabilities included in their class have the appropriate training to meet the needs of these children. We are apparently less concerned about training teachers to include gifted and talented children. Perhaps the general education curriculum needs to be reconceptualized to include the diversity of all children.

Some feel that gifted and talented children can appropriately be thought of as disadvantaged because of the lack of legislation concerning their needs and rights, the lack of government guidance relative to training teachers, and provision of services, and the lack of funding.

Defining Gifts and Talents

In many ways, what is valued is related to the sociohistorical time and the culture in which one is raised. In a society where people hunted for food, an individual who shot more accurately and from a greater distance than others might have been considered "gifted." In industrialized nations, we value other skills. In the past, we identified individuals as gifted only after they had made major contributions to society (George, 2003). In early childhood education, the goal is to identify children to provide them with a developmentally appropriate education. This is not necessarily an accelerated curriculum, any more than we try to slow down the curriculum for children with intellectual disabilities. It is a curriculum designed to meet the child's needs.

Unlike other areas covered in this text, there is no federal mandate for individualized education to meet the needs of this population. Individual states decide whether or not to have programs for them. The following definition is based on the Jacob K. Javits Gifted and Talented Students Education Act (1988) as part of the Elementary and Secondary Education Act

> Children and youth with outstanding talent perform or show the potential for performing at remarkably high levels of accomplishment when compared with others of their age, experience or environment.
>
> These children exhibit high performance capability in intellectual, creative, and/or artistic areas; possess an unusual leadership capacity, or excel in specific academic fields. They require services or activities not ordinarily provided by the schools.
>
> Outstanding talents are present in children and youth from all cultural groups, across all economic strata, and in all areas of human endeavor.

Other definitions differentiate between gifts and talents: Gifted students are those with a potential to exhibit superior performance across a range of areas or endeavors. Talented students are those with the potential to exhibit superior performance in one area of endeavor (George, 1997).

Prevalence of Gifts and Talents

Throughout this text, I have used terminology and classification to indicate the degree to which a child differs from the norms. Thus, I identify the degree to which children's development is delayed (mild, moderate, severe, or profound) or the level of supports a child needs (intermittent, limited, extensive, or pervasive). An IQ, as a measure of rate of cognitive development, also suggests the degree to which children with advanced intellectual development are developing differently from their peers. For example, a moderately gifted child with an IQ of 133 with a chronological age of 6 has a mental age of 9; and an exceptionally gifted 6 year old with an IQ of 160 has a mental age of approximately 11. This first grader would be expected to be able to understand content at the level of children in sixth grade. Some suggest that it would be useful to develop some standardized terminology and classify children based on IQ in the following way:

IQ 130–144	Moderately gifted
IQ 145–159	Highly gifted
IQ 160–179	Exceptionally gifted
IQ 180+	Profoundly gifted

In a normal distribution, approximately 1 child in 20 in a given population would be moderately gifted; 1 in 1,000 highly gifted; fewer than 9 in 100,000 could be classified as exceptionally gifted; and fewer than 1 in a million as profoundly gifted (Gross, 1993).

Reflective Practice

Think back to chapter 14 Children with Intellectual Disabilities and Developmental Delays and how these children were classified and the concerns about the levels of supports they needed in early childhood and in the future. How might you apply this information to gifted children?

Because the number of moderately gifted children is so much greater than highly, exceptionally, and profoundly gifted children, most school programs for the gifted are designed based on the characteristics, learning styles, and needs of this group (Gross, 1993). These programs rarely take into account that a child with an IQ of 190 is as different in ability level from a child with an IQ of 130 as the child with an IQ of 130 is from the child with an IQ of 70 (Gottfredson, 2003). See Table 15–1 for behaviors that may indicate advanced cognitive development.

Another way of looking at prevalence is to say that 18 percent of school children are gifted and an additional 2 percent are talented (George, 2003).

Causes of Gifts and Talents

There is debate about the causes of advanced intellectual development. With the information from brain research it is clear that the potential for giftedness is biologically rooted; however, it is also clear that the environment into which one is born shapes not only the child's expression of giftedness, but the brain itself (Shore, 1997). The brain's growth is dynamic. Appropriate stimulation increases the

Table 15–1 Early Identification of Children who are Gifted and Talented

May demonstrate a high level of language development

Asks many specific questions and seriously listens to the answers

Has an unusual capacity for memory and a greater amount of knowledge, which is well organized and accessible

Has a mature and perhaps even subtle sense of humor

Is exceptionally curious intellectually, has a passion for learning

Is interested in cause-effect relationships but may view these relationships differently from adult expectations

Has a long attention span for activities of own choosing, great powers of concentration

Has a high energy level; may be restless in mind and body, intense

Knows many things that peers are unaware of and is aware of issues at a deeper level

Learns in intuitive leaps

Is sensitive to emotional issues at an early age; empathizes, may have concerns about death, anger, love, pain, and so on

Is eager to try new activities and/or perform familiar activities in new ways

May develop a passion for a particular area of interest

May be bored in a classroom designed for typically developing children

Prefers the company of older children and adults

Has an accelerated pace of thought, rapid learning rate, extraordinary speed in processing information

Has a rapid ability to comprehend concepts and whole ideas and to identify the underlying structures and patterns in ideas and relationships

Has the ability to synthesize and think abstractly from a young age

Unevenness in their development may make children vulnerable to social isolation

Source: Clark, 1997; George, 2003; Koshy, 2002.

amount of dendrite branching in the neurons, which in turn increases the child's ability for complex thought and to see interconnections (Yaun & Keating, 2007).

The family a child is born into affects the child in two major ways: Families provide the stimulation that enables children to gain essential knowledge, skills, and mental strategies, and they transmit values and attitudes related to learning and achievement (Jackson, 2003). Biological parents also supply the child's genetic make-up.

Studies have shown some similarities among parents of young children identified as being gifted or talented. The families placed a high value on achieving. The parents introduced the child at an early age to the area in which he eventually excelled, and it was frequently an area in which at least one of the parents had talent. The child's special skills began developing in the context of home activities through informal parent teaching.

Parents were involved in the child's outside activities and made sure that the child practiced. Genes and environments work together in ways that it is almost impossible to disentangle (Jackson, 2003). A young child is precocious in an area, say reading, parents support this and use environmental print as well as reading to the child consistently at a level above what he can read independently.

There are cultural and ethnic differences in the proportion of children who are identified as gifted and talented. This raises contentious question about whether there are gender and racial-ethnic differences in mental ability or whether there are underserved gifted populations (Smutny, 2003).

Early Identification of Gifts and Talents

Unique gifts and talents appear to be a developmental phenomenon. Young children who display these gifts often show both general and unique patterns of strengths. Certainly one of the concerns that many have is the stability of the IQ over time. In general, from about ages 6 or 7 through adulthood stability is the rule rather than the exception (Gottfredson, 2003). Before school age there is more variability. So the question is what is gifted performance in early childhood? Sternberg and Zhang (2001) identified five qualities they consider to be requirements of gifted performance:

1. It must be excellent relative to the performance of same-aged peers or other who have had the same amount of instruction.
2. It must be rare among the same-aged peers.
3. It must be demonstrable or measurable on some reliable and valid assessment.
4. It must be productive or have the potential for productivity.
5. It must have some societal value.

Although initially these may not seem to be applicable to young children, however, if one considers the way a child's behavior can change his environment it becomes more apparent. The infant who talks early and well has dramatically different social opportunities than the infant who does not yet speak. The child who reads independently and fluently at age five has access to very different information than a 5 year old who does not yet read (Jackson, 2003).

Early identification of young intellectually advanced children focuses primarily on early receptive and expressive language development and positive, motivationally relevant behaviors. Identifying children who are gifted and talented is extremely unlikely until close to age three. Current infant intelligence tests do not do a good job of predicting advanced development (Gelbrich, 1998). The area that seems to hold the most promise for prediction is visual attention. When an infant is presented with an interesting visual stimulus the infant attends to it. As this stimulus is repeated and becomes familiar, the amount of attention the infant shows to the stimulus decreases. This decrement is called **habituation**. Infants who habituate faster to a redundant stimulus and recover faster to novel ones show higher scores on intelligence tests (Gelbrich, 1998).

Because children are gifted or talented does not necessarily mean that their growth or development at young ages is different from other children. However, because of *uneven* development, young children especially may appear to have deficits when in reality they are developing physically at a normal pace but not at the same pace as their intellectual development or their particular configuration of gifts and talents. Young children with exceptional intellectual resources may have a greater than average need for emotional, social, and other nonintellectual capabilities to successfully cope.

We know very little about the developmental course of giftedness until children have actually displayed these characteristics and we consequently identify them. The Fullerton longitudinal study is an exception; it chose a large sample of healthy 1 year olds. Some of the children at later ages were identified as gifted, while others were not. Hence, the study was in a good position to make comparisons between the two groups (Gottfried, Gottfried, Bathurst, & Guerin, 1994).

Verbal skills is one area where developmental differences are likely to be most apparent. The Fullerton longitudinal growth study found significant differences between gifted and nongifted children in receptive language at age 1, and differences in both receptive and expressive language were consistent from infancy onward. These were the major differences found in the early years; some questioned whether the high scores in the language area accounted for the differences in intellectual performance that were found at 18 months and continued (Gottfried et al., 1994).

The rate of development of children with advanced intellectual development is different during this period. That is, their particular pattern of gifts and talents develops more rapidly than nongifted children. Very young gifted children also appeared to be different in the testing situation itself. They showed "significantly greater goal directedness, object orientation, attention span, cooperativeness, positive emotional tone, and responsiveness to test materials" (Gottfried et al., 1994, p. 105). These characteristics are relevant to motivation and might be considered gifted motivational behaviors and be used as one means of identifying young gifted learners. Other indicators include great attentiveness, ability to concentrate,

intense interest and curiosity, and delight in the unexpected (George, 2003). Overall, however, the present research on identifying giftedness in children birth to 3 is incomplete and inconclusive, but promising. Interestingly, although there is a strong belief that young children with disabilities should be identified early and that early intervention is effective, this belief has rarely been applied to gifted and talented children. Sankar-DeLeeuw (1999) found that only half of the primary teachers responding to the survey thought that children should be identified during the early years of school. See Table 15–1 for characteristics of young gifted children.

Young children may just hint at the potential for exceptional skill that is confirmed during the preschool years. Language proficiency is still a key. Gifted children have large vocabularies that they use accurately, and they typically speak in entire sentences. Children who read before attending school are often thought to be intellectually advanced. Although parents may claim that this "just happened," that they didn't teach the child, in reality no one (adult or child) can learn to read without instruction. Children cannot teach themselves to read. Someone must draw the child's attention to the particular features and associations that reading requires. Young readers have invariably spent a good deal of time being read to by an older child or adult who has informally taught the child. They like books (Jackson, 2003).

They may also have an early interest in and proficiency in drawing, music, or other art forms. They seem to be observant and retain information they learn. They also seem to be able to concentrate for long periods of time. Many have a keen sense of humor. They are also interested in how things work and in cause-effect relationships (George, 2003).

In general, children with advanced cognitive development have physical development that is ahead of same-age children with lower IQs, but this may be due to social class differences more than any other variable (Freeman, 1985). Their coordination seems similar to their age mates. To the extent that very gifted children are accelerated in school (for example, starting first grade at age 4), their physical development may appear slower because the comparison group is actually a year or two older. Relating to others in an appropriate way is often difficult, as the child can feel (and is) different. Additionally, their tendency to choose older children as friends focuses attention on their relatively immature physical development (Gottfried et al., 1994). These differences often increase their probability of choosing noncompetitive types of physical activities.

Overall, the behavioral and emotional adjustment of children with advanced cognitive development is not distinguishable during early childhood (Gottfried et al., 1994). Advantages in the cognitive realm are not associated with disadvantages in other areas of development, although some display superior social reasoning (but not necessarily superior social behavior) and adaptive functioning.

There is a great deal of interest in the interaction of these young children with their family and family environment. Research findings in this area have been consistent since the 1920s. Gifted children are predominantly firstborn or only children. Most children with advanced intellectual development have been in consistently stimulating environments from infancy through their early elementary years (George, 2003). Their environments respond to the child's demands by providing early culturally and intellectually stimulating activities. Their families are able to provide stimulating environments in part because the families are typically high socioeconomic status, with highly educated parents. Parents are typically involved, responsive, and nurturing and have high educational aspirations for their children (George, 2003).

Children identified as having advanced intellectual development are significantly more likely to enter school at an earlier age and are not likely to be retained at any grade level through age 8 (Gottfried et al., 1994). Their teachers characterize them as working harder, learning more, and being better behaved than their nongifted counterparts. In general, they are more adapted to the demands of school. Terman (cited in Gottfried et al., 1994) found that at age 7, children identified as gifted and talented were reading an average of seven books per month, whereas nongifted children read very little. Being extensively read to in the early years is consistently associated with advanced intellectual development. Academically, these children excel and frequently skip grades during these years or are placed early into kindergarten or first grade.

As children move more clearly into the academic world, some who were not previously identified will be noted. It is not just what they do, but how they go about doing it. Gifted children seem to grasp the essence of the problem or situation or can relate the situation to an analogous one. They may skip steps in the process or are intrigued by finding alternative solutions. Again, their persistence, high ideals, self-discipline, and independence are noted (George, 2003).

Children with advanced cognitive development can be more difficult because they do not fit the norm. They are often highly curious, beyond just being interested in things. They are interested in details and ask many questions. They have a broader knowledge base than their peers and may become bored, especially during group instruction. They may be intense and highly critical, argumentative. They work with information by manipulating it, as opposed to just remembering it. They like mysteries and complexities and enjoy learning. They may have unusual or silly ideas and make keen observations. They often prefer the company of adults or older peers (George, 2003).

They may seem to be more emotionally stable, but they are not invulnerable to life circumstances. They may feel that they are different from others but are not completely aware of the cause of the differences; they may feel superior because they are "smart." They may have fewer skills in peer relationships but deal well with and prefer adults.

In the Field

My daughter, Gayle, was identified as gifted at the end of second grade. While we were initially very excited and proud, it turned out that having this label would eventually do Gayle more harm than good.

At first Gayle was very happy to be able to attend a Talented and Gifted program in school. She did very well. However, soon she would come home upset because she couldn't solve the program's daily logic problems. Gayle really felt bad that she couldn't seem to do these while the other students could. I felt she simply didn't understand what these "puzzles" were. I didn't worry about it because she did well in the rest of the TAG program, and she did well in school generally.

Soon, I got a call from the TAG teacher who told me she didn't think Gayle was ready for the program. She also mentioned the logic problems, which were a daily part of the program. I couldn't believe they were removing my daughter from TAG simply because she didn't get some puzzle. My daughter was well rounded; she played sports while also performing well on report cards and standardized tests. She was even on the school's math team. But, in the end, Gayle was removed from TAG.

I feel this hurt Gayle's self-esteem. She wondered why she wasn't smart enough to stay in TAG. She began to doubt herself in the regular classroom. She would bring home her math homework and cry because she couldn't do it. She dropped off the math team. She also cried occasionally in class when she would answer a question incorrectly. Today, I believe that TAG simply isn't for every child. I am sure TAG helps some gifted children. But, other children are gifted in ways that one program, in itself, can't identify.

Reflective Practice

What do you think went wrong in this scenario? Was Gayle not gifted or was there a problem with the program? What could you have done to intervene?

Assessment of Gifts and Talents

Some feel that high intelligence alone is not enough, that giftedness is an interaction among above-average ability, creativity, and sustained interest. Currently, we are moving away from using IQ as the only method of identifying giftedness, just as we are moving away from it as the only way of identifying children with intellectual disabilities to the concept that there are multiple talents or intelligences (George, 2003).

A more global definition of giftedness opens the door for a variety of specific areas in which unique talents might be displayed. Despite broadening of the definition, the most frequently used means of identifying gifted children is intelligence tests: *Stanford-Binet Intelligence Scale* (5th ed Roid, 2003), *Wechsler Preschool and Primary Scale of Intelligence–III* (WPPSI–III; Psychological Corporation, 2002), or the *Wechsler Intelligence Scale for Children IV* (WISC-IV; Wechsler, 2003), where they would exhibit an IQ of approximately 125 or 130 or higher. Some professionals prefer older versions of the Stanford-Binet because its construction allowed children who were gifted to not hit the ceiling of the test before they ran out of items.

Because of a lack of uniformity, state and local definitions of children who qualify as gifted and talented vary. How these terms are defined determines who is included or excluded. It is one of the most controversial areas of education, and a difficult one. Depending on the definition and method of testing, children with special needs can be included or excluded from this group.

Labels of all kinds are misleading and infer that children can be neatly divided into groups. This applies to children identified as having gifts and talents as well as those with intellectual disabilities. Generally speaking, these labels suggest variations along a continuum we refer to as intelligence. All agree that individuals vary in abilities. It is the arbitrariness with which we divide up the continuum and label individuals that is of concern. This is particularly true when we label young children as either "slow" or "fast" and use this label to project future achievement or lack thereof. In general, we look at children's present level of functioning as a prediction of future abilities. In cases where there are major changes in a child's life, we cannot accurately predict future progress.

As in other areas, there is general consensus that multimodal testing is necessary to identify children who are gifted and talented. Most recommend a combination of testing (intelligence, achievement, creativity), observations of parents and teachers, work samples, a portfolio, and so on. A professionally administered individual intelligence test is traditionally part of the battery. These measures are well designed, normed, and validated. They allow for observations by a well-trained examiner. It is useful to look not only at the total score, but at the profile. For children who achieve an IQ of 145 with particular strength in verbal and quantitative reasoning, early school entrance might be considered.

An IQ score reflects what a child has already learned and hence is a "static" approach to assessment. Another view of assessment tries to assess problem-solving ability, the interactive "dynamic" quality of learning potential. Vygotsky's (1934/1987) theory and methodology focuses not on what children can do independently but on what they can do with adult support or scaffolding. He labels this their zone of proximal development (ZPD). To use the ZPD as an assessment paradigm, children are presented a series of analogous problem-solving tasks that they cannot solve independently. The child is asked to solve the first task but is told that assistance will be available. An adult then provides hints, suggestions, and repeated trials necessary for the child to solve the problem. Once the child has mastered the problem-solving strategies, he is presented with similar and increasingly difficult problem-solving tasks. The evaluation then focuses on the child's ability to generalize and adapt the problem-solving strategy. The less help the child needs on the more difficult tasks, the broader the child's ZPD. Children with higher ability have broader ZPDs (Kanevsky, 1992).

Because of concern with the under identification of children from minority groups, those with disabilities, and less affluent families, measures such as portfolios are being used in the identification process (Kingore, 1998). In some classrooms, portfolio assessment is used with all children.

A portfolio is a collection of the child's work selected by the child (with younger children, and at the beginning of the year, there is more teacher input). These artifacts provide information about the child's attitudes, motivation, level of development, and growth over time (Kingore, 1998). The portfolio also provides important information for individualizing planning for children and conferencing with parents. Portfolios are useful for assessment for a variety of reasons, including the following:

- Portfolios must be child-driven.
- Portfolios involve a process of *collecting, selecting*, and *reflecting*. Teachers provide the guidelines for selecting ("Something you have done very well."). Children then reflect on their choice and add an artifact to that part of the portfolio. Children can dictate their reflections, write, or word process them with the understanding that creative spelling is acceptable. If children want to choose three-dimensional creations then children or teachers can photograph the artifact (ideally with a digital camera when the child can choose the appropriate view and perspective). Again, the child reflects on her choices.
- If the process of portfolio assessment is new, begin small and keep it simple.

Gardner's (1983, 1993) work on multiple intelligences has raised questions about intelligence itself and how we assess it. For many years the assessment of intelligence has been based on the assumption that there is a single "g" factor as espoused by Charles Spearman (1863–1945). Tests such as the Stanford-Binet were based on this premise. About the middle of the century David Wechsler (1896–1981) successfully proposed that there were two abilities underlying intelligence: verbal and performance. The Wechsler intelligence tests reflect these areas (2002, 2003). The latest revision of the Stanford-Binet also acknowledges at least two aspects of intelligence as it measures verbal and nonverbal abilities as separate subscales (Roid, 2003).

Acceptance of Gardner's multiple intelligences would require major changes in assessment processes. Some feel that a multiple intelligences approach to the identification of children with gifts and talents would increase the number of poor children, children from ethnic minorities, and children with disabilities who would be identified (George, 2003). They also feel that the information gleaned from the assessment process could serve to guide curriculum.

Multiple Intelligences

In some children, the potential for advanced cognitive development is identified early; in others, it is only apparent later in their development. Tests assume that children have had the same opportunity to learn. When this is not true the tests may be biased. Many children who come from lower socioeconomic-status homes or are English language learners may not be identified as gifted because they have not had the same learning opportunities as others. Likewise, children from different cultural backgrounds as well as those with disabilities are more difficult to identify. Tests that focus on divergent thinking and creativity have the potential for identifying some of these children (George, 2003). Talented students are those with a potential to exhibit superior performance in one area of endeavor (George, 1997). Gardner (1993) initially proposed seven intelligences where special talents may exist, and another one has been added. All children have a unique blend of these intelligences: talented children are especially advanced in one intelligence area.

The characteristics for multiple intelligences were gleaned from the following authors: Fisher (1998); Gardner (1983, 1993); George (1997, 2003); Goleman (1995);

Some young children are intrigued with language. They are interested in reading, have a large vocabulary, and are fascinated with writing.

Pierangelo and Giuliani (2001); Koshy (2002); Porter (1999); Reyes-Carrasquillo (2000); and Saunders and Espeland (1991).

Verbal-Linguistic Intelligence

Verbal-linguistic intelligence refers to the ability to appreciate and use language with sensitivity and clarity. Children appreciate the order, meanings and rhythm of words. Decoding words and the rules of grammar is often a game. They like to invent new languages and play with words. They have extensive vocabularies and like to communicate. These children

- speak and read early.
- have accelerated literacy skills in stories, poems, drama, and writing.
- use advanced vocabulary.
- employ longer and more advanced sentence structures (use words like *however* and *although*).
- make up elaborate, coherent stories and fantasies.
- describe experiences with unusual depth and accuracy.
- memorize and recite stories and poems.
- prefer books with more words and plot than pictures.
- may be bilingual or interested in learning a second language.
- are interested in language in its many forms.

Logical-Mathematical Intelligence

Logical-mathematical intelligence is characterized by scientific reasoning, a love for abstraction, and an interest in mathematical operations. Children use logic, deduction, reasoning, and are good problem solvers. They are interested in categorizing, hypothesizing, experimenting, and developing arguments. They are interested in graphing, counting, and manipulating numbers. They are fascinated by how things work. Young children talented in logic and mathematics:

- use advanced arithmetic skills.
- use highly original reasoning.
- ask a series of logical questions focused on solving a problem.
- apply reason to solve concrete and abstract problems.
- enjoy using hands-on tools such as Cuisenaire™ rods, Uniflex™ cubes, blocks, puzzles, and an abacus to solve logical-mathematical problems.
- enjoy computer games and applications related to logical-mathematical reasoning.

Musical-Rhythmic Intelligence

Musical-rhythmic intelligence refers to the ability to use musical elements (pitch, timbre, rhythm, timing, and tone) at an unusually sophisticated level. Some children may have perfect pitch and the ability to identify a wide range of musical scores when only a few bars are played. They enjoy creating and listening to music. Musically talented children are intrigued with and notice sounds in their environment. Musically talented young children:

- are highly motivated to practice and perform music.
- enjoy and frequently request music-related activities.
- respond emotionally to music even without clues from lyrics (might report that certain music makes them happy).
- can identify familiar songs by hearing the tune.
- sing in tune or close to it and can match pitch within their range.
- may sing to themselves and have good pitch.
- can identify the sounds of a particular instrument.
- prefer poems with sound and rhythm over narrative stories.
- dance, move, and clap in time with musical patterns and rhythms.
- have an excellent memory for melodies, music, and musical scores.
- show skill in reading music, singing complex songs, or playing difficult passages.
- are interested in composing music.

Visual-Spatial Intelligence

Visual-spatial intelligence is the ability to perceive the visual world accurately and then recreate that visual experience in art or graphics. It involves mental imagery and the ability to manipulate and transform images. These children are adept at puzzles and other spatial problem-solving activities. Visually talented young children:

- show advanced drawing, painting, and sculpting with both technical skill and fine detail.
- remember in detail items, places, and pictures they have seen.
- have advanced eye-hand coordination.
- show attention to texture, color, and balance.
- respond emotionally to photos, paintings, or sculpture.
- share feelings and moods through drawing, painting, or sculpture.

Psychomotor-Kinesthetic Intelligence

Psychomotor-kinesthetic intelligence refers to the ability to control one's body or body parts skillfully. These children move expressively (as in dance) and are good at both informal and organized games and sports. Young children with psychomotor talent:

- are skillful at movements such as running, jumping, climbing, dancing, and other movement activities.
- have an accurate and relaxed sense of both static and dynamic balance (hopping on one foot, walking a narrow line, balancing a beanbag).
- use gestures, body movements, and/or facial expression to show or mimic emotions and ideas.
- can adapt motor skills in game situations.

Intrapersonal Intelligence

Intrapersonal intelligence is the ability to form an accurate model of oneself and use this model effectively to evaluate situations. It involves detecting and distinguishing feelings. These children understand themselves well and know their own strengths and weaknesses. Young children with intrapersonal intelligence:

- are aware of their needs, problems, and emotional state and can identify their emotions.
- can express their perceptions and understandings through speaking and writing.
- can understand the cause of feelings.
- can recognize the difference between feelings and actions.

Interpersonal Intelligence

Interpersonal intelligence focuses on the ability to recognize and distinguish the moods, intentions, and motivations of other individuals. These children often emerge as effective leaders and organizers. They are empathetic and sensitive to the needs and desires of others. Young children with interpersonal talent:

- interact easily with both children and adults.
- are sought out by other children for play.
- are able to enter an already-playing group of children and be accepted.
- can influence other children toward their goals (positive or negative).
- understand cause-and-effect as it relates to behavior and consequences.
- recognize when their behavior yields certain predictable results.
- can take another child's perspective.
- are better at resolving conflicts and negotiating disagreements.
- can motivate and organize peers toward their goals (positive or negative).
- have strong leadership abilities.
- have a sense of justice and fair play for themselves and others.

Naturalist Intelligence

Naturalist intelligence is the ability to discriminate among living things (plants and animals) as well as other features of the natural world such as clouds and rock formations.

In the past this ability had great survival value. It involves a kind of pattern recognition that is valued in certain sciences. Today this ability may enable individuals to discriminate among makes and models of cars or even sneakers. Young children with naturalist intelligence:

- are interested in pets and concerned about their care.
- are curious about nature and look for and collect plants, bugs, rocks, or other natural objects.
- are interested in identifying plants and gardening.
- enjoy the outdoors and outdoor activities such as hiking, camping, and fishing.
- are curious about the human body and the way it works.
- may enjoy cooking.
- are interested in electricity and magnets and the way things work.

Other Intelligences

Gardner and his colleagues are exploring the possibility of additional intelligences including existential intelligence which is the ability to reflect on the philosophical questions about life and death.

Children with Gifts, Talents, and Special Needs

Definitions of giftedness typically involve at least two processes: a large information base and the cognitive processing skills needed to assemble, control, and execute this information (Wingenbach, 1998). That is, gifted children are aware of the knowledge they possess and know how to process that information efficiently. Additionally, they can communicate this information well in speaking and writing. They have good problem-solving skills and creative ideas.

Children with specific learning disabilities may have significant difficulties in learning to read and expressing their ideas in writing. They may show significant weaknesses in organization and in processing input. "They are not 'slow-thinkers' they are 'slow-receivers'" (Peer, 2000, p. 69). They may also have difficulty with short-term memory. These characteristics make it challenging to identify the gifted child with a specific learning disability. Further confounding identification is that these children use their strengths to compensate for their limitations. Hence, they may appear to be average learners with neither the giftedness nor the learning disability identified. The National Education Association (2006) refers to this as the twice-exceptional dilemma. They estimate that of the 6 million students aged 6 to 21 who received educational services under the IDEA in 2000–2001 school year that approximately 6 percent of these children are also academically gifted and need these unique learning needs met.

Children with specific learning disabilities and other disabilities may feel stressed as they becomes aware of the differences between their level of thinking and their ability to show others what they can do. If identified as having a specific learning disability, the focus typically moves to remediation—a focus on the deficits rather than an overall picture of the child. The academic emphasis becomes a multisensory approach to teach reading, spelling, grammar, and perhaps math. This approach "requires regular, detailed teaching, review, practice and overlearning" (Peer, 2000, p. 71). The approach is often successful in increasing the skill level of the child, but does not address the area of giftedness and, if not creatively done, may turn off the gifted learner. The child's areas of strength may not be identified and hence alternative modes of processing information are not encouraged. A strengths-based approach presents material at a high academic level in a way that is accessible to the child while at the same time spending time working on areas of deficit. However, the emphasis is not on the deficit, but rather on ways to compensate. For children with dyslexia, technology can play a key role. Computers can read to those who need it, and word process to meet the needs of others (Peer, 2000).

Children with behavioral and emotional problems present another challenge. These problems interfere with concentration, motivation, and task completion resulting in underachievement. In some cases these factors can be compounded with families who do not know the educational system well nor do they value it. Teachers may become so focused on the behavior that their expectations for the child are low and they are critical of the child. Parent-teacher relations may not be positive (Lee-Corbin & Denicolo, 1998). These problems are complex and may require therapy and medication as well as educational interventions. The focus is on finding educational tasks that the child is motivated to do using his strengths.

For children with physical and sensory disabilities the challenge involves removing the physical barriers of the disability to the greatest extent possible by using adaptive technology and focusing on the child's strengths (Sanders, 1998).

Culturally Diverse Children with Gifts and Talents

Public schools can be daunting places for both children and parents, especially those with limited English. Parents may not be aware of the opportunities for their children to participate in programs for the gifted and talented and

Using multiple intelligences may help identify culturally diverse children with gifts and talents. Having volunteer grandparents in the classroom may provide a way of enriching the environment.

children may be working so hard learning English that their other gifts and talents are overlooked. Children with limited English proficiency are underrepresented among children who are identified as gifted and talented. A variety of factors contribute to this problem. Certainly one factor is the assessment process itself. In addition to the obvious language-related issues, culture plays an important role in deciding which skills are valued. No tests are culture free. To the extent that a culture values social skills and nonverbal abilities over cognitive skills and verbal abilities, children from this culture are less likely to be identified as gifted and talented in the United States. Identification processes that use a broader definition of intelligence such as Gardner's (1983, 1993) multiple intelligences are more likely to identify gifted children. Embedding cultural factors in the specific ways in which gifts and talents are expressed may also help identify some children (Lopez, 2000). Using multiple referral sources (teachers, parents, and peers) and multiple measures of intelligence and creativity, formal and informal, increases the probability of identifying children. Teachers tend to see white children more positively and are less likely to refer African American and Hispanic children for gifted programs than white children. The difference is statistically significant and close to a full standard deviation (Tenenbaum & Ruck, 2007). Teachers and other school personnel may need training in cultural diversity to better understand the beliefs that underlie what is valued in different cultures (Fletcher & Massalski, 2003).

The Evidence Base

Mentoring Mathematical Minds (Project M³) is a project designed at the University of Connecticut to identify children in grades 3 through 5 who are capable of handling advanced mathematical concepts. They have broadened the selection process to use more than IQ scores. They selected children based on nonverbal math ability including such things as spatial sense and reasoning as well as teacher recommendations. This was done to increase the number of black and Hispanic children included in the program. The project teaches math concepts several years beyond grade level standards (O'Neil, 2006). Early results show promise. Children have made significant gains on standardized math tests compared to control groups and lower-income children have made the greatest gains. They also did well in the district level math assessments (O'Neil, 2006).

Other researchers, Briggs, Reis, and Sullivan (2008) identified five categories that contributed to the successful identification of culturally, linguistically, and ethnically diverse, and high-poverty children who could profit from gifted and talented programs. They include modified identification procedures and program support systems such as identifying high-potential children and providing advanced work prior to identification, selecting curriculum designs that support children from culturally, linguistically, ethnically diverse groups, and those who live in poverty to succeed, building home-school partnerships and using program evaluation practices that highlight student success (Briggs, Reis, & Sullivan, 2008; O'Neil, 2006).

Reflective Practice

Teacher identification plays a strong role in deciding who gets into programs for the gifted and talented. Reflect on the characteristics of children who are gifted and talented. How might these characteristics be different for children from different cultures and ethnic groups? How might you change your ideas if they did not include children from these groups?

Implications for Educators

Loyalty may confound identification. To the extent that the child feels she must emulate the majority culture when its standards and values are different from those of her family and culture, the child may suffer a conflict of identity. If the child moves in the direction of the majority culture to achieve success, she may begin to feel that she does not belong anywhere. She is "too Brazilian to be American and too American to be Brazilian." She may feel that she is not accepted at home or at school. If a child is singled out for her individual achievement in cultural groups that value affiliation, she may feel isolated and rejected (Bailey, 2000).

Using noncompetitive activities, some group work, and privately supporting children may help. Also, lending support to children who span more than one culture, helping them understand what behaviors are acceptable in particular social-cultural situations, may assist children and help them build positive relationships with gifted children from other cultures, whether or not they have been identified as gifted (Bailey, 2000). Teaching all children social-emotional skills and knowledge of other cultures may need to be included in curriculum at all levels (Goleman, 1995). Working with therapists or school counselors may help some children. A more individualized selection of books for certain children may prove useful as a springboard for discussion. Mentors from a child's culture may provide the child with both emotional support and a role model. As children increase in age, the computer can help children learn at their own pace, one based on individual ability and interest, while providing relative anonymity.

Instructional Strategies

A variety of strategies are used to meet the needs of children with gifts and talents. As with other diverse abilities, professionals support different positions. Some feel that children with gifts and talents should be included in the regular classroom to the maximum degree possible and that teachers of gifted and talented children should support regular teachers in providing an appropriate learning environment for these children. The key issue here is whether regular classroom teachers can provide an exciting and stimulating environment for children who can achieve at 3, 4, or 5 years or grade levels beyond their peers (a similar issue to what we face with children with intellectual disabilities). The record from the past in this regard is discouraging. If this *can* be done, it doesn't appear to have been done well, and some feel that

separation, especially with increasing age, is desirable. (If regular classrooms could be designed to meet the needs of all children, including gifted children, then all children would profit.) However, we do not seem to be doing that well. Although colleges and universities increasingly are requiring education students to take courses on teaching children with disabilities, few require such courses for the gifted and talented.

There are three main modifications that are used in early education to accommodate gifted learners: accelerating the pace of instruction; enrichment; which refers to a broader, more varied educational experience; or extension, which is a deepening of the curriculum (Porter, 1999). Enrichment and extension may be done together.

Acceleration

The assumption underlying acceleration is that some children learn at a consistently faster pace than others. As curriculum becomes more rigid, there is the potential for a mismatch between children's abilities and the subject matter presented. **Acceleration** is a process of moving through an educational program at a faster rate than usual or at a younger age.

Because of the range and types of acceleration options, it is difficult to be for or against them. Advocates for acceleration argue that it provides increased efficiency and effectiveness of instruction. They see it as providing bright students with appropriate educational opportunities and continuing challenges that will maintain their enthusiasm and excitement for learning. Some see it as a necessary first step in meeting the needs of gifted children (VanTassel-Baska & Stambaugh, 2006). Those opposed to acceleration are concerned about possible gaps in general knowledge. They are also concerned that children who show academic excellence at young ages may not maintain these advantages, that the accelerated demands may be too great for the young child's experience and sophistication. That is, the programming is not developmentally appropriate and children do not have enough time to play, indoors or outside. There is some concern about later social maladjustment as students reflect on lost opportunities. Some are worried about the effect of acceleration on emotional adjustment, with concern about friendship patterns, increased pressure, and lack of outlets for expression, as well as reduced opportunities for extracurricular activities. In a survey study of primary teachers only 7 percent supported the early school entrance of gifted children (Sankar-DeLeeuw, 1999). However, longitudinal studies continue to show positive results in cognitive development from acceleration and no negative impact on social and emotional development (Colangelo, Assouline, & Gross, 2004).

There are many different types of acceleration. Children can be admitted to kindergarten prior to the age specified. They can skip a grade. They can be placed in classes where two or more grade levels are combined. They can have subject or contents matter acceleration, that is, be placed at a more advanced grade level for one or more subjects (e.g., a kindergartner going to first grade for reading and math) (VanTassel-Baska & Stambaugh, 2006).

For children identified as having gifts and talents during the preschool years, certainly the most frequent option is early admission to kindergarten. This is viewed as the least-disruptive option for children who are intellectually advanced and within 6 months of the usual entry age (Koshy, 2002). Studies show that children who were *selected* for early school entrance, were within a year of the school-entrance age, and were considered mature for their age have performed well. Some feel that acceleration itself is not enough and that an enriched curriculum must be offered as well (Feldhusen, Van Winkle, & Ehle, 1996). When early school entrance is seen as the most appropriate way to provide acceleration, the following areas should be considered:

- Is the school willing to accept the child?
- Is the classroom flexibly structured and the teacher willing to include the child?
- Will any learning gaps be filled?
- Does the child have the necessary fine motor skills?
- Does the child have the prerequisite reading readiness skills?
- Does the child want to go to school?
  Do the parents want the child to go to school?
- Is the child comfortable being one of the youngest children?
- Is the child socially and emotionally ready for school?
- Is the child average or large for this age?
- Has the child had previous experience in school settings? (Braggett, 1992; George, 2003; Koshy, 2002; Porter, 1999).

At times, rather than accelerating a particular child, small groups of gifted children may be placed together.

Cluster Grouping

Cluster grouping involves placing a small group of identified children together in a classroom. By placing these children together they are included in the classroom but have the opportunity to do more complex learning as a group (Winebrenner & Devlin, 1998). They can support each other as they learn. This has the potential of meeting the learning needs of this group of children while they are in the regular classroom. This is not designed to replace other programs but a way of ensuring that gifted children get their learning needs met. Depending upon the size of the school, clusters can be of all eligible children or they can be based upon a concept such as Gardner's multiple intelligences.

Teachers of cluster groups work at both compacting the regular curriculum and differentiating it. Enrichment minicourses can help children investigate topics of interest to them. As with all children, the learning cycle begins with exploratory activities and hands-on work. All children are empowered when topics are designed around their interests. As a community of learners they can develop critical thinking skills, new knowledge, and the ability to work as a team (Schlichter et al., 1997).

In the Field

As a second-grade teacher in an inclusive program, I have struggled to provide quality extension activities for gifted and talented children in my room. Even though I tried to enrich instruction for the children with advanced

development, I felt as if I wasn't providing them with quite enough "push." I eventually came up with a system that worked.

I decided to add more centers to my program. I added a center that would be especially appropriate for children with advanced development. At the same time, children could receive more individualized instruction with the para-educators to help reinforce skills or teach unique concepts.

I assigned a learning activity to all the children in my classroom, but changed the activity slightly for different levels of children. For example, if the class was studying fruit, I would group students homogeneously and assign them to an appropriate activity. Everyone would be studying fruit, yet at a level that was appropriate. This allowed children with disabilities and children with advanced development to all work on the same topic while learning at the level each needed. I feel that through careful planning and reflection, I have improved instruction for not only children with advanced development, but also for all of my students. I just wish I felt as confident in this area as I do when I plan for the children with disabilities.

Reflective Practice

Do you feel prepared to teach children who are gifted and talented? Are you comfortable with your ability to extend and expand learning? If not, how do you plan to increase your skills?

Differentiated Teaching

Curriculum that is differentiated for each child builds on past achievements, presents challenges that allow for additional achievements, provides opportunities for success, and removes barriers to participation (George, 2003). Like universal design this system involves devising tasks that are appropriate for a range of abilities. It does not require labeling children; it does require meeting individual children's needs. Overall, the goal is to raise the achievement of all children and to ensure that all children do their personal best performance (George, 2003).

There is no single strategy for differentiation; rather, it is an approach across subject matter areas. For children who are gifted, it involves broadening the curriculum to include information that is not traditionally part of the curriculum at a particular level. George (2003) suggests that one consider the following factors before choosing a method of differentiation:

- Is the method flexible enough for children to develop at their own pace?
- Does the method support the acquisition of higher-order thinking skills?
- Is the method both intellectually stimulating and emotionally protected?
- Is the method likely to alienate a child from peers or provide information that will be repeated later?
- Does it foster teamwork or individual differences?

For children with gifts and talents many aspects of their curriculum are differentiated with enrichment of the general curriculum. Many enrichment programs use a model that increases awareness of higher-order thinking skills. Bloom's (1985) taxonomy, for example, moves from lower-level to higher-level thinking skills: knowledge, comprehension, application, analysis, synthesis, evaluation. The goal is to go beyond comprehension to ensure that children have the opportunity to use higher-level thinking skills. That is, it is not enough that a 5 year old can name several different dinosaurs (knowledge) or make a chart showing the different sizes of dinosaurs (comprehension) or even compare those who are carnivores to those who are not (application). Children who are gifted and talented need to be challenged to predict what might have happened if dinosaurs had not become extinct (analysis), write a play about life when dinosaurs lived (synthesis), or debate theories of causes for dinosaurs having become extinct (evaluation).

Other methods of adding depth to the curriculum include the design of in-depth integrated units. Units for gifted and talented children profit from an overarching theme around which long-term study can be organized. Longer units and fewer of them allow greater depth. Obviously, these themes must be chosen carefully; some considerations include:

- importance of topic and sufficient depth and breadth
- application to other learning areas
- assumptions about prior knowledge
- inclusive gender, cultural, and ethnic awareness
- outcomes in terms of products and process
- assessment and evaluation (Walker, Hafenstein, & Crow-Enslow, 1999)

Partnering with Families

Parents play a crucial role in the life and education of all children. They are their child's first and ongoing teachers, and they are vital sources of information and support. They are an invaluable resource for understanding their children. They are role models for their children. It is important that parents are empowered with knowledge, skills, and resources to support their developmentally advanced child (Moon, 2003). Teachers and families need to work collaboratively to support children's education. This is particularly true when parents have limited English and there is the possibility that the child moves into a miniature adult status because of advanced verbal skills. Gifted children need parents and parents need the support of teachers as they make decisions about their child's education so that these decisions are congruent with the family's values and the child's abilities (Moon, 2003).

The general principles of good parenting apply to parents of children who are gifted and talented. However, the challenges to parents make this problematic. Children with advanced language skills can challenge parents on issues of independence and control at an early age. Their reasoning and problem solving may place them in situations they do not have the maturity to cope with. Their advanced development in one area can foster inappropriate expectations in other areas and frustrate both children and parents.

Implications for Educators

During the early years encourage parents to devote time and energy to language, to helping their children use their imaginations, and by reading stories interactively

Children who are gifted and talented may want to use real equipment such as fishing rods, not those designed for children.

and discussing them with their children. Support parents in learning about the educational system and how it works. A positive parent-teacher relationship models parental respect for the educational system. It is a way of showing that parents openly value education and learning. Every day parents must walk a fine line between high expectations and putting so much pressure on a child that he feels like a failure even when he succeeds. This is particularly difficult when children's development is uneven and the expectation generalizes so that children are expected to do well at everything, even tasks that do not interest them or they are incapable of performing.

- Develop a regular method of communicating with parents. This can be through short conversations when children are picked up or dropped off, telephone calls, or email.
- Keep parents informed about the units and themes in your classrooms. If there is an appropriate community component tell all parents about it.
- Encourage parents to initiate communication if their child does not want to come to school or appears bored and uninterested in school or seems to be unusually stressed.
- Provide parents with a list of children's books and other materials that are developmentally appropriate yet academically challenging for their child.
- Provide parents with resources for themselves as parents to better understand the challenges in raising a gifted child.

Guidelines

Children who are gifted and talented need your help in stretching and adapting the curriculum to include and challenge them. Use your creativity to make variations on activities and to increase the cognitive demands while at the same time ensuring these children are part of the group. Emphasize similarities and differences in all children without making value judgments. Value all strengths while at the same time identifying challenges.

1. *Use open-ended activities*. Plan some activities that will take several weeks and that can go in many

directions. Ensure that what children start can remain in place until the activity has ended. It often takes more than 1 day to increase complexity.

2. *Develop independent work habits.* Don't equate independence with isolation. Use those independent work skills at home. Children come to school to learn with and about other children. Your challenge is to plan activities with a range of difficulty that allows all the children in the class to participate and learn at their particular ability level.

3. *Teach socially acceptable ways of dealing with emotions.* Many times children are frustrated if they know they are different and learn things more quickly or what they can do does not keep pace with their understanding.

4. *Provide variety and depth.* Activities and experiences that allow children to explore and find areas of interest are essential, but also allow children to concentrate their energy in one area to a depth that satisfies them.

5. *Require divergent thinking.* Provide children with activities that require divergent thinking; have them think about things they take for granted not happening such as if the earth stopped turning, rain didn't fall or didn't quit falling, and so on.

6. *Emphasize both how and why something occurs.* Go beyond what is happening to help children focus on why and to ponder how to make things happen differently.

7. *Emphasize group and individual problem solving.* Learning to work in groups is an important aspect of problem-based learning. All children need the skills to participate in group problem solving as well as individual problem solving and to even reflect on the differences.

8. *Encourage higher-level thinking skills.* Go beyond knowledge and comprehension to emphasize analysis, synthesis, evaluation, and problem solving.

9. *Use less repetition and a faster pace.* Give children important problems to solve.

10. *Offer a high degree of complexity.* Add number and variety in materials, process, and outcome.

11. *Promote intellectual risk-taking.* Support creativity and divergent thinking.

12. *Support different learning styles*: Allow students to choose and use different learning modalities to complete assignments.

There are many ways of encouraging creativity. The easiest is to tell children to be creative—obvious, yet it does work.

1. *Regard creativity as a process.* Initially do not emphasize outcomes. Encourage different ways of doing things, regardless of the results (which may look far worse than another child's more traditional product).

2. *Value creative achievement in comparison to a personal norm, not a universal one.* If a product or process is new for a child, it is creative for that child, whether or not society would see it in that light. On the other hand if a child can use materials well and is not doing so do not reward the behavior rather question it.

3. *Reward creativity.* Verbally support children who comes up with new ideas. Ask about how things could work in different ways.

4. *Encourage children to ask questions and to explore materials.* Provide new and varied materials to peak children's interest.

5. *Ask questions that stimulate creative thinking.* Here are some useful questions:

What do you think about. . . . . ?

What (who) do you see of interest?

What can you say about this?

Is there anything here worth thinking about?

Do you have any ideas?

Does this remind you of anything?

What ground rules do we need to set up?

Does this stretch your brain a little or a lot?

Does this look (sound, feel) interesting?

What else can you make out of this?

What would you like to rearrange?

Do you see any other possibilities?

What can we do with this? What else?

Can you see some place to start?

Can you find something here (in the room)?

What's funny about this?

Can you change this to make it something else?

Can you use this in a different way?

Start your mind working on this, but don't tell me for a minute.

6. *Encourage children to make the commonplace different.* Do not always ask what things are or require that products have a specific purpose.

7. *Accept failures as a natural part of the learning process.* Provide a safe, well-organized, but flexible environment where children feel safe about making mistakes and testing hypotheses.

8. *Use toys and materials with fewer details.* Encourage children to add or imagine the needed details. Support children in creating a play scenario with scenery, script, and more.

There are a number of practices you should strive to avoid with children who are gifted and talented. You want to encourage creativity, not discourage it. The following responses and procedures are great discouragers.

1. *Avoid putting pressure on children for conformity.* This does not mean the children should be excused from following class rules, but rather that they should not be judged as strange because they think differently. Discipline that demands abject compliance and discourages understanding and questioning is disastrous for these children. If children must do things "because I said so," they lose the opportunity to learn and create. Tell children why something must be done. Whether gifted or not, children like to have reasons for what must happen, and it increases the probability that the directions of a task will be completed.

2. *Avoid emphasis on traditional gender roles.* This tends to discourage creativity for both boys and girls because it narrows both roles. All children need exposure to varied nontraditional and nonsexist roles.

3. *Avoid pressuring children to succeed.* In a success-oriented culture such as ours, failures present problems. Fear of failure prevents many children from being creative.

4. *Avoid insistence on regimentation.* Having regimented activities that cannot be expanded or contracted, or requiring all children to finish projects in a specified amount of time, discourages children with advanced and delayed intellectual development. Be flexible with time limits to allow for the creativity of the process.

5. *Avoid highly structured materials.* Materials that do it all—that are brightly colored, move, make noise—don't leave as much room for imagination as those that allow the child to create the movement, function, and noise.

6. *Avoid using disparaging phrases.* Refrain from making comments that discourage creativity such as "Don't be silly," "It won't work," "That's not our problem," "Don't be so sloppy," "Do it the right way," "Do it the way I said to," "What's the matter with you?"

Judging children or their activities often discourages creativity. Parents are also in a position to encourage or discourage creativity.

In the Field

A class of 4 year olds was making reindeer out of clothespins, which required them to glue the wooden pieces together as well as add a nose and eyes. Tony proudly displayed his finished product and I said, "Tell me about it." He explained how all the other kids' reindeer had two eyes but he wanted his to only have one. I told him that there was a special name for a race of men-giants who had one eye right in the middle of their forehead: Cyclops. We looked it up in the dictionary. Tony went home and proudly told his father about making the reindeer. His father predictably asked, "Where is the other eye? All reindeer have two eyes!" To which Tony responded, "Not mine, mine is a cyclops." The father looked it up in the dictionary and brought Tony and the reindeer into school early the next day. "We have to speak," he said, handing me Tony's cyclops. "What is this? If my son is going to make a reindeer, it has to have two eyes, not one." I could almost feel Tony's hurt feelings. He was crushed that something he was proud of was maligned. Tony's father and I agreed that Tony would have time to make another reindeer with two eyes, just like all the other kids. He could keep his cyclops, and I could try to encourage creativity, but Tony would also conform when necessary. "Well, what about the other kids?" the father asked. I replied that the other children would also be given a chance to make another reindeer and that if they wanted to put three eyes on them, that would be allowed.

Tony was embarrassed after his father left and needed some reassurance. I told him that in life there are different ways to do things. He replied, "Yeah, but with my dad I'll always be making two of something: one for him and one the way I want it to be."

Reflective Practice

There are times when it is important for children to conform and times when they need the space to be creative.

A wise teacher allows time for both. What would you have done? How would you support Tony?

Curriculum Adaptations

Activities for young children who are gifted and talented need to be more varied, cover a broader range of materials, be done in greater depth and with an emphasis on higher-order thinking skills, and offer the possibility for an individualized focus.

Social Awareness: Self-Esteem, Inclusion, and Social Studies

Encourage children to practice developing social skills. Although gifted children may have greater understanding of how to solve interpersonal problems in the abstract, generating solutions and implementing them are different skills. They need to practice both. Some of the activities in the Resource Chapter 1 are specifically designed to support children who are gifted and talented. Activity 1–31w Photograph Story expands children awareness of the multiple roles people play. Activity 1–34w increases their awareness of food and cause and effect reasoning about the relationship between whole and cut-up food and the role of heat. Activity 1–39w Family Flags looks at the symbolism in flags, plaids, and coats of arms and how they relate to countries, families, and values.

Self-Esteem

All children need to feel good about themselves. Able children with advanced development, although ahead of their peers in many ways, often hold themselves to high standards that are difficult to live up to. Children who are very good in one area may expect to be good in all areas and when they are not, they quit participating.

1. Support children with realistic feedback about their performance.
2. Encourage children to try new activities and take risks in areas where they may not excel.
3. Help them learn the skill of supporting other children in areas of strength and in asking for support from their peers in other areas.
4. Encourage children in all areas of development, not just those they are good at.
5. Encourage children to take leadership roles within the classroom and school.

Inclusion

It is difficult and frustrating to be different. All children want to be included and accepted. Highlighting both similarities and differences helps all children belong.

1. Have children complete the following statements individually and talk about the differences in answers in a small group with a sensitive adult.

   I feel happy when . . .

   I feel sad when . . .

   I am frightened by . . .

I get angry when . . .

I feel proud when . . .

I am like others because . . .

I am different from others because . . .

2. Children are different. Support this as you include all children in your class. Be willing to talk about both similarities and differences but emphasize that they are all children and they have strengths as well as limitations. Use yourself as an example. You might say, "I have a little trouble with math, but I am especially good at writing."
3. Decide upon some character traits you would like all children in your classroom to display. These might include respect, self-discipline, determination, fairness, and so on. Use a different character trait each week or month. Talk about the trait. Have children reflect on themselves relative to the trait and whether or not it is one of their strengths.

Social Studies

Social studies can cover traditional and nontraditional roles and occupations and provide information on unusual ways of doing things. Lessons should be designed that give children an understanding of themselves and their role in society.

1. Cook foods from many different countries and eat them in traditional ways. Tempura and fried rice can be eaten with chopsticks, poi with two fingers, fondue with a long fork, and so on. Discuss the food and the utensils used and how they are adapted. (Be aware of safety issues. Don't use toothpicks because they are dangerous for young children.)
2. Explore varied occupations such as plumbers, computer programmers, bakers, physicists, producers, professional athletes, and pest exterminators. Let the children's interest guide your choices. Take field trips when possible. Be sure to give a nonsexist presentation of occupations and value all occupations.
3. Discuss where different foods grow and compare fresh foods with canned or frozen foods. Introduce foods that are from other parts of the country or from other parts of the world. Talk about the nutritional value of food and the concept of organic food.
4. Help children make maps of the area around the school and learn the basic elements of a map (such as legend, scale, direction). Have them find a treasure using a map.
5. Show children pictures of different types of housing and houses around the world and discuss how they are adapted to different regions.
6. Discuss the role that rules play in your class and talk about laws and the need for laws, people to obey them and others to enforce them and why.
7. Help children learn to take different perspectives. Read books such as *The True Story of the Three Little Pigs*, in which the wolf got into trouble because he had a cold.
8. Have children put themselves in the roles of historic or famous people. Ask the children what they would have done.

Language and Literacy: Speaking, Listening, Reading, and Writing

This is often an area of strength for children who are identified as gifted and talented. It is also a familiar activity for children, who usually enjoy being read to and may read independently. Reading is a strength in itself, as well as the basis for learning many academic subjects, it should be encouraged. Your job is to refine, expand, and enrich children's language skills as you continue to instill a love of reading and writing.

Speaking

Help children use descriptive, colorful, precise speech and make word pictures for people.

1. Encourage fluency and flexibility in verbal interchanges. Encourage colorful phrases, vivid descriptions, and analogies.
2. Visit the library and discuss not only its books and records, but also the events the library sponsors. Discuss how the library is organized and how people get library cards and borrow and return books as well as audio- and videotapes, cds, and dvds. Set up a lending library in your class. Follow up by sending a note home to parents about your visit and encourage them to join the library if they are not members.
3. Encourage brainstorming. Be sure not to make value judgments or belittle far out responses because children will then refrain from making comments freely.
4. Help children think creatively and then translate their thinking into expressive language by giving them situations to talk about:

   Describe your life as a 6-year-old bicycle.

   You are a gingerbread mix about to be made and then baked. How do you feel (when made and eaten)?

   You are a camera. What kind of pictures will you take? How do you work?

5. Encourage children to learn new vocabulary words by providing a life perspective that allows for differences; teach concepts such as *some, sometimes, often, frequently, rarely*, as well as *all, never*, and *always*.
6. Encourage children to expand their speaking by *substituting* a person, place, time, or situation. If they were talking about the *beach*, how would the event change if it were the *desert*? Expand children's thinking by having them imagine being on a savannah in Africa or a pass in the Andes mountains in winter. They may have to do some research to support their imagination.
7. Make a "Word Graveyard" on a bulletin board. This board should list words that are used too often in speech and writing. Also make a bulletin board of more exciting, creative, and expressive words to use.
8. Teach a second language.

Listening

Challenge children's listening skills with more complex comprehension tasks. Fingerplays combine language with motions. They are initially a listening activity that becomes responsive, and ultimately a way for children to express themselves creatively.

1. Have children act out fingerplays with their whole body (this typically takes 10 children). For example, once children know the fingerplay "Open, Shut Them," see if they can organize and act it out. It is more difficult than it seems.
2. Encourage children to make up their own fingerplays. Teach longer, more complex fingerplays to a small group of interested children.
3. Talk about listening skills and what good listeners do when others are speaking. Also talk about what to listen to in conversations and discussions.

Reading

Read to children even when they are capable of reading independently. Read "chapter" books. Children's development is uneven; what conceptually intrigues them is often beyond their reading level. In an inclusive group, it is challenging to find stories that are unusual or creative enough to intrigue all the children in your group. Provide books children can read independently as well as ones with creative illustrations.

1. After reading stories or poems, ask simple questions to evoke creative responses.
2. Have a wide range of recorded books and stories available for independent listening at learning centers. Such materials allow you to individualize programming while supporting inclusion.
3. When reading a new story, stop at a critical point and ask the children to make up an ending. Then compare their ending with the one the author wrote. Have children make up different endings to familiar stories. Pose different circumstances and see if children can make the characters respond to these.
4. Dramatize stories, songs, and poems. Provide props.
5. Have children generate stories to go with the pictures in wordless picture books.
6. Have a box of words that can be made into different compound words (clothes + line = clothesline; sun + light = sunlight). When possible, have drawings on the back.
7. Teach about Braille and sign language as forms of reading and writing.
8. Have children match labels on boxes to a shopping list, and categorize boxes and cans of food by type.
9. Teach children to use prior knowledge before reading and to use interactive strategies during reading. This will allow children to read more complex material.

Writing

Many children are fascinated by writing and by thinking about themselves as authors.

1. Children may be eager to write their own stories but lack the necessary motor skills. Have a tape recorder available for them, or write stories they dictate. Some children may want to word process their stories. Support creative spelling. However, if the spelling is too creative, you may have to ask the child to "read" the story to you. Sometimes, even a friend can read another child's story, as the friend may be far less confused than an adult in the absence of traditional language conventions.
2. Encourage writing as a joint project. Have children share ideas and help each other, as well as provide adult support. Encourage children to use mapping to organize their ideas. See Activity #2–25 Mind Mapping.
3. Help children make their personal time line and note important events in their lives:

Born	Moved	Sister born	Got dog	Visited Grand Canyon
2003	2005	2006	2007	2008

4. Encourage children to use a writing journal. Give them time to write and support them in writing on any subject that interests them. They can use the journal as a way to correspond with you and/or with other children. This supports appropriate social skills and may even start new friendships. See Activity 2–57w My Diary.
5. Help children think of themselves as writers and publishers. See Activity 2–30 Publishing and 2–56w Book Making.

Discovery: Mathematics, Science, and Technology

Discovery is encouraged by exploring the environment in a realistic way. Children can also learn the scientific method of observation, expand to theoretical concepts, and move to more abstract levels. They can learn to use reference materials to encourage and support independent problem solving.

Mathematics

Math activities should be manipulative and game-like and, at the beginning, should have a concrete experiential base. Once the basics have been established, move with the children in directions that intrigue them. Help children

Hands on materials help children discover, experiment, and manipulate materials as a way of understanding mathematical facts.

establish basic number sense and numeration. Help them think about math as a method of problem solving, give them the vocabulary to communicate about math, and help them with mathematical reasoning. Be sure to support boys and girls equally, for stereotyping often discourages girls from developing strong math skills. Don't forget to teach the basics!

1. Help children recognize patterns and relationships in their environment. Teach them the use of "pair" for a single object—pair of scissors, pair of pants, pair of glasses— and explore their ideas about why this label is used and what else they could use it for.

2. While children are in the process of mastering number and numeration skills, have them count a wide variety of objects: raisins, blocks, children, and sets made up of objects of different shapes and sizes.

3. Have children group and count by sorting and classifying: seven red buttons, three yellow buttons. Eventually, help them discover whole number operations such as addition and subtraction, and relate this to hierarchical classification:

Furniture

7 Beds + 5 Chairs + 2 Tables = 14 Pieces of Furniture

4. Fractions are fun to teach through incidental learning as the occasion arises: half an apple, a quarter of a sandwich. Give children the entire object. They can count the pieces, put them back together to make the whole, and take them apart again. Teach the relationships among fractions and have many different calibrated measuring items. Measuring tasks are easily done at a water table, in the sandbox, or when making cocoa, gelatin, or a fruit salad. Encourage children to think about units of measurement, the different ways things are measured (weight, volume, temperature), and how this is done. Use both American measures and the metric system.

5. Use **rebus** recipe cards and have children read the recipe and make different items. Encourage children to change the proportions of simple recipes and discuss the results. Children can create their own recipes or use one from a children's cookbook. See Activity 3–27 Fruit Kabobs for more ideas.

6. Once children understand easy geometric shapes, teach some of the more unusual ones, as well as the relationship between three-dimensional and two-dimensional ones: oval/egg, circle/ball/globe, combinations (oval and rectangle), cylinder, pentagon, and trapezoid. Help them describe, model, draw, and classify these as well as combine them to make other shapes.

7. To facilitate individual work in math concepts, have children use an abacus, Cuisenaire™ rods, Montessori-type materials (beads of 10), and Unifix™ cubes. These materials help children discover, experiment, and manipulate information rather than simply memorize facts. See Activities 3–3 100's Game, 3–31w Abacus, and 3–35w Variations on Cuisenaire™ Rods for additional ideas.

8. Provide activities that involve mathematics with the scientific method. This connects math and science.

Science

Science provides the structure for gaining new experiences and developing reasoning skills. Start with known concepts and expand on them. Increase the ability of children to hypothesize and make predictions. Present problems that are inherently interesting from the child's perspective. Encourage them to observe closely what they do while solving a problem. Help them learn to apply what they have learned by teaching them to see patterns, principles (general), and applications (particular) in science.

1. Use familiar concepts such as the wind, the sun, and water. On a windy day, make observations of the wind's effects. Draw on the children's experiences with the wind and their reaction to it. Share with them the tingle of the skin, the watering of eyes, the tossing of hair, and the bracing and turning of the body to cut through the blowing wind. Have them observe how clothes on a line are pushed by the wind and the differences in the way people walk facing the wind or with the wind at their back. Watch the surface of a pond or puddle as wind blows over it; watch rain change direction when the wind changes; listen to the sound of the wind. Record different wind and blowing sounds. Reenact scenes from a windy day. Have children take a pretend walk on a windy day and have other children guess the direction and strength of the wind. Demonstrate a weather vane or windmill. Discuss machines that create wind such as hair dryers and electric fans. Demonstrate how seeds travel with the wind. Blow a small boat across a pan of water. Blow ping-pong balls across the table, then try to blow a tennis ball. Make pinwheels or kites. Talk about the relationship between wind and temperature and the wind chill factor. Read books about the wind and look up wind in reference books. Talk about the role the wind plays in hurricanes.

2. Visit an orchard and pick apples. Explore the parts of the apple. Experiment with the effects of heat and cold on apples. Have children predict what will happen when apples are cooked in different ways and the same way for different lengths of time. Compare the tastes of applesauce, baked apples, apple juice, apple butter, and dried apples. Find out what happens when you drop apples and bruise them.

3. Children often enjoy learning about animals. Provide first-hand experience. Add depth to the experience by talking about where different animals live, how they protect themselves and their young, how and what they eat, and how they are adapted for their environment. Have children invent animals for particular climates or conditions, such as a lightweight animal with large, flat feet to live near quicksand. Provide reference books.

4. Help children focus on a particular problem. Encourage them to persist in trying various solutions to the problem. Try to get children to generalize the problem-solving process to new problems. Show them how to use information that was obtained to make increasingly more accurate predictions regarding outcomes.

5. Encourage children to use the scientific method before they actually do a task: state the problem; form a hypothesis; observe, experiment, gather, and record data; interpret data; and draw a conclusion. Have them determine whether their hypothesis was right or wrong, then speculate about why it was right or wrong. Then have children make new hypotheses to further test their thinking.

Technology

Technology allows children to work independently yet capture an experience to share by using a digital camera and downloading or printing the picture to share with others. Use tape recorders to capture stories told by the children. Technology holds unlimited potential for children with gifts and talents. Software can be chosen to enhance the development of children and be tailored to their individualized learning needs in a developmentally appropriate way. Computers can support independent learning as well as learning in pairs. Computers can provide the necessary scaffolding to enable children to perform tasks they could not master independently. The key is the ability of the adult to choose appropriate software and match it to the needs of the child.

1. Integrate computers into the curriculum—don't think of them as a stand-alone feature. Use creative software that allows children to make choices and be in charge, to control the flow and direction of the program and not merely respond.
2. Use a speech synthesizer to verbalize each letter or word the child types. Have the child write a story.
3. Encourage children to work at the computer in pairs or small groups.
4. Choose software that becomes increasingly complex as the children learn the basics and move on.
5. Teach children how to identify, select, and use a variety of developmentally appropriate software packages.
6. Teach children how to use a digital camera to save or share experiences or creations with other children and adults.
7. Encourage children to record stories or to leave messages for each other on a tape recorder.
8. Under supervision children might have email pen pals from other countries or other places in the United States.

Wellness: Health, Physical Education, and Sensory Motor

Children with gifts and talents, unless these lie in the motor area, will have motor skills closer to their chronological age than to their mental ability. Their ability to plan what they want to do may exceed their ability to do it. This is especially true for a child who is the youngest member of the group. There is a tendency for children who are not good at motor skills to avoid them. Children need your support to participate.

Health and Safety

Health and safety are important because children's curiosity and experimentation can lead to problems. The "what happens if I swallow a penny" or "will I bubble like the washing machine if I eat detergent and jump around" syndrome can have dangerous side effects. *So don't do it*! (A trip to the poison control center can be stimulating, but it is best to avoid making it.) Children must learn to develop a pattern of checking with adults before exploring some things. They also need feedback on how to report their specific feelings if they are sick and a clear understanding that this is not the time to be creative.

1. Help children read labels and sort them on the basis of whether or not the contents are safe to play with. Add new items and help children learn to classify unknown objects as "not to be played with" and "not to be eaten." Don't use food for art. Help them realize that unknowns are not always safe and they should check with an adult for clarification.
2. Discuss the safe use of simple tools such as hammers and screwdrivers. Have safety goggles available and discuss why they are used.
3. Talk about safety devices (helmets, seat belts, safety glasses), their use, and what can happen if you don't use them.

Large Motor

Help children understand their unevenness in conceptualizing and carrying out activities while being sure they develop fundamental motor skills.

1. Create an imaginary obstacle course. Have a child climb, dodge, or wade while other children try to guess what the obstacles are. Then have everyone do it.
2. Have children walk through imaginary substances, such as mud, deep sand, sticky paper, a swamp, or a hot sidewalk. Have others guess what the substances are and join in.
3. Have the children help create an obstacle course either inside or outside. Check for safety before children actually use the course.
4. Help children invent their own scenarios to play outside on jungle gyms and other large pieces of equipment. This is also a way of improving social skills.
5. Do yoga on a regular basis.

Small Motor

Small motor skills may be challenging if children's fine motor skills have not kept pace with their cognitive abilities. Through creative planning, motivate children to use and refine these skills.

1. Have a wide variety of materials and an abundance of them (two or three sets instead of one) so that children's creations are not limited by scarcity of materials.
2. Encourage planning and prediction by the children before they begin manipulating the materials: How many blocks do you need to make the foundation?
3. Use short pieces (under 12 inches) of heavy yarn or string, teach children knots and simple macramé.
4. Add manipulative materials to the block or dramatic play areas to encourage children to create props.
5. Provide old clocks, radios, and other equipment for children to take apart to examine or to compare the sizes and shapes of pieces and basic construction. (Be sure children know they must have permission

before experimenting at home, and note the size of the pieces if there is concern someone might swallow one.)

6. Bring in a bicycle and have the children help change the tire and wheel. Discuss air, volume, and shape. Then change the tire on a wheelchair or wagon to expand the concept.

Sensory Motor Integration

Provide opportunities for children to have a variety of experiences that allow motor skills to be integrated with visual, hearing, and kinesthetic experiences. Make activities so intriguing they want to participate.

1. Introduce children to some unusual sensory experiences that seem to defy logic or change states. Have them help you make goop (equal parts of cornstarch and water) and silly putty (one part liquid starch to two parts glue) and then play with the products they made. Help them think about the process of making and using these materials and why they are unusual. See Activity 3–13 Goop and 3–45w Flubber.

2. Encourage children to experiment with a variety of media and relate this to their control of the media and the outcome (crayons vs. markers, watercolor vs. poster paint).

3. Using just one medium, such as brushes (in varying degrees of thickness), crayons (thin, thick, cone-shaped), or paint (in a variety of densities), encourage them to think about the implications of these shapes or sizes or densities for their final product.

Creative Arts: Visual Arts, Music, Creative Movement, and Dramatic Play

Children can define problems, seek solutions, and grow in their own creative ability.

Visual Arts

Encourage children to explore their world through the visual arts. Introduce activities that allow children to make their own decisions and exert some control over their world.

1. Set up art activities with enough space to enable children to work freely either alone or in small groups. Show children art from around the world. Talk about artists and sculptors and show their work.

2. Have children draw themselves as a "creature" who is either very large or very small. Discuss with them what they could do as the creature that they can't do as a human, look at the drawbacks this creature would have based on size and configuration. See Activity 5–1 Creature.

3. Learning in the visual arts is predictably developmental. Younger children are interested more in the process; as they grow older, the outcome is more complex and more important. Do not stifle creative growth by imposing adult standards on children; however, don't give excessive praise to work that is mediocre for a particular child.

4. When you repeat activities such as easel painting or making collages, vary the shape, size, and kind of paper you use as well as the color and texture of the materials.

5. Encourage children to choose colors (paint or food color) and to predict what new colors will be made by mixing colors. Add white and black to paint so that children can experiment with shades of color as well.

6. Do art projects with several steps, like crayon etching. (Color a design with a light crayon, color over the design with black crayon, then etch with a popsicle stick. Use tough paper that resists tearing.) Try again with crayon and paint: light-colored crayon, dark paint. Discuss why the paint doesn't adhere to where the crayon is. See Activity 5–4 Crayon Rubbing.

7. Supply a variety of traditional art implements including many colors of wide and narrow crayons and paintbrushes in several widths. Use pencil grips or other assistive devices, if necessary.

8. Origami, Japanese paper folding, helps children translate ideas into three-dimensional results.

9. Repeat activities with variations and help children explore the differences. Fingerpaint with liquid laundry starch, cornstarch, whipped soap, and commercially made fingerpaint. Add texture to fingerpaint with sand, salt, coffee grounds, fine sawdust, glitter, and confetti.

10. Tie-dyeing is another good problem-solving activity. The children can put small blocks on material (or on a white t-shirt) and then make a knot with short pieces of heavy thread. The complexity of the design will depend on each child. Tie-dyed material can later be used in a sewing project. Have the children help pin the fabric together and baste it. Perhaps some can sew it, by hand or machine. Use safety needles and count them to be sure you can account for all of them.

11. Help children critique their own artistic outcomes as well as those of other artists. Discuss the dimensions of art and how different artists use these dimensions.

12. Have children write about or discuss the meaning and feelings they get from famous paintings. Go to http://www.famouspainter.com and learn about the lives and art of such painters as Pablo Picasso, Salvador Dali, Michelangelo, Leonardo da Vinci, and Vincent Van Gogh. Then have them analyze one painter and paint like that painter.

Music

Music can contribute much to a child's physical, aesthetic, and intellectual development. It provides pleasure and creative experience, develops auditory skills, encourages physical activity, and increases the range and flexibility of one's voice. There should be a wide variety of musical experiences: listening, singing, and playing musical instruments.

1. Have a variety of different musical instruments available. Help children explore and evaluate the sounds of an instrument when it is held and played in different ways. See if they can identify instruments in a recording. Talk about how instruments are alike and different (if you don't have the instruments use photographs). Have children choose an instrument

and respond to "If I were (the instrument)." Make a class book from the responses.

2. Combine music and language experiences; have children make up new verses to familiar songs or make up their own songs. Play short parts of unusual instrumental recordings and ask the children to describe what they imagined while listening.

3. Put stories to music and have children choose background music. Paint to music.

4. Have children make musical instruments (shoe box guitars, oatmeal box drums, waxed paper and comb). As they participate in this process, they will gain an understanding of how sounds are made, where they come from, and how to change them. Help them experiment with making sounds with different body parts (clapping hands, stomping feet, putting air in mouth and pressing on it with both hands, strumming finger across lower lip). See Activity 5–41w Making Tambourines and 5–42 Reeds.

5. Introduce concepts of pitch, loudness, and duration by singing echo-type songs.

6. Play a variety of music including classical, rock, jazz, blues, country, folk, big band, rap, and so on. Talk about how different music is made and help children reflect on their feelings and what they liked and didn't like when they listened to different pieces.

7. Use music that reflects different ethnic/cultural groups. Particularly listen to lyrics that tell a story.

8. Encourage children to select music to go with particular themes.

Creative Movement

Encourage children to take advantage of the creative opportunities in movement to express themselves through their body. Give them the freedom to explore this motor area without fear of failure.

1. Encourage a feeling of group belonging and, at the same time, foster creative movement. Have children "hold up the roof." Children strain together to hold up the roof; they gradually let it down and then push it back up again. They can be ice cubes melting in the hot sun or a balloon deflating. Play "people machines" with or without noises. The children can do this together or one at a time, slowly or speeding up. Repeat such creative movement experiences until the children are comfortable enough to experiment with their bodies and are interacting with each other.

2. Have two children pretend to be one machine to encourage interaction.

3. Creative movement that combines music and stories is fun and mind expanding. Introduce children to some of the classics such as *The Story of Peer Gynt*, with the recording of the *Peer Gynt Suite* by Grieg; "Cinderella," with the recording of *Cinderella* by Prokofiev; "Hansel and Gretel," with excerpts from the opera *Hansel and Gretel* by Humperdinck; stories about troubadours and Meistersingers, with excerpts from *Die Meistersinger* by Wagner; the fairy tale "Nutcracker King," with Tchaikovsky's *Nutcracker Suite*; and "Mother Goose," with the *Mother Goose Suite* by Ravel.

Dramatic Play

In the dramatic play area, too much may be worse than too little. Use props such as dolls and dishes with few details. Provide enough props to create ideas, then challenge children to create and design props they need. If you provide all the necessary props, children will not improvise and exercise their creativity.

1. Have a small-group planning session to set up a store. Discuss the props needed, how to get them, and when the store should go into business. Create the store and evaluate its success. Use play money and a cash register and/or calculators. Write signs and prices for the store's specials. Make coupons for matching and literacy skills.

2. Plan a train or airplane trip. Look at maps to determine where to go. Explain how to use a compass. Have the children investigate weather conditions, how long it will take to get there, and what they will do there. Take the class to a travel agency that is willing to answer their questions and provide schedules and brochures.

3. Have children set up their own health food store. They can make veggie burgers, baked potatoes, and chicken out of construction paper or papier-mâché. Have them decide who will be the manager, cook, order taker, bagger, and customers. (Obviously, this could be a fast-food store, but a health food store presents the opportunity to talk about nutrition.) It can also be tied into cooking and snacking.

4. Help the children set up a small tent (outside, if possible). Discuss aspects of camping and backpacking, including the equipment, and take a "hike."

Routines and Transitions

This is a good time to individualize programming while not drawing attention to a specific child.

1. If you are giving directions to others in the class, use multistep directions for these children. "Touch your nose, stamp your foot, and get your coat."

2. Because the child may have more complex projects to clean up, provide an early warning for transitions or agree that some projects don't need to be cleaned up daily but can be set aside to be continued the next day.

3. For older children, have a center available for all children who finish early. This center should include choices of diverse, creative activities for different learning styles.

Summary

It is often difficult to identify children with gifts and talents before age 3. However, early and competent use of receptive and expressive language is one clue. There is an interaction between genetics and the environment in the cause of advanced intellectual development. Development of children identified as gifted and talented, however, is strongly affected by their environment. Children who are gifted tend to have a high general intelligence, whereas children who are talented may be talented in only one area.

The field is divided over the best way to educate children who are gifted and talented. Some feel that these children should be accelerated in their education by starting school early, skipping grades, or having advanced placements in some subjects. Others feel that it is more appropriate to enrich their environment and increase the breadth, depth, and scope of their knowledge as well as their ability to do abstract thinking. This same division is apparent relative to whether children should be included in the regular classroom or separated into special classrooms.

Reflections

1. It seems that a great deal of educational money is spent today on programs for children with disabilities, including assistive technology like communication devices for children with severe and profound disabilities. Children with disabilities have a right to such support and it is fundamental to their learning. However, it seems that one facet of special education has been overlooked when it comes to funding. Children who are gifted and talented receive less funding and educational support than those with disabilities. Do you feel it is fair to give a disparate amount of money to children who are gifted and talented? Why or why not? How would you explain this to the parent of a child with advanced development? What if you were the parent?

2. As an educator, one must take a great deal of time to plan for individualized instruction. This task becomes even more complex in an inclusive classroom with children who have a wide range of abilities, knowledge, and skills. In some instances, children with advanced development receive the least individualized planning. However, they need that extra challenge to keep them interested and developing as learners. Do you expect to take the time to plan special activities for the gifted and talented children in your class? If you do, how will you design and plan these activities? Where will you find the resources, lesson plans, and activities that would be stimulating for these children? Do you think it is difficult to challenge students with advanced development in an inclusive classroom where students with disabilities may also need specialized instruction? Be a reflective practitioner; plan how you can reach children at all ability levels.

Educational Resources

Association for the Gifted, Council for Exceptional Children is a national professional association that holds annual meetings. It promotes the welfare and education of children and youth with gifts, talents, and/or high potential. (888) 232-7733 (toll-free); http://www.cectag.org

Gifted Child Society is a nonprofit organization founded by parents in New Jersey that sponsors activities designed to help gifted children, their families, and educators. It is organized into specific information for children, parents, and professionals. (201) 444-6530; http://www.gifted.org/

GT World is an on-line support community for parents of gifted and talented children. The site provides definitions, on-line materials, and many other resources of interest to parents and professionals. http://gtworld.org/

National Association for Gifted Children is a national advocacy group for gifted children and provides standards for those who teach the gifted. It has great resources for parents and professionals and is well organized. (202) 785-4268; http://www.nagc.org

National Foundation for Gifted and Creative Children provides information for parents, professionals, and children. Information includes pen pals, brochures, reading lists, message boards, testing and referrals, and links to other sites. http://www.nfgcc.org/

Odyssey of the Mind—Mastery Education Corporation sponsors competitions for gifted children that encourage cooperation and creativity and has ideas for activities and other resources for gifted children. http://www.odysseyofthemind.com/

For additional resources, visit the book companion website for this text at www.cengage.com/education/deiner.

Chapter 16

Children with Special Health Care Needs

Mary was diagnosed with Down syndrome shortly after she was born. Like many others, she also had a heart condition, but this was not what would take Mary's life. I had followed her since infancy and visited on a weekly basis. Mary was an only child and both parents loved her very much.

When Mary was about a year old she would pull to stand and then start to cry. Initially, we thought it was because she didn't know how to get down and was afraid to fall. But when we looked at her face, she seemed to be in pain and she would always fall to one side. At first, the physician said this was normal for children with low muscle tone. A few weeks went by and bruises started to appear. The family went back for further medical consultation.

With tears in their eyes, the parents met me at the door; the father had taken off work to share the news. "Mary has leukemia. They say she only has 6 months to live and we have to decide what type of treatment to do. Please help." I went in and we sat on the couch. Mary greeted me as she always did, with a huge smile, and crawled up in my lap with one of her toys. I'll never forget that day or the ones that followed. We are supposed to accept death as part of life. I had been through the death of other children and I had accepted it. I also realized that what parents and children need is not detachment, but, as the parents pleaded, help. I assured them I would be there to support them through any decision they made, but they would have to make the decisions, not me. Mary would be loved until the day she died, but it was a roller coaster of chemotherapy, radiation, and long hospitalizations, accompanied by many tears, mine included. The hospital staff was wonderful, offering emotional support and counseling for the family, making provisions for visitation whenever possible. When Mary died, her parents called and said that they were going to bury her out of state in a family cemetery and they would call me when they returned.

They did call and wanted me to come for a visit. They said that I had been part of Mary's life since birth and felt it only right that I be part of her life in death. I reluctantly agreed. I dreaded the visit at first, but it was one I'll never forget and always treasure. The parents had taken pictures of the funeral and of the grave. Some may think this morbid, but they were so tender and filled with love. Each parent dealt with Mary's death differently. Her mother wanted to take part in the funeral preparation; her father wanted little

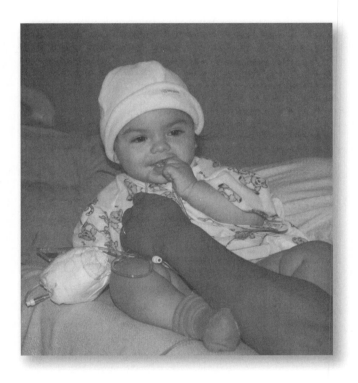

to do with it. But they respected each other's wishes. They went into detail about the service, and I listened, I cared, and I realized that I needed closure as well. And to think that these parents had no obligation to share anything with me. Her mother said, "No one can know if we will be alive tomorrow, but we do know we are alive today. We know that Mary was loved each day of her life and gave that love back in her short life. Thank you for going through the process with us." "You know," added her father, "you have been part of our family through the years as well, and we appreciate your understanding."

We may not be able to change things, but we can sincerely care, and there is nothing wrong with showing that care, while having a healthy balance of detachment when needed. I have learned more from families like Mary's than they probably ever learned from me; but we shared, we cared.

Special Health Care Needs

All children will experience sickness during their developmental years. For some children it is constant ear infections or colds while others fight pneumonia and meningitis. However, some children are born with special health care needs, while others acquire chronic health impairments. Understanding how these special health care needs affect the child's development and ability to learn is an essential task for all early childhood educators. This chapter provides you with a brief discussion of a variety of special health care needs and their implications for early childhood educators. It also provides guidelines to help you meet the needs of the children and curriculum adaptations that are designed to include children with special health care needs in the classroom.

Special health care needs pose different types of challenges for early childhood professionals. They may make us reassess our boundaries with families, look more carefully at our own role in the early intervention system, and even reflect on our personal beliefs. We may be intimidated by the terminology and feel inadequate because of our lack of medical background. However, the skills of an educator are an essential part of any team that works with children who have special health care needs.

Defining Special Health Care Needs

A health impairment interferes with normal growth and development, it continues for a long time, it is likely to have a prolonged convalescence, and it may result in death. According to the American Academy of Pediatrics, "Children with special health care needs are those who have or are at increased risk for a chronic physical, developmental, behavioral, or emotional condition and who also require health and related services of a type or amount beyond that required by children generally" (McPherson, Arango, & Fox, 1998).

Special health care needs can be defined on two levels: categorical and functional. A categorical definition (e.g., juvenile diabetes) determines whether the condition falls within stated guidelines; the functional definition looks specifically at the child and how she is affected. In most cases, the categorical definition is used for reporting purposes and the functional definition for curriculum planning.

Unlike other disabilities that directly affect the child's ability to gain or process information, most health impairments interfere with the child's learning by decreasing the body's energy, its ability to remove waste, or its ability to grow. Some special health care needs shorten the life span, whereas others do not. Many are potentially life-threatening. Some have periods of activity and remission. In some cases, the condition is progressive, getting increasingly worse, or it weakens other body systems, making the child more susceptible to other illnesses.

Children with special health care needs will miss more school, spend more time convalescing at home, and be in the hospital more frequently than most other children. Health impairments that interfere with the child's ability to learn are covered under the Individuals with Disabilities Education Improvement Act (2004):

Other health impairment means having limited strength, vitality, or alertness, including a heightened alertness to environmental stimuli, that results in limited alertness with respect to the educational environment, that—

Is due to chronic or acute health problems such as asthma, attention deficit disorder or attention deficit hyperactivity disorder, diabetes, epilepsy, a heart condition, hemophilia, lead poisoning, leukemia, nephritis, rheumatic fever, sickle cell anemia, and Tourette syndrome; and

Adversely affects a child's educational performance.

If the health impairment does not interfere with the child's educational performance, children's civil rights are protected under Section 504 of the Rehabilitation Act (1973) and the Americans with Disabilities Act (2008). Children with health impairments cannot be discriminated against in admission to early care and educational settings, and *reasonable accommodations* must be made. However, people frequently differ about what they think is reasonable.

Children who are eligible for accommodations under Section 504 of the Rehabilitation Act (1973), but require no special educational services, may have a 504 Plan. This child does not have to have an identifiable disability under IDEA but requires some accommodating. (For example, a child allergic to peanuts may require a peanut-free area at lunch and require handwashing for all children.) This plan is less complex than an IEP or IFSP. Traditionally, it is only one page; however, it requires a team determination, including an administrator or designee, and must be signed by the parents or guardian. The focus is primarily on the modifications or accommodations required and the person responsible for overseeing and/or implementing the modifications. Like the IDEA (2004), Section 504 does provide families with the right to a due process hearing if they feel their rights have been violated.

Prevalence of Special Health Care Needs

It is difficult to estimate how many children have special health care needs. At a practical level, when looking at children served under the IDEA, in 1976–1977, children classified as other health impaired constituted 3.8 percent of the school population. In 2003–2004, they constituted 7.0 percent (NCES, 2005a). Remember that children with attention-deficit/hyperactivity disorder (ADHD), when covered under the IDEA, may be placed in this category. It is likely that this accounts for some of the rise in numbers. Because a chapter was devoted to children with ADHD they are not included in this chapter. However, this number does not include children who have special health care needs that do not need educational accommodations. The National Survey of Children with Special Health Care Needs estimated that 12.8 percent of children in the United States have special health care needs (van Dyck et al., 2004).

This population is increasing not only because of children with ADHD, but because there are more children with chronic illnesses and they are living longer due to better identification procedures and technological advances. Insurance and health care programs designed to meet these children's ongoing needs are not increasing. The challenge is to provide comprehensive, coordinated health that has a **medical home** (Giardino, Turchi, & Kohrt, 2007). Although these conditions vary widely, children with special health care needs have some common characteristics that influence their quality of life.

Causes of Special Health Care Needs

The cause of specific special health care needs varies. Some result from infections, genetic factors, environmental influences, as well as prenatal and perinatal influences and factors that happen after birth. Some special health care needs are congenital and other conditions are acquired during the child's development from accidents, illnesses, or unknown causes.

Early Identification of Special Health Care Needs

Some characteristics of special health care needs interact with a given family in ways that make the illness easier or more difficult to cope with. The age at which an illness is diagnosed impacts the family. When an illness is diagnosed in infancy, the family may more easily integrate into their lifestyle the restrictive diet, complex medication regimen, frequent hospitalization, or dependence on technology. The child may know no other way of being in the world because the adjustments made in the family were done when he was so young. Children may have developed relationships and behavior patterns that allow them to adjust well until adolescence. On the other hand, children first diagnosed as having a chronic illness at age 7 may be angry about the ways they must change their activities and interact with their peers.

A child's age also impacts her understanding of the illness and the degree of dependency the child has on her family. Young children rarely have an accurate idea about how their body functions and how the prescribed medical treatment relates to their wellness. The health impairment itself may be fairly clear; however, the effects on the child's social and emotional interactions present a far more complex situation. The child's knowledge about his health condition will be based on his age, what he has been told, and what he has overheard or surmised. This information may not be complete or necessarily accurate. It is important to find out what the child knows and to ensure that the needs of the child are met without further complicating the environment.

Rolland (2002) has developed a typology of chronic illnesses and disabilities based on their psychosocial demands. These are broad areas that impact families and children. In reality, the demands are on a continuum, with the anchor points used for descriptive purposes. This is a functional approach that groups chronic illnesses and disabilities according to key biological similarities and differences that have significant implications for the children themselves, their families, and the professionals who work with them. Chronic illnesses and disabilities are not static; they have predictable patterns of development (Rolland, 2002).

Onset

Illnesses can be divided into those that have *acute* onset (such as a traumatic brain injury) and those that are more *gradual* (such as cystic fibrosis). In situations of acute onset, or where a gradual condition was not identified until an acute stage was reached (cancer), the family must rapidly mobilize itself to cope with the situation. All of the decisions and changes that must occur are compressed into a short time span. Families who have flexible roles, good crisis management and problem-solving skills, and who can call upon formal and informal support networks will manage an acute onset chronic illness better than others. When the onset is gradual, families have more time to adjust and accommodate to lifestyle changes.

Course

Chronic illnesses have three predictable patterns: progressive, constant, and relapsing/episodic (Rolland, 2002). A *progressive* illness (cystic fibrosis, muscular dystrophy, AIDS) is one where the child has symptoms of the illness and these symptoms progress in severity. There are no times when the child is symptom-free, and the progression of the illness requires constant adaptation on the part of the family. There are increasing caregiving demands and requirements to learn new caregiving tasks as the illness progresses. Families can "burn out" from the demands of care. At some point families may have to make fundamental changes in their world view to cope with the child's illness. Families may see their life mission as caring for the child and define success as keeping the child alive. If the illness is terminal, the family may see itself as a failure when the child dies, even though it was inevitable. A disability that progresses slowly (muscular dystrophy) may challenge the family's stamina, whereas a disease that progresses more quickly (brain tumor) may result in an overload of stress through the constant demands of adaptation and decision making.

A health impairment or disability that has a *constant* course after stabilization, such as a spinal cord injury or Down syndrome, is more predictable. Once a level of functioning has been determined, there is more stability over time. Once families have learned the skills needed, family members cope with the particular circumstances and adapt these to the growth and development of the child.

Some illnesses, such as asthma and hemophilia, are *relapsing* or *episodic*. Times when the child is symptom-free (or almost symptom-free) alternate with times of flare-up. Strain on the family in this instance revolves around the changing demands of crisis/non-crisis situations and the continual uncertainty of when a crisis might occur. Crisis may be brought on by stress, either positive or negative. Flare-ups may occur at holidays, birthdays, marker events such as the first day of school, and vacations, times when families are already coping with change.

It is often useful to ask the parents what they have been told about the expected course of the illness and the potential triggers that move it from a chronic state to an acute one. And, to find out what the family itself has experienced over the course of the illness and how they coped with it. Although an episodic illness may not be as severe as others, it can be the most challenging psychologically (Rolland, 2002).

Sometimes, children with special health care needs fall between the cracks in an educational system. Schools that are flexible and responsive may alter a child's day by making it shorter, making breaks for medication unobtrusive, and reducing the demand for physical activity. Episodic illnesses are the most difficult. If a child is in school 10 days, out for 5 days, back for 3, out for 8, and so on, it is difficult to keep continuity in learning. Most schools require that a child be out of school for a particular length of time before becoming eligible for homebound instruction. A child with an episodic illness may never be out long enough to qualify, yet altogether may miss a great deal of school. Some school districts have an attendance policy that automatically fails children who miss more than a particular number of days. In one district where we lived, if a child missed 28 days in an academic year, that child automatically failed the year. Such policies have implications for children with special health care needs and their families. The parents may have to be involved with bureaucratic red tape to obtain a waiver of school policy for their child, and they will almost certainly have to add home schooling to their workload.

Outcome

The extent to which a chronic illness is fatal or will shorten a child's life span has an impact on families. The expectation is that a child with allergies will live a normal life span, whereas there is the expectation that a child with AIDS will not. Other illnesses, such as cancer, can be life-threatening. Some illnesses such as cystic fibrosis, juvenile-onset diabetes, and hemophilia may shorten a child's life span.

All cultures and families give rights and privileges to those in the role of "patient," especially when the illness may be life-threatening. Those who are unsympathetic to this situation are often viewed as cold and unfeeling. Some children take advantage of this situation, called secondary gain, to avoid tasks they dislike, or to get special but unnecessary advantages. Different members of the family and team who work with a child may have very different views on the actual level of threat. It is useful to find out what different individuals believe about the child's prognosis (Rolland, 2002).

Incapacitation

The severity of the illness or involvement in more than one area also impacts the family. In young children, the severity of a particular illness may be unknown. Incapacitation results from impairments in different domains: intellectual functioning (fragile X), sensation (visual disability), movement (juvenile rheumatoid arthritis), decreased energy production (heart problems), disfigurement (severe burns), and may be exacerbated by social stigma. There is no direct correspondence between the amount of incapacitation and stress on the family. In fact, families often have the greatest stress when the disability is mild to moderate but the demands for care are ambiguous or unusual. That is, it is difficult for families to decide what they should do and how they should do it (Seligman & Darling, 2007).

Knowledge about the attributes of an illness or disability, that is, the onset, course, outcome, and incapacitation helps early childhood educators work with families and children in a more meaningful way. Regardless of the particular illness, there are predictable phases of an illness.

Phases of Illness

With chronic illness, particularly when the expectation is that the parents will outlive their child, the time phases of the illness are important variables.

Crisis

The crisis phase of a chronic illness begins when symptoms of the illness appear and includes the time when families are struggling to find out what is wrong with their child. It continues through the diagnosis and into the initial adjustment phase (Rolland, 2002). This is an unsettling time when families have to adjust to a new reality. They need to develop skills to work with a health care team, learn a vocabulary to understand their child's diagnosis, and accept the implications of that diagnosis as well as treatment-related procedures. They need to learn illness-related symptoms that accompany acute episodes and develop a flexible family system that is based on an uncertain future.

Chronic

The chronic phase is the time span, long or short, between the initial adjustment period and the time when the issue of terminal illness prevails. This is the long haul. Many parents, when asked, say they live it a day or hour at a time. Some families pull together and reorganize as a normal family in unusual circumstances; other families have less functional responses (Seligman & Darling, 2007).

Terminal

The final phase is when the inevitability of death dominates family life. Families then must deal with issues surrounding separation, death, grief and mourning, and the resumption of their family life (Rolland, 2002). Not all chronic illness shortens the life span, so some families may not move into the terminal phase. Different chronic illnesses bring different concerns and impact the child and family in different ways, but the impact of special health care needs is always present to some degree. Often, hospitals or community agencies will offer seminars on death and dying that may be helpful for educators and parents to attend. They may also have workshops for children including siblings.

Partnering with Families

Families, particularly parents play many different roles during different phases of a child's illness. They are often expected to take on the role of clinician, in addition to the traditional parental role. They perform daily much of the therapy that the specialists prescribe each week or month. They monitor the child's health, seeking medical help in acute phases. When medical treatment is required, they are the ones to chauffeur the child to and from the appointments. Extra work and responsibility may tax the parent-child relationship. Mothers seem to have the most stress. They may become overly concerned about the child's daily activities, along with managing the rest of the family, and become frustrated and angry.

Siblings, too, feel the stress and may feel neglected if their relationship with their parents has been disrupted, and then may experience guilt at feeling that way. They may show signs of irritability, social withdrawal, jealousy, guilt, behavior problems, anxiety, low self-esteem, and academic under-achievement (Seligman & Darling, 2007). If siblings are old enough they may feel resentful that the family does not have enough extra money to buy them trendy clothing, go out to eat, or to go on vacations. These problems are very real and exacerbate an already stressful situation. Long-term planning and resource management are major issues in coping with changes.

The Evidence Base

Using a survey sample of 13,792 children younger than 18 years with a response rate to a telephone survey of 65.5 percent, Newacheck, Inkelas, and Kim (2004) identified 7.3 percent of children as having special health care needs or disabilities. The definition of disabilities for the survey was "the presence of a limitation in age-appropriate social activities, such as school or play, or receipt of specialized services through the early intervention or special education programs" (p. 1). They were interested in finding out the differences in health services use and health care expenditures for children with disabilities including whose with special health care needs and those without.

It is clear that children with disabilities and special health care needs have more health care expenses than children without these needs. Children with disabilities including special health care needs accounted for 22.7 percent of the total health care expenditures for 1999–2000 while constituting only 7.3 percent of the children. Interestingly, these health care expenditures were not uniform. The median health care expenditure for children with disabilities was $462, whereas

families in the highest 10 percent income bracket spent $4,940 or more on health care for their child. This decile accounted for 64.9 percent of all health care expenses for children with disabilities. They also reported paying $644 or more in out-of-pocket expenses. Low-income families with a child with a disability were 19 times more likely to exceed 5 percent of their family income on health care. Families with an insured child with a disability spent 51 percent less of their income on health care than did families without insurance.

Reflective Practice

Clearly families who have children with disabilities spend more on health care. What do you think these figures mean for national health care policy and for families and children with disabilities and special health care needs? At a practical level, how do you think health care differs for children in high and low income families? Reflect on how this impacts the services the children receive.

The family's physical, emotional, and financial resources may be severely taxed as they attempt to cope with the effects and limitations imposed by a child's long-term condition. Families whose income places them just over the eligibility level for assistance programs may find themselves more financially strapped than others who qualify for federal or state aid. Some parents have even been advised to divorce in order to fall within the income limits for single parents. Beyond the strictly medical costs, there are many out-of-pocket costs such as transportation to clinics, meals that are eaten outside the home, babysitting for well children, toys and trinkets after procedures for the child who is ill, and lodging if hospitals are too far from home to make commuting practical. Additionally, the care requirements may keep one adult family member, usually the mother, out of the job market. Single mothers who work often lose jobs because they miss so much work. Conversely, some family members may feel chained to their jobs because they are afraid if they leave their job the child's preexisting condition will prevent health insurance coverage in a new job.

Although children's special health care needs may vary early childhood educators should use universal precautions and protective barriers with all children.

Table 16–1: Comparison of children with and without disabilities and special health care needs

Category	Children with disabilities	Children without disabilities	Comparison
Hospital days	464 days/1000	55 days/1000	8 times higher*
Physician visits	4.6 visits/year	1.9 visits/year	2 times more*
Nonphysician professsional visits	3 visits/year	0.6 visits/year	5 times more*
Home health provider days	3.8 days/year	0.04 days/year	95 times more*
Prescriptions	6.2 meds/year	1.8 meds/year	3 times more*
Health care expenditures	$2,669/year	$676/year	4 times more*
Out-of-pocket expenditure	$297/year	$189/year	1.5 times more*

*Differences are statistically significant.

Source: Newacheck, Inkelas, & Kim, 2004.

Universal Precautions and Protective Barriers

One challenge in early childhood settings is keeping children healthy and keeping disease from spreading. Because it is not possible to know who is potentially infectious, the following precautions were recommended by the Centers for Disease Control and Prevention (CDC). "Universal precautions," as defined by CDC, are a set of precautions designed to prevent transmission of human immunodeficiency virus (HIV), hepatitis B virus (HBV), and other blood-borne pathogens when providing first aid or health care. Under universal precautions, blood and certain body fluids of all patients are considered potentially infectious for HIV, HBV, and other blood-borne pathogens (CDC, 1996). Those that apply to early care and education settings follow.

Universal precautions should be taken routinely when there is bleeding (such as a nosebleed), a cut from a fall, vomiting, and even when children need to blow their nose.

- Wear disposable gloves when you come in contact with body secretions, including blood, stool, urine, and vomit, and when nonintact skin is anticipated. Avoid hand-to-mouth/eye contact when finished. Remove and dispose of gloves and wash your hands.
- Children who are sick and vomit need your love, care, and attention. Talk to them soothingly and pat their head while someone brings you gloves and probably a blanket. If a sick child is not upset, he can walk to the bathroom; if the child is upset, wrap him in a blanket and carry the child. You need a layer between you and the sick child.
- Wash with disinfectant such as household bleach (1:10 to 1:100 dilution) all toys and surfaces that have come into contact with bodily fluids or stool.
- Cover all open wounds until a scab is formed.

- Use single-use disposable tissues for runny noses and dispose of them immediately in a secure receptacle. Never share tissues. Have children deposit used tissues in a wastebasket. Don't do it for them, and don't pick them up off the floor. If you need to pick them up, use another tissue and wash your hands.
- Wash your hands when you arrive at the center, when you come in from playing outdoors, and before preparing food, eating, or feeding a child. Wash them after toileting (yourself or a child). When you wash them, use liquid soap, make a heavy lather, and wash under running water for at least 10 seconds, particularly around the nails and front and back of the hands. Rinse by holding hands so the water flows from the wrists to the fingertips. Dry hands with a paper towel, then use the paper towel to turn off the faucet and discard (adapted from CDC, 1996, National Association for the Education of Young Children [NAEYC], 2006).

Nonwater-based sanitizers are also effective and in some instances may be used instead of hand washing. Although these precautions are designed for adults, children also need to wash their hands. To help them wash for 10 seconds (which can seem like an eternity) have them sing a song as they wash. Time the song. One verse of "Mary Had a Little Lamb" takes about 10 seconds.

Using these precautions reduces the risk of spreading communicable diseases.

Categories of Special Health Care Needs

Descriptions of the most common special health care needs follow. Remember, you are *not* expected to be expert on every single health impairment, but you do need to be aware of their characteristics and how they will influence your curriculum. In the past as many as 80 percent of children died from infectious diseases such as tuberculosis, small pox, dysentery, pneumonia, typhoid fever, and diphtheria (Leung, 2003). With the advent of improved

Educators should wear disposable gloves when they come in contact with body secretions, including when helping a child blow his nose.

housing conditions, sanitation, a good water supply, and medical treatment, these diseases are no longer a major cause of death in developed countries. The special health care needs discussed in this chapter are chronic illnesses and are presented in alphabetical order. Those that you are more likely to encounter are given in greater detail.

Allergies

Allergies and asthma are determined by multiple factors including gender, race, genetic predisposition, environmental influences and even the timing of exposure (Leung, 2003). An allergy is a sensitivity to something that most other people find harmless. An allergic reaction is an inappropriate immune response. The risk of inheriting an **atopic disease**, such as allergies (**allergic rhinitis**) or asthma, is 50 percent when at least one parent has the condition (Lemanek & Hood, 1999).

Allergies affect a child's development, behavior, learning, and relationships with others. Allergies account for one-third of all chronic health conditions that occur during the preschool years. Only about 35 percent of children with allergies have been diagnosed and treated. About 10 to 24 percent of the population has serious allergies; another 26 percent experience minor allergies. Immunologic diseases account for nearly 1 out of 10 office visits to pediatricians. Most allergies begin in childhood. Allergic rhinitis is the most common allergic disease in the U. S. It affects up to 40 percent of children. Some allergic rhinitis is seasonal caused by changes outside (i.e. pollen). Although symptoms vary in occurrence and severity symptoms are often worse in the morning. Children with perennial allergic rhinitis have a chronic condition that may be triggered by such things as pet dander and dust (American College of Allergy, Asthma, and Immunology [ACAAI], 2008).

Allergens fall into four general categories based on the site of contact:

Inhalation: These substances are airborne and are taken into the body through the mouth and nose: plant pollen, fungi spores, mold, dust, feathers (down), animal dander, and perfume fall in this category.

Ingestion: These substances, food and medication, are taken into the gastrointestinal tract. Five foods account for the majority of children's food allergies: cow's milk, soy milk, soy, peanuts, and wheat (Sicherer, 1999). Seafood is another frequent allergy but it is less problematic in early care and education settings. Some oral drugs are common offenders: aspirin, sulfa drugs, and penicillin.

Skin contact: These substances come in contact with the surface of the skin: ingredients in cosmetics, starch, wool, some detergents, poison ivy, sumac, and oak, animal scratches, pollen and latex and may cause allergic reactions.

Injection: These substances enter the body through the skin by needle like penicillin, or through stings and bite from mosquitoes, bees, and other insects, and can cause allergic reactions.

Although allergies vary allergic reactions have some common characteristics (see Table 16–2).

In the Field

Jean Marie had a number of ear infections as a child and we had tubes placed in her ears. They seemed to drain continually. Then it occurred to me. A trip to the allergist provided the obvious answer: Allergies! She was young, cried through the testing, and at some point the physician decided that it wasn't worth it: Jean Marie reacted to everything.

So, we began to adapt. At first I didn't think it was going to be a big deal. Everybody I knew had allergies. My husband had asthma, I had problems with hay fever. We started in her room. We took out the rug, we took down the curtains, and all her stuffed animals went to live in the attic. We made a platform for her bed and the mattress was covered with plastic. We bought more sheets. They had to be changed every day. We bought more clothes—if it went over her head once, it was "dirty." And, we changed the way we ate. No chocolate, cheese, milk or milk products, peanuts, tomatoes, corn, and so on. The corn was actually the worst because so many things are sweetened with corn syrup. Going to the grocery store was a new experience. It took twice as long because I had to read all the labels.

Table 16–2: Signs of allergies

Nose
Frequent runny nose (clear discharge), nasal itching and stuffiness, sniffling, rubbing the nose, frequent nosebleeds, frequent sneezing (four or five times in a row), wrinkling up the nose

Mouth, Chest, and Airways
Dry hacking cough, wheezing, mouth breathing, shortness of breath or rapid breathing, chest tightness; in food allergies, itching or swelling of the lips or tongue, tightness of the throat with hoarseness, nausea, and vomiting.

Eyes
Red puffy eyes, rubbing the eyes, dark circles under the eyes, watery eyes

Skin
Skin irritations and rashes, pain, itching, swelling, hives, eczema

Source: Asthma and Allergy Foundation of America, 2005.

And then, of course, there were the allergy shots. Every Thursday afternoon at 4:00 we went to the doctor's office. Waiting was the worst. She would tell them her name and then we would sit, I would read to her, she would whimper. Then the call came. The whimpering changed to crying, and then it was over. Everyone was telling her it didn't hurt and that it wasn't that big a deal. Perhaps it wasn't to them. Then she would sit on my lap and I would talk to her. (You had to wait 15 minutes to be sure she did not have a reaction.) It got better, but every week it was an hour and a half of her life and mine.

She started to sleep through the night and, the black circles under her eyes disappeared. We struggled through birthday parties with chocolate cake (I brought a white cupcake for her), visiting friends whose houses were not allergy-free (most children came to our house to play), and wanting a pet (we settled on a turtle after several chameleons died). I assume this too will get better, but, from where we now stand, the long haul still looks pretty long.

Reflective Practice

What kinds of adaptations do you think you would have to make in your classroom if Jean Marie was in it? Reflect on how it might impact your snacks, cleaning schedule, and other aspects of your class.

An allergic reaction works something like this: The first time the allergy-prone person runs across an allergen (for example, ragweed), he makes large amounts of ragweed IgE **antibody**. The IgE molecules attach themselves to **mast cells**. The second time that person has a brush with ragweed, the IgE-primed mast cell will release its powerful chemicals, and the person will suffer the wheezing and/or sneezing, runny nose, watery eyes, and itching of allergy (Schindler, 1997). Most reactions occur within seconds or minutes after exposure to the **allergen**. The reaction can be mild or serious, confined to a small area of the body or may affect the entire body. **Anaphylaxis** is a sudden severe reaction that occurs within minutes of exposure and can get worse very quickly and may lead to death within 15 minutes if not treated (Medline Plus, 2007a).

The Evidence Base

The Pediatric Allergies in America survey obtained responses from over 500 parents of children under 18 with allergies. In an individual screen parents verified that their child had been diagnosed with nasal allergies and experienced them or had been treated for them in the past 12 months. A comparison group of 501 parents of children without allergies were also surveyed (ACAAI, 2008).

Spring is the worst time of year for children with nasal allergies 76 percent of parents reported. More parents (40 percent) of children with allergies reported that allergies interfered with their child's sleep than parents of children without allergies (8 percent) indicated that health issues interfered with their sleep. Parents (21 percent) of children with allergies indicated that allergies limited their child's activities, compared to 11 percent of parents of children without allergies. Forty percent of parent of children with allergic rhinitis reported that this condition interfered with their child's school performance compared to 10 percent of parents who attributed lower school performance to health issues. Almost half (46 percent) of parents of children with allergic rhinitis reported their children having headaches and ear and facial pain although the most bothersome symptom was a stuffy nose (27 percent) (ACAAI, 2008).

Approximately half (48 percent) of the children in the survey used prescription medication to treat allergy symptoms. Of those children who take medication over half (57 percent) have changed because they were dissatisfied with the side effects and 15 percent stopped taking the medication. (ACAAI, 2008).

Reflective Practice

As an educator it may be difficult to tell the difference between a cold and allergies. Although you do not want sick children in the class, how will you ensure that a child is experiencing allergies, not a cold? How would you modify your practice to better include children with allergies?

Food allergies are also a worry. One food allergy that causes concern in early childhood settings is peanuts and peanut butter. Although very few children have allergies that are severe enough to be life-threatening, many children do have reactions that cause swelling and breathing difficulties (an asthma-type reaction). In a severe reaction, an immediate injection of **epinephrine** will save the child's life. Most children who are allergic to peanuts know it. The problem is in the hidden sources where peanut oil is used in the preparation of products, or peanut butter is used as a thickener—again, a very low-level ingredient in a product. Children who are highly allergic can react by breathing the fumes of someone eating peanut butter and also by directly touching someone who has not washed her hands after eating peanut products. Some allergists feel that the claims are an overexaggeration, but parents of children are concerned. The Federal Department of Transportation has required airlines to set up peanut-free zones (Hartocollis, 1998), and many schools have peanut-free zones in the cafeteria.

In the Field

I walked into the gym's child care center and stopped as I stared at a 3-year-old child eating a banana smearing the yellow goopy stuff all over her face. I turned to leave—but the teacher saw me and started talking to my little girl.

"It's ok," she said. "Go enjoy your workout."

"I know this sounds weird, but I'm a little scared to leave. My daughter has a horrible allergy to bananas. If someone just touches a banana and then touches her she breaks out in hives, and then her eyes swell shut and she starts to wheeze."

"We deal with allergies all the time. Don't worry," the teacher responded.

"Alright, but I need whomever is going watch her to scrub their hands before they pick her up," I said. "And she can't play with the little girl who is eating the banana."

The teacher smiled at me. Reassured me that they deal with allergies all the time and there would be no problem. I walked away and met a friend to swim. We chatted about work and life as we swam lap after lap, but about 20 minutes into our workout, I looked at her said, "I can't do this."

I explained about the bananas, jumped out of the pool, took a fast shower and ran back to the child care center. The banana-eater had left. Serena was on the other side of the center playing quietly. She looked happy and spot-free.

And I felt both relieved and guilty. Of course, other children have allergies and I should have trusted the center to deal with my child's problems, but I still worry. I feel like I can do everything in my power to prevent allergic reactions at home, but it's very hard to do that out in public—especially when it's not a normal allergy, like to peanuts, but rather an odd one.

Reflective Practice

Allergies can be problematic in the early childhood setting. How would having a child with a food allergy influence what you do in the classroom? Do you think it is fair to not allow other children to eat foods such as bananas or peanut butter because one child is allergic to these foods? How would you discuss this with the other families?

In addition to food insect bites can be problematic and even fatal for some children. A bee sting often results in localized swelling and redness, which indicates only a mild allergy. A serious allergic reaction causes more generalized swelling and/or hotness about the face and neck, followed by difficulty in breathing and more severe bodily reactions. A sting to a severely allergic child can result in death if treatment is not immediate. If families know their child is allergic to bee stings, they will usually tell you and provide information on what to do, and perhaps even an "epi pen." This is a vial of epinephrine that can be given by injecting it into the large muscle of the thigh. The child will still need emergency care but the injection will provide more time to get it (Medline Plus, 2007a).

Implications for Educators

You play an important role in the diagnosis of allergies in young children and their treatment plan. Learn the signs of typical allergies described in Table 16–2. Ask all parents whether their children have known allergies of any kind or if they suspect they might, based on family history. The information will help you screen lunch and snack menus, choose a class pet (or not), and prepare in advance against insect bites and other potential allergens encountered during field trips. Find out what reaction the child is likely to have, what you should do if the reaction occurs, and what the side effects of the child's medication are.

Evaluate your classroom in light of what you have learned. If you have children who are allergic to airborne substances you will need to increase your awareness of the chemicals used to clean the classroom, and to think about how and when the room is cleaned. Unless you dust first and then vacuum, dusting typically only redistributes the room's dust. The vacuum cleaner needs to have a good filter or it also only redistributes the room's dust. If possible, avoid carpet with high pile, use dustless chalk, wash "soft" toys frequently, and, in general, make the area cleanable: put toys away so that surfaces can be cleaned.

If possible, avoid serving foods that are more likely to elicit allergic reactions. Plan around food allergies so that all children may be included in food-related activities. Be alert for unusual reactions to food, and convey any unusual reactions to parents. Have a written emergency plan for all children with known allergic reactions, in addition have contact information and a plan for all children, because you may be the first to encounter a severe allergic reaction.

Asthma

Asthma is the most common chronic disease of childhood (affecting more than 1 child in 20 (Asthma and Allergy Foundation of America [AAFA], 2004). It was estimated that in 2005, 6.5 million children younger than age 18 have asthma (National Center for Health Statistics, 2008). Asthma accounted for an estimate 14 million lost school days and is the most common cause of school absenteeism due to chronic disease (American Lung Association, 2006a).

Asthma is the third leading cause of hospitalization among children younger than age 15. Prevalence rates vary with a low in South Dakota and Iowa of 5.7 percent to a high in Delaware of 11.9 percent (American Lung Association, 2006b). Some studies have found the prevalence of asthma as high as 22 percent by age 4 (Tarq et al., 1998). The prevalence of asthma increased 75 percent from 1980 to 1994 and the asthma rates in children younger than age 5 increased more than 160 percent from 1980 to 1994 (Mannino et al., 1998). The increases are a cause of concern.

As you breathe in, air (oxygen) enters your lungs. Your mouth and nose rapidly warm and moisten the air to prevent it from injuring the delicate lining of the airways. They also trap large particles (dust, pollen, mold, smoke, spray) and other particles that could injure the lungs. Air then goes through smaller airways. These airways are like branches on a tree, there are millions of small airways that carry oxygen to tiny air sacs called **alveoli**. Airways have a delicate lining that is coated with a thin layer of mucus, like the nose. Some particles are trapped by the sticky mucus and eventually removed. Tiny cilia (hair or whip like structures) move the particles toward the nose and mouth. They are coughed or sneezed out or swallowed. Muscles surround the airways and it is the contraction of these muscles that selectively directs the flow of air (American Lung Association, 2006a).

Asthma is a chronic inflammatory condition of the bronchial airways that carry air to the lungs. This inflammation causes the airways to overreact, producing too much mucus, mucosal swelling, and muscle contraction. These obstruct the airway, causing chest tightness, coughing, and wheezing. They can also cause severe shortness of breath and low blood oxygen. Prolonged airway inflammation can lead to scarring (American Lung Association, 2006a). The inflammation is produced by allergy, viral respiratory infections, and airborne irritants among others. In children there is strong genetic component and 75 to 80 percent of children with asthma have significant allergies. These allergens produce both immediate and delayed reactions. The delayed reaction produces more serious injury and inflammation. Asthma breathing problems happen in episodes or attacks but the inflammation underlying asthma is continuous (American Lung Association, 2006b).

To be medically defined as asthma three components are necessary:

1. Inflammation of the airways
2. Obstruction to the airways that can be partially or completely reversed
3. Increased (hyperreactivity) airway responsiveness to stimuli (Colton & Krause, 1997)

Asthma has a variety of causes or triggers. There are two types of triggers: inflammatory triggers (allergens, chemical sensitizers, viral infections, and so on) and noninflammatory triggers (dust, cold air, and other irritants). Inflammatory triggers cause smooth muscle contraction and inflammation. Noninflammatory triggers cause a bronchospastic response that is dependent upon the level of responsiveness in the airways (Kieckhefer & Ratcliffe, 2000). The child's initial acute response happens within the first 10 to 20 minutes after encountering a trigger. An antigen binds to a specific immunoglobulin-E surface of the mast cell and histamine is released. This causes bronchospasms. Inhaled **bronchodilator** medications offer quick relief by opening up narrow air passages to relieve the wheezing, breathlessness, and tightness in the chest. There are long-acting inhaled bronchodilators that can be used at morning and night. This may be the only medication needed for children with mild asthma. They are thought of as quick relief, rescue, or emergency medicines. They are a necessary part of asthma management. The longer one delays in administering the quick relief medication, the worse the asthma attack becomes (American Lung Association, 2006c).

Anti-inflammatory medication prevents attacks by reducing the swelling and inflammation of the passageways and increasing drainage. The anti-inflammatory drugs need to be taken even if no symptoms are present. These are prescribed for children who have mild persistent, moderate, and severe asthma. Anti-inflammatory medications are the cornerstone for daily routine medical management. If taken consistently, even when the child has no symptoms, they are usually effective (American Lung Association, 2006c).

Anti-inflammatory medication includes steroids (inhaled and oral). Because of side effects, children are usually given inhaled medication. The device most frequently used with young children is a **nebulizer**, which children frequently refer to as a breathing machine. It allows them to take the medicine in a mist form and helps ensure the right dosage. As children get older, they may use a **metered-dose inhaler with spacers.** The inhaler dispenses a set amount of medication with each puff, making it easy to get the correct dosage; however, children have trouble coordinating their breaths to the burst from the inhaler. The spacers attached to the metered-dose inhaler hold the medication, which allows children to inhale it in a few breaths. Children older than 5 also frequently use

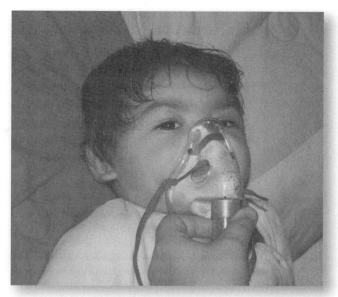

Young children who have asthma or other breathing problems often use a nebulizer to deliver needed medicine. They may think about it as their "breathing machine."

peak flow meters to measure how air moves in and out of their lungs. This allows medication to be adjusted to prevent an attack (AAFA, 2004). Children who take steroids need to be monitored carefully. The lowest possible dose should be given. Leukotriene modifiers are a new class of anti-inflammatory asthma drugs and a new drug Xolair was approved in 2003 for use with children who have serious asthma. Children with asthma are likely to be on one of these drugs (American Lung Association, 2006c). Depending upon a child's specific symptoms, different configurations are used.

Anti-asthmatic drugs are the second most frequently prescribed drug for children younger than 15. There were 7,279,000 prescriptions given to children in 1995, a number exceeded only by the number of antibiotics prescribed (National Center for Health Statistics, 1995).

Implications for Educators

One of the most important things for teachers to know is when a child is having an asthma attack, how severe it is, and what to do about it. The child's treatment is based on the severity of the symptoms and the degree of the airway obstruction. Every child has an early warning system that signals an attack is coming. Each child's pattern is unique, but good observations can identify the pattern and learn to see, hear, and feel what is happening. Early identification helps prevent symptoms from becoming severe.

All children with asthma should have a written Asthma Action Plan. This plan details personal information about the child's asthma symptoms, medications, any limitations, and specific instructions about what to do if an asthma attack occurs and what to do if it does not improve when this is done (American Lung Association, 2006e).

In a *mild* asthma attack, the breathing is mildly difficult and only slightly faster than usual; there is some wheezing, coughing, shortness of breath, or tightness in the chest. There is no "drawing in" of the muscles between the ribs; the child is alert and aware of the surroundings, can speak at his typical level, and skin color is good. If you can identify the source of the problem, remove or handle it (e.g., if child is exposed to cold dry air, bring the child inside) (American Academy of Pediatrics [AAP], 1995; American Lung Association, 2006d).

In a *moderate* asthma attack, the breathing is moderately difficult and faster than usual; there is wheezing, coughing, shortness of breath, or tightness in the chest. There is a slight to moderate "drawing in" of the muscles between the ribs. The child is alert and aware of the surroundings, can speak with difficulty, and skin color is good or may be pale. Reassure the child by your tone of voice and your confident attitude that this is something that can be taken care of. The child will look to you to decide how "bad" it is. If you can relax, he will (AAP, 1995; American Lung Association, 2006d).

In a *severe* asthma attack, the child struggles to breathe; it may be very fast or very slow and labored. The chest and neck are pulled or drawn in with each breathe. The child may become drowsy, he has trouble walking, speaks with great difficulty, stops playing and can't begin, and skin color is poor and the lips or fingernails are gray or blue (AAP, 1995; American Lung Association, 2006d). If this happens take the child to the doctor or emergency room immediately.

If you don't have asthma, but want to know how an asthmatic attack feels, "Pinch your nose closed and breathe through a drinking straw for a few minutes" (Asthma, 1997, p. 1). As the child with asthma, you may feel that you can't get enough air into your lungs. The longer you continue, the more pronounced the feeling.

If you teach children with asthma, you need to work with parents to be prepared for an asthma attack. Mild attacks can usually be handled with a child's regular medications and a break, or rest time, to recover. A note should be sent to the parents and, if possible, the trigger identified. It is expected that the child will remain in school, but activities will be monitored. Moderate attacks are more problematic and dependent upon the effects of the bronchodilator. I would notify the parents and not expect the child to remain at school. Severe asthma attacks require emergency treatment. Because asthma attacks occur with little warning, they may be frightening to the child who is having one, as well as to the other children. Children with asthma can remember prior attacks and these may trigger feelings of anxiety, which can influence perceptions of future attacks. Attacks are most likely to come in the early morning hours. Children usually have prescribed medication (in pill or inhaler form) to take. You need to have it available and to know how to help the child use it. Generally, the most comfortable positions for the child having an attack are sitting backward straddling a straight chair or planting the elbows on the knees. These positions are the easiest for breathing. Lying down flat is not helpful, and in some cases may actually be harmful.

Most children with asthma are allergic to common allergens. If possible, have the floor of your room damp-mopped rather than swept and eliminate rugs or curtains. If not possible, have the room vacuumed at night so that dust can settle. Try to balance strenuous activities with less-strenuous ones.

Bleeding and Clotting Disorders

Bleeding disorder is an umbrella term for a range of medical problems that result in poor blood clotting and continuous bleeding. When a child has a bleeding disorder he has a tendency to bleed more easily and longer than others, to bruise easily, and is particularly prone to nosebleeds. The bleeding disorder can be a result of defects in the blood vessels or from abnormalities in the blood clotting factors or in platelets (National Hemophilia Foundation, 2006a). **Blood clotting**, or coagulation, controls bleeding, that is, it changes blood from a liquid to a solid. Von Willebrand disease is the most common bleeding disorder and it is found in about 1 to 2 percent of the population of the United States. It is the result of a deficiency in the body's ability to make a protein that helps blood clot (the von Willebrand factor). It occurs equally in males and females. It is more noticeable in women due to heavy menstrual periods and after child birth. Hemophilia is an inherited bleeding disorder (X-linked) that affects about 18,000 people in the United States, primarily males. It results from deficiencies in blood clotting factors that can lead to internal bleeding (CDC, 2005b).

The problem with bleeding disorders works something like this. When there is an injury the blood vessels constrict (get smaller). Then tiny cells called platelets bunch together to stop the bleeding and then other factors, as many as 20 different plasma proteins or blood clotting factors, join to plug the clot. The clot strengthens by a complex chemical process to form a substance called **fibrin** that stops the bleeding. The clot dissolves as the wound heals. When any of these proteins, platelets, or factors don't work as they should or are missing, individuals bleed longer than usual. The disorder itself is determined by the specific factor missing. Some bleeding disorders are inherited and are present at birth, whereas others are developed because of specific illnesses or treatments.

In general, the first bleeding episode occurs before an infant is 18 months and is usually the result of a minor injury. Blood analysis is done to determine if the clotting factor is slow. Confirmation of hemophilia A is determined by testing the activity of factor VIII (National Hemophilia Foundation, 2003b). Treatment involves infusion of the missing clotting factor. This is done by injection or nasal spray. The regularity and amounts are dependent upon the child's size and the severity of the disease. The major concerns are not bleeding to death from a minor cut, but rather internal bleeding into the joints of the long bones (knees, ankles, elbows). Internal bleeding may cause deformities or intracerebral hemorrhage, which may lead to complications that can result in permanent neurologic damage or death. This is now rare.

Hemophilia B is far less common but from the perspective of a teacher is very similar to hemophilia A. In hemophilia B the deficiency is in factor IX, not VIII (National Hemophilia Foundation, 2003c). Like hemophilia A, it is treated based on the size of the individual and the severity with an infusion of the missing clotting factor.

The flip side of bleeding disorders are clotting disorders or **thrombophilia**. In this case, defects in one or more of the clotting factors in blood cause the formation of potentially dangerous blood clots (thrombosis). Approximately 5 to 8 percent of the population of the

United States has one of the clotting disorders. More than 60,000 Americans die each year from thrombophilia (CDC, 2005c). This also is an inherited condition. The symptoms relate to the part of the vascular system where they occur, the extent to which the clot breaks off and travels to another part of the body, for example, the lungs (pulmonary embolus) or the brain (embolic stroke) (National Hemophilia Foundation, 2006b). The expectation is that most children with blood or clotting disorders will lead normal, functional lives if some prudence is used.

Implications for Educators

Safety is a prime concern for children with bleeding and clotting disorders. Prevention is the first course of action. Evaluate your classroom for sharp edges or obstacles that a child might bump into. Tape or glue foam pads to the edges and remove furniture that isn't necessary. Look at push toys and determine how stable they are. Choose tricycles and other moving equipment that are stable and close to the ground as children are developing their skills. Ensure that children wear helmets when riding. Set rules about roughhousing and physical fighting and enforce them for all children. Use noncompetitive physical activities to reduce the dangers of overexertion and injury. Children can run, but don't have them run a race to see who wins.

Work with parents to encourage the child's safety by doing such things as sewing padding into the knees and seat of toddler's pants to reduce bruising. As children get older, wearing athletic elbow- and kneepads can deal with the same problem. Children need to wear shoes and high top sneakers or boots to provide support and added protection (National Hemophilia Foundation, 2006c). Talk with parents about their ideas for dealing with safety issues related to the child himself and the classroom. Jointly decide if there is any equipment the child cannot safely use (e.g., a high climber).

Respond quickly to children with bleeding disorders. If a child has a small surface cut it will usually respond to typical first aid. Take universal precautions. Put on gloves, wash the cut; apply pressure, and then bandage. The following are signs and symptoms that an internal bleed may be occurring:

- The child complains about tingling, bubbling, stiffness, or he uses a restricted **range of motion** in any limb.
- The child's joints are swollen or warm to the touch.
- The child refuses to use a limb, limps, or favors one arm or leg more than usual.

Find out what parents want you to do based on the level of the child's injury. Develop a written Action Plan and ensure that everyone knows what it is. Contact parents immediately if the child has a blow to the head, neck, or abdomen (National Hemophilia Foundation, 2003c).

Children with bleeding disorders need clear and consistent rules and the freedom to pursue their own interests and ideas. When children are young, they can tell you when they are not feeling well but it is up to the adult to try to figure out the cause. If older children see adults react to bleeds with worry, fear, or frustration, the child may not tell adults about what is happening until the pain becomes unbearable. Respond in a matter-of-fact way to information about bleeds (National Hemophilia Foundation, 2006d).

Cancer

Cancer is an umbrella term for a group of diseases related to the uncontrollable growth of cells, that is, new cells are made when the body doesn't need them and they don't die when they should. Cancer is treated with surgery, radiation, chemotherapy, or a combination of these. The prognosis depends on how early the disease is detected, what type of cancer it is, and which systems are affected.

Each day in the United States, 46 children are diagnosed with cancer. One in 330 children will develop cancer by age 20 and the number is rising. Although our ability to cure cancer is also increasing, 25 percent of children diagnosed with cancer will die within 5 years of the diagnosis. Cancer is the number one disease killer of children between infancy and age 15, more than AIDS, cystic fibrosis, and muscular dystrophy combined (Candlelighters, 2007a). Approximately 9,500 children were diagnosed with cancer in 2006. Although the incidence of cancer has increased slightly over the past 30 years, the survival rates have improved from 56 percent in the 1970s to 79 percent in the 1990s (National Cancer Institute, 2006). Only accidents result in more deaths.

Leukemia is the most common type of cancer in children. Leukemias are cancers in which abnormal white cells are produced in the bone marrow. The abnormal cells are called leukemia cells and they grow out of control. They eventually spill out of the bone marrow into the blood. They continue to multiply and eventually there are so many of them that they crowd out not only the other **white blood cells**, but the **red blood cells** and **platelets** as well. This impacts the body's ability to protect against disease, carry oxygen, and clot blood. Therefore the child looks pale, is prone to infection, and bruises easily (Candlelighters, 2007a).

There are different types of leukemia based on the course of the illness and the type of white cells affected. Acute forms get worse quickly; chronic more slowly. The white cells that can be affected are the **lymphoid** and **myeloid cells**. Although all types can happen in children the most common type, acute lymphoblastic leukemia (ALL), accounts for about 75 percent of leukemia in young children and 23 percent of all cancer diagnosed in children younger than age 15 (National Cancer Institute, 2006). Acute myeloid leukemia (AML) accounts for about 20 percent, with the other forms making up 5 percent (Candlelighters, 2007b). The incidence of ALL among children aged 2 to 3 years is approximately four times greater than that for infants and is nearly ten times greater than that for adolescents who are 19 years old. For unexplained reasons, the incidence of ALL is substantially higher for white children than for black children, but highest in Hispanic children (National Cancer Institute, 2006).

The acute form of leukemia progresses rapidly and, without treatment, life expectancy would drop to a few weeks or months. With drugs and bone marrow transplants, the life expectancy has been increased, and almost 80 percent of children are cured of cancer.

Chronic leukemia progresses more slowly but it is less amenable to cure. Treatment of children with ALL is complicated and requires intensive supportive care, such as blood transfusions, managing infectious complications, and also emotional, financial, and developmental concerns; this treatment is usually headed by a **pediatric oncologist** and is done in cancer centers or hospitals with the necessary pediatric supportive care facilities.

Signs and symptoms of leukemia include some of the following:

- Tiredness, lethargy, weakness, paleness, dizziness
- Easy bruising (black and blue marks for no apparent reason), unusual bleeding, frequent nose bleeds
- Aches in back, legs, joints, headaches
- Mild fever with or without infection
- Frequent infections
- Night sweats
- Irritability (Candlelighters, 2007a; Leukemia and Lymphoma Society, 2007)

Chemotherapy uses anticancer drugs that are taken as pills, liquids, injections, or intravenously to kill or slow the growth of abnormal cells and to replenish normal cells. For children, the side effects of the chemotherapy can be more devastating than the actual disease. The disease itself is invisible, but bodily changes are very apparent and perhaps even frightening. Children have difficulty tasting food and eat little. They may crave salt and not want meats or sugar products. Because hair follicles are affected by the drugs, their hair falls out. Because of the risk of infection, their activities may be limited.

Radiation therapy, which is usually combined with chemotherapy, uses high-energy x-rays, radium, and other ionizing radiation sources to destroy cancerous cells. The procedure is not painful; however, the room in which the therapy takes place can be frightening to children. The child is not radioactive during the treatment or after it. Side effects include some skin damage to the treated area, hair loss, nausea or vomiting, diarrhea, sleepiness, and in some cases long-term intellectual disability or hearing loss.

A bone marrow transplant may be used if a suitable donor can be found. In this case, healthy bone marrow is injected into the child's bloodstream and enters the bone and hopefully begins to produce healthy cells and platelets.

Brain cancers account for about 15 percent of pediatric cancers, and are the second-most common type of cancer in children. Because the brain controls learning, memory, the senses, and so on, symptoms vary depending on the location of the tumor. Treatment of pediatric brain cancers is very complex. Surgical removal of the tumor is not always possible; it may be inaccessible or removal could be life-threatening. Even a benign tumor in the brain can be life-threatening. It is more complicated because of the blood-brain barrier. It most cases this is helpful; in this instance it is not, as it prevents some chemicals from entering the brain and reaching the tumor. The prognosis depends on the type, grade, and size of the tumor, and its location in the brain (Candlelighters, 2007b).

Neuroblastoma is a rare form of cancer that forms in the nerve tissue. It is a solid cancer of the nerve tissue

of the sympathetic nervous system. It usually begins in the adrenal glands, which sit on top of the kidneys. It is often present at birth, but is most often diagnosed in early childhood when the child begins to show symptoms of the disease. By the time the doctor has found the cancer, it has usually spread to other parts of the body (Candlelighters, 2007b).

In the Field

When Betty was about 2 and a half she had a cold and we took her to the doctor. Because it was near the holiday we wanted to make sure our celebrations weren't interrupted with too may coughs. The doctor became alarmed when she felt her spleen. After some tests and attempts at trying to be "normal" for our 7 year old, we discovered that Betty had neuroblastoma. That was how our roller coaster ride with cancer began. I don't know where it will end. They operated to remove the cancer and then the chemo began. We know she is likely to have a hearing loss because of the chemo cocktails and some neurologic problems; if we are lucky, a learning disability. They are like eating lead paint with a few other heavy metals thrown in for good measure. She has lost her hair, but fell in love with her latest hot pink baseball hat. Not surprisingly, she has gotten clingy and does not want to be away from us. Life is a priority. When the girls are good, I'm good; when they're not, I'm not. We are truly dancing with the devil.

Reflective Practice

Betty was in preschool before the cancer was discovered. What would you do to support Betty and her family and the other children and families in the class?

Implications for Educators

Discipline should be normal at home and at school. Adequate nutrition for growth is a problem because the drugs decrease appetite. (In some cases, the drugs must be reduced so that the child's appetite can improve.) Be sure snacks and lunches are nutritious, as these children cannot afford empty calories. School, despite the dangers of infection and possible taunting by peers, has great psychological value to both the child and the family. Instilling realistic hope is the greatest asset a family can have. Being honest and open is important. However, if a child is in a terminal phase and has a prognosis of 2 months, it is *not* helpful to deny this.

Children need information, but the information they need depends on their age. The main concern for children younger than 5 is separation from their family, fear of abandonment, and fear of loneliness. They understand that they don't feel well, but they don't understand the disease. They are very egocentric in their thinking and try to relate the illness to a particular event or action. They need to be reassured that they did not do anything to become sick and that being sick is not a punishment.

Children 5 to 10 years have fears relating to physical injury and bodily harm, and perhaps even awareness of death. It is important to be honest with children, as their imaginations can do more harm than the facts. Answer the questions they ask; their questions may be very different from the questions you as an adult might have. Use analogies to help children understand that the "good" medicine is fighting the "bad" cells. Children like to be reassured that everyone is trying to make them better. Children who have been treated for cancer are at risk for long-term neurocognitive impairment. The specific treatment influences the risk; female children are at greater risk than male children. Children may experience general or more specific functional deficits.

Children typically regress when they are sick. In general, the last skill learned will be the first skill lost. Parents find this distressing. Children may have trouble sleeping and may display a range of emotions. Providing creative media such as art and dramatic play possibilities that allow them to work through their fears and concerns is helpful. The child is in a world where she feels out of control, so situations where the child can be in control and make decisions are helpful. If possible, let them decide what they want to eat, what they want to play with, and what they want you to help with.

Childhood Arthritis

Childhood arthritis is baffling and professionals disagree on the definition. At least three different clinical classifications exist: juvenile rheumatoid arthritis (JRA), juvenile chronic arthritis (JCA), and juvenile idiopathic arthritis (JLA). They are not inclusive of each other, but do include conditions that are not part of rheumatic conditions in adults. They do agree that it occurs in children younger than 16 (CDC, 2007a).

The most common term used in the United States and the most common form of juvenile arthritis is JRA. JRA is possibly caused by viral infection, autoimmunity, trauma, stress, or genetic predisposition (Hudson-Barr & Lambert, 2002). It may begin with a swollen knuckle, a spiking fever, or an unexplained rash. To be classified as JRA, the child must experience continuously active arthritis of one or more joints for at least 6 weeks with no other demonstrable disease and be younger than 16 (Hudson-Barr & Lambert, 2002). It affects approximately 50,000 children in the United States (Kids Health, 2005).

In JRA, the immune system makes a mistake and begins waging an inappropriate inflammatory attack within the joint(s) (Rennebohm, 1994). Children with JRA will experience joint inflammation until the immune system self-corrects. This generally takes a year or two. Sometimes, this remission is permanent; sometimes, the system makes the mistake again and the child will again have inflamed joints. Occasionally, the mistake is only partially corrected, and in a small number of cases the problem does not correct itself. When the disease is in remission, the joints return to normal or nearly normal size.

There are three types of JRA. The types are based on the number of joints affected, how seriously they are affected, and the length of time they are expected to be affected: pauciarticular (50 percent), polyarticular (40 percent), and systemic (10 percent) (CDC, 2007a). JRA is as prevalent among boys as girls. In addition to the expected arthritis, children can also have fevers, rash, fluid around the lungs, heart conditions, and enlarged liver and spleen. In **pauciarticular JRA**, there are four or fewer joints involved. The most common scenario is a girl between 1 and 3 years with arthritis in her knee and/or wrist; the knee is stiff and she limps, particularly in the morning. It typically goes into spontaneous remission in a year or two. However, it can persist for years and more joints can become affected; also, it can evolve into polyarticular JRA. Children with pauciarticular JRA may have an infection of the eye (iris) that can lead to blindness, so they should see an ophthalmologist on a regular basis (Kids Health, 2005).

Polyarticular JRA involves five or more joints. This is more serious because more joints are involved, they are more likely to be seriously involved, and it is likely to persist longer. It affects both large weight-bearing joints and small joints: commonly knees, hips, ankles, and neck as well as wrists and elbows (Kids Health, 2005). Children may experience chronic tiredness, poor appetite, a low-grade fever, growth retardation, and anemia. Polyarticular JRA affects twice as many girls as boys (Leet, Dormans, & Tosi, 2002). **Systemic JRA** begins with a high fever that occurs intermittently for days or weeks (another immune system mistake). The spectrum of involvement and severity in systemic onset JRA is broad and difficult to predict at the onset of the disease (Kids Health, 2005).

The drugs that are used to treat JRA do not turn off the immune system, but help by reducing the quantity and intensity of the inflammation. Mild JRA is usually treated with nonsteroidal anti-inflammatory drugs (ibuprofen, aspirin); more severe JRA usually requires prednisone or other slow-acting **antirheumatic drugs**. Children often are treated with a combination of medication, physical therapy, and exercise. In some cases, surgery is required. Exercising a painful joint can be distressing for both children and parents. (The goal is to keep the range of motion in the joints until the JRA goes into remission.) Over time, parents may have trouble paying for the medication, there is often parent-child conflict over the exercise regimen, and parents may burn out.

Implications for Educators

One of the most disturbing aspects of JRA is the pain and its management. Children may be taught self-regulatory methods such as progressive muscle relaxation, meditative breathing, or guided imagery as ways of managing the pain. Give children time to express their feelings. Include relaxation stories and other techniques in your regular repertoire of teaching (see Activity 5–25 Relaxation Stories).

A child with JRA may be tired or irritable and lack muscular strength. Allow the child time to do things. Realize that the child is probably in some pain. (The drugs reduce inflammation and pain, but don't cure them.) The child should not participate in competitive sports, in activities that continuously use the same joints, or in jarring, twisting play. Children need to maintain a regular exercise program that includes walking, swimming, and bicycling. Children need to warm up muscles by stretching before using them. It needs to be fun. The long-term impact on a child's quality of life can be considerable.

Congenital Heart Defects

Congenital heart defects are structural problems with the heart that are present at birth. The heart begins to develop shortly after conception. During development, structural defects can occur. These defects can involve the walls of the heart, the valves of the heart, and the arteries and veins near the heart. They can be relatively minor such as tiny "holes" between chambers of the heart or more severe such as the complete absence of a chamber or valve (American Heart Association, 2007). Congenital heart defects disrupt the normal flow of blood through the heart by slowing it down, having it go in the wrong direction or to the wrong place, or blocking it completely.

Congenital heart defects are the most common type of major birth defect. Approximately 35,000 infants are born with a heart defect each year; about 8 in 1,000 infants. Many of these are mild and require no treatment. They are the major cause of death from birth defects in the first year of life with twice as many children dying from heart defects than from childhood cancer, over 91,000 lives (American Heart Association, 2007).

It is more difficult to identify a heart problem in a child than in an adult. Adults can describe their experience of shortness of breath when they climb stairs or other symptoms; children may not recognize an experience as unusual—it may be the only way they have ever known. Such things as shortness of breath when feeding or crying, tiredness or sweating during feeding, blueness of the lips and fingernails that becomes more obvious when crying or involved in a physical activity, and slow growth are indications of a possible heart problem (American Heart Association, 2007). Minor defects are often diagnosed on a routine medical checkup and rarely cause symptoms.

You may encounter a child with a heart murmur. Innocent heart murmurs are heard frequently in children. When listening to the heart through a stethoscope, the normal "lub-dub, lub-dub" is the opening and closing of the heart valves. Sometimes there are extra sounds or "murmurs." These sounds are soft and variable in healthy children, but loud with a specific timing and location when there is a heart defect. Heart murmurs are harmless for most children. In other cases, restricted activity or heart surgery may be required.

Children who have either heart or lung problems are frequently given an exercise (stress) test to see whether they can safely exert themselves at the same level as other children their age without showing abnormal heart rhythms or interfering with the supply of oxygen reaching the heart. Based on the results of these tests, appropriate inclusive programs can be planned.

Implications for Educators

Although these children may need some limitations in their activity, this is generally not a problem if you let children rest when they are tired. (Find out the results of the stress test and the medical recommendation for limitations.) If you avoid strenuous competitive games, children need not exert themselves unduly to win. It's important for you to be responsive to children's needs within a framework that requires them to learn responsibility. For example, if a child says he is too tired to help pick up the dolls he played with, encourage the child to rest for a minute or two before cleaning up. If the child is genuinely tired, shorten the activity time or increase the variety of less active choices. Children need to both participate and be included. If children are tired, they can sit and hold the box while other children place toys in it, or they can sit and place toys on shelves. Help them find quiet ways to help and be part of the group.

Cystic Fibrosis

Cystic fibrosis (CF) is a hereditary disease that affects approximately 30,000 children and young adults in the United States. It occurs in 1 of every 3,900 live births in the United States, resulting in about 1,000 new cases each year. It is more prevalent in whites than in African American or Asian children. A recessive gene causes CF. To be born with CF, both parents must be carriers of this recessive gene or it is a mutation. The problem occurs on chromosome 7. An estimated 1 in 29 to 31 Americans have the CF gene. The carriers have no symptoms of the disorder. In 2005, the predicted median age of survival rose to 36.5 years, which is up from 32 years in 2000 (Cystic Fibrosis Foundation, 2007; Medline Plus, 2007b).

The defective CF gene causes the body to produce abnormally thick, sticky mucus, due to the faulty transportation of sodium and chloride (salt). When this mucus clogs the lungs, it makes breathing difficult. It also collects bacteria that cause inflammation and can lead to infection. The mucus blocks the digestive tract and pancreas and this stops digestive enzymes from getting to the intestines. These enzymes are what break down the food and provide the nutrients for growth. Children with CF need to take enzyme capsules with their meals to help with digestion.

Most children (70 percent) are diagnosed by their second birthday. A blood test is available to help detect CF or a sweat test is used. There are more than 1,500 mutations of the CF gene, so symptoms vary but in general they include:

- Salty-tasting skin
- Persistent coughing or wheezing
- Weight loss, or failure to gain weight normally; delayed growth with a good appetite
- Diarrhea and/or stools that are greasy, difficult, or foul-smelling
- Recurrent respiratory infections (Cystic Fibrosis Foundation, 2007; Medline Plus, 2007b)

Treatment is multidisciplinary. Because CF is a complex disease that affects so many parts of the body it requires specialized knowledge. There are 115 CF Foundation-accredited care centers nationwide. There is no cure for CF, but treatment, therapy, and proper nutrition go a long way to improving the quality of life for children with CF and their families. The use of airway clearance techniques helps to clear the lungs. Medications such as mucus thinners, antibiotics, anti-inflammatory drugs, and bronchodilators make breathing easier

Families who have children with CF face two major strains on their resources: time and money. The requirements of treatment and caring for the equipment may take 2 hours a day. And, the child's life is dependent upon the family's willingness and ability to do that. Although costs vary from one family to another, most families feel the financial strain of paying for necessary medication and frequent hospitalizations.

Implications for Educators

Monitor developmental progress as you would any other child. Provide and support social opportunities in an enriched environment.

Support the child who takes prescribed medication before eating. Develop a plan for maintaining contact when the child is sick. See that the child is encouraged to bring up phlegm, not stigmatized for doing so. Some signs of emotional difficulty to look for in the child are depression and withdrawal, fear of death, fear of losing control (dependence), and acting out. Have an emergency plan. Provide matter-of-fact explanations for other children: "Leroy has trouble breathing, like you do when you have a cold, only Leroy has this all the time. His tummy hurts as well."

Diabetes Mellitus: Types 1 and 2

Diabetes mellitus is one of the most frequent chronic diseases affecting children and youth; approximately 151,000 people younger than age 20 have diabetes. Next to obesity, it is the most common metabolic disorder in children and youth. In **diabetes mellitus type 1** the body does not produce insulin. The food we eat is broken down into chemicals, including a simple sugar called glucose. For glucose to get into cells, insulin must be present to

When children have diabetes they need to eat at similar times each day and have predictable food exchanges. This will affect when snack and lunch is served and may increase the probability of having healthier snacks for all.

"unlock" the cells in order to allow glucose to enter and fuel them. Insulin is a hormone made by the pancreas. The most important gene is located on the short arm of chromosome 6; however, this is a relative common genetic susceptibility and only 10 percent of the people who have this marker have type 1 diabetes. Why insulin is problematic for some individuals remains a mystery; however, the key to solving the mystery is related to both genetics and the environment (Knip, 2005).

Diabetes Mellitus Type 1

Type 1 diabetes is an autoimmune disease in which the body does not produce insulin because of the destruction of the insulin-producing beta cells of the pancreas. It accounts for 5 to 10 percent of all individuals in the United States who are diagnosed with diabetes. Each year, more than 13,000 children and youth are diagnosed with type 1 diabetes (CDC, 2005a). Researchers agree that type 1 diabetes develops through the interaction of genes and one or more environmental triggers (Juvenile Diabetes Research Foundation International [JDRF], 2003). Certain genes called HLA markers are associated with diabetes risk. These markers can be identified at birth. Although genetic, 90 percent of children who develop type 1 diabetes have no relatives with the disease. This information is particularly troubling because type 1 diabetes has increased an estimated 3 percent each year over the past 50 years (JDRF, 2003).

Although type 1 diabetes is an autoimmune disease with a genetic base the environmental factors that trigger the beginning of the disease are elusive. It can begin in infancy with the peak incidence occurring during puberty (10 to 12 for girls, 12 to 14 for boys) (American Diabetes Association, 2003). Once triggered, the body's immune system kills the insulin-producing beta cells in the pancreas and the symptoms become apparent. Symptoms include one or more of the following:

- Extreme thirst
- Frequent urination
- Drowsiness, lethargy
- Sudden vision changes
- Increased appetite, constant hunger
- Sudden weight loss
- Fruity, sweet, or wine-like odor on breath
- Heavy, labored breathing, tiring easily
- Itching
- Slow healing of cuts and scratches (JDRF, 2003; National Diabetes Information Clearinghouse, 2007)

It is possible for children to have no obvious symptoms. Some of the symptoms mimic the flu, making the diagnosis difficult. The onset of diabetes in children is usually more swift and severe than it is in adults. Children become very sick very quickly, and if treatment does not begin right away, they will lapse into a life-threatening coma. Insulin injections are necessary for almost all children with diabetes. The injections must be given daily and are probably the most hated part of the treatment. Urine testing (usually before breakfast and dinner) or blood testing may be necessary each day. This procedure is embarrassing for a child striving toward independence. Charting the test results provides the basis for changes in insulin dosage and gives clues to why some diabetics go out of control. When children are old enough, they are encouraged to do this themselves.

However, insulin pump therapy is changing how medication is given to adults, children, and even infants and toddlers (Children with Diabetes, 2007). The insulin pump is a small computerized device about the size of pager and is worn on a belt or placed in a pocket. The pump is attached to the child with a thin plastic tube that ends in a small, flexible plastic cannula or tube. The cannula is inserted through the skin (usually in the abdomen or buttocks) and taped in place. It must be changed every 48 to 72 hours (Marschilok, 2004). Pumps deliver insulin in two ways: basal insulin and bolus doses. The basal insulin is delivered in steady short-acting doses throughout the day and provides about half of the day's total insulin requirements. For the bolus doses the user pushes a button and decides how much is needed. Bolus doses are given at snack or meal time or to lower blood sugar when it is too high (Marschilok, 2004). The advantage of the pump is that it can deliver insulin in precise predictable doses on a continuous basis. It holds several days supply of insulin and the pump can be individually programmed to meet a child's needs. Additionally it can be adjusted if the child is ill or more physically active than usual. It also provides flexibility in allowing children more freedom in when, what, and how they eat (Marschilok, 2004). Obviously, if a child is on an insulin pump, educators will need to understand how the pump works and how to handle situations that may require assistance.

Children with diabetes are allowed to have slowly digestible sweets like ice cream, but are not allowed to eat candy bars and other carbohydrates that burn quickly. (An exception to this rule occurs when the child needs quick sugar to avert an insulin reaction.)

Although most insulin-dependent diabetics are on a "free" diet, it is by no means unstructured. The free exchange system used by adults is often used with children. This system divides foods into six groups based on calories and grams of carbohydrates, proteins, and fats. Thus, if the child is allowed one bread exchange, the choice of any one of the following could be made: a piece of bread, one-half cup of cereal, two graham crackers, one-half cup of mashed potatoes, or one-fourth cup of baked beans. The number of exchanges is individually determined, and parents will tell you what exchanges the child requires. This will affect what you offer at snack and how much the child eats. The child's activity level will also influence his balance of food and insulin.

The concern is when a child with type 1 diabetes' insulin is out of control. This can happen because the sugar or glucose levels are too high or too low. Hypoglycemia occurs when the level of blood sugar (glucose) is too low. It is relatively common and occurs when a child has injected too much insulin, eaten too little food, or has exercised without ingesting extra food. Symptoms include fatigue, shaking, cold sweats, dizziness, double vision, and nervousness. If caught in the early stages providing a drink of juice, or food with sugar will usually help almost immediately. Severe hypoglycemia can result in seizures or unconsciousness, called insulin shock (Medline Plus, 2007c). Hyperglycemia occurs because the blood glucose (sugar) level is too high and the child is typically dehydrated.

If this continues and glucose is not available, the body begins to break down body fat. When body fat is broken down, ketones (the by-products of fat metabolism) build up in the blood and spill over into the urine. This may be how type 1 diabetes is first diagnosed. The signs include such things as frequent urination and thirst for a day or more, fatigue, nausea and vomiting, muscular stiffness or aching, rapid breathing, and fruity breath. If caught in the beginning stages, rehydration is the first goal. This can lead to diabetic coma (Medline Plus, 2007c). Obviously, if these conditions begin and move into the more extreme, this is a medical emergency. As with asthma, there should be a written Diabetes Action Plan developed with the families.

Diabetes Mellitus Type 2

Diabetes mellitus type 2 is a metabolic disorder that results from the body's inability to make enough insulin or to use it properly. It is non–insulin-dependent diabetes, which is primarily characterized by insulin resistance, relative insulin deficiency, and hyperglycemia. In the past, this type of diabetes has been thought of as adult-onset diabetes. However, a growing number of children and adolescents are developing type 2 diabetes. Since this is a new phenomenon, we do not have accurate statistics or even common agreement on when a child has type 2 diabetes. However, reports indicate that 8 to 45 percent of children with newly diagnosed diabetes have type 2 diabetes (American Diabetes Association, 2003). Children diagnosed with type 2 diabetes frequently have a family history of this disease, are overweight at the time of diagnosis, and are older than 10 years of age (but increasing numbers of younger pre-pubescent overweight children are being identified). In a clinic I am familiar with a boy of 5 was who diagnosed with type 2 diabetes.

Obesity precedes type 2 diabetes and may cause disabilities in people who are genetically predisposed to it (Piscopo et al., 2005). There are approximately 20.8 million people in the United States (or 7 percent of the population) who have diabetes. Of these people, 14.6 million have been diagnosed and 6.2 million people are unaware that they have the disease. Diabetes has no cure. The discovery of insulin has literally made the difference between life and death for these children (American Diabetes Association, 2007). Regardless of the type of diabetes, the goal is to manage the disease by developing a predictable relationship among the child's diet, insulin, and exercise.

Implications for Educators

You need to have snack and meals at about the same times each day and they should provide about the same food values. The child need not eat the same foods every day, but the foods should be of equivalent groups and values.

Because of the possibility of insulin reaction, you must always have a source of quick-burning sugar available. Some traditional quick sugar sources are orange juice, soda, a sugar cube, and small chocolate bars. Most children have some warning signs, but young children may not be able to identify these. The child may be dizzy, shaky, trembling, or having an emotional outburst before the insulin reaction begins to occur. Find out in advance what the child's favorite sources of sugar are; you need to offer something especially tempting because the child may not feel like eating. Always carry one of these on a field trip. If you miss the warning signs and the child becomes unconscious, do not try to get the child to drink because choking might result. Discuss emergency measures with parents and have a plan for the class and for field trips. A written Diabetes Health Care Plan should be developed with the family. It should address the specific needs of the child and provide specific instructions on the following issues:

- Blood glucose monitoring
- Insulin administration (if necessary)
- Meals and snacks, including food content, amounts, and timing
- Symptoms and treatment of hypoglycemia (low blood sugar)
- Symptoms and treatment of hyperglycemia (high blood sugar)
- Testing for ketones and actions to be taken based on results (American Diabetes Association, 2003)

The parents should supervise and regulate the child's insulin and diet, and they can usually accommodate most situations if they know about them ahead of time. Send them a list of your snacks for the week or month, or at least post them on a bulletin board for the parents to check when they drop off or pick up their child. If another child will have a birthday party with cupcakes, tell the parents. This child can have one too, if it is planned. The child should wear a Medic-Alert bracelet or locket at all times.

Epilepsy and Other Seizure Disorders

Seizures are brief, stereotyped unpredictable events that alter states of consciousness in different ways. They are abnormal electrical discharges in the brain. Symptoms depend on the part of the brain involved and typically cause unusual sensations, uncontrollable muscle spasms, and loss of consciousness. They occur frequently in childhood and are isolated seizures associated with fever or acute illness. They are not seizure disorders. Seizures are a disorder of neuronal transmission and brain network interactions (Weinstein & Gaillard, 2007).

Febrile seizures, relatively common in children younger than 5, can occur when a child develops a high fever, with the temperature rising rapidly to 102°F or more (Kids Health, 2006). They are not part of the epilepsy syndrome. About 5 percent of children between 3 months and 5 years of age experience them. About 80 percent are simple febrile seizures that are brief symmetric tonic or clonic-tonic events that occur once during an illness. Complex febrile seizures are more prolonged or reoccur during an illness and they may serve as indicators of other central nervous system problems (Weinstein & Gaillard, 2007).

Seizures occur in the brain and must be understood in the context of the brain and how it works. A seizure "involves the abnormal extensive and concurrent firing of a large population of cortical neurons. This results in the interruption of usual brain-generated electrical signals, leading to an abrupt change in the person's behavior" (Weinstein & Gaillard, 2007, p. 440). The firing may continue until excitatory neurochemicals are used up, or until it is extinguished by inhibitory neurochemicals, which usually occurs in seconds to minutes. Seizures occur more frequently in children younger than 6 years of age, and in old age. It is not clear if seizures hurt the brain.

In the Field

I thought Bella was playing when she had her first seizure. As her head fell back, I waited for the smile and the giggle that usually accompanied that movement. Instead I watched her eyes roll back in her head and her body go limp. It lasted just a few seconds, but it scared me. I called my husband over to watch her, and prayed that what I'd seen was just in my imagination.

Bella laughed and cooed. She didn't exhibit signs of a seizure at all. So I decided that I had just "seen something" that looked like a seizure. But as we dropped her off with her babysitter, Debbie, so we could go to a restaurant opening that I had to attend for work, I couldn't help but feel apprehensive. If Bella starts acting weird, call me, I told Debbie, not wanting to worry her but unable to shake the feeling that something was very wrong with my baby girl.

Halfway through the entrée, my cell phone rang. "Leslie, it's Debbie," her voice sounded shaky. "I need you to come pick up the baby and I think you should take her to the emergency room. She's had four seizures in the past hour."

"We need to go," I told my husband, flagging down our waiter and then dropping a $20 on the table when he didn't come fast enough with our bill. I called our pediatrician during the 5-minute drive to our babysitter's house—he agreed with Debbie. Bella needed to go to the emergency room.

Our hospital experience was a disaster. We spent the night in the emergency room. First, they placed us in a room with a kid with meningitis, and then with a child with a violent viral infection. The nurses wouldn't tell us what was going on. No doctor appeared. Bella would have a seizure and we'd call the nurse, but she wouldn't come to check on her.

I finally snapped. I told the nurses that if they could not be responsible for caring for my child, they should send us home. I explained that my child had come in with seizures and was going to leave in a coffin if they weren't more careful about who they put us in a room with, how they did procedures, and what sorts of medicine they administered.

We were moved to a private room. The pharmacy director came upstairs and spoke to us about the medicine they were administering. Two doctors appeared at our door and I believe I made that nurse cry.

For 5 days, I refused to leave the hospital. My husband would go home to get food or take a nap but I would not leave my daughter's side because I had so little trust in the hospital. When the neurologist told me Bella was going to have to stay on Phenobarbital for up to a year but that he had no conclusive cause of her seizure, the journalist in me kicked in.

I called my friends in the newsroom and got them to look up everything they could find on Phenobarbital, and then seizures. I asked them to cross-reference the medicine Bella was taking and the occurrence of seizures. I work in a profession where we dig for information and where we know how to do it fast.

Within a couple hours my cell phone was ringing. Bella had been taking a medicine that had an ingredient in it that is known to cause seizures in children younger than 2, our health reporter said. My phone rang again. The over-the-counter version of that medicine had been taken off the market two weeks before. My source said it was because it caused seizures.

I breathed a sigh of relief. My child was having a reaction to a medicine her newly acquired and severely misinformed allergist had prescribed. I felt happy, but convincing her doctors, even with the reams of information my friends had provided, was not easy. They said she had to stay on Phenobarbital—even though I now knew it caused developmental problems, made Bella a tyrant, and when she wasn't fussing, made her incredibly sleepy.

The physicians told me that I wasn't a doctor and couldn't diagnose my own child. As more and more of the drug dripped into her veins, I felt defeated. I knew they were wrong. I started dropping the dose of Phenobarbital as soon as we got out of the hospital. I discontinued the use of all the other medications the allergist put her on. The seizures stopped.

I went back to my pediatrician to explain my theory and he listened. He said he thought I was right but wanted us to go to a different neurologist for confirmation. I did and he kept her on Phenobarbital for a month while we awaited the results of the tests. By that time we'd run out of our prescription and I told my husband I wouldn't refill it.

When we got the test results back, the doctor said my theory had been right. Bella is allergic to pseudoephedrine, a key ingredient in a prescription her allergist had prescribed.

My daughter took a potentially damaging anti-seizure medicine that she didn't need for 3 months, because some "highly qualified" doctor hadn't kept up on the research—or apparently read the newspaper. Her mistake cost us more than $1,000 in medical bills and our insurance company more than $10,000 and put my daughter through a lot of unnecessary pain and suffering.

Sometimes I wonder if Bella would still be taking that drug and suffering its consequences if I weren't a reporter. I had resources at hand that most parents don't and the mom in me told me to follow my gut, not what a doctor said. I fought tooth and nail for my daughter. I wasn't nice to incompetent nurses and I made no friends in the hospital, but I got what I needed for my child.

Reflective Practice

What happens to the children whose parents do not have the resources, intuition, or the desire to fight for what they believe for their children? Do their children follow doctor's orders? What do you think about this mother? She thought she knew more about her daughter and the problem than the medical profession. Do you think she had the right to override their advice? What would you have done?

Epilepsy is a brain disorder in which clusters of nerve cells, or neurons, in the brain sometimes signal abnormally. Somehow the normal pattern of neuronal activity becomes disturbed, causing strange sensations, emotions, and behavior or sometimes convulsions, muscle spasms, and loss of consciousness. It has many possible causes: illness, brain damage, or abnormal brain development. Epilepsy may develop because of abnormal brain wiring, an imbalance of neurotransmitters, or some combination of these factors (National Institute of Neurological Disorders and Stroke, [NINDS] (2008).

Epilepsy occurs with increased frequency in children with developmental disabilities. Epilepsy is defined as a condition involving two unprovoked seizures separated by 24 hours (Weinstein & Gaillard, 2007). For most children this is a condition that resolves itself over several years. For some children it is a chronic condition. Children with epilepsy often have learning disabilities and behavioral challenges, but so far we do not know whether problems in brain development cause these problems (as well as the epilepsy), or whether recurrent seizures cause these problems or add to them (Weinstein & Gaillard, 2007).

The effect of the seizure depends on the location of the cells and how far the discharge spreads. Seizures take many forms, but there are two major classifications: generalized, and partial. Understanding the seizure type helps to explain the child's behavior and often determines the type of intervention.

Generalized seizures account for about 35 percent of pediatric epileptic disorders. They do not have an identifiable focus and impact both hemispheres of the brain and affect widely spread cortical areas of the brain simultaneously. The cause is usually genetic. During the seizure, the child will have decreased motor activity or vigorous abnormal motor behaviors (Weinstein & Gaillard, 2007).

Absence seizures (formerly called petit mal seizures), a type of generalized seizure, are often inherited and begin between 3 and 12 years of age. They are characterized by glazed eyes, eye blinks, and/or changes in muscle tone. They last less than 30 seconds, they cannot be interrupted by touch, and they can happen hundreds of times a day (Weinstein & Gaillard, 2007). When a child is having a seizure, he can be injured by falling down stairs, or by walking into the path of an oncoming tricycle, bicycle, or car. The child is also not available for learning during seizures.

Partial seizures account for over half of all seizures. A simple partial seizure can begin anywhere in the brain, it is limited to a small region of one hemisphere and normal alertness is maintained. If it is sensory, it is called an aura. Complex partial seizures spread and alter consciousness. They usually start with auras or abrupt alterations in behavior. Children with this type of seizure will have the same aura before each seizure. Depending upon the length of the aura, there may be time for some intervention. Partial seizures may spread and become secondary generalized seizures. Children's movements slow and become purposeless during complex partial seizures. Depending upon the part of the brain in which the seizure originates, the child may appear agitated or may display unusual repetitive behaviors, such as eye blinking, lip smacking, facial grimacing, and groaning. These are caused by the brain's inability to plan and process motor and sensory input (Weinstein & Gaillard, 2007).

Some seizures have prominent motor components and can be brief or prolonged. A group of seizures called drop seizures cause abrupt changes in muscle tone. Both myoclonic and atonic seizures fall into this category. In these types of seizure, the child's loss of postural control causes him to fall. **Myoclonic seizures** are brief, single, rapid contractions of muscles that may be repeated and can involve isolated muscle groups or more general muscles of the trunk and limbs. Some are subtle, with just head nodding, while others cause sudden flexion or bending backwards that almost seem to pull the child over. In **atonic seizures**, the muscle tone is lost, which can lead to falling. Although the loss of consciousness may be brief, the child cannot protect himself during a fall (Weinstein & Gaillard 2007). Head injury is an obvious concern and children can wear helmets to protect themselves. These kinds of seizures are very disconcerting for young children, and they may cry whether or not they are hurt.

Tonic-clonic seizures (formerly called grand mal seizures) are the most disconcerting to observe. They may begin as either a partial or generalized seizure. These seizures have two components. In the clonic states there is repetitive, rhythmic jerking of extremities, with slow and rapid components. In the tonic state there is sustained stiffening, perhaps jaw clenching. The loss of consciousness may lead to an unprotected fall. Either the tonic or clonic aspect of the seizure can occur first followed by the other. During a seizure, respiration may sound raspy; an unusual cry, blueness, and incontinence may follow the seizure (Weinstein & Gaillard, 2007). Tonic-clonic seizures account for about a quarter of seizures overall (Kotagal, 2000). A period of sleep is required for the child to recover and he will rarely remember the event. Although rare, prolonged seizures—those lasting more than 15 to 30 minutes without full return to consciousness—can be considered a medical emergency. The concern here is that irreversible changes to the brain may occur.

Epilepsy syndromes are seizure disorders, but each has different clinical features and characteristic electroencephalogram patterns. Understanding a child's specific syndrome makes both educational and behavioral intervention easier.

Seizures are managed in a variety of ways and parents must make decisions they feel are in the child's best interests. The first step is to determine whether the child has epilepsy and if the seizures will reoccur. Treatment begins after a second unprovoked seizure. Some families choose to use antiepileptic drugs (AEDs). These drugs work by manipulating neurotransmitter activity. Families, in consultation with medical personnel, need to evaluate the possibility of the reoccurrence of seizures and the potential side effects of the drugs. The most common side effects are those that impact the motor and cognitive areas of the brain. They include sleepiness, decreased attention and memory, difficulty in speaking, an unstable gait, and double vision. The side effects may occur when the drug is started but then go away, or they may reoccur when dosages are increased. If side effects persist, the quest is for another drug that will regulate the seizures without side effects. There is additional concern that such drugs may have long-term adverse effects on learning, even after the drug use has been discontinued. They affect other body systems, and children can have allergic reactions to some

(Weinstein & Gaillard, 2007). The complex decisions concerning drug treatment include determining the correct dosage, and decisions about if and when drug therapy can be stopped.

Antiepileptic therapies do not always rely on medication. Some physicians find that a diet very low in sugars and carbohydrates, one that forces the brain to utilize fat rather than carbohydrates for energy, will alter neurotransmitters. Other therapies focus on making sure the child gets enough sleep and identifying and eliminating triggers. If a child's seizures do not respond to these interventions, surgery may be an option, depending on the number and severity of seizures, and their impact on the child's and family's lives.

Implications for Educators

Seizures are both embarrassing and frightening for the child having them, as well as the children who witness them. Children with seizures may be anxious, have a poor self-concept, and feel rejected and socially isolated. In early childhood, the social and emotional consequences of seizures may be the most devastating effect.

Seizures are primarily a medical problem. The management of seizures in the classroom, however, involves educational decision making. The first thing to do is to talk with the child's family and find out as much as you can about the type of seizures the child has, their frequency and length, if they are set off by identifiable environmental stimuli, and how the child reacts when having a seizure. You should also have a written Epilepsy Action Plan and follow it for any child who is identified as having epilepsy.

Obviously, it is important to know the first-aid procedure for seizures. The following information is adapted from the Epilepsy Foundation (n.d.) recommendations. It starts with *stay calm*. You can't stop a seizure once it starts. Absence seizures require no immediate action. For tonic-clonic seizures, if the child is upright, help move him to the floor, loosen clothing, and remove any nearby objects so he doesn't strike his head or body against them. Put something soft under his head. Turn the child's face to the side so saliva can flow out of the mouth, but don't otherwise interfere with movements. (A person having a seizure cannot swallow his tongue.) Time the seizure with your watch. Don't be alarmed if the child stops breathing momentarily, and don't put anything in the child's mouth. When the movements stop and the child is relaxed, cover the child and allow him to rest or sleep until he is ready to get up. Notify the child's parents that a seizure has occurred. Call for emergency medical services if the child has not had prior seizures; the child has diabetes, heat exhaustion, or a head injury; it lasts more than 5 minutes, a second seizure follows, or it is unusual in some way (Epilepsy Foundation, n.d.). The child needs to be observed until fully alert, and teachers should provide reassurance and comfort. If the child has become incontinent, he should be helped unobtrusively to change his clothing and then allowed to rest. When ready, he should be encouraged to rejoin his classmates.

In addition to knowing first aid procedures, you should note the length of the child's seizure and what the child was doing when the seizure took place. You should know the medication the child takes and its possible side effects.

Again, you are the model; to the extent that you are calm and matter of fact, the other children will be as well. If children ask you questions, answer them honestly, but simply: "Sometimes Sibyl's brain has too much energy. Her body is affected by this energy. Once the energy is gone, she is tired and wants to rest." Children who have tonic-clonic seizures are obvious to all children in the classroom. You should keep a towel and washcloth and a change of clothing for the child in your classroom.

Hepatitis

Hepatitis is an inflammation of the liver, which manifests itself in a number of different ways. It is caused by toxins, certain drugs, heavy alcohol use, and bacterial and viral infections. It is also used to identify a family of viral infections that affect the liver (CDC 2008a). Hepatitis A (HAV), often referred to as yellow jaundice, an acute liver disease, is caused by the hepatitis A virus. It is common among the very young and elderly. A fecal to oral pathogen causes HAV; the infection is best controlled through proper implementation of appropriate hygiene practices. The CDC (2008a) recommends a hepatitis A vaccination for all children starting at one year. **Hepatitis E** is a serious liver disease caused by the hepatitis E virus (HEV) that usually results in an acute infection. It is typically caused by fecal-contaminated drinking water. Although rare in the United States it is common in developing countries. There are no current approved vaccines for hepatitis E (CDC, 2008a)

Hepatitis B is a liver disease caused by the hepatitis B virus (HBV). The disease can be mild or serious and last for a few weeks to long-term liver disease or liver cancer. The CDC (2008a) recommends that children be vaccinated for Hepatitis B. Hepatitis D is a serious liver disease similar to hepatitis B, it is uncommon in the United States and there is no vaccine for HDV. Both HBV and HDV are blood-borne pathogens; they are transmitted by contact with infectious blood, semen and other bodily fluids during sex, sharing contaminated needles, and from an infected mother to her newborn. They are preventable through vaccinations (HBV) and alterations in lifestyle practices (CDC, 2008a).

Hepatitis C requires more discussion than A, B, D, or E, due to the recent rise in reported cases, and the severity of the illness. Hepatitis C (HCV) is the most common contagious blood-borne pathogen in the United States. Approximately 3.2 million people are chronically infected (CDC, 2008b). Initially, most identified cases were due to exposure of health care providers who came into contact with contaminated blood, or those individuals receiving blood transfusions prior to the establishment of appropriate screening practices in the early 1990s. HCV-infected women can spread infection to their infants. This occurs at the time of birth to about 4 out of every 100 infant births. There is no treatment to prevent this. The risk is greater if the mother is co-infected with HIV. The rate of transmission can be as high as 19 percent (CDC, 2008c). Through the proper use of universal precautions already discussed in this chapter, the risk of infections to educators and other children from hepatitis C is low and can

be controlled. Only 1.5 percent of long-term spouses of individuals with chronic HCV infection developed HCV (CDC, 2008b). There is no effective vaccine for hepatitis C (CDC, 2008a).

While blood testing is reliable, it should not be conducted during the first 18 months of life, as the mother's antibodies may still be protecting the infant (CDC, 2008c). Families may be reluctant to disclose their child as a person with HCV for fear of discrimination. It is important, however, for parents to know as soon as possible if their child has HCV, because if cirrhosis or carcinoma develops, the child will need to be placed on a waiting list for a liver transplant. Hepatitis C is the leading indication for liver transplants (CDC, 2008c).

Implications for Educators

HCV is primarily spread through direct contact with human blood. It can be spread in a household through sharing personal items that might have blood on them. It cannot be spread by sneezing, hugging, coughing, food or water, sharing eating utensils or drinking glasses, or casual contact. As an educator of young children, it is imperative that you take the time to follow good, sound, and safe hygiene practices. You may not know if a child in your class has HCV. For those who work with infants, remember that tests are not reliable until the child is at least 18 months old. Children need no special programming, just support of their social development and inclusion in the group.

Human Immunodeficiency Virus

Human immunodeficiency virus (HIV) has caused massive concern in the health care and social system. Initially, children with hemophilia who needed transfusions were more likely to get HIV than other children. Today, children with newly diagnosed HIV infection acquire it primarily from their mother (CDC, 2007b).

Between 120,000 and 160,000 women in the United States have HIV and a fourth of these women do not know it (CDC, 2007b). This places them at risk for passing the virus to their infants. Approximately 25 percent of infants born to mothers with HIV infection will become infected without intervention. Using prenatal counseling and testing for HIV, the provision of perinatal antiretroviral prophylaxis, and the use of cesarean section, and not breastfeeding can reduce the incidence of pediatric infection to 2 percent (CDC, 2007b). If it is suspected, infants should be tested within 48 hours of birth, at 1 to 2 months and again at 4 to 6 months. If negative at 6 months, the infant has a 99 percent chance of not being infected with HIV (Bell, 2007). In 2005 about 142 infants got HIV from their mothers (CDC, 2007b).

Children who are infected with HIV may have a wide spectrum of illnesses, depending on the degree of immune system dysfunction. The adoption of highly active antiretroviral treatment (HAART) regimens for pediatric use, and the development of supports for mothers and children with HIV infection helps them live longer and healthier lives (Bell, 2007, CDC, 2007b). The advent of a vaccine against *Streptococcus pneumoniae*, and the use of antibiotic prophylaxis against these infections, has also helped improve the outlook for children with HIV.

However, children are still at risk for bacterial infections that can cause complications, such as pneumonia and meningitis, as well as less serious ones that lead to middle ear infections and dental problems. Typical viral infections, such as measles and chickenpox, as well as cytomegalovirus (CMV) of the eye and herpes, also remain problems (Bell, 2007). *Pneumocystis carinii* pneumonia, or "PCP," is a severe illness that children with HIV or AIDS may get. Most children infected with this germ don't get pneumonia, because their immune systems are normal. Children whose immune systems are badly damaged by HIV can get PCP. PCP is the most common serious infection among children with AIDS in the United States (CDC, 2007c).

These changes have made tremendous differences in the quality of life for these children. However, compliance is an issue. To work, the medications need to be taken. If started and not taken, it can lead to a drug-resistant mutant HIV. There are a number of reasons why the routine is not adhered to: the large number of pills, the schedules for taking them are inconvenient, uncomfortable side effects, poor understanding of the need for the medication, taste, and caregivers who do not follow through. Once started, the therapy must be monitored both for compliance and to ensure that appropriate drug quantities are taken (Bell, 2007).

Many children with HIV infection have some form of central nervous system dysfunction. These may be mild or more significant when there is not compliance to the regime. Children may have learning disabilities and expressive language disorders, and impairments similar to cerebral palsy and seizure disorders. Some children will lose the skills they have acquired as the disability proceeds if left unmonitored (Bell, 2007).

Implications for Educators

The severe neurodevelopmental impairments of the 1980s and 1990s are less common in the United States, but they are replaced by more subtle risks, such as learning and attention disorders. Overall, infants born to women who are infected with HIV typically are of lower birth weight and length than their counterparts. They have IQ scores that fall in the low average range even when other things are factored out (Bell, 2007). Infants should have developmental assessments on a regular basis. If they are found to have delays, they are eligible for early intervention services. Children exposed to HIV have much to gain from early education.

Having a child with HIV infection in the classroom poses two serious questions: one relates to the disclosure of HIV status while the other relates to infection control. Obviously, revealing to a child that he has HIV infection is a difficult disclosure, one that must be conveyed in an age-appropriate manner if the child is to understand what it means. Because of fear of discrimination, some parents do not tell their children that they have HIV infection, so the child himself may not know. Most states have decided that the teacher does not have the need to know whether a child in her class has HIV, the rationale being that risks to others are not great enough to violate a family's rights. Even if teachers receive this information informally, they are not allowed to disseminate it.

The next obvious question, then, is, "How great is the risk?" There are no documented cases of person-to-person transmission of HIV in child care centers or schools. No special precautions need to be taken other than routine handwashing. Universal precautions should be used with all blood-related incidents because of all blood-borne diseases. A child's exposure to other, more contagious, infectious diseases may pose greater risks. Identifying infectious disease breakouts early and informing parents is good practice under any circumstances.

No single person or system can be responsive to the complex needs of children with HIV infections. Ideally, teachers work with health care providers as part of an interdisciplinary team to meet children's health, educational, and social needs. Another area of concern is the risk posed to these children for multiple placements outside the home if their parents become unable to provide a consistent and nurturing home for them as they become more ill with their own HIV infection.

Obesity and Overweight

The prevalence of children who are obese and overweight in the United States has increased markedly in the past three decades (CDC, 2006.) Individuals are considered **obese** if they have a **body mass index** (BMI) of 30 or more or are more than 30 pounds over the recommended weight for their height. The guidelines for **overweight** are a BMI of 24–29.99 or individuals who are 25–30 pounds over the recommended weight for their height (CDC, 2006). According to results of the National Health and Nutrition Examination Survey (NHANES), a large ongoing program conducted by the National Center for Health Statistics (NCHS), about 5 percent of children and adolescents aged 2 to 19 years were obese during 1971–1974 when NHANES first began collecting data (Anderson & Butcher, 2006). The 2003–2004 NHANES data show that the percentage of children and youth aged 2 to 19 classified as over-weight/obese has reached 17.1 percent (Ogden, Carroll, Curtin, McDowell, & Tabak, 2006). Increased weight gain in the early childhood years accounts for some of this increase. The prevalence of early childhood obesity showed a significant increase within one decade (Ogden,

Young children are becoming obese at earlier ages. Children need to spend less time in sedentary activities and increase the amount of time they spend in moderate to vigorous activity.

Flegal, Carroll, & Johnson, 2002). For infants and toddlers aged birth to 23 months, between 10 and 12 percent are overweight based on the Centers for Disease Control and Prevention growth charts which look at weight for length (CDC, 2007d). Among children aged 2 through 5 years, the prevalence of obesity was 7.2 percent in 1988–1994 and increased to 10 percent in 1999–2000. Among 6 through 11 year olds, the prevalence of obesity was 11.3 percent in 1988–1994 and climbed to 15.3 percent in 1999–2000. Obesity in childhood is difficult to reverse. Overweight children have a difficult time keeping up with their friends. They cannot run as far or as fast or climb as high. The social and emotional costs are great.

An individuals' weight is determined by the amount of energy they put into their body in the form of food and the amount of energy they expend in the form of physical activity or energy. If the amount of energy individuals put into their body is equal to the amount of energy they expend, then weight is maintained. If more energy is put into the body than is expended, weight gain occurs. Weight loss occurs when the amount of energy expended is greater than the amount of energy put into the body. To maintain healthy weight, individuals must learn to balance intake and expenditure. This balance requires self regulation. One aspect of self regulation is the ability to monitor one's food consumption.

Obesity causes an increased risk of health problems in early childhood and later. Increases in asthma and sleep disorders occur early. Risks for type 2 diabetes, heart disease, high blood pressure and cholesterol, liver disease, orthopedic complications, and mental health problems can occur later. However, although many of these diseases take years of damage to develop, obese children develop them at a younger age then their parents would despite advances in medicine (Daniels, 2006).

The 2002 Feeding Infants and Toddlers Study (Fox, Pac, Devaney, & Jankowski, 2004) found that 18 to 33 percent of infants and toddlers consumed no discrete servings of fruits or vegetables on a given day. French fries were the most common vegetables consumed by toddlers. Some type of dessert, sugared sweets, or sweetened beverage were consumed by almost half of 7 to 8 month olds and this percentage increased with age.

Food is part of our culture and the way we live. To reduce the risk of obesity and other chronic diseases we need to take cultural feeding practices and socioeconomic levels into account (Mennella, Ziegler, Briefel, & Novak, 2006). Many Latina mothers prefer a chubby baby. A physically heavy baby is often preferred in cultures where levels of infant mortality are high. For many families, memories of food scarcity and high rates of infant mortality linger even when food is plentiful (Clark, 2003). More Hispanic infants began eating pureed baby food around 4 to 5 months and drinking fruit juice or fruit-flavored drinks and eating fresh fruit than non-Hispanic infants. Differences at 6 to 11 months included eating fresh fruits and fruit-flavored drinks. They also ate more baby cookies, soups, and rice and beans. These differences continued into 24 months with tortillas added as a noted difference. Why the emphasis on Hispanic infants and toddlers? They are three times more likely to be overweight or are in danger of becoming overweight than white children (Mennella et al., 2006).

Although fruit juice contains some good nutrients, it contains high levels of sugar (fructose). Likewise, most fruit contains high levels of fructose. Many Hispanic cultures routinely feed their infants sweetened drinks to prevent or treat infant colic (Mennella et al., 2005). The concern is that young children will develop a heightened preference for sweet-tasting foods. Some cultures genetically prefer even higher levels of sweet tastes.

When this genetic tendency is combined with liberal feeding of sweetened beverages, gelatin, canned fruit, soft drinks and juice-heightened sweets preferences are developed in early childhood that last a lifetime (Pepino & Mennella, 2005).

By the time children are 5 years old, they are consuming most of the foods of the adult diet of their culture (Birch, 1996). However, children eat what they like and leave the rest. Therefore, food preferences are especially important determinants of the food intake of young children (Birch & Fisher, 1998). Birch (1980) found that when preschool children were provided opportunities to observe other children choosing and eating vegetables (that they themselves did not enjoy), preferences for and eating of the disliked vegetables increased. With the potential of peer modeling, early childhood settings have the potential for making nutritious foods available to children and providing models for consuming them.

During the early childhood years, children are capable of learning to like and accept a variety of foods. In addition, repeated opportunities to taste a food increased acceptance. At least 8–15 exposures may be necessary before the food is accepted (Birch, 1996). Skinner, Carruth, Bounds, and Ziegler (2002) also found children's preference for a food or flavor increased with repeated exposure. They found that foods introduced after age 4 were less likely to be liked and accepted by children. A high percentage of children's food preferences are formed as early as 2 to 3 years. As educators we need to be mindful of this information.

Beginning at 4 months, infants need to drink water if they have had breast milk or iron fortified infant formula. Infants younger than 12 months should not have cow's milk, fruit or vegetable juice, or any sweetened beverages. One to 2 year olds should only have one-fourth cup (2 ounces) of 100 percent fruit or vegetable juice per day and preschool children one-half cup (4 ounces) (Delaware Child and Adult Care Food Program[DCACFP], 2007). If it is likely that children have had juice for breakfast, then they should not have it during the school day. Children 12 to 24 months should drink either whole milk or water. Children older than 24 months should drink 1 percent or fat-free milk or water. From 1 to 3 years at least a fourth cup of fruits and or vegetables should be offered at each meal and snack. By age 3, this quantity increases to half a cup (DCACFP, 2007).

Physical activity—energy output—in infants and toddlers promotes growth and development and provides the foundation for enjoying physical activity later in childhood (Heinzer, 2005). Nutrition—energy input—during the first 3 years of life helps determine children's growth patterns and body weight (Stunkard, Berkowitz, Schoeller, Maislin, & Stallings, 2004). Eating habits established during these years may program preferences into the brain that influence adolescent and adult nutrition (Mennella, Ziegler, Briefel, & Novak, 2006).

Physical activity is part of the balance of energy in and energy out. Regular physical activity reduces the risk for many diseases and strengthens muscles, bones, and joints (CDC, 2006). Physical activity is a key component of energy balance by keeping young children active and preventing children from becoming overweight (Kohl & Hobbs, 1998). Physical activity is associated with lower risks of accelerated weight gain and excess **adiposity** among preschool-aged children (Klesges & Lisa, 1995). The Framingham children's study found that the most active children had significantly lower BMIs than their less-active counterparts (Moore, Nguyen, Rothmann, Cupples, & Ellison, 1995). Level of physical activity is also affected by being overweight. Overweight boys were significantly less active than normal-weight boys during the preschool day (Trost, Sirard, Dowda, Pfeiffer, & Pate, 2003).

The National Association for Sport and Physical Education (NASPE) classifies children's physical activity as either structured or unstructured. **Structured physical activity** for young children is "planned and directed by the parent, caregiver, or teacher and is designed to accommodate the infant, toddler, or preschooler's developmental level" (NASPE, 2002, p. 18). When physical activity is adult-directed, children obtain significant amounts of moderate and vigorous physical activity (Ward, Saunders, & Pate, 2007). Adults can also coach children to increase their skill level. **Unstructured physical activity** is "child-initiated physical activity that occurs as the child explores his or her environment" (NASPE, 2002, p. 18). Both structured and unstructured physical activity are essential.

There are no official recommendations for the amount of physical activity infants need. NASPE (2002) has recommended physical activity guidelines for toddlers and preschool children. Briefly, toddlers should accumulate at least 30 minutes daily of structured physical activity and preschoolers at least 60 minutes daily and both need at least 60 minutes to several hours per day of unstructured physical activity and should have safe indoor and outdoor space to practice skills. They should develop movement skills that are building blocks for more complex movement tasks. Early childhood educators should be aware of the importance of physical activity and facilitate movement skills (NASPE, 2002). If they are to occur, structured and unstructured physical activities need to be scheduled daily and embedded in routines.

A sedentary life style which is characterized by lack of moderate and vigorous activity and excessive screen media use (television, videos, computers) is associated with increased risks of childhood obesity (Jago, Baranowski, Baranowski, Thompson & Greaves, 2005). Screen media is negatively related to time spent in more energy expending activities and positively related to time spent in sedentary activities (Vandewater, Shim, & Caplovitz, 2004). For children as young as 3 years of age, the amount of TV viewing along with amounts of physical activity are the only significant predictors of BMI (Jago et al., 2005). Among 2,761 children aged one to five years in New York State, those who were black or Hispanic and those with a TV in their own bedroom were at greater risk of becoming overweight (Dennison, Erb, & Jenkins, 2002). A child's risk of being overweight increased by 6 percent for every hour of television watched per day. If that child had a TV in his bedroom, the odds of being overweight jumped an additional 31 percent for every hour watched. Preschool children with TVs in their bedroom watched an additional 4.8 hours of TV or videos every week (Dennison et al., 2002).

Some researchers did not find TV viewing as a direct risk factor for decreased physical activity that contributes to early childhood obesity. Vandewater, Shim, and Caplovitz (2004) found video game and print use rather than TV viewing related to children's weight status. Screen media use is a main form of sedentary behavior related to childhood overweight in direct and indirect ways.

Children 6 and younger spend an average of 2 hours a day with screen media. They primarily watch TV and videos (Rideout, Vandewater, & Wartella, 2003). Watching an excessive amount of television both decreases activity level and increases children's requests for advertised foods. Children who watched television more frequently were also more likely to eat high-calorie, low-nutrient food, ask their parents to purchase advertised foods, develop poor eating habits, become overweight, develop eating disorders, and have elevated cholesterol levels (Byrd-Bredbenner, 2002). In addition to the sedentary component of television viewing, children are also impacted by the advertisements they are processing as they watch various programs. Half to two-thirds of commercials during children's programming are about food (Comstock & Scharrer, 2003). The most common food advertisements during children's shows are for presweetened breakfast cereals and high-sugar foods. There are virtually no advertisements for vegetables, fruits, protein-rich food, and unsweetened breakfast cereals (Byrd-Bredbenner, 2002). Children younger than 6 years of age cannot distinguish between commercials and programming. They do not understand that the purpose of commercials is to persuade them to buy something or to ask their parents to (Johnson & Young, 2003). They simply know they want the advertised product. Food advertisements geared at children entice them with more than just the food.

Approximately one-third of food advertisements offer prizes and most of the advertisement focuses on the prize. If children associate getting rewards and prizes with eating fast food and snacks, they are less likely to see the benefit of consuming healthier foods (Byrd-Bredbenner, 2002).

The desire for advertised foods begins at an early age. Children as young as age 2 are more likely to choose advertised foods (Henry J. Kaiser Family Foundation, 2004) and brand preferences start in preschool and continue to strengthen through elementary school (Johnson & Young, 2003). These various influences create additional challenges in helping children establish healthy weights from an early age.

Our society looks scornfully at obesity despite the increasing numbers of children who are overweight. Even 3 year olds taunt other classmates with "Tubby," "Fats," and "Fatso." Overweight children are discriminated against by peers and teachers. They may grow up expecting rejection and usually get it. If they feel isolated and unhappy, they may react by eating more.

Implications for Educators

We need to help children get more in touch with their bodies. When children tell us they are not hungry and we require them to eat or finish the food on their plate, we are teaching them not to respond to what their body is telling them. We need to evaluate our own practices related to eating and the nutritional quality of the food served in early care and education settings.

To help children establish healthy eating habits, adults should choose meals and snacks wisely. Adults determine what foods young children have to eat. They need a variety of fruits, vegetables, whole-grain foods and bread, fluid milk products, and meat and meat alternatives, including some unsaturated fat (U. S. Departments of Health and Human Services and Agriculture, 2005; U. S. Department of Agriculture Child and Adult Care Food Program, 2002). Water needs to be available and children should be encouraged to drink water when they are thirsty.

Snacks provide about 25 percent of young children's daily energy intake (Skinner, Ziegler, Pac, & Devaney, 2004). Snacking can help children learn self-regulation by showing them how to maintain their metabolism. A stable metabolism can help children feel less hungry and thus may prevent them from overeating at meal times. To make snacking effective, snacks and meals should have balance, variety, contrast, color, and eye appeal. Snacks are also beneficial because they provide an opportunity to introduce new foods (U. S. Department of Agriculture Child and Adult Care Food Program, 2002).

Children who are overweight exercise less than other children. They seem to be able to do single, nonrhythmic activities like climbing, but have problems with repeated rhythmic activities like running. Playing loud music with a distinct beat during activities helps them improve this skill. To help burn calories and tone muscles, these children should be encouraged to participate in moderate to vigorous levels of activity in bursts of 3 to 5 minutes as many as 10 times a day. They and their parents also need education on nutrition. Praise and other noncaloric rewards should be used, never sweets.

Think about how what you need to choose for snack that will support all children's healthy eating. Go beyond juice and crackers to water and strawberries dipped in low-fat yogurt, fat-free milk and whole-grain pita with hummus, water, low-fat cottage cheese with fruit, water, and steamed or fresh vegetables dipped in fat-free sour cream. Children like to dip. However, they each need their own dipping cup.

Sickle Cell Disease

Sickle cell disease is a group of hereditary disorders that affect the red blood cells. It includes sickle cell anemia, sickle hemoglobin C disease, sickle hemoglobin D disease, sickle hemoglobin E disease, and sickle beta thalassemia (California Department of Health Care Services, 2007). It is a painful, inherited blood disorder that can be identified at birth through blood tests. Testing is offered to all families in newborn nurseries (Batshaw & Tuchman, 2002). Sickle cell disease is a problem related to the hemoglobin in the blood. **Hemoglobin** is a substance in the red blood cells that makes the blood red in color, and carries oxygen to all parts of the body. There are different variations of hemoglobin, called hemoglobin types, which are not the same as the blood type. Hemoglobin type is inherited. The most common hemoglobin type is "A." If a person has some hemoglobin A, the red blood cells stay smooth and round, and can deliver oxygen normally to the body. There is a major distinction between sickle cell trait and sickle cell disease. The trait exists when the child inherits the disease from only one parent, sickle cell disease occurs when it is inherited from both. The child with the trait is not ill, but is a carrier of the disease.

Under certain conditions, the blood cells of children with sickle cell disease become sickle-shaped, obstructing the blood vessels that lead to pain and/or damage to the tissues. The most serious problem is infections. Newborns diagnosed with sickle cell disease are placed on antibiotic therapy. Parents are given information about preventive health measures as well as signs of symptoms requiring prompt medical attention. Sickle cell disease is present in all population groups, but is more prevalent in persons of African, Mediterranean, Asian, Southeast Asian, Caribbean, and South and Central American origins (California Department of Health Care Services, 2007). The concern with infants in these countries is their susceptibility to infections such as pneumonia.

In the United States more than 70,000 people have sickle cell disease and more than 1,000 infants are born with the disease each year. One in 12 African Americans are carriers of the sickle cell gene and 1 in 500 have the disease. One in 1,000 to 1,400 Hispanic Americans have the disease. Two million people have the sickle cell trait (CDC, n.d.a).

Red blood cells are normally shaped like a doughnut with a hole in the middle that does not go through completely and they have a life span of approximately 120 days. In sickle cell disease, cells take on a crescent, or sickle, shape they are more rigid, and sticky and have a life span of about 10 to 20 days (Carroll, 2000). This impairs the oxygen-carrying capacity of the cells, is conducive to clogging, and can lead to **anemia**. The result is pain and chronic fatigue. There is no known cure, and frequent blood transfusions are necessary to replace destroyed red blood cells. Children with severe forms of the disease may die in childhood or early adulthood from a blood clot, which prevents oxygen from reaching the brain, or infections.

In sickle cell disease, children lack hemoglobin A, there is only sickle hemoglobin, called hemoglobin S, or there may be hemoglobin S and another type of hemoglobin (C, D, E, or beta thalassemia) (California Department of Health Care Services, 2007). The most common type of sickle cell disease is sickle cell anemia. Other forms of sickle cell disease include hemoglobin (*red blood cells*) sickle cell disease and sickle beta thalassemia. Hemoglobin sickle cell disease tends to be milder than sickle cell anemia. Sickle beta-thalassemia can be mild or severe. All of these types of sickle cell disease can be identified by the newborn state screening test (Ohio Sickle Cell and Health Association, 2005).

The actual proportion of the sickle-shaped cells varies from child to child. The higher the proportion and the earlier the symptoms appear, the more severe the disease is likely to be. If the diagnosis was not made at birth, it is usually made in infancy or early childhood. Infants start to have symptoms around 5 months of age when their "baby" hemoglobin is replace by "adult' hemoglobin and the cells begin to sickle. The first symptom is usually the swelling of the hands and feet along with fever. This is caused by the sickle cells getting stuck and blocking the flow of blood in and out of the hands and feet. The pain can be mild to severe and last any length of time. Stroke is also a concern. Keeping hydrated and not getting too hot or cold also helps. Pain medication is given (CDC, n. d. b).

Anemia is a complication that can cause tiredness, irritability, dizziness, trouble breathing, and slow growth. Taking iron supplements is not helpful as there are not enough oxygen-carrying red blood cells. Blood transfusions are used to treat anemia when it becomes severe. Infection is a major concern and the leading cause of death in children with sickle cell. Children should get the traditional vaccines given in early childhood as well as some extra ones (CDC, n. d. b)

Implications for Educators

Young children with sickle cell disease are more prone to crisis and hospitalization than are older children. Crises are precipitated by a variety of circumstances: infection, chilling, dehydration, strenuous exercise, sweating, and cold, damp weather. Use this knowledge to take preventive measures. These children need nutritionally dense foods. You can plan snacks and lunches to meet their needs. They also need to drink a great deal of fluid, especially water. Encourage children to drink more by having fluids readily available and ensure that there is easy access to the bathroom. Fatigue is a major factor, as children tire easily and a general lassitude is often present. Be aware of the balance of active and quiet activities in the classroom. Be sure to alternate these activities and to have alternative activities for those that are physically demanding. Stress cooperation, not competition. Help children build a good self-concept.

Tourette Syndrome

Tourette syndrome is an inherited neurologic disorder whose essential features are repetitive involuntary motor or vocal tics. A **tic** is a sudden rapid, recurrent, non-rhythmic stereotyped motor movement or vocalization (NINDS, 2005). **Simple tics** involve sudden brief, repetitive movements that use a limited number of muscle groups such as eye blinking, shoulder shrugging, throat clearing, sniffing, and so on. **Complex tics** are distinct, coordinated patterns that involve several muscle groups and may be a combination of simple tics such as facial grimacing combined with a head twist and shrugging a shoulder. They may actually appear purposeful such as hopping, bending, or twisting. Complex vocal tics involve words or phrases. The most distressing tics are those that result in self-harm either physically (punching oneself in the face) or social/emotionally such as uttering swear words or repeating the phrases of others (NINDS, 2005). The behaviors may seem voluntary and purposeful but they are not.

Tics are typically worse with excitement and anxiety and better in calm and quiet. Motor tics typically precede vocal tics and simple tics precede complex tics. First symptoms occur in the head and neck area and may proceed to the trunk and limbs. The peek period for tic severity is during the early teen years and then they show signs of improvement with approximately 10 percent lasting into adulthood (NINDS, 2005). Children with Tourette syndrome may also have other neurobiological problems such as ADHD, SLD, depression, or anxiety disorders.

The early symptoms typically begin between 7 and 10 years of age but can start as early as age 2 (APA, 2000). It is estimated that 200,000 children have the most severe form with 1 in 100 exhibiting milder and less complex symptoms such as chronic motor or vocal tics or transient tics of childhood (NINDS, 2005). To be diagnosed with Tourette syndrome, the tics must occur many times a day over a period of more than a year and the child is never tic-free for a period of more than 3 consecutive months. The tics must not be the effects of medication or of another general medical condition (APA, 2000). The causes of Tourette syndrome are not known, but are likely to be complex with research showing abnormalities in certain regions of the brain, the circuits that connect these regions, and neurotransmitters.

Implications for Educators

Because of the involuntary nature of tics, children need experiences where they have some control. They need to see themselves in positions where the environment responds to them rather than the other way around. Many children will not display tics during the early childhood years. If they do, the involuntary nature of their tics needs to be acknowledged. It is important that the children in the classroom understand that the behavior is not under their control and to learn to ignore it and continue playing.

Guidelines

Children with special health care needs cover a wide range of needs and impairments. They may require you to learn new information and develop skills that are more medical in nature. Use the following guidelines to help accommodate these differences and to support children in their growth and development:

1. *Use activities that allow children to be in control* or adapt activities so that children have more control. Let the children decide what color(s) of fingerpaint they want to use, whether they want one dab or two, and where they want these on the paper.
2. *Allow the children to do as much as possible for themselves.* Actively support age-appropriate independence.
3. *Arrange the class schedule so that vigorous activities are followed by less-strenuous ones*; during strenuous activities, provide rest periods that are built in for everyone and alternative ways for doing activities.
4. *Be flexible in scheduling the day* so that if children have to leave for medical procedures, this can become part of the routine. If you accept the children's therapy and its importance, it will be easier for them. Some children find a full day tiring, especially when they return after an illness. If possible, have them come initially for part of the day.

5. *Plan activities that are open-ended* and do not require excessive amounts of time to complete, or ones that can be completed at home. Because some children may work more slowly and miss more school than others, they may decide not to start things they never expect to complete.

6. *Be a good observer.* Watch for mood changes, as these are often cues to well-being. Be aware of the child's body language. Often, a child will grimace or give other signs that will alert you to possible pain or arouse concern about the level of medication the child is taking. Young children have trouble recognizing and verbalizing their needs; you can help them.

7. *Find out as much as you can about the illnesses children have and how it affects them.* Talk to parents, therapists, and medical personnel, read books on the subject, and check the Internet. Be informed about children's diet, physical restrictions, medication, possible side effects of the medicine, and the behaviors that indicate a chronic illness might be moving into an acute phase.

8. *Find out what a child has been told about his illness and its implications.* Be prepared to respond to comments such as, "I don't want to play with you. You have leukemia. You're going to die." You need to know how the parents are dealing with the concept of death and exactly what they call the illness. Even with that knowledge, handling the situation is not easy. Young children are not capable of abstract thinking. Death is not viewed as permanent. This doesn't mean, however, that they are any less fearful of it. Although the child's classmates may seem unfeeling, they are only displaying curiosity and lack of knowledge.

9. *Help children learn about the implications of their special health care needs.* Verbalize for them what happens under certain circumstances: "You are allergic to peanuts. If you eat them, it will be hard for you to breathe. There are other things that are crunchy like peanuts that you can eat. These are sunflower seeds. I like them. Do you?"

10. *Provide an open atmosphere where children can discuss fears and problems.* One thing that children know is that if it is taboo, it is bad. Be honest when you do not know an answer; say you don't know and then find out the answer. In general, don't tell children more than they ask. They are the best guide about what they need to know.

11. *Develop a plan for keeping in touch with absent children.* You could send get-well cards through the mail or use email. Another child could deliver an audio- or videotape. The child could be called on the phone by other children (find out good times to call or let the child phone school). Send home a "fun bag" or develop a lending library of books and toys. The best plan is tailored to your situation and the child's needs.

12. *Provide accommodations.* Certain illnesses require adaptations such as free access to the toilet, extra time for task completion, special food for snacks, scheduling time to take medication, and so on. Provide it.

13. *Play cooperative games.* Classroom stress can bring on crises in some chronic illnesses (asthma, diabetes). Do not play competitive games. Make the classroom as pressure free as possible.

14. *Prepare children for events.* Special events (holidays, birthdays, field trips) may lead to flare-ups, as there is almost always some psychosomatic element in the timing or severity of acute bouts. Talk about what is likely to happen. This is a time to watch for stress-related reactions.

15. *Learn to recognize warning signs of emergencies.* Discuss with parents what they want you to do in case of an emergency and develop a written plan that has contingencies. If you are to call, call when you suspect something is wrong—do not wait for full confirmation. Tape the numbers near the phone you will use. Know the location of the nearest emergency room and the fastest way to get there. Take a first-aid course; be sure it includes the Heimlich maneuver and cardiopulmonary resuscitation.

Curriculum Adaptations

Children with special health care needs require few curriculum adaptations as long as they are allowed to work at their own pace. While working in each curriculum area, help children feel included in the group and focus on improving their self-concept.

Social Awareness: Self-Esteem, Inclusion, and Social Studies

Many children with special health care needs have been hospitalized. They may have concerns about doctors, hospitals, and separation from their parents. One of the most frightening aspects of hospitalization is the feeling of being out of control. Giving them knowledge about the roles of professionals, including physicians, is empowering. They need to develop social skills and methods of keeping in touch with peers when they cannot attend school. Some of the activities in the Resource Chapter 1 are specifically designed to increase children's awareness of special health care needs. Activity 1–25 Medical Tools helps children become familiar with a variety of medical tools and the body part on which each tool might be used. Patient in the Hospital, Activity 1–26, is an adaptation of "The Farmer in the Dell" and children sing about the doctors, nurses, and specialists needed until the child gets better. Emergency Room, Activity 1–29, helps children understand how an emergency room is different from a doctor's office and why people go there.

Self-Esteem

Children with special health care needs become aware of their uniqueness. Because most look like other children, adults may not understand or remember their problems. As they may have periods when they are fine and periods when they are not, others wonder if it is just a game they are playing. They may be misunderstood at school. They may not be able to participate in some strenuous activities. Because of frequent absences, it may be difficult for them to build relationships with other children and to complete projects. Especially if children are experiencing pain or side effects from drugs, they may not be fun to be with. Teachers may have to remind other children of these circumstances.

1. Help children become more aware of their feelings and learn to express them. Give them the skills to work through them. See Share your Feelings (Activity 1–8) for additional ideas.
2. Have children make a list (an adult can write it) of what they can do and like to do. Focus on the positive.
3. Help children think about what makes them happy and how they can use this knowledge when they become sad or fearful.

Inclusion

Children who have spent a long time convalescing in the hospital or at home may have had fewer opportunities to learn how to play with other children. They may not function at an age-appropriate level in areas such as cooperating with others, sharing, and turn-taking. They may have fewer skills in joining and being part of groups.

1. You are a model of the behaviors that are necessary for children to join groups. To the extent that you never join groups, you don't model this behavior and it is more obvious when you try to include a child with special health care needs. Suggest roles that need filling, or parts that they could play. However, accept the reality that this sometimes does not work, and openly explain to children that this is the way it is. If this happens frequently, you may need to use a different strategy.
2. Your role should be one that changes over time. Children may initially need your active support. However, supporting them when they have the ability to act on their own creates dependency and decreases growth.
3. Emphasize ways of approaching others.

Social Studies

Although our concern about children with special health care needs focuses on medical practice and settings, children spend most of their life in the community. Children need to know and role play not only traditional occupations but also variations.

1. Help children play the roles of public health nurses who visit homes, itinerant teachers who educate children who cannot attend school, and social workers or others who may serve as a support system to families.
2. Be sure to include cultural variations and the role of extended family as well as alternative medical sources.
3. Help children understand the interconnectedness of the community in which they live. Include information about water, electricity, and waste disposal and the consequences if the community did not address these needs.
4. Have children help draw and fill in a map of the route from the classroom to the nurse's office (if that is where they go). If hospitalized, remind children that they can learn about an unfamiliar place using the skill they have in map making. Include other significant places in the map.

Language and Literacy: Speaking, Listening, Reading, and Writing

Children need to be able to communicate. Some children with special health care needs will lack the experiential basis for language because they have spent time in restrictive settings. Parents may have limited children's opportunities, both because of the illness itself and because most illnesses weaken children and increase their susceptibility to contagious diseases. In addition to expanding their overall language base, children need to develop the vocabulary to express their fears and concerns and increase their understanding of the situations they may face. They need to be aware of their symptoms and how to label them, know their body parts, and be able to put the two together to give accurate information about their current state of health. Children may have consciously tried not to listen or found that adults did not expect them to listen, so they quit attending. Adults often forget that there may be so much attention to other areas of learning that listening is neglected, or that, although children listen, they may not understand what they hear. Reading offers the child an escape into other worlds of learning. Writing affords children the opportunity to express and share feelings even when those we want to speak with are not present. It also provides a way of remembering important information.

Speaking

Encouraging children to speak about nonthreatening experiences provides the groundwork for talking about experiences that they perceive as sad or scary.

1. Take field trips to the florist, bakery, post office, and radio station to help children gain first-hand experiences they may be lacking because of their special health care needs (be sure the places you plan to visit will not trigger an episode for a child).
2. When the child is home for extended periods, exchange language experience stories. Have children write stories about "Going to the Hospital" or "Things I Can See Out My Window." Include illustrations or use pictures from a digital camera.
3. Send a "Get Well Soon" audio- or videotape to the child. Have children who want to share, send a message on the tape. If this is set up as an activity area, put a picture of the child beside the tape and encourage the children to talk to her. The child who is ill may wish to send an answering tape back. See Activity 1–2 Get Well Cards.
4. Encourage children to ask questions. Show children pictures of situations and ask them to describe what is happening in the picture; help them ask questions about what specific objects are, how they are used, and about what will happen next.
5. Show children pictures of scenes (beach, grocery store, hospital, doctor's office, classroom, and so on) and ask them about how they would feel if they were part of the picture. Show pictures with moods that may be interpreted in a variety of ways. After one child has responded, ask if others feel differently and have them describe their feelings. Ask children

what they need to change in the picture to change a negative feeling to a positive one (have a parent present, a stuffed animal, etc.).

Fingerplays can be used to teach concepts and are especially good for those who are frequently in bed. Fingerplays are active, yet not tiring. Parents can easily learn them and thus form another link with school.

1. Use fingerplays that are repetitive, so children only have to learn minor changes to participate: "Where Is Thumbkin?"
2. Use fingerplays to increase body awareness: "I Put My Finger on My Face."
3. Use fingerplays to teach concepts: "A Little Ball."

Listening

Children frequently are expected not only to listen but to understand and follow through on adult requests, especially if these come from medical personnel. Children need skills in following directions but also in asking for clarification when they do not understand what is required.

1. Play Simon Says and include requests that frequently occur in medical situations: "Say ahhh," "Take a deep breath," "Open your mouth wide," and so on.
2. Using similar phrases, put them together and have children perform a series of tasks involving their body: "Open your mouth, take a deep breath, and breathe out slowly."
3. If the child is likely to be hospitalized, make a listening tape of hospital sounds. This will make a strange place a bit more familiar. If the child has to stay in bed, make a listening tape of things one might hear from bed and find out what the sounds mean.

Stories are a great way to make the unknown a little more familiar, to help children know they are not the only ones with fears, and perhaps to help put themselves and their situation into perspective. Choose stories that relate to the specific situation the children you are teaching might face. See the Children's Bibliography.

1. Read stories about children in hospitals.
2. Read stories about children or animals who are different.
3. Have a listening center where you have appropriate books as well as recordings of those books. Help children develop the skill of independent listening, so that if they are out of school for an extended period, they have a familiar activity they can participate in. Children can use headphones and safely listen while not bothering others if the equipment has sound level governors so the children cannot play so loud it affects their hearing. Since your collection of tapes and books is likely to be more extensive than any family's, plan a system of loaning children their favorites.
4. Fatigue and illness can impair listening. If you notice children who are typically attentive listeners not paying attention, consider the appropriateness of what you are doing, but also consider health issues.
5. Read or record a story the children are familiar with. Make some obvious mistakes (change words, locations, outcomes, and so on) and have the children find your mistakes.

Reading

Reading requires not only cognitive readiness, but an experiential background, so that the reading content makes sense. Part of your role is to develop creative ways to give children the experiential background they need to read and comprehend.

1. Children with special health care needs may have limited experiences. Take them on field trips; if this is not possible, use the dramatic play area to extend their concepts. Some excellent videotapes and DVDs are also available that bring experiences to children who cannot participate in field trips.
2. Listen to the child's spoken language. If children have not had opportunities for speaking and listening that others have had, build these skills as part of your literacy program.
3. Help children focus on the relationship between printed and spoken language.
4. Encourage children to gain some control over their world through sequencing activities, especially ones that hurt or are frightening: "First we go to the doctor's office, then I tell them my name, then I wait, then I get my allergy shot, then I wait, then I get checked for a reaction, then I can go home." This makes the injection one of a series of events rather than the total focus.
5. Expose children to a wide variety of written materials. Read and recite many different types of children's books, poetry, fingerplays, and so on. It is useful, especially if what you are reciting is new to you, to have the words available in case you forget them. Point out to the children that you are doing this and why.
6. Have children match line-drawn faces showing different expressions. Then talk about what these people might be feeling or doing.
7. Play hospital or medical Lotto.

Writing

Goals for writing are to help children develop the small motor skills and eye-hand coordination necessary to write, to build a desire to write, and to connect writing with reading.

1. Make writing part of many different curriculum areas; for example, in dramatic play, encourage children to write prescriptions for the dolls who are sick.
2. Have children keep a chart about what happens to the sick doll. Discuss with children why they might do this and how this helps ensure accurate information when different people care for the doll.
3. Have some of the children make a picture menu of what the choices are for snack and then let them find out from the other children what they want from the menu. (Be sure you have enough so that children can have what they request.) After each child "writes" his name on his menu, distribute menus to children's places at the table along with their "orders." Because of the quality of the writing, it is likely that some of the orders will be wrong. Talk about the fact that mistakes happen in all restaurants, and discuss what to do about them.

Discovery: Mathematics, Science, and Technology

Children need support in investigating the world around them and in making sense out of it. They need to sort, classify, and develop the vocabulary to express themselves. They need to *do* this, not be told about it. The lives of children with special health care needs are linked to medicine and scientific discoveries. Their understanding of the scientific process can help them look at the implications of taking medicine versus not taking it. They can also explore and learn about their body and how it functions. Be sure children know the amounts of medication they need and when they need to take the medicine. Make math real and relevant. Technology can allow children to stay in touch with their classmates even when they are home. Software programs that are used at school may also be used at home. Some children with special health care needs use technology to help them move or breathe. Placing technology in the context of learning about health impairments normalizes special health care needs.

Mathematics

It is especially important for children who have special health care needs to start with a sensory motor concept of mathematics. This involves active interaction with materials like blocks, Cuisenaire™ rods, uniflex blocks, and pegs. Then move on to more abstract number concepts.

1. Use three-dimensional objects like unit blocks to teach basic math concepts; do not rely on rote memory.
2. Use music and rhythmic activities to reinforce math concepts (clap four times).
3. Make math relevant. Children need to know how many pills they must take and when. This is a step toward independence as well as toward learning number concepts.
4. Have children sort and classify familiar pieces of medical equipment (cotton balls, tongue depressors, bandages of different sizes and shapes, gauze).

Science

Because most children take medicine to alleviate symptoms, it is important to develop their cause-and-effect reasoning skills. They need to understand why they should take the medicine even when they feel well.

1. Plant seeds. Discuss conditions for growth. Put some plants in the dark. Do not water some. Discuss the implications of the various conditions and "treatments." See Activity 3–54w Planting.
2. Help children make predictions. Help them apply this skill to their particular situation: "I have trouble breathing when I run fast. If I run slower, I can run farther."
3. Help children learn about the seasons of the year, especially if they directly affect their state of health. Discuss with them how we prepare ourselves for seasonal change as well as how this happens in nature. Have children talk about the seasons' effects on them: "I can't walk as far in the winter when it is cold and windy." They need to develop this type of causal thinking.

Technology

The computer has many applications for children with special health care needs. It requires little energy to use; it is hygienic, self-paced, available when the child wants to use it, and is portable and interactive. Other technologies, such as digital cameras, can allow children to share anything from artwork to pictures of what is happening at home or in the classroom. Email and the Internet open up even more possibilities.

1. Encourage children with special health care needs to become familiar with computers. They need to establish some control over their world, and they can do that with a computer. Regardless of how rudimentary their skills, the potential for cause-effect reasoning is present.
2. There may be times when children with special health care needs cannot communicate. A communication board or computer equipped with a simple switch and a scanning program can allow children to make their needs known.
3. If children are absent from school, you might be able to loan or recommend to parents software that will help children learn some of the concepts you are teaching.
4. Technology has the possibility for helping children participate in interactive recreation. (Traditional "arcade" games typically require good fine motor coordination, but are timed, which is not helpful.) Computerized board games such as checkers and Monopoly exist, as well as many other commercially available games.

Wellness: Health, Physical Education, and Sensory Motor

All children need to learn to keep their bodies safe and healthy. They need to learn what they can and cannot do. If they become knowledgeable about their bodies and how they work, children may be able to prevent acute episodes by learning to recognize symptoms and/or avoiding situations likely to cause acute episodes. This knowledge will, in turn, make children feel more in control and help them move toward independence. Children with special health care needs must develop as much strength and endurance as they can. Respect their limits, but encourage them to participate in large motor activities. Young children will rarely overextend themselves, if programming is individualized so children can set their own limits. Opportunities for sensory motor integration are essential. Small motor activities are easily adaptable for quiet play and can be used to pace the day. Try to think of variations and new materials that will keep children interested. Be aware of the weather, especially when it is windy or very cold or hot. These extremes may cause children to tire quickly. Have some quiet activities outside also.

Health and Safety

Health and safety should be emphasized. Children need to learn about foods, those that are good for them and those they must avoid, as well as safety practices.

1. Work on the food groups, which foods are in each, and how the body uses different foods. Use the food pyramid for kids and look at the games and other supports at http://www.mypyramid.gov/kids/index.html.
2. Use illustrations to explain what happens when people eat food they are allergic to.
3. All children need to be protected from contagious diseases, so it is important that all children cover their mouths when coughing and sneezing or cough into their shoulder or elbow if nothing else is available; always wash hands after toileting and before eating, and follow forms of good hygiene by washing hands frequently.
4. Emphasize body awareness. Children need to be able to name body parts. As children's understanding increases, include the internal ones. Start with those they can feel (bones) and commonly known parts (stomach).
5. Help children analyze situations for potential injuries and talk about what can be done to prevent injuries.
6. Talk about healthy lifestyles.

Large Motor

Children with special health care needs may find large motor play challenging. Find ways of allowing different amounts of time for activities if children are not self-regulatory.

1. Keep activities noncompetitive and pressure-free.
2. Emphasize the quality of movement, not speed.
3. Modifications may need to be made to some games. Reduce the distance to be traveled. Slow the pace by having children walk, not run. Institute intermissions. (All children must clap 10 times between events.)
4. Have children jump on a trampoline (or mattress with dust cover). This improves drainage of the respiratory tract.

Small Motor

Small motor play is not physically taxing and can therefore be a potential strength builder. Many activities that fall into this category use materials that can be placed in jellyroll pans. These can serve as storage trays and can also be used in a wheelchair, on the floor, or in bed.

1. Choose toys that are washable and can be disinfected.
2. Use a variety of fine motor toys. Children need practice in this area, and without sufficient variety, they may become bored before they acquire the necessary skills.
3. Include materials that are typically used in medical settings (cotton balls, tongue depressors, small flashlights) to help children view them in a different context.

Sensory Motor Integration

Children need experience coordinating their senses. If they have not had sufficient opportunity to do this, you need to provide more activities that make them aware of their bodies and where they are in space.

1. Give verbal directions for motor activities and see whether the children can follow them. Once you have ascertained that they can, change the directions slightly.
2. Games with beach balls require little effort but a fair amount of coordination and integration.
3. Beanbags can be tossed, balanced, or caught. They are adaptable to the classroom as well as other settings.
4. Hand clapping is a simple but effective activity. When done to music or in a pattern (sequence)—especially when the hands cross the midline, the right and left hands take turns, and a partner is added—it is a challenging activity that can be used in a variety of circumstances.
5. Incorporate yoga into your daily schedule.

Creative Arts: Visual Arts, Music, Creative Movement, and Dramatic Play

Children with special health care needs may express concerns and fears through the arts that they are unable or unwilling to express otherwise. The arts also can be used as a way of releasing energy and emotions. Music can provide a good transition between home and school. Use slow music when children appear to be tiring. If a child is out of school for an extended period of time, send a musical greeting or a recording of new songs the children are learning so the child can come back to school knowing the words and thus feel included. Help children use dramatic play to better understand their world and to play through situations they may find scary. Children may be very competent at role-playing and can provide leadership, while at the same time working through some of their own feelings.

Visual Arts

The visual arts are both a means of creative expression and a tension reliever.

1. Concentrate on the process. If you can convince children to use arms and fingers they might not otherwise use, you are succeeding. As the process becomes easy, focus on variations.
2. Use many three-dimensional art materials. The initial goal is manipulation, not a final product.
3. Use art materials that require varying amounts of fine motor skills and strength.

Music

Music contributes much to a child's physical, aesthetic, and intellectual development. It provides pleasure and creative experience, develops auditory skills, encourages physical development, and increases the range and flexibility of one's voice. Provide a variety of musical experiences: listening, singing, moving to music, and playing instruments.

1. Have a variety of different instruments available. Help children explore and evaluate the sounds of an instrument when it is held and played in different ways.

2. Incorporate music and language experiences by having children make up new verses to old songs. Play instrumental recordings and ask the children to describe what they imagined while listening. See Activities 5–17 Bumblebees and 5–18 Clouds.
3. Use music for exercise, self-expression, listening, and keeping time. See Activity 5–13 Mood Songs.
4. Introduce concepts of pitch, loudness, and duration.
5. Teach songs with colors and numbers: "Who Has Red On," "Ten Little Children."
6. Sing songs that call children by name.
7. Use chants, especially if children (or adults) are self-conscious about singing.

Creative Movement

Creative movement helps children internalize their ideas about the world and their ability to respond to it.

1. Have children toss beach balls into the air and hum or sing one note until the ball touches the floor.
2. Do movement exploration activities, especially those that emphasize relaxation skills: "Move like a rag doll," "Move like a flag blowing in the breeze." See Activity 5–24 Rag Doll and 5–26 Movement Exploration.
3. Put stories to music. Have children choose background music for stories.
4. Paint to music. See 5–12 Mood Montage.
5. Music that combines creative movement and stories is fun and mind expanding.
6. Exercise to music. Select a body part (or combination) and have the children move it back and forth at a slow tempo.

Dramatic Play

Dramatic play, given appropriate props, allows children to act out fears and gives them control over frightening situations. Set up situations that children may encounter.

1. Hospital: Set up a hospital. Talk about being scared, about strange hospital sounds, about being left alone. Talk about the emergency room: Discuss and play scenes that might be going on in an emergency room, emphasizing the sense of urgency but allow the child to be in control. Extend the concept and encourage children to build a hospital, using blocks in conjunction with the dramatic play area. See Activity 1–26 Patient in the Hospital and 1–29 Emergency Room.
2. Doctor's office/clinic: Talk about routine visits and visits when children are sick. See Activity 5–28 Doctor's Office.
3. Surgery: Discuss operations. Allow the children to operate on dolls to "fix" them. Make finger casts so that children can learn that this is not a painful process.

Routines and Transitions

Transitions are often difficult times. Children who are wary of adults and who may not trust them have a particularly difficult time. Reentries into the classroom require separation from important people. Also, after a period

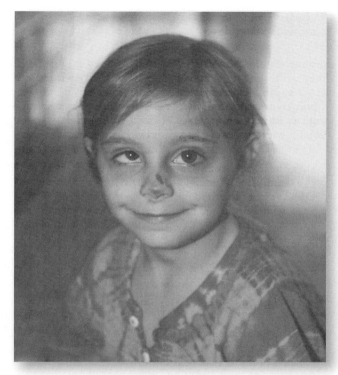

Transitions are difficult for children with special health care needs. This may be a time when a child feels as if she is lost or abandoned. She needs adult help in settling in and reentering the group.

of being absent, children may feel uncertain about their acceptance and about you. They need your support. This may be a time when children feel helpless or abandoned. They may feel hurt that they are being left again or afraid that you will hurt them. A predictable routine helps this transition.

1. Have a predictable arrival schedule, with one adult assigned to be the "greeter." At least during difficult transitions, have that be the same person each day.
2. Have the same adult help the child leave the setting and briefly talk about what will happen the next day, with the expectation that the child will return.
3. As children become more comfortable, encourage more independence—but *not* until the issue over separation has been resolved.
4. As the day is ending, try to make it positive. Find something that you can say about the day that is positive with the expectation that the next day will be even better.
5. If the child with special health care needs moves more slowly than the other children, remind her early about the transition to come. Dismiss that child early from the group.
6. Transitions may be a good time to have children take necessary medication. Other children are less likely to notice because there is a lot going on at this time and it is likely to happen if it is part of the routine.
7. This is a good time to emphasize similarities: all children with black hair and brown eyes, all children with patterned shirts, or all children with buckle shoes.

Summary

There are a variety of special health care needs that can impact the lives of children and their families. Although they are different, some of the characteristics are similar. The age of onset of the disease makes a difference. Children and their siblings may not understand the illness and its implications. Families may have a difficult time coping with the medical requirements, pain, and financial obligations of the impairment.

Special health care needs have many different manifestations. Some occur gradually, others all at once, some are acute and go into remission, some are chronic, and others are episodic. In some cases, there is the expectation that the life span will be shortened; and in still others, that the impairment will not affect the life span. The degree of incapacitation the child will have impacts the family. Some children with special health care needs will be classified as having an "other health impairment" and be covered under the IDEA, some will not meet the requirements of the IDEA but can receive accommodations under Section 504, other children will just need a sensitive teacher and a flexible routine.

There are many different special health care needs. When a child with special health care needs is in your classroom, it is important to learn more about that particular impairment, how it affects that particular child, what the child knows about the impairment, and what to do in emergency situations. Adapting the curriculum can help children work through some of their fears and give you information about their perception of their particular health care needs.

Reflections

1. There are many different special health care needs. It is challenging to learn about these. Many require accommodations that are unique, and skills that you may not have had the opportunity to develop. Reflect on the whole area of special health care needs and how you feel about having these children in your class. Are there some health problems you would find particularly challenging? Do you know why? How will you deal with your feelings? What kind of a plan do you have for finding out additional information about a child who might be in your class who has special health care needs?
2. The chapter provides information on Rolland's model of looking at chronic illness and disability. What do you see as the utility of that model? How is it useful in thinking about children and their families who have special health care needs? Does it provide you with any insights on how to work with these families, or what you might tell other children and adults?

Educational Resources

American Cancer Society has information divided into categories, such as patients, parents, survivors, and professionals. The site also allows you to search by specific cancer types. (800) ACS-2345; http://www.cancer.org/

American Heart Association contains information about children and heart disease as well as teaching tools. It is a good resource for professionals, parents, and children seeking information about heart disease and strokes. http://www.americanheart.org

American Lung Association provides a variety of information about lung diseases, including fact sheets. It is a good website for professionals, parents, and children. The site allows the user to search for information about any lung disease, including asthma and tuberculosis. http://www.lungusa.org/

Arthritis Foundation provides answers to basic questions about arthritis and has a section about children and arthritis. It also has tips for teachers, information for parents, and tips for coping with arthritis. http://www.arthritis.org/

Asthma and Allergy Foundation of America (AAFA) has basic materials related to chronic health conditions including information about children's allergies and asthma designed for parents and teachers. http://www.aafa.org

Candlelighters Childhood Cancer Foundation (CCCF) provides information about cancer, support groups and counseling for families. It has local chapters worldwide. http://candlelighters.org

Centers for Disease Control and Prevention provides information on many diseases, and is a great tool for professionals, parents, and children. It is a good starting point for gathering information, data, and statistics about diseases in general, and provides web links for additional information on specific diseases. http://www.cdc.gov

Epilepsy Foundation of America (EFA) is well organized and has a great section called the "Answer Place," which is organized by topic or by audience. A great site for professionals, parents, and children. (800) 332-1000; http://www.epilepsyfoundation.org/

Juvenile Diabetes Research Foundation International (JDRF) was started by parents with the expressed purpose of finding a cure for diabetes and its complications through research. It is a good source for up-to-date research. (800) 533-2873; http://www.jdf.org

National Dissemination Center for Children with Disabilities has funding from the U.S. Department of Education and the Office of Special Educational Programs (OSEP) to serves as the central source of information on the IDEA and No Child Left Behind (related to children with disabilities) and provides research-based information on effective educational practices. It offers fact sheets about specific disabilities and many other resources and services in English and Spanish. http://www.nichcy.org

For additional resources, visit the book companion website for this text at www.cengage.com/education/deiner.

Chapter 17

Children with Orthopedic and Neurologic Impairments

Sari is one of eight children and a twin. Her mother, Carol, is 25. Carol spends her entire day trying to feed, change, or pick up after the children. The two oldest children are in school. This leaves six at home, including Sari, who has cerebral palsy; she is very spastic. Early intervention began with home visits shortly after her birth. This was difficult, because Sari's mother had little time to pay attention to what I was saying as she tried to watch the other children. Carol's education was limited, and she didn't seem to understand what she had been told about Sari. The only thing she remembered was that Sari had "CP" and she "would never be normal." She sometimes referred to Sari as "the freak"; the other children picked this up and teased her for as long as I can remember.

Because Sari's medical treatment was very involved, she had many appointments for intervention. Some were missed because the family couldn't afford gas for the car, couldn't get a ride with someone, or couldn't find someone to watch the other children. Home visits were the mainstay of her program. Sari was a fussy child and cried frequently, but, interestingly, she almost always cried when her mother yelled at one of the other children. There were few toys; those that were there were broken. As Sari was slow, she could rarely reach a toy before someone else had snatched it up. She didn't lack verbal stimulation or visual variety with the other children around. However, she never had to speak, as someone always spoke for her. By 8 in the morning, when I came each week, Sari's mother was totally exhausted and at her wit's end. Sari had a short attention span, and her mother was happy if she was sleeping and not crying. She had to be fed slowly as she choked easily, and she would usually spill the juice or cereal as her movements were clumsy and shaky and she didn't have a high chair to give her the support she needed.

Although a diagnosis of cerebral palsy had been made shortly after birth, a full evaluation was not completed until Sari was about 6 months old. Although Sari's mother and I were part of the evaluation team I never thought they valued our input. I came for my regular home visit after Sari's mother had received a copy of the report. Carol was in a deep depression and didn't want me to come in. I persisted. I wanted to know why things had gotten worse. After a while, she told me. The team had written in their report that Carol "was a mother who neglected the needs of her child." She was trying as hard as she could just to cope through the day. Her husband worked all the time and even when he was home, he was little help. Her family lived out of state; his family "could care less." Carol admitted that she had been suicidal at times. We talked more. By the time my home visit was over, my head was splitting and I wondered how anyone could survive such a lifestyle. Carol was doing the best she could with the resources she had available to her. Her parents had divorced when she was young and she had only seen abusive parenting role models. She had no knowledge of other alternatives. As I was about the same age as this mother, I only wondered if I would have done as well in the same situation. To call this "case" a challenge was putting it mildly. I again thought of my job description, which never mentioned this type of family. It was time to become adaptive and creative as well as respectful and compassionate. I could leave and go home to a quiet, organized lifestyle and this mother could not.

Orthopedic and Neurologic Impairments

Most young children can climb and run, but children with orthopedic impairments may be limited to walking, crawling, or scooting. They may have different first-hand knowledge and experiences than their peers. Children with physical limitations often show an unevenness in physical, sensory, mental, and social-emotional growth related to this limited experience.

Defining Orthopedic and Neurologic Impairments

It is sometimes difficult to decide where particular differences should be discussed and the particular labels that should be used. Disabilities included under orthopedic and neurologic impairments are those in which nerves, muscles, and bones don't respond in a coordinated way. These include movement disorders such as developmental coordination disorder and correctable orthopedic impairments; neurologic impairments such as cerebral palsy, neural tube defects, spinal cord injuries, and traumatic brain injury; and musculoskeletal conditions including absent limbs and muscular dystrophy. Frequently, there are differences relative to definitions.

According to the Individuals with Disabilities Education Improvement Act (2004):

> Orthopedic impairment means a severe orthopedic impairment that adversely affects a child's educational performance. The term includes impairments caused by a congenital anomaly, impairments caused by disease (e.g., poliomyelitis, bone tuberculosis), and impairments from other causes (e.g., cerebral palsy, amputations, and fractures or burns that cause contractures).

Traumatic brain injury means:

> an acquired injury to the brain caused by an external physical force, resulting in total or partial functional disability or psychosocial impairment, or both, that adversely affects a child's educational performance. Traumatic brain injury applies to open or closed head injuries resulting in impairments in one or more areas, such as cognition; language; memory; attention; reasoning; abstract thinking; judgment; problem-solving; sensory, perceptual, and motor abilities; psychosocial behavior; physical functions; information processing; and speech. Traumatic brain injury does not apply to brain injuries that are congenital or degenerative, or to brain injuries induced by birth trauma.

Orthopedic and neurologic impairments are umbrella terms for a variety of different conditions and classifications.

When a disability has several aspects such as cerebral palsy, which has a neurologic base (abnormality of the immature brain) and orthopedic complications, classification is difficult. This text, and I assume your classroom, will take a functional approach to concerns such as these. It really doesn't matter what you call it; what is relevant is what the child knows and can do. The causes of specific impairments are included with information about that particular impairment.

Prevalence of Orthopedic and Neurologic Impairments

The federal government began keeping records on children with orthopedic impairments during the 1976–1977 school year. At that time 8.3 percent of children in the public schools were identified as having a disability. Of these children 0.2 percent had an orthopedic impairment. In the 2005–2006 school year 13.8 percent of children were identified as having a disability with 0.1 percent of these children having an orthopedic impairment. This number has remained relatively stable over these years. Just looking at children with disabilities in the schools they composed 2.4 percent of children with disabilities ages 3 to 21 years in 1976–1977 and the number decreased to 1.2 percent in 2003–2004 (National Center for Educational Statistics, 2006).

Causes of Orthopedic and Neurologic Impairments

Orthopedic impairments can have a variety of causes. Lack of oxygen in the child's brain either while the mother is pregnant or during birth can cause physical impairments.

Diseases that affect the brain, such as meningitis and encephalitis, and prolonged high fevers can also cause permanent brain damage. Poisoning and other conditions can lead to lack of oxygen in the brain, as well as head, neck, and back injuries, which sometimes cause paralysis or abnormal movement patterns. Some chronic health problems such as arthritis and muscular dystrophy may ultimately result in physical impairments, but, because such impairments usually occur only after repeated acute attacks, they are less likely to be apparent during the early childhood years. Automobile accidents and other injuries can also cause impairments.

Neurologic impairments are those that affect the nervous system, the brain, and the spinal cord. The neurologic impairments addressed in this chapter are those which result in orthopedic problems. That is, problems with the neuromuscular and musculoskeletal systems: the muscles, bones, and nerves of the body (Escolar, Tosi Rocha, & Kennedy, 2007). Causes that relate to specific impairments are discussed under that impairment.

Bones, Muscles, and Nerves

Knowledge of how we move and the importance of muscle tone in movement aid in the understanding of some of the problems children with physical limitations encounter. Bones form the skeleton of the body. Muscles are attached to bones by **tendons**. To move, we increase the tension in specific muscle groups. When two different bones come together they form a joint; these bones are attached by **ligaments**. Because we are concerned about both type and quality of movement there are a few more terms. **Flexion** refers to bending a joint or joints. If your elbow is flexed, your hand is near your shoulder. **Extension** is the opposite and means to straighten or stretch a joint. If your arm is extended, the elbow joint is straight.

Muscle tone is the ability of the muscle to respond to stretch, whereas **muscle strength** is the force that muscle exerts (Escolar et al., 2007). When muscle tone is too high (tight) children overreact to normal stimuli. This is called **hypertonic** or **spastic**. When muscle tone is low children have a response under what is expected and they appear floppy or **hypotonic**. Many children with orthopedic and neurologic impairments have problems with muscle tone. Muscle tone also affects the small muscles of the mouth and face that involve communication. Children's speech may be difficult to understand.

In some cases, depending on the exact area of the brain involved, a child's motor problems are compounded by faulty internal communications. The child may think, "Let go of the cup," but the brain does not send the appropriate message to the muscles in the hand for the child to let go. Children with low muscle tone (hypotonic) may have problems picking up the cup in the first place. A child who did pick it up successfully may unexpectedly drop it later because it was held too loosely. Grasping very small objects is especially difficult (it may be difficult for children with high muscle tone as well, but for different reasons).

Spasticity is the inability of the muscles to relax; it does not mean paralysis. Children with spastic cerebral palsy have voluntary movement but it is often stiff, jerky, and inaccurate. **Athetosis** refers to random, writhing, involuntary movements, especially of the hands. **Ataxia** implies irregular, uncoordinated muscular movement, especially in walking. The **range of motion** is the amount of movement present around a joint. The range of movement of the elbow is usually a little less than 180 degrees. Children may also be challenged by skills that require **rotation**, the ability to twist a part of the body. Rotation is of primary importance in learning to write because writing requires rotating the wrist. A **contracture** is a shortening of muscle fibers, which is almost always irreversible. A contracture nearly always decreases the range of motion of a joint (Escolar et al., 2007).

The **midline** of the body is an imaginary line that runs vertically through the middle of the body, dividing it in half. This is also called the **median plane**. We are interested in movements that move toward or away from this middle line. When motion moves away from the midline the movement is referred to as **abduction**; movement toward the midline is called **adduction**. (I too would have thought they could choose less confusing terms. I try to think of *add*uction as adding to the body and being centered.) Organs or body parts that are closer to the midline are called **proximal** while those that are farther away are called **distal**. The trunk of the body is proximal, whereas the fingers are distal. It is very different for muscular weakness to be in pelvic, trunk, and shoulder area than in the hands. Children with weak proximal muscles

have trouble getting up from sitting, climbing stairs, and playing on the jungle gym. Whereas children with weak distal muscles often trip because they don't lift their feet high enough when walking, have trouble holding a pencil, using scissors, or doing precise fine motor activities for a long time (Escolar et al., 2007). **Superior** means up or above, whereas **inferior** means below. The head is superior, whereas the feet are inferior. Picture the body lying down. **Prone** is lying on the stomach. **Supine** is lying on the back.

Implications for Educators

Although this may seem like a vocabulary lesson, when other professionals talk about and write reports about children with orthopedic and neurologic impairments, they use these terms. If you need to understand them further, they are all in the glossary. Let's focus on muscle tone for a minute. To get a better idea of the implications of muscle tone, lie with your back on the floor, tense all of your muscles (make fists, squint your face, tense your legs, trunk, and back), and try to sit up. You will find that your movements are jerky and stiff and that you probably cannot sit up. Now relax. Let your arms become floppy as you pretend to be a rag doll. Try to sit up without tensing any of your muscles. That doesn't work either. The first situation will give you an idea of the problems children with hypertonic muscle tone face; the second, hypotonic muscle tone. How do you feel at this point? You have only done this for a short period of time. Children who have high muscle tone, in particular, become fatigued.

If children have high, low, or inconsistent muscle tone, you can expect that they will have difficulty with many gross motor activities. The biggest issue with young children is establishing trunk stability. Try to write while constantly moving your upper body. To the extent that you move it too far and overbalance, your concern is with falling, rather than your penmanship. The focus of much early therapy is stabilizing the large muscles.

For a better understanding of rotational problems, attempt to take the lid off a container while keeping your fingers and wrists stiff. (Try handling classroom materials and doing all classroom procedures with stiff muscles to see how difficult each task is for children. In general, hard objects are more difficult to handle than soft, small more difficult than larger, and slippery more difficult than rough.) Your awareness of the child's strengths and needs and your creativity and willingness to try things that are different are the key to good programming for children with orthopedic impairments.

Early Identification of Orthopedic and Neurologic Impairments

Although children are unique, they share many commonalities in patterns of growth and development. Understanding the underlying principles of growth and development allows us to make predictions about whether or not growth and development falls within the normal patterns. We use a variety of signs and symptoms to identify impairments that relate to the growth and development of muscles, bones, and nerves.

Missed motor milestones are one of the markers we use to identify children with orthopedic impairments. In general, children with increased muscle tone (spasticity) will have delays in all antigravity positions. They may roll over or even "flip over" close to the expected time, but they will not sit unsupported and may not walk until about age 4. Children who have low muscle tone (hypotonic or floppy) may stand with support or cruise holding onto furniture, but they lack the trunk stability for independent walking and so will remain in this stage for a longer time. Because of small motor delays, children may have problems with self-feeding and dressing. Grasping objects using the pincer grasp (thumb and index finger) is difficult, as is eye-hand coordination (Miller & Bachrach, 1995).

Severely involved children may also experience delays in language and problem-solving abilities. In general, receptive language is better than expressive language (especially if a child's motor involvement effects the muscles of the speech producing organs); however, it is sometimes difficult to tell how much children understand because they may not have the physical ability to complete requested tasks. Because many developmental tests for infants and toddlers have motor components, it is difficult to determine a child's level of cognitive functioning.

By preschool age, children with physical limitations may have a difficult time keeping up with their peers. Differences are becoming more apparent to the child as well as to the other children. As children get larger and heavier and even more determined to be independent, some of the self-care tasks become more difficult. By this age, the pattern of gross and fine motor skill is clearer so the aim of intervention is to maximize a child's potential by capitalizing on what the child can do (Miller & Bachrach, 1995). Children may profit from adaptive equipment. If children are frustrated by a lack of ability to communicate, a simple communication board might help (children can show what they want if they cannot tell). Using a communication board does not discourage children from speaking.

As children enter elementary school settings they become part of a larger community. Kindergarten and certainly first grade brings a demand for more fine motor coordination. Some children find that assistive technology can compensate for lack of control in fine motor skills. Educators also need to consider the possibility of specific learning disabilities, particularly in the area of reading, when a child's performance is uneven.

Implications for Educators

It helps to be honest about abilities and limitations and to praise work that is praiseworthy. Although you can and should support effort, it should be clear that is what you are supporting. Tell a child he worked hard controlling the crayon to make the drawing, but, if he is 6 and the drawing looks like the advanced scribbles of a 3-year-old, do not tell him it is a great drawing. Children need help in developing a positive self-concept at a time when new awareness about differences and the value of a beautiful body are becoming part of the child's social world.

Some children with spinal cord injuries are in wheelchairs even during their preschool years.

Assessment of Orthopedic and Neurologic Impairments

In general, impairments are assessed or classified by severity, type, and the parts of the body that are involved. Children with *mild* impairments can walk (with or without crutches, walker, or other prosthetic device), use their arms, and communicate well enough to make their wants and needs known. They may take more time doing things, but with adaptations can do what most other children can. Their problems involve mostly fine motor skills. Children with *moderate* impairments require some special help with locomotion and need more assistance than their peers with self-help and communication skills. Children with *severe* impairments are usually not able to move from one place to another without the aid of a wheelchair. Their self-help and communication skills are usually challenging.

Types of Orthopedic and Neurologic Impairments

Some orthopedic impairments have strong neurologic components; others are related more clearly to musculoskeletal conditions. The impairments are given alphabetically.

Absent Limbs

Some children are born with deformed or absent limbs. These disorders can be caused by genetic or environmental influences such as drugs or chemicals. When congenital, the problem usually occurs during the early gestation period when limb development occurs. Young children can also have limbs surgically removed because of injury or disease. Prosthetic devices are available to assist in replacing missing limbs. There is a difference in philosophy about the age at which children should be fitted with an artificial limb or prosthesis. Some believe that children should be fitted almost immediately. They feel that the younger a child gets an artificial limb, the easier and more natural the adjustment is. Others feel that children should not be fitted for devices until they are older, when they are better able to use the device, have better control, and can take better care of it. Regardless, fit is very important, in terms of both comfort and the ability to use the device. A prosthesis must be adapted as the child grows.

Implications for Educators

You need to have some basic understanding of how the prosthesis works in case the child needs help making adjustments and so that you can plan activities that do not frustrate the child. Being accepted as a whole person is extremely important, so don't refer to the prosthesis as the child's "bad" arm or leg. If you notice abnormal postures or motor patterns developing, discuss them with the parents and physical therapist. Exercising the joints nearest an amputation is important; ask for information about that as well from the parents, medical professionals, and therapists.

Cerebral Palsy

Cerebral palsy refers to a group of neurologically related motor disorders that come in many varieties and severities. "Cerebral palsy is a disorder of movement and posture that is caused by a nonprogressive abnormality of the immature brain" (Pellegrino, 2007, p. 388). In cerebral palsy the neurologic mechanisms of posture, balance, and movement are disorganized.

Causes of Cerebral Palsy

Until the 1980s it was thought that cerebral palsy resulted from difficult births in which the blood flow to the brain was interrupted to such an extent that the brain was deprived of oxygen, which resulted in brain damage. We now believe that although still possible, that scenario only accounts for a small number of cases of cerebral palsy. Premature births, especially before 28 weeks and problems during pregnancy account for the majority of cases (Pellegrino, 2007). The number of children with cerebral palsy is about 2.0 to 2.5 per 1,000 births (Winter et al., 2002); premature infants comprise 40 to 50 percent of this group. Very low birth weight babies are the most vulnerable. A major cause of prematurity-related cerebral palsy is hemorrhaging in the brain. The hemorrhaging injures the white matter of the brain (the axons and their myelin sheaths) (Pellegrino, 2007). Brain imaging techniques are useful in identifying the location of the damage. Term infants who are diagnosed with cerebral palsy are often small for gestational age and may be part of a multiple gestation or the result of congenital malformation of the central nervous system (CNS) or have experienced birth asphyxia. Infection during pregnancy can also cause cerebral palsy (Pellegrino, 2007).

Children are often identified as having cerebral palsy when they do not walk between 12 and 15 months. Children who do walk have an unusual gait that may reflect scissoring (increased muscle tone in the inner thigh pulls the legs in toward the middle) or toe walking (because of tightness of the calf muscles and Achilles tendon).

In the Field

Greg was a preemie. He seemed to be doing well but there were always qualifiers. I finally asked the doctors what was wrong. They told me Greg had cerebral palsy. I asked them how long they had known. They were sheepish and said "for a while." They just hadn't confirmed it yet. I wanted to know what we should be doing about it while they made up their minds. Acceptance was a problem, but in some ways it was a relief. Now I could start to do something about it. I was more than just an overanxious mother.

Early intervention was a godsend. I began to learn how to work with Greg and I felt like I was making a difference. I am not sure how Greg's disability played into the divorce, and I am not sure I am really ready to look at that today. Today I am discouraged and feel hopeless and helpless.

I have never faced a harder time in Greg's life than I am facing today. Going from infant to young adult is far easier than the challenges we face as adults away from the public school system. Greg will graduate in May and would like to obtain a full-time job. I'm not sure he will be successful. Our education system failed to teach him any real skills. Because of his physical disability, he can't take a physically intensive job. Because of his spastic speech, his present employer (part-time) will not give him a job working with the public. Greg is not extremely bright, so he can't go for one of those brainy jobs either.

I had hoped that the school would have been more involved in the community by adopting a co-op program, one where the school and employer would have worked hand in hand. The school would have supplied the training and the additional aid that the employer did not have time to provide or resources to provide. Instead, the school system pushed Greg out the door so that they would have one less student to fret over. It's scary. We weren't prepared for this.

Reflective Practice

Do you think about long-term implications as you teach children in the early childhood classroom? What do you think the obligations are to prepare children for the life after school? Is this a school problem, a parent problem, or a society problem?

Early Diagnosis and Treatment

For newborns who are at high risk for developing cerebral palsy, such as premature and very low birth weight infants, close neurodevelopmental monitoring identifies cerebral palsy early. However, screening tests traditionally used with infants by the medical profession may not identify children with cerebral palsy during the first year. Often, the absence of primitive reflexes, abnormal muscle tone, and resting positions (an extended arched position for high tone and a rag doll position for low tone) give clues to the possibility of cerebral palsy (Pellegrino, 2007). Some children with cerebral palsy also have sensory impairments, speech disorders, and delayed development. Accurate developmental testing is challenging.

The question about the usefulness of medication for children with cerebral palsy has not been answered definitively. Some children with spasticity and rigidity have found drugs such as diazepam (Valium) useful, whereas others feel the side effects of drowsiness and excessive drooling outweigh the benefits. Newer therapy allows for the direct delivery of antispasticity medication (baclofen) directly into the spinal fluid using a concept similar to the insulin pump used in diabetes. In this case a disk-shaped pump is placed under the skin of the abdomen and a catheter is tunneled below the skin around to the back where it is inserted through the lumbar spine into the **intrathecal** space. The disk has a reservoir that can be refilled with a needle inserted into the reservoir (Pellegrino, 2007).

Surgery is sometimes part of the treatment process. Selective **posterior rhizomotomy** is used to reduce spasticity in some children with spastic **diplegia**. In this procedure, surgeons cut the motor fibers that cause the greatest spasticity. Spasticity is reduced, but there may be some degree of motor weakness. Orthopedic surgery may be used to increase the range of motion by lengthening the heel cord or partially releasing the hip adductor muscles. Surgeons also monitor and treat **scoliosis** (Pellegrino, 2002).

The goal of intervention is to maximize the children's functioning and minimize disability-related problems. Orthotic devices, primarily braces and splints, are used to prevent contractures of specific joints, to help provide stability, control involuntary motion, and to maintain range of motion (Pellegrino, 2007). Contractures decrease muscle joint mobility. (If you always kept your elbow bent and held your hand on your shoulder and kept your arm tight, you might develop a contracture.) Muscles that remain in shortened positions for prolonged periods are at risk of contractures. Splints and braces are used to position limbs and joints to prevent contractures. The most commonly prescribed orthotic is a short leg brace (ankle-foot orthosis) that prevents the shortening of the heel cord (Pellegrino, 2007). Most splints and braces made for young children are custom-made of plastic materials that are molded directly on the child. These must be modified as the child grows, or they can become both nonfunctional and painful.

Positioning is another key to preventing impairment. Because children spend a lot of time sitting, it is important that they sit in the most beneficial position. This is often not the easiest or most comfortable for teachers to manage. If you hold a child with cerebral palsy in your lap, have the child's legs straddle one of yours and hold the child around the middle. If the child sits on the floor, sitting cross-legged, or tailor-style is not recommended; instead, have the child sit with legs in front and together If the child has variable muscle tone the legs should be bent at the knee, if the muscle tone is tight the knees should be straight and the legs out in front. Sitting in a W position with knees forward and a foot on either side of the child's bottom is particularly disadvantageous for children with orthopedic impairments and is not recommended for any child.

Types of Cerebral Palsy

Cerebral palsy is typically classified by the motor impairment and the extremities involved. In spastic **hemiplegia**, there is involvement of the upper and lower extremities on the same side of the body with the arm more affect than the leg. If the motor neurons on the right hemisphere were affected the problem would be on left side and vice versa. In spastic **diplegia**, the whole body is involved, although the legs more so than the arms. This is the type most associated with prematurity. Spastic **quadriplegia** involves all four limbs. Head control may be poor and, in cerebral palsy, there is usually impairment of speech and eye coordination. This also indicates wider cerebral dysfunction and children may also have intellectual disability, seizures, and other medical complications (Pellegrino, 2007).

In the Field

We wanted to have a child so badly and finally I got pregnant. We were so excited and then labor started way too soon, at 24 weeks. He weighed less than a pound and a half. No one asked me if I wanted them to take extraordinary measures to save him, they just did. He spent his first year and a half in the hospital. I spent almost all of my time learning how to take care of him. The minute he was born I dedicated my life to him. I gave up my life for his; my health too.

Ravi has spastic quadriplegia because of increased muscular tension. He cannot control his bowels or urine flow. He cannot sit up without assistance; additionally he cannot walk, talk, or voluntarily move his muscles. He has epileptic seizures which happen mostly at night.

Sitting for extended time with legs is a W position should be discouraged for all children.

He has permanent brain damage. Ravi also has a tracheo-stomy, he breathes through a tube that was surgically inserted in his trachea. He is fed through a "stomach button," which is a gastric tube that carries food directly to his stomach although he eats some food as well. He can shake his head "no" and says "augh" for yes and he has a heart-stopping smile. He has a partial IEP.

He spent the first 2 years in the hospital. I went to visit him every day. When we brought him home Ravi required 24-hour-a-day care. I had some nursing help. Because of that I think of our days in shifts. The first shift is 7 A.M. to 3 P.M., the second shift is 3 P.M. until 9 P.M. and the third shift is 9 P.M. until 7 A.M.. I usually have nursing help for the third shift so I can sleep. Ravi's conditions over the years have worsened but the medical system still expects me to take care of Ravi. I am scared and I feel unqualified.

My health has deteriorated as I have cared for Ravi. My doctor says a lot of it is because I am so stressed because of caring for Ravi. I have an ulcer. I have really bad reflux that needs surgery but I can't get it because I have no one to take care of Ravi. The same is true for the two broken bones in my feet. I have migraines, irritable bowel syndrome, and chronic fatigue syndrome. My body can't take much more.

My husband helps some but he is away at work most of the day and he does a lot of traveling. It really isn't his thing. The nursing company told me that I will only have 4 days of nursing support in the whole month of January. I couldn't do it. I have gone 48 hours without sleep but that is as far as I can go. My husband is having an affair and said he is leaving. I asked him to help me one last time. On December 26th we took Ravi to the children's hospital (he had been here forty-four times in the past year and 7 months). I brought his favorite toys, some clothes, and food as well as his medical supplies. We left him in the emergency room with a note saying I could no longer care for him.

The parents were arrested the next day and charged with a misdemeanor: child abandonment.

Reflective Practice

What would you do if you were asked to testify as an expert witness in this case? What would you say? How do you make sense out of what happened?

Spastic cerebral palsy is the most common type of cerebral palsy. The abnormalities in the brain pathways originate in the gray matter of the brain. The motor cortex or pyramidal tract of the brain is damaged, resulting in limb muscles that are very tight and are difficult to move (spastic). Voluntary movements are often jerky and inaccurate. Voluntary motion is present but may be labored. Infants who are hypotonic often later develop spasticity.

In **dyskinetic** cerebral palsy, the damage is outside the pyramidal tracts and has different implications. The whole body is affected and patterns of muscle tone change from hour to hour, or day to day. Children have more problems sucking, swallowing, drooling, and speaking than children who have the spastic form. Again, the variable muscle tone makes it difficult to develop the stability needed for sitting and walking. Children may have rigid muscle tone while awake and normal or decreased muscle tone in sleep. Involuntary movements are often present (Pellegrino, 2007). A type of dyskinetic cerebral palsy, **choreoathetoid**, there are rapid, random, jerky movements (the *chorea* part) combined with slow, writhing movements (the athetosis). In **dystonic** cerebral palsy, children have rigid posturing centered in the trunk and neck (dystonic). There is one predominant level of muscle tone and a lot of involuntary posturing.

Ataxic cerebral palsy is characterized by abnormalities in voluntary movement. Children who walk use a wide base and have an unsteady gait. They have problems controlling their hands and arms accurately when reaching, and often overshoot the targeted item. They also have problems with the timing of their motor movements. Balance and controlling the position of the trunk and limbs in space are challenging. Children can have increased or decreased muscle tone (Pellegrino, 2007). In **mixed cerebral palsy**, children have damage to both the pyramidal and extrapyramidal areas of the brain and can have symptoms of both types (that is, rigidity in the arms and spasticity in the legs).

Implications for Educators

Children with cerebral palsy typically have individualized programs with a combination of consultative, home-based, or center-based intervention. The most common method of physical and occupational therapy used with young children who have cerebral palsy is neurodevelopmental therapy. The goals of this therapy are to normalize muscle tone and enhance the development of normal movement patterns during functional activities. Early childhood educators would be expected to incorporate handling techniques into the child's routine as well as provide opportunities to practice newly acquired skills. There is some question about the carryover of these techniques, and newer techniques are taking more of a systems perspective and looking at the environment, motivation, requirements of the task, cognition, and other aspects of the situation that might produce lasting changes in motor behavior. During the early years, problems related to mobility tend to be focused on and receive the most attention. As children are included in regular elementary school classes, some of the associated learning and sensory problems may receive greater attention and adaptation.

Correctable Orthopedic Impairments

A variety of relatively short-term orthopedic problems are dealt with during the early childhood years to facilitate normal future growth. These conditions usually require surgery, bracing, casting, and physical therapy. The prognosis is generally good if the condition is treated at an early age. If not treated, these problems result in some degree of orthopedic impairment.

Bowlegs and inwardly rotated feet are common when a child first begins to walk. They are usually cured by normal growth. In extreme cases, however, braces, casts, and/or surgery are used to correct the problem. Clubfeet are usually treated with casts, splints, and physical therapy or surgery. Flat feet may be treated with arch supports or corrective shoes. Congenital hip problems result from improper fit of the femur in the socket joint of the hip; they are most often treated by a webbed brace, traction, cast, or surgery. Usually, hip problems are treated in infancy. In severe cases, they can have long-term implications.

Implications for Educators

The prognosis for these correctable orthopedic impairments is very good, yet from the child's perspective, the restriction of movement is frustrating. Some children need a lot of help expressing this anger. Prepare children for medical procedures, discuss their fears and feelings, help them express emotions while they are physically restricted, give them activities they can participate in, and try to explain the purpose of the medical treatment in terms they understand.

Developmental Coordination Disorder

It is difficult to decide whether some children have movement disorders or not. When the problem relates to a physical problem such as a congenital hip problem, clubfeet, or bowed legs we expect children to have motor problems and we provide medical and educational intervention. Some problems are less obvious. We are becoming more concerned about children who are clumsy. Although it is difficult to agree on a definition of clumsy, most of us know a clumsy child when we see one.

Increasingly, children who have problems controlling their movements are recognized as having special educational needs. The *Diagnostic and Statistical Manual of Mental Disorders (DSM-IV)* added the category of Developmental Coordination Disorder to its fourth edition (APA, 1994). It remains in the *DSM-IV-TR* (APA, 2000). Like other areas, such as specific learning disabilities, there is confusion about terminology.

Developmental coordination disorder (DCD) is used synonymously with the terms **clumsy child syndrome** and **developmental dyspraxia**. The term **sensory integrative disorder** focuses on the processes of receiving and processing information. With minor variations, these terms all refer to the same group of children. This text uses the terms **developmental dyspraxia** and **developmental coordination disorder** (DCD) depending upon the source of information. This diagnostic category focuses on the relationship between age-expected norms and children who are delayed in reaching motor milestones (walking, running, and so on) or who drop things, are clumsy, do poorly at sports, and often have poor handwriting. As children increase in age, there is concern about the relationship between motor coordination and academic achievement and the activities of daily living.

It is estimated that approximately 6 percent of children between 5 and 11 years have some degree of DCD (APA, 2000). Others feel the percentage may be as high as 10 percent. Developmental dyspraxia affects children in different areas of development. It affects more boys than girls (Dyspraxia Support Group of N.Z. Inc, 2007a). It is a chronic condition that continues into adolescence and adulthood. To be identified as having DCD, children must have the following characteristics.

- Motor coordination that is substantially below expected motor milestones or clumsiness in the performance of motor tasks.
- The level of performance must be great enough that it interferes with either academic achievement or the performance of tasks of daily life.
- The disturbance is not due to a medical condition such as cerebral palsy.
- If the child has an intellectual disability, the motor problems are in excess of those expected because of the intellectual disability (APA, 2000).

There is no apparent etiology or cause of developmental dyspraxia. **Dyspraxia** is a hidden disability; the child looks like other children; however, he finds it far more difficult to accomplish the same tasks that others achieve with little effort (Dyspraxia Support Group of N.Z. Inc, 2007b).

Clumsy children have been a concern to many over the years. Dr. Samuel Orton (1937), who focused most of his work on dyslexic children, was interested in the problems of physical awkwardness. He decided that lack of motor coordination could reflect a motor planning problem or could be caused by problems with visual perception. He felt that motor dysfunction was multidimensional; that is, that children who were awkward at running also labored over printing and writing. He was concerned that poor motor coordination also led to feelings of social inferiority and low self-esteem. He believed motor awkwardness to be a most debilitating condition. He felt it was one of the six most common developmental disorders (Dyspraxia Support Group of N.Z. Inc., 2007b).

One problem is that when we look at clumsiness it is a "soft sign." Soft signs require clinical judgment as opposed to something like a temperature, which is a finite number (102 °F) and has diagnostic value. Also, some children display generalized awkwardness, whereas others are clumsy relative to only one task, such as writing or balance (Cratty, 1994). Many agree that the clumsy child syndrome is made up of several subclassifications of children, including those with and without academic problems. In some children, the problem seems to be immaturity; in other children, it is longer lasting. The literature indicates that early remediation is more likely to succeed than just

Children with dyspraxia may work with an occupational therapist to help them develop motor planning skills.

waiting, mild problems are more correctable than moderate ones, and that given the current state of knowledge, it isn't clear which problems will change because of maturation and which ones will not (Cratty, 1994). If problems are not dealt with until middle childhood, there may be a negative emotional overlay to the problems themselves. Children may develop poor self concepts because of constant feedback about dropping, spilling, running into things, knocking things over, and so on.

In the Field

"Anne, can you help me set the table for dinner?" Anne's mom asked. "Coming mom, give me two seconds," Anne replied. A few seconds later, Anne's mom heard the pitter patter of footsteps followed by an anguished oooowww.... "What happened?" asked Anne's mom, stifling a sigh. It seemed that every time her youngest daughter moved there was some ouching involved. She couldn't remember a day without dealing with tears or at least sniffles from Anne's frequent accidents. Sometimes she marveled at how her daughter injured herself walking or setting the table.

"I'm ok, mom. I just tripped," announced Anne as she appeared in the doorway.

"Good, I'm glad you didn't hurt yourself," said Anne's mom, placing a plate into Anne's hands. "Remember two hands."

Anne walked to the table as her mom asked, "How was your day, honey?"

"It was ok," Anne answered, taking another plate from her mom.

"What happened to make it just ok?"

"Stuff," said Anne reluctantly.

"What kind of stuff?" inquired her mom.

"I fell out of my chair, spilled milk all over Jeremy, tripped up the stairs, broke my science project, everybody laughed at me, even Ms. Rubenthal, the substitute, and I got sent to Mr. Theran's office 'cause I screamed at everybody," she said in one breath.

"It sounds like you had a really bad day. Mr. Theran called me today and said that you were really upset. I can see why. He said you talked about your feelings about people laughing at you and accidents."

"I don't like it when people laugh at me, mom.... I get so mad at them... I want to scream and yell and cry.... I hear the mean things they say all day," replied Anne, putting the last plate on the table.

"Is there something that we could do so they wouldn't laugh so much?" asked her mom.

"Could you talk to Ms. Dublin and tell her that I don't like it when she and her substitutes laugh at me?"

"I could do that. I will make an appointment with her tomorrow. Is there anything you could do to try to have fewer accidents at school?" she asked, handing Anne the forks. "Mr. Theran suggested that maybe we could talk about some things to do so that you might not have so many accidents. He also said he would like to meet with you once a week. How would you feel about that? Do you feel safe talking to Mr. Theran?"

Anne looked out the window for a few seconds before responding. She began in a quiet, almost introspective voice, "It would be ok with me to talk with Mr. Theran once a week; he's nice and he listens and he didn't make me feel bad for screaming. But if other people know they'll make fun of me, so I'd like to see him during lunch. 'Cause then I could eat with him and I don't think he'd be so mad if I spilled things."

"I will see if that will be okay with him," her mother responded. "Can you think of anything you could do to prevent some of the accidents?"

"Well, I could remember to use both hands when I hold my lunch tray," answered Anne, putting a fork at each place.

"What else?"

"Maybe someone could put Velcro on my chair so I wouldn't fall off so much," she said, carrying bread to the table.

"That's an idea. If not Velcro there may be something else that would work. Anything else?"

"I could make sure my projects are in my backpack and that I hold onto the railing when I climb the stairs," Anne replied, walking back into the kitchen.

"Those sound like good ideas. Do you think you can do those things?"

"Yeah, mom," said Anne, grabbing two plastic cups. Anne's mom said, "You may have to get up a little earlier to get organized before you leave for school."

"Okay."

Then Anne's mom took the cups out of her daughter's hands and placed them on the table. She wrapped her arms around Anne, hugging her close, and she whispered in her ear, "I'm sorry you had a bad day. But you know what? I love you, accidents and all."

Reflective Practice

It would be easy to classify a child such as Anne as immature, inattentive, or careless. In reality she is none of those. What might you do to support children like her in your classroom? Can you develop a plan that supports the integrity of your teaching and children's self-esteem?

Some clumsy children such as Anne are diagnosed as having developmental coordination disorder (DCD) or developmental dyspraxia. **Praxis** is a Greek word that describes the learned ability to plan and then carry out sequences of coordinated movements to attain a goal. When *dys* is used as a prefix it means "bad." Hence the term *dyspraxia* means "bad praxis." Children who have dyspraxia have trouble with learned, voluntary, skilled movements such as buttoning buttons, handwriting, using a fork, and speaking clearly. Pervasive problems in the area of motor planning lie at the heart of all of these problems (Dyspraxia Support Group of N. Z. Inc., 2007a). Praxis is the ability to organize activities in new and creative ways. It links brain and behavior to help us plan and function in our world. It has three components:

- **Ideation** is the understanding of sensory information about objects; what they feel, taste, look and smell like, what shape they are, how much they weight, whether they roll or stay put, and so on. To follow through with ideation a plan of action is needed.

- **Motor planning** involves sending the ideation information to the parietal lobe of the brain to work out how to move his body to do what he wants. This involves recalling the sensory information about the objects and information about himself. Then planning the sequence in which muscles should work. When the plan is made, motor neurons are sent out to execute the plan.
- **Execution** is carrying out the plan. Muscles can only contract or relax and the motor neurons tell the muscles what to do, for how long, and in what sequence. When the motor plan is made messages go to different parts of the brain and then to the muscles to carry out the actions (Dyspraxia Support Group of N. Z. Inc., 2007b)

These actions are interdependent. Praxis is developmental. Praxis at age 2 is different than praxis at age 5 because more connections have been made and used in the brain allowing for more complicated plans and actions. Dyspraxia is a disorder of praxis. Somewhere in the sensory information collection, storage, planning, and execution of actions there is a malfunction. Although praxis focuses on learned behavior, there is a biological component (Ripley, 2001). The cause of dyspraxia is the physical inability of the brain's neurons to effectively communicate movement instructions to the body's muscles. It may affect specific areas of growth such as large motor skill development or areas of fine motor skill development such as verbal communication, where the tongue, lips, and larynx must work together to form the sounds of the language (Wong, 1998). It is not a unitary disorder; each child is affected in different ways and to a different extent and the same child may be different on different days. It may be the only disorder a child has or it may be part of other disorders such as specific learning disabilities.

Tasks that are considered enjoyable by many, such as coloring or riding a tricycle, may be extremely difficult for the child with dyspraxia. It is understandable then that children with dyspraxia may exhibit the characteristics of a frustrated immature child. As is often the case in children with specific learning disabilities; children with dyspraxia usually have normal intelligence. They are capable of understanding what needs to be accomplished and cognitively develop at an age-appropriate rate. Once again, the problem area is the brain's inability to effectively communicate with the body. Children with dyspraxia may develop low self-esteem and behavior problems because of the amount of stress, anxiety, and failure they experience.

Developmental dyspraxia is difficult to diagnose. It must be done in the context in which the child lives and learns. It is dependent upon the demands of the environment and the child's ability to meet these demands and the adult's ability to tolerate errors as well as the child's ability to cope. It may not become apparent until the child's impaired planning and execution are overtaxed or the environmental demands are higher and less tolerant (Dyspraxia Support Group of N. Z. Inc., 2007a).

Once a skill or action is learned well enough then praxis is no longer required. Praxis is part of the learning process. So the goal of treatment is to teach the child

praxis—to form ideas for trying new things and using familiar things in new ways, that is, to plan actions and execute them. Treatment is a team approach and the treatment is very individualized depending upon the child and the demands of the environment. It is likely to include an occupational therapist who would focus on sensory integration, a speech and language therapist who will work on sounds and speech muscles, a psychologist who looks at cognitive development and learning ability, an early childhood special educator who may focus on helping the child in specific areas that are challenging, the classroom teacher whose expectations may need to be adjusted, and above all, parents who teach many skills children need to grow and learn. A child with dyspraxia will not grow out of it; the disability is a lifelong tribulation (Dyspraxia Support Group of N. Z. Inc., 2007b).

Implications for Educators

Children with dyspraxia may find it difficult to learn new things, concentrate, speak clearly, get dressed, play sports, organize ideas, or think quickly. They may need more time and more practice to develop new skills. Try to figure out where a child's major problem lies. Is it that the child doesn't understand a request, can't figure out how to do the action, or can't perform the action? Then, scaffold that area for the child. New tasks may be threatening because he can't figure out how to sequence all the actions even though he can perform all the skills. Try to sequence new tasks for him. Break down instructions into smaller simplified steps.

Children who are clumsy need to be encouraged to participate in motor activities. They need experience with motor planning in situations where they are likely to succeed and be supported. In general, to require motor planning, a task must be goal-directed. For example, just walking requires little motor planning, whereas to walk to the other end of the room, put on a hat, and skip back requires far more motor planning. Likewise, an obstacle course requires a child to motor plan. Because diagnosis is dependent upon the fit of the child and the environment you are likely to have children who have dyspraxia and have not yet been identified. The demands of kindergarten and early elementary school may challenge the child's praxis.

Muscular Dystrophies

Muscular dystrophies is an umbrella term for a group of chronic, progressive disorders that affect the voluntary muscles. It is an inherited X-linked disorder caused by a genetic mutation, which results in the absence of a critical protein, dystrophin, which stabilizes the muscle membrane during contraction (Escolar, Tosi, Rocha, & Kennedy, 2007). When this protein is deficient, muscles degenerate. The most common type, Duchenne muscular dystrophy, is not usually detected until a child is between 2 and 5. The child may experience excessive muscle cramping when exercising and begins to fall down frequently, due to muscle weakness (Escolar et al., 2007). It affects approximately 1 in 3,300 male births (Jeppesen et al., 2003). The muscles closest to the center of the body, those of the hip and shoulder area, are affected first, with the muscles in the fingers being affected later. An infant may have problems turning over to get up. The result is gradual weakness and decline in muscle strength and health. The child's intellectual functioning is not affected, although most children with this disability have lower than average intelligence. The process, which can occur quickly or slowly, leads to increased disability and death (usually in young adulthood).

We do not know how to correct the metabolic disorder or halt the progression of the disease. The earlier the symptoms appear, the more severe the disease is likely to be and the earlier death will occur. Toddlers will have a waddling gait, fall frequently, have trouble getting up, climb stairs with difficulty, and may walk on their toes. They will typically be able to walk during early childhood. As more muscles deteriorate and the child becomes weaker, a wheelchair is necessary. Once the disease has started, there is no remission and its progress over time is predictable. Patience and emotional support are an essential part of dealing with the everyday frustrations that face the child and family.

Implications for Educators

Children with muscular dystrophy have normal feeling in their limbs even though they cannot always move them (unlike a child with a spinal cord injury, who may have little or no feeling in the limbs). They cannot hold onto you very well because of muscular weakness, so be sure you are holding them securely before you pick them up. Don't lift them under the arms; because of weak shoulders, the arms may fall through your hold. Remember that the neck muscles may be very weak, so support the head when going from sitting to lying. Make sure the child has side supports when sitting. Children often depend on armrests to help hold themselves upright. As children get older and heavier, get someone to help you move the child; a two-person transfer is almost always safer for a child with muscular dystrophy. Find out from parents and physical therapists the most advantageous way to move the child. Although too much exercise is painful, appropriate stretching exercises are helpful (be sure to consult the parents and physical therapist to find the right exercises). Because the child's physical activities are limited and added weight is a problem, a low-calorie diet is recommended.

Blowing and breathing activities maintain the chest muscles, which are essential in coughing. Snacks and lunches should be planned with the child's diet in mind. At preschool age, this child looks weak, not ill, and hence may be made fun of. Work to develop both the child's self-esteem and peer relationships. School, especially at an early age, is invaluable psychologically for both the child and the parents. The child poses few problems at this age. Therapy focuses on minimizing contractures, maximizing muscle strength, and learning to compensate for weaknesses. It becomes progressively more difficult for children with muscular dystrophy to stand and walk. They need to keep their legs well stretched; a goal is to keep the child walking as long as possible. Children may also have learning disabilities and developmental delays and may need individualized educational programming to meet these needs (Leet, Dormans, & Tosi, 2002).

Neural Tube Defects

Neural tube defects is an umbrella term that refers to a group of congenital malformations of the vertebrae, spinal cord, and brain. The three major neural tube defects are spina bifida, encephalocele, and anencephaly (Liptak, 2007). The most common is spina bifida.

In spina bifida there is a split in the **vertebral arches**. This separation can be isolated such as in individuals with **spina bifida occulta** who have no symptoms and may not even know they have a split. Approximately 10 percent of the general population has this hidden separation (Liptak, 2007). A similar form of spina bifida is **occult spinal dysraphism**. In this condition the child has a visible abnormality on the lower back. This may be a birthmark, a small opening in the skin (dermal sinus), a small lump, or a dimple. If the spinal cord is connected to the surface through a sinus (opening) there is an increased risk of bacterial infection. It is important to evaluate the spinal cord and surrounding soft tissue of these children using ultrasound or an MRI. Although controversial, some believe that this should be treated surgically even in infants who show no symptoms (Liptak, 2007).

Some infants are born with a membranous sac over the spinal cord, called a **meningocele**. If the spinal cord itself is not entrapped, these children are usually symptom-free. The form of spina bifida that we typically think of is meningomyelocele (or myelomeningocele) where the spinal cord is malformed and children show an array of symptoms. The fluid-filled sac (meningocele) protrudes through the spine of the newborn above the defect in the vertebral column; it looks like a flat bubble on the infant's back and contains the malformed spinal cord. The nerves below the protrusion do not develop properly, leading to loss of sensation and paralysis below the site. Surgery is done within several days to remove the bubble, protect the exposed nerves from physical injury, and prevent infection. The surgery does not impact the neurologic functioning of the child (Liptak, 2007).

Encephalocele, another neural tube defect, involves a malformation of the skull that allows a portion of the brain to protrude. This can be at the back of the brain in the occipital region or the front. If at the back, children usually have intellectual disabilities and **hydrocephalus** (excessive fluid in the brain cavities), spastic diplegia, and/or seizures. If at the front of the head, such as the forehead, the impact is more variable (Liptak, 2007). **Anencephaly** is a more severe malformation of the skull and brain and no neural development occurs above the brainstem. About half of these fetuses are spontaneously aborted and those who live rarely survive infancy (Liptak, 2007).

Causes of Neural Tube Defects

The problem that causes neural tube defects occurs prenatally by 26 days after conception, when the **neural groove** folds over itself to become the **neural tube**, which becomes the **spinal cord** and vertebral arches. If during this process the neural groove does not close completely, the spinal cord is malformed, and the child has some form of neural tube defects (Liptak, 2007). There appears to be a genetic component and also environmental factors related to the development of neural tube defects. Treatment with folic acid during the first 12 weeks of pregnancy has been successful in decreasing the occurrences of neural tube defects. Women contemplating pregnancy are urged to take 0.4 milligrams of supplemental folic acid daily while trying to conceive and during the first 12 weeks of pregnancy (American Academy of Pediatrics, 1999). Because half of all pregnancies in the United States are unplanned (CDC, 2007a), folic acid supplements have been added to some grains, but the amount is not optimal. The presence of neural tube defects can be diagnosed by levels of alpha-fetoprotein in the mother's blood serum during the 16th to 18th week of pregnancy.

If detected this is followed by a high-resolution ultrasound focusing on the fetal head and back. Approximately half of couples choose to terminate pregnancy based on

confirmation of neural tube defects (Forrester & Merz, 2000). In the United States, the prevalence of meningomyelocele is approximately 60 in 100,000 live births, anencephaly about 20 in 100,000, and encephalocele about 10 in 100,000 (Rader & Schneeman, 2006).

Most children with myelomeningocele also have an associated malformation of the brain. In **Chiari type II** malformations, the brainstem and part of the cerebellum are lower in the neck rather than being in the skull. This is common when the meningomyelocele is above the sacral level (see Figure 17–1). This results in problems in swallowing, choking, hoarseness, breath-holding spells, apnea, disordered breathing while sleeping, and stiffness in the arms and an arched posture. Disordered sleep can cause

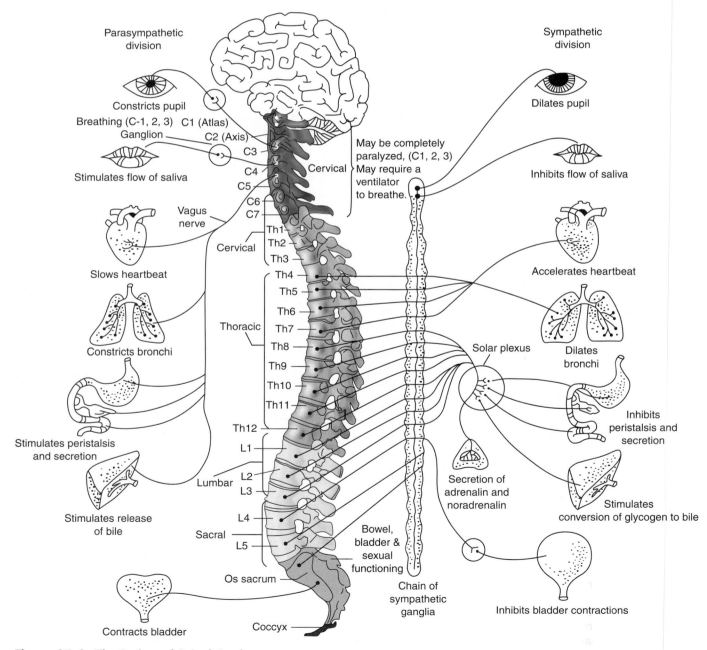

Figure 17–1: The Brain and Spinal Cord

children to be tired during the day and less available for learning (Liptak, 2007).

A related problem that occurs when the meningomyelocele is in the lumbar or thoracic region is hydrocephalus. This is diagnosed through ultrasonography in infancy and an MRI in older children. It is treated surgically with a shunt. The shunt diverts the excess cerebrospinal fluid from the brain to where it can be better absorbed, usually the abdominal cavity. A shunt consists of plastic tubing with a one-way valve that provides permanent drainage to relieve pressure on the brain. Extra tubing is left in the abdominal cavity to uncoil as the child grows. New surgical procedures to drain this fluid are being developed that do not require shunts, but they are too new to be evaluated at this time (Liptak, 2007). In young children, shunts can become blocked or infected. In infants, this results in excessive head growth and a tense "soft spot" on the top of the head. In children 2 years and older, the bones of the head have fused so the head cannot expand; symptoms can include severe headaches, lethargy, stomachaches, double vision, vomiting, and irritability (Liptak, 2007). Notify the parents if any of these occur; failure or infection of a shunt is a life-threatening condition.

There is considerable diversity in the degree of motor delay children with spina bifida may have. Although frequently late to roll over, most use belly crawling as a method of locomotion. Children's mobility is dependent on the location of the lesion. In general, the higher the level of the meningomyelocele, the more muscle weakness and the greater the impairment in ambulation.

The vertebrae of the spinal cord are divided into three major areas (see Figure 17–1). Starting from the bottom, there is the tailbone, which is connected to the **sacrum**, which has five parts, which in turn connects to the lowest lumbar vertebra, and then there are 5 **lumbar vertebrae** (L), 12 **thoracic vertebrae** (T), and 7 **cervical vertebrae** (C). The closer to the head, the more severe the injury. Each inch of spine or vertebra supports an important bodily function. Children with sacral lesions S1, S4 will walk well by age 2 or 3; S3, S4 may need minimal bracing; low lumbar (L5) will walk but may need crutches; midlumbar (L3, L4) will need braces and usually crutches. Children with thoracic or high lumbar (L1, L2) lesions will need extensive bracing at ankles, knees, and hips, and crutches or other mobility devices. They typically use a wheelchair (Liptak, 2007). As children's center of gravity changes in adolescence, more will use a wheelchair. Walking is not easy for many and is more difficult for children who also have intellectual disabilities. Walking requires physical therapy and committed parents as well as a child who wants to walk.

Children with myelomeningocele are usually incontinent and cannot tell when they are wet. During the preschool years, incontinence is not a significant problem because the child can wear diapers. The parents and surgeons make decisions about how to manage this problem. This is frequently done with a technique called clean intermittent bladder catheterization (CIC). Parents are taught how to do this and it is usually begun in infancy. Bowel problems are related to ineffective relaxation or contraction of the internal anal sphincter as well as lack of sensation. Parents make the decision how to handle this, which may include timed potty sitting after each meal. Bowel and bladder continence is a realistic and critical part of a child's development.

Implications for Educators

Intervention begins in infancy. In the sensory motor area, therapists are concerned with maintaining the range of motions of the joints, developing strength, and working toward standing and ambulation. In early childhood, many children will walk independently or with the aid of a walker or crutches.

Children with neural tube defects have decreased strength and sensations, so special care must be taken to protect their lower limbs. Their bones may not be as strong as they should be and are prone to fractures. Be alert for things that might cause skin problems, such as water that's too hot, sunburn, and insect bites. Children can develop skin sores or decubitus ulcers on weight-bearing surfaces and not know it, as they are not sensitive to pain. Socks should be worn in wading pools and shoes should be worn if the child is walking or crawling (Liptak, 2007).

Many children with spina bifida are allergic to latex. The reason is unclear, but the reaction can be life-threatening. Toys that contain significant amounts of latex, such as rubber balls, should be avoided and Band-Aids™ and Ace™ bandages should not be used. Talk with parents and therapists about alternatives.

Most children with meningomyelocele have IQ scores in the low average range. However, they frequently have problems that will eventually be labeled as specific learning disabilities. In particular, they have impairments in perceptual skills, organization, attention span, memory, speed of motor responses, and hand function (Snow, 1994). They also may have problems with executive function and adaptive skills. Executive function relates to the ability to plan, initiate, sequence, sustain, inhibit competing responses, and pace work (Burmeister et al., 2005). These learning problems are challenging. As children grow, concerns related to bowel and bladder control present health problems as well as social problems. To prevent urinary infections, children need to drink liquids; this, of course, increases the need to urinate. If this cannot be controlled beyond the preschool years, it becomes problematic for the child. Supporting children in developing a positive self-concept and feelings of autonomy and independence is imperative.

Spinal Cord Injuries

Spinal cord injuries are relatively uncommon in young children. When they do happen, they are usually the result of motor vehicle accidents when children have not been wearing seat belts.

The spinal cord sends motor and sensory messages from the brain to other parts of the body. The spinal cord is divided into four major regions and has about 25 different segments or sections (see Figure 17–1). The size of the segments vary and the delineations are clearer in discussion than they are in the spinal cord itself (Keating, Spence, & Lynch, 2002). Each segment of the spinal cord has four roots that are essentially two pairs with a ventral and dorsal root for both the left half and right half of the spinal cord. Each root is made up of smaller roots called rootlets. These rootlets take messages toward and away from the brain. The dorsal nerve roots provide the pathway for sensory input to reach the brainstem. The ventral roots deliver motor input from the brainstem to the muscles. If the spinal cord is damaged, messages do not reach beyond the impaired area and hence are not delivered or received (Keating et al., 2002).

Some infants are born with malformed spinal cords or conditions where the spinal cord deteriorates. If the spinal cord is not completely cut, some feeling may remain below the lesion, but in general, anyone who has a spinal cord injury is permanently affected and unable to feel pressure or pain below the lesion. The ultimate effect of an injury cannot be ascertained with certainty for several months.

Spinal atrophy is characterized by progressive degeneration of the motor-nerve cells, resulting in slow weakening of the body's muscle strength. The effects include skill decrease, fatigue, and decreased coordination. Congenital atrophy progresses rapidly, resulting in an early death. Acquired atrophy develops much more slowly, first affecting the legs and then progressing to the upper extremities.

Implications for Educators

Learn about what the child can and cannot do or feel. If the child lacks feeling, be concerned about sunburn, overheating, and frostbite. Insect bites or injuries may occur and not be noticed. If a child has movement in the arms and shoulders, work should be done to strengthen these because future mobility may depend on them—ultimately, the child has to learn to lift his own weight. Another important consideration is the prevention of pressure sores (decubitus ulcers). These seem innocuous, but pressure sore infections can cause death. Sometimes, it takes weeks or months for them to heal, and they may have to be closed surgically. Children with spinal cord lesions generally have poor blood circulation; therefore, injuries are slow to heal and prone to infection.

Traumatic Brain Injury

An increasingly frequent cause of neurologic impairment is head injury. This can occur from automobile accidents, falls off a bicycle, gunshot wounds, or from other accidental causes. They range from mild to profound and the effects can be temporary or permanent.

Each year, 1 child in 25 receives medical attention because of a head injury. These range from not being of medical concern to severe brain damage. Severe head injury (which injures the brain) is the most common cause of acquired disability in childhood (Schneier, et al., 2006). Traumatic brain injury (TBI) is defined as trauma sufficient to change a level of consciousness and/or having an anatomic abnormality of the brain. TBI is caused by a blow or jolt to the head or a penetrating head injury that disrupts the normal function of the brain. They range from mild, which results in a brief change in mental status or consciousness, to severe, which results in an extended period of unconsciousness or amnesia after the injury (CDC, 2007b).

TBI occurs in approximately 1 in every 500 children (Schneier et al., 2006). Boys are more likely to sustain head injuries than girls. Children from birth to age 4 are in one of the highest risks groups (CDC, 2006a). TBIs are more likely to occur in the spring and summer, on weekends, and in the afternoon (Michaud, Semel-Concepcion, Duhaime, & Lazar, 2002). Traumatic brain injury was acknowledged as a separate disability under IDEA in the 1990 reauthorization. There is also the expectation that more children will survive TBIs and be in early care and education settings.

Causes of brain injury vary. The most common causes of TBI are falls (28 percent), followed by motor vehicle-traffic crashes (20 percent), being struck by or against objects (19 percent), and assaults (11 percent) (CDC, 2007a). The number of head injuries that are not seen in an emergency room or who receive no care is unknown. Of children 14 and younger, TBI annually results in an estimated 435,000 emergency room visits, 37,000 hospitalizations, and 2,685 deaths (CDC, 2007b).

The type of head injury has implications for the impact of that injury on the child's behavior. There are two major types of injuries that are of concern: impact and inertial forces. Impact or contact forces happen when the head strikes or is struck by a moving object. Scalp injuries bleed a lot but they do not injure the brain. Focal brain bruises or contusions, usually the result of direct impact, such as a baseball striking the head, which bruises the brain. These can result in skull fractures or blood collection beneath the skull (**epidural hematomas**). These can be minor, like bruises to other parts of the body, or may require surgical removal. Inertial forces occur when the brain undergoes violent motion inside the skull. In these injuries, the concern is not with a blood clot but the nerve fibers throughout the brain that have been damaged, usually by violent motion (as in a motor vehicle accident). These too can be mild or serious. Often children have both **diffuse axonal injury** and **subdural hematomas** as a result of accidents (Michaud et al., 2007).

Epidural hematomas are the most lethal, but also the most treatable. A **hematoma** is a blood clot, in this case between the skull and the outer covering of the brain. Typically, the child falls or is injured and appears fine, but then symptoms begin to develop as the hematoma grows. These lead to headaches, confusion, vomiting, and even lethargy and coma. If treated quickly, children usually recover completely; if treatment is delayed, there can be physical and cognitive delays and even death (Michaud et al., 2002).

Acute subdural hematomas are blood clots that form beneath the **dura** or the brain covering and are often part of a more generalized injury to the brain itself. They result from sheering forces applied to the veins (acceleration-deceleration forces) that actually displace the brain from the dura to rupture these membranes (Michaud et al., 2002). A subdural hematoma may cause brain swelling and stroke. A large area of the brain is affected and, although surgery can remove the blood clot, the prognosis is not as positive.

Sometimes the brain injuries are inflicted rather than accidental. Inflicted injuries are more common with children younger than age 3 and are the leading cause of traumatic death in infancy. Confirmed abuse accounted for 33 percent of hospital admissions for head injuries for children younger than 3, and 19 percent of those younger than 6 and a half years (Reece & Sege, 2000). Shaken baby syndrome is certainly one of the factors taken into account in these figures; however, it appears that when the baby is shaken, the head also comes in contact with a surface such as a bed, wall, or floor (Salehi-Had et al., 2006).

Because timing is such an important variable, you need to know when head injuries need immediate care and when they do not. If a child hits his head and does not lose consciousness, no treatment is necessary. However, the child needs to be observed. If the child develops symptoms of an epidural hematoma (vomiting, tiredness or listlessness, irritability, changes in eating, sleep, and play, lack of interest in favorite toys or activities, loss of new skills and loss of balance or unsteady walking) the child should be evaluated by a medical professional (CDC, 2006b).

A child who has an injury and loses consciousness and then resumes normal activities may have a mild concussion. If the loss of consciousness is more than momentary, a neurologic examination and brain imaging should be done. If the child is unconscious for more than a few minutes, call 911 (Michaud et al., 2007).

When a child is in a coma, the seriousness of a brain injury is rated on the Glasgow Coma Scale within the first 6 hours. This rating scale looks at eye-opening, motor, and verbal responses. A child with a score of 3 has no eye-opening, no movement, no verbal response, and is in a deep coma. A score of 15, the highest score, reflects the ability to spontaneously look around, move limbs on request, and make relevant verbal responses. Severe head injury is a score of 8 or less (Michaud et al., 2007).

Acute medical care is the initial focus. Rehabilitation may begin when vital signs have been stabilized even if the child is still in a coma. These procedures are designed to limit secondary musculoskeletal problems by using passive range of motion and other exercises. As medical problems stabilize the extent of injury become more evident. The nature and severity of functional impairment determines the rehabilitative strategies. However, it almost always involves an interdisciplinary team.

The severity and type of injury to the brain impacts the recovery. With mild TBI, there are few if any long-term consequences in cognitive functioning. Moderate to severe TBI can cause significant cognitive impairment. Predicting how children will fare appears to be more complex than with adults. The brain of the young child is more plastic and hence has the potential for further development. However, brain injury appears to impair new learning more than the retention of old learning, and young children haven't had as much time to build a knowledge base (Michaud et al., 2007). Most recovery takes place in the first 6 months after the injury and will take place at a slower rate after that (Taylor, 1999). Goals for children are to relearn lost skills and to learn new skills to compensate for those that cannot be regained.

Whereas adults seem to develop predictable patterns after brain injury, children seem to have different patterns depending on the task. For some tasks, the child shows a progressive pattern of recovery over time; in others, the impairment is constant; in still others, there is no discernible impairment after the injury, but over time a problem appears, a delayed reaction. In young children brain damage interrupts development. Early brain damage results in cumulative defects because of the small repertoire of skills young children have making it difficult to consolidate new

skills and knowledge. Common deficits for young children include information processing, memory, and executive function (Anderson, Catroppa, Morse, Haritou, & Rosenfeld, 2000).

The Evidence Base

The goal of this research was to look a young children's cognitive ability after a TBI. Children injured before age 3 (n=27) were looked at for global intellectual skills only. Older children were divided according to age at injury (3 to 7 years; 8 to 12 years) and the severity of the injury (mild, moderate, or severe). They were evaluated at 12 and 30 months after the injury. Mild or moderate injuries were usually associated with falls whereas severe TBIs usually were the result of motor vehicle accidents.

Infants (birth to 3) with mild TBI continued to show improvements. However moderate TBI caused significant decreases in global intellectual ability (12 to 14 points below average). They showed poorer outcomes than older children. They were also more likely to lose consciousness with 78 percent having a period of coma for over an hour.

Age at injury did not predict outcomes for children over 3 with mild to moderate outcomes. Children who sustained mild TBI had IQ scores in the average range 12 months after the injury. Those with moderate TBIs were marginally lower. The trajectories were stable from 12 to 30 months.

For children older than 3 with severe TBI young children showed minimal, if any, recovery after the injury. Older children had better outcomes than younger ones showing gain in IQ of about 9 points at 12 months but less improvement from 12 to 30 months (about 2 points). Nonverbal skills had significant recovery after a severe TBI. Verbal knowledge, word knowledge, abstract thought and comprehension skills were depressed after a severe TBI (Anderson, Catroppa, Morse, Haritou, & Rosenfeld, 2005).

Reflective Practice

Reflect on what you know about the plasticity of the brain and what that means relative to brain injury. How do you make sense out of this research? How might it impact what you do if you had a child with TBI in your classroom?

Children who experienced severe diffuse axonal injuries are likely to have impairments in all areas of functioning, whereas children who had an injury in one area of the brain are likely to have more localized problems. Damage to the motor areas of the brain often results in impairments similar to pyramidal cerebral palsy: spasticity, ataxia, and tremors. Feeding disorders may result as well as impaired motor skills, sensory impairments, communication impairments (receptive, expressive, or mixed), and cognitive impairments (Michaud et al., 2007).

Children who have sustained moderate to severe TBIs often experience problems in academic learning. These may manifest themselves in reading or math, but the more pervasive effects relate to attention, problem solving, and speed of information processing (Hawley et al., 2004). Their patterns of learning differ from those of children with specific learning disabilities. Children with TBIs demonstrate highly variable performance within and across academic subjects and they continue to change over time (Michaud et al., 2007). Behavior changes can also be expected.

Children who sustain TBI must cope with psychological stress. The loss of skills is distressing to children. Families, too, may be stressed, initially with concern about whether the child will live or die, then in coping with the child himself, and the financial consequences of paying for the child's treatment.

Implications for Educators

In cases of TBI, it is important that the transition from hospital to school involves shared information. Children will typically have a difficult time attending for long periods, remembering information they had known before, and learning new information. Their greatest difficulty seems to be in the area of the organization of information. They may also find abstractions and creative thinking challenging. The loss of skills that they could perform before, that other children their age are now easily doing, is a source of frustration. It is important to maintain close contact with their families and review their IEP/IFSP every month or 6 weeks during the early recovery period, as rapid changes can take place. Children with TBI may require intervention strategies to help them relate to the social world around them. Modifications such as consistent routines, a lack of distracting elements, and clear, repetitive directions are helpful.

Requiring children to wear helmets when riding tricycles is a first step in teaching bicycle safety and in preventing traumatic brain injury.

Most childhood trauma is preventable. Teach children good safety habits such as using helmets while riding bicycles and using handrails while walking up and down stairs. As an educator actively supervise playgrounds, and ensure that equipment and surface areas are safe and at appropriate heights. Teach children rules for crossing roads. Identify child abuse and help to prevent its reoccurrence. Ensure that children ride in car seats and that restraints are appropriate for their age and weight (CDC, 2007c). Children with TBIs are challenging because of their variability and unpredictability for themselves and others.

In the Field

What I do when I learn I am getting a new child who will be challenging . . . .

The first thing I do is take a mini-mental vacation. I replay my favorite teaching moments in my mind and remind myself that I am qualified to do this job, that I like what I am doing, and that I am respected by my peers and administrators. Then, I replay my worst teaching moments and remind myself that I am still qualified to do this job, that I still like what I am doing, and that I am still respected by my peers and administrators. Then I take a moment to reflect on what I have learned from these experiences. It is not enough to have had them, but it is that I learned from them.

Next, I try to determine *why* the child is challenging, *who* has classified him as *challenging*, and *what* others have tried in the past, whether it has worked or not worked. "Challenging" is subjectively defined. I try to critically evaluate the situation, define the problem area, and determine the impact on the child's ability to learn and the possible impact on the dynamics of the classroom. Then, knowing the other children in the classroom, I try to anticipate potential problems and be proactive.

When the time comes to meet the child and the parents, I *forget* everything I have read about the child. Although I have *prepared* for the child and have become familiar with the diagnosis/classification and all the implications, I try to remain open-minded and view the child without *prejudice* or *prejudgment*.

Reflective Practice

Educators are often less familiar with children with TBI than other disabilities. Their variability makes them challenging. Think about how you will prepare yourself to teach a child who may be a challenge to you. What will you do?

Mobility Aids

Regardless of the diagnosis, many children with neurologic and orthopedic impairments use adaptive equipment for assistance in moving. Most children have a variety of mobility aids; some are simple, others are complex. It is important that you know the purpose of the equipment and the relationship among the aids. Organizationally, the equipment starts with the child and what is necessary to implement independent mobility. It then goes on to short- and long-distance mobility aids. Because children use many different types of equipment, adults must help them transfer from one to another or to a chair, the floor, or toilet.

Splinting, Bracing, and Positioning

The purpose of bracing, splinting, and positioning is to improve children's functioning. Together braces and splints are called **orthotics**. Their purpose is to maintain range of motion, prevent contractures at joints, provide stability, and control involuntary movements (Pellegrino, 2007). Splints can be either static (rigid) or dynamic (with movable parts) (Kurtz, 2002). Splints and braces are all custom-made by an **orthotist** (brace maker) or a therapist. In general, upper extremity splints may be made by occupational therapists and lower extremity splints by physical therapists. Since young children grow quickly and insurance companies may only pay for one **orthosis** per year, those made by therapists are less expensive. As children grow, their weight and use of the orthosis may require that it be made of more expensive materials and through a different process than therapists can do. There are two basic types of orthosis: plastic and metal. Plastic braces are lightweight and can be contoured to use on the trunk, legs, and arms. (A child with cystic fibrosis may even have a plastic "jacket.") Plastic braces are molded to fit the body part and keep that body part in a position that is ready to function, as well as position it for better growth. Many plastic braces have hinges at the ankles and knees to allow for movement.

Metal braces are used far less frequently today than they were in the past. For legs, braces can be short or long. If they are long, they are hinged at the knee and have locks. Young children do not have the strength or dexterity to make these locks work. The first time you work with these locks you need to do it under the supervision of the physical or occupational therapist or the parents. (The locks require a lot of pressure to change. The pressure you use needs to be against the brace and not the child's body.) When the therapist demonstrates for you how the locks work, that is only the first step. *You* need to be able to work the locks. Ask the therapist to watch and coach you while you try. You need to be able not only to work the locks, but also to put the braces on and off. (A child might get wet at the water table or have a toileting accident, and you will have to change her.) While the therapist is there, do it, and let the therapist coach you. Watching isn't the same as doing.

One of the things you will notice is that the shoes of children in braces frequently look identical, and it may be difficult to tell the right shoe from the left one. Take your handy permanent marker and mark the right and left shoes (or ask the parents to do this). Although the shoes look alike to you, they are individually fitted and feel very different to the child. If a child who is usually cheerful is unhappy or crying and you have gone through your usual repertoire of possible causes, check to see if the child's braces are on the appropriate legs. Molded plastic braces are particularly uncomfortable for the child when placed on the wrong leg. On a hectic morning, families may make a mistake.

Short-Distance Mobility Aids

Walkers, scooters, crutches, and canes are the most common mobility aids for short distances. Some or all of these may be in your classroom with the child, as they serve slightly different purposes.

Walkers are individualized to the child's ability, size, and functional level. Young children often use walkers before they use crutches. Walkers provide a broader base of support. Children can use the walker for balance and get up to it independently before they can manage the same skills with crutches. The area inside the walker is personal space for the child. If children need adult support to use the walker, place it out of the way when it is not being actively supervised. If children can use the walker independently, it needs to be accessible to the child. Know the child's individual competence level with this, as with all mobility aids. Be sure the walker has a basket so the child can transport books, puzzles, and other items.

Crutches require much better balance than walkers. They are, however, a more normalized system of transportation. They approximate a gait pattern that is similar to independent walking. Children might use crutches in therapy for a long time before they have them for general use. Children will use different types of crutches based on what is prescribed for them.

Scooters are another set of wheels that children can use for independent mobility. Some are designed to be sat upon, others to lie on. Scooters provide children with both independence and exercise when they don't have good sensation in their legs.

Long-Distance Mobility Aids

Strollers and wheelchairs constitute the most common long-distance mobility aids. When children are very young, it is fine to carry them as you would any infant or toddler. However, as children get older, this is developmentally inappropriate, except for short distances or in emergencies. For younger children, specially made strollers are designed for this time slot. These strollers offer the child a little more positioning than regular strollers and are designed for larger children. As children get older, they use wheelchairs.

For young children, a wheelchair can be thought of as a specialized source of assistance. It is necessary for fire drills, for long walks for which the child does not have enough stamina, and sometimes for seating. Wheelchairs are custom fitted to individual children by the physical therapist, **physiatrist**, or sometimes an occupational therapist, and a representative of the company that makes the wheelchair working together as a team (Pellegrino, 2007).

Wheelchairs may be totally customized or chosen from modular systems that are put together to meet the needs of an individual child. The wheelchair prescribed is based on the child's abilities, the type of seating the child needs, the level of independence, the child's age and cognitive ability, and how easy it is to get in and out of the wheelchair. Therapists are particularly concerned about children's ability to position themselves. If they can't position themselves well, the wheelchair will need more belts and padding.

All wheelchairs are different, and the expectations for the children who occupy these chairs differ also. However, there is one rule about wheelchairs that transcends types: Put on the brakes before anything else. And, when putting a child in a wheelchair, put on the child's seat belt before

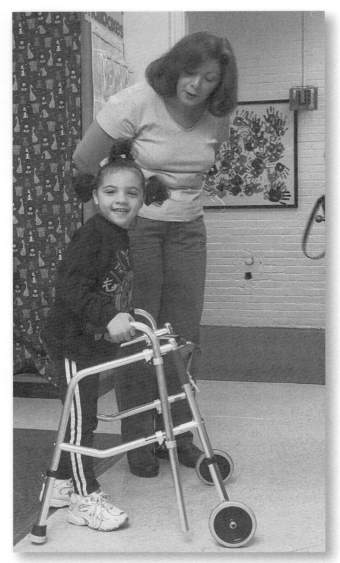

Children with orthopedic impairments need a variety of mobility aids. For short distances children frequently use walkers, for longer distances wheelchairs.

Transferring

Transferring is the term used when you move children from one piece of equipment to another. It might be from the floor to the toilet, the wheelchair to the floor, into or out of a chair, and so on. In general, transferring requires two people. One person is in charge of the trunk area and stands behind the child; the other manages the thigh area and stands in front of the child. In the case of *very small* children, one person can do the transfer. In all cases, work with therapists on transfers. The particular type of transfer that is most effective for the child and you will be determined and demonstrated by the therapists working with the child. One person transfers are not recommended for children you wouldn't normally carry, but ask a therapist how to do this in case of emergency.

Transferring happens several times each day from different positions. *Caution*: It is imperative that you know a child's level of competence in mobility. If a child does not have protective reflexes (if when she falls forward she does not put out her hands to protect herself), she needs the constant monitoring of a trained adult in all antigravity positions. Knowing the equipment is very different from knowing the child's ability to use such equipment. Children need to be an active part of the process.

When you put children with orthopedic impairments with other children, you will find that the similarities are far greater than the differences. Other children will be astonished at their creative problem-solving skills.

Technology Assistance

Assistive technology is any kind of technology that can be used by children with disabilities to enhance their functional independence. The most common mobility aids (walkers, wheelchairs, scooters, and so on) have already been discussed. With the passage of Public Law 100–407, the Technology-Related Assistance for Individuals with Disabilities Act of 1988, we began to focus more on how technology, devices, equipment, and systems could improve the capacities of children with disabilities. Training and technical assistance can support children with disabilities in their efforts to acquire and use technology as a routine part of day-to-day living.

When selecting computer software for children with orthopedic and neurologic problems software should be evaluated in the following areas:

- Directions and documentation
- Feedback and evaluation
- Content
- Individualization options
- Interface and screen design
- Accessibility (Boone & Higgins, 2007 p. 5)

Additional concerns relative to accessibility relate to ensuring that input speed does not affect the accuracy of responses and that there is the potential for alternative input devices such as a single switch (Boone & Higgins, 2007).

Guidelines

Early care and education settings can provide a broad range of experiences for children with orthopedic and neurologic impairments. Children need to be included in

taking off the brakes. For your safety and the child's, get a lesson from the child's physical therapist on how to safely transfer the child from a wheelchair and where to put the child after she is out. One obvious but crucial point: Before taking a child out of a wheelchair, know where the child is going. Children cannot stand there and wait for you to decide. In addition, you need to talk with the child before you move him: "I'm going to take you out of the wheelchair and put you on the floor." Some children may be learning to use a transfer board; if so, find out the ability of the child to independently transfer and what your role should be.

In general, young children should not be in wheelchairs in your classroom. They belong on the floor or in chairs like others sit in (with modifications, if necessary). Decide on a place to park the wheelchair, perhaps in the hall outside. Use short-distance mobility aids in the classroom (walkers, scooters, or whatever meets the child's needs) when possible.

first-hand experiences and provided with a wide variety of materials and equipment. Foster independence in any way you can.

1. *Give children tasks they can accomplish.* They learn early what others can do that they cannot.
2. *Use assistive technology routinely.* Have "reachers" in your classroom (assistive devices that individuals use to reach high objects; they usually have a grip that controls a pincer or magnet at the end to pick things up) and encourage all children to use them when they can't reach something they want. Be sure to use them yourself.
3. *Be sure children get to touch things as well as see them.* When necessary, bring materials to children so that they can actively explore them.
4. *Demonstrate how materials are used.* Some children really don't know what to do and are simply too shy to ask. Goop, a mixture of cornstarch and water, may be a new experience for children, and rather than exploring it, they avoid it. Support children through the cycle of learning; awareness (encourage children to poke, feel, and hold the goop); exploration (talk about its properties and support children in exploration); inquiry (encourage children to experiment with media in a variety of ways); and utilization (encourage children to compare goop to playdough, to fingerpaint, and so on). Expand their knowledge and talk about the uses of cornstarch in the context of cooking.
5. *Have pictures of individuals using mobility devices on your wall.* Our society is a mobile one that values beauty and strength. Because body image greatly influences self-concept, children with orthopedic impairments need help integrating body image into a healthy self-concept. Read books about children that encourage diverse abilities (see Children's Bibliography).
6. *Work on developing language skills.* Particularly support language that is necessary to express feelings and to meet personal needs. Provide creative activities that help children release energy and work out feelings.
7. *Help children establish a sexual identity.* For some reason, people with orthopedic impairments are often treated as if they are asexual. An appropriate sex-role identification is important to children's development.
8. *Keep in contact if they are absent from school.* Send get-well cards, audiotapes, videotapes, and visit if the child is out of school for an extended period of time. Send the child messages by email if the child has a computer and access to these services.

For children with orthopedic and neurologic impairments, the classroom itself needs to be evaluated for accessibility and perhaps modified.

1. *Borrow a wheelchair, sit in it, and pretend that you are teaching.* Go to the doorway to greet children, take them to their lockers and help them hang up their coats, then help them settle into the routine. Monitor different children at play in different areas of the room. Be sure to include the bathroom on your excursion. Now, reflect on what was difficult for you to do and how you feel (tired, frustrated?). How long were you in the wheelchair? Evaluate your room to determine how accessible classroom equipment is. Check doors and passageways to be sure walkers and wheelchairs can get through and turn easily. Be sure areas around activities and equipment are wide enough for mobility aids. How accessible is the class if you were on a scooter or crawling? We really don't want children in wheelchairs in the classroom, although for some children this is necessary. In general, children should be out of the wheelchair seated with other children, on the floor, in a beanbag chair, or whatever works best for that child.
2. *Use tables with adjustable legs.* These allow you to adjust the table height. Table tops that can be angled are also helpful. If not available, a wooden wedge can serve the same purpose.
3. *Include lighter equipment.* Use cardboard blocks and have a variety of manipulatives that require pushing and pulling with varying degrees of strength. Be sure that large equipment like bookshelves are heavy and stable, as children might lean against them or use them to pull upright.
4. *Move sand and activity tables away from walls.* Ensure that children can get to them from all sides. Evaluate the level of the tables so they are accessible to all children.
5. *Provide many different types of chairs.* Give children a choice of chairs they can sit in (if all the chairs are the same except one, it points out difference, not inclusion). Have bolsters, wedges, and beanbag chairs to provide a change for children. If necessary, modify a chair with the help of a physical therapist or physiatrist. An abduction block—a chunk of something padded that the child's legs can straddle—will prevent a child from sliding onto the floor, or add a seat belt. If recommended by the child's physical therapist, add a footstool so that the child's feet can be flat (this corrects the angle to obtain trunk stability).
6. *Add ramp.* This supports children's independence and helps children enter and leave the classroom.
7. *Use nonslip floor coverings.* Do not highly wax floors, use scatter rugs, or have shag carpet. If you have carpets with low pile, be sure they are attached by a metal strip so they won't slide and so children don't trip over the edges. Keep toys off the floor when not in use to prevent children from tripping.
8. *Evaluate toilet cubicles.* If you have them they should be wide enough to accommodate a child, a wheelchair, and an adult; handrails need to be at the child's height to make the transfer an easy one. A transfer pole (a movable pole that goes from floor to ceiling) may need to be added. There are also many different types of potty chairs that are designed to solve a variety of problems. Ask parents what word or sign they use for "potty" and how they deal with this issue at home.
9. *Shorten and widen the handles.* This includes handles on paintbrushes, rackets, and paddles to make them easier for children with orthopedic impairments to use. Use rubber tubing or foam around the handles

10. *Use deep-sided bowl and two-handled mugs.* These are easier for children to manage than cups and plates for meals and snacks. Serve a lot of finger foods. Use cups and plates that have rubber on the bottom (found at boat supply stores). Add rubber tubing to utensils for easier grip. Put plates on Dycem™ to keep them from moving around.

11. *Be sure the food you serve is not too hot.* Some children can't tell when something is too hot, including food, and they could burn themselves.

12. *Provide ways for children to carry things.* Be sure walkers have baskets and provide around-the-waist carriers for children on crutches. For small items, a fanny pack works well. Knapsacks also work, but children should wear them in front. Most wheelchairs have their own trays.

13. *Use both large and small versions of manipulative toys.* Especially helpful are toys that have a built-in tolerance for error (that is, blocks that fit together even if the child doesn't match them perfectly).

14. *Remove equipment that overturns easily.* Move rolling shelves if not stable.

15. *Use padded lapboards or lap trays.* These are great for children who may be more comfortable on the floor than sitting in a chair.

16. *Use a book or music stand with a page holder to keep pages of a book open.* For children who have difficulty turning pages, get a specialized page turner. Have a listening center with headphones.

17. *Prioritize tasks.* Put tasks that are most important and those that require more energy and concentration first if the child tires easily.

Curriculum Adaptations

The actual physical limitations a child has will determine the number and degree of adaptations necessary. In general, encourage children to do as much as possible independently—but not to the point of frustration. Offer help when you think it is necessary. When you give help tell the child what you are going to do and, as you do it, what you are doing.

Don't forget that children change and grow. An adaptation that may be necessary at the beginning of the year may not be needed by the middle or end of the year. As you adapt equipment and programming for children, consider whether the adaptation is developmentally and socially appropriate. Adaptations should be designed to include children, not draw attention to them.

Social Awareness: Self-Esteem, Inclusion, and Social Studies

Children need to learn about the larger world and be part of it. They need both information and skills. Children with orthopedic impairments may not move as fast as others or with the same quality of movement and need to refine skills related to speed, distance, and coordination for their own safety. Some of the activities in Resource Chapter 1 are specifically designed to increase children's awareness of orthopedic and neurologic impairments. Activity 1–9 Wheels discusses the function of wheels and encourages children to experiment moving on or using objects with wheels. Activity 1–23 Slings helps children gain an understanding of the types of adaptation that would be necessary if they could only use one arm and 1–30 Cast It increases children's understand of casts and why they are used.

Self-Esteem

Children need to be accepted for who they are. They need to be accepted for their similarities as well as their differences. They need to build a positive self-concept. Find out from the parents what they have told their child about their disability. Many parents do not talk with children about this, or give children the impression that there is a "cure" and that when they grow up the disability will be gone. It is important that children integrate their abilities and disabilities into their self-concept in a positive way.

1. Encourage children to talk about their feelings about having a disability. Be a good listener.
2. Children need to learn to deal with rejection and discrimination as it happens. Ignoring it or pretending it is not there does not work. Be sure children have the words to respond to comments such as "What's wrong with you?" An appropriate response might be, "There isn't anything wrong with me. My legs aren't strong enough to hold up my body, so I wear these braces. What's wrong with you?"
3. A full-length mirror helps develop body awareness and self-concept, as do songs and fingerplays that use body parts.
4. Provide self-help aids such as buttoners and reachers so that children can practice self-help skills with these supports.

Inclusion

All children need to feel that they are part of the group. This is especially true when equipment causes physical distance from other children. Do not exclude activities that children cannot do independently; rather, have a paraeducator help children do any movement that needs to be done to feel included. If this is not possible, adapt the movements. Encourage all children to think about how they will move before they actually do it. All children need to be part of the group.

1. Help children acknowledge obvious limitations, yet see other areas as challenges. Be realistic, but not pessimistic: "I can do ——, but I can't do ——." At the same time, help children figure out different ways they can be part of the group.
2. Children need to talk about the feelings they have about their disability. Ask open-ended questions. Children may not be able to tell you how they feel, so ask them to show you with paint or another media. Help children label feelings. For example, "I think if I needed to sit in your chair I might be scared of ——. Do you ever get scared?" Encourage all children to talk about and label feelings.
3. Talk about their role as part of the group, what they do to help others, and what others do to help them.

Social Studies

Awareness of community is important for children with orthopedic and neurologic impairments. Start by familiarizing the children with their immediate environment.

1. Get children out into the community so their knowledge is first-hand.
2. If you are doing a unit on transportation, include wheelchairs (nonpowered and electric) in your discussion.
3. Help children personalize their equipment (with parents' permission). Wheelchairs can be decorated with license nameplates, bicycle bells, or horns and streamers. Walkers may be painted or wrapped with ribbon. Casts can be decorated.
4. Have appropriate community visitors, including those who play a role in this child's life: osteopath, physical therapist, occupational therapist, orthopedic surgeon, and so forth.

Language and Literacy: Speaking, Listening, Reading, and Writing

Children develop language by actively interacting with their environment. To the extent that this first-hand experience has been limited, children may need additional experiences to spur language development. Field trips should be followed by stories, both those written by the children about the experience and those written by others to expand the experience. Children with orthopedic impairments may not be as mobile as other children. They need practice in asking for what they want, especially if they cannot reach it. Likewise, adults need practice listening and allowing children to ask rather than doing it for them. Adults particularly need to learn to give precise directions. Reading can broaden the range of experiences available to children. Writing may offer a particular challenge. Using materials that have some built-in resistance may be necessary, such as writing or drawing in sand or on clay, or using a computer with an adapted keyboard.

Speaking

Because children have physical limitations, they must rely more on speaking to get some of what they need and to convey information to others. The ability to express themselves can help compensate for lack of motor skills.

1. Use puppets to encourage expressive language. Have puppets that talk and move in many different ways. Finger puppets as well as hand puppets can encourage body awareness. Encourage children to use a puppet on each hand and having them "talk" to each other. Sock puppets or puppets on sticks with padding that just need to be moved up and down may be easier for some children to operate.
2. Expand children's utterances, especially when they use "telegraphic speech." If a child says "Get doll," you might respond, "Which doll do you want me to get you? Oh, you want the one with the red dress." When children ask for objects by pointing, help them learn vocabulary by filling in the words they need:

"That's the doll." However, if children are able to respond with only "yes" or "no," phrase your questions accordingly: "Do you want the blue one?" not "Which one do you want?"

3. If children cannot speak, support them in using a communication board. Help all children learn about different methods of communication.

Fingerplays encourage children to use both hands in a controlled fashion.

1. When you introduce a new fingerplay, keep the actions simple and slow enough for everyone to keep up.
2. Use some fingerplays that use the whole hand rather than just the fingers.
3. Remember that children may need the help of a friend to make certain movements. Use a paraeducator to assist the child if needed to include him in the activity.
4. Some fingerplays that require different motions with each hand may be too difficult. Think of variations that all children can do instead.

Listening

Be sure that books are accessible. Select stories that have a variety of characters, some of whom have visible disabilities.

1. If the children sit on the floor and the child needs to sit in a chair make some chairs available to other children as well.
2. Read stories and show pictures of children who have orthopedic impairments; choose stories that emphasize the senses the child can use. Present a balance of disabilities in your selections. Have a variety of books, including age-appropriate board books or other materials that are easier to use.
3. Use flannel board stories made of Pellon™ to focus attention and to increase participation.
4. Add background music to stories to enhance the mood for children (circus music, waves breaking).
5. As you read stories, check the vocabulary for words children might not be familiar with. If possible, add concrete examples to help children understand the story. For example, bring in types of seashells mentioned in the story to show the children.

Reading

Reading skills involving listening and visual activities can easily be adapted for children with orthopedic impairments.

1. Field trips followed by language-experience stories are good initial reading experiences. Help children establish the idea that you can learn about places by reading about them.
2. Be sure children can visually and verbally identify objects before you work on discrimination and other higher-level skills.
3. Introduce children to listening stations and recorded books as part of their reading program.
4. Make reading interactive.

Writing

Writing can present a challenge for children with coordination problems. All children need to develop trunk control before they can coordinate the small muscles of the hands and fingers necessary for writing.

1. Children may need to start activities without tools. For example, have children draw with their fingers in the sand before giving them a tool. Have them write letters with their fingers (the index and middle fingers) before using a marker.
2. The more variety you have in graphic materials and tools, the more likely it is that children will find a match between what they want to do and what the medium will allow. The variety adds to children's knowledge of the world and how they fit into it. Have a variety of sizes, shapes, and types of materials.
3. When teaching fine motor skills, have children use materials that create some resistance, such as a pencil drawing on clay, so that they can feel the resistance as well as see the results. Talk with the occupational therapist about the best adaptations for writing instruments. There are many different cushions or gripper adaptations available.
4. Children may need to warm up their muscles by squeezing clay or dough. They may need to either strengthen or loosen these muscles before using writing instruments. A short hand massage may make writing easier.
5. To teach prewriting skills, use activities that require finger and wrist movement, especially rotation with the palm of the hand down.
6. Encourage children to use the computer to write. Ask the occupational therapist about adapting the keyboard or visual display unit for the child to use it. If children lack muscle power, a smaller-sized keyboard may be useful (this is also true for one-handed users). Some keys may not be necessary. For other children, a larger keyboard with letter characters, numerals, and arrow keys may be more appropriate.

Discovery: Mathematics, Science, and Technology

This area has potential for children with orthopedic and neurologic impairments, as the approach supports and encourages the development of skills for problem solving. Concepts that relate to size, distance, and speed are especially important to children with orthopedic impairments. Because they are less mobile than others, they may require more energy to carry out tasks; thus, it is important that they learn to think through tasks before attempting them. They can learn to predict how long it will take to cross the path to the swings if someone is approaching on a tricycle. Size concepts help them understand where they can easily fit using a mobility device and still turn around. They also need to learn that, like other children, they are growing and their body is changing. They will, with time, get too big for some of their mobility aids. Technology offers children ways of communicating that have not been possible before. They need to feel comfortable with this technology at an early age. They can develop cause-and-effect

reasoning skills. Help them develop problem-solving skills to compensate for things they may not be able to do; for example, have them think of how many different ways they can get across the room, paint a picture, or play with blocks. Encourage unconventional solutions.

Mathematics

Children with orthopedic impairments have been exposed to many concepts that are classified under the heading of math. They know something about time concepts: It will take them longer to do some things than others because of different muscle tone or muscle atrophy. They know something about distance and how far they can go before they get tired. Math can help them quantify these experiences.

1. Children need to learn about the relationship between speed and distance (for example, "If I go 20 feet [here to the door] as fast as I can I'm tired. I can go 60 feet [the length of the room] slowly. It takes longer, but I can do it and I am not tired").
2. Measuring and weighing children helps them understand why braces no longer fit and need to be replaced. Weigh a child's braces and talk about how much they weigh. Bring in weights that can be attached around children's wrists, ankles, or waist and have children use these during the day and talk about the difference the weights make in how they feel and can perform tasks and the amount of energy it takes.
3. Discuss shapes that roll and those that don't. Relate them to concepts like brakes and moving: Round shapes are used for wheels; a triangular block of wood can be used to stop a wheel from moving.

Science

Science teaches the cause-and-effect reasoning that is necessary for safety and encourages children to devise adaptations to meet their needs.

1. Magnets are fun and potentially useful. Attach a string to a stick, tie a magnet on the end of the string, and go fishing. Catch fish that have paper clip mouths. Show children how to pick up metal objects with a magnet. Children can then pick up some things independently they cannot reach by using a scissors-like reacher.
2. Work on simple casual relationships: "The faster I move my hands on the wheel, the faster the wheel-chair moves. If I only move the right wheel forward, I turn left!" Children with electric wheelchairs may need practice steering them. See Activity 1–45w Creepers for additional ideas.
3. Help children learn to use simple machines such as wheels and pulleys with ropes as a way of moving objects. Demonstrate how you might use a long foam roll to move a heavy object (inflatable rollers are used to move boats).
4. Use objects that vary in weight for sorting activities. Set out a Ping-Pong™ ball, tennis ball, hard ball, empty cup, and a cupful of birdseed, and see if the children can arrange them in order. Discuss the relationships among an object's weight, the distance someone throws it, and the thrower's strength. Outside, set up a range and have each child throw

different balls (Ping-Pong™, tennis, hard ball, large rubber ball, and beach ball), mark and measure how far each goes, and relate this back to size, weight, and strength. Then have children kick the rubber ball and beach ball and see which goes farther. The focus is on relative distance, not throwing it the farthest. If children don't want to throw, have them participate in measuring.

5. Use objects that vary in shape, size, and texture. Help children decide the easiest and most difficult to use.

6. Children need to explore basic principles of physics. Use scales and balances and relate this to their body and how far they can lean without unbalancing.

7. Study the concept of energy as part of learning about children themselves and also the natural world. Children with orthopedic impairments have to expend more energy to move, so they get tired more quickly and it may take more concentration to move body parts. Read about energy as well.

8. Learning about the effects of gravity is vital because all children struggle against it as they sit and stand.

Technology

Children need to be exposed to technology early and to think about it as part of their life. Computers can be used by any child who has control over one motor part, whether that is a hand, a big toe, or the tongue. Most computers are designed with adaptations. Call the manufacturer to find out how easy adaptations will be or consult an assistive technology specialist (all states have them).

1. Computers can and should be used by all children, including those with muscular, motor, and movement disabilities. Adaptations make computers accessible to these children. The mouse can be larger and adapted to respond to different amounts of pressure. Keys can be slowed down and attached to a voice activation system that tells the child in addition to showing what is happening.

2. Computers can be equipped with foot switches and head switches. They can respond to a sip and puff straw and even the movement of an eyebrow. There are joysticks that can be operated by tongue or head movements. Because of the potential of computers for children, they need to be part of their educational environment as early as age 3 or 4.

3. As children become more competent on computers, they may be part of the child's individualized program. In this case, adults need to learn how to use the computer and software that has been chosen. This computer is likely to be customized and will travel with the child from school to home. Procedures need to be worked out for this to happen without damaging the computer.

4. Help all children understand that technology includes communication systems, switches, wheelchairs, and so on. Talk about devices in the framework of technology, and how technologies support all children.

5. Talk about editing and the use of a word processor in this process. It can find spelling errors, help with sentence structure, and remove mistakes without an erasure.

Wellness: Health, Physical Education, and Sensory Motor

Children need body awareness to achieve a good self-concept, but also to maintain their personal health and safety. Children who lack sensation in some body parts must learn to become visually aware of conditions they cannot feel. If a child uses a prosthetic device, a splint or a brace, they need to be aware of the muscles that help work the device and they also need to be aware of any irritation or pain that may indicate they are outgrowing the device or that it needs to be adjusted.

Children must be given the opportunity to discover their abilities and challenges in the motor area. Allow children to use all equipment (within realistic limits) and participate in all activities normally provided in your setting, unless you have other directives from the family, physician, or therapists. If there is *any* doubt, check. Therapists and families are prime resources for ideas on adapting equipment and activities. Have these people brainstorm with you for ideas about how to adapt activities and materials to include children with orthopedic impairments. A child's impairments will determine the extent of their ability to participate in motor play and the strategies that will be most effective. A child whose lower body is most affected needs to strengthen the upper body to allow that child to use a walker or to transfer from a wheelchair to the floor; at the same time, you do not want to ignore the child's lower body. Children need to have as much functional ability as possible so that muscles do not contract or atrophy. To adapt activities to individual differences, use lightweight plastic objects that are easily manipulated or materials that tolerate some degree of error but still work. Help children control the environment by putting

Encourage children with orthopedic impairments to use the skills they have and to participate in large and small motor activities.

smaller objects in jelly roll pans or trays with edges. Allow children time to participate.

Health and Safety

Health and safety are especially important for children with orthopedic and neurologic impairments and can make a difference not only to them, but to other children as well.

1. Teach children to put crutches or other aids in a place where they can have easy access to them. These aids are needed for independence. Teach others to walk around them. These aids belong to the child who uses them. They should not be shared. If you want to use mobility aids to increase awareness, borrow or rent them.

2. Help children identify bruises and scrapes and spot pressure sores and show them to an adult. As you care for these, talk about what you do and why you are doing it.

3. Be sure children are familiar with the procedures and the routes to be taken during safety drills. Have your own drills in preparation for the official ones. Use wagons, or if the child is light enough, lift the child up and carry him if fire occurs. Plan ahead as to who will take the child.

4. Keep extra boxes of tissues around for children to use and trash cans that are easy to get to. Distance makes a difference. Have children deposit used tissues in the trash and then wash their hands. If you help them, you need to wash your hands.

5. Children need to sit in chairs with their buttocks at the back of the chair. At this point, put the seat belt on, if necessary; it usually goes around the hips, not the waist. Check that the knees are at 90 degrees and the feet are on the floor, also at 90 degrees. Elbows should rest gently on the table.

Large Motor

Children need to use and develop their large muscles for strength and endurance.

1. Supervise children carefully. Children with poor muscular control are in danger of falling; someone must be on hand to catch them. Additionally, they need to learn to fall safely, which is vital for their health, well-being, and self-esteem—and not a bad thing for all children to know. Work with the physical therapist and parents to continue this learning process and learn how to help children transfer into unusual equipment (such as a wagon or tricycle).

2. Do not assist children in climbing higher than they can climb independently. Even then, children may climb higher than they realize and be unsure how to get down safely. They may need not only your verbal guidance, but your physical help.

3. If children can use equipment independently (get on and off a trike), encourage them to use it. However, do not assist them in using equipment beyond their skill level unless a therapist has requested this and gives you instructions on how to support the child. Use safety equipment like bicycle helmets for tricycles.

4. Where possible, have children work on vertical surfaces (chalkboard or easel) that are large enough so they can use large muscles both standing and sitting. These are antigravity positions and are necessary for children to integrate the concepts high and low, up and down, and around.

5. When you use toss games (beanbags, balls, ring throws), attach the objects to the child's chair with a string so that the child can retrieve them. Initially, keep distances short, and gradually lengthen them as children become more skillful. (Monitor the string carefully and remove it when the child has finished, as it is a potential danger.)

6. Children with poor balance and motor coordination may increase mobility if they can push something as they move, such as a weighted baby carriage.

7. Mounting toys on walls at a child's height facilitates hand coordination, balance, and grasping. If a child needs practice standing, mounted objects provide the incentive and the opportunity.

8. Children in wheelchairs can participate with little or no difficulty in any game that requires sitting down. To practice tossing and catching use yarn balls or covered foam balls for safety; underinflated beach balls are good, too. Scoopers for catching the balls can be made easily from bleach bottles.

9. If children are prone to bump into the edges of the wall, wall guards are necessary; these are plastic or metal strips on the corners of walls so that the plaster does not chip off (young children might eat the plaster chips).

Small Motor

Children need a balance of fine and gross motor skills. The ability to grasp, manipulate, and release objects is basic to using materials in the class and to lifelong independence. Most adaptive skills as well as preliteracy skills require small motor coordination.

1. Magnetic toys are great. Use the front of a conventional teacher's desk (if in the room) for small-group work; for individual work glue magnets to small toys and blocks such as 1-inch cubes, parquetry blocks, and small "people" to make them easier for the children to move on jellyroll pans. Be sure the pieces are too large to be swallowed.

2. Blocks that snap together and those that are held together with bristles can be built into structures that are not easily knocked apart unintentionally by children with poor control of their hands. Attach Velcro™ to blocks to encourage children to use them and to have them cross the midline. Although these blocks are easy to put together, they take strength to pull apart.

3. Pegboard play improves the child's ability to grasp, aim, and control voluntary motion. The size, number, and spacing of the pegs should vary according to the child's needs. Holes distantly spaced suit some children because they are less likely to knock over one peg when inserting another. Rubber pegboards with large pegs are good for strengthening fingers because they offer some resistance.

4. Playing with pop beads (both pulling them apart and putting them together) helps develop eye-hand coordination and strength.

5. If a child has trouble holding a lacing card for string-ing, you might use a stand-up pegboard or a piece of cardboard that is perpendicular to the table (and therefore does not require wrist rotation). Pasting pictures on cardboard helps to make them sturdier. Reinforce the end of the string with tape or glue so that it is stiff, or use shoelaces knotted at one end.

6. Clothespins that must be squeezed to open can be put around the edge of a can or used to hang up doll clothes. Their use develops necessary finger strength.

7. Puzzle pieces with knobs are easier to insert and remove. Start with shapes that go in easily (circles before octagons).

8. Get a variety of special scissors such as easy-grip loop scissors (they have a squeezable loop instead of finger holes) or scissors with four holes so that you can help the child cut. Use index cards or old greeting cards for cutting as they are stiffer and easier for children to handle.

9. Have children stick objects in and take them out of clay and playdough; cookie cutters and rolling pins work well for this.

10. Use a pipe cleaner instead of a shoelace to string beads. Make a loop at one end for an easier grip.

11. Blowing bubbles encourages lung usage, but be sure the bubble liquid is safe if children accidently swallow it.

Sensory Motor Integration

Integrating information that comes from the senses is critical. Give children unusual stimuli as it helps them focus.

1. Use recipes for playdough that have different consistencies, textures, and smells. Support children in using their hands to poke, pull, and roll the playdough before adding rolling pins and other tools. Encourage them to squish the playdough between their fingers.

2. Make Freddie the Frog or Katie Kangaroo or some such animal from a beanbag. Put the beanbag on the child's head and see how long it will stay there before it falls (or "jumps"). This is a fun way to strengthen neck muscles and to help children learn about the position of their head in space.

3. Activities that require performing two separate motions or a different action with each hand are difficult (holding a juice cup while pouring juice from a small pitcher). Initially, hold the cup while the child pours with two hands or vice versa. As the child's skill improves, encourage him to try both tasks (practice at the water table first).

4. Buy or make a tetherball. Using a small table as a base, secure a 30-inch pole in the center and attach a string. Attach a rubber ball to the string. The children try to wind the ball around the pole by hitting it with their hands or a paddle. This game can be played either sitting or standing. It develops children's eye-hand coordination.

5. For children who have difficulty sitting, a sandbag shaped like a large worm placed around them (like the letter *c*) on the floor provides some support and stability. Have several, so all children can try them.

These are available commercially. Talk to a physical therapist before using them.

Creative Arts: Visual Arts, Music, Creative Movement, and Dramatic Play

Creative arts offer the potential to learn about the world and different media. The emphasis is on the process and creativity. Thinking about the final product and how it will be used, the method of achieving a particular result, and the message it conveys is important. Children can use the arts to express feelings, increase body awareness, and practice fundamental motor skills. During music and movement, ensure that all children are included. Have children help you make up the rules of the game or call out "Simon Says" so that they are verbally and mentally, if not physically, included in the play. Have the child sit on your lap and gently guide her through motions to a song. If appropriate, carry the child as your partner while you play Ring Around the Rosie. Help children "visit" some places that may not be accessible to them, figure out creative ways of increasing accessibility.

Visual Arts

For some children, the visual arts are difficult and discouraging; others find in them a release.

1. Choose activities that require two hands, such as modeling playdough and finger painting. Encourage children to use both hands as a way of building strength.

2. Tape drawing paper to the table so that children can concentrate on what they are putting on the paper, not on preventing the paper from slipping. Use Dycem™, a plastic-like sheet that is tacky enough to hold objects where they are placed. (Most office or medical supply stores have it.) Also use it to keep papers and other objects from moving around. When it becomes less tacky, put it on the bottom of the chair to keep children from slipping off.

3. Use washable marking pens. They require little pressure, are easy to grip, and are colorful. Build up thin ones with masking tape or place foam hair curlers or rubber tubing around them so they are easier to use.

4. Adapt drawing materials. For easier gripping, use large pieces of chalk (on sidewalk). Encourage all children to use these variations and comment upon the effect.

5. Make paint jars easier to handle: Put a thick rubber band (or a thin sheet of foam or sponge) around them, and glue sandpaper on the lids. (Do not use rubber bands if children are younger than age 3.)

6. Use large, heavy, adjustable easels. Adjustable easels allow children many options for working. You may need to put sandbags around the legs so they won't fall if someone pulls up on them or bumps into them.

7. Paint on large paper and large objects, like boxes.

8. Outside, have children "paint" the sidewalk with a bucket of water and a broom (if a child is in a

wheelchair) or a large brush. Tape cloth or paper onto the sidewalk and have children roll wheels (wagon, wheelchair, and tricycle) in washable paint, then over the cloth (be sure the wheels are clean before the children go home). You can make tracks with water as well. (Check with parents for precautions.)

9. Make clay, varying the moisture to meet the strength and motor skills of the child (the moister the clay, the easier to manipulate). Use a rolling pin or tongue depressor to mold clay. Be sure to allow adequate time for exploration. This activity will help build strength and coordination.

10. Don't make models for children even when you are tempted. Support their attempts to control the medium, not the final product.

11. Paint with bare feet on paper on the floor (this can be done from a chair or wheelchair). Have children follow each other's footprints or go in the opposite direction.

Music

Use music to increase body awareness and encourage movement. Music can also be used to teach concepts.

1. Sing the song "Put Your Finger in the Air" and substitute words for "finger" and "air." Be sure to take into account the abilities of the children as you adapt this song. Here are some variations: nose on your shoulder, tongue on your lip, and wrist on your cheek. Other songs also teach body awareness.

2. Have children play rhythm instruments to create a mood. This is a nondemanding way for children to be part of a group.

3. Activities that require two hands to be coordinated, such as clapping, are good practice, but may be difficult, so go slowly.

4. If a child has difficulty holding on to specific instruments, adapt them. On finger cymbals, have elastic attachments that go around the hand rather than knobs. If a child cannot hold a stick to tap a xylophone, have the child wear a mitten with Velcro™ in the palm and glue Velcro™ to the stick. Weigh down objects like drums or xylophones with beanbags to help them stay in one place.

5. Use short, fat, round sticks to hit together or with the xylophone or triangle, or adapt the sticks as you did the paintbrushes and put a larger, sturdier ring on the triangle.

Creative Movement

Creative movement is just that: creative. Help children see the creative quality to movement. This involves not judging the quality of the movement, but accepting the right of individuals to interpret creatively.

1. Allow for individual differences and creativity. Make suggestions in relation to the child's abilities.

2. Plan activities where children can move creatively as part of a group. Choose some movements that the children are able to do while sitting on the floor such as swaying to music.

3. Give children time to explore the quality of their movements. Include some times of slow movement

and encourage children to do fewer of some movements (one stamp instead of five).

4. Isolate movements, based on children's ability. Have them move their eyes creatively, or arms, or another body part.

Dramatic Play

Children can use this type of activity to play different roles as well as to express fears and concerns. They need to learn to use dramatic play to acknowledge and act out their feelings. They cannot run angry feelings off; feelings that are denied take a toll.

1. Help other children become more aware of the challenges of being in a wheelchair or on crutches by having these available to play with. These should be borrowed or rented, not the child's.

2. Play hospital with casting tape (available in most drugstores). Have children cast dolls' legs or their own fingers (use blunt-nosed scissors to cut the casts off).

3. Use a full-length mirror to encourage children to explore their individual characteristics. Be sure to show children how you use the mirror to see parts of you that are difficult to see otherwise. (Put a dot or a cutout on each child's back and have the child try to see it in the mirror.)

4. You may have to demonstrate how to play some roles initially, as children may not have been exposed to them and may not know what to do. Your role is to be a coach: You can't play the game for the children, but you can encourage them, spot them, model how to do it, and teach them techniques.

Routines and Transitions

Transitions are often confusing. Be sure children know where they are going and for what purpose.

1. Use transitions to teach concepts, such as colors, numbers, prepositions, and so on.

2. If children need more time to move, dismiss them no later than the middle of the transitional activity.

3. Always tell the children what you are planning to do *before* you begin doing it. Ask children to help in the transfer—they need to be included in the process. If you simply lift them onto the rug, for example, they may become frightened at suddenly being taken out of a secure position. Even if they have limited speech, talk to them, and make them aware of any changes.

Summary

Children come into the world wanting to move. For some children, this is a challenge. One challenge is muscle tone. When children have muscle tone that is too high, their responses are spastic; when too low, it is floppy; when it is mixed, it becomes undependable and a challenge for them to control.

Increasingly, we are becoming concerned about young children who are clumsy, partly because of their developing self-concept, but also as it relates to learning differences.

There are many different types of neurologic and orthopedic impairments including cerebral palsy; neural tube defects, which are usually present at birth; and injuries to the brain or spinal column that can occur in early childhood. With the advent of new technology, increasing numbers of children with traumatic brain injury are living and returning to educational settings. Other impairments include missing limbs and other disabilities such as muscular dystrophy that relate to a progressive atrophy of the muscles.

Many children who have orthopedic impairments need mobility aids for locomotion. These aids vary from braces and splints and crutches to wheelchairs. Curriculum adaptations allow children with neurologic and orthopedic impairments to be included in regular classroom curriculum.

Reflections

1. You have a child in your kindergarten class who seems to be clumsy. You can't quite put your finger on it but he bumps into things and has trouble with writing and prewriting skills. He doesn't seem to be part of the group during outside play and you are a little concerned about his weight. Would you talk to his parents about this? If you would and they seem unconcerned what would you do?
2. Reflect on your knowledge of traumatic brain injury. Are you comfortable with your knowledge about what you would do if a child fell outside and appeared to be "out of it" for a while? What if the child was unconscious for several minutes. Develop a plan for handling these possibilities.

Educational Resources

ABLEDATA provides objective information about assistive technology products and rehabilitation equipment available from domestic and international sources. They do not sell anything but provide sources for buying. http://www.abledata.com/

Brain Injury Association of America contains facts about TBI including a "kids' corner." The site is easy to navigate for information or resources on brain injuries. http://www.biausa.org/

March of Dimes provides an online library of fact sheets about many disabilities caused by birth defects. It also provides information on current research, local chapters, and links to federal and nonfederal agencies. (914) 428-7100; http://www.marchofdimes.com/

National Clearinghouse of Rehabilitation Training Materials at Utah State University is a great resource for online materials and links to many sites and government agencies. It covers a large range of information. http://ncrtm.org/

National Easter Seal Society operates direct service programs for children with disabilities; they have an array of fact sheets on topics from accessibility and attitudes to dental care. Many of the materials are available online and would be useful to professionals and parents. http://www.easterseals.com/site/PageServer

National Spinal Cord Injury Association (NSCIA) provides information on many relevant subjects including assistive technology, resources, inclusion, and legal issues. http://www.spinalcord.org/

Traumatic Brain Injury Resource Guide provides information, newsletters, how-to manuals, and current research. http://www.neuroskills.com/

United Cerebral Palsy Association (UCP) provides information about education, parenting, and products. It has a variety of online information that would be helpful to parents and professionals. (800) USA-5-UCP; http://www.ucp.org/

For additional resources, visit the book companion website for this text at www.cengage.com/education/deiner.

Chapter 18

Children with Hearing Impairments

It's hard to know when to push and when to just agree and forget it. When I asked our pediatrician whether Erica might have a hearing loss because of her frequent ear infections, he told me he didn't think so. I wanted her seen by an ear specialist. He told me he thought it was unnecessary, but eventually gave the referral I needed. After examining her the otologist said she seemed fine. I had come this far and I wasn't giving up. I told him that he had only seen her for 15 minutes and I didn't think he could tell by what he had done whether or not she could hear. I told him her preschool teachers said that she was louder than the other children and that she seemed to "not hear" as well as the other children. Reluctantly, he agreed to the screening. I didn't want her to have a hearing loss just to prove I was right; on the other hand, I wasn't surprised. What did surprise and dismay me was that the loss they found wasn't the traditional one that accompanies fluid in the ears. It was a sensorineural loss. It was forever—it was hearing aids and speech therapy and all that. I wasn't prepared. But I did follow through. Her audiogram was pretty flat, with a loss of about 60 decibels in the speech frequencies.

It was hardest at the beginning. After all this, Erica refused to wear her hearing aids. We put them in; she took them out. She screamed, cried, and threw temper tantrums when we put them in. We tried to acknowledge her feelings, but we made the decision that she was going to wear them. We felt like meanies each time we put them back in. We even taped them in a couple times so she couldn't pull them out. I'm glad we had each other for support during this round. We kept reminding ourselves that if we didn't make her wear them, she would miss out on so much of life. She needed to begin wearing them now as a 4 year old. We couldn't wait until she was old enough to understand our explanations.

It was a war, but we eventually won the first battle. By the time we had gotten all of this sorted out, Erica was about to begin kindergarten. Putting in her hearing aids had become part of getting dressed. Mornings were no longer a war zone. During kindergarten, Erica had a speech and language pathologist visit the classroom three times a week; she helped her learn concepts that she hadn't gotten like "front" and "back." She uses both sign and speech reads. She can do this well with the help of her hearing aid as long as she can see the teacher. This teacher was really good. She would ask Erica if the volume of the video was loud enough without singling her out.

(One teacher had her in tears, as she kept asking her in front of all the other children.)

We thought we had this together. I could now sign to her and she could hear my husband's voice. We encouraged her independence and her younger brother was feeling as though we had enough time for him. The IEP meeting in May went well. The summer was a relaxing one. Erica was beginning to accept her hearing loss and the hearing aids, as were we. First grade came with a vengeance. At first, the protests were mild, but her stand was irrefutable. She refused to use the auditory trainer. She said it made things too loud; it hurt her ears, and gave her a headache. We talked, we explained, we tried to convince her what she would miss. None of it worked. We made an appointment to meet with her teacher to talk about the problem. We walked into the classroom and were warmly greeted by a voice that almost blasted us out of the classroom. We should have believed her. Erica did not need an auditory trainer in this classroom! They may not have needed a teacher in the next room or even the next school. Some things like fire drills still worry us. When sounds get really loud, like when there is a fire alarm, her ears get really sensitive and she turns off her hearing aid. She can still hear the fire alarm but not much else. I guess if next year's teacher has a soft voice I'll worry about it then.

Erica now accepts the hearing aids. They are part of her. When she takes them off, she can hear some things, like her dad's voice. It's like a mumble, but she can hear it. She can take care of the aids pretty much by herself. When kids she doesn't know ask her, "What are those?" she tells them "They're my hearing aids and they help me hear." She says it doesn't bother her when they stare. "If they stare, that's their problem. I just ignore them. I just mind my own business. It's not their fault." When she sees someone else with a hearing aid she just says, "Hi." She doesn't say anything about it until she knows them.

I think they really are a part of her now. She used to always wear her hair down to cover them. Now she wears it back in a ponytail sometimes. She even asked if she could get her ears pierced.

Reflective Practice

Reflect on the evolution of the process of learning to wear hearing aids to accepting them. Reflect on your role in this process and how you might facilitate this. Think about your voice. Would it be easy or difficult for a child with a hearing impairment to be part of your classroom? What about your style of teaching? How compatible is your teaching style with not only hearing impairments but other disabilities?

Hearing Impairments

When a child with a hearing impairment joins your class, you suddenly become aware of the many times during the day that children listen. They have to listen for their name to be called, for directions about activities, and when to cleanup. They listen during music, stories, and routines.

Hearing is important in developing communications skills. Children learn to talk by listening and imitating others and by hearing themselves. The hearing child enters kindergarten with a vocabulary of about 5,000 words. The child with a hearing impairment may understand and speak only a few basic words, and even those few words may be difficult to understand. Our society assumes that people can convey their wants and needs verbally. In school, children are expected to ask to go to the bathroom, to tell the teacher if they are hurt, and to talk with their peers. They are also expected to put away their materials when requested and to line up or come when called. Children with hearing impairments have trouble following instructions and discussions. Before their hearing impairment is identified, they may be mistaken for children who daydream or choose not to listen. They are sometimes characterized as stubborn, disobedient, and lazy.

Hearing allows a person to gain information. We use hearing to monitor our physical and social environment. Children who cannot hear danger signals may find themselves in hazardous situations that others can avoid. Being out of touch with moment-to-moment ordinary sounds has a social-emotional impact of equal magnitude. Children with hearing impairments must be taught to use other cues to keep in touch with their world.

The Auditory System

Before looking at hearing impairments, we need to understand more about sound and the auditory system.

Sound is made by an object or structure vibrating. The energy initiated by these vibrations forms sound waves. These sound waves have two distinct aspects: **intensity** and **frequency**. Sound intensity is measured by the amplitude (height and depth) of the sound waves. Loudness is not just sound intensity it is a subjective term describing the ear's perception of a sound. Intensity is measured in **decibels** (dB). The abbreviation dB is in honor of Alexander Graham Bell, hence the capital B. The softest sound a person with normal hearing can hear is 0 decibels (dB); typical conversation is about 40 to 60 dB, a shout may be 70 dB, and a rock concert could be 90 or 100 dB (Herer, Knightly, & Steinberg, 2007). The letters HL often follow the decibels and they stand for hearing level.

Frequency is determined by the number of cycles per second the sound wave has. A cycle is the distance between the top of one sound wave to the top of the next sound wave. The closer the sound waves are to each other, the higher the frequency. Pitch is the perceived frequency of sound. Frequency is measured in **hertz** (Hz): one hertz is equivalent to one cycle per second. People can hear sounds that are low (about 20 Hz) to those that are very high (about 20,000 Hz). (Dogs can hear frequencies over 40,000 Hz.) The normal speech frequencies fall between 500 and 2,000 Hz, and virtually all speech is between 250 and 6,000 Hz. Hz (Herer et al., 2007). Middle C is 261.6 Hz.

Speech is more complex than a single intensity or frequency. Some sounds, such as vowels, have lower frequencies and are more intense. Some consonants, such as the voiceless /h/, /p/, /s/, and so on, are higher in frequency (Herer et al., 2002). The interaction of speech with an individual's pattern of loss may allow some children to hear speech but not understand it because they hear only part of what is said. They may hear "Hey" as /ᵊa/.

Although there is some variation in classifying sounds, Table 18–1 will give an approximate idea of the intensity of some sounds. People can hear sounds from 0 dB HL to 120 dB HL. Listening to sounds over 100 dB HL for

Table 18–1: Approximate decibel levels of environmental and letter sounds

Decibels	Sound
0	Hearing threshold
10	Normal breathing, water dripping
20–30	Leaves rustling, whispering, /z/, /p/, /k/, /m/, /d/, /b/
40–60	Normal conversation (2 people), /a/, /o/, /r/
60–70	Telephone, baby crying
80	Vacuum cleaner
90–100	Subway train, motorcycle, large truck
110+	Airliner taking off, explosion, some bands playing

extended periods can cause hearing loss. Sounds over 120 dB HL first cause a tickle sensation, then pain and sensorineural damage.

The ear is the organ of the body that we think of when we think of hearing. However, there is rarely a problem with the outer ear or **auricle**. It is one of the least important parts of the auditory system, although it does function to keep foreign objects out of the middle ear. The external ear is one of three parts of the ear and the only one that is visible. It is connected to the **middle ear**, which is connected to the **inner ear** (see Figure 18–1).

Sound waves enter the auricle, travel through the **ear canal**, and hit the **tympanic membrane** (eardrum), causing it to vibrate. The ear canal protects the middle ear by secreting wax that catches debris and keeps it away from the eardrum. The eardrum is attached to one of the small bones in the middle ear, the **malleus** (hammer), through which vibrations are transmitted to the **incus** (anvil) and **stapes** (stirrup). Together, these are known as the **ossicles**. The stapes lies next to the **oval window**, the beginning of the inner ear. The tympanic membrane and ossicles amplify sound by about 30 dB HL, in addition to transmitting it (Herer et al., 2007).

The inner ear transforms sound from mechanical energy to electrical energy. It is about the size of a pea. As the vibrations push the oval window (a thin membrane) back and forth, the fluid in the cochlea moves. The **cochlea** is a snail-shaped structure with three chambers, which makes hearing possible. The middle chamber, the **organ of Corti**, contains about 20,000 tiny, delicate hair cells. The **hair cells** near the oval window respond to high-frequency sounds; those in the middle and end respond to low-frequency sounds. These hair cells send electrochemical impulses through the nerve fibers of the ascending auditory pathway to the **auditory cortex** in the temporal lobe of the brain. The route to the auditory cortex is complex and includes four transmitting stations. At one of these stations, the nerve fibers cross over, permitting stereophonic hearing; others fine-tune the sound and inhibit background noise. The auditory cortex combines sound with other sensory information and memory and allows perception and interpretation of sound (Herer

et al., 2007). The auditory cortex isn't needed to hear pure tones, but it is necessary to interpret language.

In addition to providing hearing, the ear serves two other functions: balance and responding to differences in pressure. The inner ear has three loop-shaped tubes, the **semicircular canals** that serve to maintain balance (vestibular sense). The **eustachian tube**, a slender tube that runs from the middle ear to the **pharynx**, equalizes pressure on both sides of the eardrum. When changing altitudes, it is the clearing of the eustachian tube by swallowing or chewing gum that keeps the eardrum from bursting. The ears essentially duplicate each other; the major benefit of having two ears is the ability to localize sound.

Modes of Hearing

We hear sound in two different ways: air conduction and bone conduction. **Air conduction** is the most common way we receive auditory input. Sound waves travels through air; when they enter the outer ear, move through the middle and inner ear, and end up at the auditory cortex, we hear. We also hear through **bone conduction**, in which the bones of the head mechanically vibrate. This vibration causes the hair cells in the cochlea to move and begins the hearing process in a way that bypasses the outer and middle ear. When we speak and hear ourselves, part of what we hear is based on bone conduction. When you hear yourself on an audiotape, you often think that it doesn't sound like you, whereas others claim it is exactly how you sound. The difference is because you are hearing just the air conduction aspect of your speaking when listening to the tape.

Defining Hearing Impairments

The most common way to define or classify hearing impairments is by their location and the severity of the loss. Knowing the exact type of loss has implications for treatment and education, as well as long-term implications. The IDEA 2004 defines both hearing impairments and deafness.

> Deafness means a hearing impairment that is so severe that the child is impaired in processing linguistic information through hearing, with or without amplification that adversely affects a child's educational performance.
>
> Hearing impairment means an impairment in hearing, whether permanent or fluctuating, that adversely affects a child's educational performance but that is not included under the definition of deafness in this section.

The term deaf is often used for children with a profound hearing loss, 70 decibels (dB) hearing level (HL), or greater. Even with hearing aids, this child may only hear the rhythm of speech, his own voice, and loud environmental sounds (Northern & Downs, 2002). The use of **cochlear implants** is changing this for children with profound losses. The terms hearing impairment or hard of hearing are used to identify children who have a loss between 25 and 70 dB HL (Herer et al., 2007).

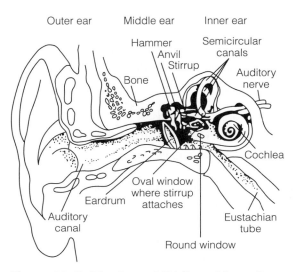

Figure 18–1: The Outer, Middle and Inner Ear

When hearing thresholds are tested, both air conduction and bone conduction tests are done. Differences in the two thresholds have important diagnostic significance.

Conductive Hearing Loss

A **conductive hearing loss** is one in which the outer or middle ear prevents sound from getting to the inner ear. This can be caused by something lodged in the ear canal, excessive earwax, or fluid in the middle ear (otitis media). The air conduction threshold indicates a hearing loss and the bone conduction indicates normal hearing. This is called a conductive hearing loss because the problem is in the conducting mechanisms of the outer and/or middle ear (Herer et al., 2002).

Sensorineural Hearing Loss

A **sensorineural hearing loss** involves damage to either the inner ear, the nerve to the brainstem, or both. Some break this apart and use the terms **sensory hearing loss** when the cochlea is implicated and **neural hearing loss** when it is the auditory nerve (Herer et al., 2007). In this case, both the air conduction and the bone conduction tests are abnormal, but the **tympanogram** is normal. Tympanometry measure the movement of the tymnpanic membrane (ear drum) and the mobility and functioning of the middle ear. Typically, **hearing aids** are prescribed to make sounds louder. Even with **amplification**, however, sounds are unclear and distorted. Children who have a profound hearing loss before they develop spoken language are likely to be 4 to 5 years behind their peers in spoken English by the time them enter high school and they are also likely to be behind in reading and writing

as well (Geers, 2006). See Figure 18–2 to compare a sensorineural loss with a conductive loss.

Mixed Hearing Loss

Children can experience a **mixed hearing loss;** both a sensorineural and a conductive loss. In this case, the conductive problem may be treated surgically, and the sensorineural problem will require a hearing aid or cochlear implant depending upon the degree of loss. These combined situations are difficult to diagnose.

Central Auditory Hearing Loss

A **central auditory hearing loss** or central **auditory processing dysfunction** occurs when children have problems understanding speech. They have additional problems related to short- and long-term auditory memory, following multistep directions, paying attention, auditory sequential memory, sounding out words, spelling, vocabulary, and reading comprehension (Herer et al., 2007). These children are particularly difficult to identify because they pass all the traditional auditory screening tests and they usually have typical intellectual development. Testing is complex, but there are standardized tests designed to identify these children.

Severity of Hearing Loss

Hearing impairments range from the inability to understand speech with amplification to problems interpreting faint speech. The effects on the child vary according to not only the type of loss, but the frequencies and severity of hearing loss as well. During early childhood years, the severity of hearing losses can be characterized as shown in Table 18–2.

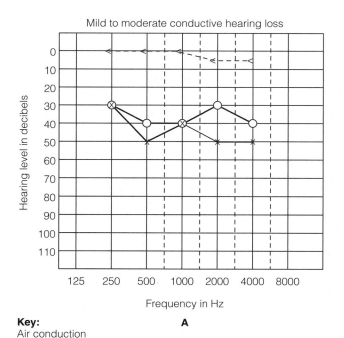

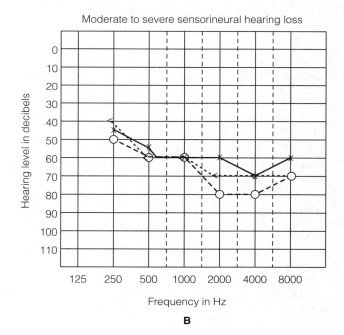

Key:
Air conduction
Right   O
Left   x
Bone conduction   <

Figure 18–2: Patterns of Conductive (A) and Sensorineural Hearing Loss (B)
In a conductive loss, the bone conduction is within normal limits, but the air conduction shows a mild to moderate loss. In a sensorineural loss, both air and bone conduction reflect this moderate to severe hearing loss.

Table 18–2: Classification of Bilateral Hearing Loss without Amplification

Normal limits: 0–15 dB HL

No difficulty hearing faint speech.

Slight hearing loss: 15–25 dB HL (at 500–2,000 Hz)

The frequencies are relevant because they are in the speech range. A loss this slight outside the speech frequencies is rarely a problem. Children with losses at this level need preferential seating.

Mild hearing loss: 25–30 dB HL

Children with a mild bilateral loss might miss distant sounds, soft speech, and as much as 25 to 40 percent of speech at conventional levels, and the unvoiced consonants such as /s/, /p/, /t/, /k/, /th/, /f/, and /sh/. This can make learning language difficult. They might miss plurals as well as stress patterns. If this loss is intermittent, like those associated with middle ear infections, it may make language confusing for children. If it is permanent hearing aids may be recommended.

Moderate hearing loss: 30–50 dB HL

Children will have some difficulty with normal speech and may hear it as a whisper. If in a group and voices are faint, they may miss most of what is said without interventions. Learning problems are frequent. Hearing aids will usually be recommended.

Severe hearing loss: 50–70 dB HL

Children with severe bilateral losses have difficulty hearing loud speech without intervention. They will hear loud environmental sounds (alarms and sirens). Hearing aids are essential. Academic supports and classroom amplification help, speech and language therapy, as well as tutoring and special educational services should be considered.

Profound hearing loss: 71 dB HL and greater

These children may hear close, loud environmental sounds. Even with amplification some consonants will be missed. Unless intervention is begun prior to 6 months, many may not develop speech spontaneously without powerful amplification. These children may profit from cochlear implants. Many parents who are deaf choose to use a visual communication strategy if their child has a loss in this range.

Source: Herer, Knightly, & Steinberg, 2007; Northern & Downs, 2002.

Keep in mind that the two ears can have different amounts of loss and, typically, the child functions at the level of the better ear. If a child had a 50 dB HL in the right ear and 80 dB HL in the left, she may function as a child with a moderate hearing loss, not a severe hearing loss.

Prevalance of Hearing Impairments

Because of definitional problems, it is difficult to reach conclusions about prevalence. The prevalence rate varies according to the method of testing and the criteria used by the audiologist. Mild hearing losses in particular are not easily detected and, consequently, the child is not referred for testing. The same is true for children who have intermittent conductive losses.

The federal government began keeping records on children with hearing impairments during the 1976–1977 school year. At that time 8.3 percent of children in the public schools were identified as having a disability. Of these children, 2.4 percent had a hearing impairment. This number decreased to 1.2 percent in 1990 as the impact of the rubella vaccine was felt. This number has remained stable since then. In the 2005–2006 school year, 13.8 percent of children were identified as having a disability with 1.2 percent of all school children having a hearing impairment (National Center for Educational Statistics, 2006). Approximately 10 to 15 percent of preschool and school age children do not pass the screening test. Most of these children have a transient conductive hearing loss (Herer et al., 2002).

Others have rated the prevalence of children having a hearing loss greater than 40 decibels as 1.2 per 1,000 well babies but it increases to 3.9 per 1,000 infants requiring hospitalization in the neonatal intensive care unit (Herer et al., 2007).

Causes of Hearing Impairments

Hearing losses that are present at birth are described as **congenital**. Those that develop after birth are **acquired**. Universal newborn hearing screening programs are identifying infants earlier than in the past; however, some disorders result in late-onset hearing loss and progressive disorders that are not present at birth (Yeargin-Allsopp, Drews-Botsch, & Van Naarden Braun, 2007). Hearing loss can be caused by hereditary factors, injury, or infection. Hearing loss is part of more than 400 syndromes; these account for about 50 percent of children who have a hearing loss. In about half of all cases of hearing loss, the cause is genetic. Of these, 75 to 80 percent are caused by autosomal-recessive inheritance and 20 to 25 percent are autosomal-dominant (Kenneson, Van Naarden Braun, & Boyle, 2002).

When the hearing loss is not genetic in nature about a third of the children have additional disabilities. For

Headphones might help some children with mild to moderate conductive losses, but even turned up loud, they do not help children with severe or profound losses.

example, a child with cleft palate is likely to have middle ear involvement, which can lead to a conductive hearing loss. The remaining children have losses resulting from pre- or postnatal infections or exposure to teratogens, anoxia,

prematurity, or other causes. Infections during pregnancy such as rubella and cytomegalovirus (CMV) can cause hearing loss. Bacterial meningitis can damage the cochlea. Even viral diseases such as mumps, measles, and chicken pox can result in hearing loss. Some children have losses because of middle ear disease. These are dealt with in detail later in this chapter.

Middle Ear Disease

Measuring the functioning of the middle ear is important in identifying the type of hearing loss and monitoring and treating middle ear disease. Tympanometry is designed to detect normal and abnormal conditions of the eardrum and middle ear. Since disorders of the middle ear are the most frequent cause of hearing loss during the early childhood years, including this screening is important. A specially designed ear probe is inserted into the child's ear canal, an airtight seal is obtained, then the middle ear pressure, tympanic membrane compliance, the mobility of the ossicles and eustachian tube function are analyzed, and the screener removed (Herer et al., 2007). When the ear probe is returned to its stand, it automatically prints out a tympanogram. A normal tympanogram looks something like a narrow pyramid. When a child has fluid in the middle ear, the tympanogram is flat. Children who have an abnormal tympanogram should be rescreened in 4 to 6 weeks or referred for further treatment, depending on the abnormality (see Figure 18–3).

Many young children who experience frequent ear infections have periodic hearing losses because of the fluid in their ear canals. This fluid interferes with the conduction of sound waves from the outer ear to the inner ear, and is hence a conductive loss. **Middle ear disease**, or **chronic otitis media**, is the build-up of thick fluid in the middle ear that doesn't drain through the eustachian tubes. Middle-ear disease or otitis media (infection and fluid) is the most common illness in young children after the common cold. The National Institute on Deafness and Other Communication Disorders (NIDCD) (2002) estimates

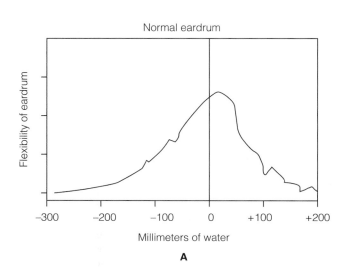

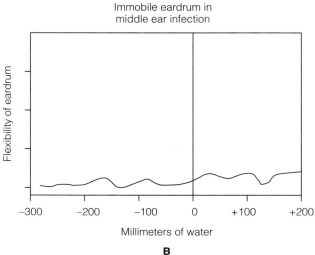

A

B

Figure 18–3: Tympanogram of a Normal Eardrum (A) and an Impaired Eardrum (B) When the tympanic membrane (eardrum) is functioning normally the tympanogram is shaped like a triangle. When the flexibility of eardrum is decreased, such as in middle ear disease, the pattern is flat.

that 75 percent of young children will experience at least one episode of otitis media by their third birthday and half of these children will have had three or more ear infections. This thick fluid, a prime target for bacterial growth, causes a hearing loss of about 60 dB HL.

Antibiotics cure the infection, but the fluid may linger on for days or even weeks, continuing the hearing loss. The cause of fluid in the middle ear is related to dysfunction of the eustachian tube. Because of the problem's intermittent nature, it can be missed even among children whose hearing is frequently tested. Sound is heard, but acuity is poor. If treated, there are usually few long-term implications from occasional ear infections (Herer et al., 2007).

More subtle, and even more difficult to diagnose, is **otitis media with effusion** (OME). This condition often follows infectious otitis media, but it occurs without the infection. This means the child has a conductive loss, but no signs of fever or pain. Some feel this condition is caused solely by the malfunctioning of the eustachian tube; others feel that it is related to allergies. Additionally, there may be a long-term relationship with learning disabilities. "Children with hearing loss due to OME constitute potentially the largest group in the world with reversible learning disorders, the significance of the link of allergy to otitis media with effusion cannot be understated" (Hurst, 2007). There is enough evidence to investigate the possibility of allergies as a cause and to look for learning disabilities in this population. As an early childhood educator you need to be aware of this connection and talk with parents about it as a possibility.

The Evidence Base

There is controversy about the relationship between allergies and chronic middle ear disease. The goal of this study was to evaluate the atopic status (**atopy** is an allergic hypersensitivity affecting parts of the body not in direct contact with the allergen) of individuals with chronic otitis media and to intervene by using allergy immunotherapy.

The subjects included 52 children under 15 years of age and 37 adults. All were evaluated for allergies using intradermal testing and all were found to be atopic. Most frequent allergies were dust (94 percent), mold (88 percent), animals (44 percent), and seasonal pollens (9 percent). Associated allergic conditions included asthma (21 percent) and allergic rhinitis (63 percent) (Hurst, 2008).

Of patients, 21 chose not to be treated for allergies. These patients served as the control group. Of the 68 subjects who participated in the allergy immunotherapy 6 percent improved significantly and 85 percent resolved their problems with otitis media with effusion. None of the controls resolved spontaneously. (Hurst, 2008)

The American Academy of Family Physicians; American Academy of Otolaryngology–Head and Neck Surgery; and American Academy of Pediatrics Subcommittee on Otitis Media with Effusion (2004) feel that there is insufficient evidence of the therapeutic efficacy or of a causal relationship between allergy and otitis media with effusion to recommend allergy management as a treatment for otitis media with effusion.

Reflective Practice

Although this study shows evidence supporting allergy treatment for patients with chronic otitis media with effusion the treating physician was also the researcher. Other medical groups have reached different conclusions about the relationship between allergies and middle ear disease. What do you do when recommendations conflict? If you had a child in your class with chronic ear infections would you suggest the possibility of allergies?

Initially, middle ear disease (MED) is treated with antibiotics. When the problem persists, MED is treated surgically by making an incision in the lower part of the eardrum, removing the fluid, and inserting a small plastic tube in the eardrum incision. The small tube, called a **pressure-equalization tube**, takes over the function of the eustachian tube by allowing air to enter the middle ear space and also allowing fluid to drain (Herer et al., 2007). The procedure is called a **myringotomy with tubal insertion**.

Implications for Educators

Be aware of children who have frequent ear infections. Monitor their speech and language development especially when they return to school after being sick with an ear infection. Focus on their learning skills especially as they relate to reading. Ensure that they are developing these skills at the expected rate. If they are not begin intervening early.

Early Identification of Hearing Impairments

We can reliably test auditory function shortly after birth, and most states universally test newborns in birthing hospitals. If not identified at birth, parents may be concerned about a hearing loss but it is often hard to pin down; just when parents think they should be concerned, the infant does something to make them think they are imagining things. Most parents don't want to appear overprotective and look foolish to their pediatricians (especially after the infant was tested for hearing loss). Additionally, many parents continually adjust to and match their child's emerging skills. As children respond to more visual communication efforts, parents automatically use more gestures and expressions. This facilitates the child's language but makes assessment more difficult. Children with mild or intermittent hearing impairments are difficult to identify at an early age. Table 18–3 highlights some signs that should alert you to suspect a hearing impairment.

Parents who note the problem usually do so because the child does not reach traditional milestones in the area of speech and language. Unless there are other disabilities present, hearing loss itself does not interfere with the attainment of physical milestones such as walking and exploring the environment. One concern is that parents and educators may interpret the child's unwillingness to verbally take turns, looking away when someone is talking, and not learning the rules that govern language as a behavior problem.

Table 18–3: Signs of hearing impairments

Speech

Speech and grammar that is delayed and immature

Speech that cannot be understood by nonfamily members beyond expected ages

Speech that is too loud or too soft for the situation

Language

Misunderstands directions or gives inappropriate answers to questions

Asks for information to be repeated or says "What?" a lot

Is hesitant in answering questions or joining conversations

Has difficulty with listening activities

Attention

Is unusually attentive to speaker's face

Short attention span, distractable

Disinterested in many activities, especially those requiring listening

Health

Frequent colds, respiratory tract infections, or ear infections

Draining ears, breathing through the mouth

Poor balance, seems clumsy

Allergies

Source: Herer, Knightly, & Steinberg, 2002; Hurst, 2007; Northern & Downs, 2002.

Infants with hearing impairments make noises and babble like other infants up until about 5 months of age. After 5 months, babbling imitates the language spoken at home. This does not happen among children with hearing impairments. They do not respond to auditory stimuli that are out of their range of hearing. An infant with a severe auditory impairment would not wake to a loud noise or try to seek out the source of sounds. The infant may, however, respond to vibrations such as approaching footsteps, making parents doubt their concerns. Adults may not recognize auditory impairments because the child does what is requested, but he may be responding to visual cues or cues from other children, not because he understands the request. As requests become more complex, the difference often becomes evident, but noncompliance may be mistaken for oppositional behavior, or a behavior disorder (Herer et al., 2007).

Auditory impairments severely impact the development of speech and language skills. Both speech and language depend upon hearing in the early years of development. Children organize language through listening, imitation, practice, and correction.

Children who are identified as having a hearing impairment before language was established are considered **prelingually hearing impaired**. They have not yet established a language base. This makes it more challenging to learn to speak. One major decision parents must make is how they are going to communicate with their child. This decision has major implications for the child, the family, and the educational system. If intervention begins before 6 months, even children with profound losses can be in contact with an auditory world, if that is what the family desires.

During the preschool years, children with hearing impairments will have delays in speech and language. They may develop unusual ways of attaining adult attention. If they cannot hear adults, they must engage them physically or visually. Misbehavior is very effective in doing this. This may be an attempt at communication. As adults, we rarely view it this way; these children may seem either extremely attentive or inattentive.

As children reach elementary school age, almost all those with moderate to profound losses, should have been identified. As children become more dependent on oral communication, those with hearing impairments are at a disadvantage in standard English. It is difficult to predict the level of communication children this age will have. If intervention began in infancy the skills children have will be very different from children who do not begin until age 3 or 4.

Assessment of Hearing Impairments

Well newborns are screened between 9 and 24 hours after birth. Infants in the neonatal intensive care unit are screened before they are discharged. Children who have identifiable risk factors should be tested semiannually until age 3 (Herer et al., 2007). Risk factors for neonates include admission to NICU for more than 48 hours, family history of hearing loss, craniofacial anomalies, low Apgar score, maternal infections such as CMV, Herpes, toxoplasmosis, or rubella, or syndromes known to include sensorineural hearing loss. For children 29 days to 2 years additional risks include adult concern, bacterial meningitis, head trauma, and infectious disease associated with hearing loss (Joint Committee on Infant Hearing, 1990).

The American Speech-Language-Hearing Association (ASHA, 1990) has developed guidelines for the screening process. These involve obtaining a case history of the child; visually inspecting the outer ear, ear canal, and eardrum; **pure-tone hearing screening**; and tympanometry. ASHA suggests that all children should be screened annually from age 3 until third grade, and high-risk children annually regardless of age.

The case history and visual inspection are often done by a school nurse, speech/language pathologist, or an audiologist. If a child has a history of ear infections or if the visual inspection shows abnormalities (excessive earwax, fluid in the middle ear, and so on), the child is referred for a medical evaluation.

Hearing screening and **hearing threshold testing** for children older than age 3 are typically done using an **audiometer**, an electronic instrument that comes in many different types. The one most commonly used in the school setting is a **pure-tone audiometer**, which can be used to screen children and also to determine hearing thresholds. Pure-tone audiometers produce discrete frequencies called **pure tones** at different intensity levels (decibels). In pure-tone testing, the tester places earphones on the child, and then the child is given sounds at 20 dB HL at frequencies of 500, 1,000, 2,000, and 4,000. These are the most important frequencies for speech, and 20 dB HL is the lower range for what we consider normal hearing. This is purely an air-conduction evaluation. Children who fail to hear at any frequency should be retested. (Before retesting, one should be sure the child understands the instructions.) Children who fail the retest should be referred to an **audiologist** or **otologist** for a pure tone threshold test.

Increasing audiologist are using **otoacoustic emissions testing** (OAE). OEA uses a probe that is placed in the ear canal. A series of sounds are presented through the probe, which contains a loudspeaker that generates the sounds and a microphone that measures the resulting OAEs that are produced in the cochlea and are transmitted through the middle ear into the outer ear canal. This resulting sound is picked up by the microphone, and digitized and processed using signal averaging methodology. To obtain an OAE one needs an unobstructed outer ear canal, absence of significant middle ear pathology, and functioning cochlear outer hair cells (Hain, 2007). Children need to sit quietly and still to obtain results but they do not need to participate in the testing.

An **otolaryngologist** is a physician who specializes in the treatment of ear disorders that can result in hearing loss. The otolaryngologist will determine whether or not medical intervention is indicated. Children younger than age 18 must have medical clearance before being fitted with hearing aids. An audiologist is a professional who has been trained in the prevention, identification, and nonmedical management of hearing loss. Audiologists can identify hearing loss and initiate treatment in children as young as neonates once medical clearance has been obtained. The audiologist may refer children to other specialists such as a speech/language pathologist or a psychologist to determine the effects of the hearing loss on other aspects of functioning.

Behavioral hearing tests are also used to determine if a hearing loss exists; the type of loss; the range of loss in each ear; and the clarity with which speech can be understood (Northern & Downs, 2002). These are typically combined with electrophysiological methods to get a better picture of the young child's hearing. For infants up to 8 months, the behavioral observations might look at turning a head in the direction of a familiar sound (mother's voice). Between 8 months and 30 months, professionals use principles of operant conditioning to determine threshold levels. This information is used to validate the electrophysiological findings. By 2 and a half, children can wear earphones and by 4 years they can typically press a button or raise a hand to indicate which ear they are hearing the sound in.

Amplification

The ears receive sound waves in the air and convert them into electrical signals the brain can understand. When the ear sends weak or distorted signals, hearing and understanding are impaired. Children, including infants, should be fitted for hearing aids as soon as a permanent loss is confirmed if parents decide that they want to use amplification (Herer et al., 2007). Audiologists are responsible for fitting **amplification devices** to particular children.

Measuring a hearing loss and understanding the implications of that loss for understanding speech are different issues. Children with mild to moderate conductive losses hear approximately what you would hear with very tight-fitting earplugs. It takes strain and much concentration to hear. Try it. Are you startled when people come up behind you quietly? Do you get tired with the effort and concentration it takes to hear? What might you do over the course of several days or weeks like this? Unless there were some good reasons for you to continue, you might tune it all out.

Children with more severe losses have an even more difficult problem. Although they may be able to hear some speech, they have trouble understanding it, even with hearing aids. They may be able to hear the low-frequency vowel sounds that carry the power of speech, but miss the high-frequency consonant sounds that make speech intelligible.

Even using a combination of hearing and vision, understanding is difficult. Try listening to a mistuned radio. You know they are speaking, but it is difficult to figure out what is being said. In classrooms where the teacher's voice is only about 5 to 10 dB HL louder than the general background noise in the classroom, children with hearing impairments have an extremely difficult time. Improving this ratio helps the child immensely. This can be done by having the teacher talk louder or modifying the classroom to make it quieter by adding carpet, drapes, and so on. Audiologists can provide information on how to improve this situation. Amplification helps but does not solve the problem.

Hearing Aids

Hearing aids have three major components: a microphone that changes sound waves into electrical energy, an amplifier (or amplifiers) that increases the intensity of the signal, and a receiver that converts the electrical signal back to an acoustical signal and projects this amplified sound through the earmold into the ear (Herer et al., 2007). Hearing aids are battery powered and have volume controls. They are individually prescribed by audiologists based on the characteristics of the loss, the child's speech and language skills, intellectual ability, situations in which the child will listen, and school performance (Herer et al., 2007). Hearing aids are purchased from commercial dealers. Prescribing a hearing aid is different for an infant or young child than it is for an adult. It is a learning process that evolves. As the aid is used, the match can be assessed in the context of the child's language development as well as the audiogram, which maps the loss. As children and technology change, the aids may change as well.

There are four basic categories of hearing aids: behind-the-ear aids, in-the-ear aids, body aids, and bone conduction aids. Because of improvements in behind-the-ear aids, body aids are less frequently used with young children than in the past. Because behind-the-ear aids are larger than in-the-ear aids, they can accommodate more circuitry and controls and allow more flexibility. This flexibility is particularly important when test data for young children are incomplete. New hearing aids are programmable and can be changed to adjust to different listening environments.

The advantage of in-the-ear aids is primarily cosmetic. Children who have problems with constant drainage into the ear canal and those with long-term conductive losses may use a bone conduction aid, which is a vibrator placed over the **mastoid** and attached to a headband to keep it in place (Herer et al., 2007).

Assistive Listening Devices

Assistive listening devices such as an FM system are used in combination with hearing aids. They are used in difficult listening situations such as classrooms to reduce the amount of background noise. These may be used in classrooms or for infants recently identified with hearing losses. If a parent wears a lapel microphone and speaks to the infant from anywhere in the room, the infant can receive vocal stimulation even when the parent is not talking directly to her. This can be used in a school situation as well. The hearing aid–FM combination helps the signal-to-noise ratio, making it easier for the child to understand the speaker. If a teacher (or parent) wears the microphone, it is as if the speaker is only about 6 to 8 inches from the child's ear (Herer et al., 2007).

A hearing aid amplifies all sounds, not just speech. Because it does not correct distortion, it is not useful for all types of hearing impairments. Using hearing aids properly requires intervention. (The child must be taught how to listen; speech may be gobbledygook to a child who has never heard it.) Hearing aids are not like eyeglasses, which can correct vision to within normal limits; hearing aids do not correct hearing impairments.

Although a hearing aid is beneficial, that doesn't ensure that the child will willingly wear it. Parents and teachers are frequently frustrated by children who pull out their hearing aids. To young children, the aid may feel strange, and they will try to make themselves more comfortable by taking it out. If children were previously unaware of most sounds and speech, the hearing aid may be delivering what to them sounds like meaningless noise. Again, their solution is to remove the aid. Once children see the advantages of hearing with the aid, they are usually willing to wear it; until then, however, encouragement is needed.

Implications for Educators

Work out an agreement with families about what to do when a child takes off the hearing aid. You need to develop some skills in working with a hearing aid. You should be able to do certain tasks younger children may not yet have mastered:

- **Put the earpiece back in when it falls out or is pulled out.**
- **Check to see if batteries are dead and replace them. (Keep a supply in the child's locker or with the school nurse.)**
- **Know how to manipulate the controls. When the hearing aid "whistles," ask the child to turn it down or, if necessary, turn it down yourself.**

Hearing aids should not be abused, but they are sturdy enough to allow the child to participate in most activities. Try to keep them from getting painted, soaked, or sandy. Remember, hearing aids do not make a child

hear perfectly. Be sure the other children understand this. Also, realize that a hearing aid works well for a radius of only 10 feet; even then, it amplifies sounds indiscriminately.

Cochlear Implants

A cochlear implant is a small, complex electronic device that can provide a sense of sound to a person who has a severe or profound hearing loss (see Figure 18–4). Cochlear implant technology is relatively new, beginning in 1984. The level of sophistication in the implants has increased dramatically since then. The Federal Food and Drug Administration (FDA) guidelines permits infants with loss of 90 dB HL or greater to have cochlear implants as young as 12 months for one type of cochlear implant and those with a loss of 70 dB HL or greater at age 2. Most children receive them between 2 and 6. At the end of 2006, approximately 23,000 adults and 15,500 children had received them (National Institute on Deafness and Other Communication Disorders [NIDCD], 2007).

The Evidence Base

Since the advent of cochlear implants the age at which they are done has become increasingly younger. The Food and Drug Administration does not allow cochlear implants in the United States for children under 12 months because of the concern that children could be misdiagnosised as having a profound loss when they do not and concerns related to the use of anesthesia. Researchers are interested in finding whether implants during the first year of life are more effective and safe.

Lesinski-Schiedat, Illg, Hearmann, Bertram, and Lenarz (2004) working out of the Medical University of

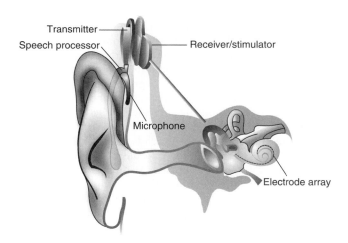

Figure 18–4: Ear with Cochlear Implant
The cochlear implant consists of a microphone to pick up sound, a speech processor to select and arrange the sounds, a transmitter and receiver/stimulator that receives signals and converts them into electrical impulses, and an electrode array that collects the impulses and sends them to different regions of the auditory nerve.

Hannover, Germany, analyzed the result of 27 infants implanted before 12 months and 89 toddlers implanted between 13 and 24 months. They found no difference between the infants and toddlers relative to surgical or anesthetic complications. At a 2-year follow-up children who were implanted as infants showed better hearing and speech development than those implanted as toddlers.

Holt and Svirsky (2008) from Indiana University conducted similar research with 96 children who were identified as having profound bilateral hearing losses who had cochlear implants before the age of 4. They had only six children in their sample who were implanted before 12 months. They followed the children for at least 2 years after the implantation. The developmental trajectory of those implanted earlier was better than children implanted later. They found that children implanted before 12 months had better receptive language but this did not carry over into expressive language or word recognition. However, it did influence the rate of both receptive and expressive language acquisition.

Both studies suggest that earlier implantation is better than later implantation and that age at implantation supports expressive and receptive language but not necessarily word recognition (Holt & Svirsky, 2008; Lesinski-Schiedat, Illg, Hearmann, Bertram, & Lenarz, 2004).

Reflective Practice

How does this research inform your practice? How might you use it in working with families? Which study do you have the most confidence in? Why? Do you think the research suggests that the first four years of life are a sensitive period for developing spoken language? How might this influence how you interact with children before age 4?

Cochlear implant systems require surgery to place the stimulating electrode array inside the cochlea and a receiver under the skin (Geers, 2006). It works like this: there is a directional microphone that is worn behind the ear that captures sound, this sound is sent to a signal processor (tiny computer) that analyzes and digitizes the sound signals into programmed electrical information and then, through a cable, sends them to the transmitter (located on the skin surface behind the ear), which then sends the signal to the receiver (implanted under the skin). The receiver sends the coded electrical signals to the electrode array that has been implanted in the cochlea and these electrodes stimulate the auditory nerve fibers at different locations along the cochlea, which then send sound sensations to the brain (Herer et al., 2007). Normally the sensory hair cells in the cochlea do this but these are damaged or reduced in number for children with severe sensorineural losses. The signal processor provides critical information contained in the auditory speech signal and consequently gives access to speech at a young age. There seems to be consensus in the field that the younger the child receives the implant, the closer the child will be to his peers in his speech and language, preferably before age 2. The cochlear implant improves the maturation of the auditory pathway (Geers, 2006; Herer et al., 2007).

Hearing aids amplify sound in order for it to be detected by damaged ears. A cochlear implant works by bypassing the damaged portions of the ear and directly stimulates the auditory nerve. The brain recognizes these signals as sound. However, it is different from normal hearing and takes time to learn how to interpret the sounds.

Like a hearing aid, a cochlear implant requires intervention in learning how to interpret what is heard and how to use visual and environmental information to clarify meaning. Children need intensive postimplantation therapy to acquire speech, language, and social skills. How effectively children can use a cochlear implant is dependent upon their cognitive abilities, the duration of their hearing loss, the age at implant, and their family structure and support (Nikolopoulos, Gibbin, & Dyar, 2004). Children need continuing contact with an audiologist to adjust the features of the cochlear implant to ensure it meets the child's needs.

In the Field

I think that many people see us as bucking the system, but we are truly trying to do what we think is best for our son. I learned a lot about cochlear implants. I thought they might be a good idea for Grady. Everyone discouraged me. They said that it might not help him at all, and questioned why I could not accept the fact that our son is deaf. I do accept that. I know he will never speak like his brothers but that doesn't mean I shouldn't do everything in my power to give him as much hearing as possible. We went to other doctors in different states with bigger cities. I found a doctor who had actually done a cochlear implant on a child about Grady's age. The physician talked to the child's parents and they gave me permission to visit. I went to visit and heard the family's story. Their son does not talk, but what gave them the most comfort was that they thought he was safe. After the implant he could hear car horns, loud bells, and other warning signals. I made my decision.

It is too soon to tell whether or not the implant will help his speech. But, like Spenser's mother, his safety is worth it to me. I'm truly not trying to buck the system. But Grady is our son, and we try to make the decisions that we feel are best for him. Sometimes I feel like I am fighting two battles, one with Grady's hearing loss and the other with the system that is supposed to be helping him.

Reflective Practice

How would you feel about having Grady in your classroom? Do you think his family is difficult or are they trying to do what they believe is best for their son? Do you think they are in denial?

Methods of Communication

There are many options available to parents relative to the communication system they choose to use with their child. Their decision is based on many different variables, including the severity and frequencies of the child's loss, whether there are other disabilities, what professional advice they have been given, what information they have sought, and their personal preferences. As educators working with children who have hearing impairments, we must understand the options available to parents; if they have not yet made a decision, help to provide information about choices, give them information about how the child communicates in the classroom, and learn enough about the chosen communication system to interact with the child.

The **total communication approach** uses the auditory, visual, and tactile senses in combination to provide children with as much information as possible. The goal is communication and to achieve that using whatever combination of methods works. Practically, it relies on a system of spoken language and sign. The sender of the message, or speaker, verbalizes the message while simultaneously signing or finger-spelling the same message. This focus allows a child to speak to hearing persons and systematically sign to others who do not hear (Gregory, Bishop, & Sheldon, 1995).

American Sign Language (Ameslan or ASL) is a language with a distinct grammatical structure that must be learned as one would learn any language. It consists of a set of standard hand signs used in relation to other parts of the body. Each sign represents an idea or concept. It uses finger-spelling for clarifying purposes and for new words that have no conventional signs. **Finger-spelling** uses 26 different finger configurations, one for each letter of the alphabet (see Figure 18–5 for an illustration of this alphabet). ASL is not a universal language. There is Japanese Sign Language (JSL), British Sign Language (BSL), French Sign Language (FSL), and so on. There is some evidence that children who learn sign language as a natural language during their early childhood years are at an advantage later socially and academically (Marschark, 1997). Many of these children live in families who use ASL as their first language.

The **oral approach** uses only spoken language (face-to-face communication), taking advantage of whatever residual hearing as child has. Because signing is much easier than speech-reading or talking, the fear is that if children are allowed to sign, they will not develop oral skills and hence will be able to communicate only with people who can sign.

Only about 30 percent of auditory information is gained from looking at the lips alone (Schwartz, 1996). Children have to find ways of filling in the missing cues based on their knowledge of the situation, past knowledge, and other cues they can extrapolate from the circumstances. Some children become competent speakers in the hearing world, while others become frustrated, lost, and confused (Gregory, Bishop, & Sheldon, 1995). The early childhood years are difficult because children are not familiar with language per se, and they have fewer experiences to draw from.

Some people feel that **cued speech** is a better system than signing. It can be used in conjunction with speaking and hearing to provide additional cues to what is being said. In this system, a hand motion depicts a particular sound and the speaker says the word as well as cuing it (the sound-related hand shapes help differentiate sounds that appear alike on the lips). As it is based on sounds in the English language, once those sounds are learned, any word can be cued. It emphasizes using residual hearing (Lim & Simser, 2005).

In the Field

I knew he was sick. When his temperature spiked we went to the emergency room. I love living in the country, but that night every mile seemed to take an eternity. The emergency room took him in and in whispered tones I heard words like "very sick" and someone even said "his brain." He had bacterial meningitis. He was only 2. At first we were just glad that he was alive. We believed that because he had lived he was fine. Because he had been so sick we expected him to regress. He did. What seemed most peculiar to us was that his walking had developed this wide stance. We didn't think he had done that before, but then we decided we really couldn't remember.

Finally Vinnie's speech started to worry me. I took him to see a friend who knew about things like this and she played with him. We had a good time and it seemed like he was doing great. She said all kinds of great things about him but also said that I should get his hearing tested. There was something in her tone that made me listen. I thought about why she said it. He didn't talk. He didn't listen either. The audiologist confirmed that he had a profound hearing loss. The meningitis had left its mark.

I read all I could about hearing loss and the different ways in which children with hearing impairments could communicate with each other. Roy and I both read them. We talked to each other about it, but didn't reach any conclusions. A few weeks later when Vinnie turned 3, we were contacted by a teacher from the School for the Deaf. We listened as she told us about the services that were available to us. At first it sounded great. The answer to our prayers. Then the ball dropped. Because we lived so far away, Vinnie would live there during the week and come home on weekends. He was 3 years old! I couldn't believe it. He needed me, his dad, and his two brothers. I fought it. I knew he would probably never speak as other children did, but this was unbelievable. I kept reading and using the Internet. I found out about cued speech.

Families decide how they want their child to communicate. It is the role of the teacher to support the family's decisions.

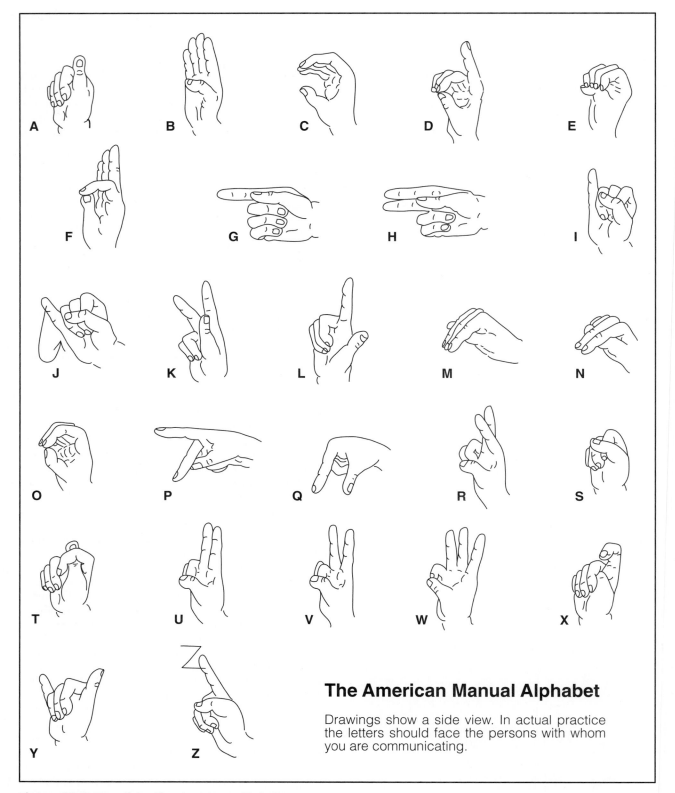

The American Manual Alphabet

Drawings show a side view. In actual practice the letters should face the persons with whom you are communicating.

Figure 18–5: American Sign Language Alphabet
The American Manual Alphabet Drawings show a side view. In actual practice the letters should face the persons who whom you are communicating

I struggled to decide if this was the right thing for Vinnie because it kept him home with us or because it was the right thing for him. I learned how to do cued speech and started. It was a beginning. I wasn't good at first. He was frustrated because he didn't understand, and I was frustrated because I so wanted him to learn and to be with his family. I felt every failure as a step toward his going away to school. Finally, it began to work. I knew he would be able to understand about the asparagus I was picking and the differences between the goat and the sheep we had. Yet I was still struggling.

I enrolled him in a church preschool. After talking with the director, she agreed to take him. One of her teachers even agreed to learn cued speech. My friend observed and thought things were going fine.

When he was 5 we had the first IEP meeting. I was frightened. Again, they wanted him to go to a school for deaf children 100 miles away. They didn't believe in cued speech and thought we were abusing our son. I kept explaining how well he was doing. All I wanted was someone in the school to be with him to help him understand. He could go to the same school his brothers did. He didn't need special transportation; all he needed was someone to help him understand the language. His friends were great. They had learned enough to communicate with him. I agree that he sometimes was frustrated and acted out, but he was still better off perfecting what he was learning and being with us. My friend again intervened. She had observed him and yes, she knew the field, and she had seen adult people who were hearing impaired. It was a battle, but one that we won. Vinnie has an aide, sorry, paraeducator who learned cued speech. He is part of the regular classroom. Some things are hard, for him and us, but we think we did what was best for all of us. I guess only time will tell.

Reflective Practice

Although you should be aware of the issues that parents face trying to make decisions related to communication, you will not have to take a side in the controversy because you will teach the child in accordance with the parents' choice. However, it is important that you keep an open mind and believe that parents make the decisions that they think are in the best interest of their child. Reflect on what you might do if this were your child.

People have very different feelings about how children with severe and profound hearing impairments should communicate. There is also controversy over whether or not inclusion during the early childhood years is ideal. Is the least-restrictive environment for a child with a profound hearing impairment a class with hearing children or a class where the child can communicate with peers who also use some type of manual communication?

Some feel that children should learn to communicate and concentrate on that skill until they have attained a level of proficiency and only then should they be included with other children.

Implications for Educators

Parents are the people who will make decisions about how their child will communicate. It is important that you know that these are difficult decisions and honor the decisions made by the parents. In reality, unless you are a trained teacher of the hearing impaired, it is likely that you will only encounter families who made the decision to educate their children in a hearing environment or they would not be in your classroom. If the child uses speech-reading, signing, finger-spelling, or cuing as aids

to communication, you need to support the child in her efforts.

- Learn to sign, fingerspell, or cue depending on the system that the child's family has chosen.
- Teach all children some signs and cues, especially the sign or cues for their name. Learn significant signs (drink, bathroom) and cues. Ask the help of the child and the family or a teacher of the hearing impaired in making up signs or cues for each child's name. Draw these on the back of your roll cards or whatever system you use.
- Look at the child when you speak even if the child has an interpreter. Talk the way you would to any other child. Do not say to the interpreter "Ask him if. . . . "

Finally, there are two points of caution. Remember: The best speech-reader only gets about one word in four. Children with hearing impairments are great bluffers. They may not want to ask you to repeat; if you ask if they understand, they will often say yes when in fact they do not. Learn to recognize when a child is bluffing; when it is important, ask the child to demonstrate or repeat the instructions.

One of the greatest skills that children with hearing impairments need to learn is to fill in missing information (what they can't understand from words). Developing ideas about their world through generalization and differentiation is difficult for children with hearing impairments because they learn primarily from direct experience. If a child is shown an armchair labeled "chair," the child may not immediately make the generalization that a rocking chair also belongs in the "chair" class. Because of this, it is important that children with hearing impairments be given a large variety of visual stimuli to help them generalize to an abstract concept. For "chair," compare many different chairs. This is the type of thinking children need to do to fill in gaps.

Guidelines

Some children with hearing impairments know how to speech-read and depend on it to understand communication. Others, with milder hearing impairments, may not have learned speech-reading but will still benefit from picking up cues and by watching lips. Regardless of the type of communication system the child is using, and whether or not there is an **interpreter** present, it is important that you as a teacher be expressive and congruent in your spoken and body language. Children with hearing impairments will watch you as a way of tuning into their environment.

1. *Face the child at the child's eye level.* Sit in front of children when helping them, not beside them. Don't talk to children from another room, while looking in a closet, or while writing on the chalkboard. Don't walk around the room or pace back and forth when you talk.
2. *Talk clearly and distinctly.* Don't obscure your lips, wear lipstick, and shave (or at least trim) a beard or mustache. If your hair is long, tie it back so that it doesn't fall in your face while you talk. Don't talk

with your hand over your mouth or anything in your mouth. Don't shout.

3. *Monitor light levels*. See that there is enough light and that it is not shining in the child's eyes.

Once you are certain the child can see your face, communication can begin.

1. *Attract the child's attention*. Before speaking, call the child's name and wait to make eye contact; otherwise, you will have to repeat your first few words.

2. *Speak in a normal voice*. It is impossible to speech-read when the mouth is distorted. Even if you whisper loudly, the sounds and lips are distorted.

3. *Use gestures*. Aid the child's understanding of your speech by using appropriate body language.

4. *Reduce background noise*. When this is not possible, realize that the child is likely to miss much of what you say.

5. *Repeat information*. Some words are more difficult to speech-read than others. If you find different ways of saying something rather than repeating the sentences, children will have a better chance of getting the information. It is important to repeat concepts; until they have been established, be consistent on word usage (cat, not kitty or kitten).

6. *Write down key words and short sentences*. Children need to develop an early knowledge that there is a relationship between what is said and what is written.

7. *Choose activities that facilitate communication*. Encourage children to play together based on a theme that sparks discussion.

8. *Use modeling for teaching*. Demonstrate how to do a specific skill and then have the child imitate what you did.

9. *Let the child take the lead*. Observe the child and see what interests him. Comment about what is important to the child—what the child wants, needs, or is interested in. Watch and interpret the child's gaze, pointing, sounds, and gestures.

Similar principles are reflected in the use of audio-visual aids.

1. *Use color codes and pictures*. Use visual aids as well as words (picture cards for daily routines, charts, and hand gestures).

2. *Use closed-captioned videos and films*. (It is not relevant that the children are not yet reading; you want them to grow up knowing this is a possibility.)

3. *Use an overhead projector or a computer and an LCD monitor*. With a chalkboard you turn your back to the children.

4. *Try not to talk in the dark*. If this is necessary, seat the child where he can see you and try to use some spot illumination.

5. *Support audio presentations with visual cues*. Don't expect the child to react to a tape recorder, record, radio, or intercom just because you turned the volume up. The child still may not understand.

During group activities, the following adaptations may help.

1. *Seat children where they have the best view of the teacher and class*. This is in front of or across from

you, not beside you and not facing a window. Use a circle.

2. *Call, sign, or cue children's names*. During discussion, use signs or gestures so the child will know who is speaking next and can follow the conversation. If the children have signs for their names, sign the speaker's name; if the child is using cued speech, cue the speaker's name. Have children raise their hands instead of calling out, it is easier for the child to identify who is speaking.

3. *Call on the child if he is comfortable*. Remember the child may be so intent on catching the main points of the discussion that he cannot think about the answer at the same time. If you call on a child give him extra time to think; don't demand an immediate answer.

4. *Summarize and repeat points other children have made*. Encourage children to use gestures, signs, and cues when they talk. Ask them to show the child what they want.

Curriculum Adaptations

The severity of the hearing impairment will determine what, if any, curriculum adaptations need to be made. The less hearing the child has, the greater the reliance on visual and tactile channels of communication.

Social Awareness: Self-Esteem, Inclusion, and Social Studies

All children need to be part of the group. They need to realize they can support each other in many ways. Given information, young children can be incredibly adept at helping each other. Be sure that the child with the hearing impairment is not always receiving help, but giving it as well. Children with hearing impairments profit from first-hand experiences, followed in the classroom by visual aids to clarify and generalize these experiences. Children may need to be taught nonverbal ways of approaching other children, and others need to be aware that that is what is happening. At an early age, they need to have signs and words that are descriptive of feelings and body parts. Some of the activities in Resource Chapter 1 are specifically designed to increase children's awareness of hearing impairments. Activity 1–3 No Words discusses how animals and people communicate without using words. Activity 1–10 Finger-Spelling Lotto teaches the children the Ameslan signs for each letter. Where as Activity 1–11 Mufflers encourages children to play together wearing earmuffs and then reflect on their feelings. Activity 1–16 Voiceless Roll Call helps children understand how difficult it is to pay attention when you cannot hear. Activity 1–35w Charades has children pantomiming to convey a message. Activity 1–27 Audiologist is designed to prepare all children to have their hearing tested. Use these activities and the additional one provided to increase children's knowledge of hearing impairments and how they might include a child with a hearing impairment.

Self-Esteem

Children need to increase their awareness of themselves as individuals and as part of a group. If children have had unsuccessful experiences in interacting with children and adults they may withdraw or avoid participating with others. If they are not aware of the tone of the events taking place, they may have inappropriate facial expressions and tone of voice. When possible, they watch for cues and follow, do not lead. They may have had more negative experiences, both medical and personal, than other children their age. They need to learn to view themselves positively and to develop skills in interacting with others.

1. Give careful thought to talking about any child's abilities and disabilities. Talk with children's families and children about how they want this handled. My choice is, after several days of school, to introduce the concept of similarities and differences. (Children conjure up fantastic ideas about what a child with a hearing impairment will look like. Sometimes, they expect the child to have no ears!) Plan a group-time game emphasizing similarities and differences. For example:

   "Will all the children with hair stand up?"

   "Will all the children with brown hair stand up?"

   "Will all the children with hearing aids stand up?"

   "Will all the children with green eyes stand up?"

   In the process, emphasize that all of the children have hair, some have brown hair, one has a hearing aid, and one has green eyes. Be nonchalant. Answer children's questions directly and honestly.

2. Because of difficulty in communicating with the outside world, children with hearing impairments may have developed self-feedback systems (such as teeth grinding, mouth breathing, masturbation). Such actions result from their need to receive information from other senses. Teach them body awareness and engage them in sensory activities that provide tactile feedback.
3. If a child has an interpreter, be sure that you and all the children talk to the child, not the interpreter.
4. Encourage children to share their style of communication with others. Talk about circumstances where signing or being able to speech-read is preferable to speaking (in a noisy place, if you want to keep something a secret, and so on).

Inclusion

When children with hearing impairments reach out, their approach may be physical. Help children develop the skills to approach others and give them cues for roles that they might play. Children need to learn skills for including others as well as skills for approaching others. They need to know that no matter who they are, these skills do not mean that they will be accepted into the group each time they ask. Including children with diverse abilities takes a type of planning you may not have done before.

1. Play games where you whisper or talk to children so softly they have difficulty hearing you; talk about how it feels.

2. Have children wear earmuffs when they play together. Keep them on long enough for children to feel the limitations, not just until the novelty wears off.
3. Talk with children about things that are difficult for them to do and what they would like others to do to help.
4. Help children understand how they might feel and behave if they could see people talking but not understand what they were saying. Have them decide what to do to include a child who might feel like this.
5. If children ask questions, answer them simply and honestly. Encourage the child with the hearing impairment to help answer the question, if possible.

"What's wrong with Carlos?" "There's nothing wrong with Carlos. He can't hear as well as others." "Why does he wear that thing in his ear?" "To help him hear better." "Does he sleep with it?" "No." "If I play with him, can I catch that?" "No, it isn't like a cold or chicken pox. Carlos was born that way" (or however the impairment occurred). "Can I have a thing like that too?" "No, ear doctors decide who needs these things just as eye doctors decide who needs glasses." "I don't like it when Carlos hits me." "I can understand that. Carlos is telling you in his way he wants to play with you. What could he do that would be better?" "Can't he talk?" "He can say some words. It is hard to learn to talk when you can't hear other people talk." "I hate Carlos." "Today, that is true for you. Someday, you might like him."

You might also give the children hints on how to communicate: "Be sure Carlos is looking at you when you talk to him." "Can you show him what you want?" "What can he do that doesn't require talking?" "What kind of game do you think Carlos would like?"

Social Studies

Children with hearing impairments have to learn the skills to cope with a hearing world.

1. Teach children to generalize by using illustrations of diverse families (those with single parents, working mothers, grandparent in the home, and so on, who are of different races and cultures).
2. Emphasize first-hand experiences but use follow-up activities as well. Take your class to a police station. Later, read stories about police and use police props in dramatic play or have a police officer visit.
3. Prepare children with hearing impairments for social situations they may encounter. Help all children learn to use social cues to decide how to act.
4. Use family celebrations and holidays to talk about similarities and differences.
5. Make maps (see Activity 1–50w Maps) to familiarize children with a new setting. Start with maps of known places (the classroom, the play yard) before you branch out into less familiar places.

Language and Literacy: Speaking, Listening, Reading, and Writing

Children with hearing impairments often have limited or impaired speech. They may run words together and have a voice quality that may be flat. When they speak, they have trouble monitoring their volume. They may use gestures or signs to express themselves. Encourage children to speak in small, informal groups first, where they feel safe. Be sure to reward their speaking even if it is labored and difficult to understand. Children need support to talk; encourage them to attempt this even if their speech is not always intelligible. If they are dependent on environmental cues help them fine-tune their ability to use contextual information. Provide many hands-on experiences. To help children use their residual hearing, pair listening with visual or kinesthetic cues. Language and literacy are challenging areas for children with impaired hearing and require adaptation.

Speaking

Help children develop experiential concepts by associating objects with words; the written word with the spoken one. Understanding and talking about abstractions is difficult for young children with hearing impairments.

1. Give children time to talk without feeling rushed.
2. Always respond to a child's communication. If you understand, reply; if not, try to have the child tell you in a different way or show you.
3. To teach concepts, use materials that interest the child. If you are teaching number concepts to a football fan, you can put the numbers on checkers, set up a checkerboard as a football field with the checkers as players, and then call the plays: "Give the ball to number 3 and have him run around number 5 and then between 1 and 7." The child scores only if she follows the correct pattern. If the child cannot hear or speech-read, use your fingers or cards to show the plays.
4. Use the concrete to demonstrate the abstract. Use conceptual matching cards in Lotto: shoe-slipper, clock-watch, lamp-flashlight, shirt-blouse, and jacket-coat.
5. Point out objects in the room that are used in the same way but look different: crayons versus paint, short versus long brushes.
6. Have children classify and reclassify objects in different ways. Using small and large shapes, some of which are black and the others white, ask the child to sort them into two piles; when the task is complete, ask the child to sort the objects another way.
7. Teach situationally and describe verbally what is happening at that moment: "I'm sitting in front of you."

Fingerplays are useful, as all children can participate and the "choral" aspect of fingerplays may reduce the children's self-consciousness about speaking. This is a good way to teach visual memory and sequencing.

1. Choose short, simple fingerplays at first.
2. Demonstrate the actions as you sing or say the words.
3. Encourage the children to imitate you; move slowly so the children can keep up.
4. Use ASL signs with fingerplays or rhymes.

Listening

Children with hearing impairments need to develop good listening skills and to use their residual hearing. They may listen with their head tilted, to favor one ear. They may have difficulty understanding the speech of others, especially in groups, when the speaker is far away, or when the speaker is looking in another direction. Be sure auditory information is presented clearly and loudly enough so children can hear it. The sequence of developing listening skills is the same for all children. Children with hearing impairments need you to match their skill level. Initially, children need to become aware of sound: They need to pay attention to sound and find its source. Then they need to make gross discrimination among sounds followed by finer ones. Finally, they have to attach meaning to sound. Children who can hear usually go through these stages within the first year of life. Children with hearing impairments may still be learning to distinguish sounds and attach meaning to them during the preschool years.

1. Help children learn to check during the day that the volume of their hearing aid is at an appropriate level.
2. Point out sounds to children when they might hear the sound and can have a visual association: "See the airplane. It went voooooom."
3. Emphasize basic vocabulary words in each curriculum area. Post words where everyone can see them or hang them on a string from the ceiling so that all educators use the same vocabulary. If you have a doctor's office in the dramatic play area, make labels for equipment and have a list of important words with pictures to support the list. Take photographs with a digital camera and label the photographs.
4. Use as many visual aids and gestures as possible to help the child understand.

Reading

Early reading literacy skills include habitually looking at words and letters from left to right, making fine visual discriminations, and recognizing a sense of pattern (letters versus spaces). Children with hearing impairments need to replace some of the auditory skills they lack with visual skills. Speech-reading also depends on fine visual discrimination. Interpreting signs and finger-spelling is both a visual task and a reading literacy skill. Plan numerous activities that require fine visual discrimination. Introduce variety into activities by using three-dimensional objects, pictures, line drawings, and even people.

1. Demonstrate left to right progression. Point a marker or your finger at the left side of a word or page before starting and move it to the right as you read.
2. When writing stories of the children's experiences, draw or paste in pictures illustrating significant words, or use a picture from a digital camera.
3. Use activities that require perceptual (visual matching) skills, such as Lotto, bingo, and puzzles.
4. Label everything in the classroom (tables, chairs, lockers, crayons, paints, and easel).
5. Emphasize activities that require fine visual discrimination (alphabet-matching Lotto or a Lotto game using the American Manual Alphabet) because this skill is needed for reading.
6. Play Concentration using the American Manual Alphabet or whatever specific method of manual communication the child is using. Play Activity 1–10 Finder-Spelling Lotto.

Stories can expand the child's world. Start with stories about familiar events and descriptive pictures before using more creative ones.

1. Choose books that depict familiar sights and actions.
2. Use illustrations that are simple, large, and uncluttered.
3. Provide the child with auditory cues and visual aids when reading. For example, when reading "The Three Little Pigs," squeal, change rhythm, and huff and puff. You might even bring in straw, wood, and bricks and let the children huff and puff at them at the science table.
4. Use flannel board stories, as these usually have simple graphics and straightforward plots.
5. Have children act out simple stories.
6. Place picture books with clear, sequential story lines in the book corner. Include some books without words.
7. Choose books with realistic illustrations when teaching language arts.
8. Encourage children to experiment with books. They may enjoy the Living Book series by Broderbund (books such as *Arthur's Birthday* and *Stellaluna*). The software can function as a storyteller or they can use it in an interactive way by hitting the hot spots, which sets off animation.

Writing

Give children a wide variety of writing tools and paper to work with. Children need to explore the media and develop the connection between the written and spoken word before writing will be meaningful. If children with hearing impairments will be more dependent on writing for communication, it is important that they have a positive view of writing.

1. Add stickers to the writing center as well as pictures that can be cut and pasted.
2. Encourage children to use creative spelling in their writing. Support all attempts at writing and illustrating. Emphasize the meaning of writing, until children become fluent writers. Accept children's creative spelling. It is extremely difficult for children who cannot hear accurately to spell accurately.
3. Encourage children to word process their writing and to use software programs that support writing such as ClarisWorks for Kids.

Discovery: Mathematics, Science, and Technology

Children need to develop the skills of inquiry, problem solving, and cause-effect reasoning. Children with hearing impairments need to learn about the parts of the body concerned with hearing and speech. They can explore how a hearing aid works by using microphones and by playing with the balance on a stereo and the volume on a tape or CD player. Technology, as well as advancements in technology, benefits children with hearing impairments by increasing their ability to hear sound and also as a potential method of communicating and connecting with others. The abstractions in math and science are more logical and based on data than in language and literacy.

Mathematics

Math goals are the same as they are for all children. The initial focus is to develop a concrete base of fundamental math concepts to prepare for abstract concepts that will come later.

1. Use three-dimensional materials (cubes, balls) before progressing to two-dimensional materials (squares, circles).
2. Develop the language skills that serve as the foundation for math, such as understanding relationships (equal/more/less).
3. Use naturally occurring situations to teach math. Cooking and sand and water play provide many opportunities for learning math concepts.
4. Measure with different instruments (ruler, metal tape, cloth tape). Compare relative amounts, using both conventional and nonconventional measures.

Science

Few other curriculum areas have the potential for discovery, satisfaction, and interaction with materials that science has. Provide children with the right materials and offer well-timed visual hints, in addition to asking questions as you normally would.

1. Help the child generalize by providing abundant materials.
2. Allow time to process hypotheses and reach conclusions.
3. Help children understand that things can exist in more than one state. Compare corn on the cob, frozen corn, canned corn, creamed corn, and popped and unpopped corn.
4. Use visual demonstrations.
5. Have the child demonstrate the actions when giving directions.
6. Use a variety of media. For example, to teach about plants, visit a farm, nursery, or plant store; plant seeds, varying the water, light, and soil; look at books on plants; show a videotape on how plants grow; and invite a florist to speak to the class.
7. Use regularly occurring natural events like seasonal changes and weather to teach a sense of predictability in the world.

Technology

Computers are very usable for children with hearing impairments. Input and output are visual and require no hearing. Computers can be used as an interactive teaching tool. They will play an important part in the lives of children with hearing impairments. Encourage children to learn about the technology that supports hearing and the ways they can use technology to communicate and enrich their understanding of the world.

1. A child can learn cause-and-effect reasoning easily on a computer: Press a key and the computer does something. Different keys cause something else to happen.
2. Encourage children to use computers. This is a good area to work with a friend so ensure there are two chairs at the computer.

3. Use a modem to access the vast resources of the Internet. Computer skills and attitudes learned now serve children for a lifetime.

4. Use closed-captioned TV and talk with children about its use and the function of the captions. Talk about foreign films with English subtitles. Show small portions of them. If other children in the class speak a language other than English encourage them to talk about the video and the challenges of learning language.

5. Teach children to use digital cameras as a method of sharing information with each other. If children cannot tell parents what they have done at school, a picture will show them.

Wellness: Health, Physical Education, and Sensory Motor

Sensory motor activities help children learn skills to become more physically fit, be more aware of where their body is in space, and fine-tune small motor skills. Emphasize safety procedures. Children must learn to recognize and respond quickly to visual signs of danger. They must be taught to respond to visual cues if they cannot hear the warning sounds of a car or tricycle horn, fire alarm, or a shout. Children with hearing impairments need practice with dynamic and static balance because the vestibular sense is located in the inner ear. They need opportunities to integrate auditory input with motor skills. Noncompetitive games that require starting, stopping, and turning are useful.

Health and Safety

If children with hearing impairments miss warning signals their safety may be jeopardized. Help children develop skills to deal with potentially dangerous situations.

1. Use traffic warning signals outside with the tricycles, wagons, and so on. Teach the meaning of traffic lights (play Red Light–Green Light). Use visual signals, not just aural ones.
2. Practice crossing streets.
3. Discuss what to do if a child is lost or hurt, then dramatize the emergency (using dialogue) or pantomime it.
4. Use snack or lunchtime to instill good eating habits, and toileting to teach good hygiene.
5. Familiarize children with the procedure for fire alarms. Incorporate a visual cue (flickering lights or a red flag) into your usual procedure. Keep this child in sight during a fire alarm to ensure the child neither wanders off nor misses later instructions. With older children, use a buddy system. Get a flashing alarm for your classroom.

Large Motor

Children with hearing impairments can enjoy and participate in large motor activities. If there is damage to the semicircular canals, the child may have problems with dizziness, with obvious implications. Discuss high climbing and rough and tumble play with families to know what limits need to be set. An adult should have an

Children with hearing impairments need opportunities to practice with skills that require static and dynamic balance.

unobstructed view of all children when outside, concern arises if the child is near a relatively dangerous area, such as swings, seesaws, a bike path and so on, and could not hear your call to warn him. Then you need to be close by.

1. Use activities that help develop the child's sense of balance—both dynamic and static.
2. Choose activities that require stopping, starting, and changing directions. (Inability to do these without losing balance is related to the inner ear.)
3. Use activities such as obstacle courses to teach language skills (crawl *through* the tunnel, jump *over* the bar, run *around* the pole).
4. Help the child perfect the fundamental motor skills of crawling, rolling, running, leaping, jumping, skipping, and so on.
5. Have the children imitate animal walks (with pictures as cues) to help them identify different styles of walking.
6. Help children use large motor skills to relieve pent-up energy and frustration.
7. Use props to help a child realize the intent of the group if it appears a change in plans is not apparent to the child.

Small Motor

Children with hearing impairments interact with the world through vision, touch, smell, and the integration of these senses as well as their residual hearing. Help them develop good fine motor control in conjunction with vision.

1. Use activities that require both visual and fine motor skills (puzzles, assorted nuts and bolts to put together, woodworking, bead stringing).
2. Use activities requiring only the sense of touch, such as sorting graded sandpaper or playing with a feely box or bag.
3. Encourage children to use activities where the hands work together such as cutting with scissors (one hand holds, the other cuts), mixing activities, using an egg beater, and so on.
4. Use tweezers or tongs to sort cotton balls, blocks, small wooden beads, or small toys. They can be used to find toys in seeds or sand and to pick up small objects.

Sensory Motor Integration

Characteristically, when children with hearing impairments explore the environment, they rely more on vision and touch than do their peers. Their visual and tactile skills need to be refined and integrated so that they can gain as much information from the environment as possible.

1. Provide a variety of unusual activities that help in processing movement information in the brain (skating, sliding, walking on different surfaces and angles).
2. Add balls to activities to help focus concentration, such as having children kick balls to each other.
3. Have children do various balancing activities with a beanbag on their head or another body part.

Creative Arts: Visual Arts, Music, Creative Movement, and Dramatic Play

Emphasis the creativity in creative arts. Use pictures and realistic props to set the mood. Children can learn by watching what others do and seeing what they make while still choosing and using materials in their own way. Music is primarily an auditory experience. For children with hearing impairments, depending on the degree of loss, music activities must be adapted to include experiences that will be meaningful to them and allow them to participate. Include visual cues so the children can clap the rhythm, stamp their feet, and so on. Include hand motions or ASL signs along with your songs so that all children can be involved. Use creative movement activities that allow children to experience rhythm. Creative movement is an excellent opportunity for children to experiment with movement. Make music and movement a release for emotions. Help children act out situations they are likely to encounter. Use as many props as you can, and keep them realistic. Help children learn what to do in a given situation through dramatic play. Use accessories to set the mood.

Visual Arts

Art needs few adaptations. Use discussions about art to provide opportunities for language input.

1. Support children with hearing impairments using art as an emotional release as well as an art form.
2. Provide three-dimensional art materials as well as two-dimensional ones.
3. If children overgeneralize as a result of limited experience, provide extra time for them to learn the qualities of materials (paint versus paste) through trial and error as well as from your demonstrations and watching peers.

Music

Support music with visual cues. Include all children by adding motions and responding to music as well as singing.

1. Use percussion instruments (children can feel vibrations and see the beat).
2. Choose songs that incorporate motions so children can participate in the movement.
3. Show pictures to set the mood for songs and creative movement. If you want the children to pretend they are walking through leaves, use a fall picture with leaves; if they are to be flowers growing, show both buds and flowers in full bloom.
4. When you sing, use your hand to show when the song goes up or down in pitch.
5. Learn to sign some favorite songs if children in your class sign. The class may find this more challenging and fun than fingerplays.

Creative Movement

Keep the focus on the process. If you are trying to convey a mood, use visual props.

1. If children are taking turns, call on children with hearing impairments in the middle when they have had the opportunity to observe other children. As children move, point out the features of the movement that help set the mood.
2. Place the child to best see how others move.
3. Use mirror movement and allow the child to be the mirror first if there is a mood. If there is just movement, be sure the child has equal opportunities to lead.
4. Use rhythmic dance and free dance.

Dramatic Play

Through dramatic play, children can express feelings and concerns. They can try out roles (mother, father, teacher, audiologist) without fear of being judged. Dramatic play provides some of the experiences necessary for developing a strong language base.

1. Include a traditional home living area in your classroom initially. (This fosters some sense of security for all children at the beginning of the year.)
2. Use the dramatic play area to expand the children's environment as well as play out situations that are familiar in their lives.
3. Provide play props appropriate to the activities.

Routines and Transitions

Transitions are rarely fun for children. They can be especially difficult for a child with a hearing impairment who may not have grasped the verbal directions or the other children's intentions.

1. Be sure that children know the daily sequence. Use a picture schedule and point to what will happen next.
2. Keep your schedule predictable once it is set. Knowing that some things are predictable gives the children a sense of predictability and security.
3. Use visual signs to announce upcoming changes (one light blink for a five-minute warning, two blinks for cleanup time).
4. Use a visual timer.
5. Post any rules, adding illustrations and the word "NO" or an X through the picture. Also, post pictures of things you want children to do. Visual reminders of how to carry scissors and put paint away help everyone.
5. Demonstrate what is going to happen next (start picking up, get your coat, and so on).

Summary

Sound travels in waves that have both frequency and intensity. It is the interpretation of these sound waves that keeps us in touch with the environment and allows communication with others. The auditory system, consisting of the outer, middle, and inner ear, as well as the auditory nerve and auditory cortex, interprets these sound waves. Because of impairments in the auditory system, some children don't hear sounds as well as others.

There are different types of hearing impairments. A conductive hearing impairment relates to the inability of the outer and middle ear to conduct sound to the inner ear. In young children, fluid in the middle ear is the most frequent cause of a conductive impairment, and drug therapy and surgery are used to remediate this situation. Sensorineural losses are permanent and are the result of an impairment in the inner ear or the auditory nerve. Increasingly children with profound losses are receiving cochlear implants in infancy. In addition to interfering with the ability to hear, a hearing loss also impacts speaking and the understanding of speech. Parents make decisions about how their child will communicate; some choose total communication, which involves both verbalizing and using sign language, others use sign alone or only just speaking, and some choose cued speech.

Some curriculum areas such as language and literacy may require modifications, whereas other areas that are dependent on vision, tactile input, and feedback need few.

Reflections

1. When a child is profoundly hearing impaired the decisions that parents make during the first years of life have a tremendous impact on the child's life and whether she will be expected to live her life in the culture of the hearing or the culture of the deaf, or both. Reflect on your own feelings; if this child was yours, how would you decide? What would you decide? What do you anticipate as the long-term outcomes of your decision making? How would you feel about a child in your class whose parents had made very different decisions from those you would make?

2. You have a child in your classroom of 3 year olds who seems to have frequent ear infections. About once every 2 weeks the child wakes up from his afternoon nap with a temperature of 103 °F. You call the mother and she comes and takes the child to the pediatrician. She is very conscientious, but because the child speaks so well she has no concern about the possibility of hearing loss. Do your feel it is your responsibility to talk with the family about this possibility? You also know that there is a relationship between frequent early ear infections and the development of learning disabilities. Again, is this your role? If you think it is, how will you go about doing this?

Educational Resources

American Sign Language Browser is a site supported by Michigan State that provides a visual dictionary for ASL both signs and finger-spelling. The signs are short videos with accompanying text. http://commtechlab. msu.edu/sites/aslweb/browser.htm

ASLPro is a site designed for teachers. It not only has ASL, but groups signs by hand shape. It also has close ups of the mouth and how it looks saying different morphemes. http://www.ASLpro.com

Alexander Graham Bell Association for the Deaf and Hard of Hearing sponsors conferences and workshops and publishes materials for parents and teachers. They have a special section for parents of children with hearing impairments. (800) 432-7543; http://www.agbell.org/

American Society for Deaf Children (ASDC) provides support, encouragement and information on the impact of a hearing impairment on children. The website has an extensive bibliography of readings that may be helpful to professionals and parents. (800) 942-2732; http://www.deafchildren.org

American Speech-Language-Hearing Association (ASHA) is a national organization and the governing body for speech-language pathologists and audiologists. The website is divided into sections for professionals, the public, and students. It is easy to navigate and is helpful to anyone looking for general information. (800) 638-TALK; http://www.asha.org

Gallaudet University is a liberal arts university for the deaf and hard of hearing. It offers programs for children with hearing impairments, distributes materials, and consults with schools throughout the country. (202) 651-5000; http://www.gallaudet.edu

John Tracy Clinic is a private non-profit education center that specializes in stimulation programs for infants who have hearing impairments. It is a great resource for parents worldwide and has courses for professionals. http://www.johntracyclinic.org/

National Association of the Deaf is a non-profit organization designed to empower Deaf and Hard of Hearing Individuals it provides online information for parents and professionals. http://www.nad.org/

National Institute on Deafness and other Communicative Disorders (NIDCD) provides online information for parents and professionals about hearing impairments. http://www.nidcd.nih.gov/

SERI Hearing Impairment Resources is part of Special Education Resources on the Internet and provides many links to valuable resources related to children with hearing impairments. http://www.seriweb.com/hearing.htm

For additional resources, visit the book companion website for this text at www.cengage.com/education/deiner.

Chapter 19

Children with Visual Impairments

One of my memories of being in first grade is of Skip, whose mother once asked our teacher whether we teased him about his patch. The teacher's startled response was, "What patch?" Skip went out of the house each morning with a patch over his left eye, took it off and put it in his pocket, and arrived at school without it. He put it back on before he got home. I don't know if we would have teased him had he worn it, but the fear of being teased or different made him avoid the possibility. It is a very powerful concern that causes a 6 year old to do that kind of planning and remembering.

Reflective Practice

Assuming Skip began to wear the patch what would you do to support him? How would you talk with the other children?

Visual Impairments

Vision helps us interpret the world around us. We form visual images of ourselves and others. Vision motivates us to reach out and touch objects, to climb a hill for the view, and to return a friendly smile. Children whose vision is impaired need to connect with their world utilizing their residual vision and other senses if their impairment is not correctable or until it is corrected. Blindness can occur as the only disability in children, however, in about half of these children, it is associated with other impairments including intellectual disability and cerebral palsy (Miller & Menacker, 2007).

Including children with visual impairments in your class involves teaching children who wear eyeglasses, lenses, or corrective patches; helping to identify children whose visual impairments have not yet been diagnosed; and adapting your programming for children who have noncorrectable visual problems including limited vision and blindness. You probably will have a number of questions about children with visual impairments.

The Visual System

Having an understanding of how the visual system works and the problems that can occur in different parts of the system helps you know what adaptations will be the most useful. The visual system is complex (see Figure 19–1). As light waves enter the eye, the colored part of the eye, the **iris**, controls the amount of light that enters the eye by opening larger to admit more light or closing smaller to limit the amount of light. The **pupil** is the opening in the center of the iris through which light enters. These light rays are first focused by the **cornea**, which covers and protects the iris, and then by the **lens**, which is behind the pupil. These light waves are focused on the inner surface of the eye, the **retina**. Images projected onto the retina are upside down and reversed. This image is sent through the **optic nerve** to the brain for interpretation (Miller & Menacker, 2007).

Given how vital vision is, the eye is protected in a variety of ways. It is protected by its position in the socket of the skull and the **sclera**, the outer thick white fibrous

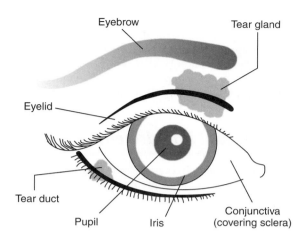

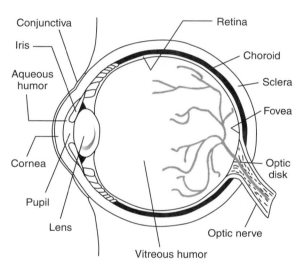

Figure 19–1: The Eye
The eye receives light and through a complex process turns light into electrical impulses and sends them through the optic nerve to the visual cortex in the brain.

covering of the eyeball. The eye maintains its round shape because of the watery **aqueous humor** in the **anterior chamber** at the front of the eye and the **vitreous humor** between the lens and the retina. Blinking removes dust and other particles from the surface of the eye, whereas the eyelashes help protect it from airborne debris. At the front of the eye the sclera is covered by the **conjunctiva**. The conjunctiva is a thin, transparent mucous membrane that contains tiny blood vessels. When someone has bloodshot eyes, it is these blood vessels that are affected. And, it is this surface that is inflamed or infected in **conjunctivitis** (Miller & Menacker, 2007).

The eye does not actually "see" any more than the ear "hears." It receives light, turns light into electrical impulses, and sends them through the optic nerve to the **visual cortex** of the **occipital lobe** of the brain. It is the brain that perceives visual images. If the relevant part

of the brain that sees is severely damaged, a child may not be able to see, even though the eye is completely normal. Defects in the eye itself are often correctable. The purpose of most visual aids is to compensate for defects in the eye so that a correct message can be sent to the brain.

Defining Visual Impairments

Visual impairments are defined in a variety of ways. They can be defined according to the legal, medical, or educational implications of the impairment. The legal and medical definitions typically emphasize visual acuity, or how clearly the child can see. The educational definition emphasizes the extent to which the child can use his visual ability to read printed material for learning. According to IDEA 2004

> Visual impairment including blindness means an impairment in vision that, even with correction, adversely affects a child's educational performance. The term includes both partial sight and blindness.

Vision may be limited in three ways: visual acuity, the field of vision, or color vision. **Visual acuity** is the resolving power of the eye, that is, the sharpness or clarity of the image viewed. We usually measure this by having children identify or match letters or pictures in various sizes while standing a standard distance from a chart; that distance is 20 feet (6.1 meters). A person who can see at 20 feet what most people see at 20 feet has normal or 20/20 vision. For children below third grade, vision of 20/40 or better in each eye or vision of 20/30 or better when using both eyes is considered normal. That is, the young child sees (with one eye) at 20 feet what an adult would see at 40 feet or with both eyes at 30 feet.

A child's **field of vision** can be restricted by lack of peripheral vision. The child may have normal central visual acuity but reduced peripheral vision. This is often called **tunnel vision**. Or the field of vision may be restricted by a **scotoma**, or blind or dark spot. This dark spot can be of various sizes and be anywhere in the field of vision. If it is in the middle of the eye, the child's **central vision** will be impaired.

Color vision involves the ability to discriminate three qualities of color: hue, saturation, and brightness. The difference between those with normal color vision and those without normal color vision is that some of the hues that appear different to a person with normal color vision appear similar to those without. **Achromatopsia, color deficiency,** or **color blindness** refers to this condition. The term color deficiency is technically correct and preferable to use because young children are often frightened by the use of the term color blindness. The total inability to see color is very rare. The most frequent problem is distinguishing between specific colors, usually red and green. For most people, it is possible to distinguish these colors when the object is large (like a car), but they have trouble with smaller items and when the colors are part of a pattern such as a plaid. Children who have color-deficient vision rarely know it. As a teacher, you may suspect it when children have difficulty identifying one or more of the primary colors. Color deficiency is an inherited

X-linked trait. It affects 1 out of 12 males and 1 out of 200 females (Salvia & Ysseldyke, 2007). We typically don't regard this as a disability as children's visual acuity is not affected; however, it is useful to be aware of it, as you are likely to encounter children with this condition. However, if you are a person who color-codes materials for children, you may need to modify your system. If you use the color red, write the letter *R* or the word *red* over the color so that you are sure all children can use the system.

Visually Limited

This term refers to children who are considered sighted children for educational purposes, but who are limited in their use of vision. They may need particular light conditions, prescriptive lenses, optic aids, or special materials to aid their vision. Although it is unlikely (but not impossible) you will have a child with no usable vision, it is more probable that you will have or help to identify a child with limited vision. Estimates about the number of school-age children who are **visually limited** vary widely—from 5 to 33 percent (Salvia & Ysseldyke, 2007). Estimates vary because of the definitions used and the screening instruments. (These estimates do not include children who have visual processing problems.) If 20 percent of the children have a visual limitation, then in every classroom of 25 children, 5 are likely to have vision problems of some sort.

Low Vision

Children who are partially sighted, or have **low vision**, have their best corrected visual acuity between 20/70 and 20/200 in their better eye (Yeargin-Allsopp, Drews-Botsch, & Van Naarden Braun, 2007). Educationally, children with low vision have enough residual vision to read large print or regular print with special assistance such as magnification. Their limitations may be greater in their distance vision. These children should *not* be referred to as blind.

Blindness

A person is considered **legally blind** who has visual acuity no better than 20/200 in the better eye, with the best possible correction, or has a field of vision restricted to 20 degrees or less (tunnel vision) in the better eye instead of the usual 105 degrees (Yeargin-Allsopp et al., 2007). The child who is legally blind sees at 20 feet what people with normal vision can see at 200 feet. For educational purposes, children are considered **blind** if they have a visual loss severe enough that it is not possible to read printed material and necessitates the use of alternative forms of written communication such as Braille. Most children who are legally blind have some useful vision. Children with 20/200 to 20/500 may be able to read large-print books or the computer screen with large fonts, some children with 20/500 to 20/800 can distinguish light and dark or detect objects that are useful in orientation and mobility. Some children will have no usable vision (Miller & Menacker, 2007). It is important to know the degree of visual impairment and how this limits what a child can do.

Reflective Practice

Terminology is important, particularly being sensitive to people first language and the needs and wants of children and their families. Ask parents what terms they use to refer to their child's visual impairment. Some parents may tell you that they prefer to use the term *blind*. Honor their preferences.

Types of Visual Impairments

Visual impairments are also categorized or defined by the part of the eye involved. There are problems related to the physical mechanisms of the eye, problems with visual acuity, impairments to the muscular structure of the eye, and problems in visual perceptions or the message pathway between the eye and brain. For many children, problems involving the physical mechanisms, acuity, and muscular structure can be corrected with medical techniques, eyeglasses or contact lenses, and/or surgery. Damage to the brain or the optic nerve is not correctable.

Visual problems can relate to the function of the eye or the mechanisms of the eye including the cornea, lens, retina, anterior chamber, eye muscles, optic nerves, and visual cortex. Damage to any of these parts can affect how light passes through the eye or is transmitted to the brain. Damage to the eye structure can result in permanent loss of vision. Large particles getting into the eye can be potentially damaging; the longer a particle remains in the eye and the deeper it becomes embedded, the greater the likelihood of permanent damage.

Refractive Errors

For clear vision, the eyeball must be the right length and the cornea must have the proper shape. Errors of refraction occur because of the shape of the eyeball or cornea or the strength of the lens. We measure the refractive power of a lens in units called **diopters**, the light-bending power of the lens. Lenses are assigned numbers according to their refractive powers. The higher the number of diopters, the stronger the prescription: a minus sign indicates concave lenses, a plus, convex lenses. A prescription for a child who is farsighted might be a –3.5 diopter correction for one eye. The other eye may have a different correction. The most common refractive error of childhood is hyperopia (Miller & Menacker, 2007).

Hyperopia

Hyperopia or farsightedness means that the child can see distant objects better than relatively close objects. When the eyeball is too short or the lens and cornea are too strong, the focused image falls behind the retina. The shorter the eyeball, the more out of focus the image will be and the more convex the lenses in the glasses will have to be to correct the problem. Often, children can use the eye's power of accommodation to focus the image and have excellent visual acuity. However, when refractive errors are over 4 diopters, corrective lenses are usually prescribed. There is a concern that children with errors over 6 diopters are at risk for both **amblyopia** and **esotropia** (Miller & Menacker, 2007).

Myopia

Myopia or nearsightedness occurs when the eye is too long, causing the image to be in focus before it reaches the retina. Myopia is corrected with the use of concave lenses. There is no mechanism to fine-tune vision for children with myopia. Therefore, these children may wear glasses from infancy if the myopia is severe.

Astigmatism

Astigmatism is an error in refraction caused by the cornea's being more football-shaped than spherical. The image does not focus because the parallel light rays do not come together at one point. Astigmatism can usually be corrected by cylindrical lenses that compensate for the irregular shape. This condition can also occur with other visual conditions. A child can be nearsighted or farsighted and also have an astigmatism (see Figure 19–2).

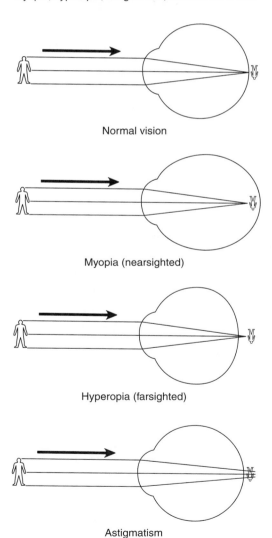

Myopia, hyperopia, astigmatism, and normal vision.

Normal vision

Myopia (nearsighted)

Hyperopia (farsighted)

Astigmatism

Figure 19–2: Refractive Errors
Refractive errors occur because of the shape of the eyeball or cornea or the strength of the lens.

From a developmental perspective, corrective lenses may not be prescribed for young children if the refractive problem does not interfere with daily functions.

Cornea

The cornea is known as "the window of the eye," because the cornea protects the lens and the iris. The cornea also focuses images on the **fovea centralis**, the most light-sensitive part of the retina. It does this by taking the parallel lines of light that reach the surface of the cornea and turning or **refracting** them so the light rays focus on the fovea and a sharp image is sent to the brain (Miller & Menacker, 2007).

Cornea damage, usually punctures or scars, results in impaired vision. A cloudy cornea can be caused by birth trauma, inborn errors of metabolism, and congenital glaucoma. It is possible in some cases to have a cornea surgically replaced.

Anterior Chamber

The anterior chamber is behind the cornea and in front of the iris. The pressure in this chamber is kept within normal limits by the drainage of fluid through a canal. If the canal becomes blocked, the intraocular pressure rises and can cause glaucoma. In children, **glaucoma** is usually a congenital anomaly, but it may be related to other diseases and syndromes or eye trauma and inflammation. Without treatment, the pressure pushes the optic nerve backward and injures it, decreasing vision.

Lens

The cornea is the first refracting surface of the eye; the second is the lens, which is located between the cornea and the retina. The lens can change its shape in response to changes in the distance of the focal object: it can be stretched or relaxed. Young children naturally have eyeballs that are too short, making them farsighted, but the ability of the lens to adjust allows most of them to compensate and not need glasses.

The major problem with the lens comes from cataracts. **Cataracts** are the clouding of the lens inside the eye, which results in blurred vision. If the lens is clouded, light cannot reach the retina. Some children are born with cataracts. Cataracts can be an isolated abnormality or part of a syndrome or disease. Most cataracts can be removed surgically. If cataracts are small and stable, they may not need to be removed, but if they become larger and denser, they will inhibit vision. Because binocular vision develops during the first 3 months, children with severe, unilateral cataracts have the best prospects of developing binocular vision if cataracts are removed before 6 weeks of age (Birch & Stager, 1996). Children who have had cataracts removed will wear very thick glasses or contact lenses that help bend and focus light rays in place of the missing lens or they may have **intraocular lenses** implanted. Intraocular lenses are now a commonly accepted treatment for cataracts in older children and are used increasingly in younger children and infants. Intraocular lenses are superior to contact lenses because they closely replicate the optics of the crystalline lens, they do not require daily ongoing care, and they ensure at least a partial optical correction all the time children are awake. However, there is still concern about postoperative complications especially in infants (National Eye Institute, 2007).

Retina

The **retina** is separated from the lens by the **vitreous humor**. It is the innermost of three layers, with the **choroid** in the middle and the **sclera** on the outside of the eyeball. Both of these layers provide support, protection, and nourishment. Images are focused on the retina and then sent to the brain. The retina has two types of sensory cells or **photoreceptors: cones** and **rods**. They respond to light through a chemical reaction. Cones are needed to see color, for detailed vision such as reading, and to see distant objects. Cones are located in the fovea centralis, or **macula**. Each cone is sensitive to one of three colors: red, green, or blue. (**Color deficiency** is a disorder of the cones.) Rods function in low-light conditions and are necessary for night vision (Miller & Menacker, 2007).

Injury can cause the retina to come loose from the back of the eye. As a result, the retina loses its ability to function. This can be corrected by burning the retina back onto the eye with a laser beam. There will be a permanent blind spot where the laser beam reattaches the retina, but vision will be restored.

Retinopathy of Prematurity (ROP)

The most common cause of retinal damage is ROP. Because more premature infants survive the number of children with ROP has increased as almost 25 percent of infants weighing less than 2,500 grams will have some degree of ROP (Hameed et al., 2004). Premature infant's blood vessel growth is incomplete and as they catch up blood vessels grow to the center of the eye rather than along the back surface. The scar tissue can constrict and pull on the retina, in some cases detaching it and causing loss of vision (Miller & Menacker, 2007). However, the number of children becoming blind due to ROP is decreasing because of early diagnosis and treatment (Khan, O'Keefe, Kenny, & Nolan, 2007).

Optic Nerves

Over a million nerve cells join at the **optic disk** (blind spot) to form the **optic nerve**. Because there are nerve fibers there, not cones and rods, there is no vision. One optic nerve is joined to each eye. At one point along the path to the brain, some nerve fibers cross over (**optic chiasm**) on their way to the **occipital lobe** (Miller & Menacker, 2007).

Damage to the optic nerve itself is usually associated with incomplete development or damage from disease or trauma. The optic nerve carries the electrical impulses from the eye to the brain for processing. If this nerve is not developed properly, it will not be possible for the signals to get to the brain so the child can see. The effects on vision vary depending on the amount and place of the damage.

Amblyopia

Sometimes referred to as "lazy eye," amblyopia is a reduction in visual acuity that only occurs in children younger than age 9 and is a consequence of long spans of time when there are no retinal images or blurred ones. The visual system of young children is immature and susceptible to being turned off. Unless it is identified and treated with patching, blurry eye drops or glasses vision could be permanently impaired (Miller & Menacker, 2007).

When young children have amblyopia the eye with the best vision is patched forcing children to use the weaker eye to make it stronger. When the strength is even the child will wear corrective lenses

Visual Cortex

Visual information passes through the optic nerves to the **visual cortex** in the occipital lobe of the brain. It is then sent to the temporal and parietal lobes. For some children, the visual process appears to work accurately until the message gets to the brain. These children have **cortical visual impairments**, most commonly caused by oxygen deprivation, infection, or traumatic brain injury (Miller & Menacker, 2007).

Eye Muscles

Muscular problems involve the inability of the six muscles controlling the eyes to work in coordination with each other to result in clear vision. **Binocular vision** is produced by the brain fusing the images seen from both eyes into one. Correct fusion of these images depends on the eyes being straight and moving in synchrony. Disruption in either causes visual problems.

Strabismus

In **strabismus**, the eyes are not able to focus simultaneously on one point. This occurs in 3 to 4 percent of children and more frequently (15 percent) in children who were born prematurely (Olitsky & Nelson, 1998). There are two main forms of strabismus. In **esotropia**, the most common problem, the eyes (or weak eye) turn in toward the nose (cross-eyed), whereas in **exotropia**, the eyes (or weak eye) turn away from the nose (walleyed). Healthy infants whose eyes cross after 3 months of age will often need surgery (Miller & Menacker, 2007).

Prevalence of Visual Impairments

The federal government began keeping records on children with visual impairments during the 1976–1977 school year. At that time 8.3 percent of children in the public schools were identified as having a disability. Of these children 1.0 percent had a visual impairment. In the 2005–2006 school year, 13.8 percent of children were identified as having a disability with 0.4 percent of these children having a visual impairment. This percentage has remained the same since 1994–1995. Children with identified visual impairments constitute 0.1 percent of the total school population of children between 3 and 21 years of age (National Center for Educational Statistics, 2006).

Although this represents the number of children who were identified with visual impairments the question remains about the undiagnosised visual conditions effecting young children.

The Evidence Base

Ganz, Xuan, and Hunter (2006) used the 48,304 individuals who responded to the Medical Expenditure Panel Surveys from 1996 through 2001 to look at the prevalence of children with diagnosed eye and visual conditions. On average 7 percent of children younger than 18 years had a diagnosed eye or visual condition. Excluding conjunctivitis the most common conditions were refractive disorder, potentially blinding disorders, trauma or injury and other nonclassified disorders.

Interestingly, white children with more educated mothers who had higher incomes were more likely to have children with diagnosed eye and vision conditions. Hispanic children, children in very good to excellent health, and uninsured children were less likely to have any self-reported eye and vision conditions. These results provide some evidence that some children may be underdiagnosed, undertreated and at risk for future problems.

Reflective Practice

How does this evidence affect how you might look at children who may potentially have visual impairments? What might you think about differently based on this evidence?

Causes of Visual Impairments

Although the causes of blindness vary prenatal causes account for 43 percent of low vision with an additional 27 percent of the causes occurring during the **perinatal period**, which includes the first month of life (Rahi & Dezateux, 1998). Causes of blindness fall into four major etiologies: genetic, prenatal, perinatal, and childhood.

The genetic group makes up 33 percent of the total, prenatal 27 percent, perinatal 26 percent, and childhood 12 percent (Khan et al., 2007).

In the United States the three leading causes of visual impairment are **cortical visual impairment, retinopathy of prematurity**, and **optic nerve hypoplasia** (Hatton, 2001). Of infants born with severe visual impairments, about a fourth have no usable vision, another fourth can distinguish some light, and the remaining half have enough vision that they can read enlarged type (Miller, Menacker, & Batshaw, 2002). Other causes of visual impairments include traumatic brain injury, severe eye infection and trauma to the eye, and tumors.

Early Identification of Visual Impairments

Unless parents have a reason to suspect that a child has a visual problem, it usually doesn't occur to them to take a young child to an ophthalmologist. Children themselves are usually no help, because they assume that whatever vision they have is normal. See Table 19–1 for signs of a visual impairment.

Implications for Educators

As you observe children, be aware of the behaviors and complaints that may indicate vision problems. Preschool children have a tendency to see things better at a distance than they do at close range. When doing close work such as looking at books, puzzles, or games, a child with a visual impairment may blink continually, hold a book (or place himself) too close or too far away, keep changing the distance of the book, or over- or underestimate distance when working with puzzles or pegboards. When doing visual work at a distance (such as when a book is being read during group time), the child may seem inattentive or lose interest after a brief time. Some children experience **double vision** if the images sent to the brain cannot be fused into one image.

Other symptoms to look for are the inability to identify parents, friends, or teachers at a distance; not noticing objects from across the room or playground; difficulty in such activities as calendar reading or chalkboard games; bumping into things; and misjudging distances in games. The child may also move slowly so as not to bump into things. Vocabulary may be limited for things like birds, which are usually in the distance. If your observations support your suspicion, ask parents if they have considered this; if not, encourage them to observe more closely. After they have observed, share your concerns and encourage them to take the child to an eye doctor (ideally, a pediatric, developmental, or neuro-ophthalmologist).

Many infants and young children with correctable visual problems function as if they had low vision until their vision is corrected. They often show delays in reaching developmental milestones and tend to sit later and may not crawl but hitch. **Hitching** is a method of moving where the child's bottom is on the floor and she scoots, using her legs for propulsion. Hitching makes the head less vulnerable. Children will typically walk with a wide

Table 19–1: Signs of visual impairments

Medical/Physical
Eyes that are red, watery, or have a discharge
Itchy, scratchy, burning eyes
Uncoordinated eyes (one eye remains still while the other follows the object; eyes cross or one eye wanders)
Eyelids that are red, swollen, crusted, or droopy
Swelling of eyes
A white pupil
Frequent or recurring styes
Excessive blinking
Eyes that appear out of focus

Behavioral
Frequent frowning, squinting, or eye rubbing
Widening or squinting eyes when looking in the distance
Holding books or objects too close
Shutting or covering one eye
Consistently tilting head to one side or the other
Frequent headaches, stomachaches, or dizziness
Not alert to surroundings; few attempts at locomotion or communication
Problems judging distance when using small objects
High sensitivity to light
Inability to recognize familiar faces from a distance

stance for added support, but may not walk until age 2 or later. Speech also develops later, often with less body and facial expression, and little nonverbal communication.

The infant who is born with no vision not only misses the visual aspects of the environment, but also misses the ability to form visual images about the world. Therefore, the child may not be attracted to people, objects, or even the exploration of his own body; unless the child can experience these through taste, touch, or sound, he does not know they exist. A conscious effort has to be made to link the child to the environment by building mental concepts through language. Young children who cannot see babble, smile, and laugh when sighted infants do, but infants with sight see the responses that their parents make to these behaviors and they are reinforced. The tonal pattern of voices must convey to young infants what they cannot see. As infants become familiar with the people and objects in their environment, they will form concepts through their senses of hearing and touch. They will recognize the voices and footsteps of family members. This is the time that an infant is building connections. Name whatever the infant touches, whatever she does, and whatever is done for her. Pick out the salient features of the experience and put them into words. Objects that make sounds need to be placed in their hands. They need to learn to touch their nose and toes. They need to learn "up" as they are being picked "up" and obviously "down" in the same way. At first words and associations are difficult, initially use the same objects and the same words during routines.

Infants who do not respond to visual stimuli need other stimulation. They need to *feel* a smile; they need sounds and singing as their day progresses. Call infants so they raise their heads; rattle noisemakers in different positions to entice them to move; place them in different positions; and call to infants from above, beside, and below them. Encourage infants to move. Place noisemaking objects in their hands and then slightly out of reach to intrigue them to reach for these objects. Prop infants in a sitting position or place them in a contained area where they can sit, and place a variety of noisemaking toys with them. (This makes the toys easier to locate.) Periodically, squeak a toy to help maintain interest. Teach infants to localize and attend to sound. This is a precursor to learning to look at the person who is talking. They need the same learning experiences as sighted children they just need them presented in a nonvisual way (California Department of Education, 2006).

Children who cannot see may not want to explore their world. They might become discouraged as they bump into things and it hurts. When children are learning to walk, they can learn about the process of walking by standing on your feet, their back to your front, and walking with you. This gives information about bending their knees as well as information that walking is safe.

Walking, although wonderful, poses additional challenges. Children must now rely on their memory of space and hope that things remain in the same place. Initially, rubber soles give security; however, once walking has been mastered, leather soles provide more feedback. Climbing up stairs is easier than going down; help by placing their feet on the treads. Use snack time to help toddlers develop hand-mouth coordination. Use small bits of food in a contained area to help children both grasp the food and then eat it. This is messy, but practice works. The ability to develop accurate eye-hand coordination is based on stereopsis. **Stereopsis** is the sensation and perception of depth based on the slight difference between retinal images from the eyes because of their horizontal separation.

Prepare children for new experiences and changes by providing auditory cues. This is not just verbally telling children what will happen next, but consciously thinking about the natural environmental cues that provide information. Before giving an infant a bottle, shake the bottle, let the infant feel it, walk "heavy," and talk to the infant to let her know you are near. Perhaps "drop" children's boots in front of them and then say, "You need to put your boots on," or "Listen, I'm pouring your juice," and so on.

Play games in which children need to crawl or walk toward sound sources. Use environmental sounds such as running water in the sink (with comments like, "It sounds as though some of the children are washing their hands") as well as sounds of toys. Then, of course, name the sound, put the child's hands in the water, and help her experiment with turning the water on and off.

A child with little sight may need to be taught how to explore an object placed in her hands. Teach children to explore the length of a spoon with their fingertips, then the bowl of it, as well as feeling the weight, texture, and temperature. Help them turn it over and feel the bowl from the back. These are the qualities of "spoonness" they must learn, but labeling them as they are learning "spoon" is confusing. Just say the word "spoon." As children become more competent encourage them to explore groups of objects which can be perceived with one or two hands and to compare the relative size of groups of things (Kapperman & Sticken, 2006).

Until children are about 3, they may not be aware that others see differently than they do. If they "see" using their hands, they may expect that you see that way as well and give you things to feel (i.e., see). The realization begins gradually as children discover discrepant behavior. Others may comment on a child's new watch without feeling the child's arm, or talk about something the child realizes he is not experiencing. At some point during the preschool years, children come to an understanding of the meaning of having limited sight. Children react differently to this discovery; some children become angry, others depressed.

Children need help putting their feelings into words, and adults need to provide acceptance with words as well. Adults need to ask such questions as, "Does it make you angry that you can't see the picture the other children are talking about?" Children with visual impairments need support in play skills. Interactive play develops more slowly, and their play tends to lack imagination. Describing, explaining, and helping them experience their world helps them understand it better.

Children with very limited vision rely on hearing as their most important link with the other children; instead of facial expressions, this is how a child knows if another child is serious, angry, or joking. Loud sounds, too much noise, and constant auditory stimulation may cause children to tune out, losing a major source of contact with the environment.

One decision that needs to be discussed during the preschool years is how children will learn to read and write: with **Braille**, print, or a combination. Children need early instruction in both so that a decision can be made while a child is at an appropriate age to learn the necessary preliteracy skills. Classrooms should have both large-print books and Braille books available for children. Braille is also essential in teaching mathematics. Young children who will learn Braille should be immersed in a Braille-rich environment just as sighted children are immersed in a print-rich environment (California Department of Education, 2006).

As children with visual impairments reach school age, they continue to need support with social development and interaction. Their language may be more self-centered than other early elementary school children because they don't see what others do to talk about it or comment on it. Peers need support in communication. Perhaps the best analogy for children this age is to have them pretend they are talking on the telephone when they communicate with a child who is visually impaired and have them fill in the necessary details in that way. Initial social relationships may be awkward, but children adapt.

Listening skills are extremely important for children with low vision, especially as they move into elementary school where children are expected to follow directions and do many teacher-directed tasks. Children with visual impairments need extra time to respond, as it takes them longer to make the necessary connections among words, people, objects, activities, experiences, and other information.

Watch for gaps in general knowledge and experience. Children may fail to perceive similarities, differences, and invariances, so they mix up concepts that are perceptually different but functionally the same. For example, a young child who is familiar with houseplants might assume that the bark of a large tree is the tree's pot.

In elementary school, children need access to the content of more formal lessons and this requires adapting teaching materials and different teaching approaches. Most children can use some form of print. Where regular print cannot be seen, a low-vision aid must be employed. These devices use one or more lenses to magnify the print; all use enlarged photocopies (these can get a bit bulky, depending on the degree of enlargement). Some children who need low-vision aids are reluctant to use them because they believe it will draw attention to them. Other problems include skill in using the materials. Some children read Braille; others use a combination, often writing on a Braille writing machine. With assistive technology, the range of input and output devices has expanded to the point that a specialist in this area is necessary to determine the best match for the particular child and the classroom situation.

Children vary in how good their orientation and mobility skills are. "**Orientation** is the ability to create and maintain a mental map of one's environment and the relationship of oneself to that environment. Mobility . . . is the ability to travel safely and efficiently through the environment" (Tuttle & Tuttle, 1996, p. 21). **Trailing** is a method that young children use to learn about their environment. They learn to hold the back of their hand at waist level and gently maintain contact with the walls and furniture as they walk.

Assessment of Visual Impairments

Tests of visual acuity fall into two general categories: those based on an examiner's assessment or eye chart, and those that utilize high technology, which require special training and equipment. Most early care and education settings and elementary schools provide some kind of basic vision screening.

Vision Screening

The most common screening test for elementary school children is the standard Snellen Wall Chart. The child is asked to read standard-sized letters at a distance of 20 feet. Although a good screening test, some children may fail or pass this test based on variables other than vision. Children who don't know their letters may not pass the test for this reason. Some children may memorize the order of the letters if they hear many other children say them; some letters of the alphabet are easier to discriminate than others, which leads to guessing.

The Snellen E Test is used with preschool children who don't know the letters of the alphabet. The letter *E* is shown in different spatial arrangements and the child either identifies the direction, points, or holds up the letter *E* to match the stimulus. Neither test identifies children with near-vision problems, and near vision is critical for learning to read. The criterion for referral is acuity of 20/40 for children kindergarten through third grade (Salvia & Ysseldyke, 2007). (To help prepare young children for a vision screening use Activity 1–28, Eye Doctor.)

In the Field

I was once called by a mother who was concerned because her 18-month-old son only ate what was on the top half of his plate. She found that very strange. I went for a home visit at lunchtime. Sure enough, the little boy only ate from the top of his plate. He didn't appear full, but he also didn't touch the food on the bottom of the plate. So, we turned the plate around so that the remaining food was at the top, and that too was then eaten. The mother was baffled. "But why? This makes no sense." I agreed and told her I would think about it. It nagged me. There was something obvious I was missing, but for the life of me I couldn't figure out what it was. The child wasn't physically impaired or autistic. It was truly strange. It continued to nag. Then the light broke. I called and said, "I think I have an idea. I think Seth may be farsighted and perhaps doesn't see the food when it is too close to him. Can you take him for an eye examination?" She replied, "Well, I guess, but wouldn't his physician already have noticed this?" I then said, "He needs to see an ophthalmologist, not a pediatrician." She agreed to take him. She called back several weeks later, elated, saying, "Seth now has glasses. He was farsighted. He eats all the food on his plate. I'm so pleased. But, do you think he would ever have learned to read if we hadn't figured this out?"
Scary, isn't it?

Reflective Practice

Being a good observer is an important characteristic for an early childhood educator. The ability to connect that observation to creativity and developmental knowledge is imperative. Would you have thought of that possibility? What other hypothesizes might you have generated?

An **ophthalmologist** has higher technology for following up with children who do not pass visual screening tests and for determining the visual acuity of children who do not give verbal responses or recognize characters. There are a variety of techniques they use depending upon the specific concern and what they are trying to rule out.

Implications for Educators

You want to find out from the parents how much functional vision a child has. On a practical note, you want to know if the child can participate in everyday classroom activities you currently have, or the types of adaptations that will allow the child to be included. You might have questions about the arrangement of your room and safety concerns about how to best protect the child from injuries. Your role as an educator is to help children use the vision they have and the vision aids they need while being included in the activities of your classroom.

Assistive Technology

Increasingly, technology is being used to help those with limited vision. Depending on the amount of vision a child has, a ViewScan may be helpful. This is a machine that uses a camera to project an image. It is able to project the pages of a book in many sizes of print and contrast. An Optacon is a device that scans print and converts it into patterns transmitted by 144 tactile pins that produce an image of the letter that can be felt against a finger. Another system, VersaBraille, can convert information from the computer into Braille. Other computer programs provide speech capacity to a personal computer, and computer printouts can be converted into speech by using a Kurzweil Reading Machine and Total Talk. There are talking calculators, talking watches, and talking clocks. This is all in addition to talking books that are available from Recording for the Blind and Dyslexic (http://www.rfbd.org) and other individualized tools that children can profit from. The traditional long cane is being replaced by laser/ultrasound wave processing, and the global position system (GPS) allows individuals to be verbally guided to their destination.

Guidelines

The modifications that you will need to make in your classroom depend on the needs of the particular children you have. The following guidelines are divided into two sections. The first deals with techniques to encourage children to use corrective vision aids. The second section provides guidance in how to modify your room for children whose corrected vision still qualifies them as being partially sighted or blind.

Corrected Visual Impairments

When you are working with a child with correctable vision problems, the dilemma is that you want the child to wear the patch or glasses and to enjoy learning. You can't afford to be cast in the role of the villain who makes the child wear these things. First check with the parents or, if necessary, the ophthalmologist to be certain what the child is supposed to do. Then the trick is to make the child want to do what she is supposed to do.

1. *Find out when and for how long visual aids should be used.* Check with parents to find out if glasses are to be worn at all times. Sometimes the correction is for a specific use only. A nearsighted child wears glasses to see at a distance, but because this correction may distort the child's vision for close work, it may be inappropriate to keep the glasses on during close work.
2. *Observe the child's behavior using the visual aids.* Does the child continually take the glasses off or look over them? Such actions may mean the correction is not helping and further consultation is necessary.
3. *Support children using corrective lenses.* If a child refuses to wear glasses, try to create a situation in which the child needs to wear the glasses to succeed. How you do this actually depends on the problem. If, for example, a child is farsighted, find an intriguing book or game that requires close vision. Then, depending on the circumstances, say something like, "Before you got your glasses, we couldn't have played this," or, "I'd like to play this game with you, but you forgot your glasses. If you wear them tomorrow, we

Some children willingly wear glasses because they can see better and they may prevent headaches. Other children are reluctant to wear them.

can play." You might also make appropriate statements like, "You've learned to do this so much faster since you got your glasses," or, "I like the way you look with your glasses." The child will feel rewarded not only by the activity, but also by your attention. Help children become assertive. Children must learn to say, "I don't like it when you call me Four Eyes."

In the Field

I don't mind wearing glasses. I am the same on the inside, in my heart. Everyone has something she has to go through. I just pretend they aren't on my face, and my friends don't even notice them. Some kids teased me at first—but now no one cares.

Reflective Practice

Even when children's vision can be corrected they pay a price for that correction. Teasing hurts whether it is glasses, hearing aids, or braces. Reflect on how you will handle this for all children.

4. *Create a need to see.* For example, if a nearsighted child dislikes wearing glasses, you might have that child sit as far away from you as possible during group time. Then, when the child realizes that there is a need to see (in the middle of a story with pictures or during a fingerplay), have the child get the glasses if that won't disrupt the group; otherwise, have someone bring the child's glasses.

This sounds like a manipulative thing to do, and the child will have a harder time learning, but if you and the parents agree that it is important to wear the glasses, you must create a definite need and then reinforce the change in behavior that occurs. This process will have to be repeated many times before the behavior is established. Be careful to do this subtly and in a matter-of-fact way so as not to focus the group's attention on the child. But you also have to be realistic and say, "Tommy, you can't come any closer, but you can see better if you get your glasses." You may need to remind him where the glasses are, but you want him to be responsible. It is your job to make the activity so enticing that the child will want to get his glasses or he'll miss something others are enjoying. Don't let this become a power struggle. If he chooses not to comply, he won't see as well. Some children who don't want to wear glasses may purposefully lose them.

5. *Plan a unit on sight.* This helps all children better understand how they see. Discuss the sense of vision as well as a variety of visual problems. Simulating various visual needs creates awareness and is educational as well. Use cameras and focus to help explain sight.
6. *Support essential learning with or without glasses.* If it is important that a child learn a particular thing, such as safety rules, make sure the child can learn it with or without glasses. Don't fall into the trap of saying, "I'll bet you can see much better since you got your glasses." A child who doesn't want to wear glasses will probably respond, "No, I can't," even when you are sure he can. Sometimes, reality is irrelevant.

In the Field

I know to the teachers I must have seemed like a witch, but it got to me. I got his eyes tested like they said and he needed glasses. I got the first pair. They were lost in a week. The kids called him "Four Eyes." He lost them. They sent letters home. I got another pair, not as pretty, but it was all I could afford. He lost them on the way to school. I can't keep doing this. I bought another pair and they were broken on the playground in 2 days. I can't get him any more glasses until the beginning of the month. They don't even need him to come with me anymore to have them fitted. They know his size. All I have to do is pay and I'm all out of money. And I'm all out of patience. I know what my responsibility is in this: I pay. But what is your responsibility?

Reflective Practice

What is your responsibility? The question is a real one. You obviously want the child to see, as does his mother. How would you work with this child and the others in the class to ensure this child's full participation? What do you feel is the mother's responsibility?

Uncorrected Visual Impairments

Some children with uncorrected visual impairments will have limited vision, whereas others will have little or no usable vision.

Children with Low or Limited Vision

Children who have low or limited vision need accommodations. Fostering visual skills means encouraging children to use their vision in a way most advantageous to them. Remember, children will not hurt their eyes through use.

1. *Teach children visual discrimination within their ability to see.* Start with gross discrimination paired with tactile reinforcement, then progress to finer distinctions. Some children may miss details, so help them make better guesses about what is missing.
2. *Regulate light levels.* This helps some children compensate for reduced vision. Be aware of lighting conditions and sources of light. Use shades or Venetian blinds to regulate the amount of natural light in your room. (Ideally, illumination should be between 70 and 100 foot-candles. Foot-candles are the unit of measurement used to calculate adequate lighting levels of schools and workspaces. Light switches with dimmers can be helpful (but most cannot be used with fluorescent lights). Do not stand or sit with your back to the light source or in outside doorways; there is too much contrast between the bright light of outside and your figure.
3. *Arrange seating to favor the lighting conditions.* (Check the specialist's report. For some children, maximum illumination is best, and for others lower-than-normal levels are optimal.) Some children use tinted lenses to reduce glare.
4. *Use matte or flat finishes and nonglare glass or contact paper on framed pictures.*
5. *Choose light-colored tables (or dishes) with a dull finish.* Glare is fatiguing.
6. *Change or improve color contrast.* Where possible, paint the rims of bookcases, tables, and door frames with a lighter or darker color that will make the edges easier to see. Use a dark light switch against light-colored walls so it will stand out.
7. *Mark boundaries.* Use a heavy black marking pen to outline the boundaries of the paper so that the child knows where the edges are.
8. *Provide clear, simple pictures and large-print books.* Look at the books you have in your reading area to ensure accessibility for all children.
9. *Use materials with distinctive shapes and textures.* Use bright, high-contrast colors.
10. *Keep the general noise level down.* A child with low visual ability relies on auditory cues, and these will be masked by noise.
11. *Avoid excessive detail on bulletin boards.* Be aware of the child's vision when you display the children's work. Hang all children's work at their eye level so that they can see it displayed and can point it out to others.
12. *Use auditory and tactile cues to reinforce children's behavior.* Do you rely on smiles, gestures, body cues, and eye contact to reinforce behavior? These are visual cues. With children who have partial sight, you need to talk and touch for reinforcement in addition to using visual cues. You may need to draw attention to the visual cues with words and gestures.
13. *Enlarge images and objects.* Print information large. Regularly use different types of magnifiers.

In the Field

As a teacher I have worked with children who have had a variety of challenges. One child I remember, Lucas, was being raised by his great-grandparents. Lucas had multiple medical challenges when he was born. As a result, the family had difficulty meeting his medical needs. The family frequently missed medical appointments and there were concerns that he was being neglected. Lucas was taken away from his mother and placed in the custody of his father's grandmother when he was 2 years old.

Lucas has a degenerative eye disease, a kidney disorder, and many dietary restrictions. When I had Lucas in my class his eyesight had deteriorated to the point that he was legally blind. His kidney disorder was relatively under control.

Lucas has to live with his medical conditions and has learned skills to cope with them. However, each time he visited his mother and siblings for the weekend, Monday was a nightmare for him and me. I learned to give Lucas time to talk about what happened, how it made him feel, and spent one-on-one time playing with him during center time. Generally, Lucas was not able to choose or attend any activity during center time unless an adult was with him. He complained that no one liked him or wanted to play with him, and he became easily frustrated whenever he encountered difficulty in his play.

Lucas's difficulty seeing caused him to misinterpret the actions and intentions of his peers, resulting in many conflicts. It was difficult to explain to Lucas that he did not see what happened correctly. He was very strong-willed and refused to listen when I tried to help him to solve a conflict. What finally worked was to remove him from the situation until he calmed down, explain what happened, and then have each child talk to the other, using teacher scripts to solve the problem.

When Lucas had difficulty telling another child what he wanted, I would provide words for him to use, then he would repeat them to the child. For example, "Lucas, tell him that you would like to have a turn when he is done." Then Lucas would repeat my sentence to the child.

In addition to having difficulty with his peers, Lucas's vision provided challenges with the setup of the classroom space. Lucas was unaware that he had difficulty seeing. In fact, he frequently ran in the room. This usually ended with him tripping or knocking down furniture or even me. I had to be sure there were large spaces between centers for him to maneuver around.

Finding accommodations for activities was challenging, because I had to make sure Lucas could see what I was planning for the class. Some of the things I did were to enlarge the print on the copy machine, use bigger objects, give him verbal cues when completing a task, pair him with a partner to be his eyes, and I incorporated a lot of multisensory activities into my themes.

Reflective Practice

How would you work with a child like Lucas? How do you think he would impact your classroom? How does his environment impact his development? Do you think the accommodations this teacher made were adequate?

Children with Little or No Vision

Children who have very little or no usable vision need additional accommodations. The following guidelines will help you support children who have little or no usable vision in the classroom and those who need corrective lenses but have not been identified or do not use the lenses. Obviously, the less vision the child has, the more you will need to adapt and stabilize the classroom environment.

1. *Eliminate clutter and confusion.* A well-arranged classroom helps all children, but especially those with severe visual impairments. Keep things neat and make sure that toys are picked up as soon as children are finished with them. Be sure that chairs are pushed under the tables. Eliminate unnecessary obstacles in the classroom. Be aware of protruding objects such as puzzles or blocks that have been placed on a shelf but still stick out. Rearrange these so they no longer protrude. Consolidate items where possible. (Have one large wastebasket rather than many small ones.) Keep doors fully open or completely shut. Even children with excellent vision tend to run into partly opened doors. Round tables are safer than rectangular ones because there are no corners to bump into. If rectangular ones are all you have, pad sharp edges with foam. If you are a person who likes to arrange and then rearrange your classroom, don't! It takes a while for children to establish permanent reference points and feel comfortable in a room. If possible, give children with visual disabilities a chance to

become acquainted with the arrangement of the room before other children come in by having them visit the classroom before school starts or in the evening when other children are not present. Verbally describe the classroom and spatial relationships as the child explores. Then ask for specific feedback: "Can you show me where the puzzles are?" Don't assume that just because you told the child and he had time for free exploration that he will understand and remember. Use auditory, olfactory, and tactile cues to structure the room. The bubbling of an aquarium might identify the science area, a rug could mark the story area provided it is firmly attached to the floor, wind chimes could indicate that the outside door is open, and so on.

2. *Encourage independence.* When you assign lockers or coat hooks, give this child one that is easy to locate, perhaps one on the end, out of the traffic pattern. Don't move objects around after the child has placed them without telling the child. Moving something 2 inches may mean that it is "gone" if a child can't visually scan the area.

3. *Label materials with raised letters.* Use a label maker to put raised labels on materials where possible or use Braille. It is more important to label favorite toys with something easy to find than to make a descriptive label. (A puzzle of different types of fruit might have just the raised letter *F* on it rather than the entire title or label in Braille.) Make sure materials are put away so that the label is facing out. With older children, use rubber bands as labels on round objects. Put one rubber band on the red paint, two on the blue, and three on the yellow. This helps children with color deficiencies also. Using rubber bands with children under three is not safe, as they might swallow them.

4. *Use props children can feel.* Be careful not to give children unnecessary special treatment. Before you give a child help you would not give others, ask if it is needed. Offer help, but don't take over or allow other children to do the task for a child with visual impairments. Teach other children in the class how to offer help as well.

5. *Adapt your teaching techniques.* Identify yourself when you enter a room or area, especially if the child is alone. Tell the child specifically where you are: "I'm standing behind your chair." Encourage the other children to do the same. Also make it clear when you leave, especially if you are wearing soft-soled shoes. Use children's names during group time and when they are playing in small groups. Teach children in the group to do this as well. Have you ever talked to an unidentified person on the telephone who assumes you know who is speaking? It's disconcerting until you identify the person. It is important for a child with visual limitations to know who is present, especially at the beginning of the year. Use auditory cues—a short tune, a chord on the piano, or a song—to signal regular activities, such as cleanup time. Be consistent in using the signals, so the child learns to associate the activities and cues. Help with an ongoing monologue about what is happening during an activity. If the class is

making cookies, say, "Tanika has finished sifting the flour, and now Harry is going to beat the batter." Include children by asking, " Jesusa, what are you doing now?" This helps the child learn to identify sounds and encourages all children to participate in the experience.

6. *Keep your voice within normal limits.* (Some assume that those who don't see well also don't hear well.) Give careful attention to the tone of your voice. Talk directly to a child, not about her. Don't ask Maria's father if she wants to play in the block area; ask her. (Her father may answer, but that is a different problem.) Don't eliminate the words "see" and "look" from your vocabulary—use them when they are appropriate. Make directions clear and concise. Use characteristics that can be felt, heard, or counted rather than seen.

7. *Address the child by name.* Before giving instructions identify the child and make sure that the instructions you give really help. "It is right over there" is not enough. You have to name places and specify ways of doing things. It helps if the child knows right from left. If not, have the child wear something (rings, bracelet, watch, ribbon) on one hand or arm so that you can say, "Reach up with the hand with the bracelet on it."

8. *Teach directions.* Teach children the concepts of left and right early. Use the word "correct" when something is accurate, not "right," as this is confusing. Older children use the image of a clock for location. Use this image to identify where items are located: "The cup is at 2 o'clock." This is also useful when children are sitting in a circle. If the child knows that the teacher is at 12 o'clock and the child is at 3 o'clock, it is useful to say, "Jason is sitting at 6 o'clock."

9. *Walk slightly in front of the child.* When walking with a child who has very limited vision, walk in front, never behind the child. If you walk alongside, let the child hold your arm or wrist; don't hold the child's. This allows a greater sense of the movement of your body, especially when you turn or go up or down steps. As you walk, be sure to describe what you are passing: "Now we're going by the swings. Can you hear Terry and Bahira talking while they swing?"

10. *Provide many opportunities to ask questions.* Because children don't see objects to say, "What is that?", they ask questions less frequently. If adults always anticipate their needs, they don't have the opportunity to ask questions and may not gain this skill.

11. *Give accurate feedback.* If a child is not able to evaluate her own work, she is dependent on you for this information. If feedback is always positive, the child will not have an incentive to improve and may build a false sense of confidence.

12. *Increase other children's awareness.* Include a unit on feelings and emotions and openly talk about taunting and teasing. At first, you may have to lead the discussion and state some typical reactions, but you should gradually help children to speak up. Perhaps a session on assertiveness training will help.

Some children with visual impairments have vision as their only disability; others have additional impairments. If children have additional impairments be sure to check the curriculum adaptations and guidelines for those disabilities.

Curriculum Adaptations

The amount of functional vision a child has will determine what, if any, curriculum modifications have to be made. The less vision the child has, the more the auditory and tactile channels must be used. The use of any residual vision is encouraged.

Social Awareness: Self-Esteem, Inclusion, and Social Studies

All children need to be part of the group and learn about the strengths and needs of others. As adults, we are familiar with aids to vision such as glasses; younger children are not as familiar, and they need to learn. Personal worth and adequacy is a fundamental need for all children. Self-esteem is a personal judgment of worthiness that children feel about themselves; it is shaped by self-perception and the perception of others. Some of the activities in Resource Chapter 1 are specifically designed to increase children's awareness of visual impairments. The activity Simulated Glasses 1–19 helps all children understand the impact of different types of visual impairments. Moving in the Dark 1–21 helps children learn safe ways to move when they cannot see. Eye Doctor 1–28 teaches children the basic process of matching the "three-legged stool," the capital letter E, to an eye chart on the wall to prepare them to get their eyes examined.

Self-Esteem

Children with limited vision tend to develop body awareness more slowly because of lack of confidence and having fewer examples to emulate. Visual memory is the basis for such things as pretend play. If children do not have visual memory, alternative ways of developing memory need to be explored. A child may learn words without having a clear understanding of their social significance. Many social skills are learned through observation. If a child cannot see others, he may need to be taught skills other children learn from observation.

1. Children with visual impairments need role models who wear glasses and use optical devices. They need to use the correctable vision they have and to learn the skills to explain to others why these particular devices help them. Look around your classroom and be sure the pictures include children with visual impairments and visual aids.
2. Sometimes, children with visual impairments make faces that are socially unpleasant. These faces offend both children and adults and may be followed by teasing and name-calling. Address the problem directly. Describe the problem: "When you move your tongue like that, you look unpleasant (or silly). Do you want to look silly now? If not, please put your tongue back in your mouth."
3. Often, children with visual impairments have fewer facial expressions and less obvious body movements. They may turn their face away when others are talking and appear inattentive when in reality they are listening carefully. Reinforce them when their face is more expressive and tell them, "I like it when your face is turned toward me when I speak to you."
4. Help children label their body parts. Use exercises and songs in naming body parts and discuss the ways these parts move. Hold the child's hands in your own as you point and demonstrate, but tell the child what you are going to do before you do it.
5. Teach children the vocabulary to explain how they feel as well as how to use auditory cues to understand others' emotions.
6. Encourage children to explore a variety of methods of moving from place to place. Have them talk about when they could use these different methods. They need to become more aware of their bodies in relation to their surroundings.
7. Confidence and positive self-esteem come from learning age-appropriate adaptive skills. This is an important part of group acceptance and motivates further exploration. Give children time and opportunity to develop these skills.
8. Provide an environment of acceptance and experimentation that will build children's self-confidence.

Inclusion

Your expectations of a child with a visual impairment will set the tone for the class. If you do not require the child to clean up, or if you are apprehensive or overprotective, the other children will quickly pick this up.

1. Teach children to identify themselves when they begin a conversation; otherwise, the child's energy is spent on figuring out who the speaker is rather than what that person is saying.
2. Explain to other children the impact of having limited vision; sometimes, children do not approach children with visual impairments because they seem unresponsive and lack curiosity.
3. Encourage children to invite a child with low vision to play by suggesting or bringing specific toys and materials for both of them to use.
4. Children with low vision often learn about their environment through their tactile/kinesthetic senses. They may want to touch their classmates. Help them find acceptable ways to work this out. See Activity 1–17, Who is It?
5. As children get older, have them use blindfolds or masks that simulate various visual impairments. See Activity 1–19, Simulated Glasses. Support children in pretending they have different visual impairments and give them specific tasks to do (go to specific places in the room, find particular objects, write their name, eat a snack). Discuss with children how this felt and how they could make it easier. If teasing is an issue, bring it up.

Social Studies

All children need to learn about the world around them, and field trips are a pleasant and effective way to accomplish this. Children with visual impairments can use many hands-on experiences to make accurate generalizations. Even children who have fully corrected vision have spent some portion of their life without optimal vision. (If corrective lenses were worn at age 3 and the child is 6, that is *half* of the child's lifetime.)

1. Plan field trips with small groups of children so that each of them can participate in the experience. It isn't enough just to see a cow, especially if the child can't see it well. The child has to feel it and feel enough of it to form an accurate perception of a cow.
2. Provide follow-up activities with stories and dramatic play after field trips. Have the children describe with all their senses what they remember. Drink milk, smell and handle hay, make farm sounds, and sing farm songs.
3. When naming objects for a child, differentiate between the representation and the real thing: "We saw a real cow on the field trip. This is a toy cow. How are they different?"
4. Tapes, CDs, DVDs, and videos help children expand their social world. Children may be more sensitive to auditory signals than visual ones. These resources must be linked to meaningful experiences if they are to expand the child's knowledge base.

5. Help children become aware of the role the medical profession plays in assessing visual acuity and prescribing corrective lenses. This can be done with a field trip, or a visit from an eye doctor followed up with dramatic play. See Resource Chapter 1, Activity 1–28, Eye Doctor.

6. If you know a person with a visual impairment who would be comfortable with the children, have the person visit. (A seeing eye dog always makes an impression and provides an important learning experience.)

Language and Literacy: Speaking, Listening, Reading, and Writing

The area of language and literacy is challenging yet essential for children with visual impairments. Language is their major source of acquiring knowledge, of "seeing" the world, and of communicating with others. Children with visual impairments usually depend on verbal skills to communicate and listening skills to learn about their environment. If they can't find a needed object, they may ask others. They need practice in giving and following directions with children and adults. They are more dependent on auditory cues and auditory memory. Children who have visual losses miss some of the nonverbal qualities of attending and eye contact. They need help focusing on intonation patterns, volume, and speed of language for additional cues. They require an individualized literacy program. Encourage children to refine the visual skills they use.

Speaking

Children with visual impairments rely more on auditory cues to learn speech, whereas other children can more easily see and imitate movements of the lips, mouth, and jaw. Encourage children to ask what things are and help them to broaden their understanding of labels used. Encouraging feedback from the children about their perceptions will enable you to clarify misunderstandings and foster increased verbalization.

1. Following verbal directions is an important language skill. Start with simple one- or two-step directions. Remember to keep them concrete.

2. Children with visual impairments depend more on words to express or understand feelings. Help them learn these words.

3. Many young children talk to themselves; this is normal for all children. Children with visual impairments may also talk to imaginary friends. This is fine, unless they become more interested in imaginary friends than real ones.

Fingerplays incorporate language as well as fine motor skills.

1. Begin with simple, short fingerplays that have more large than small movements. (Teach "Head, Shoulders, Knees, and Toes" before "Where is Thumbkin.")

2. Write down fingerplays and send them home. Teach the parents the fingerplays so that the children can practice them at home or while traveling. (If you don't demonstrate the fingerplay, you can get some amazing variations.)

3. A child with low vision may find fingerplays difficult because he cannot see some of the finer details. When teaching fingerplays, have a paraeducator or volunteer help the child respond at the appropriate time so that the child begins to associate the movement with the words.

Listening

Children who have visual impairments have a greater need for understanding speech because they are dependent on verbal information to perform certain tasks. Even children with corrected vision problems do not always wear their glasses. It is important that they learn to identify and discriminate among sounds. Help children develop skills in this area through differentiating similar sounds and listening to tapes or CDs. Often children who are visually impaired tune out language because it is based on what others have seen and it makes no sense to them.

1. Because children with visual impairments may not be able to clearly see the speaker, they may not look at the person speaking. Encourage them to look by saying, "Please look at me." Give them an opportunity to respond. If they don't, say, "I'll help by turning your head so it faces me. People like it when you look at them when they are speaking." Then gently turn it.

2. Children need practice locating sounds. Play listening games. Make a sound and see if the child can locate the source of the sound. Once the source is located, the child needs to feel the object that makes the sound and tell how it is used.

3. Have children match sounds by placing objects in pairs of small containers (with taped lids) and shaking them.

4. Children have to learn fine auditory discrimination. Describe and explain what children hear but cannot see. Use this as a game (describe noises and their implications and have the children guess the source from your description). Use an activity such as Sound Cues (2–9).

5. Use tapes and CDs of stories and music for classifying sounds (long, short, high, low) and for identifying who or what might make that sound and in what situation.

6. Where possible, give children replicas of what you are talking about. Don't worry about size relationships at this point—you can describe those verbally—but clearly identify the object as a toy, so children know it is not the real thing.

7. "Where," "why," and "what" are difficult for all children to comprehend. Demonstrate, where possible, the meaning of these words. If possible, take the child to a location, or let the child feel "what" is making the sound.

8. The most difficult words for children to use and understand are those that cannot be experienced through vision such as colors, the sky, and so on. Use these words in context so children have additional cues. Literature often does this well.

9. Use language to help children focus their vision, as well as to get feedback: "Can you see that wheel? Do you see what's inside the wheel? Those are spokes. Can you count them by touching each one?"

10. Use words that refer to things that can be smelled, touched, heard, seen, tasted, or experienced directly. Try to make the words you use as concrete as possible, using real examples whenever you can. Then move on to more abstract language concepts such as "time," "friendship," and so on.

11. Use functional definitions of objects as well as descriptive ones. "A ball rolls" or "a ball bounces" should be used in addition to the definition "a ball is round." Reinforce the concept by letting the child roll and bounce the ball.

12. To move freely, the child with low vision needs to be able to follow verbal directions. Words like "stop/go," "high/low," "big/little," "in/out/on," and "hard/soft" are useful. Other important spatial terms include "side by side," "back to back," "full turn, half turn, quarter turn," "top/bottom," "in front of," and so on. Games like Simon Says, May I, Hokey Pokey, and Follow the Leader work well for teaching directions.

Reading

Stories can expand the children's world, provided you start with themes children are familiar with. It is preferable to use pictures that illustrate the story's major points in a simple way. Point out to children the relationship of the picture to the story. Create a need to see within their ability to discriminate. In the area of reading literacy, one emphasis is on developing and refining visual discrimination skills.

1. When you read stories, pass around small replicas of the major objects (rabbits, carrots, trains) for the children to look at and feel. Do the same with textures and smells.

2. Use cassette tapes, or CDs of books at a listening center. These allow more individualization and choice in the books available. Make your own recordings of favorite books, and bring in blank cassettes so children can dictate their own books.

3. Have books with large type and in Braille. Even if the child does not require Braille, it broadens the range of experience and understanding to develop the idea that Braille is a form of writing. Sometimes refer to books on tape as "talking books" or audiobooks to expand children's ideas about books.

4. Start with large objects that have gross distinctions. Simple shapes are fine, such as circles, triangles, and squares. Encourage children not only to label and distinguish among shapes, but also to point out salient characteristics (a circle doesn't have any corners, a triangle has three). Have children trace the shapes with their index and third fingers to gain a kinesthetic as well as a visual sense of these distinctions.

5. When children can make gross distinctions, work on finer ones. When you teach these, try to point out significant features. Use large wooden letters and have the children trace them with their index and third fingers. Teach them that *A* has straight lines,

O has curved lines, and *P* has straight and curved lines. Teach by contrasting *A*, *O*, and *P* and use other contrasting groups of shapes before you have the children differentiate among letters such as *N*, *M*, and *W*, for example, which have only straight lines. Help children fine tune tactile skills and introduce Braille to those children who will be using it.

6. Children with low vision may have to combine their usable vision with tactile skills to develop reading readiness. If the amount of usable vision decreases, the need for more tactile discrimination will increase because this is a pre-Braille skill. Among the things that can be used to help children develop these skills are sandpaper letters and texture cards (for matching). See Sandpaper Letters 2–23.

7. Use the computer or overhead projector to increase the contrast and size of print children are exposed to.

8. Increase their awareness of print by helping them feel books and identify the different parts of books.

9. Show children different written languages (Spanish, Chinese, and Russian), including Braille, and talk about how different children learn to read using different written representations.

10. Read books about children who have visual impairments. (See the Children's Bibliography for suggestions.)

Writing

All children need to develop the link between the ability to speak a word and the ability to write it so others can understand. The form this takes depends on the child.

1. For children who are partially sighted, choose wide black markers so they can easily see what they are marking.

2. If the child cannot use visual feedback, then you need to employ media with more tactile feedback. Start without tools. Have children air write. Encourage them to hold their two writing fingers together (the index finger and longest finger of their dominant hand), then, using their whole arm, write letters. (This gives them body feedback.)

3. Provide children with sandpaper or wooden letters they can trace with two fingers. Provide auditory cues to support the visual or tactile experience.

4. Use writing media that have different tactile properties. Have children "write" in sand in a jelly roll pan, and mark clay that has been rolled flat, or, using their fingers, "write" on black felt on which you have taped white lines (narrow masking tape is fine).

5. As children get older, they will probably use a computer or word processor for written work. Provide children with experiences for learning the position of letters on the keyboard; if necessary, use a Braille keyboard. A speech synthesizer and appropriate software provide children with auditory feedback about their keystrokes. See Activity 3–25, My Keyboard for more ideas.

6. A good way to prepare for reading and writing Braille is using pegs and a pegboard. First, allow a child to explore the entire pegboard by feeling the holes. Then, cover with tape or cardboard all except the lines you want the child to use. If it is a horizontal

line, have the child move from left to right; if vertical, top to bottom. Children who are right-handed should use the index finger of their left hand as a guide to find the hole and the right hand to place the peg into the hole. Then find the next hole with their index finger and continue. Work to the point that children can copy adult patterns.

Discovery: Mathematics, Science, and Technology

Discovery experiences need to start with the familiar and concrete and work toward the less familiar and more abstract. Start with natural situations and real objects that are meaningful to the children: two socks and two shoes, one coat with two arms, and so on. Help children feel round balls and square boxes. Use sandpaper outlines of circles and squares. Help children pace off and count distances to and from various places in the room: 5 steps from the locker to the circle area, compared with 10 steps from the locker to the blocks. Provide additional time for children to touch the equipment and materials. Be sure to include equipment that magnifies. Computer literacy is an excellent long-term resource for children. Computers can be designed to have large print, speech, or Braille output. Computers with a voice synthesizer are extremely useful. Learning to make predictions about what will happen under a specified set of circumstances is important as a way of developing independence and creating a sense of predictability in the world.

Mathematics

Number concepts are necessary for all children. The fun is in using them creatively to help children explore and classify their world. For children with low vision, the tactile-motor aspect of learning these concepts can be added with a few modifications.

1. Teach children to tactilely discriminate and match materials of various shapes, sizes, and weights. Have children sort matching buttons into ice cube trays.
2. When teaching number concepts and geometric shapes, start with real objects. Food works well. Everyone gets *1* glass of milk, *2* pieces of fruit, *10* raisins, and so on. An abacus is also useful for counting. One can both see and feel the placement of the beads and check back if necessary. Encourage children to count.
3. Matching large dominoes with indented dots is a good activity that teaches fine motor skills as well as number concepts. Play dominoes.
4. Have children use their bodies and other devices to measure. Record these measurements. Special modifications should be made to help children with low vision understand distances: an arm's length, two paces, three hand spans. Glue pieces of string on the paper or use glue lines to make graphs that can be felt (see Measuring Tools 3–7).
5. Use physical boundaries to delimit the block area, and put the blocks in a tub so the child can locate them easily. Show and tell the child the dimension of the blocks in the tub. Start with individual block building.

6. Teach children about patterns and relationships by using a variety of repeating tactile patterns (rough, smooth, rough, smooth; rough, rough, smooth, and so on).
7. Provide children with many experiences matching, sorting, categorizing, sequencing, and patterning with a wide variety of materials.

Science

Science helps children learn about the sense of vision and the other senses as well as the natural world. Emphasize creative problem solving, decision making, and discovery.

1. Help children learn about the eye and how it works. Get a model of the eye and use the concept of a camera to help children understand vision.
2. Talk about the purpose of lenses. Have a variety of magnifying glasses and binoculars available in the science area. Talk about the difference in the amount of detail that can be seen with the naked eye and with magnification.
3. Have children participate in experiences in which materials change form, such as making butter or melting ice. Let children with low vision feel the changes as well.
4. Discuss the weather and appropriate dress for different types of weather. Talk about and feel fabrics used in warm-versus cold-weather clothing. Experiment with materials designed for specific uses (rain, sun, cold).
5. Help children develop thermic (temperature) and baric (weight) sensitivity by sequencing and matching plastic bottles full of water of differing temperatures and containers of varying weights.
6. Children need to refine their senses to identify pleasant and unpleasant tastes and smells. These are important cues. Some smells might mean that something is going bad (like sour milk), some provide environmental information (damp earth means it rained recently), some are clues to locations (flowers are near a garden), and so on. Other smells indicate whether something or someone is clean or dirty, such as smells of clothing and babies. Children can refine these senses by matching cinnamon, cloves, basil, nutmeg, ginger in small plastic containers and tasting a variety of foods.

Technology

Initially, computers may be difficult for young children with visual impairments because so much of computing is visual. For children with enough vision to see the keyboard and the monitor, the problems are few. Most adults with visual impairments have learned touch-typing and to use a numeric keypad. This learning begins when children are young.

1. Use a voice synthesizer with the computer.
2. Use a 25-inch monitor so the letters displayed on the screen are large. Programs are also available that enlarge the type on the screen. It may be easier to read a video screen than a piece of paper because the light source is coming from the back of the screen and is not reflected light.

3. Computers also allow us to change text and background colors. Some children with partial sight do better with certain color combinations. Find the best combination.
4. Experiment with digital cameras and the contrast in printing pictures to enhance visual discrimination.

Wellness: Health, Physical Education, and Sensory Motor

Children with limited vision may face health and safety issues other children do not. Be aware of the environment and the feedback it potentially provides children. Try to increase the auditory and kinesthetic information available.

Although vision may be limited, the coordination of hearing and tactile/kinesthetic senses provides an avenue of learning combined with available vision. Children with visual impairments are dependent on motor skills and also have more limited opportunities to practice them. They need to learn where they are and to develop safe ways of moving through unknown spaces. This requires sensory motor integration. Children who lack the visual aspect of sensory integration need to learn ways of compensating for, as well as refining, their residual vision. The refinement of fine motor skills will aid Braille reading (if needed). Body awareness and motor planning are an integral part of orientation and mobility training. Children with limited vision need encouragement and a safe place to practice developing skills. Outdoor activities may be a challenge. With temperature changes, glasses sometimes fog up, so have tissues handy to wipe them off. For children with low vision, watch for safety concerns. Be sure that paths for moving vehicles are well delineated and that there is a boundary around swings, seesaws, and other moving equipment so that children cannot accidentally walk into them.

Health and Safety

Health and safety is an important and difficult area of learning for all young children. It requires them to consciously inhibit their spontaneous curiosity and think through the implications of actions *before* doing them. For children with low vision, the possibility of falling or bumping into things or stooping over and hitting something is greater than for other children, yet the price of overprotection is great also. Greater coordination problems exist when learning skills because children are more dependent on tactile and auditory cues for learning than on visual ones. They may not see another child riding a tricycle toward them or the swing in motion. They need to use their residual vision and hearing to compensate.

1. Help all children develop independence in adaptive (self-help) skills. Use buttoning, lacing, and snapping frames to teach these skills. Montessori materials are excellent, but you can make your own fairly easily. Keep soap, paper towels, and the wastebasket in the same places and at a level the child can reach.
2. Teach safety, looking, and listening skills. Make sure children can identify such sounds as cars, sirens, and fire alarms and know what to do when they hear these sounds.

3. Teach children to do deep knee bends as a way of getting down to pick things up. It is especially important when they lift heavy objects, and it decreases bumped heads.
4. When children are playing very actively, have those wearing eyeglasses use a safety strap to keep their glasses from falling off.
5. In outdoor play areas, fence in the swings, seesaws, and any other heavy moving equipment. Keep tricycles, bicycles, and wagons on specified paths. Add bells to moving objects (tricycles, wagons, even balls) and encourage children to use them appropriately.
6. Teach children with limited vision to use their sense of touch to determine if they have rashes or cuts or to tell if their hands are clean.

Large Motor

Using the large muscles of the body is one way for children to increase their knowledge of their own bodies, as well as a way to explore their environment. Children who have recently had visual correction and those with low vision will probably have less refined skills in this area than their age-mates. They may need encouragement as well as practice.

1. Balancing "tricks" are especially useful. Start with static balance: The child stands or sits still and balances a particular object. (Beanbags are easier to start with than books.) For dynamic balance, have the child walk, jump, or crawl while balancing an object on her head or other body part. As the child becomes more skillful, see how long or how far the child can balance objects. Walk on a balance board or beam. See Variations on Balancing 4–9.
2. Relay races where children run, walk, jump, hop, or skip while holding hands with a partner are great for developing both large motor skills and cooperating with peers.
3. Walking between the rungs of a ladder placed flat on the ground or floor helps children establish spacing, and they learn to realize whether or not they are walking in a straight line. Spot children so they don't fall.
4. Encourage children to do motor tasks blindfolded (use half-face Halloween masks and cover the eye openings) and talk about the implications of not being able to see. See Activity 1–21, Moving in the Dark to make it a learning experience for all children.
5. If children are having trouble conceptualizing a particular movement, have them feel the outline of an adult's body (or that of a willing peer) before they do a movement. An adult may need to help children position their bodies until they get the feel of the movement.

Small Motor

The development and refinement of fine motor skills and eye-hand coordination requires practice. Start with experiences that are likely to be successful so that children do not get discouraged. Success is especially important for those who are just learning to use corrective visual aids. They may tell you they can do it better without the aids and, if they have learned good compensatory skills, they may be right!

1. Fit-in puzzles (those with large pieces that go into specific places) and knob puzzles work well.
2. Three-dimensional building toys are very helpful (but get the type that interlock in some way, so they won't fall apart when bumped). Encourage children to start with larger pieces and work toward using the smaller ones. Keep the pieces in a tray so that children can keep track of them.
3. Sewing cards with large holes around the perimeter of the image allow a child to both feel and see the outline of the images. These cards can be easily made by pasting pictures on cardboard and using a hole punch.
4. Teach children to discriminate among textures. Begin with pleasant-feeling textures such as satin and velvet. Then move on to fleece, cotton, and so on. These fabrics can also be used for texture-matching games. Try different grades of sandpaper, which the children can try to arrange in order of fineness.

Sensory Motor Integration

If children do not have accurate visual feedback, they need to develop a motor memory for moving their bodies through space.

1. An obstacle course that requires children to crawl over, under, and through different-sized obstacles is a great way to teach spatial orientation. You might start a human obstacle course, where the "course" itself can provide help and support.
2. Emphasize tactile-motor and auditory-motor activities.
3. Use the vision children have, but be aware that it may vary from day to day. Children who are anxious or tired may not have as much ability to focus their vision as they do when they are relaxed and rested.

Creative Arts: Visual Arts, Music, Creative Movement, and Dramatic Play

Creative arts provide children with the opportunity to explore their world in a safe way. They can gain experiences inside the classroom that can prepare them for what will happen outside. Children with visual impairments may need obvious boundaries for work on paper, such as a thick, black line marking the outside of the paper, or a larger, high-contrast piece of paper underneath the paper being worked on. As long as the emphasis is on process, there are few limitations on what children can do. It is often useful to add textured materials to paint and playdough. Three-dimensional materials such as clay and playdough are particularly good because the children can feel the results.

Music can be used to enhance listening skills and auditory discrimination. Moving to music is an excellent way to acquire body awareness, but be sure to have an area without physical obstacles. Give children boundaries they can trust, such as adults who can cue them if their movements are too large. Creative movement supports orientation and mobility skills. Children with limited vision must learn a variety of ways of moving safely. Have children move with partners. Use music to help them localize sound and distinguish one voice from another. Let them feel vibrations of instruments and voices. Sound will be vital in the life of these children, so use music to train their hearing.

Children with visual impairments profit from acting out situations and having realistic props. Be sure to keep the props in the same place so they are easy to find.

Visual Arts

Although children with very little residual vision face limitations in some areas of art, there are many highly tactile materials that allow a great deal of manipulation. The potential that art activities and materials offer for the release of emotions makes them doubly valuable experiences for all children with visual impairments.

1. Use a variety of modeling materials to provide different tactile experiences. Among the most popular materials are playdough (made of salt and flour), clay (use the powdered type and let the children help mix it), cornstarch, papier-mâché, and plastic-coated wire.
2. Have children fingerpaint right on the table if they are using actual finger paint. You can then print the picture when a child makes one he wants to keep. Finger painting to music is a good variation.
3. Add textured materials such as sand or sawdust to easel paint and fingerpaint. Make the paint thicker so that it can be more easily felt and controlled.
4. Make textured boundaries for work areas. (This is a good idea for any child who tends to use too much space.) Use masking tape to divide the table into areas, depending on your needs. Use placemats to define each child's space: Put glue around the outside edge of a sheet of paper and sprinkle a little sand on it as a tactile boundary.
5. If you are using white paper on the easel, first cover the easel with dark construction paper so that the child can easily see where the paper ends. If the child cannot see, use a textured material for the board, such as coarse sandpaper or cork, so the child can feel the boundaries.
6. Use thick, dark marking pens to print names on papers and remember *print big* for all children to help them recognize their name and the names of others.
7. Hang the child's artwork in a place where she can find it easily, see it, and point it out to others. Hang it low and near the beginning or the end.
8. Make a texture collage with a specific theme; for example, for *nature*, use feathers, pine needles, leaves, and grass.
9. Tape paper to the table so it stays in one place.

Music

Music is often a particularly enjoyable activity for children with low vision and, with the number of famous musicians who are visually impaired (such as Ray Charles,

Stevie Wonder, and Joaquin Rodrigo) it is not difficult to find encouragement to do well. However, don't assume that children with visual impairments will automatically be good at music. Music study develops finer auditory discrimination and facilitates the development of memory skills.

1. Play an instrument or ring a bell and have the children (who have their backs to you and eyes closed) guess what area of the room you are in. A variation of this is to have them search for a ticking kitchen timer or music box.
2. Teach the concepts of *high* and *low* with music pitch games. Have children practice using *loud* and *soft* volume as cues to distance (for example, for finding a hidden object). *Fast* and *slow* are also easily taught through musical games: The faster the music, the closer the child is to the hidden object.
3. Songs that have motions teach names, actions, and labels. Extra time, however, must be devoted (at school or home) to teaching children with low vision the motions that go with songs.
4. Sing songs that promote body awareness and songs that describe what children are doing: "This is the way we put on our boots/climb the stairs/ride our trike" and so on. Adapt and make up songs to fit your needs.
5. Use a variety of musical instruments and allow children time to experiment with them.
6. Have children move around the room while music is being played. When the music stops, the child has to follow the teacher's directions: "Make yourself into a ball"; "Make yourself as tall (or as short) as you can"; "Be as still as you can."

Creative Movement

Combining movement and an idea helps children learn abstract concepts. It is also a way of finding out about a child's concepts of the world. If you ask children to be leaves blowing in the wind, you will see their interpretation of what this is like. It can serve as the foundation for future planning.

1. Start with ideas that are simple and familiar to children and provide props that support these ideas, but do not dictate how an activity is done. Talk about being a group marching in a parade and play music to march by.
2. When you ask children to move in a particular way, be sure to verbally discuss "how" this will happen and to give clear, precise details about the event the children are portraying. Using the example of leaves, ask children what would make the leaves fall, then talk about how they would move in response to falling off the tree versus being blown by a strong wind.
3. Talk about personal space and how to figure out where they can move without bumping into each other.
4. Provide props such as scarves or hats to make an experience more concrete. Props help set the stage for children who cannot see well. They can expand on an idea that has been established.

5. Moving creatively to music encourages a variety of movements and gracefulness, and there is no right or wrong. Dancing, from the waltz to the twist to the macarena, is good exercise and great for developing coordination.

Dramatic Play

Dramatic play allows children to learn about, experience, and control situations. They can make new experiences more familiar by playing through them first. Working through potentially frightening experiences may make them easier to handle.

1. Provide a lot of props. Be sure that at least some of them give obvious cues (tactile as well as visual) about the activity going on. For example, teacups and saucers mean a tea party; adding a teapot and appropriate clothing sets the mood.
2. When children dress up, check to be sure there are no dangling belts or scarves that could cause tripping.
3. Set up an optometrist's office and have children test each other's vision. See 1-28 Eye Doctor.
4. Be sure to include eyeglass frames as props for a variety of activities.

Routines and Transitions

Transition times are difficult for all children because a lot of movement and change occurs. Use routines to support IEP/IFSP goals.

1. Use nonvisual cues as one means of dismissal, for example, "Everyone with a shirt that buttons can get their coats." You can use types of clothing, fabrics, or the first letters of names.
2. Dismiss children with visual impairments either early or late, when there will be the least amount of confusion.
3. Allow enough time for children to use their adaptive skills. If children are slow or need more help, provide additional support.

Summary

The visual system is a complex one, and disease or injury to the system can cause visual impairments. Early signs of a visual impairment include lack of attention to objects, holding objects too close or too far away, and inattention. The degree of the impairment determines the accommodations that are needed. Problems in different parts of the visual system have different implications for the child and his learning.

For educational purposes, we are concerned with the amount of usable vision a child has. Children with little functional vision are dependent on auditory and tactile sources for learning. Children with low vision need accommodations such as larger print or particular lighting. There are many assistive devices that are available to children with visual impairments to help compensate for their lack of vision.

Young children are difficult to assess visually, and some of the standard screening tests are unlikely to identify children who are myopic. This is a drawback, as we are most concerned about children who lack the near-vision necessary for reading and other close work. Children have a variety of needs depending on the amount of vision they have available to them. Some activities must be modified to allow them to participate; other concerns relate to safety.

Reflections

1. I know now that some children who are blind have been in public schools for a long time, but I never thought I would have one. There are really so few of them, I just thought I wouldn't have to deal with this. I am a visual person. I think that way. That is the way I am. I think if a child is blind she just shouldn't be in this class. My classroom is exciting. I don't want to change it. I don't think I should have to include her if I have to change my program so much that I really don't feel comfortable with it. I can deal with other disabilities, but I just don't want to do this one. Reflect on this position.

2. Well, wearing glasses might be a problem but I can't really see it as one. I wear glasses. I tried contacts once but didn't like them. I can't really understand why kids can't want to see better. I don't know why it is my problem to make them wear their glasses. If the parents were really committed they would want to do it. It really disrupts what I am trying to do with all the other children. I think it is asking too much of me. What should I tell the parents?

Educational Resources

American Council of the Blind is the largest organization for individuals who are visually impaired. It has guidelines on how to make material accessible. (800) 424-8666; https://www.acb.org/

American Foundation for the Blind (AFB) serves as a clearinghouse for information on visual impairments. They have information on blindness, Braille, reviews of books, links to laws, and information that is useful to professionals, parents, and children. (800) 232-5463; http://www.afb.org/

American Printing House for the Blind (APH) is a resource for educational materials in large print and Braille; sells children's Braille books; manufactures and sells equipment and assistive devices. It is easy to navigate and has useful information for professionals, parents, and children. (800) 223-1839; http://www.aph.org/

Lighthouse International is a comprehensive site for both visually impaired and blind resources. There is information on types of resources that would be helpful to professionals, parents, and children. http://www.lighthouse.org/

National Association for Parents of the Visually Impaired (NAPVI) provides information to adults to support children with visual impairments. It has practical suggestions for teaching games and activities to young children and information about resources. It provides links to a variety of sites. http://www.spedex.com/napvi/

National Center to Improve Practice in Special Education through Technology, Media and Materials; Technology for Students who are Visually Impaired Collection lists resources that relate to the visually impaired, including products, research, organizations, and publications. Products and resources were developed from 1992 to 1998. http://www2.edc.org/NCIP/library/vi/toc.htm

National Library Service for the Blind and Physically Handicapped, Library of Congress provides talking and large print books for individuals with visual or physical impairments. All services and publications are free. The Kids Zone has books that start at preschool. (800) 424-8567; (800) 424-8572 (Reference); http://www.loc.gov/nls/

National Braille Press is a non-profit organization that produces Braille books for children. (617) 266-6160; http://www.nbp.org

Visually Impaired Preschool Services provides resources for families and also produced a series of videotapes, *Can Do Video Series*, about preschool children and their families. (502) 636-3207; http://www.vips.org/

For additional resources, visit the book companion website for this text at www.cengage.com/education/deiner.

PART

III

Resources and Practice for Inclusive Early Childhood Education

Using the Resources

Although it is important to highlight each curriculum area individually, it is also important to integrate the curriculum to provide a context for learning. The impact of content and performance standards and cultural diversity has changed how all educators plan and carry out curriculum. Early childhood curriculum has moved from interesting activities to meeting state or national standards by choosing goals and implementing activities that take into account the abilities, needs, strengths, likes, and dislikes of each child in the classroom. Although some children in your class will have disabilities, the curriculum will reflect the concepts and skills needed to satisfy the requirements of the general education curriculum and are of interest to *all* the children.

continued

Activities and Record Keeping

In addition to designing a curriculum and choosing appropriate materials for the children in your classroom, you need a record-keeping system to track children's learning and chart their progress. (Refer back to Chapter 3 for additional information about record keeping.) Be clear *why* you need to keep the records. If it is to support an individual educational program (IEP) goal, the system is relatively straightforward: identify the goal and the benchmarks you are working on with space to show the activities you have chosen, the duration of that goal, and the quality of the child's behavior, noting increasing competence to signal when the goal will be met.

Before choosing activities, review information about where children spend time and their likes and dislikes. Choose activities that support the scope and sequence of reaching goals and are in areas children enjoy. The skill is figuring out how to teach what children need to learn in such a way that children want to learn it. Use activities that include a range of skills to pinpoint where children are in the learning cycle and this becomes their present level of academic achievement (PLAA) and their functional performance. This information is necessary for all children. It is part of the teaching-learning-assessment cycle. The indexes at the beginning of each Resource Chapter list the goals each activity supports in that curriculum area. The list of activities at the end of this section lists all the activities in the book that are designed to meet a particular goal regardless of curriculum area. Using these indexes effectively helps you meet the general education curriculum requirements, the national standards developed by professional organizations, and a child's individualized needs through meeting IEP/IFSP goals.

Organization of Activities

The activities in Resource Chapter 1 through Resource Chapter 6 are organized by developmental/curriculum areas such as "Language and Literacy Activities." Within these chapters this focus is broken into curriculum strands such as speaking, listening, reading, and writing. And finally, these are divided up into goals for each strand, for example, "to increase vocabulary." Activities are numbered, these numbers identify the chapter they are in and the activity. When activities have more than one goal, they appear in the index under each goal. When activities are followed by a "w" this means that they are on the book companion website and can be assessed at www.cengage.com/education/deiner. For example, if you were interested in looking up the activity "Input-Output" you would find it in the list of activities as 3–22 indicating that it was in Resource Chapter 3 and it was number 22, whereas "Creepers" would be identified as 1–45w indicating that it was in Resource Chapter 1, but that it would be found on the web rather than in the book. The activities numbered 1 through 30 are in the text. Activity numbers higher than 30 are in the book companion website.

Resource Chapter 1

Goal
To increase cultural awareness

Activities
1–1, 1–7, 1–14, 1–18, 1–24
1–38w, 1–39w, 1–44w, 1–48w

If you look up activity 1–18, you will find it is called "Foreign Languages." If you look up 1–39w in the book companion website it is called "Family Flags." Both of these activities have as their goal to increase cultural awareness. The initial table in the Resource Chapters in both the text and the online companion, index the activities and their location. For the activities in the book companion website go to www.cengage.com/education/deiner.

The organization of the activities section is designed to aid you in record keeping as well as in day-to-day curriculum planning. The activities have a standard format:

> Curriculum Area: Group Size
> Activity Number and Name
> Goals
> Materials
> Procedure
> Assessment
> Accommodations and Integration

The Assessment section provides specific information about how to evaluate a child's performance. The Accommodations and Integration section provides information for modifying or adapting the level of difficulty of the activity and integrating it into other curriculum areas. This is done to adapt for individual children, to expand the age range, and to meet the goals of the general curriculum.

Using Activities in the IEP/IFSP

If a child has an IEP, look at the annual goals and the benchmarks that support reaching these goals, locate these and related ones in the list of activities, and use the activities to help implement the IEP. If you are in charge of writing the IEP, use the goals to help you write and carry out the plan.

Activities designed for infants and toddlers are in Resource Chapter 6. They are organized by both goals and the age of the infant or toddler. If an infant or toddler has an IFSP, use the goals and supporting activities to meet child outcomes. Share activities with families if they want this type of information.

Using the Activities

Most of the activities in this book are designed to meet the goals of children with diverse abilities (5–30 Circus; 2–12 Alphabet Lotto). Other activities are designed to increase all children's awareness of professionals in the field and how specific disabilities affect behavior (1–27 Audiologist; 1–23 Slings). Adapt these activities to suit your class, and use them as a springboard to make up your own activities. The Educational Resources section after each activity chapter provides additional sources.

As an educator of young children, you have much to keep in mind. Because you have the strengths and needs of all the children in your class to consider, you must find activities that foster the strengths of children with special needs but are appropriate and enriching for all children. As important as your curriculum is, remember that you are a model for the children. Your behavior toward children—your acceptance, consideration, and respect—speaks louder to the class than anything you deliberately set out to teach.

Guidelines for Adapting Activities for Children with Special Needs

Tables PIII–1 through PIII–12 provides guidelines for including children with special needs.

Table PIII–1: Guidelines: Children with specific learning disabilities

---

- Build self-esteem by matching materials to ability level and scaffolding learning.

- Provide immediate feedback, and encourage the use of self-correcting materials.

- Find children's strengths and provide opportunities for increasing them.

- Keep instruction short; use simple vocabulary and short sentences. Use questions to involve children. Use visual aids to support what you are saying. Keep the pace lively.

- Have written (and picture) rules for behavior. Identify consequences. Be consistent.

- Be patient. Give children time to learn.

- Begin with children's preferred method of learning (visual, tactile, or auditory), but don't exclude other modalities; instead, work to strengthen them.

- Support children's interest and comprehension by reading to them as they are learning to read. Teach prereading and reading skills in interesting creative ways.

- Identify children who are not learning at the expected rate and provide more intense and individualized instruction in reading and math.

Table PIII–2: Guidelines: Children with social, emotional, and behavioral disorders

---

- Remove toys that might be dangerous or cause problems (hammers or mallets that might be thrown).

- Analyze the daily schedule and if problematic make adjustments.

- Remove children from situations if they are unable to cope and the situation is escalating. Give the child time to think (time should be based on the child's age and situation, 2 minutes may be long enough), and then talk about what happened and how the child can get back in control.

- Set clear, precise expectations: "In this class, we use words to say how we feel."

- Teach the difference between feelings and behavior. All children have feelings and should be in touch with them. However, the way they express their feelings (behavior) should not hurt themselves or others.

- Be alert. If possible, intervene before a situation becomes a problem.

- Arrange the environment to enhance learning. Balance active with less active times. Provide quiet alternatives when children need them.

- Keep noise levels reasonable.

- Develop a plan for dealing with aggressive behavior and follow it.

- Simplify, shorten, and structure activities when necessary.

- Utilize and arrange space to enhance your goals and prevent problems.

- Plan to specifically teach skills others might learn informally.

- Make learning meaningful and be respectful of children's work.

- Limit the number of transitions where possible.

Table PIII–3: Guidelines: Children with attention-deficit/hyperactivity disorder

---

- Be consistent.

- Follow an established routine so children can anticipate what will happen next (snack, free play, outside).

- Plan for transitions; prepare children for changes by giving them a 5-minute warning.

- Eliminate distractions. Keep noise levels down and confusion to a minimum.

- Make eye contact; keep directions short, simple, and clear.

- Confirm that a child has prerequisite skills before teaching new skills.

- Work from hands-on experiences to characteristics and properties.

- Provide numerous learning experiences with interesting planned variations.

- Teach prosocial skills. Develop a plan to address challenging behavior.

- Motivate children to attempt demanding activities.

- Provide children with fidget objects and two options of places to work.

Table PIII–4: Children with communication disorders

- Simplify your grammar and vocabulary. Use shorter sentences, but don't "talk down."

- Be a good communications model by using clear diction and correct grammar.

- Include children in group activities, but don't call on a child unless he volunteers.

- Set aside a specific time each day for language and literacy but also incorporate language into routines and other activities.

- Encourage children to communicate by increasing their self-confidence and interest in their environment.

- Select activities that support noncompetitive peer interaction.

- Create a need for speech. Do not always respond to a child who is just pointing if he can speak.

- Talk with children about what they are doing; build vocabulary.

- Reinforce learning through visual and tactile experiences.

- Be an attentive listener.

- If you can't understand a child's speech, reinforce the child's attempts at communication and then be honest and say, "I'm having trouble understanding you. Can you tell me in different words?"

Table PIII–5: Children who are English language learners

- Support children in learning their home language as well as learning English.

- Label items in the classroom in English and the home languages of the children in the class.

- If possible, have educators in the classroom who are bilingual and bicultural.

- Be a good language model. Use correct English supported by props and gestures as needed.

- Keep large group times short and encourage small group learning.

- Support demonstrations or modeling with appropriate language.

- Have a language-rich, culture-rich environment.

- Provide books in the languages of the children in the class.

- Teach about the culture and traditions of the children in the class.

Table PIII–6: Children with autistic spectrum disorders

- Make your face and your voice congruent. When you are happy, look and sound happy. When you are not happy, use a stern voice and grumpy facial expression.

- Give clear, specific directions for all tasks, one step at a time.

- Simplify your language.

- Use many visual cues. Present tasks visually, highlight written information, and provide visual (tape) boundaries for sitting.

- Eliminate visual distractions.

- Check the environment for auditory distractions.

- Teach social skills.

- Allow children to be alone some of the time.

- Give children a fidget item to play with when they are listening.

- Ask (or tell) children before you touch them. Use deep pressure.

- Be patient. Learning and relationships take time to build.

Table PIII–7: Children with intellectual disabilities

- Use as many senses to teach as possible.

- Help children over-learn concepts by presenting interesting variations of principles.

- Teach a concept for a short time each day for many days rather than a long time for a few days.

- Evaluate the utility of materials, tasks, and skills and begin with the most functional ones. Learning should be essential and fun.

- Teach concepts that are relevant and familiar first, and then work toward the less familiar.

- Use several examples to teach a concept (*red*: apples, balls, books, crayons).

- Sequence learning from simple to complex.

- Use a task analysis to break down complex tasks into their component parts.

- Use backward chaining so children have the satisfaction of completing a task.

- Support the child in learning at a rate that is possible for that child, while at the same time including him in group activities and planning.

- Encourage children to participate in the same activity at different levels.

Table PIII–8: Children who are gifted and talented

- Plan activities that children can work on together but at different levels of complexity.

- Avoid pressure to conform by asking open-ended questions, not yes-no questions.

- Teach socially acceptable ways of handling emotions.

- Model acceptance. Smile, clap, use verbal praise, and high fives, to support children.

- Provide a variety of activities and experiences that encourage exploration of interests and allow depth and concentration.

- Increase complexity by adding materials and expanding the time frame.

- Provide activities and problems that require divergent thinking.

- Emphasize how and why things occur and what children (or others) can do to change them.

- Make up new endings for stories, take a different perspective, and so on.

- Emphasize group and individual brainstorming and problem solving.

- Encourage children to do activities in different ways and reflect on the differences.

- Allow children to choose some themes.

Table PIII–9: Children with special health care needs

- Find out as much as possible about a child's health (diet, physical restrictions, medication and its possible side effects, and behaviors indicating an illness is becoming acute).

- Find out what children have been told about their illness and its implications.

- Use activities that allow children to be in control or adapt activities so that children have more control.

- Encourage age-appropriate independence and allow the children to do as much as possible for themselves.

- Arrange the schedule so that vigorous activities are followed by less strenuous ones. If necessary, provide short breaks for everyone.

- Organize your routine so that children can leave for medical procedures. Treat these departures as you would any transition.

- Allow children returning from an illness to come initially for part of the day, working back up to a full day.

- Plan some open-ended activities and some that can be completed at home if necessary.

- Observe children. Watch for mood changes and body language indicating pain, fatigue, or reactions to medication.

- Help children learn about the implications of their special health care needs. Verbalize this for them.

- Provide an atmosphere where children can discuss fears and problems.

Children with special health care needs can be active
participants in the classroom with the needed supports.

Table PIII–10: Children with orthopedic and neurologic impairments

- Learn about a child's particular disability and the objectives of therapy. Know the child's competence in independent mobility and transferring.

- Learn how to safely lift and transfer a child with another adult, and alone if necessary.

- Learn how wheelchairs work in general and how the particular wheelchair a child uses works. Regardless of type, *put on the brakes* before placing a child in or taking a child out of a wheelchair.

- Learn what equipment children can use for variety in positioning and how to use it (beanbag chairs, bolsters, wedges).

- Attach baskets to walkers or have bags with shoulder straps or knapsacks available to carry materials.

- Have assistive devices available to reach objects, turn pages, and so on.

- Have large versions of manipulative toys and puzzles with knobs.

- Keep toys and materials picked up and off the floor.

- Encourage tactile exploration.

- Demonstrate how to explore new materials. Support children in learning about new materials and exploring them.

- Provide spaces wide enough for activities and movement, including space for mobility aids.

- Evaluate classroom doors, bathrooms, and passageways for accessibility as well as the building itself. Do this for field trips, too.

Table PIII–11: Children with hearing impairments

- Face the child, and bring yourself to the child's eye level.

- Make your lips clearly visible (wear lipstick, trim or shave a mustache or beard).

- Keep bright lights out of children's eyes. Avoid fluorescent lights, if possible.

- Attract the child's attention *before* you begin speaking. Make eye contact or use a visual signal or touch to get the child's attention, but don't scare the child.

- Speak in a normal voice to aid speech reading.

- Use appropriate expressive body language, including gestures and pointing.

- Reduce background noise; ask other children to talk or play more quietly. Remember that a hearing aid does not correct a hearing impairment.

- If you repeat a word that is not understood, try a different one.

- Use as many visual aids as possible.

- If a child cannot see to read your lips when you are using audiovisual aids, be sure the child sits close to the sound source. Use closed-captioned aids, when possible.

- In group activities, place the child across from you (where she has the best view), with the child's back to the windows.

- Learn significant signs or cues to communicate with the child.

- Learn how to work with and use an interpreter.

Table PIII–12: Children with visual impairments

Corrected Visual Impairments

- Find out when and for how long corrective lenses must be worn.

- Observe and record the child's behavior with the visual aids (removing eyeglasses, position relative to materials, headaches) and share these observations with parents.

- Create a need to see and a reason for a child to wear glasses to see better.

- Support children wearing glasses. Discuss name-calling and alternatives.

Visual Limitations

- Find out the level of a child's usable vision.

- Use verbal and tactile supports and rewards.

- Be aware of lighting conditions; arrange seating to benefit from lighting. Use natural light but regulate it with blinds.

- Use black marker to outline paper; other surfaces that need to stand out should be high contrast.

- Have a variety of books, including some with large print, and Braille.

- Use materials with distinctive shapes and textures that have high-contrasting colors.

- Keep furniture in the same place and materials picked up.

- Have children practice giving and following directions.

- Teach location by referring to the numbers on a clock face.

Use these guidelines to further adapt activities to include all children.

List of Activities

Activity Goals and Activity Numbers in Text and Online
Goals Activity Numbers (w indicates activities on the web)

Social Awareness

To improve self-concept   1–1, 1–2, 1–5, 1–6, 1–8, 1–25, 1–26, 1–29
1–31w, 1–32w, 1–33w, 1–34w, 1–36w, 1–37w, 1–39w

To increase awareness of roles people play   1–2, 1–5, 1–25, 1–26, 1–27, 1–28, 1–29, 1–30, 5–27, 5–28, 5–29
1–31w, 1–32w, 1–33w, 1–36w, 1–37w, 1–46w, 1–47w, 1–48w, 1–49w, 5–48w

To broaden concepts of family   1–1, 1–5, 1–6, 1–14, 1–24
1–31w, 1–32w, 1–33w, 1–34w, 1–37w, 1–38w, 1–39w

To increase inclusion   1–2, 1–3, 1–8, 1–9, 1–10, 1–11, 1–12, 1–13, 1–14, 1–15, 1–16, 1–17, 1–19, 1–20, 1–21, 1–22, 1–23, 1–25, 1–26, 1–27, 1–28, 2–2, 2–3, 2–5, 2–10, 2–24, 4–18, 4–19, 4–20, 5–9, 5–10, 5–23, 5–26, 5–30
1–40w, 1–42w, 1–43w, 1–44w, 1–45w, 1–46w, 1–47w, 2–32w, 4–31w, 5–45w

To increase awareness of individual differences and similarities   1–3, 1–7, 1–10, 1–11, 1–13, 1–15, 1–16, 1–17, 1–18, 1–19, 1–20, 1–21, 1–22, 1–23, 1–30
1–38w, 1–40w, 1–41w, 1–42w, 1–43w, 1–45w, 1–46w

To increase cultural awareness   1–1, 1–7, 1–14, 1–18, 1–24
1–38w, 1–39w, 1–44w, 1–48w

To understand geography concepts   1–9
1–47w, 1–50w, 1–51w

Language and Literacy

To improve expressive communication   1–4, 2–1, 2–2, 2–3, 2–5
1–36w, 1–44w, 2–31w, 2–32w, 2–33w, 2–34w, 2–35w, 2–36w, 2–37w, 2–40w, 2–41w

To improve listening skills   2–7, 2–8, 2–9, 2–10, 2–11
2–31w, 2–43w, 2–44w, 2–45w, 2–46w, 2–47w, 2–48w, 2–49w, 2–50w, 2–51w

To increase knowledge of the structure of language   2–4, 2–7, 2–14, 2–15, 2–21, 2–25
2–32w, 2–37w, 2–38w

To improve receptive communication   2–1, 2–7, 2–13
2–42w, 2–43w, 2–45w, 2–46w, 2–47w

To improve reading literacy   2–4, 2–12, 2–13, 2–14, 2–15, 2–16, 2–17, 2–18, 2–19, 2–20, 2–21, 2–22, 2–23, 2–24, 2–28, 2–29, 2–30, 3–1, 3–3, 3–5, 3–11, 3–24, 3–25, 3–26, 3–27, 3–28, 3–29
2–53w, 2–52w, 2–55w, 2–56w, 2–58w, 3–31w, 3–32w, 3–33w, 3–40w

To increase vocabulary   2–1, 2–6, 2–13, 3–1, 3–2, 4–3, 4–15, 4–16, 4–24, 4–27
2–34w, 2–38w, 2–39w, 2–40w, 2–41w, 3–56w, 4–33w

To increase respect for diversity in modes of communication   1–7, 1–10, 1–11, 1–16, 1–18, 1–22, 2–10, 2–12
1–35w, 1–49w, 2–45w

To use diverse print and nonprint sources and genres   2–2, 2–27, 2–28, 2–29, 2–30
2–33w, 2–54w, 2–56w, 2–57w

To increase phonemic awareness   2–4, 2–12, 2–13, 2–14, 2–16, 2–23
2–38w

To increase writing literacy   2–19, 2–25, 2–26, 2–27, 2–28, 2–29, 2–30
2–56w, 2–57w

To increase comprehension   2–6, 2–8, 2–15, 2–25, 5–17, 5–18
2–36w, 2–42w, 2–44w, 2–46w, 2–47w, 2–52w, 2–53w, 5–47w

To follow directions   2–18, 3–23, 3–28, 3–29, 3–30
2–37w, 2–42w, 3–40w, 3–44w

To improve memory skills   2–11, 2–17, 2–20, 2–22, 2–24
2–52w

Discovery

To improve number sense and numeration   3–1, 3–2, 3–3, 3–4, 3–5, 3–10
3–31w, 3–32w, 3–13w, 3–34w, 3–35w, 3–43w

To improve geometric and spatial sense   3–6
3–33w, 3–34w, 3–36w, 3–37w, 3–38w, 3–39w, 3–40w, 3–41w

To improve measurement concepts   3–7, 3–17, 3–30
3–35w, 3–36w, 3–37w, 3–39w, 3–42w

To improve estimation skills   3–5, 3–8, 3–10, 3–11, 3–12
3–32w, 3–42w, 3–46w, 3–47w, 3–49w

To identify and understand patterns and relationships   2–17, 2–18, 2–21, 3–4, 3–6, 3–8, 3–19, 3–25, 3–26, 3–27, 4–29, 5–7, 5–19
2–50w, 2–51w, 2–53w, 3–35w, 3–36w, 3–37w, 3–41w, 4–41w, 4–42w, 4–43w, 5–31w, 5–33w, 5–37w, 5–43w, 5–48w

To improve knowledge of whole number operations and computations   3–3, 3–8, 3–9, 3–11
3–31w, 3–43w, 3–46w, 3–47w, 3–48w

To improve knowledge of fractions and decimals   3–2
3–44w, 3–45w

To improve observational skills   1–19, 3–10, 3–13, 3–14, 3–15, 3–16, 3–17, 3–21
1–35w, 3–45w, 3–49w, 3–50w, 3–51w, 3–52w, 3–53w

To improve classification skills   2–8, 3–6, 3–7, 3–15, 3–18, 3–19, 3–20
2–31w, 2–36w, 2–40w, 3–34w, 3–38w, 3–41w, 3–42w, 3–49w, 3–50w

To improve cause-and-effect reasoning   1–9, 1–12, 1–13, 2–9, 3–9, 3–13, 3–11, 3–20, 3–22, 3–23, 4–1, 4–2, 4–4, 4–5, 4–25, 5–1, 5–5, 5–6, 5–11, 5–25, 5–29
1–34w, 1–48w, 1–51w, 2–35w, 2–48w, 2–49w, 3–50w, 3–51w, 3–52w, 3–53w, 3–54w, 3–55w, 4–32w, 5–37w, 5–42w, 5–45w, 5–48w

To improve generalization skills   3–14, 3–18, 3–19, 3–21, 3–22, 3–24
3–37w

To increase knowledge of the natural world   3–14, 3–15, 3–18, 3–21
3–47w, 3–49w, 3–54w, 3–56w

To make predictions   2–11, 2–20, 2–22, 3–9, 3–16, 3–20, 4–6, 4–8, 4–12
2–48w, 2–49w, 2–51w, 3–51w, 3–52w, 3–54w, 3–55w, 3–56w, 4–31w, 4–34w

To improve technology skills   3–17, 3–22, 3–23, 3–24, 3–25, 3–26, 3–27, 3–28, 3–29, 3–30
3–43w, 3–55w

To increase thinking and reasoning skills   1–4, 3–7, 3–12
1–40w, 3–38w

Wellness

To improve health literacy   4–1, 4–2, 4–3, 4–4, 4–5, 4–26
4–31w, 4–32w, 4–33w, 4–34w

To increase adaptive skills   4–1, 4–2, 4–4, 4–5, 4–15, 4–16, 4–17
4–31w, 4–32w, 4–33w, 4–34w, 4–42w

To improve locomotor skills   1–21, 4–6, 4–7, 4–8, 4–10, 4–13
1–45w, 4–35w, 4–37w

To improve gross motor manipulative skills   4–11, 4–12, 4–23, 4–24
4–36w, 4–40w, 4–44w

To improve stability skills   4–9, 4–13, 4–21, 4–24, 4–25
4–38w

To improve physical fitness   4–6, 4–7, 4–10, 4–13
4–38w, 4–39w, 4–40w

To improve sensory motor integration   2–16, 2–19, 2–23, 2–26, 2–27, 3–4, 3–12, 3–13, 4–9, 4–14, 4–20, 4–21, 4–22, 4–23, 4–25, 4–26, 4–27, 4–28, 4–29, 4–30, 5–15, 5–21, 5–22, 5–24, 5–25, 5–30
2–41w, 2–44w, 2–50w, 2–54w, 2–55w, 3–39w, 3–44w, 3–45w, 3–48w, 3–53w, 4–35w, 4–36w, 4–38w, 4–39w, 4–44w, 5–46w

To improve motor planning   4–7, 4–8, 4–9, 4–11, 4–20, 4–21, 4–22, 4–23
4–35w, 4–36w, 4–37w, 4–39w, 4–40w, 4–44w

To increase body awareness   1–17, 1–20, 1–23, 4–3, 4–10, 4–18, 4–19, 4–22, 4–26, 5–24, 5–25, 5–26
1–41w, 4–38w, 5–44w

To improve fine motor manipulative skills   4–14, 4–15, 4–16, 4–17, 4–18, 4–19, 4–28, 4–30
4–42w, 4–43w

To improve eye-hand coordination   4–11, 4–12, 4–17, 4–29
4–41w, 4–43w

To improve tactile skills   4–14, 4–27, 4–28, 4–30
4–41w

Creative Arts

To use different art media, techniques, and processes   5–1, 5–2, 5–3, 5–4, 5–5, 5–6, 5-7, 5–8, 5–9, 5–10, 5–11
5–31w, 5–32w, 5–33w, 5–34w, 5–35w, 5–36w, 5–37w, 5–38w

To understand the structures and functions of art   5–2, 5–3
5–31w, 5–34w, 5–35w

To understand art in a cultural and historical context   5–4, 5–5
5–32w, 5–33w, 5–41w

To use the arts to express a range of subject matter, symbols, and ideas   5–2, 5–3, 5–4, 5–6, 5-7, 5–8, 5–12
5–36w, 5–39w

To connect the arts and other disciplines   5–1, 5–10, 5–11
5–32w, 5–38w, 5–39w

To listen, analyze, describe, and respond to music   5–13, 5–14, 5–15, 5–17, 5–18, 5–20, 5–21, 5–22
5–40w, 5–41w, 5–43w, 5–46w

To read and interpret music   5–14, 5–16
5–40w

To perform on instruments alone and with others   5–14, 5–16, 5–20
5–41w, 5–42w

To sing alone and with others   5–19, 5–20, 5–23
5–43w, 5–44w

To appreciate a varied repertoire of music   5–16, 5–17, 5–18, 5–19, 5–21, 5–23
5–40w, 5–42w, 5–44w

To develop creative movement   5–13, 5–15, 5–22, 5–24, 5–26
5–45w

To encourage problem solving   1–3, 1–4, 1–29, 5–27, 5–28, 5–29
1–35w, 1–50w, 1–51w, 5–34w, 5–38w, 5–47w

To encourage creativity   2–6, 5–8
2–33w, 2–34w, 2–35w, 2–39w, 2–43w 5–35w, 5–36w, 5–46w

To improve self-concept   5–9, 5–12, 5–30
5–47w

To express feelings   1–8, 1–12, 1–15, 2–3, 2–5, 5–12, 5–13, 5–27, 5–28
1–42w, 1–43w, 2–55w, 5–39w

Goals and Activity for Infants and Toddlers

To increase social awareness   6–1, 6–2, 6–3, 6–4, 6–5, 6–6, 6–15, 6–25, 6–30
6–31w, 6–32w, 6–33w, 6–34w, 6–36w, 6–42w, 6–43w, 6–52w, 6–54w, 6–63w

To increase language and communication skills   6–3, 6–5, 6–7, 6–8, 6–9, 6–10, 6–11, 6–12, 6–16, 6–18, 6–23, 6–28
6–32w, 6–34w, 6–35w, 6–36w, 6–37w, 6–38w, 6–39w, 6–40w, 6–41w, 6–42w,
6–52w, 5–53w, 6–58w

To increase cognitive development   6–1, 6–7, 6–8, 6–13, 6–14, 6–15, 6–16, 6–17, 6–18, 6–19, 6–20, 6–21, 6–22, 6–24
6–35w, 6–38w, 6–43w, 6–44w, 6–45w, 6–46w, 6–47w, 6–48w, 6–49w, 6–50w, 6–51w,
6–55w, 6–56w, 6–57w

To increase sensory motor skills   6–2, 6–4, 6–5, 6–6, 6–9, 6–10, 6–12, 6–13, 6–14, 6–17, 6–18, 6–19, 6–20, 6–21, 6–22, 6–23,
6–24, 6–25, 6–26, 6–27, 6–29
6–31w, 6–32w, 6–33w, 6–34w, 6–35w, 6–36w, 6–39w, 6–40w, 6–41w, 6–44w, 6–45w, 6–46w,
6–47w, 6–48w, 6–49w, 6–50w, 6–51w, 6–52w, 6–53w, 6–54w, 6–55w, 6–56w, 6–57w, 6–58w,
6–59w, 6–60w, 6–61w, 6–62w

To increase creative development   6–10, 6–11, 6–25, 6–26, 6–27, 6–28, 6–29, 6–30
6–58w, 6–59w, 6–60w, 6–61w, 6–62w, 6–63w

Infant and Toddler Activities by Age

Young infants (birth to 9 months)   6–1, 6–2, 6–7, 6–8, 6–13, 6–14, 6–18, 6–20, 6–25, 6–26
6–31w, 6–32w, 6–35w, 6–43w, 6–44w, 6–49w, 6–50w

Mobile infants (8 to 18 months)   6–3, 6–4, 6–9, 6–10, 6–15, 6–16, 6–21, 6–22, 6–27, 6–28
6–33w, 6–45w, 6–46w, 6–51w

Mobile infants and toddlers (8 to 36 months)   6–52w, 6–53w, 6–54, 6–58w, 6–59w

Toddlers (16 to 36 months)   6–5, 6–6, 6–11, 6–12, 6–17, 6–18, 6–23, 6–24, 6–29, 6–30
6–36w, 6–37w, 6–38w, 6–39w, 6–40w, 6–41w, 6–42w, 6–43w, 6–47w, 6–48w, 6–55w, 6–56w,
6–57w, 6–60, 6–61w, 6–62w, 6–63w

Social Awareness Activities:

Self-Esteem, Inclusion, and Social Studies

Social awareness for young children is designed to help them understand and function in the world in which they live. During their early years, children are developing their values and attitudes about themselves, other children, and their family and community, and the world. They are developing a concept of self. It is important that they have a broad range of experiences and are exposed to people and materials without gender, racial, ability, or cultural bias. People with disabilities must be portrayed accurately, including both their abilities and disabilities.

Activity Goals

Activities are organized by the goals they support. Activities that focus directly on social awareness are given first. The activity number is provided after the goal to make finding the activity more efficient. The activities that are in the book have their number identified; those that are in the Online Companion are followed by a "w" (refer to Table R1-1).

Social Awareness Guidelines

The following guidelines will be helpful as you think about adapting social awareness activities to meet the needs of children with diverse abilities.

Adapting activities for children with:	
Specific learning disabilities	Encourage them to use a variety of solutions to problems. Actively promote prosocial skills. Focus on what children can do and support their doing it.
Social, emotional, and behavioral disorder	Make school a familiar, safe, and predictable place. Prepare children for change. Discuss ways of dealing with feelings.
Attention-deficit/hyperactivity disorder	Work on conflict resolution skills. Use short activities, brief lessons, and break information into small chunks. Present information sequentially rather than all at once.
Communication disorders	Plan a language rich environment that increases children's knowledge of the roles people play and the variety of ways people communicate.
English language learners	Use field trips to provide first-hand cultural and language experiences. Discuss the cultural and ethnic groups of the children in the class and the languages they speak at home as a way of including all children.

Autism spectrum disorders	Help children engage in relationships with other children and adults. Support children in taking an interest in the sights, sounds, and sensations of the environment. Help children learn to self-regulate their behavior.
Intellectual disabilities	Give children tasks they can accomplish and roles to help them be part of the group. Build on familiar experiences. Highlight what children can accomplish.
Gifts and talents	Promote social skills, help children take different perspectives on social situations. Support children who take intellectual risks.
Special health care needs	Expand children's knowledge of the medical community in ways that give them some control. Develop methods (notes, telephone calls, e-mail) of keeping children in touch with their peers.
Orthopedic and neurologic impairments	Use field trips to help children learn about their environment and technology, and visitors to support learning about inaccessible places. Teach about accessibility and how it is important to many groups of people (babies in strollers, older people, and so on).
Hearing impairments	Teach children verbal and nonverbal ways of approaching others. Use visual aids to clarify and generalize experiences.
Visual impairments	Include a variety of role models, including those who wear glasses and use optical devices. Use technology to expand children's world. Help children learn to use their residual vision. Provide many opportunities to develop the sense of touch.

Table R1–1: Activity goals and activity numbers in text and online

Goals	Activity Numbers
• To improve self-concept	1–1,1–2,1–5,1–6, 1–8, 1–25, 1–26, 1–29 1–31w, 1–32w, 1–33w,1–34w, 1–36w, 1–37w, 1–39w
• To increase awareness of roles people play	1–2, 1–5, 1–25, 1–26, 1–27, 1–28, 1–29, 1–30 1–31w, 1–32w, 1–33w, 1–36w, 1–37w, 1–46w, 1–47w, 1–48w, 1–49w
• To broaden concepts of family	1–1, 1–5, 1–6, 1–14, 1–24 1–31w, 1–32w, 1–33w, 1–34w, 1–37w, 1–38w, 1–39w
• To increase inclusion	1–2, 1–3, 1–8, 1–9, 1–10, 1–11, 1–12, 1–13, 1–14, 1–15, 1–16, 1–17, 1–19, 1–20, 1–21, 1–22, 1–23, 1–25, 1–26, 1–27, 1–28 1–40w, 1–42w, 1–43w, 1–44w, 1–45w, 1–46w, 1–47w
• To increase awareness of individual differences and similarities	1–3, 1–7, 1–10, 1–11, 1–13, 1–15, 1–16, 1–17, 1–18, 1–19, 1–20, 1–21, 1–22, 1–23, 1–30 1–38w, 1–40w, 1–41w, 1–42w, 1–43w, 1–45w, 1–46w
• To increase cultural awareness	1–1, 1–7, 1–14, 1–18, 1–24 1–38w, 1–39w, 1–44w, 1–48w
• To understand geography concepts	1–9 1–47w, 1–50w, 1–51w
• To increase thinking and reasoning skills	1–4 1–40w
• To encourage problem solving	1–3, 1–4, 1–29 1–35w, 1–50w, 1–51w
• To express feelings	1–8, 1–12, 1–15 1–42w, 1–43w
• To improve expressive communication	1–4 1–36w, 1–44w

- To increase respect for diversity in modes of communication

  1–7, 1–10, 1–11, 1–16, 1–18, 1–22

  1–35w, 1–49w

- To improve observational skills

  1–19

  1–35w

- To improve cause-and-effect reasoning

  1–9, 1–12, 1–13

  1–34w, 1–48w, 1–51w

- To improve locomotor skills

  1–21

  1–45w

- To increase body awareness

  1–17, 1–20, 1–23

  1–41w

Social Awareness Activities

Self-Esteem: Large Group

1-1 Celebrations

Goals: To improve self-concept; to broaden concepts of family; to increase cultural awareness

Materials: None (unless the child wants to bring in something)

Procedure: Talk with children about how their families celebrate particular holidays. Then choose one or two children to act out their families' celebrations for the group. Include different holidays, birthdays, and celebrations. Be sure to discuss feelings, excitement, and expectations. Discuss how families have different ways of celebrating as well as different occasions that are celebrated. Encourage children to have family members or others come to talk about the celebrations as well. Plan some special activities and snacks that support the learning experience.

Assessment: The child will verbally describe one occasion celebrated in her family.

Accommodations and Integration: Discuss celebrations, why people look forward to them, their significance, and why they can be stressful events. Talk about appropriate ways to deal with the stress that accompanies both joy and disappointment. Talk about the role of marker events and the various reasons for celebration. Discuss both formal and informal celebrations. If there are children in your class who do not celebrate holidays find out from them and their families how they want to share this information.

Self-Esteem: Small Group

1-2 Get Well Cards

Goals: To improve self-concept; to increase awareness of roles people play; to increase inclusion

Materials: Construction paper, crayons or markers, computer, digital camera

Procedure: Have the children make drawings or paintings of their choice on a folded piece of construction paper. They can make either two pictures (front and inside of card) or one picture with a written message. Talk with the children about the particular illness the child has and the kinds of activities that child particularly likes. Encourage children to write (or dictate) a message.

Assessment: The child will write or dictate an appropriate message for a card.

Accommodations and Integration: Use a computer and printer to generate the card or take a picture with a digital camera, print it, and add a message. Be specific about the purpose of the card and the types of messages that are appropriate. Make the first card for a specific child; then start a collection of get-well cards so you will always have a card to send when the occasion arises. After a while, children may notice that certain members of the class are absent more often than others. Talk about this.

Self-Esteem: Small Group

1-3 No Words

Goals: To increase awareness of individual differences and similarities; to increase inclusion; to encourage problem solving

Materials: None

Procedure: Have a discussion about how animals and people communicate without using words.

Bees	dance to help other bees find honey
Dogs	bark, wag tails
Birds	chirp, sing
People	gesture

Give one child in the class instructions for a task the group must perform. Have this child get the other children to carry out the task without using words. Initially, all the children could do the same thing, for example, go to the bathroom and wash their hands. Make the tasks easy and have a pair of children convey the message. As the children get better, assign more difficult tasks.

Assessment: The child will use body language to communicate with classmates and then discuss how the experience made him feel.

Accommodations and Integration: Discuss specific traditional nonverbal strategies used to communicate (waving for good-bye, throwing a kiss, making a circle of the thumb and index finger, high five) and ensure that children know their meaning. Talk about cultural variations in nonverbal language (eye contact, open or closed hand gestures) and their meaning during interactions. Talk about American Sign Language and why it is used. Teach children some signs. Discuss the differences between nonverbal and verbal "language," especially as they relate conveying information. Discussion communication in general and how difficult it is to express yourself when you do not know the right words to say.

Self-Esteem: Small Group

1-4 One More

Goals: To encourage problem solving; to improve expressive communication; to increase thinking and reasoning skills

Materials: None

Procedure: Make up hypothetical situations or use actual problems that have occurred in the classroom. The situations can relate to peer relationships, sharing materials, time with the teacher, and so forth. For example, if two children want the same toy, ask them for a solution, and then ask, "What else could you do?" See if children can generate at least four different alternatives to consider. Do not give children solutions or judge their answers as inappropriate, although they may seem outlandish to you—unless they are dangerous. It is important that children learn to generate alternatives as a way of coping. Expand the scope of the problems. Help children evaluate the probable outcome of each solution and decide which they might try first.

Assessment: The child will state four solutions to a problem described by the teacher.

Accommodations and Integration: Children with diverse abilities may encounter more challenges than other children may. They need a repertoire of potential solutions and consequences. Use this technique to deal with problems that occur in your classroom. Have children role-play the situation, trying out different solutions. Have children coach each other and provide feedback. The more complex situations children are in, the more likely they will need to find solutions to problems. They may need to try several options before they find one that works. Give them the foundation for generating solutions to problems and thinking them through.

1-5 Family Book

Goals: To improve self-concept; to broaden concepts of family; to increase awareness of the roles people play

Materials: Three-ring binder, plastic sleeve protectors, black construction paper to fit inside sleeve protectors, tape and pictures of family members for each child in the class, digital camera

Procedure: Have children bring in pictures of family, friends, and themselves. Give them a piece of black paper and tape and ask them to make a collage with the pictures keeping the faces visible. Place the picture-covered papers into plastic sleeve protector and into a three-ring binder. Encourage children to look at and talk about the pictures.

Support children in talking about their families and how they have fun together.

Assessment: The child will tape pictures of her family and friends onto a piece of paper and add the paper to a class book about families and friends.

Accommodations and Integration: Help children with the selection and pasting process. Encourage children who do not bring pictures from home to draw their family members and friends, or take digital pictures of their friends at school to include in the book. Encourage children to look at these pictures with other children when they are concerned about family members or miss them during the school day. This allows children to talk about important people in their lives, as well as important people in their classmates' lives.

1-6 Family Collage

Goals: To improve self-concept; to broaden concepts of family; to increase awareness of the roles people play

Materials: Magazines, scissors, construction paper, glue or glue stick

Procedure: Give children magazines, scissors, glue sticks, and a piece of construction paper. Explain that they are going to create families. Talk about what members might constitute a family. Encourage children to have a broad definition of family. Let the children cut out a variety of pictures from magazines and paste them onto construction paper. Have children discuss why they included different members in their families, and the roles of included members.

Assessment: The child will cut out pictures of people from magazines and paste them on a piece of paper to form families.

Accommodations and Integration: Encourage children to make pictures of different families they know, and ask them to compare and contrast the families with their own family. Let children choose pictures but help them cut out or tear out the people they choose if necessary. This helps children realize that families are unique as well as similar.

1-7 Hello Poem

Goals: To increase awareness of individual differences and similarities; to increase cultural awareness; to increase respect for diversity in modes of communication

Materials: None

Procedure: Talk with the children about how people can speak differently but say the same things. Introduce the "Hello Poem," using motions to help the children get involved. Replace "hello" with "hello" in Spanish, Chinese, or another language including the languages of the children in the classroom.

Hello (poem)

Hello's a handy word to say,
At least 100 times a day.
Without hello what would I do
Whenever I bumped into you?
Without hello where would you be
Whenever you bumped into me?
Hello's a handy word to know.
Hello. Hello. Hello. Hello.

HELLO IN OTHER LANGUAGES

Mandarin—kneeha	Korean—anyorg
Asian Indian—key ayo	German—guten tag
Japanese—ohay o	Turkish—marhabah
Russian—pree veyet	Finnish—tear vay
Spanish—hola	French—bonjour

Assessment: The children will sing the "Hello Poem," substituting the English "hello" with "hello" in other languages.

Accommodations and Integration: Shorten the poem. Have children become familiar with the poem before they try it in other languages. Fingerspell hello. This allows children to hear and speak different languages and still be understood. Use this as a platform to talk about other languages. Be sure to include the languages of all children in the class.

Inclusion: Small Group

1-8 Share Your Feelings

Goals: To increase inclusion; to improve self-concept; to express feelings

Materials: None

Procedure: After the children have discussed feelings and expressions, ask them to share a feeling with the other children, for example, liking. Some ways the children might share this are to hold hands, smile, hug, say "I like you," and so on. Support children in expressing feelings with their peers and knowing that they are valued members of the class. Give children the vocabulary they need to express their feelings accurately. Help them think of a variety of ways to share feelings, both verbal and nonverbal.

Assessment: The child can perform the appropriate actions for a variety of feelings.

Accommodations and Integration: Model feelings and behaviors as you state what you are doing. "I'm so glad to see Richea I am giving her a high five." Coach children on expressing their feelings. Encourage children to ask others for feedback or clarification about how they interpret the behavior. Sharing feelings is not usual in some cultures. At first, older children might feel self-conscious doing this, but if you demonstrate and support them, they may learn that they can share feelings at school.

Inclusion: Small Group or Individual

1-9 Wheels

Goals: To increase inclusion; to improve cause-and-effect reasoning; to understand geography concepts

Materials: Familiar objects with wheels: inline skates, wagons, tricycles, roller skates, skateboards, wheelchairs, creepers, scooters, suitcases, backpacks, dollies

Procedure: Discuss the function of wheels and encourage children to experiment moving on or using things with wheels. If you have shelves on wheels, compare moving those shelves with shelves not on wheels. Help children experiment by using rollers to move objects. When you are outside, keep the wheels of a tricycle or wagon from turning by putting something through the spokes and discuss how this affects its movement. Be sure to include a wheelchair. Talk about brakes and the function they serve. Map out a course that requires turns, and have children use wheeled objects to traverse the course. Ask about what is easy and difficult for them.

Assessment: The child will state the function of wheels and how they are useful.

Accommodations and Integration: Encourage children to experiment with the wheelchair, to go from one place to another. Be sure it includes going up and down a ramp (with close adult supervision). Talk about the energy it takes to use a wheelchair and how this is different from using a tricycle or a scooter. If possible, have someone who does wheelchair sports visit and demonstrate his skills. Children can learn about the functions wheels play in moving and become aware of the implications of using a wheelchair, of curb cuts, and so on.

Inclusion: Small Group

1-10 Finger Spelling Lotto

Goals: To increase awareness of individual differences and similarities; to increase inclusion; to increase respect for diversity in modes of communication

Materials: Alphabet Lotto cards with Ameslan signs for each letter

Procedure: Make a Lotto game using the letters of the alphabet and the manual signs for those letters. Encourage the children to make the sign with their hands as they match the cards. Have the children fingerspell their names.

Assessment: The child will match letters to Ameslan signs for the letters.

Accommodations and Integration: Start with fewer letters where the signs have a visual resemblance to the letters they represent (*c, d, l, m, n, o, v*). Have the children spell words using the signs. This shows children a potential avenue of communication and another representation of language.

Inclusion: Small Group

1-11 Mufflers

Goals: To increase awareness of individual differences and similarities; to increase inclusion; to increase respect for diversity in modes of communication

Materials: Earmuffs or cotton balls, tapes or CD and tape recorder or CD player

Procedure: Set up the dramatic play area in the usual way. Have the children wear earmuffs or put cotton balls in their ears and tell them to whisper while playing instead of talking out loud. Have a tape playing in the background to make it more difficult to hear. Follow this activity with a discussion at group time where you talk softly while the music is playing. If the children get frustrated or restless, go back to your normal style. Talk about how hard it is to cooperate with others and to pay attention when you can't hear.

Assessment: The child will communicate how he feels when it is difficult to hear.

Accommodations and Integration: Do this only for a short time. Help children focus on what they do differently when they cannot hear. Children will begin to understand the implications and frustrations of not being able to hear or understand what is going on around them.

Inclusion: Small Group

1-12 Feelings

Goals: To increase inclusion; to express feelings; to improve cause-and-effect reasoning

Materials: Paper, crayons, markers, scissors, old magazines

Procedure: Have children make a book about situations in which they were sad (or angry, unhappy, or mad). Have a group discussion and talk about how children might feel if a lot of sad things happen at one time, how hard it would be to be happy, and how they might be scared and expect sad things to happen. Talk about what children can do to help themselves when they feel sad. Encourage children to talk in greater depth and to distinguish short- and long-term emotions. Have them discuss how the actions and reactions of others influence their response.

Assessment: The child will draw a picture of a person and/or situation to show anger, sadness, and/or other negative emotions.

Accommodations and Integration: Start with pictures of two relatively obvious situations and ask children which one they think would make them feel happy. Do the same with other emotions. Move from the more obvious (happy, sad, angry) to embarrassed, jealous, and so on. This helps children realize that all people, including adults, have bad days. Help them differentiate a bad day from a pattern of negative emotions that might cause children to either withdraw or become aggressive.

Inclusion: Large or Small Group

1-13 Tired

Goals: To increase awareness of individual differences and similarities; to increase inclusion; to improve cause-and-effect reasoning

Materials: None

Procedure: Encourage children to run jump, march vigorously until they are tired (at least breathless). This will require your support and participation. It will take 3 to 6 minutes depending upon the age of the children. Then have them list the activities they would not want to do right away (run more, climb fast) and those they would do (listen to a story or music). Talk about how children differ in how easily they get tired and how it is not fun to play actively when you are tired. Encourage children to talk about the difference between what they do not want to do because of lack of energy and tasks they just do not like (cleaning their room, picking up in general). Ask them if they ever use being tired as an excuse. Do they ever not believe others who say they are tired?

Assessment: The child will state two activities that she might not want to do when she is tired, and give reasons why.

Accommodations and Integration: Point out the specific characteristics of being tired and how they vary with different activities: running legs might feel wobbly, heart rate up, and shortness of breath. Talk about medicine and how you can be tired from taking medicine. Discuss the body's reactions to different medicine (listlessness, sleepy, low energy, difficulty sleeping at night, and so on). Start with what children want to do then expand the discussion to what would be difficult if they could not sleep, or were tired. Then address how the class might respond to children who were tired (Allow the child to sleep in class? Provide quiet areas? and so on). Children know how it feels to be tired. They need to learn that others may feel tired when they do not and some of the reasons why (reactions to medicine, not feeling well, and so on). Encourage children to tell each other when they are tired and suggest things they can still do together.

Inclusion: Large Group

1-14 Family Heirlooms

Goals: To increase inclusion; to broaden concepts of family; to increase cultural awareness

Materials: None

Procedure: Talk with the children about special objects that families pass down. Discuss the special meanings that make these objects important to families. Invite children to bring in a family heirloom. Have children describe the object, and explain why the object is important to their families. Display the items on a special table.

Assessment: The child will bring in a meaningful object for his family and state its significance.

Accommodations and Integration: If children do not have family heirlooms help them develop some. What would they like to have? Take pictures of the child or his work. Write a story about the child. It is important for children to develop a sense of permanence. This allows children to learn more about their families and their heritage. It also allows children to see how families are different.

Inclusion: Large or Small Group

1-15 Tongue Twisters

Goals: To increase awareness of individual differences and similarities; to increase inclusion; to express feelings

Materials: None

Procedure: Teach children some tongue twisters, and then encourage them to say them fast. This often results in both laughter and the realization that some things are difficult for all of us to say. For example:

> The bootblack brought the book back.
> Beth brought a big blue bucket of blueberries.
> Big black bugs buckle and bulge beneath the big blue bundle.
> Betty Balder bought some butter for her bread batter.
> Greek grape growers grow great grapes.
> Peter Piper picked a peck of pickled peppers.
> Suzy sells seashells down by the seashore.
> The sixth sheik's sixth sheep's sick.
> Red roosters read riddles rapidly.

Assessment: The child will attempt to say a tongue twister and communicate her feelings about the difficulty of saying the tongue twister.

Accommodations and Integration: Make the tongue twisters shorter. Write the words out and point to each word as you say it. Have children make up their own tongue twisters. This promotes an understanding that speech can be difficult for some children. Done slowly, it is an interesting way of practicing specific initial sounds.

Inclusion: Large Group

1-16 Voiceless Roll Call

Goals: To increase awareness of individual differences and similarities; to increase inclusion; to increase respect for diversity in modes of communication

Materials: None

Procedure: Call the children's names but mouth the names instead of speaking them out loud. Discuss how difficult voiceless roll call is, especially how hard it is to keep paying attention. When the children get the idea, tell them voicelessly what activities are available and ask them to make choices.

Assessment: The child will watch the teacher's mouth as she says the names of the children and respond appropriately when his name is called voicelessly.

Accommodations and Integration: If children do not understand their name, whisper it. Increase the length and complexity of the information you give them voicelessly. You may have to practice a bit before you are comfortable calling roll this way. Discuss how difficult it is to pay attention when you can not hear and why it might be challenging for a child who has a hearing impairment to participate. Help them decide how to include children who cannot hear.

Inclusion: Small Group

1-17 Who Is It?

Goals: To increase awareness of individual differences and similarities; to increase inclusion; to increase body awareness

Materials: A blindfold, scarf, or half mask with eye holes covered

Procedure: Blindfold one child and have him touch another child. You will have to give some guidance at first on the appropriate ways to touch another person. You might even guide the child's hand to feel the length of hair, height, type of shoes and clothes, facial features, and so on. Help the child by stating what to feel for: "Let's see. Who is about as tall as you are? Who has long, straight hair, and high cheek bones? Who is wearing a sweatshirt and tie shoes?" (Children may have to use clothing as clues until they become more precise in their ability to touch.) Initially, choose a child to identify who has very obvious features or one who is a good friend. Have the child talk. As children become more proficient, give fewer clues.

Assessment: The child will use her hands to feel an object or person and communicate what or whom it is.

Accommodations and Integration: Just tell children to close their eyes (they can talk). Have the children spend more of their day blindfolded. Encourage children to work in pairs, with one child blindfolded, and talk about what is helpful and what is not. This gives children the experience of "seeing" with their hands as a child who is blind might. It also shows them some of the difficulties such children face. Encourage children to look in the mirror and figure out what would feel different about different faces (bone structure, how deeply set the eyes are, shape of the nose, and so on).

Inclusion: Large or Small Group

1-18 Foreign Languages

Goals: To increase awareness of individual differences and similarities; to increase cultural awareness; to increase respect for diversity in modes of communication

Materials: Tape or CD, tape or CD player (CDs from the Putumayo Kids series)

Procedure: Sing or play a cassette or CD of a familiar song in a foreign language. Ask children what the words mean and discuss how some words are the same or similar in several languages. Then teach the English version. "Frère Jacques" is one of the most familiar songs. Discuss with the children how hard it is to listen and pay attention when you do not understand. Have children work on differentiating English from non-English. Use a variety of languages so children understand that there are many different languages. If children or their families speak another language, invite them to come and talk to the class, but be sure they talk about the culture as well. If there is a foreign language TV or radio station in your area, ask the children to listen to it. Help children become more aware of other languages and how difficult and valuable it is to learn another language.

Assessment: The child will listen to an unfamiliar foreign language and communicate the difficulty of understanding it.

Accommodations and Integration: Teach children words in another language first so they have some familiarity of the underlying concept. Encourage children to listen to language-learning tapes, CDs, and videos. Use interactive computer programs so that children can hear themselves speaking words in another language and compare it to a model. Encourage children to think about their dependence on language to communicate and the problems encountered when you do not speak the language of the people around you. Have a children's picture dictionary that labels pictures in two languages so they not only hear that the language is different but see it as well.

Provide many hands-on experiences for children who are English language learners. They are the fastest growing population of children and they need support in learning English and in validating their home language and culture.

Inclusion: Small Group or Individual

1-19 Simulated Glasses

Goals: To increase awareness of individual differences and similarities; to increase inclusion; to improve observational skills

Materials: Glasses, frames or sunglasses, gauze, half-face Halloween masks, cellophane, adhesive tape

To Make: *To simulate different visual conditions use inexpensive sunglasses or half-face Halloween masks, putting cellophane over the inside opening or a variety of coverings over the outside (see Figure R1–1).*

Procedure: Encourage children to wear the glasses and play as they usually do during the day. Talk with them about what is easy to do with the glasses, what is difficult, and what they can and cannot see with the glasses on.

Assessment: The child will wear different types of glasses and describe the differences she sees when using them.

Accommodations and Integration: Use the glasses for a shorter time. Provide magnifying glasses and binoculars and talk about the changes these make in what they see. Have the glasses available for several days so children can continue to experiment with them. Children can progress from being aware of what a particular visual impairment means to the implications it has for daily life.

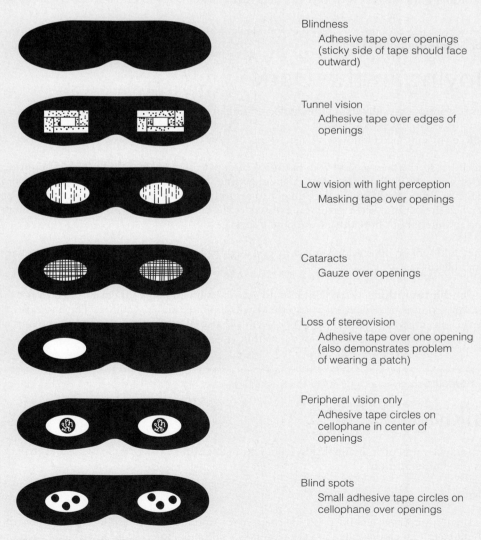

Blindness
   Adhesive tape over openings
   (sticky side of tape should face
   outward)

Tunnel vision
   Adhesive tape over edges of
   openings

Low vision with light perception
   Masking tape over openings

Cataracts
   Gauze over openings

Loss of stereovision
   Adhesive tape over one opening
   (also demonstrates problem
   of wearing a patch)

Peripheral vision only
   Adhesive tape circles on
   cellophane in center of
   openings

Blind spots
   Small adhesive tape circles on
   cellophane over openings

Figure R1–1: Simulated Glasses
Make simulated glasses with the instructions provided. Use adhesive or electrical tape by first putting the tape on the inside of mask (sticky side out) and then put the tape on the outside in the same places.

Inclusion: Small Group or Individual

1-20 Mittens

Goals: To increase awareness of individual differences and similarities; to increase inclusion; to increase body awareness

Materials: Mittens, a variety of small objects and typical small manipulatives (puzzles, blocks that join together, and so on)

Procedure: Have the children bring mittens to school or provide them. They can be worn throughout the day or used just to demonstrate fine motor skills such as stacking small blocks, interlocking shapes, eating snacks, stringing beads, coloring, and so on. If they take the mittens off, ask why and discuss how they felt before and after. Encourage children to put them on again when they change tasks. Have children discuss how they feel after an activity.

Assessment: The child will attempt different fine motor activities with mittens on his hands, and communicate the difficulty of accomplishing the tasks.

Accommodations and Integration: Allow children to take the mittens off if they become frustrated. But encourage them to put them back on as they try new tasks. Encourage some children to wear the mittens for the whole day. As children become more aware of how useful their fingers are, they also gain an appreciation of the difficulties faced by children with fine motor coordination problems provided you help them make the connection.

Inclusion: Large or Small Group

1-21 Moving in the Dark

Goals: To increase awareness of individual differences and similarities; to increase inclusion; to improve locomotor skills

Materials: Blindfolds or half face Halloween masks with the eyes covered, sunglasses with the lenses taped over.

Procedure: Make up a story about a child who has to go somewhere in the dark and is afraid of hitting her head. Have the children think of ways the child could move to avoid getting hurt, and then demonstrate these. Make it relevant to the children by suggesting they could get up in the night to try to find something. See if they can learn specific techniques for moving safely when they cannot see. Create some obstacles the children have to go around or through to add interest. Encourage children to think about how others could help them.

Assessment: The child will be blindfolded and move through obstacles. She will state two ways that people can help her when she is not able to see.

Accommodations and Integration: Have children do activities in pairs. Encourage children to put on blindfolds and try out techniques. Have others provide feedback so that the technique can be modified. This increases children's awareness of where their head is in space and the need to protect it. It also illustrates the problem of moving when you cannot see and what others can do that is helpful and not as helpful.

Inclusion: Large or Small Group

1-22 Talking

Goals: To increase awareness of individual differences and similarities; to increase inclusion; to increase respect for diversity in modes of communication

Materials: None

Procedure: In a small group, give a child a specific thing to say and then tell the child how to use her mouth. If you do not think she will understand, demonstrate the various ways of talking before asking them to do each one. For example:

Keep your teeth clenched while you talk.
Keep your lips closed.
Keep your tongue behind the lower teeth.

Have the children continue trying to make themselves understood until they experience some frustration. Discuss how it feels when others do not understand them. Help children focus on the function of the various parts of their mouths in speech. Help them specify how speech changes based on the parts of the mouth that they cannot use.

Assessment: The child will talk in designated ways and communicate the difficulty in understanding others when they speak differently.

Accommodations and Integration: Have children begin by speaking extremely slow, fast, loud, or soft. Then have children speak into a tape recorder, and listen to themselves. Have children do this in pairs to see if they can understand each other, or talk in such a way they cannot see the other child's mouth. Have a speech/language pathologist visit and talk about where different sounds are made in the mouth and discuss speech and the process of talking.

Inclusion: Large and Small Group

1-23 Slings

Goals: To increase inclusion; to increase body awareness; to increase awareness of individual differences and similarities

Materials: A piece of material or scarf for each child, large enough to make a sling

Procedure: During group time, talk about what it is like to be able to use only one arm. (Some children are born with only one arm, others break their arms.) Have the children think about what things are difficult to do with just one arm. Encourage them to participate in activities with one arm in a sling. Help children who participated talk about their feelings and difficulties they had. If they become frustrated and take the sling off, use their experience of frustration to make your point.

Assessment: The child will state the reason for using slings and three things that are difficult to do when wearing a sling.

Accommodations and Integration: First put the sling on the child's non-dominant arm, then move it to the dominant arm. Help children think about the kinds of adaptations having only one arm might require. Encourage them to think about adaptive devices, skills they would have to develop, and what they would do differently.

Social Studies: Large Group

1-24 International Snack

Goals: To broaden concepts of family; to increase awareness of roles people play; to increase cultural awareness

Materials: Flour tortillas, pupu, fondue, crêpes, Irish soda bread, pita bread

Procedure: Make a snack that is not traditionally American. Start with foods that, although from other countries originally, are familiar to many of the children (tofu, pita bread, crêpes), then work in foods that are increasingly different. Discuss what the foods are made of and where they come from, and then eat them. Include children in the preparation and discuss the foods used, the culture, and the people. Use families as a resource.

Assessment: The child will state the name of different snacks and make accurate statements about the regions from which they come.

Accommodations and Integration: Check for allergies, particularly if the foods are unusual and children may not have eaten the ingredients. Help children think of differences without judgment. Have them look at the broad geographic features of a region such as temperature, rainfall, and elevation, and look at the foods eaten in relation to those variables. Children will often participate in experiences with food at school that they would not try at home, especially if they participated in its preparation.

1-25 Medical Tools

Goals: To increase awareness of roles people play; to improve self-concept; to increase inclusion

Materials: Medical equipment, or pictures of medical equipment, and pictures of the parts of the body where these are most commonly used:

mouth	tongue depressor	arm	blood pressure cuff
throat	throat swab	eyes, ears, throat	small flashlight
knee	rubber hammer	lungs, heart	stethoscope
arm	intravenous system	bottom, arm, thigh	syringe

Procedure: Demonstrate and discuss how the equipment is used on a child or doll. Begin with the most familiar ones. Have the children match the pictures of medical equipment to pictures of the appropriate body parts. This often leads to discussion about doctors and medical procedures. Include information on what doctors look for and why. Have a medical dictionary available so you can look up information.

Assessment: The child will state the names of a variety of medical equipment and the body part on which each tool might be used.

Accommodations and Integration: Start with the most obvious and work toward more specific types of equipment. Invite a physician to visit and share information with the children. Perhaps show them x-rays of a hand, then talk about what they do and the significance of different conditions on the movement and use of a hand. Use the equipment children in your class are most likely to encounter. This should help make all children's contact with the medical profession less frightening, and help them realize that some of their classmates must see doctors more frequently than they do.

1-26 Patient in the Hospital

Goals: To increase awareness of roles people play; to improve self-concept; to increase inclusion

Materials: None

Procedure: Adapt the song "The Farmer in the Dell" to your specific purposes relative to the medical profession:

> There's a child whose sick,
> There's a child whose sick.
> Hi Ho the Office O.
> There's a child who is sick.

"There's a child going to the doctor" and "There's a child going to the hospital" can also be used. In the following stanzas, the child chooses someone to accompany him to the hospital (mother, father, grandmother, aunt); that person chooses the doctor; the doctor chooses the nurse (or specialists). Then:

> They all stand together,
> They all stand together.
> Hi Ho the Office O.
> Until the child gets better.

Have each children hold a picture or piece of equipment (stethoscope, thermometer) as a clue to their role. You might follow the song by talking about some of the various specialists and what they do. Include the speech/language pathologist, occupational and physical therapists, psychologist, family therapist, and different types of doctors.

Change the song to "My Doctor" and sing it to the tune of "Mary Had a Little Lamb":

> My doctor has a stethoscope,
> Stethoscope, stethoscope

My doctor has a stethoscope
To listen to my heart.

Continue with other tools. The order does not matter:

Thermometer . . . to take my temperature
Reflex hammer . . . to check my knees
Otoscope . . . to look in my ears (can also look in other parts)
Blood pressure cuff . . . to see how my blood is moving
(use other people and specialists as they seem to fit)

Assessment: The child will sing the adapted song and state what types of equipment might be used when visiting a doctor or hospital, and state their purpose.

Accommodations and Integration: Start with equipment all children are familiar with but do not find threatening. Have appropriate equipment on hand to demonstrate what you will sing in the song. Children encounter many members of the health profession. This activity helps frame the potential interaction as informational rather than threatening. Let the children choose whom to include.

Social Studies: Large and Small Group

1-27 Audiologist

Goals: To increase awareness of roles people play; to increase inclusion; to improve self-concept

Materials: Props for an audiologist's office: bells, earmuffs, a box with knobs, buzzers

Procedure: During group time, introduce the concept of an audiologist and what she does. Talk about how and why people get their hearing tested. Explain that there is an audiologist's office set-up. Use a box with knobs on it; bells, buzzers, or anything that makes noise; and earmuffs for earphones. Have the children "test" each other's hearing. They can raise a hand when they hear a noise or they can do a task, such as stack a circle on a stick, each time they hear a noise. Once children understand the process, erect a barrier so one child can't see what is happening and has to rely on sound to respond. Ask children to identify the sound.

Assessment: The child will state what an audiologist does and why she does it.

Accommodations and Integration: Model the role of the audiologist so children know what an audiologist does. Use this to prepare all children to have their hearing tested by a school nurse or audiologist. Allow children for whom this is a common practice to take a leadership role and work through any feelings that they have about the procedure.

Social Studies: Large and Small Group

1-28 Eye Doctor

Goals: To increase awareness of roles people play; to increase inclusion; to improve self-concept

Materials: Props for an eye doctor's office: vision chart, card with a "three-legged stool" (Figure R1–2), glasses, index card, frames, pointer, mirror

Procedure: During group time, discuss eye doctors and what they do. Explain you have set up an eye doctor's office. Encourage one child to be the doctor and point to the chart, another to be an assistant and help with glasses and the testing process. Initially concentrate on the matching aspect of this experience at a distance where you are sure children can see. Encourage children to experiment with the relationship between distance and seeing, and have them find where in the room they can no longer see accurately. Have them measure this distance.

Assessment: The child will state what an eye doctor does and why he does it.

Accommodations and Integration: Model the role of the eye doctor. Help children chart the responses of other children to the doctor's eye chart. If children do not understand the process, give them extra time to play the role of the "patient." Follow this activity with vision screening by a nurse or other qualified person. Help children see an eye doctor as helping identify children who need visual follow-up to help them see better.

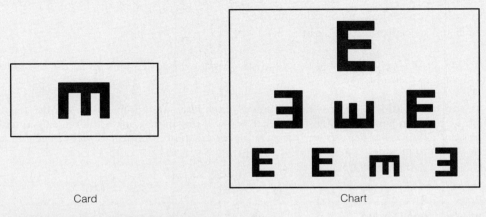

Card   Chart

Figure R1–2: Eye Chart and Card

Social Studies: Small Group

1-29 Emergency Room

Goals: To increase awareness of roles people play; to encourage problem solving; to improve self-concept

Materials: Emergency room setup: table, paper, chairs, pencils, bandages, lab coat

Procedure: During group time, talk about reasons for going to the emergency room: a broken bone, a bad cut or burn, as opposed to a headache or a cold. Talk to children about what might happen: Someone would ask for their name and insurance number, and they would have to wait. Also discuss what they could do while they wait, what the doctor might do, and the possibility that they would not know the doctor. Emphasize that there is an emergency. Stress the importance of time, and how those with life-threatening conditions are treated first, regardless of when people arrived.

Assessment: The child will state what an emergency room is, and why people go.

Accommodations and Integration: The purpose of this activity is to familiarize children with a set of procedures so that the fear of the emergency room is not added to the medical problem. Have an element of realism as well as creativity. See this as a variation on the doctor's office, although the element of time, the reasons for going to the emergency room, and the other people in the waiting room are different.

Social Studies: Small Group

1-30 Cast It

Goals: To increase awareness of roles people play; to increase awareness of individual differences and similarities; to increase inclusion

Materials: Plaster tape (available at most drugstores), water, scissors without points, dolls, broken chicken bone, x-ray

Procedure: Talk about broken bones; show one from an animal and talk about what a cast does for a bone. Set up the dramatic play area with plaster tape (just soak it in water to use it), a bucket of water, and dolls. First, have the children experiment with a doll. Some children may just explore the plaster tape as an art medium. Then, have them put a cast on a thumb or finger. The cast will slip off, but have some blunt-nosed fingernail scissors so you can cut off any stubborn ones. Discuss with the children that breaking bones hurts, but casting doesn't. Bring in an x-ray of a broken bone and show it to the children. Help them understand the purpose of setting and casting broken bones.

Assessment: The child will make a cast and state what it does.

Accommodations and Integration: Help the child begin the cast. Cut the tape into shorter pieces. Make a thinner cast. Talk about different types of casts (walking cast, straight leg cast, foot cast, and so on). Discuss plastic casts and more temporary casts made out of plastic and Velcro. Warn parents about this project so they will know their child's thumb is not broken if he wears the cast home. Children who know how and why casts are put on and taken off are less fearful when they need a cast. If most children cast their thumbs or finger make an art project out of decorating the casts.

Summary

Social awareness activities cover a broad range and are useful to all children in learning about themselves and the global world they live in. Many of these activities are focused on helping all children become aware of specific disabilities and how to include children who are different from them because of the culture they come from or the way they look, move, or talk.

Educational Resources

Resources on Early Learning: Illinois Early Learning Standards provide benchmarks for working toward the standards as well as ideas for tips and activities for meeting the standards. http://www.illinoisearlylearning.org/

Intercultural E-Mail Classroom Connection is a listserv to encourage partnerships with classrooms for the exchange of international and cross-cultural email. http://www.iecc.org/

Link Library at Education Place, supported by Houghton Mifflin, connects to an incredible number of websites related to art, math, social studies, and cross-cultural curriculum themes and as well as disabilities. http://www.eduplace.com/linklibrary/

National Council for the Social Studies has information about social studies standards and suggestions for activities to support the standards as well as other resources. http://www.socialstudies.org/

Social Studies for Kids has articles, current events and fun facts and games about cultures, holidays, languages, religions as well as U. S. government, economics, and geography. http://www.socialstudiesforkids.com/

For additional resources, visit the book companion website for this text at www.cengage.com/education/deiner.

Language and Literacy Activities:

Speaking, Listening, Reading, and Writing

Learning to communicate is one of the major tasks facing all young children. Learning language is a dynamic process that is affected by the language heard in the environment and the way that adults respond to language development. Speaking, listening, reading, and writing are the major components of the language and literacy curriculum. These skills are interdependent.

Activity Goals

Activities are organized by the goals they support. Goals that focus directly on language and literacy are given first. The activity number is provided after the goal to make finding the activity more efficient. The activities that are in the book have their number identified; those that are in the book companion website are followed by a "w" (refer to Table R2–1).

Language and Literacy Guidelines

The following guidelines will be helpful as you think about adapting language and literacy activities to meet the needs of children with diverse abilities.

Adapting activities for children with:	
Specific learning disabilities	Play sequencing and memory games to develop language skills. Support phonemic awareness daily in a variety of ways. Ensure that children have the readiness skills to move into reading. Read to children at their level of understanding rather than the level they can read and help them develop a love of books.
Social, emotional, and behavioral disorders	Help children develop a vocabulary to verbalize their feelings and to communicate with others. Use writing and illustrating as potential outlets for feelings. Use reading as a springboard to talk about emotions.
Attention-deficit/hyperactivity disorder	Read short, high-interest books. Read books and talk about feelings and emotions. Use the computer to develop literacy skills. Work on the language skills necessary to join and maintain group memberships.

Communication disorders	Give children many hands-on experiences so they have something to talk about. Be a good speech model. Encourage and support children when they talk by listening and responding. Ask children open-ended questions. Expand and extend their speech.
English language learners	Support children in developing proficiency in both their home language and English. If children use languages that do not use the standard English alphabet, ensure that children see the letters of the alphabet used in their home language. For example, Spanish has an ll and rr. Also, show markings such as accents and umlauts. Show languages such as Chinese that use a symbol system and Russian, which uses the Cyrillic alphabet.
Autism spectrum disorders	Work on nonverbal aspects of language (eye contact) as well as vocabulary. Teach concepts of verbal turn-taking. Use a picture communication system to support language.
Intellectual disabilities	Work on developing a functional vocabulary. Be sure children have prerequisite skills as you introduce new literacy tasks. Do a task analysis to teach these.
Gifts and talents	Support children in thinking about themselves as authors and illustrators. Introduce reference books and use the Internet to supplement classroom literacy work.
Special health care needs	Help children develop a vocabulary to increase their understanding of situations they may face and to express their feelings. Use reading to prepare children for new situations. Support children in learning to use e-mail to communicate with peers.
Orthopedic and neurologic impairments	Help children learn to give precise directions. Work on connecting sounds to sources and comprehending these relationships. Use materials with some built-in resistance such as clay or sand in emerging writing skills.
Hearing impairments	Provide many hands-on activities to develop inner language. Pair listening with visual and tactile experiences. Help children learn to use residual hearing and refine their auditory skills. Support reading and writing especially with the computer. Help children learn to read nonverbal cues. Use American Sign Language to support learning for all children.
Visual impairments	Encourage children to refine the visual skills they have. Include audio books as well as large-print and Braille books on your bookshelves. Include writing media that have tactile properties. Emphasize the verbal and tonal aspects of language.

Table R2–1: Activity goals and activity numbers in text and online

Goals	Activity Numbers
• To improve expressive communication	2–1, 2–2, 2–3, 2–5
	2–31w, 2–32w, 2–33w, 2–34w, 2–35w, 2–36w, 2–37w, 2–40w, 2–41w
• To improve listening skills	2–7, 2–8, 2–9, 2–10, 2–11
	2–31w, 2–43w, 2–44w, 2–45w, 2–46w, 2–47w, 2–48w, 2–49w, 2–50w, 2–51w
• To increase knowledge of the structure of language	2–4, 2–7, 2–14, 2–15, 2–21, 2–25
	2–32w, 2–37w, 2–38w
• To improve receptive communication	2–1, 2–7, 2–13
	2–42w, 2–43w, 2–45w, 2–46w, 2–47w
• To improve reading literacy	2–4, 2–12, 2–13, 2–14, 2–15, 2–16, 2–17, 2–18, 2–19, 2–20, 2–21, 2–22, 2–23, 2–24, 2–28, 2–29, 2–30
	2–53w, 2–52w, 2–55w, 2–56w, 2–58w

- To increase vocabulary

  2–1, 2–6, 2–13

  2–34w, 2–38w, 2–39w, 2–40w, 2–41w

- To increase respect for diversity in modes of communication

  2–10, 2–12

  2–45w

- To use diverse print and nonprint sources and genres

  2–2, 2–27, 2–28, 2–29, 2–30

  2–33w, 2–54w, 2–56w, 2–57w

- To increase phonemic awareness

  2–4, 2–12, 2–13, 2–14, 2–16, 2–23

  2–38w

- To increase writing literacy

  2–19, 2–25, 2–26, 2–27, 2–28, 2–29, 2–30

  2–56w, 2–57w

- To increase comprehension

  2–6, 2–8, 2–15, 2–25

  2–36w, 2–42w, 2–44w, 2–46w, 2–47w, 2–52w, 2–53w

- To follow directions

  2–18

  2–37w, 2–42w

- To increase inclusion

  2–2, 2–3, 2–5, 2–10, 2–24

  2–32w

- To improve memory skills

  2–11, 2–17, 2–20, 2–22, 2–24

  2–52w

- To identify and understand patterns and relationships

  2–17, 2–18, 2–21

  2–50w, 2–51w, 2–53w

- To improve classification skills

  2–8

  2–31w, 2–36w, 2–40w

- To improve cause-and-effect reasoning

  2–9

  2–35w, 2–48w, 2–49w

- To make predictions

  2–11, 2–20, 2–22

  2–48w, 2–49w, 2–51w

- To improve sensory motor integration

  2–16, 2–19, 2–23, 2–26, 2–27

  2–41w, 2–44w, 2–50w, 2–54w, 2–55w

- To encourage creativity

  2–6

  2–33w, 2–34w, 2–35w, 2–39w, 2–43w

- To express feelings

  2–3, 2–5

  2–55w

Language and Literacy Activities

Speaking: Small Group

2-1 Synonyms

Goals: To improve expressive communication; to improve receptive communication; to increase vocabulary

Materials: Pictures or objects that have more than one name (see synonyms, p. R-28)

Procedure: Define synonyms: words that mean the same thing but sound different. Then present children with the objects or pictures of objects, and see how many synonyms they can think of. It is not important that these be exact synonyms in a dictionary sense. The point is for the children to know that one object can have several different names. Start with familiar objects in your classroom and community:

rug/carpet/floor covering	store/shop	chair/seat
couch/sofa/davenport	road/street	bed/cot
scissors/shears	bathing suit/swimsuit	shirt/top

Assessment: The child will state two different names for a given object.

Accommodations and Integration: Use the analogy of nicknames to help children learn the concept. Talk about regional differences in language usage. Children need to know that objects often have several names even in the same language. Show children a thesaurus as a book or on the computer and encourage them to use it to think of synonyms. Help children build vocabulary by learning synonyms as they provide context.

Speaking: Small Group

2-2 Shoe Theater

Goals: To improve expressive communication; to use diverse print and nonprint sources and genres; to increase inclusion

Materials: Pairs of shoes and socks (men's, women's, children's, babies')

Procedure: Have the children pretend the objects are puppets. Use one hand for each shoe or sock and have a shoe or sock theater.

Assessment: The child will use familiar objects as puppets and participate in a play.

Accommodations and Integration: Start with easy obvious roles using familiar items. Help less skillful children find roles that allow them to participate but require less language, such as a visiting pair of shoes or the baby's shoes. Children can develop a script for their play and dictate it into a tape recorder or write (or have someone write) it down. Encourage them to make props and scenery. Because shoes suggest ideas but no particular theme, this activity encourages creativity. Roles are undefined, so it is easy to include children with varying skill levels. Help children learn about the ways in which plays are different from other types of literature and the many different support roles people have to produce a play (prompter, set designer, and so on).

Speaking: Large Group

2-3 Weekend News

Goals: To improve expressive communication; to increase inclusion; to express feelings

Materials: None

Procedure: During group time, give each child (or a designated smaller group of children) an opportunity to talk about things that happened to them over the weekend. Write down briefly what the children say and encourage them to look at it during the day. As you write, be sure to include each child's name. For example,

Trisha said, "Mary Beth slept over at my house."
"I saw a fire," Carlos said.

When children have gotten comfortable sharing what happened to them over the weekend, ask them to talk about the best and worst things that they encountered. Be respectful of the variety of comments:

WORST	BEST
coming to school	going out to dinner
falling down	staying up later than usual
hearing a scary noise at night	having a special food
Inti hit me	Nana's coming to visit
being teased or yelled at	playing with Mommy
a sibling's birthday	getting my hair cut

Assessment: The child will share an important event that happened to him.

Accommodations and Integration: These topics can lead to discussions about all children's concerns. Children are surprisingly candid about and responsive to this. With the help of sensitive adults, children can safely talk about their worst experiences without shame or ridicule and perhaps gain ideas for handling future problems. They also learn that all people have best and worst things, including you. For variation, have the children draw pictures of what happened to them over the weekend and talk about their picture individually. Children can also "write" their weekend news and read it to the class. Having children discuss the best and worst events can help others see that children with disabilities have many of the same problems all children do.

Speaking: Large or Small Group

2-4 Rhyming Words

Goals: To improve reading literacy; to increase knowledge of the structure of language; to increase phonemic awareness

Materials: None

Procedure: Define rhyming words: words that end with the same sound. Give lots of examples before asking the children for words. Read stories such as Dr. Seuss's *Green Eggs and Ham* and point out the rhyming words to the children. See if they can generate some as well. Say familiar fingerplays that use rhyming words. List both real and nonsense words. Praise the children for finding a rhyme, even if it is a nonsense word, but point out that it isn't a real word—look it up in a children's dictionary.

ACE	DARE	HEAD	BUMP	COW	BED
brace	care	read	stump	now	fed
trace	stare	bread	lump	how	led
pace	flare	dead	jump	pow	red
place	bare	tread	grump	plow	sled

Use the opportunity to expand the children's vocabularies by asking them to define the words. Have the children repeat the rhyming words quickly and slowly. Encourage children to make a "Have You Seen a . . . " book of rhyming words they can illustrate: Have you seen a red bed, bare mare, cow plow, fake cake.

Assessment: The child will say one rhyming word for each word presented.

Accommodations and Integration: Read books and poems, pointing out rhyming words. Give words for children to find rhymes for. Start with ones where you can help children with hints—What rhymes with red? (Point to your head.) Help children explore the structure of language using different parts of speech and longer words that rhyme. Make cards with pictures of words that rhyme (red, bed, sled) and see if you can help children isolate the initial sound and add the rhyme. Rhyming can be built into routines. As each child leaves, ask the child to give a word that rhymes with yours: "Tomás, give me a word that rhymes with cat." "Sat." "Sally, another word." "Hat."

Speaking: Large Group

2-5 Interviews

Goals: To improve expressive communication; to increase inclusion; to express feelings

Materials: A play microphone

Procedure: Do a takeoff on some of the popular talk shows: "Good morning, today is Tuesday, February 2, and we are delighted to have as our guest today Miss Suling. Miss Suling, can you tell our listeners some of the things that you really like to do? Do you have any favorite foods?"

Assessment: The child will answer questions about herself when asked by the teacher and classmates.

Accommodations and Integration: If children are hesitant, make the questions easy, and keep the interview short. Be sure to have a "mike" as a prop. Explain this is Suling's first appearance and she is a bit shy. Encourage children to talk about their interests and whatever they want to share. It is great for children to feel special and to highlight what is unique about them. If you really get into it, you can take questions from the "audience" and also share with the "audience" what you find so special about this particular child and why you "invited" her.

Speaking: Small or Large Group

2-6 Word Associations

Goals: To increase comprehension; to increase vocabulary; to encourage creativity

Materials: None

Procedure: Teach the children the game of word associations: "I'll say a word, and I want you to tell me what other words you think of." Start with something easy, such as colors—red: fire, hot, tomatoes, anger. Have children look around the room for ideas if they are having problems. Encourage children to say as many things as they can think of that they associate with the color. Use more obscure ideas. Listen to their rationale for why they associate those words. Encourage them to think of several associations.

Assessment: The child will listen to a word stated by a teacher and state three words that can be associated with the stated word.

Accommodations and Integration: If children don't say some of the obvious words you want to explore, say, "It reminds me of . . . ." Then share with them your rationale. This encourages and supports divergent thinking. Children need many solutions to problems and many ways of dealing with a particular situation.

Listening: Large Group

2-7 Say It

Goals: To improve listening skills; to improve receptive communication; to increase knowledge of the structure of language

Materials: None

Procedure: During group time, say various words or sentences and have the children imitate you. Using the same words, change your voice pitch, intonation, speed, or stress.

Sentence Variations
I like juice. (normal, loud, soft/whisper, fast, slow, puckered mouth)
I like juice. (stress)
I *like* juice. (stress)
I like *juice*. (stress)
raise your voice for a question
hold your nose

As the children imitate you and change their voices, verbalize for them what you (they) did: "Great, you all said it as loud as I did." Explore with children the impact that tone and intonation patterns have for meaning. Discuss where you might use different voices. Ask children how they would say something at a sports event as compared to inside time.

Assessment: The child will repeat the teacher's words with the same intonation, pitch, stress, or speed.

Children need experience speaking and listening. Engaging group times can provide both.

Accommodations and Integration: Use gestures to reinforce the tonal pattern. Have children use longer sentences and have other children imitate them and give them feedback about different intonation patterns. Because so much of meaning is passed through the nonverbal aspect of language, it is important that children are aware of it from an early age.

Listening: Large Group

2-8 Sound and Tell

Goals: To improve listening skills; to increase comprehension; to improve classification skills

Materials: A screen (could be a rectangular table on its side); a paper bag for each child in the class; a noisemaker (an object from class or one brought from home):

whistle	dishes	bell
two blocks	spoons	pen that clicks
timer	scissors	book (to close or drop)

Procedure: Ask each child to bring a noisemaker from home or to find an object in the classroom that makes a noise and can fit in a bag. Hide the noisemaker in a bag and have each child go behind the screen and make the sound and the other children guess what it is. Or, while hidden, have children make noises with various body parts behind the screen (e.g., clap, stomp).

Assessment: The child will listen and identify the sound-making object.

Accommodations and Integration: Have the child make the sound so everyone can see. Make a chart classifying the sounds. Classify noises as loud, soft, sharp, and so on. Discuss the properties of objects that make noise and those that do not. Classifying sounds helps children become aware of the environment and personal safety.

Listening: Large Group

2-9 Sound Cues

Goals: To improve listening skills; to improve cause-and-effect reasoning; to improve receptive communication

Materials: Tape recorder, tapes of sounds, pictures of items making the sound

Procedure: Record a variety of sounds. Have the children identify them. Then have them decide where they might hear each sound and what might be happening.

Indoor sounds	*Outdoor street sounds*
mixer: cooking	brakes: car stopping
vacuum cleaner: cleaning	engine: car starting
toilet flushing: going to the bathroom	car door closing: getting in or out of a car
washing machine: washing clothes	seat belt clinking: putting on seat belt
water: hand washing	horn: warning of danger

Assessment: The child will identify a variety of sounds and relate each sound to a possible action.

Accommodations and Integration: Give the child pictures of two objects, one of which made the sound. Then, using the car noises as an example, see if the children can sequence the sounds of events as they might normally happen. Give the child a tape recorder, have the child record sounds in the classroom and outside, and have others identify them. Help children identify the sounds in familiar sequences such as washing hands and brushing teeth. Provide photographs of these to sequence.

Listening: Large Group

2-10 Quiet Donald

Goals: To improve listening skills; to increase respect for diversity in modes of communication; to increase inclusion

Materials: None

Procedure: At group time, talk with the children about how people talk to each other. Ask the children what happens when someone can't talk. How do they communicate with others? Introduce "Quiet Donald" as a new poem. Read through it and let the children watch. Ask the children questions about what is happening in the poem. Say the poem again with the children joining in. Talk about American Sign Language, ASL, and the many ways people communicate if they do not share a common language.

> **Quiet Donald (poem)**
> *[I love you when in italics use ASL].*
> Quiet Donald met Talky Sue
> But *[I love you]* was all that he could do.
> And Sue said, Donald I sure like you.
> But *[I love you]* was all that he could do.
> And Sue asked Donald, Do you like me too?
> But *[I love you]* was all that he could do.
> Good-bye then Donald I am leaving you.
> But *[I love you]* was all that he could do.
> And she left forever, so she never knew
> That *[I love you]* means, I love you.

Assessment: The child will say the words of the poem and sign *I love you* in ASL.

Accommodations and Integration: Demonstrate the signs several times slowly. Go to http://comtechlab.msu.edu/sites/aslweb/browser.htm for ASL signs and how to do them. If children are interested have them look at this site and learn additional words. Encourage children to look at other forms of communication and acknowledge differences among people.

Listening: Small Group

2-11 Tape It

Goals: To improve listening skills; to improve memory skills; to make predictions

Materials: Video recorder, videotape, pictures of children

Procedure: Over the course of several days, videotape each child talking about what the child is doing for about a minute or two. Using only the audio portion of the tape, have a small-group listening time when the children try to predict who is talking and explain their rationale (it's a boy, voice quality, etc.).

Assessment: The child will listen to a tape of classmates talking and identify the voices of different classmates.

Accommodations and Integration: Give children pictures of several classmates who might be talking and ask them to choose which one it is. Have children try to disguise their voices. Encourage children to identify the features in a voice that make it recognizable. Then turn on the video portion so they can see if they are right. Send this tape to a child who has been out of school for a while. The child can practice identifying voices at home as well as keeping in touch with classmates. Encourage children to send videotaped messages to friends who are not in school and have them returned. Audiotapes do the same thing, but are not as effective with younger children.

Reading Literacy: Individual

2-12 Alphabet Lotto

Goals: To improve reading literacy; to increase phonemic awareness; to increase respect for diversity in modes of communication

Materials: Alphabet lotto board and letters.

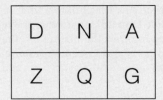
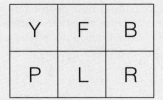
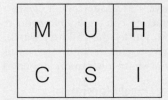

FIGURE R2–1: Alphabet Lotto Board with Printed Capital Letters

To Make: *Divide pieces of posterboard (9″ × 12″) into six rectangles (4″ × 4 1/2″). Print a letter of the alphabet (not necessarily in order) in each rectangle. Make four cards with different letters on each (see Figure R2–1).*

Cut 24 4″ × 4 1/2″ pieces, also out of posterboard. Print a letter on each small rectangle to match the larger boards. (*Note:* Because our alphabet has 26 letters, two will be missing. If you make two sets like this, omit different letters from each one.) If children are having trouble matching particular letters, design cards to meet these problems. For lowercase letters, make a card that has letters with reversible lines and curves (see Figure R2–2).

Procedure: Play the game as you would any Lotto game. Put the individual letters into a box to draw from so children can match them to the board with six letters. Children can play this as a matching game alone. With all these combinations, there will be five cards for each letter on the board. When children are learning, make a board out of letters that are very dissimilar (for example, *A, W, O, S, T, D*). Don't have letters such as *M* and *W* or *O* and *C* on the same board, as they might be confused initially.

Assessment: The child will accurately match alphabet letters.

FIGURE R2–2: Alphabet Lotto Board with Printed Small Letters with Reversible Lines and Curves

Accommodations and Integration: First work on letter identification using the boards. Then play Lotto. To expand the letter concept, make Lotto combinations as in Figure R2–3. You can add alphabets from other languages. the American Sign Language alphabet, the Braille alphabet, as well as sandpaper letters.

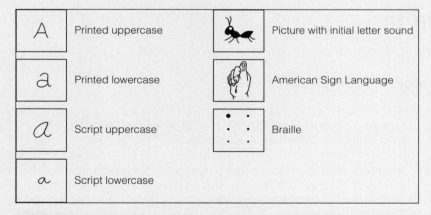

FIGURE R2–3: Alphabet Lotto Cards in Print, Script, Pictures for Initial Sounds, ASL, and Braille

---

Reading Literacy: Small Group

2-13 Body Sounds

Goals: To improve reading literacy; to increase vocabulary; to increase phonemic awareness

Materials: None

Procedure: Name a part of the body and then ask the children to name a part that has the same beginning sound (or letter).

   toe: teeth, tongue, tendons
   eye: elbow, eyebrow, ears, earlobe

hair: hand, head, heart, hips
fingers: fingernails, foot, forearm, follicle
legs: lips, lungs

Assessment: The child will name two body parts that have the same beginning sound as the body part stated by the teacher.

Accommodations and Integration: Have children choose between two parts that you name or have them name things in the room or anything they can think of that has the same initial sound or letter. Encourage children to think of less obvious body parts (internal ones) such as muscles, joints, and blood vessels. Use pictures or models to help children learn about parts they cannot see. Give them functional clues. This is a fun way of teaching children the names of body parts and the functions they serve. Children need the vocabulary to talk about their body with precision.

Reading Literacy: Large Group

2-14 Sound Bingo

Goals: To improve reading literacy; to increase phonemic awareness; to increase knowledge of the structure of language

Materials: Bingo cards with letters rather than numbers (see Figure R2–4)

Procedure: Using a regular bingo game format play the game and ask children to identify the letters as you call them out. As you move to letter sounds, pair the children so they can work together. A few letters will have to be eliminated, as they sound the same as others (/c/ and /k/), or give words that start with that sound as a clarifying clue. Have the children put a marker on the letter for each sound as it is called out. The winner is the first child to have a horizontal, vertical, or diagonal row. Continue to play until most children have completed a row.

Assessment: The child will listen to the sound of a letter and identify that letter on his bingo card.

B	I	N	G	O
a	u	r	b	o
s	h	b	c	i
w	y	free	g	v
m	j	n	l	d
e	f	t	p	z

FIGURE R2–4: Bingo Card for Sound Bingo

Accommodations and Integration: Show children the card after you have said the sound to allow them to match visually if they do not know the name or sound of the letter. Instead of letter sounds, call out words and have the children mark the initial letter sound. This can also be done with the final letter sound, but you need to check the words for silent letters and those that are misleading, such as *penny*, where the *y* sounds like an *e*. As you work toward developing words for games such as this, you begin to appreciate the problems in learning English, which has so many exceptions to rules. Talk with children about why some sounds cannot be used in this game.

Reading Literacy: Large Group

2-15 Title

Goals: To improve reading literacy; to increase comprehension; to increase knowledge of the structure of language

Materials: A made-up story or a printed story with the title hidden

Procedure: Read or tell a story or use a paragraph from a longer story. Explain that it has no title and that you want their help in deciding on one. Ask them to suggest titles and write them down. Talk with the children about the titles and have them explain which titles would be good or not as good as others.

Assessment: The child will listen to a story and choose an appropriate title for it.

Accommodations and Integration: Choose simple stories. Use more complex stories as children become more proficient. Appropriate titles require high-level abstract reasoning skills. Challenge children to think this way.

Reading Literacy: Large or Small Group

2-16 Letter Day

Goals: To improve reading literacy; to increase phonemic awareness; to improve sensory motor integration

Materials: Alphabet letters made of sandpaper and wood, objects that begin with each letter

Procedure: Pick a letter of the alphabet. Expose the children to that letter in many ways. Write the letter *P*; trace a sandpaper letter *P*; feel your breath with your hand as you say /*P*/; point to *P* in a group of letters; think of words that start with *P*; make cookies or clay in the shape of *P*; eat *p*retzels for snack. Emphasize the sound of the letter. This is important for letters that have more than one sound, such as *g* (*George* versus *Gary*), as well as long and short vowel sounds.

Children need many and varied reading readiness activities.

Assessment: The child will identify a letter by sight, sound, and touch.

Accommodations and Integration: Concentrate on letter identification. Start with the vowels and leave the most difficult consonants until last. You can do any letter. Granted, *X* is a challenge! Use both upper- and lowercase letters.

Reading Literacy: Small Group

2-17 Changing Objects

Goals: To improve reading literacy; to identify and understand patterns and relationships; to improve memory skills

Materials: Small objects such as blocks, doll furniture, toy cars, and a screen

Procedure: Put three objects in a row and ask the children to look at them. Put a screen in front of the objects and rearrange them. Ask one of the children to put them in the original order. Initially, use objects that are less similar, such as cup/doll/block. For variation, take one object away and have the children name the missing object.

> Easier: red block/blue airplane/green cup/orange crayon
> Hard: Red block/blue block/green block/orange block
> Harder: Red stocking cap/red baseball cap/red ski hat/red felt hat

Assessment: The child will view three objects in a row and put them in order after they have been rearranged.

Accommodations and Integration: Start with two dissimilar objects. Using the screen either rearrange them or leave them the same. Work on same and different. As children improve increase the number of objects and their similarity. The objects you choose can be based on the theme you are working on (hospital: tongue depressor, little flashlight, stethoscope, bandages) or as a way of introducing a topic that has unfamiliar materials or materials that children might be concerned about. Encourage the children to touch and handle the materials.

Reading Literacy: Large or Small Group

2-18 Color Graphs

Goals: To improve reading literacy; to follow directions; to identify and understand patterns and relationships

Materials: Paper, crayons. Draw a pattern of squares on a piece of paper and duplicate it so each child has one.

Procedure: Give the children directions to follow in coloring in the squares: "Color the first two squares on the top left green. Color the next square red. Color the square below the second green square yellow," and so on.
   Move from left to right in your directions.

Assessment: The child will listen to directions for coloring and color the shapes the designated colors.

Accommodations and Integration: Have children color each "car" on the train in order. Make the first square somewhat different as a starting place. Give children additional time to color. As they improve, you can have children skip a particular number of squares, if that is useful, and use more squares. Have the children describe the pattern to you using both color and number. Vary your rate of presentation to match the skill of the children. If you are very creative, the design can be made to look like an object when it is colored accurately. This is not art, it is literacy.

Reading Literacy: Small Group

2-19 Alphabet Line

Goals: To improve reading literacy; to improve writing literacy; to improve sensory motor integration

Materials: Clothesline, marking pen, paper, pictures, wooden clothespins with an alphabet letter on each

Procedure: Have the children put each clothespin on the clothesline in alphabetical order using a guide, or put up each letter or sound you or another child request. Print the letter or sound on a separate piece of paper. Have the children match the paper letters or initial sounds of pictures to the clothespin, then hang them.

Assessment: The children will find a designated letter from a pile and put it on a clothesline.

Accommodations and Integration: Use this as a letter identification task and have the children find the clothespin letter and put it on the clothesline. Have children make words with the clothespins (you will need additional letters) or copy words that you have printed on cards. Although simple, this activity is a useful way of developing finger strength while teaching a variety of skills relating to the alphabet. Identifying letters and sounds is essential for reading.

Reading Literacy: Small Group

2-20 Color Concentration

Goals: To improve reading literacy; to make predictions; to improve memory skills

Materials: A set of cards with matching pairs of colors on one side

Procedure: This is a variation of the game Concentration. Lay out the cards face down. Each child takes a turn and chooses two cards. The objective is to turn over two cards that are the same color.

Assessment: The child will remember where specific colored cards are when turned over and match two cards of the same color.

Accommodations and Integration: Start with four or five pairs of cards. Use primary colors and/or simple shapes. First, have the children match the cards, then demonstrate how the game is played. Gradually add more cards. As children become more proficient, add shades of colors and more cards. You can use a regular deck of cards for numbers, or pairs of pictures of any kind. The more cards you add, the more difficult the activity becomes. Also, the more detailed the pictures, the more difficult the game. This can also be done with letters of the alphabet. You can even match capital and small letters, a more difficult variation.

Reading Literacy: Small Group or Individual

2-21 Follow That Line

Goals: To improve reading literacy; to increase knowledge of the structure of language; to identify and understand patterns and relationships

Materials: Posterboard, markers (red, green, black).

To Make: *Cut posterboard into 3″ × 3″ squares and arrange these squares in a pattern on a large table or the floor. (This is only for your ease in drawing.) Using black, red, and green markers, draw a pattern of lines, stopping and starting colors and using straight and curved lines.*

Procedure: Have the children build a track with the cards in a variety of patterns (see Figure R2–5). Talk with the children about punctuation, especially periods, and their function in language. Discuss how the period represented on the cards is also a stop. Encourage them to make a variety of patterns.

Assessment: The child will make a pattern using the squares and explain how he made the pattern.

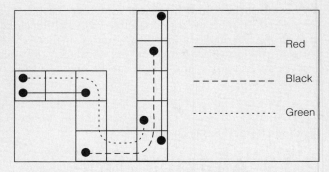

FIGURE R2–5: Cards with Lines and Punctuation Marks

Accommodations and Integration: Use squares with only one color. The more squares you have available and the more colors and patterns, the more complicated the task is. It is also more challenging when children must make a designated pattern. Punctuation and spacing make important contributions to both reading and writing and may be overlooked as we teach children the structure of language.

Reading Literacy: Large or Small Group

2-22 What Is It?

Goals: To improve reading literacy; to make predictions; to improve memory skills

Materials: Large (8″ × 10″) pictures of familiar objects, large envelopes

Procedure: Put a picture of a familiar object in an envelope. Pull it out slowly until part of the picture is exposed. Have the children guess what it is. Keep exposing more of the picture until it is correctly identified. Encourage the children to guess and give you the reasons for their guesses. Start with pictures of simple, familiar objects (boats, cars, trains, animals). Pull about half of the picture out before you stop. You can use a screen and gradually push objects out as well.

Assessment: The child will correctly identify an object while viewing less than 50 percent of it.

Accommodations and Integration: Use 8″ × 10″ pictures of all children in the class to add interest at the beginning of the year. Add pictures of less familiar objects or ones that have more ambiguous cues (an armchair and sofa). Children need to develop skills in the area of visual closure. They need to be able to use partial information to infer what they cannot see and focus on relevant details. Encourage children to talk about guesses they make and their rationale for them.

Reading Literacy: Individual

2-23 Sandpaper Letters

Goals: To improve reading literacy; to increase phonemic awareness; to increase sensory motor integration

Materials: Sandpaper, glue, cardboard, pictures.

To Make: *Cut the letters of the alphabet out of sandpaper and glue each on a cardboard square. Glue or draw a picture of something that begins with that letter on the back.*

Procedure: Have the child trace the letter with index and middle fingers as you talk about the structure of the letter: "This is the letter *A*. It has three straight lines. One, two, three. The third connects the first two in the middle." Show the child the picture on the back to connect the letter with a sound.

Assessment: The child will trace an alphabet letter, name it, and say the letter sound.

Accommodations and Integration: Start with the easiest letters based on the configuration of the letter and the child's knowledge. Have the child identify the letters blindfolded.

Reading Literacy: Small Group

2-24 Changes

Goals: To improve reading literacy; to increase inclusion; to improve memory skills

Materials: None

Procedure: Begin by focusing the children's attention on a category—for example, clothing—and make obvious changes. It helps if you are "it" first and give some clues. Then, have one child turn around and close his eyes while the child who is "it" changes something about her appearance (unties shoe, rolls up pant leg, removes glasses, or unbuttons shirt). The first child must name or point to the change. As children improve, make the changes more subtle.

Assessment: The child will look at another child and state what aspect of the other child 's appearance has changed.

Accommodations and Integration: Have the child who is "it" state where or what the category of change will be (clothing, facial expression, and so on). This allows the child who is "it" to be in control of the change and to be part of the group, yet the child does not have to speak. Children become aware that they can change some aspects of themselves.

Writing: Large or Small Group

2-25 Mind Mapping

Goals: To improve writing literacy; to increase comprehension; to increase knowledge of the structure of language

Materials: Paper, pencil or marker

Procedure: After a topic has been chosen, encourage children to make a mind map before they begin to write. Start with the topic in the center of the page. Draw a balloon around it. Surround it with related ideas connected to it or to each other with lines. The lines show the relationship between the central theme and the topics mentioned. If there appear to be tangents, put these in the corners of the page. If they eventually become related, attach them; if not, they will not be part of the writing. A mind map of the ocean is pictured in Figure R2–6.

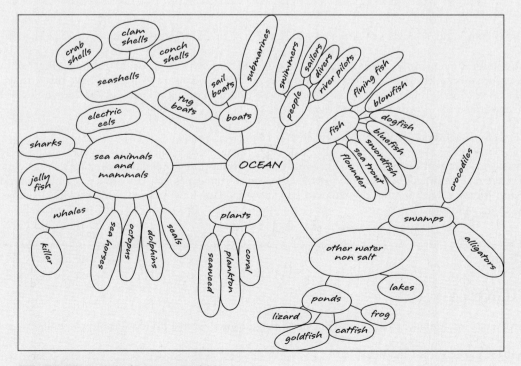

FIGURE R2–6: Mind Map or Webbing

Assessment: The child will contribute ideas to create a mind map.

Accommodations and Integration: Do the mind map as a group project and have the adult do the mapping while scaffolding the children's ideas. Have a small group of children make more complex maps on topics of their choice. Have reference materials available. Children need to organize their ideas for writing, but traditional outlines are rarely useful with young children. Mind mapping, or clustering ideas, is more useful and helps set the flow for the writing. Initially, each balloon will probably only be a phrase or sentence.

Writing: Individual or Small Group

2-26 Air Writing

Goals: To improve writing literacy; to improve sensory motor integration

Materials: None

Procedure: Have children write letters and words in the air before they put them on paper. Using the dominant hand, have children keep their elbow straight, point their index finger, and write the letter or word in the air. Be sure children use the large muscles of the arm, not wrist muscles. Write large letters. Cursive works better than printing.

Assessment: The child will write cursive upper- and lowercase letters accurately in the air.

Accommodations and Integration: Guide the child's arm through the motions or stand next to the child and model the motion while talking about the strokes. Have children write large letters on the chalkboard after writing them in the air, and then on large paper. As children become interested in writing, they need to develop a sensory motor base. For some children, writing comes easily; others need support. Children who have trouble writing with paper and pencil may need additional work with their large muscles before practice with a pencil and paper is useful.

Writing: Small Group

2-27 Sand Printing

Goals: To improve writing literacy; to improve sensory motor integration; to use diverse print and nonprint sources and genres

Materials: Jellyroll pan, sand, stick or unsharpened pencil, cards with an individual letter or word printed on each

Procedure: Fill a jellyroll pan (cookie sheet with sides) about 1/4″ deep with sand. Using the index finger of their dominant hand, have children write letters, sounds, their name, or words in the sand. For variation have them use a stick after they have gained skill with their finger. Sort the letters into those that have straight lines, curved lines, and combinations. Give children cards with simple words printed on them.

Assessment: The child will write letters in the sand with his finger or a stick.

Accommodations and Integration: Begin with words that are important to children yet short. After children have written individual letters, encourage them to copy words in the sand from cards that you have written. The sand provides some resistance and leaves a mark so that the children can see what they have printed. This provides feedback on fine motor control in an unusual way.

Writing: Small Group

2-28 Tickets

Goals: To improve writing literacy; to improve reading literacy; to use diverse print and nonprint sources and genres

Materials: Markers, paper, press-on labels

Procedure: Have the children make tickets for snack or lunch using the labels as a base. Tell children that today they need tickets to eat and encourage them to make them. (Have a few extras and a marker for those who do not.) Be sure to collect and comment on the tickets as you distribute the snack.

Assessment: The child will write, distribute, and read the tickets.

Accommodations and Integration: Support any writing on the ticket. Encourage children to make "identical" tickets (numbers are easiest) and have one ticket for snack and the other to mark where the child is to sit. Then have the children find their place at the table by matching the ticket to the place marker. Children need to practice writing, especially numbers. Use this to support dramatic play by giving out railroad and airline tickets. Give tickets for using an obstacle course or riding tricycles. There can be tickets for puppet shows, group time, and stories. Make writing fun and varied.

Writing: Small Group

2-29 Writing Center

Goals: To improve writing literacy; to improve reading literacy; to use diverse print and nonprint sources and genres

Materials: Variety of paper: manila paper, wide-lined paper, plain white paper, paper folded in half, small notepads, paper cut into interesting shapes, colored paper, and stationery; writing tools: thin and thick water soluble markers, pencils and colored pencils, a supply of interesting erasers, a pencil sharpener; copy of the alphabet; writing folder with each child's name

Procedure: Encourage children to think about an experience or feeling they would like to write about. Discuss writing as a process that involves writing, editing, and publishing. When you talk with children at the writing center, use the terms *author*, *editor*, and *publisher* with them. Writing is a small-group activity, where children can discuss their ideas and try them out on others. It is not a quiet solitary activity. Emphasize the process of writing. Encourage children to work in small groups and support each other in the process. Discuss illustrating and how it is different from drawing.

Assessment: The child will write and illustrate a story using a variety of writing media.

Accommodations and Integration: Accept all attempts at writing and support the discussion of what will be written about. Encourage children to write more detailed and longer stories; increase the variety of writing genres to include poetry and plays. Have children read their work to others and publish their work. Discuss the different but related aspects of writing, editing, and publishing. Encourage children who want to to use a word processor to write or illustrate their stories. As children begin to think about themselves as authors, their interest in writing increases. When they see writing as a process, and the details of editing as separate from writing, they can focus on the aspects of spelling and punctuation that are important in a final product but ought not to interfere with creativity.

Writing: Small Group

2-30 Publishing

Goals: To improve writing literacy; to improve reading literacy; to use diverse print and nonprint sources and genres

Materials: Three ring notebook, plastic sleeves, paper ($8\,1/2'' \times 11''$) and markers, pencils, or crayons

Procedure: Talk with children about the parts of a book and the purposes they serve. Show them a copyright symbol and talk about the meaning of it. Show them copyright pages, dedications, acknowledgments, and indexes. Then write a class book to which each child contributes a page. The contributions can vary with the ability and interest of the children. Encourage children to use their knowledge of books and their parts in their own writing when appropriate.

Assessment: The child will contribute to a class book.

Accommodations and Integration: Encourage all writing and illustrating. Book contributions can also include digital pictures. Help children add additional stories to their personal book or create new books on other topics. Include photographs as well as illustrations. After children have written the text for their book, have them put the paper in the plastic sleeve protector and then in the notebook. Encourage them to use a title page and, if there is more than one story, a table of contents. Children like to think of themselves as authors who produce a product that is called a book that can be kept, read, and placed on a bookshelf. Learning at an early age that one edits and reflects on what one writes is a lifelong skill.

Summary

Language and literacy is an area in itself, yet many other areas of learning are dependent on these basic skills. Many children with disabilities have challenges in this area. Ensuring that language and literacy experiences occur every day in a variety of contexts with interesting variations provides needed support. Young children need to develop the literacy skills for further learning as well as a commitment to literacy.

Educational Resources

Child Literacy Centre: Reading to Babies, Toddlers and Young Children. The Why? The What? and the How? The title really cover it. It also includes information on choosing books and tips on using them with children of different ages. http://www.childliteracy.com/babies.html

Children's Literature Web Guide provides information about available literature for children with many links. It also has lists of children's book that have received awards. http://www.ucalgary.ca/~dkbrown/index.html

Little Explorers by Enchanted Learning is set up like a children's picture dictionary in eight different languages. Although you need to subscribe to enjoy all of the advantages many of them are available free. http://www.EnchantedLearning.com/Dictionary.html

iLoveLanguages contains 2,400 links to languages and literature from around the world from Aboriginal to Yiklamu. http://www.ilovelanguages.com/

International Reading Association (IRA) seeks to improve the quality of reading instruction through studying the reading processes and teaching techniques, and serving as a clearinghouse for the dissemination of reading research. IRA publishes a journal *Reading Online* about reading. http://www.reading.org/

For additional resources, visit the book companion website for this text at www.cengage.com/education/deiner.

Discovery Activities:
Mathematics, Science, and Technology

Mathematics, science, and computers are taught as hands-on experiences in the early childhood curriculum. Young children are beginning to think logically and moving into more abstract concepts. However, simply telling them about their world is rarely effective. They need to develop a solid base of internalized experiences as a foundation for later abstract scientific and mathematical thinking.

Activity Goals

Activities are organized by the goals they support. Goals that focus directly on discovery are given first. The activity number is provided after the goal to make finding the activity more efficient. The activities that are in the book have their number identified; those that are in the book companion website are followed by a "w" (refer to Table R3–1).

Discovery Guidelines

The following guidelines will be helpful as you think about adapting discovery activities to meet the needs of children with diverse abilities.

Adapting activities for children with:	
Specific learning disabilities	Emphasize the role of technology and software, particularly in the areas of reading and math. Support children in learning word processing skills and using such supports as spell and grammar check.
Social, emotional and behavioral disorders	Use a discovery-based approach. Reduce stress. For some children warm water may be relaxing, so teach relevant concepts using it. Use software that helps children be in control and is responsive to them.
Attention-deficit/hyperactivity disorder	Talk about the brain and how it works. Teach children skills to use the computer independently and help them choose appropriate programs.
Communication disorders	Emphasize the vocabulary that goes with math and science. Teach children about body parts that are involved with making sound. Use the speech synthesizer to help children speak if appropriate.
English language learners	Use context for teaching math and science vocabulary in both English and the home language. Teach computer skills and use computer programs that support both English and the home language.
Autism spectrum disorders	Use the digital cameras and computer to take advantage of visual learning skills. Make your own picture menus about your class and choices children have. Help children sequence activities.

Intellectual disabilities	Start with the concrete and allow children to repeat experiences and to do variations. Help them generalize what they have learned to real situations.
Gifts and talents	Encourage children to expand on themes and explore them in more depth. Have more complex interactive computer programs, and encourage the use of technology to solve problems. Explore perspective through a digital camera and help children capture some of the complex projects they have made in this way as well.
Special health care needs	Help children understand the scientific process and how science may impact their health. Have children become more independent by counting pills, and learning the times they are taken. Work on safety and hygiene and their understanding of how disease is spread.
Orthopedic and neurologic impairments	Help children relate the concepts of size, distance, speed, and time to themselves, any equipment they might use, and their safety. Focus on some of the mechanical aspects of sciences such as pulleys and magnets that may help them reach objects. Support their use of adaptive technology.
Hearing impairments	Help children learn about body parts involved in hearing. Use microphones and other aids that control volume. Use computers that can translate printed input into verbal output.
Visual impairments	Help children learn about body parts involved in vision. Use magnifying glasses and other forms of magnification. Help children learn to measure by stepping things off. Use computer fonts to change the size of print. Scan materials and have them made larger (or do this with a copier). Use digital cameras with zoom lenses.

Table R3–1: Activity goals and activity numbers in text and online

Goals	Activity Numbers
• To improve number sense and numeration	3–1, 3–2, 3–3, 3–4, 3–5, 3–10 3–31w, 3–32w, 3–33w, 3–34w, 3–35w, 3–43w
• To improve geometric and spatial sense	3–6 3–33w, 3–34w, 3–36w, 3–37w, 3–38w, 3–39w, 3–40w, 3–41w
• To improve measurement concepts	3–7, 3–17, 3–30 3–35w, 3–36w, 3–37w, 3–39w, 3–42w
• To improve estimation skills	3–5, 3–8, 3–10, 3–11, 3–12 3–32w, 3–42w, 3–46w, 3–47w, 3–49w
• To identify and understand patterns and relationships	3–4, 3–6, 3–8, 3–19, 3–25, 3–26, 3–27 3–35w, 3–36w, 3–37w, 3–41w
• To improve knowledge of whole number operations and computations	3–3, 3–8, 3–9, 3–11 3–31w, 3–43w, 3–46w, 3–47w, 3–48w
• To improve knowledge of fractions and decimals	3–2 3–44w, 3–45w
• To improve observational skills	3–10, 3–13, 3–14, 3–15, 3–16, 3–17, 3–21 3–45w, 3–49w, 3–50w, 3–51w, 3–52w, 3–53w
• To improve classification skills	3–6, 3–7, 3–15, 3–18, 3–19, 3–20 3–34w, 3–38w, 3–41w, 3–42, 3–49w, 3–50w
• To improve cause-and-effect reasoning	3–9, 3–13, 3–11, 3–20, 3–22, 3–23 3–50w, 3–51w, 3–52w, 3–53w, 3–54w, 3–55w

- To improve generalization skills

  3–14, 3–18, 3–19, 3–21, 3–22, 3–24

  3–37w

- To increase knowledge of the natural world

  3–14, 3–15, 3–18, 3–21

  3–47w, 3–49w, 3–54w, 3–56w

- To make predictions

  3–9, 3–16, 3–20

  3–51w, 3–52w, 3–54w, 3–55w, 3–56w

- To improve technology skills

  3–17, 3–22, 3–23, 3–24, 3–25, 3–26, 3–27, 3–28, 3–29, 3–30

  3–43w, 3–55w

- To increase thinking and reasoning skills

  3–7, 3–12

  3–38w

- To follow directions

  3–23, 3–28, 3–29, 3–30

  3–40w, 3–44w

- To improve reading literacy

  3–1, 3–3, 3–5, 3–11, 3–24, 3–25, 3–26, 3–27, 3–28, 3–29

  3–31w, 3–32w 3–33w 3–40w

- To increase vocabulary

  3–1, 3–2

  3–56w

- To improve sensory motor integration

  3–4, 3–12, 3–13

  3–39w, 3–44w, 3–45w, 3–48w, 3–53w

Discovery Activities

Mathematics: Small Group or Individual

3-1 Matching Symbols

Goals: To improve number sense and numeration; to improve reading literacy; to increase vocabulary

Materials: Cards numbered 1 through 20, cards with up to 20 symbols

Procedure: Have the children match the number and symbol cards. As children begin, make the cards large and only use the numbers 1 through 5.

Assessment: The child will match numeral cards from 1–20 to the appropriate number symbol cards.

Accommodations and Integration: Initially use cards to count and identify numbers. Encourage children to point to or touch the symbols as they count. Cardboard or laminated cards are easier to handle (see Figure R3–1). Add cards that have different shapes or pictures on them (small animal stickers); include cards that have different symbols on the same card (dot, square, sticker) with different spatial arrangements (see Figure R3–2). Encourage children to put all of the cards with the same number of symbols in a pile. Help children learn that the number value does not change based on specific symbols or their arrangement on the card. Emphasize the language of equivalency—"same as," "equals"—and the concepts "more," "less," and so on. Use sandpaper or felt numbers and shapes to provide tactile cues.

FIGURE R3–1: Cards with Symbols and Numbers

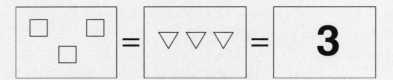

FIGURE R3–2: Cards with Different Spatial Configurations and Different Symbols and Numbers

---

Mathematics: Small Group or Individual

3-2 Fractions

Goals: To improve number sense and numeration; to improve knowledge of fractions and decimals; to increase vocabulary

Materials: Box or bag to contain whole objects; and those objects cut in half, thirds, and fourths:

pieces of cardboard	cards	pieces of felt	drinking straws
paper plates	pieces of note paper	pieces of paper or poster board of different sizes	

Procedure: Show the children the whole objects and then the same object cut in pieces. Talk about how the pieces go together to form a whole (as if a puzzle). Identify the names of the different fractions (half, thirds, fourths, and so on).

Assessment: The child will put pieces of objects together to make a whole; count the number of pieces; and identify the fraction based on the number of pieces.

Accommodations and Integration: Let children use the pieces like a puzzle, with fewer pieces and materials that are more dissimilar. As children get the idea of putting the pieces together, introduce the idea of fractions, starting with half. Use the vocabulary "half" and "whole." Talk about the mathematical properties that make something *half*. When children understand the concept of half, introduce other fractions and have children cut some objects into thirds and fourths. Introduce the term "equals." Use the vocabulary of "whole" and "half" during snack, asking children to eat half of their apple slices or raisins. As they consume some, ask them to eat half again to help them see the relative nature of fractions.

Mathematics: Small Group

3-3 100's Game

Goals: To improve number sense and numeration skills; to improve reading literacy; to improve knowledge of whole number operations and computations

Materials: Unifix™ cubes (6 colors), a color die, a number die, Unifix™ number track

Procedure: In a small group have children play a game with Unifix™ cubes. Each child takes a turn rolling a set of dice. After rolling the dice, the child stacks the appropriate number and color of Unifix™ cubes together. Then the child places the cubes on a Unifix™ number track starting at the number 1. Each child follows the same procedure. The children add their stacks of Unifix™ cubes to the ones on the number track until they reach 100.

Assessment: The child will roll a set of dice (one with colors and one with numbers), and look at the dice to determine what color and how many Unifix™ cubes to stack and stack them.

Unifix™ cubes offer the potential for developing many aspects of number sense and numeration.

Accommodations and Integration: Start with only one color of Unifix™ cubes and only use the number die. As children become more competent add an additional number die so the children must add the dice together to obtain the number of Unifix™ cubes needed or add the color die. Providing a noncompetitive game allows children to focus on the outcome of the game rather than competing with peers.

Mathematics: Small Group

3-4 Number Line

Goals: To improve number sense and numeration; to identify and understand patterns and relationships; to improve sensory motor integration

Materials: A 20-foot length of fabric marked into 20 1-foot areas and numbered consecutively from 1 to 20, a spinner or dice

Procedure: Spin a spinner or roll dice and have children move on the fabric the designated number of spaces.

Assessment: The child will accurately move the specified number of spaces.

Accommodations and Integration: Use only one die or numbers up to 6. As children become more competent using the board game format, increase the complexity by adding "wild cards" and the child who lands on an occupied space sends the other child back to "start." This is a variation of a board game, with the children as the playing pieces. Although this may initially be a teacher-directed game, once children learn the rules, encourage them to play independently. Children can gain a sensory motor feeling for numbers by playing while they participate with peers.

Mathematics: Large Group

3-5 Bead Estimation

Goals: To improve number sense and numeration; to improve estimation skills; to improve reading literacy

Procedure: During a group time show children a bag of wooden beads or other objects. Ask children to estimate how many there are and what color there is the most of in the bag. Record each child's answer. Have children break up into groups and give each group a portion of the bag. The children are to sort the beads by color and count them. When all the children have had a chance to sort, come back together as a group and combine all the group's findings to discover what color there is the most of and how many beads there are all together.

Assessment: The child will look at a bag of beads, estimate how many there are in the bag, and determine what color there is the most of in the bag. The child will sort the beads by color, count the beads, and record the results.

Accommodations and Integration: Use colored 1-inch blocks instead of beads and only have two colors with twice as many of one color. As children become more proficient, have two different kinds of objects that vary in size (for example, Unifix™ cubes and Cuisenaire™ rods). Repeat this activity with various other bags of items until the children have a good sense of estimation.

Mathematics: Large Group

3-6 Picture Shapes

Goals: To improve geometric and spatial sense; to identify and understand patterns and relationships; to improve classification skills

Materials: Geometric shapes cut from cardboard, pictures of common objects with definite geometric shapes mounted on cards (ball, house, ice cream cone, bed)

Procedure: Have children match their geometric shapes with the shapes in the picture or drawing.

Assessment: The child will match the appropriate shape(s) with the picture. The child will sort the pictures by the shapes they contain.

Accommodations and Integrations: Choose pictures with little detail and help children place shapes over the pictures to find a shape in the picture. Then have the children sort the pictures according to shape. Use more complex pictures with several shapes and have children find shapes in a picture containing several shapes. This activity helps children recognize and classify geometric shapes in their world. It requires visual generalization and application of knowledge of shapes to pictures of real objects. Talk with children about why a particular shape is functional for a particular purpose; the pitch of roofs (or angle of a triangle) and the north-south orientation of a structure relative to snow and its weight; a roof overhang to keep the sun from shining in regions that are very hot.

Mathematics: Small Group

3-7 Measuring Tools

Goals: To improve measurement concepts; to improve classification skills; to increase thinking and reasoning skills

Materials: Timer, ruler, food scale, hourglass, stopwatch, tape measure, bathroom scale, alarm clock, calendar, yardstick, balance scale, meter stick, paper, pencils

Procedure: Place one group of measuring devices on a table with appropriate suggestions for things to be measured, timed, or weighed. Encourage children to use and explore the tools. Discuss with children the efficacy of their choices, what worked, and what did not work as well. Encourage children to record and graph their results and to make predictions about other measurements.

Assessment: The child will choose an appropriate measuring tool.

Accommodations and Integration: Begin with just one type of measurement such as time. Brainstorm with children different ways of measuring time and why some methods work better than others depending upon the purpose. Contrast a watch with a calendar and help children make other comparisons. Talk about why people carry date books and their uses. Be sure to include the children's daily schedule as a measure of time. When there are special events discuss how they are noted. Have children order objects and events based on principles of measurement. This is a good activity for children working in pairs. It encourages inclusion and teaches math concepts.

Mathematics: Small Group

3-8 Number Dog

Goals: To improve estimation skills; to identify and understand patterns and relationships; to improve knowledge of whole number operations and computations

Materials: Picture of a Dachshund dog with the body separated into 10 segments with varying numbers of dots within each segment, construction paper cut to the sizes of each segment on the dog with a numeral written on it that corresponds to the number of dots on the dog.

Procedure: Encourage children to explore this activity in small groups or individually. Have children estimate the number of dots in each segment, count them, and find the matching numeral to fit over the segment. For variation, have the segments make a repeating pattern and the children add segments to make the dog longer.

Assessment: The child will estimate the number of dots in each section of the dog, count them, attach the correct numeral, and add up the number of dots on the dog.

Accommodations and Integration: Make the number of dots in each section small. Have children only count the dots and match the segment with an equal set of dots, not the numeral. Creating an animal or other figure like the number dog that incorporates one to one correspondence helps ensure it is part of the curriculum.

Mathematics: Small Group

3-9 The Bottle Game

Goals: To improve knowledge of whole number operations and computations; to make predictions; to improve cause-and-effect reasoning

Materials: 28 small plastic water bottles filled with colored water (12 yellow, 9 blue, 6 red, and 1 green), 1 piece each of yellow, blue, red, and green construction paper (2 pieces of each if teams are playing), dice (oversized)

Procedure: Set up the game as shown in Figure R3–3. The floor provides more room to move. Two children can play at a time or there can be two teams of two children each. Each participant gets a turn to roll the die. The child collects the appropriate number of yellow bottles with each roll and places them on his yellow sheet of paper. When a child has three yellow bottles, he can trade them in for one blue bottle. When the child has traded enough yellow bottles in to get three blue bottles, he can trade the blue bottles in for a red bottle. When the child has collected three red bottles, he can trade them in for the green bottle and the game is over.

Assessment: The child will roll the number die and collect the appropriate number and color of bottles while trading in his number and color of bottles until he gets the green bottle.

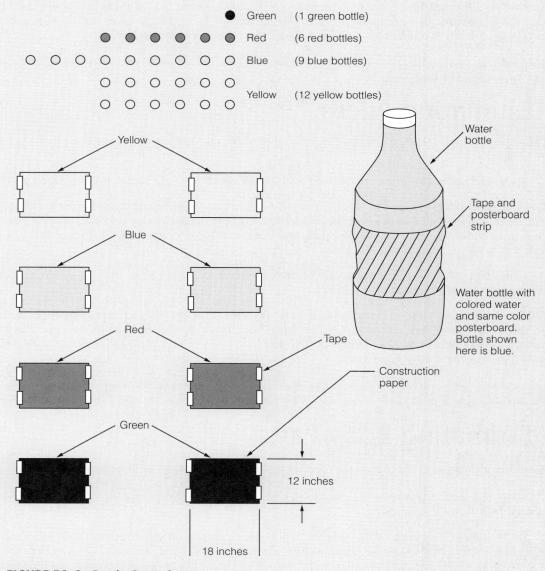

FIGURE R3–3: Bottle Game Set up

Accommodations and Integration: Children can use the bottles to indicate the number on the die. This activity provides an opportunity for children to problem-solve on various levels and work with others to win the game. It requires counting, making sets, trading, predicting, and deductive reasoning (with permission of Nancy Edwards).

Mathematics: Small Group

3-10 Counting Jars

Goals: To improve number sense and numeration; to improve observational skills; to improve estimation skills

Materials: Four to five jars of the same size, a variety of common objects (markers, wooden cubes, crayons, wooden beads, and so on), paper, pencils

Procedure: Set up a table with four to five jars filled with various numbers of different objects. Encourage children to carefully look at each jar. Ask children to estimate the number of objects in each jar and write down their estimates. Then have children count the items in the jars and compare this with their estimations. Talk about the variables considered in estimating.

Assessment: The child will estimate the number of items, count them, compare the total to his estimation, and reflect on the process.

Accommodations and Integration: Keep the numbers small until children get the idea. Talk about the relationship between object size and the number of objects in containers. Estimation is a skill that takes practice. Use different-sized items and encourage children to think about size as a variable that influences estimation.

Mathematics: Small Group or Individual

3-11 Estimating Prices

Goals: To improve estimation skills; to improve knowledge of whole number operations and computations; to improve reading literacy

Materials: Variety of items with a price value between $0.01 and $0.99 with price tags on them, paper, pencils

Procedure: Have the children choose four or five items from the variety of items displayed. Have the children estimate how much the items will cost all together. Let the children add up the items together and compare the total with the estimated total. Talk with the children about the differences between the two amounts. Encourage them to reflect on the differences.

Assessment: The child will look at the prices of four items, estimate the total cost of the items, compare his estimate with the arithmetic total, and reflect on the process.

Accommodations and Integration: Have children start with two items and make the prices low. Take children on a field trip to the grocery store, buy several inexpensive items, and have the children estimate the cost. This encourages children to estimate the amount of money they will need to purchase items. It is concrete and useful. It could be integrated into a dramatic play area that sells various items.

Mathematics: Small Group or Individual

3-12 Estimating Body Parts

Goals: To improve estimation skills; to increase thinking and reasoning skills; to increase sensory motor integration

Materials: Copies of a picture of a body with two lines next to each body part that needs to be measured, chain links, blue and red crayons, string

Procedure: Show children the picture of the body and talk about measuring different parts of their body. Let them work with each other to use string to measure the length of their arms, legs, head, hand, and foot. Cut and label the string for each part for each child. Then have children estimate the number of chain links they will need to create the same length as their pieces of string. Have the children write their estimation in blue next to the body part on their papers. After making the estimations have the children use the chain links to determine the actual length of the string. Have the children write the actual length in red next to the appropriate body part. When the children are finished discuss with them the differences in the numbers, which were easy to estimate, which were hard, and why.

Assessment: The child will estimate how many chain links it will take to equal the length of his arm, head, leg, hand, and foot. Compare this with the actual measurements and reflect on the differences.

Accommodations and Integration: Have an adult assist the child in determining the length of the string. Encourage children to measure body parts held straight and bent. Have children use this method to measure furniture, dolls, and stuffed animals as well. Providing concrete and interesting items to measure enables children to be more involved and work together to accomplish the tasks.

Science: Individual or Small Group

3-13 Goop

Goals: To improve observational skills; to improve cause-and-effect reasoning; to improve sensory motor integration

Materials: Water, cornstarch, flour, sugar, bowls, or jelly roll trays

Procedure: Have children mix approximately equal amounts of cornstarch and water to make goop. Allow children to experiment with the proportions and observe the results. Help children think about the different and confusing states of the goop. Then, use equal proportions of flour and water and compare the results to the goop. Then combine sugar and water. Help children learn about the different properties and reactions of materials that look similar.

Assessment: The child will make goop and describe the properties of goop.

Accommodations and Integration: Goop requires little strength to manipulate and defies coordination. It is a soothing, yet intriguing media. It is edible (although this is not advised) and relatively easy to clean up. It can be used on a bed tray, and it is clean.

Science: Individual or Small Group

3-14 Ant Farm

Goals: To improve observational skills; to improve generalization skills; to increase knowledge of the natural world

Materials: Sets of two clear glass jars (one small enough to fit inside the other), loose or sandy soil, sugar, water, ants

Procedure: Put the smaller jar inside the large one, open side down. Fill the larger one with loose soil—don't pack it down. (You want to be able to see the ants, so you want the space relatively narrow.) Collect ants from one ant colony only for each jar (otherwise, they may fight). Collect about 20 ants, put them in the jar, and screw on the lid. Once a week, feed the ants a few drops of sugar water; add a few grains of birdseed, if you wish.

Assessment: The child will describe what she thinks happens on an ant farm.

Accommodations and Integration: Concentrate on the observation process. Point out what is going on in the ant farm. Then make a second ant farm and encourage the children to compare the two. Have them draw the configuration of tunnels. Encourage them to look up ants in reference books and on the Internet to learn how ants live and work. Discuss the survival needs of animals and how ants are both different and the same as other animals. It is possible to get commercially available ant farms, but the process of making your own is part of the children's learning.

Science: Large or Small Group

3-15 Nature Board

Goals: To improve observational skills; to improve classification skills; to increase knowledge of the natural world

Materials: Objects found on a nature walk, cardboard, glue, small bags, rubber gloves

Procedure: On a nature walk, help the children pick up objects such as nuts, sticks, stones, leaves, twigs, and so on. Start by labeling objects for the children. While you are on the walk, point out obvious relationships: "Look, you found a leaf. Let's look up in the tree and see if there are more like it. I think this leaf fell from this tree. This is called an oak tree. You have a green oak leaf." Try to get at least two of each object. In addition to picking up natural objects, using gloves, pick up environmental pollutants as well: Styrofoam, aluminum cans, plastic bags, cigarette butts. Put these in a separate bag. When you get back to the class, glue each of the natural objects onto a separate, small piece of cardboard. Put the "pairs" to these objects in a bag, and have children see if they can match the designated object. Have children try to remember where they found certain objects and why they might be there, for example, acorns and pine cones under trees. Classify the objects found in as many different ways as possible. Talk with children about pollutants and the problems they cause in the environment. Have them help figure out some potential solutions to these problems.

Encourage children to examine what they find on a nature walk and to think about the relationship between what they find (pinecones) and where they find them (under pine trees).

Assessment: The child will collect items and classify them in a variety of ways.

Accommodations and Integration: Help children focus on the walk itself. Take digital pictures of the various items collected and the areas from which they were found and let children use these as clues for their classification. Have children make a map of the nature walk and draw significant landmarks. Help them mark where objects were found and glue some of the objects to the map. Classifying objects makes them more relevant. And, it is never too early to begin environmental education.

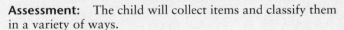

Science: Small or Large Group

3-16 Pollution

Goals: To improve observational skills; to make predictions; to improve cause-and-effect reasoning

Materials: Three sticks of fresh celery with leaves, or white carnations, three glasses of water, red and blue food coloring

Procedure: Cut off the bottoms of celery sticks or carnation stems. Put a few drops of red food coloring in one glass of water and blue in a second. Leave the water in the third glass clear. Put one stick of celery (or carnation) in each glass. Do this early in the day and check at the end of the day. Cut the celery sticks and see how the ones in colored water are different from the one in fresh water. One needs only observe the carnations to see the effects. Discuss the effects of pollution and how it can get into plants and animals including people.

Assessment: The child will predict what color the celery will turn when set in colored water and explain how pollution can affect the food we eat.

Accommodations and Integration: Help children think about pollution in a more concrete way. Have them think about drinking the water they wash their hands in. The carnations may look beautiful, but it is important that children see beyond the visual effect. Talk with children about pollution in underground water. Tell them how it gets into the plants we eat. Have them begin to think about ways of preventing pollution. Pollution is a relatively abstract concept, and children may learn only about the principle of osmosis. Talk about the implications of increasing populations and conservation. Help children generate ideas for actions to take at school and home to decrease pollution. It is important to make this global, abstract problem relevant to children.

Science: Small Group

3-17 Maps

Goals: To improve observational skills; to improve measurement concepts; to improve technology skills

Materials: Cardboard, water, paper, crayons, a container, masking tape, papier-mâché, string or yarn

Procedure: Have the children choose an area of the classroom (block, dramatic play) or playground and draw it on cardboard with crayons. Divide the area and paper into quarters. Discuss with the children where things are in their drawing and how they decide where to put them. Make large graph paper for the children (1 inch equals 1 square foot) and use string or yarn to mark off the area the children are mapping in 1-foot-square sections. (If you have floor tiles that are 1 foot square, this helps.) Ask the children what in the area is flat and what should stand up from the surface (tables, swings, and so on). Use papier-mâché to help children make maps that reflect these contours. Talk about relative size as it relates to both area and height.

Assessment: The child will draw a picture of the classroom, divide the picture into quarters, and describe what objects are in different quarters of his map.

Accommodations and Integration: Using a digital camera take a picture of the four quarters of the room to help children figure out what objects are in which areas. Tape the four pictures together. Then make another map. Do this project over several days; they need not be consecutive.

Science: Small Group

3-18 Food Lotto

Goals: To improve classification skills; to improve generalization skills; to increase knowledge of the natural world

Materials: A Lotto game with four sets of pictures of fruits or vegetables

To Make: *Take two identical pictures of each fruit or vegetable in the following states:*
whole fruit or vegetable as it grows (for example, apple on an apple tree, squash on a plant)
whole fruit (vegetable) to be matched with a picture of the same fruit (vegetable) cut in half and smaller pieces
whole fruit (vegetable) to be matched with a picture of the same fruit (vegetable) in a different state
(for example, apple/applesauce; orange/orange juice; pumpkin/pumpkin pie; corn on the cob/corn in a bowl)
Use the photographs to make a lotto game

Procedure: Let the children first have experience looking at and tasting the fruits and vegetables, then go on to the Lotto game. Start with a traditional Lotto game in which children match the identical pictures. Then have the child match the other sets. This can be done individually or in small groups.

Assessment: The child will match the sets of food pictures correctly.

Accommodations and Integration: Choose less familiar fruits and vegetables (star fruit, yard-long beans, yucca, etc.). Use seed catalogues. Two or three of the same kind are especially useful. Some children may have trouble recognizing the source of less familiar food.

Science: Individual or Small Group

3-19 Sorting

Goals: To improve classification skills; to improve generalization skills; to identify and understand patterns and relationships

Materials: Three containers for each child and objects that can be sorted into two categories, blocks, fruits, animals, furniture, vegetables, vehicles, kitchen utensils, balls:

OBJECTS	CATEGORY A	CATEGORY B
buttons	rough	smooth
buttons	two holes	four holes
silverware	forks	knives
silverware	big spoons	little spoons
shapes	circles	squares
shapes	oval	rectangle

Procedure: Anchor three containers to a board or place them in a row (coffee cans with lids work well). Vary the size of the can based on the size of the objects to be sorted. Put the objects in the middle container. Then have the children sort the objects into the two empty containers.

Assessment: The child will sort the objects into two containers using a classification system.

Accommodations and Integration: Start with simple objects with obvious differences (blocks and balls) that are large enough to handle easily and few enough to complete the task. Have children sort the objects into categories and tell you the basis for their sorting. Then have them resort the same objects using a different classification system. Have them sort the objects into three categories. For children who rely on tactile cues, choose objects that have tactile cues (rough and smooth, one or two holes).

Science: Small Group

3-20 Magnets

Goals: To make predictions; to improve cause-and-effect reasoning; to improve classifications skills

Materials: Magnets of varying sizes, shapes, and strengths; assorted small nonmetal objects (plastic milk bottle tops, plastic clips); assorted small metal objects (not aluminum) paper clips (large and small), nails, washers, safety pins (large and small), staples; shallow box of metal filings covered with plexiglass (metal filings are available from hardware stores that cut pipes)

Procedure: Give the children a variety of magnets and materials to experiment with. Encourage them to use the magnet both on the top and bottom of the box with metal filings. Ask them to sort objects according to the object's response to the magnet. Ask them to predict whether specific objects will be attracted by the magnet. Have them discover objects in the room that are attracted to the magnet.

Assessment: The child will predict and sort materials based on which will be attracted to magnets and which ones will not respond to the magnet.

Accommodations and Integration: Allow children to explore the magnets and their properties. Teach them to modify objects so that they will be attracted to the magnet (attach a paper clip to a small piece of paper). Encourage children to chart the results of their investigations. Have them explore the strength of different magnets by finding out how many paper clips each magnet can pick up. Introduce paper clips of different sizes including plastic coated paper clips and see how many of each size can be picked up. Weigh or balance the different clips. Graph the results. Encourage children to think of ways that magnets might be useful. Add a magnet to the end of a stick. Have children sit in a chair and use it as an extension of their arm to get things they cannot reach such as paper clips. This activity is an initial step in showing how devices can help those with physical impairments. *Note:* This activity should not be used if there are children under three and even with older children this requires close teacher supervision.

Science: Large and Small Group

3-21 Insect Aquarium

Goals: To increase knowledge of the natural world; to improve observational skills; to improve generalization skills

Materials: Small, clear containers with lids that have holes in them, aquarium, dirt, dish of water, plants/grass/flowers

Procedure: Show the children an aquarium with nothing in it. Tell them that they are going to collect insects to put into the aquarium so that the class can observe them. Ask the children what things they might need in the aquarium before they collect the insects and why. Discuss that dirt, water, plants, grass, flowers, and so on are all appropriate (have these items ready to add when the children state them). If there are items that the children state are not available tell the children that they can look for more materials when they go to collect insects. Make the aquarium. Give each child a container. Outside, encourage children to collect a variety of insects for the aquarium. Discuss with children how an aquarium works. Talk about the natural environment of insects and how they can try to make it as much like their natural home as possible.

Assessment: The child will catch an insect and place it in the aquarium, observe interactions between the insects within the aquarium and record them.

Accommodations and Integration: If children are wary of picking up insects, encourage them to think of ways to deal with this (let them crawl up a stick, wear gloves, and so on). Use magnifying glasses to identify insects and observe them. Use reference books and the Internet to learn more about insects in the aquarium to ensure the environment will sustain them. This activity enables children to search for insects and learn about their needs and to provide an appropriate environment for them.

Technology: Large Group

3-22 Input-Output

Goals: To improve technology skills; to improve cause-and-effect reasoning; to improve generalization skills

Materials: Chalkboard, chalk outline of a person

Procedure: Talk with the children about how they learn information. For example, how did they decide what to wear today? If they looked outside and saw the sun was shining, that was visual *input*. If their mother told them what to wear, that was auditory *input*. That input went into their central processing unit (CPU), or brain. They all came with clothes on; that is *output*. Help children think about how they learn in terms of an *input-CPU-output* framework. Ask the children, "Who is absent today?" (input). The children look around, and in their CPU (brain), they compare who they see with their memory of who is in the class. They process the information. Then they decide that Lanie is absent (output). Use the chalkboard to draw further illustrations for the children. Use a simple machine such as a drinking straw dispenser. Explain how pressing the lever is an *input*, the movement inside the CPU causes the straw to fall, and the straw is the *output*. Or turn the handle of the jack-in-the-box (input), something happens inside (CPU), the figure pops up (output). Encourage children to design their own processors based on the principle of input-CPU-output. Help them think of simple machines that work on this principle (water and juice machines, jukeboxes). Now help children go a step further and think about the automatic teller at the bank and the computer at the fast-food restaurant. (*Note:* Tell children they must put money in before they can take it out!)

Assessment: The child will accurately identify at least one input and one output.

Accommodations and Integration: Take children on a field trip to an automatic teller, juice machine, or other place close by where they can experience the input-CPU-output experience. Encourage parents to talk about this with children when the occasions arise. This is a basic introduction to the concepts of input-CPU-output, some basic computer terminology, and logical thinking. It is important for children to know that if they don't put anything in the computer, nothing will come out. They can use a software program, but somebody had to put all the information into the computer.

Technology: Small Group

3-23 Robot-Controller

Goals: To improve technology skills; to improve cause-and-effect reasoning; to follow directions

Materials: None

Procedure: Have one child be the controller of a robot and another (or the teacher) be the robot. The controller's job is to command the robot. The robot could initially work like a toggle switch (on or off). If the child says, "Jump," the robot jumps until the child says, "Stop jumping." When the teacher is the robot, she can lead the child into more complexity: "Shall the robot jump fast or slow?" "Shall the robot jump in place or around the room?" If the commands are unclear ("Robot walk"), send back a message: "That does not compute. Robot needs to know whether to walk forward, backward, or sideways." The feedback will help children expand their vocabulary and be more specific in their speech, as well as gain practice giving commands. Have the children take turns so that they get practice in both commanding and following directions. The children need to learn that the computer will not do anything unless they give the commands. They also need to learn that commands must be specific and some commands "will not compute," so they need to find ones that will.

Assessment: The child will give computable directions to a classmate.

Accommodations and Integration: Start with simple commands, which the teacher gives and the children respond to as a group. Then have children give two- and three-step commands at one time and increase the complexity of the cues: "Take three steps to the right and then raise your hands and clap twice." Modify the robot-controller for any situation in which someone is in charge and telling another what to do. It could be an animal trainer in the circus; a dog in (pet) obedience school; ground control to someone in a space capsule, and so on. This activity is an excellent way for children to see the results of their commands.

3-24w Buried Treasure

Goals: To improve technology skills; to improve generalization skills; to improve reading literacy

Materials: Large, flat box with top, or sand table; sand or birdseed; string or yarn; masking tape; nine small treasures; clay; marker; cards with coordinates on one side and a drawing or picture of the treasure in those coordinates on the other

To Make: *Using four pieces of string, divide the box into nine equal segments (or start with two pieces of string and four segments). Tape the string so that it goes on top of the open box. In each segment, put a small piece of clay to keep the treasure from moving around, and stick the treasure in the clay. Add sand to the box, making sure the treasure stays in the designated segment. Divide the top of the box in the same way, using a marker to divide it into sections. Add a narrow section across the left side and the bottom; put the numbers 1, 2, and 3 on the sides and A, B, and C on the top and bottom.*

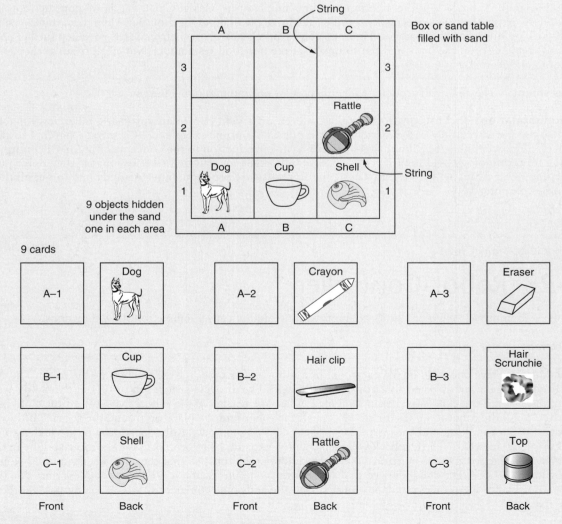

FIGURE R3–4: **Design and Cards for Buried Treasure**

Give the children a card with a set of coordinates (2-B) and see if they can find the right treasure. Draw a simple picture of the treasure on the back of the card so they can check themselves (see Figure R3–4).

Procedure: Have children predict what they will find. Then, have children find the treasures. Once they have the idea, bury the treasures, give them a drawing of the area marked off, and have them chart the location of the treasures.

Assessment: The child will follow the picture directions and find the buried treasure.

Accommodations and Integration: Use string to make only four areas with hidden objects. Help children use the coordinates to bury treasure for others to find. This helps children learn to move in a systematic way between vertical and horizontal planes, a skill that is necessary not only for the computer but for copying from the chalkboard. It also helps children learn to read the coordinates of a graph.

Technology: Individual

3-25 My Keyboard

Goals: To improve technology skills; to identify and understand patterns and relationships; to improve reading literacy

Materials: Posterboard, keyboard markers, Velcro™

To Make: *Using the computer keyboard as a guide (see Figure R3–5), make a keyboard out of posterboard by using a large piece (12″ × 15″) for the base and smaller pieces (3/4-inch squares) for the keys. Write the letters and numbers on the keys. Place four 15-inch strips of Velcro™ across the base and attach Velcro™ to the back of each of the keys.*

If you have computers use them and ensure that children see computing as something to be shared with a friend. If you do not, build computer skills with off computer concepts.

Procedure: Place the keys in a container and have the children place the keys on the keyboard in the correct order, using a keyboard as a guide. Add a guide strip with the letters or numbers for each row of the computer keyboard for the child. Making the keyboard is a difficult task in itself, but you might add some of the additional keys, such as the return, shift, control, alternate, and delete. Choose keys that are meaningful in the software packages you use.

Assessment: The child will place letters and numbers in the correct location and identify the function of the control keys on a keyboard.

Accommodations and Integration: Initially use this as an exercise in matching letters. Place the guide strip above the Velcro.™ At the beginning, have some of the letters in place so that the children only have to find three or four missing

FIGURE R3–5: Computer Keyboard

ones. Increase the number of missing letters until the children can place all the letters. You can encourage children to locate letters and take them off the keyboard. Whether or not your classroom has a computer, this activity provides a good foundation in computing and reading literacy. Use discarded keyboards to help children become familiar with the sequences. If you have computers, use them. Ensure that computing is not seen as a solitary activity, but rather one that is to be shared with friends.

Technology: Individual or Small Group

3-26 Spell It

Goals: To improve technology skills; to identify and understand patterns and relationships; to improve reading literacy

Materials: Keyboard from My Keyboard with letters and numbers and guide strips in place, 3-inch × 15-inch poster board with a 15-inch long Velcro™ piece, basket with children's names printed on posterboard, basket with words printed on cards or posterboard

Procedure: Have children decide on a word they want to "type" and place it above the keyboard. The children can then take the letters off the keyboard and place them on the blank strip. Encourage children to replace the letters when they are finished. The guide strip is essential for this part of the process. Print words that children request and place them in the basket. Encourage children to work with a friend. As children get better, put short sentences on cards.

Assessment: The child will find letters on a Velcro™ keyboard and use them to "type" three different words.

Accommodations and Integration: Help the child find the letters on the keyboard. As this is only a pretend keyboard, words that use a letter twice will not be able to be typed. Help children think through this logic and figure out what they can do to solve the problem. This activity does not require an actual computer (although having one available is great) and supports reading literacy skills.

Technology: Small Group

3-27 Fruit Kabob

Goals: To improve technology skills; to identify and understand patterns and relationships; to improve reading literacy

Materials: Wooden skewers, cut-up apples, pineapple cubes, grapes, banana slice, rebus picture menus

Procedure: Design several rebus picture menus (these are pictures designed for nonreaders that resemble international road signs) using varying amounts of fruit (1 apple piece, 3 half grapes, 2 pineapple cubes, 1 banana slice) on a skewer or a repeating pattern of fruit (1 apple piece, 1 pineapple cube, 1 half grape, 1 apple piece, 1 pineapple cube, 1 half grape, and so on; see Figure R3–6). Let children choose the menu they want and make it. Eat the fruit kabob for snack.

Assessment: The child will look at a rebus picture menu and follow the pictures to make a fruit kabob.

Accommodations and Integration: Include a picture that uses a simple repeating pattern with just two different fruits. Cut grapes in half for younger children. Check for allergies. Increase the complexity of some of the menus by having additional fruits and more difficult patterns. Have a word menu as an alternative for children who can read. This activity gives children practice selecting from menus and interpreting rebus pictures. Use this procedure for adding fruit to a fruit salad or making trail mix, and for other food projects.

Step 1: Put name on plate

Step 2 : Decide on a pattern for the fruit

Step 3: Choose fruit to match pattern

Step 4: Get stick and put fruit on stick in pattern and put fruit stick on plate

Step 5: Eat for snack

FIGURE R3–6: **Rebus Directions for Fruit Kabob**

Technology: Large or Small Group

3-28 Alphabet Keyboard

Goals: To improve technology skills; to follow directions; to improve reading literacy

Materials: Picture of a computer keyboard for each child, a separate card of each letter of the alphabet and the numbers 0 to 9, basket, crayon or marker

Procedure: Place the cards in the basket. Draw a card and read the number or letter. Give children time to locate the letter or number and identify it. After you read the first card, give children time to locate the next item and draw a line between the first and second letter or number. Continue this process.

Assessment: The child will connect the designated letters and numbers on a drawing of a keyboard as they are drawn or read.

Accommodations and Integration: Hold up the letter or number for the children to see as you call out the letter. Give the letter or number to the child so he can match it to the keyboard or let children play this game individually choosing the letters or numbers themselves to control the pace of the activity. Vary the activity so that you call out letter sounds instead of letter names. This off-computer activity stresses keyboard skills. Children can connect the letters of their name. They can even color in the connecting shapes.

Computers: Individual or Small Group

3-29 Computer Bingo

Goals: To improve technology skills; to follow directions; to improve reading literacy

Materials: A bingo card made with the designations for a computer keyboard (see Figure R3–7), individual cards with corresponding designations, basket

Procedure: Play as you would bingo. Draw a card out of the basket, call out the information on the card (3-H), and have the children find the square and mark it.

Assessment: The child will find and place a marker on the correct letter or number on a keyboard like bingo card when the letter or number is called or shown.

Accommodations and Integration: Children can play this alone or in pairs. Point out for children the two-step decision making. (The number designates the row and then they must look for the right letter.) Have children figure out how they can call out letters that make words as they play. This off-computer activity stresses keyboard skills. Although structured like bingo, obviously all the children who follow the instructions accurately will "win."

1–1	1–2	1–3	1–4	1–5	1–6	1–7	1–8	1–9	1–0
2–Q	2–W	2–E	2–R	2–T	2–Y	2–U	2–I	2–O	2–P
3–A	3–S	3–D	3–F	3–G	3–H	3–J	3–K	3–L	3–;
4–Z	4–X	4–C	4–V	4–B	4–N	4–M	4–,	4–.	4–/

FIGURE R3–7: Computer Bingo Card

Technology: Small Group or Individual

3-30 Banana Snack

Goals: To improve technology skills; to follow directions; to improve measurement concepts

Materials: Bananas, wheat germ, plastic knives, plastic sandwich sized bags that zip closed, small paper plate and marking pen.

Procedure: Make a rebus menu for the children to follow as they make their snack (see Figure R3–8). First peel the banana and then cut it in half. Next the children take their half and cut it into small pieces (about 1/2 inch), then they measure about a tablespoon of wheat germ into the plastic bag and place the banana pieces in the bag. Seal the bag and shake the pieces of banana to get them coated with the wheat germ. When the banana is coated the children put their banana pieces on the paper plate with their name on it and eat it for snack.

Assessment: The child will follow the rebus directions to make the banana snack.

Accommodations and Integration: Make the banana snack but only have the children put the bananas in the bag and shake them. Talk to the children about recipes and how rebus recipes are much like computer menus. Encourage children to write a recipe for something they want to make. Help them identify each step in the process. Look at cookbooks

Step 1: Put name on plate

Step 2: Cut banana half

Step 3: Peel banana

Step 4: Cut banana in pieces

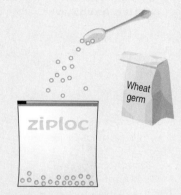

Step 5: Get plastic bag. Fill with 1 tablespoon wheat germ

Step 6: Put banana piece in bag and shake

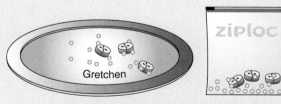

Step 7: Put banana piece on plate. Put another banana piece in bag and shake

Step 8: Eat bananas for snack

FIGURE R3–8: Rebus Directions for Bananas Snack

designed for children. Following sequential, multistep directions is an important computing skill. Using rebus pictures for illustration reinforces the concept as well. Use words that imply the sequence: "First we are going to cut the banana. Second … third …." *Note:* Be sure no children are allergic to bananas.

Summary

Young children need a solid foundation in discovery activities. In addition to doing math activities, play math games while waiting or during transitions. Children can learn as much from activities that are fun as from those that seem "academic." The arithmetic problems that we so commonly associate with school are a formalization of experiences that relate to numbers, geometry, measurement, time, and money. Many activities in this area require 2 days or more. The second time the materials are out, some children will continue to explore the materials; others will need more structure to expand their explorations. It is important that children view science as part of their world and that they see the cause-and-effect relationships rather than "teacher magic." Technology has tremendous potential for positive change for children with disabilities. They need adult scaffolding to make the system work. The educator's role is to help children see technology as a natural part of everyday life and to help them develop the skills to use it.

Educational Resources

Children's Technology Revue provides timely, accurate, and objective information about children's software and access to reviews of the software. You can see a sample but you have to subscribe to get all their reviews. http://www.childrenssoftware.com/

Discovery Channel contains lesson plans for children K indexed by grade level and topic and has a school clip art gallery that is useful when writing newsletters. http://school.discoveryeducation.com/lessonplans/index.html

Frank Potter's Science Gems provides science lesson plans for educators and links to other sources of lesson plans. http://www.sciencegems.com/

National Geographic, a resource for teachers and children, is interesting and up to date. http://www.nationalgeographic.com/education/

Smithsonian Institution describes exhibits and has places to visit virtually and in person. http://www.si.edu/

For additional resources, visit the book companion website for this text at www.cengage.com/education/deiner.

Wellness Activities:
Health, Physical Education, and Sensory Motor

Having adequate motor abilities is important for young children. They learn from the sensations acquired through movement. The acquisition of new sensations occurs through active participation in the environment. Because children with disabilities, like others, spend increasing amounts of time watching television, they may need encouragement and support to develop motor skills. They need to participate in activities that expose their muscles to demanding tasks. We must resist the temptation to do too many things for children with disabilities and must allow them to participate in enough resistance and power activities to develop strength.

Activity Goals

Activities are organized by the goals they support. Goals that focus directly on health, physical education, and sensory motor are given first. The activity number is provided after the goal to make finding the activity more efficient. The activities that are in the book have their number identified; those that are in the book companion website are followed by a "w" (refer to Table R4–1).

Wellness Guidelines

The following guidelines will be helpful as you think about adapting health, physical education, and sensory motor activities to meet the needs of children with diverse abilities.

Adapting activities for children with:	
Specific learning disabilities	Ensure the children can read safety signals and pair illustrations with words. Work on sensory motor integration. Choose activities that support fundamental motor activities especially those that develop trunk strength and stability.
Social, emotional and behavioral disorders	Remind children about health and safety rules. Play noncompetitive games. Teach children to vent energy using large motor activities. Support children in refining small motor skills.
Attention-deficit/hyperactivity disorder	Provide opportunities to respond to safety signals. Help children learn to evaluate their environment relative to health and safety. Encourage children to use active play to release energy.

Communication disorders	Teach children the vocabulary that goes with health and safety. Focus fine motor skills on movements associated with speech (breath control, lip and tongue action), visual discrimination, and writing skills. Help children recognize when they are tense and teach them how to relax voluntarily.
English language learners	Teach safety skills with verbal and visual cues. Role play them as well. Use motor skills to teach prepositions (on, under, in front of, behind, and so on) and other important vocabulary in the home language and English.
Autism spectrum disorders	Monitor health and safety practices. Visually post health and safety rules. Coach children through motor tasks. Simplify activities and use relatively large objects with fewer pieces.
Intellectual disabilities	Make good health and safety practices part of the routine. Do a task analysis and support children in attaining adaptive skills independently. Simplify activities and have children repeat these with minor variations.
Gifted and talented	Teach children to recognize a variety of safety signs and to respond to these appropriately. Although physical development is within the normal range support the development of fundamental motor skills. Scaffold skills as needed.
Special health care needs	Work on body awareness and the early identifications of symptoms. Teach children the events that might trigger a reaction. Work on developing strength and endurance while respecting physical limits. Teach children to pace themselves and to learn to use fine motor activities for times they need a break.
Orthopedic and neurologic impairments	Teach children body awareness. Adapt activities to help children control their environment (put small objects in a jellyroll pan or tray). Help children strengthen body parts that are under their control and will increase mobility. Use lightweight materials (cardboard blocks) and materials that tolerate some degree of error (Bristle™ blocks).
Hearing impairments	Teach children to recognize and respond to visual signs of danger as well as the auditory sounds within their range of hearing. Focus on activities that promote body awareness and balancing (starting, stopping, turning). Help children integrate visual and tactile input with motor skills.
Visual impairments	Teach children to use their sense of touch to tell if their hands are clean. Help children integrate visual and tactile input with motor skills. Teach children how to move through unknown areas safely. Work on body awareness and motor planning, as they relate to orientation and mobility training. Help children learn when they need visual aids and how to use them. If children wear glasses decide how they can be safely worn during active play.

Table R4–1: Activity goals and activity numbers in text and online

Goals	Activity Numbers
• To improve health literacy	4–1, 4–2, 4–3, 4–4, 4–5, 4–26 4–31w, 4–32w, 4–33w, 4–34w
• To increase adaptive skills	4–1, 4–2, 4–4, 4–5, 4–15, 4–16, 4–17 4–31w, 4–32w, 4--33w, 4–34w, 4–42w
• To improve locomotor skills	4–6, 4–7, 4–8, 4–10, 4–13 4–35w, 4–37w
• To improve gross motor manipulative skills	4–11, 4–12, 4–23, 4–24 4–36w, 4–40w, 4–44w
• To improve stability skills	4–9, 4–13, 4–21, 4–24, 4–25 4–38w

- To improve physical fitness

  4–6, 4–7, 4–10, 4–13

  4–38w, 4–39w, 4–40w

- To improve sensory motor integration

  4–9, 4–14, 4–20, 4–21, 4–22, 4–23, 4–25, 4–26, 4–27, 4–28, 4–29, 4–30

  4–35w, 4–36w, 4–38w, 4–39w, 4–44w

- To improve motor planning

  4–7, 4–8, 4–9, 4–11, 4–20, 4–21, 4–22, 4–23

  4–35w, 4–36w, 4–37w, 4–39w, 4–40w, 4–44w

- To increase body awareness

  4–3, 4–10, 4–18, 4–19, 4–22, 4–26

  4–38w

- To improve fine motor manipulative skills

  4–14, 4–15, 4–16, 4–17, 4––18, 4–19, 4–28, 4–30

  4–42w, 4–43w

- To improve eye-hand coordination

  4–11, 4–12, 4–17, 4–29

  4–41w, 4–43w

- To identify and understand patterns and relationships

  4–29

  4–41w, 4–42w, 4–43w

- To make predictions

  4–6, 4–8, 4–12

  4–31w, 4–34w

- To increase inclusion

  4–18, 4–19, 4–20

  4–31w

- To improve cause-and-effect reasoning

  4–1, 4–2, 4–4, 4–5, 4–25

  4–32w

- To improve tactile skills

  4–14, 4–27, 4–28, 4–30

  4–41w

- To increase vocabulary

  4–3, 4–15, 4–16, 4–24, 4–27

  4–33w

Wellness Activities

Health and Safety: Large Group

4-1 Seasonal Clothing

Goals: To improve health literacy; to increase adaptive skills; to improve cause-and-effect reasoning

Materials: Articles of clothing or pictures of them, pictures of scenes of the seasons labeled by season, pictures of events that happen in various seasons

Procedure: Have the children sort the clothes or pictures into piles by season. Include fabric swatches to sort as well. The seasons described are characteristic of the Northeast. Choose seasons that are relevant to the area the children live in. There might be a rainy season and a dry one, or even a windy one. Change is based on altitude in some areas. Use these ideas to expand the concept. Discuss why certain clothes and fabrics are chosen for different seasons:

SPRING	SUMMER	FALL	WINTER
long pants	swimsuit	long pants	snowsuit
sweater	sleeveless top	jacket	mittens
jeans	shorts	knee socks	boots
flannels	eyelet	knit	fake fur
gabardine	cotton	wool	velvet

Be sure to agree that some clothes for cool weather can be worn in spring or fall or all seasons. It is the reasoning that matters. Have the children try on the clothing and sort it into boxes. Make comments to support children's choices: "When you put mittens on, I can't see your hands. Mittens keep your hands warm." Have children classify seasonal events and also include appropriate clothing to be worn at the events. Use pictures of events to be classified as well:

SPRING	SUMMER	FALL	WINTER
trees bud	people swim	school starts	animals hibernate
birds build nests	people take vacations	leaves change colors	snow falls
		apples and pumpkins are harvested	people ice skate

Assessment: The child will sort clothing and fabric by the season that it is worn: winter, spring, summer, fall, or other designations. The child will state one reason why each fabric is worn during a specific season.

Accommodations and Integration: Start with obvious comparisons such as a swimsuit and a snowsuit. Talk about clothing children are wearing based on the season you are currently having. Encourage children to dress for a particular season or event and have others guess the season or event. Help children explain the rationale for their choices. Expand the concept of seasons to other regions of the world. This provides an opportunity for children to talk about the predictability of seasonal change and how seasons are different in various climates. Children need to learn to be responsive to the weather as they choose their clothing. They can also learn about the protective quality of clothing.

Health and Safety: Small Group

4-2 Smell Cues

Goals: To improve health literacy; to increase adaptive skills; to improve cause-and-effect reasoning

Materials: Small containers, each holding a cotton ball saturated with a familiar-smelling substance (paint, food, perfume, liquid smoke, and so on)

Procedure: Have the children guess what the smells are, in what situations they would find them, and how they could respond:

paint, wet paint, don't touch
food, mealtime, set the table
smoke, danger, leave
ammonia, cleaning time, pick up toys
perfume, going out, say good-bye

A variety of behaviors is possible in all these situations. Support all appropriate behaviors and help children think of many different ways to respond.

Assessment: The child will identify and name different substances by smell. The child will state how each substance might be used and which substances are dangerous and should not be touched.

Accommodations and Integration: Tell children to just smell (caution them not to taste the substances); initially, use only substances that would be safe if ingested. When children are familiar with the procedure, increase the variety of smells under careful supervision. Where possible, include smells of dangerous substances. Be very clear that these are dangerous and supervise the activity closely. Because of experience and visual association, small cues are meaningful to us, but they are not necessarily meaningful to children or those who have sensory impairments. Children need to be taught when smells indicate a situation is dangerous. They must learn some things in the environment that are not safe to experiment with, and that one clue is smell.

Health and Safety: Small Group

4-3 Symptoms

Goals: To improve health literacy; to increase vocabulary; to increase body awareness

Materials: Dolls

Procedure: Help children develop their vocabulary to describe their symptoms and to give some information on the area and degree of the "hurt."

BODY PARTS	MEDICAL TERMS	CONDITIONS	DEGREE TERMS
tummy, stomach	vomit, throw up	swollen, puffy	little, a lot
head	pain, hurts	dizzy	big, small
arms, legs	swollen	blood, bleeding	sharp, dull
throat, neck	sore	cut	hot, cold

Role-play situations in which a child who is "hurt" tells you or another child what's wrong. Decide what to do in the case of various symptoms (dizzy—lie down; cut—wash it; swollen part—put ice on it).

Assessment: The child will name the body part and the type and severity of the pain.

Accommodations and Integration: Use both the child's body and a doll to teach body parts. Role-play the most likely events a child might encounter (a cut or a stomachache). Help children learn more internal body parts as well as where they are located. This activity provides useful information for a child *before* he becomes ill. Include specific terms children will need, based on their impairments. Be sure that children understand that their objective is to be accurate, not creative.

Health and Safety: Small Group

4-4 Stop and Go

Goals: To improve health literacy; to increase adaptive skills; to improve cause-and-effect reasoning

Materials: Red, green, and yellow pieces of construction paper; tricycles

Procedure: Adapt the traditional game of red light/green light by having the children walk or ride when you hold up a piece of green paper and stop when you hold up a piece of red paper. Once children learn the process, vary the time between changes from red to green, making some very short and others long so children must pay close attention. Use yellow to slow them down.

Assessment: The child will look at red, yellow, and green papers and stop, slow down, and go in response to the color of the paper, while riding a tricycle or walking.

Accommodations and Integration: Say the word "stop" with red and "go" with green. Using this procedure, introduce the concept of caution to children. When holding up the yellow paper, have them walk or ride more slowly and be ready for change. Have a child be the traffic director and regulate the tricycles with the red, yellow, and green "lights." Stop and go are important safety concepts. Children need practice learning to wait for the signal to change as well as identifying the basic relationship between color and their behavior. Introduce "one way" signs as well. Have children wear helmets when they ride tricycles or bicycles and talk about why they are important.

Health and Safety: Small or Large Group

4-5 Warning Signs

Goals: To improve health literacy; to increase adaptive skills; to improve cause-and-effect reasoning

Materials: Pictures of familiar warning signs (stop, yield, one-way, railroad crossing, traffic lights, walk signals, and so on)

Procedure: Introduce the various warning signs; be sure to include ones near your setting. Discuss with the children what each signs mean and what the children should do when they see them. Role-play situations. Use the signs in the play yard to direct traffic flow. Change their locations and direction frequently, so children have to look. Follow this with a walk in the community and have children identify the signs. Include more signs such as those that give information about places to camp, sleep, eat, and buy gas.

Assessment: The child will identify warning signs and how she should respond.

Accommodations and Integration: Focus on the signs necessary for survival. Initially verbalize for children what they should do to respond to the sign. Have children help make signs to add to the play yard that include additional information about the area (swinging, no trikes, picnic area, and so on). Encourage children to think of significant ways of portraying the information they want to convey. Obeying safety signs is necessary for all children. Those with sensory impairments may need specific help learning the cues; others may have difficulty waiting for the sign and readjusting when the signs change. This is an important experience for all children. Help children pair sounds with warning signs for additional information.

Large Motor: Small Group

4-6 Variations on Jumping

Goals: To improve locomotor skills; to improve physical fitness; to make predictions

Materials: Masking tape

Procedure: Have the children participate in various styles of jumping. Encourage children to think about the names of some of the jumps and make up new names with a rationale. Have children estimate how long, how high, how far, and how many times they can jump. If they work in pairs one child can check the other's prediction by writing it down and graphing it. Put the graph in their portfolio. Encourage them to repeat this activity after several weeks and compare the results.

Pairs jumping: Children face each other, hold hands and jump together

Line jumping: Children jump forward and backward across a taped line.

Step jumping: Children jump from a step to a line on the floor.

Long jump: Children jump forward for distance from standing (crouched) position.

Kangaroo jump: Children do knee bends and jump up with feet together, elbows bent, and hands away from body.

Rabbit jump: Children squat low on heels, palms on floor and fingers pointing forward, jumping with feet coming forward between hands, like a rabbit.

Mattress jump: Children jump forward and backward on a partially filled air mattress or regular mattress. For safety, put mattress on a $5' \times 8'$ rug with adult spotters.

Jumping Jacks and Jills: Children start with feet together and arms by side; they jump so their feet go to each side and arms come up to shoulder height, then jump and return to starting position.

Assessment: The child will jump in a variety of ways. The child will graph how long, how high, how far, and how many times she can jump each way.

Accommodations and Integration: Begin with easier jumps and accept all attempts at jumping. Hold children's hands as they jump. Keep the activity short; as it is easy for children to become fatigued however, the goal is for them to jump until they are breathless. When children are seated, have them use their arms and hands to help their bottom jump off the floor. Have children think about how realistic their predictions were. Children like to see personal improvement, and by graphing their jumping, they can look at their personal growth as well as have a base from which to estimate when they do the activity again.

Jumping is a fundamental motor skill. Encourage children to jump in a variety of different ways and to continue jumping until they are breathless.

Large Motor: Small Group

4-7 Variations on Running

Goals: To improve locomotor skills; to improve physical fitness; to improve motor planning

Materials: Tape, yarn, rope, cones, string

Procedure: Have the children run and try some of the following variations. Focus on the quality of children's movement and coach them to increase efficiency and coordination. Use variations to refine skills as well as to build endurance. As children run for longer distances, have them stretch to warm up and walk to cool down. Encourage all children to run until they are breathless. Help them challenge their limits. Videotape children and discuss variation differences. Have children run in the following ways:

> slowly, quickly, quietly, noisily, lightly, heavily
> stop on a signal; change direction on the signal; change from running to walking on a signal
> walk, run, walk; repeat
> slowly talking to a friend
> on a designated path
> in pairs, with one child running blindfolded

Assessment: The child will run following the adult's directions.

Accommodations and Integration: Decrease (or increase) the length, time, distance, and speed children run and use fewer variations. As children become more skilled, change the variations while children are running. Encourage children to think about the relationship between speed and endurance; help them decide which is more important in various situations.

Large Motor: Small Group

4-8 Obstacle Course

Goals: To improve locomotor skills; to improve motor planning; to make predictions

Materials: Barrels, boxes, boards, chairs, hoops, balance beam

Procedure: Set up an obstacle course (inside or outside) that requires a variety of movement skills and is long enough so several children can participate at the same time. Use obstacles that require children to move over, under, around, and through them. Encourage children to explore the course and discuss how they plan to move through it. Point out strategies different children use.

Assessment: The child will state how she will go through the course, and estimate how long it will take, do it, and reflect on what she planned and what happened.

Accommodations and Integration: Provide pictures and models for how children might move through each obstacle (use a digital camera as a child moves through the course). Walk beside the child and coach him. Keep the course simple and short. Add activities that are more complex: picking up a beanbag or walking through a hoop on the balance beam. Add music to set the pace. Have children time their trip through the course and estimate their completion time (it is not a race, it is a prediction). Add a rope guide and have children do the course blindfolded. Encourage children to work out adaptations to include scooters and wheelchairs and to try them and decide if they are easier or more difficult. Children can learn about their body, spatial relationships (over, under, around, or through), and the vocabulary to support movement.

Large Motor: Individual

4-9 Variations on Balancing

Goals: To improve stability skills; to improve sensory motor integration; to improve motor planning

Materials: Tape; balance beams: 6-inch and 4-inch wide, 6 inches off the ground

Procedure: Dynamic balance is an important skill for children. Begin by using 6-inch wide lines taped on the floor. Then use a balance beam that is 6 inches wide, then 4 inches wide. Move the 4-inch beam higher off the floor so that you can add dips. Have children walk between the taped lines or across the beam in the following ways:

forward, backward, sideways	forward, turning at each end
touching heel against toe	holding an object (short pole) in hands
to middle, touch board with hand	to middle, pick up a small object
to middle, catch a ball	to middle, touch board with knee

Assessment: The child will walk on a balance beam independently while following adult directions.

Accommodations and Integration: Begin with the lines taped on the floor. Hold the child's hand as he walks and coach him through the variations. Help children focus on different techniques. Talk to children about gravity, their center of gravity, and how it affects movement. Have the children perform some of the tasks using a scooter or wheelchair. Learning to move in a confined area is valuable. Children redefine straight and narrow and look at activities they considered easy from a new perspective.

Large Motor: Small Group

4-10 Variations on Hopping

Goals: To improve locomotor skills; to improve physical fitness; to increase body awareness

Materials: Hopping stones made of tiles or carpet squares, tape or chalk

Procedure: Hopping is challenging. Help the child count the number of hops she can make without putting down the other foot. For older children, try variations that are more complex. Play hopping games on patterns of tiles: The children hop on the tiles in an obstacle course fashion according to your directions. Play hopscotch. Have children hop in the following ways:

left foot; right foot	quietly; noisily
high; low	as far as they can
change feet	with a partner
as long as they can (time it, record it, and compare it to the next time)	

Assessment: The child will accurately follow adult directions for hopping.

Accommodations and Integration: Hold the child's hand while he hops. Have children practice hopping while holding on the back of a chair. Hopping is a basic locomotor skill that is part of many games. As children gain proficiency, combine hopping with other skills and use them in games.

Large Motor: Small Group

4-11 Target Bounce

Goals: To improve gross motor manipulative skills; to improve motor planning; to improve eye-hand coordination

Materials: Tape, 8-inch or 10-inch ball

Procedure: Tape a target on the floor, large at first (3 feet square). Have the children see how often they can hit the target and have their partner catch the ball. Have the children stand about 3 feet on either side of the target and bounce the ball to each other, hitting the target with the ball. Have children throw the ball overhand and underhand. Establish a rhythm by singing a song.

Assessment: The child will bounce a ball onto a target, analyze his mistake if he does not hit the target, and state his new strategy.

Accommodations and Integration: Use a larger ball and a larger target. Have children sit in chairs and play. After a number of successful bounces, have them move back 6 inches. Modify the size and weight of the ball and target. Have children count how often they can catch the ball or hit the target. Use a ball that has a bell inside and see if children can catch and throw the ball blindfolded. Many games use throwing and catching skills. Help children develop upper body strength and skill to use in games and in combination with other skills.

Large Motor: Small Group

4-12 Variations on Throwing

Goals: To improve gross motor manipulative skills; to improve eye-hand coordination; to make predictions

Materials: 8-inch or 10-inch ball, tennis ball, Nerf ball, beach ball, 15-inch or 24-inch wastebasket, hula hoop, cans of varying sizes

Procedure: Have the children participate in various types of ball-throwing activities. Discuss the differences in skills required to throw large and small balls. Have children measure the distances they can throw and make a graph, or count the number of times they can throw and catch a ball with another child. Have children throw the ball:

as high as they can	as low as they can without hitting the ground
as far as they can	softly to another child
in a high arc to another child	into a round wastebasket from 2´ to 5´ away
at a target of stacked cans	through a hula hoop from varying distances

Assessment: The child will follow adult directions and throw different balls for height, distance, and accuracy, and discuss the strategy he used.

Accommodations and Integration: Use an underinflated beach ball as children are learning to catch. Increase the distance children stand from the target or a partner. Encourage children to predict how different balls will influence throwing. Encourage children to play ball-throwing games with others so that they practice both throwing and catching. Have some balls available with bells inside. *Note:* These activities are most easily done outside.

Large Motor: Individual

4-13 Fitness Course

Goals: To improve physical fitness; to improve locomotor skills; to improve stability skills

Materials: Cards with pictures of the exercise and numbers of repetitions:

5 bent knee sit-ups	10 knee lifts
4 toe touches	count to 15 running in place
3 push-ups	10 double leg jumps

Procedure: Place cards around the room or an outside area and have children go to each area and perform the activity. Vary the activities. Coach children as they perform the activities, and modify the activities and repetitions to meet the children's needs.

Assessment: The child completes the exercises and the number of repetitions.

Accommodations and Integration: Decrease or increase the activities and number of repetitions, or choose easier or more difficult activities. Have children keep a fitness log so they can see how frequently they "work out." Talk with children about the role of a coach and help them think about physical fitness as part of their active lifestyle.

4-14 Buttons

Goals: To improve fine motor manipulative skills; to improve sensory motor integration; to improve tactile skills

Materials: 12 pairs of large buttons (with tactile differences), a bowl or bag, an egg carton or ice cube tray, a blindfold

Procedure: Collect pairs of buttons that feel different. Put one button of each pair in an egg carton or ice cube tray section and put the other in a bowl or bag. Initially, choose buttons that are larger and more dissimilar. Have the children match the pairs while blindfolded. If children do not like blindfolds, put the buttons in a bag and have the children find the matching buttons by touching them.

Assessment: The child will match the pairs of buttons visually and then by touch.

Accommodations and Integration: Have the children match very dissimilar buttons visually. As children become proficient, use smaller, more similar buttons. Use this procedure with fabric, textured wallpaper disks, or small objects. We often neglect to isolate the tactile sense and it needs to be fine-tuned. Ensure that an adult is near this activity as some buttons are small enough they could be swallowed.

4-15 Progressive Dress Up

Goals: To improve fine motor manipulative skills; to improve adaptive skills; to improve vocabulary

Materials: Adult clothing: sweaters, sweatshirts, pants, shirts, skirts, shorts, dresses, socks, shoes, and so on

Procedure: Divide the clothing into three piles: tops, bottoms, and footwear. Put the piles in three different places. Have the children walk, jump, or skip to each pile, find and put on that article of clothing, and then go on to the next pile until they are "dressed." Then have each child describe his outfit.

Assessment: The child will put on various parts of clothing, describe the article he is wearing, and what makes it easy or difficult to put on or take off.

Accommodations and Integration: Include oversized clothing without buttons and with cutoff sleeves, as well as clothing that is closer to the children's actual size. Add accessories such as gloves, ties, scarves, and hats. Have children dress for a particular occasion, particular weather, or a particular profession, and discuss why they chose those clothes. Help children focus on aspects of clothing that make it more or less difficult to put on, and how clothing can be adapted for individuals with disabilities.

4-16 Tools

Goals: To improve fine motor manipulative skills; to increase adaptive skills; to improve vocabulary

Materials: Tub with birdseed, small and tiny objects, chopsticks, spatula, spaghetti spoon, pierced serving spoons, tongs, tweezers, needle-nose pliers, magnifying glass

Procedure: Place small objects in the tub with birdseed. Have the child retrieve the objects using different tools. Once picked up, encourage children to explore them under a magnifying glass, turning them with tweezers. When children find them, encourage the children to describe and classify the objects and tools used to retrieve them.

Assessment: The child will name and classify a variety of tools she used to pick up hidden objects and reflect on the tools used and how their characteristics influenced use.

Accommodations and Integration: Have children use their hands to find the objects, then tools such as a spoon, that are relatively easy to manipulate. Encourage children to think about the match between the tool they use and the type of material they are picking up. Children need practice using many different tools.

Small Motor: Individual

4-17 Busy Box

Goals: To improve fine motor manipulative skills; to improve eye-hand coordination; to increase adaptive skills

Materials: A busy box

Procedure: Buy or make a variety of busy boxes. All require fine motor skills, but some teach more needed skills (such as locking and unlocking See Figure R4–1) and are more intriguing.

Assessment: The child will open the different types of locks and state where he might find each type of lock.

Accommodations and Integration: Start with a busy box that requires simpler skill so that children learn the concept then add ones that are more challenging. After using the lock box, talk with children about the purpose of locks: privacy and safety. Discuss when to unlock doors and when not to. Talk about locks on car doors and how locks might keep you safe. Also, talk about being locked in a place like a bathroom and how you might be able to get out of locked places if you had a key; discuss how someone might get a key to someone who is locked in.

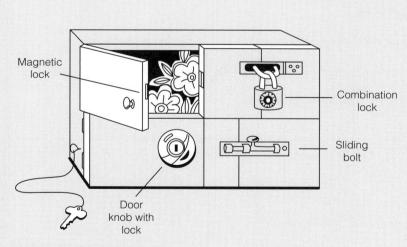

Figure R4–1: Lock Box

Locking and unlocking different kinds of locks helps children practice fine motor skills and also teaches adaptive behavior.

Small Motor: Individual or Small Group

4-18 My Puzzle

Goals: To improve fine motor manipulative skills; to increase inclusion; to increase body awareness

Materials: A 8″ × 10″ picture of each child and a group picture, scissors or jigsaw.

To Make *Take digital pictures of all the children in class doing something they enjoy as well as a group picture. Keep a small picture of all children for a class collage. Laminate or cover a large photograph of each child with clear contact paper and glue it to heavy cardboard. Draw lines on the back and cut it with heavy scissors or a jigsaw. No matter how you cut it, it will fit back together. (Put the child's initials on the back of each puzzle piece so they can be sorted if they are mixed up. Number the back pieces of the child group puzzle.)*

Procedure: Encourage children to put the puzzles together in small groups and discuss how they are each similar and different, and what each child enjoys doing. Have several different group puzzles and encourage children to talk about others in the group.

Assessment: The child will put her picture puzzle together and state three characteristics about herself.

Accommodations and Integration: Cut the picture into fewer pieces (you can always cut it into more pieces later). Have a frame to help children know where pieces might go (a piece of mat board cut the right size works well). This can also be done with children's drawings, or buy blank puzzles that are already cut and have children draw on them.

Small Motor: Individual

4-19 Body Pictures

Goals: To improve fine motor manipulative skills; to increase body awareness, to increase inclusion

Materials: Large butcher paper (big enough for a child to lie on), crayons, markers, paint, mirrors

Procedure: Talk with the children about what they look like, the clothes they wear, their hair, eye, and skin color. Encourage them to look in the mirror. Have each child lie down on the paper and have an adult or other child trace their outline. Have the children paint or color their paper body.

Assessment: The child will draw or paint clothing and facial features on her paper body that resemble her.

Accommodations and Integration: Point out relevant features of clothing as well as facial characteristics of each child or have a peer do it. Encourage children to be very detailed and accurate on facial features, coloring, and clothing. Have children look at their peers' pictures and discuss differences and similarities.

Sensory Motor Integration: Small Group

4-20 Hand Clapping

Goals: To improve sensory motor integration; to improve motor planning; to increase inclusion

Materials: Cassette or CD; cassette or CD player

Procedure: Have children clap slow and fast, loud and soft, and then to a constant rhythm. Then progress to a two-step sequence: clap hands, clap thighs, clap hands, clap thighs. (Choose any body parts: head, feet, shoulders.) Make the pattern more difficult: clap hands twice, clap thighs twice, repeat. Or, do it three or four times. For variation have children clap hands, clap their left thigh with their right hand, clap hands, clap their right thigh with their left hand. (The objective is crossing the body's midline, not learning right and left.) Have children clap hands with a partner using the patterns given.

Assessment: The child will follow the adult's directions and clap his hands in the designated pattern alone and with a partner.

Accommodations and Integration: These patterns are ordered in increasing levels of difficulty. Start at the beginning and use increasingly more complex patterns with partners. Enhance traditional children's songs and games by clapping.

Sensory Motor Integration: Small Group

4-21 Balance It

Goals: To improve sensory motor integration; to improve stability skills; to improve motor planning

Materials: Beanbags, books, paper plates, paintbrushes, feathers, crayons, plastic drinking glasses

Procedure: Have children balance a beanbag on their head. Encourage them to stand up and sit down, walk fast and slow while balancing it. Coach children how to move to make balancing easier. Then have them balance the beanbags using other body parts: shoulders, elbow, knee, foot. As children become more competent have them balance other objects.

Assessment: The child will balance the beanbag on her head and on three different parts of her body while moving for increasing periods of time.

Accommodations and Integration: Start with something easy to balance, a beanbag, and have children balance it on the back of their hand so they can see what they are doing. Coach them on ways to move their hand. Encourage children to balance a variety of objects and have them predict how long they can balance each object, or what movements they can make without its falling off. These activities require static and dynamic balance and concentration.

Sensory Motor Integration: Small Group

4-22 Mirroring

Goals: To improve sensory motor integration; to improve motor planning; to increase body awareness

Materials: String

Procedure: Have the children work in pairs facing each other. One child initiates a movement (this is easier) and the other child mirrors it. As children become more skillful, the movements can be faster and more subtle (such as facial movements).

Assessment: The child will accurately copy (mirror) the motions of another child. The child will initiate movements for another child to follow.

Accommodations and Integration: Encourage children to use slow, simple movements. Blindfold one child or tie a 12˝ string between the children's wrists and have them move gently to respond to the pressure on their hands or the string. Mirroring requires the child to look at another child to figure out what to do. It requires a child to "read" and respond to another child's body language.

Sensory Motor Integration: Individual

4-23 Big Balls

Goals: To improve sensory motor integration; to improve motor planning; to improve gross motor manipulative skills

Materials: Various sizes of inflatable beach balls or yoga balls

Procedure: Have the children participate in a variety of ball handling activities. Discuss with children the concepts of spatial awareness, force, and direction using these activities.

Toss: Throw the ball up in the air with two hands and catch it. As children gain skill, have them toss it to another child.

Tap: Tap the ball with hands and forearms several times without letting it hit the floor; tap the ball from one hand to the other. Count the number of taps.

Kick: Kick the ball using the feet; kick the ball while sitting or in a crab-like position.

Tools: Have children pick a variety of tools (rackets, rods, and so on) to move the ball.

Balance: (Be sure the ball is sturdy enough.) Have children sit on the ball, put their belly on the ball, bounce on the ball, and rotate their hips while sitting. See if they can figure out how to move while on the ball. (Be sure to spot the child so he does not fall.)

Assessment: The child will move the ball and reflect on his actions and the ball's movement.

Accommodations and Integration: Begin with slightly underinflated beach balls. Encourage children to experiment. Children need to develop and refine fundamental movement skills during the early childhood years. They need to practice these skills with variations until they become competent.

Sensory Motor Integration: Small Group

4-24 Foam

Goals: To improve stability skills; to improve gross motor manipulative skills; to increase vocabulary

Materials: A piece of 4-inch- or 5-inch-thick covered foam or a mattress

Procedure: Put the foam on the floor in the center of a piece of carpet. Have children walk, roll, jump, and so forth on the foam. Encourage them to experiment by doing these activities on the floor and then on the foam.

Assessment: The child will perform the activities and describe how performing them on the foam differs from performing them on a hard surface.

Accommodations and Integration: Have the child perform simple tasks, such as walking, across the foam and hold the child's hand. Use tasks that involve both **dynamic** and **static balance**. Encourage children to combine skills that involve locomotion (such as walking), axial stability (bending, twisting), static stability (upright balancing), and dynamic stability (rolling) into a routine, write it down, and repeat the routine.

Sensory Motor Integration: Large Group

4-25 Freeze

Goals: To improve stability skills; to improve sensory motor integration; to improve cause-and-effect reasoning

Materials: Drum, gong, or cassette, CD; cassette, or CD player

Procedure: Have the children move around the room (walking, skipping, hopping, jumping, spinning). Play music or beat a drum or gong, then stop suddenly. Call out "Freeze" until they get the idea. The children should maintain their position. As you unfreeze them (by touching them), talk about the positions they are in. As a variation, have all the children melt to the ground before the music starts again.

Assessment: The child will stop moving on a signal and maintain her position.

Accommodations and Integration: Initially, unfreeze children who have trouble balancing first. Encourage children to move in ways that will be harder to hold when frozen and discuss these. Use a visual signal, flicking the lights or waving your hands, to freeze children. Help children understand some of the basic principles of balance and why some postures are easier to hold. Have them experiment with block designs and see which ones are more stable, and help them draw analogies.

Sensory Motor Integration: Large Group

4-26 Tense Me

Goals: To improve sensory motor integration; to increase body awareness; to improve health literacy

Materials: None

Procedure: Have all the children lie or sit on the floor. (Initially, sitting is easier because everyone can see well.) Have children tense and relax both arms and then both legs. You may need to touch the tensed part to see if the child understands the request. Then have the children make a tight fist or muscle in one arm and feel that arm with the other hand. Tell them that feeling is *tense*. Ask if they can squeeze harder and make it more tense. Have them hold it to a count of five. Then tell them to see how loose (relaxed) they can make that arm. Again, have them feel it with their other hand. Discuss the difference in feeling. Have them make the arm even floppier. Repeat with the other arm. Do different body parts (legs and face) on different days. Words like "tight," "loose," and "floppy" may work better than the words "tense" and "relax," but be sure to use these too. Use your voice to mirror both the tension and relaxation. Help children learn to isolate and tense specific body parts (tense their right fist, left fist relaxed). Before children can voluntarily relax, they need to learn the feeling of what relaxation is.

Assessment: The child will tense and relax the designated body parts.

Accommodations and Integration: Encourage the children to touch your arm when it is relaxed and then tense. See if they can feel the change. Gradually try to teach them to isolate the sides of the body and individual body parts. Children need to tune in to their body for self-knowledge and to monitor their behavior. Teach them the relationship between body tension and behavior, what they do when they are tense, and how to recognize tension.

Sensory Motor Integration: Individual

4-27 Feely Bag

Goals: To improve sensory motor integration; to improve tactile skills; to increase vocabulary

Materials: Several small fabric bags, two identical objects that can be identified by touch: cups or glasses, cars and trucks, blocks, doll furniture, balls, dishes, and so on

Procedure: Place one object in the bag and have the children feel through the bag to figure out what the object is. Use only one object per bag. Place a duplicate set of objects on the table and ask the child to point to or name the one she feels. Encourage children to talk about the objects they feel and their descriptive characteristics. Use any object that fits in the bag and has obvious tactile features. Avoid sharp objects.

Assessment: The child will identify objects through her sense of touch and verbally describe them and their significant characteristics.

Accommodations and Integration: Point out salient characteristics of different possible objects that might be in the bag. As children become more skilled choose objects that are more similar and without a duplicate to compare it visually. Have children put only one hand inside the bag to touch what is there. Touch can provide children with information. They need to learn to link touch to awareness of what might be happening and implications for behavior.

Sensory Motor Integration: Small Group

4-28 Draw It On

Goals: To improve sensory motor integration; to improve tactile skills; to improve fine motor manipulative skills

Materials: Paper, markers, cards with simple shapes, numbers, or letters

Procedure: Demonstrate the procedure by having an adult tap out numbers or finger-draw simple designs (square, circle, triangle) on a child's back. Have the children sit in pairs front to back and give the child in back a card with a design. Using his finger, this child draws the design on the back of the other child. When completed, the child in front draws the design on the paper with a marker or identifies the number or shape verbally. The children then compare the design drawn with the one on the card.

Assessment: Given a card with a design on it, the child will draw the design on another child's back. He will also identify a design drawn on his back, and draw or name it.

Accommodations and Integration: Start by having an adult draw a design on the child's back and the child identify the design or choose from possible designs. As children become more skilled increase the complexity of the designs or use a series of designs (letters or numbers) or simple words. Children need to integrate information from all body parts. This provides an unusual way to identify and draw geometric shapes, numbers, and letters.

Sensory Motor Integration: Individual

4-29 Follow That Light

Goals: To improve sensory motor integration; to improve eye-hand coordination; to identify and understand patterns and relationships

Materials: Two flashlights

Procedure: Make the room as dark as possible. Turn on two flashlights. Give a flashlight to each of two children. One child makes simple designs with the light on the wall, floor, or ceiling, and the other child repeats the design when it is completed, or "shadows" the design as it is being done.

Assessment: The child will use a flashlight to create a design on a wall or repeat the design another child makes.

Accommodations and Integration: Have an adult use one flashlight and move it slowly in a simple pattern for the child to follow. Make the designs more complex and move the flashlight faster. Encourage children to use the button on the flashlight to make long and short flashes in a repeating pattern. Children who are in bed can make or follow these patterns. Talk about patterns such as Morse code, and signal lights and how ships use patterns of light for communication. Show children these symbol systems.

Sensory Motor Integration: Individual

4-30 Pick-a-Pair

Goals: To improve sensory motor integration; to improve tactile skills; to improve fine motor manipulative skills

Materials: Fake fur, cardboard, flannel, felt, sandpaper, sponge, nylon, corduroy, dotted Swiss, wool, silk, ultra suede

To Make   *Cut each piece of fabric in two 2 × 2-inch pieces. Glue one piece of each fabric on cardboard. Place the matching piece of fabric in a feely bag or box.*

Procedure: Choose a piece of fabric on the cardboard and ask the child to find that piece in the feely bag and match it. Discuss the different textures and classify them in some way: woven/not woven, soft/hard, rough/smooth, and so on. Have children explain how they found the match.

Assessment: The child will identify and match fabrics by touch.

Accommodations and Integration: Make the differences among the materials obvious (cardboard, fake fur, nylon) and have fewer materials. As children become more skillful have them order 2-inch-square pieces of sandpaper from coarse to fine. Talk with children about fabric and the qualities of different fabrics. Help them think about the qualities of materials that relate to their use.

Summary

Health, physical education, and sensory motor activities support the development of large and small motor skills and the integration of these skills with sensory information. Wellness activities support learning. All children need to develop and maintain a physically active lifestyle. Variations on activities increases motivation while providing necessary practice and the need to adjust to different conditions. Fundamental motor activities are the basic skills for participating in sports as well as the precision of movement necessary for academic activities such as writing.

Educational Resources

American Alliance for Health, Physical Education, Recreation and Dance (AAHPERD) is a national organization that shares current research findings and opportunities for professional development in this area. http://www.aahperd.org

Kids Health created by the Nemours Foundation promotes health. Professionals such as physicians and nutritionists check all entries. It is a good resource to share with parents. http://www.kidshealth.org

National Dairy Council provides information about nutrition and suggestions for hands-on nutrition and food tasting activities. http://www.nutritionexplorations.com/

PE Central provides information about developmentally appropriate physical education programs for children and youth as well as assessments and lesson ideas for early childhood educators in physical/health education and adaptive physical education. http://www.pecentral.org

P.E. Links 4 U provides information about physical education practices, book reviews, and health and nutritional information and links curriculum ideas, federal news and national organizations. http://www.pelinks4u.org/

For additional resources, visit the book companion website for this text at www.cengage.com/education/deiner.

Creative Arts Activities:

Visual Arts, Music, Creative Movement, and Dramatic Play

All children are creative. Some are more creative than others. Some children are more creative in one area than in other areas. Educators have an important role in the development of creativity. They can actively support creativity or squelch it. The response children receive about their creative efforts plays a large part in their creative development. Educators can enhance the experience by having children think more about the process, as it will affect the product.

Activity Goals

Activities are organized by the goals they support. Goals that focus directly on the creative arts are given first. The activity number is provided after the goal to make finding the activity more efficient. The activities that are in the book have their number identified; those that are in the book companion website are followed by a "w" (refer to Table R5–1).

Creative Arts Guidelines

The following guidelines will be helpful as you think about adapting creative arts to meet the needs of children with diverse abilities.

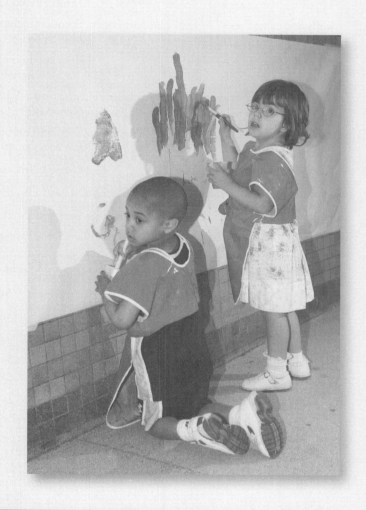

Adapting activities for children with:	
Specific learning disabilities	Promote creative problem solving. Use music to develop memory skills. Focus on relationships between the child's behavior and the outcome. Use the arts to build literacy skills. Use dramatic play to learn about new situations.
Social, emotional and behavioral disorders	Use creative arts activities to help children increase awareness of their moods and express their feelings. Provide large materials and an expansive work area. Use music to set a tone. Support children in playing out their fears and anxieties through puppets and dramatic play.

Attention-deficit/hyperactivity disorder	Match activities to the child's energy level. Use creative arts to support and sustain attention. Help children organize creative experiences. Encourage children to think about the arts as leisure time activities.
Communication disorders	Provide opportunities for children to speak, imitate peers, and use expressive language through choral activities and play. Use context to expand and extend vocabulary and language development.
English language learners	Provide art materials that are used in different cultures. Use puppets, music, and other dramatic play experiences to support language development in the home language and English. Encourage children to use the arts to express themselves.
Autism spectrum disorders	Use visual signs to cue participation. Join and expand on idiosyncratic movements. Provide play scripts, use realistic props.
Intellectual disabilities	Provide familiar themes and settings. Keep activities simple and realistic. Teach functional skills using dramatic play.
Gifts and talents	Encourage divergent thinking and unconventional solutions to problems. Add articles and information that increase the depth of all creative arts.
Special health care needs	Help children express concerns and fears through art and music. Use dramatic play to help children gain some control of medical experiences.
Orthopedic and neurological impairments	Adapt materials by making them larger or smaller, and add grips to make objects easier to hold. Have materials in different shapes, sizes, and textures.
Hearing impairments	Use hand motions and signs with music and songs. Role-play situations, use accessories to set moods.
Visual impairments	Provide obvious boundaries for work (texture, high contrast, or people). Add texture to materials and use three-dimensional materials.

Creative Arts Activities

Table R5–1: Activity goals and activity numbers in text and online

Goals	Activity Numbers
• To use different art media, techniques, and processes	5–1, 5–2, 5–3, 5–4, 5–5, 5–6, 5-7, 5–8, 5–9, 5–10, 5–11 5–31w, 5–32w, 5–33w, 5–34w, 5–35w, 5–36w, 5–37w, 5–38w
• To understand the structures and functions of art	5–2, 5–3 5–31w, 5–34w, 5–35w
• To understand art in a cultural and historical context	5–4, 5–5 5–32w, 5–33w, 5–41w
• To use the arts to express a range of subject matter, symbols, and ideas	5–2, 5–3, 5–4, 5–6, 5-7, 5–8, 5–12 5–36w, 5–39w
• To connect the arts and other disciplines	5–1, 5–10, 5–11 5–32w, 5–38w, 5–39w
• To listen, analyze, describe, and respond to music	5–13, 5–14, 5–15, 5–17, 5–18, 5–20, 5–21, 5–22 5–40w, 5–41w, 5–43w, 5–46w
• To read and interpret music	5–14, 5–16 5–40w
• To perform on instruments alone and with others	5–14, 5–16, 5–20 5–41w, 5–42w
• To sing alone and with others	5–19, 5–20, 5–23 5–43w, 5–44w

• To appreciate a varied repertoire of music	5–16, 5–17, 5–18, 5–19, 5–21, 5–23
	5–40w, 5–42w, 5–44w
• To develop creative movement	5–13, 5–15, 5–22, 5–24, 5–26
	5–45w
• To encourage problem solving	5–27, 5–28, 5–29
	5–34w, 5–38w, 5–47w
• To encourage creativity	5–8
	5–35w, 5–36w, 5–46w
• To improve self-concept	5–9, 5–12, 5–30
	5–47w
• To express feelings	5–12, 5–13, 5–27, 5–28
	5–39w
• To increase comprehension	5–17, 5–18
	5–47w
• To improve cause-and-effect reasoning	5–1, 5–5, 5–6, 5–11, 5–25, 5–29
	5–37w, 5–42w, 5–45w, 5–48w
• To increase body awareness	5–24, 5–25, 5–26
	5–44w
• To improve sensory motor integration	5–15, 5–21, 5–22, 5–24, 5–25, 5–30
	5–46w
• To increase inclusion	5–9, 5–10, 5–23, 5–26, 5–30
	5–45w
• To increase awareness of roles people play	5–27, 5–28, 5–29
	5–48w
• To identify and understand patterns and relationships	5–7, 5–19
	5–31w, 5–33w, 5–37w, 5–43w, 5–48w

Visual Arts: Small Group

5-1 Creature

Goals: To use different art media, techniques, and processes; to connect the arts and other disciplines; to improve cause-and-effect reasoning

Materials: Papier-mâché.

To Make: *Tear newspaper into very small pieces and pour a little boiling water over it. Stir until it forms a pulp. Cool. Then add about 6 tablespoons of wheat paste for every 2 cups of pulp. Mix first with a spoon, then with the hands.*

Procedure: Have children think about different environments and how animals adapt or are adapted to these. Have children decide on a particular environment. Talk about aspects of the creature they are going to make that will help him survive there. Help children think about how it moves, what and how it eats, where it lives, and so on. Then have the children mold the papier-mâché into the creature-like form they have envisioned. When the creatures are dry, encourage the children to use the construction area to build an environment for them.

Assessment: The child will design and make a creature, describe its environment, and how it is adapted to live there.

Accommodations and Integration: Focus on the papier-mâché and having children tear the paper for it and make it. Help children focus on the adaptations creatures (and people) make to the environment or how they can adapt the environment to them. Talk about mobility aids, prosthetic devices, and eyeglasses. Precede this activity by discussing how people and animals are adapted to their environments (a monkey's tail is for climbing; polar bears are white for protective coloration; a cheetah's sleek body and long legs are used for speed in catching prey).

Visual Arts: Small Group

5-2 Tissue Paper Art

Goals: To use different art media, techniques, and processes; to understand the structures and functions of art; to use the arts to express a range of subject matter, symbols, and ideas

Materials: Small pieces of tissue paper, light-colored construction paper, paste, books illustrated by Eric Carle such as *The Very Hungry Caterpillar, I See a Song, The Tiny Seed.*

Procedure: Read a book illustrated by Eric Carle. Talk with the children about how Eric Carle created his pictures (overlapping tissue paper). Have children think about what they want to create and encourage them to overlap the pieces to see new colors emerge.

Assessment: The child will make a picture using overlapping tissue paper.

Accommodations and Integration: Demonstrate the technique of overlapping pieces. Encourage children to explore the concept and resulting colors before pasting. Have children predict the outcome and then verify their predictions. Have the children create and illustrate a story using tissue paper art.

Visual Arts: Small Group

5-3 Woodworking

Goals: To use different art media, techniques, and processes; to understand the structures and functions of art; to use the arts to express a range of subject matter, symbols, and ideas

Materials: Small pieces of soft wood, nails (long enough to hold two pieces of the wood together, but short enough that the point does not stick out), hammers, woodworking table, markers

Procedure: Set up a center where children can use hammers and nails; be sure it is large enough for children to hammer their creations together. Encourage children to use different materials and try to hammer two pieces of wood together to make something and to describe what they are making. Encourage children to color or paint their creations.

Assessment: The child will hammer a nail into wood attaching it to another piece of wood and describe what it looks like or what she is making.

Accommodations and Integration: Use safety glasses and have a vise and clamps to hold the wood in place. Use wood glue and clamps if hammering is not advisable. Encourage children to make projects that are more complex by allowing them to work on the project for several days. Woodworking is an empowering activity for children to feel in control and independent. It encourages children who may not participate in art to become involved.

Visual Arts: Small Group

5-4 Crayon Rubbing

Goals: To use different art media, techniques, and processes; to use the arts to express a range of subject matter, symbols, and ideas; to understand art in a cultural and historical context

Materials: Paper, masking tape, thick crayons, objects with various textures

Procedure: Talk to children about rubbings and how people rub tombstones, temples, and other interesting objects as mementos. Show children examples of rubbings. Talk about various surfaces that the children touch and how they would describe them (soft, furry, scratchy), then about surfaces that they see (shiny, hairy, has ridges or patterns), and then about the two combined (something that feels bumpy and looks rough). Demonstrate rubbing techniques to the children. Help children rub the edges of objects first to determine their shape. Initially, help children pick objects with distinctive shapes and textures by providing a variety of textured objects. Tape the corners of the paper to the table with the object under it. The tape keeps the paper from moving as the children rub. Write the name of the article rubbed on the backside of the paper. During group time, ask the children to look at the papers and guess what article was rubbed. (The name on the back helps for those "creative" rubbings.)

Assessment: The child will choose an object to rub, make predictions about what it will look like, do the rubbing, and discuss the ways rubbings are used.

Accommodations and Integration: Choose relatively small objects with distinctive shapes and textures. Have two of the objects, placing one under the paper and the other for the child to look at to see if it is "coming up." Have children predict how a rubbing will look before they begin and then see if they were accurate. This requires little coordination, yet helps develop finger strength and sensory motor integration and gives the children feedback about how hard they are pressing the crayon. It is an interesting way to include history and culture into the curriculum in a very concrete way. You might show children rubbings from other cultures. Talk about how fossils relate to rubbings.

Visual Arts: Large Group

5-5 Making Dyes

Goals: To use different art media, techniques, and processes; to understand art in a cultural and historical context; to improve cause-and-effect reasoning

Materials: Large pot, stove or hot plate, red cabbage, onion peels, spinach, tea, beets, white cotton fabric cut into small pieces, tongs

Procedure: As a small group have the children examine the various foods. Discuss with the children how people used food to create different colors for fabrics. They would put the food into boiling water, add the fabric, and let it soak until it was the color they wanted. Have children take turns making predictions about what color the fabric will turn when placed in a pot with different foods for different amounts of time. After making the predictions, let the children experiment with the different food dyes. Discuss the outcomes with the children.

Assessment: The child will help prepare dye, place the fabric into the dye and predict the color the fabric will turn.

Accommodations and Integration: Use only one or two foods that have the fastest, most obvious effects (beets). Encourage children to experiment with leaving the material in the dye for different lengths of time and chart the outcome. Have them predict what will happen if they tie a knot in the material or put the cloth in several different dyes. Children can use the fabric to make something. They can make pickled beets, eggs and onions and talk about other foods that change color.

Visual Arts: Individual or Small Group

5-6 Texture Paint

Goals: To use different art media, techniques, and processes; to use the arts to express a range of subject matter, symbols, and ideas; to improve cause-and-effect reasoning

Materials: Add texture to one color of easel paint with one of the following:

flour: lumpy (do not stir it too much)	salad oil: oily
sugar: shiny, grainy (use right away)	sawdust: rough
salt: shiny, grainy (table or Epsom salts)	syrup: sticky
sand: gritty	

Procedure: Have the children experiment with various paint textures. Experiment with making different colors and different textures. Focus on the cause-effect relationship in the materials added and the change in texture. Talk with children about how the change in the paint will change their picture (outcome). Have them think about what this means relative to what they will do.

Assessment: The child will describe the texture of different paints based on what was added and how it affects the picture.

Accommodations and Integration: Experiment with only one color and texture at a time. Experiment with making different colors and textures and have children paint with them (red: rough-sawdust; blue: oily salad oil; yellow: lumpy-flour). Have children not only describe the different visual features of the picture but also the tactile ones. This activity provides both tactile and visual variations of a familiar substance.

Texture adds another dimension to painting.

Visual Arts: Small Group

5-7 Stencils

Goals: To use different art media, techniques, and processes; to use the arts to express a range of subject matter, symbols, and ideas; to identify and understand patterns and relationships

Materials: Construction paper, scissors, paint, posterboard, cotton ball, colored chalk, crayons, tape or bits of adhesive

Procedure: Talk with children about the problems of making identical pictures. Talk about stencils and how they are used. Give the children posterboard and have them cut holes or designs for a stencil in the posterboard. If they want a symmetrical design (for example, heart, flower, person), it is easiest if they fold the paper or posterboard in half first. Encourage them to think about how they will use the stencil. When they have completed the stencil, place it on construction paper and use tape or bits of adhesive to keep the stencil in one place as the children color it. Have children use colored chalk or crayons to color the opening (or rub the colored chalk with the cotton ball). Demonstrate how to work from the edge of the stencil to the center of the opening, have them color until they have a clear print. Then have them move the stencil and make a repeating pattern.

Assessment: The child will create a stencil and use it as a guide to make a repeating pattern.

Accommodations and Integration: Have simple stencils available for the children to use. Add stencils where two or three stencils (one for each color) must be used to make the desired object. Talk with children about using stencils to make repeating patterns. Show them commercially made stencils and how they are used. If they want to use more than one color, explain how this is done.

Visual Arts: Small Group

5-8 Torn Paper Flowers

Goals: To use different art media, techniques, and processes; to use the arts to express a range of subject matter, symbols, and ideas; to encourage creativity

Materials: A pot or vase of flowers, construction paper, colored paper scraps, paste, crayons

Procedure: Show the children the flowers. Discuss the parts that make up the flower (stem, petals, leaves, and so on). Help them experiment with pieces of paper of different sizes and shapes for different purposes. Have them paste paper petals and other flower parts. (If children are not interested in flowers, choose something else.) Once the children understand the concept, allow them the freedom to make *their* flower. Provide crayons and markers to complete details.

Assessment: The child will identify the different parts of the flower and create her own flower using torn paper and paste.

Accommodations and Integration: Let children experiment by tearing the paper and pasting it. Encourage children to both cut and tear the paper and show them how to curl the paper around a pencil so it curls away from the paper to add depth. Tearing is satisfying for children who have trouble cutting. It is also an artistic technique that offers the potential for three-dimensional pictures.

Visual Arts: Large Group

5-9 Hand Print Mural

Goals: To use different art media, techniques, and processes; to improve self-concept; to increase inclusion

Materials: Paint, butcher paper, paint brush, construction paper

Procedure: Decide on the purpose for the mural (get-well or thank-you card, part of a bulletin board display and so on). Have the children generate an appropriate message. Put the mural paper on a separate table. Put the paint on a sponge and have children press their hand on the sponge, and then print it. Then identify their handprint. Encourage them to be creative perhaps paint the palm one color and the area between each knuckle another. Supply additional small paper so children can try out their print first or make another project.

Assessment: The child will make handprints, examine her print and compare it to other handprints.

Accommodations and Integration: Help the child by pressing his hand into the sponge and then onto the paper. Point out the salient characteristics. Have children add finger and thumbprints and look at both hand- and fingerprints with a magnifying glass. The concept of printing is different from fingerpainting. This project is an easy one for children to participate in and, if hung on the wall, a reminder that all children are part of the class. Some communities encourage all children to be fingerprinted. This is a good way to prepare children for this process.

Visual Arts: Small Group

5-10 Finger Puppets

Goals: To connect the arts and other disciplines; to use different art media, techniques, and processes; to increase inclusion

Materials: Papier-mâché (see Activity 5–1, Creature, for the recipe)

Procedure: Help children focus on what they want their puppet to do or be when the puppet is finished. Help them think about how this influences the size and shape of the puppet, and how they will dress it. As children mold their creation; have them insert their finger to make the finger hole.

Assessment: The child will create a finger puppet for a specific role using papier-mâché.

Accommodations and Integration: Focus more on the process than the character of the puppet. Wait for the puppets to dry and then have children paint them. Have children take them into the dramatic play area and use them together. Encourage children to think about the roles they envisioned for each puppet. Finger puppets require less manipulation than other puppets, but children supply more of the dramatic energy. Talk about how dramatic productions need set design as well as the puppets to perform. They may need a script, narrator, and additional characters (finger puppets).

Visual Arts: Small Group

5-11 Tracing Pictures

Goals: To use different art media, techniques, and processes; to connect the arts and other disciplines; to improve cause-and-effect reasoning

Materials: Paper, glue, crayons, saltshakers full of sand

Procedure: Have the children draw a simple shape (circle, triangle, square), pattern, or picture (kite, table, cup, balloon, maze) on heavy paper. Tell the children to outline the shape with glue (try to avoid ending up with puddles of glue that take days to dry). Have them sprinkle sand on the glue. Putting the sand in a saltshaker makes it easier to control. Point out where the sand stays and where it doesn't. When the glue is dry, shake off the excess sand and have the children trace the outline with their fingers and fill in the spaces if they choose.

Assessment: The child will draw a simple shape, outline the shape with glue, and sprinkle sand on it.

Accommodations and Integration: Use glitter glue or a type made to "write" with and outline the shape. Have children make designs that are more complex and trace the outline blindfolded. Talk to children about the tactile quality of their picture. Help them think about how they could share this picture with a person who can not see.

Visual Arts: Small Group

5-12 Mood Montage

Goals: To use the arts to express a range of subject matter, symbols, and ideas; to improve self-concept; to express feelings

Materials: Pictures, magazines, scissors, crayons, paper, glue, or paste

Procedure: Give the children pictures, magazines, and crayons. Have them pick a mood or feeling, find pictures that match or create that mood, and paste the pictures on a piece of paper. They can use the crayons to personalize and finish the pictures. Encourage children to "write" a book about "The Many Moods of Me." Children can illustrate moods as well as write about them. The book illustrations should help set and convey different moods.

Assessment: The child will state a mood and find pictures that depict that mood and paste the pictures on a piece of paper stating why the pictures describe the mood chosen.

Accommodations and Integration: Have pictures already cut out so children only have to choose appropriate ones. Make a class mural instead of individual pictures. Have children write or dictate stories about moods to go with the pictures they have chosen. Help children become more aware of moods, the situations in which moods may occur, and how to convey moods through the visual arts, music, and movement.

Music: Large Group

5-13 Mood Songs

Goals: To listen, analyze, describe, and respond to music; to develop creative movement; to express feelings

Materials: Audiotape, or CD; audiotape or CD player

Procedure: Choose songs that have specific moods: lullabies, jazz, rock, easy listening, and traditional children's music. Start with familiar, obvious songs and help children focus on the mood of the music before they begin to move. After moving to a song, talk about when they might want to listen to this type of music. Then, have them sing a familiar song the "wrong" way (a loud, fast lullaby).

Assessment: The child will listen to different types of music and move his body to the mood of the music.

Accommodations and Integration: Identify the mood and tell children how to move. Model appropriate movements. As children become more skillful, use songs that are not familiar to the children. Have children identify some of the musical characteristics that are used to create the mood. Help them identify how different instruments contribute to the mood. Children learn to become more aware of their own moods and can perhaps match music to these as a way of learning to control them. Children need to develop the skills of analyzing and describing music.

Music: Small Group or Individual

5-14 Color Notes

Goals: To listen, analyze, describe, and respond to music; to read and interpret music; to perform instruments alone and with others

Materials: Sheet music of familiar songs, crayons or markers to color in the notes on the sheet music, colored stickers to stick onto the piano keys

Procedure: Encourage children to explore a piano or keyboard. Have them press different keys to hear sounds they can make (soft, hard, high, low). Provide sheet music with the notes colored in different colors that correspond to colored keys on the piano. Show the children how to look at the sheet music and then press the appropriate keys.

Assessment: The child will look at the colored music notes and press the corresponding color key on the piano.

Accommodations and Integration: Start with one sheet of music where the notes directly correspond to the order of the notes on the piano like a scale. Place the music directly above the keyboard. Increase the number of lines and complexity of the music. Talk about different types of notes (whole or half) and their relationship to playing music. This activity encourages children to start to understand the written "language" of music and exposes them to another symbol system.

Music: Large Group

5-15 Rhythm Walk

Goals: To listen, analyze, describe, and respond to music; to develop creative movement; to increase sensory motor integration

Materials: Drum or piano

Procedure: Set up a path around the room (or outside) and have the children walk to a beat you establish. Initially, warn the children before changing the rhythm: "Listen, I'm going to change now. Is it faster or slower?"

Assessment: The child will response to the beat of the music (fast, slow, soft, hard).

Accommodations and Integration: Be sure the children can see you and the beat; play dramatically. Then, vary the beat and see if the children change with you. As children's skill increases, make the changes more quickly. Do not let the children see what you are doing; this takes away the visual cue. Sometimes beat slowly enough for their movements to become a balancing activity. Instead of walking, children can participate in many different movement activities. Use music from different cultures that have different beats and moods. Talk about these differences.

Music: Small or Large Group

5-16 Conductor

Goals: To read and interpret music; to perform on instruments alone and with others; to appreciate a varied repertoire of music

Materials: Rhythm band instruments, videotape of a concert

Procedure: Play a short videotape of a concert and point out to the children the motions the conductor uses to direct the orchestra. Teach children some of the simpler signals used:

> softer: palms toward the group (up and down)
> louder: palms toward you (large gesture)
> slow: waving slowly (circular)
> fast: waving fast (circular)
> expand: pass arm in front of body parallel to floor
> staccato: cut in the air (vertically)

Your signals don't have to be the actual signals, but you and the children should agree on their meanings: Make a picture of the signals, with the word written below.

Start with the teacher being the "director." Use sounds like *me, me, me, me; la, la, la, la; see, see, see, see*. Then go to two or more syllables. Names are always fun: *Ja*—expand (use horizontal hand movement), *mie*—staccato (vertical hand movement). Be sure a child knows the process before choosing her to be the conductor. Encourage children to figure out what happens with each different motion.

Assessment: The child will give or follow visual musical symbols.

Accommodations and Integration: Have the child hold up a picture of a particular signal for the group to follow. Have the children use their instruments with a conductor. Instruments are far more challenging to control than voices. This can be a positive experience even if the child only discovers that other children will start and stop on their hand signals.

Music: Small or Large Group

5-17 Bumblebees

Goals: To appreciate a varied repertoire of music; to listen, analyze, describe, and respond to music; to increase comprehension

Materials: "Flight of the Bumblebee" by Rimsky-Korsakov; cassette, or CD player; toothpicks; wax paper; construction paper; glue; black pipe cleaners; crayons or markers; pictures of bumblebees; yarn, yellow and black cut into strips; Styrofoam balls

Procedure: Talk with children about bees, notably their characteristics and function. Include information about how bumblebees fly. Listen to "Flight of the Bumblebee." Talk about the music with the children. Give the children the materials to make a bumblebee and encourage them to talk about the music while they make their bumblebee. Encourage the children to use the materials creatively. Listen to "Flight of the Bumblebee" again and have children pretend they are bumblebees and dance to the music. Talk in more detail about bumblebees.

Assessment: The child will listen to "Flight of the Bumblebee," make a bumblebee, and identify some of its characteristics.

Accommodations and Integration: Describe only the most salient characteristics of bumblebees and support any product the child makes. Talk in more detail about how bumblebees fly and communicate with each other. Point out details from a picture of the bumblebee. Encourage children to talk about why this is not called "Flight of the Hawk" or other animals they might have some knowledge of.

Music: Small or Large Group

5-18 Clouds

Goals: To appreciate a varied repertoire of music; to listen, analyze, describe, and respond to music; to increase comprehension

Materials: Cassette, or CD player; "Nuages" (Clouds) by Claude Debussy; *The Cloud Book* by Tomie DePaola; cotton balls; paste; construction paper; crayons, markers

Procedure: Read *The Cloud Book* before playing the selection. Discuss clouds with the children. If possible, go outside and have the children lie down on the ground and watch the clouds as they listen to "Nuages." Have children move as they listen and then make a cloud drawing.

Assessment: The child will listen to *The Cloud Book* and then to "Nuages" and move like a cloud. He will state how the movement felt and if the musical title is appropriate.

Accommodations and Integration: Play only a portion of the selection if children get restless. Have some of the children listen a second time and move as if they were clouds. Encourage children to make pictures of clouds and write about their feelings. Children can develop another way of enjoying and thinking about nature. They can begin to tie sound, whether in nature or as an interpretation of nature, into a context.

Music: Large Group

5-19 Sequencing Songs

Goals: To sing alone and with others; to appreciate a varied repertoire of music; to identify and understand patterns and relationships

Materials: None

Procedure: Sing songs that require the children to remember a particular sequence such as "Old MacDonald," "This Old Man," "If You're Happy," "I Know an Old Lady Who Swallowed a Fly," and "Hush, Little Baby."

Assessment: The child will sing at least three items in the sequence.

Accommodations and Integration: Make pictures for the different words the children have to remember and hold them up as visual reminders. For "Old MacDonald," these would be pictures of the different animals. When you sing "Old MacDonald," pause after "and on his farm he had a … " to see if they can remember the sequence without your help. As children become more skillful, add more words for the children to remember.

Music, movement, and sequences help children focus on mood and rhythm and provide the opportunity for all children to be active.

Music: Large Group

5-20 Mitch the Fish

Goals: To listen, analyze, describe, and respond to music; to perform on instruments alone or with others; to sing alone and with others

Materials: Tambourines (one for each child), book *Mitch the Fish*

Procedure: Tell the children about a fish you know that can change colors when he wishes. Read *Mitch the Fish*. Give the children the background of how he changes color (i.e., "I'm Mitch the fish, I swim and I swish and I can change my color if I wish"). Let the children know that Mitch needs help to change his color and that they can help him. Give each child a tambourine. (Require the tambourine to stay on the floor until the appropriate part of the story.) When the time comes let the children shake their tambourines saying, "I'm Mitch the fish, I swim and I swish and I can change my color if I wish."

Assessment: The child will listen to *Mitch the Fish* and shake his tambourine at the appropriate times while saying the correct words.

Accommodations and Integration: Read *Mitch the Fish* and have the children clap their hands at the appropriate time. Let the children develop their own stories in which to use the tambourines or other instruments. After the story set out the tambourines to allow the children to explore them.

Music: Large or Small Group

5-21 Musical Colors

Goals: To appreciate a varied repertoire of music; to listen, analyze, describe, and respond to music; to improve sensory motor integration

Materials: A variety of colored shapes, one for each child, backed with cardboard, and placed in a circle. Have simple shapes (square, triangle, rectangle) and more difficult shapes (oval, cross, trapezoid) in shades of colors (pink, violet, and so on)

Procedure: Play music and have the children move around the outside of the circle of colored shapes. When the music stops, have the children sit on the nearest shape. Ask them to name the color and the shape. As a variation, use numbers and letters instead of colors and shapes. Have children move like various animals around the circle.

Assessment: The child will stand on a colored shape when the music stops and name the color and shape she is on.

Accommodations and Integration: Choose slower music and give all children time to find a color to sit on. Only ask a few children to name the colors and shapes they are sitting on. Foster a spirit of cooperation, not competition. Include more unusual shapes and colors. This is an adaptation of musical chairs based on color and shape recognition but without the mad scramble. Since speed is not important, all children can play and no one is eliminated.

Music: Large Group

5-22 Tempo

Goals: To listen, analyze, describe, and respond to music; to improve sensory motor integration; to develop creative movement

Materials: Drum or piano

Procedure: Have the children lie down on the floor, spaced so that they can stretch and not touch each other. As they are lying there, tell them that you want them to listen to the beat and move according to how fast or slow the beat is. They can move any body parts they want in any way as long as they remain in one place on their backs. Start with a slow beat so you can watch and make comments to the children about their movements.

Assessment: The child will move her body part to different musical tempos.

Accommodations and Integration: Warn children before you change the tempo. If they move with you, make finer gradations to your changes and make them more abrupt. Change the beat frequently and introduce some intermediate tempos. Also, vary the loudness and sometimes use more difficult rhythms or patterns: soft but fast or loud but slow. See if the children can focus on the tempo. This activity can be used to quiet excited children. Pace your periods of vigorous beat so that the children don't become too tired. Unless you want excited children, be sure to end on a slow tempo.

Music: Large Group

5-23 My Song

Goals: To sing alone and with others; to appreciate a varied repertoire of music; to increase inclusion

Materials: None

Procedure: Sing songs in which you can substitute the name of a child from your group, or adapt a song to include a name.

"BINGO"	"PAW-PAW PATCH"
There was a farmer had a son	Where, oh, where is pretty little Sherry?
and Michael was his name—O.	Where, oh, where is pretty little Laura?
M-I-C-H-AEL	Where, oh, where is handsome Juan?
M-I-C-H-AEL	They're in the block corner
M-I-C-H-AEL	picking up blocks.
And Michael was his name—O.	

"HEY BETTY MARTIN"	"WHO HAS RED ON?"
Hey, Jenny Gilbert	T. R. has a red shirt,
tippy toe tippy toe.	red shirt, red shirt,
Hey, Dante Turner	T. R. has a red shirt
tiptoe fine.	in school today.

Assessment: The child will recognize her name when sung or look at the child being sung about.

Accommodations and Integration: Point to the child whose name you are singing. Use songs that require children to sing back a response such as "Here I am." These songs are great at the beginning of the year, when children are getting to know each other. Also, use them when you are trying to get a group together and you have a few wanderers ("Hey, Gabi O'Day, come join us").

Creative Movement: Small or Large Group

5-24 Rag Doll

Goals: To develop creative movement; to increase body awareness; to improve sensory motor integration

Materials: Rag doll

Procedure: Show the children a rag doll and demonstrate how it moves. Start with the children lying down and show them what happens to the rag doll when the legs and arms are lifted. Then go around the class and check out your collection of "rag dolls." Raise limbs an inch or two and see how floppy children can be. (Don't drop a leg very far or the children will tense!) It takes practice to relax.

Assessment: The child will move her body like a rag doll.

Accommodations and Integration: Ensure that the environment is safe; use soothing music to create a mood, dim the lights, and allow children to feel relaxed. As the children learn to relax lying down, see if they can gain skill in locating just the muscles they need; that is, they can sit up while keeping their arms and head relaxed. Then have them try standing. Eventually add music. See if children can alternate between being floppy rag dolls and tense, marching tin soldiers on your command. Call out to the children what you want them to be. Help children learn to relax specific body parts on command. Tension increases pain, so anything you can teach children about relaxing is useful. Tension may also be the precursor to aggression.

Creative Movement: Large Group

5-25 Relaxation Stories

Goals: To increase body awareness; to improve sensory motor integration; to improve cause-and-effect reasoning

Materials: None

Procedure: Have the children lie down and shut their eyes. Begin by using this activity to teach body parts and lightly touch the parts as you talk or have someone else do that. Tell them a story while they listen and relax. The actual content of the story may vary with what your class has done and the experiences your children are familiar with. An example follows:

There was a little boy who was tired, but he could not go to sleep; he had the wiggles. Every time a part of him was tired, another part would start to wiggle, and he'd giggle, and then he couldn't go to sleep. So he decided to tell himself a sleepy story. He started with his toes and said, "Toes, don't wiggle," but they kept wiggling. Then he said, "Toes, we're going to the beach and we are going to walk through so much sand that you'll be glad not to wiggle." And he walked and he walked and he walked and finally he was so tired that he sat down and his toes weren't wiggling. They were too tired. His ankles were tired and so were his knees. They felt heavy. Even his legs felt heavy. It just felt nice to be sitting down. Maybe even lying down. Oh, stretch out. ... Umm. Rest your head back, get comfortable, and close your eyes. ... Oh, relax those tired feet again, all the way up the leg. Now your hip. Now your middle. Let your shoulders touch the floor if they want to; your elbows too. Now your hands. Uncurl your fingers. Even that little finger is heavy. Now let's go back up. The wrists, elbows, and shoulders are all heavy and relaxed. Move your head up and lay it down; roll it a little to find a comfortable place. Open your mouth. Now close it. Yawn. Close your eyes. (Pause.) Breathe deeply. (Pause.) You're waking up. Roll your head, open your eyes. Sit up and wiggle just a little.

Assessment: The child will listen to a story with her eyes closed and relax her body in response to the story.

Accommodations and Integration: Keep the stories short until children feel comfortable with the process. Make your pauses short. As children learn the process, increase the length of the pauses and incorporate more visual images. Make a recording of the story and encourage children to make up their own stories. Point out the relevant variables of pace and tone as well as content. The relaxation portion of this is best spoken in a slow, placid monotone. In addition to providing a tone of relaxation, it exposes children to another type and use of storytelling.

5-26 Movement Exploration

Goals: To develop creative movement; to increase body awareness; to increase inclusion

Materials: None

Procedure: Ask the children to move in unusual ways using any three parts:

> 1 hand, 2 feet; 2 hands, 1 foot; 1 hand, 2 knees.
> holding your feet with your hands and pretend they are connected
> moving across the floor without touching your feet on the ground

Assessment: The child will move his body in different ways based on the directions.

Accommodations and Integration: Encourage children to make up ways to move. Have them do this in pairs. Verbally describe their adaptations. After one child has responded to a request, see if children can respond to the same request in a different way. Given appropriate choices, all children may be very skillful in moving in different ways. With discussion, others may become aware of the challenges of not being able to use one or more limbs.

5-27 Dentist's Office

Goals: To increase awareness of roles people play; to encourage problem solving; to express feelings

Materials: Props for a dentist's office:

dental floss	lab coat	cloth for around neck
table	tongue depressors	small mirrors
cups	pretend drill	rubber gloves
mask	chair	glasses

Procedure: Set up a dentist's office. Allow children to play the dentist, dental hygienist, nurse, receptionist, patient, parent of patient, and so on. Encourage them to explore the different materials and how they are used. Also talk about why it is important to go to the dentist. Precede (or follow) this with a trip to a dentist's office and some information on teeth and food. Talk about the care of the teeth and mouth area as well as their function in speech. Support children in cooperative play and role-taking. Provide them with pictures and additional equipment. Have them use the mask and rubber gloves and talk about why these are used. Talk about the dentist and their feelings about going.

Assessment: The child will play the role of a dentist or patient and discuss how he feels when he goes to the dentist.

Accommodations and Integration: Encourage children to explore the equipment and materials. Have this out for several days if the materials are unfamiliar to children. Talk about teeth and their role in health. If appropriate, talk about teeth that "fall out." Discuss the role teeth play in speech. Some children may not have been to the dentist's office. They may have many questions. For children who are fearful of trips to the dentist this activity might help them work through some of their concerns. Be sure that all materials that might get into children's mouths are disinfected and disposable ones are thrown away immediately.

5-28 Doctor's Office

Goals: To increase awareness of roles people play; to encourage problem solving; to express feelings

Materials: Props for a doctor's office: stethoscope, lab coat, flashlight, syringes (without needles), dolls, tongue depressors

Procedure: Set up the dramatic play area as a doctor's office. Have the children examine "sick" dolls and/or peers. Be sure to include information on routine procedures, such as immunization and regular checkups, in addition to sick calls.

Assessment: The child will play the role of doctor or patient.

Accommodations and Integration: Encourage children to explore the equipment by having it available for several days. Give children information on different types of medical specialties. Talk about pediatricians, surgeons, ophthalmologists, family practice physicians, and allergists, and how you might need several doctors to handle a particular problem. Include the specialties that are most relevant to your classroom. The doctor's office will probably be a familiar setting because most of the children will have been to the doctor for a checkup. Introduce this activity with a book or a visit from a doctor. You can expand this activity into a hospital setup noting the differences. Talk about health and staying healthy as well as illness.

Dramatic Play: Small Group

5-29 Shoe Store

Goals: To encourage problem solving; to improve cause-and-effect reasoning; to increase awareness of roles people play

Materials: Shoes for different purposes:

walking shoes	baby shoes	bowling shoes
high heels	toe shoes	baseball shoes with plastic cleats
steel-toed shoes	hiking boots	flip flops
golf shoes	running shoes	boots
clogs	ballet slippers	bedroom slippers

Procedure: Set up a shoe store. Discuss the function of shoes and how some shoes are designed for certain situations. Have some examples and talk about how these shoes make it easier. Use obvious examples:

steel toes:	won't hurt if something gets dropped on the toes
baseball cleats:	get better traction running, less likely to slip
flip flops:	cool in hot weather

Once children have grasped the idea, have them use it in dramatic play to choose the shoes they need.

Assessment: The child will select and buy a pair of shoes appropriate for her purpose.

Accommodations and Integration: Have children pair up the different shoes as they become mixed up. Help them compare shoes for differences in color, size, and purpose. Use the concept of shoes to help children think of a variety of ways we can adapt to changing situations. This activity not only teaches the principles of buying and selling but also teaches specialized ways of coping with environments. For children who rely on visual cues, add pictures of the places where the shoes might be used and have children match the shoes to the pictures.

Dramatic Play: Large Group

5-30 Circus

Goals: To improve self-concept; to participate in the democratic process; to increase inclusion

Materials: Props for a circus: hats, balance beam, scarves, stuffed animals, costumes, mats

Procedure: Read a book about the circus and talk about animal trainers, acrobats, tightrope walkers, and so on. Then have a circus in the class. Encourage children to decide how they will organize their circus, how many events they will have, and in what order they will appear, the events themselves, necessary props, and so on. Have children practice for their events before putting on the circus.

Assessment: The child will assist in setting up a pretend circus and participate in at least one event.

Accommodations and Integration: Include some undemanding acts. Provide children with alternative roles if they are uncomfortable performing, such as handing out tickets. Help other children play organizational roles. Encourage them to develop a program and print it on the computer. This provides an opportunity for children to practice skills of negotiating and participating in a group process that needs a resolution, which includes all children.

Summary

The creative arts are an integral part of the early childhood curriculum. They provide opportunities for problem solving and develop skills for working in groups. Children develop an appreciation for other cultures and more global connections. They provide children with lifelong skills as well as a way of learning about themselves and others in an atmosphere of exploration.

Educational Resources

Best Children's Music provides reviews and commentary on music by age group, including infants and toddlers. You can even listen before you choose to buy something. http://www.bestchildrensmusic.com/

Bright Ideas for Learning is a publishing company who believes that "it's the process, not the product." They list art activities taken from the books they sell as a way to preview the books. (800) 480-4278; http://www.brightring.com/Fun%20Activities.html

Children's Music Web is a non-profit resource for children, families and educators as a source for music and an index of websites related to music for children. http://www.childrenmusic.org/

Getty, a museum, provides lesson plans and curriculum ideas. It is particularly useful in helping children analyze art and other experiences. http://www.getty.edu/education/

Kinderart Littles is a website designed especially for preschool children. It provides activities, information on books, music, videos, and more. It also provides teaching tips and the opportunities to share ideas. http://www.kinderart.com/littles/index.html

For additional resources, visit the book companion website for this text at www.cengage.com/education/deiner.

Infant and Toddler Activities:

Young Infants, Mobile Infants, and Toddlers

Because infants change and grow so quickly curriculum must adjust to their new developmental level. For this reason, activities are designed as prototypes for young infants, birth to 9 months, mobile infants, 8 to 18 months, and toddlers, 16 to 36 months. If infants or toddlers are in the younger range or their disability affects this particular area, use activities from a lower age range. If they are in the older range or activities seem too easy, move into the activities for older children, in Resource Chapters 1 through 5.

Activity Goals

The activities for infants and toddlers are divided into five broad areas: social awareness, language and communication skills, cognitive development, sensory motor skills, and creative development. Activities are organized by the goals they support. The targeted age group for each activity is designated: young infants (birth to 9), mobile infants (8 to 18), and toddlers (16 to 36). If it is appropriate for a broader age range, the designation includes that information. A birth to 18 designation would include children from birth to 18 months. All activity areas begin with activities for young infants, then activities for mobile infants, and finally, activities for toddlers. The activities that are in the book have their number identified; those that are in the book companion website are followed by a "w" (refer to Tables R6–1 and R6–2).

Infant and Toddler Guidelines

Because infants and toddlers have a small repertoire the accommodations needed can be applied in general to all the listed activities. The following list highlights

accommodations. They are more functional than accommodations for older children. The accommodations for regulatory problems relate to children who may later be identified with specific learning disabilities, attention-deficit/hyperactivity disorder, and social, emotional, and behavioral disorders as well as some children on the autism spectrum.

Adapting activities for infants and toddlers with:	
Regulatory problems: Detached	Focus on one behavior at a time. Teach body awareness, especially tension.
Regulatory problems: Underreactive	Use massage. Direct and redirect children. Actively teach items you might assume others would learn. Use brief, focused lessons. Engage children; model and reinforce appropriate eye contact, facial expressions, and gestures. Model interactions. Use multimodal methods.

Regulatory problems: Hypersensitive	Reduce excess stimuli (light, noise, activity). Be consistent. Teach adaptive skills.
Regulatory problems: Motorically disorganized/impulsive skills	Do a functional behavior assessment if undesirable behaviors continue and do not respond to traditional guidance. Try reinforcing quiet behavior with a special audiotape (turn off the tape if the child cries and so on). Redirect behavior. Give intermittent reinforcement. Work on self-control and self-image.
Regulatory problems: Dysregulated	Ignore inappropriate crying. Reinforce appropriate responses to situations. Be available. Develop a predictable schedule, especially as it relates to sleeping and eating. Teach infants and toddlers to self-comfort. Use music to set a mood. Gradually increase environmental demands.
Communication disorders	Talk to infants and toddlers. Support all communication. Build language and vocabulary. Help children respond to people and environmental stimuli. Look at communication as social interaction.
English language learners	Support children in developing vocabulary and language in their home language and English. Provide context for language learning. If helpful, use a simple picture communication system for toddlers to show how they are feeling or what they want.
Intellectual disabilities	Use toys that respond (shake rattle, it makes noise). Use verbal and physical prompts. Support and enhance a child's capabilities. Model desired behavior. Work toward independence in eating, dressing, and grooming. Use a picture-task analysis.
Gifted and talented	Provide activities with cause-effect relationships. Increase complexity while keeping activities at a developmentally appropriate level (read books with more details). Encourage and support motor skills. Be flexible.
Special health care needs	Normalize the educational setting within the medical aspects of health. Adapt to physical limitation, stamina, and endurance levels by flexible schedules. Learn danger signs and side effects of treatments (appetite loss, mood swings, hair loss, and so on) and develop a plan to deal with these. Have an emergency care plan.
Orthopedic and neurologic	Help children move as normally as possible. Work toward symmetry (using both sides of the body equally). Check with a physical or occupational therapist for the best way to position children. Actively promote peer interaction.
Hearing impairments	Use visual and tactile stimulation. Promote the use of auditory aids. Talk to children and use the communication system the family has chosen. Supplement this with pictures and photographs for choices and to support learning tasks.
Visual impairments	Use auditory and tactile stimulation. Promote the use of visual aids. Help children develop appropriate responses to auditory stimulation (look at speaker). Promote social interaction and mobility.

Table R6–1: Activity goals and activity numbers in text and online

Goals	Activity Numbers
• To increase social awareness	6–1, 6–2, 6–3, 6–4, 6–5, 6–6, 6–15, 6–25, 6–30 6–31w, 6–32w, 6–33w, 6–34w, 6–36w, 6–42w, 6–43w, 6–52w, 6–54w, 6–63w
• To increase language and communication skills	6–3, 6–5, 6–7, 6–8, 6–9, 6–10, 6–11, 6–12, 6–16, 6–18, 6–23, 6–28 6–32w, 6–34w, 6–35w, 6–36w, 6–37w, 6–38w, 6–39w, 6–40w, 6–41w, 6–42w, 6–52w, 5–53w, 6–58w

• To increase cognitive development	6–1, 6–7, 6–8, 6–13, 6–14, 6–15, 6–16, 6–17, 6–18, 6–19, 6–20, 6–21, 6–22, 6–24
	6–35w, 6–38w, 6–43w, 6–44w, 6–45w, 6–46w, 6–47w, 6–48w, 6–49w, 6–50w, 6–51w, 6–55w, 6–56w, 6–57w
• To increase sensory motor skills	6–2, 6–4, 6–5, 6–6, 6–9, 6–10, 6–12, 6–13, 6–14, 6–17, 6–18, 6–19, 6–20, 6–21, 6–22, 6–23, 6–24, 6–25, 6–26, 6–27, 6–29
	6–31w, 6–32w, 6–33w, 6–34w, 6–35w, 6–36w, 6–39w, 6–40w, 6–41w, 6–44w, 6–45w, 6–46w, 6–47w, 6–48w, 6–49w, 6–50w, 6–51w, 6–52w, 6–53w, 6–54w, 6–55w, 6–56w, 6–57w, 6–58w, 6–59w, 6–60w, 6–61w, 6–62w
• To increase creative development	6–10, 6–11, 6–25, 6–26, 6–27, 6–28, 6–29, 6–30
	6–58w, 6–59w, 6–60w, 6–61w, 6–62w, 6–63w

Table R6–2: Age and reference numbers

Age	Activity Numbers
• Young infants (B to 9 months)	6–1, 6–2, 6–7, 6–8, 6–13, 6–14, 6–18, 6–20, 6–25, 6–26
	6–31w, 6–32w, 6–35w, 6–43w, 6–44w, 6–49w, 6–50w
• Mobile infants (8 to 18 months)	6–3, 6–4, 6–9, 6–10, 6–15, 6–16, 6–21, 6–22, 6–27, 6–28
	6–33w, 6–45w, 6–46w, 6–51w
• Mobile infants and toddlers (8 to 36 months)	6–52w, 6–53w, 6–54w, 6–58w, 6–59w
• Toddlers (16 to 36 months)	6–5, 6–6, 6–11, 6–12, 6–17, 6–18, 6–23, 6–24, 6–29, 6–30
	6–33w, 6–36w, 6–37w, 6–38w, 6–39w, 6–40w, 6–41w, 6–42w, 6–47w, 6–48w, 6–55w, 6–56w, 6–57w, 6–60w, 6–61w, 6–62w, 6–63w

Infant and Toddler Activities

Social Awareness: Individual, birth to 9 months

6-1 Anticipation

Goals: To increase social awareness; to increase cognitive development

Materials: None

Procedure: Before beginning an event such as giving an infant a bottle, picking him up, or changing him, tell the infant what is going to happen. Show the infant the bottle and say, "Are you hungry? I have your bottle ready. Do you want it?" Then pause to give the infant time to respond. (Don't expect him to say "yes," you are giving him the time and respect to process information rather than just putting the bottle in his mouth.) Before picking up an infant hold out your arms and say, "I'm going to pick you up." Then pause so the infant can anticipate what will happen. Keep the gestures and words you use consistent so the infant knows what to expect. Follow through with the action quickly; if you show him the bottle and he responds, then feed him right away; do not wait several minutes. Respond to the infant's cues. If he quiets when approaching him say, "You know I'm going to pick you up." Then do it.

Assessment: The infant increases the amount of time he can wait for an anticipated activity without fussing.

Integration: As infants learn that their world is predictable they are willing to wait longer for events to happen because they are developing trust.

Social Awareness: Individual, B to 9 months

6-2 Tummy Time

Goal   To increase social awareness, to increase sensory motor skills

Materials: None

Procedure: Tummy time is whenever infants are not on their backs or sitting in seats or other containers. Carrying infants in different ways changes their view of the world and also helps them strengthen needed muscles. As you carry young infants point out items they can see, talk, or sing to them.

- Stomach down: To carry an infant stomach down place one arm underneath his chest with the hand supporting his chin and neck. The other arm goes around his entire body.
- Back to front vertical: Pick up the infant so his back is toward your front. Carry him in a vertical position so his head is up and he is looking out. For young babies keep their head centered as you hold them. As infants get older have them put their arms out and pretend to fly. As a variation put one arm under the infant to make a seat and the other arm around his middle for support.
- Back to front horizontal: Pick up the infant so his back is toward your front. Carry him in a horizontal position with his head in the elbow of your right arm as he is looking out. Your right arm goes under his head and your left arm goes between his legs to hold the infant's side. Your hands will meet in front.

Assessment: The infant will look around when held in various positions and carried.

Integration: Tummy time is adaptable and infants need to spend more time actively moving. By carrying them in different positions you give them the opportunity to increase muscular strength. Lack of tummy time may lead to flat areas on the back of the head, muscles that are tight or weak on one side of the neck, and delayed motor skills.

Social Awareness: Individual, 8 to 18 months

6-3 My Book about Me

Goals: To increase social awareness; to increase language and communication skills

Materials: Plastic sleeve covers, three-ring binders, markers, digital or regular camera, photographs of the infant, construction paper, paste

To Make: *Take photographs of the infant doing various activities throughout the day. Print them or have them developed. Cut construction paper or posterboard into 8 1/2″ × 11″ pieces so that each fits the plastic sleeve cover. Paste the pictures of the infant on both sides of the construction paper and put each page in a plastic sleeve. Make a beginning page to identify the infant's book. Place in a 3-ring binder. Pictures can also be laminated or covered with clear contact paper.*

Procedure: With the infant on your lap, look through the book with him and talk about each picture, what he is doing, and how wonderful he is. For younger infants, keep the book short and if possible have the pictures of the child alone doing everyday things (eating, sleeping, playing, and so on). As children get older have more pictures in the book with a wider range of events or make several shorter, more specific books such as "Shalini at Home," "Shalini at School," "Shalini Playing with Her Friends."

Assessment: The infant will look at the book.

Integration: Infants enjoy looking at these books. Take pictures of infants at school or ask parents to send in pictures, whichever is most appropriate. A digital camera makes it easy to add to books as infants change and grow. Photographs can also be used for assessment and to document developmental milestones.

Social Awareness: Individual, 8 to 18 months

6-4 Cups and Spoons

Goals: To increase social awareness; to increase sensory motor skills

Materials: A variety of plastic cups with handles, plastic spoons

Procedure: Place the infant in a highchair and place a cup and spoon on the tray. Encourage the infant to explore each item. Demonstrate how you can use the spoon to hit the cup or to stir, and then give the item back to the infant. Encourage her to pick up the cup with the handle and pretend to drink from it or eat with the spoon. Repeat this using a slightly different cup. For younger infants introduce the cup and spoon separately before pairing them. As infants gain experience, give them several different cups and spoons to play with at the same time.

Assessment: The infant will explore the materials and occasionally use the cups and spoons appropriately.

Integration: It is useful for infants to have experience playing with and exploring the properties of cups and spoons before they use them to eat and drink.

Social Awareness: Small Group, 16 to 36 months

6-5 Dolls

Goals: To increase social awareness; to increase language and communication skills; to increase sensory motor skills

Materials: Multiethnic dolls

Procedure: Encourage exploration of the dolls. Help toddlers gently feel the dolls' hair, eyes, and clothing, and to move body parts. Name body parts and clothing for toddlers. Encourage them to play with dolls in different ways. Toddlers may want to carry, cuddle, bottle-feed, sing to, or rock the doll baby. When they are ready, introduce new ways of playing with the doll. Encourage two children to play together and talk about what each is doing and why. Encourage them to think about what the doll baby might want or need. See if toddlers can imitate skills that are more difficult: pretending to feed with a spoon, sprinkling powder or rubbing lotion on body parts, and combing the doll's hair. Help toddlers use their imagination with the doll. Take the doll for a walk in a wagon or stroller. Wash the baby in a small tub, using soap and a washcloth, and then dry the doll with a towel. Help children develop adaptive skills by practicing undressing and dressing, not only themselves, but also a doll.

Assessment: The toddler will demonstrate at least three different types of caregiving activities using the doll.

Integration: Teach children caregiving skills. They are often more willing to practice adaptive skills in play.

Social Awareness: Small Group, 16 to 36 months

6-6 Washing Dishes

Goals: To increase social awareness; to increase sensory motor skills

Materials: Plastic dishes, basin, water (lukewarm)

Procedure: Put the dishes in the basin and have toddlers explore the dishes. Encourage them to put the dishes in the basin, swish the water, and take them out. Talk about their actions. Ask them questions. Have at least two basins so that children can interact. Say "out" as you take a dish out and "in" as you put the dishes in. Physically guide the child's hand, if needed. Say, "Good, you took it out!" Fill the basin with a small amount of water and add a small amount of soap. Let children "wash" dishes. Add a sponge or handled scrubber for them to wash dishes. Have several towels available to dry dishes. Encourage appropriate actions; that is, placing cups on saucers, pouring, and stirring the cup with a spoon. Have children sort utensils in a storage unit. Encourage them to match items by color. Have children set the table and use dishes to serve snack.

Assessment: The toddler will parallel play with others while washing and drying dishes.

Integration: Toddlers enjoy pretending with familiar objects. The lukewarm water is soothing.

Language Development: Individual, birth to 9 months

6-7 Talking Walk

Goals: To increase language and communication skills; to increase cognitive development

Materials: None

Procedure: Pick the infant up and hold him so he can see over your shoulder. Walk around the room and point out objects and events that are taking place and what other infants and toddlers are doing. "That's the telephone. Sometimes it rings and I talk to people on it. There is Roxanna, she is playing with Dot. This is one of my favorite pictures. Aura painted it. See the beautiful red she used." For younger infants make the walk shorter and talk less. Use items that the infant is familiar with and start out with what she knows, like her own coat, then let her touch it. Use disparate items to continue such as a book; allow her to touch this also. Only label one or two items and then stop. With older infants label more items and talk about their function. Encourage the infant to touch the items and try to imitate what you say. Vary what you say to include a "What is that?" Wait a few seconds and then say something like "Those are Nathan's boots!" Use similar items such as sneakers, boots, slippers, and shoes to make it even more difficult and talk about the properties of footgear and why they are different.

Assessment: The infant will participate in the walk and focus on the identified items.

Integration: Infants need to learn about and feel comfortable in their environment. The view from your shoulder is very different from their view from the floor, so it is important they see this too. Although infants will not understand all the words you use, they will hear the different tones of your voice and begin to make associations, especially if you demonstrate what the objects do.

Carrying infants in different ways, showing them different objects in their environment, and talking to them about what they see supports learning in young infants.

Language Development: Individual, birth to 9 months

6-8 Signs

Goals: To increase language and communication skills; to increase cognitive development

Materials: None

Procedure: Look at the sign for "more." Learn how to do the sign so you feel comfortable teaching infants the sign. Show the infant the sign for "more" during an activity or feeding when you want to know whether or not the infant wants more. Use the sign for more before or during feeding and show the infant the sign every time you feed her. Consistency is key. Use the sign for more until the infant begins to sign back to you. Once infants know the sign "more" begin to add additional signs.

Assessment: The infant will use the sign for "more" when she wants more.

Integration: Infants can control their hands before they can talk. Being able to give adults feedback about their needs helps everyone. Having all children learn useful signs is particularly helpful for infants with developmental delays, hearing impairments, and English language learners. The more signs they learn the earlier they can communicate. This can also be helpful in toilet training if children know the signs for wet and dry.

Language Development: Individual, 8 to 18 months

6-9 My Active Activity Book

Goals: To increase language and communication skills; to increase sensory motor skills

Materials: Three-hole plastic sleeves, markers, a digital camera or camera with film, photographs of mobile infants' being active, construction paper or poster board, paste, three-hole binders (optional)

To Make: *Take photographs of mobile infants engaged in active activities throughout several days. Some examples are crawling, rolling, walking, dancing, clapping and so on. Print the photographs or have them developed. Cut construction paper or poster board into 8 1/2″ × 11″ pieces so each fits inside the plastic sleeve. Paste the photographs of the mobile infants on both side of the construction paper (one or two per side) and put each page into a separate sleeve. Make a name page to identify the mobile infant and fasten them together with yarn or place them in a three-hole binder. Add photographs as mobile infants learn new skills.*

Procedure: Place the mobile infant on your lap or sit beside him. Look through the book with him and talk about each photograph and what he is doing, how important physical activity is in making him strong and healthy and how wonderful he is. After reading the book encourage him to move like some of the photographs. If time has passed point out how much farther or faster he can move now. Encourage him to see how far he can walk or run and for how long.

Assessment: The mobile infant will look at the book and perform the requested activities.

Integration: "Book babble" is an important preliteracy skill. Mobile infants jabber in a tone and pattern that sounds like reading if they have been read to. They are practicing language in a new and different way. In addition to literacy this encourages mobile infants to practice emerging skills. Practice helps the mobile infants' efficiency and coordination. Although you do not need to teach mobile infants to move, movement opportunities enhance the ongoing maturation of motor pathways in the infant's brain and spinal cord.

Language Development: Individual, 8 to 18 months

6-10 Nursery Rhymes and Chants

Goals: To increase language and communication skills; to increase sensory motor skills; to increase creative development

Materials: Books with simple nursery rhymes such as I'm a little teapot; This little piggy; Baa, baa, black sheep; Hickory dickory dock; and so on

Procedure: Read, chant, or sing nursery rhymes as you turn the pages of the books with a mobile infant. Use the books frequently so infants continue to hear the rhymes and chants. Add silly rhymes and ones that you play the leader and the children follow your actions such as

Up to the ceiling (raise hands up)
Down to the floor (put hands down)
Left to the window (point left with left hand)
Right to the door (point right with right hand)
This is my right hand – (wave it vigorously)
Raise it up high (raise right hand and stretch)
This is my left hand – (wave it vigorously)
Reach for the sky (raise left hand up, keep right up and stretch)
Right hand, left hand (wave both hands)
Twirl them around (twirl hands over one another)
Left hand, right hand (keep twirling)
Pound, pound, pound (reach down and pound the ground)

Do not expect mobile infants to know their right hand from their left, it is the motion and rhyme that is important. Make up motions to songs, and continue to pair language and movement.

Assessment: The mobile infant will listen to the book and participate in acting out the rhyme or chant.

Integration: Do not expect mobile infants to follow the directions as they are said. Mobile infants can increase their physical activity by acting out imaginative nursery rhymes and chants. They can develop creativity and language while increasing their activity level. When songs or rhymes with actions are done in a series they help build endurance and increase brain activity.

Language Development: Individual, 16 to 36 months

6-11 Puppets

Goals: To increase language and communication skills; to increase creative development

Materials: Duck or bunny puppets (or other animal puppets)

Procedure: With the puppet on your hand, talk to the toddler and encourage the toddler to talk with the duck or bunny: "I'm a duck. I say 'quack, quack.' " Encourage the toddler to imitate sounds, words, or actions. Then let the toddler experiment with putting the puppet on his hand. Use the puppet to have a "conversation" with the toddler. Give the toddler time to respond.

Assessment: The toddler will respond to overtures by the puppet and will socially interact with the puppet.

Integration: Talking with puppets encourages peer interaction as well as fostering language development. Simple puppets that use whole-hand movements are best at this age.

Language Development: Individual, 16 to 36 months

6-12 Dressing Book

Goals: To increase language and communications skills; to increase sensory motor skills

Materials: A book about dressing

Procedure: Begin by using children's clothing and ask toddlers to point to the part of themselves that the clothing would cover. If necessary, give them a choice. Then point to the picture and back to the clothing as you name each. Name and point to the articles of clothing. Ask the toddler to point to the correct picture as you name each article. Then ask him to name the article of clothing shown in the picture and find the piece of clothing if he is wearing that article. Encourage toddlers to "read" the book to you. Then ask them to show you where each article goes, for instance: "Where do the shoes go? Yes, that's right! Shoes go on your feet!"

Assessment: The toddler will point to the articles of clothing named and show where they go on his body.

Integration: This activity fosters adaptive behavior as well as language development. There is no expectation that toddlers will dress themselves, rather, that their awareness is increased and that they frame these experiences as positive.

Cognitive Development: Individual, birth to 9 months

6-13 Scrunches

Goals: To increase cognitive development; to increase sensory motor skills

Materials: Brightly colored scrunches (what women use to hold ponytails) or commercially available baby wrist and ankle elastics

Procedure: Put scrunches around the infant's wrists or ankles. Point these out to the infant by holding the infant's hand and saying, "Look at you, this hand looks great!" Check to see if the infant's eyes focus on the hand (or on the scrunches). For young infants use scrunches made out of black-and-white striped or highly contrasting, patterned materials. Securely attach a large bell to a scrunche or circle of elastic that can go over the baby's feet. Encourage the infant to bring his hands or feet to his mouth. Help him focus on the scrunches for longer periods of time.

Assessment: The infant will attend to the ankles or wrists with the scrunches for increasing periods.

Integration: Infants need to become aware of and explore their own bodies before they can reach and grasp objects. Brightly colored or striped socks also call infants' attention to their feet. *Note:* Adding a bell for sound provides an additional stimulus. It is a safety hazard if it is small enough to be swallowed. Use a large bell, attach it securely, check it regularly and use it only under adult supervision.

Cognitive Development: Individual, birth to 9 months

6-14 Infant Massage

Goals: To increase cognitive development; to increase sensory motor skills

Materials: Lotion, changing table, floor, couch, or bed

Procedure: Place the infant on a changing table or other surface. Undress the infant (be sure it is warm enough). Place some lotion in one hand to warm it, and then put the lotion on the infant's body. As you massage the infant's body with the lotion, talk to the infant about his body. "Adolfo, now I'm going up and down your arm. Let's check out that hand. You've got five fingers. I'm going to count them. One, two, three, four, oh, actually this one is a thumb." Continue to talk to the infant as you massage his body. Just do one area of the infant's body such as the arms or legs. As children respond, talk in more detail about what you are doing.

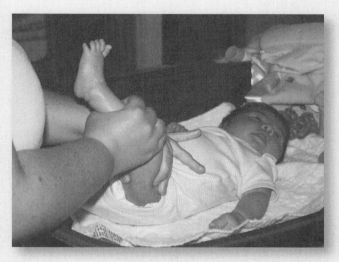

Infant massage increases body awareness, helps the infant relax, and establishes a close trusting relationships between the infant and her caregiver.

Assessment: The infant attends to and responds to the massage by increased body awareness.

Integration: Massaging the infant's body increases body awareness. It is also good for relaxation and for establishing closeness between infants and their caregivers. Occupational therapists often use massage with children to increase awareness before performing skills (a hand massage before doing fine motor skills). It can also be used to decrease tension in muscles for children with high muscle tone. Talk to occupational therapists about how to use this to benefit the children you are working with. *Note:* Talk with parents about infant massage. Some parents are very comfortable with your massaging their infants while others may not be as comfortable. Support parents in learning about infant massage and encourage them to do it at home if they do not wish to have it done in the classroom. Some parents find massage to be a very personal thing so check with parents first.

Cognitive Development: Individual, 8 to 18 months

6-15 Hidden Toys

Goals: To increase cognitive development; to increase social awareness

Materials: A small toy, several cloths

Procedure: Get the infant intrigued with a toy. Then cover the toy completely with cloth and say, "Oh, where did it go?" Encourage the infant to find it. Start by partly covering the toy with cloth. If the infant does not attempt to get it, point to the toy and again encourage her. If she still does not find it, take the cloth off dramatically and say, "Here it is!" If the infant is willing, play the game again. If the infant easily finds the toy, hide it first under one cloth, and then move it to the other, covering the toy completely. Initially, expect that the infant will hunt under the first cloth and then go to the second.

Assessment: The infant will successfully find the hidden toy.

Integration: Activities such as these help infants develop the concept of object permanence. Play peek-a-boo and other games that focus on hiding and finding as well.

Cognitive Development: Individual, 8 to 18 months

6-16 Mimic

Goals: To increase cognitive development; to increase language and communication skills

Materials: Three vegetables of different colors (e.g., broccoli, carrots, and mushrooms) steamed for about 10 minutes and cut into very small pieces, plates

Procedure: A serving size for a mobile infant is approximately 2 tablespoons. Put each color of vegetable on a small plate and encourage mobile infants to pass the plate (with your help) and choose a piece(s) of vegetable to put on their plate (or make individual plates but mobile infants are more likely to try things if they can choose). Eat with the mobile infants and talk about the vegetables and how you enjoy them. Help them learn the names of the foods they are eating.

Assessment: The mobile infant will try at least one of the vegetables or fruits.

Integration: Provide a similar snack with fruit. Mobile infants are just learning healthy eating habits. Nutrient-dense age appropriate foods for snack include fruit, vegetables, cheese, yogurt and water. Juice has too much sugar. Making eating a social experiences helps all mobile infants to see others eating and choosing.

Cognitive Development: Individual, 16 to 36 months

6-17 Shape Sorter

Goals: To increase cognitive development; to increase sensory motor skills

Materials: Shape sorter

Procedure: Present the toy to the child and encourage the toddler to lift the top off, remove the shapes, and then replace the top. Encourage them to place the shapes in appropriate holes. If needed, demonstrate how the shapes fit into the holes. If this is difficult, have toddlers put in and take out the shapes without the lid. Then cover one or two spaces with your hand or a piece of cardboard or tape so children have fewer choices. As toddlers become more skillful, use a shape sorter with more shapes, name the shapes, and ask toddlers to put in the shapes you name.

Assessment: The toddler will put the shapes in the correct holes.

Integration: Help toddlers learn about the shapes in their environment. Play games looking for round, square, or tri-angular shapes in the room. Use form boards.

Cognitive Development: Individual, 16 to 36 months

6-18 Take-Apart Toys

Goals: To increase cognitive development; to increase language and communication skills; to increase sensory motor skills

Materials: Toys (animals) that come apart

Procedure: Present the toy to the toddler to explore. If she doesn't take it apart on her own, show her how. Talk about the toy's body parts. Ask, "Where's his head?" and so on. Use the toy to stimulate language development while you do the more difficult taking apart and putting together. Ask, "Is this where the head goes?" Or ask the child to show you where the head goes and then you put it on. Take off one part at a time, such as the head or tail. Encourage the toddler to replace that piece. Gradually remove more and more pieces for the toddler to replace or encourage the toddler to pull the toy apart. Help put the toy back together as needed.

Assessment: The toddler will take the toy apart, identify the body parts, and put it back together.

Integration: This activity helps toddlers think about body parts as well as part-whole relationships.

Sensory Motor Development: Individual, birth to 9 months

6-19 Keys

Goals: To increase sensory motor skills; to increase cognitive development

Materials: Plastic keys

Procedure: Call the infant's name and shake keys. Gently place the keys in her hand. Help her mouth, look at, or shake the keys, if necessary. Keep the keys close to the midline. Then offer keys for her to reach and grasp from different angles (up, down, right, left). Have her reach across her midline to get the keys. (This can be encouraged by having the child hold a toy in one hand while you offer the keys.) Increase the distance the keys are from the infant so that it is a long reach. Put the keys out of the infant's field of vision and call, "Get the keys," so she has to turn and reach.

Assessment: The infant will reach for and grasp the keys, crossing her midline.

Integration: Any small toy that intrigues the infant can be used. Reaching across her midline helps the sides of an infant's brain communicate with each other.

Sensory Motor Development: Individual, birth to 9 months

6-20 Yoga for Infants

Goals: To increase sensory motor skills; to increase cognitive development

Materials: None

Procedure: Lie down on the floor (or a bed or couch) with your legs bent. Place the infant on your bet legs facing you. Smile and talk to him and tell him what you will be doing. Gently take his right arm and move it across his body to his left waist. Hold it for about five seconds and then return it to his side. Do the same thing with the left arm and then the legs. As you are doing this activity, keep saying things like "I'm moving your arm." "I'll take it across your body and touch your waist." "Doesn't that stretch feel good?"

For variation place the infant supine on a mat or blanket. Place one hand on each of the infant's legs and gently lift the legs up and bring them toward the infant's chest. Hold this pose for 5 seconds, then slowly put the infant's legs back down to the floor. Repeat this several times. And, keep talking.

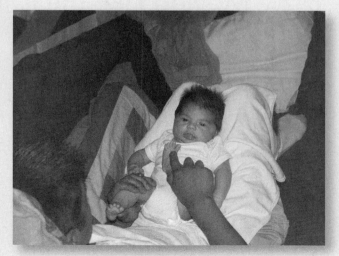

Assessment: The infant will participate in yoga and hold the poses with adult help.

Integration: Cross-lateral movements require the two hemispheres of the brain to work together. When infants do movements that cross the midline of the body such as reaching the right arm to the left leg these communications increase. Yoga can help infants sleep, improve digestion, ease gas pains and colic, stimulate neuromuscular development, and boost the immune system. It is a great way to teach body awareness.

The cross-lateral movements in yoga help the sides of the brain to communicate with each other. In some cultures yoga-type movements are an expected part of child rearing.

6-21 Grab It

Goals: To increase sensory motor skills; to increase cognitive development

Materials: A variety of small blocks of different sizes

Procedure: With the child in a sitting position, hold a small block just outside of the infant's reach and see if he will reach for it. If not, place the block closer to the infant's midline or preferred hand, if established. If the infant takes the block, offer a second and then a third to see what he does. Vary where you place the block for reaching. Sometimes place it close to the center of the infant's body, sometimes more to the right or left so he has to maintain balance while reaching. Give the infant two blocks and keep two matching blocks. Clap them together or bang them and see if the infant will imitate you.

Assessment: The infant will grasp the blocks, explore them, and use two blocks together in some way.

Integration: Some children need to be encouraged to reach, grasp, and imitate.

6-22 Variations on Push and Pull

Goals: To increase sensory motor skills; to increase cognitive development

Materials: A variety of push and pull toys

Procedure: First allow the infant to explore the toy and then roll the toy slightly out of his reach. Encourage him to crawl after the toy. As he reaches it push it a little farther, then encourage him to push it rather than retrieve it. (Don't do this to the point where he is frustrated.) Help push the toy in front of the infant. Move it slowly so he can crawl after it. Choose toys that move slowly with a small push, and encourage the infant to follow it as quickly as he can. When the child understands about pushing toys, introduce toys that can be pulled as well. When the child is comfortable using push and pull toys, encourage him to push or pull them to a specific location.

Assessment: The child will push or pull a toy to a designated location.

Integration: Use push toys before pull toys. Some pull toys are a challenge to beginning walkers, as the child must concentrate on holding onto the toy, know where the toy is relative to where he is, and walk at the same time.

6-23 Moving Like the Animals

Goals: To increase sensory motor skills; to increase language and communication skills

Materials: Pictures of familiar animals

Procedure: See if toddlers can identify the animals in the picture. Help them decide if the animals are large or small and how they move. Have the children move as they think the animal would move. As toddlers become more proficient, choose less familiar animals with obvious movement patterns. Talk about animals and where they live.

Assessment: The child will move like the designated animal.

Integration: This activity helps children learn more about the world in which they live and even think about it differently.

6-24 Dump and Fill

Goals: To increase sensory motor skills; to increase cognitive development

Materials: Dishpans, rice, oatmeal, beans, plastic measuring cups, measuring spoons

Procedure: Put about 2 inches of rice, oatmeal, or beans in a dishpan. Add a variety of cups and spoons. If necessary, place children's hands in the container and help them explore the medium. Encourage them to fill the container with their hands and dump them. Have toddlers dump the contents from one container into another.

Integration: This activity is a precursor to pouring liquids, but far less messy. It has the potential for simple exploration as well as for building concepts about measurement and size. With older children, I would not use edible products but with infants and toddlers, they are likely to eat whatever they use.

Creative Arts: Individual, birth to 8 months

6-25 Touching Songs

Goals: To increase creative development; to increase social awareness; to increase sensory motor skills

Materials: None

Procedure: Sing or chant songs or rhymes where you touch the infant such as "This little piggy went to market," "I'm going to get your nose," and "Hickory Dickory Dock." Sing or hum a song while you hold the infant and move him to the rhythm of the song such as "Rock-A-Bye Baby." Help him do the motions to songs or rhymes like "Pat-A-Cake" or "Johnny Hammers with One Hammer" by holding him on your lap and gently moving his body.

Assessment: The infant enjoys the song and anticipates what is going to happen next.

Integration: Infants learn to feel secure through close sensitive contact.

Creative Arts: Individual, birth to 9 months

6-26 Textured Mat

Goals: To increase creative development; to increase sensory motor skills

Materials: Mat made of various materials (satin, cotton, fake fur, velvet, terry cloth, Lycra, knit fabric, suede, leather-like, and so on) (commercially available)

To Make: *Sew together squares of various materials. Nine squares of 12 inches each makes a good size mat (36″ × 36″).*

Procedure: Place the infant prone on mat. If it is warm enough, have her in diapers. Take a corner of the mat and stroke her hand with it and talk with her about the texture of the material and how it feels. Talk about how the squares are different in color, pattern, and texture. Discuss how they look and feel. Place her in different positions on the mat so it is easier to reach other textures. As infants become older, they can use 6-inch fabric squares to explore by themselves.

Assessment: The infant will explore the mat and respond to the different textures.

Integration: Some infants might not like some of the textures, so go gently, using smooth, soft textures first. Help the infant explore the fabrics and gently rub one piece of fabric on her arm and talk about how it looks and feels.

Creative Arts: Individual, 8-18 months

6-27 Row, Row, Row Your Boat

Goals: To increase creative development; to increase sensory motor skills

Materials: None

Procedure: Place the mobile infant in an upright sitting position facing you. Place her so she is sitting between your outstretched legs so you can provide her with support for sitting if needed. Take her hands in yours and beginning singing "Row, row, row your boat." As you sing, rock back and forth with the infant—this will feel like you are actually rowing a boat together.

Assessment: The mobile infant will rock back and forth in tune to the music with adult support.

Integration: Infants with low muscle tone may need additional support. Place them on your lap with their back toward your front. Extend your hands and theirs and gently rock back and forth. For infants who want more activity row more vigorously and make some variations such "Row, row, row your boat quickly down the stream, faster, faster, faster now until we catch your dream."

Creative Arts: Individual, 8 to 18 months

6-28 Doing it Songs

Goals: To increase creative development; to increase language and communication skills

Materials: None

Procedure: Talk to mobile infants about what they do during the day. Tell them that you are going to make up a song about what they do. Encourage them to decide on motions to go with the words. If this is taking a long time, suggest appropriate movements to go with the verse. Try to get several related concepts. Ask them what they do in the morning or what they do when they get up. (Have a sequence that will work in your mind before you start and only do as many verses as there is interest.) Sing to the tune of "Here we go round the mulberry bush."

> This is the way we wash our hands, wash our hands, wash our hands.
> This is the way we wash our hand so early in the morning.

Morning

Get out of bed	Wash our hands
Brush our teeth	Comb our hair
Put on our clothes	Eat our breakfast
Come to school	

Substitute an activity theme such as cleaning house

Sweep the floors	Vacuum the rugs
Make our beds	Wipe the table

Another variation is to ask mobile infants what they like to do and incorporate their name into the song.

> This is the way Claudia plays with the ball, plays with the ball, plays with the ball.
> This is the way Claudia plays with the ball, and plays with all her friends.

To promote healthy eating you can peel bananas, eat peas, and any other healthy foods.

Assessment: The mobile infant will participate in some of the motions with adult support.

Integration: Mobile infants begin to sing by "tagging on" that is, at the end of the songs they copy what they hear sung. They just lag a bit. Hearing more complex language and music develops more sophisticated language skills. Music uses many senses simultaneously, it makes mobile infants brains "light up" in many different areas. These growing neural networks become the foundation of learning in many areas such as math and language. Whether or not children participate accurately is not as relevant as if they participate actively and with purpose. Ensure that you include the music and words that reflect the culture of the children in the class.

Creative Arts: Individual or Small Group, 16 to 36 months

6-29 Painting with Water

Goals: To increase creative development; to increase sensory motor skills

Materials: 1-inch and 2-inch paintbrushes, buckets, water

Procedure: On a warm day, fill buckets with water and encourage toddlers to paint the sidewalk or building. Encourage them to draw faces or pictures and then watch as the sun makes them disappear.

Assessment: The toddler will paint with the water and brushes.

Integration: This is a clean painting activity. Toddlers are free to experiment with the water and brush.

6-30 Big Pictures

Goals: To increase creative development; to increase social awareness

Materials: Large sheet of newsprint, water-based markers, large crayons, large chalk

Procedure: Cover a table with paper; tape it down. Be sure each toddler has space to draw with markers, crayons, and chalk while encouraging him to be part of a group. Make the picture have a theme and have the toddlers' scribble something related to that theme. If toddlers desire, label the scribble and write what they say about it.

Assessment: The toddler will place a mark on the group paper.

Integration: Leave the paper out long enough so toddlers can leave and come back. Young toddlers often leave an activity and return to it later.

Summary

Infants change and grow rapidly and educators adapt the curriculum and activities to their needs. Their repertoire is small so variations on experiences predominate for young infants (birth to 9 months). Mobile infants (8 to 18 months) reach major developmental milestones. Their curriculum is driven by their interest in moving and the development of language. Toddlers (16 to 36 months) are predictably mobile and are experiencing bursts of cognitive and language growth. They are curious and want to learn about themselves and their world. Experiences and activities are designed to meet these needs.

Educational Resources

Better Baby Care Campaign, a nationwide effort to improve the quality of infant and toddler child care, provides up-to-date information on research and resources about infant and toddler care. The website also provides information on federal, state, and local policy initiatives. http://www.betterbabycare.org

Clearinghouse on Early Education and Parenting (CEEP) is part of the Early Childhood and Parenting (ECAP) Collaborative at the University of Illinois at Urbana-Champaign. CEEP provides publications and information to the worldwide early childhood and parenting communities. http://ceep.crc.uiuc.edu/index.html

Early Head Start Nation Resource Center at Zero to Three has information about Early Head Start as well as ideas for teaching young infants, mobile infants, and toddlers. Their goal is to share knowledge with infant-toddler teachers and home visitors. http://www.ehsnrc.org

Healthy Child Care America (HCCA) supported by the American Academy of Pediatrics, with the Department of Health and Human Services, the Child Care Bureau, and the Maternal and Child Health Bureau, sponsors the Healthy Child Care America Campaign that has resources for parents and early childhood educators. Launched in 1995, HCCA seeks to maximize the health, safety, well-being, and developmental potential of all children so that each child experiences quality child care within a nurturing environment and has a medical home. http://www.healthychildcare.org

ZERO TO THREE provides information on brain development, learning during everyday routines, the developmental assessment process, parenting tips, professional journal articles, policy briefs, A-Z topic listings, a search engine, and a list of Spanish materials. http://www.zerotothree.org

For additional resources, visit the book companion website for this text at www.cengage.com/education/deiner.

Children's Bibliography

The Children's Bibliography was chosen to support the topics in the text. It is not intended to be inclusive and focuses only on topics that relate directly to children with disabilities and their families.

The Children's Bibliography is arranged by topic. The first section supports the topics covered by Part I of the book. These children's books focus on different types of families, family relationships, cultural diversity, and challenges that are faced by the children you will teach. The remainder of the children's bibliography supports Part II of the book and is arranged in the same order as the chapters with books chosen to support each chapter. Like the disabilities themselves, some topics overlap so scan several areas to find potential books. The age range of each book is given in parentheses. The final section of the Children's Bibliography is the Educational Resources which will help you find good sources for additional books. There are more books annotated on the web as well as additional Educational Resources that you can access at www.cengage.com/education/deiner.

Table CB–1 identifies the categories of books and the order in which they appear to make finding them easier.

Table CB–1: Books about children with special needs and their families

BOOKS ABOUT FAMILIES AND THEIR CULTURE

    Latino Families and Children

    African American Families and Children

    Asian and Pacific Islander Families and Children

    American Indian and Native Alaskan Families and Children

    Anglo-European American Families and Children

        Jewish Families

    Interracial/Intercultural Families

    Other Families

BOOKS ABOUT DIFFERENT TYPES OF FAMILIES AND THEIR CHILDREN

    Families Who Separate and Divorce

        Families who are Separated

    Remarried Families

    Foster and Adoptive Families

    Gay and Lesbian Families

    Parents with Disabilities

    Siblings with Disabilities

    Grandparents and Relatives with Disabilities

BOOKS ABOUT FAMILIES WHO FACE CHALLENGES

    Poverty

    Disasters

Please look in several places to find books that are relevant to your teaching needs as well as on the web. More general books and books written before the early 1990s are on the web. There are some topics that have an extensive selection of children's books. Additional books for these topics are also on the web.

Books About Families and Their Culture

Kincade, S. and the Global Fund for Children (2006). *My Family*. Watertown, MA: Charlesbridge Publishing.

(3–8) A photo-essay that shows loving families across the world having fun together with only the name of the country in which they live.

Kuklin, S. (2006). *Families*. New York: Hyperion Books for Children

(4–8) 15 children tell about their families and the bonds that connect them.

Simon, N. (2003). *All families are special*. Morton Grove, IL: Albert Whitman.

(5–8) Many examples of contemporary families are represented including blended, international, extended and lesbian.

Smith, Jr., C. R. (2003). *I am America*.

(3–8) Vibrant photographs of the many faces of children in America today.

Latino Families and Children

Dominguez, K. K. (2002). *The perfect piñata /La piñata perfecta*. Morton Grove, IL: Albert Whitman.

(6–8) A bilingual book about Marisa's sixth birthday, her butterfly piñata, her unwillingness to break it on her birthday, and her mother's solution.

Garza, C. L. (2005). *Family pictures: 15th anniversary edition*. San Francisco, CA: Children's Book Press.

(4–8) A classic in the field of Latino children's literature since its original release in 1990. Day-to-day

Books help children learn about a variety of family cultures and configurations.

experiences are told through art and narrative about different aspects of traditional Mexican American culture (English/Spanish).

Helmer, D. S. (2003). *The cat who came for tacos*. Morton Grove, IL: Albert Whitman.

(6–8). When Flynn, a stray cat, is welcomed into the house Señora Rosa and Señor Tomás must explain some house rules about eating. Flynn also has ideas about how cats and people can live together.

Jimenez, F. (2000). *The Christmas gift/ El regalo de navidad*. New York: Houghton Mifflin.

(4–8) The author shares a poignant Christmas memory and shows how a child draws strength from family bonds (English/Spanish).

Levy, J. (2007). *Celebrate! It's Cinco de Mayo / ¡Celebremos! ¡Es el Cinco de Mayo!* Morton Grove, IL: Albert Whitman.

(3–8) A very simple history of the holiday is interspersed with the story of a young boy celebrating Cinco de Mayo with his family (English/Spanish).

Levy, J. (2007). *I remember abuelito / Yo recuerdo a abuelito: A day of the dead story / Un cuento del dia de los muertos*. Morton Grove, IL: Albert Whitman.

(3–8) In this bilingual book a young girl prepares to honor those who have died and she remembers her uncle and is excited for his spirit to visit (English/Spanish).

Paul, A. W. (2004). *Mañana iguana*. New York: Holiday House.

(3–8) Iguana is planning a fiesta but his friends want to come but not help. A clever update of *Little Red Hen* with a sprinkling of Spanish words.

Sacre, A. (2003). *The barking mouse*. Morton Grove, IL: Albert Whitman.

(3–8) A Cuban tale of the Ratón family going for a picnic, teasing a cat, and running back to the protection of Mama.

African American Families and Children

Nelson, K. (2005). *He's got the whole world in his hands*. New York: Dial Books for Young Readers.

(3–8) The well-known spiritual shows the interconnectedness of people, community, and nature portrayed through an African American family in its home.

Nikola-Lisa, W. (1994). *Bein' with you this way*. New York: Lee & Low.

(3–6) An African American girl gathers a diverse group of friends and they discover that their similarities are more important than their differences. They celebrate friendship and cooperation.

Riggio, A. (1997). *Secret signs: Along the Underground Railroad*. Honesdale, PA: Boyds Mills.

(3–8) An intriguing, suspenseful story about a young boy with a hearing impairment who carries a message to the next safe house when his mother is detained.

Saint James, S. (1997). *The gifts of Kwanzaa*. Morton Grove, IL: Albert Whitman.

(3–8) This simple text (with pronunciation guide) helps young children learn about the seven-day African American celebration.

Asian and Pacific Islander Families and Children

Balouch, K. (2006). *Mystery bottle*. New York: Hyperion Books for Children.

(3–8) A boys receives a package from his grandfather in Iran. The bottle is a gust of wind that takes him from Brooklyn into the arms of his grandfather and makes the Persian culture come to life.

Chang, A. (2003). *Goldfish and chrysanthemums*. New York: Lee and Low.

(3–8) Nancy's NiNi, grandmother, is sad because her childhood home is being torn down in China. She remembers the fish pond and Nancy comes up with an idea to keep her memories alive.

Choi, Y. (2006). *Behind the mask*. New York: Farrar, Straus and Giroux.

(4–8) Kimin says he will be his grandfather (a Korean mask dancer) for Halloween. He finds a link to his grandfather behind the mask.

Lee, H. V. (2000). *In the snow*. New York: Henry Holt.

(4–8) A mother and son practice writing Chinese characters in the snow. (Shows the characters for 10 simple words.)

Lee, H. V. (2005). *In the leaves*. New York: Henry Holt.

(4–8) Xiao Ming can't wait to show his friends the Chinese characters he has learned. He helps them discover one of the oldest picture languages in the world.

Lin, G. (2001). *Dim sum for everyone*. New York: Knopf.

(3–8) Shares with children the joy of eating dim sum, a tasty tradition.

Lo, G. (2005). *Mahjong all day long*. New York: Walker Books for Young Readers.

(4–8) JieJie and DiDi see their parents playing mahjong all the time as the family has fun together.

Look, L. (2001). *Henry's first moon birthday*. New York: Atheneum.

(4–8) Jenny's brother is one month old and the family is celebrating his first moon birthday.

Look, L. (2006). *Uncle Peter's amazing Chinese wedding*. New York: Atheneum.

(4–8) Jenny's favorite uncle is getting married with a traditional Chinese wedding. She is unhappy because she will not be his number one girl any more.

Noguchi, R. & Jenks, D. (2001). *Flowers from Mariko*. New York: Lee and Low.

(4–8) Mariko's family has been freed from a Japanese-American interment camp but they cannot start up their gardening business because they do not have a truck. Mariko has an idea that brings flowers and happiness back.

Park, L. S. (2005). *Bee-bim bop*! New York: Clarion Books.

(4–8) Bee-bim bop (mix-mix-rice) is a traditional Korean dish of rice topped and mixed with meat and vegetables. The story is about a hungry child helping her mother make the dish and the family eating it (recipe included).

Robles, A. R. (2003). *Lakas and the Manilatown fish*. San Francisco, AC: Children's Book Press.

(6–8) A bilingual English/Tagalog story in which an all-American boy of Filipino descent, some amusing Filipino elders, and a fish romp through Manilatown, San Francisco.

Sheth, K. (2007). *My Dadima wears a sari*. Peachtree.

(4–8) Rupa's grandmother wears a beautiful sari and shares the wonderful things that saris can do. It also provides a view of Indian culture and traditions.

Tucker, K. (2003). *The seven Chinese sisters*. Morton Grove, IL: Albert Whitman.

(3–8) Seven Chinese sisters lived together and each had a special talent. When the seventh sister is snatched by a hungry dragon, her sisters use their talents to save her.

Uegaki, C. (2003). *Suki's kimono*. Tonawanda, NY: Kids Can Press.

(6–8) Suki's favorite possession is her Japanese kimono and she decides she is going to wear it to school on the first day no matter what anyone says.

Wells, R. (2001). *Yoko's paper cranes*. New York: Hyperion Books for Children.

(3–8) Yoko learns about Japanese cranes from her Obaasan (grandmother). When she doesn't have money for a present she sends her folded paper cranes.

American Indian and Native Alaskan Families and Children

Andrews, J. (2003). *Very last first time*. Toronto, Ontario, Canada: Groundwood Books.

(6–8) This book discusses the daily routine for Inuits of Northern Canada, as told through a young girl and her mother who belong to this nation.

Bouchard, D. (2003). *The song within my heart*. Vancouver, BC: Raincoast Books.

(6–8) Sapp's paintings, which show a young First Nations boy preparing for his first powwow with the help of his Nokum (grandmother), depict life on the reservation in Saskatchewan.

Bruchac, J. (2003). *How chipmunk got his stripes*. London: Puffin.

(3–8) A Native American tale, Brown Squirrel challenges prideful Bear to keep the sun from rising. When the sun does rise, and Brown Squirrel teases Bear, Bear threatens to eat Brown Squirrel, and his claw marks transformed Brown Squirrel into a Chipmunk.

Krasilovsky, P. (2003). *Benny's flag*. Boulder, CO: Roberts Rinehart.

(3–8) Benny was an Aleut Indian boy living in Alaska before it became a state. His teacher asks everyone in his class to create a design for the flag, and Benny's design wins.

Lind, M. (2003). *The bluebonnet girl*. New York: Henry Holt.

(6–8) Lind presents a colorful retelling of the Comanche legend that explains why bluebonnets grow in Texas. When summer brings a drought, the buffalo disperse and the people grow thin. When the Spirit Talker receives a message that this happened because of greed, many people do not want to sacrifice things in their life.

Littlechild, G. (2003). *This land is my land*. Berkeley, CA: Children's Book Press.

(6–8) Taking bits of his own observations, the author writes about the history of the Plains Cree Nation, the largest nation in Canada.

McCain, B. (2001). *Grandmother's dreamcatcher*. Morton Grove, IL: Albert Whitman.

(6–8) A sensitive story about Kimmy who stays with her Chippawa grandmother and learns to make a dreamcatcher.

Williams, S. (2003). *The Cherokee*. (Native Americans). Barrington, IL: Heinemann Library.

(6–8) Giving great detail to the culture of the Cherokee Indians, this book gives young readers insight to Native American culture.

Anglo-European American Families and Children

Kane, T. (2001). *Fairy Houses*. Lee, NH: Light-Beams Publishing.

(3–8) Kristen's family spends a week on a small island off the coast of Maine. Kristen learns about nature and, of course, fairies.

McClintock, B. (2006). *Adele and Simon*. New York: Frances Foster Books; Farrar, Straus and Giroux.

(4–8) Adele picks up her brother Simon and makes him promise not to lose things as they tour 20th-century Paris.

Shelby, A. (1995). *Homeplace*. New York: Scholastic Inc.

(4–8) A multigenerational pictorial history and story about a family in the house that great- great- great- great-grandpa built.

Jewish Families

Glaser, L. (2001). *The borrowed Hanukkah latkes*. Morton Grove, IL: Albert Whitman.

(6–8) As more people call to say they are coming, Rachel's mother has to borrow ingredients from their neighbor and talks her into joining them.

Glaser, L. (2004). *Mrs. Greenberg's messy Hanukkah*. Morton Grove, IL: Albert Whitman.

(6–8) Mrs. Greenberg's tidy kitchen becomes a mess as she and Rachael make latkes. Rachael is afraid she has ruined a friendship, but Mrs. Greenberg thinks it is a wonderful mess.

Kimmelman, L. (2000). *The runaway latkes*. Morton Grove, IL: Albert Whitman.

(3–8) A Jewish version of *The gingerbread man* has latkes rolling around town to avoid being eaten.

Rosenthal, B. R. (2006). *It's not worth making a tzimmes over*. Morton Grove, IL: Albert Whitman.

(6–8) A warm celebration get an extra kick when Sara accidentally adds extra yeast to the challah and the dough grows and starts to take over the neighborhood. A Yiddish glossary is appended as well as a recipe for challah.

Interracial/Intercultural Families

Ada, A. F. (2002). *I love Saturdays y Domingos*. New York: Athenaeum.

(5–8) On Saturdays, she visits Grandma and Grandpa, who come from a European-American background, and on Sundays—los domingos—she visits Abuelito y Abuelita, who are Mexican American; all love their granddaughter.

Adoff, A. (2002). *Black is Brown is Tan*. New York: HarperCollins Children's Books.

(4–8) With a brown-skinned mama and a white-skinned daddy their two children are the beautiful colors of both.

Haugaard, K. (2006). *The day the dragon danced*. Auburn, CA: Shen's Books.

(4–8) Sugar and her Grandma go to the Chinese New Year's Day parade and her quick thinking saves the day. She watches her neighbors and even her African American daddy emerges from under the dragon.

Hall, B. E. (2004). *Henry and the Kite Dragon*. New York: Philomel/Penguin Young Readers Group.

(4–8) Henry loves to visit the kite maker in Chinatown. But when the boys from little Italy throw rocks and destroy the kites Henry and his friends decide to do something.

Michelson, R. (2006). *Across the Alley*. New York: Penguin.

(4–8) Abe and Willie live across the alley. Willie is black and Abe is Jewish. During the day they don't talk, but at night they are best friends.

Thompson, H. (2007). *The Wakame gatherers*. Auburn, CA: Shen's Books.

(4–8) Nanami has two grandmothers: Baachan, who lives with her family in Japan, and Gram, who lives in Maine. When Gram visits Japan for the first time, Baachan takes her and Nanami on a trip to the seaside to gather Wakame. Nanami translates for the grandmothers as they talk about how each uses seaweed.

Wahl, J. (2004). *Candy Shop* Watertown, MA: Charlesbridge.

(4–8) While shopping Daniel and his aunt find the Taiwanese owner of the Candy Shop in tears because someone has writen hateful words in front of the store. Daniel gets a bucket and scrubs the words away.

Wing, N. (1996). *Jalapeño bagels*. New York: Athenaeum Books for Young Readers.

(4–8) For international day Pablo wants to bring something that reflects both his Jewish and Mexican culture.

Other Cultures

Brown, T. (2006). *Salaam: A Muslim American boy's story*. New York: Henry Holt.

(4–8) Inram, a young Muslim American boy, likes to do what boys his age do. The book also provides information about the Muslim faith.

Kimmel, E. A. (1999). *The bird's gift: A Ukrainian Easter story*. New York: Holiday House.

(4–8) Villagers take a flock of golden birds to a nearly frozen pond and are rewarded with beautiful eggs the next spring.

Books About Different Types of Families and Their Children

Families Who Separate and Divorce

Adams, E. K. (2003). *On the day his daddy left*. Morton Grove, IL: Albert Whitman.

(6–8) Danny writes down a question asking if it is his fault when his parents leave. All the adults reassure him with a big "NO."

Masurel, C. (2001). *Two homes*. Cambridge, MA: Candlewick Press.

(6–8) Young Alex's parents are divorced, and he spends time with each of them. He has two rooms, two favorite chairs, two sets of friends, two of everything. He loves both of them no matter where he is, and they love him, no matter where they are.

Pickhardt, C. (1998). *The case of the scary divorce*. Washington, DC: Magination Press.

(6–8) Professor "Skye" assists a 10-year-old boy in understanding the many issues of life, including divorce.

Pristine, J. (1996). *Mom and dad break up*. St. Paul, MN: Redleaf Press.

(3–8) A boy deals with his feelings and the reality of his parents' separation.

Ransom, J. (2000). *I don't want to talk about it*. Washington, DC: Magination Press.

(3–8) When a child's parents announce that they want to divorce, she wants to scream and shout, but with the help of her parents, she realizes that their love for her will remain the same.

Rogers, F. (1996). *Let's talk about it: Divorce*. New York: G. P. Putnam.

(3–6) Through pictures and easy reading, Mr. Rogers talks about divorce and the concerns of children. This book can provide the impetus for helpful talk and careful listening.

Schindel, J. (1995). *Dear daddy*. Morton Grove, IL: Albert Whitman.

(6–8) Jesse's father lives across the country from him, but his letters bring them closer.

Spelman, C. (1998). *Mama and daddy bear's divorce*. Morton Grove, IL: Albert Whitman.

(3–6) Dinah Bear feels sad and scared when her parents say they are getting divorced.

Van Leeuwen, J. (1996). *Blue sky, butterfly*. New York: Dial.

(6–8) After the separation, Twig's mother sits and does nothing. Twig, an 11-year-old, assumes responsibility for the family. Her grandmother arrives and gradually the family begins to rebuild.

Families who are Separated

Lindsay, J. W. (1991). *Do I have a daddy? A story about a single-parent child*. Buena Park, CA: Morning Glory Press.

(4–8) Erik's friends ask him where his father is. His mother explains that he was not ready to get married.

McElory, L. T. (2005). *Love, Lizzie: Letters to a military mom*. Morton Grove, IL: Albert Whitman.

(6–8). Lizzie's mom is in the military overseas and she misses her. She doesn't know exactly where her mom is but they wish on the same star.

Pelton, M. (2004). *When dad's at sea*. Morton Grove, IL: Albert Whitman.

(6–8) Emily's dad is in the military and he is gone for months at a time. She makes a paper chain to count down the days of his trip.

Remarried Families

Best, C., & Palmisciano, D. (1996). *Getting used to Harry*. New York: Orchard Books.

(6–8) Cynthia is left home when her mother and stepfather Harry go on their honeymoon. When they return, Harry is home all the time. Cynthia wants Harry to go home, but remembers—he is home.

Casley, J. (1995). *Priscilla twice*. New York: Greenwillow Books.

(6–8) Priscilla has two of everything, but what she really wants is a family. This is a heartwarming and funny story of Priscilla as she realizes there's more than one kind of family and what makes a family is love.

Cook, J. T. (1995). *Room for stepdaddy*. Morton Grove, IL: Albert Whitman.

(6–8) The more Joey's stepfather tries to connect with him, the more he misses his dad. After seeing the positive relationship between his mom, dad, and stepfather, Joey realizes that there's room for them all.

Sherman, C. (1996). *Eli and the swampman*. New York: HarperCollins.

(6–8) Eli leaves the home of his mother and stepfather to visit his father in Alaska. As he travels through an old swamp, he develops a brief relationship with the swampman who helps him understand that two fathers are better than none.

Foster and Adoptive Families

Coste, M. (2006). *Finding Joy*. Honesdale, PA: Boyds Mill Press.

(3–8) An upbeat but realistic international adopting story showing the heartbreak of those giving up a child in China and the joy of those receiving her.

Lears, L. (2005). *Megan's birthday tree*. Morton Grove, IL: Albert Whitman.

(3–8) Megan is adopted but she keeps in touch with her birth mother who decorates a tree on her birthday and sends her a picture. Her mother writes that she is getting married and moving and Megan worries that she will forget her without the tree.

Lin, G. (2007). *The red thread: An adoption fairy tale*. Morton Grove, IL: Albert Whitman.

(3–8) A king and queen who should be full of joy feel a strange pain that worsens each day. A peddler reveals a red thread pulling at their hearts that they must follow.

Peacock, C. A. (2000). *Mommy far, mommy near*. Morton Grove, IL: Albert Whitman.

(3–8) Elizabeth feels a range of emotions when she learns that she has one mommy in China and one in America. They make up the "Adopt-me" game.

Thomas, P. (2003). *My New Family: A first look at adoption*. Hauppauge, NY: Barrons Educational Series, Inc.

(3–8) Children are sometimes upset by discovering that they have been adopted. This book helps them understand more about adoptive parents—and how lucky their parents are to have them.

Young, E. (2006). *My Mei Mei*. New York: New York: Philomel.

(4–8) Antonia wanted a little sister, Mei Mei, to call her own. When they fly to China to get her, she is not all like Antonia imagined her.

Gay and Lesbian Families

Elwin, R., & Paulse, M. (1990). *Asha's mums*. Toronto: Women's Press.

(3–8) When Asha brings a form signed by two mothers, the teacher is confused until Asha and her mothers explain.

Heron, H., & Maran, M. (1991). *How would you feel if your dad was gay?* New York: Alyson.

(6–8) Jasmine faces problems with her classmates because she has three dads: her stepfather, her natural father, and his lover.

Newman, L. (1991). *Heather has two mommies*. Los Angeles: Alyson Publications.

(3–6) Three-year-old Heather sees nothing unusual about having two mommies. When she joins a playgroup and discovers "daddies," her confusion is dispelled by a caring adult and other children who describe their families.

Parents with Disabilities

Andrews, B. (2002). *Why are you so sad?* Washington, DC: Magination Press.

(3–8) A child's book about parental depression. This book defines depression and explains to the child how the parent feels, as well as exploring how the child feels about her parent's depression.

Maciachian, P. (1992). *Mama one, mama two*. New York: Trumpet.

(6–8) When mama one becomes severely depressed, Maudie goes to a foster parent until her mother gets well.

Sherkin-Langer, D. S. (1995). *When mommy is sick*. Morton Grove, IL: Albert Whitman.

(6–8) A girl shares her feelings and fears about her mother's frequent hospitalizations.

Siblings with Disabilities

Dwight, L. (2005). *Brothers and sisters*. New York: Bright Star Books

(3–8) A diverse set of families with one child in each who has a disability. The stories are told by their siblings. A bit stiff but all want to laugh, play, and be loved.

Gifaldi, D. (2001). *Ben, king of the river*. Morton Grove, IL: Albert Whitman.

(6–8) Ben was born with a developmental disability. Chad hopes he won't ruin the camping trip because Ben does not like new things. He loves the water and is surprised when he introduces Ben to others.

Stuve-Bodeen, S. (1998). *We'll paint the octopus red*. Bethesda, MD: Woodbine House.

(3–8) Emma anxiously awaits the birth of her new brother. When the baby is born with Down syndrome, Emma is disappointed and worried. With her dad's help, Emma realizes that she and her brother will be able to share their experiences.

Grandparents and Relatives with Disabilities

Bunting, E. (1994). *Sunshine home*. New York: Clarion.

(6–8) Timmie's grandmother is in a nursing home recovering from a broken hip. At first everyone in the family seems happy, then Timmie helps them express their feelings of sadness.

Cruise, R. (2006). *Little mama forgets*. New York: Farrar, Straus and Giroux.

(4–8) Lucy's grandmother is losing her memory but she still remembers stories from Mexico and how to give hugs and kisses.

Books About Families Who Face Challenges

Poverty

Borton, L. (1997). *Junk pile*. New York: Philomel Books.

(3–6) Jamie, an Appalachian child, doesn't notice her poverty. Others notice but accept her because of her ingenuity and imagination.

McCully, E. A. (2001). *Four hungry kittens*. New York: Dial Books for Young Readers.

(3–6) A wordless picture book where children can help problem solve a dilemma faced by some hungry little kittens.

Butterworth, O. (1993). *A visit to the big house*. Boston: Houghton Mifflin.

(3–8) Along with her mother and younger brother, Rose visits her dad in prison.

Guthrie, D., & Hockerman, D. (1997). *A rose for Abby*. Nashville, TN: Abingdon Press.

(6–8) A great story about a young girl who is tired of seeing homeless people and starts a soup kitchen.

Disasters

Bunting, E. (1995). *Smoky night*. Cedar Falls, L.A: Perfection Learning.

(4–8) This is a story about cats and people who couldn't get along until the smoky and fearful night of the Los Angeles riots brings them together.

Calhoun, M. (1997). *Flood*. New York: Morrow.

(3–8) A picture book that describes a young girl's experiences preparing for and dealing with a flood. The book is based on a 1993 flood in the Midwest.

Abuse and Neglect

Girard, L. (1995). *My body is private*. Seattle, WA: Bay Press.

(6–8) The book discusses what is appropriate and inappropriate touching between adults and children using simple language. It also gives suggestions about what a child can do if he or she has been inappropriately touched.

Riggs, S. (2007). *Not in room 204*. Morton Grove, IL: Albert Whitman.

(6–8) Regina is doing well but is very quiet in school and at home. As her teacher reads about inappropriate touching Regina wonders if she should tell.

Drugs and Alcohol

Vigna, J. (1990). *I wish daddy didn't drink so much*. Morton Grove, IL: Albert Whitman.

(3–8) A story about a father's alcoholism.

Vigna, J. (1990). *My big sister takes drugs*. New York: Albert Whitman.

(3–8) A story about an older sibling's involvement with drugs and alcohol.

Books About Infants and Toddlers At-Risk

Global Fund for Children (2008). *Global babies*. Watertown, MA: Charlesbridge Publishing.

(birth to 3) Great photos of babies from 17 cultures around the globe depicting differences in clothing, daily life, and traditions and similarities in the joy of love, caring, and nurturing.

Hathon, E. (1994). *Let's go to the doctor*. New York: Grosset & Dunlap.

(birth–3) A small board book about a toddler going to the doctor to get an inoculation.

Pitzer, M. W. (2004). *I can, can you?* Bethesda, MD: Woodbine House.

    (birth–3) A delightful board book full of babies and toddlers with Down syndrome having fun.

Williams, V. B. (1990). *"More, more, more," said the baby*. New York: Greenwillow Books.

    (birth–6) This book contains short stories about three multiethnic babies who want attention. A mother, father, and grandmother lovingly respond.

Gentieu, P. (2000). *Baby! Talk!* Crown Books for Young Readers.

    (birth–3) Multicultural babies, clad only in colorful diapers, are doing what babies love to do.

Books About Children With Specific Learning Disabilities

Robb, D. B. (2004). *The alphabet war*. Morton Grove, IL: Albert Whitman.

    (6–8) Adam started kindergarten and confused letters with tails. Other children were learning to read but Adam wasn't. By second grade he was so frustrated he got into trouble. At last he got help and actually found himself reading a book.

Books About Children With Social, Emotional, and Behavioral Disorders

Making Friends

Hahn, M. (1996). *Following my own footsteps*. New York: Clarion.

    (6–8) Gordy, a troublemaker, and his family move in with his grandparents after his abusive father is arrested. An inspiring story of a grandmother's love.

Hess, D. (1994). *Wilson sat alone*. New York: Simon & Schuster.

    (3–8) Wilson is shy and lonely until a new girl comes to school. She pretends to be a monster and roars. Wilson roars back and becomes accepted into a new group.

Fears and Anxiety

Brown, M. (1994). *Arthur's first sleepover*. Boston: Little, Brown & Company.

    (3–8) This is a good book for children who may be preparing for their first overnight stay.

Henkes, K. (1996). *Sheila Rae, the brave*. New York: Greenwillow Books.

    (3–8) Sheila Rae is not afraid of anything. Her little sister on the other hand is not quite so brave. One day when caught in a bind, her little sister helps her out and proves that she is not a "scaredy cat" after all.

Hamm, D. J. (1991). *Laney's Lost Momma*. Morton Grove, IL: Albert Whitman.

    (3–6) Laney loses herself in a store and when her mother finds her she sweeps her up and holds her close.

Slate, J. (2001). *Miss Bindergarten gets ready for kindergarten*. New York: Puffin Books.

    (3–6) The book shows 26 animals (one for each letter of the alphabet) getting ready for kindergarten. The book talks about their fears and expectations for the first day of school.

Wells, R. (1995). *Edward unready for school*. New York: Dial Books for Young Readers.

    (3–6) Edward, a timid bear, resists going to nursery school. He has problems separating and is unhappy, vulnerable, and fearful. This book allows children to identify with emotions and parents and educators to acknowledge that some children are not ready for particular experiences.

Wells, R. (1996). *Edward's overwhelming overnight*. New York: Dial Books.

    (3–6) Describes a new experience for young children—sleeping over at a friend's house.

Wing, N. (2001). *The night before kindergarten*. New York: Grosset & Dunlap.

    (3–6) As kindergarten begins, children address their fears and excitement.

Anger

Agassi, M. (2000) *Hands are not for hitting*. Minneapolis, MN: Free Spirit Publishing.

    (3–8) The refrain that "hands are not for hitting" is accompanied by numerous better uses for them, such as waving, helping, drawing, and making music.

Bang, M. (1999). *When Sophie gets angry—really, really, angry*. New York: Scholastic Trade.

    (3–8) A book about sharing and dealing with strong emotions.

Books About Children With Attention-Deficit/Hyperactivity Disorder

Carpenter, P., & Ford, M. (2000). *Sparky's excellent misadventures. My ADD journal, by me (Sparky)*. Washington, DC: Magination Press.

    (3–8) A lovable and funny boy keeps track of his days with ADD and how he manages all of his "wiggles" and "giggles."

Galvin, M. (2001). *Otto learns about his medicine: A story about medicine for children with ADHD*. Washington, DC: Magination Press.

    (3–8) Otto, a young car, visits a special engine mechanic and receives an engine treatment to help him run at the right speed. Otto's experience reflects a multiple treatment approach to ADHD.

Janover, C. (1997). *Zipper, the kid with ADHD*. Bethesda, MD: Woodbine House.

    (6–8) Zipper is bright, but his impulsive behavior gets him into trouble at school and at home. He earns a drum set by becoming more organized and learning to control his actions.

Moss, D. (2006). *Shelly the hyperactive turtle.* (2nd ed.) Bethesda, MD: Woodbine House.

(3–8) Shelly has been updated to reflect more current practices. The story follows Shelly through some bumpy times at school, on the bus and with other kids.

Offill, J., & Carpenter, N. (2007). *17 things I'm not allowed to do any more.* New York: Schwartz and Wade Books.

(6–8) A young girl lists 17 things she cannot do anymore such as walking home from school backward or setting Joey Whipple on fire.

Books About Children With Communication Disorders

Lears, L. (2000). *Ben has something to say: A story about stuttering.* Morton Grove, IL: Albert Whitman.

(3–8) To help a neglected dog he meets in a junkyard Ben, who stutters, confronts his fears. Additional information about stuttering is included.

Lester, H. (1999). *Hooway for Wodney Wat.* Houghton Mifflin/Walter Lorraine Books.

(3–8). His classmates tease Rodney because he can't say his name but he drives away the class bully.

Lester, H. (1997). *Listen Buddy.* Houghton Mifflin/Walter Lorraine Books.

(3–8) A silly tale about a bunny who just can't seem to listen—until he takes the wrong turn, and meets up with the "Scruffy Varmint".

Rahaman, V. (1997). *Read for me, Mama.* Honesdale, PA: Boyds Mills.

(3–8) A young boy is unhappy because his mother never has time to read to him. She is distressed because she is illiterate.

Books About Children Who Are English Language Learners

Arguenta, J. (2001). *A movie in my pillow/Una pelicula en mi almohada.* San Francisco, CA: Children's Book Press.

(6–8) Jorgito has come to live in San Francisco, but he remembers El Salvador and his confusion and delight in his new urban home through his inner world and dreams—the movie in his pillow.

Arguenta, J. (2003). *Xochitl and the flowers/ Xochitl, la nana de las flores.* San Francisco, CA: Children's Book Press.

(6–8) Xochitl and her family, arriving in San Francisco from El Salvador, create a beautiful plant nursery in place of the garbage heap behind their apartment, and celebrate with their friends and neighbors.

Bunting, E. (1999). *A picnic in October.* New York: Voyager Books: an imprint of Harcourt Children's Books.

(4–8) Tony thinks it's dumb to go all the way to Liberty Island for a birthday picnic. But that's before he understands what the Statue of Liberty means to Grandma.

Choi, Y. (2001). *The name jar.* New York: Alfred A. Knopf.

(6–8) Having just moved from Korea Unhei hopes the children will like her. She tells the class she will choose a name by the following week.

Cohn, D. (2002). *Si Se Puede! Yes we can!: Janitor strike in L.A.* El Paso, TX: Cinco Puntos Press.

(4–8) Carlitos, a Mexican immigrant child, whose widowed mother cleans offices tells Carlitos she is helping to organize a janitors' strike. Carlitos gets support at school and he joins the march with a sign "I love my Mama. She is a janitor!" (English/Spanish)

Cumpiano, I. (2005). *Quinito's neighborhood/El vecindario de Quinto.* San Francisco, CA: Children's Book Press.

(3–6) Quinito goes on a neighborhood journey and introduces various jobs as well as friends and family members who hold them.

English, K. (2000). *Speak English for Us, Marisol!* Morton Grove, IL: Albert Whitman.

(6–8) Marisol speaks for all of her family who cannot speak English.

Iyengar, M. (2007). *Romina's Rangoli.* Auburn, CA: Shen's Books

(4–8) Romina's class is learning about immigration and she must come up with a project that represents her culture: Her father is from India and her mother is from Mexico. She blends art forms that are just like her.

Jimenez, F (1998). *La Mariposa. (The butterfly).* New York: Houghton Mifflin.

(6–8) Because he only speaks Spanish, Francisco has trouble when he begins first grade but his fascination with the caterpillar helps him begin to fit in (English/Spanish).

Leventhal, D. (1998). *What is your language?* New York: Puffin Books.

(3–6) A boy travels the world asking each person he encounters, "What is your language?" Many languages are represented including Spanish, German, and Arabic.

McCunn, R, L. (1998). *Pie-biter.* Auburn, CA: Shen's Books.

(6–8). A young Chinese immigrant, after working on the Continental Railroad, turned his hand to making pies. It is in a trilingual format: English/Spanish/Chinese.

Miller, E. I. (2003). *Just like home/Como en mi tierra.* Morton Grove, IL: Albert Whitman.

(6–8) In English and Spanish a young girl shares the story of arriving in the United States and how her experiences are just like home or not like home until she feel at home.

Pak, S. (2002). *A place to grow.* New York: Arthur A. Levine Books.

(4–8) A South Korean father explains to his daughter that families are like seeds and need a place to grow and flourish.

Park, F., & Park, G. (2005). *The have a good day café.* New York: Lee & Low.

(4–8) Having arrived recently from Korea, Mike's family sets up a food cart. When competition arrives Mike decides they should serve Korean food at the Have A Good Day Café cart.

Perez, A. I. (2002). *My diary for here to there. Mi diario de aqui hasta alla.* San Francisco, CA: Children's Book Press.

(6–8) Amada tell the story of her family's move from Mexico to Los Angeles. She confides her hopes and dreams in her diary. (Includes a teacher's guide)

Recorvits, H. (2003). *My name is Yoon*. New York: Frances Foster Books.

(4–8) Yoon's name means Shining Wisdom and looks happy in Korean but in English it looks like lines and circles which stand alone, which is how she feels. At her new school she tries out different names.

Williams. L. E. (2006). *The best winds*. Honesdale, PA: Boyds Mill Press.

(6–8) Jinho gets involved in kite making to please his Korean grandfather who still follows the old ways. He gets caught up in the excitement of the craft when the best winds approach.

Wong, J. S. (2000). *The trip back home*. New York: Harcourt.

(4–8) A young girl and her mother visit extended family in Korea and discover that even when family members speak different languages there is much to share.

Yang, B. (2004). *Hannah is my name*. Somerville, MA: Candlewick Press.

(6–8) Hannah's family has emigrated from Taiwan to San Francisco to make America their home. The book talks about the very real struggle with documentation as they wait and hope for the arrival of their green card.

Books About Children with Autism Spectrum Disorders

Aitman, A. J. (2008). *Waiting for Benjamin: A story about autism*. Morton Grove, IL: Albert Whitman.

(3–8) Benjamin doesn't do things the way his brother Alexander thinks he should. He stares at the wall and does not want to play. His friends think he is "wacko." He is diagnosed with autism and Alexander works though his feelings.

Ellis, M. (2005). Keisha's Doors/Las Puertas de Keisha, An autism story, Book 1. Austin, TX: Speech Kids Texas Press.

(3–8) Keisha's older sister can't understand why she will not play with her. She is diagnosed with autism and a therapist helps them understand what autism means.

Ellis, M. (2005).¿*Tacos anyone?/ Alguien quire tacos? An autism story, Book 2*. Austin, TX: Speech Kids Texas Press.

(3–8) This is a very simple to read, yet factually accurate, story of Michael, a four year old boy with autism, and his older brother. English and Spanish.

Lears, L. (2003). *Ian's Walk: A Story About Autism*. Morton Grove, IL: Albert Whitman & Company.

(6–8) Three children walk, tie a shoe, or feed the ducks. As Tara and Julie take Ian on a walk to the park, Julie describes how Ian acts differently from most people.

Luchsinger, D. F. (2007). *Playing by the rules*. Bethesda, MD: Woodbine House.

(3–8) When her Aunt Tilda come to take care of them she unknowingly breaks some of Josh's rules. Jody, his big sister, helps her understand more about autism.

Peralta, S. (2002). *All about my brother*. Autism Asperger Publishing Co.

(3–8) Sarah, the young author of this book draws a portrait of her day-to-day life with her brother, Evan, who has autism, and her family's love and acceptance of him.

Shally, C. (2007). *Since we're friends: An autism picture book*. Centerton, AR: Awaken Specialty Press.

(3–8) This book is about two boys: one has autism, the other does not. The story of their relationship provides examples of how to make such a friendship work.

Children with Intellectual Disabilities and Developmental Delays

Bunnett, R. (2006). *Friends at school*. Long Island, NY: Star Bright Books.

(3–6) A light, informal book featuring children of different abilities working and playing at an inclusive school setting.

Byrd. L. M. (2003). *The treasure on gold street/ El Tesoro en la calle oro: A neighborhood story in Spanish and English*. El Paso, TX: Cinco Puntos Press.

(4–8) One of Hannah's best friends, Isabel, is an adult with an intellectual disability. Hannah doesn't know or mind because she is a wonderful playmate.

Dwight, L. (2005). *We can do it*. Star Bright Books.

(3–8) A lively book of photographs about children with Down syndrome, spina bifida, visual impairments, and cerebral palsy having fun.

Girnis, M. (2000). *ABC for you and me*. Morton Grove, IL: Albert Whitman.

(3–8) Full-color photographs of multicultural children, most with Down syndrome, to illustrate the ABCs.

Shriver, Maria. (2001). *What's wrong with Timmy?* Boston: Little Brown Children's Books.

(6–8) A young girl named Kate sees Timmy on the playground. Timmy has an intellectual disability and Kate wonders a lot about him. Eventually the two children become friends.

Stuve-Bodeen, S. (2005). *The best worst brother*. Bethesda, MD: Woodbine House.

(4–8) Emma's almost 3-year-old bother Isaac spits out food and knocks down blocks. His low pace is maddening but he is learning to sign. Isaac has Down syndrome.

Wojahn, R. H. (2006). *Evan Early*. Bethesda, MD: Woodbine House.

(4–8) Natalie is eager for her new brother but Evan was born too early and his first home is in the hospital NICU. It is a scary place to visit. Natalie is hurt and angry over the way her parents are preoccupied with Evan but agrees that big sisters can help a lot.

Woloson, E. (2003). *My friend Isabelle*. Bethesda, MD: Woodbine House.

(2–6) Isabelle and Charlie both like to draw, dance, read and play at the park. Like friends they are also different. Isabelle has Down syndrome, Charlie doesn't.

Books About Children who are Gifted and Talented

Fern, E. (1991). *Pepito's story*. New York: Yarrow Press.

(3–8) A young boy, who likes to dance, overcomes his friends' teasing.

Gauch, P. (1992). *Bravo, Tanya*. New York: Putnam.

(3–8) Young Tanya encounters difficulties when she begins taking ballet lessons.

Hoff, S. (1994). *Duncan the dancing duck*. New York: Clarion Books.

(3–6) Duncan dances his way to celebrity status but eventually misses home and goes back to his pond.

Hru, D. (1993). *Joshua's Masai mask*. New York: Lee & Low.

(3–8) Joshua gains self-esteem playing the kalimba, an African musical instrument, in his school's talent show.

Johnson, A. (1993). *The girl who wore snakes*. New York: Orchard Books.

(6–8) An African American girl loves snakes and wears them wherever she goes. She defends her rights and finds an aunt who shares her passion.

Lester, H. (1996). *Three cheers for Tacky*. Boston: Houghton Mifflin.

(3–8) Tacky, a penguin, is different but ends up stealing the show because of his special abilities.

Rand, G. (2002). *Little Flower*. New York: Henry Holt.

(4–8) Little Flower is a very smart pig. She has learned lots of tricks, but one of them is really special: she can play dead! When Miss Pearl falls and hurts herself nobody hears her calls for help. Little Flower uses her trick to get help for Miss Pearl and becomes a hero.

Rockwell, N. (1994). *Willie was different*. Stockbridge, MA: Berkshire House Publishers.

(4–8) Willie, a wood thrush, discovers his genius at composing beautiful variations of his native song.

Shannon, M. (1993). *Elvira*. New York: Ticknor & Fields.

(3–8) Elvira, a dragon, is different and doesn't want to do dragon-like things. She would rather make daisy chains. She eventually discovers she can be accepted for being herself.

Spinelli, E. (1993). *Boy, can he dance*! New York: Macmillan.

(6–8) Tony's father wants him to become a chef, but for Tony dancing is his world.

Books About Children with Special Health Care Needs

Allergies and Asthma

Carter, A. S. (1996). *I'm tougher than asthma*! Morton Grove, IL: Albert Whitman.

(5–8) Siri leads an active life that is sometimes interrupted by her asthma. She explains to readers about her first attack, and what she does to treat attacks when they occur.

Ellis, M., & Loehr, J. (2008). *Busy bees: A sensory defensiveness story*. Austin, TX: Speech Kids Texas Press.

(3–8) A young girl talks about how input from her senses can make her upset and how by working with an occupational therapist, she is overcoming her sensory dysfunction (hypersensitive to food textures).

Harrison, T. (1998). *Aaron's awful allergies*. Buffalo, NY: Kids Can Press.

(3–6) Aaron loves animals but is allergic to them. He is unhappy until his mother gives him a surprise.

Kroll, V. (2005). *Brianna breathes easy: A story about asthma*. Morton Grove, IL: Albert Whitman.

(6–8) Brianna, an African American girl, gets the lead in the school play. She has a cough, which is ultimately diagnosed as asthma. She learns about the disease, how to manage it, and her triggers.

London, J. (1997). *The lion who has asthma*. Morton Grove, IL: Albert Whitman.

(3–8) In his imagination, asthmatic Sean becomes a variety of animals to suit different situations. When using a nebulizer, Sean imagines he is a jet pilot.

Smith, N. S. (1999). *Allie the allergic elephant: A children's story of peanut allergies*. Colorado Springs, CO: Jungle Communication Incorporated.

(3–8) Allie helps children learn about peanut allergies, and how important it is not to share food with your friends, just in case they are allergic.

AIDS

Forbes, A. (2003). *Heroes against AIDS*. (The AIDS Awareness Library). New York: Powerkids Press.

(3–8) Providing information on AIDS in a developmentally appropriate way, the author includes words from such people as Magic Johnson, who speaks about the strength needed in dealing with AIDS.

Forbes, A. (2003). *Kids with AIDS*. (The AIDS Awareness Library). New York: Powerkids Press.

(3–8) The author gears this book toward educating young children that AIDS cannot be transmitted just by touching someone, and discusses how people live with this virus in everyday situations.

Forbes, A. (2003). *Where did AIDS come from*? (The AIDS Awareness Library). New York: Powerkids Press.

(3–8) Discussing the seriousness of AIDS, the author makes the point of letting young readers know that people with AIDS have feelings and need love and support like everyone else.

Cancer

Chamberlain, S. (1990). *My ABC book of cancer*. New York: Synergistic Press.

(3–8) An A-B-C description of cancer.

Krisher, T. (1992). *Kathy's hats: A story of hope*. New York: Westcott.

(3–8) When Kathy undergoes chemotherapy for cancer, she finds a new reason to wear her hats.

When books are also recorded they can be used to individualize instruction to allow children to pursue some topics in greater depth.

Chronic Illness

Kruszka, B. J. (2004). Eating gluten-free with Emily. Bethesda, MD: Woodbine House.

(3–6) Emily has celiac disease and she talks about what food she can and cannot eat and how she copes with restaurants and birthday parties.

Mills, J. (1993). *Gentle willow*. Washington, DC: Magination Press.

(3–6) Little Tree and her friend Amanda the squirrel help address feelings of disbelief, anger, and sadness, along with love, as they discuss issues geared toward children who may not survive their illness, or for children who know friends like these.

Diabetes

Pirner, C. (1994). *Even little kids get diabetes*. Morton Grove, IL: Albert Whitman.

(3–6) A young patient relates her hospital stay, and explains how she must have injections every day (and will eventually give them to herself), and states her frustration at never being able to eat sweets, even at a birthday party.

Overweight and Obesity

Durant, A. (2006). *Burger boy*. New York: Houghton Mifflin

(3–8) Benny only eats Bigga Burgers and balloons into a burger. Being a burger has some downfalls as hungry people want to eat him. A funny story in which Benny eats a variety of fruits and vegetables to recover his shape.

Death and Dying/Grief

Bohlmeijer, A. (1996). *Something very sorry*. Boston: Houghton Mifflin.

(6–8) A tragic car accident kills Rosemyn's mother and leaves other family members with serious injuries. Rosemyn's inner turmoil and emotions are shared.

Johnston, T. (2002). *That summer*. San Diego, CA: Harcourt.

(6–9) Two brothers begin a summer like any other they had before, until Joey becomes terminally ill, and both boys discover that he is dying. This book is particularly geared toward children dealing with loss in their life.

Old, W. (1995). *Stacy had a little sister*. Morton Grove, IL: Albert Whitman.

(6–8) When Stacy's baby sister dies of SIDS she has many fears and questions. Her parents, although sad, are reassuring and loving.

Spelman, C. (1996). *After Charlotte's mom died*. Morton Grove: IL: Albert Whitman.

(6–8) This concept book features a 6-year-old dealing with the recent death of her mother. Charlotte feels angry with Mom, estranged from her grieving and preoccupied dad, and afraid that she, or her father, may also die. Dad arranges for her to talk with a therapist, who helps her to acknowledge these feelings and develop a more positive outlook toward the future.

Willner-Pardo, G. (1996). *Hunting grandma's treasures*. New York: Clarion.

(6–8) Seven grandchildren try to enjoy a family vacation, but it is not the same since their grandmother died. They discover that she has left one last treasure.

Books About Children with Orthopedic and Neurologic Impairments

Orthopedic Impairments

Ellis, M., & Loehr, J. (2008). *Sitting on letters: A story about low muscle tone*. Austin, TX: Speech Kids Texas Press.

(3–8) A young girl with low muscle tone learns from her uncle, an occupational therapist, how sitting positions affect how she works and plays. The positions remind her of letters of the alphabet.

Meyers, C. (1999). *Rolling along with Goldilocks and the three bears*. Bethesda, MD: Woodbine House.

(3–8) The beginning starts with the traditional story of the three bears but in this story baby bear uses a wheelchair, goes to physical therapy and makes friends with Goldilocks.

Senisi, E. (2002). *All kinds of friends, even green*. Bethesda, MD: Woodbine House.

(6–8) Moses' teacher asks the class to write a story about a special friend. Moses, who uses a wheelchair, writes about Zaki, his baby-sitter's toeless iguana. Moses realizes that even though people are different they are still special.

Shirley, D. (2008). *Best friend on wheels*. Morton Grove, IL: Albert Whitman.

(6–8) A teacher asks a student to show a new girl around the school. She is surprised she is in a wheelchair but discovers they both collect rocks.

Thomas, P. (2002). *Don't call me special: A first look at disability*. Hauppauge, NY: Barrons Educational Series, Inc.

(3–8) This picture book explores questions and concerns about physical disabilities in a simple and reassuring way. Children find out about individual disabilities and special equipment.

Willis, J. (2001) *Susan Laughs*. London, UK: Red Fox Picture Books.

(3–8) Susan laughs, she sings, she rides, she swings. She gets angry, she gets sad, she is good, she is bad. In fact, Susan is no different from any other child. It is not until the last page that the reader realizes that Susan is in a wheelchair.

Cerebral Palsy

Debear, K. (2001). *Be quiet Marina*. Long Island, NY: Star Bright Books.

(3–6) This photographic book is about Marina and Moira, both 3 years old, but Marina screams and is very noisy. Moira likes quiet, and Marina's noise scares her away. One has cerebral palsy the other Down syndrome. They learn to play together and become friends.

Heelan, J. R. (2000). *Rolling along: The story of Taylor and his wheelchair*. Atlanta, GA: Peachtree Publishers.

(6–8) This book proves glimpses into the life of a boy with cerebral palsy. Taylor describes his cerebral palsy what he does at home, at school, in physical therapy, and his desire for independence. He likes his wheelchair as it enables him to go faster and not tire as quickly.

Lears, L. (2005). *Nathan's wish: A story about cerebral palsy*. Morton Grove, IL: Albert Whitman.

(6–8) Nathan struggles with cerebral palsy. As he helps an owl named Firefly, he helps himself as well.

Epilepsy

Lears, L. (2002). *Becky the brave. A story about epilepsy*. Morton Grove, IL: Albert Whitman.

(6–8) While Becky's family and teacher know about her condition with epilepsy, she is afraid to tell her classmates out of fear that they will laugh at her and tease her.

Physical Differences

Mitchel, R. (1993). *Hue boy*. New York: Dial Books for Young Readers.

(6–8) Hue boy is so slow in growing that he worries he will be small forever.

Books About Children with Hearing Impairments

Fain, K. (1993). *Handsigns*. San Francisco, CA: Chronicle Books.

(birth–6) A classic ABC book that contains no words, but the alphabet letter, a clear sign, and an illustrated picture of an animal that begins with that letter of the alphabet.

Lakin, P. (1994). *Dad and me in the morning*. Morton Grove, IL: Albert Whitman.

(6–8). A young boy wakes to a special alarm clock, puts in his hearing aids, dresses, and wakes his dad to see the sunrise.

Millman, I. (1998). *Moses sees a play*. New York: Farrar, Straus & Giroux.

(3–8) Moses's class of hearing impaired children is joined by a group of hearing children from another school and see *Cinderella* by the Little Theatre of the Deaf. Moses meets Manuel, a new immigrant who does not yet speak English. The two boys develop a rapport, and they communicate through gestures.

Okimoto, J. (1995). *A place for Grace*. Seattle, WA: Sasquatch Books.

(3–8) Grace is disappointed that her size keeps her from becoming a Seeing Eye dog, but through hard work and persistence, she finds that she has strengths that allow her to help those with hearing impairments.

Books About Children with Visual Impairments

Hoban, T. (1996). *Just look*. New York: Greenwillow Books.

(3–8) This picture book provides a visual mystery as children attempt to identify a photograph through a small hole in each page.

Faustino, L. R. (2001). *The hickory chair*. Arthur A. Levine Books.

(3–8) Louis loves his grandmother and even though he can't see her because he has been blind since birth, he feels her. When she is gone, his love for her helps him through.

Kostechi-Shaw, J. S. (2008). *Traveling eye*. New York: Henry Holt, and Co.

(3–8) Jenny Sue's eyes are not the same as other people's eyes. Her right eye looks in one direction, while her left eye sometimes wanders. Jenny Sue has a lazy eye. Although it makes her different, it also helps her see the world in a special way.

Moon, N. (1994). *Lucy's picture*. New York: Dial Books.

(3–6) Lucy makes a collage that her grandfather, who is blind, enjoys through touch.

Turk, R. (1998). *The doll on the top shelf*. Los Altos, CA: Owl's House Press. (Book is presented in text and Braille.)

(3–8) An enchanting story of a girl with a visual impairment's favorite Christmas and a lesson on giving.

Educational Resources

Albert Whitman and Company specializes in timely books for children about topics such as divorce, disability, and cultural diversity. http://www.awhitmanco.com

Barahona Center for the Study of Books in Spanish for Children and Adolescents at California State University-San Marcos has a very searchable data base of over 10,000 books in Spanish or in English about Hispanic topics. New books are updated weekly. http://www.csusm.edu/csb/intro_eng.html

International Children's Digital Library wants all children to have books available to them and to members of the global community. The books are from many different countries and in many different languages. Book pages are displayed on the computer. Books are available on line at no charge. http://www.childrenslibrary.org/

Parent's Choice reviews children's books, TV shows, web sites, videos, and more. Their Doing & Learning section provides ideas for activities and explorations. http://www.parents-choice.org/default.cfm

Woodbine House has a special needs collection of over 50 books on specific disabilities and related topics. http://www.woodbinehouse.com

Glossary

A

Abduction is motion away from the midline.

Acceleration is the process of moving through an educational program at a faster rate than usual (skipping grades) or at a younger age (starting school early).

Acculturation supports the adoption of the host country's values without relinquishing all ethnic/culture and values.

Achievement tests measure the extent that a child has mastered a certain body of knowledge.

Achromatopsia is a rare hereditary visual disorder where individuals are unable to see color.

Acquired is the term used for a medical condition that originates after birth.

Active initiation is a type of attachment that begins around 8 or 9 months and is characterized by the infant's initiative in seeking proximity and contact with the attachment figure.

Adaptive skills are self-help skills.

Adduction is movement toward the midline.

Adiposity is the fat found in adipose (fatty) tissue of the body.

Air conduction is the process of transmitting sound waves to the cochlea by way of the outer and middle ear.

Aggressive behaviors are behaviors that are intended to harm another individual, even if the attempt to harm fails.

Alleles are a pair or series of genes that occupy a particular location on a chromosome that is usually a coding sequence.

Allergen is an antigenic substance capable of producing an immediate hypersensitivity reaction in individuals.

Allergic rhinitis is an inflammation of the nasal passages caused by an allergic reaction to airborne substances.

Alveoli are tiny air sacs in the lungs that expand the lung's surface area for the exchange of oxygen and carbon dioxide.

Amblyopia is a disorder of the visual system caused by either no or poor transmission of visual images to the brain for an extended time.

American Sign Language (Ameslan or ASL) is a language that consists of a set of standard hand signs used in relation to other parts of the body with each sign representing a word, idea, or concept.

Amnion is a membranous sac that surrounds and protects the developing embryo and fetus during pregnancy.

Amniotic fluid is the clear liquid that helps to protect the developing fetus and is contained by the amnion or amniotic sac.

Amniotic sac is a thin transparent pair of membranes that hold the embryo and then the fetus during pregnancy.

Amphetamine stimulants are medications designed to release the neurotransmitter dopamine into the synaptic cleft and may be used to treat ADHD.

Amplification is a process that makes a signal stronger or louder.

Amplification devices are products (such as hearing aids that increase the level of sound) that make a signal stronger or louder.

Amygdala is part of the limbic system and a primitive arousal area that is central to the "fight or flight" response and is involved in producing and responding to nonverbal signs of anger, avoidance, defensiveness and fear.

Anaphylaxis is a severe allergic reaction that occurs within minutes of exposure and may lead to death if not treated.

Anemia is a deficiency of red blood cells and/or hemoglobin that reduces the ability of blood to transfer oxygen to the tissues.

Anencephaly is severe malformation of the skull and brain with no neural development above the brainstem.

Anterior chamber is the fluid-filled space inside the eye between the iris and the cornea's innermost surface.

Anti-bias curriculum is a curriculum approach used in early childhood education that attempts to combat forms of prejudice such as racism, sexism, handicapism, and other isms.

Antibodies are gamma globulin proteins found in blood and other bodily fluids that are part of the immune system that identify and neutralize germs, such as bacteria and viruses.

Antigravity postures are all postures where some part of the body is in an upright position such as sitting or standing.

Anti-inflammatory medication is medication that decreases pain by reducing inflammation as opposed to opioids that affect the brain.

Antirheumatic drugs are a category of drugs used in many autoimmune disorders to slow disease progression and reduce the rate of damage to bone and cartilage.

Antisocial behaviors are behaviors that violate social norms; the violation may be minor or major.

Anxiety is generalized worry.

Anxiety disorders are different forms of abnormal anxiety, fears, and phobias that are irrational or illogical worry not based on fact.

Apnea is the suspension of external breathing for 20 seconds or more.

Apnea monitor is a machine that checks the heart rate and respiration of an infant and when either falls below normal levels, the monitor beeps.

Apraxia is a neurological disorder of motor planning that involves the inability to carry out learned purposeful movements.

Aqueous humor is a thick watery substance that fills the space between the lens and the cornea of the eye.

Assessment is the process of collecting information for the purpose of making decisions about children or groups of children or to evaluate a program's effectiveness.

Assimilate is the process of taking in new information to develop a schema or concept.

Assistive listening devices are products designed to improve audibility; some work with hearing aids or cochlear implants, others are used independently.

Assistive technology device is any item, piece of equipment, or product system that increases, maintains, or improves the functional capabilities of a child with a disability.

Associative play is play where children are playing together but the play is not goal oriented and there is no leader.

Astigmatism is an error in refraction caused by the cornea of the eye being more football-shaped than spherical, therefore the parallel light rays do not come together at one point so the image is not in focus.

Ataxia is irregular, uncoordinated muscular movement, especially in walking.

Ataxic cerebral palsy is an impairment characterized by abnormalities in voluntary movement that cause increased or decreased muscle tone, resulting in problems in balance and in controlling the position of the trunk and limbs.

Athetosis refers to random, writhing, involuntary movements, especially of the hands.

Atopy is an allergic hypersensitivity affecting parts of the body not in direct contact with the allergen.

Atopic disease is a heredity predisposition toward developing specific hypersensitivity reactions such as asthma, hay fever, and other allergies.

Attachment is the development of the human bond between infants, children, and adults.

Atonic seizures or drop seizures consist of a brief abrupt loss of muscle tone.

Audiologist is a professional who has been trained in the prevention, identification, and nonmedical management of hearing loss. Audiologists can identify hearing loss and initiate treatment (fit hearing aids) in children once medical clearance has been obtained.

Audiometer is a machine used for evaluating hearing loss.

Auditory cortex is the region of the brain responsible for processing of auditory (sound) information.

Auditory discrimination is the identification of differences between sounds on the basis of variations in their complexity, pattern, pitch, or intensity.

Auditory memory is part of memory that allows individuals to retrieve information that was heard through remembering the auditory information over time.

Auditory processing dysfunction is a receptive language impairment that affects the way sounds are interpreted by the brain

Auricle is the outer, or external, ear.

Autosomes are paired chromosomes that are the same for both sexes. Humans have 22 pairs.

Axons are long snakelike fibers that reach out from the cell to conduct electrical impulses away from the cell body.

B

Baclofen is a drug used to treat spasms of skeletal muscles that involuntarily contract due to sudden stretching of the muscle, rigidity, and pain.

Backward chaining is teaching the last step in a task analysis first and working toward the first step.

Basal ganglia are a large collection of nuclei with a variety of functions that modify movement. They also play a role in cognition, emotions, and learning.

Behavioral disorders are disorders that focus on disruptive behavior.

Behavioral intervention plan is a written plan based on a functional behavioral assessment designed to address problematic behavior.

Bias is a preference for a particular perspective or ideology that interferes with the ability to be objective or impartial.

Bicultural adaptation involves honoring the home culture and adding experiences from the broader community to this base.

Biculturalism is a way of adapting to the environment that incorporates aspects of the home culture with the mainstream culture.

Bilirubin is a product of the breakdown of the hemoglobin in red blood cells and if levels are too high it can cause brain damage.

Binocular vision is vision using two eyes simultaneously.

Bipolar disorder, or manic-depression disorder, is a mental illness characterized by mood instability that moves between manic behavior and depression.

Blastocyte is the second stage in development that begins 5 days after fertilization and lasts until implantation when it becomes an embryo.

Blended families are stepfamilies where one or both adults have children from a prior union.

Blind, for educational purposes, is a visual loss severe enough so that it is not possible to read printed material and necessitates the use of alternative forms of written communication such as Braille.

Blindisms are socially inappropriate behaviors such as eye pressing, spinning, head banging, and rocking or bouncing that children who are blind may do for stimulation.

Blood clotting, or coagulation, changes blood from a liquid to a solid.

Body mass index, a number calculated based on a person's weight and height, is an indicator of body fatness and is used to identify weight categories.

Bone conduction is the transmission of sound to the inner ear through the bones of the skull.

Boomerang generation is a generation of young adults, born between about 1975 and 1985, named because of their tendency to move back into their parents' home after living independently for a while.

Bradycardia is a drop in a fetal or infant heart rate to below 80 to 100 beats per minute.

Braille is a system of reading and writing used by people who cannot see print. Braille cells are made up of six dot positions, arranged in a rectangle to form sixty-four different patterns.

Brain stem is the lower part of the brain that connects to the spinal column and controls reflexive and involuntary activities such as blood pressure, heart rate, and the regulation of body temperature, breathing, and other automatic processes.

Bronchodilator is an asthma medication that dilates the bronchi and bronchioles thus widening the air passages of the lungs to make breathing easier. It is used as an emergency drug for children with asthma.

C

Cannula is a tube that is inserted into the body to deliver or remove fluids.

Cardiovascular system is the system that carries oxygenated blood away from the heart, to the body, and then returns deoxygenated blood back to the heart.

Cataracts are a clouding of the natural lens, a part of the eye responsible for focusing light and producing clear, sharp images.

Catheterize is the process of threading a flexible tube (catheter) through a channel in the body to inject drugs or a bladder catheter goes through the urethra into the bladder to relieve the bladder.

Central auditory hearing loss, or central auditory processing dysfunction, describes a variety of problems with the brain that interfere with processing auditory (sound) information when hearing is within normal limits.

Central nervous system consists of the brain, the spinal cord, and the nerves that control voluntary and involuntary body functions.

Central vision is straight-ahead vision produced by light rays falling directly on the fovea centralis of the eye.

Cephalocaudal is a pattern of development that goes from the head to the tail with the upper part of the body (head) developing before the lower part (legs).

Cerebral cortex of the brain is the outer portion of the cerebrum that is responsible for higher brain functions such as language, cognition, and memory. It is often referred to as grey matter because of the color of the neurons and unmyelinated fibers it is made of.

Cerebrum is the largest part of the brain residing in both the left and right hemispheres. It has four lobes: frontal, parietal, temporal, and occipital. It is what most people think of when they think of the brain.

Cervical vertebrae are those vertebrae immediately behind the skull connecting the skull and spine. They are the smallest of the true vertebrae going from C-1 to C-7.

Cesarean section is a form of childbirth where a surgical incision is made through the mother's abdomen and uterus to deliver one or more infants.

Chaining is the process of ordering a task analysis into a sequence that starts at the beginning of a task (forward chaining) or at the end (backward chaining).

Chiari type II is a congenital malformation of the brainstem and part of the cerebellum that causes them to be lower in the neck rather than being in the skull. It occurs only in children with spina bifida.

Child development specialists are individuals who are trained in developmental principles and work with children in a variety of settings.

Child Find is a system for identifying, locating, and evaluating children with disabilities who need early intervention, special education, and related services.

Child of an immigrant parent is a child younger than 18 years of age who is either foreign-born or was born in the United States with at least one foreign-born parent.

Child life staff are early childhood professionals who work with children in hospital settings.

Child with a disability, according to the IDEA, is a child with mental retardation, hearing impairments, speech or language impairments, visual impairment, emotional disturbance, orthopedic impairments, autism, traumatic brain injury, other health impairments, or specific learning disabilities, and because of these impairments needs special education and related services.

Children without disabilities are children who do not receive services based on the IDEA.

Choreoathetoid is a type of dyskinetic cerebral palsy, where there are rapid, random, jerky movements (chorea) combined with slow, writhing movements (athetosis).

Chorionic gonadotrophin is a hormone that is measured in blood or urine to determine if a woman is pregnant and it helps maintain the pregnancy.

Choroid is the vascular layer of the eye that contains the blood vessels and lies between the retina and the sclera and provides oxygen and nourishment to the outer layers of the retina.

Chromosomes are long, single continuous pieces of DNA that contain many genes, regulatory elements, and other nucleotide sequences.

Chronic otitis media is a reoccurring inflammation of the middle ear.

Cleavage is the early successive splitting of a zygote into smaller cells by mitosis.

Clinical judgment or opinion is the recommendation of qualified personnel relative to areas of expertise.

Clumsy child syndrome, also called developmental dyspraxia, is a disorder characterized by impairment in the ability to plan and carry out sensory and motor tasks.

Cluster grouping is the practice of placing a small group of identified gifted children together in a classroom and providing more complex activities for them.

Cochlea is a snail-shell-like structure in the inner ear whose core component is the organ of Corti. It is important for hearing and also balance and equilibrium.

Cochlear implants are small, complex electronic devices that can help provide a sense of sound to a child who is profoundly deaf or severely hard of hearing.

Code-switching is using more than one language or dialect in a conversation.

Cognitive behavioral therapy is a psychotherapy that has an objective to identify irrational or maladaptive thoughts, assumptions, and beliefs related to negative emotions that are not helpful, and to find more flexible ways to respond to break the pattern.

Cohabitation is an emotionally and physically intimate relationship between two adults that includes a common living place that exists without legal or religious sanction.

Cohort is a group of subjects, usually people, from a given population defined by experiencing an event (typically birth) in a particular time span. All the children born in a particular hospital or city during a particular year would be a cohort.

Collaboration is the dynamic process of connecting families' resources, motivation, and knowledge/skills to an empowering context to make decisions collectively.

Color blindness is a lay term used instead of color deficiency and it means the same thing.

Color deficiency is the inability to differentiate among some colors.

Color vision is the capacity of the child to distinguish objects based on the wavelengths of the light they reflect or emit.

Comorbid is the occurrence of more that one disease or disorder in a child.

Comorbidity refers to the presence of one or more diseases or disorders in addition to the primary disease or disorder.

Complex tics are tics with distinct, coordinated patterns that involve several muscle groups and may be a combination of simple tics such as facial grimacing combined with a head twist and shrugging a shoulder.

Compliance is the process of ensuring that individuals and systems adhere to relevant laws and regulations, particularly the IDEA.

Conductive hearing loss is a failure in the efficient conduction of sound waves through the outer ear, eardrum, or middle ear.

Cones, or cone cells, are photoreceptor cells in the retina of the eye that function best in relatively bright light and are needed to see color, to see distant objects, and for detailed vision such as reading. There are three kinds of cones. Each one is sensitive to one of three colors: red, green, or blue.

Congenital is a medical condition that is present at birth.

Congenital malformations are anomalies that are present at birth.

Conjunctiva is the thin, transparent mucous membrane in the eye that contains tiny blood vessels. It is the outermost layer of the eye and the inner surface of the eyelids.

Conjunctivitis, "pink eye," is an inflammation of the conjunctiva, due to an allergic reaction or an infection.

Constructivism is an approach to teaching and learning based on the belief that learning is the result of mental construction, that children learn by fitting new information into what they already know, and that learning is active and affected by context.

Constructivist approach is the approach used by those who support constructivism.

Consultant is a professional who provides advice in a particular area of expertise such as early childhood special education.

Content standards are standards that specify what children should know and be able to do.

Content validity is concerned with the relationship between the items in an assessment and the intended use of the assessment.

Contingency contracting is part of a behavior plan where children can decide on the rewards they will get after they have accomplished specific goals.

Contractions are the movements of the muscles in the wall of the uterus that push the fetus through the birth canal.

Contracture is a shortening of muscle fibers that is usually irreversible and decreases the range of motion of a joint.

Cooperative play is play where children have a common goal and are interacting using similar materials or materials related to a common theme.

Cornea is the transparent front part of the eye that covers the iris, pupil, and anterior chamber, providing most of an eye's optical power. Together with the lens, the cornea refracts light and helps the eye to focus.

Corpus callosum is a broad band of nerve fibers, axons of cells in the cerebral cortex that connect the left and right hemispheres of the brain.

Cortex is the outermost layer of an organ.

Cortical visual impairments are temporary or permanent visual impairments caused by an abnormality of the visual cortex or the visual pathways of the brain. They are caused by oxygen deprivation, infection, or traumatic brain injury.

Corticospinal tract is a massive collection of long motor axons that go between the brain and the spinal column.

Co-teaching model is when an early childhood educator and an early childhood special educator teach in the same classroom together.

Criterion-referenced is a system of comparing performance to an absolute standard.

Criterion-referenced measures are measures that use an absolute standard for determining scores. Children perform certain tasks and their score is based on their level of competency in completing the tasks.

Critical care unit is a specialized department in a hospital that provides intensive care medicine.

Cued speech is a visual communication system that uses eight hand shapes in four different placements near the face in combination with the mouth movements of speech to make the sounds of spoken language look different from each other.

Cuing is warning children before they are expected to do something.

Curriculum-based assessments are measures used in schools to determine the instructional needs of students.

D

Decibel (dB) is a measure of the magnitude or intensity of sound.

Decoding is the process of transforming information from one format into another, such as the written word into sound.

Decubitus ulcers, pressure sores or bedsores, are lesions caused by unrelieved pressure to any part of the body, usually over bony or cartilaginous areas.

Dendrites are branched projections of a neuron that conduct electrical impulses to the cell body.

Depression is a psychiatric disorder that is characterized by a pervasive low mood, loss of interest in usual activities, and diminished ability to experience pleasure.

Developmental delay is a condition that represents a significant delay in the developmental processes, not a slight or momentary lag in development, which will continue without intervention.

Depressive disorders are disorders that are characterized by severe and persistent sadness.

Developmental coordination disorder is a disorder of childhood characterized by physical awkwardness and clumsiness.

Developmental dyspraxia is a disorder characterized by impairment in the inability to plan and carry out sensory and motor tasks and may include poor balance and coordination, clumsiness, vision problems, perception difficulties, emotional and behavioral problems, difficulty with reading, writing, and speaking, poor social skills, poor posture, and poor short-term memory.

Developmental quotients (DQs) are scores obtained on developmental assessments for young children with a mean of 100. They are used similarly to intelligent quotients IQs for older children.

Developmental tests are age-related, norm-referenced measures of skills and behaviors that compare the scores of children of a given age.

Developmentally appropriate practices is a way of teaching that has three basic components: knowledge about development and learning, knowledge about individual children, and knowledge about the social and cultural context in which children learn and grow.

Diabetes mellitus type 1 is an autoimmune disease where the body does not produce insulin because of the destruction of the insulin-producing beta cells of the pancreas.

Diabetes mellitus type 2 is a metabolic disorder that is characterized by insulin resistance, insulin deficiency, and hyperglycemia; it is typically managed by increasing exercise and modifying the diet, although insulin may be needed.

Dialogic reading is a shared reading practice where the adult and the child switch roles so the child learns to become the storyteller with the assistance of the adult who functions as an active listener and questioner.

Diffuse axonal injury is widespread brain damage with extensive lesions in the white matter of the brain.

Diopter is a unit of measurement of the optical power of a lens. The higher the number of diopters, the stronger the glasses prescription: a minus sign indicates concave lenses and a plus sign indicates a convex lens.

Diplegia is an impairment that involves the whole body, although the legs more so than the arms.

Direct language stimulation is communication where an adult questions a child to elicit responses in a way that the child cannot answer with just a yes or no.

Disability is a general term referring to a condition or functional limitation that interferes with major life activities such as walking, hearing, or learning.

Discipline is actions or words that help children self-monitor their behavior so it is appropriate and acceptable and to encourage self control.

Discretionary, as opposed to mandated services, are those services that may incur a cost to those using the service and do not have to be provided.

Discriminate attachment is a type of attachment that begins about 3 to 4 months and goes to about 8 or 9 months where infants respond differently to one (or a few) familiar individuals than they do to strangers.

Disproportionality compares the racial and ethnic backgrounds of the school population with the population who are identified as needing special education services.

Dissociation is a mental state where certain thoughts, sensation, or memories are compartmentalized because they are too overwhelming for the conscious mind.

Distal organs or body parts are those away from the midline, such as the fingers.

Dizygotic twins, or fraternal twins, result from two separate fertilized eggs in one pregnancy.

Dopamine is a hormone and a neurotransmitter in the brain.

Double vision, or diplopia, is the simultaneous perception of two images of a single object as a result of the misalignment of the eyes.

DSM-IV-TR is the fourth text revision of the *Diagnostic and Statistical Manual of Mental Disorders* published by the American Psychiatric Association and is used to classify mental disorders.

Dual-language learners are children who are learning two or more languages at the same time.

Due process is the legal right families of children with disabilities have to ensure that the services their child is suppose to receive are granted by having a due process hearing with impartial hearing officers and, if necessary, a court of law.

Dura is the tough and inflexible outermost of the three layers of the meninges surrounding the brain and spinal cord.

Dyscalculia is the inability to understand the processes associated with mathematical calculation and reasoning.

Dysgraphia is a neurologic disorder characterized by the profound inability to form meaningful symbols.

Dyskinetic is a form of cerebral palsy that is characterized by abnormal involuntary movements.

Dyslexia, or reading disability, is a difficulty with written language, particularly reading and spelling, based on how the brain processes written language.

Dyspraxia is a poor ability to conceive, plan, organize or carry out novel actions or sequences of coordinated movements to attain a goal.

Dysthymia is a mood disorder that is part of the depression spectrum and is characterized by being sad or "down in the dumps" for a long time, perhaps a year.

Dystonia is a form of cerebral palsy in which there are rapid involuntary changes in muscle tension or tone.

E

Ear canal is a tube that goes from the outer ear to the middle ear.

Early care and education is the education and caregiving for children from birth through age 8.

Early childhood special education is the education of children with disabilities from birth through age 8.

Early childhood special education consultants are early childhood special educators who give advice to educators and caregivers in a variety of settings to ensure that children who need early intervention or special education receive needed educational services.

Early Head Start is a program for children ages 3 and younger funded as a set-aside of the Head Start program whose mission is to promote healthy prenatal outcomes for pregnant women, enhance the development of very young children and promote healthy family functioning.

Early intervention is a service designed for infants and toddlers with disabilities. It promotes development and learning, supports families and helps with service coordination with the goal of reducing or eliminating the need for special programs later.

Early interventionist is a person, typically a nurse, child development specialist, and/or early childhood special educator, who provides educational services for children with disabilities and those at risk.

Echolalia is the repetition of vocalizations made by another person.

Eclampsia is a serious complication of pregnancy that is associated with high blood pressure and can result in seizures or convulsions.

Ectoderm is the outermost of the three germ layers of the embryo. It becomes the nervous system, skin, hair, teeth, and other body parts.

Ectopic pregnancy is when a fertilized egg implants in tissue other than the uterine wall, most frequently the fallopian tube.

Edema is swelling caused by excess fluid in body tissues.

Electroencephalogram (EEG) is a test that measures and records the electrical activity of the brain.

Embryo is a developing organism from the time of implantation in the uterus wall until the end of 8 weeks.

Emotional disorders are disorders that relate to mood.

Encephalocele is a neural tube defect where the skull is malformed so that it allows a portion of the brain to protrude at the back or front of the brain.

Endoderm is the innermost of the three germ layers of the embryo from which the respiratory and digestive systems develop.

Endometrium is the mucus membrane lining the uterus.

Engagement is a time during labor and delivery when the largest part of the fetal head has passed through the mother's pelvic rim and into the true pelvis.

English language learners are children who, because of foreign birth or ancestry, speak a language other than English, and either understand or speak little or no academic English.

Entitlement is a guarantee of access to benefits or services because of rights or by agreement through law.

Epidural hematoma is a type of traumatic brain injury where a blood clot develops between the skull and the outer covering of the brain (dura mater).

Epicanthic fold is a skin fold of the upper eyelid that covers the inner corner of the eye caused by weak eyelid muscles.

Epilepsy is a brain disorder where clusters of nerve cells, or neurons, in the brain sometimes signal abnormally.

Epinephrine, also called adrenaline, is a hormone and neurotransmitter.

Esotropia is the most common form of strabismus where the eyes are deviated inward; turned in toward the nose (cross-eyed).

Ethnic or ethnicity is a part of an individual's identity based on cultural, linguistic, religious, behavioral, or biological traits.

Ethnographic is a scientific way of describing human cultures.

Etiology is a branch of medical science that studies the cause of diseases and the accumulated knowledge we have about them.

Eustachian tube is a slender tube that runs from the middle ear to the pharynx.

Evaluation is using assessment information to make decisions.

Execution is carrying out a course of action or conduct to its completion.

Executive function is the ability to maintain appropriate problem-solving procedures to attain future goals. It includes the ability to plan, to wait and to control one's impulses, to store relevant information for future use, to think creatively, and to problem solve.

Exotropia, is a form of strabismus where the eyes are deviated outward; turned away from the nose (wall-eyed).

Expansion is the process of extracting meaning from a child's utterance and putting it in a more complex form. ("Up" "Do you want me to pick you up?").

Expertise is a level of mastery beyond literacy for children who want to become mini-experts in a field.

Extension is the opposite of flexion and means to straighten or stretch a joint. If your arm is extended, the elbow joint is straight.

Extinction is a way of extinguishing behavior by the lack of any consequence following a behavior, either favorable or unfavorable, so that the behavior occurs with less frequency.

F

Fallopian tubes are a pair of slender ducts going from the ovaries into the uterus.

Fast mapping is a mental process where children form a working hypothesis about word meaning after a single exposure and gradually refine it, thus allowing them to increase their vocabulary very quickly.

Federal Bureau of Indian Affairs is a federal agency whose responsibility is the administration and management of 55.7 million acres of land held in trust by the United States for American Indians, Indian tribes, and Alaska Natives.

Fetus is what the developing organism is called from the time the major structures have formed (about the ninth week after fertilization) until birth.

Fibrin is a substance made by a complex chemical process to form a clot that stops bleeding.

Field of vision is the angular extent of the observable world that is seen at any given moment.

Fill-ins require the child to complete the statement on a test.

Finger-spelling is the representation of the letters and numbers of a written language using only the hands.

First stage of labor begins with contractions and ends when the cervix is dilated and effaced.

Flexion is the bending of a joint. If your elbow is flexed, your hand is near your shoulder.

Foot-candles are a measure of the amount of light that falls on a given surface. Technically, 1 foot-candle is equal to 1 lumen per square foot.

Foreign-born parents means that one or both of a child's parents were born outside of the United States.

Foster care is a living arrangement for children when a court decides they cannot safely live at home with their biological parent(s).

Fovea centralis or fovea, a part of the eye located in the center of the macula region of the retina, is needed for sharp central vision.

Frequency is the pitch of a sound and is measured by the number of sound waves per unit of time. The more frequent the sound waves, the higher the frequency.

Function is analyzing the purpose of a particular action and what a child gains by continuing the particular behavior.

Functional behavioral assessment is a systematic assessment that analyzes the connection between problematic behavior and its function in the child's life.

Functional skills are those skills the child needs to function independently in the environment and that can be taught during activities or routines in the classroom or in routines at home.

Fundamental movement skills are movements that provide the foundation to build more complex motor skills.

G

Gastroesophageal reflux is a disease caused by a muscle at the end of the esophagus not closing properly, which allows the stomach contents to leak back, or reflux, into the esophagus and irritate it.

Generalized anxiety disorder is excessive anxiety and worry about a variety of things and results in fatigue, restlessness, difficulty concentrating, irritability, tension, and sleep disturbance.

Generalized seizures are seizures that do not have an identifiable focus, impact both hemispheres of the brain, affect widely spread cortical areas of the brain simultaneously, and usually have a genetic base.

Genetic counseling is the process of advising individuals of the consequence of a disorder, the probability of developing it and transmitting it, and about ways the disorder can be prevented or ameliorated.

Genotype is the specific genetic genome of a person or his DNA.

Gestation is carrying an embryo or fetus.

Gestational age is the time from conception plus 2 weeks. (Gestational age is counted from the mother's last menstrual cycle.)

Gestational diabetes is a condition where women who did not previously have diabetes exhibit high blood glucose levels during the latter part of pregnancy.

Glaucoma is a group of diseases of the optic nerve that can lead to permanent damage of the optic nerve, loss of visual field, and blindness.

Glial cells (Greek for "glue") are non-neuronal cells that provide support and nutrition for neurons, maintain homeostasis, form myelin, and participate in signal transmission in the nervous system. They out number neurons by about 10:1.

Glucose is a simple sugar that cells use as a source of energy.

Goal-directed attachment is a type of attachment that appears at about 30 to 36 months and is characterized by toddlers using attachment figures for a particular purpose.

Grammar is concerned with the rules for using the smallest units of language that contain meaning (*morphemes*) and word order (*syntax*) to convey meaning.

Gray matter is nerve cell bodies that are grayish in color, and that covers the white matter (myelinated axons) and together make up the cerebral cortex of the brain.

Growth cone is the tip of an axon that provides guidance for the growing axon and helps it reach its destination.

Guidance is a process approach to guiding children's behavior, rather than an isolated act of punishment, that is designed to facilitate the development of self-esteem, prosocial behaviors, and the ability to control one's own behavior.

Guided reading is a process where teachers introduce a book and guide children through it, children think about what will happen in the book, teachers introduce key vocabulary and reading strategies, children read the book independently and then discuss the book with the teacher, and finally re-read the book.

H

Habituate is to become familiar with a stimulus and then not respond to it.

Hair cells are the sensory receptors of the auditory and vestibular systems. There are two types of hair cells: Outer hair cells amplify low-level sound that enters the cochlea and inner hair cells transform the sound vibrations in the fluids of the cochlea into electrical signals and relay them via the auditory nerve to the auditory brainstem and auditory cortex.

Handicap is the cumulative result of the barriers imposed by society that come between an individual and the environment of an activity that the person wants to do.

Head Start is a national program that promotes school readiness by enhancing the social and cognitive development of children through the provision of early care and education to children in low-income families.

Hearing aids are small electronic devices worn in or behind the ear that make some sounds louder.

Hearing threshold testing is testing of hearing to determine the softest sound a child is able to hear at different frequencies.

Hematoma is a collection of blood, generally the result of internal bleeding, also called a blood clot.

Hemiplegia is severe or complete paralysis of one side of the body.

Hemoglobin is the oxygen transport system in red blood cells.

Hepatitis is an infectious disease of the liver that manifests itself in a number of different strands, and is caused by viruses.

Hertz (symbol Hz) is the base unit of frequency. One hertz is one cycle per second, 50 hertz is 50 cycles per second. The term Hertz replaced cycles per second (cps).

Heterozygous is when one possesses two different forms of a particular gene.

Hippocampus is a small structure at the base of the temporal lobe of the brain that plays a role in memory and in the ability to rapidly learn and process new information.

Hitching is a method of moving where the child's bottom is on the floor and she scoots, using her legs for propulsion.

Homeless people are those who lack a fixed, regular, and adequate nighttime residence.

Homozygous is a condition where the genes in two specific chromosomes are the same.

Householder is the person in whose name a housing unit is owned or rented.

Hydrocephalus is excessive fluid in the brain cavities.

Hyperglycemia, or high blood sugar, is a condition where an excessive amount of glucose (sugar) circulates in the blood plasma.

Hyperlexia is a set of unusual splinter skills, such as perfect pitch and the ability to perform rapid mathematical calculations, which children with specific learning disabilities, ADHD, or autism may sometimes display.

Hypertension, or high blood pressure, is a medical condition in which the blood pressure is chronically elevated.

Hypertonic is muscle tone that is too high (tight) causing children to overreact to normal stimuli.

Hypertonicity is increased tension of the muscles with the muscle tone abnormally tight or rigid.

Hypoglycemia is a condition characterized by an abnormally low blood sugar (glucose) level.

Hypothermia is a condition where a person's temperature drops below that required for normal metabolism and bodily functions.

Hypotonic is when muscle tone is low, less responsive than expected, or floppy.

Hypoxia is a condition where some or all of the body is deprived of adequate oxygen.

I

Ideation is the process of forming or relating ideas and planning actions.

Illegal immigrants are individuals who cross national borders in a way that violates the immigration laws of the destination country, or a foreigner who entered legally but overstayed his or her visa.

Immigrant children are children who were born outside the United States and currently live in the United States.

Immigrant parents are parents who were born outside of the United States and currently reside in the United States.

Impulse control disorders are disorders characterized by an inability to resist the impulse to take actions that are harmful to self or to others.

Incus is the anvil-shaped small bone or ossicle in the middle ear that connects the malleus to the stapes.

Indiscriminate attachment is a form of attachment that is present from birth to 4 to 6 months where infants enjoy social interactions with almost all adults.

Indirect language stimulation is the language the child hears and overhears that is not directed to him.

Infant mortality is the number of deaths of infants 1 year of age or younger per 1,000 live births.

Infant or toddler with a disability is a child younger than 3 years of age who needs early intervention services because she is experiencing developmental delays, has a diagnosed physical or mental condition that has a high probability resulting in developmental delay, or in some states is at risk of developing delays.

Inferior is below; the feet are inferior to the waist.

Inner ear is a bony labyrinth in the skull that starts at the oval window and contains the cochlea and the vestibular apparatus that consists of three semicircular canals and the vestibule.

Intelligence quotient (IQ) is a score derived from a standardized test designed to measure intelligence.

Intensity is the noise measurement of sound intensity in the air at a listener's location.

Interpreter is an individual who is certified by the National Registry of Interpreters for the Deaf who translates spoken English into American Sign Language.

Interactive shared reading involves an adult reading a book to a child or a small group of children and using a variety of techniques to engage the children in the text.

Intermittent catheterization is the temporary placement of a catheter (tube) to remove urine from the body.

Intraocular lenses are lenses that are implanted in the eye because the existing lenses were removed (usually because of cataracts).

Intrathecal is the space surrounding the spinal cord, the spinal canal.

Intraventricular hemorrhage (IVH) is bleeding into or near the normal fluid spaces (ventricles) of the brain.

Iris is the part of the eye that controls the amount of light that enters by opening wider to let in more light or closing to decrease the amount of light.

J

Jargon is terminology that relates to a specific activity, profession, or group; also professional slang or shorthand.

Jaundice, or icterus, is a yellowish discoloration of the skin, whites of the eyes, and mucous membranes caused by high levels of bilirubin in the blood.

K

Karyotyping is a laboratory test where chromosomes are separated from cells, stained and arranged from largest to smallest so that their number and structure can be studied under magnification.

Kinship care is a situation when children who cannot safely live at home live in a foster home with relatives or other adults whom they know.

Kinship foster care occurs when a child welfare agency places children in the care of relatives.

L

Labor is the process of regular uterine contractions that result in child birth.

Lead is a heavy metal that can get into the blood and cause a medical condition, lead poisoning, which can lead to irreversible neurological problems.

Least restrictive environment is an environment where to the maximum extent appropriate, children with disabilities are educated with children who do not have disabilities.

Legally blind is visual acuity no better than 20/200 in the better eye, with the best possible correction, or with a field of vision restricted to 20 degrees or less (tunnel vision) in the better eye instead of the usual 105 degrees.

Lens is a transparent structure in the eye located behind the pupil that helps to focus light rays on the retina.

Ligaments are fibrous bands or sheets of tissues that connect bones to other bones. They provide stability to a joint during rest and movement.

Lightening is the descent of the uterus and fetus into the pelvic cavity changing the contour of the abdomen and facilitating breathing by lessening pressure under the diaphragm.

Limbic system is part of the brain involved in controlling emotions, emotions associated with memories and motivation, and emotional reactions to stress.

Limited English proficiency (LEP) is the term used by the public schools, the IDEA, and No Child Left Behind to identify children who do not understand or speak academic English well.

Linguistically isolated is a home situation where no one older than the age of 13 speaks English fluently or exclusively.

Literacy is the minimum level of knowledge and skills that children need in a particular academic or developmental area to continue moving toward becoming competent adults.

Low vision is visual acuity between 20/70 and 20/200 in the better eye with the best corrected vision.

Lumbar vertebrae are the largest and lowest segments of the movable part of the spinal cord L-1 to L-5.

Lymphoid cells are white blood cells that are part of the lymphatic system.

M

Macula is an oval yellow spot near the center of the retina of the human eye. The fovea is in its center and it is responsible for central vision and visual acuity.

Malleability is the plasticity of some parts of the brain to change.

Malleus is a hammer-shaped small bone in the middle ear that connects with the incus and is attached to the inner surface of the eardrum. It transmits sound vibrations from the eardrum to the incus.

Mandate is a requirement to provide a free appropriate public education.

Mandated services are those that must be provided.

Mania is an abnormal mental state characterized by an elevated or irritable mood, exaggerated self-importance, racing thoughts, and hyperactivity.

Manic episode is the period when an individual is in a manic state.

Manifestation of the disability is an educational distinction between behavior that is caused by the disability and behavior that is unrelated to the disability. The determination is also related to appropriate implementation of the IEP.

Mast cells are cells that reside in several types of tissues and contains many granules rich in histamine and heparin and play a role in allergic reactions.

Median is the middle number in an array of numbers.

Median plane is an imaginary line that runs vertically through the middle of the human body, dividing it in half.

Medicaid is a health program for children and families with low incomes in the United States.

Medical home is a setting that provides accessible, continuous and comprehensive health care to a child in a family-centered way.

Medulla oblongata is the lower portion of the brainstem and controls autonomic functions.

Meiosis is the process of cell division where the genetic material in the chromosome is mixed and divided into sex cells, the number of chromosomes in a cell is divided in half, and then recombined with the sex cell to form an offspring with 23 chromosome pairs.

Meningitis is an inflammation of the protective membranes (meninges) that cover the brain and spinal cord.

Meningocele is a form of spina bifida where there is a membranous sac over the spinal cord. If the spinal cord is not entrapped children are usually symptom-free.

Mesoderm is the middle of the three germ layers in embryos that becomes the circulatory system, bones, muscles, and other parts.

Metaphase is a stage in mitosis where the chromosomes align in the middle of the cell before being separated into daughter cells.

Metered-dose inhaler with spacers is a method of dispensing drugs to children that gives a set amount of medication with each puff. The spacers attached to the metered-dose inhaler holds the medication, allowing children to inhale it in a few breaths instead of just one.

Methylphenidate stimulants are medications that block dopamine transporters; because there are fewer available transporters, there is increased dopamine at the synapses.

Midbrain, part of the brainstem, is the nerve pathway of the cerebral hemispheres and contains auditory and visual reflex centers.

Middle ear is the portion of the ear between the eardrum and the oval window containing three ossicles.

Middle ear disease is an inflammation of the middle ear and is associated with fluid in the middle ear space that may or may not have a bacterial infection.

Midline is an imaginary line that runs vertically through the middle of the body, dividing it in half.

Mind reading is assuming to know what another person is thinking or feeling without asking.

Minimal brain damage is a neurologic condition characterized by learning and behavioral disorders, a former name for attention-deficit/hyperactivity disorder.

Minority is a subordinate political group that is disadvantaged; it is not necessarily a numerical minority.

Mitosis is the process of cell division that results in two genetically identical cells.

Mixed cerebral palsy is an impairment that results from damage to both the pyramidal and extrapyramidal areas of the brain. Children with mixed cerebral palsy can have symptoms of both rigidity and spasticity (rigidity in the arms and spasticity in the legs).

Mixed hearing loss is a hearing loss that includes both a sensorineural and a conductive loss.

Mixed-status families are families where some members are legally in the United States and others are not.

Modeling is demonstrating behavior that is appropriate in a variety of situations.

Modulation is the ability to regulate responses in the context of ongoing events.

Monozygotic twins, or identical twins, occur when a single egg is fertilized to form one zygote, which then divides into two separate embryos.

Mood disorders are conditions where the common emotional state is distorted or inappropriate to the circumstances; they include depression as well as alternating states of depression and mania.

Morbidity refers to the occurrence of complications such as disease, disability, and chronic illness.

Morphemes are the smallest meaningful units of language. They include words or meaningful word parts. Prefixes and suffixes are morphemes.

Morphology looks at how adding or deleting parts of words (prefixes and suffixes) changes their meaning.

Morula is an early stage of embryonic development when it is a solid ball consisting of 12 to 32 cells.

Mosaicism is a condition where a child has two or more cell populations that have a different genetic makeup.

Mosaic trisomy is a condition that occurs when extra chromosomal material exists in some but not all of the cells.

Mosaic trisomy 18 is a rare genetic disorder where a piece of chromosome 18 becomes attached to another chromosome (caused by translocation) before or after conception.

Motor planning is the ability to originate, organize, plan, initiate, sequence, and then execute new or unpracticed fine or gross motor activity.

Muscle tone is the ability of the muscles to respond to stretch.

Multiple intelligences refer to an educational theory showcasing eight kinds of intelligence in children, which was developed by Howard Gardner.

Mutation is damage or change to the DNA of a gene that alters the genetic message it carries.

Myelin sheath is an electrically insulating layer of glial cells that surrounds the axons of many neurons.

Myeloid cells are cells that originate in the bone marrow or spinal cord and the term is used to describe leukocytes that are not lymphocytes and related to the classification of cancers.

Myoclonic seizures are brief, single, rapid contractions of muscles that may be repeated and can involve isolated muscle groups or more general muscles of the trunk and limbs. Some are subtle, with just head nodding, while others cause sudden flexion or bending backwards that almost seem to pull the child over.

Myopia, or nearsightedness, is a refractive defect of the eye where parallel lines of light focus the image in front of the retina because the eyeball is too long, or the cornea is too steep.

Myringotomy with tubal insertion is the process of inserting grommets, tiny ventilation tubes, into the eardrum to allow air to pass freely into the middle ear to keep the pressure at atmospheric levels. A grommet is needed if the Eustachian tube is not working properly.

N

Natural environments are educational, social, and recreational environments that are as close to what they would be if children were typically developing.

Nebulizer is a device used to administer medication to children in the form of a liquid mist. It is commonly used in treating cystic fibrosis, asthma, and other respiratory diseases.

Necrotizing enterocolitis is a medical condition primarily seen in premature infants, where portions of the bowel undergo necrosis (tissue death).

Neonatal deaths are deaths that occur during the first 28 days after birth.

Neonatal intensive care unit (NICU) is a hospital unit in specially designated hospitals with highly trained staff and technological equipment designed for the acute care of very sick newborns.

Neonatal nurses are nurses who specialize in caring for newborn infants, particularly at-risk neonates.

Neonatologists are pediatricians with a subspecialty in neonatology who provide medical care of newborn infants, especially ill or premature newborns.

Neural fold is caused by rapid growth of neurons that allows the ectoderm to fold.

Neural groove is a shallow groove between the neural folds. It gradually deepens as the neural folds elevate and meet, which converts the groove into a closed tube, for example, the neural tube or canal.

Neural hearing loss is a hearing loss that occurs because the auditory nerve is damaged or absent.

Neural plate is a layer of ectoderm that forms into a thin flat plate. Its rapid growth causes it to fold.

Neural tube is the embryo's forerunner of the brain and spinal cord, the central nervous system.

Neurons are the specialized nerve cells that make up the central nervous system and they receive and transmit messages.

Neurotransmitters are chemicals released from one neuron that cross the synaptic cleft to a receiving neuron.

No Child Left Behind Act (P.L. 107–110) is a federal law that is the reauthorization of the Elementary and Secondary Education Act.

Nondisjunction, or not coming apart, is the failure of a chromosome to separate properly during cell division. When a single chromosome is lost it is called monosomy, when one is gained it is called trisomy.

Norepinephrine is a neurotransmitter that affects parts of the brain where attention and responding actions are controlled.

Normal development is development that follows a typical pattern.

Normalization is an approach that ensures that children who require special services are not separated from experiences of normal life, that is, educational, social, and recreational environments are as close to natural environments as possible.

Norm-referenced is the process of comparing the scores of one individual to the scores of all those who have taken the test (the norm).

Norm-referenced measures compare assessment scores of one child to all those who have taken that particular assessment.

Not Otherwise Specified (NOS) is a designation used when a child does not meet the specific criteria set forth by the APA for a particular disability but is identified as having the disorder.

O

Obesity is having a body mass index (BMI) of 30 or more or being more than 30 pounds over the recommended weight for height.

Objective-referenced assessments look at how a child is performing relative to specific objectives that have been designed for that particular child.

Objectivity is an aspect of testing that assumes that others administering the test would get the same results provided the requirements of the measure were adhered to.

Occipital lobe is one of four lobes of the brain; it contains the primary visual receptive cortex and is the visual processing center of the brain.

Occult spinal dysraphism is a form of spina bifida where the child has a visible abnormality on the lower back; this may be a birthmark, a small opening in the skin, a small lump, or a dimple.

Occupational therapists are specialists who work from a developmental base. Their therapy emphasizes vestibular, tactile, kinesthetic or proprioception, and perceptual motor development, fine motor coordination, and self-help/adaptive skills.

Onlooker play is when a child is watching other children play but is not actively participating.

Oppositional defiant disorder is a disorder characterized by an ongoing pattern of disobedient, hostile, and defiant behavior toward authority figures.

Ophthalmologist is a medical doctor who specializes in diseases and surgery of the visual pathways, including the eye, brain, and areas surrounding the eye.

Optic chiasm is the part of the brain where the optic nerves partially cross.

Optic disk, blind spot, is where ganglion cell axons exit the eye to form the optic nerve.

Optic nerve (cranial nerve II) is the nerve that transmits visual information from the retina to the brain.

Optic nerve hypoplasia is a medical condition that results in underdevelopment of the optic nerves.

Oral approach, or auditory-oral approach, is a way of teaching children with hearing impairments with the goal of the child learning spoken language and communicating verbally by looking at the speaker's face and mouth to speech read, and using hearing aids to take advantage of residual hearing.

Organ of Corti is an organ in the inner ear that contains auditory sensory cells, or "hair cells."

Orientation and mobility specialists are vision specialists who help children learn to move about their home, school, and community with confidence.

Orthotics is a medical field concerned with the application and manufacture of orthoses, devices such as braces that support or correct human function.

Ossicles are the three smallest bones in the human body (malleus, incus, and stapes) that are within the middle ear space and transmit sound from the air to the fluid-filled cochlea.

Otoacoustic emissions testing is a computerized hearing screening test that evaluates the cochlear (inner ear) function and detects hearing loss without the child's participation.

Otolaryngologist is a physician who specializes in the treatment of diseases of the ear, nose, and throat.

Otologist is another word for otolaryngologist.

Ovary is the female organ that produces reproductive cells, eggs, or ova.

Oval window is a membrane-covered opening that leads from the middle ear to the vestibule of the inner ear.

Overweight is having a body mass index (BMI) of 24 to 29.99 or being between 25 to 30 pounds over the recommended weight for height.

Oxytocin is a synthetic form of a natural hormone that causes the uterus to contract and can be used to increase the strength of contractions.

P

Palilalia is the repetition of one's own words.

Paradigm is a way of looking at the world.

Paraeducators are individuals who work under the supervision of educators in the classroom to provide additional instruction, particularly in inclusive classrooms. Paraeducators include paraprofessionals such as teacher's aides, educational assistants, instructional assistants, and other members of the special education team.

Parallel play is when the child is playing near other children using similar materials but playing in his own way.

Parallel talk is a method of adult speech where the adult gives words to the child's behavior and describes what the child is doing, seeing, or hearing.

Partial seizures can begin anywhere in the brain, are limited to a small region of one hemisphere, and allow continuance of normal alertness. If the partial seizure becomes complex, it can spread and alter consciousness.

Patent ductus arteriosus (PDA) is a congenital heart defect caused by the lack of closure of the ductus arteriosus after birth.

Pauciarticular JRA is the most common form of juvenile rheumatoid arthritis where four or fewer joints are involved.

Pediatric nurse is a registered nurse who specializes in young children. She usually has additional training in developmental screening tools, family counseling, child care, and early intervention.

Pediatric oncologist is a medical professional who treats children with cancer.

People first language is a way of using language so that the term disability is not placed in a preceding adjectival phrase, people and conditions are not confused, and groups of people are not put into categories such as the disabled.

Perception is the cognitive process of receiving information from the senses and organizing and interpreting it.

Perceptual-motor development is the ability to mentally organize, interpret, and respond to sensory information.

Performance standards are standards that specify at what level children need to know and demonstrate their understanding of a concept to meet the standard.

Perinatal is the time around the time of birth.

Perinatal period is 5 months before until 1 month after birth.

Pharynx is the part of the neck and throat that is behind the mouth and nasal cavity.

Phenotype is an individual's physical appearance and constitution.

Phobia is a marked and persistent fear that is excessive or unreasonable, and set off by anticipating, seeing, or coming into contact with a particular object or situation.

Phonemes are letter-sound combinations. English has 44 phonemes: each letter has a sound, vowels have two sounds (short and long), and some letter combinations have their own sound.

Phonemic awareness is the child's understanding and conscious awareness that speech is composed of identifiable units, such as spoken words, syllables, and sounds.

Phonology is the study of phonemes and the rules for combining types of phonemes, pauses, and stress to form words.

Photoreceptors, or photoreceptor cells, are specialized types of neurons found in the retina of the eye that convert light into electrical signals.

Physical therapists are state-licensed health professionals, largely medically based, whose skills are directed toward preventing disability by developing, improving, or restoring more efficient muscular functioning and maintaining maximum motor functioning for a child.

Pincer grip is the ability to hold objects neatly between the thumb and index finger, which typically develops in infants between 12 and 15 months of age.

Placenta is formed out of the endometrium; it supplies the embryo with oxygen and nutrients and takes away wastes.

Platelets are cells circulating in the blood that are involved in the formation of blood clots.

Polyarticular JRA is a form of juvenile rheumatoid arthritis that involves five or more joints and is serious because of the number of joints involved, the seriousness of the involvement, and the length of time it lasts.

Pons, part of the brainstem, plays a role in relaying messages in the brain, controls arousal, and regulates respiration.

Posterior rhizomotomy is a surgical procedure that cuts motor fibers that cause the greatest spasticity in the legs. Spasticity is reduced, but there may be some degree of motor weakness.

Postterm is a pregnancy that lasts more than 42 weeks or more than 294 days after the first day of the last menstrual cycle.

Posttraumatic stress disorder is a disorder that results from exposure to an extreme traumatic stressor, such as actual or threatened death or serious injury; it usually involves feelings of intense fear, helplessness, or horror, and in young children this may result in disorganized or agitated behavior.

Poverty line is a governmentally determined dollar amount used to identify individuals and families who live in poverty.

Pragmatics is the personal and social use of language. It includes eye contact, turn taking in conversation, use of appropriate words in social conversation, taking the perspective of the listener, as well as understanding and appropriately using body language and expressions.

Praxis is the learned ability of the brain to conceive of, organize, and carry out a sequence of unfamiliar actions to attain a goal. Praxis has three components: ideation, motor planning, and execution.

Predictive validity is a type of validity concerned with the ability to predict the same or related characteristics in the future.

Preeclampsia is a condition that only occurs during pregnancy and is characterized by a rapidly progressive high blood pressure and protein in the urine.

Preterm is labor that begins before 37 weeks of pregnancy.

Prefixes are morphemes that come at the beginning of words.

Prelingually hearing impaired is when a hearing impairment occurs before children have established a language base.

Pressure-equalization tube is the Eustachian tube that links the pharynx to the middle ear. If the tube does not work well, fluid can collect in the middle ear.

Primary intervention site is the place where most early intervention takes place. It can be a school, home, early care and education center, or other location.

Private kinship care is an arrangement of caring for children by kin that occurs without the involvement of a child welfare agency.

Progesterone is a steroid hormone that helps prepare the female body for pregnancy and when pregnant to maintain the pregnancy.

Prone is lying face down on the stomach.

Prosthesis is an artificial extension that replaces a missing body part.

Prosthetic management training is the education individuals need to care for a prosthesis.

Proximal is close to the center or midline.

Proximodistal is a pattern of development that goes from the center of the body to the extremities with the trunk of the body developing before arms and the arms before hands and fingers.

Psychometric issues are concerns that relate to the design, administration, and interpretation of tests.

Punishment is a negative consequence that causes a behavior to occur with less frequency.

Pupil is the opening in the center of the iris of the eye through which light enters.

Pure-tone audiometer is an electroacoustical generator that produces pure tones at selected frequencies with an output that is calibrated to test hearing thresholds.

Pure-tone hearing screening is a basic test to find out if a hearing loss is present or not by using pure tones at different frequencies (typically 1000, 2000, and 4000 Hz).

Pure tones are particular sine waves used to identify hearing thresholds.

Pyramidal tract is a massive collection of long motor axons that go between the brain and the spinal column.

Q

Quadriplegia is an impairment that involves the motor control of all four limbs. Head control may be poor, and in cerebral palsy, there is usually impairment of speech and eye coordination.

R

Racial refers to the characteristics of a race.

Radiation is energy in the form of waves or particles.

Range of motion is the measurement of the achievable distance of movement between the flexed position and the extended position of a particular joint or muscle group; the range of motion of the elbow is a little less than 180 degrees.

Reading is the cognitive process of decoding written symbols to determine meaning.

Rebus is a representation of a word or phrase by pictures or symbols. Directions using a rebus menu are often used with prereading children.

Red blood cells are the most common type of blood cell and they deliver oxygen from the lungs to body tissues via the blood.

Referral is a formal process requiring parents to fill out specific forms requesting assessment by a team of professionals to determine whether a child's academic, behavioral, or physical development qualifies him for special education services.

Refracting is changing the direction of light waves using lenses.

Refractive errors, nearsightedness and farsightedness, are caused by the inability of the eye to focus light effectively.

Registration is the point at which an individual knows he has touched or smelled something; awareness.

Regulations are the codification of rules published in the Federal Register by federal departments and agencies.

Reinforcement is a consequence that causes a behavior to occur with greater frequency.

Reliability is the consistency of a measure, that is, the degree that scores are consistent, dependable, or repeatable. If a measure is reliable, the results should be the same or very close to the same each time it is given to the same individual.

Remarried families are families that occur upon the legal remarriage of a person who was divorced or widowed and who is actively involved with a biological or adopted child from a prior union.

Renal is an adjective that relates to the kidney and kidney functioning.

Repetitions are when an adult repeats all or part of a child's phrase, particularly when he has made an incorrect utterance.

Respite care is a system of care designed to give adult caregivers a break from caring for a child with a disability.

Response to instruction is the core educational programming for children or what is happening everyday to all children in a classroom with the expectation that 80 percent of the children are learning at the expected rate.

Response to intervention is more specific programming for children who are not learning at the expected rate and this intervention is a substantial change in programming for about 20 percent of children.

Reticular activating system is the name of the part of the brain (the reticular formation and its connections) believed to be the center of arousal and motivation in individuals.

Retina is a thin layer of neural cells that lines the back of the eyeball.

Retinopathy of prematurity is a disease of the eye that affects prematurely born infants. It may be caused by the disorganized growth of retinal blood vessels and can result in scarring and retinal detachment.

Rods, or rod cells, are cylindrically shaped photoreceptor cells in the retina of the eye that can function in less light than cone cells. Rods are responsible for night vision.

Role release is the process of transferring information and skills traditionally associated with one discipline (for example, occupational therapy) to team members of other disciplines (early childhood).

Root words are real words that can be made into new words by adding prefixes and suffixes.

Rotation is movement of an object in a circular motion such as the ability to twist or turn a part of the body such as the wrist.

Routines are events that must be completed on a regular basis and often involve the opportunity to practice adaptive skills and embed IEP/IFSP goals.

S

Sacrum is a large, triangular bone at the base of the spine. Its upper part connects with the last lumbar vertebra. It has five parts, with the bottom part connecting to the coccyx or tailbone.

Scaffolding is a dynamic system of learning as adults provide children with support that allows them to complete tasks they are interested in but could not do alone.

Schedules refer to who will do what and when they will do it in the classroom.

Sclera is the opaque fibrous, protective, outer layer of the eye.

Scoliosis is a condition that involves complex lateral and rotational curvature and deformity of the spine.

Scotoma is a type of visual loss where there is an area of impaired visual acuity (blind spots) surrounded by a field of normal vision.

Second stage of labor is the stage of labor that begins when the cervix is fully dilated and effaced, and ends with the birth of the infant.

Secondhand smoke is smoke breathed by a person in the environment who is not smoking; also called environmental tobacco smoke.

Seizures are abnormal electrical discharges in the brain. Symptoms depend on the part of the brain involved and may cause unusual sensations, uncontrollable muscle spasms, and loss of consciousness.

Self-talk is when a child talks to himself about what he is doing as a method of self-regulation.

Semantics is the psycholinguistic system that governs the relationship between words or phrases and their meanings—the intent and meaning of utterances.

Semicircular canals are three half-circular, interconnected tubes located inside each ear that help maintain balance (vestibular sense).

Sensorineural hearing loss is a type of hearing loss where the auditory nerve (cranial nerve VIII), the inner ear, or central processing centers of the brain malfunction are defective.

Sensory hearing loss is hearing loss due to poor hair cell function. The hair cells in the cochlear may be abnormal at birth, or damaged because of an illness such as bacterial meningitis.

Sensory integrative disorder is a disorder where the processes of receiving and processing sensory information accurately is dysfunctional.

Sepsis, sometimes referred to as blood poisoning, is a generalized systemic response to infection instead of a localized response at the site of the infection.

Serotonin is a neurotransmitter that may play a role in the regulation of anger, aggression, body temperature, mood, sleep, vomiting, sexuality, and appetite.

Service coordinator is a designated individual, who in addition to being part of the IFSP team, has the specific role of communicating with the family, setting up meetings, and coordinating information and events.

Shared reading involves an adult reading a book to one child or a small group of children without requiring extensive interactions from them.

Sight vocabulary is the number of words a child can read without sounding them out.

Simple tics are tics that are sudden brief, repetitive movements using a limited number of muscle groups such as eye blinking, shoulder shrugging, or throat clearing.

Small for gestational age is a designation used for infants whose weight is below the 10th percentile for their age.

Sociohistorical time looks at a particular event (birth of a child with a disability) in the context of what is happening in society and the world.

Social disorders, or anxiety disorders, are disorders related to attachment, separation, and social situations.

Social networks are systems consisting of individuals and the ties between the individuals within their social system.

Social phobia is a marked and persistent fear of situations that expose a child to strangers or when a child feels she might be embarrassed.

Solitary play is when a child is playing alone with materials that are different from other children's.

Somatic problems are problems that affect the body such as an illness.

Sound is vibrations made by an object or structure vibrating that causes the transmission of mechanical energy that moves through the air in waves and can be heard.

Spastic is when muscle tone is too high (tight) and children overreact to normal stimuli.

Spasticity is the inability of the muscles to relax; it does not mean paralysis.

Special education is specially planned instruction at no cost to the parents designed to meet the unique needs of a child with a disability.

Speech/language pathologists are state licensed specialists who have completed a degree program with an accredited college. They provide assessments and intervention for children with feeding and swallowing problems and communication delays and disorders.

Spina bifida occulta is a split in the vertebral arches of the spinal column. Individuals have no symptoms and may not even know they have the split.

Spinal atrophy is the progressive degeneration of the motor-nerve cells, resulting in slow weakening of the body's muscle strength.

Spinal cord is a thin, tubular bundle of nerves that is part of the central nervous system. It is enclosed in and protected by the bony vertebral column. It is divided into four major regions and has about 30 different segments or sections. It sends motor and sensory messages from the brain to other parts of the body.

Stages are qualitatively different periods of development.

Standards are a way of determining a common definition and application of a particular area of study.

Stapes is the stirrup-shaped small bone in the middle ear that attaches the incus to the oval window. It transmits sound vibrations from the incus to the membrane of the inner ear inside the oval window. It is the smallest and lightest bone in the human body.

Stepfamilies are families where one or both of the adults have a child from a previous union.

Sterilize is a surgical technique used to make a male or female unable to procreate.

Stereopsis is the sensation of depth based on the slight difference between retinal images from the eyes because of their horizontal separation on the face.

Stimulants are medications that increase the activity of the sympathetic nervous system or the central nervous system or both.

Strabismus is a condition where the eyes are not properly aligned with each other. It is caused by a lack of coordination between the muscles that prevents the gaze of each eye from coming to the same point in space and thus preventing proper binocular vision. It may affect depth perception.

Structured physical activity is planned and directed by an adult and is designed to accommodate the child's developmental level.

Subthreshold conditions are conditions that do not meet the full diagnostic criteria for a particular disorder.

Subdural hematomas are blood clots that form beneath the dura (brain covering) and are often part of a more generalized injury to the brain itself. They result from sheering forces applied to the veins (acceleration-deceleration forces) that displace the brain from the dura to rupture these membranes.

Substance disorder are disorders that are characterized by the inappropriate use of drugs, alcohol, or nicotine with or without dependence.

Successive approximation describes behavior that is not the target behavior but is reinforced because it is increasingly moving closer to the target behavior.

Suffixes are morphemes that come at the end of words.

Superior means up or above; the head is superior to the shoulders.

Supine is the condition of lying on the back with the face upward.

Synapses are very small gaps separating neurons. The synapse consists of a presynaptic ending that contains neurotransmitters and other cell materials, a postsynaptic ending that contains receptor sites for neurotransmitters and a synaptic cleft between the presynaptic and postsynaptic endings.

Synaptic cleft is the gap between neuron cell membranes.

Synaptic vesicles store the various neurotransmitters that are released at the presynaptic terminal into the synaptic cleft of a synapse.

System accountability is the requirement that not only children but systems must be assessed and evaluated for their service delivery.

Systemic JRA is a form of juvenile rheumatoid arthritis that begins with a high fever and has a spectrum of involvement and severity that is broad and difficult to predict at the onset of the disease.

Syntax is the set of linguistic rules that govern the arrangement of words into phrases or sentences, and the relationship between these elements in a sentence.

T

Technology dependence is dependence upon technology to provide life-supporting assistive therapies because of limitations in normal body functions, such as eating or breathing.

Tendons are tough, flexible, ropelike fibers that connect muscle to bone. They vary in size and shape, and glide smoothly over muscles as the body moves.

Teratogens are nongenetic, extraneous substances (e.g., drugs, nicotine, and alcohol) that can cause malformations in the developing fetus.

Third stage of labor is the expulsion of the placenta.

Thoracic vertebrae make up the middle segment of the vertebral column, between the cervical and lumbar vertebrae T-1 to T-12. They are intermediate in size with the upper vertebrae being much smaller than those in the lower part of the region

Thrombophilia is a blood clotting disorder in which the blood clots easily or excessively due to an abnormality in the system of coagulation.

Tonic-clonic seizures (formerly called grand mal seizures) are seizures that may begin as either a partial or generalized seizure. These seizures have two components: in the clonic state there is repetitive, rhythmic jerking of extremities, with slow and rapid components and in the tonic state there is sustained stiffening, perhaps jaw clenching.

Total communication is an approach to working with individuals with severe or profound hearing impairments that makes use of a number of different modes of communication such as signed, oral, auditory, written, and visual aids, depending on the particular needs and abilities of the child.

Total communication approach uses the auditory, visual, and tactile senses in combination to provide children with as much information as possible about a communication.

Tourette syndrome is an inherited neurologic disorder whose essential features include repetitive involuntary motor or vocal tics.

Toxomoplasmosis is a disease caused by the protozoan parasite *Toxoplasma gondii*. It is usually asymptomatic; however, in pregnant women it can have devastating consequences in immunodeficient and congenitally infected infants.

Trailing is a method of moving that young children who are visually impaired use to learn about their environment, by holding the back of their hand at waist level and gently maintaining contact with the walls and furniture as they walk.

Transcultural is the ability to adapt to more than one culture.

Transferring is moving (or being moved) from one piece of equipment to another or to the floor or other surface typically starting from a wheelchair.

Transitions are the times between events.

Translocation is the transfer of a portion of one chromosome to a different chromosome. (A portion of chromosome 21 may attach to chromosome 14).

Tunnel vision is the loss of peripheral vision with retention of central vision (20 degrees or less in the better eye; a typical eye has 105 degrees), resulting in a constricted circular tunnel-like field of vision.

Tympanogram is a graphic representation of the function of the tympanic membrane and ossicles of the middle ear obtained by tympanometry.

Tympanic membrane, or eardrum, is a thin membrane that separates the external ear from the middle ear and transmits sound from the air to the ossicles inside the middle ear.

Tympanometry is a testing process used to detect disorders of the middle ear.

Typically developing is development that is within the normal range.

U

Umbilical cord is the connecting cord between the developing embryo, or fetus and the placenta.

Unauthorized migrants are foreigners who either have illegally crossed an international political border or who have entered the country legally but then overstayed their visa.

Undocumented refers to individuals who do not have the legal documents to be in a country.

Undocumented immigrants are foreigners who either have illegally crossed an international political border or who have entered the country legally but then overstayed their visa.

Unoccupied play is when the child is not participating in an activity or watching other children.

Unstructured physical activity is child-initiated physical activity that occurs as the child explores the environment.

Uterus, or womb, is the major female reproductive organ. It is connected to the Fallopian tubes on both sides and the cervix which opens into the vagina.

V

Validity is whether a test measures what it claims to measure.

Vertebral arches, or neural arches, are the posterior projection from the body of a vertebra that encloses the vertebral foramen.

Visual acuity is the sharpness or clarity of the image viewed.

Visual closure is the ability to recognize an object from partial or limited stimulus; it focuses on perceiving part-whole relationships.

Visual cortex is the region of the cerebral cortex that occupies the entire surface of the occipital lobe and receives visual data.

Visual discrimination is the ability to perceive letters and words accurately by noting the likenesses and differences in their written form.

Visual memory is an aspect of memory that allows individuals to place a mental image where it can be retrieved through remembering the mental image of the original letter, word, animal, object, and so on.

Visual perception is the ability to interpret information from light reaching the eyes.

Visual tracking is the ability to focus the eyes on one point and then move them rhythmically from side to side, up and down, and diagonally.

Visually limited is a type of visual impairment where children are considered sighted children for educational purposes, but who are limited in their use of vision.

Vitreous humor is a clear gel that fills the space between the lens and the retina of the eyeball.

Voluntary kinship care is when a child welfare agency tells parent(s) it will seek a foster care placement for a child unless the child is placed with kin outside of their house.

Volunteers are people who work for free because they choose to do so.

W

White blood cells or leukocytes, are cells of the immune system defending the body against both infectious disease and foreign materials to protect against disease.

White matter consists of myelinated axons that connect gray matter areas to each other and carry nerve impulses. The axons are covered in a protective fatty coating of glial cells.

Word families are related words built by using a root word.

Z

Zone of proximal development (ZPD) is the gap between what a child can do independently and what he can do with adult scaffolding.

References

A status report on hunger and homelessness in American cities. (1998). The United States Conference of Mayors, Washington, DC.

Abrams, B., Altman S. L., & Pickett, K. E. (2000). Pregnancy weight gain: still controversial. American Journal of Clinical Nutrition, 71, 1233S–1241S.

Achenbach, T. M. (1992). Child Behavior Checklist/2-3 Years (CBICL/2-3). Burlington, VT: University of Vermont, Department of Psychiatry.

Achenbach, T. M. (1991). Manual for the Child Behavior Checklist/4-18. Burlington, VT: University of Vermont, Department of Psychiatry.

Ada, A. F. (1993). Mother-tongue, literacy as a bridge between home and school cultures: The power of two languages. New York: McGraw-Hill.

Ada, A. F. (2002). Biliteracy for personal growth and social participation. (Foreword). In B. Perez & M. E. Torres-Guzman (Eds.), Learning in two worlds: An integrated Spanish/English biliteracy approach (3rd ed., pp. viii–x). Boston: Allyn & Bacon.

ADA Amendments Act of 2008, Pub. L. No. 110-325, § 122 Stat. 3553.

Administration for Children and Families. (2003). U.S. census counts adopted children for the first time. Retrieved May 17, 2007, from http://cbexpress.acf.hhs.gov/articles.cfm?issue_id=2003-10&article_id=717.

Administration for Children and Families. (2006a). Early Head Start benefits children and families. Early Head Start Research and Evaluation Project: Author.

Administration for Children and Families (ACF). (2006b). Trends in foster care and adoption. Retrieved May 17, 2007, from http://www.acf.hhs.gov/programs/cb/stats_research/afcars/trends.htm.

Aicardi, J. (1998). The etiology of developmental delay. Seminars in Pediatric Neurology, 5, 15–20.

Ainsworth, M. D. (1963). The development of infant-mother interaction among the Ganda. In B. M. Foss (Ed.), Determinants of infant behavior (Vol. 2, pp. 67–102). London: Methuen.

Ainsworth, M. D. (1969). Object relations, dependency, and attachment: A theoretical review of the infant-mother relationship. Child Development, 40, 969–1025.

Akinbami, L. (2008). Asthma prevalence, health care use and mortality: United States, 2003-05, National Center for Educational Statistics. Retrieved September 20, 2008, from http://www.cdc.gov/nchs/products/pubs/pubd/hestats/ashtma03-05/asthma03-05.htm.

Alaskan Native Heritage Center. (2000). Information about Alaska Native cultures. Retrieved November 17, 2007, from http://www.alaskanative.net/2.asp.

Al-Chalabi, A., Turner, M. R., & Delamont, R. S. (2006). The brain: A beginner's guide. Oxford, England: One World.

Allen, M. C. (2002). Preterm outcomes research: A critical component of neonatal intensive care. Mental Retardation and Developmental Disabilities Research Reviews, 8, 221–232.

Amato, P. R. (2004). Divorce in social and historical context: Changing scientific perspectives on children and marital dissolution. In M. Coleman & L. H. Ganong, (Eds.), Handbook of contemporary families: Considering the past, contemplating the future (pp. 265–281). Thousand Oaks, CA: Sage.

American Academy of Family Physicians; American Academy of Otolaryngology—Head and Neck Surgery; and American Academy of Pediatrics Subcommittee on Otitis Media with Effusion. (2004). Otitis media with effusion. Pediatrics, 113(5), 1412–1429.

American Academy of Pediatrics. (1995). How to help your child with asthma: Guidelines for parents. Elk Grove Village, IL: Author.

American Academy on Pediatrics, Committee on Genetics. (1999). Folic acid for prevention of neural tube defects. Pediatrics, 104, 325–327.

American Association for the Advancement of Science. (1989). Science for all Americans: Project 2061 report on literacy goals in science, mathematics, and technology. Washington, DC: Author.

American Association on Intellectual and Developmental Disabilities AAIDD. (2008). Frequently asked questions on intellectual disability and the AAIDD definition. Retrieved November 15, 2008 from http://www.aamr.org/Policies/pdf/AAIDDFAQonID.pdf

American Association on Mental Deficiency. (1992). Mental retardation: Definition, classification, and systems of supports (9th ed.). Washington, DC: Author.

American Association on Mental Retardation. (2002). Mental retardation: Definition, classification, and systems of supports (10th ed.). Washington, DC: Author.

American College of Allergy, Asthma, and Immunology. (2008). Landmark "pediatric allergies in America" survey uncovered negative impact of allergy symptoms on children. Retrieved September 11, 2008, from http://www.acaai.org/public/linkpages/Pediatric_Allergies_America_031708.htm.

American College of Obstetricians and Gynecologists. (2001). Prenatal diagnosis of fetal chromosomal abnormalities. Washington, DC: American College of Obstetricians and Gynecologists, Bulletin No. 27.

American Diabetes Association. (2003). Position statement on care of children with diabetes in the school and day care setting. Retrieved September 3, 2007, from http://care.diabetesjournals.org/cgi/content/full/26/suppl_1/s131.

American Federation of Teachers. (2004). Early screening is at the heart of prevention. Retrieved July 30, 2007, from http://www.ldonline.org/aarticle/11336.

American Heart Association. (2007). *Congenital heart defects in children fact sheet*. Retrieved September 3, 2007, from http://www.americanheart.org/presenter.jhtml?identifier= 12012.

American Lung Association. (2006a). *Childhood asthma overview*. Retrieved September 1, 2007, from http://www.lungusa.org/site/ppasp?c=dvLUK9O0E&b=22782.

American Lung Association. (2006b). *Asthma and children fact sheet*. Retrieved September 1, 2007, from http://www.lungusa.org/site/ppasp?c=dvLUK9O0E&b=44352.

American Lung Association. (2006c). *Asthma medication for kids*. Retrieved September 2, 2007, from http://www.lungusa.org/site/ppasp?c=dvLUK9O0E&b=22883.

American Lung Association. (2006d). *Early warning signals*. Retrieved September 1, 2007, from http://www.lungusa.org/site/ppasp?c=dvLUK9O0E&b=22880.

American Lung Association. (2006e). *Back-to-school with asthma: The basics for parents*. Retrieved September 1, 2007, from http://www.lungusa.org/site/ppasp?c=dvLUK9O0E&b=2019829.

American Psychiatric Association. (1994). *Diagnostic and statistical manual of mental disorders (DSM-IV)* (4th ed.). Washington, DC: Author.

American Psychiatric Association. (2000). *Diagnostic and statistical manual of mental disorders: DSM-IV-TR* (text revision). Washington, DC: Author.

American Speech-Language-Hearing Association (ASHA) (1990). Guidelines for audiometric symbols. *ASHA, 32* (Suppl. 2), 25–30.

American Speech-Language-Hearing Association (ASHA) (1997–2007a). *What is language? What is speech?* Retrieved September 19, 2007, from http://www.asha.org/public/speech/development/LanguageSpeech.htm.

American Speech-Language-Hearing Association (ASHA) (1997–2007b). *Aphasia*. Retrieved December 24, 2007, from http://www.asha.org/public/speech/disorders/Aphasia.htm?print=1.

Americans with Disabilities Act of 1990, Pub. L. No. 101–336, § 2, 104 Stat. 328 (1991).

Anderson, P. M., & Butcher, K. F. (2006). Childhood obesity: Trends and potential causes. *The Future of Children, 16*(1), 19–45.

Anderson, V., Catroppa, C., Morse, S., Haritou, F., & Rosenfeld, T. (2000). Recovery of intellectual ability following TBI in childhood: Impact of injury severity and age at injury. *Pediatric Neurosurgery, 32*, 282–290.

Anderson, V., Catroppa, C., Morse, S., Haritou, F., & Rosenfeld, T. (2005). Functional plasticity or vulnerability after early brain injury? *Pediatrics, 116*(6), 1374–1382. Retrieved September 27, 2008, from http://pediatrics.aappublications.org/cgi/content/full/116/6/1374.

Andress, B. (1995). Transforming curriculum in music. In S. Bredekamp & T. Rosegrant (Eds.), *Reaching potentials: Transforming early childhood curriculum and assessment* (Vol. 2, pp. 99–108). Washington, DC: NAEYC.

Annie E. Casey Foundation. (2003). *Kids count data book: State profiles of child well-being*. Baltimore: Author.

Annie E. Casey Foundation. (2005). *Kids count data book: State profiles of child well-being*. Baltimore: Author.

Annie E. Casey Foundation. (2006). *Kids count data book: State profiles of child well-being*. Baltimore: Author. Retrieved December 2, 2007, from http://www.kidscount.org/sld/compare_results.jsp?i=191.

Annie E. Casey Foundation (2007). *Kids count data center: Children in immigrant families: Comparison by topic*. Retrieved April 4, 2008, from http://www.kidscount.org/datacenter/compare_results.jsp?i=750.

Annie E. Casey Foundation. (2007a). *Kids count data center: Children in poverty by state*. Retrieved April 4, 2008, from http://www.kidscount.org/datacenter/compare_results.jsp?i=190.

Annie E. Casey Foundation. (2007b). *Kids count data center: Children in poverty by race*. Retrieved April 4, 2008, from http://www.kidscount.org/datacenter/compare_results.jsp?i=191.

Anzalone, M. E. (1993). Sensory contributions to action: A sensory integrative approach. *Zero to Three, 14*(2), 17–20.

Aronen, E. T., & Arajarvi, T. (2004). Effects of early intervention on psychiatric symptoms of young adults in low-risk and high-risk families. In M. A. Feldman (Ed.), *Early intervention: The essential readings* (pp. 214–235). Malden, MA: Blackwell Publishing Ltd.

Asherson, P., Kuntsi, J., & Taylor, E. (2005). Unraveling the complexity of attention-deficit/hyperactivity disorder: A behavioural genomic approach. *British Journal of Psychiatry, 187*, 103–105.

Association for the Gifted. (2008). CEC-NAGC initial knowledge and skill standards for gifted and talented education. Retrieved September 26, 2008, from http://www.cectag.org/.

Asthma and Allergy Foundation of America. (2004). *Asthma*. Retrieved January 8, 2004, from http://www.aafa.org.

Asthma and Allergy Foundation of America. (2005). *Allergy Overview*. Retrieved December 29, 2007, from http://www.aafa.org.

Asthma: What is asthma? (1997). *Medical treatment*. Retrieved September 8, 2002, from http://www.thriveonline.com@IQ. . .th/asthma/seek/omfp.framewhat.html.

Atreya, C., Mohan, K., & Kulkarni, S. (2004). Rubella virus and birth defects: Molecular insights into the viral teratogenesis at the cellular level. *Birth Defects Research, 70*, 431–437.

Attwood, T. (2007). *The complete guide to Asperger's syndrome*. London: Jessica Kingsley Publishers.

Autism and Developmental Disabilities Monitoring Network; Surveillance Year 2002 Principal Investigators; Centers for Disease Control and Prevention. (2007). Prevalence of autism spectrum disorders – Autism and Developmental Disabilities Monitoring Network, 14 sites, United States, 2002. *Morbidity and Mortality Weekly Report Surveillance Summaries, 56*(1), 12–28.

Bailey, S. (2000). Culturally diverse gifted students. In M. J. Stopper (Ed.), *Meeting the social and emotional needs of gifted and talented children* (pp. 80–99). London: David Fulton.

Bandura, A. (1992). Social cognitive theory. In R. Vasta (Ed.), *Six theories of child development* (pp. 1–60). London: Jessica Kingsley Publishers.

Barkley, R. A. (1998). *Attention deficit hyperactivity disorder: A handbook for diagnosis and treatment* (2nd ed.). New York: Guilford.

Barnett, S. S., Hustedt, J. T., Friedman, A. H., Boyd, J., & Ainsworth, P. (2008). *The state of preschool 2007*. National Institute for Early Education Research (NIEER). Retrieved August 22, 2008, from http://nieer.org/yearbook/pdf/yearbook.pdf.

Barnett, W. S., & Yarosz, D. J. (2007). Who Goes to Preschool and Why Does it Matter? *Preschool Policy Matters*, Issue 15. New Brunswick, NJ: National Institute for Early Education Research.

Baron-Cohen, S., Allen, J., & Gillberg, C. (1992). Can autism be detected at 18 months? The needle, the haystack, and the CHAT. *British Journal of Psychiatry, 161*, 839–843.

Batshaw, M. L. (2007). Genetics and developmental disabilities. In M. L. Batshaw, L. Pellegrino & N. J. Rosen (Eds.), *Children with disabilities* (6th ed., pp. 3–21). Baltimore: Paul H. Brookes.

Batshaw, M. L., Shapiro, B., & Farber, M. L. Z. (2007). In M. L. Batshaw, L. Pellegrino & N. J. Rosen (Eds.), *Children with disabilities* (6th ed., pp. 245–261). Baltimore: Paul H. Brookes.

Bayley, N. (2005). *The Bayley scales of infant and toddler development, Third Edition (Bayley III)*. New York: Psychological Corporation.

Biemiller, A., & Slonim, N. (2001). Estimating root word vocabulary growth in normative and advantaged populations: Evidence for a common sequence of vocabulary acquisition. *Journal of Educational Psychology, 93*, 498–520.

Beker, L. T., Farber, A. F., & Yanni, C. C. (2002). Nutrition and children with disabilities. In M. L. Batshaw (Ed.), *Children with disabilities* (5th ed., pp. 141–164). Baltimore: Paul H. Brookes.

Bell, M. J. (2007). Infections and the fetus. In M. L. Batshaw, L. Pellegrino & N. J. Rosen (Eds.), *Children with disabilities* (6th ed., pp. 71–82). Baltimore: Paul H. Brookes.

Benokraitis, N. V. (2005). *Marriages and Families: Changes, choices, and constraints.* (5th ed.) Upper Saddle River, NJ: Pearson/Prentice Hall.

Berg, A. O., & U.S. Preventive Services Task Force. (2003). *Counseling to prevent tobacco use and tobacco-caused disease. Recommendation Statement.* Rockville, MD: Agency for Health Care Research and Quality.

Berger, E. H. (2004). *Parents as partners in education.* Columbus, OH: Pearson Merrill Prentice Hall.

Berk, L. E. (2002). *Infants, children, and adolescents* (4th ed.). Boston: Allyn & Bacon.

Berkson, G. (1993). *Children with handicaps: A review of behavioral research.* Hillsdale, NJ: Erlbaum.

Birch, L. L. (1980). Effects of peer models' food choices and eating behaviors on preschoolers' food preferences. *Child Development, 51*, 489–496.

Birch, L. L. (1996). Children's food acceptance patterns. *Nutrition Today, 31*(6), 234–241.

Birch, L. L., & Fisher, J. O. (1998). Development of eating behaviors among children and adolescents. *Pediatrics, 101*, 539–349.

Birch, E. E., & Stager, D. R. (1996). The critical period of surgical treatment of dense congenital unilateral cataract. *Investigative Ophthalmology and Visual Science, 37*, 1532–1538.

Blaska, J. (1993). The power of language: Speak and write using "person first." In M. Nagler (Ed.), *Perspectives on disability* (2nd ed., pp. 25–32). Palo Alto, CA: Health Market Research.

Blazer, B. (1999). Developing 504 classroom accommodation plans: A collaborative systematic parent-student-teacher approach. *Teaching Exceptional Children, 32, 2.*

Retrieved July 21, 2002, from http://www.ldonline.org/ld_indepth_teaching_techniques/504_plans.html.

Bloom, B. S. (1985). *Developing talent in young people.* New York: Ballantine Books.

Board of Education of the Hendrick Hudson Central School District v. Rowley, 453 U.S. 176 (1982).

Boone, R., & Higgins, K. (2007). The software check-list: Evaluating educational software for use by students with disabilities. *Technology in Action 3*(1), 1–16.

Bowlby, J. (1989). The role of attachment in personality development and psychopathology. In S. I. Greenspan & G. H. Pollock (Eds.), *The course of life: Vol. 1 Infancy* (pp. 229–270). Washington, DC: U.S. Government Printing Office.

Braggett, E. J. (1992). *Pathways for accelerated learners.* Melbourne, Australia: Hawker Brownlow Education.

Bredekamp, S., & Copple, C. (Eds.). (1997). *Developmentally appropriate practice in early childhood programs serving children from birth through age 8* (Rev. ed.). Washington, DC: NAEYC.

Bredekamp, S., & Rosegrant, T. (1995). Reaching potentials through transforming curriculum, assessment, and teaching. In S. Bredekamp & T. Rosegrant (Eds.), *Reaching potentials: Transforming early childhood curriculum and assessment* (Vol. 2, pp. 15–22). Washington, DC: NAEYC.

Bredekamp, S., & Rosegrant, T. (Eds.). (1992). *Reaching potentials: Appropriate curriculum and assessment for young children (Vol. 1).* Washington, DC: NAEYC.

Bretherton, I. (2005). In pursuit of the internal working model construct and its relevance to attachment relationships. In K. E. Grossmann, K. Grossmann, & E. Waters (Eds.), *Attachment from infancy to adulthood: The major longitudinal studies* (pp. 13–47). New York: The Guilford Press.

Briere, J. (1992). *Child abuse trauma: Theory and treatment of the lasting effects.* Newbury Park, CA: Sage.

Briggs, C. J., Reis, S. M., & Sullivan, E. E. (2008). A national view of promising programs and practices for culturally, linguistically, and ethnically diverse gifted and talented students. *Gifted Child Quarterly, 52*(2), 131–145.

Brinkmeyer, M., & Eyberg, S. M. (2003). Parent-child interaction therapy for oppositional children. In A. E. Kazdin & J. R. Weisz (Eds.), *Evidence-based psychotherapies for children and adolescents* (pp. 204–223). New York: Guilford.

Brown, P. M., Remine, M. D., Prescott, S. J., & Rickards, F. W. (2000). Social interactions of preschoolers with and without impaired hearing in integrated kindergarten. *Journal of Early Intervention, 23*, 200–211.

Brown, M. J., & Chattopadhyay, S. (2006). Lead, elevated blood lead level evidence-statement. In K. P. Campbell, A. Lanza, R. Dixon, S. Chattopadhyay, N. Molinari, & R. A. Finch (Eds.), *A purchaser's guide to clinical preventive services: Moving science into coverage* (pp. 165–169). Washington, DC: National Business Group on Health. Retrieved August 10, 2008, from http://www.businessgrouphealth.org/benefitstopics/topics/purchasers/part3.pdf.

Brown, J. E., & Satin, A. J. (2007). Having a baby: The birth process. In M. L. Batshaw, L. Pellegrino, & N. J. Roizen (Eds.) *Children with disabilities* (6th ed. pp. 35–45) Baltimore: Paul H. Brookes Publishing.

Brazelton Institute. (2005). *Understanding the baby's language*. Retrieved April 14, 2007, from http://www.brazelton-institute.com/intro.html.

Brazelton, T. B., & Nugent, J. K. (1995). *The neonatal behavioral assessment scale*. Cambridge, MA: Mac Keith Press.

Brown v. Board of Education, 347 U.S. 483 (1954).

Bulotsky-Shearer, R., Fantuzzo, J. F., & McDermott, P. A. (2008). An investigation of the situational dimensions of preschool emotional and behavioral adjustment: A study of problems within the classroom context. *Developmental Psychology, 44(1)*, 139–154.

Bumpass, L. L., & Lu, H. H. (2000). Trends in cohabitation and implications for children's family contexts in the United States. *Population Studies, 54*, 29–41.

Bumpass, L. L., & Raley, R. K. (1995). Redefining single-parent families: Cohabitating and changing family reality. *Demography, 32*, 97–109.

Burbacher, T. M., & Grant, K. S. (2006). Neurodevelopmental effects of alcohol. In P. W. Davidson, G. J. Meyers, & B. Weiss (Eds.), *International review of mental retardation research: Vol. 30. Neurotoxicology and developmental disabilities* (pp. 1–46). San Diego, CA: Elsevier Academic Press.

Burd, L. (n.d.a). *Drinking during pregnancy*. Retrieved August 10, 2008, from http://www.cjsids.com/art/DRNKGRPH.pdf.

Burd, L. (n.d.b). *Smoking during pregnancy*. Retrieved August 10, 2008, from http://www.cjsids.com/art/SMOKGRPH.pdf.

Burmeister, R., Hannay, H. J., Copeland, K. et al. (2005). Attention problems and executive function in children with spina bifida and hydrocephalus. *Child Neurology: A Journal on Normal and Abnormal Development in Childhood and Adolescence, 11*, 265–283.

Burns, E. (2004). *The special education consultant teacher: Enabling children with disabilities to be educated with nondisabled children to the maximum extent appropriate*. Springfield, IL: Charles C. Thomas.

Burns, E. (2006). IEP-2005: *Writing and implementing individualized education programs (IEPs)*. Springfield, IL: Charles C. Thomas.

Byrd-Bredbenner, C. (2002). Saturday morning children's television advertising: A longitudinal content analysis. *Family and Consumer Sciences Research Journal, 30(3)*, 382–403.

California Department of Education. (2006). *Braille mathematics standards*. Retrieved September 29, 2008, from http://www.cde.ca.gov/sp/se/sr/documents/braillemathstand.pdf.

California Department of Health Care Services. (2007). *Newborn screening program*. Retrieved December 30, 2007, from http://www.dhs.ca.gov/pcfh/gdb/htm/NBS/SCDParents.htm.

Campbell, K. P., Grosse, S., & Chattopadhyay, S. (2006). Prenatal diagnosis of chromosomal abnormalities and neural tube defects evidence-statement: Screening and testing. In K. P. Campbell, A. Lanza, R. Dixon, S. Chattopadhyay, N. Molinari & R. A. Finch (Eds.), *A purchaser's guide to clinical preventive services: Moving science into coverage* (pp. 284–290). Washington, DC: National Business Group on Health. Retrieved August 10, 2008, from http://www.businessgrouphealth.org/benefitstopics/topics/purchasers/part3.pdf.

Campbell, K. P., Rosenthal, A. C., & Chattopadhyay, S. (2006). Tobacco use treatment during pregnancy evidence-statement: Screening and counseling. In K. P. Campbell, A. Lanza, R. Dixon, S. Chattopadhyay, N. Molinari, & R. A. Finch (Eds.), *A purchaser's guide to clinical preventive services: Moving science into coverage* (pp. 305–310). Washington, DC: National Business Group on Health. Retrieved August 10, 2008, from http://www.businessgrouphealth.org/benefitstopics/topics/purchasers/part3.pdf.

Candlelighters: Childhood Cancer Foundation. (2007a). *Childhood cancer facts*. Retrieved September 2, 2007, from http://www.candlelighters.org.

Candlelighters: Childhood Cancer Foundation. (2007b). *Leukemias*. Retrieved September 2, 2007, from http://www.candlelighters.org/leuk.stm.

Capps, R., & Fix, M. E. (2007). *Undocumented immigrants: Myths and reality*. Retrieved December 1, 2007, from http://www.urban.org/publications/900898.html.

Capps, R., Fix, M. E., & Passel, J. S. (2002). *The dispersal of immigrants in the 1990s* (Policy Brief). Washington, DC: Urban Institute. Retrieved September 21, 2008, from http://www.urban.org/publications/410589.html.

Capps, R., Fix, M., Ost, J., Reardon-Anderson, J., & Passel, J. S. (2005). *The health and well-being of young children of immigrants*. Washington, DC: The Urban Institute. Retrieved October 27, 2008, from http://www.urban.org/UploadedPDF/311139_ChildrenImmigrants.pdf.

Capps, R., Fix, M. E., Murray, J., Ost, J., Passel, J. S., & Herwantoro, S. (2005). *The new demography of America's schools: Immigration and the No Child Left Behind Act*. Washington, DC: The Urban Institute. Retrieved September 21, 2008, from http://www.urban.org/UploadedPDF/311230_new_demography.pdf.

Carrera-Carrollo, L., & Smith, A. R. (2006). *7 steps to success in dual language immersion: A brief guide for teachers and administers*. Portsmouth, NH: Heinemann.

Carroll, B. A. (2000). Sickle cell disease. In P. L. Jackson & J. A. Vessey (Eds.), *Primary care of the child with a chronic condition* (3rd ed., pp. 808–836). St Louis, MO: Mosby, Inc.

Carter, B., & McGoldrick, M. (1999). *The expanded family life cycle: Individual, family, and social perspectives* (3rd ed.). Boston, MA: Allyn & Bacon.

Carey, S., & Bartlett, E. (1978). Acquiring a single new word. *Proceedings of the Stanford Child Language Conference, 15*, 17–29.

Carrasquillo, O., Lantigua, R. A., & Shea, S. (2000). Differences in functional status of Hispanic versus non-Hispanic white elders: Data from the medical expenditure panel survey. *Journal of Aging and Health, 12(3)*, 342–361.

CAST. (2007). *What is universal design for learning?* Retrieved December 6, 2007, from http://www.cast.org/research/udl/index.html.

Castellanos, F. X., Giedd, J. N., Berquin, P. C., et al. (2001). Quantitative brain magnetic resonance imaging in girls with ADHD. *Archives of General Psychiatry, 58*, 289–295.

Center on Addiction and Substance Abuse. (1996). *Substance abuse and the American woman*. New York: Columbia University.

Center for Civic Education. (1994). *National standards for civics and government*. Calabasas, CA: Author.

Center for Civic Education. (2007). *National standards for civics and government*. Retrieved August 1, 2008, from http://www.civiced.org/index.php?page=k4toc.

Centers for Disease Control and Prevention. (n.d.a). *Sickle cell disease: Health care professionals: Data and statistics.* Retrieved September 5, 2007, from http://www.cdc.gov/ncbddd/sicklecell/hcp_data.htm.

Centers for Disease Control and Prevention. (n.d.b). *Sickle cell disease: Facts about sickle cell disease.* Retrieved September 5, 2007, from http://www.cdc.gov/ncbddd/sicklecell/faq_sicklecell.htm.

Centers for Disease Control and Prevention. (1995). Economic costs of birth defects and cerebral palsy – United States, 1992. *Morbidity and Mortality Weekly Report, 44*(37): 649–694.

Centers for Disease Control and Prevention. (1996). *Universal precautions for prevention of transmission of HIV and other bloodborne infections.* Retrieved August 31, 2007, from http://www.cdc.gov/ncidod/dhqp/bp_universal_precautions.html#.

Centers for Disease Control and Prevention. (2003). *Overview of Hepatitis B in healthcare settings.* Retrieved September 3, 2007, from http://www.cdc.gov/ncidod/dhqp/bp_hepatitisb.html.

Centers for Disease Control and Prevention. (2005a). *Attention-Deficit/Hyperactivity Disorder.* Retrieved August 8, 2007, from http://www.cdc.gov/ncbddd/adhd/.

Centers for Disease Control and Prevention. (2005b). *Bleeding disorders.* Retrieved September 3, 2007, from http://www.cdc.gov/ncbddd/hbd/hemophelia.htm.

Centers for Disease Control and Prevention. (2005c). *Diabetes projects.* Retrieved September 3, 2007, from http://www.cdc.gov/diabetes/projects/cda2.htm.

Centers for Disease Control and Prevention. (2005d). *Intellectual disability.* Retrieved September 23, 2008, from http://www.cdc.gov/ncbddd/dd/mr3.htm.

Centers for Disease Control and Prevention. (2005e). *Preventing smoking during pregnancy.* Retrieved April 12, 2007, from http://www.cdc.gov/nccdphp/publications/factsheets/Prevention/smoking.htm.

Centers for Disease Control and Prevention. (2005f). *Thrombophilia/clotting disorders.* Retrieved September 3, 2007, from http://www.cdc.gov/ncbddd/hbd/clotting.htm.

Centers for Disease Control and Prevention. (2006a). *BMI – body mass index: About BMI for children and teens: Home.* Retrieved April 15, 2006, from http://www.cdc.gov/nccdphp/dnpa/obesity/.

Centers for Disease Control and Prevention. (2006b). *Chlamydia fact sheet.* Retrieved April 12, 2007, from http://www.cdc.gov/std/chlamydia/STDFact-Chlamydia.htm.

Centers for Disease Control and Prevention. (2006c). *Fetal alcohol spectrum disorders.* Retrieved August 23, 2007, from http://www.cdc.gov/ncbddd/fas/fasask.htm.

Centers for Disease Control and Prevention. (2006d). *Overview.* Retrieved September 8, 2007, from http://www.cdc.gov/ncipc/tbi/Overview.htm.

Centers for Disease Control and Prevention. (2006e). *Signs and symptoms.* Retrieved September 8, 2007, from http://www.cdc.gov/ncipc/tbi/Sings_and_Symptoms.htm.

Centers for Disease Control and Prevention. (2007a). *Fetal alcohol spectrum disorders.* Retrieved April 12, 2007, from http://www.cdc.gov/ncbddd/fas/default.htm.

Centers for Disease Control and Prevention. (2007b). *Hurricanes – special populations, Effects on pregnant women: Environmental exposures.* Retrieved April 12, 2007, from http://www.cdc.gov/ncbddd/hurricanes/environmental.htm.

Centers for Disease Control and Prevention. (2007c). *Epidemiology briefs: Childhood arthritis.* Retrieved September 3, 2007, from http://www.cdc.gov/arthritis/data_statistics/epi_briefs/childhood.htm.

Centers for Disease Control and Prevention. (2007d). *Malaria during pregnancy.* Retrieved April 12, 2007, from http://www.cdc.gov/malaria/pregnancy.htm.

Centers for Disease Control and Prevention. (2007e). *Newborns and group B strep.* Retrieved April 12, 2007, from http://www.cdc.gov/groupBstrep/general/gen_public_faq.htm.

Centers for Disease Control and Prevention. (2007f). *Overweight and obesity: Introduction.* Retrieved June 12, 2007, from http://www.cdc.gov/nccdphp/dnpa/obesity/index.htm.

Centers for Disease Control and Prevention. (2007g). *Pregnancy and childbirth.* Retrieved September 20, 2008, from http://www.cdc.gov/hiv/topics/perinatal/.

Centers for Disease Control and Prevention. (2007h). *Prevention.* Retrieved September 8, 2007, from http://www.cdc.gov/ncipc/tbi/Prevention.htm.

Centers for Disease Control and Prevention. (2007i). *Prevalence of overweight, infants and children less than 2 years of age: United States, 2003–2004.* Retrieved June 12, 2007, from http://www.cdc.gov/nccdphp/dnpa/obesity/childhood/prevalence.htm.

Centers for Disease Control and Prevention. (2007j). *Single gene disorders and disabilities.* Retrieved April 12, 2007, from http://www.cdc.gov/ncbddd/single_gene/default.htm.

Centers for Disease Control and Prevention. (2007k). *What is traumatic brain injury?* Retrieved September 8, 2007, from http://www.cdc.gov/ncipc/tbi/TBI.htm.

Centers for Disease Control and Prevention. (2007l). *You can prevent PCP in children.* Retrieved September 20, 2008, from http://www.cdc.gov/hiv/resources/brochures/pcp-kidz.htm.

Centers for Disease Control and Prevention. (2007m). *Pregnancy and childbirth.* Retrieved September 7, 2007, from http://www.cdc.gov/hiv/topics/perinatal/overview_partner.htm.

Centers for Disease Control and Prevention. (2008a). *Frequently asked questions: Hepatitis C.* Retrieved September 20, 2008, from http://www.cdc.gov/hepatitis/HCV/HCVfaq.htm.

Centers for Disease Control and Prevention. (2008b). *Hepatitis C.* Retrieved September 19, 2008, from http://www.cdc.gov/hepatitis/HCV.htm.

Centers for Disease Control and Prevention. (2008c). *Intellectual disabilities among children.* Retrieved September 23, 2008, from http://www.cdc.gov/ncbddd/dd/documents/IntellectualDisabilitiesFactSheet.pdf.

Centers for Disease Control and Prevention. (2008d). *Viral hepatitis.* Retrieved September 19, 2008, from http://www.cdc.gov/hepatitis/index.htm.

Centers for Disease Control and Prevention, Centers for Autism and Developmental Disabilities Research and Epidemiology (CADDRE). (2008). *Study to explore early development.* Retrieved September 23, 2008, from http://www.cdc.gov/ncbddd/autism/seed_faqs.htm#seed.

Chakrabarti, S., & Fombonne, E. (2001). Pervasive developmental disorders in preschool children. *Journal of the American Medical Association, 285*(24), 3092–3099.

Chakrabarti, S., & Fombonne, E. (2005). Pervasive developmental disorders in preschool children: Confirmation of high prevalence. *American Journal of Psychiatry, 162,* 1133–1141.

Chan, S., & Lee, E. (2004). Families with Asian roots. In E. W. Lynch & M. J. Hanson (Eds.), *Developing cross-cultural competence: A guide for working with children and their families* (3rd ed., pp. 219–298). Baltimore: Paul H. Brookes.

Chan, R. W., Raboy, B., & Patterson, C. J. (1998). Psychosocial adjustment among children conceived via donor insemination by lesbian and heterosexual mothers. *Child Development, 69,* 443–457.

Charlesworth, R., & Lind, K. K. (1999). *Math and science for young children* (3rd ed.). Albany, NY: Delmar Publishers.

Charlesworth, R., & Lind, K. K. (2003). *Math and science for young children* (4th ed.). Clifton Park, NY: Delmar Learning.

Chase, R. M., & Eyberg, S. M. (2008). Clinical presentation and treatment outcome for children with comorbid externalizing and internalizing symptoms. *Journal of Anxiety Disorders, 22,* 273–282.

Chess, S. (1983). Basic adaptations required for successful parenting. In V. Sasserath (Ed.), *Minimizing high-risk parenting* (pp. 5–11). Skillman, NJ: Johnson & Johnson.

Chess, S., & Thomas, A. (1977). Temperamental individuality from childhood to adolescence. *Journal of Child Psychiatry, 16,* 218–226.

Chess, S., & Thomas, A. (1990). The New York Longitudinal Study (NYLS): The young adult periods. *Canadian Journal of Psychiatry, 16,* 218–226.

Children with Diabetes. (2007). *Insulin pump therapy.* Retrieved September 3, 2007, from http://www.childrenwithdiabetes.com/pumps/.

Child and Adolescent Bipolar Foundation. (2002). *About pediatric bipolar disorder.* Retrieved December 20, 2007, from http://www.bpkids.org/site/PageServer?pagename=lrn_about.

Children's Defense Fund. (1975). *Washington research report.* Washington, DC: Author.

Children's Defense Fund. (2000). *The state of America's children yearbook.* Washington, DC: Author.

Children's Defense Fund. (2002). *The state of children in America's union. A 2002 action guide to leave no child behind.* Washington, DC: Author.

Children's Defense Fund. (2007). *Nine million uninsured children need a solution now.* Retrieved May 19, 2007, from http://www.childrensdefense.org/site/PageServer.

Cicchetti, D., & Lynch, M. (1993). Toward an ecological/transaction model of community violence and child maltreatment: Consequences for child development. In D. Reiss, J. E. Richters, & M. Radke-Yarrow (Eds.), *Children and violence* (pp. 96–118). New York: Guilford Press.

Chiriboga, C. A. (1996). Cocaine and the fetus: Methodological issues and neurological correlates. In R. J. Koukol & G. D. Olsen (Eds.), *Prenatal cocaine exposure* (pp. 1–21). Boca Raton, FL: CRC Press.

Chugani, H. T. (1998). Biological basis of emotions: Brain systems and brain development. *Pediatrics, 102(5),* Supplement, November, 1225–1229.

Clark, B. (1997). *Growing up gifted: Developing the potential of children at home and at school* (5th ed.). Upper Saddle River, NJ: Prentice Hall.

Clark, L. (2003). Making new choices possible: Understanding differences in infant feeding practices between Latina mothers and Anglo health care providers. *Zero to Three, 23(5),* 22–27.

Clements, D. (2002, November). *Content standards for early childhood education—from ideas to implementation.* Paper presented at the annual conference of the National Association for the Education of Young Children, New York.

Colangelo, N., Assouline, S. G., & Gross, M. U. M. (2004). *A nation deceived: How schools hold back America's brightest students.* Iowa City, IA: Belin-Blank Center.

Coleman, M. R., Buysse, V., & Neitzel, J. (2006). *Recognition and response: An early intervening system for young children at-risk for learning disabilities.* University of North Carolina: Frank Porter Graham Child Development Institute.

Colton, H. R., & Krause, J. E. (1997). Clinical implications of basic research: Pulmonary inflammation—a balancing act. *New England Journal of Medicine, 336(15),* 1094–1096.

Columba, L., & Dolgos, K. A. (1995). Portfolio assess in mathematics. *Reading Improvement, 32(3),* 174–176.

Combating Autism Act of 2006, Pub. L. No. 109–416, 120 Stat. 2821, 42 U.S.C. 201 note.

Committee on the Prevention of Reading Difficulties in Young Children. (1998). Predictors of success and failure in reading. In C. E. Stone, M. S. Burns & P. Griffin (Eds.), *Preventing Reading Difficulties in Young Children* (pp. 100–134). Washington, DC: National Academy Press.

Comstock, G., & Scharrer, E. (2003). Meta-analyzing the controversy over television violence and aggression. In D. A. Gentile (Ed.), *Media Violence and Children* (pp. 205–226). Westport, CT: Praeger Publishers.

Conners, C. K. (1997). *Conners' rating scales–revised.* North Tonawanda, NY: Multi-Health Systems.

Conners, C. K. (2000). *Conners' rating scales–revised.* Boston: Pearson Education Inc.

Connor, D. F. (2002). Preschool attention deficit hyperactivity disorder: A review of prevalence, diagnosis, neurobiology, and stimulant treatment. *Developmental and Behavioral Pediatrics, 23,* S1–S9.

Consentinode Cohen, C., Deterding, N., & Clewell, B. (2005). *Who's left behind? Immigrant children in high and low LEP schools.* Washington, DC: The Urban Institute. Retrieved September 10, 2008, from http://www.urban.org/UploadedPDF/411231_whos_left_behind.pdf.

Consortium of National Arts Education Associations. (1994). *National standards for arts education.* Reston, VA: Music Educators National Conference.

Copple, C., & Bredekamp, S. (Eds.). (2009). *Developmentally appropriate practice in early childhood program: Serving children from birth through age 8* (3rd ed.). Washington, DC: NAEYC.

Cote, S. M., Vaillancourt, T., LeBlanc, J. C., Nagin, S. S., & Tremblay, R. E. (2006). The development of physical aggression from toddlerhood to pre-adolescence: A nation wide longitudinal study of Canadian children. *Journal of Abnormal Child Psychology, 34(1),* 71–86.

Courchesne, E., Carper, R., & Aksoomoff, N. (2003). Evidence of brain overgrowth in the first year of life in autism. *Journal of the American Medical Association, 290*(3), 337–344.

Covington, C. Y., Nordstrom-Klee, B., Ager, J., Sokol, R., & Delaney-Black, V. (2002). Birth to age 7 growth of children prenatally exposed to drugs: A prospective cohort study. *Neurotoxicology and Teratology, 24*(4), 489–496.

Cratty, B. J. (1994). *Clumsy child syndromes: Descriptions, evaluation, and remediation.* Chur, Switzerland: Harwood Academic.

Crawford, J. (2002). *The Bilingual Education Act: 1968–2002.* Retrieved September 21, 2008, from http://ourworld.compuserve.com/homepages/jwcrawford/T7obit.htm.

Creasy, R. K., Resnik, R., & Iams, J. (2004). *Maternal-fetal medicine: Principles and practice* (5th ed.). Philadelphia: W.B. Saunders.

Crocker, A. D., & Orr, R. R. (1996). Social behaviors of children with visual impairments enrolled in preschool programs. *Exceptional Children, 62,* 451–462.

Crosbie-Burnett, M., & McClintic, K. M. (2000). Remarriage and recoupling. In P. C. McKenry & S. J. Price (Eds.), *Families and change: Coping with stressful events and transitions* (pp. 303–332). Thousand Oaks, CA: Sage.

Cumine, V., Leach, J., & Stevenson, G. (1998). *Asperger syndrome: A practical guide for teachers.* London: David Fulton.

Cunningham, F. G., Leveno, K. J., Boom, S. L., et al. (2005). *Williams obstetrics* (22nd ed.). New York: McGraw-Hill.

Cystic Fibrosis Foundation. (2007). *About cystic fibrosis.* Retrieved September 2, 2007, from http://www.cff.org/AboutCF/.

Daniels, S. R. (2006). The consequences of childhood overweight and obesity. *The Future of Children, 16*(1), 47–67.

Davidson, P. W., & Myers, G. J. (2007). Environmental toxins. In M. L. Batshaw, L. Pellegrino & N. J. Rosen (Eds.), *Children with disabilities* (6th ed., pp. 61–70). Baltimore: Paul H. Brookes.

Davis, S. (1997). *Child labor in agriculture.* ERIC Digest (Las Cruces, N.M.): EDO-RC-96-10.

DeBey, M., & Bombard, D. (2007). An approach to second-language learning and cultural understanding. *Young Children, 62*(2), 88–93.

Dedman, B. (2000, October 15–16). Secret Service findings overturn stereotypes. In *Chicago Sun-Times* Exclusive Report, Deadly lessons: School shooters tell why (pp. 8–12).

Deiner, P. L., Hardacre, L., & Dyck, L. (1999). *Educating children with diverse abilities, Birth through 12.* Toronto, Ontario: Harcourt Brace Canada.

Delaware Child and Adult Care Food Program (DCACFP). (In press). *Best practices for healthy eating: A guide to help children grow up healthy.*

Demonet, J. F., Taylor, M. J., & Chaix, Y. (2004). Developmental dyslexia. *The Lancet, 363,* 1451–1460.

Denckla, M. B. (2003). ADHD: Topic update. *Brain and development, 25*(6), 383–389.

Dennison, B. A., Erb, T. A., & Jenkins, P. L. (2002). Television viewing and television in bedroom associated with overweight risk among low-income preschool children. *Pediatrics, 109*(6), 1028–1035.

Department of Health and Human Services. (2007). *Children and secondhand smoke exposure: Excerpts from the health consequences of involuntary exposure to tobacco smoke.* Retrieved August 10, 2008, from http://www.surgeongeneral.gov/library/smokeexposure/report/fullreport.pdf.

Developmental Disabilities Task Force. (n.d.). *Inclusive education: A background paper for state legislators* (1–11). National Conference of State Legislatures.

DeWolfe, N. A., Byrne, J. M., & Bawden, H. N. (1999). Early clinical assessment of attention. *The Clinical Neuropsychologist, 13,* 458–473.

Diana v. State Board of Education of Monterey County, No. C-70-37 (N.D. Cal., Feb. 5, 1970).

Division for Early Childhood. (1996). *Inclusion.* Position Statement. Retrieved August 2, 2008, from http://ww.dec-sped.org/pdf/positionpapers/PositionStatement_Inclusion.pdf.

Division for Early Childhood, Council for Exceptional Children, National Association for the Education of Young Children, & Association of Teacher Educators. (1995). Personnel standards for early education and early intervention: Guidelines for licensure in early childhood special education. *Communicator, 21*(3), 1–16.

Dozier, M., Dozier, D., & Manni, M. (2002). Attachment and biobehavioral catch-up: The ABC's of helping foster infants cope with early adversity. *Zero to Three, 22*(5), 7–13.

Drews, C. D., Yeargin-Allsopp, M. Decoufle, P., et al. (1995). Variation in the influence of selected sociodemographic risk factors for mental retardation. *American Journal of Public Health, 85,* 329–334.

Duarte, G., & Rafanello, D. (2001). The migrant child: A special place in the field. *Young Children, 56*(2), 26–34.

Dumont-Mathew, T., & Fein, D. (2005). Screening for autism in young children: The Modified Checklist for Autism in Toddlers (M-CHAT) and other measures. *Mental Retardation and Developmental Disabilities Research Reviews, 11,* 253–262.

Dunst, C. J., Trivette, C. M., Masiello, T., Roper, N., & Robyak, A. (2006). Framework for developing evidence-based early literacy learning practices. *CELL Papers, 1*(1), 1–12. Retrieved August 23, 2008, from http://www.earlyliteracylearning.org/cellpapers/cellpapers_v1_n1.pdf.

Dunst, C. J., Trivette, C. M., & Hamby, D. W. (2007). Predictors of and interventions associated with later literacy accomplishments. *CELL Reviews, 1*(3), 1–12. Retrieved August 23, 2008, from http://earlyliteracylearning.org/cellreviews/cellreviews_v1_n3.pdf.

DuPaul, G. J., McGoey, K. E., Eckert, T. L., & Vanbrakle, J. (2001). Preschool children with attention-deficit/hyperactivity disorder: Impairments in behavior, social, and school functioning. *Journal of the American Academy of Child and Adolescent Psychiatry, 40,* 508–516.

Dyspraxia Support Group of N.Z. Inc. (2007a). *Developmental dyspraxia.* Retrieved September 6, 2007, from http://www.dyspraxia.org.nz/.

Dyspraxia Support Group of N.Z. Inc. (2007b). *What is developmental dyspraxia?* Retrieved September 6, 2007, from http://www.dyspraxia.org.nz/.

Early Connections-Preschool. (n.d.). *Learning and Technology.* Retrieved December 17, 2007, from http://www.netc.org/earlyconnections/preschool/technology.html.

Early Learning Accomplishment Profile, Third Edition (E-LAP). (2002). Kaplan Early Learning Company and Chapel Hill Training Outreach Project, Inc.

Education Act Amendments of 1978, Pub. L. No. 95–561, Title IX, Gifted and Talented Children's Act, 92 Stat. 2292, 20 U.S.C. § 2701.

Education for All Handicapped Children Act of 1975, Pub. L. No. 94–142, 89 Stat. 773–796, 20 U.S.C. § 1400.

Education for All Handicapped Children Act of 1983, Pub. L. No. 98–199, 97 Stat. 1357–1377, 20 U.S.C. § 1400.

Education for All Handicapped Children Act of 1986, Pub. L. No. 99–457, 100 Stat. 1145–1211, 20 U.S.C. § 1400.

Eicher, P. S. (2007). Feeding. In M. L. Batshaw, L. Pellegrino & N. J. Rosen (Eds.), *Children with disabilities* (6th ed., pp. 479–497). Baltimore: Paul H. Brookes.

Electronic Code of Federal Regulations. (2007). *Emotional Disturbance*. Retrieved August 25, 2008, from http://ecfr.gpoaccess.gov/cgi/t/text/text-idx?c=ecfr&tpl=%2Findex.tpl.

Epilepsy Foundation. (n.d.) *First aid*. Retrieved September 19, 2008, from http://www.epilepsyfoundation.org/about/firstaid/.

Eschbach, K. (1993). Changing identification among American Indians and Alaska Natives. *Demography, 30,* 635–652.

Escolar, D. M., Tosi, L. L., Rocha, A. C. T., & Kennedy, A. (2007). Muscles, bones, and nerves. In M. L. Batshaw, L. Pellegrino & N. J. Rosen (Eds.), *Children with disabilities* (6th ed., pp. 203–215). Baltimore: Paul H. Brookes.

Eshleman, J. R. (2000). *The family* (9th ed.). Needham Heights, MA: Allyn & Bacon.

Espy, K. A., Kaufman, P. M., & Glisky, M. L. (1999). Neuropsychological function in toddlers exposed to cocaine in utero: A preliminary study. *Developmental Neuropsychology, 15,* 447–460.

Fagerheim, T., Raeymaekers, P., Tonessen, F. E., Pedersen, M., Tranebjaerg, L., & Lubs, H. A. (1999). A new gene (DYX2) for dyslexia is located on chromosome 2. *Journal of Medical Genetics, 36*(9), 664–669.

Federal Interagency Forum on Child and Family Statistics. (2007). *America's Children: Key national indicators of well being, 2007*. Federal Interagency Forum on Child and Family Statistics, Washington, DC: U.S. Government Printing Office. Retrieved November 18, 2007, from http://www.childstats.gov/americaschildren/index.asp.

Federal Register. (January 24, 2007). *Poverty*. Vol. 72, No. 15, pp. 3147–3148. Retrieved May 14, 2007, from http://aspe.hhs.gov/poverty/07poverty.shtml.

Feldhusen, J. F., Van Winkle, L., & Ehle, D. A. (1996). Is it acceleration or simply inappropriate instruction for precocious youth? *Teaching Exceptional Children, 28*(3), 48–51.

Fields, J. (2003). *Children's living arrangements and characteristics: March 2002*. Current Population Reports, P20-547. U.S. Census Bureau, Washington, DC. Retrieved November 28, 2006, from http http://www.census.gov/prod/2003pubs/p20-547.pdf.

Fineberg, R. C. (2002). *Bilingual education: A reference handbook*. Santa Barbara, CA: ABC-CLIO, Inc.

Finkelhor, D. (1995). The victimization of children: A developmental perspective. *American Journal of Orthopsychiatry, 65*(2), 177–193.

Fisher, M. D. (1998). A sensibility approach to identifying and assessing young gifted children. In J. F. Smutny (Ed.), *The young gifted child: Potential and promise, an anthology* (pp. 52–61). Cresskill, NJ: Hampton Press.

Fix, M., Zimmermann, W., & Passel, J. S. (2001). *The integration of immigrant families in the United States*. Washington, DC: The Urban Institute. Retrieved July 30, 2008, from http://www.urban.org/url.cfm?ID=410227.

Fletcher, T. V., & Massalski, D. C. (2003). Poised on the threshold of a new paradigm for giftedness: Children from culturally and linguistically diverse backgrounds. In J. F. Smutny (Ed.), *Underserved gifted populations: Responding to their needs and abilities* (pp. 157–177). Cresskill, NJ: Hampton Press, Inc.

Flores, G., Abreu, M., & Tomany-Korman, C. (2005). Limited English proficiency, primary language at home, and disparities in children health care: How language barriers are measured matters. *Public Health Reports, 120*(4), 418–430.

Florida State University. (1996). *Teen pregnancy final report*. Tallahassee, FL: Author.

Florida State University Center for Prevention and Early Intervention Policy. (1997). *Florida's children: Their future is in our hands*. Tallahassee, FL: The Task Force for Prevention of Developmental Handicaps, Florida Developmental Disabilities Council.

Ford, L., & Dahinten, V. S. (2005). The use of intelligence tests in the assessment of preschool children. In Flanagan, D. P. & Harrison, P. L (Eds.), *Contemporary intellectual assessment: Theories, tests, and issues (2nd ed)*. (pp. 487–503). New York: Guildford Press.

Forrester, M. B., & Merz, R. D. (2000). Prenatal diagnosis and elective termination of neural tube defects in Hawaii, 1986–1997. *Fetal Diagnosis and Therapy, 15,* 146–151.

Forum on Child and Family Statistics. (2007). *Infant Mortality*. Retrieved August 11, 2008, from http://www.childstats.gov/americaschildren/health2.asp.

Fox, M. K., Pac, S., Devaney, B., & Jankowski, L. (2004). Feeding infants and toddlers study: What foods are infants and toddlers eating? *Journal of the American Dietetic Association, 104*(1), 22–30.

Frank Porter Graham Child Development Institute. (2005a). Who goes to pre-k and how are they doing? *Early Developments, 9*(1), 10–12.

Frank Porter Graham Child Development Institute. (2005b). How is quality measured? *Early Developments, 9*(1), 20–21.

Frank Porter Graham Child Development Institute. (2005c). How is the pre-k day spent? *Early Developments, 9*(1), 22–27.

Freeman, J. (1985). A pedagogy for the gifted. In J. Freeman (Ed.), *The psychology of gifted children: Perspectives on development and education* (pp. 1–22). Chichester, England: Wiley.

French, L. (1996). Language, listening, and literacy. *Young Children, 51*(2), 17–20.

Frick, P. J. (1998). *Conduct disorders and severe antisocial behavior*. New York: Plenum Press.

Fried, V., Prager, K., MacKay, A., et al. (2003). *Chartbook on the trends in the health of Americans*. Hyattsville, MD: National Center for Health Statistics.

Frost, L., & Bondy, A. (2002*). PECS: The picture exchange communication system* (2nd ed). Newark, DE: Pyramid Educational Consultants, Inc.

Fry, R. (2007). *How far behind in math and reading are English language learners?* Washington, DC: Pew Hispanic Center. Retrieved September 5, 2008, from http://pewhispanic.org/files/reports/76.pdf.

Fry, R. (2008). *The role of schools in the English language learner achievement gap.* Washington, DC: Pew Hispanic Center. Retrieved September 5, 2008, from http://pewhispanic.org/files/reports/89.pdf.

Gaitatzes, C., Chang, T., & Baumgart, S. (2007). The first weeks of life. In M. L. Batshaw, L. Pellegrino & N. J. Rosen (Eds.), *Children with disabilities* (6th ed., pp. 47–69). Baltimore: Paul H. Brookes.

Gammeltoft, L., & Nordenhof, M. S. (2007). *Autism, play and social interaction.* London: Jessica Kingsley Publishers.

Ganz, M. L., Xuan, Z., & Hunter, D. G. (2006). Prevalence and correlates of children's diagnosed eye and vision conditions. *Ophthalmology, 113*(12), 2298–2306.

Gardner, H. (1983). *Frames of mind: The theory of multiple intelligences.* New York: Basic Books.

Gardner, H. (1993). *The theory in practice.* New York: Basic Books.

Garnett, K. (1998). *Math learning disabilities.* Retrieved July 28, 2002, from http://www.ldonline.org/ld_indepth/math_skills/garnett.htm.

Gartrell, D. (2002). *The power of guidance and a guidance approach for the encouraging classroom* (3rd ed.) Albany, NY: Thomson Delmar Learning.

Gates, F., Badgett, L. M. V., Macomber, J. E., & Chambers, K. (2007). *Adoption and foster care by lesbian and gay parents in the United States.* The Urban Institute. Retrieved July 20, 2007, from http://www.urban.org/publications/411437.html.

Gearheart, B., Mullen, R. C., & Gearheart, C. (1993). *Exceptional individuals: An introduction.* Belmont, CA: Brooks/Cole.

Geary, D. C. (1999). *Mathematical disabilities: What we know and don't know.* Retrieved August 4, 2002, from http://www.ldonline.org/ld_indepth/math_skills/geary_math_dis.htm.

Geers, A. E. (2006). Spoken language in children with cochlear implants. In P. E. Spencer & M. Marschark (Eds.), *Advances in the spoken language development of deaf and hard-of-hearing children* (pp. 244–270). New York: Oxford University Press.

Gelbrich, J. A. (1998). Identifying the gifted infant. In J. F. Smutny (Ed.), *The young gifted child: Potential and promise, an anthology* (pp. 16–30). Cresskill, NJ: Hampton Press.

Genesse, F., Paradis, J., & Crago, M. B. (2004). *Dual language development and disorders: A handbook on bilingual and second language learning.* Baltimore: Paul H. Brookes.

Geography Education Standards Project. (1994). *Geography for life, national standards.* Washington, DC: National Geographic Research and Exploration.

George, D. R. (1997). *The challenge of the able child.* (2nd ed). London: David Fulton Publishers.

George, D. R. (2003). *Gifted education: Identification and provision* (2nd ed.) London: David Fulton Publishers.

Gersten, R., Jorden, N. C., & Flojo, J. R. (2005). Early identification and interventions for students with mathematics difficulties. *Journal of Learning Disabilities, 38,* 293–304.

Gersten, R., Baker, S. K., Shanahan, T., Linan-Thompson, S., Collins, P., & Scarcella, R. (2007). *Effective literacy and English language instruction for English learners in the elementary grades:* A practice guide (NCEE 2007–4011). Washington, DC: National Center for Education Evaluation and Regional Assistance, Institute of Education Sciences, U.S. Department of Education. Retrieved September 21, 2008, from http://ies.ed.gov/ncee/wwc/practiceguides.

Giardino, A. P., Turchi, R, M., Korth, A. E. (2007). Health care delivery systems and financing issues. In M. L. Batshaw, L. Pellegrino & N. J. Rosen (Eds.), *Children with disabilities* (6th ed., pp. 623–633). Baltimore: Paul H. Brookes.

Gillberg, C., Persson, E., Grufman, M., et al. (1986). Psychiatric disorders in mildly and severely mentally retarded urban children and adolescents: Epidemiological aspects. *British Journal of Psychiatry, 149,* 68–74.

Gilliam, W. S. (2005). *Prekindergarteners left behind: Expulsion rates in state prekindergarten systems.* New Haven, CT: Yale University Child Study Center. Retrieved July 21, 2008, from http://www.fcd-s.org/usr_doc/ExpulsionPolicyBrief.pdf.

Glanzman, M. M., & Blum, N. J. (2007). Attention Deficits and Hyperactivity. In M. L. Batshaw, L. Pellegrino & N. J. Rosen (Eds.), *Children with disabilities* (6th ed., pp. 345–365). Baltimore: Paul H. Brookes.

Goals 2000: Educate America Act of 1994, Pub. L. No. 103–227, 108 Stat. 125.

Golden, M., Marra, C., & Holmes, K. (2003). Update on syphilis. *Journal of the American Medical Association, 290,* 1510–1514.

Goldman, R., & Fristoe, M. (2000). *Goldman-Fristoe Test of Articulation* (2nd ed.). Circle Pines, MN: American Guidance Service.

Goleman, D. (1995). *Emotional intelligence: Why it can matter more than IQ.* New York: Bantam Books.

Gonzalez-Mena, J. (2005). *Diversity in early care and education: Honoring differences.* (4th ed.). Boston: McGraw Hill.

Gottfredson, L. S. (2003). The science and politics of intelligence in gifted education. In N. Colangelo & G. A. Davis (Eds.), *Handbook of gifted education* (3rd ed., pp. 24–40). Boston: Pearson Education, Inc.

Gottfried, A. W., Gottfried, A. E., Bathurst, K., & Guerin, D. W. (1994). *Gifted IQ: Early developmental aspects: The Fullerton longitudinal study.* New York: Plenum Press.

Graham, G., Holt-Hale, S. A., & Parker, M. (2005). *Children moving: A reflective approach to teaching physical education* (7th ed.). New York: McGraw Hill.

Green, R. (2004). The evolution of kinship care policy and practice. *The Future of Children, 14*(1), 131–194. Retrieved May 18, 2007, from http://thefutureofchildren.org/usr_doc/8-green.pdf.

Greenspan, S. I., & Wieder, S. (2006). *Infant and early childhood mental health: A comprehensive developmental approach to assessment and intervention.* Washington, DC: American Psychiatric Publishing, Inc.

Gregory, S., Bishop, J., & Sheldon, L. (1995). *Deaf young people and their families.* New York: Cambridge University Press.

Grisham-Brown, J., & Hemmeter, M. L. (1998). Writing IEP goals and objectives: Reflecting an activity-based approach for instruction for young children with disabilities. *Young Exceptional Children, 1*(3), 1–10.

Gronlund, G. (1998). Portfolios as an assessment tool: Is collection of work enough? *Young Children, 53*(3), 4–10.

Gross, M. U. M. (1993). *Exceptionally gifted children.* London: Routledge & Kegan Paul.

Grosse S. D., Matte, T. D., Schwartz, J., & Jackson, R. J. (2002). Economic gains resulting from the reduction in children's exposure to lead in the United States. *Environmental Health Perspectives, 110,* 563–569.

Groves, B. M., Lieberman, A. F., Osofsky, J. D., & Fenichel, E. (2000). Protecting young children in violent environments—A framework to build on. *Zero to Three, 20*(5), 9–13.

Guitar, B., & Conture, E. G. (2007). *Seven ways to help the child who stutters.* Retrieved May 4, 2007, from http://www.stutteringhelp.org/Default.aspx?tabid=38.

Guralnick, M. J., Connor, R. T., Hammond, J. M., Gottman, J. M., & Kinnish, K. (1996). The peer relations of preschool children with communication disorders. *Child Development, 67,* 471–489.

Guralnick, M. J. (2004). Effectiveness of early intervention for vulnerable children: A developmental perspective. In M. A. Feldman (Ed.), *Early intervention: The essential readings* (pp. 9–50). Malden, MA: Blackwell Publishing, Ltd.

Guralnick, M. J. (Ed.). (2005). *The developmental systems approach to early intervention.* Baltimore: Paul H. Brookes.

Haffner, W. H. J. (2007). Development before birth. In M. L. Batshaw, L. Pellegrino & N. J. Rosen (Eds.), *Children with disabilities* (6th ed., pp. 23–33). Baltimore: Paul H. Brookes.

Hagerman, R. J. (2007). Fragile X syndrome: A genetic model for autism with targeted treatments. Retrieved November 16, 2008 from http://www.iancommunity.org/cs/articles/fragile_x_syndrome_a_genetic_model_for_autism_with_targeted_treatments

Hain, T. C. (2007). *OEA Testing (otoacoustic emissions).* Retrieved January 4, 2008, from http://www.dizziness-and-balance.com/testing/OAE.htm.

Halgunseth, L. C. (2004). Continuing research on Latino families: El pasado y el futuro. In M. Coleman & L. H. Ganong (Eds.), *Handbook of contemporary families: Considering the past, contemplating the future* (pp. 333–351). Thousand Oaks, CA: Sage.

Hameed, B., Shyamanur, K., Kotecha, S., et al. (2004). Trends in the incidence of severe retinopathy of prematurity in a geographically defined population over a 10-year period. *Pediatrics, 113,* 1653–1657.

Han, M., Roskos, K., Christie, J., Mandzuk, S., & Vukelich, C. (2005). Learning words: Large group time as a vocabulary development opportunity. *Journal of Research in Childhood Education, 4*(19), 333–345.

Hanson, M. J. (2004). Families with Anglo-European roots. In E. W. Lynch & M. J. Hanson (Eds.), *Developing cross-cultural competence: A guide for working with children and their families* (3rd ed., pp. 81–108). Baltimore: Paul H. Brookes.

Harjo, S. S. (1993). The American Indian experience. In H. P. McAdoo (Ed.), *Family ethnicity: Strength in diversity* (pp. 199–207). Thousand Oaks, CA: Sage.

Hart-Shegos, E. (1999). *Homelessness and it effects on children: A report prepared for the family housing fund.* Hart-Shegos and Associates, Inc. Retrieved May 17, 2007, from http://fhfund.org/dnldreports/Supportive Children.pdf.

Hartocollis, A. "Nothing's Safe: Some Schools Ban Peanut Butter as Allergy Threat," *New York Times,* September 23, 1998.

Haskins, R., & Rouse, C. (2005). Closing the achievement gap. *The Future of Children,* (Policy Brief). Retrieved July 23, 2008, from http://www.brookings.edu/es/research/projects/wrb/publications/pb/20050301foc.pdf.

Hatton, D. D. (2001). Model registry of early childhood visual impaired collaborative group: First year results. *Journal of Blindness and Visual Impairments, 95,* 418–433.

Haugland, S. W. (2002). *Selecting developmentally appropriate software.* Retrieved December 29, 2002, from http://www.childrenandcomputers.com.

Hausman, M. S., & Reed, J. R. (1991). Psychological issues in relocation: Response to change. *Journal of Career Development, 17,* 247–258.

Hawley, C. A., Ward, A. B., Magnay, A. R., et al. (2004). Return to school after brain injury. *Archives of Disease in Childhood, 89*(2), 136–142.

Hebbeler, K., Smith, B., & Black, T. (1991). Federal early childhood special education policy: A model for the improvement of services for children with disabilities. *Exceptional Children, 58*(2), 104–112.

Hebbeler, K., Spiker, D., Bailey, D., Scarborough, A., Mallik, S., Simeonsson, R., et al. (2007). *Early intervention for infants and toddlers with disabilities and their families: Participants, services, and outcomes.* Retrieved December 14, 2007, from http://www.sri.com/neils/pdfs/NEILS_Report_02_07_Final2.pdf.

Hegde, M. N. (2001). *Introduction to communicative disorders* (2nd ed.). Austin, TX: Pro-Ed.

Heinzer, M. M. (2005). Obesity in infancy: Questions, more questions, and few answers. *Newborn and Infant Nursing Reviews, 5*(4), 194–202.

Hendricks, C., & Smith, C. J. (1995). Transforming health curriculum. In S. Bredekamp & T. Rosegrant (Eds.), *Reaching potentials: Transforming early childhood curriculum and assessment* (Vol. 2, pp. 65–79). Washington, DC: NAEYC.

Henry J. Kaiser Family Foundation. (2004). *The role of media in childhood obesity.* (Issue Brief). Menlo Park, CA: Author.

Hepburn, K. S. (2004). *Building culturally and linguistically competent services to support young children, their families, and school readiness.* Baltimore: Annie E. Casey Foundation. Retrieved March 15, 2008, from http://www.aef.org/upload/publicationfiles/ha3622h.

Herer, G. R., Knightly, C. A., & Steinberg, A. G. (2007). Hearing: Sounds and silences. In M. L. Batshaw, L. Pellegrino & N. J. Rosen (Eds.), *Children with disabilities* (6th ed., pp. 157–183). Baltimore: Paul H. Brookes.

Herer, G. R., Knightly, C. A., & Steinberg, A. G. (2002). Hearing: Sounds and silences. In M. L. Batshaw (Ed.), *Children with disabilities* (5th ed., pp. 193–227). Baltimore: Paul H. Brookes.

Hernandez, D. J. (2004). Demographic change and the life circumstances of immigrant families. *The Future of Children, 14*(2), 17–39.

Hernandez, D. J. (2006). Young Hispanic children in the U.S.: A demographic portrait based on Census 2000. *National Task Force on Early Childhood Education for Hispanics. New York: Foundation for Child Development.* Retrieved May 15, 2007, from http://www.ecehispanic.org/work/September_update_2006.doc.

Hetherington, E. M., & Kelly, J. (2002). *For better or worse.* New York: Norton.

Hill, J. B., & Haffner, W. H. J. (2002). Growth before birth. In M. L. Batshaw (Ed.), *Children with Disabilities.* (5th ed., pp. 243–262). Baltimore: Paul H. Brookes.

Holt, R. F., & Svirsky, M. A. (2008). An exploratory look at pediatric cochlear implantation: Is earliest always best? *Ear and Hearing 29*(4), 492–511.

Honig, A. S. (1993). Mental health for babies: What do theory and research teach us? *Young Children, 48*(3), 69–76.

Hoover, H. D., Dunbar, S. B., & Frisbe, D. A. (2007). *Iowa Tests of Basic Achievement.* Rolling Meadows, IL: Riverside Publishing.

Houk, F. A. (2005). *Supporting English language learners: A guide for teachers and administrators.* Portsmouth, NH: Heinemann.

Howard, P. J. (2000). *The owner's manual for the brain* (2nd ed.). Marietta, GA: Bard Press.

Howard, S., Shaughnessy, A., Sanger, D., & Hux, K. (1998). Let's talk! Facilitating language in early elementary classrooms. *Young Children, 53,*(3), 34–39.

Hoyert, D. L., Freedman, M. A., Strobino, D. M., et al. (2001). Annual summary of vital statistics: 2000. *Pediatrics, 108,* 1241–1255.

Hudson-Barr, D., Capper-Michel, B., Lambert, S. et al. (2002). Validation of the Pain Assessment in Neonates (PAIN) scale with the Neonatal Infant Pain Scale (NIPS). *Neonatal Network, 21,* 15–21.

Huestis, M. A., & Choo, R. E. (2002). Drug abuse's smallest victims: In utero drug exposure. *Forensic Science International, 128* (1–2), 20–30.

Hulit, L. M., & Howard, M. R. (2006). *Born to talk: An introduction to speech and language development* (4th ed.). Boston: Pearson Education, Inc.

Huncharek, M., Kupelnick, B., & Klassen, H. (2001). Paternal smoking during pregnancy and the risk of childhood brain tumors: Results of a meta-analysis. *In Vivo, 15*(6), 535–541.

Hundert, J., Mahoney, B., Mundy, F., & Vernon, M. L. (1998). A descriptive analysis of developmental and social gains of children with severe disabilities in segregated and inclusive preschools in southern Ontario. *Early Childhood Research Quarterly, 13,* 49–65.

Huppke, P., & Gartner, J. (2005). Molecular diagnosis of Rett syndrome. *Journal of Child Neurology, 20,* 732–736.

Hurst, D. S. (2007). *Middle ear disease and allergy: Why allergy?* Retrieved April 25, 2007, from http://www.ear-allergy.com/.

Hurst, D. S. (2008). Efficacy of allergy immunotherapy as a treatment for patients with chronic otitis media with effusion. *International Journal of Pediatric Otorhinolarngology, 72*(8), 1215–1223.

Hurth, J., Shaw, E., Iseman, S., Whaley, K., & Rogers, S. (1999). Areas of agreement about effective practices among programs serving very young children with autism spectrum disorders. *Infants and Young Children, 12*(2), 17–26.

Hyman, S. L., & Towbin, K. E. (2007). Autism Spectrum Disorders. In M. L. Batshaw, L. Pellegrino & N. J. Rosen (Eds.), *Children with disabilities* (6th ed., pp. 325–343). Baltimore: Paul H. Brookes.

Iglesias, A., & Quinn, R. (1997). Culture as a context for early intervention. In S. K. Thruman, J. R. Cornwell, & S. R. Gottwald (Eds.), *Contexts of early intervention: Systems and settings* (pp. 55–72). Baltimore: Paul H. Brookes.

Individuals with Disabilities Education Act of 1990, Pub. L. No. 101–476, 104 Stat. 1103, 20 U.S.C. § 1400.

Individuals with Disabilities Education Act of 1991, Pub. L. No. 102–119, 105 Stat. 587, 20 U.S.C. § 1400.

Individuals with Disabilities Education Act of 1997, Pub. L. No. 105–17, 111 Stat. 37–157, 20 U.S.C. § 1400.

Individuals with Disabilities Education Improvement Act of 2004, Pub. L. No. 108–446, 118 Stat 2647, 20 U.S.C. § 1400.

Inlow, J. K., & Restifo, L. L. (2004). Molecular and comparative genetics of mental retardation. *Genetics, 166,* 835–881.

Interactive Autism Network. (2007). Environmental aspects of autism. Retrieved December 26, 2007, from http://www.iancommunity.org/cs/understanding_research/environmental_aspects.

International Dyslexia Association. (2003). Dyslexia and related disorders. Retrieved August 3, 2007, from http://www.interdys.org/fact%20sheets/Dys&RelDis%20FS%20N.doc.

International Reading Association. (1998). *Phonics in the early reading program: A position statement.* Newark, DE: Author.

International Reading Association and the National Association for the Education of Young Children. (1998). *Learning to read and write: Developmentally appropriate practices for young children. Overview.* Retrieved August 1, 2008, from http://www.naeyc.org/about/positions/psread0.asp.

International Reading Association and the National Council of Teachers of English. (1996). *Standards of the English language arts.* Newark, DE: International Reading Association.

International Society for Technology in Education. (2007). *Educational technology standards for students.* Retrieved August 2, 2008, from http://www.iste.org/Content/NavigationMenu/NETS/ForStudents/2007Standards/NETS_for_Students_2007.htm.

Isaacs, J. S. (2007). Nutrition and children with disabilities. In M. L. Batshaw, L. Pellegrino & N. J. Rosen (Eds.), *Children with disabilities* (6th ed., pp. 125–136). Baltimore: Paul H. Brookes.

Ishii-Kuntz, M. (2004). Asian American families: Diverse history, contemporary trends and the future. In M. Coleman & L. H. Ganong, *Handbook of contemporary families: Considering the past, contemplating the future* (pp. 369–384). Thousand Oaks, CA: Sage.

Jacob K. Javits Gifted and Talented Students Education Act (1988) of the Elementary and Secondary Education Act Pub. L. No.100-297, 102 Stat 237, 20 U.S.C. §§ 3061 et. seq. 1988.

Jackson, N. R. (2003). Young gifted children. In N. Colangelo & G. A. Davis (Eds.), *Handbook of gifted education* (3rd ed., pp. 470–482). Boston: Pearson Education, Inc.

Jago, R., Baranowski, T., Baranowski, J. C., Thompson, D., & Greaves, K. A. (2005). BMI from 3-6 years of age is predicted by TV viewing and physical activity, not diet. *International Journal of Obesity, 29*(6), 557–564.

Jencks, C., & Phillips, M. (1998). The black-white test score gap: An introduction. In C. Jencks & M. Phillips (Eds.), *The black-white test score gap* (pp. 1–51). Washington, DC: Brookings Institution Press.

Jensen, E. (2006). *Enriching the brain: How to maximize every learner's potential.* San Francisco, CA: Jossey-Bass.

Jeppesen, J., Green, A., Steffensen, B. F., et al. (2003). The Duchenne muscular dystrophy populations in Denmark, 1977–2001: Prevalence, incidence and survival in relation to the introduction of ventilator use. *Neuromuscular Disorders, 13*(10), 804–812.

Joe, J. R., & Malach, R. S. (2004). Families with American Indian roots. In E. W. Lynch & J. Hanson (Eds.), *Developing cross-cultural competence: A guide for working with children and their families* (3rd ed., pp. 109–139). Baltimore, MD: Paul H. Brookes.

Johnson, C. P., & Meyers, S. M. and the Council on Children with Disabilities. (2007). Identification and evaluation of children with autism spectrum disorders. *Pediatrics* (October 29, 2007), 1–34.

Johnson, M. D., & Young, M. B. (2003). Advertising history of televisual media. In E. L. Palmer & B. M. Young (Eds.), *The faces of televisual media: Teaching, violence, selling to children* (2nd ed., pp. 265–285). Mahwah, NJ: Lawrence Erlbaum Associates.

Joint Committee on Infant Hearing. (1990). *Joint Committee on Infant Hearing Position Statement 1990.* Retrieved September 10, 2007, from http://www.jcih.org/JCIH1990.pdf.

Joint Committee on National Health Education Standards. (1995). *National health education standards: Achieving health literacy.* Atlanta, GA: American Cancer Society.

Jones, S. (1996). *Accommodations and modifications for students with handwriting problems and/or dysgraphia.* Retrieved July 28, 2002, from http://www.ldonline.org/ld_indepth/writing/dysgraphia.html.

Jordan, N. C., Hanich, L. B., & Kaplan, D. (2003). A longitudinal study of mathematical competencies in children with specific mathematical difficulties versus children with comorbid mathematics and reading difficulties. *Child Development, 74,* 834–850.

Jordan, N. C., Kaplan, D., Oláh, L. N., & Locuniak, M. N. (2006). Number sense growth in kindergarten: A longitudinal investigation of children at risk for mathematics difficulties. *Child Development, 77*(1), 153–175. Retrieved August 23, 2008, from http://www.udel.edu/cmp2/kindergartenpaper.pdf.

Jordan, N. C., Kaplan, D., Locuniak, M. N., & Ramineni, C. (2007). Predicting first-grade math achievement from developmental number sense trajectories. *Learning Disabilities Research and Practice, 22*(1), 36–46. Retrieved August 23, 2008, from http://www.udel.edu/cmp2/jordan_LDRP2007.pdf.

Jordan, N. C., Glutting, J., & Remineni, C. (2008). A number sense assessment tool for identifying children at risk for mathematical difficulties. In A. Dowker (Ed.), *Mathematical difficulties: Psychology and intervention* (pp. 45–58). San Diego, CA: Academic Press. Retrieved August 23, 2008, from http://www.udel.edu/cmp2/jordan_number%20sense.pdf.

Jovanovic, G., & Johnsen, M. (2006). Restraint and seclusion: Can they become obsolete practices? *Issue Brief: Center for Mental Health Services Research, University of Massachusetts Medical School, 3*(2).

Juvenile Diabetes Research Foundation International. (2003). *Paths to a cure.* Retrieved January 3, 2004, from http://www.jdrf.org/index.

Kandall, S. R., Doberczak, T. M., Jantunen, M., & Stein, J. (1999). The methadone-maintained pregnancy. *Clinics in Perinatology, 26*(1), 173–183.

Kanevsky, L. (1992). The learning game. In P. S. Klein & A. J. Tannenbaum (Eds.), *To be young and gifted* (pp. 204–244). Norwood, NJ: ABLEX.

Kanner, L. (1943). Autistic disturbances of affective contact. *Nervous Child, 2,* 217–250.

Kaplow, J. B., & Widom, C. S. (2007). Age of onset of child maltreatment predicts long-term mental health outcomes. *Journal of Abnormal Psychology, 116*(1), 176–187.

Kapperman, G., & Sticken, J. (2006). *Project Math Access.* Retrieved September 29, 2008, from http://s22318.tsbvi.edu/mathproject/.

Kawamoto, W. T., & Cheshire, T. C. (2004). A seven-generation approach to American Indian families. In M. Coleman & L. H. Ganong, *Handbook of contemporary families: Considering the past, contemplating the future* (pp. 385–393). Thousand Oaks, CA: Sage.

Kazdin, A. E. (1995). *Conduct disorders in childhood and adolescence* (2nd ed.). Mountain View, CA: Mayfield.

Khan, R. I., O'Keefe, M., Kenny, D., & Nolan, L. (2007). Changing patterns of childhood blindness. *Irish Medical Journal, 100*(5), 458–461.

Kea, C., & Campbell-Whatley, G. D., & Richards, H. V. (2006). *Becoming culturally responsive educators: Rethinking teacher education pedagogy.* Retrieved June 4, 2008, from http://www.nccrest.org/Briefs/Teacher_Ed_Brief.pdf?v_document_name=Teacher%20Ed%20Brief.

Keating, R., Spence, C. A., & Lynch, D. (2002). The brain and nervous system: Normal and abnormal development. In M. L. Batshaw (Ed.), *Children with disabilities* (5th ed., pp. 243–262). Baltimore: Paul H. Brookes.

Keity, B., Walsh, S., & Ziegler, D. (October, 2007). IDEA Essentials: What you need to know to know. Paper given at the Division for Exceptional Children Annual Conference, Niagara Falls, Ontario, Canada.

Kelly, A.E., Haddix, A.C., Scanlon, K.S., Helmick, C.G., & Mulinare, J. (1996). Cost-effectiveness of strategies to prevent neural tube defects. In M. R. Gold, J. E. Siegel, L. B. Russell & M. C. Weinstein (Eds.), *Cost-Effectiveness in Health and Medicine* (pp. 312–349). New York, Oxford: Oxford University Press.

Kendall, J. S., & Marazano, R. J. (1996). *Content knowledge: A compendium of standards and benchmarks for K–12 education.* Aurora, CO: McREL.

Kenneson, A., Van Naarden Braun, K., & Boyle, C. (2002). GJB2 (connexin 26) variants and nonsyndromic sensorineural hearing loss. *Genetics in Medicine, 4*(4), 258–274.

Kids Health. (2005). *Juvenile rheumatoid arthritis.* Retrieved September 3, 2007, from http://kidshealth.org/PageManager.jsp?dn=KidsHealth&lic=1&ps=107&cat_id=133&article.

Kids Health. (2006). *Seizures*. Retrieved September 19, 2008, from http://kidshealth.org/parent/firstaid_safe/emergencies/seizure.html.

Kids Health. (2008). *Down syndrome*. Retrieved September 25, 2008, from http://kidshealth.org/parent/medical/genetic/down_syndrome.html.

Kieckhefer, G., & Ratcliffe, M. (2000). Asthma. In P. L. Jackson & J. A. Vessey (Eds.), *Primary care of the child with a chronic condition* (3rd ed. pp. 164–190), St Louis, MO: Mosby, Inc.

Klesges, R. C. K., & Lisa, M. (1995). A longitudinal analysis of accelerated weight gain in preschool children. *Pediatrics, 95*(1), 126.

Klesges, L. M., Johnson, K. C., Ward, K. D., & Barnard, M. (2001). Smoking cessation in pregnant women. *Obstetrics Gynecology Clinics of North America, 28*(2), 269–282.

Klug, M. G., & Burd, L. (2003). Fetal alcohol syndrome prevention: Annual and cumulative cost savings. *Neurotoxicology and Teratology, 25*(6), 763–765.

Kindler, A. (2002). *Survey of the states' limited English proficient students and available educational programs and services: 2000–2001 summary report*. National Clearinghouse for English Language Acquisition and Language Instruction Educational Programs, Washington, DC: Office of English Language Acquisition, Language Enhancement and Academic Achievement for Limited English Proficient Students.

Kingore, B. (1998). Seeking advanced potentials: Developmentally appropriate procedures for identification. In J. F. Smutny (Ed.), *The young gifted child: Potential and promise, an anthology* (pp. 31–51). Cresskill, NJ: Hampton Press.

Knip, M. (2005). Etiopathogenetic aspects of type 1 diabetes. In F. Chiarelli, K. Dahl-Jorgensen & W. Kiess (Eds.), *Diabetes in childhood and adolescence* (pp. 1–27). Basel, Switzerland: Karger.

Kohl, H. W. III, & Hobbs, K. E. (1998). Development of physical activity behaviors among children and adolescents. *Pediatrics, 101*(3), 549–554.

Kohn, A. (2001). Fighting the tests: Turning frustration into action. *Young Children, 56*(2), 19–24.

Kopan, J., Liverman, C. T., & Kraak, V. I. (2005). *Preventing childhood obesity: Health in the balance*. Washington, DC: National Academics Press.

Koshy, V. (2002). *Teaching gifted children 4-7: A guide for teachers*. London: David Fulton Publishers.

Kotagal, P. (2000). Tonic-clonic seizures. In H. O. Luders & S. Noachtar (Eds.), *Epileptic seizures: Pathophysiology and clinical semiology* (pp. 425–432). New York: Churchill Livingstone.

Kreider, R. M. (2003). *Adopted children and stepchildren: 2000*. Census 2000 special reports. U.S. Census Bureau. Retrieved May 18, 2007, from http://www.census.gov/prod/2003pubs/censr-6.pdf.

Kronenberger, W. G., & Dunn, D. W. (2003). Learning disorders. *Neurological Clinics, 21*, 941–952.

Kranowitz, C. S. (1998). *The out-of-sync child: Recognizing and coping with sensory integration dysfunction*. New York: Skylight Press.

Kuhl, P., Coffey-Corina, S., Padden, D., & Dawson, G. (2005). Links between social and linguistic processing of speech in preschool children with autism: Behavioral and electrophysiological measures. *Developmental Science, 8*, 617–620.

Kuntsi, J., Rijsdijk, F., Ronald, A., Asherson, P., & Plomin, R. (2005). Genetic influences on the stability of attention-deficit/hyperactivity disorder symptoms from early to middle childhood. *Biological Psychiatry, 57*, 647–654.

Kurdek, L. A. (2004). Gay men and lesbians. In M. Coleman & L. H. Ganong (Eds.), *Handbook of contemporary families: Considering the past, contemplating the future* (pp. 97–115). Thousand Oaks, CA: Sage.

Kurtz, L. A. (2002). Rehabilitation: Physical therapy and occupational therapy. In M. L. Batshaw (Ed.), *Children with disabilities* (5th ed., pp. 647–657). Baltimore: Paul H. Brookes.

Laird, J. (2003). Lesbian and gay families. In F. Walsh (Ed.), *Normal family processes* (3rd ed., pp. 176–209). New York: Guilford Press.

Lally, J. R., & Mangione, P. (2006). The uniqueness of infancy demands a responsive approach to care. *Young Children, 61*(4) 14–20.

Lambie, R. (2000). *Family systems within educational contexts: Understanding at-risk and special-needs students* (2nd ed.). Denver, CO: Love.

Lamme, L. (1985). *Growing up writing*. Washington, DC: Acropolis Books.

Landrigan, P. J., Schechter, C. B., Lipton, J. M., Fahs, M. C., & Schwartz, J. (2002). Environmental pollutants and disease in American children: Estimates of morbidity, mortality, and costs for lead poisoning, asthma, cancer and developmental disabilities. *Environmental Health Perspectives, 110*(7), 721–728.

Learning Accomplishment Profile, Third Edition (LAP-3). (2004). Kaplan Early Learning Company and Chapel Hill Training Outreach Project, Inc.

Learning Disabilities Roundtable. (2002, July). *Specific learning disabilities: Finding common ground*. Division of Research to Practice, Office of Special Education Programs, U.S. Department of Education, Washington, DC.

Lee-Corbin, H., & Denicolo, P. (1998). *Able children in primary schools*. London: David Fulton.

Leet, A. I., Dormans, J. P., & Tosi, L. L. (2002). Muscles, bones, and nerves: The body's framework. In M. L. Batshaw (Ed.), *Children with disabilities* (5th ed., pp. 263–284). Baltimore: Paul H. Brookes.

Lemanek, K. L., & Hood, C. (1999). Asthma. In R. T. Brown (Ed.), *Cognitive aspects of chronic illness in children* (pp. 78–104). New York: Guilford.

Lengua, L. J., Wolchik, S., Sandler, I. N., & West, S. G. (2000). The additive and interactive effects of parenting and temperament in predicting problems of children of divorce. *Journal of Clinical Psychology, 29*, 232–244.

Lesinski-Schiedat, A., Illg, A., Hearmann, R., Bertram, B., & Lenarz, T. (2004). Paediatric cochlear implantation in the first and in the second year of life: A comparative study. *Cochlear Implants International, 5*(4), 146–159.

Lester, B. M. (2000). Prenatal cocaine exposure and child outcome: A model for the study of the infant at risk. *Israel Journal of Psychiatry and Related Sciences, 37*, 223–235.

Leukemia and Lymphoma Society. (2007). *Leukemia*. Retrieved September 2, 2007, from http://www.leukemia-lymphoma.org/all_page?item_id=7026.

Leung, D. Y. M. (2003). Epidemiology of allergic disease. In D. Y. M. Leung, H. A. Sampson, R. S. Geha, & S. J. Szefler (Eds.). *Pediatric allergy: Principles and practices* (pp. 1–7). St. Louis, MI: Mosby.

Lewin, L. (1999). Childhood social predictors of adolescent antisocial behavior: Gender differences in predictive accuracy and efficacy. *Journal of Abnormal Child Psychology, 27*(4), 212–230.

LD OnLine. (2007). *The ABCs of LD.* Retrieved July 30, 2007, from http://www.ldonline.org/article/5613.

Lim, S., & Simser, J. (2005). Auditory-verbal therapy for children with hearing impairment. *Annals Academy of Medicine Singapore, 34,* 307–312.

Linder, T. W. (2008a). *Transdisciplinary play-based assessment* (2nd. ed.) Baltimore: Paul H. Brookes Publishing Co.

Linder, T. W. (2008b). *Transdisciplinary play-based intervention* (2nd. ed.) Baltimore: Paul H. Brookes Publishing Co.

Lipsky, D. K., & Gartner, A. (1997). *Inclusion and school reform: Transforming America's classrooms.* Baltimore: Paul H. Brookes.

Liptak, G. S. (2002). Neural tube defects. In M. L. Batshaw (Ed.), *Children with disabilities* (5th ed., pp. 467–492). Baltimore: Paul H. Brookes.

Liptak, G. S. (2007). Neural tube defects. In M. L. Batshaw, L. Pellegrino & N. J. Rosen (Eds.), *Children with disabilities* (6th ed., pp. 419–438). Baltimore: Paul H. Brookes.

Loesch, D. Z., Huggins, R. M., Bui, Q. M., et al. (2002). Effect of the deficits of fragile X mental retardation protein on cognitive status of fragile X males and females assessed by robust pedigree analysis. *Journal of Developmental and Behavioral Pediatrics, 23*(6), 416–424.

Lopez, E. C. (2000). Identifying gifted and creative linguistically and culturally diverse children. In G. B. Esquivel & J. C. Houtz (Eds.), *Creativity and giftedness in culturally diverse students* (pp. 125–148). Cresskill, NJ: Hampton Press.

Lord, C., Risi, S., Lambrecht, L., et al. (2000). The autism diagnostic observation schedule-generic: A standard measure of social and communication deficits associated with the spectrum of autism. *Journal of Autism and Developmental Disorders, 30,* 205–223.

Lord, C., Rutter, M., Goode, S., Heemsbergen, J., Jordan, H., & Mawhood, L. (1989) Autism diagnostic observational schedule: A standardized observation of communicative and social behavior. *Journal of Autism and Developmental Disorders, 24,* 659–685.

Lord, C., Rutter, M., & Le Couteur, A. (1994). Autism diagnostic interview-revised: A revised version of a diagnostic interview for caregivers of individuals with possible pervasive developmental disorders. *Journal of Autism and Developmental Disorders, 19,* 185–212.

Lovaas, O. I. (1987). Behavioral treatment and normal intellectual and educational functioning in autistic children. *Journal of Consulting and Clinical Psychology, 55,* 3–9.

Lowdermilk, D. L., & Perry, S. E. (2003). *Maternity Nursing* (6th ed.). St. Louis, MO: Mosby.

Lutz, M. N., Fantuzzo, J., & McDermott, P. (2002). Multidimensional assessment of emotional and behavioral adjustment problems of low-income preschool children: Development and initial validation. *Early Childhood Research Quarterly, 17*(3), 338–355.

Lynch, E. W. (2004a). Conceptual framework. In E. W. Lynch & M. J. Hanson (Eds.), *Developing cross-cultural competence: A guide for working with children and their families* (3rd ed., pp. 19–39). Baltimore: Paul H. Brookes Publishing Co.

Lynch, E. W. (2004b). Developing cross-cultural competence. In E. W. Lynch & M. J. Hanson (Eds.) *Developing cross-cultural competence: A guide for working with children and their families* (3rd ed. pp. 41–80). Baltimore: Paul H. Brookes Publishing Co.

Lynch, E. W., & Hanson, M. J. (Eds.) (2004). *Developing cross-cultural competence: A guide for working with children and their families* (3rd ed.). Baltimore: Paul H. Brookes Publishing Co.

Lyons-Ruth, K. (1996). Attachment relationships among children with aggressive behavior problems: The role of disorganized attachment patterns. *Journal of Consulting and Clinical Psychology, 64,* 64–73.

Macfie, J., Cicchetti, D., & Toth, S. L. (2001). Dissociation in maltreated versus nonmaltreated preschool-aged children. *Child Abuse and Neglect, 25*(9), 1253–1267.

Mandlazwitz, M. (2007). *What every teacher should know about IDEA 2004 laws and regulations.* Boston, MA: Pearson Education, Inc.

Mannino, D. M., Homa, D. M., Pertowski, C. A., Ashizawa, A., Nixon, L. L., Johnson, C. A., et al. (1998). *Surveillance for asthma—United States, 1960–1995.* Retrieved December 29, 2007, from http://www.medscape.com/medline/9580746?src=emed_ckb_ref_0.

Marini, Z., Fairbairn, L., & Zuber, R. (2001). Peer harassment in individuals with developmental disabilities: Towards the development of a multidimensional bullying identification model. *Developmental Disabilities Bulletin, 29,* 170–195.

Marion, M. (2002, November 20). *Good decision making: Your key to helping children with challenging behaviors.* Paper presented at the National Association for the Education of Young Children annual conference, New York.

Marks, J. S., Koplan, J. P., Hogue, C. J. R., & Dalmat, M.E. (1990). A cost-benefit/cost-effectiveness analysis of smoking cessation for pregnant women. *American Journal of Preventive Medicine 5,* 282–291.

Marshak, L. E., & Prezant, F. (2007). *Married with special needs children: A couple's guide to keeping connected.* Bethesda, MD: Woodbine House.

Marschark, M. (1997). *Raising and educating a deaf child.* New York: Oxford University Press.

Marschilok, C. (2004). *Update on insulin pump therapy.* Retrieved September 3, 2007, from http://indep.nih.gov/diabetes/pubs/snn_March_2004.pdf.

Martin, J. A., Kochanek, K. D., Strobino, D. M., Guyer, B., & MacDorman, M. F. (2005). Annual Summary of Vital Statistics—2003. *Pediatrics, 115,* 619–634.

Martin, M. T., Emery, R. E., & Peris, T. S. (2004). Single-parent families: Risks, resilience, and change. In M. Coleman & L. H. Ganong, *Handbook of contemporary families: Considering the past, contemplating the future* (pp. 282–301). Thousand Oaks, CA: Sage.

Mason, E., & Lee, R. V. (1995). Drug abuse. In W. M. Barron & M. D. Lindheimer (Eds.), *Medical disorders during pregnancy* (2nd ed., pp. 465–486). St. Louis, MO: Mosby.

Matson, J. L., & Minshawi, N. F. (2006). *Early intervention for autism spectrum disorders: A critical analysis.* Oxford, England: Elsevier Ltd.

Matthews, H., & Ewen, D. (2006). *Reaching all children? Understanding early care and education participation among immigrant families*. Center for Law and Social Policy. Retrieved September 21, 2008, from http://www.clasp.org/publications/child_care_immigrant.pdf.

Mayesky, M. (2002). *Creative activities for young children* (7th ed.). Clifton Park, NY: Delmar/Thomson Learning.

McDowell, J. (2004). *The nervous system and sense organs*. Westport, CT: Greenwood Press.

McGoldrick, M. (1993). Ethnicity, cultural diversity, and normality. In F. Walsh (Ed.), *Normal family processes* (2nd ed., pp. 331–360). New York: Guilford Press.

McKusick, V. A., et al. (2005). *Online Mendelian Inheritance in Man*. Retrieved August 26, 2007, from http://www.ncbi.nlm.nih.gov/sites/entrez?db=OMIM.

McPherson, M., Arango, P., & Fox H. B. (1998). A new definition of children with special health care needs. *Pediatrics 102*, 137–140.

Medline Plus. (2007a). *Medical encyclopedia: Allergic reactions*. Retrieved September 1, 2007, from http://www.nlm.nih.gov/medlineplus/ency/article/000005.htm.

Medline Plus. (2007b). *Medical encyclopedia: Cystic Fibrosis*. Retrieved September 2, 2007, from http://www.nlm.nih.gov/medlineplus/ency/article/000107.htm#Definition.

Medline Plus. (2007c). *Medical Encyclopedia: Hypoglycemia*. Retrieved September 3, 2007, from http://www.nlm.nih.gov/medlineplus/ency/article/000386.htm.

Meisels, S. J., & Atkins-Burnett, S. (2000). The elements of early childhood assessment. In J. P. Shonkoff & S. J. Meisels (Eds.), *Handbook of early childhood intervention* (2nd ed., pp. 231–257). Cambridge, England: Cambridge University Press.

Meisels, S. J., & Shonkoff, J. P. (2000). Early childhood intervention: A continuing evolution. In J. P. Shonkoff & S. J. Meisels (Eds.), *Handbook of early childhood intervention* (2nd ed., pp. 3–34). Cambridge, England: Cambridge University Press.

Mendola, P., Selevan, S. G., Gutter, S., et al. (2002). Environmental factors associated with a spectrum of neurodevelopmental deficits. *Mental Retardation and Developmental Disabilities Research Reviews, 8*(3), 188–197.

Mennella, J. A., Ziegler, P., Briefel, R., & Novak, T. (2006). Feeding infants and toddlers study: The types of foods fed to Hispanic infants and toddlers. *Journal of the American Dietetic Association, 106*(Suppl. 1), s96–s106.

Mesibov, G. B., Shea, V., & Schopler, E. (2005). *The TEACCH approach to autism spectrum disorders*. New York: Kluwer Academic/Plenum Publishers.

Meyer, G. A. (2007). X-linked syndromes causing intellectual disability. In M. L. Batshaw, L. Pellegrino & N. J. Rosen (Eds.), *Children with disabilities* (6th ed., pp. 275–283). Baltimore: Paul H. Brookes.

Miller, L. C., & Hendrie, N. W. (2000). Health of children adopted from China. *Pediatrics, 105*(6), E76.

Michaud, L. J., Duhaime, A. C., Wade, S. L., Rabin, J. P., Jones, D. O., & Lazar, M. F. (2007). Traumatic brain injury. In M. L. Batshaw, L. Pellegrino & N. J. Rosen (Eds.), *Children with disabilities* (6th ed., pp. 461–476). Baltimore: Paul H. Brookes.

Michaud, L. J., Semel-Concepcion, J., Duhaime, A. C., & Lazar, M. F. (2002). Traumatic Brain Injury. In M. L. Batshaw (Ed.), *Children with disabilities* (5th ed., pp. 525–545). Baltimore: Paul H. Brookes.

Miller, F., & Bachrach, S. J. (1995). *Cerebral palsy: A complete guide for caregiving*. Baltimore: Johns Hopkins University Press.

Miller, L. C., Chan, W., Comfort, K., & Tirella, L. (2005). Health of children adopted from Guatemala: Comparison of orphanage and foster care. *Pediatrics, 115*(6): e710–e717.

Miller, M. M., & Menacker, S. J. (2007). Vision: Our window on the world. In M. L. Batshaw, L. Pellegrino & N. J. Rosen (Eds.), *Children with disabilities* (6th ed., pp. 137–155). Baltimore: Paul H. Brookes.

Miller, M. M., Menacker, S. J., & Batshaw, M. L. (2002). Vision: Our window to the world. In M. L. Batshaw (Ed.), *Children with disabilities* (5th ed., pp. 165–192). Baltimore: Paul H. Brookes.

Miller, P. S., & Stayton, V. D. (2005) DEC recommended practices: Personnel preparation. In S. Sandall, M. L. Hemmeter, B. J. Smith, & M. E. McLean (Eds.), *DEC recommended practices: A comprehensive guide for practical application in early intervention/early childhood special education.* (pp. 189–208). Missoula, MT: Division for Early Childhood.

Miller, S., Nunnally, E. W., & Wackman, D. B. (1975). *Alive and aware: How to improve your relationships through better communications*. Minneapolis, MN: Interpersonal Communications Programs.

Minshew, N. J., Sweeney, J. A., Bauman, M. L., & Webb, S. J. (2005). Neurologic aspects of autism. In F. Volkmar et al. (Eds.), *Handbook of Autism and Pervasive Developmental Disorders* (pp. 473–514). Hoboken, NJ: John Wiley and Sons.

Moffitt, T. E. (1993). The neuropsychology of conduct disorder. *Development and Psychopathology, 5*, 135–151.

Mokuau, N., & Tauili'ili, P. (2004). Families with Native Hawaiian and Samoan roots. In E. W. Lynch & M. J. Hanson (Eds.), *Developing cross-cultural competence: A guide for working with children and their families* (3rd ed., pp. 345–372). Baltimore: Paul H. Brookes.

Montoya, J., & Liesenfeld, O. (2004). Toxoplasmosis. *The Lancet, 363*, 1965–1976.

Moon, S. M. (2003). Counseling families. In N. Colangeol & G. A. Davis (Eds.), *Handbook of Gifted Education* (3rd ed., pp. 388–402). Boston: Pearson Education, Inc.

Moore, L. L., Nguyen, U.S. D. T., Rothman, K. J., Cupples, L. A., & Ellison, R. C. (1995). Preschool physical activity level and change in body fatness in young children: The Framingham children's study. *American Journal of Epidemiology, 142*(9), 982–988.

Moore, M. L. (2003). Preterm labor and birth: What have we learned in the past two decades? *Journal of Obstetric, Gynecologic, and Neonatal Nursing, 32*(5), 638–649.

Morey, A., & Kitano, M. K. (1997). *Multicultural course transformation in higher education: A broader truth*. Needham Heights, MA: Allyn and Bacon.

Msall, M. E., & Tremont, M. R. (2002). Measuring functional outcomes after prematurity: Developmental impact of very low birth weight and extremely low birth weight status on childhood disability. *Mental Retardation and Developmental Disabilities Research Reviews, 8*, 258–272.

Muhle, R., Trentatcoste, S. V., & Rapin, I. (2004). The genetics of autism. *Pediatrics, 113*(5), e472–e486.

Mundy, P., & Burnette, C. (2005). Joint attention and neurodevelopmental models of autism. In F. Volkmar et al. (Eds.), *Handbook of Autism and Pervasive Developmental Disorders* (pp. 650–681). Hoboken, NJ.: John Wiley and Sons.

Music Educators National Conference. (1994a). *Opportunity to learn standards for music instruction: Grades preK–12.* Reston, VA: Author.

Music Educators National Conference. (1994b). *The school music program: A new vision.* Reston, VA: Author.

Myles, B. S., Cook, K. T., Miller, N. E., Rinner, L., & Robbins, L. A. (2000). *Asperger syndrome and sensory issues: Practical solutions for making sense of the world.* Shawnee Mission, KS: Autism Asperger Publishing Co.

Naglieri, J. A., LeBuffe, P. A., & Pfeiffer, S. I. (1993). *Devereux Behavior Rating Scale-School Form.* San Antonio, TX: Psychological Corporation.

National Academy of Sciences. (1995). National science education standards. Retrieved August 1, 2008, from http://www.nap.edu/readingroom/books/nses/html/6c.html.

National Association for the Education of Young Children (NAEYC). (2003). *Early childhood curriculum, assessment, and program evaluation: Building an effective, accountable system in programs for children birth through age 8.* Position Statement with expanded resources. Retrieved July 20, 2007, from http://www.naeyc.org/about/positions/cape.asp.

National Association for the Education of Young Children (NAEYC). (2005). *Screening and assessment of young English-language learners: Supplement to the NAEYC position statement on early childhood curriculum, assessment and program evaluation.* Retrieved July 22, 2007, from http://www.naeyc.org/about/positions/ELL_Supplement.asp.

National Association for the Education of Young Children (NAEYC). (2006a). *New NAEYC Early Childhood Program Standards and Accreditation Performance Criteria.* Retrieved May 24, 2007, from http://www.naeyc.org/about/releases/20050426.asp.

National Association for the Education of Young Children (NAEYC). (2006b). *Children's illnesses and child care.* Retrieved August 31, 2007, from http://www.naeyc.org/ece/1997/01.asp.

National Association for the Education of Young Children (NAEYC). (2006c). *Developmentally appropriate practice in early childhood programs serving children from birth through age 8.* Retrieved May 21, 2007, from http://www.naeyc.org/about/positions/dap7.asp.

National Association for the Education of Young Children (NAEYC). (2006d). *NAEYC position statement: Technology and young children—ages three through eight.* Retrieved July 26, 2007, from http://www.naeyc.org/about/positions/PSTECH98.asp.

National Association for the Education of Young Children (NAEYC) and National Association of Early Childhood Specialists in State Departments of Education. (2006). *Position statement on curriculum, assessment, and program evaluation.* Retrieved December 15, 2007, from http://www.naeyc.org/about/positions/pdf/CAPEexpand.pdf.

National Association for the Education of Young Children and the National Council of Teachers of Mathematics. (2002). *Early childhood mathematics: Promoting good beginnings.* Retrieved August 1, 2008, from http://naeyc.org/about/positions/pdf/psmath.pdf.

National Association for the Education of Young Children (NAEYC) & International Reading Association. (2005). *Where we stand on learning to read and write.* Retrieved August 1, 2008, from http://www.naeyc.org/about/positions/pdf/WWSSLearningToReadAndWriteEnglish.pdf.

National Association of Early Childhood Specialists in State Departments of Education. (NAECS/SDE). (2000). *Still unacceptable trends in kindergarten entry and placement: A position statement developed by NAECS/SDE.* Retrieved July 23, 2008, from http://www.naeyc.org/about/positions/PsUnacc.asp.

National Association for Music Education. (2002). *National standards for music education.* Retrieved February 3, 2004, from http://www.menc.org/publication/books/standards.htm.

National Association for Music Education. (2008). *National standards for music education.* Retrieved August 3, 2008, from http://menc.org/resources/view/national-standards-for-music-education.

National Association for Sport and Physical Education. (2002). *Active Start: A Statement of Physical Activity Guidelines for Children: Birth to Five Years.* Reston, VA: Author.

National Cancer Institute. (2006). *A snapshot of pediatric cancer.* Retrieved September 2, 2007, from http://www.cancer.gov/cancertopics/types/childhoodcancers.

National Center for Complementary and Alternative Medicine. (2007). *What is CAM?* Retrieved September 22, 2008, from http://nccam.nih.gov/health/whatiscam/.

National Center for Educational Statistics. (2005). *Children 3 through 21 years old served in federally supported programs for the disabled, by type of disability: Selected years, 1976–77 through 2003–04.* Retrieved August 17, 2007, from http://nces.ed.gov/programs/digest/d05/tables/dt05_050.asp.

National Center for Educational Statistics. (2006). *Children with disabilities in public schools.* Retrieved July 30, 2007, from http://nces.ed.gov/programs/coe/2007/section1/table.asp?tableID=671.

National Center for Health Statistics (CD-ROM). (1995). *National Survey of Family Growth.* Hyattsville, MD: U.S. Department of Health and Human Services, Public Health Services, Centers for Disease Control, and National Center for Health Statistics.

National Center for Health Statistics. (2000). *Births: Final data for 1998.* National vital statistics reports, 48(4). Washington, DC: U.S. Government Printing Office.

National Center for Health Statistics. (2007). *Infant Health.* Retrieved April 14, 2007, from http://www.cdc.gov/nchs/fastats/infant_health.htm.

National Center for History in Schools. (1994). *National standards: History for grades K–4.* Los Angeles, CA: Author.

National Center for Learning Disabilities. (2008). *Dysgraphia.* Retrieved August 23, 2008, from http://www.ncld.org/index.php?option=content&task=view&id=468.

National Center of Improving Science Education. (1990). *Getting started in science, a blueprint for elementary school science education.* A report for the National Center for Improving Science Education. Colorado Springs, CO: Author.

National Comorbidity Survey. (2005). *Lifetime prevalence of DSM-IV/WMH-CIDI disorders by sex and cohort.* Retrieved May 18, 2007, from http://www.hcp.med.harvard.edu/ncs/publications.php.

National Council for Geographic Education. (1994). *National geography standards.* Retrieved August 1, 2008, from http://www.ncge.org/publications/tutorial/standards/.

National Council for the Social Studies. (2008). *Expectations of excellence—Curriculum standards for social studies. NCSS curriculum standards revision.* Retrieved August 1, 2008, from http://communities.ncss.org/standardsrevision.

National Council of Teachers of Mathematics. (2003). *Standards for school mathematics.* Retrieved February 4, 2004, at http://www.nctm.org/.

National Council of Teachers of Mathematics. (2004). *Curriculum and evaluation standards for school mathematics.* Reston, VA: Author.

National Diabetes Information Clearinghouse. (2007). *Information on children and young people.* Retrieved September 2, 2007, from http://diabetes.niddk.nih.gov/index.htm.

National Dissemination Center for Children with Disabilities. (2004). *Mental retardation.* Retrieved September 23, 2008, from http://old.nichcy.org/pubs/factshe/fs8txt.htm.

National Education Association. (2006). *The twice-exceptional dilemma.* Washington, DC: Author.

National Educational Technology Standards for Students. (2007). *Profiles for technology literate students.* Retrieved July 24, 2008, from http://www.iste.org/.

National Eye Institute. (2006). *Retinopathy of prematurity.* Retrieved April 14, 2007, from http://www.nei.nih.gov/health/rop/index.asp.

National Forum on Early Childhood Program Evaluation. (2007). *A decision-maker's guide.* Retrieved July 23, 2008, from http://www.developingchild.harvard.edu/.

National Fragile X Foundation. (2008). *Autism and fragile X syndrome.* Retrieved September 25, 2008, from http://www.fragilex.org/html/autism_and_fragile_x_syndrome.htm.

National Hemophilia Foundation. (2003a). *Bleeding disorders info center: Hemophilia A: Factor VIII deficiency.* Retrieved January 4, 2004, at http://www.hemophilia.org/bdi/bdi_types1.htm.

National Hemophilia Foundation. (2003b). *Bleeding disorders info center: Hemophilia B: Factor IX deficiency.* Retrieved January 2, 2004, from http://www.hemophilia.org/bdi/bdi_types2.htm.

National Hemophilia Foundation. (2003c). *Bleeding disorders info center: Information for teachers and childcare providers.* Retrieved January 2, 2004, from http://www.hemophilia.org/bdi/bdi_providers2.htm.

National Hemophilia Foundation. (2006a). *What is a bleeding disorder?* Retrieved September 3, 2007, from http://www.hemophilia.org/NHFWeb/MainPgs/MainNHF.aspx?menuid=26&contentid=5&rptname=bleeding.

National Hemophilia Foundation. (2006b). *What are clotting disorders?* Retrieved September 3, 2007, from http://www.hemophilia.org/NHFWeb/MainPgs/MainNHF.aspx?menuid=176&contentid=378.

National Hemophilia Foundation. (2006c). *Baby and toddler tips.* Retrieved September 3, 2007, from http://www.hemophilia.org/NHFWeb/MainPgs/MainNHF.aspx?menuid=194&contentid=66.

National Hemophilia Foundation. (2006d). *Child Raising.* Retrieved September 3, 2007, from http://www.hemophilia.org/NHFWeb/MainPgs/MainNHF.aspx?menuid=195&contentid=67.

National Human Genome Research Institute (HGP). (2007). *All about the human genome project.* Retrieved April 9, 2007, from http://www.genome.gov.

National Institute on Deafness and Other Communication Disorders (NIDCD). (2002a). *Stuttering.* Retrieved December 23, 2007, from http://www.nidcd.nih.gov/health/voice/stutter.htm.

National Institute on Deafness and Other Communication Disorders (NIDCD). (2002b). *Aphasia.* Retrieved December 23, 2007, from http://www.nidcd.nih.gov/health/voice/aphasia.htm.

National Institute on Deafness and Other Communication Disorders (NIDCD). (2002c). *Apraxia of speech.* Retrieved December 23, 2007, from http://www.nidcd.nih.gov/health/voice/apraxia.htm.

National Institute on Deafness and Other Communication Disorders (NIDCD). (2004). *Auditory processing disorder in children.* Retrieved December 23, 2007, from http://www.nidcd.nih.gov/health/voice/auditory.htm.

National Institute on Deafness and Other Communication Disorders (NIDCD). (2007). *Cochlear implants.* Retrieved April 9, 2008, from http://www.nidcd.nih.giv/health/hearing/coch.asp.

National Institute of Neurological Disorders and Stroke (NINDS). (2005). *What is Tourette syndrome?* Retrieved September 5, 2007, from http://www.ninds.nih.gov/disorders/tourette/detail_tourette.htm?css=print.

National Institute of Neurological Disorders and Stroke (NINDS). (2007). *NINDS dysgraphia information page.* Retrieved August 23, 2008, from http://www.ninds.nih.gov/disorders/dysgraphia/dysgraphia.htm.

National Institute of Neurological Disorders and Stroke (NINDS). (2008a). *Epilepsy.* Retrieved September 19, 2008, from http://www.ninds.nih.gov/disorders/epilepsy/epilepsy.htm.

National Institute of Neurological Disorders and Stroke (NINDS). (2008b). *Rhett syndrome fact sheet.* Retrieved September 22, 2008, from http://www.ninds.nih.gov/disorders/rett/detail_rett.htm.

National Joint Committee on Learning Disabilities. (2006). *Learning disabilities and young children: Identification and intervention.* Retrieved July 30, 2007, from http://www.ldonline.org/article/11511.

National Professional Development Center on Inclusion. (2007). *Research synthesis points on early childhood inclusion.* Retrieved December 6, 2007, from http://www.fpg.unc.edu/Xnpdci/assest/media/products/NDPIC_ResearchSynthesis_9-2007.pdf.

National Research Council and Institute of Medicine. (2000). *From neurons to neighborhoods: The science of early childhood development.* Committee on Integrating the Science of Early Childhood Development. J. P. Shonkoff & D. A. Phillips (Eds.). Board on Children, Youth, and Families, Commission on Behavioral and Social Sciences and Education. Washington, DC: National Academy Press.

National Science Teachers Association (1996). *National science education standards*. Retrieved July 26, 2007, from http://www.nsta.org/about/positions/standards.aspx.

National Task Force on Early Childhood Education for Hispanics. (2007a). *Expanding and improving early education for Hispanics*. Retrieved June 6, 2008, from http://www.ecehispanic.org/work/expand_MainReport.pdf.

National Task Force on Early Childhood Education for Hispanics. (2007b). *Hispanic children gain an academic edge when their education starts early*. Retrieved May 15, 2007, from http://www.ecehispanic.org/work/expand_PR.pdf.

Newacheck, P. W., Inkelas, M., & Kim, S. E. (2004). Health services use and health care expenditures for children with disabilities. *Pediatrics, 114*(1), 79–85. Retrieved December 29, 2007, from http://www.pediatrics.org/cgi/content/full/114/1/79.

Newborg, J. (2004). *Battelle developmental inventory, second edition*. Rolling Meadows, IL: Riverside Publishing.

Newcomer, P., & Hammill, D. (1999). *Test of Language Development – Primary* (3rd ed.). Austin, TX: Pro-Ed.

Newman. B. M. (2000). The challenges of parenting infants and young children. In P. C. McKenry & S. H. Price (Eds.), *Families and change: Coping with stressful events and transitions* (2nd ed., pp. 45–70). Thousand Oaks, CA: Sage.

Newschaffer, C. J., Croen, L. A., Daniels, J., Giarelli, E., Grether, J. K., Levy, S. E., et al. (2007). The epidemiology of autism spectrum disorders. *Annual Reviews of Public Health, 28*, 235–258.

Nichol, A. R., Stretch, D., & Fundudis, T. (1993). *Preschool children in troubled families: Approaches to intervention and support*. Oxford, England: John Wiley & Sons.

Niehoff, D. (1999). *The biology of violence*. New York: The Free Press.

Nihira, K., Leland, H., & Lambert, N. (1993). *AAMD adaptive behavior scale–school* (2nd ed.). Austin, TX: Pro-Ed.

Nikolopoulos, T., Gibbin, K., & Dyar, D. (2004). Predicting speech perception outcomes following cochlear implantation using Nottingham children's implant profile (NChIP). *International Journal of Pediatric Otorhinolaryngology, 68*, 137–141.

No Child Left Behind Act of 2001, Elementary and Secondary Education Act, Pub. L. No. 107–110 (2002).

Nolan, E. D., Gadow, K. D., & Sprafkin, J. (2001). Teacher reports of DSM-IV ADHD, ODD, and CD symptoms in schoolchildren. *Journal of Child and Adolescent Psychiatry, 40*, 241–249.

Northern, J. L., & Downs, M. P. (2002). *Hearing in children* (5th ed.). Philadelphia: Lippincott, Williams & Wilkins.

Norwitz, E., Robinson, J., & Challis, J. (1999). The control of labor. *New England Journal of Medicine, 341*, 660–666.

O'Brien, T. (2005). Social, emotional and behavioural difficulties. In A. Lewis & B. Norwich (Eds.), *Special teaching for special children? Pedagogies for inclusion* (pp. 166–179). Berkshire, England: Open University Press.

Office of English Language Acquisition, Language Enhancement, and Academic Achievement for Limited English Proficient Students (OELA). (2008). *Welcome to OELA's home page*. Retrieved September 21, 2008, from http://www.ed.gov/about/offices/list/oela/index.html?src=mr.

Office of Head Start. (2007). *About Head Start*. Administration for Children and Families. Retrieved July 17, 2007, from http://www.acf.hhs.gov/programs/hsb/about/index.htm.

Ogden, C. L., Carroll, M. D., Curtin, L. R., McDowell, M. A., & Tabak, C. J., et al. (2006). Prevalence of overweight and obesity in the United States, 1999–2004. *Journal of the American Medical Association 295*(13), 1549–1555.

Ogden, C. L., Flegal, K. M., Carroll, M. D., & Johnson, C. L. (2002). Prevalence and trends in overweight among U.S. children and adolescents, 1999–2000. *Journal of the American Medical Association, 288*(14), 1728–1732.

Ohio Sickle Cell and Health Association. (2005). *Is sickle cell disease a common disease?* Retrieved December 30, 2007, from http://www.ohiosicklecell.org/population.html.

Okagaki, L., & Diamond, K. E. (2000). Responding to cultural and linguistic differences in the beliefs and practices of families with young children. *Young Children, 55*(4), 74–80.

Olitsky, S. E., & Nelson, L. B. (1998). Common ophthalmologic concerns in infants and children. *Pediatric Clinics of North America, 45*, 993–1012.

Oller, D., Eilers, R. D., Urbano, R., & Cobo-Lewis, A. B. (1997). Development of precursors to speech in infants exposed to two languages. *Journal of Child Language, 24*, 407–425.

Olweus, D. (2001). Peer harassment: A critical analysis and some important issues. In J. Juvonen & S. Graham (Eds.). *Peer harassment in school: The plight of the vulnerable and victimized* (pp. 3–20). New York: The Guilford Press.

Olweus, D., Limber, S., & Mihalic, S. (1999). *Blueprints for violence prevention, Book Nine: Bullying prevention program*. Boulder, CO: Center for the Study and Prevention of Violence.

O'Neil, J. (January, 2006). Beautiful minds. *NEA Today*, 34–36. Retrieved September 13, 2008, from http://www.gifted.uconn.edu/projectm3/pdf/NEA%20article%20Beautiful%20Minds.pdf.

Onslow, M. (May, 2000). Stuttering: Treatment for preschoolers. *Current Therapeutics*, 52–56.

Orton, S. T. (1937). *Reading, writing, and speech problems in children*. New York: Norton.

O'Shea, M. (2005). *The brain: A very short introduction*. Oxford, England: Oxford University Press.

Osofsky, J. D. (1994). Introduction. In J. D. Osofsky & E. Fenichel (Eds.), Hurt, healing, hope: Caring for infants and toddlers in violent environments. *Zero to Three, 14*(3), 3–6.

Ostrosky, M. M., Jung, E. Y., Hemmeter, M. L., & Thomas, D. (n.d.). *Helping children understand routines and classroom schedules*. Center on the Social and Emotional Foundations for Early Learning. What Works Briefs #3. Retrieved August 11, 2008, from http://www.vanderbilt.edu/csefel/briefs/wwb3.html.

Owens, R. E. (2005). *Language development: An introduction* (6th ed.). Boston, MA: Allyn & Bacon.

Palley, E. (2002). *The implementation of the federal special education policy related to discipline at the state and local level: A case study of Delaware public schools*. Dissertation, Brandeis University.

Parten, M. (1932). Social participation among preschool children. *Journal of Abnormal and Social Psychology, 27,* 243–269.

Passel, J. S. (2006). *The size and characteristics of the unauthorized migrant population in the U.S.: Estimates based on the March 2005 current population survey.* Retrieved December 2, 2007, from http://pewhispanic.org/files/reports/61pdf.

Passel, J. S., Capps, R., & Fix, M. (2004). *Undocumented immigrants: Facts and figures.* Washington, DC: The Urban Institute. Retrieved December 2, 2007, from http://www.urban.org/UploadedPDF/1000587_undoc_immigrant_facts.pdf.

Pathways Awareness. (2008). *Pathways sets standards for tummy time.* Retrieved August 11, 2008, from http://www.pathwaysawareness.org/?q=node/319.

Paul, R., Chawarska, K., Fowler, C., Cicchetti, D., & Volkmar, F. (2007). "Listen my children and you shall hear:" Auditory preference in toddlers with autism spectrum disorders. *Journal of Speech, Language, and Hearing Impairment, 50,* 1350–1364.

Peer, L. (2000). Gifted and talented children with dyslexia. In M. J. Stopper (Ed.), *Meeting the social and emotional needs of gifted and talented children* (pp. 65–79). London: David Fulton.

Pellegrino, L. (2002). Cerebral palsy. In M. L. Batshaw (Ed.), *Children with disabilities* (5th ed., pp. 443–466). Baltimore: Paul H. Brookes.

Pellegrino, L. (2007). Cerebral palsy. In M. L. Batshaw, L. Pellegrino, & N. J. Rosen (Eds.), *Children with disabilities* (6th ed., pp. 387–408). Baltimore: Paul H. Brookes.

Pennington, B. F. (1991). *Diagnosing learning disorders: A neuropsychological framework.* New York: Guilford Press.

Pennsylvania Association of Retarded Children v. Commonwealth of Pennsylvania, 334 F. Supp. 1257 (E.D. Pa. 1971).

Pepino, M. Y., & Mennella, J. A. (2005). Factors contributing to individual differences in sucrose preference. *Chemical Senses, 30,* 319–320.

Perez, B., & Torres-Guzman, M. E. (2002). *Learning in two worlds: An integrated Spanish/English biliteracy approach* (3rd ed.) Boston: Allyn & Bacon.

Perry Preschool Study. (2005). *Lifetime effects: The High/Scope Perry preschool study through age 40.* Retrieved December 1, 2007, from http://www.highscope.org/Content.asp?ContentId=219.

Perry Study. (2004). *Long-term study of adults who received high-quality early childhood care and education shows economic and social gains, less crime.* Retrieved December 1, 2007, from http://www.highscope.org/Content.asp?ContentId=282.

Peter Mills v. Board of Education of the District of Columbia, 348 F. Supp. 866 (D.C. D.C. 1972).

Petito, L. A., Katerelos, M., Levy, B. G., Gauna, K., Tetrealto, K., & Ferraro, V. (2001). Bilingual signed and spoken language acquisition from birth: Implications for the mechanisms underlying early bilingual language acquisition. *Journal of Child Language, 28,* 453–496.

Piaget, J. (1967). *The language and thought of the child.* Cleveland, OH: World.

Piaget, J. (1970). Piaget's theory. In P. H. Mussen (Ed.), *Carmichael's manual of child psychology. Vol. 1.* (3rd ed., pp. 703–732). New York: John Wiley.

Pierangelo, R., & Giuliani, G. A. (2001). *What every teacher should know about students with special needs.* Champaign, IL: Research Press.

Piscopo, M. A., Rigamonti, A., Chiesa, G. B., Bettini, S., Azzinari, A., Bonfanti, R., et al. (2005). Type 2 diabetes mellitus in childhood. In F. Chiarelli, K. Dahl-Jorgensen, & W. Kiess (Eds.), *Diabetes in childhood and adolescence* (pp. 347–361). Basel, Switzerland: Karger.

Plauche Johnson, C. P., Meyers, S. M., & the Council on Children with Disabilities. (2007). Identification and evaluation of children with autism spectrum disorders. *Pediatrics, 120,* 1183–1215.

Pliszka, S. R. (2003). Psychiatric comorbidities in children with attention deficit hyperactivity disorder: Implications of management. *Pediatric Drugs, 5,* 741–750.

Plucker, J. A., & Yecke, C. P. (1999). The effect of relocation on gifted students. *Gifted Child Quarterly, 43*(2), 95–106.

Popham, W. J. (2000). *Testing! testing! What every parent should know about standardized testing.* Boston: Allyn & Bacon.

Porter, L. (1999). *Gifted young children: A guide for teachers and parents.* Buckingham, England: Open University Press.

Powers, M. D. (1989). What is autism? In M. D. Powers (Ed.), *Children with autism: A parents' guide* (pp. 1–30). Rockville, MD: Woodbine House.

Prentice, A., & Goldberg, G. (1996). Maternal obesity increases congenital malformations. *Nutritional Review, 54*(5), 146–150.

Pretti-Frontczak, K., & Bricker, D. (2004). *An activity-based approach to early intervention* (3rd ed.). Baltimore: Paul H. Brookes.

Psychological Corporation. (2002). *Wechsler Preschool and Primary Scale of Intelligence – III.* San Antonio, TX: Author.

Putnam, F. W. (1991). Dissociative disorders in children and adolescents: A developmental perspective. *Psychiatric Clinics of North America, 14,* 519–531.

Putnam, F. W., & Trickett, P. K. (1993). Child sexual abuse: A model of chronic trauma. In D. Reiss, J. E. Richters, & M. Radke-Yarrow (Eds.), *Children and violence* (pp. 96–118). New York: Guilford Press.

Rader, J. I., & Schneeman, B. O. (2006). Prevalence of neural tube defects, folate status, and folate fortification of enriched cereal-grain products in the United States. *Pediatrics, 117,* 1394–1399.

Rahi, J. S., & Dezateux, C. (1998). Epidemiology of visual impairment in Britain. *Archives of Disease in Childhood, 78*(4), 381–386.

Rainforth, B., & York-Barr, J. (1997). *Collaborative teams for students with severe disabilities: Integrating therapy and educational services* (2nd ed.). Baltimore: Paul H. Brookes Publishing Co.

Rais-Bahrami, J., & Short, B. L. (2007). Premature and small-for-dates infants. In M. L. Batshaw, L. Pellegrino & N. J. Rosen (Eds.), *Children with disabilities* (6th ed., pp. 107–122). Baltimore: Paul H. Brookes.

Raskind, W. H. (2001). Current understanding of the genetic basis of reading and spelling disability. *Learning Disability Quarterly, 24,* 141–158.

Reece, R. M., & Sege, R. (2000). Childhood head injuries: Accidental or inflicted? *Archives of Pediatric and Adolescent Medicine, 154,* 11–15.

Rehabilitation Act of 1973, Pub. L. No. 93–112, 87 Stat. 355 U.S.C. §701.

Reid, R., Casat, C. D., Norton, H. J., Anastopoulos, A. D., & Temple, E. P. (2001). Using behavior rating scales for ADHD across ethnic groups: The IOWA Conners. *Journal of Emotional and Behavioral Disorders, 9*, 210–218.

Rennebohm, R. M. (1994). Arthritis. In R. A. Olson, L. L. Mullins, J. B. Gillman & J. M. Chaney (Eds.), *The source book of pediatric psychology* (pp. 70–74). Boston: Allyn & Bacon.

Reschly, D. J. (2005). Learning disabilities identification: Primary intervention, secondary intervention, and then what? *Journal of Learning Disabilities 38*(6), 510–515.

Restrepo, M. A., Schwanenflugel, P. J., Blake, J., Neuharth-Pritchett, S., Cramer, S. E., & Ruston, H. P. (2006). Performance on the PPVT-III and the EVT: Applicability of the measures with African American and European American preschool children. *Language, Speech, and Hearing Services in Schools, 37*, 17–27.

Reyes-Carrasquillo, A. (2000). The culturally and linguistically diverse school population in the United States. In G. B. Esquivel & J. C. Houtz (Eds.), *Creativity and giftedness in culturally diverse students* (pp. 3–28). Cresskill, NJ: Hampton Press.

Rice, K., & Groves, B. (2005). *Hope and Healing: A caregivers' guide to helping young children affected by trauma.* Washington, DC: Zero to Three.

Richards, R. G. (1999). *Strategies for dealing with dysgraphia.* Retrieved August 4, 2002, from http://ldonline.org/ld_indepth/writing/dysgraphia_strategies.htm.

Rideout, V. J., Vandewater, E. A., & Wartella, E. A. (2003). *Zero to six: Electronic media in the lives of infants, toddlers, and preschoolers.* A Keiser Family Foundation Report. Retrieved September 20, 2008, from http://www.kff.org/entmedia/upload/Zero-to-Six-Electronic-Media-in-the-Lives-of-Infants-Toddlers-and-Preschoolers-PDF.pdf.

Rind, E., & Rind, P. (2003). *The stutter in the classroom: A guide for the teacher.* New Rochelle, NY: Stuttering Resource Foundation. Retrieved December 28, 2003, from http://www.mankato.msus.edu/dept/comdis/kuster/InfoPWDS/Classroom.html.

Ripley, K. (2001). *Inclusion for children with dyspraxia/DCD.* London: David Fulton.

Robb, A., & Reber, M. (2007). Behavioral and psychiatric disorders in children with disabilities. In M. L. Batshaw, L. Pellegrino & N. J. Rosen (Eds.), *Children with disabilities* (6th ed., pp. 297–311). Baltimore: Paul H. Brookes.

Robyak, A., Masiello, T., Trivette, C. M., Roper, N., & Dunst, C. J. (2007). Mapping the contemporary landscape of early literacy learning. *CELL Reviews, 1*(1), 1–11. Retrieved August 23, 2008, from http://www.earlyliteracylearning.org/cellreviews/cellreviews_v1_n1.pdf.

Rock, D. A., & Stenner, A. J. (2005). Assessment issues in the testing of children at school entry. *The Future of Children, 15*–34. Retrieved July 23, 2008, from http://www.futureofchildren.org/usr_doc/pg_15_rock-stenner.pdf.

Roid, G. (2003). *Stanford-Binet Intelligence Scale* (5th ed.). Chicago, IL: Riverside Publishing.

Roizen, N. J. (2007). Down Syndrome. In M. L. Batshaw, L. Pellegrino & N. J. Rosen (Eds.), *Children with disabilities* (6th ed., pp. 263–273). Baltimore: Paul H. Brookes.

Rolland, J. S. (2002). *Families, illness, and disability: An integrative treatment model.* New York: Basic Books.

Rose, D. H., & Meyer, A. (2002). *Teaching every student in the digital age: Universal design for learning*, Alexandria, VA: Association for Supervision and Curriculum Development.

Rothenberg, D. (1998). *With these hands: The hidden world of migrant farm workers today.* Berkeley: University of California Press.

Roush, W. (1995). Arguing over why Johnny can't read. *Science, 267*, 1896–1898.

Rubin, K. H., & Coplan, R. J. (1998). Social and nonsocial play in childhood: An individual differences perspective. In O. N. Saracho & B. Spodek (Eds.), *Multiple perspectives on play in early childhood* (pp. 144–170). Albany, NY: State University of New York Press.

Rutter, M. (1994). Beyond longitudinal data: Causes, consequences, changes and continuity. *Journal of Consulting and Clinical Psychology, 62*, 928–940.

Safford, P. L., & Safford, E. J. (1996). *A history of childhood and disability.* New York: Teachers College Press.

Salehi-Had, H., Brandt, J. D., Rosas, A. J., et al. (2006). Findings in older children with abusive head injury: Does shaken-child syndrome exist? *Pediatrics, 117*(5), e1039–e1044.

Salvia, J., & Ysseldyke, J. (2007). *Assessment in special and inclusive education.* (10th ed.) Boston: Houghton Mifflin.

Sandall, S., & Smith, B. J. (2005). An introduction to the DEC recommended practices. In S. Sandall, M. L. Hemmeter, B. J. Smith & M. E. McLean (Eds.), *DEC recommended practices: A comprehensive guide for practical application in early intervention/early childhood special education.* (pp. 11–18). Missoula, MT: Division for Early Childhood.

Sandall, S., McLean, M. E., Santos, R. M., & Smith, B. J. (2005). DEC's recommended practices: The context for change. In S. Sandall, M. L. Hemmeter, B. J. Smith & M. E. McLean (Eds.), *DEC recommended practices: A comprehensive guide for practical application in early intervention/early childhood special education.* (pp. 19–26). Missoula, MT: Division for Early Childhood.

Sandall, S., Hemmeter, M. L., Smith, B. J., & McLean, M. E. (Eds.) (2005). *DEC recommended practices: A comprehensive guide for practical application in early intervention/early childhood special education.* Missoula, MT: Division for Early Childhood.

Sanders, J. H. B. (1998). Gifted special populations: Overcoming hindrances, developing gifts. In J. F. Smutny (Ed.), *The young gifted child: Potential and promise, an anthology* (pp. 199–207). Cresskill, NJ: Hampton Press.

Sanford, A. R., Zelman, J. G., Hardin, B. J., & Peisner-Feinberg, E. (2004). *The learning accomplishment profile* (3rd ed). Chapel Hill, NC: Kaplan Early Learning Company and Chapel Hill Training-Outreach Project, Inc.

Sankar-DeLeeuw, N., (1999). Gifted preschoolers: Parent and teacher views on identification, early admission and programming. *Roeper Review, 21* (3), 174–179.

Santos, R. M., & Chan, S. (2004). Families with Pilipino roots. In E. W. Lynch & M. J. Hanson (Eds.), *Developing cross-cultural competence: A guide for working with children and their families* (3rd ed., pp. 299–344). Baltimore: Paul H. Brookes.

Saracho, O. N., & Spodek, B. (2004). Historical perspectives in language policy and literacy reform. In O. N. Saracho & B. Spodek (Eds.) *Contemporary perspectives on language policy and literacy instruction in early childhood education* (pp. 1–27). Greenwich, CN: Information Age Publishing.

Saunders, J., & Espeland, P. (1991). *Bringing out the best: A resource guide for parents of young gifted children.* Minneapolis, MN: Free Spirit.

Schindler, L. W. (1997). Understanding the immune system's role. In A. R. Cook (Ed.), *Allergies sourcebook* (pp. 31–35). Detroit, MI: Omnigraphics.

Schmidley, D. (2003). The foreign-born population in the United States: March 2002. Current Population Reports, pp. 20–539. Washington, D.C.: U.S. Census Bureau.

Schneier, A. J., Shields, B. J., Hostetler, S. G., et al. (2006). Incidence of pediatric traumatic brain injury and associated hospital resource utilization in the United States. *Pediatrics, 118*(2), 483–492.

Schneider, H., & Eisenberg D. (2006). Who receives a diagnosis of attention-deficit/hyperactivity disorder in the United States elementary school population? *Pediatrics, 117*(4), e601–609.

Schlichter, C. L., Larkin, M. J., Casareno, A. B., Ellis, E. S., Gregg, M., Mayfield, P., et al. (1997). Partners in enrichment: Preparing teachers for multiple ability classrooms. *Teaching Exceptional Children, 29*(4), 4–9.

Schonberg, R. L., & Tifft, C. J. (2007). Birth defects and prenatal diagnosis. In M. L. Batshaw, L. Pellegrino & N. J. Rosen (Eds.), *Children with disabilities* (6th ed., pp. 83–96). Baltimore: Paul H. Brookes.

School Board of Nassau County, Florida et al. v. Arline, 480 U.S. 273 (1987).

Schopler, E., Reichler, R. J., & Renner, B. R. (1993). *Childhood autism rating scale (CARS)* Circle Pines, MN: AGS Publishing.

Schwartz, S. (Ed.). (1996). *Choices in deafness: A parent's guide to communication options* (2nd ed.). Bethesda, MD: Woodbine House.

Seefeldt, C. (1995). Transforming curriculum in social studies. In S. Bredekamp & T. Rosegrant (Eds.), *Reaching potentials: Transforming early childhood curriculum and assessment* (Vol. 2, pp. 109–124). Washington, DC: NAEYC.

Seligman, M., & Darling, R. B. (2007). *Ordinary families, special children: A systems approach to childhood disability.* (3rd ed.) New York: The Guilford Press.

Seltzer, J. A. (2000). Families formed outside of marriage. *Journal of Marriage and the Family, 62,* 1247–1268.

Shalev, R. S. (2004). Developmental dyscalculia. *Journal of Child Neurology, 19,* 765–771.

Shapiro, B. K., Church, R. P., & Lewis, M. E. B. (2002). Specific learning disabilities. In M. L. Batshaw (Ed.), *Children with disabilities* (5th ed., pp. 417–442). Baltimore: Paul H. Brookes.

Shapiro, B., Church, R. P., & Lewis, M. E. B. (2007). Specific learning disabilities. In M. L. Batshaw, L. Pellegrino & N. J. Rosen (Eds.), *Children with disabilities* (6th ed., pp. 367–385). Baltimore: Paul H. Brookes.

Shaywitz, B. A., & Shaywitz, S. E. (1991). Comorbidity: A critical issue in attention deficit disorder. *Journal of Child Neurology, 6* (Suppl.), S13–S22.

Shaywitz, S. E. (1998). Dyslexia. *New England Journal of Medicine, 338*(5), 307–312.

Shaywitz, S. E., & Shaywitz, B. A. (2005). Dyslexia (specific reading disability). *Biological Psychiatry, 57,* 301–309.

Shepard, L. A., Kagan, S. L., & Wurtz, E. (1998). Goal 1 early childhood assessments resource group recommendations. *Young Children, 35*(3), 52–54.

Sholevar, G. P. (1995). *Conduct disorders in children and adolescents.* Washington, DC: American Psychiatric Press.

Shore, R. (1997). *Rethinking the brain: New insights into early development.* New York: Families and Work Institute.

Sicherer, S. (1999). Manifestation of food allergy: Evaluation and management. *American Family Physician, 59,* 415–424.

Silver, L. B. (1995). *ADHD—Attention deficit-hyperactivity disorder and learning disabilities* [A booklet for parents]. Summit, NJ: Ciba-Geigy.

Silver, L. B. (2002). *What is ADHD? Is it a type of LD?* Retrieved July 21, 2002, from http://www.ldonline.org/ld_indepth/add_adhd/what_is_adhd.html.

Silver, L. B. (2004). *Attention-deficit/hyperactivity disorder: A clinical guide to diagnosis and treatment for health and mental health professionals* (3rd ed.). Washington, DC: American Psychiatric Publishing, Inc.

Singer, L. T., Arendt, R., Minnes, S., Farkas, K., Salvator, A., Kirchner, H. L., et al. (2002). Cognitive and motor outcomes of cocaine-exposed infants. *Journal of the American Medical Association, 287,* 1952–1960.

Skinner, B. F. (1953). *Science and Human Behavior.* New York: The Free Press.

Skinner, J. D., Carruth, B. R., Bounds, W., & Ziegler, P. J. (2002). Children's food preferences: A longitudinal analysis. *Journal of the American Dietetic Association,* 102 (11), 1638–1647.

Skinner, J. D., Ziegler, P., Pac, S., & Devaney, B. (2004). Meal and snack patterns of infants and toddlers. *Journal of American Dietetic Association, 104*(1), 65–70.

Smith, B. J., & Fox, L. (2003). *Systems of service delivery: A synthesis of evidence relevant to young children at risk of or who have challenging behavior.* Center for Evidence-Based Practice: Young Children with Challenging Behavior. Retrieved August 2, 2008, from http://challengingbehavior.fmhi.usf.edu/resources/smith-fox-jan03.pdf.

Smith, K., & Corkum, P. (2007). Systematic review of measures used to diagnose attention-deficit/hyperactivity disorder in research on preschool children *Topics in Early Childhood Special Education, 27,* 164–173.

Smutny, J. F. (Ed.) (2003). *Underserved gifted populations: Responding to their needs and abilities.* Cresskill, NJ: Hampton Press, Inc.

Snell, M., & Janney, R. (2000). Teacher's problem-solving about children with moderate and severe disabilities in the elementary classrooms. *Exceptional Children, 66*(4), 472.

Snow, J. H. (1994). Memory functions for children with spina bifida: Assessment in rehabilitation and exceptionality. *Pediatrics, 1,* 20–27.

Solnit, A. J., & Nordhaus, B. F. (1992). *When home is not a haven: Child placement issues.* New Haven, CT: Yale University Press.

Sparrow, S., Balla, D., & Cicchetti, D. (2005). *Vineland adaptive behavior scales.* Circle Pines, MN: American Guidance Service.

Spiegel, H. M. L., & Bonwit, A. M. (2002). HIV infection in children. In M. L. Batshaw (Ed.), *Children with disabilities* (5th ed., pp. 123–140). Baltimore: Paul H. Brookes.

Spencer, T., Wilens, T., Biederman, J., Wozniak, J., & Harding-Crawford, M. (2000). Attention-deficit/hyperactivity disorders with mood disorders. In T. E. Brown (Ed.), *Attention-deficit disorders and comorbidities in children, adolescents, and adults* (pp. 79–124). Washington, DC: American Psychiatric Press.

Sroufe, L. A., Egeland, B., Carlson, E., & Collins, W. A. (2005). Placing early attachment experiences in developmental context: The Minnesota longitudinal study. In K. E. Grossmann, K. Grossmann & E. Waters (Eds.), *Attachment from infancy to adulthood: The major longitudinal studies* (pp. 48–70). New York: The Guilford Press.

Stahl, S. (1999). Universal design: Ensuring access to the general education curriculum. U.S. Office of Special Education Programs and the ERIC Clearinghouse on Disabilities and Gifted Education. *Research Connections in Special Education, 7,* 1–2.

Stechuk, R. A., Burns, A. S., & Yandian, S. E. (2006). *Bilingual infant/toddler environments: Supporting language and learning in our youngest children—a guide for migrant and seasonal Head Start programs.* AED Center for Early Care and Education. Retrieved May 3, 2007, from http://www.aed.org/toolsandPublications/upload/BITE_web1106.pdf.

Stein, M. A., Efron, L. A., Schiff, W. B., & Glanzman, M. (2002). Attention deficits and hyperactivity. In M. L. Batshaw (Ed.), *Children with disabilities.* (5th ed., pp. 389–416). Baltimore: Paul H. Brookes.

Sternberg, R. J., & Zhang, L. F. (Eds.) (2001). *Perspectives on thinking, learning, and cognitive styles.* Mahwah, NJ: Lawrence Erlbaum Associates.

Stevenson, R. E., & Schwartz, C. E. (2002). Clinical and molecular contributions to the understanding of X-linked mental retardation. *Cytogenetic Genome Research, 99*(1–4), 265–275.

Strain, P. S. (1990). LRE for preschool children with handicaps: What we know, what we should be doing. *Journal of Early Intervention, 14,* 291–296.

Stuart, S. (2007). Communication: Speech and language. In M. L. Batshaw, L. Pellegrino & N. J. Rosen (Eds.), *Children with disabilities* (6th ed., pp. 229–241). Baltimore: Paul H. Brookes.

Stunkard, A. J., Berkowitz, R. I., Schoeller, D., Maislin, G., & Stallings, V. A. (2004). Determinants of body size in the first two years of life. *International Journal of Obesity, 28*(4), 503–513.

Stuttering Foundation. (2007). *Facts on stuttering.* Retrieved May 4, 2007, from http://www.stutteringhelp.org/Default.aspx?tabid=17.

Substance Abuse and Mental Health Services Administration. (2005a). *The NHSDA Report: Substance use during pregnancy 2002 and 2003.* Retrieved April 12, 2007, from http://oas.samhsa.gov/2k5/pregnancy/pregnancy.htm.

Substance Abuse and Mental Health Services Administration. (2005b). *Marijuana use and characteristics of users.* Retrieved April 12, 2007, from http://oas.samhsa.gov/marijuana.htm.

Sullivan, P. M., & Knutson, J. F. (2000). Maltreatment and disabilities: A population-based epidemiological study. *Child Abuse & Neglect, 24*(10), 1257–1273.

Takanishi, R. (2004). *Leveling the playing field: Supporting immigrant children from birth to eight.* New York: Foundation for Child Development. Retrieved March 20, 2007, from http://fcd-us.org/uploadDocs/RTPackard06_11_04.pdf.

Tarq, S. M., Matthews, S. M., Hakim, E. A., et al. (1998). The prevalence of and risk factors from atopy in early childhood: A whole population birth cohort study. *Journal of Allergy and Clinical Immunology, 101,* 587–593.

Taylor, H. G., Yeates, K. O., Wade, S. L., et al. (1999). Influences on first-year recovery from traumatic brain injury in children. *Neuropsychology, 13*(1), 76–89.

Technology-Related Assistance for Individuals with Disabilities Act of 1988, Pub. L. No. 100–407, 29 U.S.C. § 2201.

Tenenbaum, R. R., & Ruck, M. D. (2007). Are teacher's expectations different for racial minority than for European American students? A meta-analysis. *Journal of Educational Psychology, 99,* 253–273.

The Kennedy Center. (2008). *ARTSEDGE: The national standards for arts education.* Retrieved August 3, 2008, from http://www.artsedge.org/teach/standards/standards_k4.cfm.

Thomas, A., & Chess, S. (1980). *The dynamics of psychological development.* New York: Brunner/Mazel.

Thomas, A., Chess, S., & Birch, C. (1968). *Temperament and behavior disorders in children.* New York: New York University Press.

Through the Looking Glass. (2007). *Parents with disabilities.* Retrieved May 18, 2007, from http://lookingglass.org/parents/.

Thurlow, M. L., & Bolt, S. (2001). *Empirical support for accommodations most often allowed in state policy* (Synthesis Report 41). Minneapolis, MN: National Center on Education Outcomes.

Tien, K. (2008). Effectiveness of the picture exchange communication system as a functional communication intervention for individuals with autism spectrum disorders: A practice-based research synthesis. *Education and Training in Developmental Disabilities, 43*(1), 61–76.

Tinker v. Des Moines Independent Community School District, 393 U.S. 503 (1969).

Toossi, M. (2002, May). A century of change: The U.S. labor force, 1950–2050. *Monthly Labor Review,* 15–28.

Travers, J. (2006). Current views of life span development. In K. Thies & J. Travers (Eds.), *Handbook of Human Development for Health Care Professionals,* pp. 3–18. Sudbury, MA: Jones and Bartlett Publishers.

Trivette, C. M., & Dunst, C. J. (2005). DEC recommended practices: Family-based practices. In S. Sandall, M. L. Hemmeter, B. J. Smith & M. E. McLean (Eds.), *DEC recommended practices: A comprehensive guide for practical application in early intervention/early childhood special education.* (pp. 107–126). Missoula, MT: Division for Early Childhood.

Trivette, C. M., & Dunst, C. J. (2007). Relative effectiveness of dialogic, interactive, and shared reading interventions, *CELL Reviews 1*(2), 1–11. Retrieved August 23, 2008, from http://www.earlyliteracylearning.org/cellreviews/cellreviews_v1_n2.pdf.

Trost, S. G., Sirard, J. R., Dowda, M., Pfeiffer, K. A., & Pate, R. R. (2003). Physical activity in overweight and nonoverweight preschool children. *International Journal of Obesity, 27*(7), 834–839.

Tuchman, R. (2000). Treatment of seizure disorders and EEG abnormalities in children with autism spectrum disorders. *Journal of Autism and Developmental Disorders, 30,* 491–495.

Tucker, M. B., Subramanian, S. K., & James, A. D. (2004). Diversity in African American families: Trends and projections. In M. Coleman & L. H. Ganong, *Handbook of contemporary families: Considering the past, contemplating the future* (pp. 352–368). Thousand Oaks, CA: Sage.

Turnbull, A. P., & Turnbull, H. R., III. (1997). *Families, professionals, and exceptionalities* (3rd ed.). Upper Saddle River, NJ: Merrill.

Turnbull, A. P., Turnbull, H. R., III, Erwin, E. J., & Soodak, L. C. (2005) *Families, professionals, and exceptionality: Positive outcomes through partnership and trust* (5th ed.). Upper Saddle River, NJ: Pearson/Prentice Hall.

Tuttle, D. W., & Tuttle, N. R. (1996). *Self-esteem and adjusting with blindness: The process of responding to life's demands* (2nd ed.). Springfield, IL: Thomas.

Ullman, R., Sleator, S., Sprague, R., & MetriTech Staff. (1996). *Manual for the comprehensive teacher's rating scale: Parent form.* Champaign, IL: MetriTech.

U.S. Bureau of the Census. (1995). *Top 25 American Indian tribes for the United States: 1990 and 1980.* Retrieved May 15, 2007, from http://www.census.gov/population/socdemo/race/indian/ailang1.txt.

U.S. Bureau of the Census. (1998). *Marital status and living arrangements: March 1996* (Current Population Reports, Series P20-496). Washington, DC: U.S. Government Printing Office.

U.S. Bureau of the Census. (1999). *Region of birth of the foreign-born population: 1850–1930; 1960–1990.* Retrieved May 19, 2007, from http://www.census.gov/population/www/documentation/twps0029/tab02.html.

U.S. Bureau of the Census. (2000). *The Hispanic population in the United States: Current population characteristics, March 1999* (Current population Reports, Series P20–527). Washington, DC: U.S. Government Printing Office.

U.S. Census Bureau. (2002). *Introduction to Census 2000 data products – American Indian and Alaska Native.* Retrieved May 15, 2007, from http://factfinder.census.gov/home/aian/mso01icd.pdf.

U.S. Census Bureau. (2004). *Projected population of the United States by race and Hispanic origin: 2000 to 2050.* Retrieved May 19, 2007, from http://www.census.gov/ipc/www/usinterimproj.

U.S. Census Bureau. (2005a). *Hispanic population passes 40 Million Census Bureau Reports.* Retrieved May 14, 2007, from http://www.census.gov/Press-Release/www/releases/archives/population/005164.html.

U.S. Census Bureau. (2005b). *Income, poverty, and health insurance coverage in the United States: 2005.* Retrieved May 14, 2007, from http://www.infoplease.com/ipa/A0104688.html.

U.S. Census Bureau. (2005c). *Poverty: 2005 highlights.* Retrieved May 14, 2007, from http://www.census.gov/hhes/www/poverty/poverty05/pov05hi.html.

U.S. Census Bureau. (2006). *Geographic mobility between 2004 and 2005.* Retrieved August 8, 2008, from http://www.census.gov/population/www/pop-profile/files/dynamic/Mobility.pdf.

U.S. Census Bureau. (2007). *Annual estimates of the population by age and sex for the United States: April 1, 2000–July 1, 2006.* Retrieved November 10, 2007, from http://www.census.gov/popest/national/asrh/htm.

U.S. Department of Agriculture. (2002). *Child and Adult Care Food Program.* Author.

U.S. Department of Defense. (2008). *Military child education agreement now in effect.* Retrieved July 19, 2008, from http://www.defenselink.mil/releases/release.aspx?releaseid=12062.

U.S. Department of Education and U.S. Department of Justice. (1999). *The 1999 annual report on school safety.* Washington, DC: Author.

U.S. Department of Education. (2006). Building the legacy: IDEA 2004. Retrieved August 16, 2008, from http://idea.ed.gov/.

U.S. Department of Education. (2007a). *History: Twenty-five years of progress in educating children with disabilities through IDEA.* Retrieved November 27, 2007, from http://www.ed.gov/policy/speced/leg/idea/history.html.

U.S. Department of Education. (2007b). *IDEA – Building the legacy of IDEA 2004 Q and A: Questions and Answers on Response to Intervention (RTI) and Early Intervening Services (EIS).* Retrieved April 5, 2008, from http://idea.ed.gov/explore/view/p/%2Croot%2Cdynamic%2CQaCorner%2C8%2C.

U.S. Department of Education, Office of Special Education Programs. (2006). *IDEA – Building the legacy of IDEA 2004, Identification of Specific Learning Disabilities* Retrieved August 22, 2008, from http://idea.ed.gov/explore/view/p/%2Croot%2Cdynamic%2CTopicalBrief%2C23%2C.

U.S. Department of Education, Office of Special Education and Rehabilitative Services, Office of Special Education Programs. (2007). *Part B Individualized Education Program.* Retrieved April 5, 2008, from http://idea.ed.gov/download/modelform1_IEP.doc.

U.S. Department of Health and Human Services. (2003a). *Ending chronic homelessness: Strategies for action.* Retrieved May 17, 2007, from http://aspe.hhs.gov/hsp/homelessness/strategies03/.

U.S. Department of Health and Human Services. (2003b). *Fetal alcohol syndrome.* Retrieved December 7, 2006, from http://www.cdc.gov/ncbddd/factsheets/FAS_alcoholuse.pdf.

U.S. Department of Health and Human Services. (2004). *The health consequences of smoking: A report of the surgeon general.* Atlanta, GA: U.S. Department of Health and Human Services, Centers for Disease Control and Prevention, National Center for Chronic Disease Prevention and Health Promotion, Office on Smoking and Health.

U.S. Department of Health and Human Services and Agriculture. (2005). *Dietary Guidelines for Americans 2005.* Retrieved June 22, 2007, from http://www.health.gov/dietaryguidelines/dga2005/document/.

U.S. Government Accountability Office (USGAO). (2001). *Public education: Meeting the needs of students with limited English proficiency.* GAO-06-807. Retrieved March 12, 2008, from http://purl.access.gpo.gov/GPO/LPS49122.

U.S. Government Accountability Office. (2005). *Special Education: Children with Autism.* Retrieved September 22, 2008, from http://www.gao.gov/new.items/d05220.pdf.

U.S. Government Accountability Office. (2006a). *No Child Left Behind Act: Assistance from education could help states better measure progress of students with limited English proficiency.* GAO-06-815. Retrieved March 12, 2008, from http://purl.access.gpo.gov/GPO/LPS73081.

U.S. Government Accountability Office. (2006b). *Child care and early childhood education: More information sharing and program review by HHS could enhance access for families with limited English proficiency.* GAO-06-807. Retrieved March 12, 2008, from http://purl.access.gpo.gov/GPO/LPS65832.

U.S. Preventive Services Task Force. (2003). *Counseling to prevent tobacco use.* Rockville, MD: Agency for Healthcare Research and Quality. Retrieved August 10, 2008, from http://www.ahrq.gov/clinic/uspstf/uspstbac.htm.

Van Dyck, P. C., Kogan, M. D., McPherson, M. G., et al. (2004). Prevalence and characteristics of children with special health care needs. *Archives of Pediatric and Adolescent Medicine, 158,* 884–890.

Vandewater, E. A., Shim, M., & Caplovitz, A. G. (2004). Linking obesity and activity level with children's television and video game use. *Journal of Adolescence, 27*(1), 71–85.

Vanidivere, S., Chalk, R., & Moore, K. A. (2003*). Children in foster homes: How are they faring?* Research Brief, Publication #2003023. Washington, DC: Child trends. Retrieved May 17, 2007, from http://childtrends.org/files/FosterHomesRB.pdf.

VanTassel-Baska, J., & Stambaugh, T. (2006). *Comprehensive curriculum for gifted learners.* (3rd ed.). Boston: Pearson Education, Inc.

VORT Corporation. (1995). *HELP for preschoolers charts.* Palo Alto, CA: Author.

Vygotsky, L. S. (1934/1987). Thinking and speech. In R. Rieber & A. S. Carton (Eds.), *The collected works of L. S. Vygotsky: Vol. 1. Problems of general psychology* (pp. 37–285). New York: Plenum.

Vygotsky, L. S. (1978). *Mind in society: The development of higher psychological processes* (14th ed.). Cambridge, MA: Harvard University Press.

Walker, B., Hafenstein, N. L., & Crow-Enslow, L. (1999). Meeting the needs of gifted learners in the early childhood classroom. *Young Children, 54*(1), 32–36.

Walker, H. M., Ramsey, E., & Gresham, F. M. (2004). *Antisocial behavior in school: Evidence-based practices.* Belmont, CA: Thomson/Wadsworth.

Wallerstein, J., Lewis, J., & Blakeslee, S. (2000). *The unexpected legacy of divorce: A twenty-five year landmark study.* New York: Hyperion Press.

Walsh, F. (2003). Changing families in a changing world: Reconstructing family normality. In F. Walsh (Ed.), *Normal family processes* (3rd ed., pp. 3–26). New York: Guilford Press.

Waltz, M. (1999). *Pervasive developmental disorders: Finding a diagnosis and getting help.* Sebastopol, CA: O'Reilly.

Wamboldt, M. A., & Wamboldt, F. S. (2000). Role of the family in the onset and outcome of childhood disorders: Selected research findings. *Journal of the American Academy of Child and Adolescent Psychiatry, 39*(10), 1212–1219.

Wang, P. P., & Baron, M. A. (1997). Language: A code for communicating. In M. L. Batshaw (Ed.), *Children with disabilities* (4th ed., pp. 275–292). Baltimore: Paul H. Brookes.

Ward, D. S., Saunders, R. P., & Pate, R. R. (2007). *Physical activity interventions in children and adolescents.* Champaign, IL: Human Kinetics.

Warren, S. L. (2004). Anxiety disorders. In R. DelCarmen-Wiggins & A. Carter (Eds.). *Handbook of infant, toddler, and preschool mental health assessment* (pp. 355–375). Oxford, England: Oxford University Press.

Watson, J. B. (1926). What the nursery has to say about instincts. In C. Murchison (Ed.) *Psychologies of 1925.* Worchester, MA: Clark University Press.

Waxmonsky, J. (2003). Assessment and treatment of attention deficit hyperactivity disorder in children with comorbid psychiatric illness. *Current Opinion in Pediatrics, 15,* 576–482.

Webster-Stratton, C. (1998). Preventing conduct problems in Head Start children: Strengthening parenting competencies. *Journal of Consulting and Clinical Psychology, 66,* 715–730.

Wechsler, D. (2003). *Wechsler intelligence scale for children* (4th ed.). San Antonio, TX: Psychological Corporation.

Weinstein, S. L., & Gaillard, W. D. (2007). Epilepsy. In M. L. Batshaw, L. Pellegrino & N. J. Rosen (Eds.), *Children with disabilities* (6th ed., pp. 439–460). Baltimore: Paul H. Brookes.

Wesson, K. A. (2001). The "Volvo effect"—Questioning standardized tests. *Young Children, 56*(2), 16–18.

Weyandt, L. L. (2006). *An attention deficit hyperactivity disorder primer* (2nd ed.) Manwah, NJ: Lawrence Erlbaum Associates.

What Works Clearinghouse (2007). *Character education.* Retrieved August 25, 2008, from http://www.positive-action.net/content/PDFs/Character-education-topic-report.pdf.

Widom, C. S., & Maxfield, M. G. (2001). *An update on the "cycle of violence."* National Institute of Justice. Research in Brief. Office of Justice Programs. Retrieved May 17, 2007, from http://www.ncjrs.giv/txtfiles1/nij/184894.txt.

Wiggs, L., & Stores, G. (2004). Sleep patterns and sleep disorders in children with autistic spectrum disorders: Insights using parent report and actigraphy. *Developmental Medicine and Child Neurology, 46,* 372–380.

Williams, K. C., & Cooney, M. H. (2006). Young children and social justice. *Young Children, 61*(2), 75–82.

Williamson, G. G., & Anzalone, M. E. (2001). *Sensory integration and self-regulation in infants and toddlers: Helping very young children interact with their environment.* Washington, DC: Zero to Three Press.

Willis, W. (1998). Families with African American Roots. In E. W. Lynch & J. Hanson (Eds.), *Developing cross cultural competence: A guide for working with children and their families* (2nd ed., pp. 165–208). Baltimore: Paul H. Brookes.

Winebrenner, S., & Devlin, B. (1998). Cluster grouping of gifted students: How to provide full-time services on a part-time budget. *Teaching Exceptional Children, 30*(3), 62–65.

Wingenbach, N. (1998). The gifted-learning-disabled child: In need of an integrative education. In J. F. Smutny (Ed.), *The young gifted child: Potential and promise, an anthology* (pp. 190–198). Cresskill, NJ: Hampton Press.

Winter, S., Autry, A., Boyle, C., et al. (2002). Trends in the prevalence of cerebral palsy in a population-based study. *Pediatrics, 110*(6), 1220–1225.

Winzer, M. A. (1993). *The history of special education: From isolation to integration.* Washington, DC: Gallaudet University Press.

Wolery, M. (2005). DEC recommended practices: Child-focused practices. Introduction. In S. Sandall, M. L. Hemmeter, B. J. Smith & M. E. McLean (Eds.), *DEC recommended practices: A comprehensive guide for practical applications in early intervention/early childhood special eduction* (pp. 71–76). Missoula, MT: Division for Early Childhood.

Woodcock, R. (1997). *Woodcock Diagnostic Reading Battery.* Allen, TX: DLM.

Wong, B. (1998). *Learning about learning disabilities* (2nd ed.). San Diego, CA: Academic Press.

Wunsch, M. J., Conlon, C. J., & Scheidt, P. C. (2002). Substance abuse: A preventable threat to development. In M. L. Batshaw (Ed.), *Children with disabilities.* (5th ed., pp. 107–122). Baltimore: Paul H. Brookes.

Yatvin, J. (1995). Flawed assumptions. *Phi Delta Kappan, 76*(6), 482–485.

Yaun, A. L., & Keating, R. (2007). The brain and the nervous system. In M. L. Batshaw, L. Pellegrino & N. J. Rosen (Eds.), *Children with disabilities* (6th ed., pp. 185–202). Baltimore: Paul H. Brookes.

Yeargin-Allsopp, M., Drews-Botsch, C., & Van Naarden Braun, K. (2007). Epidemiology of Developmental Disabilities. In M. L. Batshaw, L. Pellegrino & N. J. Rosen (Eds.), *Children with disabilities* (6th ed., pp. 231–243). Baltimore: Paul H. Brookes.

Yeargin-Allsopp, M., Rice, C., Karapurkar, T., et al. (2003). Prevalence of autism in a U.S. metropolitan area. *Journal of the American Medical Association, 289*(1), 49–55.

Zeph, L., Gilmeer, D., Brewer-Allen, D., & Moulton, J. (Eds.) (1992). Kids talk about inclusive classrooms: Creating inclusive educational communities: A monograph series (No.3) Orono: LEARNS, College of Education, University of Maine.

Zero to Three. (2007). *Research summary: Children exposed to violence.* RetrievedMay 17, 2007, from http://www.zerotothree.org/sit4e/DocServer/children_Exp_to_Violence.pdf?docID=2502.

Zero to Three. (2008). Military Projects at Zero to Three. Retrieved August 8, 2008, from http://www.zerotothree.org/site/PageServer?pagename=key_military.

Zito, J. M., Safer, D. J., DosReis, S., Gardner, J. F., Boles, M., & Lynch, F. (2000). Trends in the prescribing of psychotropic medications to preschoolers. *Journal of the American Medical Association, 23,* 1025–1030.

Zito, J. M., Safer, D. J., DosReis, S., Gardner, J. F., Magder, L. Soeken, K., et al. (2003). Psychotropic practice patterns for youth: A 10-year perspective. *Archives of Pediatric and Adolescent Medicine, 157,* 17–25.

Zoccolillo, M. (1993). Gender and the development of conduct disorder. *Development and Psychopathology, 5,* 65–78.

Zuniga, M. E. (2004). Families with Latino roots. In E. W. Lynch & J. Hanson (Eds.), *Developing cross cultural competence: A guide for working with children and their families* (3rd ed., pp. 179–217). Baltimore: Paul H. Brookes.

Index